WOMEN'S VOICES, FEMINIST VISIONS

Classic and Contemporary Readings

SUSAN M. SHAW   JANET LEE

Oregon State University

Mc Graw Hill Education

WOMEN'S VOICES, FEMINIST VISIONS: CLASSIC AND CONTEMPORARY READINGS, SIXTH EDITION

Published by McGraw-Hill Education, 2 Penn Plaza, New York, NY 10121. Copyright © 2015 by McGraw-Hill Education. All rights reserved. Printed in the United States of America. Previous editions © 2012, 2009, and 2007. No part of this publication may be reproduced or distributed in any form or by any means, or stored in a database or retrieval system, without the prior written consent of McGraw-Hill Education, including, but not limited to, in any network or other electronic storage or transmission, or broadcast for distance learning.

Some ancillaries, including electronic and print components, may not be available to customers outside the United States.

This book is printed on acid-free paper.

2 3 4 5 6 7 8 9 0 DOC/DOC 1 0 9 8 7 6 5 4

ISBN 978-0-07-802700-0
MHID 0-07-802700-4

Managing Director: *Gina Boedeker*
Director: *Matthew Busbridge*
Brand Manager: *Courtney Austermehle*
Executive Director of Development: *Lisa Pinto*
Managing Editor: *Sara Jaeger*
Marketing Specialist: *Alexandra Schultz*
Brand Coordinator: *Adina Lonn*
Content Production Manager: *Faye Schilling*
Content Project Manager: *Lisa Bruflodt*
Buyer: *Nichole Birkenholz*
Cover Designer: *Studio Montage, St. Louis, Mo.*
Cover Image: *Courtesy Janet Lee*
Compositor: *Cenveo® Publisher Services*
Typeface: *10/12 Times LT Std*
Printer: *R. R. Donnelley*

All credits appearing on page or at the end of the book are considered to be an extension of the copyright page.

Cataloging-in-Publication Data is on file with the Library of Congress

The Internet addresses listed in the text were accurate at the time of publication. The inclusion of a website does not indicate an endorsement by the authors or McGraw-Hill Education, and McGraw-Hill Education does not guarantee the accuracy of the information presented at these sites.

www.mhhe.com

*Dedicated to all our WS 223 "Women: Self
and Society" students
with thanks for all they have taught us.*

Contents

Preface

We decided to create this book after finding our students were increasingly not reading the assigned material in our introductory women's studies course. Our students found the texts to be mostly inaccessible, or alternatively, they enjoyed reading the more testimonial first-person accounts included in some texts but were not getting the theoretical framework necessary to make sense of these more experiential readings. We were tired of creating packets of readings, and students were tired of having to access alternative readings on top of purchasing a textbook. This book was crafted to include a balance of recent contemporary readings with historical and classic pieces as well as both testimonial and more theoretical essays that would speak to the diversity of human experience. Each chapter has an introduction that provides an overview of the topic and provides a framework for the readings that follow. Additionally, each chapter provides a variety of learning activities, activist profiles, ideas for activism, and other sidebars that can engage students with the material in various ways.

Although students of women's and gender studies today are in many ways like the students who have preceded them, they are also characterized by certain distinctions from the students of the past. Many of today's students come to our classes believing the goals of the women's movement have already been accomplished, and, although most will say they believe in gender equity of some sort, few identify with feminism as a political theory or social movement. Even among students who are supportive of feminist thought, there is a distinct sense of a "third wave" of feminism that reflects the interests of young women who have come of age benefiting from the gains made by their feminist foremothers. Moreover, as women's and gender studies has become institutionalized on college campuses and is fulfilling baccalaureate core requirements, more students are being exposed to women's and gender studies than ever before. Many of these students "choose" women's and gender studies from a menu of options and come to the discipline with varying levels of misunderstanding and resistance. Some of these students have been influenced by the backlash efforts of the 1980s and 1990s and by conservative religious ideologies that seek a return to traditional gender relations. All of these distinctions call for a new, relevant, and accessible introductory women's and gender studies text.

As is typical of contemporary students, students in women's and gender studies today are the kind of visual learners who often prefer reading and interacting in front of a computer screen or a smartphone or watching video clips to reading traditional texts. They are unlikely to wade through long, dense, theoretical readings because they deem them "boring" and "irrelevant." We know from experience that a large percentage of students in introductory women's and gender studies classes only read a fragment of the required readings and that our required readings end up as "fragmented texts."

Our intention in this book is to address these challenges by presenting a student-friendly text that provides short, accessible readings which reflect the diversity of women's experiences and offer a balance of classic/contemporary and theoretical/experiential pieces. The goal is to start where students are rather than where we hope they might be, and to provide a text that enriches their thinking, encourages them to read, and relates to their everyday experiences. We have chosen accessible articles that we hope are readable. They are relatively short, to the point, and interesting in terms of both topics and writing styles. Although most articles are quite contemporary, we have also included several earlier classic articles that are "must-reads." And although the articles we have chosen cover the breadth of issues and eras in women's and gender studies, we hope students will read them and enjoy reading them because of their accessibility, style of presentation, and relevance to their lives. Many are written by young feminists, many are testimonial in format, and, on the whole, they avoid dense, academic theorizing. The cartoons, we hope, bring humor to this scholarship.

We also structure opportunities for students to reflect on their learning throughout the text, and, in this sense, the book is aimed at "teaching itself." It includes not only articles and introductions but also a number of features designed to engage students in active learning around the content. For example, we address students' tendencies to lose interest by creating a format that presents smaller, self-contained, more manageable pieces of knowledge that hold together through related fields and motifs that are woven throughout the larger text as boxes. This multiple positioning of various forms of scholarship creates independent but related pieces that enable students to read each unit in its entirety and make connections between the individual units and the larger text. We see this subtext as a way to address students' familiarity and comfort with contemporary design, multiple windows (as on web pages), and "sound bytes." By also presenting material in these familiar formats, we intend to create a student-friendly text that will stimulate their interest. We encourage them actually to read the text and then be actively engaged with the material.

Pedagogy is embedded within the text itself. In addition to the textual narrative, we include in each chapter learning activities, activism ideas that provide students with examples and opportunities for the practical implementation of the content, questions for discussion that help students explore chapter themes critically, and suggestions for further reading. Instructors will be able to utilize the various pedagogical procedures suggested in the text (and those in the accompanying instructor's manual found on the Online Learning Center at: www.mhhe.com/shaw6e) to develop teaching plans for their class sessions. By embedding the pedagogy within the text, we are creating a classroom tool that enables a connection between content and teaching procedure, between assigned readings and classroom experience. Thus, students and instructors should experience the text as both a series of manageable units of information and a holistic exploration of the larger topics.

We hope that this text will address the needs and concerns of students and instructors alike by speaking to students where they are in relation to feminist issues. Our hope is that the innovations included in this book will invite students into productive dialogue with feminist ideas and encourage personal engagement in feminist work.

Like other women's and gender studies text-readers, this book covers the variety of issues that we know instructors address in the introductory course. We do not isolate race and racism and other issues of difference and power as separate topics, but thoroughly integrate them throughout the text into every issue addressed. We have also chosen not to present groups of chapters in parts or sections but to let the individual chapters stand alone. Pragmatically, this facilitates instructors being able to decide how they want to organize their own courses. At the same time, however, the chapters do build on each other. For example, after introducing students to women's studies, Chapter 2 presents the systems of privilege and inequality that form the context of women's lives and then Chapter 3 explores the social construction of gender, building on the previous chapter by introducing the plurality of sex/gender systems. The following chapters then examine how sex/gender systems are expressed and maintained in social institutions.

For this new edition, we have revised chapter framework essays to reflect the most up-to-date research and theory in the field. We've also included new readings that are contemporary and exciting. With each new edition, we strive to keep the textbook fresh and interesting for our students.

New readings for this edition include:

ACKNOWLEDGMENTS

Writing a textbook is inevitably a community project, and without the assistance of a number of people this project would have been impossible. We would like to thank Karen Mills, administrator for the School of Language, Culture, and Society, for her support.

We also would like to acknowledge the work of the many reviewers who provided insights and suggestions for this edition:

Karen M. Booth, University of North Carolina at Chapel Hill

Emily Bowles, University of Wisconsin at Fox Valley

Elizabeth R. Canfield, Virginia Commonwealth University

Brian R. Jara, West Virginia University

Mel Michelle Lewis, Goucher College

Diane Perpich, Clemson University

Alicia Mischa Renfroe, Middle Tennessee State University

Beth Younger, Drake University

Finally, we want to thank Sara Jaeger and Erin Guendelsberger, our editors at McGraw-Hill, who have provided invaluable support and encouragement. We'd also like to thank Serina Beauparlant, who initiated the first edition of the book with us when she was an editor at Mayfield Publishing.

About the Authors

Susan M. Shaw is professor of women, gender, and sexuality studies and director of the School of Language, Culture, and Society at Oregon State University. Her research interests are in women and rock 'n' roll, women and HIV/AIDS, and women in religion, and she teaches courses in systems of oppression, women and sexuality, feminist theology, and women and pop culture. She is author of *Storytelling in Religious Education* (Religious Education Press, 1999) and *God Speaks to Us, Too: Southern Baptist Women on Church, Home, and Society* (University Press of Kentucky, 2008), and co-author of *Girls Rock! Fifty Years of Women Making Music* (University Press of Kentucky, 2004). She is an avid racquetball player, reader of murder mysteries, and hot tubber.

Janet Lee is professor of women, gender, and sexuality studies at Oregon State University where she teaches a variety of courses on gender and feminism. Research interests include women's history and biography, feminist theories and pedagogy, and issues concerning women and the body. She is author of *War Girls: The First Aid Nursing Yeomanry* (FANY) in the First World War (Manchester University Press, 2005), *Comrades and Partners: The Shared Lives of Grace Hutchins and Anna Rochester* (Rowman and Littlefield, 2000), and co-author of *Blood Stories: Menarche and the Politics of the Female Body in Contemporary U.S. Society* (Routledge, 1996). She enjoys gardening, riding her horses, and playing tennis.

Janet Lee and Susan Shaw are also co-authors and co-editors of *Women Worldwide: Transnational Feminist Perspectives on Women,* published by McGraw-Hill in 2010. This introductory-level textbook brings global perspectives to the study of women, gender, and feminism.

Women's and Gender Studies: Perspectives and Practices

WHAT IS WOMEN'S AND GENDER STUDIES (WGS)?

WGS is an interdisciplinary academic field devoted to topics concerning women, gender, and feminism. It focuses on gender arrangements (the ways society creates, patterns, and rewards our understandings of femininity and masculinity) and examines the multiple ways these arrangements affect everyday life. In particular, WGS is concerned with gender as it intersects with multiple categories, such as race, ethnicity, social class, age, and sexuality. Exploring how we perform femininity and masculinity and how this interacts with other aspects of our identities, WGS focuses on the ways women and other feminized bodies experience discrimination and oppression. Simply put, WGS involves the study of gender as a central aspect of human existence.

The goal of WGS, however, is not only to provide an academic framework and broad-based community for inquiry about the impacts of gender practices on social, cultural, and political thought and behavior, but also to provide advocacy and work toward social change. This endeavor is framed by understandings of the social, economic, and political changes of the past half century that include a rapid increase in globalization and its impacts locally, including the deindustrialization of the global north, the blurring and dispersal of geopolitical boundaries and national identities, and the growth of new technologies that have not only transformed political and economic institutions, but supported mass consumerism. Such changes shape contemporary imperialism (economic, military, political, and/or cultural domination over nations or geopolitical formations) with implications for people in both local and global communities.

In this way, WGS seeks understanding of these issues and realities with the goal of social justice. In this endeavor it puts women and other marginalized peoples at the center of inquiry as subjects of study, informing knowledge through these lenses. This inclusion implies that traditional notions regarding men as "humans" and women as "others" must be challenged and transcended. Such a confusion of maleness with humanity, putting men at the center and relegating women to outsiders in society, is called *androcentrism*. By making women and other marginalized peoples the subjects of study, we assume that our opinions and thoughts about our own experiences are

LEARNING ACTIVITY   **Why Are We Reading These Essays?**

By Margaret Stetz
University of Delaware

Imagine that you, not Susan Shaw and Janet Lee, have final responsibility for *Women's Voices, Feminist Visions*. Shaw and Lee have finished arranging all the contents, and those are in their current order. Everything is ready to go to press and, at this point, you cannot move anything around. Nonetheless, you have just received an urgent message from the publisher, who wants one additional essay in the book. That essay is Pandora L. Leong's "Living Outside the Box" from *Colonize This!* (2002). Your instructor will let you know how to access this article.

Now it is up to you to figure out where to place Leong's essay in the existing volume. Leong discusses a number of feminist issues, which means that the essay could go into any one of several different sections of *Women's Voices, Feminist Visions*. You will have to decide which is the most significant of the topics that Leong raises, as that will determine into which one of the chapters of *Women's Voices, Feminist Visions* you will insert "Living Outside the Box."

But you will also have to choose where, within the chapter, to put "Living Outside the Box," and that, too, will be an important matter. If you place it at the start of a section, how might that affect readers' feelings about the essays that follow it, especially about the one that comes right after it? If you place it at the end of a section, how will its presence implicitly comment on the earlier essays in the section and perhaps color readers' reactions to the essay immediately preceding it? And if you sandwich it between two essays, midway through a section, how will that influence the way readers look at both the essay that comes before it and the one that comes after? You have a lot of power here, and you must think about how to exercise it.

Write a report to the publisher. In your report, you will need to do the following:

1. Identify the issue in Leong's "Living Outside the Box" that you think is most worth highlighting and describe what she says about it.
2. Explain how you have chosen a place for "Living Outside the Box" in *Women's Voices, Feminist Visions* and make a case for your choice.
3. Discuss the possible implications of its placement, talking briefly about the essays that will surround it.

What do you think this activity suggests about the construction of an introductory women's studies textbook? What kinds of decisions do you think Shaw and Lee had to make in developing *Women's Voices, Feminist Visions*? If you were a co-author/co-editor, would you make similar or different decisions?

central in understanding human society generally. Adrienne Rich's classic essay from the late 1970s, "Claiming an Education," articulates this demand for women as subjects of study. It also encourages you as a student to take seriously your right to be taken seriously and invites you to understand the relationship between your personal biography and the wider forces in society that affect your life. As authors of this text, we also invite your participation in knowledge creation, hoping it will be personally enriching and vocationally useful.

HOW DID WGS ORIGINATE?

The original manifestation of WGS was the emergence of women's studies programs and departments in response to the absence, misrepresentation, and trivialization of women in the higher education curriculum, as well as the ways women were systematically excluded from many positions of power and authority as college faculty and administrators. This exclusion was especially true for women of color, who experienced intersecting obstacles based upon both race and gender. In the late 1960s and early 1970s, students and faculty began demanding that the knowledge learned and shared in colleges around the country be more inclusive of women's issues, and they asked to see more women in leadership positions on college campuses. It was not unusual, for example, for entire courses in English or American literature to not include a single novel written by a woman, much less a woman of color. Literature was full of men's ideas about women—ideas that often continued to stereotype women and justify their subordination. History courses often taught only about men in wars and as leaders, and sociology courses primarily addressed women in the context of marriage and the family. Similarly, entire departments often consisted exclusively of men with perhaps a small minority of (usually white) women in junior or part-time positions. Although there have been important changes on most college campuses as women's and multicultural issues are slowly integrated into the curriculum and advances are made in terms of leadership problems, unfortunately, these problems still exist in higher education today. What kinds of people hold leadership positions on your campus?

It is important to note in terms of the history of WGS that making women subjects of study involved two strategies that together resulted in changes in the production of knowledge in higher education. First, it rebalanced the curriculum. Women as subjects of study were integrated into existing curricula through the development of new courses about women. This shifted the focus on men and men's lives in the traditional academic curriculum and gave some attention to women's lives and concerns by developing, for example, courses such as "Women and Art" and "Women in U.S. History" alongside "regular" courses that sometimes claimed to be inclusive but focused on (usually white) men. In addition, not

SYLVIA   **by Nicole Hollander**

Copyright © 1991 by Nicole Hollander. Used by permission of Nicole Hollander.

only did traditional academic departments (such as Sociology or English) offer these separate courses on women, but the development of women's studies programs and departments offered curricula on a variety of issues that focused specifically on (initially, mostly white) women's issues.

Second, the integration of women as subjects of study resulted in a transformation of traditional knowledge (what Beverly Guy-Sheftall, author of "Origins," the first essay in the reading "Forty Years of Women's Studies," calls "mainstreaming"). People began questioning the nature of knowledge, how knowledge is produced, and the applications and consequences of knowledge in wider society. This means that claims to "truth" and objective "facts" are challenged by new knowledge integrating the perspectives of marginalized people. It recognizes, for example, that a history of the American West written by migrating whites is necessarily incomplete and differs from a history written from the perspective of indigenous native people who had their land taken from them. Although the first strategy was an "add women and stir" approach, this second involved a serious challenge to traditional knowledge and its claims to truth. In this way, women's studies aimed not only to create programs of study where students might focus on women's issues and concerns, but also to integrate a perspective for looking at things that would challenge previously unquestioned knowledge. This perspective questions how such knowledge reflects women's lives and concerns, how it maintains patterns of male privilege and power, and how the consequences of such knowledge affect women and other marginalized people. As Guy-Sheftall explains in the above-mentioned essay, this approach fostered heightened consciousness and advocacy about gendered violence and was also central in the development of other academic fields such as gay and lesbian and gender studies.

Women's studies has its origins in the women's movement of the 1960s and 1970s, known as the "second wave" women's movement. The second wave refers to this twentieth-century period of social activism from the 1960s through the 1980s that addressed formal and informal inequalities associated, for example, with the workplace, family, sexuality, and reproductive freedom. The second wave movement can be distinguished from "first wave" mid-nineteenth-century women's rights and suffrage (voting) activity, which sought to overturn legal obstacles to women's participation in society, and more contemporary "third wave" movements, discussed in more detail below. As an academic discipline, women's studies was influenced by the American studies and ethnic studies programs of the late 1960s. The demand to include women and other marginalized people as subjects of study in higher education was facilitated by broad societal movements in which organizations and individuals (both women and men) focused on such issues as work and employment, family and parenting, sexuality, reproductive rights, and violence against women. The objective was to improve women's status in society and therefore the conditions of women's lives. The U.S. women's movement emerged at a moment of widespread social turmoil as various social movements questioned traditional social and sexual values, racism, poverty and other inequities, and U.S. militarism. These social movements, including the women's movement and the civil rights movement, struggled for the rights of people of color, women, the poor, gays and lesbians, the aged and the young, and the disabled, and fought to transform society through laws and policies as well as changes in attitudes and consciousness.

Two aspects of the women's movement—a commitment to personal change and to societal transformation—helped establish women's studies. In terms of the personal, the

HISTORICAL MOMENT **The First Women's Studies Department**

Following the activism of the 1960s, feminists in academia worked to begin establishing a place for the study of women. In 1970 women faculty at San Diego State University (SDSU) taught five upper-division women's studies classes on a voluntary overload basis. In the fall of that year, the SDSU senate approved a women's studies department, the first in the United States, and a curriculum of 11 courses. The school hired one full-time instructor for the program. Other instructors included students and faculty from several existing departments. Quickly, many other colleges and universities around the nation followed suit, establishing women's studies courses, programs, and departments. In 1977 academic and activist feminists formed the National Women's Studies Association (NWSA) to further the development of the discipline. NWSA held its first convention in 1979.

U.S. women's movement involved women asking questions about the cultural meanings of being a woman. Intellectual perspectives that became central to women's studies as a discipline were created from the everyday experiences of people both inside and outside the movement. Through consciousness-raising groups and other situations where some women were able to come together to talk about their lives, participants realized that they were not alone in their experiences. Problems they thought to be personal (like working outside the home all day and then coming home to work another full day doing the domestic tasks that are involved with being a wife and mother) were actually part of a much bigger

Education for All

Education for All (EFA) is an international initiative first launched in Jomtien, Thailand, in 1990 to bring the benefits of education to "every citizen in every society." In order to realize this aim, a broad coalition of national governments, civil society groups, and development agencies committed to achieving six specific education goals:

- Expand and improve comprehensive early childhood care and education, especially for the most vulnerable and disadvantaged children.
- Ensure that by 2015 all children, particularly girls, those in difficult circumstances, and those belonging to ethnic minorities, have access to, and complete, free and compulsory primary education of good quality.
- Ensure that the learning needs of all young people and adults are met through equitable access to appropriate learning and life-skills programs.
- Achieve a 50% improvement in adult literacy by 2015, especially for women, and equitable access to basic and continuing education for all adults.
- Eliminate gender disparities in primary and secondary education by 2005, and achieve gender equality in education by 2015, with a focus on ensuring girls' full and equal access to and achievement in basic education of good quality.
- Improve all aspects of the quality of education and ensure the excellence of all so that recognized and measurable learning outcomes are achieved by all, especially in literacy, numeracy and essential life skills.

Source: http://web.worldbank.org/WBSITE/EXTERNAL/TOPICS/EXTEDUCATION/0,,contentMDK:20374062~menuPK:540090~pagePK:148956~piPK:216618~theSitePK:282386,00.html.

picture of masculine privilege and female subordination. Women began to make connections and coined the phrase *the personal is political* to explain how things taken as personal or idiosyncratic have broader social, political, and economic causes and consequences. In other words, situations that we are encouraged to view as personal are actually part of broader cultural patterns and arrangements. In addition, the idea that the personal is political encouraged people to live their politics—or understandings of the world and how it is organized—in their everyday lives: to practice what they preach, in other words. This concept is illustrated in the essay (originally presented as a leaflet) "No More Miss America," written in 1968 by members of an organization called the New York Radical Women. It accompanied a protest against the 1968 Miss America beauty pageant and was one of the the first women's liberation's protest covered widely by the national media. The 10 points in the leaflet present a feminist critique of the objectification of female "beauty" and its connection to sexism, racism, and consumerism. Is this critique still relevant today? Particularly interesting about the 1968 protest was the way the media produced the idea that women were "burning their bras." Even though none took place here, and there is no evidence that any bra-burnings ever took place, the notion has survived many decades and still exists as a fabricated, yet still iconic, aspect of feminism. Why do you think this is the case? Perhaps you will burn your bras in this class. :)

By the 1970s questions were being raised about this generic notion of "woman" and the monolithic way "women's experiences" were being interpreted. In particular, critiques of the women's movement and women's studies centered on their lack of inclusivity around issues of race, class, sexual identity or orientation, and other differences. These critiques fostered, among other developments, a field of Black Women's Studies that encouraged a focus on intersectionality which continues to transform the discipline. As Bonnie Thornton Dill explains in "Intersections," the second essay in "Forty Years of Women's Studies," intersectionality involves the ways all people's experiences of gender are created by the intersection or coming together of multiple identities like race, ethnicity, social class, and so forth. The need to provide more inclusive curricula involves the necessity of incorporating knowledge by and about people of color and those who do not identify with the the binaries of gender (masculinity/femininity) or sexuality (heterosexuality/homosexuality) or who represent marginalized communities like immigrants, migrants, or the disabled. As this essay emphasizes, although intersectionality is most easily understood as multifaceted identities, it also helps explain the organization of power in society and can be used as a tool of social justice. As readings in Chapter 2 also illustrate, intersectional analyses have shown how systems of power maintain patterns of privilege and discrimination.

Within the last few decades the emergence of WGS represents not only the inclusion of intersectional analyses as mentioned above, but the movement away from a stable and fixed idea of "woman" as in "women's studies" towards a more inclusive focus on gender as "gender studies." The latter encourages the study of gender as socially constructed, historically and culturally variable, and subject to change through social and political action. Recognizing that "woman" and "man" are changeable and contested categories is central in the study of the ways gendered personhood is mapped onto physical bodies. In particular, gender studies provides knowledge and advocacy for understanding the ways bodies and gender expressions (as feminine or masculine) do not necessarily adhere to the typical female/male binary (implied in what is known as "trans" and discussed more in later chapters). However, while such a study emphasizes the ways social practices produce bodies that perform gender, it is important to note that gender performances are privileged and constrained by institutional structures that affect people who actually identify as "real" women and men. This means that even though gender studies may provide a more inclusive approach, there are social and political consequences of identifying as a woman, or living with a feminized body, that result in certain experiences and outcomes (for example, being more likely to live in poverty, or experience violence and sexual assault). The importance of understanding the experience of living as women in society, alongside the recognition of inclusivity and intersectionality, means that "women's studies" tends not to have been changed to "gender studies," but instead transformed into "women's and gender studies." This move recognizes the historical development and contemporary reality of the field of women's studies as a site for social justice for those who live and identify as women in the world.

A key term for WGS writers and activists is *patriarchy,* defined as a system where men and masculine bodies dominate because power and authority are in the hands of adult men. Discussions of patriarchy must recognize the intersectional nature of this concept whereby someone may be simultaneously privileged by gender, but face limitations based upon other identities. Men of color, for example, may benefit from patriarchy, but their expressions of masculine privilege are shaped by the politics of racism. It is important to remember that many men are supporters of women's rights and that many of the goals of the women's movement benefit men as well, although being a supporter of women's rights does not necessarily translate into men understanding how everyday privileges associated with masculinity maintain entitlements in a patriarchal society. It is one thing to feel indignant about inequality or compassion for marginalized people, and another to recognize that one's privilege is connected to the oppression of others. Connecting with the personal as political encourages men to potentially function as allies on a deeper, more authentic level. The concept of the personal is political has relevance for those with masculine privilege as

LEARNING ACTIVITY   **What's in a Name?**

Is the program that sponsors this introductory course at your institution called "Women's Studies," "Gender Studies," "Women's and Gender Studies," "Women, Gender, and Sexuality Studies," "Feminist Studies," or some other name? Have you ever stopped to think about the history and politics of the name of that unit?

In this chapter we have discussed how in its early years, women's studies tended to focus on women as an essential category and explored the ways women experienced discrimination based on sex or recovered the ways women had contributed to society. Soon a number of critiques and realizations challenged this understanding of the discipline, emphasizing that sex and gender are socially constructed ways of relating within systems of domination and subordination. This realization that gave rise to "Gender Studies" as an interdisciplinary field examines the complex interactions of biology and society, sex and gender, with a specific emphasis on how gender is constituted across forms of difference. Another contested area of study that related to but was not always central to Women's Studies and Gender Studies was sexuality. While many early second wave feminists made important connections between women's oppression and the control of sexuality, others feared the intrusion of lesbian politics. As Queer Studies emerged, debates also arose about the place of gay men, transgendered people, and queer-identified people in the Women' Studies and Gender Studies curricula.

Different colleges and universities have grappled with the controversies and developments in different ways. At Oregon State University, our program came into being in late 1972 as Women Studies. Notice the absence of the apostrophes. In the archives we have a number of memos back and forth between the founder of our program and university administrators about this. The founder argued (successfully) that women were the subject of study, not the owners of the discipline. Therefore, she contended, the program should be "Women Studies," not "Women's Studies." This name lasted for 40 years, even as the focus of our program shifted with changes in the discipline. From about 2008 to 2012 we added faculty members with expertise in multicultural, transnational, and queer feminisms, and so in 2013 we changed our name to reflect both growth in the discipline and in our specific program, and we became Women, Gender, and Sexuality Studies. As our proposal to change our name moved through the approval process, we were asked several times why we wanted to keep the word "women." Our response was two-fold: We did not want women to become invisible in our identity, and we wanted to acknowledge our history. So, as you can see, politics played a very important role in the naming of our program and shaping of our identity 40 years ago and just last year.

What about your program? Find out why your institution made the decisions it did about your program's name. Discover the history of your program's name. Has it changed over the years? Why or why not? Ask your professors how they think those choices have affected the courses and degrees the program offers. What difference do you think the name makes for you?

understandings are made about the connections between social institutions that reward men and personal experiences of gendered entitlement.

In terms of societal change, the U.S. women's movement and other social movements, have improved, and continue to improve, the lives of marginalized people through various forms of activism. The legal changes of the second wave include the passage of the Equal Pay Act of 1963 that sought equal pay for equal work, Title VII of the Civil Rights Act of 1964 that forbade workplace discrimination, and the creation of the Equal Employment Opportunity Commission (EEOC) in 1965 to enforce antidiscrimination laws (although this enforcement did not occur until 1972). Rulings in 1978 and 1991 prohibited discrimination against pregnant women and provided women workers the right to damages for sex discrimination, respectively. The Family Medical Leave Act of 1993 provides 12 weeks of unpaid, job-protected leave for workers to care for children or ill relatives (although it is required only for businesses with more than 50 employees and for workers with at least a year's tenure in their job). Affirmative action as a legal mechanism to combat discrimination was first utilized in 1961 and was extended to women in 1967, although it is increasingly under attack. Similarly, though legislation such as *Roe v. Wade* legalized abortion and provided reproductive choices for women and the FACE (Freedom of Access to Clinic Entrances) Act of 1994 protected reproductive health care workers and patients accessing these services, such gains are currently under attack as well. In terms of legal changes directly aimed at higher education, Title IX of the Education Amendments of 1972 supported equal education and forbade gender discrimination, including in sports, in schools. Since that time the Civil Rights Restoration Act of 1988 reversed a Supreme Court decision gutting Title IX, and more recent rulings (*Fitzgerald v. Barnstable School Committee*, 2009) established parents' right to sue for sex discrimination in schools under both Title IX and the Equal Protection Clause of the 14th Amendment to the Constitution. Women's right to fight in combat positions and the overturning of the anti-gay military policy "don't ask, don't tell" in 2012 also reflect the activism of the women's and other civil rights' movements, especially LGBTQ (lesbian, gay, trans, queer) activism. These examples of civil rights legislation, often taken for granted today, are the result of organized resistance and a concerted effort to democratize the legal structure of U.S. society.

Legal changes in the United States have been accompanied by relatively significant increases in the numbers of women and people of color running for political office; taking positions of authority in government, business, education, science, and the arts; and becoming more visible and active in all societal institutions. These societal changes have strengthened the demand for alternative educational models: Not only is it the right thing to include women in college life, but it is illegal to prevent their participation. Alongside Jennifer Baumgardner and Amy Richards' classic essay that encourages you to think about these second wave gains in the reading "A Day Without

Feminism," is Marge Piercy's plea to recognize the "heroines" who continue working every day in their families and communities to improve women's everyday lives. This poem/reading, titled "My Heroines," emphasizes that it is these people who write our future.

WHAT WERE THE ORIGINS OF WOMEN'S RIGHTS ACTIVISM IN THE UNITED STATES?

Although the original women's studies programs emerged out of the second wave of mid- to late-twentieth-century social activism, that activism itself was a part of an ongoing commitment to women's liberation that had its roots in late-eighteenth-century and nineteenth-century struggles for gender equity. Women had few legal, social, and economic rights in nineteenth-century U.S. society. They had no direct relationship to the law outside of their relationships as daughters or wives; in particular, married women lost property rights upon marriage. Women were also mostly barred from higher education until women's colleges started opening in the mid-nineteenth century. However, when socioeconomically privileged white women started to access higher education in the late-nineteenth century, most women of color still faced obstacles that continued through the twentieth century and into the present. Despite this, African American women like Ida B. Wells, Mary Church Terrell, and Anna Julia Cooper (see "Activist Profile") offered strategies of resistance that provided an explicit analysis of patriarchy to address racial domination.

Most early women's rights activists (then it was referred to as "woman's" rights) in the United States had their first experience with social activism in the Abolition Movement, the struggle to free slaves. These activists included such figures as Elizabeth Cady Stanton, Lucretia Mott, Susan B. Anthony, Sojourner Truth, Sarah M. and Angelina Grimké, Henry Blackwell, Frederick Douglass, and Harriet Tubman. Many abolitionists became aware of inequities elsewhere in society. Some realized that to improve women's status a separate social movement was required. In this way, for many abolitionists, their experiences with abolition inspired their desire to improve the conditions of all women's lives.

English philosopher Mary Wollstonecraft's book *A Vindication of the Rights of Woman* (1792) is seen as the first important expression of the demand for women's equality, although the beginning of the women's movement in the United States is usually dated to the Seneca Falls Convention of 1848. This convention was conceived

LEARNING ACTIVITY **The National Women's Hall of Fame**

How many significant American women can you name? Most students cannot name 20 women from American history. To learn more about some of the women who have made important contributions in the United States, visit the National Women's Hall of Fame at *www.greatwomen.org*. What is the mission of the Hall of Fame? Select five inductees and read their biographies. Why do you think they were selected for the Hall of Fame? What do you think is the significance of having a National Women's Hall of Fame?

ACTIVIST PROFILE **Anna Julia Cooper**

Anna Julia Cooper was born in North Carolina in 1858 to an enslaved woman and her white slave owner. By the later part of the nineteenth century, she had become a profound voice for the rights and dignity of black women. Even as a child, she protested the unequal treatment of women and girls, and when she attended Oberlin College, she refused to take the less rigorous course set out for women and insisted on enrolling in the men's course. By 1887, she had earned a master's degree in math, and she moved to Washington, DC, to work at the only all-black high school in the city. She became the school's principal in 1902.

Cooper saw education as the path to uplift and empowerment for black women. She insisted on preparing students for college rather than for the trades, and she was successful in sending many students on to prestigious universities. She also founded the Colored Women's League of Washington and helped begin the first black women's chapter of the YWCA.

Her book, *A Voice from the South*, offered an early analysis of the intersections of gender and race. In it she wrote, "only the BLACK WOMAN can say when and where I enter, in the quiet, undisputed dignity of my womanhood, without violence and without suing or special patronage, then and there the whole Negro race enters with me."

In 1924, Cooper became only the fourth black woman in the United States to earn a PhD. In 1930, she became president of Frelinghuysen University, a DC institution founded to provide access to education for local residents. She died in 1964 at the age of 105.

Learn more by visiting the website for the Anna Julia Cooper Project at www.cooperproject.org.

Stone Soup © 1992 Jan Eliot. Reprinted with permission of Universal Press Syndicate. All Rights Reserved.

as a response to the experience of Lucretia Mott and Elizabeth Cady Stanton, who, as delegates to the World Anti-Slavery Convention in London in 1840, were refused seating, made to sit behind a curtain, and not allowed to voice their opinions because they were women. Their experience fueled the need for an independent women's movement in the United States and facilitated the convention at Seneca Falls, New York, in July 1848. An important document, the "Declaration of Sentiments and Resolutions," came out of this convention. Authored primarily by Elizabeth Cady Stanton, it used the language of the U.S. Declaration of Independence and included a variety of demands to improve women's status in the family and in society. Woman's suffrage, the right of women to vote, was included. Other conventions were held across the country, and national organizations were formed to promote women's rights generally and suffrage in particular. These organizations included the National Woman Suffrage Association (NWSA) formed in 1869 and the National American Woman Suffrage Association (NAWSA) in 1890. NAWSA was formed from the merging of NWSA and the American Woman Suffrage Association and continues today as the League of Women Voters. Throughout all this history it is important to understand that the rights of women of color were often subordinated and "women's rights" came to mean the liberation of white women. In some cases movement leaders conspired with racist forces to keep women of color subordinated, arguing, for example, for literacy requirements for voters that enhanced the status of economically privileged women and undermined the poor, ex-slaves, and many immigrants and migrants. Despite these serious problems, the first wave women's movement fought for political personhood—a struggle that continues today. The "Anthony Amendment," the women's suffrage amendment, was introduced into Congress in 1878; it took another 42 years for this amendment to be ratified as the Nineteenth Amendment in 1920, granting women the right to vote.

WHAT IS THE STATUS OF WGS ON COLLEGE CAMPUSES TODAY?

As the reading "Forty Years of Women's Studies" explains, WGS has steadily become institutionalized, or established as a regular custom, on many college campuses. From a scattering of courses (often taught for free by committed faculty when colleges did not want to spend money on these courses) have come whole programs and departments with minors and majors of study and graduate degrees at both the master's and doctoral levels. Although most campuses adopted women's studies, some have gone with gender studies and others with feminist studies, and many have been renamed as women's and gender studies. These different names reflect different perspectives concerning knowledge about and for women. As the Learning Activity: The National Women's Hall of Fame asks, how is it institutionalized on your campus?

Professors of WGS might teach only in WGS, or they might do most of their work in another department like anthropology or history. This illustrates the multidisciplinary nature of our field: It can be taught from the point of view of many different disciplines. For the most part, however, WGS is *interdisciplinary;* that is, it combines knowledge and methodologies from across many academic disciplines. Knowledge integration has occurred at a more rapid rate in the humanities and social sciences than in the biological and physical sciences. This is primarily because these sciences are considered "objective" (free of values), with topics of study immune from consideration of issues of gender, race, and class. However, as scholars have pointed out, science is a cultural product and its methodologies are grounded in historical practices and cultural ideas. There are now courses on many campuses examining the history and current practices of science that integrate knowledge about science as a human (gendered and racialized) product.

A list of the goals or objectives of WGS might look like this:

- To understand the social construction of gender: the ways gendered personhood is mapped on to physical bodies.
- To examine the intersection of gender with other systems of inequality in women's lives, including the effects of imperialism and globalization.
- To learn about the status of women and other marginalized peoples in society and ways to improve that status through individual and collective action for social change.
- To experience how institutions in society affect individual lives and to be able to think critically about the role of patterns of privilege and discrimination in our own lives.
- To develop critical thinking skills, improve writing and speaking skills, and empower self and others.

WHAT DOES WGS HAVE TO DO WITH FEMINISM?

WGS is generally associated with feminism as a paradigm for understanding self and society. Although there are many definitions of feminism and some disagreement concerning a specific definition, there is agreement on two core principles underlying any concept of feminism. First, feminism concerns equality and justice. Because feminism is politics of equality and a social movement for social justice, it anticipates a future that guarantees human dignity and equality for all. A social movement can be defined as a sustained, collective campaign that arises as people with shared interests come together in support of a common goal. Second, feminism is inclusive and affirming of women and expressions of femininity; it celebrates women's achievements and struggles and works to provide a positive and affirming stance toward women and expressions of the feminine. As longtime feminist advocate and *Ms* magazine co-founder Gloria Steinem explains in the interview with Rachel Graham Cody titled "The Power and the Gloria," feminism is about social, economic, and political equality. Steinem makes the case that reproductive freedom is the key to women's equality, emphasizing its role in explaining poverty, educational attainments, and health outcomes.

Feminism is a personal perspective as well as a political theory and social movement that has worked as a central force in advocating women's rights and making room for other liberatory possibilities. Put this way, feminism is hardly a radical notion. In terms of transforming social inequality in a broad sense, however, it is important to note that feminism has worked alongside other social movements such as immigrant and migrant rights and indigenous peoples' movements that may or may not identify as feminist. And, while feminism is usually at the center of WGS and has embodied the discipline with advocacy for social justice and cultural plurality, the concept itself, and the often accompanying (although not always or necessarily present) "baggage" of its ideological location in the global north, can exclude those who do not identify as feminist from movements for the improvement of women's lives.

It is also important to understand that although this chapter addresses the origins of U.S. feminism, the movement for social justice takes different forms in societies around the world, and certainly feminism's multiple origins do not necessarily reside in the U.S. In addition, transnational feminism, the movement for the social, political, and economic equality of women across national boundaries, is alive and well. Transnational feminism recognizes opportunities associated with the development of alliances and networks for the emancipation of marginalized peoples worldwide. It also educates about the problems of claiming a "universal sisterhood" that ignores differences between women and claims solidarity based on shared conditions, experiences, or concerns. Such claims often result in women in the global north or "First World" societies (those with political and economic privilege in the world order) making decisions for those in developing countries of the global south or "Third World" nations. Note how the terms "First World" and "Third World" imply a hierarchical ordering. The problematic nature of these terms is underscored by the phrase "Two-Thirds World" to emphasize that the global north has defined most of the world as coming in third.

In this way, feminism recognizes both the similarities and differences in women's status worldwide. This status in developing and nonindustrialized countries is often very low, especially in societies where strict religious doctrines govern gendered behaviors. Although women in various countries around the world often tend to be in subordinate positions, the form this subordination takes varies. As a result, certain issues, like the ability of women to maintain subsistence agriculture and feed their families—matters of personal survival—take priority over the various claims to autonomy that characterize women's issues in the global north or what is often termed "westernized" societies. What are considered feminist issues in the United States are not necessarily the most important concerns of women in other parts of the world. As already mentioned, it is important to understand this in order to avoid overgeneralizing about feminism's usefulness globally, even though the notion of global feminism or transnational feminism is real and useful for political alliances across national borders. It is also important to recognize that any claims for "Western" feminisms are necessarily interpreted internationally in the context of U.S. militarism, a history of colonialism, and international "development," as well as in regard to the power of U.S.-based corporations, consumerism, and popular culture. Nonetheless, transnational feminisms underscore the similarities women share across the world and seek strategies that take into account the interdependence of women globally. And, as communication technologies have advanced, the difficulties of organizing women in all parts of the world have decreased, despite issues of access for many people.

Some feminist peace and social justice movements have used the concept of the personal is political to make the case that diverse personal narratives shared within and across cultures encourage political awareness and have the potential to foster opportunities for communication and networking in an increasingly globalized world. Indeed, transnational feminist groups have worked against militarism, global capitalism, and racism, and for issues identified by local women in specific communities worldwide. Such actions were reflected in the United Nations Fourth World Conference on Women held in Beijing, China, in 1995 and the post-Beijing gatherings of the last decades. More than 30,000 women attended the Beijing conference, and 189 governments signed the "Platform for Action." This platform was a call for concrete action to include the human rights of women and girls as part of universal human rights, thus eradicating poverty of women, removing the obstacles to women's full participation in public life and decision making, eliminating all forms of violence against women, ensuring women's access to educational and health services, and promoting actions for women's economic autonomy.

Currently, much transnational feminist emphasis is on the passage of CEDAW (Convention on the Elimination of All Forms of Discrimination Against Women), adopted by the United Nations (UN) General Assembly in 1979, and already ratified by 186 countries (over 90 percent of UN countries). CEDAW prohibits all forms of discrimination against women by legally binding the countries that ratify it to incorporate equality of men and women into their legal systems. Measures include abolishing discriminatory laws and adopting new ones, establishing tribunals to ensure the protection of women, and eliminating acts of discrimination against women by persons, organizations, or enterprises. As of this writing, although U.S. President Obama and Secretary of State Kerry support the resolution and have made ratification a priority, the measure needs 67 votes in the U.S. Senate to pass. As a result, the United States is the only industrial society that has still not yet ratified the convention because of fear among some that it would give the UN power over U.S. legal statutes and institutions.

Various kinds of feminist thought (while embracing the two core concepts described above) differ in terms of their specific explanations for understanding the social organization of gender and their ideas for social change. An important distinction among U.S. feminisms is that between liberal and radical feminisms. Liberal feminists believe in the viability of the present system (meaning the system is okay) and work within this context for change in such public areas as education and employment. Liberal feminists attempt to remove obstacles to women's full participation in public life. Strategies include education, federal and state policies, and legal statutes.

Whereas liberal feminists want a piece of the pie, and have been critiqued as conservative reformists on account of this perspective, radical feminists (sometimes known as radical cultural feminists or difference feminists) want a whole new pie. Radical feminists recognize the oppression of women as a fundamental political oppression wherein women are categorized as inferior based upon their gender. It is not enough to remove barriers to equality; rather, deeper, more transformational changes need to be made in societal institutions (like the government or media) as well as in people's heads. Patriarchy, radical feminists believe, shapes how women and men think about the world, their place in it, and their relationships with one another. Radical feminists assert that reformist solutions like those liberal feminism would enact are problematic because they work to maintain rather than

LEARNING ACTIVITY **Global Feminisms, Transnational Activism**

Feminism is not simply a U.S. phenomenon. Indigenous feminisms have arisen all over the world to address the specific issues facing women in particular places. For example, in Botswana in the early 1990s a human rights attorney named Unity Dow challenged her country's Citizenship Act. That Act, authorized in 1984, conferred citizenship on children born in Botswana only if the father was a citizen of Botswana. If the mother was a citizen of Botswana but the father was not, the children did not receive citizenship. Dow believed the law violated Botswana's constitution and challenged it in Botswana's high court. She won her case after four years of fighting for this right for women. Another Motswana woman, Musa Dube, is a biblical critic and professor at the University of Botswana. Dube uses her perspective as an African woman as a lens for interpreting the Bible. So, for example, when she reads the story of the hemorrhaging woman in Mark 5: 24–43 from an African postcolonial feminist perspective, she imagines the bleeding woman as Mama Africa, who is oppressed by sexism as well as colonialism and yet survives and participates in her own healing. Other feminists in Botswana have worked diligently to support people living with HIV/AIDS and to stop the spread of the virus through the empowerment of women.

Choose one of the nations below and research feminisms in that country. What issues facing women do feminists confront? What forms does feminist activism take? How do these feminisms and forms of activism connect with feminist issues and activism in other countries? How do feminists work together across national borders to support one another's efforts?

- Australia
- Chile
- China
- Costa Rica
- Egypt
- Ghana
- India
- Korea
- Lesotho
- Russia
- South Africa
- Turkey

undermine the system. The "No More Miss America" manifesto by the radical feminist social organization New York Radical Women illustrates these points.

Not surprisingly, although the focus of liberal feminism is on the public sphere, the focus of this radical approach is the private sphere of everyday individual consciousness and change. Radical feminist offshoots include lesbian feminism, which focuses on how compulsory heterosexuality (the cultural norm that assumes and requires heterosexuality) and heterosexual privilege (the rights and privileges of heterosexuality, such as legal marriage and being intimate in public) function to maintain power in society. Radical feminist thought also includes ecofeminism, a perspective that focuses on the association of women with nature and the environment and the simultaneous relationships among patriarchy, global economic expansion, and environmental degradation. Radical feminism tends to have a relatively fixed or biologically based idea of who is a "woman" and is often guilty of essentialism in treating all women as having common attributes and in minimizing differences among them.

Other feminist perspectives of "late modernity" (the latter part of the twentieth century) include Marxist feminism, a perspective that uses economic explanations from traditional Marxist theory to understand women's oppression. For Marxist feminists, the socioeconomic inequities of the class system are the major issues. This can be distinguished from socialist feminism, a perspective that integrates both Marxist and radical feminism. Socialist feminists use the insights of class analysis alongside radical feminist explanations of gender oppression. Contemporary socialist feminists seek to understand the workings of capitalist patriarchal institutions and often incorporate an environmental analysis that sees capitalism's push for private profits as the major cause of environmental degradation.

Many of these feminist approaches have been critiqued by the perspectives of women of color, who insist that theory be inclusive of *all* women's lives. Multiracial feminism or women of color feminism, for example, asserts that gender is constructed by a range of interlocking inequalities that work simultaneously to shape women's experience. This is the concept of intersections mentioned above. It brings together understandings drawn from the lived experiences of diverse women and influences all feminist writing today. The reading by bell hooks, "Feminist Politics: Where We Stand," fits into this genre. Indeed, expressions of feminism grounded in the lives of women of color have included *womanism*, a social change perspective rooted in the lives of black women and other women of color that emphasizes that social change begins with self-change, and critiques the location of feminism in the ivory towers of academia. This perspective was coined in 1983 by writer Alice Walker, who sought to distinguish this approach from that of white feminism. More recently, such moves by Latina/Chicana feminists include *xicanista* to represent their indigenous roots and postcolonial histories.

Finally, some feminists have utilized a postmodern perspective that focuses on the relationship between knowledge and power. Postmodern approaches question the assumption that reality has an inherent order that is discernible through scientific inquiry, reject binaries or dualistic thinking like male/female and heterosexual/homosexual, and attempt to destabilize such fixed identities. This approach recognizes changes in the organization of contemporary social life as a result, for example, of virtual technologies and increasing globalization and capitalist development. It also pays attention to how language constructs reality. Postmodernism emphasizes that humans actively construct or shape their lives in the context of various social systems, and often in the face of serious constraints. Queer theory is influenced by postmodernsim and makes the case that gender and sexuality are socially produced and used as instruments of power. "Queer," once a derogatory term, is claimed back and celebrated in this approach that emphasizes fluid notions of power and identity and seeks to dismantle the binaries of gender and sexuality.

Many writers now refer to a "third wave" of feminist activity influenced by postmodernism, queer theory, and multiracial feminism, which problematizes the universality and potential inclusivity of the term "woman." Third wave feminism has its origins in the 1990s and reflects the thinking, writing, and activism of those who came of age taking for granted the gains of second wave feminism, as well as the resistance or backlash to it. Third wave perspectives are shaped by the material conditions created by globalization and technoculture, and tend to focus on issues of sexuality and identity. Contemporary third wave activity has been important in fueling feminist activism, especially through musical and art forms, such as "zines" (consciousness-raising magazines produced locally and often shared electronically), and through social networking and other virtual technologies. C.V. Harquail writes about social networking in the reading "Facebook for Women vs. Facebook Designed by Feminists." This author imagines social networking sites as activism to improve women's lives.

Despite the advantages of using a "wave" metaphor to characterize the developments in feminism, the metaphor distracts attention from the continuity of feminist activity and runs the risk of setting up distinctions and potential intergenerational divisiveness between a more stodgy second wave generation, devoid of sexuality and unwilling to share power, and a younger, self-absorbed generation obsessed with popular culture and uncritically sexualized. And, although third wave feminism is accessible for many young women in the United States and is energizing in its focus on media, popular culture, sexuality, and so

Thank a Feminist

Thank a feminist if you agree that . . .

- Women should have the right to vote.
- Women should have access to contraceptives.
- Women should have the right to work outside the home.
- Women should receive equal pay for equal work.
- Women should have the right to refuse sex, even with their husbands.
- Women should be able to receive a higher education.
- Women should have access to safe, legal abortion.
- Women should be able to participate in sports.
- Women should be able to hold political office.
- Women should be able to choose any career that interests them.
- Women should be free from sexual harassment in the workplace.
- Women should be able to enter into legal and financial transactions.
- Women should be able to study issues about women's lives and experiences.

One hundred years ago, none of these statements was possible for women in the United States. Only through the hard work and dedication of women in each decade of the twentieth century did these rights become available to women.

Imagine a world without feminism. If you are a woman, you would not be in college. You would not be able to vote. You could not play sports. Contraception is illegal. So is abortion. You're expected to marry and raise a family. If you must work, the only jobs available to you are in cleaning, clerical services, or teaching. And you have no legal protection on the job if your boss pressures you for sex or makes lewd comments. Your husband can force you to have sex, and, if you were sexually abused as a child, most likely no one will believe you if you tell. If you are sexually attracted to women, you are considered mentally ill and may be subjected to an array of treatments for your illness.

Today, young women who claim, "I'm not a feminist, but . . ." benefit from the many gains made by feminists through the twentieth century. So the next time you go to class or vote or play basketball, thank a feminist!

IDEAS FOR ACTIVISM **Two-Minute Activist**

Many important legislative issues related to women come before elected officials regularly. You can make your voice to support women heard by contacting your senators and representatives. To become a two-minute activist ("one minute to read, one minute to act"), visit the website of the American Association of University Women (AAUW) at *www.aauw.org.* Click the "Act" button to find the Two-Minute Activist link. There, you'll find links to information about the latest issues before Congress and to prewritten AAUW messages that you can personalize and send to your representatives.

forth, it is critiqued as an "anything goes" movement. Some critics question its transformation of self rather than society, in part because of its potential ineffectiveness for collective action and structural change. In addition, they suggest third wave feminism distorts the history of the second wave and fabricates a victim and/or anti-sex feminism that actually never existed. These issues and the problems associated with the "wave" metaphors are discussed in more detail in a reading in Chapter 13 by Katha Pollit titled "Amber Waves of Blame." In this way, just as feminism encompasses diversity, so feminists do not all agree on what equality looks like or how to get there. As a social movement, feminism has always thrived on differences of ideology and practice. In "A Day Without Feminism," self-proclaimed third wavers Jennifer Baumgardner and Amy Richards actively claim feminism as relevant to their lives and do underscore the gains of second wave feminist activism.

WHAT ARE THE MYTHS ASSOCIATED WITH FEMINISM?

The most recent nationwide poll on feminism was published by CBS Broadcasting Inc. in 2009. Seventy-seven percent of people polled indicated they had more opportunities than their mother, 82 percent said their status was increased compared to 25 years ago, and 69 percent declared that the women's movement had improved their lives (80 percent of those aged 36 to 44 years indicated this). When women were asked if they identified as a feminist, however, only 24 percent agreed (and 22 percent classified this as an insult), although when the definition of feminist was included ("someone who supports the political, economic, and social equality of women"), the percentage of women identifying as feminists rose to 65 percent. An earlier poll from 2003 also found that when respondents were asked their opinion of the movement to strengthen women's rights, not the "women's rights movement," people's support was much higher. The misleading and negative connotations associated with the words "feminism" and "women's movement" play a central role in backlash, or organized resistance, and encompass what some call the "battered-word syndrome." The organized backlash to feminism also involves, for example, the ways certain groups who believe they would lose from a redistribution of power have worked hard to discredit and destroy the feminist movement and brand feminists in negative ways. This perspective is known as anti-feminism. Although such anti-feminist activity includes conservative groups and politicians, it also involves women who claim to be feminists yet are resistant to its core principles. These women, whose careers in part have been fueled by the gains brought about by the feminist movement, include such successful female academics as Christina Hoff Summers (featured in a reading in Chapter 3), Camille Paglia, Daphne Patai, Katie Roiphe, and Rene Denfield, and syndicated journalists like Mona Charen.

One result of this backlash has been the coining of the term *postfeminism* by those who recognize feminism as an important perspective but believe its time has passed and it is now obsolete. "We're already liberated" is the stance they take. The way this notion is accepted by public opinion is evidenced above by the number of people who believe the goals of the women's movement have already been met. Like other broad generalizations, there is some small truth to this: Things have improved for some women in some areas. Although generally it is accurate to say that women's status in the United States at the beginning of the twenty-first century is markedly improved, we still have a long way to go to reach full equality. In terms of the issues of poverty, violence, pornography, and health and HIV/AIDS (to name just a few), things are worse for many women than they ever have been. There are still many areas in which women's status might be enhanced, and, for the majority of the world's women, life is very difficult indeed.

The idea that women have achieved equality is reinforced by the capitalist society in which we live. Surrounded by consumer products, we are encouraged to confuse liberation

LEARNING ACTIVITY **The Dinner Party**

In *Manifesta: Young Women, Feminism, and the Future,* Jennifer Baumgardner and Amy Richards tell the story of a dinner party they had, reminiscent of the consciousness-raising meetings of the 1970s during which women shared the stories and frustrations of their lives, most of which were directly related to sexism. The point of consciousness raising was to radicalize women, to help them develop the consciousness and motivation needed to make personal and political change in the world. One night many years ago, Jennifer and Amy brought together six of their friends around a dinner table to talk about current issues for women and directions needed for the contemporary women's movement. They found that the conversation wound its way around personal experiences and stories and their political implications and strategies. Their dinner party offered the beginnings of a revolution. They write, "Every time women get together around a table and speak honestly, they are embarking on an education that they aren't getting elsewhere in our patriarchal society. And that's the best reason for a dinner party a feminist could hope for."

Have a dinner party! Invite five or six of your friends over for dinner to discuss issues related to women. What are the experiences of the people around the table in terms of sexuality, work, family, body image, media, and religion? What are the political implications of these experiences? What can be done to make the world better around these issues?

After your dinner party, write about what happened. What issues came up? What did various guests have to say about the issues? What strategies for change did the group identify? What plans for action did the group make? What did you learn from the experience?

with the freedom to purchase products or to choose among a relatively narrow range of choices. Often personal style is mistaken for personal freedom as the body becomes a focus for fashion, hair, piercing, exercise, tattoos, and so forth. We are often encouraged to confuse such freedoms of expression with freedom in the sense of equality and social justice. Of course, popular culture and media play a large part in this. We are encouraged to enjoy the freedoms that, in part, feminism has brought, often without recognition of this struggle or allegiance to maintaining such freedoms. Feminist writers explain that cultural changes exacerbated by virtual technologies often encourage young women to participate in their own objectification (being made into objects for male pleasure). They emphasize that these young women (who might consider themselves feminists) confuse their freedom to objectify themselves with authentic freedom. This is one of the points made by Susan Douglas in the Chapter 5 reading "Enlightened Sexism."

Many people, groups, and institutions have attempted to discredit feminism (and therefore WGS) in other ways. Feminism has been subject to the following associations: (1) Feminists are angry, whiny women who have an axe to grind, who have no sense of humor, and who exaggerate discrimination against women; (2) feminists hate men or want to be like men and selfishly want to create new systems of power *over* men; (3) all feminists are said to be lesbians, women who choose romantic relationships with other women; (4) feminists are said to reject motherhood, to consider children a burden, and to have rejected all things feminine; and (5) feminism is dismissed as a white, middle-class movement that draws energy away from attempts to correct social and economic problems and discourages coalition building.

While several of these myths contain grains of truth, as a whole they can easily be shattered. First, although there are some feminists who respond, some would say rightly, to societal injustices with anger, most feminists work patiently with little resentment. Men as a social group demonstrate much more anger than women, feminists included. Even though male rage comes out in numerous acts of violence, wars, school shootings, and so on, men's anger is seen merely as a human response to circumstance. Note the androcentrism at work here. Because a few angry feminists get much more publicity than the majority of those working productively to change the status quo, a better question might be why women are not more angry, given the levels of injustice against women both in the United States and worldwide. Feminists do not exaggerate this injustice; injustice is a central organizing principle of contemporary society. We should also ask why women's anger provokes such a negative response. The cause of the relatively intense reaction to women's anger is grounded in a societal mandate against female anger that works to keep women from resisting their subordination—that is, it keeps them passive. Anger is seen as destructive and inappropriate, going against what we imagine to be feminine. As a result, organized expressions of anger are interpreted as hostile.

Second, it is often said that feminists hate men. It is accurate to say that, in their affirmation of women and their desire to remove systems of inequality, feminists ask men to understand how gender privilege works in men's lives. Many men are more than willing to do this because the same social constructions of masculinity that privilege men also limit them. Because the demand for the examination of gender privilege is not synonymous with hating men, we might ask why these different concepts are so easily conflated. A more interesting question is why men are not accused more often of hating women, given the high levels of violence perpetrated by men against women. Certainly the world is full of *misogyny,* the hatred of, or contempt for, women, and every day we see examples of the

Yes, I Am

ways misogyny influences, and sometimes destroys, the lives of women. The reality, of course, is that most feminists are in relationships with men, and some feminists *are* men. Some men eagerly call themselves pro-feminist because feminism is a perspective on life. The reading by Byron Hurt, "Feminist Men," illustrates this practice. Nonetheless, the man-hating myth works to prevent many women who want to be in relationships with men from claiming feminism. They are encouraged to avoid a political stance that suggests antagonism toward men.

Feminists often respond to the declaration that they hate men with the observation that the statement illustrates a hypersensitivity about the possibility of exclusion and loss of power on the part of men. Only in a patriarchal society would the inclusion of women be interpreted as a potential threat or loss of men's power. It is a reflection of the fact that we live in a competitive patriarchal society when it is assumed that the feminist agenda is one that seeks to have power over men. Only in an androcentric society where men and their reality is center stage would it be assumed that an inclusion of one group must mean the exclusion of another. In other words, male domination encourages the idea that affirming women means hating men and interprets women's request for power sharing as a form of taking over. This projection of patriarchal mentality equates someone's gain with another's loss.

In response to the assertion that feminists want to be men, it is true to say that feminists might like to share some of the power granted to men in society. However, feminism is not about encouraging women to be like men; it's about valuing women for being women and respecting expressions of femininity no matter what body these expressions are mapped upon. People opposed to feminism often confuse *sameness* and *equality* and say that women will never be equal to men because they are different (less physically strong, more emotional, etc.) or they say that equality is dangerous because women will start being like men. Feminism, of course, affirms and works to maintain difference; it merely asks that these differences be valued equally. That is the basis of social justice.

Third, feminists are accused of being lesbians in an effort to discredit feminism and prevent women both from joining the movement and from taking WGS classes. The term for this is *lesbian baiting*. Feminism affirms women's choices to be and love whomever

"I'm really proud of my daughter. She's a thorn in the side of the patriarchy."

they choose. Although some lesbians are feminists, many lesbians are not feminists, and many feminists are heterosexual. Feminists do not interpret an association with lesbianism as an insult. Nonetheless, *homophobia,* the societal fear or hatred of lesbians and gay men, functions to maintain this as an insult. There is considerable fear associated with being called a lesbian, and this declaration that all feminists are lesbians serves to keep women in line, apart from one another, and suspicious of feminism and WGS. Note that this myth is related to the above discussion on men-hating because it is assumed that lesbians hate men too. Again, although lesbians love women, this does not necessitate a dislike of men.

Fourth, feminism does not reject motherhood but instead attempts to improve the conditions under which women mother. Contemporary legislation to improve working mothers' lives and provide safe and affordable health care, childcare, and education for children (to name just a few examples) has come about because of the work of feminists. In terms of rejecting femininity, feminists have rejected some of the constraints associated with femininity such as corsets and hazardous beauty products and practices. Mostly they strive to reclaim femininity as a valuable construct that should be respected.

Fifth, feminism has been critiqued as a white, middle-class perspective that has no relevance to the lives of women of color. The corollary of this is that WGS is only about the lives of white, bourgeois women. This critique is important because, as discussed above, the history of the women's movement provides examples of both blatant and subtle racism, and white women have been the ones to hold most positions of power and authority in those movements. Similarly, working-class women have been underrepresented. This is also reflected in the discipline of WGS as faculty and students have often been disproportionately white and economically privileged. Much work has been done to transform the women's movement into an inclusive social movement that has relevance for all people's lives. WGS departments and programs today are often among the most diverse

U.S. Suffrage Movement Timeline

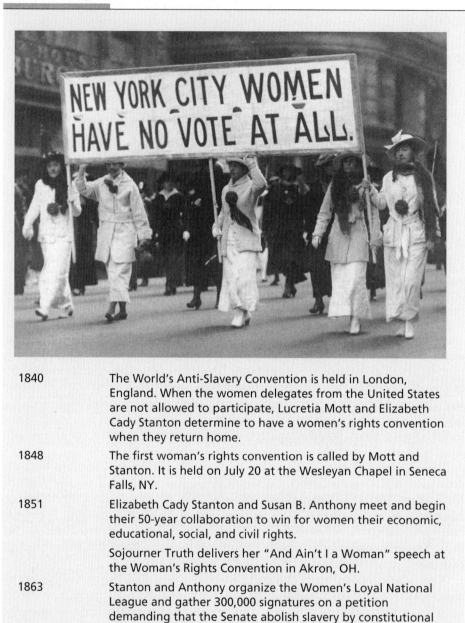

1840	The World's Anti-Slavery Convention is held in London, England. When the women delegates from the United States are not allowed to participate, Lucretia Mott and Elizabeth Cady Stanton determine to have a women's rights convention when they return home.
1848	The first woman's rights convention is called by Mott and Stanton. It is held on July 20 at the Wesleyan Chapel in Seneca Falls, NY.
1851	Elizabeth Cady Stanton and Susan B. Anthony meet and begin their 50-year collaboration to win for women their economic, educational, social, and civil rights.
	Sojourner Truth delivers her "And Ain't I a Woman" speech at the Woman's Rights Convention in Akron, OH.
1863	Stanton and Anthony organize the Women's Loyal National League and gather 300,000 signatures on a petition demanding that the Senate abolish slavery by constitutional amendment.
1866	The American Equal Rights Association is founded with the purpose to secure for all Americans their civil rights irrespective of race, color, or sex. Lucretia Mott is elected president. To test women's constitutional right to hold public office, Stanton runs for Congress, receiving 24 of 12,000 votes cast.

1867	Stanton, Anthony, and Lucy Stone address a subcommittee of the New York State Constitutional Convention requesting that the revised constitution include women's suffrage. Their efforts fail.
	Kansas holds a state referendum on whether to enfranchise blacks and/or women. Stone, Anthony, and Stanton traverse the state speaking in favor of women's suffrage. Both black and women's suffrage is voted down.
1868	The Fourteenth Amendment to the U.S. Constitution is adopted. The amendment grants suffrage to former male African American slaves, but not to women. Anthony and Stanton bitterly oppose the amendment, which for the first time explicitly restricts voting rights to "males." Many of their former allies in the abolitionist movement, including Lucy Stone, support the amendment.
1869	The National Woman Suffrage Association (NWSA) is founded with Elizabeth Cady Stanton as president.
	The American Woman Suffrage Association (AWSA) is founded with Henry Ward Beecher as president.
	Wyoming Territory grants suffrage to women.
1870	Utah Territory grants suffrage to women.
1871	Victoria Woodhull addresses the Judiciary Committee of the House of Representatives arguing that women have the right to vote under the Fourteenth Amendment. The Committee issues a negative report.
1872	In Rochester, NY, Susan B. Anthony registers and votes contending that the Fourteenth Amendment gives her that right. Several days later she is arrested.
1873	At Anthony's trial the judge does not allow her to testify on her own behalf, dismisses the jury, rules her guilty, and fines her $100. She refuses to pay.
1874	In *Minor v. Happersett,* the Supreme Court decides that citizenship does not give women the right to vote and that women's political rights are under the jurisdiction of each individual state.
1876	Stanton writes a "Declaration and Protest of the Women of the United States" to be read at the centennial celebration in Philadelphia. When the request to present the Declaration is denied, Anthony and four other women charge the speakers' rostrum and thrust the document into the hands of Vice President Thomas W. Ferry.
1882	The House of Representatives and the Senate appoint Select Committees on Woman Suffrage.
1887	The first three volumes of the *History of Woman Suffrage,* edited by Susan B. Anthony, Matilda Joslyn Gage, and Elizabeth Cady Stanton, are published.

(continued)

1890	After several years of negotiations, the NWSA and the AWSA merge to form the National American Woman Suffrage Association (NAWSA) with Elizabeth Cady Stanton, Susan B. Anthony, and Lucy Stone as officers.
	Wyoming joins the union as the first state with voting rights for women. By 1900 women also have full suffrage in Utah, Colorado, and Idaho.
	New Zealand is the first nation to give women suffrage.
1895	Elizabeth Cady Stanton publishes *The Woman's Bible,* a critical examination of the Bible's teaching about women. The NAWSA censures the work.
1896	Mary Church Terrell, Ida B. Wells-Barnett, Margaret Murray Washington, Fanny Jackson Coppin, Frances Ellen Watkins Harper, Charlotte Forten Grimké, and former slave Harriet Tubman meet in Washington, D.C., to form the National Association of Colored Women (NACW).
1902	Elizabeth Cady Stanton dies.
	Women of Australia are enfranchised.
1906	Susan B. Anthony dies. Women of Finland are enfranchised.
1910	The Women's Political Union holds its first suffrage parade in New York City.
1912	Suffrage referendums are passed in Arizona, Kansas, and Oregon.
1913	Alice Paul organizes a suffrage parade in Washington, D.C., the day of Woodrow Wilson's inauguration.
1914	Montana and Nevada grant voting rights to women.
	Alice Paul and Lucy Burns organize the Congressional Union for Woman Suffrage. It merges in 1917 with the Woman's Party to become the National Woman's Party.
	The National Federation of Women's Clubs, which by this time includes more than two million white women and women of color throughout the United States, formally endorses the suffrage campaign.
1915	Suffrage referendum in New York State is defeated.
	Women of Denmark are enfranchised.
1916	Jeannette Rankin, a Republican from Montana, is elected to the House of Representatives and becomes the first woman to serve in Congress.
1917	Members of the National Woman's Party picket the White House. Alice Paul and 96 other suffragists are arrested and jailed for "obstructing traffic." When they go on a hunger strike to protest their arrest and treatment, they are force-fed.

	Women win the right to vote in North Dakota, Ohio, Indiana, Rhode Island, Nebraska, Michigan, New York, and Arkansas.
1918	Women of Austria, Canada, Czechoslovakia, Germany, Hungary, Ireland, Poland, Scotland, and Wales are enfranchised.
	The House of Representatives passes a resolution in favor of a woman suffrage amendment. The resolution is defeated by the Senate.
1919	Women of Azerbaijan Republic, Belgium, British East Africa, Holland, Iceland, Luxembourg, Rhodesia, and Sweden are enfranchised.
	The Nineteenth Amendment to the Constitution granting women the vote is adopted by a joint resolution of Congress and sent to the states for ratification.
	New York and 21 other states ratify the Nineteenth Amendment.
1920	Henry Burn casts the deciding vote that makes Tennessee the thirty-sixth, and final, state to ratify the Nineteenth Amendment.
August 26	The Nineteenth Amendment is adopted and the women of the United States are finally enfranchised.

Source: Anthony Center for Women's Leadership: US Suffrage Movement Timeline, prepared by Mary M. Huth, Department of Rare Books and Special Collections, University of Rochester Libraries, February 1995. Obtained from *http://www.rochester.edu/SBA/timeline1.html,* August 2002.

units on college campuses, although most still have work to do. It is absolutely crucial that the study of women and other marginalized peoples as subjects both recognizes and celebrates diversity and works to transform all systems of oppression in society. In "Feminist Politics," bell hooks claims back feminism as the movement to do just that. She emphasizes that any call to sisterhood must involve a commitment on the part of white women to examine white privilege and understand the interconnections among gender, race, and class domination.

Although the women's movement has had a profound impact on the lives of women in the United States and great strides have been made toward equality, real problems still remain. Women continue to face discrimination and harassment in the workplace, domestic violence, rape and abuse, inequities in education, poverty, racism, and homophobia. Anna Quindlen responds to this in the short reading "Still Needing the F Word." WGS provides a forum for naming the problems women face, analyzing the root causes of these problems, envisioning a just and equitable world, and developing strategies for change. As you read the following articles, keep these questions in mind: What does the author identify as problems women face? What does the author suggest is the root of these problems? What strategies does the author suggest for bringing about change to improve the lives of women?

Claiming an Education

Adrienne Rich (1979)

For this convocation, I planned to separate my remarks into two parts: some thoughts about you, the women students here, and some thoughts about us who teach in a women's college. But ultimately, those two parts are indivisible. If university education means anything beyond the processing of human beings into expected roles, through credit hours, tests, and grades (and I believe that in a women's college especially it *might* mean much more), it implies an ethical and intellectual contract between teacher and student. This contract must remain intuitive, dynamic, unwritten; but we must turn to it again and again if learning is to be reclaimed from the depersonalizing and cheapening pressures of the present-day academic scene.

The first thing I want to say to you who are students is that you cannot afford to think of being here to *receive* an education; you will do much better to think of yourselves as being here to *claim* one. One of the dictionary definitions of the verb "to claim" is *to take as the rightful owner; to assert in the face of possible contradiction.* "To receive" is *to come into possession of; to act as receptacle or container for; to accept as authoritative or true.* The difference is that between acting and being acted-upon, and for women it can literally mean the difference between life and death.

One of the devastating weaknesses of university learning, of the store of knowledge and opinion that has been handed down through academic training, has been its almost total erasure of women's experience and thought from the curriculum, and its

exclusion of women as members of the academic community. Today, with increasing numbers of women students in nearly every branch of higher learning, we still see very few women in the upper levels of faculty and administration in most institutions. Douglass College itself is a women's college in a university administered overwhelmingly by men, who in turn are answerable to the state legislature, again composed predominantly of men. But the most significant fact for you is that what you learn here, the very texts you read, the lectures you hear, the way your studies are divided into categories and fragmented one from the other—all this reflects, to a very large degree, neither objective reality, nor an accurate picture of the past, nor a group of rigorously tested observations about human behavior. What you can learn here (and I mean not only at Douglass but any college in any university) is how *men* have perceived and organized their experience, their history, their ideas of social relationships, good and evil, sickness and health, etc. When you read or hear about "great issues," "major texts," "the mainstream of Western thought," you are hearing about what men, above all white men, in their male subjectivity, have decided is important.

Black and other minority peoples have for some time recognized that their racial and ethnic experience was not accounted for in the studies broadly labeled human; and that even the sciences can be racist. For many reasons, it has been more difficult for women to comprehend our exclusion, and to realize that even the sciences can be sexist. For one thing, it is only within the last hundred years that higher education has grudgingly been opened up to women at all, even to white, middle-class women. And many of us have found ourselves poring eagerly over books with titles like *The Descent of Man; Man and His Symbols; Irrational Man; The Phenomenon*

This talk was given at the Douglass College Convocation, September 6, 1977, and first printed in *The Common Woman,* a feminist literary magazine founded by Rutgers University women in New Brunswick, New Jersey.

of Man; The Future of Man; Man and the Machine; From Man to Man; May Man Prevail?; Man, Science and Society; or *One-Dimensional Man*—books pretending to describe a "human" reality that does not include over one-half the human species.

Less than a decade ago, with the rebirth of a feminist movement in this country, women students and teachers in a number of universities began to demand and set up women's studies courses—to *claim* a woman-directed education. And, despite the inevitable accusations of "unscholarly," "group therapy," "faddism," etc., despite backlash and budget cuts, women's studies are still growing, offering to more and more women a new intellectual grasp on their lives, new understanding of our history, a fresh vision of the human experience, and also a critical basis for evaluating what they hear and read in other courses, and in the society at large.

But my talk is not really about women's studies, much as I believe in their scholarly, scientific, and human necessity. While I think that any Douglass student has everything to gain by investigating and enrolling in women's studies courses, I want to suggest that there is a more essential experience that you owe yourselves, one which courses in women's studies can greatly enrich, but which finally depends on you, in all your interactions with yourself and your world. This is the experience of *taking responsibility toward your selves.* Our upbringing as women has so often told us that this should come second to our relationships and responsibilities to other people. We have been offered ethical models of the self-denying wife and mother; intellectual models of the brilliant but slapdash dilettante who never commits herself to anything the whole way, or the intelligent woman who denies her intelligence in order to seem more "feminine," or who sits in passive silence even when she disagrees inwardly with everything that is being said around her.

Responsibility to yourself means refusing to let others do your thinking, talking, and naming for you; it means learning to respect and use your own brains and instincts; hence, grappling with hard work. It means that you do not treat your body as a commodity with which to purchase superficial intimacy or economic security; for our bodies and minds are inseparable in this life, and when we allow our bodies to be treated as objects, our minds are in mortal danger. It means insisting that those to whom you give your friendship and love are able to respect your mind. It means being able to say, with Charlotte Brontë's *Jane Eyre:* "I have an inward treasure born with me, which can keep me alive if all the extraneous delights should be withheld or offered only at a price I cannot afford to give."

Responsibility to yourself means that you don't fall for shallow and easy solutions: predigested books and ideas, weekend encounters guaranteed to change your life, taking "gut" courses instead of ones you know will challenge you, bluffing at school and life instead of doing solid work, marrying early as an escape from real decisions, getting pregnant as an evasion of already existing problems. It means that you refuse to sell your talents and aspirations short, simply to avoid conflict and confrontation. And this, in turn, means resisting the forces in society which say that women should be nice, play safe, have low professional expectations, drown in love and forget about work, live through others, and stay in the places assigned to us. It means that we insist on a life of meaningful work, insist that work be as meaningful as love and friendship in our lives. It means, therefore, the courage to be "different"; not to be continuously available to others when we need time for ourselves and our work; to be able to demand of others—parents, friends, roommates, teachers, lovers, husbands, children—that they respect our sense of purpose and our integrity as persons. Women everywhere are finding the courage to do this, more and more, and we are finding that courage both in our study of women in the past who possessed it, and in each other as we look to other women for comradeship, community, and challenge. The difference between a life lived actively, and a life of passive drifting and dispersal of energies, is an immense difference. Once we begin to feel committed to our lives, responsible to ourselves, we can never again be satisfied with the old, passive way.

Now comes the second part of the contract. I believe that in a women's college you have the right to expect your faculty to take you seriously. The education of women has been a matter of debate for centuries, and old, negative attitudes about women's role, women's ability to think and take leadership, are still rife both in and outside the university. Many male professors (and I don't mean only at Douglass) still feel that teaching in a women's college is a second-rate career. Many tend to eroticize their women students—to treat them as sexual objects—instead of demanding the best of their minds. (At Yale a legal suit [*Alexander v. Yale*] has been brought against the university by a group of women students demanding a stated policy against sexual advances toward female students by male professors.) Many teachers, both men and women, trained in the male-centered tradition, are still handing the ideas and texts of that tradition on to students without teaching them to criticize its antiwoman attitudes, its omission of women as part of the species. Too often, all of us fail to teach the most important thing, which is that clear thinking, active discussion, and excellent writing are all necessary for intellectual freedom, and that these require *hard work*. Sometimes, perhaps in discouragement with a culture which is both antiintellectual and antiwoman, we may resign ourselves to low expectations for our students before we have given them half a chance to become more thoughtful, expressive human beings. We need to take to heart the words of Elizabeth Barrett Browning, a poet, a thinking woman, and a feminist, who wrote in 1845 of her impatience with studies which cultivate a "passive recipiency" in the mind, and asserted that "women want to be made to *think actively:* their apprehension is quicker than that of men, but their defect lies for the most part in the logical faculty and in the higher mental activities." Note that she implies a defect which can be remedied by intellectual training—*not* an inborn lack of ability.

I have said that the contract on the student's part involves that you demand to be taken seriously so that you can also go on taking yourself seriously. This means seeking out criticism, recognizing that the most affirming thing anyone can do for you is demand that you push yourself further, show you the range of what you *can* do. It means rejecting attitudes of "take-it-easy," "why-be-so-serious," "why-worry-you'll-probably-get-married-anyway." It means assuming your share of responsibility for what happens in the classroom, because that affects the quality of your daily life here. It means that the student sees herself engaged *with* her teachers in an active, ongoing struggle for a real education. But for her to do this, her teachers must be committed to the belief that women's minds and experience are intrinsically valuable and indispensable to any civilization worthy [of] the name; that there is no more exhilarating and intellectually fertile place in the academic world today than a women's college—*if* both students and teachers in large enough numbers are trying to fulfill this contract. The contract is really a pledge of mutual seriousness about women, about language, ideas, methods, and values. It is our shared commitment toward a world in which the inborn potentialities of so many women's minds will no longer be wasted, raveled-away, paralyzed, or denied.

R E A D I N G   2

Forty Years of Women's Studies

Origins

Beverly Guy-Sheftall (2009)

Women's studies, as a distinct entity within U.S. higher education, made its debut in 1970 with the establishment of the first program at San Diego State University. Forty years later, there are more than 900 programs in the U.S., boasting well over 10,000 courses and an enrollment larger than that of any other interdisciplinary field. And women's studies has gone international in a big way: Students can find programs and research centers everywhere from Argentina to India to Egypt to Japan to Uganda—more than 40 countries in all, from nearly every region of the globe.

As it has developed on individual campuses, women's studies has also reached out to a wider audience by creating a wealth of scholarship in print. The U.S. can now boast more than 30 refereed women's studies journals, and hundreds of monographs in the field have been published by university presses and trade houses.

Want to earn a doctorate in women's studies? You have 13 choices of programs in the U.S. plus those in Canada, Australia and England. Want to teach? Colleges and universities across the nation routinely advertise faculty searches in women's studies programs and departments, and award prestigious endowed professorships in the field. Want to put your degree to work outside of higher education? There is a growing domestic and international market for women's studies graduates in government, policy and research institutes, foundations and nonprofit organizations.

During the 1970s, the pioneers of women's studies focused on establishing the field as a separate discipline with autonomous programs. In the 1980s, the focus expanded to include "mainstreaming" women's studies throughout the established curriculum, incorporating feminist scholarship within many academic disciplines. In that way, women's studies wouldn't remain in an academic ghetto, but could begin to transform and gender-balance every aspect of the curriculum.

Also in the 80s, women of color began to critique both women's studies and gender-focused curriculum projects for their relative lack of attention to questions of race, ethnicity, class and cultural differences. One of the hardest-hitting examinations of the insensitivity of women's studies to difference can be found in the pioneering work of feminist theorist bell hooks, especially her book *Feminist Theory: From Margin to Center* (1984), in which she illuminated the impact of employing a monolithic conception of women's experiences in the new scholarship on gender and sexuality.

Responding to such critiques, a new field of study emerged—black women's studies, which now

provides a framework for moving women of color from the margins of women's studies to its center. The 1982 book *All the Women Are White, All the Blacks Are Men, but Some of Us Are Brave* (edited by Gloria Hull, Patricia Bell Scott and Barbara Smith) helped catalyze this transformation of women's studies, providing a theoretical rationale for incorporating "minority women's studies" and "intersectional" analyses into all teaching and research on women.

In these 40 years since its inception, women's studies has revamped and revitalized major disciplines in the academy. It has challenged curricular and pedagogical practice. It has disrupted the male-centered canon. It has altered or blurred the boundaries between disciplines. It has introduced the social construction of gender and its intersections with race, class, ethnicity and sexuality as a major focus of inquiry And it has experienced phenomenal and unanticipated growth, becoming institutionalized on college and university campuses, spurring the hiring of feminist faculty, adding graduate courses of groundbreaking content, generating a large body of educational resources and providing the impetus for the establishment of feminist research centers. It has stimulated the development of *other* academic fields as well: gay and lesbian studies, cultural studies, gender studies, men's studies, peace studies and more.

Even more compelling, perhaps, are the profound changes that have occurred over the past 40 years as a result of the feminist activism, teaching and research stimulated by women's studies. There is heightened consciousness and advocacy around rape, incest, battering, sexual harassment, sex trafficking, the feminization of poverty, and health disparities related to race, gender and class. In addition, there is more intense dialogue about government-subsidized child care, health-care reform, sex equity in education and spousal leave. It is unfortunately still the case that empowerment strategies for women do not necessarily address the particular experiences and needs of women of color or poor women, but this just gives women's studies scholars and activists a challenge for the future.

Because of its potential for societal transformation, women's studies should be supported more than ever during this paradoxical period of assault or backlash, on the one hand, and increased demand from students plus the growing imperatives of diversity and inclusion on the other. A well-organized right-wing movement, inside and outside of higher education, still employs outmoded but persistent racist, sexist and homophobic schemes to try and reverse progressive reforms. We cannot let that happen. We need to advocate even more loudly and clearly for the revamping of mainstream curricula that remain insensitive to racial, ethnic, cultural, sexual and class differences—a campaign in which women's studies plays a crucial role.

Women's studies must also work more closely with other interdisciplinary programs, and provide expertise—along with ethnic studies—to the important multicultural initiatives taking place on many campuses. Feminist scholars must continue to conduct research and generate data to inform public policy debates and decision-making that will affect women and families in the U.S. and around the globe.

This is the greatest challenge for our field: to transcend the boundaries of race, ethnicity, class, sexuality, age, geography and language in the interest of a feminism that is expansive and responsive. After 40 years, we know that women's studies is more than up to it.

Intersections

Bonnie Thornton Dill (2009)

As a black scholar writing about women's issues in the late 1970s, I joined others in arguing that women's studies needed to incorporate a more complex approach to understanding women's lives. My colleagues and I contended that the gender analyses of that period were too often derived from the experiences of White middle-class women, and ignored the oft-untold stories of women of color and those without economic privilege. We wanted feminist theory to incorporate the notion of difference, beginning with race, ethnicity, class and culture.

Today, one of the *first* things students learn in women's studies classes is how to look at women's lives through these multiple lenses. The concept of *intersectionality* has been a key factor in this transition. Intersectionality has brought the distinctive knowledge and perspectives of previously ignored groups of women into general discussion and awareness, and has shown how the experience of gender differs by race, class and other dimensions of inequality.

For example, one impact of gender in schools is that girls are more likely than boys to be steered away from math and science. Class differences then compound the effects of gender, because low-income girls interested in math and science are likely to attend schools with poorly equipped labs and fewer certified teachers—thus their training may make it harder for them to compete successfully at higher levels. Race adds another layer of differentiation because White and middle-class teachers—who are the majority of educators—are likely to have higher expectations of White girls than of Black girls. As research has shown, they give White girls tasks that develop their academic abilities while giving Black girls tasks that focus on their social maturity and caretaking competencies.

Women's studies students tend to grasp the concept of intersectionality most readily in relationship to personal identity. They understand immediately that their sense of self is multifaceted, that they have been shaped by a number of different (and sometimes conflicting) social factors and that their behaviors cannot be understood in a one-dimensional manner.

Yet intersectionality is also an important way of understanding the organization of society—the distribution of power within it and the relationship of power and privilege to individual experience. At the societal level, intersectional analysis seeks to reveal the ways systems of power are used to develop and maintain privileges for some groups and deprivations for others. As an example, well-financed and -equipped public services—schools, health and recreational facilities, libraries—are more likely to be located in communities with high concentrations of middle- and upper-income white people.

Finally, intersectionality is a tool for social justice. Its focus is to transform knowledge by fully incorporating the ideas, experiences and critical perspectives of previously excluded groups. That knowledge can then be used to advocate for policies and practices that will eliminate inequality.

No More Miss America

New York Radical Women (1968)

1. *The Degrading Mindless-Boob-Girlie Symbol.* The Pageant contestants epitomize the roles we are all forced to play as women. The parade down the runway blares the metaphor of the 4-H Club county fair, where the nervous animals are judged for teeth, fleece, etc., and where the best "Specimen" gets the blue ribbon. So are women in our society forced daily to compete for male approval, enslaved by ludicrous "beauty" standards we ourselves are conditioned to take seriously.

2. *Racism with Roses.* Since its inception in 1921, the Pageant has not had one Black finalist, and this has not been for a lack of test-case contestants. There has never been a Puerto Rican, Alaskan, Hawaiian, or Mexican-American winner. Nor has there ever been a *true* Miss America—an American Indian.

3. *Miss America as Military Death Mascot.* The highlight of her reign each year is a cheerleader-tour of American troops abroad— last year she went to Vietnam to pep-talk our husbands, fathers, sons and boyfriends into dying and killing with a better spirit. She personifies the "unstained patriotic American womanhood our boys are fighting for." The Living Bra and the Dead Soldier. We refuse to be used as Mascots for Murder.

4. *The Consumer Con-Game.* Miss America is a walking commercial for the Pageant's sponsors. Wind her up and she plugs your product on promotion tours and TV-all in an "honest, objective" endorsement. What a shill.

5. *Competition Rigged and Unrigged.* We deplore the encouragement of an American myth that oppresses men as well as women: the win-or-you're-worthless competitive disease. The "beauty contest" creates only one winner to be "used" and forty-nine losers who are "useless."

6. *The Woman as Pop Culture Obsolescent Theme.* Spindle, mutilate, and then discard tomorrow. What is so ignored as last year's Miss America? This only reflects the gospel of our Society, according to Saint Male: women must be young, juicy, malleable-hence age discrimination and the cult of youth. And we women are brainwashed into believing this ourselves!

7. *The Unbeatable Madonna-Whore Combination.* Miss America and Playboy's centerfold are sisters over the skin. To win approval, we must be both sexy and wholesome, delicate but able to cope, demure yet titillatingly bitchy. Deviation of any sort brings, we are told, disaster: "You won't get a man!!"

8. *The Irrelevant Crown on the Throne of Mediocrity.* Miss America represents what women are supposed to be: inoffensive, bland, apolitical. If you are tall, short, over or under what weight The Man prescribes you should be, forget it. Personality, articulateness, intelligence, and commitment—unwise. Conformity is the key to the crown—and, by extension, to success in our Society.

9. *Miss America as Dream Equivalent To—?* In this reputedly democratic society, where every little boy supposedly can grow up to be President, what can every little girl hope to grow to be? Miss America. That's where it's at. Real power to control our own lives is restricted to men, while women get patronizing pseudo-power, an ermine clock and a bunch of flowers; men are judged by their actions, women by appearance.

10. *Miss America as Big Sister Watching You.* The pageant exercises Thought Control, attempts

to sear the Image onto our minds, to further make women oppressed and men oppressors; to enslave us all the more in high-heeled, low-status roles; to inculcate false values in young girls; women as beasts of buying; to seduce us to our selves before our own oppression.

R E A D I N G   4

A Day Without Feminism

Jennifer Baumgardner and Amy Richards (2000)

We were both born in 1970, the baptismal moment of a decade that would change dramatically the lives of American women. The two of us grew up thousands of miles apart, in entirely different kinds of families, yet we both came of age with the awareness that certain rights had been won by the women's movement. We've never doubted how important feminism is to people's lives—men's and women's. Both of our mothers went to consciousness-raising-type groups. Amy's mother raised Amy on her own, and Jennifer's mother, questioning the politics of housework, staged laundry strikes.

With the dawn of not just a new century but a new millennium, people are looking back and taking stock of feminism. Do we need new strategies? Is feminism dead? Has society changed so much that the idea of a feminist movement is obsolete? For us, the only way to answer these questions is to imagine what our lives would have been if the women's movement had never happened and the conditions for women had remained as they were in the year of our births.

Imagine that for a day it's still 1970, and women have only the rights they had then. Sly and the Family Stone and Dionne Warwick are on the radio, the kitchen appliances are Harvest Gold, and the name of your Whirlpool gas stove is Mrs. America. What is it like to be female?

Babies born on this day are automatically given their father's name. If no father is listed, "illegitimate" is likely to be typed on the birth certificate. There are virtually no child-care centers, so all preschool children are in the hands of their mothers, a baby-sitter, or an expensive nursery school. In elementary school, girls can't play in Little League and almost all of the teachers are female. (The latter is still true.) In a few states, it may be against the law for a male to teach grades lower than the sixth, on the basis that it's unnatural, or that men can't be trusted with young children.

In junior high, girls probably take home ec; boys take shop or small-engine repair. Boys who want to learn how to cook or sew on a button are out of luck, as are girls who want to learn how to fix a car. *Seventeen* magazine doesn't run feminist-influenced current columns like "Sex + Body" and "Trauma-rama." Instead, the magazine encourages girls not to have sex; pleasure isn't part of its vocabulary. Judy Blume's books are just beginning to be published, and *Free to Be . . . You and Me* does not exist. No one reads much about masturbation as a natural activity; nor do they learn that sex is for anything other than procreation. Girls do read mystery stories about Nancy Drew, for whom there is no sex, only her blue roadster and having "luncheon." (The real mystery is how Nancy gets along without a purse and manages to meet only white people.) Boys read about the Hardy Boys, for whom there are no girls.

In high school, the principal is a man. Girls have physical-education class and play half-court basketball, but not soccer, track, or cross country; nor do they have any varsity sports teams. The only prestigious physical activity for girls is cheerleading, or being a drum majorette. Most girls don't take calculus or physics; they plan the dances and decorate the gym. Even when girls get better grades than their male counterparts, they are half as likely to qualify for a National Merit Scholarship because many of the test questions favor boys. Standardized tests refer to males and male experiences much more than to females and their experiences. If a girl "gets herself pregnant," she loses her membership in the National Honor Society (which is still true today) and is expelled.

Girls and young women might have sex while they're unmarried, but they may be ruining their chances of landing a guy full-time, and they're probably getting a bad reputation. If a pregnancy happens, an enterprising gal can get a legal abortion only if she lives in New York or is rich enough to fly there, or to Cuba, London, or Scandinavia. There's also the Chicago-based Jane Collective, an underground abortion-referral service, which can hook you up with an illegal or legal termination. (Any of these options are going to cost you. Illegal abortions average $300 to $500, sometimes as much as $2,000.) To prevent pregnancy, a sexually active woman might go to a doctor to be fitted for a diaphragm, or take the high-dose birth-control pill, but her doctor isn't likely to inform her of the possibility of deadly blood clots. Those who do take the Pill also may have to endure this contraceptive's crappy side effects: migraine headaches, severe weight gain, irregular bleeding, and hair loss (or gain), plus the possibility of an increased risk of breast cancer in the long run. It is unlikely that women or their male partners know much about the clitoris and its role in orgasm unless someone happens to fumble upon it. Instead, the myth that vaginal orgasms from penile penetration are the only "mature" (according to Freud) climaxes prevails.

Lesbians are rarely "out," except in certain bars owned by organized crime (the only businessmen who recognize this untapped market), and if lesbians don't know about the bars, they're less likely to know whether there are any other women like them. Radclyffe Hall's depressing early-twentieth-century novel *The Well of Loneliness* pretty much indicates their fate.

The Miss America Pageant is the biggest source of scholarship money for women. Women can't be students at Dartmouth, Columbia, Harvard, West Point, Boston College, or the Citadel, among other all-male institutions. Women's colleges are referred to as "girls' schools." There are no Take Back the Night marches to protest women's lack of safety after dark, but that's okay because college girls aren't allowed out much after dark anyway. Curfew is likely to be midnight on Saturday and 9 or 10 p.m. the rest of the week. Guys get to stay out as late as they want. Women tend to major in teaching, home economics, English, or maybe a language—a good skill for translating someone else's words. The women's studies major does not exist, although you can take a women's studies course at six universities, including Cornell and San Diego State College. The absence of women's history, black history, Chicano studies, Asian-American history, queer studies, and Native American history from college curricula implies that they are not worth studying. A student is lucky if he or she learns that women were "given" the vote in 1920, just as Columbus "discovered" America in 1492. They might also learn that Sojourner Truth, Mary Church Terrell, and Fannie Lou Hamer were black abolitionists or civil-rights leaders, but not that they were feminists. There are practically no tenured female professors at any school, and campuses are not racially diverse. Women of color are either not there or they're lonely as hell. There is no nationally recognized Women's History Month or Black History Month. Only 14 percent of doctorates are awarded to women. Only 3.5 percent of MBAs are female.

Only 2 percent of everybody in the military is female, and these women are mostly nurses. There are no female generals in the U.S. Air Force, no female naval pilots, and no Marine brigadier generals. On the religious front, there are no female cantors or rabbis, Episcopal canons, or Catholic priests. (This is still true of Catholic priests.)

Only 44 percent of women are employed outside the home. And those women make, on average, fifty-two cents to the dollar earned by males. Want ads are segregated into "Help Wanted Male" and "Help Wanted Female." The female side is preponderantly for secretaries, domestic workers, and other low-wage service jobs, so if you're a female lawyer you must look under "Help Wanted Male." There are female doctors, but twenty states have only five female gynecologists or fewer. Women workers can be fired or demoted for being pregnant, especially if they are teachers, since the kids they teach aren't supposed to think that women have sex. If a boss demands sex, refers to his female employee exclusively as "Baby," or says he won't pay her unless she gives him a blow job, she has to either quit or succumb—no pun intended. Women can't be airline pilots. Flight attendants are "stewardesses"—waitresses in the sky—and necessarily female. Sex appeal is a job requirement, wearing makeup is a rule, and women are fired if they exceed the age or weight deemed sexy. Stewardesses can get married without getting canned, but this is a new development. (In 1968 the Equal Employment Opportunity Commission—EEOC—made it illegal to forcibly retire stewardesses for getting hitched.) Less than 2 percent of dentists are women; 100 percent of dental assistants are women. The "glass ceiling" that keeps women from moving naturally up the ranks, as well as the sticky floor that keeps them unnaturally down in low-wage work, has not been named, much less challenged.

When a woman gets married, she vows to love, honor, and obey her husband, though he gets off doing just the first two to uphold his end of the bargain. A married woman can't obtain credit without her husband's signature. She doesn't have her own credit rating, legal domicile, or even her own name unless she goes to court to get it back. If she gets a loan with her husband—and she has a job—she may have to sign a "baby letter" swearing that she won't have one and have to leave her job.

Women have been voting for up to fifty years, but their turnout rate is lower than that for men, and they tend to vote right along with their husbands, not with their own interests in mind. The divorce rate is about the same as it is in 2000, contrary to popular fiction's blaming the women's movement for divorce. However, divorce required that one person be at fault, therefore if you just want out of your marriage, you have to lie or blame your spouse. Property division and settlements, too, are based on fault. (And at a time when domestic violence isn't a term, much less a crime, women are legally encouraged to remain in abusive marriages.) If fathers ask for custody of the children, they get it in 60 to 80 percent of the cases. (This is still true.) If a husband or a lover hits his partner, she has no

shelter to go to unless she happens to live near the one in northern California or the other in upper Michigan. If a woman is downsized from her role as a housewife (a.k.a. left by her husband), there is no word for being a displaced homemaker. As a divorcée, she may be regarded as a family disgrace or as easy sexual prey. After all, she had sex with one guy, so why not *all* guys?

If a woman is not a Mrs., she's a Miss. A woman without makeup and a hairdo is as suspect as a man with them. Without a male escort she may be refused service in a restaurant or a bar, and a woman alone is hard-pressed to find a landlord who will rent her an apartment. After all, she'll probably be leaving to get married soon, and, if she isn't, the landlord doesn't want to deal with a potential brothel.

Except among the very poor or in very rural areas, babies are born in hospitals. There are no certified midwives, and women are knocked out during birth. Most likely, they are also strapped down and lying down, made to have the baby against gravity for the doctor's convenience. If he has a schedule to keep, the likelihood of a cesarean is also very high. *Our Bodies, Ourselves* doesn't exist, nor does the women's health movement. Women aren't taught how to look at their cervixes, and their bodies are nothing to worry their pretty little heads about; however, they are supposed to worry about keeping their little heads pretty. If a woman goes under the knife to see if she has breast cancer, the surgeon won't wake her up to consult about her options before performing a Halsted mastectomy (a disfiguring radical procedure, in which the breast, the muscle wall, and the nodes under the arm, right down to the bone, are removed). She'll just wake up and find that the choice has been made for her.

Husbands are likely to die eight years earlier than their same-age wives due to the stress of having to support a family and repress an emotional life, and a lot earlier than that if women have followed the custom of marrying older, authoritative, paternal men. The stress of raising kids, managing a household, and being undervalued by society doesn't seem to kill off women at the same rate. Upon a man's death, his beloved gets a portion of his Social Security. Even if she has worked outside the home for her entire adult life, she is probably better off with that portion than with hers in its entirety, because she has earned less and is likely to have taken time out for such unproductive acts as having kids.

Has feminism changed our lives? Was it necessary? After thirty years of feminism, the world we inhabit barely resembles the world we were born into. And there's still a lot left to do.

Feminist Politics
Where We Stand

bell hooks (2000)

Simply put, feminism is a movement to end sexism, sexist exploitation, and oppression. This was a definition of feminism I offered in *Feminist Theory: From Margin to Center* more than 10 years ago. It was my hope at the time that it would become a common definition everyone would use. I liked this definition because it did not imply that men were the enemy. By naming sexism as the problem it went directly to the heart of the matter. Practically, it is a definition which implies that all sexist thinking and action is the problem, whether those who perpetuate it are female or male, child or adult. It is also broad enough to include an understanding of systemic institutionalized sexism. As a definition it is open-ended. To understand feminism it implies one has to necessarily understand sexism.

As all advocates of feminist politics know, most people do not understand sexism, or if they do, they think it is not a problem. Masses of people think that feminism is always and only about women seeking to be equal to men. And a huge majority of these folks think feminism is anti-male. Their misunderstanding of feminist politics reflects the reality that most folks learn about feminism from patriarchal mass media. The feminism they hear about the most is portrayed by women who are primarily committed to gender equality—equal pay for equal work, and sometimes women and men sharing household chores and parenting. They see that these women are usually white and materially privileged. They know from mass media that women's liberation focuses on the freedom to have abortions, to be lesbians, to challenge rape and domestic violence. Among these issues, masses of people agree with the idea of gender equity in the workplace—equal pay for equal work.

Since our society continues to be primarily a "Christian" culture, masses of people continue to believe that god has ordained that women be subordinate to men in the domestic household. Even though masses of women have entered the workforce, even though many families are headed by women who are the sole breadwinners, the vision of domestic life which continues to dominate the nation's imagination is one in which the logic of male domination is intact, whether men are present in the home or not. The wrongminded notion of feminist movement which implied it was anti-male carried with it the wrongminded assumption that all female space would necessarily be an environment where patriarchy and sexist thinking would be absent. Many women, even those involved in feminist politics, chose to believe this as well.

There was indeed a great deal of anti-male sentiment among early feminist activists who were responding to male domination with anger. It was that anger at injustice that was the impetus for creating a women's liberation movement. Early on most feminist activists (a majority of whom were white) had their consciousness raised about the nature of male domination when they were working in anti-classist and anti-racist settings with men who were telling the world about the importance of freedom while subordinating the women in their ranks. Whether it was white women working on behalf of socialism, black women working on behalf of civil rights and black liberation, or Native American women working for indigenous rights, it was clear that men wanted to lead, and they wanted women to follow. Participating in these radical freedom struggles awakened the spirit of rebellion and resistance in progressive females and led them towards contemporary women's liberation.

As contemporary feminism progressed, as women realized that males were not the only group in our society who supported sexist thinking and behavior—that females could be sexist as well—anti-male sentiment no longer shaped the movement's consciousness. The focus shifted to an all-out effort to create gender justice. But women could not band together to further feminism without confronting our sexist thinking. Sisterhood could not be powerful as long as women were competitively at war with one another. Utopian visions of sisterhood based solely on the awareness of the reality that all women were in some way victimized by male domination were disrupted by discussions of class and race. Discussions of class differences occurred early on in contemporary feminism, preceding discussions of race. Diana Press published revolutionary insights about class divisions between women as early as the mid-70s in their collection of essays *Class and Feminism*. These discussions did not trivialize the feminist insistence that "sisterhood is powerful," they simply emphasized that we could only become sisters in struggle by confronting the ways women—through sex, class, and race—dominated and exploited other women, and created a political platform that would address these differences.

Even though individual black women were active in contemporary feminist movement from its inception, they were not the individuals who became the "stars" of the movement, who attracted the attention of mass media. Often individual black women active in feminist movement were revolutionary feminists (like many white lesbians). They were already at odds with reformist feminists who resolutely wanted to project a vision of the movement as being solely about women gaining equality with men in the existing system. Even before race became a talked about issue in feminist circles it was clear to black women (and to their revolutionary allies in struggle) that they were never going to have equality within the existing white supremacist capitalist patriarchy.

From its earliest inception feminist movement was polarized. Reformist thinkers chose to emphasize gender equality. Revolutionary thinkers did not want simply to alter the existing system so that women would have more rights. We wanted to transform that system, to bring an end to patriarchy and sexism. Since patriarchal mass media was not interested in the more revolutionary vision, it never received attention in mainstream press. The vision of "women's liberation" which captured and still holds the public imagination was the one representing women as wanting what men had. And this was the vision that was easier to realize. Changes in our nation's economy, economic depression, the loss of jobs, etc., made the climate ripe for our nation's citizens to accept the notion of gender equality in the workforce.

Given the reality of racism, it made sense that white men were more willing to consider women's rights when the granting of those rights could serve the interests of maintaining white supremacy. We can never forget that white women began to assert their need for freedom after civil rights, just at the point when racial discrimination was ending and black people, especially black males, might have attained equality in the workforce with white men. Reformist feminist thinking focusing primarily on equality with men in the workforce overshadowed the original radical foundations of contemporary feminism which called for reform as well as overall restructuring of society so that our nation would be fundamentally anti-sexist.

Most women, especially privileged white women, ceased even to consider revolutionary feminist visions, once they began to gain economic power within the existing social structure. Ironically, revolutionary feminist thinking was most accepted and embraced in academic circles. In those circles the production of revolutionary feminist theory progressed, but more often than not that theory was not made available to the public. It became and remains a privileged discourse available to those among us who are highly literate, well-educated, and usually materially privileged. Works like *Feminist Theory: From Margin to Center* that offer a liberatory vision of feminist transformation never receive mainstream attention. Masses of people have not heard of this book. They have not rejected its message; they do not know what the message is.

While it was in the interest of mainstream white supremacist capitalist patriarchy to suppress visionary feminist thinking which was not anti-male or concerned with getting women the right to be like men, reformist feminists were also eager to silence these forces. Reformist feminism became their route to class mobility. They could break free of male domination in the workforce and be more self-determining in their lifestyles. While sexism did not end, they could maximize their freedom within the existing system. And they could count on there being a lower class of exploited subordinated women to do the dirty work they were refusing to do. By accepting and indeed colluding with the subordination of working-class and poor women, they not only ally themselves with the existing patriarchy and its concomitant sexism, they give themselves the right to lead a double life, one where they are the equals of men in the workforce and at home when they want to be. If they choose lesbianism they have the privilege of being equals with men in the workforce while using class power to create domestic lifestyles where they can choose to have little or no contact with men.

Lifestyle feminism ushered in the notion that there could be as many versions of feminism as there were women. Suddenly the politics was being slowly removed from feminism. And the assumption prevailed that no matter what a woman's politics, be she conservative or liberal, she too could fit feminism into her existing lifestyle. Obviously this way of thinking has made feminism more acceptable because its underlying assumption is that women can be feminists without fundamentally challenging and changing themselves or the culture. For example, let's take the issue of abortion. If feminism is a movement to end sexist oppression, and depriving females of reproductive rights is a form of sexist oppression, then one cannot be anti-choice and be feminist. A woman can insist she would never choose to have an abortion while affirming her support of the right of women to choose and still be an advocate of feminist politics. She cannot be anti-abortion and an advocate of feminism. Concurrently there can be no such thing as "power feminism" if the vision of power evoked is power gained through the exploitation and oppression of others.

Feminist politics is losing momentum because feminist movement has lost clear definitions. We have those definitions. Let's reclaim them. Let's share them. Let's start over. Let's have T-shirts and bumper stickers and postcards and hip-hop music, television and radio commercials, ads everywhere and billboards, and all manner of printed material that tells the world about feminism. We can share the simple yet powerful message that feminism is a movement to end sexist oppression. Let's start there. Let the movement begin again.

R E A D I N G   **6**

The Power and the Gloria

Rachel Graham Cody (2012)

Like most icons, Gloria Steinem is smaller than you would expect, fine boned and angular.

She still parts her hair down the center, but her trademark tinted glasses are gone. She does not work to make you comfortable, nor indulge clichéd questions. But once she gets talking, she is a fount of ideas: books you should read, people to Google, a deep sense of history, and sharp commentary on current events. It doesn't take long before she shows you why she has become a giant.

Steinem has been the public face of American feminism since its heyday in the 1970s, and many of the movement's landmarks owe their origins to her. Steinem coined the term "reproductive freedom," created "Take Our Daughters to Work Day" and, in 1972, cofounded *Ms.* magazine. At a time when American women were still classed as "good girls" or "bad," Steinem offered herself as an example of the independent woman—and her magazine as the only one for those who wanted to be like her.

Steinem wasn't the only feminist around writing, leading marches and testifying before Congress, but she was the one America knew best.

A native of Ohio, she began her career as a free-lance writer (her mother was a journalist before suffering a nervous breakdown), working for *New York* magazine, the satirical TV show *That Was the Week That Was, Esquire* and *Show* magazine, for which she went undercover as a Playboy bunny. Editors' reluctance to publish the stories Steinem wanted to write—those not based on cleavage and fluffy tails—led her to co-found *Ms.*

The first issue of *Ms.* featured a list of prominent women who'd had abortions (Steinem included), almost a year before *Roe v. Wade.* It sold out within eight days. *Ms.*—where Steinem remains a consulting editor—went on to be the first national magazine to feature a battered woman on its cover, and to talk about sexual harassment in the workplace, equal pay, lesbianism as anything other than obscene, unfair divorce laws, sexism in child-rearing, and gender inequity in marriage. Steinem became the public face and the candid, relentless voice on these and many other issues.

She is now 78, and as the status of women steadily rises, Steinem's prominence has waned. Another generation of feminists (and young women who reject the term) has grown up with legal abortion, birth control, Title IX, and public awareness of and legal recourse against sexual harassment, date rape and domestic violence. In other words, a world very different from the one Steinem grew up in and helped transform.

This new generation has criticized Steinem for focusing on gender, assuming a singular female point of view, and overlooking the varieties of women's racial, class and sexual identities.

Steinem has rolled with the changes, remaining outspoken and busy as a writer and activist. She's currently working on a memoir of her 40-plus years of feminist organizing, *Road to the Heart: America As if Everyone Mattered.* She visited Portland last weekend for NARAL Pro-Choice Oregon's annual gala.

Steinem sat down for an extended interview with *WW (Willamette Week).* In addition to talking about her life and the current state of women's issues, Steinem revealed her early fear of public speaking, laughed about funny feminists (and one humorless one), and discussed the late Helen Gurley Brown's focus on sex as the primary source of female power.

WW: What is your definition of feminism now?
Gloria Steinem: The dictionary's.

Hasn't it changed?
No, not at all. It is the belief in the social, economic, political equality of males and females. A feminist is the person, male or female, who believes in that. I would like to add acts on it. There are other words that mean the same thing: womanism, women's liberation, girrls—with two r's, which I love—and mujerista.

Do you think the mainstream media uses the label too much?
They put us in a silo. Reporters for 40 years off and on have said, "Aren't you interested in anything other than the women's movement?" And for 40 years I have been saying, "Name me one thing that is separate." They've never been able to come up with anything that would not be transformed by looking at it as if everyone mattered.

What's the issue most important to American women that's least understood?
The deep anthropological, political reason for controlling women is to control reproduction.

Reproductive freedom, gaining reproductive freedom, is the key to unraveling this structure that has falsely created feminine and masculine, subject/object kind of roles.

And reproductive freedom, the right to decide for yourself when and whether to have children, is the single greatest determinant of whether you are healthy or not, whether you are poor or not, how long you live, whether you are educated, are you able to be active outside the home.

You think that's not well understood?
Yes. The impulse to think of women in reproductive terms makes it hard to imagine a world in which the center of authority is within each woman.

Even our legal structure, in general, penalizes the invasion of private property more than the invasion of bodies. Our legal world was built on a law that saw women as possessions, as objects. We've come up with a legal system that now penalizes men, too, because men should be protected from bodily invasion.

So what are the issues that people remain unaware of?
We talk about economic stimulus all the time. I have never seen in any print, other than us, that the most effective economic stimulus would be equal pay. It would put about $200 billion more a year into the economy.

It would be a stimulus exactly where that money is most likely to be spent. Those women are not going to put their money into Swiss bank accounts. They are going to spend it and create jobs.

I have yet to see equal pay for equal work spoken of as an economic stimulus. And, of course, Romney won't even say he is for equal pay.

It seems what the mainstream media present as debate about feminism has to do with privileged women who already have choices, rather than . . .
Real life. But the virtue of those issues is that they divide women. They are always trying to divide us. I mean, many fewer women are thinking about, "Can I have it all?" than are thinking about, "Will I lose it all?"

I'm thinking of *The Atlantic* cover story from this summer, "Why Women Still Can't Have It All."
That's ridiculous. It is not relevant for most women. And also it puts the burden on the woman: Can she have it all?

My question is, can we have a country and a culture in which it is possible for people to make a living and to have a family life? We work longer hours than any other modern democracy in the world, we have less child care than any modern democracy in the world, less flexible time, shorter vacations.

If I had a dollar for every time *Ms.* magazine tried to declare "superwoman" dead, I would have enough to go out and have a vacation.

Nobody can be superwoman, nobody can do it all. And no man can do it, either. The point is to change the structure so we can all have a life.

Whom do you see now carrying this message of awareness to younger women?
Everybody. Younger women are much more willing to support feminist issues than older women. The word feminism has been demonized. But if you look at the polls, young women are much more supportive than older women.

But we hear it is the reverse. The same people who used to say to me, "Oh, this is against biology, nature, Freud, God, something," now are saying, "Well, it used to be necessary, but it is not anymore." It is a new form of obstructionism.

We're seeing a lot about funny, no-BS feminism—Tina Fey and Caitlin Moran.
Which is great. I used to write for *That Was the Week That Was*. I was their only girl writer.

It turns out laughter is the only free emotion. You can compel fear. You can also compel love, because if people are kept isolated and dependent in order to survive—like the Stockholm syndrome—they will attach to their captor and even believe they love their captor.

You can't compel laughter. You laugh when you understand something—aha!—when two things come together and form a third unexpectedly.

There used to be this idea, I think it is past, that feminists have no sense of humor. We once did a *Ms.* cover with a cartoon and this guy is saying to this woman, "Do you know feminists have no sense of humor?" And she says, "No, but hum a few bars and I'll fake it."

We were not so enthusiastic anymore about laughing at dumb-blonde jokes, mother-in-law jokes, farmer's daughter jokes—because they were really insulting. But to see women in possession of not only our own laughter but also the ability to make other people laugh is a big power, actually.

There was a Katie Roiphe article in Slate that talked about it as mockery taking the place of anger.

Katie Roiphe has no sense of humor. That is not a legitimate source. We need somebody who laughs.

When you were younger, what was your biggest personal challenge?

Speaking in public. I was terrified. It was only the women's movement that got me to do it, and then only because I couldn't get articles published about the women's movement. I was always a freelance writer and my editors were, to put it mildly, not interested. I was so frustrated by that.

Because I was a journalist, people had occasionally asked me from time to time to speak. So I got myself to do it but only with another woman. For years, I went with Dorothy Pitman Hughes and then Flo Kennedy. It was good, because it was one white woman and one black woman together. We had a much more inclusive audience.

When did you overcome your fear?

It's like malaria—it still comes back. I think it helped a lot to spend a decade or so speaking with another woman. I realized I didn't die. They were standing there, so if I really fucked up, they were there next to me and could help me. So that helped a lot.

I had the idea that writing was a superior form of communication, more than speaking. Out of experience I came to realize that something happens in a room, when you are physically present, that cannot happen on the printed page and can't happen on a computer screen. The oxytocin, or whatever it is called, the chemical that allows us empathy, is only possible when we are together.

There isn't a hierarchy of expression. It made me realize they can fuel each other. If I am by myself writing for a long time, I overwrite and I lose faith. If you are speaking, you understand people's brains do work on narrative. Simple things are helpful. It doesn't have to be all that complicated.

What is your biggest personal challenge now?

I am trying very hard to understand I am not immortal. It is hard to realize one's own age, and especially if you are doing what you love, because you forget what time it is. And if you don't have children, you don't have a marker of age, exactly. If you really think you are immortal, you don't plan very well. I keep saying to myself, "You have to finish this book." I don't want to die saying, "But, but . . ."

Speaking of mortality: Longtime *Cosmopolitan* editor Helen Gurley Brown died this year. Often, you were placed at one pole of women's empowerment and she was the other. What is your take on her legacy and the two of you being set against each other?

She was a great girlfriend. She was a very generous, good person. At the same time, she really saw sex as the only way a woman could get ahead.

She called me up once and said, "You have to help me. Your people are demonstrating in my lobby." I said, "What do you mean, 'your people'?" She said, "Women. They are demonstrating against *Cosmo*." It turns out the guy who wrote the regular sex column had been convicted of sexually assaulting his patients. She didn't fire him, he was still writing the column. I said, "But, Helen, no wonder they are demonstrating against you." And she said, "Oh, but he's such a nice man."

She certainly stood for a woman's right to determine her own personal and sexual life, which was a big step forward for women's magazines, because they had a formula that said if you had sex before marriage, even in a fiction story, you had to be punished. But she didn't see the rest of it.

She was the one who helped her girlfriends find an abortion, but she didn't campaign to change the laws against abortion. Maybe she did, but I wasn't aware of it.

What public figures do you see energizing a new generation?

Ai-jen Poo. She is the head of the [National Domestic Workers Alliance], the organization that has been working about a decade so that household workers are included under minimum wage in New York—and almost in California, but Gov. [Jerry] Brown vetoed it. She is a genius organizer. She is amazing. She does it in a way that is a whole human way unlike Saul Alinsky. Saul Alinsky was very good at it, but he did it in a hostile way. She does it in an inclusive way.

You are an icon. What makes you yell at the TV or newspaper when you see yourself discussed? First of all, it's an accident who gets to be known and who doesn't. If I were an engineer instead of a media worker. . . . It just came with the territory because I was always already working in media when the movement came along. I think the most frustrating single article, though it was meant in a positive way, so I'm not complaining, was the recent *New York Times* article ["Gloria Steinem, a Woman Like No Other," March 16, 2012] saying, who is the next Gloria Steinem? As if it were not a movement. As if there was only one person.

R E A D I N G 7

Facebook for Women vs. Facebook Designed by Feminists: Different vs. Revolutionary

C.V. Harquail (2010)

What would Facebook be like if it were designed by women?

In my earlier post, I proposed that Facebook would look, feel and function differently if it had been designed by "women." What I actually was writing about was what Facebook might look like if it had been designed by Feminists—but I used "women" in the title to enhance SEO (Search Engine Optimization). Sometimes we make tradeoffs, and write headlines that prioritize discoverability over precision.

DISTINGUISHING BETWEEN WOMEN AND FEMINISTS

Clarifying how a facebook designed for women is different from a facebook designed by feminists is an important place to begin the conversation, because so many people struggle to distinguish between "women" and "feminists/feminism."

"Women" is a social category, based on a person's gender self-definition. When we talk about "Women" we're talking about a social category with predictable, empirically verifiable, modal preferences. We can measure what women as a group prefer, and we can design to appeal to these preferences. "Feminists" is a social category, based on a person's political orientation. Many women advocate feminism and many feminists are women. Some feminists are men, and some feminists choose to define themselves without using the terms like man or woman. Feminist have values they want to "build in" to products, services and organizations.

When it comes down to distinguishing between women and feminists, we need to separate marketing and politics.

Marketing to Women

Designing something "for women" is a marketing challenge. Products designed for women are intended to appeal to women by reflecting the preferences of women as a social group. If you want to get lots of women to like, buy, use your product, you identify empirically what kinds of features "women" prefer, you design your product to have these features, and *voilà*, you've got a product "for Women."

Feminist Design

Feminist design of a product is a political action. Products designed by feminists are intended to change power relationships and advance social change, on behalf of women and men. Facebook was not and is not designed "for women." It is not designed in ways that reflect what women prefer in terms of the tool's appearance, functionality, and *raison d'etre*.

A facebook designed "for Women" might have begun with some research into how women might want to create, sustain and recreate social relationships in an online forum. That research might have included what kinds of visual appearance they'd like the site to have, as well as what kinds of functions they'd like the site to enable, and what different ways they'd like their social relationships categorized, organized and represented.

Women would have been asked:

- What do you want to be able to share, see and do with your "friends"? (Would we even call them "friends"?)
- How do you understand the variety of your relationships?
- How can relationships best be presented graphically/visually and over time?

Maybe Facebook for women would have been pink, with flowery text and pictures of cats; maybe not. Maybe a facebook designed by women would display the romantic relationship status of each user; maybe it would have displayed each person's answer to the question "If I could make the world a better place, I would _____."

Facebook for women might have had:

- Ways to evoke and express emotion.
- Ways to personalize the look and feel to make it more "us."
- Ways to rate men on how supportive and mature they are (just kidding).

Who knows—no one seems to have asked women what they might prefer to find on Facebook, either in terms of appearance or functionality.

FACEBOOK DESIGNED BY FEMINISTS: FEMINIST HCI

A Facebook designed by Feminists would be a much different "product."

I am not an expert in Feminist HCI (Human Computer Interface) so I'll just give you the general, layfeminist/layperson's view.

There is a feminist approach to software design, a feminist model of social community, a feminist political and economic ideology, a feminist technology movement, and a feminist social movement. All of these are engaged and reflected in feminist design. As a movement, feminism focuses on changing power relationships to bring about social, economic, and ecological justice. (While feminism initially focused on changing gender relations, the movement and ideology have expanded dramatically.) A social network platform designed by feminists would aim to facilitate egalitarian and inclusive social relationships, distribute authority and responsibility, encourage collaboration, honor individual agency and self-definition, and more. A Feminist Social Network Platform would "give the user a tool to express her choice and the truth of her existence."

A feminist social network would not be a "product" to be sold to users, but would instead be a service that was supported by users. We tend to forget that Facebook is a product because we don't pay anything to use it—as far as we know. But we users generate a great deal of profit for Facebook not only by looking at profiles and feeds, but also by creating content ourselves.

Some additional ideas? A "facebook" designed by feminists:

- Would show relationships between people as more flexible and dynamic, represented more like these twitter tools than like a hierarchy.
- Would involve users in the creation process, perhaps not as Free Libre Open Source Software (FLOSS) experts but certainly as experts in what they want.
- Would put privacy decisions in the hands of each user.
- Would not own people's data or people's content. It would not aim to profit from this data

and content without an explicit profit sharing agreement.

- Would not sell people's private information to companies that want to market to those people, without the explicit, ongoing, informed consent of those users.
- Would not be privately owned by individual shareholders, although it might be privately owned by members or by a for-purpose organization.
- Would be created and sustained through feminist design processes and feminist "management" (a topic for another post).
- Would be socially, economically, politically inclusive.
- Would allow for privacy and identity protections related to political action.
- Would from the very start have embraced accessibility issues for people with vision-related and other ability challenges.
- Would have default settings that are inclusive and self-presentation choices that are more varied.
- Would have terms of service (TOS) and regulations about what is and is not allowed that did not reinforce sexism and racism.

Feminists would approach the project with a political goal in mind. The overall intent of the platform might be "general social networking," just as with the current Facebook. But the driving interest might have been for creating friendships, affinity groups and social movements, not checking out chicks to evaluate whether you want to date them.

A feminist social network would be designed on open-source software (as Facebook is), as a political value driven choice, not (only) because open source is less expensive, more malleable and often more reliable than proprietary software resources. The processes through which a feminist Facebook would be created would also be different—feminists would approach the very project of building a platform very differently from the way that Facebook was

designed. As other commenters have mentioned, there are some alternatives out there—some alive, some defunct, some in alpha, some in wireframes—that are trying to do things differently. Not many of these are explicitly feminist designed, but some like Diaspora have political and economic justice as a driving value.

WHERE DO WE GO FROM HERE?

I'm excited by the thoughtfulness and complexity of the comments shared after the last post, and I will take them up in future posts. Thank you all so much for these insights. From my research, it looks like the conversation about values and technology is confined within expert tech communities, and I think it needs to come further out into the mainstream social media conversation. Any suggestions about how to do this? I'm open. . . .

The general point to remember is that any piece of technology reflects implicit assumptions of the people/business that designed it, along with the explicit design/commercial goals of the product. We often miss this, because we take for granted the male-ness of our dominant approach to technology. And, we take for granted that profit motives will dominate what is included and excluded from a product—unless we set different priorities.

These last few weeks there's been a great conversation about whether social networks can facilitate advocacy and social change. The answer is obvious, although more complex than some make it seem. No technology is neutral. Every technology reflects values and a political stance towards the social world. Many technologies can be co-opted so that they facilitate unintended purposes. Truly revolutionary technology has social justice and liberation built in. Facebook is changing our world, that's for sure. But is it truly revolutionary? Not the way a social network designed by feminists would be.

Still Needing the F Word

Anna Quindlen (2003)

Let's use the F word here. People say it's inappropriate, offensive, that it puts people off. But it seems to me it's the best way to begin, when it's simultaneously devalued and invaluable.

Feminist. Feminist, Feminist, Feminist.

Conventional wisdom has it that we've moved on to a postfeminist era, which is meant to suggest that the issues have been settled, the inequities addressed, and all is right with the world. And then suddenly from out of the South like Hurricane Everywoman, a level 03 storm, comes something like the new study on the status of women at Duke University,* and the notion that we're post-anything seems absurd. Time to use the F word again, no matter how uncomfortable people may find it.

Fem-i-nism *n. 1. Belief in the social, political and economic equality of the sexes.*

That wasn't so hard, was it? Certainly not as hard as being a female undergraduate at Duke, where apparently the operative ruling principle is something described as "effortless perfection," in which young women report expending an enormous amount of effort on clothes, shoes, workout programs and diet. And here's a blast from the past: they're expected "to hide their intelligence in order to succeed with their male peers."

"Being 'cute' trumps being smart for women in the social environment," the report concludes.

That's not postfeminist. That's prefeminist. Betty Friedan wrote *The Feminine Mystique* exactly 40 years ago, and yet segments of the Duke report could have come right out of her book. One 17-year-old girl told Friedan, "I used to write poetry. The guidance office says I have this creative ability and I should be at the top of the class and have a great future. But things like that aren't what you need to be popular. The important thing for a girl is to be popular."

Of course, things have changed. Now young women find themselves facing not one, but two societal, and self-imposed, straitjackets. Once they obsessed about being the perfect homemaker and meeting the standards of their male counterparts. Now they also obsess about being the perfect professional and meeting the standards of their male counterparts. In the decades since Friedan's book became a best seller, women have won the right to do as much as men do. They just haven't won the right to do as little as men do. Hence, effortless perfection.

While young women are given the impression that all doors are open, all boundaries down, empirical evidence is to the contrary. A study from Princeton issued at the same time as the Duke study showed that faculty women in the sciences reported less satisfaction in their jobs and less of a sense of belonging than their male counterparts. Maybe that's because they made up only 14 percent of the faculty in those disciplines, or because one out of four reported their male colleagues occasionally or frequently engaged in unprofessional conduct focusing on gender issues.

Californians were willing to ignore Arnold Schwarzenegger's alleged career as a serial sexual bigot, despite a total of 16 women coming forward to say he thought nothing of reaching up your skirt or into your blouse. (Sure, they're only allegations. But it was Arnold himself who said that where there's smoke, there's fire. In this case, there was a conflagration.) The fact that one of the actor's defenses was that he didn't realize this was objectionable—and that voters were OK with that—speaks volumes about enduring assumptions about women. What if he'd habitually publicly humiliated black men, or Latinos, or Jews? Yet the revelation that the guy

---

*In the Fall, 2003, Duke University published a comprehensive Women's Initiative Report that documented the full range of women's experiences at the university.

often demeaned women with his hands was written off as partisan politics and even personal behavior. Personal behavior is when you have a girlfriend. When you touch someone intimately without her consent, it's sexual battery.

The point is not that the world has not changed for women since Friedan's book lobbed a hand grenade into the homes of pseudohappy housewives who couldn't understand the malaise that accompanied sparkling Formica and good-looking kids. Hundreds of arenas, from government office to the construction trades, have opened to working women. Of course, when it leaks out that the Vatican is proposing to scale back on the use of altar girls, it shows that the forces of reaction are always waiting, whether beneath hard hats or miters.

But the world hasn't changed as much as we like to tell ourselves. Otherwise, *The Feminine Mystique* wouldn't feel so contemporary. Otherwise, Duke University wouldn't find itself concentrating on eating disorders and the recruitment of female faculty. Otherwise, the governor-elect of California wouldn't be a guy who thinks it's "playful" to grab and grope, and the voters wouldn't ratify that attitude. Part fair game, part perfection: that's a tough standard for 51 percent of everyone. The first women's-rights activists a century ago set out to prove, in Friedan's words, "that woman was not a passive empty mirror." How dispiriting it would be to those long-ago heroines to read of the women at Duke focused on their "cute" reflections in the eyes of others. The F word is not an expletive, but an ideal—one that still has a way to go.

R E A D I N G 9

My Heroines

Marge Piercy (2010)

When I think of women heroes,
it's not Joan of Arc or Molly Pitcher
but mothers who quietly say
to their daughters, *you can.*
Who stand behind attempts
to open doors long bolted shut
to teams or clubs or professions.

I think of women who dress
'respectably' and march and march
and march again, for the ability
to choose, for peace, for rights
their own or others. Who form
phone banks, who stuff envelopes
who do the invisible political work.

They do not get their faces on
magazine covers. They don't get fan
mail or receive awards. But without
them, no woman or liberal man

would ever be elected, no law
would be passed or changed. We
would be stuck in sexist mud.

It's the receptionist in the clinic,
the escorts to frightened women,
the volunteers at no kill shelters,
women sorting bottles at the dump,
women holding signs in the rain,
women who take calls of the abused,
of rape victims, night after night.

It's the woman at her computer
or desk when the family's asleep
writing letters, organizing friends.
Big change turns on small pushes.
Heroes and heroines climb into
history books, but it's such women
who actually write our future.

DISCUSSION QUESTIONS FOR CHAPTER 1

1. How does the inclusion of women as subjects transform the nature of knowledge and the means of producing knowledge? How does consideration of differences among women complicate the transformation and production of knowledge?

2. How do gender arrangements foster oppression, and how do these arrangements intersect with race/ethnicity, sexual identity, nation of origin, social class, and other forms of difference?

3. What is feminism and what is its relationship to WGS?

4. How does the notion that women have already achieved equality intersect with capitalist concerns of consumption and personal style?

5. What does Adrienne Rich mean by "claiming an education" and what does that concept have to do with WGS?

SUGGESTIONS FOR FURTHER READING

Berger, Michele Tracy, and Cheryl Radeloff. *Transforming Scholarship: Why Women's and Gender Studies Students are Changing Themselves and the World.* New York: Routledge, 2011.

Collins, Gail. *When Everything Changed: The Amazing Journey of American Women from 1960 to the Present.* New York: Little, Brown, 2009.

Collins, Patricia Hill. *On Intellectual Activism.* Philadelphia: Temple University Press, 2012.

Freedman, Estelle B. *No Turning Back: The History of Feminism and the Future of Women.* New York: Ballantine, 2002.

Hernandez, Daisy, and Bushra Rheman, eds. *Colonize This! Young Women of Color on Today's Feminism.* New York: Avalon, 2002.

hooks, bell. *Feminism Is For Everybody: Passionate Politics.* Boston: South End, 2000.

Kaufman, Michael and Michael Kimmel. *The Guy's Guide to Feminism.* Berkeley, CA: Seal Press, 2011.

Mohanty, Chandra Talpade. *Feminism Without Borders: Decolonizing Theory, Practicing Solidarity.* Durham, NC: Duke University Press, 2003.

Orr, Catherine M., and Ann Braithwaite, eds. *Rethinking Women's and Gender Studies.* New York: Routledge, 2012.

Mann, Susan. *Doing Feminist Theory: From Modernity to Postmodernity.* New York: Oxford University Press, 2012.

Siegel, Deborah, and Jennifer Baumgardner. *Sisterhood, Interrupted: From Radical Women to Girls Gone Wild.* New York: Palgrave Macmillan, 2007.

Sudbury, Julia, and Margo Okazawa-Ray. *Activist Scholarship: Antiracism, Feminism, and Social Change.* Boulder, CO: Paradigm, 2009.

Valenti, Jessica. *Full Frontal Feminism: A Young Woman's Guide to Why Feminism Matters.* Emeryville, CA: Seal Press, 2007.

Wiegman, Robyn. *Object Lessons.* Durham, NC: Duke University Press, 2012.

CHAPTER 2

Systems of Privilege and Inequality

"Women" are as different as we/they are alike. Although sharing some conditions, including having primary responsibility for children and being victims of male violence, individual lives are always marked by difference. This is a result of the varying conditions and material practices of women's existence in global communities and the societies in which these communities are embedded. We inhabit different cultures whose norms or cultural expectations prescribe different ways of acting as women and men and impose different sanctions if these norms are broken. It is therefore important to recognize difference and, as already discussed in Chapter 1, avoid using "woman" as a universal or homogeneous category that assumes sameness. Many of the readings in this chapter are essays illustrating how power in society works, how differences are ranked or valued differently, and how privilege and discrimination operate. Although several may seem "dated" because they were written during the critique of second wave feminism in the 1980s, they are used intentionally here as examples of classic scholarship in WGS. They make suggestions for change in both personal and social lives. They emphasize that what it means to identify as a "woman" is a complex interaction of multiple identities.

In the United States our differences are illustrated by the material conditions of our lives; the values, cultures, behavioral practices, and legal structures of the communities in which we live; and even the geographic region of the country we inhabit. In particular, we inhabit different identities in terms of race and ethnicity, religion, age, looks, sexual identity, socioeconomic status, and ability. For people in the United States these identities are also situated within a global context that positions the United States within the world order. In particular, this means understanding colonialism and imperialism: the practices that subordinate one society to another and exercise power through military domination, economic policies, and/or the imposition of certain forms of knowledge. As discussed in Chapter 1, just as it is important to question the homogenizing notions of sameness in terms of the category "woman" across societies, it is also important to understand that these universalizing tendencies work against our understanding of women in the United States as well. Often we tend to think of women in comparison to a *mythical norm:* white, middle-class, heterosexual, abled, thin, and a young adult, which is normalized or taken for granted such that we often forget that whites are racialized and men are gendered. Asking the question "Different from what?" reveals how difference gets constructed against what people think of as "normal." "Normality" tends to reflect the identities of those in power. This is especially apparent in the issue of disability where it is impossible for someone to be "disabled" or "impaired" without reference to a constructed idea of "normal." As many disability scholars emphasize, any notion of "normal" is an artifact or by-product produced by the discipline that measures it. In other words this normality is created and has no physical reality apart from that practice that constructs the idea of normality in the first place. This concept is illustrated in "The Social Construction of Disability" by Susan Wendell.

In this way it is important to recognize that the *meanings* associated with differences are socially constructed. These social constructions would not be problematic were they not created against the notion of the mythical norm. Being a lesbian or identifying as "queer" would not be a "difference" that invoked cultural resistance if it were not for *compulsory heterosexuality,* the notion that everyone should be heterosexual and have relationships with the opposite sex. Implicit here, of course, is also the idea that sexuality must be categorized into the binaries of heterosexuality and homosexuality in the first place.

In this chapter we focus on differences among women and explore the ways systems of privilege and inequality are created out of these differences. Such systems, however, are shaped by broader forces of *imperialism* at home and abroad. As already mentioned, imperialism refers to the economic, political, and cultural domination over nations or communities. Early forms of imperialism (such as the U.S. conquest of Hawaii) subjugated indigenous populations and extracted resources. Contemporary imperialism continues to do this, but also destroys indigenous forms of production by usurping and privatizing land and forcing economies into market or capitalist production. Often this involves military occupation or the use of colonized land for strategic military use. Also included is cultural imperialism, the destruction of indigenous languages, and the imposition of certain forms of knowledge: a particularly insidious problem with the rapid growth of digital and other technologies. In this way, although imperialism often involves *colonialism* (the building and maintenance of colonies in one region by people from another region), it must be understood in terms of broader economic, military, and cultural practices of domination. June Jordan discusses imperialism in the reading, "Report from the Bahamas." These forces of imperialism provide the global context for our discussion of systems of inequality and privilege in the United States. It is also important to consider the privileges afforded citizens of the global north as a result of this global structuring. Privileges include the availability of cheap goods produced elsewhere (often under problematic conditions) and the ability to remain "innocent" of the consequences of U.S. economic and military policies abroad.

In addition, however, we must consider the notion of *internal colonialism* (sometimes called settler colonialism) that has colonized indigenous people in North America. Colonizing processes include the following: assimilation of the dominant group's culture and language; denial of citizenship rights; relegation to subordinate labor markets; and entrance into a host country by force. We can recognize the history of U.S. racism in this brief discussion of internal colonialism. Examples include the importation of black slaves forced to leave their African homelands; the removal from indigenous lands of native people who are forced into reservations; and the construction of "illegal" to describe immigrants and migrants who lost their land in Mexico through military conquest and yet are needed by the economic system to participate in menial and often dangerous work.

DIFFERENCE, HIERARCHY, AND SYSTEMS OF PRIVILEGE AND INEQUALITY

Simply put, society recognizes the ways people are different and assigns group membership based on these differences; at the same time, society also ranks the differences and institutionalizes them into the fabric of society (Figure 2.1). *Institutionalized* means officially placed into a structured system or set of practices. In other words, institutionalized means to make something part of a structured and well-established system. For example, there may be feelings and attitudes that women do not belong in certain aspects of higher education, but these beliefs and practices that disparage women become institutionalized if standardized tests (such as SATs, GREs, and intelligence tests) contain language and gendered content that is less accessible for girls and more familiar to boys, thus facilitating lower scores for girls and women that provide the "evidence" or justification for these beliefs. This would be an example of institutionalized sexism. The concept of institutionalization in this context also implies that meanings associated with difference exist beyond the intentions of individual people. This distinction between the "micro" (focusing on the level of individuals) and "macro" (focusing on the large-scale, societal level) is important. Your experience of reading this chapter as a class assignment, for example, centers on the individual micro level, but it is embedded in, and part of, a more macro, systematically organized set of practices associated with education as an institution. Whether you actually read or study this on the micro level is independent of the fact that education as an institution functions in certain ways. In other words, studying course readings is institutionalized into education (whether you actually study your reading or not).

Even though differences associated with various identities intersect, they are also ranked. Masculine is placed above feminine, thin above fat, economically privileged above poor, and so forth. These rankings of groups and their members create a hierarchy in which some ways of being, like being abled or heterosexual, are valued more than others, like being disabled or gay or lesbian. Some have advantages in accessing resources whereas others are disadvantaged by unequal access to economic opportunities; some are unable to exercise the rights of citizenship and others have clearer access to right to life and happiness. For example, U.S. rights of citizenship include equal participation in the political process to ensure that laws reflect the will of the people with the knowledge that the government exists to serve the people, and to serve all equally. Although civil

LEARNING ACTIVITY **Unpack Your Knapsack**

In the readings "White Privilege" and "Cisgender Privilege," Peggy McIntosh and Evin Taylor list the ways entitlement is experienced. Choose from the various nontarget statuses below and make lists of the ways you experience the following categories of privilege:

White	Male	Heterosexual
Middle or upper class	Young	Able-bodied

FIGURE 2.1 Intersecting Axes of Privilege, Domination, and Oppression

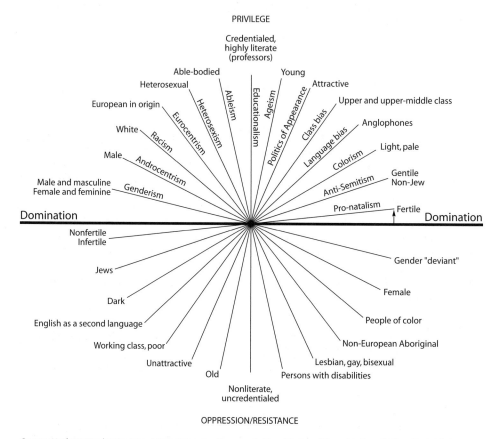

Source: Kathryn Pauly Morgan, "Describing the Emperor's New Clothes: Three Myths of Educational (In) Equality." In *The Gender Question in Education: Theory, Pedagogy & Politics,* Ann Diller et al. Boulder, CO: Westview, 1996.

LEARNING ACTIVITY   **Test for Hidden Bias**

The Implicit Association Test, developed by researchers at Harvard University, tests for unconscious bias. Even though most of us believe we view everyone equally, we still may hold stereotypes and biases of which we are unaware. These tests can check to see if perhaps you hold hidden biases concerning race, sexual identity, age, gender, or body image. To take one or more of these tests, go to Project Implicit's website at *www.implicit.harvard.edu/implicit.* After you finish the tests, take a few minutes to write about what you learned about yourself. Were there any surprises? Do you hold hidden biases? How do you feel about your test results? Now that you know about your hidden biases, what can you do?

rights legislation removed many of the barriers set up to prevent non-whites from voting, intimidation (such as discarding votes for various reasons and requiring different ID for certain voters) and restructuring (drawing voting district lines in a way that neutralizes the power of non-white voters) still occur.

LEARNING ACTIVITY **Five Faces of Oppression**

Iris Young identifies characteristics of systems of oppression listed below. Think about a group of people—American Indian women or queer Chicanas, for example. How might these categories apply? Why, according to Young's categories, would young, heterosexual white men not qualify as an oppressed group?

1. EXPLOITATION

- A steady process of the transfer of the results of the labor of one social group to benefit another.
- Social relations produced and reproduced through a systematic process in which the energies of the subordinate group are continuously expended to maintain and augment the power, status, and wealth of the dominant group.

2. MARGINALIZATION

- The expulsion of entire groups of people from useful participation in social life that potentially subjects them to severe material deprivation and possible extermination.
- Even those with material resources experience feeling useless, bored, and lacking self-respect.

3. POWERLESSNESS

- The powerless lack authority; they are those over whom power is exercised without their exercising it; they are situated so that they must take orders and rarely have the right to give them.
- The powerless have little or no work autonomy, exercise little creativity or judgment in their work, and do not command respect.
- A lack of "respectability"—respect is not automatically given.

4. CULTURAL IMPERIALISM

- The universalization of a dominant group's experience and culture—its establishment as the norm.
- These norms render the experiences and cultures of subordinate groups invisible and create stereotypes about the group, marking it as the Other.

5. VIOLENCE

- Members of subordinate groups live with the threat of violence based on their status as group members.
- To a great extent, this violence is legitimated because it is tolerated.

Source: Iris Young, "Five Faces of Oppression," in *Readings for Diversity and Social Justice*, (2nd. edition), ed. Maurianne Adams, et al. (New York: Routledge, 2010), 35–45.

The hierarchical ranking of difference is constructed through social processes such that patterns of difference become systems of privilege and inequality. Inequality for some and privilege for others is the consequence of these processes. *Privilege* can be defined as advantages people have by virtue of their status or position in society. This can be distinguished from earned privilege that results, for example, from earning a degree or fulfilling responsibilities. In "White Privilege and Male Privilege," Peggy McIntosh writes that white privilege is the "invisible package of unearned assets" that white people can count on cashing in every day. And, as McIntosh explains, it is easier to grant that others are disadvantaged than to admit being privileged. Men might be supportive of women's rights but balk at the suggestion that their personal behavior is in need of modification. Whites might be horrified by the stories of racial injustice but still not realize that taken-for-granted white privilege is part of the problem. This is similar to the discussion in Chapter 1 where being supportive of women's rights does not necessarily translate into an understanding of how the entitlements of masculine privilege work.

Systems of oppression can be understood as systems that discriminate and privilege based on perceived or real differences among people. Systems that facilitate privilege and inequality, subordination and domination, include *sexism* based upon gender: something you will be reading a lot about in this book. However, although sexism is understood and lived as discrimination against women, it is also important to understand that gender conformity itself entails privilege. What this means is that people who are recognized as fitting into the gender binary of "female" and "male" receive collective advantages. *Cisgender* people are those whose gender identity or expression matches their assigned gender by societal standards. Those who change or cross these gender binaries are *transgender* individuals who do not enjoy the privileges that cisgender individuals do. This is the topic of Evin Taylor's short piece titled "Cisgender Privilege," an essay originally published in the anthology *Gender Outlaws* by Kate Bornstein and S. Bear Bergman. The essay invokes Peggy MacIntosh's invisible knapsack to explore the question of cisgender privilege. The author encourages readers to adapt the questionnaire to suit their own gender positioning and to come up with questions that can be added to the list.

Systems of inequality and privilege also include *racism* based upon racial/ethnic group membership (African American, Asian American, Latino/a, Native American—note this also includes anti-Semitism, or discrimination against Jews, as well as discrimination against Muslims and Arab Americans); *classism* associated with socioeconomic status; *ageism* relating to age; *looksism* and *sizeism,* concerning body size and looks; and *ableism,* about physical and mental ability. Also included is *heterosexism,* which concerns sexual identity or orientation. As already mentioned, systems function by discriminating and privileging based upon perceived or real differences among people. Given this, sexism discriminates and privileges on the basis of gender, resulting in gender stratification; racism discriminates and privileges on the basis of racial and ethnic differences; and so forth for classism, heterosexism, ageism, looksism, and ableism. *Homophobia,* the fear and dislike of those who do not identify as heterosexual or "straight," functions to support heterosexism as well as sexism. The latter occurs, for example, through misogyny directed at gay men and as a threat to encourage women to give up the love of other women to gain male approval. It is important to understand that homophobia is an example of prejudice, and, although it plays a part in the maintenance of heterosexism, it is not equivalent to it as a structured system of power. A similarly functioning concept is *transphobia,* the fear and dislike of transgender individuals.

As introduced in the discussion of intersectionality in Chapter 1, all people are in multiple places vis-à-vis these systems. A person might not have access to race and gender privilege because she is African American and a woman; she might have access to heterosexual privilege because she is heterosexual, and class privilege because she lives in a

COMPLEX IDENTITIES   **Thinking Outside the Check-Box**

Heather Montes Ireland

Multiracial Americans had the option to select "more than one race" for the very first time on the U.S. Census in 2000. According to *The New York Times,* the multiracial population in the United States has increased almost fifty percent to 4.2 million people since that time, with 1 in 7 couples comprised of individuals from different ethno-racial origins. Universities have seen a marked rise in the number of incoming students checking "multiracial" as their racial/ethnic identity. Mixed race studies has emerged as a viable field of inquiry, and the 2nd biennial Critical Mixed Race Studies conference held at DePaul University in 2012 attracted over 400 attendees from across the U.S. and Canada, the UK, Brazil, Australia, and Ukraine.

Yet multiracial people are still often seen as divisive, irrelevant, or secondary in importance to monoracial groups. Mixed race individuals are often told to choose between ethno-racial categories, or that if they cannot, they are confused about their "true" identities. However, multiracial writers, 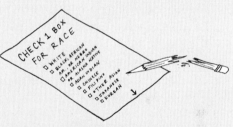 ethnic studies scholars, and mixed race bloggers are all challenging those representations by researching and writing about the experiences of this growing population. The now-celebrated "Bill of Rights for People of Mixed Heritage" by Dr. Maria P. P. Root (1993) was one of the first writings that provided validation for mixed race people to not feel compelled to "choose" between narrow or binary racial categories.

Today's critical mixed race studies scholarship emphasizes that we must critique and analyze the institutionalization of the very racial and ethnic categories that are mistaken as natural—and pure. Race and ethnicity are social constructions that are co-constituted with gender, sexuality, (dis)ability and other identity vectors. In other words, racial boundaries are much too fluid, porous, and complex than can be ascertained with rigid check-boxes. This does not mean that racial categories that exist in society do not matter. Indeed, understanding critical mixed race studies affords a specific approach to oppose structural racism and critique social stratification based on race. Today there are many resources for those who are interested in learning more about the experiences of multiracial people and feminist perspectives on critical mixed race studies.

(continued)

BOOKS

- Barry, Lynda. *One Hundred Demons*. Seattle: Sasquatch Books, 2002.
- Durrow, Heidi W. *The Girl Who Fell from the Sky*. Chapel Hill: Algonquin Books, 2010.
- Lopez, Erika. *Flaming Iguanas: An Illustrated All-girl Road Novel Thing*. New York: Simon & Schuster, 1997.
- Prasad, Chandra, and Rebecca Walker, eds. *Mixed: An Anthology of Short Fiction on the Multiracial Experience*. New York: W.W. Norton, 2006.
- Shepard, Sadia. *The Girl from Foreign: A Memoir*. New York: Penguin Press, 2009.

WEB

- DrMariaRoot.com—Information on the topics of multiracial families, multiracial identity, and more. Includes the new "Multiracial Oath of Social Responsibility."
- CriticalMixedRaceStudies.org—A biennial conference, a journal, a field of study, and a scholarly/activist/artistic community.
- Swirlinc.org—A multiracial community committed to initiating and sustaining cross-racial, cross-cultural dialogue.
- MixedHeritageCenter.org—Resources relevant to the lives of people who are multiracial, multiethnic, transracially adopted, or otherwise impacted by the intersections of race and culture.

Illustration by Louise Leong http://louleo.tumblr.com/

family that is financially secure. This is the intersection or confluence, the flowing together of various identities. As Patricia Hill Collins explains in "Toward a New Vision," it is not as useful to think of these various identities as being stacked or arranged in a cumulative manner. Lives are not experienced as "Here I'm a woman, here I'm abled, here I'm poor," as if all our various statuses are all stacked up; we experience ourselves as ordinary people who struggle daily with the inequities in our lives and who usually take the privileges for granted. Various identities concerning these systems of equality and privilege are usually thoroughly blended and potentially shifting depending on subjective orientation and cultural context. This means that cultural forces of race and class, and others such as age and ability, all shape gender expression. It is important to emphasize that people experience race, class, gender, and sexual identities differently depending on their social location in various structures of inequality and privilege. This means that people of the same race or same age, for example, will experience race or age differently depending on their location in gendered structures (whether they are women or men) or class structures (such as working class, professional class, or unemployed), as well as structures associated with sexual identity (whether they identify as heterosexual, bisexual, lesbian, gay, or queer), and so on. This is also Audre Lorde's point in the reading "There Is No Hierarchy of Oppression." She writes about these intersections and advocates solidarity among multiple intersecting identities.

"Intersectionality" is the topic and title of the essay by Vivian M. May. She describes the approach as incorporating an intersecting matrix that allows an understanding of simultaneous privilege and oppression. Among her vision of future possibilities for this

LEARNING ACTIVITY   **Queer Disruptions**

Queer is one of those tricky words that has a particular historical meaning (its denotation) and specific cultural meanings (its connotations) that can be either positive or negative. Originally, *queer* just meant "odd," but in the early twentieth century it was applied to gays in a derogatory way. In the 1980s people who in many ways were part of nonheteronormative categories began to reclaim the word to mean "sexually dissident" and to reflect a growing activism that challenged fixed sexual categories and heteronormativity. In academic circles, queer theory became a method of analysis that disrupted fixed meanings and exposed underlying contradictions and structures of power, particularly as they pertained to the regulation of sexual behavior and the oppression of people who do not conform to societal expectations around sexuality. Beyond the goals of acceptance and equal treatment pursued by gay and lesbian rights activists, queer theory seeks to destabilize cultural ideas and norms that are used to oppress nonconforming people.

Let's look at an example: queer theology. Queer theology seeks to deconstruct and disrupt normative theologies, especially heteronormative theologies. It is a transgressive theology. So a simple question queer theology asks of sacred texts is about the reader's assumption that the characters in the text are heterosexual. Queer theology also imposes present-day cultural norms about sexuality and sexual identity on characters from ancient texts. This opens up space to understand, for example, the relationship of David and Jonathan from the Hebrew Bible or Jesus and the apostle John from the Christian testament in ways that do not force contemporary understandings of sexuality on the text. How might we understand these as queer relationships, as relationships that contest heteronormative standards? This is not to say that we are arguing that these characters had sex with one another. Rather, we are asking how these relationships reflect a larger continuum of intimate behaviors than traditional masculinity (in these cases) might allow. Queer theology asks questions of how we might understand Divinity from queer perspectives or how we might use "coming out" as a metaphor in Christianity to understand Jesus as the incarnation of God's love or how we might through the character of the Virgin Mary understand the sexual oppression/denial of women in the contemporary world.

Queering Your Discipline: Identify an important text (a book, a story, a movie, a song, a painting) in your own discipline. Think about how you might do a queer reading of this text:

- How might you challenge the heteronormative assumptions of the text?
- What are the underlying norms of power and domination in the text?
- How does the text (and its typical reading) regulate sexual behavior?
- How might the text be read to disrupt essential notions of gender and sexuality?

Challenging Your Assumptions

Read the following sentences and identify the assumptions inherent in each regarding age, ability, appearance, ethnicity, gender, race, religion, sexual identity, and socioeconomic power or status.

Identify the "norm" (a standard of conduct that should or must be followed; a typical or usual way of being or behaving, usually said of a certain group), and discuss how the assumptions reflect this norm.

Discuss how these assumptions operate in your cultural situation. How are you affected by cultural assumptions about the "norm"?

Our founding fathers carved this great state out of the wilderness.

Mrs. Imoto looks remarkably good for her age.

Fashion tights are available in black, suntan, and flesh color.

Someday I intend to visit the third world.

We need more manpower.

Our facilities all provide handicapped access.

I'm just a person.

The network is down again. We'd better get Kevin in here to do his voodoo on it.

Our boys were having a rough time of it, and the black regiment was, too.

How Neandertal man existed for so long is a mystery. He must have had the ability to adapt to his environment.

I see she forgot to sign her time sheet. She's acting a little blonde today.

Mitochondrial DNA testing should help us determine when our race split off from the lower creatures.

Confined to a wheelchair, Mr. Garcia still manages to live a productive life.

Pat really went on the warpath when the budget figures came out.

I won't be associated with you and your pagan behaviors!

The Academy now admits women and other minorities.

We have a beautiful daycare center where women can leave their children while they work.

See if you can Jew him down to $50.

Personally, I don't think it's right that the foreign students come in here before term and buy up all the insignia bags. Our kids don't get a chance at them.

I completely forgot where I put my car keys. I must be having a senior moment.

Win a fabulous lovers' weekend in Hawaii! Prizes include a day at the spa for her and a relaxing game of golf for him.

That is not a very Christian attitude.

We welcome all guests, their wives, and their children.

May I speak to Mr. or Mrs. Williams?

Source: Janet Lockhart and Susan Shaw, *Writing for Change: Raising Awareness of Issues of Difference, Power, and Discrimination, www.teachingtolerance.org.*

approach is a focus on lived experience and a shift toward this more complex subjectivity as central to both theory construction and liberatory strategies. June Jordan also makes this case in "Report from the Bahamas." Jordan illustrates the multilayered tensions associated with intersecting identities in the context of global inequality, and the shifting limitations/ privileges that shift again when a citizen of the global north visits colonized, "westernized" locations.

Systems of inequality interconnect and work together to enforce inequality and privilege, each mostly supporting the other. The intersections of racism and classism, for example, are demonstrated by the fact that according to 2012 U.S. Census data, 25 percent of Latino/as and 28 percent of African Americans compared to 10 percent of white Americans are living in poverty. As Felice Yeskel explains in the reading "Opening Pandora's Box: Adding Classism to the Agenda," social class always intersects with other identities, but is particularly intertwined with race. While about half of all poor people are white, wealthy people are disproportionately white. Similarly, although ageism or age discrimination is very much connected to classism, it is also intertwined with sexism as well as with looksism. Women learn to "age pass"; that is, we do not want to be mistaken for 40 when we are in our 30s, or mistaken for 70 when only 60. This is part of the pursuit for youth and beauty that encourages women to participate as agents of ageism as we fulfill the expectations of gender. Ellie Mamber rejects such ideas in the poem "Don't Laugh, It's Serious, She Says." She refers to the "double standard of aging" whereby society interprets women's aging differently than men's (remembering too that "women" and "men" imply intersections of various identities with age and other identities and not just gender). Mamber observes the cultural acceptance of men being able to romantically pursue much younger women, but refuses to let this affect her sense of self.

Awareness of intersecting inequalities and advocacy for social justice was inspired by civil rights, feminist, and other social movements of the late twentieth century. In particular, intersectionality theory was shaped by the theoretical writings of women of color who, as described in Chapter 1, decried the lack of inclusivity and racism of the white women's movement. Intersectionality was applied to disability studies, for example, as a result of the work of the disability rights movement that worked to ensure the passage of the Americans with Disabilities Act in 1990, which protected the disabled from discrimination

IDEAS FOR ACTIVISM

- Find out how your university ensures access for people with disabilities. If some structures on your campus are inaccessible, advocate with your administration to create accessibility.
- Plan a celebration of black women during Black History Month.
- Find out what programs your university offers to recruit and retain students and faculty of color. If programs are not in place, advocate with your administration to develop such programs.
- Find out if your university's antidiscrimination policy includes sexual identity as a protected classification, and find out if your university provides benefits for domestic partners. If not, advocate with your administration to include sexual identity in its policy and/or to provide domestic partner benefits.

in employment, transportation, and other spaces such as public accommodations. Like other intersectionality theorists, disability scholars like Rosemarie Garland-Thompson emphasize that integrating understandings of ableism is not an additive endeavor but a "conceptual shift that strengthens our understanding of how these multiple oppressions intertwine, redefine, and mutually constitute each other."

DISCOURSE, POWER, AND KNOWLEDGE

A focus on difference, hierarchy, and systems of inequality and privilege implies the study of power. In this chapter we have presented this discussion of power as something individuals or groups have—or have not. It is important, however, to recognize that power does not necessarily operate in a binary or top-down fashion. Rather, power can be dispersed, multidimensional, and can function in all aspects of our everyday lives. Postmodern scholar Riki Wilchins calls this "small power exercised in hundreds of everyday transactions." And, instead of imagining power as something individuals acquire, share, or demand, we can imagine a concept of power as diffused and embedded in "discourse." This notion is central to Evin Taylor's discussion of the ways cisgender privilege involves a "cultural currency" or power enjoyed by people who possess desired characteristics such as "normal" gender expressions.

Discourse is the process of creating knowledge or a culturally constructed representation of reality. It involves language and other categories of meaning that work with social, material practices to produce "regimes of truth." These regimes of truth tell us what is "appropriate" in any given context. This involves the taken-for-granted rules about what people can say, who it is possible to be, and what it is possible to do (or not say or not do). In this way, discourse provides a range of being ("subjectivity") that we recognize as identity. This is what is meant by identities being produced through discourse. In other words, power produces discourses of difference, normality, and truth that shape bodies and identities. Moving beyond the notion of hierarchies, postmodern theorists focus on the diffuse and microlevel powers that produce multiple "truths" about gender, desire, and bodies.

Importantly, each community or society has its regimes of truth connected to power that inform what counts as knowledge. Imagine, for example, the different knowledge accepted among your family, or different groups of friends; your academic classes; or in your church, mosque, or synagogue, if you attend one. Regimes of truth are shaped by general truths/discourses such as "science," for example; other levels of discourse, such as patriotism, are framed by these broader, general discourses like religion. There are also discursive fields such as law that provide meaning and organize social institutions and processes. Scholars who focus on discourse are interested in understanding the ways some discourses have created meaning systems that have gained the status of "truth" and shape how we define and organize our social world (such as science) when other discourses are marginalized. These marginalized discourses offer a site for challenge and resistance. In this way it is interesting to consider how some discourses maintain their authority, how some "voices" get heard when others are silenced, and who benefits and how. These are all questions addressing issues of power/empowerment/disempowerment associated with knowledge, power, and discourse. We know this is a more complicated notion of power, but it is one you will encounter as you take more classes in the humanities and the social sciences.

Language, or the symbolic means by which we communicate, is a key aspect of regimes of truth as described above. Language is an incredibly sophisticated process of symbols that we learn at an early age and mostly take for granted unless we are confronted with trying to communicate in a language not our own. Because language allows us not only to name the objects of our experience but also to typify them (experience them as similar to something of a similar type), it creates as well as reflects our reality. It shapes as well as expresses thought. And because language helps us sort and anticipate our experiences, it has a primary influence on our lives. Language influences how its speakers focus their attention, remember events and people, and think about the world. This shapes how we understand space, time, and even justice. English, for example, tends to assign an agent to an action regardless of the agent's intent. In Japanese or Spanish, however, intent matters and requires different verb forms. Language maintains sexism and racism, for instance, by shaping our understandings and limiting options for self-definition. In this way it is important to consider how language shapes our reality and helps structure the everyday realities of our lives. When you grow up knowing 20 different words synonymous with "slut," and fewer, more positive words for men who have multiple sexual partners, for example, you learn something powerful about gender and sexuality.

These categories of meaning or regimes of truth discussed above involve ideas and values (such as stereotypes and jokes) or sets of beliefs (sometimes called ideologies) that provide rationale for injustice. Hill Collins calls this the "symbolic dimension" of systems of domination and subordination. For example, media often reinforce negative stereotypes about women such as dumb blondes, passive Asian Americans, or pushy African Americans. Another example of gendered messages comes from the institution of religion. This institution is especially powerful because it implies the notion of divine sanction. Traditional religious texts tell stories (for instance, Eve's behavior that led to the banishment from the Garden of Eden or the chaste role of the Virgin Mary) that convey important messages about moral thought and behavior as well as women's place in society. These messages tend to be strongly gendered and often support different behaviors for women and men. A central code of such religious teaching is that women should be subordinate to men in their spiritual and everyday lives.

An example of discourse supported by institutional power is the *bootstrap myth* concerning economic success. Yeskel addresses such ideologies in her article on classism and emphasizes how these truth claims ("regimes of truth") are propagated by economic systems that paint economic success as a result of hard work and ambition. People, if properly motivated and willing to work hard, can pull themselves up by their bootstraps. Given this set of ideas, those individuals who are not able to provide for their families must have deficiencies. Perhaps they were unmotivated, did not work hard enough, or were not smart enough. Such ideas encourage blaming the poor for their poverty rather than understanding the wider societal forces that shape people's existence and maintain classism. Notwithstanding the fact that of course hard work and ambition may facilitate some measure of success in the short term, it does not guarantee such success, nor does it tend to transform the bigger picture of structural inequalities. Notice that a particular truth claim need not be supported unanimously for it to influence society. Many people would disagree vehemently with the bootstrap myth; yet, still, this is a key part of the ideology of capitalist countries. In this way, institutions construct and are constructed by truth claims that provide authority about how people should be and live.

Copyright © Judy Horacek. www.horacek.com.au. Reprinted with permission.

Discourses that result in marginalization involve prejudices. *Prejudice* means, literally, to prejudge and involves making premature judgments without adequate information or with inaccurate information. Often prejudice is adopted when there is no other basis for understanding. For example, many white people have little contact with people of color, and many young people do not interact on an everyday basis with old people. As a result, there is a lack of accurate information to destabilize oppressive regimes of truth, and stereotypes or images from movies or other media are used instead. This kind of ignorance and misinformation breeds prejudice. Prejudices are *internalized* (assimilated, integrated, or incorporated into our thoughts and behavior) by all of us and as already mentioned in the discussion of homophobia and transphobia, they play a part in maintaining systems of inequality and privilege. However, because humans have active agency and will, prejudices can be resisted. Generally we can say that individuals negotiate these ideologies, accepting, resisting, and/or modifying them. If we are members of the *target group,* the group against whom the prejudice is aimed, it can lead to low self-esteem, self-loathing, and shame. Sadly, it can mean individuals are encouraged to believe they are not worthy of social justice and therefore are less likely to seek equality. Although members of target groups may accept oppressive regimes of truth, members of *nontarget groups,* groups (often part of the mythical norm) against whom the prejudice is not aimed, also internalize these messages as well as messages about their own privilege. This can encourage or justify hostility.

Internalizing oppression means that we self-police ourselves as a result of discourses that "discipline" bodies and encourage self-surveillance. In addition, however, we also police one another, encouraging compliance with institutions that may oppress. When individuals direct the resentment and anger they have about their situation onto those who are of equal or of lesser status, this process is called *horizontal hostility*. As a strategy, it is similar to the military tactic of "divide and conquer" in which groups are encouraged to fight with one another in order to avoid alliances that might collaboratively overpower an enemy. Women might do this when they are in competition about each other's looks or put other women down with verbal and/or nonverbal behavior.

INSTITUTIONS

Postmodern notions of power described above transcend the practices of who acquires what and how by seeing power as an everyday embodied phenomenon. This discursive notion of power as everywhere replaces the notion of institutions set apart from the systems of meanings they create. Some postmodern scholars, including Michel Foucault, still prioritize themes of institutionalized power, and it is to these that we now turn.

Institutions are social organizations that involve established patterns of behavior organized around particular purposes. They function through social norms (cultural expectations), which as explained above are institutionalized and patterned into organizations and sometimes established as rules and/or laws. Major institutions in our society include the family, marriage, the economy, government and criminal justice systems, religion, education, science, health and medicine, mass media, the military, and sports. Usually patterns of rules and practices implicit in major societal institutions have a historical component and reflect political, military, legal, and socioeconomic decisions made over decades and centuries. Although institutions are intended to meet the needs of society generally, or people in particular, they meet some people's needs better than others. These social organizations are central in creating systems of inequality and privilege because they pattern and structure differences among women in relatively organized ways. Institutions are important channels for the perpetuation of what Hill Collins calls "structures of domination and subordination." Note that institutions may resist systems of inequality and privilege through, for example, positive portrayals of women and marginalized people in media or the activities of some churches for civil rights.

Institutions encourage the channeling of various systems of gendered inequality to all aspects of women's lives. In terms of the patterning of resources and practices, institutions function to support systems of inequality and privilege. First, institutions assign various roles to women and men and are also places of employment where people perform gendered work. K-12 educational institutions, for example, employ a considerable number of women. However, as the prestige of the teaching position increases, the number of white males in these positions increases, along with higher salaries. Additionally, it is very difficult for openly lesbian teachers to find employment in some schools, and some states have attempted to pass laws preventing lesbians and gay men from teaching in state-funded educational establishments.

Second, to return to a more resource-based notion of power where the latter is imagined as something people acquire, own, or share, institutions distribute resources and extend privileges differentially to different groups. Sports are a good example of this. As an institution, athletics has traditionally been male dominated. Men's sports are more highly valued than women's sports and are a major focus for sports entertainment. Compared to men's

LEARNING ACTIVITY   **Women in Science and Engineering**

In 2005 Harvard University President Lawrence H. Summers created an uproar when he made the comment at an academic conference that the reasons fewer women than men succeed in science, technology, engineering, and math may be more related to innate differences than to socialization or discrimination. Many feminists responded by pointing to the wealth of research that indicates that girls and women are just as capable but their performances are often affected by social factors.

Certainly, the numbers do indicate a persistent dearth of women in science and engineering careers, although more women than ever are completing degrees in these areas. Still, women earn only 18% of degrees in engineering. Additionally, studies demonstrate that few white women are in tenured and tenure-track faculty positions in science, technology, and engineering, and the numbers are even bleaker for women of color. U.S. women are half the workforce but hold less than 25% of STEM jobs. Women are 27% of the computer and math workforce, but only one in seven engineers is a woman.

Why do you think white women and women and men of color are underrepresented in science, technology, and engineering?

Visit the websites of the professional organizations listed below that are dedicated to increasing the success of white women and women and men of color in various science, technology, and engineering fields. What do these sites suggest about the reasons for underrepresentation? How do they suggest addressing the problem of underrepresentation?

   Society of Women Engineers *www.swe.org*

   Association for Women in Computing *www.awc-hq.org*

   Association for Women in Mathematics *www.awm-math.org*

   Association for Women in Science *www.awis.org*

   National Action Council for Minorities in Engineering *www.nacme.org*

professional sports, women's are grossly underrepresented. Despite Title IX of the Educational Amendments of 1972, which barred discrimination in education, many colleges still are not in compliance and spend considerably more money on men's sports than on women's. Female athletes on some campuses complain that men receive better practice times in shared gymnasiums and more up-to-date equipment. And, within women's sports, some are more "white" than others. Examples that immediately come to mind are gymnastics, ice skating, equestrian sports, tennis, golf, and to some extent soccer (all relatively expensive pursuits). Most women's sports—outside of basketball and track—are dominated by white women. In this way, sports and athletics are an example of an institution where resources are inequitably distributed.

    Another blatant example of inequitable distribution concerns the economic system. Other than inherited wealth, the major way our economic system distributes resources is in terms of remuneration for the work that we do. Women tend to work in jobs that are

HISTORICAL MOMENT **Women of Color Feminism**

Acutely aware of the intersections of gender, race, sexual identity, and social class were women of color who daily experienced the material realities of the confluence of oppressions. From the beginning of the women's movement, women of color participated actively, although their specific concerns were often overlooked by some of the middle-class white women in the movement. In the early 1970s, women of color spoke out about their experiences of racism, sexism, and heterosexism. Barbara Smith co-founded the Combahee River Collective, a black feminist group that confronted racism and homophobia in the women's, gay, and black movements. The Collective took its name from a river in South Carolina where Harriet Tubman led a military action that freed hundreds of slaves.

In the late 1970s, Smith joined forces with Cherríe Moraga to found Kitchen Table/Women of Color Press when Moraga and Gloria Anzaldúa could not find a publisher for *This Bridge Called My Back: Writings by Radical Women of Color*. Kitchen Table/Women of Color Press was the first independent press to publish exclusively works by feminists of color. *This Bridge Called My Back* won an American Book Award from the Columbus Foundation.

In 1983 poet and novelist Alice Walker coined the term *womanism* to describe black feminism in contrast to *feminism,* which has generally been associated with white women. Walker situates womanists in a long line of black women who have struggled for social change and liberation. Womanists are, in her words, "outrageous, audacious, courageous, and willful, responsible, in charge, serious." They love black women's culture, black women's beauty, and themselves.

heavily occupied by women; examples include clerical work, service and retail sales, and professional occupations such as teaching and nursing. These jobs are undervalued in our society, contributing to the fact that a woman's average salary generally for all occupations tends to be less than a man's average salary. Some women work under deplorable conditions at minimum wage levels; some work with hazardous chemicals or have to breathe secondhand smoke throughout their workday. Old women and women of color own a tiny percentage of the wealth in this society—another example of the inequitable distribution of resources by an intersection or confluence of multiple identities.

Third, major institutions in society are interconnected and work to support and maintain one another. Often this means that personnel are shared among major institutions; more likely it means that these institutions mutually support one another in terms of the ways they fulfill (or deny) the needs of people in society. For example, close ties to economic institutions include the military (through the military-industrial complex), the government (corporate leaders often have official positions in government and rely on legislative loopholes and taxation systems to maintain corporate profits), health and medicine (with important ties to pharmaceutical companies), the media (whose content is controlled in part by advertising), and sports (through corporate sponsorship).

Stark Intersections: Gender, Race, Class, and HIV/AIDS

"We must address power imbalances in every single policy, strategy, and pro-gramme related to prevention, treatment and care if we seriously want to tackle this global challenge. [Gender] equality is not simply a matter of justice or fair-ness. Gender inequality is fatal."

—Noeleen Heyzer, UNIFEM

Gender inequality is fueling the HIV/AIDS epidemic: it deprives women of the ability to say no to risky practices, leads to coerced sex and sexual violence, keeps women uninformed about prevention, puts them last in line for care and life-saving treatment, and imposes an overwhelming burden for the care of the sick and dying. These fundamental threats to women's lives, health, and well-being are critical human rights issues—when women's human rights are not promoted, protected, and fulfilled, gender inequality is the dangerous result. Guaranteeing women's human rights is an indispensable component of the international strug-gle to combat HIV/AIDS. To combat today's scourge, we must understand the multiple intersections between gender, racial and ethnic discrimination, and the epidemiology of HIV/AIDS.

This intersectional approach derives from the realization that discriminations based on gender, race, ethnicity, caste, and class are not discrete phenomena, but compound one another in almost all socioeconomic circumstances.[1] Nine points are critical with regard to HIV/AIDS:

- Economic dependence and social subordination limit the ability of women and members of racial and ethnic minorities to demand safe and responsible sexual practices, including the use of condoms.
- Groups already subject to socioeconomic discrimination—including racial and ethnic minorities, migrant populations, and refugees—rank high among those most vulnerable to HIV infection. In all these groups, women are hardest hit.
- Racial and ethnic identities operate in complicated ways to increase women's vulnerability to sex trafficking, a major factor in women's growing infection rates.
- The culture of silence that surrounds female sexuality in many societies pre-vents women and girls from accessing information and services for protec-tion or treatment.
- In many countries, especially among racial and ethnic minorities, men receive preferential treatment in anti-retroviral therapies.
- Gender-based violence, both inside and outside the household, increases women's vulnerability to HIV/AIDS. HIV-positive women are frequently shunned by families and communities—and often subjected to further violence.
- This vulnerability mounts because of practices such as polygyny and wife-inheritance, as well as mistaken beliefs, such as that sex with a virgin can cure AIDS.
- Because women are primarily responsible for caregiving, caring for people with HIV/AIDS typically falls to widows and grandmothers or older girl chil-dren. Caregiving responsibilities increase as health and social services decrease and increasingly privatized services require a higher proportion of household income.

- Because women often care for communities as well as families, their illness or absorption in sheer survival activities weakens the vital informal support systems on which poor and marginalized communities depend, deepening and perpetuating poverty.[2]

These intersections are more alarming in light of the gender dimensions of HIV/AIDS:

- In 2014, an estimated 35 million people are living with HIV worldwide; more than half of adults living with HIV are women.
- Only about half of the countries that provide funding for HIV/AIDS programs include monies for programs specifically for women.
- Women represent approximately 60 percent of the people in Sub-Saharan Africa who are living with HIV/AIDS.
- Most caregivers are women. In particular in Africa, older women often care for sick children and orphaned grandchildren. These caregivers face serious financial and emotional stress from the burdens of caregiving.
- In India, women constitute approximately 39 percent of adult HIV infections; 80 percent of married women infected with HIV were monogamous.

Moreover, these statistics represent underestimations due to the personal reluctance to report the disease as well as government reluctance to acknowledge its extent. In addition, medical studies often do not disaggregate data according to race and gender, nor do they examine the specific health issues affecting women from racial and ethnic minorities or indigenous women as a matter of course. Thus, they may fail to uncover medical problems specific to particular groups of women.[3]

[1]For discussion of the concept of intersectionality, see *Gender and Racial Discrimination: Report of the Expert Group Meeting,* November 2000, Zagreb. UN Division for the Advancement of Women, 2001.
[2]Mercedes González de la Rocha and Alejandro Grinspun, "Private Adjustments: Household, Crisis and Work," in Grinspun, ed., *Choices for the Poor: Lessons from National Poverty Strategies.* New York: UNDP, 2001.
[3]UNIFEM, 2000. "Integrating Gender into the Third World Conference Against Racism, Racial Discrimination, Xenophobia and Related Intolerance." Background Paper prepared for the *Gender and Racial Discrimination: Report of the Expert Group Meeting,* November 2000, Zagreb, Croatia.

Source: www.unaids.org.

CONCLUSION

In closing, we have emphasized that systems of inequality and privilege are maintained through institutionalized power and various regimes of truth. However, it is also important to recognize the ways hate crimes (also known as bias-motivated crimes) are central to these power relations. Hate crimes reflect the ways power produces regimes of truth, difference, and normalcy that regulate people's lives. As already explained, we are expected to police ourselves and indulge in self-surveillance, often to keep ourselves in narrow boxes of "appropriate" behavior. However, in addition, disciplinary acts to regulate others who are perceived as not conforming (for example, not dressing like a woman is "supposed" to dress, or not acting like a man is supposed to act, or a person of color not showing the

ACTIVIST PROFILE **Fannie Lou Hamer**

She began life in Mississippi in 1917 as the granddaughter of slaves and the daughter of sharecroppers, but Fannie Lou Hamer was to become one of the most important leaders of the U.S. civil rights movement. Although Hamer became a sharecropper herself, by 1962 she'd had enough of the second-class life of the segregated South. She joined 17 other African Americans taking a bus to the county seat to register to vote. On the way home, they were stopped by police and arrested. After Hamer returned home, she was visited by the plantation owner, who told her that if she insisted on voting, she would have to get off his land, which she did that same day.

The next year, when Hamer joined other civil rights workers in challenging the "whites only" policy at a bus terminal diner, she was arrested and jailed. The police ordered two other African American prisoners to beat her with a metal-spiked club. Hamer was blinded in one eye from the beating and suffered permanent kidney damage.

In 1964 Hamer helped organize the Mississippi Freedom Democratic Party (MFDP) to challenge the all-white Mississippi delegation to the Democratic Convention. Hamer spoke to the credentials committee of the convention, and although her live testimony was preempted by a presidential press conference, it was aired by national networks in its entirety later that evening. The MFDP and the credentials committee reached a compromise, giving voting and speaking rights to two MFDP delegates and seating the others as honored guests. Hamer responded, "We didn't come all this way for two seats when all of us is tired." In 1968 the Mississippi Democratic Party did seat an integrated delegation.

Throughout her life, Hamer continued to work for justice, supporting Head Start for black schools and jobs for poor African Americans, opposing the Vietnam War, and helping to convene the National Women's Political Caucus in the 1970s.

Hamer died in 1977 and was buried in Mississippi. Her tombstone reads, "I am sick and tired of being sick and tired."

appropriate amount of defence expected by whites who hold racist views about people of color) result in hate crimes. And for some, the very act of living and being in a certain body is enough to cause anger and resentment. This kind of foundational bigotry is often at the heart of hate crimes.

Hate crimes include the threat of coercion and violence as well as the actual practice of it, and their motives are hate and bigotry. Evidence shows that perpetrators of hate crimes are most likely to be heterosexual white males. For example, there has been a substantial increase in hate crimes in the last decade, especially against people of color, lesbians, gays, and transgendered and transsexual people, although improved reporting systems are also increasing awareness of this social problem and providing hate-crime statistics. Hate groups include the Ku Klux Klan, racist Skinhead, Christian Identity Movement, Neo-Confederate, and Neo-Nazi (including Aryan Nations). One of the best sources for understanding hate crimes is the Southern Poverty Law Center at *www.splcenter.org*. It is important to emphasize that gender as a category is omitted from most hate-crime statutes despite the fact that women, transgendered, and queer/ gay men suffer from crimes of misogyny. People are often hurt and killed because they are perceived as women, or are expressing feminine behavior. In the case of transgender individuals, this reflects the ways regimes of truth discipline bodies that do not perform in expected ways. The United Nations now recognizes crimes against women, and the United States is starting to recognize crimes against non-U.S. women as basis for asylum. Hate crimes against women just because they are women, as well as hate crimes against, for example, lesbians or women of color, often involve *sexual terrorism,* the threat of rape and sexual assault that controls a woman's life whether or not she is actually physically or sexually violated.

In concluding this chapter we underscore the need for social change and transformation to improve the conditions of women's lives. Almost all the readings focus on this need. Patricia Hill Collins, for example, writes about awareness and education, the need to build empathy for one another, and the need to work to form coalitions for structural change around common causes. June Jordan also writes of the power of empathy and the possibilities of friendship for alliance building and social transformation. Peggy McIntosh and Evin Taylor tell us to recognize our privilege and work on internalized prejudices and privileges. Ellie Mamber suggests identifying and acknowledging sources of inequality and specifically the ways we are taught contempt for aging women. Felice Yeskel presents

LEARNING ACTIVITY **Combating Hate**

Many web pages provide valuable information about hate, hate crimes, and hate groups in the United States. Go to the Southern Poverty Law Center's homepage at *www.splcenter.org*. Click on "Hate Map." Then enter your state to discover which hate groups operate where you live. Then click on "Intelligence Files" to learn more about these hate groups. You may also want to visit these websites as well: *www.wiesenthal.com, www.adl.org, www.campuspride.org/ stop-the-hate, www.hrc.org,* and *www.hatewatch.org*. Using information from these sites, make a list of ways you can help stop hate.

LEARNING ACTIVITY   **Transgendered Experiences Around the World**

Go to YouTube and find videos made by transgendered people in the following countries:

- Brazil
- India
- Kenya
- Ukraine
- United States

What common experiences do these people have? How have they experienced being transgendered differently? What difficulties and forms of oppression do they face? What do they celebrate about their lives?

How do their lives and experiences offer challenges to fixed notions of gender identity?

The United Nations adopted the Universal Declaration of Human Rights in 1948: *http://www.un.org/en/documents/udhr/*. In 2012 the UN Secretary-General called for an end to discrimination based on gender identity. Take a look at the UN declaration and identify cultural and social changes that would be needed to bring about equity for transgendered people.

ways to challenge classism that involve confronting the behavior in ourselves, making demands on behalf of poor communities, and learning from the skills and strengths of working-class people. All authors, and especially the late Audre Lorde, hope for alliances across our differences. The message in all these articles is the need to recognize difference, to understand how the meanings associated with intersecting differences and the material conditions of everyday lives get translated into privilege and inequality, and to celebrate difference through coalitions for social justice and other expressions of personal and social concern.

Challenging the Pseudogeneric "Man"

Examine the following phrases that use male nouns as "generic." Describe the mental image created for you by each phrase. Do you see yourself and people like you in the images?

Next, choose a term representing a group of people of a specific age, religion, class, or ethnicity, and substitute that term for the male noun (example: "mankind" becomes "childkind"). Does use of the new, specific term sound incongruous or unusual? Why?

Describe the mental images created by using the substitute terms. Do you see yourself and people like you in the images?

Finally, suggest a gender-free, inclusive term for each (example: for "mankind," "humanity" or "people").

For the benefit of all mankind

"All men are created equal"

May the best man win

Prehistoric man

Man the pumps!

The first manned mission to Mars

Chairman of the Board

We need more manpower

Not fit for man or beast

The relationship between men and machines

Man's best friend

"To boldly go where no man has gone before"

Man of the Year

"Peace on Earth, goodwill toward men"

The founding fathers

"Crown thy good with brotherhood"

"Friends, Romans, countrymen; lend me your ears"

Source: Janet Lockhart and Susan M. Shaw, *Writing for Change: Raising Awareness of Difference, Power, and Discrimination, www.teachingtolerance.org.*

Toward a New Vision

Race, Class, and Gender as Categories of Analysis and Connection

Patricia Hill Collins (1993)

The true focus of revolutionary change is never merely the oppressive situations which we seek to escape, but that piece of the oppressor which is planted deep within each of us.

—*Audre Lorde,* Sister Outsider, *123*

Audre Lorde's statement raises a troublesome issue for scholars and activists working for social change. While many of us have little difficulty assessing our own victimization within some major system of oppression, whether it be by race, social class, religion, sexual orientation, ethnicity, age or gender, we typically fail to see how our thoughts and actions uphold someone else's subordination. Thus, White feminists routinely point with confidence to their oppression as women but resist seeing how much their White skin privileges them. African-Americans who possess eloquent analyses of racism often persist in viewing poor White women as symbols of white power. The radical left fares little better. "If only people of color and women could see their true class interests," they argue, "class solidarity would eliminate racism and sexism." In essence, each group identifies the type of oppression with which it feels most comfortable as being fundamental and classifies all other types as being of lesser importance.

Oppression is full of such contradictions. Errors in political judgment that we make concerning how we teach our courses, what we tell our children, and which organizations are worthy of our time, talents and financial support flow smoothly from errors in theoretical analysis about the nature of oppression and activism. Once we realize that there are few pure victims or oppressors, and that each one of us derives varying amounts of penalty and privilege from the multiple systems of oppression that frame our lives, then we will be in a position to see the need for new ways of thought and action.

. . .

[This discussion] addresses this need for new patterns of thought and action. I focus on two basic questions. First, how can we reconceptualize race, class and gender as categories of analysis? Second, how can we transcend the barriers created by our experiences with race, class and gender oppression in order to build the types of coalitions essential for social exchange? To address these question[s] I contend that we must acquire both new theories of how race, class and gender have shaped the experiences not just of women of color, but of all groups. Moreover, we must see the connections between these categories of analysis and the personal issues in our everyday lives, particularly our scholarship, our teaching and our relationships with our colleagues and students. As Audre Lorde points out, change starts with self, and relationships that we have with those around us must always be the primary site for social change.

HOW CAN WE RECONCEPTUALIZE RACE, CLASS, AND GENDER AS CATEGORIES OF ANALYSIS?

To me, we must shift our discourse away from additive analyses of oppression (Spelman 1982; Collins 1989). Such approaches are typically based on two key premises. First, they depend on either/or, dichotomous thinking. Persons, things and ideas are conceptualized in terms of their opposites. For example, Black/White, man/woman, thought/feeling, and fact/opinion are defined in oppositional terms. Thought and feeling are not seen as two different and interconnected ways of approaching truth that can coexist in scholarship and teaching. Instead, feeling is defined as antithetical to reason, as its opposite. In spite of the fact that we all have "both/and" identities (I am both a college professor and a mother—I don't stop being a mother when I drop my child off at school, or forget everything I learned while scrubbing the toilet), we persist in trying to classify each other in either/or categories. I live each day as an African-American woman—a race/gender specific experience. And I am not alone. Everyone has a race/gender/class specific identity. Either/or, dichotomous thinking is especially troublesome when applied to theories of oppression because every individual must be classified as being either oppressed or not oppressed. The both/and position of simultaneously being oppressed and oppressor becomes conceptually impossible.

A second premise of additive analyses of oppression is that these dichotomous differences must be ranked. One side of the dichotomy is typically labeled dominant and the other subordinate. Thus, Whites rule Blacks, men are deemed superior to women, and reason is seen as being preferable to emotion. Applying this premise to discussions of oppression leads to the assumption that oppression can be quantified, and that some groups are oppressed more than others. I am frequently asked, "Which has been most oppressive to you, your status as a Black person or your status as a woman?" What I am really being asked to do is divide myself into little boxes and rank my various statuses. If I experience oppression as a both/and phenomenon, why should I analyze it any differently?

Additive analyses of oppression rest squarely on the twin pillars of either/or thinking and the necessity to quantify and rank all relationships in order to know where one stands. Such approaches typically see African-American women as being more oppressed than everyone else because the majority of Black women experience the negative effects of race, class and gender oppression simultaneously. In essence, if you add together separate oppressions, you are left with a grand oppression greater than the sum of its parts.

I am not denying that specific groups experience oppression more harshly than others—lynching is certainly objectively worse than being held up as a sex object. But we must be careful not to confuse this issue of the saliency of one type of oppression in people's lives with a theoretical stance positing the interlocking nature of oppression. Race, class and gender may all structure a situation but may not be equally visible and/or important in people's self-definitions. In certain contexts, such as the antebellum American South and contemporary South America, racial oppression is more visibly salient, while in other contexts, such as Haiti, El Salvador and Nicaragua, social class oppression may be more apparent. For middle class White women, gender may assume experiential primacy unavailable to poor Hispanic women struggling with the ongoing issues of low-paid jobs and the frustrations of the welfare bureaucracy. This recognition that one category may have salience over another for a given time and place does not minimize the theoretical importance of assuming that race, class and gender as categories of analysis structure all relationships.

In order to move toward new visions of what oppression is, I think that we need to ask new questions. How are relationships of domination and subordination structured and maintained in the American political economy? How do race, class and gender function as parallel and interlocking systems that shape this basic relationship of domination and subordination? Questions such as these promise to move us away from futile theoretical struggles concerned with ranking oppressions and towards analyses that assume race, class and gender are all present in any given setting, even if one appears more visible and salient than the others. Our task becomes redefined as one of reconceptualizing oppression by uncovering the connections among race, class and gender as categories of analysis.

1. The Institutional Dimension of Oppression

Sandra Harding's contention that gender oppression is structured along three main dimensions—the institutional, the symbolic, and the individual—offers a useful model for a more comprehensive analysis encompassing race, class and gender oppression (Harding 1986). Systemic relationships of domination and subordination structured through social institutions such as schools, businesses, hospitals, the workplace, and government agencies represent the institutional dimension of oppression. Racism, sexism and elitism all have concrete institutional locations. Even though the workings of the institutional dimension of oppression are often obscured with ideologies claiming equality of opportunity, in actuality, race, class and gender place Asian-American women, Native American men, White men, African-American women, and other groups in distinct institutional niches with varying degrees of penalty and privilege.

Even though I realize that many . . . would not share this assumption, let us assume that the institutions of American society discriminate, whether by design or by accident. While many of us are familiar with how race, gender and class operate separately to structure inequality, I want to focus on how these three systems interlock in structuring the institutional dimension of oppression. To get at the interlocking nature of race, class and gender, I want you to think about the antebellum plantation as a guiding metaphor for a variety of American social institutions. Even though slavery is typically analyzed as a racist institution, and occasionally as a class institution, I suggest that slavery was a race, class, gender specific institution. Removing any one piece from our analysis diminishes our understanding of the true nature of relations of domination and subordination under slavery.

. . .

A brief analysis of key American social institutions most controlled by elite White men should convince us of the interlocking nature of race, class and gender in structuring the institutional dimension of oppression. For example, if you are from an American college or university, is your campus a modern plantation? Who controls your university's political economy? Are elite White men overrepresented among the upper administrators and trustees controlling your university's finances and policies? Are elite White men being joined by growing numbers of elite White women helpmates? What kinds of people are in your classrooms grooming the next generation who will occupy these and other decision-making positions? Who are the support staff that produce the mass mailings, order the supplies, fix the leaky pipes? Do African-Americans, Hispanics or other people of color form the majority of the invisible workers who feed you, wash your

dishes, and clean up your offices and libraries after everyone else has gone home?

If your college is anything like mine, you know the answers to these questions. You may be affiliated with an institution that has Hispanic women as vice-presidents for finance, or substantial numbers of Black men among the faculty. If so, you are fortunate. Much more typical are colleges where a modified version of the plantation as a metaphor for the institutional dimension of oppression survives.

2. The Symbolic Dimension of Oppression

Widespread, societally-sanctioned ideologies used to justify relations of domination and subordination comprise the symbolic dimension of oppression. Central to this process is the use of stereotypical or controlling images of diverse race, class and gender groups. In order to assess the power of this dimension of oppression, I want you to make a list, either on paper or in your head, of "masculine" and "feminine" characteristics. If your list is anything like that compiled by most people, it reflects some variation of the following:

Masculine	*Feminine*
aggressive	passive
leader	follower
rational	emotional
strong	weak
intellectual	physical

Not only does this list reflect either/or, dichotomous thinking and the need to rank both sides of the dichotomy, but ask yourself exactly which men and women you had in mind when compiling these characteristics. This list applies almost exclusively to middle class White men and women. The allegedly "masculine" qualities that you probably listed are only acceptable when exhibited by elite White men, or when used by Black and Hispanic men against each other or against women of color. Aggressive Black and Hispanic men are seen as dangerous, not powerful, and are often penalized when they exhibit any of the allegedly "masculine" characteristics. Working-class and poor White men fare slightly better and are also denied the allegedly "masculine" symbols of leadership, intellectual competence and human rationality. Women of color and working class and poor White women are also not represented on this list, for they have never had the luxury of being "ladies." What appear to be universal categories representing all men and women instead are unmasked as being applicable to only a small group.

It is important to see how the symbolic images applied to different race, class and gender groups interact in maintaining systems of domination and subordination. If I were to ask you to repeat the same assignment, only this time, by making separate lists for Black men, Black women, Hispanic women and Hispanic men, I suspect that your gender symbolism would be quite different. In comparing all of the lists, you might begin to see the interdependence of symbols applied to all groups. For example, the elevated images of White womanhood need devalued images of Black womanhood in order to maintain credibility.

. . .

Assuming that everyone is affected differently by the same interlocking set of symbolic images allows us to move forward toward new analyses. Women of color and White women have different relationships to White male authority, and this difference explains the distinct gender symbolism applied to both groups. Black women encounter controlling images such as the mammy, the matriarch, the mule and the whore, that encourage others to reject us as fully human people. Ironically, the negative nature of these images simultaneously encourages us to reject them. In contrast, White women are offered seductive images, those that promise to reward them for supporting the status quo. And yet seductive images can be equally controlling. Consider, for example, the views of Nancy White, a 73-year-old Black woman, concerning images of rejection and seduction:

> My mother used to say that the black woman is the white man's mule and the white woman is his dog. Now, she said that to say this: we do the heavy work and get beat whether we do it well or not. But the white woman is closer to the master and he pats them on the head and lets them sleep in the house, but he ain't gon' treat neither one like he was dealing with a person. (Gwaltney 1980, 148)

Both sets of images stimulate particular political stances. By broadening the analysis beyond the confines of race, we can see the varying levels of rejection and seduction available to each of us due to our race, class and gender identity. Each of us lives with an allotted portion of institutional privilege and penalty, and with varying levels of rejection and seduction inherent in the symbolic images applied to us. This is the context in which we make our choices. Taken together, the institutional and symbolic dimensions of oppression create a structural backdrop against which all of us live our lives.

3. The Individual Dimension of Oppression

Whether we benefit or not, we all live within institutions that reproduce race, class and gender oppression. Even if we never have any contact with members of other race, class and gender groups, we all encounter images of these groups and are exposed to the symbolic meanings attached to those images. On this dimension of oppression, our individual biographies vary tremendously. As a result of our institutional and symbolic statuses, all of our choices become political acts.

Each of us must come to terms with the multiple ways in which race, class and gender as categories of analysis frame our individual biographies. I have lived my entire life as an African-American woman from a working-class family, and this basic fact has had a profound impact on my personal biography. Imagine how different your life might be if you had been born Black, or White, or poor, or of a different race/class/gender group than the one with which you are most familiar. The institutional treatment you would have received and the symbolic meanings attached to your very existence might differ dramatically from what you now consider to be natural, normal and part of everyday life. You might be the same, but your personal biography might have been quite different.

I believe that each of us carries around the cumulative effect of our lives within multiple structures of oppression. If you want to see how much you have been affected by this whole thing, I ask you one simple question—who are your close friends? Who are the people with whom you can share your hopes, dreams, vulnerabilities, fears and victories? Do they look like you? If they are all the same, circumstance may be the cause. For the first seven years of my life I saw only low-income Black people. My friends from those years reflected the composition of my community. But now that I am an adult, can the defense of circumstance explain the patterns of people that I trust as my friends and colleagues? When given other alternatives, if my friends and colleagues reflect the homogeneity of one race, class and gender group, then these categories of analysis have indeed become barriers to connection.

I am not suggesting that people are doomed to follow the paths laid out for them by race, class and gender as categories of analysis. While these three structures certainly frame my opportunity structure, I as an individual always have the choice of accepting things as they are, or trying to change them. As Nikki Giovanni points out, "we've got to live in the real world. If we don't like the world we're living in, change it. And if we can't change it, we change ourselves. We can do something" (Tate 1983, 68). While a piece of the oppressor may be planted deep within each of us, we each have the choice of accepting that piece or challenging it as part of the "true focus of revolutionary change."

HOW CAN WE TRANSCEND THE BARRIERS CREATED BY OUR EXPERIENCES WITH RACE, CLASS, AND GENDER OPPRESSION IN ORDER TO BUILD THE TYPES OF COALITIONS ESSENTIAL FOR SOCIAL CHANGE?

Reconceptualizing oppression and seeing the barriers created by race, class and gender as interlocking categories of analysis is a vital first step. But we must transcend these barriers by moving toward race, class and gender as categories of connection, by building relationships and coalitions that will bring about social change. What are some of the issues involved in doing this?

1. Differences in Power and Privilege

First, we must recognize that our differing experiences with oppression create problems in the relationships among us. Each of us lives within a system that vests us with varying levels of power and privilege. These differences in power, whether structured along axes of race, class, gender, age or sexual orientation, frame our relationships. African-American writer June Jordan describes her discomfort on a Caribbean vacation with Olive, the Black woman who cleaned her room:

> . . . even though both "Olive" and "I" live inside a conflict neither one of us created, and even though both of us therefore hurt inside that conflict, I may be one of the monsters she needs to eliminate from her universe and, in a sense, she may be one of the monsters in mine. (1985, 47)

Differences in power constrain our ability to connect with one another even when we think we are engaged in dialogue across differences. . . .

In extreme cases, members of privileged groups can erase the very presence of the less privileged. When I first moved to Cincinnati, my family and I went on a picnic at a local park. Picnicking next to us was a family of White Appalachians. When I went to push my daughter on the swings, several of the children came over. They had missing, yellowed and broken teeth, they wore old clothing and their poverty was evident. I was shocked. Growing up in a large eastern city, I had never seen such awful poverty among Whites. The segregated neighborhoods in which I grew up made White poverty all but invisible. More importantly, the privileges attached to my newly acquired social class position allowed me to ignore and minimize the poverty among Whites that I did encounter. My reactions to those children made me realize how confining phrases such as "well, at least they're not Black," had become for me. In learning to grant human subjectivity to the Black victims of poverty, I had simultaneously learned to demand White victims of poverty. By applying categories of race to the objective conditions confronting me, I was quantifying and ranking oppressions and missing the very real suffering which, in fact, is the real issue.

One common pattern of relationships across differences in power is one that I label "voyeurism." From the perspective of the privileged, the lives of people of color, of the poor, and of women are interesting for their entertainment value. The privileged become voyeurs, passive onlookers who do not relate to the less powerful, but who are interested in seeing how the "different" live. Over the years, I have heard numerous African-American students complain about professors who never call on them except when a so-called Black issue is being discussed. The students' interest in discussing race or qualifications for doing so appear unimportant to the professor's efforts to use Black students' experiences as stories to make the material come alive for the White student audience. Asking Black students to perform on cue and provide a Black experience for their White classmates can be seen as voyeurism at its worst.

Members of subordinate groups do not willingly participate in such exchanges but often do so because members of dominant groups control the institutional and symbolic apparatuses of oppression. Racial/ethnic groups, women, and the poor have never had the luxury of being voyeurs of the lives of the privileged. Our ability to survive in hostile settings has hinged on our ability to learn intricate details about the behavior and worldview of the powerful and adjust our behavior accordingly. I need only point to the difference in perception of those men and women in abusive relationships. Where men can view their girlfriends and wives as sex objects, helpmates and a collection of stereotyped categories of voyeurism—women must be attuned to every nuance of their partners' behavior. Are women "naturally" better in relating to people with more power than themselves, or have circumstances mandated that men and women develop different skills? . . .

Coming from a tradition where most relationships across difference are squarely rooted in relations of domination and subordination, we have much less experience relating to people as different but equal. The classroom is potentially one powerful and safe space where dialogues among individuals of unequal power relationships can occur. . . .

2. Coalitions Around Common Causes

A second issue in building relationships and coalitions essential for social change concerns knowing the real reasons for coalition. Just what brings people together? One powerful catalyst fostering group solidarity is the presence of a common enemy. African-American, Hispanic, Asian-American, and women's studies all share the common intellectual heritage of challenging what passes for certified knowledge in the academy. But politically expedient

relationships and coalitions like these are fragile because, as June Jordan points out:

> It occurs to me that much organizational grief could be avoided if people understood that partnership in misery does not necessarily provide for partnership for change: When we get the monsters off our backs all of us may want to run in very different directions. (1985, 47)

Sharing a common cause assists individuals and groups in maintaining relationships that transcend their differences. Building effective coalitions involves struggling to hear one another and developing empathy for each other's points of view. The coalitions that I have been involved in that lasted and that worked have been those where commitment to a specific issue mandated collaboration as the best strategy for addressing the issue at hand.

. . .

None of us alone has a comprehensive vision of how race, class and gender operate as categories of analysis or how they might be used as categories of connection. Our personal biographies offer us partial views. Few of us can manage to study race, class and gender simultaneously. Instead, we each know more about some dimensions of this larger story and less about others. . . . Just as the members of the school had special skills to offer to the task of building the school, we have areas of specialization and expertise, whether scholarly, theoretical, pedagogical or within areas of race, class or gender. We do not all have to do the same thing in the same way. Instead, we must support each other's efforts, realizing that they are all part of the larger enterprise of bringing about social change.

3. Building Empathy

A third issue involved in building the types of relationships and coalitions essential for social change concerns the issue of individual accountability. Race, class and gender oppression form the structural backdrop against which we frame our relationship—these are the forces that encourage us to substitute voyeurism . . . for fully human relationships. But while we may not have created this situation, we are each responsible for making individual, personal choices concerning which elements of race, class and gender oppression we will accept and which we will work to change.

One essential component of this accountability involves developing empathy for the experiences of individuals and groups different than ourselves. Empathy begins with taking an interest in the facts of other people['s] lives, both as individuals and as groups. If you care about me, you should want to know not only the details of my personal biography but a sense of how race, class and gender as categories of analysis created the institutional and symbolic backdrop for my personal biography. How can you hope to assess my character without knowing the details of the circumstances I face?

Moreover, by taking a theoretical stance that we have all been affected by race, class and gender as categories of analysis that have structured our treatment, we open up possibilities for using those same constructs as categories of connection in building empathy. For example, I have a good White woman friend with whom I share common interests and beliefs. But we know that our racial differences have provided us with different experiences. So we talk about them. We do not assume that because I am Black, race has only affected me and not her or that because I am a Black woman, race neutralizes the effect of gender in my life while accenting it in hers. We take those same categories of analysis that have created cleavages in our lives, in this case, categories of race and gender, and use them as categories of connection in building empathy for each other's experiences.

Finding common causes and building empathy is difficult, no matter which side of privilege we inhabit. Building empathy from the dominant side of privilege is difficult, simply because individuals from privileged backgrounds are not encouraged to do so. For example, in order for those of you who are White to develop empathy for the experiences of people of color, you must grapple with how your white skin has privileged you. This is difficult to do, because it not only entails the intellectual process of seeing how whiteness is elevated in institutions and symbols, but it also involves the often painful process of seeing how your whiteness has shaped your personal biography. Intellectual stances against the institutional and symbolic dimensions of racism

are generally easier to maintain than sustained self-reflection about how racism has shaped all of our individual biographies. Were and are your fathers, uncles, and grandfathers really more capable than mine, or can their accomplishments be explained in part by the racism members of my family experienced? Did your mothers stand silently by and watch all this happen? More importantly, how have they passed on the benefits of their whiteness to you?

These are difficult questions, and I have tremendous respect for my colleagues and students who are trying to answer them. Since there is no compelling reason to examine the source and meaning of one's own privilege, I know that those who do so have freely chosen this stance. They are making conscious efforts to root out the piece of the oppressor planted within them. To me, they are entitled to the support of people of color in their efforts. Men who declare themselves feminists, members of the middle class who ally themselves with antipoverty struggles, heterosexuals who support gays and lesbians, are all trying to grow, and their efforts place them far ahead of the majority who never think of engaging in such important struggles.

Building empathy from the subordinate side of privilege is also difficult, but for different reasons. Members of subordinate groups are understandably reluctant to abandon a basic mistrust of members of powerful groups because this basic mistrust has traditionally been central to their survival. As a Black woman, it would be foolish for me to assume that White women, or Black men, or White men or any other group with a history of exploiting African-American women have my best interests at heart. These groups enjoy varying amounts of privilege over me and therefore I must carefully watch them and be prepared for a relation of domination and subordination.

Like the privileged, members of subordinate groups must also work toward replacing judgments by category with new ways of thinking and acting. Refusing to do so stifles prospects for effective coalition and social change. Let me use another example from my own experiences. When I was an undergraduate, I had little time or patience for the theorizing of the privileged. My initial years at a private, elite institution were difficult, not because the course work was challenging (it was, but that wasn't what distracted me) or because I had to work while my classmates lived on family allowances (I was used to work). The adjustment was difficult because I was surrounded by so many people who took their privilege for granted. Most of them felt entitled to their wealth. That astounded me.

I remember one incident of watching a White woman down the hall in my dormitory try to pick out which sweater to wear. The sweaters were piled up on her bed in all the colors of the rainbow, sweater after sweater. She asked my advice in a way that let me know that choosing a sweater was one of the most important decisions she had to make on a daily basis. Standing knee-deep in her sweaters, I realized how different our lives were. She did not have to worry about maintaining a solid academic average so that she could receive financial aid. Because she was in the majority, she was not treated as a representative of her race. She did not have to consider how her classroom comments or basic existence on campus contributed to the treatment her group would receive. Her allowance protected her from having to work, so she was free to spend her time studying, partying, or in her case, worrying about which sweater to wear. The degree of inequality in our lives and her unquestioned sense of entitlement concerning that inequality offended me. For a while, I categorized all affluent White women as being superficial, arrogant, overly concerned with material possessions, and part of my problem. But had I continued to classify people in this way, I would have missed out on making some very good friends whose discomfort with their inherited or acquired social class privileges pushed them to examine their position.

Since I opened with the words of Audre Lorde, it seems appropriate to close with another of her ideas. . . .

> Each of us is called upon to take a stand. So in these days ahead, as we examine ourselves and each other, our works, our fears, our differences, our sisterhood and survivals, I urge you to tackle what is most difficult for us all, self-scrutiny of our complacencies, the idea that since each of us believes she is on the side of right, she need not examine her position. (1985)

I urge you to examine your position.

REFERENCES

Collins, Patricia Hill. 1989. "The Social Construction of Black Feminist Thought." *Signs*. Summer 1989.

Gwaltney, John Langston. 1980. *Drylongso: A Self-Portrait of Black America*. New York: Vintage.

Harding, Sandra. 1986. *The Science Question in Feminism*. Ithaca, NY: Cornell University Press.

Jordan, June. 1985. *On Call: Political Essays*. Boston: South End Press.

Lorde, Audre. 1984. *Sister Outsider*. Trumansberg, NY: The Crossing Press.

———. 1985. "Sisterhood and Survival." Keynote address, conference on the Black Woman Writer and the Diaspora, Michigan State University.

Spelman, Elizabeth. 1982. "Theories of Race and Gender: The Erasure of Black Women." *Quest* 5: 36–32.

Tate, Claudia, ed. 1983. *Black Women Writers at Work*. New York: Continuum.

READING **11**

Intersectionality

Vivian M. May (2012)

The struggle to comprehend and implement intersectionality is epistemologically and politically significant for Women's and Gender studies (WGS), and suggests a problem of understanding that must be accounted for. As Susan Babbitt describes it, unpacking a problem of understanding entails first examining how "dominant expectations"—about rationality, subjectivity, narrative style, or form—tend to "rule out the meaningfulness of important struggles" and impede their ability to be understood (2001, 298). Some discourses "are not able to be heard" (300); they seem unimaginable because of power asymmetries and injustices (308). Moreover, this implausibility is rarely questioned. Often, "people *think* they have understood . . . when they have not in fact understood what most needs to be understood" (303), so that, any difficulty in understanding (i.e., that there is something important that is still *not yet understood* from a normative stance) and the fundamental differences in worldview are thereby put to the side. The alternative way of seeing becomes characterized merely as different or illogical: its meaning is flattened. I would argue that intersectionality's recursiveness signifies the degree to which its practices go against the grain of prevailing conceptualizations of personhood, rationality, and liberation politics, even in WGS.

PROBLEMS OF UNDERSTANDING AND NOMINAL USE

To better illustrate how elusive this shift in thinking can be, and because I am interested in well-intended applications of intersectionality that fall short, I first turn to a text that is widely taught in Women's and Gender Studies: Marilyn Frye's essay, "Oppression"—regularly included across the WGS curriculum because Frye's delineation of systemic "double-binds" (1983, 2) is useful. . . . Yet despite Frye's important contributions to examining oppression, and notwithstanding her intent to focus on how gender is interwoven with race, class, and sexuality, she slips away from developing the multifaceted analyses she sets out to undertake.

For example, Frye concludes her essay with a gender-universal analysis of patriarchy that posits the divide between men and women as primary, since, she argues, "men" are never denigrated or oppressed "as men." Frye explains, "whatever assaults and harassments [a man] is subject to, being male is not what selects him for victimization; . . . men are not oppressed *as men*" (1983, 16). To be taken up, Frye's analysis requires a form

of "pop-bead" logic (Spelman 1988, 136, 186), wherein the gender "bead" of masculinity can be pulled apart from race, sexuality, social class, and other factors. Masculinity seems, therefore, not to be impacted by or intersected with disability, race, sexuality, or citizenship status, in an inextricable, dynamic way.

This atomization of multiplicity is also evident in that Frye is confident, in analyzing the politics of anger or of the smile, that "it is [her] being a woman that reduces the power of [her] anger to a proof of [her] insanity" (1983, 16). Perhaps Frye can presume it is her "being a woman" alone that is causal because she is white, able-bodied, and middle class—since people who are marked as "different" by means of race, disability, and social class, for instance, are also often stereotyped as more irrationally "angry" than are members of privileged groups. Some Women are perceived as "angrier" (or as inappropriately angry) in comparison to other women; likewise, some women are expected to show docility or compliance via smiles or silences to other women because of interwined factors of (and asymmetries of power related to) race, class, sexuality, and ability.

Additionally, Frye's analysis of how women's dependency (4, 7-10) is derogated (while structurally reinforced) obscures how different forms of gendered dependency are differently derogated because gender is not isolatable from other facets of identity. Some forms of dependence (heteronormative, middle class) are more idealized (e.g., women's dependence on men who are their fathers or husbands for protection and care), whereas others are stigmatized as deviant and in need of remediation (e.g., poor women's dependency on the state via welfare). Both types of institutionalized dependency can be understood as oppressive, but differently so; one carries social stigma, the other social approval (even if, as feminist scholars, we may think it should not). Throughout her analysis of the workings of oppression, Frye includes reference to (and seeks to acknowledge) differences among women (of race, class, and sexuality), yet reverts to statements about women as a general group and to analyses of gender processes as not only homogenized but also isolatable from other factors and processes.

A SNAPSHOT OF INTERSECTIONALITY

Rather than assume "everyone understands intersectionality," I want to pause to summarize some of its central insights. Intersectionality calls for analytic methods, modes of political action, and ways of thinking about persons, rights, and liberation informed by multiplicity. It is both metaphorical and material, in that it seeks to capture something not adequately named about the nature of lived experience and about systems of oppression. Intersectionality adds nuance to understanding different sites of feminism(s) and the multiple dimensions of lived experience, it lends insight into the interrelationships among struggle for liberation, and . . . it shifts what "counts" as a feminist issue and what is included as gendered experience. Intersectionality offers a vision of future possibilities that can be more fully realized once a shift toward the multiple takes place. Its critical practices include:

- *Considering lived experience as a criterion of meaning:* Intersectionality focuses on how lived experience can be drawn upon to expose the partiality of normative modes of knowing (often deemed neutral) and to help marginalized groups articulate and develop alternative analyses and modes of oppositional consciousness, both individually and collectively.[1]
- *Reconceptualizing marginality and focusing on the politics of location:* Intersectionality considers marginalization in terms of social structure and lived experience and redefines "marginality as a potential source of strength," not merely "tragedy" (Collins 1998,128). Lugones and Price insist that the marginalized, "create a sense of ourselves as historical subjects, not exhausted by intermeshed oppressions" (2003, 331). While hooks characterizes the margins as a "site of radical possibility, a space of resistance" (1990, 149), Lugones describes marginality as a site of the "resistant oppressed" wherein "you have ways of living in disruption of domination" (2006, 78, 79). Methodologically, attending to the politics of location entails accounting for the contexts of knowledge production (Bowleg 2008, 318; Jordan-Zachery 2007, 259) and

thinking about the relevance of the knower to the known—factors usually considered outside the realm of knowledge "proper."[2]

- *Employing "both/and" thinking and centering multiracial feminist theorizing:* Moving away from "dichotomized" thought (Lugones 1990, 80) and "monolithic" analyses of identity, culture, and theory (Christian 1990a, 341), intersectionality theorizes from a position of "simultaneity" (Nash 2008, 2; V. Smith 1998, xv).[3] Bridging the theoretical and empirical (McCall 2005, 1780), and using "double vision" (Lugones 2006, 79), intersectionality "refers to both a normative theoretical argument *and* an approach to conducting empirical research that emphasizes the interaction of categories" (Hancock 2007, 63). While it is *not* merely the descriptive for which intersectionality was developed, it is often reduced to this.[4] As Shields explains: "Most behavioral science research that focuses on intersectionality . . . employs as a perspective on research rather than as a theory that drives the research question. . . . [Intersectionality's] emergent properties and processes escape attention" (2008, 304).
- *Shifting toward an understanding of complex subjectivity:* Alongside an epistemological shift toward simultaneity and both/and reasoning is a shift toward subjectivity that accounts for "compoundedness" (Crenshaw 2000, 217); critiques of unitary knowledge and the unitary subject are linked (McCall 2005, 1776). Rather than approach multiple facets of identity as "non-interactive" and "independent" (Harnois 2005, 810), an intersectional approach focuses on indivisibility, a "complex ontology" (Phoenix and Pattynama 2006, 187) conceptualized as woven (Alarcón 1990, 366), kneaded (Anzaldúa 1990e, 380), and shifting (Valentine 2007, 15). This approach "denies any *one* perspective as the only answer, but instead posits a shifting tactical and strategic subjectivity that has the capacity to re-center depending upon the forms of oppression to be confronted" (Sandoval 2000, 67).
- *Analyzing systems of oppression as operating in a "matrix":* Connected to complex subjectivity

are analyses of domination that account for relationships among forms of oppression. As Pauli Murray aptly put it, "The lesson of history that all human rights are indivisible and that the failure to adhere to this principle jeopardizes the rights of all is particularly applicable" (1995, 197). The Combahee River Collective insists on "the development of an integrated analysis and practice based upon the fact that the major systems of oppression are interlocking" (1983, 261).[5] A "single axis" approach "distorts" and "theoretically erases" differences within and between groups (Crenshaw 2000, 209-17); multiple systems of power must therefore be addressed simultaneously.

- *Conceiving of solidarity or coalition without relying on homogeneity:* Rather than sameness as a foundation for alliance, Lorde attests, "You do not have to be me in order for us to fight alongside each other" (1984, 142).[6] Intersectionality pursues "'solidarity' through different political formations and . . . alternative theories of the subject of consciousness" (Alarcon 1990, 364). Mohanty advocates thinking about feminist solidarity in terms of mutuality, accountability, and the recognition of common interests as the basis for relationships among diverse communities. Rather than assuming an enforced commonality of oppression, the practice of solidarity foregrounds communities of people who have chosen to work and fight together. . . . [It] is always an achievement, the result of active struggle (2003, 78). This requires acknowledging that marginalization does not mean "we" should "naturally" be able to work together. Lugones urges us to "craft coalitional gestures" both communicatively and politically, since there is no guarantee of "transparency" between us, even margin to margin (2006, 80, 83).
- *Challenging false universals and highlighting omissions built into the social order and intellectual practices:* Intersectionality exposes how the experiences of some are often universalized to represent the experiences, needs, and claims of all group members. Rather than conceptualize group identity via a common denominator framework that subsumes within-group

differences, creates rigid distinctions between groups, and leads to distorted analyses of discrimination, intersectionality explores the politics of the unimaginable, the invisible, and the silenced. Intersectionality understands exclusions and gaps as meaningful and examines the theoretical and political impact of such absences.[7]

- *Exploring the implications of simultaneous privilege and oppression:* In addition to focusing on the "relational nature of dominance and subordination" (Zinn and Dill 1996, 327)[8] and breaking open false universals, intersectionality focuses on how personhood can be structured on internalized hierarchies or "arrogant perception" (Lugones 1990); thus "one may also 'become a woman' in opposition to other women" not just in opposition to "men" (Alarcon 1990, 360).[9] Normative ideas about identity categories as homogenous "limit[s] inquiry to the experiences of otherwise-privileged members of the group," and "marginalizes those who are multiply-burdened and obscures claims that cannot be understood as resulting from discrete sources of discrimination" (Crenshaw 2000, 209). Intersectionality seeks to shift the logics of how we understand domination, subordination, personhood, and rights.
- *Identifying how a liberatory strategy may depend on hierarchy or reify privilege to operate:* Intersectionality offers tools for seeing how we often uphold the very forms of oppression that we seek to dismantle.[10] For instance, Crenshaw identifies how the court's normative view of race and sex discrimination means that the very legal frameworks meant to address inequality require a certain degree of privilege to function (2000, 213). She lays bare the court's "refusal to acknowledge compound discrimination" (214) and highlights the problem Lugones characterizes as a collusion with divide and conquer thinking (2006, 76).

We must ask some difficult questions. Do nods to intersectionality in WGS provide a "conceptual warrant" to avoid, if not suppress, multiplicity? Has intersectionality's critical lexicon, forged in struggle, been co-opted and flattened rather than engaged with as an epistemological and political lens? We must address the common notion that "everyone" already "does" intersectionality; even if one agrees, for the sake of argument, that "we" all "do" intersectional work, the question remains, *how*? Does intersectionality shape research, pedagogy, or curriculum structure from the start, or is it tacked on or tokenized? How does intersectionality translate into methodology, be it qualitative, quantitative, literary, or philosophical? Is it reduced to a descriptive tool or conceptualized as impossible? Do its key insights slip away, even in well-intended applications? Statements about intersectionality's having "arrived" beg the question Collins raises when she wonders whether it is being adopted primarily as the latest "overarching" terminology to explain both the matrices of identity and of systems of oppression, but in a way that obscures complexities. She writes: "If we are not careful, the term 'intersectionality' runs the . . . risk of trying to explain everything yet ending up saying nothing" (2008, 72).

NOTES

1. See Anzaldua 1999; Christian 1990; Collins 1990; Crenshaw 2000; Combahee 1983; Guy-Sheftall 1995b.
2. See Anzaldúa 1999; Zinn and Dill 1996, 328; Lugones 2006, 76–78; Sandoval 2000, 86.
3. See Anzaldúa 1990b, 145 and 1990c, 378; Henderson 1989, 117; Phoenix and Pattynama 2006, 187; Sandoval 2000, 88; Yuval-Davis 2007.
4. See Bowleg 2008, 316–18; Hancock 2007, 66; Harnois 2005, 813; Jordan-Zachery 2007, 261.
5. See Bcalc 1970, 92–93; Collins 2008, 72 and 2004, 95–96; Jordan-Zachery 2007, 259; King 1988; Lemons 2001, 87; Lorde 1984, 140; B. Smith 1983, xxxii–xxviii; Zinn and Dill 1996, 237.
6. See Alarcón 1990, 366; Lemons 2001, 87; B. Smith 1983, xliii.
7. See Alarcón 1990, 356; Bowleg 2008, 312; Crenshaw 2000, 223; A. Davis 1984; DuCille 2001, 254; Henderson 1989, 117; Jordan-Zachery 2007, 254; Ringrose 2007, 267; Sandoval 2000, 75–76.
8. See Anzaldúa 1990d, xix; and Minh-ha 1990, 375.
9. See Crenshaw 2000, 209-13; Lorde 1984, 67, 132; Cole 2008, 446; Lemons 2001, 86–87; Marable 2001, 124; Neal 1995.
10. See Alarcón 1990; Anzaldúa 1990d and 1990e; McCall 2005; Murray 1995; Nnacmeka 2003.

REFFERENCES

Alarcón, Norma. 1990. "The 'Theoretical Subject(s) of This Bridge Called My Back and Anglo American Feminism." In *Making Face, Making Soul* Haciendo Caras: *Creative and Critical Perspectives by Feminists of Color,* edited by Gloria E. Anzaldúa, 356–69. San Francisco: Aunt Eute Books.

Babbitt, Susan E. 2001. "Objectivity and the Role of Bias." In *Engendering Rationalities*, edited by Nancy Tuana, and Sandra Morgen, 297–314. Albany: SUNY Press.

Bailey, Alison. 1998. "Privilege: Expanding on Marilyn Frye's 'Oppression'." *Journal of Social Philosophy* 29 (3): 104–19.

Bowleg, Lisa. 2008. "When Black + Lesbian + Woman ≠ Black Lesbian Woman: The Methodological Challenges of Qualitative and Quantitative Intersectionality Research." *Sex Roles 59* (5–6): 312–25.

Carbado, Devon W. 1999. *Black Men on Race, Gender, and Sexuality.* New York: New York University Press.

Christian, Barbara. 1990a. "The Race for Theory." In *Making Face, Making Soul* Haciendo Caras: *Creative and Critical Perspectives by Feminists of Color* edited by Gloria E. Anzaldúa, 335–45. San Francisco: Aunt Lute Books.

———. 1998. *Fighting Words: Black Women and the Search for Justice.* Minneapolis: University of Minnesota.

———. 2004. *Black Sexual Politics: African Americans, Gender, and the New Racism,* New York: Routledge.

———. 2008, "Reply to Commentaries: *Black Sexual Politics Revisited.*" *Studies in Gender and Sexuality* 9: 68–85.

Combahee River Collective. 1983. "The Combahee River Collective Statement." In *Home Girls: A Black Feminist Anthology,* edited by Barbara Smith, 272–82. New York: Kitchen Table Press. First Published 1977.

Cooper, Anna Julia. 1988. *A Voice from the South by a Black Woman of the South,* New York: Oxford University Press. First Published 1892.

_____. 1925. *L'Attitude de la France á l'égard de l'esclavage pendant la Révolution.* Paris: impr. de la cour d'appel, L. Maretheux.

Crenshaw, Kimberlé. 2000. "Demarginal-izing the Intersection of Race and Sex: A Black Feminist Critique of Antidis-crimination Doctrine, Feminist Theory, and Antiracist Politics." In *The Black Feminist Reader,* edited by Joy James and T. Denean Sharpley–Whiting, 208–38. Maiden: Blackwell.

Davis, Kathy. 2008. "Intersectionality as Buz-zword: A Sociology of Science Perspective on What Makes a Feminist Theory Successful." *Feminist Theory* 9 (1): 67–85.

Frye, Marilyn. 1983. "Oppression." In *The Politics of Reality: Essays in Feminist Theory,* 1–16, Trumansburg: Crossing Press.

Giddings Paula J. 2006. "Editor's Introduction." *Meridians* 7 (1) v–vii.

_____. 1995b. "The Evolution of Feminist Consciousness Among African American Women." In *Words of Fire,* 1–22. New York: New Press.

Hancock, Ange-Marie. 2007. "When Multiplica-tion Doesn't Equal Quick Addition: Examin-ing Intersectionality as a Research Paradigm." *Perspectives Politics* 5 (1): 63–79.

Harnois, Catherine. 2005. "Different Paths to Different Feminisms? Bridging Multiracial Feminist Theory and Quantitative Sociological Gender Research" *Gender & Society* 19 (6): 309–28.

Holloway, Karla F. C. 2006. "'Cruel Enough to Stop the Blood': Global Feminisms and the U.S. Body Politic, Or: 'They Done Taken My Blues and Gone'." *Meridians: Feminism, Race, Transnationalism* 7 (1): 1–18.

_____. 1990. *Yearning: Race, Gender, and Cul-tural Politics.* Boston: South End Press.

Jordan-Zachery, Julia. 2007. "Am I a Black Woman or a Woman Who Is Black? A Few Thoughts on the Meaning of Intersectionality." *Politics & Gender* 3 (2): 254–63.

Lorde, Audre. 1984. *Sister Outsider: Essays and Speeches by Audre Lorde.* Berkeley: The Crossing Press.

Lugones, Maria. 1990. "Playfulness, 'World'–Traveling and Loving Perception." In *Making Face, Making Soul* Haciendo Caras: *Creative and Critical Perspectives by Feminists of Color,* edited by Gloria E. Anzaldúa, 390–402. San Francisco: Aunt Lute Books.

_____. 2006. "On Complex Communication." *Hypatia* 21 (3): 75–85.

Lugones, María, and Joshua Price. 2003, "The Inseparability of Race, Class, and Gender." *Latino Studies Journal* 1 (2): 329–32.

Lugones, María, and Elizabeth Spelman. 2005. "Have We Got a Theory for You!: Feminist Theory, Cultural Imperialism and the Demand For 'The Woman's Voice'." In *Feminist The-ory: A Reader,* edited by Wendy Kolmar and Frances Bartkowski, New York: McGraw Hill.

Maparyan, Layli. 2012. *The Womanist Idea.* New York; Routledge.

McCall, Leslie. 2005. "Tie Complexity of Intersec-tionality." *Signs: Journal of Women in Culture and Society* 30 (3): 1771–1800.

_____. 2003. *Feminism without Borders: Decolo-nizing Theory, Practicing Solidarity.* Durham, NC: Duke University Press.

Murray, Pauli. 1995. "The Liberation of Black Women." In *Words of Fire: An Anthology of African-American Feminist Thought,* edited by Beverly Guy-Sheftall, 186–97. New York: New Press.

Nash, Jennifer. 2008. "Re-Thinking Intersectional-ity." *Feminist Review* 89 (1) 1–15.

Nnaemeka, Obioma. 2003. "Nego-Feminism: Theorizing, Practicing, and Pruning Africa's Way." Signs: *Journal of Women in Culture and Society* 29 (2): 357–85.

Phoenix, Ann, and Pamela Pattynama. 2006. "Intersectionality." *European Journal of Women's Studies* 13 (3): 187–92.

_____. 2000. *Methodology of the Oppressed.* Minneapolis: University of Minnesota Press.

Shields, Stephanie. 2008. "Gender: An Intersectionality Perspective." *Sex Roles* 59 (5–6): 301–11.

_____, ed. 1983, *Home Girls: A Black Feminist Anthology.* New York: Kitchen Table, Women of Color Press.

Simith, Valerie. 1998. *Not Just Race, Not Just Gender: Black Feminist Readings.* New York: Routledge.

Spelman, Elizabeth V. 1988. *Inessential Woman: Problems of Exclusion in Feminist Though*t. Boston: Beacon.

Valentine, Gill. 2007 "Theorizing and Researching Intersectionality: A Challenge for Feminist Geography." *The Professional Geographer* 59 (1): 10–21.

Zinn, Maxine Bace, and Bonnie Thornton Dill. 1996. "Theorizing Difference from Multiracial Feminism." *Feminist Studies* 22 (2): 321–33.

R E A D I N G **12**

There Is No Hierarchy of Oppression

Audre Lorde (2009)

I was born Black, and a woman. I am trying to become the strongest person I can become to live the life I have been given and to help effect change toward a livable future for this earth and for my children. As a Black, lesbian, feminist, socialist, poet, mother of two, including one boy, and a member of an interracial couple, I usually find myself part of some group in which the majority defines me as deviant, difficult, inferior, or just plain "wrong."

From my membership in all of these groups I have learned that oppression and the intolerance of difference come in all shapes and sizes and colors and sexualities; and that among those of us who share the goals of liberation and a workable future for our children, there can be no hierarchies of oppression. I have learned that sexism (a belief in the inherent superiority of one sex over all others and thereby its right to dominance) and heterosexism (a belief in the inherent superiority of one pattern of loving over all others and thereby its right to dominance) both arise from the same source as racism—a belief in the inherent superiority of one race over all others and thereby its right to dominance.

"Oh," says a voice from the Black community, "but being Black is NORMAL!" Well, I and many Black people of my age can remember grimly the days when it didn't used to be!

I simply do not believe that one aspect of myself can possibly profit from the oppression of any other part of my identity. I know that my people cannot possibly profit from the oppression of any other group which seeks the right to peaceful existence. Rather, we diminish ourselves by denying to others what we have shed blood to obtain for our children. And those children need to learn that they do not have to become like each other in order to work together for a future they will all share.

The increasing attacks upon lesbians and gay men are only an introduction to the increasing attacks upon all Black people, for wherever oppression manifests itself in this country, Black people are potential victims. And it is a standard of right-wing cynicism to encourage members of oppressed groups to act against each other, and so long as we are divided because of our particular identities we cannot join together in effective political action.

Within the lesbian community I am Black, and within the Black community I am a lesbian. Any attack against Black people is a lesbian and gay issue, because I and thousands of other Black women are part of the lesbian community. Any attack against lesbians and gays is a Black issue, because thousands of lesbians and gay men are Black. There is no hierarchy of oppression.

It is not accidental that the Family Protection Act,[1] which is virulently antiwoman and antiblack, is also antigay. As a black person, I know who my enemies are, and when the Ku Klux Klan goes to court in Detroit to try and force the board of education to remove books the Klan believes "hint at homosexuality," then I know I cannot afford the luxury of fighting one form of oppression only. I cannot afford to believe that freedom from intolerance is the right of only one particular group. And I cannot afford to choose between the fronts upon which I must battle these forces of discrimination, wherever they appear to destroy me. And when they appear to destroy me, it will not be long before they appear to destroy you.

NOTE

[1] A 1981 congressional bill repealing federal laws that promoted equal rights for women, including coeducational school-related activities and protection for battered wives, and providing tax incentives for married mothers to stay at home.

R E A D I N G **13**

White Privilege and Male Privilege

Peggy McIntosh (1988)

Through work to bring materials and perspectives from Women's Studies into the rest of the curriculum, I have often noticed men's unwillingness to grant that they are overprivileged in the curriculum, even though they may grant that women are disadvantaged. Denials that amount to taboos surround the subject of advantages that men gain from women's disadvantages. These denials protect male privilege from being fully recognized, acknowledged, lessened, or ended.

Thinking through unacknowledged male privilege as a phenomenon with a life of its own, I realized that since hierarchies in our society are interlocking, there was most likely a phenomenon of white privilege that was similarly denied and protected, but alive and real in its effects. As a white person,

I realized I had been taught about racism as something that puts others at a disadvantage, but had been taught not to see one of its corollary aspects, white privilege, which puts me at an advantage.

I think whites are carefully taught not to recognize white privilege, as males are taught not to recognize male privilege. So I have begun in an untutored way to ask what it is like to have white privilege. This paper is a partial record of my personal observations and not a scholarly analysis. It is based on my daily experiences within my particular circumstances.

I have come to see white privilege as an invisible package of unearned assets that I can count on cashing in each day, but about which I was "meant" to remain oblivious. White privilege is like an invisible weightless knapsack of special provisions, assurances, tools, maps, guides, codebooks, passports, visas, clothes, compass, emergency gear, and blank checks.

Since I have had trouble facing white privilege, and describing its results in my life, I saw parallels here with men's reluctance to acknowledge male privilege. Only rarely will a man go beyond acknowledging that women are disadvantaged to acknowledging that men have unearned advantage, or that unearned privilege has not been good for men's development as human beings, or for society's development, or that privilege systems might ever be challenged and *changed.*

I will review here several types or layers of denial that I see at work protecting, and preventing awareness about, entrenched male privilege. Then I will draw parallels, from my own experience, with the denials that veil the facts of white privilege. Finally, I will list forty-six ordinary and daily ways in which I experience having white privilege, by contrast with my African American colleagues in the same building. This list is not intended to be generalizable. Others can make their own lists from within their own life circumstances.

Writing this paper has been difficult, despite warm receptions for the talks on which it is based.[1] For describing white privilege makes one newly accountable. As we in Women's Studies work [to] reveal male privilege and ask men to give up some of their power, so one who writes about having white privilege must ask, "Having described it, what will I do to lessen or end it?"

The denial of men's overprivileged state takes many forms in discussions of curriculum change work. Some claim that men must be central in the curriculum because they have done most of what is important or distinctive in life or in civilization. Some recognize sexism in the curriculum but deny that it makes male students seem unduly important in life. Others agree that certain *individual* thinkers are male oriented but deny that there is any *systemic* tendency in disciplinary frameworks or epistemology to overempower men as a group. Those men who do grant that male privilege takes institutionalized and embedded forms are still likely to deny that male hegemony has opened doors for them

personally. Virtually all men deny that male over-reward alone can explain men's centrality in all the inner sanctums of our most powerful institutions. Moreover, those few who will acknowledge that male privilege systems have overempowered them usually end up doubting that we could dismantle these privilege systems. They may say they will work to improve women's status, in the society or in the university, but they can't or won't support the idea of lessening men's. In curricular terms, this is the point at which they say that they regret they cannot use any of the interesting new scholarship on women because the syllabus is full. When the talk turns to giving men less cultural room, even the most thoughtful and fair-minded of the men I know will tend to reflect, or fall back on, conservative assumptions about the inevitability of present gender relations and distributions of power, calling on precedent or sociobiology and psychobiology to demonstrate that male domination is natural and follows inevitably from evolutionary pressures. Others resort to arguments from "experience" or religion or social responsibility or wishing and dreaming.

After I realized, through faculty development work in Women's Studies, the extent to which men work from a base of unacknowledged privilege, I understood that much of their oppressiveness was unconscious. Then I remembered the frequent charges from women of color that white women whom they encounter are oppressive. I began to understand why we are justly seen as oppressive, even when we don't see ourselves that way. At the very least, obliviousness of one's privileged state can make a person or group irritating to be with. I began to count the ways in which I enjoy unearned skin privilege and have been conditioned into oblivion about its existence, unable to see that it put me "ahead" in any way, or put my people ahead, overrewarding us and yet also paradoxically damaging us, or that it could or should be changed.

My schooling gave me no training in seeing myself as an oppressor, as an unfairly advantaged person, or as a participant in a damaged culture. I was taught to see myself as an individual whose moral state depended on her individual moral will. At school, we were not taught about slavery in any depth; we were not taught to see slaveholders as damaged people. Slaves were seen as the only group at risk of being dehumanized. My schooling followed the pattern which Elizabeth Minnich has pointed out: whites are taught to think of their lives as morally neutral, normative, and average, and also ideal, so that when we work to benefit others, this is seen as work that will allow "them" to be more like "us." I think many of us know how obnoxious this attitude can be in men.

After frustration with men who would not recognize male privilege, I decided to try to work on myself at least by identifying some of the daily effects of white privilege in my life. It is crude work, at this stage, but I will give here a list of special circumstances and conditions I experience that I did not earn but that I have been made to feel are mine by birth, by citizenship, and by virtue of being a conscientious law-abiding "normal" person of goodwill. I have chosen those conditions that I think in my case *attach somewhat more to skin-color privilege* than to class, religion, ethnic status, or geographical location, though these other privileging factors are intricately intertwined. As far as I can see, my Afro-American co-workers, friends, and acquaintances with whom I come into daily or frequent contact in this particular time, place, and line of work cannot count on most of these conditions.

1. I can, if I wish, arrange to be in the company of people of my race most of the time.
2. I can avoid spending time with people whom I was trained to mistrust and who have learned to mistrust my kind or me.
3. If I should need to move, I can be pretty sure of renting or purchasing housing in an area which I can afford and in which I would want to live.
4. I can be reasonably sure that my neighbors in such a location will be neutral or pleasant to me.
5. I can go shopping alone most of the time, fairly well assured that I will not be followed or harassed by store detectives.
6. I can turn on the television or open to the front page of the paper and see people of my race widely and positively represented.
7. When I am told about our national heritage or about "civilization," I am shown that people of my color made it what it is.
8. I can be sure that my children will be given curricular materials that testify to the existence of their race.
9. If I want to, I can be pretty sure of finding a publisher for this piece on white privilege.
10. I can be fairly sure of having my voice heard in a group in which I am the only member of my race.
11. I can be casual about whether or not to listen to another woman's voice in a group in which she is the only member of her race.
12. I can go into a book shop and count on finding the writing of my race represented, into a supermarket and find the staple foods that fit with my cultural traditions, into a hairdresser's shop and find someone who can deal with my hair.
13. Whether I use checks, credit cards, or cash, I can count on my skin color not to work against the appearance that I am financially reliable.
14. I could arrange to protect our young children most of the time from people who might not like them.
15. I did not have to educate our children to be aware of systemic racism for their own daily physical protection.
16. I can be pretty sure that my children's teachers and employers will tolerate them if they fit school and workplace norms; my chief worries about them do not concern others' attitudes toward their race.
17. I can talk with my mouth full and not have people put this down to my color.
18. I can swear, or dress in secondhand clothes, or not answer letters, without having people attribute these choices to the bad morals, the poverty, or the illiteracy of my race.
19. I can speak in public to a powerful male group without putting my race on trial.
20. I can do well in a challenging situation without being called a credit to my race.
21. I am never asked to speak for all the people of my racial group.
22. I can remain oblivious to the language and customs of persons of color who constitute the world's majority without feeling in my culture any penalty for such oblivion.

23. I can criticize our government and talk about how much I fear its policies and behavior without being seen as a cultural outsider.

24. I can be reasonably sure that if I ask to talk to "the person in charge," I will be facing a person of my race.

25. If a traffic cop pulls me over or if the IRS audits my tax return, I can be sure I haven't been singled out because of my race.

26. I can easily buy posters, postcards, picture books, greeting cards, dolls, toys, and children's magazines featuring people of my race.

27. I can go home from most meetings of organizations I belong to feeling somewhat tied in, rather than isolated, out of place, outnumbered, unheard, held at a distance, or feared.

28. I can be pretty sure that an argument with a colleague of another race is more likely to jeopardize her chances for advancement than to jeopardize mine.

29. I can be fairly sure that if I argue for the promotion of a person of another race, or a program centering on race, this is not likely to cost me heavily within my present setting, even if my colleagues disagree with me.

30. If I declare there is a racial issue at hand, or there isn't a racial issue at hand, my race will lend me more credibility for either position than a person of color will have.

31. I can choose to ignore developments in minority writing and minority activist programs, or disparage them, or learn from them, but in any case, I can find ways to be more or less protected from negative consequences of any of these choices.

32. My culture gives me little fear about ignoring the perspectives and powers of people of other races.

33. I am not made acutely aware that my shape, bearing, or body odor will be taken as a reflection on my race.

34. I can worry about racism without being seen as self-interested or self-seeking.

35. I can take a job with an affirmative action employer without having my co-workers on the job suspect that I got it because of my race.

36. If my day, week, or year is going badly, I need not ask of each negative episode or situation whether it has racial overtones.

37. I can be pretty sure of finding people who would be willing to talk with me and advise me about my next steps, professionally.

38. I can think over many options, social, political, imaginative, or professional, without asking whether a person of my race would be accepted or allowed to do what I want to do.

39. I can be late to a meeting without having the lateness reflect on my race.

40. I can choose public accommodation without fearing that people of my race cannot get in or will be mistreated in the places I have chosen.

41. I can be sure that if I need legal or medical help, my race will not work against me.

42. I can arrange my activities so that I will never have to experience feelings of rejection owing to my race.

43. If I have low credibility as a leader, I can be sure that my race is not the problem.

44. I can easily find academic courses and institutions that give attention only to people of my race.

45. I can expect figurative language and imagery in all of the arts to testify to experiences of my race.

46. I can choose blemish cover or bandages in "flesh" color and have them more or less match my skin.

I repeatedly forgot each of the realizations on this list until I wrote it down. For me, white privilege has turned out to be an elusive and fugitive subject. The pressure to avoid it is great, for in facing it I must give up the myth of meritocracy. If these things are true, this is not such a free country; one's life is not what one makes it; many doors open for certain people through no virtues of their own. These perceptions mean also that my moral condition is not what I had been led to believe. The appearance of being a good citizen rather than a troublemaker comes in large part from having all sorts of doors open automatically because of my color.

A further paralysis of nerve comes from literary silence protecting privilege. My clearest memories of finding such analysis are in Lillian Smith's unparalleled *Killers of the Dream* and Margaret Andersen's review of Karen and Mamie Fields' *Lemon Swamp*. Smith, for example, wrote about walking toward black children on the street and knowing they would step into the gutter; Andersen contrasted the pleasure that she, as a white child, took on summer driving trips to the south with Karen Fields' memories of driving in a closed car stocked with all necessities lest, in stopping, her black family should suffer "insult, or worse." Adrienne Rich also recognizes and writes about daily experiences of privilege, but in my observation, white women's writing in this area is far more often on systemic racism than on our daily lives as light-skinned women.[2]

In unpacking this invisible knapsack of white privilege, I have listed conditions of daily experience that I once took for granted, as neutral, normal, and universally available to everybody, just as I once thought of a male-focused curriculum as the neutral or accurate account that can speak for all. Nor did I think of any of these perquisites as bad for the holder. I now think that we need a more finely differentiated taxonomy of privilege, for some of these varieties are only what one would want for everyone in a just society, and others give license to be ignorant, oblivious, arrogant, and destructive. Before proposing some more finely tuned categorization, I will make some observations about the general effects of these conditions on my life and expectations.

In this potpourri of examples, some privileges make me feel at home in the world. Others allow me to escape penalties or dangers that others suffer. Through some, I escape fear, anxiety, insult, injury, or a sense of not being welcome, not being real. Some keep me from having to hide, to be in disguise, to feel sick or crazy, to negotiate each transaction from the position of being an outsider or, within my group, a person who is suspected of having too close links with a dominant culture. Most keep me from having to be angry.

I see a pattern running through the matrix of white privilege, a pattern of assumptions that were passed on to me as a white person. There was one main piece of cultural turf; it was my own turf, and I was among those who could control the turf. I could measure up to the cultural standards and take advantage of the many options I saw around me to make what the culture would call a success of my life. *My skin color was an asset for any move I was educated to want to make.* I could think of myself as "belonging" in major ways and of making social systems work for me. I could freely disparage, fear, neglect, or be oblivious to anything outside of the dominant cultural forms. Being of the main culture, I could also criticize it fairly freely. My life was reflected back to me frequently enough so that I felt, with regard to my race, if not to my sex, like one of the real people.

Whether through the curriculum or in the newspaper, the television, the economic system, or the general look of people in the streets, I received daily signals and indications that my people counted and that others *either didn't exist or must be trying, not very successfully, to be like people of my race.* I was given cultural permission not to hear voices of people of other races or a tepid cultural tolerance for hearing or acting on such voices. I was also raised not to suffer seriously from anything that darker-skinned people might say about my group, "protected," though perhaps I should more accurately say *prohibited,* through the habits of my economic class and social group, from living in racially mixed groups or being reflective about interactions between people of differing races.

In proportion as my racial group was being made confident, comfortable, and oblivious, other groups were likely being made unconfident, uncomfortable, and alienated. Whiteness protected me from many kinds of hostility, distress, and violence, which I was being subtly trained to visit in turn upon people of color.

For this reason, the word "privilege" now seems to me misleading. Its connotations are too positive to fit the conditions and behaviors which "privilege systems" produce. We usually think of privilege as being a favored state, whether earned or conferred by birth or luck. School graduates are reminded they are privileged and urged to use their (enviable) assets well. The word "privilege" carries the connotation of being something everyone must want. Yet some of the conditions I have described here work to systemically overempower certain groups. Such privilege simply *confers dominance,* gives permission to control, because of one's race or sex. The kind of privilege that gives license to some people to be, at best, thoughtless and, at worst, murderous should not continue to be referred to as a desirable attribute. Such "privilege" may be widely desired without being in any way beneficial to the whole society.

Moreover, though "privilege" may confer power, it does not confer moral strength. Those who do not depend on conferred dominance have traits and qualities that may never develop in those who do. Just as Women's Studies courses indicate that women survive their political circumstances to lead lives that hold the human race together, so "underprivileged" people of color who are the world's majority have survived their oppression and lived survivors' lives from which the white global minority can and must learn. In some groups, those dominated have actually become strong through *not* having all of these unearned advantages, and this gives them a great deal to teach the others. Members of so-called privileged groups can seem foolish, ridiculous, infantile, or dangerous by contrast.

I want, then, to distinguish between earned strength and unearned power conferred systemically. Power from unearned privilege can look like strength when it is, in fact, permission to escape or to dominate. But not all of the privileges on my list are inevitably damaging. Some, like the expectation that neighbors will be decent to you, or that your race will not count against you in court, should be the norm in a just society and should be considered as the entitlement of everyone. Others, like the privilege not to listen to less powerful people, distort the humanity of the holders as well as the ignored groups. Still others, like finding one's staple foods everywhere, may be a function of being a member of a numerical majority in the population. Others have to do with not having to labor under pervasive negative stereotyping and mythology.

We might at least start by distinguishing between positive advantages that we can work to spread, to the point where they are not advantages at all but simply part of the normal civic and social fabric, and negative types of advantage that unless rejected will always reinforce our present hierarchies. For example, the positive "privilege" of belonging, the feeling that one belongs within the human circle, as Native Americans say, fosters development and should not

be seen as privilege for a few. It is, let us say, an entitlement that none of us should have to earn; ideally it is an *unearned entitlement.* At present, since only a few have it, it is an *unearned advantage* for them. The negative "privilege" that gave me cultural permission not to take darker-skinned Others seriously can be seen as arbitrarily conferred dominance and should not be desirable for anyone. This paper results from a process of coming to see that some of the power that I originally saw as attendant on being a human being in the United States consisted in *unearned advantage* and *conferred dominance,* as well as other kinds of special circumstance not universally taken for granted.

In writing this paper I have also realized that white identity and status (as well as class identity and status) give me considerable power to choose whether to broach this subject and its trouble. I can pretty well decide whether to disappear and avoid and not listen and escape the dislike I may engender in other people through this essay, or interrupt, answer, interpret, preach, correct, criticize, and control to some extent what goes on in reaction to it. Being white, I am given considerable power to escape many kinds of danger or penalty as well as to choose which risks I want to take.

There is an analogy here, once again, with Women's Studies. Our male colleagues do not have a great deal to lose in supporting Women's Studies, but they do not have a great deal to lose if they oppose it either. They simply have the power to decide whether to commit themselves to more equitable distributions of power. They will probably feel few penalties whatever choice they make; they do not seem, in any obvious short-term sense, the ones at risk, though they and we are all at risk because of the behaviors that have been rewarded in them.

Through Women's Studies work I have met very few men who are truly distressed about systemic, unearned male advantage and conferred dominance. And so one question for me and others like me is whether we will be like them, or whether we will get truly distressed, even outraged, about unearned race advantage and conferred dominance and if so, what we will do to lessen them. In any case, we need to do more work in identifying how they actually affect our daily lives. We need more down-to-earth writing by people about these taboo subjects.

We need more understanding of the ways in which white "privilege" damages white people, for these are not the same ways in which it damages the victimized. Skewed white psyches are an inseparable part of the picture, though I do not want to confuse the kinds of damage done to the holders of special assets and to those who suffer the deficits. Many, perhaps most, of our white students in the United States think that racism doesn't affect them because they are not people of color; they do not see "whiteness" as a racial identity. Many men likewise think that Women's Studies does not bear on their own existences because they are not female; they do not see themselves as having gendered identities. Insisting on the universal "effects" of "privilege" systems, then, becomes one of our chief tasks, and being more explicit about the *particular* effects in particular contexts is another. Men need to join us in this work.

In addition, since race and sex are not the only advantaging systems at work, we need to similarly examine the daily experience of having age advantage, or ethnic advantage, or physical ability, or advantage related to nationality, religion, or sexual orientation. Professor Marnie Evans suggested to me that in many ways the list I made also applies directly to heterosexual privilege. This is a still more taboo subject than race privilege: the daily ways in which heterosexual privilege makes some persons comfortable or powerful, providing supports, assets, approvals, and rewards to those who live or expect to live in heterosexual pairs. Unpacking that content is still more difficult, owing to the deeper embeddedness of heterosexual advantage and dominance and stricter taboos surrounding these.

But to start such an analysis I would put this observation from my own experience: the fact that I live under the same roof with a man triggers all kinds of societal assumptions about my worth, politics, life, and values and triggers a host of unearned advantages and powers. After recasting many elements from the original list I would add further observations like these:

1. My children do not have to answer questions about why I live with my partner (my husband).

2. I have no difficulty finding neighborhoods where people approve of our household.

3. Our children are given texts and classes that implicitly support our kind of family unit and do not turn them against my choice of domestic partnership.

4. I can travel alone or with my husband without expecting embarrassment or hostility in those who deal with us.

5. Most people I meet will see my marital arrangements as an asset to my life or as a favorable comment on my likability, my competence, or my mental health.

6. I can talk about the social events of a weekend without fearing most listeners' reactions.

7. I will feel welcomed and "normal" in the usual walks of public life, institutional and social.

8. In many contexts, I am seen as "all right" in daily work on women because I do not live chiefly with women.

Difficulties and dangers surrounding the task of finding parallels are many. Since racism, sexism, and heterosexism are not the same, the advantages associated with them should not be seen as the same. In addition, it is hard to isolate aspects of unearned advantage that derive chiefly from social class, economic class, race, religion, region, sex, or ethnic identity. The oppressions are both distinct and interlocking, as the Combahee River Collective statement of 1977 continues to remind us eloquently.[3]

One factor seems clear about all of the interlocking oppressions. They take both active forms that we can see and embedded forms that members of the dominant group are taught not to see. In my class and place, I did not see myself as racist because I was taught to recognize racism only in individual acts of meanness by members of my group, never in invisible systems conferring racial dominance on my group from birth. Likewise, we are taught to think that sexism or heterosexism is carried on only through intentional, individual acts of discrimination, meanness, or cruelty, rather than in invisible systems conferring unsought dominance on certain groups. Disapproving of the systems won't be enough to change them. I was taught to think that racism could end if white individuals changed their attitudes; many men think sexism can be ended by individual changes in daily behavior toward women. But a man's sex provides advantage for him whether or not he approves of the way in which dominance has been conferred on his group. A "white" skin in the United States opens many doors for whites whether or not we approve of the way dominance has been conferred on us. Individual acts can palliate, but cannot end, these problems. To redesign social systems, we need first to acknowledge their colossal unseen dimensions. The silences and denials surrounding privilege are the key political tool here. They keep the thinking about equality or equity incomplete, protecting unearned advantage and conferred dominance by making these subjects taboo. Most talk by whites about equal opportunity seems to me now to be about equal opportunity to try to get into a position of dominance while denying that *systems* of dominance exist.

Obliviousness about white advantage, like obliviousness about male advantage, is kept strongly inculturated in the United States so as to maintain the myth of meritocracy, the myth that democratic choice is equally available to all. Keeping most people unaware that freedom of confident action is there for just a small number of people props up those in power and serves to keep power in the hands of the same groups that have most of it already. Though systemic change takes many decades, there are pressing questions for me and I imagine for some others like me if we raise our daily consciousness on the perquisites of being light-skinned. What will we do with such knowledge? As we know from watching men, it is an open question whether we will choose to use unearned advantage to weaken invisible privilege systems and whether we will use any of our arbitrarily awarded power to try to reconstruct power systems on a broader base.

NOTES

I have appreciated commentary on this paper from the Working Papers Committee of the Wellesley College Center for Research on Women, from members of the Dodge seminar, and from many individuals, including Margaret Andersen, Sorel Berman, Joanne Braxton, Johnnella Butler, Sandra Dickerson, Marnie Evans, Beverly Guy-Sheftall, Sandra Harding, Eleanor Hinton Hoytt, Pauline Houston, Paul Lauter, Joyce Miller, Mary Norris, Gloria Oden, Beverly Smith, and John Walter.

1. This paper was presented at the Virginia Women's Studies Association conference in Richmond in April 1986, and the American Educational Research Association conference in Boston in October 1986, and discussed with two groups of participants in the Dodge seminars for Secondary School Teachers in New York and Boston in the spring of 1987.

2. Andersen, Margaret, "Race and the Social Science Curriculum: A Teaching and Learning Discussion." *Radical Teacher,* November 1984, pp. 17–20. Smith, Lillian, *Killers of the Dream,* New York: W. W. Norton, 1949.

3. "A Black Feminist Statement," The Combahee River Collective, pp. 13–22 in G. Hull, P. Scott, B. Smith, Eds., *All the Women Are White, All the Blacks Are Men, But Some of Us Are Brave: Black Women's Studies,* Old Westbury, NY: The Feminist Press, 1982.

R E A D I N G   **14**

Cisgender Privilege

Evin Taylor (2010)

The latin prefix "cis," loosely translated, means "on this side," while the prefix "trans" is generally understood to mean "change, crossing, or beyond" Cisgender people are those whose gender identity, role, or expression is considered to match their assigned gender by societal standards. Transgender people are individuals who change, cross, or live beyond gender.

Privilege is the "cultural currency" afforded to a person or group of persons who are recognized as possessing a desired social or political characteristic. Privilege is the stability society affords us when we don't rock the boat

Gendered privilege is the collective advantages that are accepted, most often unknowingly, by those who are not positioned in opposition to the dominant ideology of the gender binary. Simply put: A person who is able to live in a life and/or body that is easily recognized as being either man/male or woman/female generally needs to spend less energy to be understood by others. The energy one need not expend to explain their gender identity and/or expression to others is gendered privilege.

The following questionnaire was inspired by Peggy Mcintosh's article "Unpacking the Invisible White Knapsack" (1988). This questionnaire is intended to inspire some insight into the privileges of those who are, for the most part, considered to be performing normative gender. It is certainly not an exhaustive list, nor can it be generalized to people in every social position. Gendered privilege is experienced differently depending on the situation and the individual people involved. Readers of this article are encouraged to adapt the questions to suit their own positioning and to come up with questions that can be added to the list.

1. Can you be guaranteed to find a public bathroom that is safe and equipped for you to use?
2. Can you be sure to find a picture of someone whose gender expression resembles yours somewhere on a magazine rack?
3. Can you be reasonably sure whether to check the M or F box on a form?
4. Can you be reasonably sure that your choice of checked box on such forms will not subject you to legal prosecution of fraud or misrepresentation of identity?
5. Are you able to assume that your genitals conform relatively closely to portrayals of "normal" bodies?
6. Can you expect to find a doctor willing to provide you with urgent medical care?
7. Are you able to make a decision to be a parent without being told that you are confused about your gender?
8. Can you be confident that your health care providers will not ask to see your genitals when treating you for a sore throat?
9. Can you be confident that your health care providers will provide treatment for your health concerns without assuming that you chose to be ill?
10. Can you obtain a passport and travel without government employees asking explicit questions regarding your genitals?
11. Do people often act as if they are doing you a favor by using the appropriate pronouns for your gender?
12. Can you undress in a public changing room without risk of being assaulted or reported?
13. Are you able to discuss your childhood without disguising your gender?
14. Can you provide government identification without risking ridicule for your name or legal sex status?
15. Do you need to prove your gender before others will refer to you with your chosen name and pronouns?
16. Can you wear a socially acceptable bathing suit?
17. Does the government require proof of the state of your genitals in order to change information on your personal identification?
18. Are incidental parts of your identity defined as a mental illness?
19. Can you reasonably expect to be sexual with your consenting partner of choice without being told you have a mental illness?
20. Do other people consider your lifestyle a mental illness?
21. How many mental illnesses can be put into total remission through medical surgeries?
22. Can you expect that your gender identity will not be used against you when applying for employment?
23. Do your sexual preferences cause people to assume that your gender identity is mistaken?
24. Can you expect to be reasonably eligible to adopt children if you should choose to?
25. Do people assume that they know everything about you because they saw an investigative news episode about plastic surgery?
26. On most days, can you expect to interact with someone of a gender similar to your own?

27. Can you expect to find a landlord willing to rent to someone of your gender?
28. Do teachings about your national and cultural history acknowledge the existence of people of your gender identity?
29. Can you be sure that your children will not be harassed at school because of your gender?
30. Can you be sure that school teachers will not try to convince your children that their understanding of their family members' bodies is incorrect?
31. Are you able to use your voice and speak in public without risk of being ridiculed?
32. Can you discuss feminism with others without the appearance of your genitals being called into question?
33. Can you freely use checks, credit cards, or government-issued ID in a grocery store without being accused of using stolen finances?
34. Can you wait at a bus stop at noon without passers-by assuming that you are working in the survival sex trade?
35. If you are asked for proof-of-age in order to purchase tobacco or alcohol, can you be reasonably sure that the cashier is trying to prove your age, not your gender?
36. Can you be reasonably sure that, when dating someone new, they will be interested in getting to know your personality over and above your medical history?
37. Can you smile at a young child without their parents scorning or explaining you to the child?
38. Can you be sure that your gender identity doesn't automatically label you as an outsider, an anomaly, abnormal, or something to be feared?
39. Can you argue for gender equality without your right or motivation to do so being questioned?
40. Does the state of your genitals cause you to fear violence if they are discovered?
41. Are your height, weight, muscle mass, or hair follicles used as "proof" that your gender identity is mistaken?
42. Are your height, weight, muscle mass, or hair follicles consistently pointed out as being incongruent with your gender?
43. Are your basic healthcare needs minimized by others who contrast them in priority with life-saving surgeries?
44. Can you find a religious community that will not exclude you based upon your genital or hormonal structures?
45. If you are having a difficult time making new friends, can you generally be sure that it is not because of your gender identity?
46. Can you choose whether or not to think of your gender as a political or social construct?
47. When you tell people your name, do they ask you what your "real" name is?
48. Can you consider social, political, or professional advancements without having to consider whether or not your gender identity will be called into question as being appropriate for advancement?
49. Do people assume that they have a right to hear, and therefore ask, about your intimate medical history or future?
50. Can you find gendered privilege in other places?

R E A D I N G   **15**

Opening Pandora's Box: Adding Classism to the Agenda

Felice Yeskel (2007)

Imagine sitting in a room in a circle of chairs. Across from you is someone who grew up in a small mansion where servants, responding to a bell, served meals. Her current net worth is over 14 million dollars. To your left is someone with a net worth significantly less than zero, due to health care debts.

He grew up in a trailer and never attended college. She was raised with unexamined and unaware class privilege, while he was raised with the humiliation of public assistance. Six other people, with various class experiences, also sit around the circle.

Most of us had never really discussed our own class experiences with anyone, nor shared our feelings about our class differences with others. I helped form this Cross-Class Dialogue Group[1] a little over ten years ago when eight of us began a journey of dialogue about class issues. Four of us were millionaires and brought up in privileged families. Four of us were raised poor or working class/lower middle class. We all passionately desired a world with greater equality and justice.

We began this journey with the belief that we had to talk to each other across our differences if we wanted to really understand one another. We believed we must know each other if we are to allow compassion, rather than fear, guilt, anger and resentment, to determine our strategies for social change. We wondered if there was a way to make sense of our diverse experiences and emotions and bridge the class divide. Starting with an attitude of experimentation, we weren't sure what we would find or how useful it might ultimately be.

Our group met monthly for about six hours over six and a half years and became a learning laboratory for understanding class differences and dynamics. Although I had been an activist, teacher and author for many years—exploring class issues on a personal level, experiencing some cross-class relationships, organizing activities on issues of economic inequality—never before had I explored the depth of feelings and experiences as I did during those six and a half years.

At the age of five, I was sent from my neighborhood in New York City to Hunter College Elementary School on 68th Street and Park Avenue, to a school for "intellectually gifted" kids. I not only crossed the miles on the way to school, but the cultures too. I learned to act differently, talk differently and basically to pass as middle class. I never invited anyone home from school because I was ashamed of where I lived. In our dialogue group I met someone who came from a super-privileged family who never invited anyone home either because she was

embarrassed by her big, fancy house. I was surprised we shared that common ground.

We learned that the person who came from the most poverty wasn't saving for retirement, not because they couldn't have done so financially, but because it was hard to imagine living that long. Most of his family members had died well before 60 due to work-related causes. It was an illuminating and liberating experience for all of us in the group. As our group came to a close, we wondered how we might bring some of the lessons we learned out into the world so that others, who weren't likely to spend six and a half years in dialogue, could benefit from what we were learning. It was out of that experience that Class Action[2] was born.

CLASS: OUR COLLECTIVE FAMILY SECRET

Walk into any hospital cafeteria and you'll seldom see the class lines broken. At lunch or dinnertime there will be tables of nurses, tables of doctors and tables of working crews (maintenance, food service, security, etc.). This same dynamic is replicated in many other workplaces across the U.S. The divisions aren't only based on race or gender; they are based on class—what Noam Chomsky calls "the unmentionable five-letter word."

Class is our collective family secret. We pretend it doesn't exist and if it doesn't exist how can we talk about it? This invisibility and lack of attention, unfortunately, is often as true among diversity professionals as it is in society at large. The idea of adding issues of classism to our existing list of issues causes discomfort. We worry about what might happen when we open this Pandora's box.

Workplaces are one of the few places where there is any cross-class contact. Most of us tend to live in a class segregated world. Because of the way housing works, our immediate neighborhoods are usually homogenous. So, too, are our social circles. Even those of us who regularly socialize with folks of varied races, ethnicities, religions and sexual orientations don't typically spend social time with folks different from us class-wise.

In many of the workshops I facilitate, I ask people how many have graduated from a four-year college.

I then ask those who have a college degree or more, how many have friends who didn't go to or graduate from college. Very few hands are raised. Since only 28 percent of those over age 25 have graduated from a four-year college,[3] random odds tell us we would have a decent percentage of friends who didn't go to college. But there is nothing random operating; we are experiencing the systemic effects of class segregation and classism.

When I recently asked this question of diversity professionals in a train-the-trainer session focused on class issues the response was the same. If we are the folks who make a living teaching others the importance of valuing diversity and how to eliminate systemic barriers and discrimination, then why isn't this on our agendas? There are many reasons for this and one is the lack of clarity and consensus about what we mean by class. Fifteen years ago I wanted to write my dissertation on anti-classist training and education. After spending eight months trying to define "class" to the satisfaction of my committee, I switched topics.

There are no commonly agreed upon definitions because different disciplines focus on different aspects of class. Some economists focus on income strata as the main criteria, such as whether someone is in the bottom or middle quintile. Some sociologists tend to focus primarily on occupational status; is someone white collar, blue/pink collar, etc.? Still others focus on the issue of ownership, power or control; does someone sell their labor or own the means of production? For others it is how much control does someone have in the workplace and over the conditions under which they work? Still others talk about class as culture, which includes values, cultural capital (what you know) and social capital (who you know). If we don't have clarity about class, social class or socio-economic class how can we tackle classism?

Many Americans take pride and comfort in the belief that all people have boundless opportunity. We believe that since there are no landed gentry, aristocracy and titles based on birth, that class no longer matters today—that class was a problem of a different time and place. However, the gap between rich and poor in the U.S. is the greatest it has been since 1929. Since the late 1970s, the wealthy have gained a bigger share of the nation's private wealth; the richest one percent of the population now have more wealth than the bottom 90 percent. Income inequality has grown as well. Average Americans were actually making less, on an hourly basis, at the end of the 1990s than they made in 1980.[4]

CLASSIST IDEOLOGY AND MYTHOLOGY

In addition to these material realities, classist ideology and mythology shape the beliefs that provide the rationale for such excessive inequality. The American Dream—the belief that people in this country can attain enough income to own their own homes and provide comfortably for their families if only they work hard enough—is pervasive. The fact that most Americans can point to at least one example where this is true reinforces the myth of class mobility and the assumption that those who don't move up the class ladder lack a strong work ethic. We locate the credit and blame for success or lack of success solely in the individual.

While it is true that there is some class fluidity, and that our class position may change over the course of a lifetime, the current reality is that economic class is much less fluid than most people think. A series on class in America[5] reviewed research on class mobility and concluded that, "mobility . . . has lately flattened out or possibly even declined." At the same time, according to a *New York Times* poll conducted in 2005, "More Americans than 20 years ago believe it is possible to start out poor, work hard and become rich." There is a cruel irony to this situation; people are more likely to believe that they can make it, while in fact they are less able to succeed economically. People in this situation, without an adequate systemic understanding of how class works, often internalize classism and blame themselves. They find scapegoats and blame others. They buy lottery tickets and engage in some level of fantasy that they too will some day be rich.

Particularly during periods of social and economic stress, in the absence of a framework for understanding classism, people often turn to scapegoats and distractions. Thus the underlying factors[6] that create vast inequalities in wealth, along with the beneficiaries of these policies, remain largely invisible.[7] Instead, people on welfare are blamed for causing our budget woes; urban young men of color are blamed for crime; immigrants are blamed for taking away jobs; working women, gays and lesbians are held responsible for the breakdown of the nuclear family and the moral decay of society.

Issues of class and classism also intersect with every other form of oppression. Race and class in particular are very intertwined in the U.S. While about half of all poor people are white, wealthy people are disproportionately white. Poor people are disproportionately black, Latino/a and Native American. The racial wealth divide is even wider than the income gap: for every dollar of assets owned by Whites, people of color own about 18 cents of that dollar.[8]

People living in poverty are more likely than others to be disabled, and disabled people are more likely than able-bodied people to be poor. A far higher percentage of people with disabilities live in households that are below the poverty level (29 versus 10 percent overall), and a similarly disproportionate number report not having adequate access to health care or transportation.[9]

The feminization of poverty over the last 30 years has increased the classism and sexism connection. There is the two-job phenomenon for women, who still perform endless hours of unpaid work caring for children and the elderly at home on top of their paid work out in the world.[10] Men are socialized to equate self-worth with what they produce (their net worth) and women performing comparable work to men are still not paid an equal amount.

BEYOND THE ECONOMIC REALM

The harms from classism, however, extend far beyond the economic realm. Prejudice exists in our language, in words such as "trailer trash," "white trash," "redneck," "ghetto," "low-class" and "classy." The same prejudice is manifested in the treatment of service workers; underpaying them, disregarding their humanity and often creating unnecessary tasks for them to do. Popular culture and the U.S. media are full of classist stereotypes.

Working-class people are often portrayed as dumb buffoons while poor people are depicted as criminals, tragic victims or heartwarming givers of wisdom. Wealthy people are rendered as shallow and vain or as evil villains. "Normal" is portrayed as an expensive upper-middle-class lifestyle that no more than 10 percent of American families can actually afford. This combines with manipulative advertising to fuel consumerism, the overemphasis on buying more and better things as a component of happiness, which in turn fuels excessive consumer debt.[11]

The lives of many working-class people, especially those of people in poverty, are full of stress. The shortage of options and scarce resources take an emotional toll.[12] Bad health outcomes, such as shorter life expectancy, higher infant mortality and more preventable diseases, are prevalent among working-class and poor people. These stem not only from inferior health care, poor diet, long hours and physical work that take a toll on workers' bodies, but also from the stress of living in a society that looks down on them. Disrespect is harmful.[13] Interestingly, it is not just poverty that creates bad health outcomes. In a given population where basic needs are met, greater levels of economic inequality correlate with negative health outcomes for everyone. People higher up the economic spectrum as well as those lower down have worse health outcomes when the inequality is greater.[14]

Classism, like other forms of oppression, can be internalized causing self-blame, shame, low expectations, discouragement and self-doubt, particularly about one's intelligence. Internalized classism[15] can also be manifested through disrespect towards other poor and working-class people, in the form of harsh judgments, betrayal, violence and other crimes. Upward mobility, far from bringing relief from classism, can bring culture shock and painful divided loyalties.[16]

Professional middle-class people are harmed when they're isolated from working-class people and taught they are superior to them and should be in charge. They are harmed by misinformation about how society works (they are sometimes less clued in to social and economic trends than working-class, poor or rich people), and by conditioning that shapes their behavior to a narrow "proper" range.[17]

In addition to the same isolation and lack of awareness that impacts middle-class people, wealthy people also find that others sometimes connect with them primarily in relation to their money, and they may have trouble trusting others' motivations. Some develop a sense of entitlement and arrogance that makes them unable to connect across class differences.

Many of the ways we "read" someone's class, or "size someone up" in terms of class (a process that can be quite unconscious), are based on our own class culture, which includes normative behaviors such as language use, manner of dress and the "proper" guidelines for conducting ourselves. While these things can be learned, the process is not easy. We also judge others' cultural capital, which refers to their familiarity with cultural objects such as books, fine art, theater, restaurants, vacation spots and jewelry.

ENCOURAGING DIVERSITY PROFESSIONALS TO STEP UP

Part of the challenge of adding issues of class and classism to the agenda is the prohibition on talking about it. In the U.S., discussions involving issues of class and money are often more taboo than discussing sexuality. Deep-seated prohibitions about disclosing the facts of one's class identity are learned quite early in our lives. Shame of being poorer or richer than others leads to secrecy and silence. This silence powerfully maintains the invisibility of class. Issues of class may be less familiar than other issues of oppression partly due to secrecy about the personal aspects of class identity and the confusion surrounding the societal and economic aspects. Diversity professionals with math anxiety or who are unfamiliar with the economic basics, e.g., the difference between income and wealth, or between salary and wages or the meaning of terms like Gross National Product (GNP), often feel overwhelmed while tackling issues of class.

A central reason most diversity professionals don't add classism to the agenda may be because classism is a different type of "ism." It is possible to imagine working for equality between the sexes, or equality for gays and lesbians or people of color, without necessarily eliminating gender, sexual orientation or race as identities. However, by definition it is impossible to have equality between classes while still having different classes. You can't have an owning class without having a working class, a serf without nobility or a slaveholder without slaves. The existence of class necessitates class inequality. I think it is because of this that the rationales that underlie class inequality are so strong and persistent.

Ultimately, I don't think we will be successful in any of our work against racism, sexism, heterosexism, etc., until we begin to take on the issue of classism. I encourage you to add issues of classism to your work.

ENDNOTES

1. I would like to acknowledge Jennifer Ladd, who started the group with me.
2. Class Action has developed a variety of resources including a wonderful web site full of useful resources. We publish a monthly e-newsletter that highlights resources, actions and events. If you are interested in subscribing please visit our web site. Class Action helps organizations better fulfill their missions by reducing class barriers and facilitating cross-class connections.
3. In 2005, 85 percent of all adults 25 years or older reported they had completed at least high school. More than one-quarter (28 percent) of adults age 25 years and older had attained at least a bachelor's degree. October 26, 2006 Census Bureau News Release, "Census Bureau Data Underscore Value of College Degree."
4. Collins, Chuck & Yeskel, Felice, "Economic Apartheid in America: A Primer on Economic Inequality and Insecurity," New York: The New Press, 2005.
5. The *New York Times,* May 2005
6. For example, domestic tax and spending policies, U.S. imperialism, war, global trade policies, multinational corporate power, etc.
7. Collins & Yeskel, 2005; Kivel, "You Call This a Democracy?" New York: The Apex Press, 2004.

8. Lui et al., "The Color of Wealth: The Story Behind the U.S. Racial Wealth Divide," New York: The New Press, 2006.

9. National Organization on Disabilities, 2000.

10. Folbre, "The Invisible Heart: Economics and Family Values," New York: The New Press, 2001.

11. Degraaf, Wann, & Naylor, "Affluenza: The All-Consuming Epidemic," San Francisco: Berrett-Koehler Publishers, 2001; and Frank, "Luxury Fever," Princeton University Press, 2000.

12. Sennett & Cobb, "The Hidden Injuries of Class," Vintage Press, 1973.

13. Lawrence-Lightfoot, "Respect: An Exploration," Perseus Books Group 2000; and Miller & Savoie, "Respect and Rights: Class, Race, and Gender Today," Rowman & Littlefield Publishers, Inc. 2002.

14. Wilkinson, Richard G., "The Impact of Inequality: How to Make Sick Societies Healthier," New York: The New Press, 2005.

15. People who are poor/working-class often internalize the dominant society's beliefs/attitudes toward them, and act them out on themselves and others of a similar class. The acceptance and justification of classism by working-class and poor people, plays out in feelings of inferiority to higher-class people and feelings of superiority to people lower on the class spectrum. Often hostility and blame is projected on other working-class or poor people, including beliefs that classist institutions are fair.

16. Lubrano, Limbo, "Blue Collar Roots, White Collar Dreams," Wiley: 2003.

17. Leondar-Wright, "Class Matters: Cross-Class Alliance Building for Middle Class Activists," New Society Publishers, 2005.

R E A D I N G **16**

Don't Laugh, It's Serious, She Says

Ellie Mamber (1985)

At 55, I'm trying to meet men.
But though I look my best
(beautiful say some
of my friends) & am spirited
& very interesting (you can
tell this, can't you?)
most men look at me with blank eyes,
no part of them flickering.
At parties they talk around me
as though I weren't there,
choose less attractive
partners to dance or talk with.
Such a puzzle! I try
so hard not to let them know
that I am smarter, more
talented, classier & more

interesting than they. Nicer, too.
I cover this so well
with a friendly smile
& a cheerful word
that they could never tell
I want them to pursue me
so I can reject them.
Bug off, you bastards,
balding middle-aged men with paunches
hanging around women 20 years
younger, who the hell
do you think you are?
You'd better hurry up
and adore me or
it will be too late.

The Social Construction of Disability

Susan Wendell (1996)

I maintain that the distinction between the biological reality of a disability and the social construction of a disability cannot be made sharply, because the biological and the social are interactive in creating disability. They are interactive not only in that complex interactions of social factors and our bodies affect health and functioning, but also in that social arrangements can make a biological condition more or less relevant to almost any situation. I call the interaction of the biological and the social to create (or prevent) disability "the social construction of disability."

Disability activists and some scholars of disability have been asserting for at least two decades that disability is socially constructed. Moreover, feminist scholars have already applied feminist analyses of the social construction of the experience of being female to their analyses of disability as socially constructed. Thus I am saying nothing new when I claim that disability, like gender, is socially constructed. Nevertheless, I understand that such an assertion may be new and even puzzling to many readers, and that not everyone who says that disability is socially constructed means the same thing by it. Therefore, I will explain what I mean in some detail.

I see disability as socially constructed in ways ranging from social conditions that straightforwardly create illnesses, injuries, and poor physical functioning, to subtle cultural factors that determine standards of normality and exclude those who do not meet them from full participation in their societies. I could not possibly discuss all the factors that enter into the social construction of disability here, and I feel sure that I am not aware of them all, but I will try to explain and illustrate the social construction of disability by discussing what I hope is a representative sample from a range of factors.

SOCIAL FACTORS THAT CONSTRUCT DISABILITY

First, it is easy to recognize that social conditions affect people's bodies by creating or failing to prevent sickness and injury. Although, since disability is relative to a person's physical, social, and cultural environment, none of the resulting physical conditions is necessarily disabling, many do in fact cause disability given the demands and lack of support in the environments of the people affected. In this direct sense of damaging people's bodies in ways that are disabling in their environments, much disability is created by the violence of invasions, wars, civil wars, and terrorism, which cause disabilities not only through direct injuries to combatants and noncombatants, but also through the spread of disease and the deprivations of basic needs that result from the chaos they create. In addition, although we more often hear about them when they cause death, violent crimes such as shootings, knifings, beatings, and rape all cause disabilities, so that a society's success or failure in protecting its citizens from injurious crimes has a significant effect on its rates of disability.

The availability and distribution of basic resources such as water, food, clothing, and shelter have major effects on disability, since much disabling physical damage results directly from malnutrition and indirectly from diseases that attack and do more lasting harm to the malnourished and those weakened by exposure. Disabling diseases are also contracted from contaminated water when clean water is not available. Here too, we usually learn more about the deaths caused by lack of basic resources than the (often life-long) disabilities of survivors.

Many other social factors can damage people's bodies in ways that are disabling in their environments, including (to mention just a few) tolerance of high-risk working conditions, abuse and neglect of children, low public safety standards, the degradation of the environment by contamination of air, water, and food, and the overwork, stress, and daily grinding deprivations of poverty. The social factors that can damage people's bodies almost always affect some groups in a society more than others because of racism, sexism, heterosexism, ageism, and advantages of class background, wealth, and education.

Medical care and practices, traditional and Western-scientific, play an important role in both preventing and creating disabling physical damage. (They also play a role in defining disability. . . .) Lack of good prenatal care and dangerous or inadequate obstetrical practices cause disabilities in babies and in the women giving birth to them. Inoculations against diseases such as polio and measles prevent quite a lot of disability. Inadequate medical care of those who are already ill or injured results in unnecessary disablement. On the other hand, the rate of disability in a society increases with improved medical capacity to save the lives of people who are dangerously ill or injured in the absence of the capacity to prevent or cure all the physical damage they have incurred. Moreover, public health and sanitation measures that increase the average lifespan also increase the number of old people with disabilities in a society, since more people live long enough to become disabled.

The *pace of life* is a factor in the social construction of disability that particularly interests me, because it is usually taken for granted by nondisabled people, while many people with disabilities are acutely aware of how it marginalizes or threatens to marginalize us. I suspect that increases in the pace of life are important social causes of damage to people's bodies through rates of accident, drug and alcohol abuse, and illnesses that result from people's neglecting their needs for rest and good nutrition. But the pace of life also affects disability as a second form of social construction, the social construction of disability through expectations of performance.

When the pace of life in a society increases, there is a tendency for more people to become disabled, not only because of physically damaging consequences of efforts to go faster, but also because fewer people can meet expectations of "normal" performance; the physical (and mental) limitations of those who cannot meet the new pace become conspicuous and disabling, even though the same limitations were inconspicuous and irrelevant to full participation in the slower-paced society. Increases in the pace of life can be counterbalanced for some people by improvements in accessibility, such as better transportation and easier communication, but for those who must move or think slowly, and for those whose energy is severely limited, expectations of pace can make work, recreational, community, and social activities inaccessible.

Let me give a straightforward, personal illustration of the relationship between pace and disability. I am currently just able (by doing very little else) to work as a professor three-quarter time, on one-quarter disability leave. There has been much talk recently about possible increases in the teaching duties of professors at my university, which would not be accompanied by any reduction in expectations for the other two components of our jobs, research and administration. If there were to be such an increase in the pace of professors' work, say by one additional course per term, I would be unable to work more than half-time (by the new standards) and would have to request half-time disability leave, even though there had been no change in my physical condition. Compared to my colleagues, I would be more work-disabled than I am now. Some professors with less physical limitation than I have, who now work full-time, might be unable to work at the new full-time pace and be forced to go on part-time disability leave. This sort of change could contribute to disabling anyone in any job.

Furthermore, even if a person is able to keep up with an increased pace of work, any increase in the pace of work will decrease the energy available for other life activities, which may upset the delicate balance of energy by which a person manages to participate in them and eventually exclude her/him from those activities. The pace of those other activities may also render them inaccessible. For example, the more the life of a society is conducted on the assumption of quick travel, the more disabling are those physical conditions that affect movement and travel, such as needing to use a wheelchair or having a kind of epilepsy that prevents one from driving a car, unless compensating help is provided. These disabling effects extend into people's family, social, and sexual lives and into their participation in recreation, religious life, and politics.

Pace is a major aspect of expectations of performance; non-disabled people often take pace so much for granted that they feel and express impatience with the slower pace at which some people with disabilities need to operate, and accommodations of pace are often crucial to making an activity accessible to people with a wide range of physical and mental abilities. Nevertheless, expectations of pace are not the only expectations of performance that contribute to disability. For example, expectations of individual productivity can eclipse the actual contributions of people who cannot meet them, making people unemployable when they can in fact do valuable work. There are often very definite expectations about *how* tasks will be performed (not the standards of performance, but the methods). For example, many women with disabilities are discouraged from having children because other people can only imagine caring for children in ways that are impossible for women with their disabilities, yet everything necessary could be done in other ways, often with minor accommodations. Furthermore, the expectation that many tasks will be performed by individuals on their own can create or expand the disability of those who can perform the tasks only in cooperative groups or by instructing a helper.

Expectations of performance are reflected, because they are assumed, in the social organization and physical structure of a society, both of which create disability. Societies that are physically constructed and socially organized with the unacknowledged assumption that everyone is healthy, non-disabled, young but adult, shaped according to cultural ideals, and, often, male, create a great deal of disability through sheer neglect of what most people need in order to participate fully in them.

Feminists talk about how the world has been designed for the bodies and activities of men. In many industrialized countries, including Canada and the United States, life and work have been structured as though no one of any importance in the public world, and certainly no one who works outside the home for wages, has to breast-feed a baby or look after a sick child. Common colds can be acknowledged publicly, and allowances are made for them, but menstruation cannot be acknowledged and allowances are not made for it. Much of the public world is also structured as though everyone were physically strong, as though all bodies were shaped the same, as though everyone could walk, hear, and see well, as though everyone could work and play at a pace that is not compatible with any kind of illness or pain, as though no one were ever dizzy or incontinent or simply needed to sit or lie down. (For instance, where could you rest for a few minutes in a supermarket if you needed to?) Not only the architecture, but the entire physical and social organization of life tends to assume that we are either strong and healthy and able to do what the average young, non-disabled man can do or that we are completely unable to participate in public life.

A great deal of disability is caused by this physical structure and social organization of society. For instance, poor architectural planning creates physical obstacles for people who use wheelchairs, but also for people who can walk but cannot walk far or cannot climb stairs, for people who cannot open doors, and for people who can do all of these things but only at the cost of pain or an expenditure of energy they can ill afford. Some of the same architectural flaws cause problems for pregnant women, parents with strollers, and young children. This is no coincidence. Much architecture has been planned with a young adult, non-disabled male paradigm of humanity in mind. In addition, aspects of social organization that take for granted the social expectations of performance and productivity, such as inadequate public transportation (which I believe assumes that no one who is needed in the public world needs public transportation), communications systems that are inaccessible to people with visual or hearing impairments, and inflexible work arrangements that exclude part-time work or rest periods, create much disability.

When public and private worlds are split, women (and children) have often been relegated to the private, and so have the disabled, the sick, and the old. The public world is the world of strength, the positive (valued) body, performance and production, the non-disabled, and young adults. Weakness, illness, rest and recovery, pain, death, and the negative (devalued) body are private, generally hidden, and often neglected. Coming into the public world with illness, pain, or a devalued body, people encounter resistance to mixing the two worlds; the split is vividly revealed. Much of the experience of disability and illness goes underground, because there is no socially acceptable way of expressing it and having the physical and psychological experience acknowledged. Yet acknowledgement of this experience is exactly what is required for creating accessibility in the public world. The more a society regards disability as a private matter, and people with disabilities as belonging in the private sphere, the more disability it creates by failing to make the public sphere accessible to a wide range of people.

Disability is also socially constructed by the failure to give people the amount and kind of help they need to participate fully in all major aspects of life in the society, including making a significant contribution in the form of work. Two things are important to remember about the help that people with disabilities may need. One is that most industrialized societies give non-disabled people (in different degrees and kinds, depending on class, race, gender, and other factors) a lot of help in the form of education, training, social support, public communication and transportation facilities, public recreation, and other services. The help that non-disabled people receive tends to be taken for granted and not considered help but entitlement, because it is offered to citizens who fit the social paradigms, who by definition are not considered dependent on social help. It is only when people need a different kind or amount of help than that given to "paradigm" citizens that it is considered help at all, and they are considered socially dependent. Second, much, though not all, of the help that people with disabilities need is required because their bodies were damaged by social conditions, or because they

cannot meet social expectations of performance, or because the narrowly-conceived physical structure and social organization of society have placed them at a disadvantage; in other words, it is needed to overcome problems that were created socially.

Thus disability is socially constructed through the failure or unwillingness to create ability among people who do not fit the physical and mental profile of "paradigm" citizens. Failures of social support for people with disabilities result in inadequate rehabilitation, unemployment, poverty, inadequate personal and medical care, poor communication services, inadequate training and education, poor protection from physical, sexual, and emotional abuse, minimal opportunities for social learning and interaction, and many other disabling situations that hurt people with disabilities and exclude them from participation in major aspects of life in their societies.

. . .

CULTURAL CONSTRUCTION OF DISABILITY

Culture makes major contributions to disability. These contributions include not only the omission of experiences of disability from cultural representations of life in a society, but also the cultural stereotyping of people with disabilities, the selective stigmatization of physical and mental limitations and other differences (selective because not all limitations and differences are stigmatized, and different limitations and differences are stigmatized in different societies), the numerous cultural meanings attached to various kinds of disability and illness, and the exclusion of people with disabilities from the cultural meanings of activities they cannot perform or are expected not to perform.

The lack of realistic cultural representations of experiences of disability not only contributes to the "Otherness" of people with disabilities by encouraging the assumption that their lives are inconceivable to non-disabled people but also increases non-disabled people's fear of disability by suppressing knowledge of how people live with disabilities. Stereotypes of disabled people as dependent, morally depraved, super-humanly heroic, asexual, and/or pitiful are still the most common cultural portrayals of people with disabilities. Stereotypes repeatedly get in the way of full participation in work and social life. For example, Francine Arsenault, whose leg was damaged by childhood polio and later by gangrene, describes the following incident at her wedding:

> When I got married, one of my best friends came to the wedding with her parents. I had known her parents all the time I was growing up; we visited in each other's homes and I thought that they knew my situation quite well.
>
> But as the father went down the reception line and shook hands with my husband, he said, "You know, I used to think that Francine was intelligent, but to put herself on you as a burden like this shows that I was wrong all along."

Here the stereotype of a woman with a disability as a helpless, dependent burden blots out, in the friend's father's consciousness, both the reality that Francine simply has one damaged leg and the probability that her new husband wants her for her other qualities. Moreover, the man seems to take for granted that the new husband sees Francine in the same stereotyped way (or else he risks incomprehension or rejection), perhaps because he counts on the cultural assumptions about people with disabilities. I think both the stigma of physical "imperfection" (and possibly the additional stigma of having been damaged by disease) and the cultural meanings attached to the disability contribute to the power of the stereotype in situations like this. Physical "imperfection" is more likely to be thought to "spoil" a woman than a man by rendering her unattractive in a culture where her physical appearance is a large component of a woman's value; having a damaged leg probably evokes the metaphorical meanings of being "crippled," which include helplessness, dependency, and pitifulness. Stigma, stereotypes, and cultural meanings are all related and interactive in the cultural construction of disability. . . .

SOCIAL DECONSTRUCTION OF DISABILITY

In my view, then, disability is socially constructed by such factors as social conditions that cause or fail to prevent damage to people's bodies; expectations of performance; the physical and social organization of societies on the basis of a young, non-disabled, "ideally shaped," healthy adult male paradigm of citizens; the failure or unwillingness to create ability among citizens who do not fit the paradigm; and cultural representations, failures of representation, and expectations. Much, but perhaps not all, of what can be socially constructed can be socially (and not just intellectually) deconstructed, given the means and the will.

A great deal of disability can be prevented with good public health and safety standards and practices, but also by relatively minor changes in the built environment that provide accessibility to people with a wide range of physical characteristics and abilities. Many measures that are usually regarded as helping or accommodating people who are now disabled, such as making buildings and public places wheelchair accessible, creating and respecting parking spaces for people with disabilities, providing American Sign Language translation, captioning, and Telephone Devices for the Deaf, and making tapes and Descriptive Video services available for people who are visually impaired, should be seen as preventive, since a great deal of disability is created by building and organizing environments, objects, and activities for a too-narrow range of people. Much more could be done along the same lines by putting people with a wide variety of physical abilities and characteristics in charge of deconstructing disability. People with disabilities should be in charge, because people without disabilities are unlikely to see many of the obstacles in their environment. Moreover, they are likely not to see them *as obstacles* even when they are pointed out, but rather as "normal" features of the built environment that present difficulties for "abnormal" people.

Disability cannot be deconstructed by consulting a few token disabled representatives. A person with a disability is not likely to see all the obstacles to people with disabilities different from her/his own, although s/he is likely to be more aware of potential inaccessibility. Moreover, people with disabilities are not always aware of the obstacles in our environment *as obstacles,* even when they affect us. The cultural habit of regarding the condition of the person, not the built environment or the social organization of activities, as the source of the problem, runs deep. For example, it took me several years of struggling with the heavy door to my building, sometimes having to wait until someone stronger came along, to realize that the door was an accessibility problem, not only for me, but for others as well. And I did not notice, until one of my students pointed it out, that the lack of signs that could be read from a distance at my university forced people with mobility impairments to expend a lot of energy unnecessarily, searching for rooms and offices. Although I have encountered this difficulty myself on days when walking was exhausting to me, I interpreted it, automatically, as a problem arising from my illness (as I did with the door), rather than as a problem arising from the built environment having been created for too narrow a range of people and situations. One of the most crucial factors in the deconstruction of disability is the change of perspective that causes us to look in the environment for both the source of the problem and the solutions.

. . .

OBSTACLES TO THE DECONSTRUCTION OF DISABILITY

. . .

Attitudes that disability is a personal or family problem (of biological or accidental origin), rather than a matter of social responsibility, are cultural contributors to disability and powerful factors working against social measures to increase ability. The attitude that disability is a personal problem is manifested when people with disabilities are expected to overcome obstacles to their participation in activities by their own extraordinary efforts. The public adoration of a few disabled heroes who are believed to have "overcome their handicaps" against great odds both demonstrates and contributes to this expectation. The attitude that disability is a family matter is manifested when the families of people with disabilities are expected to provide whatever they need, even at great personal sacrifice by other family members. Barbara Hillyer describes the strength of expectations that mothers and other caregivers will do whatever is necessary to "normalize" the lives of family members, especially children, with disabilities—not only providing care, but often doing the work of two people to maintain the illusion that there is nothing "wrong" in the family.

These attitudes are related to the fact that many modern societies split human concerns into public and private worlds. Typically, those with disabilities and illnesses have been relegated to the private realm, along with women, children, and the old. This worldwide tendency creates particularly intractable problems for women with disabilities; since they fit two "private" categories, they are often kept at home, isolated and overprotected. In addition, the confinement of people with disabilities in the private realm exploits women's traditional caregiving roles in order to meet the needs of people with disabilities, and it hides the need for measures to make the public realm accessible to everyone.

There also seem to be definite material advantages for some people (people without disabilities who have no disabled friends or relatives for whom they feel responsible) to seeing disability as a biological misfortune, the bad luck of individuals, and a personal or family problem. Accessibility and creating ability cost time, energy, and/or money. Charities for people with disabilities are big businesses that employ a great many non-disabled professionals; these charities depend upon the belief that responding to the difficulties faced by people with disabilities is superogatory for people who are not members of the family—not a social responsibility to be fulfilled through governments, but an act of kindness. Moreover, both the charities and most government bureaucracies (which also employ large numbers of non-disabled professionals) hand out help which would not be needed in a society that was planned and organized to include people with a wide range of physical and mental abilities. The potential resistance created by these vested interests in disability should not be underestimated.

The "personal misfortune" approach to disability is also part of what I call the "lottery" approach to life, in which individual good fortune is hoped for as a substitute for social planning that deals realistically with everyone's capabilities, needs and limitations, and the probable distribution of hardship. In Canada and the United States, most people reject the "lottery" approach to such matters as acute health care for themselves and their families or basic education for their children. We expect it to be there when we need it, and we are (more or less) willing to pay for it to be there. I think the lottery approach persists with respect to disability partly because *fear,* based on ignorance and false beliefs about disability, makes it difficult for most non-disabled people to identify with people with disabilities. If the non-disabled saw the disabled as potentially themselves or as their future selves, they would want their societies to be fully accessible and to invest the resources necessary to create ability wherever possible. They would feel that "charity" is as inappropriate a way of thinking about resources for people with disabilities as it is about emergency medical care or basic education.

The philosopher Anita Silvers maintains that it is probably impossible for most non-disabled people to imagine what life is like with a disability, and that their own becoming disabled is unthinkable to them. Certainly many people without disabilities believe that life with a disability would not be worth living. This is reflected in the assumption that potential disability is a sufficient reason for aborting a fetus, as well as in the frequent statements by non-disabled people that they would not want to live if they had to use a wheelchair, lost their eyesight, were dependent on others for care, and so on. The belief that life would not be worth living with a disability would be enough to prevent them from imagining their own disablement. This belief is fed by stereotypes and ignorance of the lives of people with disabilities. For example, the assumption that permanent, global incompetence results from any major disability is still prevalent; there is a strong presumption that competent people either have no major physical or mental limitations or are able to hide them in public and social life.

It seems that the cultural constructions of disability, including the ignorance, stereotyping, and stigmatization that feed fears of disability, have to be at least partly deconstructed before disability can be seen by more people as a set of social problems and social responsibilities. Until that change in perspective happens, people with disabilities and their families will continue to be given too much individual responsibility for "overcoming" disabilities, expectations for the participation of people with disabilities in public life will be far too low, and social injustices that are recognized now (at least in the abstract), such as discrimination against people with disabilities, will be misunderstood.

To illustrate, let me look briefly at the problem of discrimination. Clearly, when considering whether some action or situation is an instance of discrimination on the basis of ability, the trick is to distinguish ability to do the relevant things from ability to do irrelevant things. But, given that so many places and activities are structured for people with a narrow range of abilities, telling the two apart is not always easy. No one has to walk to be a typist, but if a company is housed in a building that is inaccessible to wheelchairs, and therefore refuses to hire a competent typist who uses a wheelchair because it would be expensive to fix the building, has it discriminated against her on the basis of her disability? Laws may say yes, but people will resist the laws unless they can see that the typist's inability to work in that office is not solely a characteristic of her as an individual. Most people will be ready to recognize refusal to hire her to work in a wheelchair-accessible office, provided she is the most competent typist who applied, as discrimination against her because of her disability; they will regard her disability (like her race) as a personal characteristic irrelevant in the circumstances. But will they be ready to require a company to create wheelchair accessibility so that it can hire her? This is being tested now in the United States by the 1990 Americans with Disabilities Act. Although I expect the Act to have an invaluable educational function, I predict that it will be very difficult to enforce until more people see accessibility as a public responsibility. Only then will they be able to recognize inabilities that are created by faulty planning and organization as irrelevant.

Consider these sentiments expressed in the Burger King case, as described in *The Disability Rag and Resource:*

> When deaf actress Terrylene Sacchetti sued Burger King under the ADA for refusing to serve her when she handed the cashier a written order at the pickup window instead of using the intercom, Stan Kyker,

executive vice-president of the California Restaurant Association, said that those "people (with disabilities) are going to have to accept that they are not 100 percent whole and they can't be made 100 percent whole in everything they do in life."

Had a woman been refused service because she used a cane to walk up to the counter, her treatment would, I think, have been recognized at once as discrimination. But since Ms. Sacchetti was refused service because she was unable to perform the activity (ordering food) in the way (orally) that the restaurant required it to be performed, the refusal to serve her was not immediately recognized as discrimination. Indeed, the representative of the restaurant association apparently felt comfortable defending it on the grounds that her individual characteristics were the obstacles to Ms. Sacchetti's being served.

When I imagine a society without disabilities, I do not imagine a society in which every physical and mental "defect" or "abnormality" can be cured. On the contrary, I believe the fantasy that someday everything will be "curable" is a significant obstacle to the social deconstruction of disability. Instead, I imagine a fully accessible society, the most fundamental characteristic of which is universal recognition that all structures have to be built and all activities have to be organized for the widest practical range of human abilities. In such a society, a person who cannot walk would not be disabled, because every major kind of activity that is accessible to someone who can walk would be accessible to someone who cannot, and likewise with seeing, hearing, speaking, moving one's arms, working for long stretches of time without rest, and many other physical and mental functions. I do not mean that everyone would be able to do everything, but rather that, with respect to the major aspects of life in the society, the differences in ability between someone who can walk, or see, or hear, and someone who cannot would be no more significant than the differences in ability among people who can walk, see, or hear. Not everyone who is not disabled now can play basketball or sing in a choir, but everyone who is not disabled now can participate in sports or games and make art, and that sort of general ability should be the goal in deconstructing disability.

I talk about accessibility and ability rather than independence or integration because I think that neither independence nor integration is always an appropriate goal for people with disabilities. Some people cannot live independently because they will always need a great deal of help from caregivers, and some people with disabilities, for example the Deaf, do not want to be integrated into non-disabled society; they prefer their own, separate social life. Everyone should, however, have access to *opportunities* to develop their abilities, to work, and to participate in the full range of public and private activities available to the rest of society.

R E A D I N G **18**

Report from the Bahamas

June Jordan (1985)

I am staying in a hotel that calls itself The Sheraton British Colonial. One of the photographs advertising the place displays a middle-aged Black man in a waiter's tuxedo, smiling. What intrigues me most about the picture is just this: while the Black man bears a tray full of "colorful" drinks above his left shoulder, both of his feet, shoes and trouserlegs, up to ten inches above his ankles, stand in the also "colorful" Caribbean salt water. He is so delighted to serve you he will wade into the water to bring you Banana Daquiris while you float! More precisely, he will wade into the water, fully clothed, oblivious to the ruin of his shoes, his trousers, his health, and he will do it with a smile.

I am in the Bahamas. On the phone in my room, a spinning complement of plastic pages offers handy index clues such as CAR RENTAL and CASINOS. A message from the Ministry of Tourism appears among these travellers' tips. Opening with a paragraph of "WELCOME," the message then proceeds to "A PAGE OF HISTORY," which reads as follows:

New World History begins on the same day that modern Bahamian history begins—October 12, 1492. That's when Columbus stepped ashore— British influence came first with the Eleutherian Adventurers of 1647—After the Revolutions. American Loyalists fled from the newly independent states and settled in the Bahamas. Confederate blockade-runners used the island as a haven during the War between the States, and after the War, a number of Southerners moved to the Bahamas.

There it is again. Something proclaims itself a legitimate history and all it does is track white Mr. Columbus to the British Eleutherians through the Confederate Southerners as they barge into New World surf, land on New World turf, and nobody saying one word about the Bahamian people, the Black peoples, to whom the only thing new in their island world was this weird succession of crude intruders and its colonial consequences.

This is my consciousness of race as I unpack my bathing suit in the Sheraton British Colonial. Neither this hotel nor the British nor the long ago Italians nor the white Delta airline pilots belong here, of course. And every time I look at the photograph of that fool standing in the water with his shoes on I'm about to have a West Indian fit, even though I know he's no fool; he's a middle-aged Black man who needs a job and this is his job—pretending himself a servile ancillary to the pleasures of the rich. (Compared to his options in life, I am a rich woman. Compared to most of the Black Americans arriving for this Easter weekend on a three nights four days' deal of bargain rates, the middle-aged waiter is a poor Black man.)

We will jostle along with the other (white) visitors and join them in the tee shirt shops or, laughing together, learn ruthless rules of negotiation as we, Black Americans as well as white, argue down the price of handwoven goods at the nearby straw market while the merchants, frequently toothless Black women seated on the concrete in their only presentable dress, humble themselves to our careless games:

"Yes? You like it? Eight dollar."

"Five."

"I give it to you. Seven."

And so it continues, this weird succession of crude intruders that, now, includes me and my brothers and my sisters from the North.

This is my consciousness of class as I try to decide how much money I can spend on Bahamian gifts for my family back in Brooklyn. No matter that these other Black women incessantly weave words and flowers into the straw hats and bags piled beside them on the burning dusty street. No matter that these other Black women must work their sense of beauty into these things that we will take away as cheaply as we dare, or they will do without food.

We are not white, after all. The budget is limited. And we are harmlessly killing time between the poolside rum punch and "The Native Show on the Patio" that will play tonight outside the hotel restaurant.

This is my consciousness of race and class and gender identity as I notice the fixed relations between these other Black women and myself. They sell and I buy or I don't. They risk not eating. I risk going broke on my first vacation afternoon.

We are not particularly women anymore; we are parties to a transaction designed to set us against each other.

"Olive" is the name of the Black woman who cleans my hotel room. On my way to the beach I am wondering what "Olive" would say if I told her why I chose The Sheraton British Colonial; if I told her I wanted to swim. I wanted to sleep. I did not want to be harassed by the middle-aged waiter, or his nephew. I did not want to be raped by anybody (white or Black) at all and I calculated that my safety as a Black woman alone would best be ensured by a multinational hotel corporation. In my experience, the big guys take customer complaints more seriously than the little ones. I would suppose that's one reason why they're big; they don't like to lose money anymore than I like to be bothered when I'm trying to read a god-damned book underneath a palm tree I paid $264 to get next to. A Black woman seeking refuge in a multinational corporation may seem like a contradiction to some, but there you are. In this case it's a coincidence of entirely different self-interests: Sheraton/cash = June Jordan's short run safety.

Anyway, I'm pretty sure "Olive" would look at me as though I came from someplace as far away as Brooklyn. Then she'd probably allow herself one indignant query before righteously removing her vacuum cleaner from my room; "and why in the first place you come down here without your husband?"

I cannot imagine how I would begin to answer her.

My "rights" and my "freedom" and my "desire" and a slew of other New World values; what would they sound like to this Black woman described on the card atop my hotel bureau as "Olive the Maid"? "Olive" is older than I am and I may smoke a cigarette while she changes the sheets on my bed. Whose rights? Whose freedom? Whose desire?

And why should she give a shit about mine unless I do something, for real, about hers?

It happens that the book that I finished reading under a palm tree earlier today was the novel *The Bread Givers,* by Anzia Yezierska. Definitely autobiographical. Yezierska lays out the difficulties of being both female and "a person" inside a traditional Jewish family at the start of the twentieth century....

. . .

I am thinking about the boy who loaned this novel to me. He's white and he's Jewish and he's pursuing an independent study project with me, at the State University where I teach whether or not I feel like it, where I teach without stint because, like the waiter, I am no fool. It's my job and either I work or I do without everything you need money to buy. The boy loaned me the novel because he thought I'd be interested to know how a Jewish-American writer used English so that the syntax, and therefore the cultural habits of mind expressed by the Yiddish language, could survive translation. He did this because he wanted to create another connection between us on the basis of language, between his knowledge/his love of Yiddish and my knowledge/my love of Black English.

He has been right about the forceful survival of the Yiddish. And I had become excited by this further evidence of the written voice of spoken language protected from the monodrone of "standard" English, and so we had grown closer on this account. But then our talk shifted to student affairs more generally, and I had learned that this student does not care one way or the other about currently jeopardized Federal Student Loan Programs because, as he explained it to me, they do not affect him. He does not need financial help outside his family. My own son, however, is Black. And I am the only family help available to him. . . .

. . .

It's time to pack it up. Catch my plane. I scan the hotel room for things not to forget. There's that white report card on the bureau.

"Dear Guests:" it says, under the name "Olive." "I am your maid for the day. Please rate me: Excellent. Good. Average. Poor. Thank you."

I tuck this momento from the Sheraton British Colonial into my notebook. How would "Olive" rate *me?* What would it mean for us to seem "good" to each other? What would that rating require?

But I am hastening to leave. Neither turtle soup nor kidney pie nor any conch shell delight shall delay my departure. I have rested, here, in the Bahamas, and I'm ready to return to my usual job, my usual work. But the skin on my body has changed and so has my mind. On the Delta flight home I realize I am burning up, indeed.

So far as I can see, the usual race and class concepts of connection, or gender assumptions of unity, do not apply very well. I doubt that they ever did. Otherwise, why would Black folks forever bemoan our lack of solidarity when the deal turns real. And if unity on the basis of sexual oppression is something natural, then why do we women, the majority people on the planet, still have a problem?

The plane's ready for takeoff. I fasten my seatbelt and let the tumult inside my head run free. Yes: race and class and gender remain as real as the weather. But what they must mean about the contact between two individuals is less obvious and, like the weather, not predictable.

And when these factors of race and class and gender absolutely collapse is whenever you try to use them as automatic concepts of connection. They may serve well as indicators of commonly felt conflict, but as elements of connection they seem about as reliable as precipitation probability for the day after the night before the day.

It occurs to me that much organizational grief could be avoided if people understood that partnership in misery does not necessarily provide for partnership for change: *When we get the monsters off our backs all of us may want to run in very different directions.*

And not only that: even though both "Olive" and "I" live inside a conflict neither one of us created, and even though both of us therefore hurt inside that conflict, I may be one of the monsters she needs to eliminate from her universe and, in a sense, she may be one of the monsters in mine.

I am reaching for the words to describe the difference between a common identity that has been imposed and the individual identity any one of us will choose, once she gains that chance.

That difference is the one that keeps us stupid in the face of new, specific information about somebody else with whom we are supposed to have a connection because a third party, hostile to both of us, has worked it so that the two of us, like it or not, share a common enemy. *What happens beyond the idea of that enemy and beyond the consequences of that enemy?*

I am saying that the ultimate connection cannot be the enemy. The ultimate connection must be the need that we find between us. It is not only who you are, in other words, but what we can do for each other that will determine the connection.

I am flying back to my job. I have been teaching contemporary women's poetry this semester. One quandary I have set myself to explore with my students is the one of taking responsibility without power. We had been wrestling ideas to the floor for several sessions when a young Black woman, a South African, asked me for help, after class.

Sokutu told me she was "in a trance" and that she'd been unable to eat for two weeks.

"What's going on?" I asked her, even as my eyes startled at her trembling and emaciated appearance.

"My husband. He drinks all the time. He beats me up. I go to the hospital. I can't eat. I don't know what/anything."

In my office, she described her situation. I did not dare to let her sense my fear and horror. She was dragging about, hour by hour, in dread. Her husband, a young Black South African, was drinking himself into more and more deadly violence against her.

Sokutu told me how she could keep nothing down. She weighed 90 lbs. at the outside, as she spoke to me. She'd already been hospitalized as a result of her husband's battering rage.

I knew both of them because I had organized a campus group to aid the liberation struggles of Southern Africa.

Nausea rose in my throat. What about this presumable connection: this husband and this wife fled from that homeland of hatred against them, and now what? He was destroying himself. If not stopped, he would certainly murder his wife.

She needed a doctor, right away. It was a medical emergency. She needed protection. It was a security crisis. She needed refuge for battered wives and personal therapy and legal counsel. She needed a friend.

I got on the phone and called every number in the campus directory that I could imagine might prove helpful. Nothing worked. There were no institutional resources designed to meet her enormous, multifaceted, and ordinary woman's need.

I called various students. I asked the Chairperson of the English Department for advice. I asked everyone for help.

Finally, another one of my students, Cathy, a young Irish woman active in campus IRA activities, responded. She asked for further details. I gave them to her.

"Her husband," Cathy told me, "is an alcoholic. You have to understand about alcoholics. It's not the same as anything else. And it's a disease you can't treat any old way."

I listened, fearfully. Did this mean there was nothing we could do?

"That's not what I'm saying," she said. "But you have to keep the alcoholic part of the thing central in everybody's mind, otherwise her husband will kill her. Or he'll kill himself."

She spoke calmly. I felt there was nothing to do but to assume she knew what she was talking about.

"Will you come with me?" I asked her, after a silence. "Will you come with me and help us figure out what to do next?"

Cathy said she would but that she felt shy: Sokutu comes from South Africa. What would she think about Cathy?

"I don't know," I said. "But let's go."

We left to find a dormitory room for the young battered wife.

It was late, now, and dark outside.

On Cathy's VW that I followed behind with my own car, was the sticker that reads BOBBY SANDS FREE AT LAST. My eyes blurred as I read and reread the words. This was another connection: Bobby Sands and Martin Luther King Jr. and who would believe it? I would not have believed it; I grew up terrorized by Irish kids who introduced me to the word "nigga."

And here I was following an Irish woman to the room of a Black South African. We were going to that room to try to save a life together.

When we reached the little room, we found ourselves awkward and large. Sokutu attempted to treat us with utmost courtesy, as though we were honored guests. She seemed surprised by Cathy, but mostly Sokutu was flushed with relief and joy because we were there, with her.

I did not know how we should ever terminate her heartfelt courtesies and address, directly, the reason for our visit: her starvation and her extreme physical danger.

Finally, Cathy sat on the floor and reached out her hands to Sokutu. "I'm here," she said quietly, "Because June has told me what has happened to you. And I know what it is. Your husband is an alcoholic. He has a disease. I know what it is. My father was an alcholic. He killed himself. He almost killed my mother. I want to be your friend."

"Oh," was the only small sound that escaped from Sokutu's mouth. And then she embraced the other student. And then everything changed and I watched all of this happen so I know that this happened: this connection.

And after we called the police and exchanged phone numbers and plans were made for the night and for the next morning, the young South African woman walked down the dormitory hallway, saying goodbye and saying thank you to us.

I walked behind them, the young Irish woman and the young South African, and I saw them walking as sisters walk, hugging each other, and whispering and sure of each other and I felt how it was not who they were but what they both know and what they were both preparing to do about what they know that was going to make them both free at last.

And I look out the windows of the plane and I see clouds that will not kill me and I know that someday soon other clouds may erupt to kill us all.

And I tell the stewardess No thanks to the cocktails she offers me. But I look about the cabin at the hundred strangers drinking as they fly and I think even here and even now I must make the connection real between me and these strangers everywhere before those other clouds unify this ragged bunch of us, too late.

R E A D I N G **19**

Our Grandmothers

Maya Angelou (1990)

She lay, skin down in the moist dirt,
the canebrake rustling
with the whispers of leaves, and
loud longing of hounds and
the ransack of hunters crackling the near
branches.

She muttered, lifting her head a nod toward freedom,
I shall not, I shall not be moved.

She gathered her babies,
their tears slick as oil on black faces,
their young eyes canvassing mornings of madness.

Momma, is Master going to sell you
from us tomorrow?

Yes,
Unless you keep walking more
and talking less.
Yes.
Unless the keeper of our lives
releases me from all commandments.
Yes.
And your lives,
never mine to live,
Will be executed upon the killing floor
    of innocents.
Unless you match my heart and words,
saying with me,

I shall not be moved.

In Virginia tobacco fields,
leaning into the curve
of Steinway
pianos, along Arkansas roads,
in the red hills of Georgia,
into the palms of her chained hands, she
cried against calamity,
You have tried to destroy me
and though I perish daily,

I shall not be moved.

Her universe, often
summarized into one black body
falling finally from the tree to her feet,
made her cry each time into a new voice.
All my past hastens to defeat,
and strangers claim the glory of my love,
Iniquity has bound me to his bed,

yet, I must not be moved.

She heard the names,
swirling ribbons in the wind of history:
nigger, nigger bitch, heifer,
mammy, property, creature, ape, baboon,
whore, hot tail, thing, it.
She said, But my description cannot
fit your tongue, for
I have a certain way of being in this world,

and I shall not, I shall not be moved.

No angel stretched protecting wings
above the heads of her children,
fluttering and urging the winds of reason
into the confusion of their lives.
They sprouted like young weeds,
but she could not shield their growth
from the grinding blades of ignorance, nor
shape them into symbolic topiaries.
She sent them away,
underground, overland, in coaches and
shoeless.

When you learn, teach.
When you get, give.
As for me,

I shall not be moved.

She stood in midocean, seeking dry land.
She searched God's face.
Assured,
she placed her fire of service
on the altar, and though
clothed in the finery of faith,
when she appeared at the temple door,
no sign welcomed
Black Grandmother, Enter here.

Into the crashing sound,
into wickedness, she cried,
No one, no, nor no one million
ones dare deny me God, I go forth
alone, and stand as ten thousand.

The Divine upon my right
impels me to pull forever
at the latch on Freedom's gate.

The Holy Spirit upon my left leads my
feet without ceasing into the camp of the
righteous and into the tents of the free.

These momma faces, lemon-yellow, plum-purple,
honey-brown, have grimaced and twisted
down a pyramid for years.
She is Sheba the Sojourner,
Harriet and Zora,

Mary Bethune and Angela,
Annie to Zenobia.

She stands
before the abortion clinic,
confounded by the lack of choices.
In the Welfare line,
reduced to the pity of handouts.
Ordained in the pulpit, shielded
by the mysteries.
In the operating room,
husbanding life.
In the choir loft,
holding God in her throat.

On lonely street corners,
hawking her body.
In the classroom, loving the
children to understanding.

Centered on the world's stage,
she sings to her loves and beloveds,
to her foes and detractors:
However I am perceived and deceived,
however my ignorance and conceits,
lay aside your fears that I will be undone,

for I shall not be moved.

DISCUSSION QUESTIONS FOR CHAPTER 2

1. How is difference socially constructed?

2. What is intersectionality? How is this concept helpful as a tool of feminist analysis?

3. Give examples of the ways "regimes of truth" operate in everyday lives, focusing, for example on media or religion or family. How is your behavior shaped by these? In what ways do you accept and/or resist these discourses?

4. What role do hate crimes play in maintaining systems of inequality? Can you offer an example?

SUGGESTIONS FOR FURTHER READING

Allison, Dorothy. *Trash*. Ithaca, NY: Firebrand, 1989.

Ange-Marie Hancock. *Solidarity Politics for Millennials: A Guide to Ending the Oppression Olympics*. New York: Palgrave Macmillan, 2011.

Anzaldúa, Gloria. *Borderlands/La Frontera: The New Mestiza*. San Francisco: Aunt Lute, 1987.

———. 1990c. "*La conciencia de la mestiza*: Towards a New Consciousness" In *Making Face, Making Soul* Haciendo Caras: *Creative and Critical Perspectives by Feminists of Color,* edited by Gloria E. Anzaldúa, 377-89. San Francisco: Aunt Lute Books.

Basu, Amrita, ed. *Women's Movements in the Global Era: The Power of Local Feminisms*. Boulder, CO: Westview Press, 2010.

Blee, Kathleen M. *Inside Organized Racism: Women in the Hate Movement*. Berkeley: University of California Press, 2002.

Chow, Esther Ngan-Ling, Marcia Texler Segal, and Tan Lin, eds. *Analyzing Gender, Intersectionality, and Multiple Inequalities: Global-Transnational and Local Contexts*.

Cole, Johnnetta, and Beverly Guy-Sheftall. *Gender Talk: The Struggle for Women's Equality in African American Communities*. New York: One World/Ballantine, 2003.

Hall, Kim Q., ed. *Feminist Disability Studies*. Bloomington: Indiana University Press, 2011.

hooks, bell. *Where We Stand: Class Matters*. New York: Routledge, 2002.

Kafer, Alison. *Feminist, Queer, Crip*. Bloomington: Indiana University Press, 2013.

Kristof, Nicholas D., and Shery WuDunn. *Half the Sky: Turning Oppression into Opportunity for Women Worldwide*. New York: Vintage, 2010.

Lorde, Audre. *Sister Outsider*. Freedom, CA: Crossing Press, 1984.

Mihesuah, Devon A. *Indigenous American Women: Decolonization, Empowerment, Activism*. Lincoln, NE: Bison Books, 2003.

Stein, Arlene. *The Stranger Next Door: The Story of a Small Community's Battle over Sex, Faith, and Civil Rights*. Boston: Beacon Press, 2002.

CHAPTER 3

Learning Gender

Our typical in-class exercise while teaching a unit on the social construction of gender is to ask how many students identified as "tomboys" when they were growing up. A sea of hands usually results as many remember resisting traditional notions of femininity. When students are asked whether they identified as "sissies," usually the whole group laughs as one lone male-identified student sheepishly raises his hand and remarks that he's always been a sissy. Why is it so easy to say you were a tomboy and so difficult to admit to being a sissy? This has a lot to do with the meanings associated with masculinity and femininity and the ways these are ranked in society. In this chapter we focus specifically on gender and sexism, keeping in mind two important points: first, how gender is constructed through intersection with other differences among women such as race, ethnicity, and class, and second, how sexism as a system of oppression is related to other systems of inequality and privilege.

GENDER, CULTURE, AND BIOLOGY

In Chapter 1 we explained gender as the way society creates, patterns, and rewards our understandings of femininity and masculinity, or the process by which certain behaviors and performances are ascribed to "women" and "men." Society constructs and interprets perceived differences among humans and gives us "feminine" and "masculine" people. These words are intentionally placed in quotation marks to emphasize that notions of femininity and masculinity are fluid and socially constructed—created by social processes that reflect the various workings of power in society. Therefore gender is culturally and historically changeable. There is nothing essential, intrinsic, or static about femininity or masculinity; rather, they are social categories that might mean different things in different societies and in different historical periods.

It is important to emphasize that gender is embedded in culture and the various forms of knowledge associated with any given community. What it might mean to be "feminine" or "masculine" in one culture may be different from meanings in another. This implies that people growing up in different societies in different parts of the world at different historical moments perform different gender expressions. As the boxed insert in this chapter called "Rites of Passage" suggests, gender performances vary around the world.

In addition, contemporary life in the twenty-first century, which involves global systems of production, consumption, and communication, means that patterns of gender in the United States are exported worldwide and are increasingly linked to patterns of global economic restructuring. This encourages us to consider the ways the social and economic dynamics of globalization (including economic and political expansion, militarism and colonial conquest and settlement, disruption/appropriation of indigenous peoples and resources, and the exportation of ideas through world markets, etc.) have shaped global gender arrangements and transformed gender relations. Whatever our global locations, it is important to consider the ways we interact with globalized cultures and particularly the ways in which products of world media feature in our lives and shape our ideas about femininity and masculinity.

Femininities and masculinities are performed by bodies in a series of repetitive acts that we usually take for granted and tend to see as "natural." As we "do" gender, these practices (such as walking, speaking, or sitting in a certain way) are always shaped by discourses or regimes of truth that give these actions meaning. However, it is important not to reduce this "performativity" associated with gender to a voluntary act or understand it as something over which we have perfect control. In this sense it is not merely a theatrical performance. Rather performativity is constrained by social norms. What this means is that gender is not only what we "do"; it is a process by which we "are" or "become."

In addition, the relationship between biology and culture is more complicated than the assertion that sex is a biological fact and gender is the societal interpretation of that fact. First, there is greater gender diversity in nature than once thought. Many species are not just female or male, but can be both female and male at the same time, or be one or the other at different times. As discussed below, this ambiguity relates to humans too. Some children are born without distinct sex characteristics and are assigned one at birth. The classic reading by Anne Fausto-Sterling, "The Five Sexes, Revisited," critiques the traditional binaries we call female and male. Second, while biology may imply some basic physiological "facts," culture gives meaning to these in such a way that we must question whether biology can exist except within the society that gives it meaning in the first place. This implies that sex, in terms of raw male or female, is already gendered by the culture

LEARNING ACTIVITY   **Tomboys and Sissies**

Take an informal poll on your campus. Ask the women if they ever wanted to be a boy when they were growing up. Note their reaction to the question. Then ask why or why not. Also ask the women if they were considered tomboys growing up and how they felt about it if they were. Record responses and observations in a research journal.

Ask men on your campus if they ever wanted to be a girl when they were growing up. Again, note their reaction to the question. Ask why or why not. Then ask if they were considered sissies growing up and, if so, how they felt about it. Record responses and observations.

Once you've completed your poll, compare and contrast the responses you received from women and men. What do you notice? Why do you think responses may have been the way they were? What do responses suggest about gender in American society?

within which these physiological facts of biology exist. In other words, although many people make a distinction between biological sex (female/male) and learned gender (feminine/masculine), it is really impossible to speak of a fixed biological sex category outside of the sense that a culture makes of that category.

We know this is a complicated idea, but basically it is saying that we must no longer understand biological femaleness and maleness as the fixed foundation upon which gender is imposed. The body is given meaning by preexisting beliefs about gender, including that of medical and scientific authorities. Science is a human (and necessarily gendered) product. This is what it means to say that "sex" as in "male/female" is actually gender all along.

An example that highlights how biology is connected to culture concerns the processes by which ambiguous sex characteristics in children are handled. When "intersex" children (those with reproductive or sexual anatomies that do not seem to fit the typical binary definitions of "female" or "male") are born, families and health professionals often make an immediate sex determination. Hormone therapy and surgeries may follow to make such a child fit normative constructed binary categories, and gender is taught in accordance with this decision. In other words, physicians and others use gendered norms to construct the sexed bodies of ambiguously-sexed infants. This is an example of the way a breakdown in taken-for-granted tight connections between natural biology and learned gender is interpreted as a medical and social emergency. As already mentioned, Anne Fausto-Sterling's reading, "The Five Sexes, Revisited," questions this tidy organization of human sex into the two categories female and male, emphasizing that sex is not as easy as genetics and genitalia and arguing for theories that allow for human variation.

Another illustration of the variable relationships between gender, biology, and culture is exemplified by indigenous "Two Spirit" status, whereby people with multiple or integrated genders held/hold places of honor in native communities. The Navajo, for instance, have believed that to maintain harmony, there must be a balanced interrelationship between the feminine and the masculine within the individual, in families, in the culture, and in the natural world. Two Spirit reveals how these beliefs are expressed in a broad range of gender diversity that is accepted as normative within certain communities.

"Why does he *always get to be the boy?"*

A focus on gender assignment, identity, and expression involves three ways to understand the forces shaping gender and how we experience and express gender as individuals. *Gender assignment* is usually given to us at birth and determined by our physical body type to be male or female. This assignment, decided by doctors and parents, is the first classification an individual receives. Corresponding gender performances (behavior, dress, activities that one may participate in, etc.) are usually enforced based on the individual's gender assignment at birth. *Gender identity* concerns how one feels internally about one's own gender. This is a gendered sense of self that comes from within and may or may not match one's assigned gender at birth. The ways we present ourselves to the world are our expression of gender. Our *gender expression* is how we perform and express gender to those around us. In this way, gender is a pervasive theme in our world, shaping social life and informing attitudes, behavior, and individual's sense of self. Basically, it is one of the foundational ways that societies are organized.

Gender is always experienced, however, in intersection with other identities. As emphasized in Chapter 2, a person's sense of self is multifaceted and shaped by multiple (and sometimes conflicting) social patterns and practices. In other words, experiences of gender differ by race, class, age, and other factors. For example, due to historical and cultural reasons, many African American women have not internalized the association of femininity with passivity and dependency characteristic of white femininities. The reading by Isis Settles, Jennifer Pratt-Hyatt, and NiCole Buchanan titled "Through the Lens of Race" illustrates how experiences of gender differ. This article discusses how differences in black and white women's perceptions of womanhood reflect socio-historical factors and experiences of gender discrimination, as well as stereotypes and gender norms.

The pervasiveness of gender is a focus of Judith Lorber's article "The Social Construction of Gender." She explains gender as a process that involves multiple patterns of interaction created and re-created constantly in human interaction. Lorber also makes the important point that because gender is so central in shaping our lives, much of what is gendered we do not even recognize; it's made normal and ordinary and occurs on a subconscious level. In other words, the differences between "femininity" (passive, dependent, intuitive, emotional) and "masculinity" (strong, independent, in control, out of touch emotionally) are made to seem natural and inevitable despite the fact that gender is a social script that individuals learn. Cordelia Fine also addresses this "naturalizing" of gender in the reading "Unraveling Hardwiring," an excerpt from her book *The Delusions of Gender* that focuses on research in gendered brain chemistry. She disputes the belief that gendered traits are "hardwired" into the brain and critiques the "biology is destiny" argument that claims innate psychological differences between the minds of women and men.

In reality, gender is a practice in which all people engage; it is something we perform over and over in our daily lives. As already mentioned, gender is something we "do" rather than "have." Through a process of *gender acquisition,* we practice the performative aspects of gender and learn the "appropriate" thinking and behaviors associated with our assignments as girls and boys. Sometimes there are harsh responses to children who do not follow these patterns, and as mentioned earlier, especially to boys who embrace "girly" things such as nail polish or pink clothes. As an aside, it is interesting to note that the association of color options with gender is a relatively recent phenomenon. Traditionally, pink had been associated with males as a diminutive of the reds favored in men's clothing. It was not until the 1940s that manufacturers dictated specific color options for boys and girls.

LEARNING ACTIVITY **More Genders**

Across history, many cultures have recognized more than two genders. Take a closer look at this PBS Map of Gender-Diverse Cultures at http://www.pbs.org/independentlens/two-spirits/map.html. Follow each of the map pins to learn more about people who inhabit other genders than male and female. For example, in Albania, the *burrnesha* are "sworn virgins." These people are born with typical female bodies, but they take a vow of chastity and, in exchange, can live as men. Until very recently, women's roles in Albania were severely limited. Becoming *burrnesha* allowed women to escape their restraints and gain freedom and power. By taking the oath of virginity, *burrnesha* became patriarchs of their families. They wear men's clothing, carry weapons, own property, and move about society freely. As women have gained status in recent years, the tradition of *burrnesha* has diminished, leaving only a small number of them in Albania. In Samoa, *fa'afafine* are people born with typical male bodies raised as girls by their families. Historically, parents chose to raise a child as a *fa'afafine* when the family had many boys in it and few or no girls. In recent years, parents my recognize more traditionally feminine behaviors in a young boy and acknowledge him as *fa'afafine*. Other boys may choose to become *fa'afafine* and then may begin to adopt more traditionally feminine behaviors, dressing as women and learning the traditional duties of Samoan women.

What do these additional genders suggest about our dominant notion of only two genders? Why is the dominant culture so invested in maintaining the illusion of only two genders? How does the dominance of the ideology of only two genders intersect with the history and legacy of colonialism? What are the implications for liberation of all people in the recognition of many genders?

Our gender expression is not always the same as our gender identity and may or may not match our assigned gender at birth. As discussed in Chapter 2, transgender people, in the words of Evin Taylor, are individuals "who change, cross, or live beyond gender." Transgender individuals who claim a gender identity or expression different from the one assigned at their birth by their family and community resist the social construction of gender into two distinct binary categories, masculinity and femininity, and subvert these taken-for-granted categories that in most cultures are set in opposition to each other. Transgender people push at the boundaries of gender and help reveal its constructed nature by refusing to identify in any distinct category. Evelyn Blackwood writes about this in her reading "Trans Identities and Contingent Masculinities: Being Tombois in Everyday Practice." She discusses female-bodied individuals in Indonesia who perform masculinity, but whose identity as men is complex and integrated into their role in communities. In comparison to transgender, cisgender identity is one where gender identity and expression match the gender assignment given at birth. Cisgender individuals can be said to experience conformity between gender assignment, identity, and expression.

Although transgender illustrates the ways a person's gender identity might not match the gender assignment given at birth based upon physical or genetic sex characteristics, it is often used interchangeably with the term *transsexual* (and simply labeled *trans*). However, you are more likely to see the term *transsexual* in describing transgendered people who believe they

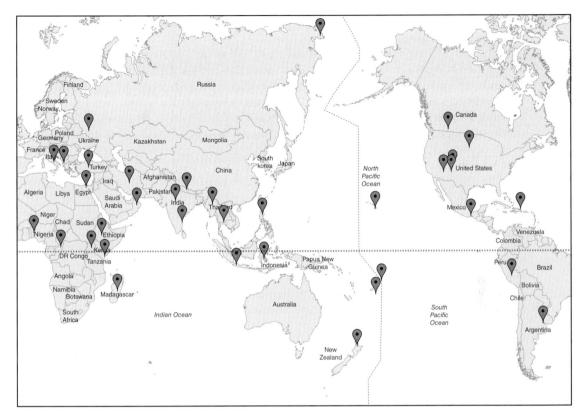

On nearly every continent, and for all of recorded history, thriving cultures have recognized, revered, and integrated more than two genders. Terms such as transgender and gay are strictly new constructs that assume three things: that there are only two sexes (male/female), as many as two sexualities (gay/straight), and only two genders (man/woman).

Yet hundreds of distinct societies around the globe have their own long-established traditions for third, fourth, fifth, or more genders. Fred Martinez, for example, was not a boy who wanted to be a girl, but both a boy and a girl—an identity his Navajo culture recognized and revered as nádleehí. Most Western societies have no direct correlation for this Native "two-spirit" tradition, nor for the many other communities without strict either/or conceptions of sex, sexuality, and gender. Worldwide, the sheer variety of gender expression is almost limitless. Take a tour and learn how other cultures see gender diversity.

are born with the bodies of the wrong sex and who desire chemical or surgical altering in the form of hormone therapies or sex reassignment surgeries. They transition from female to male (FtM, F2M, or "transman") and male to female (MtF, M2F, or "transwoman"). As a category, transgender also overlaps with cross-dressing, the practice of wearing the clothes of the opposite sex, or the sex different from that to which a person was assigned in childhood. Cross-dressing is different from fetishistic transvestism, which involves occasional wearing of the other sex's clothes for sexual self-arousal or pleasure. In addition, the category of transgender cross-dressers does not necessarily include impersonators who look upon dressing as solely connected to their livelihood or actors undertaking roles. Similarly, drag performances that involve makeup and clothing worn on special occasions for theatrical or comedic purposes are not necessarily transgender behavior, although within the genre of drag there are gender illusionists who do pass as another gender and are very active in the transgender community. Drag queens are men doing female impersonation and drag kings are women doing male impersonation.

As a concept, transgender is different from androgyny, although in practice, one performance of a transgender identity might be androgyny. *Androgyny* can be defined as a lack of gender differentiation or a balanced mixture of recognizable feminine and masculine traits. It is an example of transgender behavior because it attempts to break down the binary categories of femininity and masculinity. It is interesting to note that contemporary ideas about androgyny tend to privilege the "andro" (masculine) more than the "gyny" (feminine), with the presentation of androgyny looking a lot more like masculinity than femininity. The trappings of femininity seem to be the first things that are shed when a body is constructed as androgynous. This is related to androcentrism and the ways masculinity more closely approximates our understanding of (nongendered) "human."

It is also interesting to consider the ways the Internet and other virtual technologies have facilitated transgender identities through a disruption of the expected relationship between self and body ("feminine" identity/"female" body). These technologies remove physical, bodily cues and potentially allow "gender swapping," or the creation of identities that attempt to avoid the binaries of "femininity" and "masculinity" (see box, "Gender Swapping on the Web"). This supports the postmodern view of gender as performative and identity as multiple and fluid.

Transgender does not imply any specific form of sexual identity: Transgender people may identify as heterosexual, gay, lesbian, bisexual, or asexual. It is important not to confuse gender and sexuality here. Transgender identities are about gender performance and might involve any sexual identity. It can be confusing, however, because on many campuses there are LGBTQ (Lesbian/Gay/Bisexual/Trans/Queer) alliances or centers where resources for transgender students are incorporated into a coalition about sexual rights. In addition, transgender theory has been heavily influenced by queer theory and its insistence on fluid identities (discussed in Chapter 1). Both trans and queer theory emphasizes that "woman" and "man" are changeable, evolving, and contested categories that must not be seen as fixed, static, normalized, and taken-for-granted. Both are interested in the ways diverse notions of personhood are mapped onto the physical body.

Another potential confusion that encourages the merging of gender and sexuality is the term *genderqueer*, which combines alternative gender identities and sexualities, although you might see it used to imply someone who is transgendered without concern for sexual identity. Generally, genderqueer describes a person who is a nonconformist in challenging existing constructions and identities. You might also see it used to describe a social movement resisting the traditional categories of gender. In other words, although genderqueer focuses on the integration of gender and sexual identities and therefore is a useful concept in terms of individual empowerment, social commentary, and political change, again, it is important to understand that, conceptually, these identities (gender and sexuality) are distinct from each other even though they are lived simultaneously. Gender performances are associated with meanings about femininity and masculinity (this chapter), whereas sexuality concerns sexual desire, feelings, and practices (discussed more fully in Chapter 6). A person could potentially combine any combination of gendered performances with sexual identities.

We actively learn the skills and practices of gender, accepting, rejecting, and negotiating them until most of us become very accomplished in our various performances. For example, throwing a ball is a learned act and one that any body can perform. However, because girls are less likely to be taught this skill, even today, the ways they do throw is often the object of derision. Throwing "like a boy" is learned, then performed again and again until it becomes a skill valued in organized sports. Men are not necessarily better athletes than women; rather, sports as an institution has developed to reflect the particular athletic competencies of men, even though upper-body strength is only one aspect of athleticism. For example, if long-distance swimming or balance beam (activities where women generally outperform men) were popular national sports, then we might think differently about the athletic capabilities of women and men. Sporting activities where upper-body strength is a plus and where women perform less well than men are most valued in the United States. This gendering of sport is the focus of the reading "Wrestling with Gender" by Deborah Brake. She explains the ways wrestling embodies a "precarious" masculine identity and explores the accelerated entry of girls into the sport in the last decade.

LEARNING ACTIVITY　**Speaking of Women and Men**

Think about the adjectives we typically use to describe women and men and list these words in the columns below. A couple of examples are provided to get you started.

WOMEN	MEN
Passive	Active
Nurturing	Strong

What do you notice about the words we use to describe women and men? How does our language reinforce stereotypical notions about women and men?

Think about the words we use to designate women and list these names in the columns below. Also, try to find parallel names for women and men. And think about the profanities we use as well. Again, a couple of examples are provided.

WOMEN	MEN
Slut	Stud
Chick	

What do you notice here about the terms we use to name women and men? What is the significance of the words for which you could not identify parallels?

How do you think language plays a role in shaping the ways we think about and "do" gender?

In addition to sports, there are many other major U.S. institutions that support gendered practices. You need only go to a toy store and cruise the very different girls' and boys' aisles to witness the social construction of gender in contemporary U.S. society. What does it mean to get a child-size ironing board instead of a toy gun, and what kinds of behaviors and future roles do these toys help create and justify? Increasingly, and at earlier ages, children are preoccupied with video and cell phone games and computerized activities that also teach lessons about gender.

HISTORICAL MOMENT **Gender Testing**

In 1966 the European Athletics Championships in Budapest required the first sex testing of women athletes. Earlier, charges had been leveled suggesting that some women competitors were really men. In 1966 the first sex test was a visual examination of the naked athletes. Later, this test was replaced by a test that detected the athletes' chromosomal pattern (XX for female and XY for male).

In 1967 Polish sprinter Ewa Klobukowska failed the sex test and was banned from competition. Later, doctors found that she had a condition that once identified would have allowed her to compete.

In 1985 Spanish hurdler Maria Patino expected to compete in the World University Games in Kobe, Japan. Patino had lived her entire life as a woman, and her body type and sex characteristics were typically female. Unfortunately, for Patino, however, her sex test revealed that she did not have two X chromosomes. She was barred from the competition. A few months later, she competed in Spain and won her event. Following her win, however, she was kicked off the Spanish national team, stripped of her titles, and banned from all future competition. Her fight to be reinstated by the International Amateur Athletics Federation took 2½ years.

While our society generally operates under the assumption that people are either male or female, variations from typical biological patterns are common. Some form of intersexuality may occur in as many as 1 in 100 births. Generally, 1 in 400 female athletes will fail the sex test. For many years, women athletes engaged in activism to stop the sex test. Finally, the test was suspended for the 2000 Olympics, although the Olympic Committee reserved the right to reinstate the test at any point in the future.

In 2009 18-year-old South African runner Caster Semenya was subjected to nearly a year of gender scrutiny after she blew away her competitors in the 800-meter race at the world track and field championships in Berlin. Eventually, she was cleared to run as a woman but only after a barrage of psychological, gynecological, and endocrine tests and negative comments about her gender and appearance.

Notice that sex testing has been used only for female athletes. Why do you suppose this is true? How does the existence of people who do not fit neatly into one or the other of the biological categories of male and female disrupt notions of fixed sexes and fixed genders?

This discussion of gender identities and practices does not imply that all men in contemporary North American society are ambitious and independent and all women domestic and emotional. Far from it! However, this discussion clarifies the social norms or shared values associated with the two kinds of human beings our society has created. Regimes of truth about gender and other identities provide the standards or parameters through which thoughts and behaviors are molded.

MASCULINITY

In mainstream contemporary North American society, the "regimes of truth" associated with masculinity are constructed from the classical traits of intelligence, courage, and honesty, with the addition of two other key dimensions. One of these dimensions revolves around potent sexuality and an affinity for violence: the machismo element. *Machismo* involves breaking rules, sexual potency contextualized in the blending of sex and violence, and contempt for women (*misogyny*). To be a man is to *not* be a woman. Weakness, softness, and vulnerability are to be avoided at all costs. Boys are often socialized into contemporary masculinity through shaming practices that ridicule expressions of femininity. As Michael Kimmel explains in the reading "What's Up with Boys?" where his dialogue with Christina Hoff Sommers is reported, boys are relentlessly policing each

Calvin and Hobbes

by Bill Watterson

other, "pressured to conform to a narrow definition of masculinity by the constant spectre of being called a fag or gay." Kimmel's solution to the academic disengagement of boys (as evidenced by the fact that girls do better in school) is "to empower boys' resilience in the face of this gender policing." He emphasizes that there are actually more differences among boys than between boys and girls, emphasizing that the stereotype of the rough and tumble, boys will be boys type of boy, flattens the differences among boys and crushes those who do not conform to the stereotype.

It is no coincidence that the symbol of male ♂ represents Mars, the Roman god of war. A second dimension of masculinity is the *provider role,* composed of ambition, confidence, competence, and strength. Early research by Deborah David and Robert Brannon characterized four dictates of masculinity that encompass these key dimensions. The dictates include (1) "no sissy stuff," the rejection of femininity; (2) the "big wheel," ambition and the pursuit of success, fame, and wealth; (3) the "sturdy oak," confidence, competence, stoicism, and toughness; and (4) "give 'em hell," the machismo element.* Although these scripts dictate masculinity in a broad sense, there are societal demands that construct masculinity differently for different kinds of men. Of course, again masculinity is also experienced through intersections with other identities. Middle-class masculinities, for example, put emphasis on the big-wheel dimension, the dictates of white masculinity often involve the sturdy oak, and men of color often become associated with the machismo element (with the exception of Asian American men, who are sometimes feminized, when they are not being portrayed as karate warriors).

The last decades have seen changes in the social construction of contemporary masculinity. Although the machismo element is still acted out by countless teenage boys and men, it is also avoided by many men who genuinely do not want to be constrained by its demands. Often these men have realized that moving away from the machismo does not necessarily imply a loss of power. In fact, it seems contemporary women may prefer men who are a little more sensitive and vulnerable. In part, these changes have come about as a result of the focus on gender provided by the women's movement and as a result of the work

*Deborah S. David and Robert Brannon, eds., *The Forty-Nine Percent Majority: The Male Sex Role* (Reading, MA: Addison-Wesley, 1976), pp. 13–35.

Rites of Passage

In almost every culture, adolescents participate in some rite of passage to mark entry into adulthood. Quite often, these rites reinforce gender distinctions. Most rites of passage share four basic elements: (1) separation from society; (2) preparation or instruction from an elder; (3) transition; and (4) welcoming back into society with acknowledgment of changed status.* Notice in the following examples how gender is reinforced through rites of passage:

- Among the Okrika of Africa, girls participate in the Iria, a rite that begins in the "fatting rooms" where the girls are fed rich foods to cause the body to "come out." The girls learn traditional songs from the elderly women, and these songs are used to free the girls from their romantic attachments to water spirits so they can become marriageable and receive mortal suitors. On the final day of their initiation, the water spirits are expected to try to seize the girls, but the Osokolo (a male) strikes the girls with sticks and drives them back to the village, ensuring their safety and future fertility.*
- The Tukuna of the Amazon initiate girls into womanhood at the onset of menstruation through the Festa das Mocas Novas. For several weeks, the girl lives in seclusion in a chamber in her family's home. The Tukuna believe that during this time, the girl is in the underworld and in increasing danger from demons, the Noo. Near the end of the initiation period, the girl is painted with black genipa dye for 2 days to protect her from the Noo, while guests arrive, some wearing masks to become incarnations of the Noo. On the third day, she leaves the chamber to dance with her family until dawn. The shaman gives her a firebrand to throw at the Noo to break the Noo's power and allow her to enter into womanhood.*
- In Ohafia in Nigeria, a father provides his son with a bow and arrows around age 7 or 8. The boy practices shooting at targets until he develops the skill to kill a small bird. When this task is accomplished, the boy ties the dead bird to the end of his bow and marches through his village singing that his peers who have not yet killed their first bird are cowards. His father, then, dresses him in finery and takes him to visit, often for the first time, his maternal family. His new social role distinguishes him from the "cowards" and marks his entrance into manhood.[†]

What are some rites of passage in the United States? How do these rites reinforce gender? How might rites of passage be developed that acknowledge entrance into adulthood without reinforcing gender distinctions?

*Cassandra Halle Delaney, "Rites of Passage in Adolescence," *Adolescence* 30 (1995): 891–987.
[†] *www.siu.edu/~anthro/mccall/children.html.*

LEARNING ACTIVITY **Performing Gender in the Movies**

Many movies offer gender-bending performances. Choose one or more of the following movies to watch. During the movie, record your observations about how the various characters learn and perform gender. Also note the ways race intersects with gender in these performances. How does sexual identity get expressed in the performance of gender?

- *Victor/Victoria*
- *Tootsie*
- *Mrs. Doubtfire*
- *To Wong Foo, Thanks for Everything! Julie Newmar*
- *The Adventures of Priscilla, Queen of the Desert*
- *Switch*
- *The Birdcage*
- *Orlando*
- *Shakespeare in Love*
- *Boys Don't Cry*
- *Big Momma's House*
- *Sorority Boys*
- *Nutty Professor*
- *Nutty Professor II: The Klumps*
- *Connie and Carla*
- *White Chicks*
- *Yentl*
- *The Associate*
- *Transamerica*
- *Albert Nobbs*
- *Tomboy*

of such organizations as the National Organization of Men Against Sexism (NOMAS). As feminist writer and activist Gloria Steinem once said, gender is a prison for both women and men. The difference, she explained, is that for men it's a prison with wall-to-wall carpeting and someone to bring you coffee. An interview with Steinem is included in Chapter 1 readings. Understanding the limitations associated with masculine social scripts has encouraged some men to transform these scripts into more productive ways of living. Many pro-feminist men and men's organizations have been at the forefront of this work.

Some men have responded to the limitations of masculinity and the advances of women brought about by feminism by focusing on themselves as victims, as demonstrated by the mytho-poetic men's movement, which encourages men to bond and reclaim their power. While this may empower individual men, private solutions to social problems do little to transform patriarchal social structures. Other men more overtly express their desire to take back the power they believe they have lost as a result of changes in contemporary notions of femininity and the gains of the women's movement. These include the Promise Keepers, a group of Christian-affiliated men who want to return men to their rightful place in the family and community through a strong re-assertion of traditional gender roles. They believe that men are to rule and women are to serve within the traditional family system.

ACTIVIST PROFILE   **Qwo-Li Driskill**

Qwo-Li Driskill is a Queer Two-Spirit Cherokee poet, performer, and activist and our colleague at Oregon State University, where he is an assistant professor of Queer Studies in the Women, Gender, and Sexuality Studies program. Raised in Colorado, Qwo-Li earned a B.A. from the University of Northern, Colorado; an M.A. from Antioch University, Seattle; and a PhD from Michigan State University.

Qwo-Li explains, "My activism is committed to radical social transformation and intersectional politics. It is deeply rooted in and informed by Native decolonization movements, Queer/Trans/GLBT communities of color, feminisms, poor/working-class politics, and (dis)ability movements. My work as a poet, performer, scholar, and educator (both inside and outside of the university) is entwined with struggles for social justice and healing."

Her first book of poetry, *Walking with Ghosts: Poems* (2005), confronts the forced removal of the Cherokee from their native lands, as well as the ongoing attacks on the LGBTQ community. As reviewer Janice Gould commented, "Qwo-Li Driskill's poetry, part lament and part manifesto, is haunted by ghost dancers. It is a record of those we've lost to the irrational hatred and fear of racism and homophobia. The voice within these poems chants, croons, sasses, and sings, for this is poetry meant to be spoken into being. In the tradition of other queer, socially-conscious poets, like Chrystos, Pat Parker, and Audre Lorde, the question of whether justice exists for all—especially for the poorest and most despised among us—burns at the center of this fine first collection." The book was named Book of the Month by *Sable: The LitMag for New Writing* and was nominated for the Griffin Poetry Prize. More of Qwo-Li's poems have appeared in a variety of journals and anthologies. S/he also published co-edited volumes including *Scars Tell Stories: A Queer and Trans (Dis)ability Zine* (2007) and *Queer Indigenous Studies: Critical Interventions in Theory, Politics, and Literature* (2011), a collection of essays that critique the intersections of colonialism and heteropatriarchy.

FOR MARSHA P. (PAY IT NO MIND!) JOHNSON

by Qwo-Li Driskill

found floating in the Hudson River shortly after NYC Pride, 1992

"You are the one whose spirit is present in the dappled stars."

-- Joy Harjo, from "For Anna Mae Pictou Aquash . . ."

Each act of war
is whispered from
Queen to Queen
held like a lost child

(continued)

then released into the water below.
Names float into rivers
gentle blooms of African Violets.

I will be the one that dangles
from the side but
does not let go.

The police insisted you leapt
into the Hudson
driftwood body
in sequin lace
rhinestone beads
that pull us to the bottom.
No serious investigation -- just another
dead Queen.

I am the one who sings Billie Holiday
as a prayer song to you, Marsha P.

We all choke on splintered bones,
dismembered screams,
the knowledge that each
death is our own.

I pour libations of dove's blood,
leave offerings of yam and corn
to call back all of our lost spirits.

Marsha P, your face glitters with
Ashanti gold
as you sashay across the moonscape
in a ruby chariot ablaze.
Sister, you drag
us behind you.

We are gathered on the bridge between
survival and despair.
I will be the one wearing gardenias
in my hair,
thinking about
how we all go back to water.
Thinking about
the night
you did not jump.

I will make voodoo dolls
of the police and other thugs,
walk to the edge,
watch the river rise to meet them.

I will be the one
with the rattlesnake that binds
my left arm and
in my right hand I will carry
a wooden hatchet to
cut away at the
silence of your murder.

Each of us go on,
pretend to pay it no mind,
bite down hard on the steel of despair.

We will be the ones that gnaw off our own
legs rather than let them win.

We will be the ones mourning
the death of yet another Queen.

Girl, I will put your photo
on my ancestral altar
to remember all of us
who never jumped.

Miss Johnson, your meanings
sparkle like stars dappled
across the piers of the
Hudson River.

Gathered on the bridge
we resist the water.

(published in *Lodestar Quarterly,* Fall 2004)

FEMININITY

Adjectives associated with traditional notions of femininity in contemporary mainstream North American society include soft, passive, domestic, nurturing, emotional, dependent, sensitive, as well as delicate, intuitive, fastidious, needy, fearful, and so forth. These are the qualities that have kept women in positions of subordination and encouraged them to do the domestic and emotional work of society. Again, no surprise that the symbol of female ♀ represents Venus, the goddess of love. "Doing gender" in terms of femininity involves speaking, walking, looking, and acting in certain ways: in feminine ways. The performative quality involved in being a drag queen (a man who is acting out normative femininity) highlights and reveals the taken-for-granted (at least by women) affectations of femininity. Yet femininity, like masculinity, varies across cultures and intersects with other identities. As already discussed, African American women may not identify with some aspects of femininity more readily associated with white femininity such as

LEARNING ACTIVITY   **Gender Swapping on the Web**

The virtual world of the Internet has provided a fascinating environment in which people often play with gender, although, given the social relations of power in contemporary society, this virtual world can also be a place where individuals use gender as a source of power over, or harassment against, other people. Still, in many text-based virtual environments, Web users are able to take on another gender. Men create "feminine" identities for themselves, and women create "masculine" identities for themselves. As Web users engage in this process of gender swapping, they are able to explore the ways that human interactions are structured by gender and to experience in some ways what life is like as another gender.

Create a virtual identity for yourself as another gender and join a chat room or game on the Web as that person. How does it feel to experience the world as another gender? Do you notice ways you act or are treated differently as this gender? What do your experiences suggest to you about how gender structures the ways humans interact with one another?

Men, by far, gender swap on the Web more than women. Why do you think this is true? Do you think gender swapping on the Web has the potential to challenge gender stereotypes? Or do you think it reinforces them? How might the technology of the Internet be used to challenge the limitations of gender? How might the technology of the Internet be used to reinforce male dominance?

Learn more: The following books offer in-depth exploration of these issues. What do these authors suggest about the nature of gender on the Web?

Baldwin, Dianna, and Julie Achterberg, eds. *Women and Second Life: Essays on Virtual Identity, Work and Play.* Jefferson, NC: McFarland and Co., 2013.

Kendall, Lori. *Hanging Out in the Virtual Pub: Masculinities and Relationships Online.* Berkeley: University of California Press, 2002.

Nayar, Pramod K. *The New Media and Cyberculture Anthology.* Hoboken, NJ: Wiley-Blackwell, 2010.

Paasonen, Susanna. *Figures of Fantasy: Internet, Women, and Cyberdiscourse.* New York: Peter Lang, 2005.

Ray, Audacia. *Naked on the Internet: Hookups, Downloads, and Cashing In on Internet Sexploration.* New York: Seal Press, 2007.

passivity. Asian American women, on the other hand, often have to deal with societal stereotypes that construct femininity very much in terms of passivity and dependence: the "exotic gardenia" or "oriental chick" described in Nellie Wong's poem "When I Was Growing Up."

A key aspect of femininity is its bifurcation or channeling into two opposite aspects. These aspects involve the chaste, domestic, caring mother or madonna and the sexy, seducing, fun-loving playmate or whore (sometimes known in popular mythology as women you marry and women with whom you have sex). These polar opposites cause tension as women navigate the implications of these aspects of femininity in their everyday lives. A woman may discover that neither sexual activity nor sexual

LEARNING ACTIVITY   **Walk like a Man, Sit like a Lady**

One of the ways we perform gender is by the way we use our bodies. Very early, children learn to act their gender in the ways they sit, walk, and talk.

Try this observation research:

- Observe a group of schoolchildren playing. Make notes about what you observe concerning how girls and boys act, particularly how they use their bodies in their play and communication.
- Find a place where you can watch people sitting or walking. A public park or mall may offer an excellent vantage point. Record your observations about the ways women and men walk and sit.

Also try this experiment: Ask a friend who identifies with the "opposite sex" to participate in an experiment with you. Take turns teaching each other to sit and to walk like the opposite gender assignment. After practicing your newfound gender behaviors, write your reflections about the experience.

inactivity is quite right. If she is too sexually active, she will be censured for being too loose, the whore; if she refrains from sexual activity, she might similarly be censured for being a prude or frigid. Notice there are many slang words for both kinds of women: those who have too much sex and those who do not have enough. This is the double bind: You're damned if you do and potentially damned if you don't. These contradictions and mixed messages serve to keep women in line.

Unlike contemporary masculinity, which is exhibiting very small steps into the realms of the feminine, femininity has boldly moved into areas that were traditionally off-limits. Today's ideal woman (perhaps from a woman's point of view) is definitely more androgynous than the ideal woman of the past. The contemporary ideal woman might be someone who is smart, competent, and independent; beautiful, thin, athletic, and sexy; yet also loving, sensitive, competent domestically, and emotionally healthy. Note how this image has integrated characteristics of masculinity with traditional feminine qualities at the same time that it has retained much of the feminine social script. The contemporary ideal woman is strong, assertive, active, and independent rather than passive, delicate, and dependent. The assumption is that she is out in the public world rather than confined to the home. She has not completely shed her domestic, nurturing, and caring dimension, however, or her intuitive, emotional, and sensitive aspects. These attributes are important in her success as a loving and capable partner to a man, as indeed are her physical attributes concerning looks and body size.

To be a modern woman today (we might even say a "liberated woman") is to be able to do *everything:* the superwoman. It is important to ask who is benefiting from this new social script. Women work in the public world (often in jobs that pay less, thus helping employers and the economic system) and yet still are expected to do the domestic and emotional work of home and family as well as stay fit and "beautiful." In many ways, contemporary femininity tends to serve both the capitalist economic system and individual men better than the traditional, dependent, domestic model.

GENDER RANKING

Gender encompasses not only the socially constructed, intersecting differences prescribed for different kinds of human beings but also the values associated with these differences. Recall the sissy/tomboy exercise at the beginning of this chapter. Those traits assigned as feminine are less valued than those considered masculine, illustrating why men tend to have more problems emulating femininity and trans people moving into femininity are viewed with somewhat more hostility than those transitioning toward masculine identities. It is okay to emulate the masculine and act like a boy, but it may not be okay to emulate the feminine. This is *gender ranking* (the valuing of one gender over another). "When genders are ranked," writes Judith Lorber in "The Social Construction of Gender," the "devalued genders have less power, prestige, and economic rewards than the valued genders." Just as white is valued above brown or black, and young (though not too young) above old, and heterosexual above homosexual, masculinity tends to be ranked higher than femininity. To be masculine is to have privileges vis-à-vis gender systems; to be feminine means to identify with members of a target group. As already discussed, the social system here that discriminates and privileges on the basis of gender is sexism, although any one person experiencing entitlements or obstacles associated with sexism may also experience entitlements and/or obstacles associated with other intersecting differences or identities. Sexism works by viewing the differences between women and men as important for determining access to social, economic, and political resources. As defined in Chapter 2, sexism is the system that discriminates and privileges on the basis of gender and that results in gender stratification. Given the ranking of gender in our society, sexism works to privilege men and limit women. In other words, men receive entitlements and privilege in a society that ranks masculinity over femininity even while they may be limited by virtue of other intersecting identities such as race or social class.

This discussion, however, must be nuanced by an understanding that masculine privilege tends to be granted first and foremost to cisgendered masculinity. Transgender individuals often face transphobia as well as hate crimes as a result of their gender expressions. It can be especially difficult for male-bodied individuals to identify as girls since their gender performances are ranked both as a result of breaking gender norms and identification with a target group. This encourages us to pay attention to the varied forms of regulation and violence associated with gender ambiguity and transgender identification. Gender expressions that do not adhere to traditional female/male binaries are often subject to discipline in a society that expects and enforces "opposite" genders.

Although women are limited by sexism as a system of power that privileges men over women, the social category "woman," as you recall from Chapter 2, is hardly homogeneous and constantly in flux. Location in different systems of inequality and privilege shapes women's lives in different ways; they are not affected by gender in the same ways. As Settles et al. discuss in the reading in this chapter on black and white women's perceptions of femininity and womanhood, other systems based on class, race, sexual identity, and so forth interact with gender to produce different experiences for individual women. This means that the effects of gender and understandings of both femininity and masculinity are mediated by other systems of power. This is another way that ranking occurs. Forms of gender-based oppression and exploitation depend in part on other social characteristics in people's lives, and gender practices often enforce other types of inequalities. This reflects the confluence that occurs as gender categories are informed/constructed through social relations of power associated with other identities and accompanying systems of inequality and privilege (such as racial identities and racism, sexual identities and heterosexism, and so forth). These identities cannot be separated, and certainly they are lived and performed through a tangle of multiple (and often shifting) identities. In this way, ranking occurs both *across* gender categories (masculinity is valued over femininity) and *within* gender categories (for example, as economically privileged women are represented differently than poor women and receive economic and social entitlements, or as abled women live different lives than disabled women, and so forth).

Examples of this latter type of gender ranking also include the ways African American women may be characterized as promiscuous or matriarchal and African American men are described as hyperathletic and sexually potent. Jewish women are painted as materialistic and overbearing, whereas Jewish men are supposedly very ambitious, thrifty, good at business, yet still tied to their mothers' apron strings. Latinas and Chicanas are stereotyped as sexy and fun loving, and, likewise, Latinos and Chicanos are seen as oversexed, romantic, and passionate. Native American women are portrayed as silent and overworked or exotic and romantic, whereas Native American men are stereotyped as aloof mystics, close to nature, or else as "savages" and drunks. Asian Americans generally are often portrayed as smart and good at science and math while Asian American women have also been typed as exotic, passive, and delicate. Such stereotypes are part of regimes of truth that keep power systems intact. Remember that you will always find examples of people who may fit a certain stereotype to some extent; rather, stereotypes are used to shape meaning about, and often denigrate, a whole category of humans without respect to accurate information about them.

Finally, other examples of this gender ranking include the ways certain women (the poor and women of color) were historically regarded as carrying out appropriate womanhood when they fulfilled the domestic labor needs of strangers. Upper-class femininity meant that there were certain jobs these privileged women could not perform. This demonstrates the interaction of gender with class and race systems. Old women endure a certain brand of femininity that tends to be devoid of the playmate role and is heavy on the mother aspect. Sexually active old women are violating the norms of femininity set up for them: This shows the influence of ageism in terms of shaping gender norms. Other stereotypes that reveal the interaction of gender with societal systems of privilege and inequality include disabled women's supposedly relatively low sexual appetite or lesbians' lack of femininity (they are presumed to want to be like men at the same time they are said to hate them).

All these problematic constructions are created against the norm of whiteness and work to maintain the privileges of the mythical norm. This concept is illustrated in Nellie Wong's poem. She longed to be white, something she saw as synonymous with being a desirable woman. Note there are ethnic and regional stereotypes for white women (such as the dizzy blonde, Southern belle, sexually liberated Scandinavian, or hot-tempered Irish), even though whites are encouraged not to see white as a racial category. Whiteness is just as racialized as any other racial group. The fact that being white can be claimed the mythical norm, strips whiteness from the historical and political roots of its construction as a racial category. As discussed in Chapter 2, this ability for nontarget groups to remain relatively invisible is a key to maintaining their dominance in society.

IDEAS FOR ACTIVISM

- Be a gender traitor for a day. Act/dress in ways that are not generally considered to be appropriate for your gender.
- Develop and perform on campus a street theater piece about gender performance.
- Plan, create, publish, and distribute a zine challenging traditional gender roles.
- Examine how masculinity is valued above femininity on your campus. Write a letter about your findings to your campus newspaper.

The Five Sexes, Revisited

Anne Fausto-Sterling (2000)

As Cheryl Chase stepped to the front of the packed meeting room in the Sheraton Boston Hotel, nervous coughs made the tension audible. Chase, an activist for intersexual rights, had been invited to address the May 2000 meeting of the Lawson Wilkins Pediatric Endocrine Society (LWPES), the largest organization in the United States for specialists in children's hormones. Her talk would be the grand finale to a four-hour symposium on the treatment of genital ambiguity in newborns, infants born with a mixture of both male and female anatomy, or genitals that appear to differ from their chromosomal sex. The topic was hardly a novel one to the assembled physicians.

Yet Chase's appearance before the group was remarkable. Three and a half years earlier, the American Academy of Pediatrics had refused her request for a chance to present the patients' viewpoint on the treatment of genital ambiguity, dismissing Chase and her supporters as "zealots." About two dozen intersex people had responded by throwing up a picket line. The Intersex Society of North America (ISNA) even issued a press release: "Hermaphrodites Target Kiddie Docs."

It had done my 1960s street-activist heart good. In the short run, I said to Chase at the time, the picketing would make people angry. But eventually, I assured her, the doors then closed would open. Now, as Chase began to address the physicians at their own convention, that prediction was coming true. Her talk, titled "Sexual Ambiguity: The Patient-Centered Approach," was a measured critique of the near-universal practice of performing immediate, "corrective" surgery on thousands of infants born each year with ambiguous genitalia. Chase herself lives with the consequences of such surgery. Yet her audience, the very endocrinologists and surgeons Chase was accusing of reacting with "surgery and

shame," received her with respect. Even more remarkably, many of the speakers who preceded her at the session had already spoken of the need to scrap current practices in favor of treatments more centered on psychological counseling.

What led to such a dramatic reversal of fortune? Certainly, Chase's talk at the LWPES symposium was a vindication of her persistence in seeking attention for her cause. But her invitation to speak was also a watershed in the evolving discussion about how to treat children with ambiguous genitalia. And that discussion, in turn, is the tip of a biocultural iceberg—the gender iceberg—that continues to rock both medicine and our culture at large.

Chase made her first national appearance in 1993, in *The Sciences,* announcing the formation of ISNA in a letter responding to an essay I had written for the journal, titled "The Five Sexes" [March/April 1993]. In that article I argued that the two-sex system embedded in our society is not adequate to encompass the full spectrum of human sexuality. In its place, I suggested a five-sex system. In addition to males and females, I included "herms" (named after true hermaphrodites, people born with both a testis and an ovary); "merms" (male pseudohermaphrodites, who are born with testes and some aspect of female genitalia); and "ferms" (female pseudohermaphrodites, who have ovaries combined with some aspect of male genitalia).

I had intended to be provocative, but I had also written with tongue firmly in cheek. So I was surprised by the extent of the controversy the article unleashed. Right-wing Christians were outraged, and connected my idea of five sexes with the United Nations–sponsored Fourth World Conference on Women, held in Beijing in September 1995. At the same time, the article delighted others who felt constrained by the current sex and gender system.

Clearly, I had struck a nerve. The fact that so many people could get riled up by my proposal to revamp our sex and gender system suggested that change—as well as resistance to it—might be in the offing. Indeed, a lot has changed since 1993, and I like to think that my article was an important stimulus. As if from nowhere, intersexuals are materializing before our very eyes. Like Chase, many have become political organizers, who lobby physicians and politicians to change current treatment practices. But more generally, though perhaps no less provocatively, the boundaries separating masculine and feminine seem harder than ever to define.

Some find the changes under way deeply disturbing. Others find them liberating.

Who is an intersexual—and how many intersexuals are there? The concept of intersexuality is rooted in the very ideas of male and female. In the idealized, Platonic, biological world, human beings are divided into two kinds: a perfectly dimorphic species. Males have an X and a Y chromosome, testes, a penis and all of the appropriate internal plumbing for delivering urine and semen to the outside world. They also have well-known secondary sexual characteristics, including a muscular build and facial hair. Women have two X chromosomes, ovaries, all of the internal plumbing to transport urine and ova to the outside world, a system to support pregnancy and fetal development, as well as a variety of recognizable secondary sexual characteristics.

That idealized story papers over many obvious caveats: some women have facial hair, some men have none; some women speak with deep voices, some men veritably squeak. Less well known is the fact that, on close inspection, absolute dimorphism disintegrates even at the level of basic biology. Chromosomes, hormones, the internal sex structures, the gonads and the external genitalia all vary more than most people realize. Those born outside of the Platonic dimorphic mold are called intersexuals.

In "The Five Sexes" I reported an estimate by a psychologist expert in the treatment of intersexuals, suggesting that some 4 percent of all live births are intersexual. Then, together with a group of Brown University undergraduates, I set out to conduct the first systematic assessment of the available data on intersexual birthrates. We scoured the medical literature for estimates of the frequency of various categories of intersexuality, from additional chromosomes to mixed gonads, hormones and genitalia. For some conditions we could find only anecdotal evidence; for most, however, numbers exist. On the basis of that evidence, we calculated that for every 1,000 children born, seventeen are intersexual in some form. That number—1.7 percent—is a ballpark estimate, not a precise count, though we believe it is more accurate than the 4 percent I reported.

Our figure represents all chromosomal, anatomical and hormonal exceptions to the dimorphic ideal; the number of intersexuals who might, potentially, be subject to surgery as infants is smaller—probably between one in 1,000 and one in 2,000 live births. Furthermore, because some populations possess the relevant genes at high frequency, the intersexual birthrate is not uniform throughout the world.

Consider, for instance, the gene for congenital adrenal hyperplasia (CAH). When the CAH gene is inherited from both parents, it leads to a baby with masculinized external genitalia who possesses two X chromosomes and the internal reproductive organs of a potentially fertile woman. The frequency of the gene varies widely around the world: in New Zealand it occurs in only forty-three children per million; among the Yupik Eskimo of southwestern Alaska, its frequency is 3,500 per million.

Intersexuality has always been to some extent a matter of definition. And in the past century physicians have been the ones who defined children as intersexual—and provided the remedies. When only the chromosomes are unusual, but the external genitalia and gonads clearly indicate either a male or a female, physicians do not advocate intervention. Indeed, it is not clear what kind of intervention could be advocated in such cases. But the story is quite different when infants are born with mixed genitalia, or with external genitals that seem at odds with the baby's gonads. Most clinics now specializing in the treatment of intersex babies rely on case-management principles developed in the 1950s by the psychologist John Money and the psychiatrists Joan G. Hampson and John L. Hampson, all of Johns Hopkins University in Baltimore, Maryland. Money believed that gender identity is completely malleable for about eighteen months after birth. Thus, he argued, when a treatment team is presented with an infant who has ambiguous genitalia, the team could make a gender assignment solely on the basis of what made the best surgical sense. The physicians could then simply encourage the parents to raise the child according to the surgically assigned gender. Following that course, most physicians maintained, would eliminate psychological distress for both the patient and the parents. Indeed, treatment teams were never to use such words as "intersex" or "hermaphrodite"; instead, they were to tell parents that nature intended the baby to be the boy or the girl that the physicians had determined it was. Through surgery, the physicians were merely completing nature's intention.

Although Money and the Hampsons published detailed case studies of intersex children who they said had adjusted well to their gender assignments, Money thought one case in particular proved his theory. It was a dramatic example, inasmuch as it did not involve intersexuality at all: one of a pair of identical twin boys lost his penis as a result of a circumcision accident. Money recommended that "John" (as he came to be known in a later case study) be surgically turned into "Joan" and raised as a girl. In time, Joan grew to love wearing dresses and having her hair done. Money proudly proclaimed the sex reassignment a success.

But as recently chronicled by John Colapinto, in his book *As Nature Made Him,* Joan—now known to be an adult male named David Reimer—eventually rejected his female assignment. Even without a functioning penis and testes (which had been removed as part of the reassignment) John/Joan sought masculinizing medication, and married a woman with children (whom he adopted).

Since the full conclusion to the John/Joan story came to light, other individuals who were reassigned as males or females shortly after birth but who later rejected their early assignments have come forward. So, too, have cases in which the reassignment has worked—at least into the subject's mid-twenties. But even then the aftermath of the surgery can be problematic. Genital surgery often leaves scars that reduce sexual sensitivity. Chase herself had a complete clitoridectomy, a procedure that is less frequently performed on intersexuals today. But the newer surgeries, which reduce the size of the clitoral shaft, still greatly reduce sensitivity.

The revelation of cases of failed reassignments and the emergence of intersex activism have led an increasing number of pediatric endocrinologists, urologists and psychologists to reexamine the wisdom of early genital surgery. For example, in a talk that preceded Chase's at the LWPES meeting, the medical ethicist Laurence B. McCullough of the Center for Medical Ethics and Health Policy at Baylor College of Medicine in Houston, Texas, introduced an ethical framework for the treatment of children with ambiguous genitalia. Because sex phenotype (the manifestation of genetically and embryologically determined sexual characteristics) and gender presentation (the sex role projected by the individual in society) are highly variable, McCullough argues, the various forms of intersexuality should be defined as normal. All of them fall within the statistically expected variability of sex and gender. Furthermore, though certain disease states may accompany some forms of intersexuality, and may require medical intervention, intersexual conditions are not themselves diseases.

McCullough also contends that in the process of assigning gender, physicians should minimize what he calls irreversible assignments: taking steps such as the surgical removal or modification of gonads or genitalia that the patient may one day want to have reversed. Finally, McCullough urges physicians to abandon their practice of treating the birth of a child with genital ambiguity as a medical or social emergency. Instead, they should take the time to perform a thorough medical workup and should disclose everything to the parents, including the uncertainties about the final outcome. The treatment mantra, in other words, should be therapy, not surgery.

I believe a new treatment protocol for intersex infants, similar to the one outlined by McCullough, is close at hand. Treatment should combine some basic medical and ethical principles with a practical but less drastic approach to the birth of a mixed-sex child. As a first step, surgery on infants should be performed only to save the child's life or to substantially improve the child's physical well-being. Physicians may assign a sex—male or female—to an intersex infant on the basis of the probability that the child's particular condition will lead to the formation of a particular gender identity. At the same time, though, practitioners ought to be humble enough to recognize that as the child grows, he or she may reject the assignment—and they should be wise enough to listen to what the child has to say. Most important, parents should have access to the full range of information and options available to them.

Sex assignments made shortly after birth are only the beginning of a long journey. Consider, for instance, the life of Max Beck: Born intersexual, Max was surgically assigned as a female and consistently raised as such. Had her medical team followed her into her early twenties, they would have deemed her assignment a success because she was married to a man. (It should be noted that success in gender assignment has traditionally been defined as living in that gender as a heterosexual.) Within a few years, however, Beck had come out as a butch lesbian; now in her mid-thirties, Beck has become a man and married his lesbian partner, who (through the miracles of modern reproductive technology) recently gave birth to a girl.

Transsexuals, people who have an emotional gender at odds with their physical sex, once described themselves in terms of dimorphic absolutes—males trapped in female bodies, or vice versa. As such, they sought psychological relief through surgery. Although many still do, some so-called transgendered people today are content to inhabit a more ambiguous zone. A male-to-female transsexual, for instance, may come out as a lesbian. Jane, born a physiological male, is now in her late thirties and living with her wife, whom she married when her name was still John. Jane takes hormones to feminize herself, but they have not yet interfered with her ability to engage in intercourse as a man. In her mind Jane has a lesbian relationship with her wife, though she views their intimate moments as a cross between lesbian and heterosexual sex.

It might seem natural to regard intersexuals and transgendered people as living midway between the poles of male and female. But male and female, masculine and feminine, cannot be parsed as some kind of continuum. Rather, sex and gender are best conceptualized as points in a multidimensional space. For some time, experts on gender development have distinguished between sex at the genetic level and at the cellular level (sex-specific gene expression, X and Y chromosomes); at the hormonal level (in the fetus, during childhood and after puberty); and at the anatomical level (genitals and secondary sexual characteristics). Gender identity presumably emerges from all of those corporeal aspects via some poorly understood interaction with environment and experience. What has become increasingly clear is that one can find levels of masculinity and femininity in almost every possible permutation. A chromosomal, hormonal and genital male (or female) may emerge with a female (or male) gender identity. Or a chromosomal female with male fetal hormones and masculinized genitalia—but with female pubertal hormones—may develop a female gender identity.

The Medical and Scientific Communities have yet to adopt a language that is capable of describing such diversity. In her book *Hermaphrodites and the Medical Invention of Sex,* the historian and medical ethicist Alice Domurat Dreger of Michigan State University in East Lansing documents the emergence of current medical systems for classifying gender ambiguity. The current usage remains rooted in the Victorian approach to sex. The logical structure of the commonly used terms "true hermaphrodite," "male pseudohermaphrodite" and "female pseudohermaphrodite" indicates that only the so-called true hermaphrodite is a genuine mix of male and female. The others, no matter how confusing their body parts, are really hidden males or females. Because true hermaphrodites are rare—possibly only one in 100,000— such a classification system supports the idea that human beings are an absolutely dimorphic species.

At the dawn of the twenty-first century, when the variability of gender seems so visible, such a position is hard to maintain. And here, too, the old medical consensus has begun to crumble. Last fall the pediatric urologist Ian A. Aaronson of the Medical University of South Carolina in Charleston organized the North American Task Force on Intersexuality (NATFI) to review the clinical responses to genital ambiguity in infants. Key medical associations, such as the American Academy of Pediatrics, have endorsed NATFI. Specialists in surgery, endocrinology, psychology, ethics, psychiatry, genetics and public health, as well as intersex patient-advocate groups, have joined its ranks.

One of the goals of NATFI is to establish a new sex nomenclature. One proposal under consideration replaces the current system with emotionally neutral terminology that emphasizes developmental processes rather than preconceived gender categories. For example, Type I intersexes develop out of anomalous virilizing influences; Type II result from some interruption of virilization; and in Type III intersexes the gonads themselves may not have developed in the expected fashion.

What is clear is that since 1993, modern society has moved beyond five sexes to a recognition that gender variation is normal and, for some people, an arena for playful exploration. Discussing my "five sexes" proposal in her book *Lessons from the Intersexed,* the psychologist Suzanne J. Kessler of the State University of New York at Purchase drives this point home with great effect:

The limitation with Fausto-Sterling's proposal is that . . . [it] still gives genitals . . . primary signifying status and ignores the fact that in the everyday world gender attributions are made without access to genital inspection. . . . What has primacy in everyday life is the gender that is performed, regardless of the flesh's configuration under the clothes.

I now agree with Kessler's assessment. It would be better for intersexuals and their supporters to turn everyone's focus away from genitals. Instead, as she suggests, one should acknowledge that people come in an even wider assortment of sexual identities and characteristics than mere genitals can distinguish. Some women may have "large clitorises or fused labia," whereas some men may have "small penises or misshapen scrota," as Kessler puts it, "phenotypes with no particular clinical or identity meaning."

As clearheaded as Kessler's program is—and despite the progress made in the 1990s—our society is still far from that ideal. The intersexual or transgendered person who projects a social gender—what Kessler calls "cultural genitals"—that conflicts with his or her physical genitals still may die for the transgression. Hence legal protection for people whose cultural and physical genitals do not match is needed during the current transition to a more gender-diverse world. One easy step would be to eliminate the category of "gender" from official documents, such as driver's licenses and passports. Surely attributes both more visible (such as height, build and eye color) and less visible (fingerprints and genetic profiles) would be more expedient.

A more far-ranging agenda is presented in the International Bill of Gender Rights, adopted in 1995 at the fourth annual International Conference on Transgender Law and Employment Policy in Houston, Texas. It lists ten "gender rights," including the right to define one's own gender, the right to change one's physical gender if one so chooses and the right to marry whomever one wishes. The legal bases for such rights are being hammered out in the courts as I write and, most recently, through the establishment, in the state of Vermont, of legal same-sex domestic partnerships.

No one could have foreseen such changes in 1993. And the idea that I played some role, however small, in reducing the pressure—from the medical community as well as from society at large—to flatten the diversity of human sexes into two diametrically opposed camps gives me pleasure.

Sometimes people suggest to me, with not a little horror, that I am arguing for a pastel world in which androgyny reigns and men and women are boringly the same. In my vision, however, strong colors coexist with pastels. There are and will continue to be highly masculine people out there; it's just that some of them are women. And some of the most feminine people I know happen to be men.

The Social Construction of Gender

Judith Lorber (1994)

Talking about gender for most people is the equivalent of fish talking about water. Gender is so much the routine ground of everyday activities that questioning its taken-for-granted assumptions and presuppositions is like thinking about whether the sun will come up.[1] Gender is so pervasive that in our society we assume it is bred into our genes. Most people find it hard to believe that gender is constantly created and re-created out of human interaction, out of social life, and is the texture and order of that social life. Yet gender, like culture, is a human production that depends on everyone constantly "doing gender" (West and Zimmerman 1987).

And everyone "does gender" without thinking about it. Today, on the subway, I saw a well-dressed man with a year-old child in a stroller. Yesterday, on a bus, I saw a man with a tiny baby in a carrier on his chest. Seeing men taking care of small children in public is increasingly common—at least in New York City. But both men were quite obviously stared at—and smiled at, approvingly. Everyone was doing gender—the men who were changing the role of fathers and the other passengers, who were applauding them silently. But there was more gendering going on that probably fewer people noticed. The baby was wearing a white crocheted cap and white clothes. You couldn't tell if it was a boy or a girl. The child in the stroller was wearing a dark blue T-shirt and dark print pants. As they started to leave the train, the father put a Yankee baseball cap on the child's head. Ah, a boy, I thought. Then I noticed the gleam of tiny earrings in the child's ears, and as they got off, I saw the little flowered sneakers and lace-trimmed socks. Not a boy after all. Gender done.

. . .

For the individual, gender construction starts with assignment to a sex category on the basis of what the genitalia look like at birth.[2] Then babies are dressed or adorned in a way that displays the category because parents don't want to be constantly asked whether their baby is a girl or a boy. A sex category becomes a gender status through naming, dress, and the use of other gender markers. Once a child's gender is evident, others treat those in one gender differently from those in the other, and the children respond to the different treatment by feeling different and behaving differently. As soon as they can talk, they start to refer to themselves as members of their gender. Sex doesn't come into play again until puberty, but by that time, sexual feelings and desires and practices have been shaped by gendered norms and expectations. Adolescent boys and girls approach and avoid each other in an elaborately scripted and gendered mating dance. Parenting is gendered, with different expectations for mothers and fathers, and people of different genders work at different kinds of jobs. The work adults do as mothers and fathers and as low-level workers and high-level bosses, shapes women's and men's life experiences, and these experiences produce different feelings, consciousness, relationships, skills—ways of being that we call feminine or masculine.[3] All of these processes constitute the social construction of gender.

. . .

To explain why gendering is done from birth, constantly and by everyone, we have to look not only at the way individuals experience gender but at gender as a social institution. As a social institution, gender is one of the major ways that human beings organize their lives. Human society depends on a predictable division of labor, a designated allocation of scarce goods, assigned responsibility for children and others who cannot care for themselves, common values and their systematic transmission to new members, legitimate leadership, music, art, stories, games, and other symbolic productions. One way of choosing people for the different tasks of society is on the basis of their talents, motivations, and competence—their demonstrated achievements. The other way is on the basis of gender, race, ethnicity—ascribed membership in a category of people. Although societies vary in the extent to which they use one or the other of these ways of allocating people to work and to carry out other responsibilities, every society uses gender and age grades. Every society classifies people as "girl and boy children," "girls and boys ready to be married," and "fully adult women and men," constructs similarities among them and differences between them, and assigns them to different roles and responsibilities. Personality characteristics, feelings, motivations, and ambitions flow from these different life experiences so that the members of these different groups become different kinds of people. The process of gendering and its outcome are legitimated by religion, law, science, and the society's entire set of values.

GENDER AS PROCESS, STRATIFICATION, AND STRUCTURE

As a social institution, gender is a process of creating distinguishable social statuses for the assignment of rights and responsibilities. As part of a stratification system that ranks these statuses unequally, gender is a major building block in the social structures built on these unequal statuses.

As a *process,* gender creates the social differences that define "woman" and "man." In social interaction throughout their lives, individuals learn what is expected, see what is expected, act and react in expected ways, and thus simultaneously construct and maintain the gender order. . . .

Gendered patterns of interaction acquire additional layers of gendered sexuality, parenting, and work behaviors in childhood, adolescence, and adulthood. Gendered norms and expectations are enforced through informal sanctions of gender-inappropriate behavior by peers and by formal punishment or threat of punishment by those in authority should behavior deviate too far from socially imposed standards for women and men.

. . .

As part of a *stratification* system, gender ranks men above women of the same race and class. Women and men could be different but equal. In practice, the process of creating difference depends to a great extent on differential evaluation. . . . The dominant categories are the hegemonic ideals, taken so for granted as the way things should be that white is not ordinarily thought of as a race, middle class as a class, or men as a gender. The characteristics of these categories define the Other as that which lacks the valuable qualities the dominants exhibit.

In a gender-stratified society, what men do is usually valued more highly than what women do because men do it, even when their activities are very similar or the same. In different regions of southern India, for example, harvesting rice is men's work, shared work, or women's work: "Wherever a task is done by women it is considered easy, and where it is done by [men] it is considered difficult" (Mencher 1988, 104). A gathering and hunting society's survival usually depends on the nuts, grubs, and small animals brought in by the women's foraging trips, but when the men's hunt is successful, it is the occasion for a celebration. Conversely, because they are the superior group, white men do not have to do the "dirty work," such as housework; the most inferior group does it, usually poor women of color (Palmer 1989).

. . .

When gender is a major component of structured inequality, the devalued genders have less power, prestige, and economic rewards than the valued genders. In countries that discourage gender discrimination, many major roles are still gendered; women still do most of the domestic labor and child rearing, even while doing full-time paid work; women and men are segregated on the job and each does work considered "appropriate"; women's work is usually paid less than men's work. Men dominate the positions of authority and leadership in government, the military, and the law; cultural productions, religions, and sports reflect men's interests.

In societies that create the greatest gender difference, such as Saudi Arabia, women are kept out of sight behind walls or veils, have no civil rights, and often create a cultural and emotional world of their own (Bernard 1981). But even in societies with less rigid gender boundaries, women and men spend much of their time with people of their own gender because of the way work and family are organized. This spatial separation of women and men reinforces gendered differences, identity, and ways of thinking and behaving (Coser 1986).

Gender inequality—the devaluation of "women" and the social domination of "men"—has social functions and social history. It is not the result of sex, procreation, physiology, anatomy, hormones, or genetic predispositions. It is produced and maintained by identifiable social processes and built into the general social structure and individual identities deliberately and purposefully. The social order as we know it in Western societies is organized around racial, ethnic, class, and gender inequality. I contend, therefore, that the continuing purpose of gender as a modern social institution is to construct women as a group to be the subordinates of men as a group.

THE PARADOX OF HUMAN NATURE

To say that sex, sexuality, and gender are all socially constructed is not to minimize their social power. These categorical imperatives govern our lives in the most profound and pervasive ways, through the social experiences and social practices of what Dorothy Smith calls the "everday/evernight world" (1990, 31–57). The paradox of human nature is that it is *always* a manifestation of cultural meanings, social relationships, and power politics; "not biology, but culture, becomes destiny" (J. Butler 1990, 8). Gendered people emerge not from physiology or sexual orientations but from the exigencies of the social order, mostly, from the need for a reliable division of the work of food production and the social (not physical) reproduction of new members. The moral imperatives of religion and cultural representations guard the boundary lines among genders and ensure that what is demanded, what is permitted, and what is tabooed for the people in each gender is well known and followed by most (C. Davies 1982). Political power, control of scarce resources, and, if necessary, violence uphold the gendered social order in the face of resistance and

rebellion. Most people, however, voluntarily go along with their society's prescriptions for those of their gender status, because the norms and expectations get built into their sense of worth and identity as [the way we] think, the way we see and hear and speak, the way we fantasy, and the way we feel.

There is no core or bedrock in human nature below these endlessly looping processes of the social production of sex and gender, self and other, identity and psyche, each of which is a "complex cultural construction" (J. Butler 1990, 36). *For humans, the social is the natural. . . .*

NOTES

1. Gender is, in Erving Goffman's words, an aspect of *Felicity's Condition:* "any arrangement which leads us to judge an individual's . . . acts not to be a manifestation of strangeness. Behind Felicity's Condition is our sense of what it is to be sane" (1983, 27). Also see Bem 1993; Frye 1983, 17–40; Goffman 1977.
2. In cases of ambiguity in countries with modern medicine, surgery is usually performed to make the genitalia more clearly male or female.
3. See J. Butler 1990 for an analysis of how doing gender is gender identity.

REFERENCES

Bem, Sandra Lipsitz. 1993. *The Lenses of Gender: Transforming the Debate on Sexual Inequality.* New Haven: Yale University Press.

Bernard, Jessie. 1981. *The Female World.* New York: Free Press.

Butler, Judith. 1990. *Gender Trouble: Feminism and the Subversion of Identity.* New York and London: Routledge.

Coser, Rose Laub. 1986. "Cognitive structure and the use of social space." *Sociological Forum* 1:1–26.

Davies, Christie. 1982. "Sexual taboos and social boundaries." *American Journal of Sociology* 87:1032–63.

Dwyer, Daisy, and Judith Bruce (eds.). 1988. *A Home Divided: Women and Income in the Third World.* Palo Alto, Calif.: Stanford University Press.

Frye, Marilyn. 1983. *The Politics of Reality: Essays in Feminist Theory.* Trumansburg, N.Y.: Crossing Press.

Goffman, Erving. 1977. "The arrangement between the sexes." *Theory and Society* 4:301–33.

Mencher, Joan. 1988. "Women's work and poverty: Women's contribution to household maintenance in South India." In Dwyer and Bruce 1988.

Palmer, Phyllis. 1989. *Domesticity and Dirt: Housewives and Domestic Servants in the United States, 1920–1945.* Philadelphia: Temple University Press.

Smith, Dorothy. 1990. *The Conceptual Practices of Power: A Feminist Sociology of Knowledge.* Toronto: University of Toronto Press.

West, Candace, and Don Zimmerman. 1987. "Doing gender." *Gender & Society* 1:125–51.

R E A D I N G   **22**

Unraveling Hardwiring

Cordelia Fine (2010)

A member of my family, who shall remain nameless, refers to all newborns as "blobs." There's a certain, limited truth to the description. Certainly, research continues to reveal just how sophisticated the neonate mind really is: already tuned to prefer its mother tongue, seek out facelike stimuli, time its waking up to coincide precisely with when its parents have just fallen most deeply into sleep. But it would not be an overstatement to say that newborns still have much to learn. Ideas about how this happens have been changing in important ways in neuroscience.

For decades, brain development has been thought of as an orderly adding in of new wiring that enables you to perform evermore-sophisticated cognitive functions. According to this maturational viewpoint, gene activity at the appropriate time (and with the necessary experience and environment) brings about the maturation of new bits of neural circuitry. These are added in, enabling the child to reach new developmental milestones. Everyone, of course, acknowledges the essential role of experience on development. But when we think of brain development as a gene-directed process of adding in new circuitry, it's not difficult to see how the concept of hardwiring took off. It's been helped along by the popularity of evolutionary psychology, versions of which have promoted the idea that we are the luckless owners of seriously outdated neural circuitry that has been shaped by natural selection to match the environment of our hunter-gatherer ancestors.

But our brains, as we are now coming to understand, are changed by our behavior, our thinking, our social world. The new neuroconstructivist perspective of brain development emphasizes the sheer exhilarating tangle of a continuous interaction among genes, brain, and environment. Yes, gene expression gives rise to neural structures, and genetic material is itself impervious to outside influence. When it comes to genes, you get what you get. But gene *activity* is another story: genes switch on and off depending on what else is going on. Our environment, our behavior, even our thinking, can all change what genes are *expressed.*[1] And thinking, learning, sensing can all change neural structure directly. As Bruce Wexler has argued, one important implication of this neuroplasticity is that we're not locked into the obsolete hardware of our ancestors:

> In addition to having the longest period during which brain growth is shaped by the environment, human beings alter the environment that shapes their brains to a degree without precedent among animals. . . . It is this ability to shape the environment that in turn shapes our brains that has allowed human adaptability and capability to develop at a much faster rate than is possible through alteration of the genetic code itself. This transgenerational shaping of brain function through culture also means that processes that govern the evolution of societies and cultures have a great influence on how our individual brains and minds work.[2]

It's important to point out that this is not a starry-eyed, environmentalist, we-can-all-be-anything-we-want-to-be viewpoint. Genes don't determine our brains (or our bodies), but they do constrain them. The developmental possibilities for an individual are neither infinitely malleable nor solely in the hands of the environment. But the insight that thinking, behavior, and experiences change the brain, directly, or through changes in genetic activity, seems to strip the word "hardwiring" of much useful meaning. As neurophysiologist Ruth Bleier put it over two decades ago, we should "view biology as potential, as capacity and not as static entity. Biology itself is socially influenced and defined; it changes and develops in interaction with and response to our minds and environment, as our behaviors do. Biology can be said to define possibilities but not determine them; it is never irrelevant but it is also not determinant."[3]

And so, what do popular writers, scientists, and former presidents of Harvard *mean* when they refer to gender differences as "hardwired," or "innate," or "intrinsic," or "inherent"? Some philosophers of biology, so far as I can tell, devote entire careers to the concept of innateness and what, if anything, it might mean. As cognitive neuroscientist Giordana Grossi points out, terms like *hardwired*—on loan from computer science where it refers to fixedness—translate poorly to the domain of neural circuits that change and learn throughout life, indeed, in *response* to life.[4]

Certainly, there is far more acknowledgment now of the role of experience and environment compared with a century or so ago. In the early twentieth century, "[g]enius was considered an innate quality which would naturally be manifested if it were possessed," as psychologist Stephanie Shields summarized.[5] No one now, I should think, would agree with this. And yet there remains, in some quarters, a Victorian-style attachment to notions of innate, immutable, inevitable qualities. How else to explain why the Greater Male Variability hypothesis—the idea that men are more likely to be outliers, good or bad ("more prodigies, more idiots"[6])—appears to be no less appealing now than it was over a century ago?[7] In the early twentieth century, the Greater Male Variability hypothesis offered a neat explanation of why men so outnumbered women in eminence, despite the fact that there was little sex difference in the average scores of men and women on psychological tests. As Edward Thorndike explained it in 1910:

> In particular, if men differ in intelligence and energy by wider extremes than do women, eminence in and leadership of the world's affairs of whatever sort will inevitably belong oftener to men. They will oftener deserve it.[8]

And today, it seems, they oftener deserve high-ranking positions in mathematics and science, according to Lawrence Summers:

> It does appear that on many, many different human attributes—height, weight, propensity for criminality, overall IQ, mathematical ability, scientific ability ... there is a difference in the standard deviation and variability [statistical measures of the spread of a population] of a male and a female population. And that is true with respect to attributes that are and are not plausibly, culturally determined. If one supposes, as I think is reasonable, that if one is talking about physicists at a top twenty-five research university ... small differences in the standard deviation will translate into very large differences in the available pool.[9]

I'd love to know, by the way, how extreme *non*-criminality manifests itself. (Number of Supreme Court judges, perhaps?) But more to the point, the assertion that males are more variable in all regards—whether you're talking weight, height, or SAT scores—certainly helps to frame variability as "a guy thing" across the board. The implication is that there is something *inevitable* and immutable about greater male variability in mathematical and scientific ability. Certainly, in the furor that followed, Steven Pinker defended the idea of the timeless, universal nature of greater male variability ("biologists since Darwin have noted that for many traits and many species, males are the more variable gender").[10] Susan Pinker also plays the argument that "[m]en are simply more variable" in the shadow of the Summers controversy.[11] Her book displays a graph showing the findings from a report published by psychologist Ian Deary and his colleagues—a massive IQ study of 80,000 Scottish children born in 1921. Boys' and girls' average IQs were the same, the study found, but the boys' scores were more variable. But as the educational psychologist Leta Stetter Hollingworth pointed out in 1914, and as Ian Deary and his colleagues felt compelled to reiterate nearly 100 years later, "the existence of sex differences either in means or variances in ability says nothing about the source or inevitability of such differences or their potential basis in immutable biology."[12] This should be more obvious to us now than it was a hundred years ago when capacity for eminence was regarded as something that was simply "in there." We realize that, as Grossi has pointed out, "[m]athematics and science are learned in a period of time that spans across several years; passion and application need to be constantly nurtured and encouraged."[13]

And, as it turns out, contemporary investigations of variability—both in the general population and in the most intellectually blessed pockets—have been showing that "inevitable" and "immutable" are adjectives that need not apply when it comes to describing greater male variability in mental ability. One cross-cultural study, published several years before the Summers debacle, compared sex differences in variability in verbal, math, and spatial abilities to see if the greater male variability in the United States was invariably seen in other countries. It was not. In each cognitive domain, there were countries in which females' scores were more variable than males'.[14]

More recently, several very large-scale studies have collected data that offer tests of the Greater Male Variability hypothesis by investigating whether males are inevitably more variable in math performance, and always outnumber females at the high end of ability. The answer, in children at least, is no. In a *Science* study of over 7 million United States schoolchildren, Janet Hyde and her team found that across grade levels and states, boys were modestly more variable than girls. Yet when they looked at the data from Minnesota state assessments of eleventh graders to see how many boys and girls scored above the 95th and 99th percentile (that is, scored better than 95 percent, or 99 percent, of their

peers) an interesting pattern emerged. Among white children there were, respectively, about one-and-a-half and two boys for every girl. But among Asian American kids, the pattern was different. At the 95th percentile boys' advantage was less, and at the 99th percentile there were more girls than boys.[15] Start to look in other countries and you find further evidence that sex differences in variability are, well, variable. Luigi Guiso's cross-cultural *Science* study also found that, like the gender gap in mean scores, the ratio of males to females at the high end of performance is something that changes from country to country. While in the majority of the forty countries studied there were indeed more boys than girls at the 95th and 99th percentiles, in four countries the ratios were equal or even reversed. (These were Indonesia, the UK, Iceland, and Thailand.)[16] Two other large cross-cultural studies of math scores in teenagers have also found that although males are usually more variable, and outnumber girls at the top 5 percent of ability, this is not inevitably so: in some countries females are equally or more variable, or are as likely as boys to make it into the 95th percentile.[17]

Of course, scoring better than 95 or 99 percent of your school peers in mathematical ability is probably a baseline condition for eventually becoming a tenured Harvard professor of mathematics: like having hands, if you want to be a hairdresser. Top scorers on standardized math tests may be what one group of researchers, rather stingily, refers to as "the merely gifted."[18] But also changeable proportion of girls identified in what's called the Study Mathematically Precocious Youth (SMPY), which gives the quantitative section of the Scholastic Aptitude Test (the SAT) to kids who, theoretically, are way too young to take it. Children who score at least 700 (on a 200 to 800 scale) are defined as "highly gifted." In the early 1980s, highly gifted boys identified by the SMPY outnumbered girls 13 to 1. By 2005, this ratio had plummeted to 2.8 to 1.[19] That's a big change.

Being highly gifted is, I imagine, rather nice, but at the risk of swelling the head of any research mathematicians in top-ranked institutions who happen to be reading this book, they need to have made it onto the next rung of the giftedness ladder, and be "profoundly gifted." And here again—in this literally one-in-a-million category—there can be striking differences in female representation, depending on time, place, and cultural background. The International Mathematical Olympiad (IMO) is a nine-hour exam, taken by six-person teams sent from up to ninety-five countries. The length of the exam is off-putting enough, but the six problems within it are also so difficult that every year just a few students (or sometimes even none) get a perfect score. We tend not to hear that much about math competitions (perhaps in part because, let's be honest, live televised coverage of a nine-hour math exam would not make for compelling viewing). So it's probably worth pointing out that these competitions are not female-free zones. Girls are among those who achieve perfect scores. Girls, like U.S. team member Sherry Gong, win medals for outstanding performance. Gong won a silver medal in the 2005 IMO and a gold medal in 2007. The girl can do math—and she's not alone. As the researchers point out, "numerous girls exist who possess truly profound ability in mathematical problem solving."[20]

But an equally important insight from their analysis is what a difference where you come from makes for your chances of being identified and nurtured as a math whiz. Between 1998 and 2008 *no* girls competed for Japan. But next door, seven girls competed for South Korea (which, by the way, ranks higher than Japan). A profoundly gifted young female mathematician in Slovakia has a five times greater chance of being included on the IMO team than her counterpart in the neighboring Czech Republic. (Again, Slovakia outperforms the Czech Republic. I say this not to be competitive, but merely to show that teams with more girls have not been scraping the bottom of the barrel.) The ratio of female members on IMO teams among the top 34 participating countries ranges from none at all, to 1 in 4 (in Serbia and Montenegro). This is not random fluctuation, but evidence of "socio-cultural, educational, or other environmental factors" at work.[21]

In fact, we can see this very clearly even within North America. Being underrepresented on the IMO team, or the Mathematical Olympiad Summer Program (MOSP), is not, as you might assume, a *girl* problem. It's more subtle and interesting than that.

First of all, if you're Hispanic, African American, or Native American, it matters not whether you have two X-chromosomes or one—you might as well give up now on any dreams of sweating for nine hours over some proofs. Then within girls, interesting patterns emerge. Asian American girls are *not* underrepresented, relative to their numbers in the population. But that doesn't mean that it's even simply a *white girl* problem. Non-Hispanic white girls born in North America are sorely underrepresented: there are about twenty times fewer of them on IMO teams than you'd expect based on their numbers in the population, and they virtually never attend the highly selective MOSP. But this isn't the case for non-Hispanic white girls who were born in Europe, immigrants from countries like Romania, Russia, and the Ukraine, who manage on the whole to keep their end up when it comes to participating in these prestigious competitions and programs. The success of this group of women continues into their careers. These women are a *hundred times more likely* to make it into the math faculty of Harvard, MIT, Princeton, Stanford, or University of California–Berkeley than their native-born white counterparts. They do every bit as well as white males, relative to their numbers in the population. As the researchers conclude:

> Taken together, these data indicate that the scarcity of USA and Canadian girl IMO participants is probably due, in significant part, to socio-cultural and other environmental factors, not race or gender *per se*. These factors likely inhibit native-born white and historically underrepresented minority girls with exceptional mathematical talent from being identified and nurtured to excel in mathematics. Assuming environmental factors inhibit most mathematically gifted girls being raised in most cultures in most countries at most times from pursuing mathematics to the best of their ability, we estimate the *lower* bound on the percentage of children with IMO medal-level mathematical talent who are girls to be in the 12%–24% range [i.e., the levels seen in countries like Serbia and Montenegro]. . . . In a gender-neutral society, the real percentage could be significantly higher; however, we currently lack ways to measure it.[22]

That's a lot of squandered talent, and among boys, too. As the researchers acknowledge, the data they collected can't answer the question of whether females—in a perfectly gender-equal environment—could match (or, why not be bold, perhaps even surpass) males in math. But the gender gap is narrowing all the time, and shows that mathematical eminence is not fixed, or hardwired or intrinsic, but is instead responsive to cultural factors that affect the extent to which mathematical talent is identified and nurtured, or passed over, stifled, or suppressed in males and females.

And so this is all good news for Lawrence Summers, who said that he "would far prefer to believe something else" than the "unfortunate truth" that, in part, "differing variances" lie behind women's underrepresentation in science.[23] And for Pinker, too, who warned Summers' detractors that "[h]istory tells us that how much we want to believe a proposition is not a reliable guide as to whether it is true."[24] Evidence for the malleability of the gender gap in ability and achievement is there. And this is important because, as we learned in the first part of the book, it makes a difference what we believe about difference. Stanford University's psychologist Carol Dweck and her colleagues have discovered that what you believe about intellectual ability—whether you think it's a fixed gift, or an earned quality that can be developed—makes a difference to your behavior, persistence, and performance. Students who see ability as fixed—a gift—are more vulnerable to setbacks and difficulties. And stereotypes, as Dweck rightly points out, "are stories about gifts—about who has them and who doesn't."[25] Dweck and her colleagues have shown that when students are encouraged to see math ability as something that grows with effort—pointing out, for example, that the brain forges new connections and develops better ability every time they practice a task—grades improve and gender gaps diminish (relative to groups given control intervention).[26] The Greater Male Variability hypothesis, of course, endorses the view that very great intellectual ability is indeed a fixed trait, a gift bestowed almost exclusively on men. Add a little talk of women's insufficient white matter volumes,

or their plump corpora callosa, and the ingredients for a self-fulfilling prophecy are all in place.

The sensitivity of the mind to neuroscientific claims about difference raises ethical concerns.[27] A recent study by University of Exeter psychologist Thomas Morton and his colleagues asked one group of participants to read the kind of passage that is the bread-and-butter of a certain type of popular gender science book. It presented essentialist theories—that gender differences in thinking and behavior are biological, stable, and immutable— as scientifically established facts. A second group read a similar article, but one in which the claims were presented as being under debate in the scientific community. The "fact" article led people to more strongly endorse biological theories of gender difference, to be more confident that society treats women fairly, and to feel less certain that the gender status quo is likely to change. It also left men rather more cavalier about discriminatory practices: compared with men who read the "debate" article, they agreed more with statements like, "If I would work in a company where my manager preferred hiring men to women, I would privately support him," and "If I were a manager in a company myself, I would believe that more often than not, promoting men is a better investment in the future of the company than promoting women." They also felt better about themselves—a small consolation indeed to women, I think you'll agree.

Interestingly, for men who tend to the view that sex discrimination is a thing of the past, the appeal of essentialist research is enhanced by evidence that the gender gap is closing, Morton and his colleagues also found. Participants were asked to rate research that investigated the genetic basis of sex differences in mouse brains, as well as claiming that similar factors may underlie psychological gender differences in humans. Beforehand they read an article, supposedly from a national newspaper, arguing either that gender inequality was stable, or closing. After reading about women's gains these men more readily agreed that "this type of research should continue, deserved more funding, was good for society, represented the facts about gender differences, and made a major contribution to understanding human nature."[28]

Taken together, Morton's findings suggest that women's gains will, in certain quarters, increase demand for essentialist research. As this research trickles back into society, people will turn away from social and structural explanations of gender difference. They will give up on the idea of further social change. And, to help the belief in the inevitability of inequality come true, workplace discrimination against women will increase.

It is, I think, time to raise the bar when it comes to the interpretation and communication of sex differences in the brain. How long, exactly, do we need to learn from the mistakes of the past?

As we've seen, speculating about sex differences from the frontiers of science is not a job for the faint-hearted who hate to get it wrong. So far, the items on that list of brain differences that are thought to explain the gender status quo have always, in the end, been crossed off.[29] But before this happens, speculation becomes elevated to the status of fact, especially in the hands of some popular writers. Once in the public domain these supposed facts about male and female brains become part of the culture, often lingering on well past their best-by dates. Here, they reinforce and legitimate the gender stereotypes that interact with our minds, helping to create the very gender inequalities that the neuroscientific claims seek to explain.[30]

NOTES

1. For details, and contrast with maturational viewpoint, see (Westermann et al., 2007), in particular figure 4, p. 80. Also (Lickliter & Honeycutt, 2003; Mareschal et al., 2007).
2. (Wexler, 2006), pp. 3 and 4.
3. (Bleier, 1984), p. 52, footnote removed.
4. (Grossi, 2008).
5. (Shields, 1982), pp. 778 and 779. See also (Shields, 1975).
6. As Steven Pinker put it (Edge, 2005b).
7. For a history of the Greater Male Variability hypothesis see (Shields, 1982).
8. E. L. Thorndike, *Educational Psychology* (1910), p. 35. Quoted in (Hollingworth, 1914), p. 510.
9. (Summers, 2005), para. 4.
10. Quoted in (Edge, 2005b).
11. (Pinker, 2008), p. 13.
12. (Hollingworth, 1914). Wendy Johnson, Andrew Carothers, and Ian Deary published a reanalysis of these data in 2008. They concluded that males were *especially* variable at lower levels of IQ. They also noted that, with a ratio of about 2 boys to 1 girl at the very highest levels of intelligence, this did not go very far in explaining the much steeper ratios for high-level academic physical science, math, and engineering positions (Johnson, Carothers, & Deary, 2008), p. 520.
13. (Grossi, 2008), p. 98.
14. (Feingold, 1994).
15. (Hyde et al., 2008).
16. (Guiso et al., 2008).
17. (Penner, 2008; Machin & Pekkarinen, 2008). These latter authors stress the strong pattern of greater male variability, but the boy/girl ratio (shown in parentheses) at the top 5 percent of math ability was more-or-less equal in Indonesia (0.91), Thailand (0.92), Iceland (1.04), and the UK (1.08). Penner found greater female variability in the Netherlands, Germany, and Lithuania. For useful discussion of these data, see (Hyde & Mertz, 2009).
18. (Andreescu et al., 2008), p. 1248.
19. See (Andreescu et al., 2008), p. 1248.
20. (Andreescu et al., 2008), p. 1251.
21. (Andreescu et al., 2008), p. 1252.
22. (Andreescu et al., 2008), pp. 1253 and 1254. See table 7, p. 1253.
23. (Summers, 2005), para. 4.
24. (Pinker, 2005), para. 3.
25. (Dweck, 2007), p. 49.
26. See (Blackwell, Trzesniewski, & Dweck, 2007; Dweck, 2007; Good, Aronson, & Inzlicht, 2003).
27. This has been surprisingly little discussed in the academic literature, but see (Chalfin, Murphy, & Karkazis, 2008; Fine, 2008).
28. (Morton et al., 2009), pp. 661 and 656 (reference removed), respectively.
29. This is thanks, in no small part, to books aimed at a general audience that have critiqued popular myths of gender. Recent examples of such efforts include (Barnett & Rivers, 2004; Cameron, 2007; Fausto-Sterling, 1985, 2000; Rogers, 1999; Tavris, 1992).
30. This is a point made in a general way by the instigators of the Critical Neuroscience project, which "holds that while neuroscience potentially discloses facts about behaviour and its instantiation in the brain, the cultural context of science interacts with these knowledge claims, adds new meaning to them and influences the experience of the people to whom they pertain" (Choudhury, Nagel, & Slaby, 2009), p. 66, references removed.

Trans Identities and Contingent Masculinities: Being Tombois in Everyday Practice

Evelyn Blackwood (2009)

Tombois in West Sumatra, Indonesia, are female-bodied individuals who lay claim to the social category "man," by which I mean the ideologically dominant conception of manhood that circulates through much of Indonesia. In speaking of themselves as men, tombois state that they not only dress and act like men but that they physically embody masculinity as well. One tomboi told me, "You can tell by the way they walk, like a guy, and the way they talk, which is coarser and more firm [than women's speech]." Yet, their self-positioning as men is not uncomplicated. Despite articulating a sense of self that they consider to be nearly the same as other men's, tombois take up different subject positions in different spaces, engaging with and reproducing a version of femininity when they move within family and community spaces.

Tombois, whose gender expression exceeds or transgresses normative gender categories, may be included in the category of transgender people, if "transgender" is defined broadly, following Susan Stryker, as "an umbrella term that refers to all identities or practices that cross over, cut across, move between, or otherwise queer socially constructed sex/gender binaries."[1] However, the word "transgender" is not a term that tombois I interviewed use for themselves; it began to circulate as an adopted term in *lesbi* and *gay* (the Indonesian terms) activist communities in Indonesia only since the late 1990s.

This article focuses on a group of tombois in Padang, West Sumatra. The city of Padang, with a population of over 700,000 in 2000, is neither a global metropolis nor a nonmetropolitan area, which makes it an intriguing site to study global sexualities.[2] Although I focus on tombois in a particular locale in Indonesia, I am not making any claims that they are representative of all tombois in West Sumatra or Indonesia.

Several excellent studies in Southeast and East Asia document the nuances and complexities of masculinities among such female-bodied individuals, who identify variously as hunters, toms, tombois, TBs, and butches. The English-derived terms speak to the influence of global LGBT signifiers, but these masculine subjectivities are far from identical. Sharon Graham Davies classifies hunters, or calalai, in South Sulawesi, Indonesia, as a distinct gender because they are female-bodied, but they do not identify as women nor do they aspire to be men. Megan Sinnott argues that toms in Thailand are transgendered females who strategically appropriate and manipulate cultural stereotypes of Thai masculinity and emergent sexualities to create a hybrid form of masculinity. Older butches whom Saskia E. Wieringa studied in Jakarta, Indonesia, refer to themselves as men and see themselves as possessing a male soul in a female body.[3] The versions of masculinity represented in these studies point to the complexities of each situation; they highlight the asymmetrical reception of global and national discourses that produces not homogeneous national or international queer identities but a plethora of dynamic subjectivities that exceed any simple categorization.

TOMBOIS PRAXIS AND SELF-UNDERSTANDING

In research for this project in Indonesia, . . . I met twenty-eight individuals, who were either tombois or girlfriends of tombois, and formally interviewed sixteen (eight tombois and eight girlfriends). These girlfriends, whom I also refer to as "femmes," identify as normatively gendered women who are attracted to men. These individuals came from a range of socioeconomic backgrounds, from quite poor to well-to-do, although most were of average means. Their education levels ranged from middle school to high school; most, but not all, were Muslim. Their ages spanned the late teens to early thirties; the average age in 2004 was closer to thirty. Using friendship networks to make contacts meant that most of the individuals I eventually met were of the same age cohort. Further, most of the tombois I interviewed belonged to two groups of friends. Members of each group spent time together and had been friends, in some cases, from when they were in middle and high school. They had developed and negotiated their identities together and relied on each other for knowledge about being tombois. One tomboi in particular provided several of the key stories in this article, but h/er[4] experiences and self-positioning were echoed in the interviews I conducted with other tombois.

First I examine tombois' practices of masculinity in the context of family and community spaces; then I move to the contexts in which tombois perform some version of femininity. Tombois generally had close relationships with their natal families. Most of them lived in the same residences with their parents or kin and maintained close ties with married and unmarried siblings. I use the word "kin" to indicate that Padang families extend beyond and encompass more than parents and children, usually comprising three generations linked by emotional, economic, and lineal ties. Several of the tombois worked with close kin in family businesses; most relied on their families for access to jobs or financial support to start businesses or purchase things such as motorcycles.

Despite the fact that kin thought of tombois as female based on their knowledge of tombois' physical bodies during the period when they were growing up, they did not force tombois to appear in feminine attire within familial spaces. The tombois whom I visited at their homes did not change their appearance around family but wore the same clothes they always wore: pants, T-shirts, belts, and shoes, common attire for young men. The first time I was invited to eat at Dedi's house, however, I was not sure what to expect. Dedi, which is not h/er real name, met me at h/er family's business and then took me to h/er mother's house, which was off the main road in a small group of houses nestled next to rice fields. Dedi was dressed in h/er typical men's attire and appeared to be quite comfortable around h/er family. H/er mother and older sister had prepared the meal for us without Dedi's assistance. S/he and h/er close friend, Tommi, carried the food to the half-finished house next door where we ate. On this occasion as well as other times when I visited Dedi at home or at the family business, I saw no change in Dedi's appearance, although her behavior was more tempered in front of h/er elders.

The tombois I interviewed explained that they have the same privileges as their brothers in terms of mobility and autonomy. In fact, their movement in public (men's) spaces helped to confirm their masculinity. Dedi said, "My family doesn't restrict me. I'm free to hang out with whomever I want. At home I'm the only one who has this much freedom." In this statement s/he contrasts h/erself with h/er unmarried sister and sickly brother. Tommi, who also lived at h/er family home, told me, "Since I was little I hung out with guys so my family understands that I'm more like a guy. After high school I was given my freedom because I promised to protect myself. . . . I can go out at night, like guys do. And I can also sleep wherever I want to, like guys." Dedi said that h/er habit of sleeping "here and there," meaning at different friends' houses, is one reason h/er family recognizes h/er as a tomboi. Sal, who is in h/er early twenties and has a room at h/er maternal aunt's house, commented, "I like my freedom and don't want to be tied down." S/he is often away from h/er aunt's house visiting other tombois or at the local coffee shop (warung). Tombois' abilities to move freely in space and to sleep wherever they want, which are encoded as men's privileges, signify their masculinity and their families' acknowledgment of that masculinity.

Tombois' narratives underscore the attributes that are associated with men. When asked to talk about themselves, tombois laid claim to men's feelings, characteristics (sifat), spirit/soul (jiwa), actions (tingkah laku), and appearance (penampilan). They described masculine behaviors that are typical for young men, including heavy drinking, smoking, and staying out late without supervision. Robi, one of the tombois, said, "There is no difference between me and other men"; Tommi said that s/he does not see anything womanly in h/erself. Tombois feel that they possess the characteristics associated with men and convey these characteristics through what they do. They talked about being in men's spaces at night without fear of physical or sexual violence. One of the girlfriends' comments about tombois' behavior makes this point clearly: "But those [tombois], they're not afraid, they're very tough (jantan sekali). They look (tampilannya) just like guys. People don't know if they're guys or not, and they act so tough, other guys are afraid of them. So they're not afraid to go out at night at all." For tombois, their ability to handle themselves in public spaces is proof of their status as men.

Through their day-to-day activities, tombois perform masculinity within and across household, community, and public spaces. I use performance in Judith Butler's sense of practices expressed in bodily gestures, movements, and styles, through which gendered meanings are constructed.[5] Tombois' performance does more than put into effect what it names (masculinity); it attaches masculinity to what tombois consider to be, and what is culturally read as, a female body. Johnson's quare theory suggests that performance not only enunciates a self for others to interpret, give meaning to, or impose meaning on, it also has "the potential to transform one's view of self in relation to the world." By performing masculinity, tombois enunciate a self that comes to be recognized by themselves and their families. It is not through discursive claims that tombois are recognized as such, because tombois do not speak about their gendered selves to family; their performance of proper masculinity creates a space for them within the family context. As Tommi told me, "My family trusts me not to get in trouble. If I'm out at night, they know I can protect myself and would not embarrass them." Although the movements of unmarried women are closely monitored by their families as a way to protect their reputation, tombois' abilities to navigate public and masculine spaces (*dunia laki-laki*) without problems helps to

confirm for their families that their performance of masculinity is fitting and permissible.

HETEROSEXUAL MARRIAGE EXPECTATIONS

Despite the legitimacy tombois have within family spaces, they face certain obstacles in enacting their masculinity. Although they see themselves, as they say in their own words, "the same as men," at the same time cultural understandings of female bodies situate them somewhat precariously within the social category "man," because the dominant gender ideology in Indonesia equates sex with gender.

Tombois' kin may respond to and treat them as men in many ways but they retain knowledge of tombois' female bodies by virtue of having raised them or having grown up with them.

Tombois' everyday performance of masculinity does not erase for their kin the gendered expectations assigned to female bodies, in particular the duty to marry a man and bear children. . . . Becoming a wife (or husband) is necessary to fulfill familial duties and obligations as well as to gain the full respect of society and national belonging.

Consequently, families seek to provide marriage partners for their tomboi daughters in the only way that they understand: by finding husbands for them. According to Boellstorff, many Indonesian lesbians and gays have no opposition to marriage, finding it "a source of meaning and pleasure allowing them to enjoy homosexual relationships while pleasing their parents . . ."[6] For tombois, however, marriage is the most troubling challenge to their positionality as men. Marriage places them irrevocably in the social category "woman" and forces them to constantly perform a feminine gender as a consequence of having husbands and in-laws. The prospect of tombois marrying evoked the strongest reactions from Dayan, one of the tombois, who asserted that it was just wrong for a tomboi to marry a man. . . . Efforts by families in Padang to marry off their tomboi daughters were met with varying degrees of resistance. Tombois I interviewed understood that their families would be ashamed (*mah*) if they did not marry, yet most tombois that I knew told me stories about finding ways to put off marriage indefinitely.

A "WOMAN" AT HOME

Although expectations of marriage create the greatest problems for tombois and are consciously resisted, it is not the only instance in family space in which expectations associated with femininity and female bodies recall their culturally designated sex/gender. In the context of everyday life with their families, tombois I interviewed accommodated kin expectations by engaging with and reproducing femininity to a certain extent despite presenting themselves as men. In these instances, tombois do not insist on a proper performance of masculinity.

Dedi was talking about h/er family one day and commented that at h/er mother's house, s/he is "a woman at home" (wanita di rumah). Struck by that comment, which I thought was so out of character for a tomboi, I asked h/er to explain what s/he meant. Dedi said it means "doing feminine duties around the house, like washing dishes, sweeping, keeping my room clean." At the same time that Dedi is careful to perform some feminine tasks, s/he is not just like other women at home, because there are limits to what s/he feels comfortable doing. When I asked h/er if h/er feminine duties included cooking or washing clothes, she said, "No. I won't do that." In West Sumatra, the mantra of womanhood, as told repeatedly to me, is "a woman cooks, sews, and takes care of her husband and family." In light of this expectation, Dedi's lack of knowledge about cooking would not be interpreted simply as lack of interest or ability but as lack of femininity. Dedi proudly told me that s/he is asked to do repair work and painting around the house, which are considered men's jobs.

The care taken at home to perform some feminine practices and to hide those practices that are not considered appropriate for women is meant to show respect for and preserve relationships with families. In recounting these stories Dedi never suggested that s/he felt burdened or angered by the need to conceal h/er masculine behaviors. By being "a woman at home," Dedi said, s/he was able to maintain a good relationship with h/er mother. Dedi's story is indicative of the feelings expressed by other tombois I interviewed. Tombois asserted the importance of upholding kin expectations to a certain degree

because loyalty and duty to family and kin carry a great deal of weight. In Indonesia, kin ties provide individuals with a social identity and sense of belonging that they rely on throughout their lives. In addition, kin are a source of emotional and financial support, paving the way for future opportunities by paying for education, extending loans, and helping find jobs. To act in a way that would create a rift between oneself and one's family is neither advisable nor acceptable. Thus, couched within the context of maintaining good relations at home, Dedi acts in ways that are congruent with h/er concerns about family and kin.

By acting with restraint and politeness within the house, Dedi demonstrates respect for h/er mother, as would be expected of a daughter. Dedi's feelings of respect and loyalty are expressed materially by washing dishes, keeping h/er room clean, and sweeping floors, duties that sons typically would not perform. At the same time, h/er refusal to perform certain tasks, such as cooking, which would position h/er uncomfortably as a woman, suggests that a feminine performance can only be taken so far, beyond which it begins to seriously challenge h/er masculine subject position. H/er relationship with h/er family is managed by maintaining some aspects of femininity, while refusing others. Like Dedi, tombois perform a version of femininity within household space, taking on some tasks that are considered feminine and avoiding certain markers of masculine behavior, such as smoking. In other words, tombois' actions at home speak to the contingency of their subject positions.

VERSIONS OF FEMININITY IN COMMUNITY SPACE

Tombois' performance of femininity extends to their immediate surroundings, which I have called community space. This space is interspersed with kin and long-time acquaintances who knew tombois when they were growing up and attending school in girls' uniforms. As in household spaces, tombois present a complex positionality in community spaces that both calls on their masculinity and recalls their female bodies.

Dedi is friends with many of the men who come to the family business where s/he and other family members work. S/he talks to them easily and at length, unlike h/er unmarried sister, who is polite and courteous to male customers but spends little time in conversation with them. When asked why s/he has more freedom than women, Dedi said, "If a woman hangs out with guys, people will say she is bad, but for tombois, they understand. They say it's natural—of course a tomboi has men friends. Nobody is bothered by that." According to Dedi, even the wives of married men are unconcerned about their husbands spending time with tombois, the implication being that because s/he is a tomboi, wives do not perceive h/er as a potential threat to their marriage in the way that they would if s/he were a woman. Dedi said that many of the men confide (curhat) in h/er. "They even ask me about their problems with girlfriends—what do I think about this or that girl. Because, you know, I'm a female too, so of course I would know more about women." During this conversation, Dedi asserts the naturalness of h/er interactions with other men, which is corroborated by others around h/er. Yet Dedi suggests at the same time that s/he has a better understanding of women than men do, which s/he attributes to h/er female body and h/er consequent knowledge of what girls are like. Here Dedi recalls h/er female body as part of h/erself, giving voice to a cultural expectation that female bodies produce female ways of knowing. Having a female body then is not seen as a contradiction of her masculinity but as part of h/er self, h/er experiences, and h/er understanding of the world.

Despite their masculine appearance and behavior, tombois are constantly reminded of their female bodies as they interact with others in community spaces. Terms of address used in conversation in Indonesia are based on the age, sex, and status of both speakers, effectively slotting people into gendered categories. People tend to employ gender-marked kin terms when addressing acquaintances or close friends, bringing an idiom of sibling relationships and seniority into their interactions.[7] Robi mentioned to me that s/he is called aunt by h/er younger kin. Dedi is called Aunt Di (*tante* Di) by younger kin and "older sister" (*uni*) by customers at h/er family

business. Tommi is called "Uni" at work. Because some family members use h/er nickname, Tomboi, or call h/er "older brother" (*uda*), I asked h/er why s/he was addressed like that at work. S/he said simply, "Because it's the workplace." By calling her Uni, the employee marked Tommi as a woman, which s/he did not contest, despite the fact that as a manager, Tommi might have been addressed by other terms. These gendered terms of address mark tombois as women and tip off casual bystanders who hear them being addressed that way.

Within community space, where interactions with kin and close acquaintances are frequent, tombois are likely to be called on as kinswomen, marking not only their gender but also their sex, according to Indonesian understandings of sex/gender as a unitary construct. Because of the presence of kin and acquaintances in this space, tombois are unwilling to demand male terms of address; in fact, they do not find it important to do so. Robi shrugged off the apparent inconsistency by saying, "It doesn't matter. At home we have to follow the rules." For Tommi, being called Uni is expected and unproblematic at work. Similarly, one of the calalai Davies interviewed said "it is not really important" whether s/he is called Miss or Mister.[8] In everyday practice, terms of address invoke ties of kinship based on the cultural nexus between sex and gender, thus reminding tombois of their female bodies. Those terms are considered unproblematic, because they reflect and substantiate one's kinship and solidarity with family and community, a position that produces a sense of well-being through relationality. The reminder of their female bodies is also a reminder of the security kinship offers.

TOMBOIS, TRANS IDENTITIES, AND CONTINGENT MASCULINITIES

The awareness of tombois' female bodies that is shared by their kin and community carries with it certain consequences for tombois. Within household and community spaces, tombois' female bodies are called upon by family members and recalled by tombois. Despite positioning themselves as men, tombois manifest particular practices congruent with those spaces and accede to certain interpretations and cultural expectations that are attached to female bodies. The femininity a tomboi invokes at home and in community spaces suggests that tomboi masculinity is a contingent masculinity that takes into account the culturally dictated positioning attached to female bodies and the material effects of that positioning.

Tombois I interviewed demonstrated their masculinity through everyday practices, as well as in their dress, appearance, posture, and language; but in certain contexts they performed a version of femininity when expectations of filial duty and proper womanhood were unavoidable. Not only did tombois consciously hide certain masculine behaviors, such as smoking, to avoid bringing shame to their families, but they also permitted themselves to be read as women within household and community spaces. Actions within family and community spaces pointed to the context specificity of tomboi praxis. Although tombois saw themselves "the same as men," thereby defining themselves in accordance with dominant gender norms, family and community spaces required other practices that expressed femininity as well as masculinity. Social relations of kinship and family connected tombois with discourses of femininity. Because subjects are embedded in multiple social relations, these relations provided the meaning and offered the efficacy that tombois attained as intelligibly gendered beings.

By identifying tombois' masculinity as contingent masculinity, I am not suggesting that it is a partial masculinity or an intermediate gender identity. Tombois' masculinity is one of many versions of masculinity in Southeast Asia that transgresses normative categories of "woman" and "man," in this case through an explicit referral to and performance of feminine and masculine behaviors. Tombois also strategically manipulated cultural gender codes of femininity to create space for themselves and their partners. Tombois spoke of having female bodies and doing feminine things while at the same time they declared that they were the "same as" or "just like" men. By situating tombois' masculinity as contingent, I offer a concept of trans identities that takes into account the social relations and cultural frameworks within which people live and make sense of their self-understandings.

NOTES

1. Susan Stryker, "My Words to Victor Frankenstein above the Village of Chamounix: Performing Transgender Rage," GLQ: Journal of Lesbian and Gay Studies 1, no. 3 (1994): 251 n 2; see also definitions offered by Kate Bornstein in Gender Outlaw: On Men, Women, and the Rest of Us (New York: Vintage Books, 1994); and Riki Anne Wilchins, Read My Lips: Sexual Subversion and the End of Gender (Ithaca, N.Y.: Firebrand Books, 1997).

2. Sumatera Barat dalam Angka (West Sumatra in Figures) (Padang: Badan Pusat Statistik Propinsi Sum-Bar, 2000).

3. Sharon Graham Davies, Challenging Gender Norms: Five Genders among the Bugis in Indonesia (Belmont, Calif.: Thomson Wadsworth, 2007), and "Hunting Down Love: Female Masculinities in Bugis South Sulawesi," in Women's Sexualities and Masculinities in a Globalizing Asia, 139-57; Megan Sinnott, Toms and Dees: Transgender Identity and Female Same Sex Relationships in Thailand (Honolulu: University of Hawaii Press, 2004), and "Gender Subjectivity.? Dees and Toms in Thailand," in Women's Sexualities and Masculinities in a Globalizing Asia, 119-38; Saskia E. Wieringa, "Desiring Bodies or Defiant Cultures: Butch-Femme Lesbians in Jakarta and Lima," in Female Desires: Same-Sex Relations and Transgender Practices across Cultures, ed. Evelyn Blackwood and Saskia E. Wieringa (New York: Columbia University Press, 1999), 206-31, and "If There Is No Feeling . . . ': The Dilemma between Silence and Coming Out in a Working-Class Butch/Femme Community in Jakarta," in Love and Globalization: Transformations of Intimacy in the Contemporary World, ed. Mark Padilla et al. (Nashville: Vanderbilt University Press, 2007), 70-90. See also Thomas Boellstorff, The Gay Archipelago: Sexuality and Nation in Indonesia (Princeton, N.J.: Princeton University Press, 2005); Mark Johnson, "Living Like Men, Loving Like Women: Tomboi in the Southern Philippines," in Changing Sex and Bending Gender, ed. Alison Shaw and Shirley Ardener (Oxford, U.K.: Bergahn Books, 2005), 85-102; and Ara Wilson, The Intimate Economies ofBanghk: Tomboys, Tycoons, and Avon Ladies in the Global City (Berkeley: University of California Press, 2004).

4. When referring to tombois, I use the pronominal constructions "s/he" and "h/er" as a way to disrupt the binary genders of the English language. No English pronouns adequately convey the Indonesian usage, in which the third person pronoun is gender neutral.

Other scholars have chosen to use the English pronoun that seems to most closely resemble the person's gender identity, but to my mind that has the potential to reinsert transgressively gendered individuals into fixed genders.

5. Judith Butler, Gender Trouble: Feminism and the Subversion of Identity (New York: Routledge, 1990).

6. 23. Boellstorff, Gay Archipelago, 111.

7. J. Joseph Errington, Shifting Languages: Interaction and Identity in Javanese Indonesian (Cambridge, U.K.: Cambridge University Press, 1998).

8. Davies, Challenging Gender Norms, 59.

R E A D I N G 24

What's Up with Boys?

Michael Kimmel and Christina Hoff Sommers (2013)

When it comes to education, are boys the new girls? Are they facing more discrimination than their female peers, just because they are sexually different? According to recent studies, boys score as well as or better than girls on most standardized tests, yet they are far less likely to get good grades, take advanced classes or attend college. We asked Michael Kimmel and Christina Hoff Sommers to hash this one through in HuffPost's latest "Let's Talk" feature.

Michael: Christina, I was really impressed with your recent *op-ed* in the *Times*.

The first edition of your book, *The War Against Boys: How Misguided Policies Are Harming Our Young Men,* came out in 2000. Maybe I've optimistically misread, but it seemed to me that the change in your subtitle from "misguided feminism" (2000) to "misguided policies" indicates a real shift in your thinking? Does it? What's changed for boys in the ensuing decade? Have things gotten worse? Why revise it now? And what's changed for feminism that it's no longer their fault that boys are continuing to fall behind?

Christina: Thank you Michael. I am delighted you liked the op-ed. Boys need allies these days, especially in the academy. Yes, I regret the subtitle of the first edition was "How Misguided Feminism is Harming Our Young Men." My emphasis was on *misguided*—I did not intend to indict the historical feminist movement, which I have always seen as one of the great triumphs of our democracy.

But some readers took the book to be an attack on feminism itself, and my message was lost on them. Indeed, many dismissed the book as culture war propaganda. In the new edition (to be published this summer), I have changed the subtitle and sought to make a clear distinction between the humane and progressive feminist movement and a few hard-line women's lobbying groups who have sometimes thwarted efforts to help boys. I have also softened the tone: the problem of male underachievement is too serious to get lost in stale cultural debates of the 1990s.

Groups like the American Association of University Women and the National Women's Law Center continue to promote a girls-are-victims narrative and sometimes advocate policies harmful to boys. But it is now my view that boys have been harmed by many different social trends and there is plenty of blame to go round These trends include the decline of recess, punitive zero-tolerance policies, myths about armies of juvenile "super-predators" and a misguided campaign against single-sex schooling. As our schools become more feelings-centered, risk-averse, competition-free and sedentary, they have moved further and further from the characteristic sensibilities of boys.

What has changed since 2000? Back then almost no one was talking about the problem of male disengagement from school. Today the facts are well-known and we are already witnessing the alarming social and economic consequences. (Have a look at a recent report from the Harvard Graduate School of Education—"Pathways to Prosperity"—about the bleak economic future of inadequately educated young men.) The problem of school disengagement is most serious among boys of color and white boys from poor backgrounds—but even middle-class white boys have fallen behind their sisters. My new book focuses on solutions.

The recent advances of girls and young women in school, sports, and vocational opportunities are cause for deep satisfaction. But I am persuaded we can address the problems of boys without undermining the progress of women. This is not a zero-sum contest. Most women, including most feminist women, do not see the world as a Manichean struggle between Venus and Mars. We are all in this together. The current plight of boys and young men is, in fact, a women's issue. Those boys are our sons; they are the people with whom our daughters will build a future. If our boys are in trouble, so are we all.

Now I have a question for you, Michael. In the past, you seem to have sided with a group of gender scholars who think we should address the boy problem by raising boys to be more like girls. Maybe I am being overly optimistic, but does your praise for my *New York Times* op-ed indicate a shift in your own thinking?

Michael: Not at all. I'm not interested in raising boys to be more like girls any more than I want girls to be raised more like boys. The question itself assumes that there is a way to raise boys that is different from the way we raise girls. To me this is stereotypic thinking. I want to raise our children to be themselves, and I think that one of the more wonderful components of feminism was to critique that stereotype that all girls are supposed to act and dress in one way and one way only. Over the past several decades, girls have reduced the amount of gender policing they do to each other: for every "You are such a slut," a young woman is now equally likely to hear "You go girl!" (Note: I am not saying one has replaced the other; this is not some either/or, but a both/and.) The reforms initiated in the 1970s for girls—Title IX, STEM programs—have been an incontesible success. We agree there, I think—and also that we need to pay attention also to boys,

because many are falling behind (though not upper- and middle-class white boys as much, as you rightly point out.)

I think cultural definitions of masculinity are complex and often offer boys contradictory messages. Just as there are parts that may be unhealthy—never crying or showing your feelings, winning at all costs, etc.—there are also values associated with manhood such as integrity, honor, doing the right thing, speaking truth to power, that are not of "redeemable" but important virtues. I wouldn't want to get rid of them in some wholesale "Etch-a-Sketch" redefinition.

Our disagreement, I think, comes from what we see as the source of that falling behind. My interviews with over 400 young men, aged 6–26, in *Guyland*, showed me that young men and boys are constantly and relentlessly policed by other guys, and pressured to conform to a very narrow definition of masculinity by the constant spectre of being called a fag or gay. So if we're going to really intervene in schools to ensure that boys succeed, I believe that we have to empower boys' resilience in the face of this gender policing. What my interviews taught me is that many guys believe that academic disengagement is a sign of their masculinity. Therefore, re-engaging boys in school requires that we enable them to reconnect educational engagement with manhood.

My question to you: In your essay, you list a few reforms to benefit boys, that strike me as unproblematic, such as recess, and some that seem entirely regressive, like single-sex classes in public schools or single-sex public schools. Is your educational vision of the future—a return to schools with separate entrances for boys and girls—a return to the past?

Christina: I hereby declare myself opposed to separate entrances for boys and girls at school. And I agree that we should raise children to be themselves. But that will often mean respecting their gender. Increasingly, little boys are shamed and punished for the crime of being who they are. The typical, joyful play of young males is "rough and tumble" play. There is no known society where little boys fail to evince this behavior (girls do it too, but far less). In many schools, this characteristic play of little boys is no longer tolerated. Intrusive and intolerant adults are insisting "tug of war" be changed to "tug of peace"; games such as tag are being replaced with "circle of friends"—in which no one is ever out. Just recently, a seven-year-old Colorado boy named Alex Evans was suspended from school for throwing an imaginary hand grenade at "bad guys" so he could "save the world." Play is the basis of learning. And boys' superhero play is no exception. Researchers have found that by allowing "bad guy" play, children's conversation and imaginative writing skills improved. Mary Ellin Logue (University of Maine) and Hattie Harvey (University of Denver) ask an important question: "If boys, due to their choices of dramatic play themes, are discouraged from dramatic play, how will this affect their early language and literacy development and their engagement in school?"

You seem to think that single-sex education is "regressive." This tells me that you may not have been keeping up with new developments. Take a close look at what is going on at the Irma Rangel Young Women's Leadership School and the Barack Obama Male Leadership Academy in Dallas. There are hundreds of similar programs in public schools around the country and they are working wonders with boys and girls. Far from representing a "return to the past," these schools are cutting edge.

An important new study by three University of Pennsylvania researchers looked at single-sex education in Seoul, Korea. In Seoul, until 2009, students were randomly assigned to single-sex and coeducational schools; parents had little choice on which schools their children attended. After controlling for other variables such as teacher quality, student-teacher ratio, and the proportion of students receiving lunch support, the study found significant advantages in single-sex education. The students earned higher scores on their college entrance exams and were more likely to attend four-year colleges. The authors describe the positive effects as "substantial." With so many boys languishing in our schools, it would be reckless not to pay attention to the Dallas academies and the Korean school study. No one is suggesting these schools be the norm—but they may be an important part of the solution to male underachievement. For one thing, they seem

to meet a challenge you identify: connecting male educational engagement with manhood.

Finally, a word about Title IX, which you call an "incontestable success." Tell that to all the young men who have watched their swimming, diving, wrestling, baseball and gymnastic teams eliminated. Title IX was a visionary and progressive law; but over the years it has devolved into a quota regime. If a college's student body is 60 percent female, then 60 percent of the athletes should be female—even if far fewer women than men are interested in playing sports at that college. Many athletic directors have been unable to attract the same proportions of women as men. To avoid government harassment, loss of funding, and lawsuits, they have simply eliminated men's teams.

Michael, I think you focus too much on vague and ponderous abstractions such as "cultural definitions of masculinity." Why not address the very real, concrete and harsh prejudice boys now face every day in our nation's schools? You speak of "empowering boys to resist gender policing." In my view, the most aggressive policing is being carried out by adults who seem to have ruled conventional masculinity out of order.

Michael: Well, my earlier optimism seems somewhat misplaced; it's clear that you changed the subtitle, and want to argue that it's not a zero sum game—these give me hope. But then you characterize Title IX exactly as the zero sum game you say you no longer believe in. I think some of the reforms you suggest—increased recess, for example—are good for both boys and girls. Others, like reading more science fiction, seem to touch the surface, and then only very lightly. Some others, like single-sex schools strike me as, to use your favorite word, misguided. (There is little empirical evidence that the sex of a teacher has a demonstrable independent effect on educational outcomes.) It seems to me you mistake form for content.

I'd rather my son go to a really great co-ed school than a really crappy single-sex one. (It happens that single-sex schools, whether at the secondary or tertiary level, are very resource-rich, with more teacher training and lower student-teacher ratios. Those things actually do matter.) It's not the form, Christina, but the content.

And the content we need is to continue the reforms initiated by feminist women, reforms that suggested *for the first time* that one size doesn't fit all. They didn't change the "one size," and impose it on boys; they expanded the sizes. Those reforms would have us pay attention to differences *among* boys and differences among girls, which, it turns out, are far larger than any modest mean difference that you might find between males and females. You'd teach to the stereotype—that rambunctious roll-in-the-mud "boys will be boys" boy of which you are so fond—and not the mean, that is some center of the distribution. Teaching to the stereotype flattens the differences among boys, which will crush those boys who do not conform to that stereotype: the artistic ones, the musical ones, the soft-spoken ones, the ones who aren't into sports.

If you'd actually talked to boys in your research, instead of criticizing Bill Pollack or Carol Gilligan, I think you'd see this. The incredible research by Niobe Way, for example, in her book *Deep Secrets,* shows that prior to adolescence, boys are emotionally expressive and connected in ways that will surprise you. Something happens to those exuberant, expressive, emotional boys in middle school or so, and what happens to them is masculinity, the ideology of gender, which is relentlessly policed by other guys.

In my more than 400 interviews with boys this was made utterly clear to me. I've done workshops with literally thousands of boys, and asked them about the meaning of manhood and where they get those ideas they have. The answer is overwhelming: it is other guys who police them, with the ubiquitous "that's so gay" and other comments.

I've said this above, so I'll use my last word to reiterate. Boys learn that academic disengagement is a sign of their masculinity. If we want to re-engage boys in education, no amount of classroom tinkering and recess and science fiction reading is going to address that. We will need to enable boys to decouple the cultural definition of masculinity from academic disengagement. We need to acknowledge the vast differences among boys; their beauty lies in their diversity. We need to stop trying to force them into a stereotypic paradigm of rambunctiousness and let them be the individuals they are. And the really good research that talks to boys, all sorts of boys, suggests to me that they are waiting for us to do just that.

R E A D I N G   **25**

When I Was Growing Up

Nellie Wong (1981)

I know now that once I longed to be white.
How? you ask.
Let me tell you the ways.

> when I was growing up, people told me
> I was dark and I believed my own darkness
> in the mirror, in my soul, my own narrow vision

> > when I was growing up, my sisters
> > with fair skin got praised
> > for their beauty, and in the dark
> > I fell further, crushed between high walls

when I was growing up, I read magazines
and saw movies, blonde movie stars, white skin,
sensuous lips and to be elevated, to become
a woman, a desirable woman, I began to wear
imaginary pale skin

> when I was growing up, I was proud
> of my English, my grammar, my spelling
> fitting into the group of small children
> smart Chinese children, fitting in,
> belonging, getting in line

when I was growing up and went to high
school,
I discovered the rich white girls, a few
yellow girls,
their imported cotton dresses, their
cashmere sweaters,
their curly hair and I thought that I too
should have
what these lucky girls had

when I was growing up, I hungered
for American food, American styles,
coded: white and even to me, a child
born of Chinese parents, being Chinese
was feeling foreign, as limiting,
was unAmerican

when I was growing up and a white man
wanted
to take me out, I thought I was special,
an exotic gardenia, anxious to fit
the stereotype of an oriental chick

when I was growing up, I felt ashamed
of some yellow men, their small bones,
their frail bodies, their spitting
on the streets, their coughing,

their lying in sunless rooms,
shooting themselves in the arms

when I was growing up, people would ask
if I were Filipino, Polynesian, Portuguese.
They named all colors except white, the shell
of my soul, but not my dark, rough skin

when I was growing up, I felt
dirty. I thought that god
made white people clean
and no matter how much I bathed,
I could not change, I could not shed
my skin in the gray water

when I was growing up, I swore
I would run away to purple mountains,

houses by the sea with nothing over
my head, with space to breathe,
uncongested with yellow people in an area
called Chinatown, in an area I later learned
was a ghetto, one of many hearts
of Asian America

I know now that once I longed to be white.
How many more ways? you ask.
Haven't I told you enough?

R E A D I N G **26**

Through the Lens of Race: Black and White Women's Perceptions of Womanhood

Isis H. Settles, Jennifer S. Pratt-Hyatt, and NiCole T. Buchanan (2008)

Gender is socially constructed, and how women conceptualize their own gender is shaped by numerous factors, such as gender-role socialization, interpersonal interactions, media messages, and personal experiences as women (e.g., Abrams, 2003; Baker, 2005; Tenenbaum & Leaper, 2003; Witt, 1997). Some of these external forces and personal experiences may create similar perceptions of gender for women of different backgrounds. Yet, women's perceptions of their gender reflect significant within-group heterogeneity (e.g., Abrams, 2003; Boisnier, 2003; Rederstorff,

Buchanan, & Settles, 2007). One factor that may contribute to these differences is race. Specifically, socio-historical differences in Black and White women's options for work, family, and domestic labor, as well as experiences of discrimination and stereotyping, have created a set of race-related gender norms that are likely to influence how women from these groups perceive and value their own gender. Employing focus-group methodology to attain rich, detailed, qualitative data, we drew upon an intersectional theoretical framework to examine how race influences Black and White women's perceptions of womanhood.

CONCEPTUALIZATIONS OF GENDER AND RACE

Gender and race have sometimes been described as master statuses or superordinate groups that influence other group memberships and identities (Frable, Blackstone, & Scherbaum, 1990). As a result of the prominence and visibility of race and gender, individuals may be especially likely to think about themselves in terms of these groups (Cooley, 1922; Deaux, Reid, Mizrahi, & Ethier, 1995; Frable, 1997; Mead, 1925), and others are likely to categorize and stereotype them based on their membership in these groups (Fiske & Neuberg, 1990; Lott & Saxon, 2002). In addition to their importance singly, gender and race intersect to place individuals into unique positions based on the combination of these groups (e.g., Black women, White men, Latina women; Crenshaw, 1995; Hurtado, 1989; Settles, 2006). This joint social position is sometimes referred to as "ethgender" (Ransford & Miller, 1983) and is theorized to create experiences and perceptions that are distinct from those of individuals with other combinations of group memberships (Hurtado & Stewart, 1997).

Further, individuals' understanding and experience of one identity (e.g., gender) may be shaped by the context and experiences created by the other (e.g., race). For example, although both Black and White women may experience sexual harassment, Black women are more likely to experience sexual harassment that has a racial component (racialized sexual harassment; Buchanan, 2005; Buchanan & Ormerod, 2002). Another example of intersectionality is the finding that feminist attitudes buffered psychological outcomes for sexually harassed White women, but exacerbated psychological outcomes for sexually harassed Black women (Rederstorff et al., 2007). Thus, we regard gender and race as often internalized group memberships (i.e., identities) that intersect in many ways; one way is that women's racial group membership creates a unique lens that informs how their gender is viewed.

THE ROLE OF RACE IN WOMEN'S EXPERIENCE OF WOMANHOOD

For all women, gender is devalued and ascribed a low status (Katz, Joiner, & Kwon, 2002; Kessler, Mickelson, & Williams, 1999) and such experiences can impact one's own value and perception of womanhood (e.g., feminist consciousness, internalized sexism; Schmitt, Branscombe, Kobrynowicz, & Owen, 2002). As a result, women of different ethnic backgrounds may face similar forms of gender-based mistreatment, such as gender discrimination and sexism. For example, research has found that Black and White women report similar experiences of sexist treatment (Lott, Asquith, & Doyon, 2001) and pay inequity compared to men (U.S. Department of Labor, Bureau of Labor Statistics, 2006). Overt sexism, in which women are expected to adhere to traditional gender roles, persists, and subtle forms that tend to discount the existence of gender inequality may be increasing (Click & Fiske, 1997, 2001; Swim, Aikin, Hall, & Hunter, 1995). The ambiguity and subtlety of modern-day sexism may present additional challenges to women by creating uncertainty about whether they have been the target of mistreatment.

These and other types of gender-based mistreatment of women are prevalent. For example, a large national study found that 48% of women attributed their perceived daily discriminatory experiences to their gender (Kessler et al., 1999). Similarly, studies suggest that at least 50% of women will experience sexual harassment (i.e., unwanted sex-related behaviors and comments; Fitzgerald, 1996) during college and their working lives (Fitzgerald & Shullman, 1993; Huerta, Cortina, Pang, Torges, & Magley, 2006; Hies, Hauserman, Schwochau, & Stibal, 2003; Paludi & Paludi, 2003). Because gender-based experiences such as sexism, discrimination, sexual harassment, and rape are associated with numerous psychological well-being and job and/or academic outcomes (e.g., Buchanan & Fitzgerald, 2008; Fitzgerald, Drasgow, Hulin, Gelfand, & Magley, 1997; Gutner, Rizvi, Monson, & Resick, 2006; Settles, Cortina, Malley, & Stewart, 2006), they are likely to affect profoundly how women see themselves, regardless of whether they have been directly targeted.

Although Black and White women are both devalued on the basis of their gender, *double jeopardy theory* (Beal, 1970; King, 1988) suggests that Black women may face additional challenges because their race is also devalued. This double marginalization of Black women makes them targets of both sexism and racism (Hurtado, 1989; King, 1988; Perkins, 1983; Reid & Comas-Diaz, 1990; Smith & Stewart, 1983; St. Jean & Feagin, 1997) and creates a unique social space for Black women (or other groups with multiple devalued identities). Consistent with the idea of double marginalization, studies have found that, compared to White women, Black women experience higher rates of sexual harassment (e.g., Berdahl & Moore, 2006; Bergman & Drasgow, 2003; Buchanan, Settles, & Woods, 2008; Mecca & Rubin, 1999; Nelson & Probst, 2004), report more systematic discrimination and barriers to their career goals (Browne & Kennelly, 1999; Lopez & Ann-Yi, 2006), and experience greater disability and mortality due to health care disparities, even controlling for socioeconomic status (Andresen & Brownson, 2000; Green, Ndao-Brumblay, Nagrant, Baker, & Rothman, 2004).

Within the United States, socio-historical factors have created differences in the gender-role norms typically held for Black and White women. Many of these differences grew out of the *cult of true womanhood* (Perkins, 1983; Welter, 1966), a notion of womanhood that emerged for White (middle-class) women in the mid-1800s. This ideal emphasized modesty, purity, and domesticity for White women and identified wife and mother as their primary and most important roles. Historically, Black women were viewed in contrast to this norm for middle-class White women. Black women were not seen as "true" women, but rather as animalistic and hypersexed, which was then used to justify their enslavement and rape (Collins, 2000; West, 2004). There is evidence that these historical ideals persist in the stereotypes of Black and White women. For example, compared to Black women, White women are stereotyped as more nurturing, domestic, dependent, submissive, and emotional (Baker, 2005; Coltrane & Messineo, 2000; Kilbourne, 1999; Landrine, 1985). Thus, White women continue to be seen in terms of domestic ideals and as objects of men's sexual desire. In contrast, stereotypes of Black women (e.g., Jezebel, Mammy) tend to present Black women as hypersexual yet hypofeminine, which further reinforces the perception that White women are the norm (Bell, 2004; Collins, 2000; Fuller, 2004; West, 2004).

These historical differences in gender-role norms and ideals have led to the stratification of Black and White women in multiple domains. For example, historically, White middle-class women were expected to end their work or schooling after marriage so they could devote themselves to their domestic roles. Today, White women have significantly increased their presence in the labor force, but frequently work in sex-segregated occupations (Reskin, 1999; U.S. Department of Labor, Bureau of Labor Statistics, 2006) and are still primarily defined by their family and caretaking roles. In contrast, since slavery, Black women have been expected to work while taking care of their families (Davis, 2002; Pascale, 2001). Compared to White women, Black women with young children are more likely to be in the labor force (75% of Black women vs. 63% of White women with children under 6 years old; 71% of Black women vs. 59% of White women with children under 3 years old) and are more likely to be employed in jobs with less flexibility (U.S. Department of Labor, Bureau of Labor Statistics, 2006). Further, discrimination has limited the economic opportunities for many Black men, which may contribute to Black women's greater likelihood of being single parents (White & Cones, 1999). Thus, Black women commonly combine their work and family roles.

Further, Glenn (1992) described that, although paid and unpaid "reproductive labor"—maintenance of the household and relationships and care of children and other adults—is perceived as the responsibility of women, this role is also "racialized." Specifically, whereas Black women have been, and continue to be, relegated to the "dirtier" and least valued aspects of reproductive labor (e.g., cooking and cleaning), White women have traditionally held more skilled positions related to this work (e.g., supervisory, technical, and administrative support roles). As a result of these differences in work and family norms, Black and White women may come to view womanhood as having different requirements related to work and domestic roles.

THE CURRENT STUDY

The current study seeks to examine similarities and differences in the perceptions of womanhood for Black and White women. . . . Although there is extant research on differences in the experiences of Black and White women (e.g., sexism, sexual harassment, health outcomes), there is little or no empirical research that focuses simultaneously on Black and White women's thoughts and feelings about their experiences as women and how those perceptions shape their sense of self and the world. Further, past research has tended to ignore issues of race or to focus exclusively on racial differences; the current study seeks to identify both similarities and differences in Black and White women's conceptualization of womanhood. Thus, we used qualitative focus groups to encourage women to speak about their lived experiences rather than our imposing preconceived notions upon them (Madriz, 2000; Wilkinson, 1999). Additionally, we used an intersectional theoretical framework because, by considering how race and gender depend upon one another for meaning and uniquely position individuals within the social structure, we are able to gain a fuller picture of how racial contexts shape experiences of gender for Black and White women (Crenshaw, 1995; Settles, 2006; Stewart & McDermott, 2004).

. . .

Five primary themes emerged for both Black and White women: Gender-Based Mistreatment, Perceived Advantage, Friendships and Community, Caretaking, and Work and Family Options. An additional theme, Inner Strength, emerged only for Black women. . . .

GENDER-BASED MISTREATMENT

Black and White women described experiences of sexism, harassment, or gender-based discrimination. Such experiences were diverse and affected participants' lives in a variety of ways. White women, more than Black women, expressed having been discriminated against at school. Most often, they described not being offered the same number of options and level of encouragement they felt men received, especially in male-dominated areas of study. For example, a White 24-year-old law student said about her mathematics education:

> People really weren't pushing me and I really had the feeling it was because I was a woman. And I saw there was another guy who was in my grade, they let skip a couple of the classes and skip a couple of levels and go to the college . . . and take advanced classes and I was as smart as this kid and they never afforded me these opportunities.

Black and White women shared experiences of gender discrimination in the workplace. They discussed the "glass ceiling," the pay discrepancy between men and women, difficulty being hired or promoted, and a preference for men over women in positions of power and authority. . . .

Some women felt that even if they held the same position as male employees they were still treated differently. For example, a Black 23-year-old woman described her previous experience as a used car salesperson:

> I knew those cars good, but they didn't take me seriously until my numbers got serious. When I first put on my suit and went out on the floor it was a joke . . . but I didn't get their respect until later. Whereas, when guys start they're respected immediately.

Four White women articulated their belief that discrimination against them was due to employers' expectations about their likelihood of becoming mothers. A White 54-year-old woman said, "I was passed over for a promotion because they said, 'Well, you're just going to be quitting and having kids.'" . . .

Some White women also described sexual harassment in school and the workplace, sometimes with lasting effects on their career and educational choices. . . .

Both Black and White women described experiences of sexual harassment in the community, concerns about their safety, and fears of rape. Black and White women both described being approached or groped by strangers. . . . However, only White women described being harassed and groped by acquaintances or in social settings (e.g., bars, parties). . . .

Black and White women also noted various forms of sexism. A Black 20-year-old student shared an experience at work, when her ability was questioned because of her gender:

> This summer I was workin' at [a warehouse] . . . everything is in bulk, heavy boxes you have to train to lift. And there was this one particular guy that works there, and every time he walks by he makes it a point to just harass me . . . he always makes it a point, "Oh you can't lift that. I don't even know why they let women work in here, transporting this and lifting this. Little ladies can't handle this. Let me get this for you, little lady." Just because I don't have muscles rippling all down my body does not mean that I can't lift this. He got on my nerves, my last nerve 'cause every day, every day it was something.

Slightly more Black women than White women expressed frustration with experiences that might be termed "benevolent sexism" (Glick & Fiske, 1997, 2001), which they described as men acting as if women need to be protected. . . .

Both groups also described other more common forms of sexism and unequal treatment. These included feeling bullied by men who perceive women as weaker and more vulnerable than they are. Others talked about being cheated by service providers and the need to have a man around to prevent this mistreatment, placing men in the dual roles of protector and perpetrator and women in the role of being dependent on men to protect them from the abuses of other men. The sexist portrayal of women in the media—on magazine covers and on television—also emerged as a concern, especially for Black women. In its totality, the discussion of gender-based mistreatment was the most extensive theme that emerged and covered a wide range of experiences, contexts, and consequences for both Black and White women.

PERCEIVED ADVANTAGE

Despite their awareness of gender discrimination and harassment, many participants also felt that as women they had certain benefits and freedoms that made their lives easier than men's. Although Black and White women described similar types of advantages, more than twice as many White women than Black women discussed this topic, suggesting that White women may perceive more benefits of gender than do Black women. Some examples of relative advantage included female-only scholarships, accessibility to certain jobs (e.g., sales and restaurant jobs, jobs where "pretty girls" are desired), protection from male relatives and friends, and acts of male chivalry (e.g., men opening doors and buying drinks for women). Women's ability to express their emotions was also perceived as an advantage, but it was primarily raised by White women. . . .

A few Black and White women talked about being afforded more leniencies from men in power (e.g., supervisors, police officers) than their male counterparts. Further, two White women perceived that women were particularly advantaged now because they have greater equality with men, while retaining benefits traditionally given to women (e.g., chivalry from men). . . .

Thus, many of the women felt that, compared to men, some aspects of life were easier. Some of these advantages provided economic benefits (e.g., scholarships, free drinks, avoiding traffic fines) and others related to freedom of expression (e.g., being able to cry or make "smart ass" comments). Finally, two White women felt that women were especially fortunate in modern times due to a combination of "old-fashion" privileges and newer postfeminism benefits. However, whereas over three-quarters of White women identified sources of advantage, fewer than one-third of Black women did so.

FRIENDSHIPS AND COMMUNITY

A theme related to women's friendships and sense of community with other women emerged for both groups; however, whereas only half of Black women discussed issues related to this topic, every White woman commented on this theme. Of them, more than half of White women, but only one Black woman, noted that, compared to men, women value and nurture their same-sex friendships, leading to deeper relationships than those between men. This closeness was attributed, in part, to women's sense that some things (e.g., emotions, romantic relationship issues) can be shared only with other women. Similarly, nearly all of the White women, but only one Black woman, talked about the sense of emotional support and encouragement they receive from their female friends. . . .

Although many women (mostly White women) expressed the importance of their same-sex friendships and connections with other women, both Black and White women discussed some difficulties in their relationships with other women. . . .

Other women, even those who easily formed and valued their friendships, shared this participant's sense that female friendships can have a dark side. One negative aspect of female friendships mentioned by a few White women was related to the pressure to stand by and support friends, no matter the reason. . . .

These themes suggest that friendship is relevant to both groups, although White women discussed both positive and negative aspects much more than did Black women. Positive aspects of friendships with women included emotional support, encouragement, and a sense of understanding that relationships with men often do not provide. Impediments to the formation of such friendships included female "cattiness" and deviations from traditional female roles (e.g., being a tomboy). Women also discussed drawbacks of female friendships, such as having one's reputation damaged by friends and obligatory loyalty.

CARETAKING

Being a caretaker within the family was a theme that emerged for large numbers of both Black and White women. Although most participants talked about this theme in terms of being a mother, the roles of wife, grandmother, and foster parent were also discussed in much the same way. In the quotations below, we note statements by child-free women (those who are past childbearing age or those who say they will not/cannot have children) and women who have not yet had children but intend to do so, because these groups of women likely have different perceptions of motherhood.

To a large extent, women described caretaking as a positive, desirable aspect of their womanhood;

however, this positive conceptualization of caretaking was more common for White women than Black women. For some of the White women, being a caretaker (e.g., being a wife and/or mother) was a meaningful role that created psychological changes in their sense of self, by giving them a sense of purpose in life or creating a new identity (usually mother). Along with this new role of caring for others came personal growth and a shift in focus from the self to others. . . .

Some of the Black and White women who did not yet have children, but who intended to, spoke about that role being important in how they envisioned their future selves. A Black 19-year-old student stated that "I think part of my purpose, not the whole entire purpose, but a little part of it, is to have some kids or one kid [group laughs]."

Although many of the women described caretaking as including things they wanted and desired, participants also described some of the burdens of caretaking. Black women, more than White women, described the difficulties and challenges associated with this role. One such burden younger women reported was the pressure they felt from other women (especially older women) to be mothers and homemakers. As a Black 20-year-old woman without children put it:

> From my grandmother's point of view . . . every woman's purpose should be to have kids, be a mother, you know, take care of your husband and I believe that is not all I'm here for. I believe if I want to be an attorney, I'll be an attorney. If I want to be a doctor, I'll be a doctor. Whatever I aspire to be, that's what my purpose in life should be. . . . But, my grandmother is like, "This is the only reason you're here on this earth is to take care of a man and kids," and I do not believe that at all.

Other women who were wives and mothers (or wanted to be someday) noted that this role was accompanied by many other expectations that were less than desirable, such as cooking, cleaning, and organizing events with extended family. Although many women noted that more men now take on caregiving and housekeeping roles than in the past, some expressed frustration with the ways in which household labor is often divided between men and women. . . .

WORK AND FAMILY OPTIONS

The work and family options theme focused on women's decisions to work or stay at home (and not engage in paid labor) and emerged much more frequently for White women than Black women. Further, the nature of the discussion of work and family was different for Black and White women. For White women, the discussion was focused on the decision-making process related to work and family choices. Two Black women discussed this theme (each mentioned it only once) and, despite being aware of the option to stay at home to care for family or to work for pay, they did not describe thinking about which of these options they would follow. Instead, both indicated that they intended to work regardless of their caretaking roles.

Some White women discussed valuing their work and family choices, noting that recent generations of women have more career options. Further, they contrasted their work–family choices with those of men. A 48-year-old White woman said: "Guys never go through all of that mental stuff. . . . They never have the options. The guy goes to college, gets a job or just gets outta high school and gets a job." Further, some women felt that they could more easily choose to stay home with their children than men, as society views stay-at-home moms more positively than stay-at-home dads. Nevertheless, some White women felt that having to choose work, family, or a combination of the two was difficult and often led to conflicting emotions and desires.

. . .

As demonstrated by the work–family options theme, Black and White women were aware of their options regarding work and family, yet White women elaborated on this far more than Black women. White women noted that the career options available to women have increased substantially in their lifetimes and provide them more work and family choices than men. Despite appreciating these freedoms, many White women also noted that career and family choices are often difficult to make and combining both roles could be stressful and challenging.

INNER STRENGTH

A final theme of inner strength emerged only for Black women. For Black women, discussion of their personal and emotional strength combined their race and their gender, that is, they explicitly attributed their strength to being Black women (rather than attributing it to their race or gender alone). Half of the Black women spoke of learning to be strong women through the example of their mothers and other Black women around them.

> Basically, I grew up in a household with my mother, and my grandmother lived around the corner. So I was around women. And so that's all I know is to be a strong woman. That's all I was raised around. So I think it comes naturally for me. (19-year-old Black student)

In some of these cases, women explicitly noted the role of single mothers as models of strength. An 84-year-old Black grandmother said, "My father died when I was three, so my mother raised me. . . . I guess naturally my mother was a strong person and she worked every day and so therefore, by her being a strong woman it made me that way, too."

Black women described strength as having the courage to stand up for oneself, persevere, and refuse to be taken advantage of by others (specifically men or White people). That is, strong women were defined as those who are self-reliant, able to withstand the challenges placed before them, and unwilling to depend on others to take care of them. . . .

Some Black women felt that their strength was necessitated by the challenges presented to them in a racist society. Further, a few participants perceived that Black women needed to be strong to fill the void created by Black men, who were viewed as being especially harmed by discrimination against Black people in the United States. And although participants largely accepted their perceived role in maintaining the Black community, there was also acknowledgement of the pressure this creates.

Being a Black woman, I feel like we are the back-bone. I really honestly think that Black women are the only thing that is really kind of keeping this race together right now. And I think that is a huge burden. (26-year-old Black law student)

Thus, inner strength was a personal characteristic that most of the Black women in the study felt they possessed. The idea of inner strength was not raised by any of the White women, suggesting that this trait is unique to Black women's self-conceptions. Although Black women reflected on the importance and necessity of their strength, some of them simultaneously noted that the need to always be strong could be emotionally difficult.

DISCUSSION

The current study examined our assertion that race is a marker for certain types of life experiences that shape how women view their gender. The data suggested that Black and White women view womanhood as comprising many of the same broad components: gender-based mistreatment, perceived advantages, community and friendships, and caretaking. However, there were more substantial differences in the importance and nature of subthemes for each group. Further, two themes were relevant primarily to only one group. Specifically, it was principally White women who described how being a woman encompassed having to make decisions about whether and how to combine work and family. Further, Black women perceived inner strength to be an important characteristic common to many Black women. Following, we will discuss the similarities and differences in the themes and subthemes that emerged.

GENDER-BASED MISTREATMENT

For both Black and White women, the most detailed discussion of what it is to be a woman centered on experiences and concerns about gender-based mistreatment, reflecting both the frequency of such events (e.g., Hics et al., 2003; Kessler et al., 1999) and women's perceptions that they may be potential victims. Women described ways that men attempted

to assert their power and control through bullying; overprotection from friends, brothers, and fathers; sexist comments about women's abilities and competence; and multiple types of sexual harassment. Gender-based mistreatment occurred in a variety of contexts, including families, schools, workplaces, and the community. Thus, it seems that women are vulnerable to being mistreated in most domains of their lives, which likely intensifies the negative impact of such experiences. Women described the practical consequences of gender-based mistreatment for their lives personally, academically, and professionally. Further, the psychological impact of gender-based mistreatment included feelings of fear, anger, and mistrust.

Although there were far more similarities than differences between Black and White women's discussion of gender-based mistreatment, one notable difference was that some White women, but no Black women, identified part of the discrimination they experienced at work to being put on the "mommy-track." That is, they were not placed on the career track that would lead to the most advancement because of assumptions by employers that they would leave the workforce when they had children. . . .

In addition, White women, but not Black women, described experiences with coworkers and acquaintances in social settings that could be defined as sexual harassment, perhaps reflecting men's inappropriate and sexualized attempts to form relationships with them (Adams, 1997; Baker, 2005; Fuller, 2004). More Black women than White women expressed concern about the negative sexualized portrayal of women in the media. Because most of the representations of Black women in the media are negative (e.g., sexually promiscuous, welfare queen; Collins, 2000; Stephens & Phillips, 2003; West, 2004), this group may be particularly conscious of how all women are depicted.

PERCEIVED ADVANTAGE

In contrast to the discussion of gender-based mistreatment, women, particularly younger women, asserted that, compared to men, some things were easier for them because they were women. However, many of the examples provided reflected sexist beliefs and practices. In particular, women described characteristics of benevolent sexism, which refers to being taken care of by men (Glick & Fiske, 1997, 2001). They also described ways in which they could use their femininity and sexuality to "get away with things" when dealing with men. These behaviors may reflect the internalization of sexist beliefs or they may be deliberate strategies to redress a relative lack of power in many life domains. However, a potential cost is that such behaviors may reify the belief that women will use their sexuality to gain power over men. Such actions are conceptualized as a component of hostile sexism, and both benevolent and hostile sexism are status-legitimizing ideologies that satisfy men's and women's notions of men as protectors and women as in need of protection (Glick & Fiske, 1997, 2001).

Because sexism serves to maintain the status quo and women's lower status and power (Glick & Fiske, 1997, 2001), it is particularly troubling that these women perceived benefits of womanhood as including behaviors that might be defined as sexist. Similarly, women identified some areas of employment that were more readily available to them as a type of privilege; however, these were typically low-wage and low-prestige jobs with little opportunity for upward mobility, such as retail and service positions. By comparing the gender-based mistreatment and perceived advantages themes, we can identify some ambivalence in the gender-related worldview of young women. For example, the idea of being protected by men was raised in both themes; women appreciated being cared for and made to feel safer by men while also resenting men's attempts to restrict them. This ambivalence may occur because many of women's perceived advantages actually reflected sexist practices rather than any real advantage.

FRIENDSHIPS AND COMMUNITY

Within the theme of friendships and community, only half of the Black women in the sample discussed related issues, whereas all of the White women did. Further, only one Black woman noted the positive, supportive aspects of friendship. It may be that, when Black women think about their friendships and community, they think about other Black people or Black women, rather than women generally. For White women, thinking about women generally likely brings to mind relationships with other White women.

White women described valuing their friendships with other women and perceived them as providing emotional support, camaraderie, and a connection to others. Nevertheless, both Black and White women, even those with close female friendships, described negative aspects of their relationships with other women, although this segment of the theme also seemed more salient to White women. . . .

CARETAKING AND WORK-FAMILY OPTIONS

Caretaking was another significant aspect of womanhood raised by participants. Rewarding aspects of caretaking included the positive emotions and personal growth gained from holding the role of mother and grandmother. In contrast, caretaking was also linked to less desirable role requirements, including pressure from self and others to have children (because this is seen as defining womanhood), as well as the psychological and practical burden of being responsible for others in terms of housework, childcare, and the maintenance of extended family relationships. Women attribute some of their sense of burden to their caretaking responsibilities being seen as "second shift" work that often was not shared equally by male partners (Hochschild, 1989).

Despite the many similarities in the caretaking issues raised by participants, White women described more of the rewards of caretaking, whereas Black women noted more of the burdens. This contrast may reflect real differences in the lived experiences of these two groups; Black women may be more likely to do "second shift" work because they are more likely to work while having young children, and Black women's extended family networks may create more ties to maintain (Sarkisian & Gerstel, 2004). . . .

INNER STRENGTH

The final theme, inner strength, emerged only for the Black women in our study. Participants discussed the idea of inner strength in terms of the image of the "Strong Black Woman" (Romero, 2000; Wallace, 1978), thereby explicitly linking this concept to their intersected gender and racial status. Consistent with the stereotyped image, being a strong Black woman entailed certain behaviors (e.g., caring for one's family while working and supporting the family economically) and certain personality characteristics (e.g., resolve, persistence, and self-reliance). For the participants, these traits acted as a sort of armor against a society in which Black people have been historically mistreated and where racism is expected as a matter of course. Further, some participants felt that racism directed toward Black men has made it more common for adult males to be absent from Black households, furthering the need for Black women to be strong and self-reliant.

At the same time, some participants noted the emotional burden they experienced as a result of always having to be strong. The idea of the strong Black woman has also been termed the "Superwoman" stereotype and is associated with emotional and psychological costs. For example, endorsement of the Superwoman stereotype has been linked to unhealthy overeating (as a coping mechanism) and lower self-esteem for Black women (Beauboeuf-Lafontant, 2003; Thomas, Witherspoon, & Speight, 2004). Thus, the internalization of the strong Black woman stereotype may be a practical defensive strategy for dealing with daily hassles and challenges; yet, this inner strength can have negative psychological consequences for Black women when their caring for others is done at the expense of attending to their own needs.

OTHER FINDINGS, LIMITATIONS, AND FUTURE DIRECTIONS

Although not the focus of the present study, we found interesting generational differences in perceptions of gender-based mistreatment across racial groups. Specifically, some of the younger women in the study expressed surprise and disbelief about personal experiences of sexual harassment and discrimination. They commented that prior to their negative experiences they believed that women had gained equality in most areas and that discrimination was no longer a societal problem. Thus, they suffered a disruption to their worldview that required them to revise their notions about the place of women in society and their relationship to men. Older women were more likely to have noted that women's social position had improved during their lives, but without the belief that women had achieved equality with men. . . .

One area in which we observed little variability was in the sexual orientation of the women in the study (90% were heterosexual). Lesbian and bisexual women may have more negative experiences because of the heterosexist bias that exists in our society. Additionally, White women were of a higher social class than Black women, which may explain why they perceived having more advantages as women than did Black women. Although race and social class are confounded in our study, these differences reflect actual economic disparities between racial groups (U.S. Department of Labor, Bureau of Labor Statistics, 2006), thereby increasing the ecological validity of the results.

We focused the current study on the exploration of Black and White women's gender perceptions. Latinas, Asian women, and other women of color may be similar to the Black women in our study in that, as a result of their devalued racial/ethnic identity, they may also experience double jeopardy. However, it is likely that interesting differences would also emerge because of the particular stereotypes and histories of these groups in the United States. Future work should expand on our results through the study of other groups of women of color. . . .

REFERENCES

Abrams, L. S. (2003). Contextual variations in young women's gender identity negotiations. *Psychology of Women Quarterly, 27,* 64–74.

Adams, J. H. (1997). Sexual harassment and Black women: A historical perspective. In O'Donohue (Ed.), *Sexual harassment: Theory, research, and treatment* (pp. 213–224). Boston: Allyn & Bacon.

Andresen, E. M., & Brownson, R. C. (2000). Disability and health status: Ethnic differences among women in the United States. *Journal of Epidemiological Community Health, 54,* 200–206.

Baker, C. N. (2005). Images of women's sexuality in advertisements: A content analysis of Black- and White-oriented women's and men's magazines. *Sex Roles, 52,* 13–27.

Beal, F. M. (1970). Double jeopardy: To be Black and female. In T. Cade (Ed.), *The Black ivoman: An anthology* (pp. 90–100). New York: Signet.

Beauboeuf-Lafontant, T. (2003). Strong and large Black women? Exploring relationships between deviant womanhood and weight. *Gender and Society, 17,* 111–121.

Bell, E. L. (2004). Myths, stereotypes, and realities of Black women: A personal reflection. *The Journal of Applied Behavioral Science, 40,* 146–159.

Berdahl, J. L., & Moore, C. (2006). Workplace harassment: Double jeopardy for minority women. *Journal of Applied Psychology, 91,* 426–436.

Bergman, M. E., & Drasgow, F. (2003). Race as a moderator in a model of sexual harassment: An empirical test. *Journal of Occupational Health Psychology, 8,* 131–145.

Boisnier, A. D. (2003). Race and women's identity development: Distinguishing between feminism and womanism among Black and White women. *Sex Roles, 49,* 211–218.

Browne, I., & Kennelly, I. (1999). Stereotypes and realities: Images of Black women in the labor market. In I. Browne (Ed.), *Latinas and African American women at work: Race, gender, and economic inequality* (pp. 302–326). New York: Russell Sage Foundation.

Buchanan, N. T. (2005). The nexus of race and gender domination: The racialized sexual harassment of African American women. In P. Morgan & J. Gruber (Eds.), *In the company of men: Re-discovering the links between sexual harassment and male domination* (pp. 294–320). Boston: Northeastern University Press.

Buchanan, N. T., & Fitzgerald, L. F. (2008). The effects of racial and sexual harassment on work and the psychological well-being of African American women. *Journal of Occupational Health Psychology, 13,* 137–151.

Buchanan, N. T., & Ormerod, A. J. (2002). Racialized sexual harassment in the lives of African American Women. *Women & Therapy, 25,* 107–124.

Buchanan, N. T., Settles, I. H., & Woods, K. C. (2008). Comparing sexual harassment subtypes for Black and White women: Double jeopardy, the Jezebel, and the cult of true womanhood. *Psychology of Women Quarterly, 32,* 347–361.

Collins, P. H. (2000). *Black feminist thought: Knowledge, consciousness and the politics of empowerment* (2nd ed.). New York: Routledge.

Coltrane, S., & Messineo, M. (2000). The perpetuation of subtle prejudice: Race and gender imagery in 1990s television advertising. *Sex Roles, 42,* 363–389.

Cooley, C. H. (1922). *Human nature and the social order.* New York: Schocken Books.

Crenshaw, K. W. (1995). Mapping the margins: Intersectionality, identity politics, and violence against women of color. In K. W. Crenshaw, N. Gotanda, G. Peller, & K. Thomas (Eds.), *Critical race theory: The key writings that formed the movement* (pp. 357–383). New York: The New Press.

Davis, A. (2002). "Don't let nobody bother yo' principle": The sexual economy of American Slavery. In S. Harley & The Black Women and Work Collective (Eds.), *Sister circle: Black women and work* (pp. 103–127). New Brunswick, NJ: Rutgers University Press.

Deaux, K., Reid, A., Mizrahi, K., & Ethier, K. A. (1995). Parameters of social identity. *Journal of Personality and Social Psychology, 68,* 280–291.

Fiske, S. T., & Neuberg, S. L. (1990). A continuum of impression formation, from category-based to individuating processes: Influences of information and motivation on attention and interpretation. In M. P. Zanna (Ed.), *Advances in experimental social psychology* (pp. 1–74). San Diego, CA: Academic Press.

Fitzgerald, L. F. (1996). Sexual harassment: The definition and measurement of a construct. In M. A. Paludi (Ed.), *Sexual harassment on college campuses: Abusing the ivory power* (pp. 21–44). Albany, NY: University of New York Press.

Fitzgerald, L. F., Drasgow, F., Hulin, C. L., Gelfand, M. J., & Magley, V. J. (1997). Antecedents and consequences of sexual harassment in organizations: A test of an integrated model. *Journal of Applied Psychology, 82,* 578–589.

Fitzgerald, L. F., & Shullman, S. L. (1993). Sexual harassment: A research analysis and agenda for the 1990s. *Journal of Vocational Behavior, 42,* 5–27.

Frable, D. E. S. (1997). Gender, racial, ethnic, sexual, and class identities. *American Review of Psychology, 48,* 139–162.

Frable, D. E. S., Blackstone, T., & Scherbaum, C. (1990). Marginal and mindful: Deviants in social interactions. *Journal of Personality and Social Psychology, 59,* 140–149.

Fuller, A. A. (2004). What difference does difference make? Women, race-ethnicity, social class, and social change. *Race, Gender, & Class, 11,* 8–24.

Glenn, E. N. (1992). Historical continuities in the racial division of paid reproductive labor. *Signs, 18,* 1–43.

Glick, P., & Fiske, S. T. (1997). Hostile and benevolent sexism: Measuring ambivalent sexist attitudes toward women. *Psychology of Women Quarterly, 21,* 119–135.

Glick, P., & Fiske, S. T. (2001). An ambivalent alliance: Hostile and benevolent sexism as complementary justifications for gender inequality. *American Psychologist, 56,* 109–118.

Green, C. R., Ndao-Brumblay, K., Nagrant, A. M., Baker, T. A., & Rothman, E. (2004). Race, age, and gender influences among clusters of African American and White patients with chronic pain. *The Journal of Pain, 5,* 171–182.

Gutner, C. A., Rizvi, S. L., Monson, C. M., & Resick, P. A. (2006). Changes in coping strategies, relationship to the perpetrator, and posttraumatic distress in female crime victims. *Journal of Traumatic Stress, 19,* 813–823.

Hochschild, A. (1989). *The second shift.* New York: Viking.

Huerta, M., Cortina, L. M., Pang, J. S., Torges, C. M., & Magley, V. J. (2006). Sex and power in the academy: Modeling sexual harassment in the lives of college women. *Personality and Social Psychology Bulletin, 32,* 616–628.

Hurtado, A. (1989). Relating to privilege: Seduction and rejection in the subordination of White women and women of color. *Signs, 14,* 833–855.

Hurtado, A., & Stewart, A. J. (1997). Through the looking glass: Implications of studying Whiteness for feminist methods. In M. Fine, L. Weis, L. C. Powell, & L. M. Wong (Eds.), *Off white: Readings on race, power, and society* (pp. 297–311). New York: Routledge.

Ilies, R., Hauserman, N., Schwochau, S., & Stibal, J. (2003). Reported incidence rates of work-related sexual harassment in the United States: Using meta-analysis to explain reported rate disparities. *Personnel Psychology, 82,* 578–589.

Katz, J., Joiner, T. E., Jr., & Kwon, P. (2002). Membership in a devalued social group and emotional well-being: Developing a model of personal self-esteem, collective self-esteem, and group socialization. *Sex Roles, 47,* 419–431.

Kessler, R. C., Mickelson, K. D., & Williams, D. R. (1999). The prevalence, distribution, and mental health correlates of perceived discrimination in the United States. *Journal of Health and Social Behavior, 40,* 208–230.

Kilbourne, J. (1999). *Deadly persuasion: Why women and girls must fight the addictive power of advertising.* New York: Free Press.

King, K. (1988). Multiple jeopardy, multiple consciousness: The context of Black feminist ideology. *Signs, 14,* 42–72.

Landrine, H. (1985). Race X class stereotypes of women. *Sex Roles, 13,* 65–75.

Lopez, F. G., & Ann-Yi, S. (2006). Predictors of career indecision in three racial/ethnic groups of college women. *Journal of Career Development, 33,* 29–46.

Lott, B., Asquith, K., & Doyon, T. (2001). Relation of ethnicity and age to women's responses to personal experiences of sexist discrimination in the United States. *Journal of Social Psychology, 141,* 309–322.

Lott, B., & Saxon, S. (2002). The influence of ethnicity, social class, and context on judgments about U.S. women. *Journal of Social Psychology, 142,* 281–299.

Madriz, E. (2000). Focus groups in feminist research. In N. K. Denzin & Y. S. Lincoln (Eds.), *Handbook of qualitative research* (2nd ed., pp. 835–850). Thousand Oaks, CA: Sage.

Mead, G. H. (1925). The genesis of the self and social control. In C. Gordon & K. J. Gergen (Eds.), *The self in social interaction* (pp. 51–59). New York: Wiley.

Mecca, S. J., & Rubin, L. J. (1999). Definitional research on African American students and sexual harassment. *Psychology of Women Quarterly, 23,* 813–817.

Nelson, N. L., & Probst, T. M. (2004). Multiple minority individuals: Multiplying the risk of workplace harassment and discrimination. In J. L. Chin (Ed.), *The psychology of prejudice and discrimination: Ethnicity and multiracial identity* (pp. 193–217). Westport, CT: Praeger/Greenwood.

Paludi, M., & Paludi, C. (2003). *Academic and workplace sexual harassment: A handbook of cultural, social science, management, and legal perspectives.* Westport, CT: Praeger/Greenwood.

Pascale, C. (2001). All in a day's work: A feminist analysis of class formation and social identity. *Race, Gender & Class, 8,* 34–59.

Perkins, L. (1983). The impact of the "Cult of True Womanhood" on the education of Black women. *Journal of Social Issues, 39,* 17–28.

Ransford, H. E., & Miller, J. (1983). Race, sex, and feminist outlooks. *American Sociological Review, 48,* 46–59.

Rederstorff, J. C., Buchanan, N. T., & Settles, I. H. (2007). The moderating roles of race and gender role attitudes in the relationship between sexual harassment and psychological well-being. *Psychology of Women Quarterly, 31,* 50–61.

Reid, P. T., & Comas-Diaz, L. (1990). Gender and ethnicity: Perspectives on dual status. *Sex Roles, 22,* 397–408.

Reskin, B. F. (1999). Occupational segregation by race and ethnicity among women workers. In I. Browne (Ed.), *Latinas and African American women at work: Race, gender, and economic inequality* (pp. 183–206). New York: Russell Sage Foundation.

Romero, R. E. (2000). The icon of the strong Black woman: The paradox of strength. In L. C. Jackson & B. Greene (Eds.), *Psychotherapy with African American women: Innovations in psychodynamic perspective and practice,* (pp. 225–238). New York: Guilford.

Sarkisian, N., & Gerstel, N. (2004). Kin support among Blacks and Whites: Race and family organization. *American Sociological Review, 69,* 812–837.

Schmitt, M. T., Branscombe, N. R., Kobrynowicz, D., & Owen, S. (2002). Perceiving discrimination against one's gender group has different implications for well-being in women and men. *Personality and Social Psychology Bulletin, 28,* 197–210.

Settles, I. H. (2006). Use of an intersectional framework to understand Black women's racial and gender identities. *Sex Roles, 54,* 589–601.

Settles, I. H., Cortina, L. M., Malley, J., & Stewart, A. J. (2006). The climate for women in academic science: The good, the bad, and the changeable. *Psychology of Women Quarterly, 30,* 47–58.

Smith, A., & Stewart, A. J. (1983). Approaches to studying racism and sexism in Black women's lives. *Journal of Social Issues, 39,* 1–15.

St. Jean, Y., & Feagin, J. R. (1997). Racial masques: Black women and subtle gendered racism. In N. V. Benokraitis (Ed.), *Subtle sexism: Current practice and prospects for change.* Thousand Oaks, CA: Sage.

Stephens, D. P., & Phillips, L. D. (2003). Freaks, gold diggers, divas, and dykes. *Sexuality and Culture, 7,* 3–49.

Stewart, A. J., & McDermott, C. (2004). Gender in psychology. *Annual Review of Psychology, 55,* 519–544.

Swim, J. K., Aikin, K. J., Hall, W. S., & Hunter, B. A. (1995). Sexism and racism: Old-fashioned and modern prejudices. *Journal of Personality and Social Psychology, 68,* 199–214.

Tenenbaum, H. R., & Leaper, C. (2003). Parent-child conversations about science: The socialization of gender inequalities? *Developmental Psychology, 39,* 34–47.

Thomas, A. J., Witherspoon, K. M., & Speight, S. L. (2004). Toward the development of the Stereotypic Roles for Black Women Scale. *Journal of Black Psychology, 30,* 426–442.

Wallace, M. (1978/1990). *Black macho and the myth of the super-woman.* New York: Verso.

Welter, B. (1966). The cult of true womanhood: 1820–1860. *American Quarterly, 18,* 151–174.

West, C. (2004). Mammy, Jezebel, and Sapphire: Developing an "oppositional gaze" toward the image of Black women. In J. C. Chrisler, C. Golden, & P. D. Rozee (Eds.), *Lectures on the psychology of women* (3rd ed., pp. 220–233). New York: McGraw-Hill.

White, J. L., & Cones III, J. H. (1999). *Black man emerging.* New York: Routledge.

Wilkinson, S. (1999). Focus groups: A feminist method. *Psychology of Women Quarterly, 23,* 221–244.

Witt, S. D. (1997). Parental influence on children's socialization to gender roles. *Adolescence, 32,* 253–259.

Wrestling with Gender

Deborah H. Brake (2013)

In February of 2011, a high school boy captured national media attention when he refused to wrestle a girl at the Iowa State wrestling championship tournament. Two girls had qualified for the state tournament that year in Iowa, a state where wrestling has an ardent following. But, when Joel Northrup was paired against one of the girls, Cassy Herkelman, in the first round of the 112-pound weight class, he decided to forfeit the match rather than wrestle a girl. According to media reports, before he forfeited, Northrup had been a favorite to win his weight class.[1] The incident launched a brief but intense media frenzy, with coverage in major television and print outlets. The general tenor of the stories portrayed the boy and his father who supported him as heroes in a drama about sacrificing a boy's chance to be a state champion for the welfare of a girl.[2] The storyline set up a familiar conflict juxtaposing the religious values of the boy and his family against the girl's quest for equal opportunity.[3] This is a common frame for neutralizing a gender equality claim, by offsetting it with the assertion of contrary religious beliefs. At the same time, the stories about the incident diffused this conflict by casting doubts about the girl's agency, suggesting that the boy and his father were acting in her real best interests.[4] Other aspects of the incident also fueled the backlash narrative that emerged from the story: the semblance of formal equality (the boy opted out, neither Joel nor Cassy had the opportunity to wrestle), and the appropriation of feminist-sounding messages toward nonfeminist ends (men should not hit women; girls deserve their own matches).[5] Lost in the media's framing of the story arc the deep and implicit connections between sport and masculinity that lie at the heart of this episode.

GOING TO THE MAT: GIRLS, WRESTLING, AND RESISTANCE

The sport of wrestling has always been a volatile one for gender relations. Wrestling is a sport rife with gender tensions and contradictions. On the one hand, it is a quintessential contact sport, one of the warrior sports, with strong associations with masculinity.[6] Wrestlers grapple face to face, using strength, force, and skillful moves to battle their opponents at close range.[7]

Like other contact sports, participants risk injury and must have a high threshold for pain.[8] At the same time, the sport's masculine identity is a precarious one. Wrestling tends to draw boys who are too short or lightweight to be competitive in sports with the strongest connection to masculinity, football and basketball. Since wrestlers are grouped into weight classes, smaller, lighter boys are not held back by their body type.[9]

The sport also struggles with what might look to an outsider like a homoerotic aesthetic. Wrestlers wear body-hugging lycra singlets, and up-close bodily encounters are a major part of the sport, requiring all kinds of intimate and (to observers) awkward positions. In the culture of sport that has taken hold since sports were first introduced in U.S. schools (largely for the very purpose of inculcating masculinity in boys), a sport's masculine identity is inextricably bound up in its power to confer on its male participants a prized hetero-masculinity.[10] For wrestling especially, this has required the sport to actively distance itself from any suggestion of sexuality or homoeroticism. And yet, the sport's susceptibility to a sexualized understanding can make the uninitiated spectator uncomfortable and its participants defensive. Even the lingo of the sport is loaded with possible double entendres suggesting an undercurrent of sexuality (e.g., "wrestling up the backside," "high crotch takedown," the "butt grab"). Wrestlers themselves, along with their coaches and educated fan base, know that the extraordinary, undivided focus required to compete in the sport leaves little room for distracting feelings of attraction or desire in the heat of a match. Still, more so than for other sports, the potential is there for sexualizing the sport in a way that is inconsistent with maintaining a strong hetero-masculine identity for the sport and its participants.[11]

According to sport and gender scholars Theresa Walton and Michelle Helstein, wrestling's role in recent decades as the leader of the opposition to Title IX is indicative of the sport's "gender trouble."[12] Wrestling has taken the lead in advocacy blaming Title IX for cuts to men's sports, including and especially to the sport of wrestling itself. Walton and Helstein explain this dynamic in terms of the gendered hierarchy within men's sports, in which wrestling is subordinated to the more masculine sports of football and basketball.[13] On average, these sports consume the vast majority of the total men's athletic operating budget in universities.[14] Since Title IX sets limits on cutting women's sports where women already have fewer opportunities to play than men, the excesses of football and men's basketball budgets tend to squeeze out the budgets of other men's sports such as wrestling.[15] And yet, by choosing to align itself with the "big boys" of football and men's basketball in the Title IX culture wars, wrestling bolsters its masculine credentials, building "community" among wrestlers through an identity that is oppositional to girls' and women's participation in sport, and in line with hegemonic masculinity.[16] In keeping with this stance, and more so than other sports, many wrestlers and supporters of wrestling have reacted strongly and negatively to the increasing participation of girls and women in the sport.

In recent years, the accelerating entry of girls and women into the sport of wrestling has added fuel to these fires of gender conflict. Girls' and women's participation in wrestling has grown rapidly in recent years, sparked by the addition of women's freestyle wrestling as a new Olympic Sport in the 2004 Olympics, and five years earlier, by the U.S.

women winning the 1999 world championship title in women's wrestling.[17] Despite growing interest in the sport, however, girls and women typically do not have their own teams. In order to participate in the sport, they have to wrestle male opponents. This has provoked a great deal of resistance, including most recently in the form of forfeiture by male wrestlers.

A quick look at the numbers shows girls' wrestling on a steep upward trajectory. In 1990, 112 high school girls participated in competitive wrestling nationwide.[18] By 2011, that number was over 7000.[19] The areas where girls' wrestling numbers are highest, however, are not the same as the hotbeds of boys' wrestling (the Midwest and East Coast).[20] Girls' wrestling has had its greatest growth in areas where wrestling is not as emphasized, such as California (near the top of the list, with 1,910 high school girls participating), and in states that offer a separate girls' championship tournament, such as Texas (with more than 1,700 girls in high school wrestling).[21] However, most states do not have separate wrestling championships or separate competitions for girls.[22] And, despite their growing numbers, girls are still only two percent of all high school wrestlers.[23] As a result, girls must wrestle boys if they are to have the opportunity to participate in the sport.[24]

Girls who stay in contact sports like wrestling must overcome negative cultural stereotypes associated with women in the sport and weather a variety of forces that coalesce to suppress female sports participation in early adolescence. Sport scholars have long known that girls' athletic participation declines in adolescence, and especially so for sports identified as "masculine."[25] Girls are less confident than boys in performing masculine-typed tasks, and gender stereotypes begin to influence physical activity choices at a young age.[26] The research in sport and gender studies also documents differential parental support and encouragement of sons and daughters, with parents spending more time and effort supporting and playing sports with their sons than their daughters.[27]

For girls and women to participate in a male gender-typed sport such as wrestling, they must perceive enough positive benefits to overcome these negative cultural influences.[28] For the girls who do, they are drawn to wrestling for a variety of reasons. Through wrestling, girls learn to defend themselves and be more assertive, showing boys that they can be strong and worthy opponents.[29] As one woman training with the U.S. Olympic Training Center (USOTC) said, "[i]t kinda pushes me and makes me feel like I can do anything I put my mind to."[30] Many girls say that they are drawn to the sport because it suits their body type and their temperament. One female wrestler tapped for Olympic training explained, "I was looking for something to do to work out over the winter and I kind of always wanted to try wrestling because I am a very hands-on, physical person."[31] Others explain that they chose the sport because it provides them with the ultimate mental and physical challenge.[32] It is also attractive as a sport that allows athletes to stand out individually while still being part of a team; and as a newer sport, it offers relatively high chances for Olympic success in comparison to other, more established sports.[33] These distinctive features make wrestling a potentially rewarding sport for girls and women. In one of the few studies of female wrestlers' experiences, researchers found that the girls and women in the study expressed a greater degree of comfort with their bodies and experienced wrestling as a source of both physical and mental empowerment.[34] Interestingly, this study turned up a finding that departs from other research findings that female athletes engage in what sport scholars call an "apologetic," in which female athletes emphasize their femininity to compensate for a gender role conflict that arises when they participate in sports, especially in sports gender-typed as masculine.[35] The female wrestlers in this study did not perceive such a role conflict, and did not consciously try to overcome negative stereotypes associated with female wrestlers by ramping up their femininity off the mat.[36] In contrast to the low figure of six percent of female wrestlers in this study who said that they were concerned about being labeled "lesbian" because of their sports participation, a majority of the subjects in other studies of female athletes (soccer players and boxers) have expressed this concern.[37] Speculating on the reasons for this, the researchers noted several possible explanations for this discrepancy, including the fact that female wrestlers may be better able to resist a perceived gender role conflict.[38] Notably, the wrestlers in the study claimed that they viewed wrestling as a sport that is appropriate for women, and not a masculine sport at all, while nevertheless acknowledging that the general population perceives it as a masculine sport.[39] The study portrayed these women as actively resisting popular gendered understandings of wrestling and substituting their own views of the sport's suitability for girls and women.

Another study of female wrestlers, this one focusing on elite women wrestlers training for the U.S. Olympic tryouts, likewise found that the female wrestlers in the study built a strong and empowering identity for themselves as wrestlers.[40] These women too were aware that wrestling is stereotyped as a masculine sport, but persisted in the sport anyway, choosing for themselves alternative definitions of what it means to be feminine.[41] As one female wrestler explained: "I know that society thinks that girls' wrestling is not feminine. My dad thinks being feminine is wearing a dress, but my mom thinks it's being in charge of yourself and being confident."[42] Another wrestler added her own redefinition of femininity: "I think femininity is about how you carry yourself on and off the mat. I don't have to have my nails done and wear makeup everyday to be feminine. Even though I'm sweating and my shirt is all torn up, I'm still feminine."[43] This study too found the female wrestlers actively engaged in a process of constructing their own identities and resisting interpretations of female wrestling as inconsistent with femininity.[44]

The findings of these studies are consistent with how female wrestlers describe themselves and their decision to wrestle in news reports on female wrestlers. As one high school wrestler said, defending her right to compete, "I think it's really important, because you shouldn't stereotype a sport. Guys and girls can do any sport they want." [45] The two female wrestlers interviewed in the story said that the sport made them "stronger, better athletes and more goal-oriented."[46]

Still, even if the female apologetic is more variable now than when it first surfaced in the literature, and even if female athletes differ in how they experience and navigate gender role conflict, female wrestlers too must navigate conflicting expectations about ideal femininity (an ideal with implicitly white and heterosexual markers, such as having long hair, and being attractive to and attracted to men) while engaging in athletic performances that clash with this ideal. As the sport/gender scholarship has shown, even though the dominant cultural ideal of femininity has expanded to embrace fitness, firm bodies, and athleticism, it still punishes women whose athletic performances and/or bodies go too far in pressing against the boundaries of white hetero-feminine norms.[47] Girls and women who play masculine-typed sports are especially likely to be caught in this role conflict and to engage in "impression management" in order to avoid or mitigate the stigmas of mannishness and lesbianism.[48] This dynamic in the sport/gender literature is similar to the discussion of identity performance and "covering" discussed in legal scholarship—efforts undertaken by members of subordinated groups in a variety of settings and in context-specific ways to make their identities more palatable to controlling majority groups.[49]

Notwithstanding the study (discussed above) of elite female wrestlers claiming that they did not engage in actions to compensate for their participation in wrestling, news stories abound with examples of what could be called "identity management" by female wrestlers. For example, one story about a female high school wrestler in Pennsylvania softened its account of a female wrestler's proficiency with a quote from the girl saying, "I may be a little rougher than some of my girl friends, but when I'm not wrestling, I go to the mall, I talk about boys, and I worry about my hair."[50]

The persistence of gender role conflict for girls and women who wrestle can also be seen in defenses of female wrestlers by their supporters. Proponents of girls' wrestling almost invariably feel compelled to defend the girls' femininity, and implicitly, their heterosexuality. For example, one wrestling coach who had coached girls on his team wrote a letter to the local newspaper in the wake of the Iowa forfeiture controversy responding to comments by other readers wondering, "what kind of girls would wrestle?" The coach responded that the four girls he coached grew up to be "solid citizens," emphasizing that "[a]ll of them got married."[51] He also confided that he himself had asked the girls why they wanted

to wrestle, and shared one girl's answer that she was not good enough to make the varsity team in any other school sport.[52] In this exchange, the girl's lack of competence in other sports serves the purpose of making her decision to wrestle more acceptable. Although the coach expressed his support for girls in wrestling, his defense ultimately reinforced the cultural ambivalence about girls' wrestling by reaffirming that a girl's decision to wrestle requires an explanation.[53] He also, tellingly, expressed the wish that there were enough girls in the sport so that girls did not have to wrestle boys.[54] It is a common refrain of supporters of girls' wrestling, even as they defend girls' right to wrestle boys, that it would be better if girls had their own teams.[55] Girls themselves often deflect criticisms of their participation in the sport by emphasizing that they had no choice but to wrestle boys, since the lack of female competition meant that they could not otherwise participate in the sport.[56]

Other signs of ambivalence, if not outright hostility, to girls' participation in wrestling abound. Mixed-sex wrestling matches often prompt negative publicity,[57] and the NCAA still has not recognized wrestling as an emerging women's sport, despite their recognition of "emerging sports" with much lower levels of female high school participation.[58] And, despite the likely illegality of such practices under the Equal Protection Clause there have been numerous attempts to impose outright bans on girls from participating on boys' wrestling teams. One such attempt took a dramatic turn when hearings before a committee of the Minnesota legislature took "testimony" in the form of a live wrestling exhibition between two high school boys to demonstrate the physical intimacies involved in certain wrestling moves.[59] This "testimony" was offered in support of a bill that the Minnesota legislature considered in 2002 to repeal a state law requiring that girls be allowed to try out for boys' teams if they did not have a team of their own in that sport.[60] The bill was motivated by opposition to mixed-sex wrestling, and its proponents sounded the alarm of sex-panic. The bill was ultimately defeated but takes its place among other widespread efforts to stop girls from wrestling boys.[61]

Where girls have not been kept off boys' wrestling teams, forfeiture has become a potent method of resistance. As more girls have gone into wrestling, there have been increasing reports of boys refusing to wrestle female opponents. Boys' stated reasons vary, but typically include the explanation that they would not want to hurt a girl or that it would seem sexually inappropriate. Such refusals result in the boy's forfeiture of the match but are otherwise permitted by schools and athletic associations without penalty—that is, the boy is not disqualified from the tournament, just tagged with a loss.

Wrestling is unlike most other sports in which girls and women participate in that female wrestlers must rely on competition from male opponents in order to develop their skills and compete at a high level.[62] Male wrestlers who forfeit matches against girls are therefore a significant impediment to female wrestlers' competitive opportunities and a potent form of resistance to girls' entry in the sport. When widespread, such forfeitures can decimate girls' competitive opportunities in the sport. As one high school wrestling coach said of the first girl he ever coached: "I bet she had a dozen forfeits. (Boys) just don't want to be beaten by a girl."[63] Stories abound of female athletes whose competitive opportunities, and therefore skills development, were significantly impaired because of forfeits by male opponents.[64] One high school wrestler lamented that, as she got better, she had a harder time finding opponents willing to wrestle her:

> What I hate the most though is when people forfeit to me. . . . That's something I've kind of had to deal with ever since I started wrestling, just because I'm a girl.

> In eighth grade, I was on a junior league team, and in about my first 10 matches I got forfeits, and it was because I was a girl. I was really disappointed about that. You put in a lot of effort, and then people just forfeit to you. It didn't happen before I got good, that's the worst part.[65]

Another high school coach recalled how "one of his former female star wrestlers get [sic] credited with a bunch of forfeit wins because male wrestlers didn't want to be embarrassed by losing to a talented female wrestler."[66] Even women training for the U.S. Olympic team, who had reached the highest levels in their sport, identified lack of competition as a major impediment to their development in the sport, and expressed frustration at being dependent on the men for competition and at having to wait for the men's team to finish their workouts in order to have an opponent to wrestle.[67] Despite their lukewarm and sometimes outright hostile reception, girls have achieved increasing success on the mat in recent years. Girls have qualified for the state championship in as many as forty-nine states and have placed in at least ten states.[68] To date, three girls have won state title championships, including, most recently, a Vermont high school girl who beat a boy in the final round to win her state's title match for her weight class just a week after the Iowa forfeiture debacle.[69] Unlike the male forfeiter in the celebrated Iowa forfeiture, this Vermont state champion was not heralded in an in-depth interview aired on the Cable News Network (CNN).

NOTES

1. Mara Gray, *High School Wrestler Forfeits Match Rather Than Face Girl,* AOL News (Feb. 17, 2011, 5:09 PM), http://www.aolnews.com/2011/02/17/high-school-wrestler-joel-northrup-forfeits-match-rather-than-fa/.

2. *See* Editorial, *A Matter of Conscience, Respect,* GAZETTE (Iowa) (Feb. 19, 2011, 12:57 AM), http://thegazette.com/2011/02/19/a-matter-of-conscience-respect/; Fred Bowen, *Honoring Your Beliefs Makes You a Winner,* WASH. Post, Feb. 24, 2011, at C10.

3. *See* Bowen *supra* note 2, at C10; Luke Meredith, *Boy Opts Not to Wrestle Girl at Iowa Tourney,* TEL. HERALD (Iowa), Feb. 18, 2011, at A1; Jere Longman, *On Mat, Girls Still Face Uphill Struggle,* N.Y. Times, Feb. 28, 2011, at D1.

4. Betsy Hart, *In Iowa, Chivalry Goes to the Mat,* CHI. SUN-TIMES, Mar. 2, 2011, at 4.

5. *See* Elizabeth Scalia, *Is Society Purposely Messing with Boys' Heads?,* Anchoress (Mar. 18, 2011, 7:14 PM), http://www.patheos.com/blogs/theanchoress/2011/03/18/is-society-purposely-messing-with-boys-heads/; Brian Preece, *Girls Have Wrestled in Utah for Nearly Two Decades,* DESERET MORNING NEWS (Salt Lake City), Feb. 19, 2011.

6. *See* Laurel Halloran, *Wrestling Injuries,* 27 ORTHOPAEDIC NURSING 189, 189 (2008); Mari Kristin

Sisjord & Elsa Kristiansen, *Elite Women Wrestlers' Muscles: Physical Strength and a Social Burden,* 44 INT'L REV. FOR THE SOC. OF SPORT 231, 231 (2009).

7. *Id.*

8. *Id.*

9. *Id.*

10. *See* Marie Hardin & Jennifer D. Greer, *The Influence of Gender-Role Socialization, Media Use and Sports Participation on Perceptions of Gender-Appropriate Sports*, 32 J. SPORT BEHAV. 207, 209 (2009) (discussing the process by which sports acquire a gender identity); *see also* Sally R. Ross & Kimberly J. Shinew, *Perspectives of Women College Athletes on Sport and Gender*, 58 Sex Roles 40, 41–42 (2007).

11. Theresa Walton, *Pinned by Gender Construction?: Media Representations of Girls' Wrestling*, 14 WOMEN SPORT & PHYSICAL ACTIVITY J. 52, 58 (2005).

12. Theresa A. Walton & Michelle T. Helstein, *Triumph of Backlash: Wrestling Community and the "Problem" of Title IX*, 25 SOC. SPORT J. 369, 378 (2008); *see generally* JUDITH BUTLER, GENDER TROUBLE (2007).

13. *Id.*

14. *Id.* at 381.

15. *See* DEBORAH L. BRAKE, GETTING IN THE GAME: TITLE IX AND THE WOMEN'S SPORTS REVOLUTION 74, 217-18 (2010).

16. Walton & Helstein, *supra* note 15, at 377.

17. Moira E. Stuart & Diane E. Whaley, *Resistance and Persistence: An Expectancy-Value Approach to Understanding Women's Participation in a Male-Defined Sport*, 14 WOMEN IN SPORT & PHYSICAL ACTIVITY J. 24, 25 (2005).

18. Gary Mihoces, *Girls Grapple with Success Against Boys*, USA Today (Mar. 3, 2005, 11:34 PM), http://usatoday30.usatoday.com/sports/preps/wrestle/2005-03-03-girls-wrestling_x.htm.

19. *2011–2012 High School Athletics Participation Survey*, NAT'L FED'N OF STATE HIGH SCH. ATHLETIC ASS'NS, http://www.nfhs.org/WorkArea/linkit.aspx?LinkIdentifier=id&ItemID=5751&libID=5773 (last visited Jan. 8, 2013) (8,235 is likely a low number, since the numbers come from competition at the high school level, and many schools report zero girls in wrestling. While the numbers in those schools may be low, they are likely not zero).

20. Walton, *supra* note 14, at 56.

21. *2011–2012 High School Athletics Participation Survey*, *supra* note 22; Walton, *supra* note 14, at 57 (stating that Texas created separate wrestling competitions for girls specifically to keep boys and girls from wrestling together).

22. Longman, *supra* note 3, at D1 (citing California, Hawaii, Tennessee, Texas and Washington as the only states that offer separate high school wrestling teams and championships for girls).

23. *Id.* (stating that the number of male high school wrestlers is 270,000, while 6,000 women competed in high school wrestling in 2009–10).

24. Tamar Lewin, *In Twist for High School Wrestlers, Girl Flips Boy*, N.Y. TIMES, Feb. 17, 2007, at A1.

25. *See* Stuart & Whaley, *supra* note 20, at 24 for a research study on female members of USA women's wrestling team on why they wrestle.

26. *Id.* at 25–26.

27. *Id.* at 37.

28. *Id.* at 26 (discussing the literature on motivation and the expectancy-value theory, which takes into account the influence of gender role beliefs and cultural beliefs).

29. *See* Walton, *supra* note 14, at 63–64.

30. Stuart & Whaley, *supra* note 20, at 35. *See also* Vincent Thomas, *They're Holding Strong; More Female Wrestlers Going to the Mat Despite Mixed-Sex Issues*, wash. post, Mar. 26, 2004, at D1 (statement of female wrestler on why she wrestles: "Wrestling is such a dynamic sport . . . It's like a clash of wills, and it forces you to learn how to conquer yourself and be in control mentally and physically.").

31. Harold Raker, *High School Wrestling: Selinsgrove's Spiegel Closer to Olympic Dream*, DAILY ITEM (Sunbury, Pa.), June 30, 2010.

32. Lewin, *supra* note 27, at B4 ("Jessica, a soft-spoken girl who braids and pins up her hair before each match, says wrestling has helped build her confidence, challenging both her body and her mind.").

33. Paige Parker, *Taking Down the Naysayers: Pacific University's Women Wrestlers Win Respect from Their Male Counterparts*, SUNDAY OREGONIAN, Jan. 6, 2002, at D1 (citing these reasons why women choose the sport).

34. Ellen Macro, Jennifer Viveiros & Nick Cipriano, *Wrestling with Identity: An Exploration of Female Wres[t]lers' Perceptions*, 18 WOMEN IN SPORT & PHYSICAL ACTIVITY J. 42, 48 (2009). The subjects of the study were forty-seven Canadian female wrestlers at the high school, college, and club/community level. *Id.* at 42. Although the subjects were Canadian and their experiences might differ from female wrestlers in the U.S., the authors noted similarities in the position of female wrestlers in the two countries. As in the U.S., Canadian girls and women are newer and nontraditional participants in the sport, and, due to

insufficient numbers of female opponents, must typically compete against boys and men. The finding on the wrestlers' comfort with their bodies was based on measures of their expressed comfort showering in the presence of others (including three different groups of "others": teammates, wrestlers not on their own team, and non-wrestlers) and their comfort levels in other situations (being in a sauna, being weighed, and being seen by others while being weighed, and being seen in public while wearing a singlet). *Id.* at 45. The wrestlers also expressed high levels of satisfaction with how they looked in general. *Id.* at 46.

35. *Id.* at 48–49. The researchers contrasted their findings with previous research on soccer players (citing studies from 2000 and 2005), finding female soccer players felt more inhibited about their bodies and expressed greater anxiety about their body fat. *Id.* at 47. Compared to these findings, the wrestlers were more confident about their bodies, and attributed their confidence to wrestling. *Id.*

36. *Id.* at 48. Among the data relevant to this finding, ninety-four percent of the female wrestlers in the study said that they were not worried about personally being stereotyped as lesbian because of their participation in wrestling, and seventy-four percent said that they did not try to compensate for being a wrestler by playing up their femininity (wearing long hair, feminine clothes, make-up, etc.). *Id.* at 46–47.

37. *Id.* at 47. Similarly, fewer than half of the wrestlers said it was important to them to be perceived as feminine, contrasting with much larger numbers on research on other athletes. *Id.* at 48.

38. *Id.* at 49.

39. *Id.* at 48.

40. Stuart & Whaley, *supra* note 20, at 36.

41. *Id.* at 33.

42. *Id.*

43. *Id.*

44. *Id.*

45. Meera Patel, *Girls Grapple with Sexism in Sports*, Indianapolis Star, Apr. 20, 2008, at 4.

46. *Id.*

47. Macro, *supra* note 37, at 43; *see also* Ross & Shinew, *supra* note 13, at 53; Amanda Roth & Susan A. Basow, *Femininity, Sports, and Feminism: Developing a Theory of Physical Liberation*, 28 J. SPORT & SOC. ISSUES 245, 252 (2004).

48. Macro, *supra* note 37, at 44.

49. *See* Devon W. Carbado & Mitu Gulati, *The Fifth Black Woman*, 11 J. CONTEMP. LEGAL ISSUES 701, 701–03 (2001); Kenji Yoshino, *Covering*, 111 YALE L.J. 769, 772 (2002).

50. Deborah Weisberg, *Hampton Girl Making a Name for Herself*, PITTSBURGH POST-GAZETTE, June 14, 2000, at N12.

51. Preece, *supra* note 5.

52. *Id.*

53. *Id. See also* Parker, *supra* note 36, at D1 (quoting a wrestling coach who "finds himself reassuring startled listeners that women wrestlers aren't ugly, masculine or dumb," when he mentions that he coaches women, adding, "These aren't the dregs of society. . . . These are girls you'd be proud to have your sons going with.").

54. Preece, *supra* note 5.

55. *See, e.g.*, Lewin, *supra* note 27, at B4 (statement of coach of a successful female wrestler, "I think it's better if it's girl and girl. . . . If boys and girls wrestle together, it's physically harder for the girl, but mentally harder for the boy.").

56. *See, e.g.*, Stuart & Whaley, *supra* note 20, at 33.

57. *Id.* at 25; Parker, *supra* note 36, at D1 ("Articles about women's wrestling are rife with snide asides about mud and Jell-O.").

58. Karen Price, *NCAA Program Keeps Emerging Sports Alive*, Trib.-Rev Oct. 11, 2011 (the current list of NCAA emerging sports is equestrian, rugby, and sand volleyball, with a proposal pending for triathlon. None of these sports has anywhere near the numbers of female high school participation as wrestling). Women's wrestling is not a recognized sport by the NAIA (National Association of Intercollegiate Athletics), either. *NAIA Championship Sports*, THE NAIA ELIGIBILITY CENTER, http://www.playnaia.org/page/sports.php (last visited Jan. 8, 2013) (women's wrestling not listed).

59. Mark Brunswick, *A Touchy Issue: Should Girls Wrestle Boys?; Panel Moves to Repeal Law that Allows for Co-ed Teams*, STAR TRIB. (Minneapolis), Feb. 20, 2002, at 1B.

60. *Id.*

61. *See, e.g.*, Ellen Nakashima, *Girls Getting a New Hold on an Old Sport: Some Boys Forfeit Rather than Wrestle*, Wash. Post, Feb. 24, 1999, at A1 (identifying two states, South Dakota and Wyoming, with bans on mixed-sex wrestling, and noting as another example of rules against mixed-sex wrestling that the Lutheran High School Association of Greater Detroit requires boys to forfeit matches against girls); H.F. 2437, 2001 Leg., 82d Sess. (Minn. 2002) (Minnesota House Committee recommended

that the bill pass on Feb. 20, 2002, but there was no Senate action, and it was not enacted).

62. Stuart & Whaley, *supra* note 20, at 34.

63. Chad Garner, *Local Athletes, Coaches Debate Issue of Co-ed Competition*, SENTINEL & ENTERPRISE (Fitchberg, MA), Feb. 26, 2011 (alteration in original).

64. Stuart & Whaley, *supra* note 20, at 34.

65. Ryan Young, *Wrestling for Respect, One Victory at a Time; Maroulis Excels but Still Searches for Acceptance*, WASH. POST, Feb. 16, 2006, at ME18.

66. Garner, *supra* note 66.

67. Stuart & Whaley, *supra* note 20, at 34 (statement of one woman training with USOTC: "It's difficult . . . the way we have to be dependent on the guys to train with us, because there are so few women in my weight class. In some ways it's hard because women seem to fight different than men."). *See also* Raker, *supra* note 34 (interviewing a Pennsylvania wrestler recently tapped for Olympic training who described her high school wrestling experience saying that her only wins against boys came by forfeit).

68. Longman, *supra* note 3, at D1 (citing U.S. Girls Wrestling Association); E-mail from Kent Bailo, founder and CEO of U.S. Girls' Wrestling Assoc., to author (Apr. 5, 2012) (on file with author).

69. Longman, *supra* note 3, at D1 (The other two were from Alaska, also winning their title matches against male opponents).

DISCUSSION QUESTIONS FOR CHAPTER 3

1. How do notions of sex and gender take shape within a cultural context?

2. How are dominant notions of masculinity and femininity in the U.S. racialized? How does this intersection help maintain both sexism and racism?

3. How do transgender identities disrupt fixed notions of sex and gender?

4. How does gender ranking reinforce sexism?

5. How is gender reinforced by patterns of interaction in society?

SUGGESTIONS FOR FURTHER READING

Benshoff, Harry M., and Sean Griffin. *America on Film: Representing Race, Class, Gender, and Sexuality at the Movies,* Second Edition. Hoboken, NJ: Wiley-Blackwell, 2009.

Boylan, Jennifer Finney. *She's Not There: A Life in Two Genders.* New York: Broadway, 2003.

Butler, Judith. *Undoing Gender.* New York: Routledge, 2004.

Fausto-Sterling, Anne. *Sexing the Body: Gender Politics and the Construction of Sexuality.* New York: Basic Books, 2000.

Feinberg, Leslie. *Transgender Warriors.* Boston: Beacon, 1996.

Green, Eileen. *Virtual Gender: Technology, Consumption and Identity.* London: Taylor & Francis, 2007.

Halberstam, Jack. *Gaga Feminism: Sex, Gender, and the End of Normal.* Boston: Beacon Press, 2012.

Howey, Noelle. *Dress Codes: Of Three Girlhoods—My Mother's, My Father's, and Mine.* New York: St. Martin's Press, 2002.

Kane, Emily W. *The Gender Trap: Parents and the Pitfalls of Raising Boys and Girls.* New York: NYU Press, 2012.

Roughgarden, Joan. *Evolution's Rainbow: Diversity, Gender, and Sexuality in Nature and People.* Berkeley: University of California Press, 2004.

CHAPTER 4

Inscribing Gender on the Body

Human bodies illustrate the most obvious expressions of gender. Indeed, this inscription of gender onto bodies is the key to gender identities as we recognize bodies as "masculine" or "feminine." Bodies that are not easily and immediately recognizable as fitting within this binary often cause anxiety and consternation when we cannot place them neatly into either masculine/male or feminine/female boxes. This binary aspect of bodies as "either this or that" is so thoroughly taken for granted that we rarely question these binary aspects. If you have ever attended a drag show or parade where bodies act outside gender expectations, you might have noted these exaggerated gender performances. They are especially instructional because drag performances accentuate traditional gendered bodies through the clothes people wear and the ways they walk and talk. They help illustrate how gender is normalized and usually experienced as "natural." When gender is performed in these ways, it can be entertaining, in part because it emphasizes this "taken-for-grantedness" of most individuals' experiences of gender. As emphasized in the previous chapter, there is nothing "natural" about gender at all. Instead it is constructed and repeated over and again every minute of the day. However, as also explained in Chapter 3, "performativity" must not be reduced to a voluntary act or something that is totally willful. Rather, performativity is constrained by social norms.

Actions performed by our bodies provide a sense of agency (the "me" that separates me from "you") and are shaped by social forces that give them meaning. Gender performances are not only what we "do"; they are also who we "are" or "become." This implies that we are what we do, and what we do is shaped by cultural ideas, social practices, and structured institutions that give those everyday actions meaning. In addition, remember that all bodies are racialized. "White" is a racialized concept too. The mythical norm serves to assume race is just about people of color, but white is a diverse category also constructed through history, culture, and politics. In terms of bodies, however, the stereotype of the hypersexualized black male body, for example, has been used to control communities of color, just as the expectation that certain bodies are "naturally" good at sports or science and so forth has functioned to reinscribe racialized discourses on human bodies. As already mentioned, there are also discourses or regimes of truth about the aging body that regulate behaviors, just as there are many discourses in contemporary societies about ability and disability that provide meaning about the body. As discussed in Chapter 2, these include the very notions of disability or differently abled as bodily "impairment" that implies a lack or pathology

LEARNING ACTIVITY **Considering Body Size, Shape, and Movement**

Take a tour examining the public facilities of your school or campus, which may include:

Telephone booths or stalls

Drinking fountains

Bleachers

Sinks and stalls in public restrooms

Curbs, ramps, and railings

Chairs and tables

Turnstiles

Elevators and escalators

Stairs and staircases

Vending machines

Doors and doorways

Fire alarm boxes

Answer the following questions:

What assumptions about the size and shape of the users (height, weight, proportionate length of arms and legs, width of hips and shoulders, hand preference, mobility, etc.) are incorporated into the designs?

How do these design assumptions affect the ability of you and people you know to use the facilities satisfactorily?

How would they affect you if you were significantly:

Wider or narrower than you are?

Shorter or taller?

Heavier or lighter?

Rounder or more angular?

More or less mobile/ambulatory?

Identify any access or usage barriers to people with physical disabilities. Answer the following questions:

Are classrooms accessible to people who can't walk up or down stairs?

Are emergency exit routes usable by people with limited mobility?

Are amplification devices or sign language interpreters available for people with hearing impairments?

Are telephones and fire alarms low enough to be reached by people who are seated in wheelchairs or who are below average height?

Are audiovisual aids appropriate for people with hearing or vision impairments?

Describe the experience of a person in your class or school who has a mobility, vision, speech, or hearing impairment.

Variation 1. Identify one assumption incorporated into the design of one of the facilities (drinking fountain, phone booth, etc.). Gather formal or informal data about the number of people on campus that might not be able to use the facility satisfactorily, based on the design assumption. Suggest one or two ways to make the facility more useful to those people.

Variation 2. Choose one of the access or usage barriers you have identified and suggest a way to remove the barrier. Research the cost involved. Identify one or two ways of funding the access strategy you have suggested.

Source: Janet Lockhart and Susan M. Shaw, *Writing for Change: Raising Awareness of Difference, Power, and Discrimination, www.teachingtolerance.org.*

rather than a different set of attributes. "Impaired" only has meaning against something that is defined as "normal." In this way bodies, and the ways bodies are interpreted, are contextualized in cultural meanings informed by our ideas about gender and other identities. Many of these cultural ideas, for example, come from contemporary media, the focus of the next chapter. Indeed, bodies are foundational for many issues discussed in this book: sexuality, reproductive justice, health, violence, to name just a few.

In this chapter we focus on this social construction of the body and go on to explore "beauty": one of the most powerful discourses associated with gendered bodies that regulates our lives, affecting what we do and how we think. Everyone knows what a beautiful person, and especially a beautiful woman, looks like, even though this notion is constantly in flux and varies across time and culture. We close the chapter with a discussion of eating disorders and methods for negotiating "beauty" ideals.

THE SOCIAL CONSTRUCTION OF THE BODY

A social constructivist approach to understanding the body recognizes attributes as arising out of cultures in which the body is given meaning. For example, in some communities large-bodied women are considered more beautiful than slim women, illustrating that there is no fixed idea of "beauty." Contrary to this is the concept of *biological determinism* where a person's biology or genetic makeup, rather than culture or society, determines her/his destiny. This approach sees people in terms of their reproductive and biological bodies and allows men to avoid the constraints of biological determinism through a construction of the male body as less grounded in, and able to transcend, nature (as evident in mythology, art, and philosophy). This association of women with the body, earth, nature, and the domestic is almost universal and represents one of the most basic ways that bodies are gendered. Males, because of historical and mythological associations with the spirit and sky, have been associated with culture and the mind rather than the body, and with abstract reason rather than with earthly mundane matters.

In addition, many societies have not only incorporated a distinction between nature and culture, but often a domination of culture and mind over nature and body. In particular, imperialist notions of "progress" have involved the taming and conquering of nature in favor of "civilization." As a result, the female/nature side of this dichotomy is valued less and often denigrated and/or controlled.

A prime example of this association and denigration of women with the body is the way menstruation has often been seen as smelly, taboo, and distasteful. Menstruation has often been regarded negatively and described with a multitude of derogatory euphemisms like "the curse" and "on the rag," and girls are still taught to conceal menstrual practices from others (and men in particular). As Gloria Steinem suggests in the classic essay "If Men Could Menstruate," the experience would be something entirely different if men menstruated. Advertisements abound in magazines and on television about tampons, pads, douches, feminine hygiene sprays, and yeast infection medicines that give the message that women's bodies are constantly in need of hygienic attention. Notice we tend not to get ads for jock itch during prime-time television like we do ads for feminine "ailments." In this way, there is a strange, very public aspect to feminine bodily processes at the same time that they are coded as very private. This is an example of the discourses or regimes of truth that shape bodies in contemporary culture.

In this way, although the body is an incredibly sophisticated jumble of physiological events, our understanding of the body cannot exist outside of the society that gives it meaning. Take for example the ways we recognize "the heart," not just as a physiological organ, but also as symbolic of cultural meaning: in this case love and care. "Head" is sometimes opposed to "heart." In this way, even though bodies are biophysical entities, what our bodies mean and how they are experienced is intimately connected to the meanings and practices of the society in which we reside. And, while meanings about the body are always contextualized in local communities, ideas about bodies are transported around the globe and their commercialization supports imperialism and global capitalism alongside sexism and misogyny.

The favoring of certain looks (including size, shape, and color, as well as certain clothes or fashion) associated with the global north are examples of how imperialism and globalization frame meanings about the body, as well as shape bodies in a more literal sense. As we emphasize in this chapter and others in the book, this is about power and control over women through practices associated with the body. An example is female genital cutting (FGC), practiced in some parts of North Africa and the Middle East, as well as other regions, that ensures a girl's marriageability. The cutting varies from ritually "nicking" the clitoris to full infibulation in which external genitalia are removed and the labia stitched together. Advocates against FGC argue its detrimental health consequences and decry the inability of girls to give consent. It is important for feminists of the global north to understand the cultural and economic contexts in which FGC occurs. In addition, we must recognize the surgical modifications of genitalia that occur in the global north, such as labia remodeling and vaginoplasty (discussed later in this chapter), as well as the surgical assignment of "sex" that may occur with intersex children.

Bodies are thus cultural artifacts; culture becomes embodied and is literally inscribed or represented through the body. Gender and other identity performances are scripted, for example, by the ways more women (and particularly white women) want to shrink their bodies compared to men, who are more likely to want bigger bodies, especially in terms of height and muscle mass. The fact that many more women than men would willingly want to be characterized as "petite" is an example of gender norms associated with the body. Indeed, scholars suggest that women's decisions for cosmetic surgery reflect their desire to attain normative standards of "beauty," whereas men are more likely to want cosmetic changes in order to be more competitive in the marketplace. Again, remember that these discussions of "men" and "women" assume intersection with other identities. They also assume a symmetry between identification as a man or woman and a masculine or feminine body, respectively. Transgender individuals identify with identities that may not match the bodily assignment given at birth or they may portray an androgynous mixture in the same body. Trans bodies illustrate the ways bodies may subvert taken-for-granted social norms and practices. This is illustrated in the reading by Dan Frosch, "Bodies and Bathrooms," about a 6-year-old who identifies as a girl, yet was prevented from using the girls' bathroom. Her case tested Colorado's anti-discrimination law, which expanded protections for transgender individuals in 2008.

An essential aspect of the gendering of bodies is *objectification* (seeing the body as an object and separate from its context) as supported by media and entertainment industries as well as by fashion. Both female- and male-identified bodies are objectified, although the context for objectification of female-identified bodies is different. This means that the turning of women into objects is contextualized in what (in her reading in Chapter 6) Andrea Smith calls a racist hetero-patriarchy. In other words, there is broad institutional support for the objectification of multifaceted femininities in our culture. This does not mean that men cannot be objectified, but rather that the contexts for, and thus the consequences of, such objectification are different. You might also note that this is a key point in the reading by Kimberly Springer on "Queering Black Female Heterosexuality," also in Chapter 6. She writes: "Know that our bodies are our own—our bodies do not belong to the church, the state, our parents, our lovers, our husbands, and certainly not Black Entertainment Television (BET)."

In this way, the assertion "our bodies are our own" reminds us that alongside objectification is the opportunity for the body as a site of identity and self-expression. When Muslim women, for example, choose to wear the *hijab* or headscarf, they are responding to personal desires that may include identity and self-reliance, piety, and safety. When transwomen don feminine attire, they are presenting themselves to the world as women: This is their identity and their sense of agency. This concept of agency is discussed by Minh-Ha T. Pham in the reading, "If the Clothes Fit: A Feminist Take on Fashion." She claims the politically conscious understanding of fashion as a source of empowerment, and also cites feminist fashion blogs as ways to celebrate nonnormatively raced, gendered, sexed, and sized bodies.

As our lives become more complex and we have less power over the way we live them, we are encouraged to focus more on the body as something we *can* control and as something we can use to express our identity. As a result, the body becomes something to be fashioned and controlled; at the same time, this control over body—and the ability to shape, clothe, and express it—becomes synonymous with personal freedom. We might question whether the ability to change and adorn the body in new ways is really "freedom," as is political or economic freedom. Indeed, scholars discussing backlash (organized resistance) have emphasized that the contemporary preoccupation with the body illustrates the ways society encourages us (members of marginalized groups in particular) to focus on the body and its management as a "distraction" from real economic and political concerns.

ACTIVIST PROFILE   **Maggie Kuhn**

Most people are getting ready to retire at 65. Maggie Kuhn began the most important work of her life at that age. In 1970 Kuhn was forced to retire from her career with the Presbyterian Church. In August of that year, she convened a group of five friends, all of whom were retiring, to talk about the problems faced by retirees—loss of income, loss of social role, pension rights, age discrimination. Finding new freedom and strength in their voices, they also concerned themselves with other social issues, such as the Vietnam War.

The group gathered in Philadelphia with college students opposed to the war at the Consultation of Older and Younger Adults for Social Change. A year later, more than 100 people joined the Consultation. As this new group began to meet, a New York television producer nicknamed the group the Gray Panthers, and the name stuck.

In 1972 Kuhn was asked at the last minute to fill in for someone unable to speak during the 181st General Assembly of the United Presbyterian Church. Her stirring speech launched the Gray Panthers into national prominence, and calls began to flood the organization's headquarters. Increased media attention came as the Gray Panthers became activists. They co-sponsored the Black House Conference on Aging to call attention to the lack of African Americans at the first White House Conference on Aging, and they performed street theater at the American Medical Association's 1974 conference, calling for health care as a human right. At the core of Panther activities was the belief that older people should seize control of their lives and actively campaign for causes in which they believe.

The Gray Panthers have been instrumental in bringing about nursing home reform, ending forced retirement provisions, and combating fraud against the elderly in health care. Kuhn, who was active with the Panthers until her death at age 89, offered this advice to other activists: "Leave safety behind. Put your body on the line. Stand before the people you fear and speak your mind—even if your voice shakes. When you least expect it, someone may actually listen to what you have to say. Well-aimed slingshots can topple giants."

Body Art

Across practically all times and cultures, humans have practiced various forms of body modification for such differing reasons as warding off or invoking spirits, attracting sexual partners, indicating social or marital status, identifying with a particular age or gender group, and marking a rite of passage (Lemonick et al.). People all over the world have pierced, painted, tattooed, reshaped, and adorned their bodies, turning the body itself into an artistic canvas.

The earliest records of tattoos were found in Egypt around the time of the building of the pyramids. Later, the practice was adopted in Crete, Greece, Persia, Arabia, and China. The English word *tattoo* comes from the Polynesian *tatau*, a practice observed by James Cook when he visited Tahiti on his first voyage around the world. In the Marquesas, Cook noted that the men had their entire bodies tattooed, but women tattooed only their hands, lips, shoulders, ankles, and the area behind the ears.

Today, many of the Maori men of New Zealand are returning to the practice of wearing the elaborate tattoos of their ancestors. In Morocco, henna designs on the hands and feet are an integral part of significant celebrations, such as weddings and religious holidays. In Ethiopia, Hamar men earn raised scars made by cutting with a razor and then rubbing ash into the wounds for killing a dangerous animal or enemy. Surma girls have their earlobes stretched by clay plates and paint their faces during courtship season.

As you may have noted, body art is a gendered practice. Tattooing, piercing, painting, and reshaping the body also serve the purpose of marking gender. What are common body modification practices in the United States? How do these practices express and reinforce gender?

Sources: Monica Desai, "Body Art: A History," *Student BMJ* 10 (2002):196–97. Michael Lemonick et al., "Body Art," *Time South Pacific* (12/13/99), 66–68. Pravina Shukla, "The Human Canvas," *Natural History* 108 (1999): 80.

LEARNING ACTIVITY **On the Rag**

Collect a wide variety of women's magazines such as *Cosmopolitan, Glamour, Vogue, Elle,* and so on. Identify advertisements for "feminine hygiene products"—tampons, pads, douches, feminine hygiene sprays, yeast infection medicines. What do the visual images in the ads suggest? What do the words tell readers? What messages do these advertisements send about women's bodies? Now collect a variety of men's magazines such as *GQ, Maxim, Men's Journal,* and so on. Identify advertisements for "masculine hygiene products." What do you find? What does the difference imply about women's bodies in contrast to men's bodies? How does this implication reinforce structures of gender subordination?

Tattoos and piercing among young women are examples of a trend toward self-expression in the context of mass-market consumerism. Having a tattoo or multiple tattoos—traditionally a masculine or an outlaw, rebellious act—is a form of self-expression for many. Similarly, multiple piercing of many body parts, including erogenous and sexually-charged areas of the body, can be seen as a form of rebellion against the constraints of gender and sexuality. This expression is certainly less rebellious from society's point of view than activities for real social and political justice, especially when trends involve the purchase of products and services that support the capitalist economy and make someone rich. Indeed, both tattooing and piercing can also be interpreted as reactionary trends and as examples of the many ways women are encouraged to mutilate and change parts of their bodies. Note that these "rebellious" behaviors have now been appropriated as relatively ordinary fashion practices. You can buy nose and belly-button rings, for example, that clip on without ever having to pierce anything, just as you can buy temporary tattoos. In fact, the self-consciousness involved in the parody of the real thing is now a form of self-expression all its own. This issue of body image and its consequences for women's lives is a central issue for third wave feminism, mobilizing many young women and men.

THE "BEAUTY" IDEAL

In contemporary U.S. society we are surrounded by images of "beautiful," thin (although fit, sculpted, and large breasted), young, abled, smiling women. Most of these bodies are white, and when women of color are depicted, they tend to show models with more typically white features or hair. Obviously, real women come in all shapes and sizes. Our diversity is part of our beauty! Nonetheless, these images set standards for appearance and "beauty" that are internalized—standards that affect how we feel about our own bodies. Such internalization is mediated though multifaceted identities arising out of diverse community memberships. Although different communities have different standards and expectations associated with how bodies should look, the permanence of some standard means that most of us grow up disliking our bodies or some parts of them. Many of us are especially troubled by parts of our bodies perceived as larger than societal ideals or, in the case of breasts and perhaps bottoms, we might be troubled because these parts are not big enough.

As men are increasingly tapped as a market for beauty and body management products, they are also increasingly confronted with idealized images. Anxiety over the presence of back hair or baldness is a case in point, as is the anxiety among some men that they are not muscled enough. Penis size, of course, while a source of amusement in popular culture, is a sensitive issue that is supported by extensive industries catering to penis enlargements as advertised on TV and in your email inbox. In addition, the *metrosexual* market is one marketing niche for men's consumption. Metrosexual is derived from "metropolitan" and "heterosexual" and alludes to men who are meticulous about grooming and have disposable income to spend on clothes and other products. Again all these standards of how bodies should look are mediated through communities that interpret for people who identify as men what a masculine body should look like. However, because women's worth is more tied to bodily appearances than men's worth, portrayals of female "beauty" are more significant in women's lives. This is called the *double standard* associated with "beauty" or normative bodily standards. What this means is that despite the increasing focus on male bodies in society and popular culture, women are particularly vulnerable to the cultural preoccupation with, and the measuring of their worth against, the body. Physical appearance is more important in terms of the way women are perceived and treated. This is especially true in terms of the aging body; there is a much stronger mandate for women than for men to keep their bodies looking young. In U.S. society men's beer bellies, for example, provoke less aversion than women's tummy fat (either by traditional cultural definitions or by individuals themselves). Again, while we attempt to trouble these binary categories of "women" and "men" with a discussion of gender and the ways gender is inscribed onto bodies, the reality that most people in the world identify as women and as men, and experience the consequences of that identification in terms of privilege and limitations or discriminations, means that these categories are experienced as relatively fixed.

In this section we discuss four points associated with the "beauty" ideal: (1) the changeable, fluid notion of beauty; (2) the ways beauty ideals illustrate power in society; (3) the ways beauty standards are enforced in complex ways; and (4) the relationship between contemporary beauty standards and consumerism and the growth of global capitalist expansion.

First, contemporary images of female beauty are changeable. What is considered beautiful in one society is different from standards in others: Practices in one society might ostracize you—or might certainly prevent your getting a date—in another. Some societies encourage the insertion of objects into earlobes or jawline or other mechanics to increase neck length or head shape. Others consider large women especially attractive and see their fat as evidence of prosperity; again, in most contemporary societies of the global north, thin is closer to standards of ideal beauty, although there are differences within specific communities within the United States. In other words, what is considered beautiful is culturally produced and changes across different cultures. In addition, as already discussed, standards of body appearance are exported along with fashion and other makeup products. A poignant example of this is the trend in limb-lengthening surgeries where bones are broken and then stretched. In some cultures the painful and expensive procedure is seen as an investment in the future, especially for men. Minimum heights, for example, are often quoted in personal and job advertisements in China, and to join the foreign service men are required to be at least 5' 7". Although this controversial surgery was banned in China in 2006, surgeries are still performed in many countries, including the United States. Such procedures reinscribe certain ideals of beauty and body standards.

What is considered "beautiful" also varies across historical periods. Most adult women can clearly see these changes in feminine "beauty" even within their own lifetimes. Fashion trends are particularly implicated in these practices. Minh-Ha Pham writes about this in "If the Clothes Fit." She explains how fashion industries shape how we're perceived by others, especially in terms of gender, class, race, and sexual identity across different time periods. "That most ordinary and intimate of acts, getting dressed, has very real political and economic consequences," writes Pham.

For example, a focus on standards of "Western" female beauty over time reveals that in the nineteenth century white, privileged women were encouraged to adopt a delicate, thin, and fragile appearance and wear bone-crushing (literally) corsets that not only gave them the hourglass figure but also cramped and ruptured vital organs. Such practices made women faint, appear frail, delicate, dependent, and passive—responses to notions of middle-class femininity. Victorian furniture styles accommodated this ideal with special swooning chairs. Standards for weight and body shape changed again in the early twentieth century when a sleek, boyish look was adopted by the flappers of the 1920s. Women bound their breasts to hide their curves. Although more curvaceous and slightly heavier bodies were encouraged through the next decades, body maintenance came to dominate many women's lives. Fueled by the fashion industry, the 1960s gave us a return to a more emaciated, long-legged look, but with very short skirts and long hair. At the beginning of

HISTORICAL MOMENT **The Disability Rights Movement**

Much like the other civil rights movements of the late twentieth century, the disability rights movement sought to provide equal access and equal opportunity for people living with disabilities. This movement had its roots in earlier actions directed toward improving the lives of people with disabilities. In 1817, the American School of the Deaf in Hartford, Connecticut, opened as the first educational institution to use sign language. The New England Asylum for the Blind opened in 1829, and Braille was introduced in 1832. In 1911, the U.S. government approved compensation for disabled workers and in 1946 passed the Hill-Burton act that provided assistance for rehabilitation. Social Security Disability insurance was created in 1950.

Unfortunately, the progression of disability rights was not smooth. In the 1880s, eugenics, a pseudo-science with the goal of "improving" the genetic composition of humanity discouraged reproduction by people considered "undesirable," including people with disabilities (as well as people of color, immigrants, and the poor). Many disabled people underwent forced sterilization as a result, and in 1927 the U.S. Supreme Court upheld the constitutionality of forced sterilization. By the 1970s, tens of thousands of people with disabilities had been sterilized without their consent.

Throughout the twentieth century, disability rights advocates continued to organize. The Blinded Veterans Association, the Cerebral Palsy Society of New York City (which became the United Cerebral Palsy Associations), the National Mental Health Foundation, Paralyzed Veterans of America, the National Wheelchair Basketball Association, Little People of America, the National Association of the Physically Handicapped, and the American Council of the Blind are just a few of the organizations founded in the 1940s through 1960s. In 1963 President John F. Kennedy called for the de-institutionalization of the mentally ill and increased community services for them.

More radical disability rights groups formed in the 1970s and pushed for greater legislation and accommodation. In 1972, the first independent living center opened and sparked the independent living movement. In 1973, Congress passed the Rehabilitation Act that for the first time addressed discrimination against people with disabilities, and the litigation coming from the act gave rise to concepts such as "reasonable modification," "reasonable accommodation," and "undue burden." In 1990, the most comprehensive legislation about disabilities became law—the Americans with Disabilities Act. The act mandates accessibility and reasonable accommodations in government and public areas.

While such legislation has improved conditions for people with disabilities, disability rights activists continue to advocate for access and change. Cultural groups such as theater for the deaf and sports groups such as the Paralympics provide opportunities for people with disabilities to participate in social activities, and these events also function as consciousness-raisers about disabilities. Universal access to buildings continues to be an issue, even on college campuses, as many old buildings do not provide easy access for people in wheelchairs or blind people who need Braille signage. Individuals with mental disabilities still face stigma, and, as the population ages, the need for greater attention to disabilities in the elderly grows.

The successes of the disability rights movement are many, but, as in other civil rights movement, work remains to be done. For more information, visit the website of the National Disability Rights Network at *ndrn.org*.

this new century, we see a more eclectic look and a focus on health and fitness, but norms associated with ideal female beauty still construct the thin, large-breasted, white (tanned, but not too brown) body as the most beautiful. Note the body type that has a slender, thin frame with large breasts is quite rare and represents a very small minority of women in the United States. Most large-breasted women also have larger hips and waist. Nonetheless the slender, large-breasted body type is still the standard of beauty to which most women aspire. This is reflected in the increasing numbers of cosmetic surgeries involving breast augmentation among fashion models, celebrities, and the general population, as already mentioned.

A *second* point concerning beauty ideals is that such ideals reflect various relations of power in society. Culture is constructed in complex ways, and groups with more power and influence tend to set the trends, create the options, and enforce the standards. As Janna Fikkan and Esther Rothblum suggest in the reading "Is Fat a Feminist Issue?: Exploring the Gendered Nature of Weight Bias," sizeism and the discrimination against fat people remain one of the final socially acceptable forms of discrimination." They review the literature on weight-based stigma across numerous domains that include education, employment, health, and romantic settings, and explain how fat women fare worse than thinner women and worse than men, whether men are fat or thin. As explained in Chapter 2, these deleterious outcomes as a result of weight bias have a significant impact on health, quality of life, and socioeconomic outcomes.

In U.S. culture, beauty standards are very much connected to the production and consumption of various products, and beauty product and fashion industries are multi-billion-dollar enterprises. As the reading excerpted from Joan Jacobs Brumberg's *The Body Project* explains, garment industries in the United States helped sexualize women's breasts through their development of the bra. Corporate powers, advertising, and the fashion, cosmetics, and entertainment industries all help create standards for us and reinforce gender relations. Even the "natural look" is sold to us as something to be tried on, when obviously the real natural look is devoid of marketing illusions in the first place. Most of these industries are controlled by white males or by other individuals who have accepted what many scholars call ruling-class politics. The main point is that most of us get offered beauty and fashion options constructed by other people. Although we have choices and can reject them, lots of resources are involved in encouraging us to adopt the standards created by various industries.

In this way, beauty ideals reflect white, abled, and middle-class standards. Lisa Miya-Jervis understands the racial politics of appearance and explains in "Hold That Nose" why she avoided surgery to change the shape of her nose. Such standards of beauty can humiliate fat or non-white women as well as the poor, the aged, and the disabled. These norms help enforce racism, classism, ableism, ageism, and fat oppression, as well as sexism generally. Many communities, however, have alternative notions of feminine beauty and actively resist such normalizing standards of Anglo culture. Fikkan and Rothblum, for example, in the reading "Is Fat a Feminist Issue?" review literature that suggests Latinas and African American women are less likely to rely on others' approval, less likely to idealize (white, thin) cultural norms about "beauty," and less likely to experience body dissatisfaction than white women. However, the authors caution against an "overly optimistic" reading. They suggest in part that other sources of discrimination might overshadow those attributable to body size. Still, this "resilience" to traditional beauty norms seems to occur as women of color experience a decreased self-relevance associated with these norms. In other words, Latinas and African American women are less likely to indulge in social comparisons with typical (white, thin) media images precisely because they do not see themselves in such images. However, when they do indulge in comparisons, they are just as susceptible as white women to body dissatisfaction. Dara N. Greenwood and Sonya Dal Cin explore this phenomenon in the reading "Ethnicity and Body Consciousness." They surveyed young African Americans' and white women's social comparisons with their favorite media personae and found no ethnic differences. All women indulged in wishful identification and body surveillance when comparing themselves to their favorite media personae.

Physically challenged individuals are also claiming the right to redefine beauty and the body. Aimee Mullins, a spokeswoman for high-tech prosthetics and an activist for disability rights, illustrates this goal in the reading "Prosthetic Power." Although she was born without fibular bones and both her legs were amputated when she was an infant, she learned to use prosthetics and competed as a champion sprinter in college. She writes that a prosthetic limb "doesn't represent the need to replace loss anymore. It can stand as a symbol that wearers have the power to create whatever it is that they want to create in that space. So people once considered disabled can now become the architects of their own identities and indeed continue to change those identities by designing their bodies from a place of empowerment." It is also important to point out that Mullins is a fashion model and actress and very closely fits the normative standard of feminine beauty in the global north. These characteristics do not detract from her important message, but they are important features in terms of understanding how her message is received.

The *third* point concerning beauty practices is that standards are enforced in complex ways. Of course, "enforcement" does not mean, as feminist scholar Sandra Bartky has said, that someone marches you off to electrolysis at gunpoint. Instead, we adopt various standards and integrate them as "choices" we make for ourselves. Self-objectification, seeing ourselves through others' eyes, impairs women's body image. At the same time that young girls are sexualized and objectified by contemporary media, they also learn that their body is a project that must be altered before they can attract others. It is estimated that the average woman is exposed to hundreds of advertisements a day, in part a result of the Internet and especially advertising on social networking sites. At the same time that girls and women "police" themselves, they also learn to regulate one another in a general sense. The surveillance of women by other women around body issues (such as imposing standards and sanctions like negative talk, withdrawing friendship, or exclusion from a group or party) is an example of horizontal hostility (see Chapter 2). Norms (cultural expectations) of female beauty are produced by all forms of contemporary media and by a wide array of products. For example, Victoria's Secret, a lingerie company, sells more than underwear. Models are displayed in soft-porn poses and the company's advertisements shape ideas about gender, sexuality, and the body. Other companies have emphasized body acceptance, paralleling a surge in the acceptance of "plus size" models. It is interesting to note that these models, although called "plus size," more closely mirror average U.S. women's bodies than do traditional fashion models.

Beauty norms are internalized, and we receive various positive and negative responses for complying with or resisting them. This is especially true when it comes to hair. Hair plays significant roles in women's intimate relationships, as the reading "What We Do for Love" by Rose Weitz suggests. It is interesting to think about these everyday behaviors that maintain the body: the seemingly trivial routines, rules, and practices. Some scholars call these *disciplinary body practices*. They are "practices" because they involve taken-for-granted routinized behaviors such as shaving legs, applying makeup, or curling/straightening/coloring hair; and they are "disciplinary" because they involve social control in the sense that we spend time, money, and effort, and imbue meaning in these practices that regulate our lives. Again, disciplinary beauty practices are connected to the production and consumption of various products. Of particular concern is the connection between practices associated with weight control and smoking. A recent study from the National Institutes of Health reported that weight concerns and a "drive for thinness" among both black and white girls at ages 11 to 12 years were the most important factors leading to subsequent daily smoking.

You can probably think of many disciplinary beauty practices in which you or your friends take part. Men have their practices too, although generally these tend to be simpler and involve a narrower range of (usually less-expensive) products. Alongside fashion and various forms of cosmetics and body sculpting, women are more likely to get face-lifts, eye tucks, rhinoplasties (nose reshaping), collagen injections to plump up lips, Botox injections, liposuction, tummy tucks, stomach bands and stapling, and, of course, breast augmentation (implants) as well as breast reductions. The American Society of Plastic Surgeons reports twice as many women electing to have breast augmentation than a decade ago, even though the U.S. FDA (Food and Drug Administration) has been concerned about the safety of both silicone-gel-filled and saline-filled breast implants and banned the widespread use of silicone-gel-filled implants some years ago. Known risks involve leakage and rupture, loss of sensation in the nipples, permanent scarring, problems with breast-feeding, potential interference with mammography that may delay cancer diagnoses, and fibrositis, or pain and stiffness of muscles, ligaments, and tendons.

Breast implants require ongoing maintenance and often need periodic operations to replace or remove the devices. In 2006 the FDA again approved the marketing of silicone-gel-filled implants by two companies for breast reconstruction in women of all ages and breast augmentation in women aged 22 years and older. The companies are required to conduct postapproval studies of potential health risks.

Another surgery that has increased in popularity is vaginal cosmetic surgery. It includes labiaplasty (a procedure to change the shape and size of the labia minora [inner lips of the vagina] and/or labia majora [outer lips], although most often it involves making the labia minora smaller), vaginoplasty (creating, reshaping, or tightening the vagina; the latter procedure is often called "vaginal rejuvenation"), and clitoral unhooding (exposing the clitoris in an attempt to increase sexual stimulation). There is no agreement, for example, on what is the "normal" size for labia and no reliable studies on the impact of labia size on sexual functioning and sexual pleasure. The most recent data from the American Society for Aesthetic Plastic Surgery reports a 64 percent increase in vaginal cosmetic surgeries in 2012 (from 2,142 performed in 2011 to 3,521 in 2012). Although these surgeries are sometimes performed for medical reasons, their increase is related to what has been called "aesthetic" motivations. It is important to understand that the aesthetics of the pelvic area are related to norms about gender, the body, and sexuality, and especially norms created by media and contemporary pornography.

A 2013 report from the American Society for Aesthetic Plastic Surgery cites more than 10 million U.S. cosmetic procedures were performed in 2012, with breast augmentation the number one, closely followed by liposuction. In particular, the number of African American women electing cosmetic surgery has increased (with most favored procedures being rhinoplasty, liposuction, and breast reduction), reflecting the imposition of white standards of beauty as well as increases in disposable income and acceptance of cosmetic surgery among some groups in the African American community. The report shows more than $11 billion was spent in the United States in 2012 on cosmetic procedures that include surgery and other practices such as laser hair removal and skin rejuvenation. Women account for 90 percent of all individuals undergoing procedures, although rates of men electing cosmetic procedures have increased by more than 100 percent since the late 1990s. In order to understand all these trends, it is necessary to recognize the crucial role of the media. Celebrities, for example, often set trends that "ordinary" people try and emulate. It is known that Jennifer Lopez, for instance, had three cosmetic surgery procedures when she was just 15 years old that included liposuction, breast implants, and buttock fillers.

The enormous popularity of "reality" television shows like "The Biggest Loser," plus the increased number of websites encouraging young girls to change the way they look, has fueled these changes. These shows take people (especially women) out of communities, isolate them, and then transform their bodies through surgery, cosmetics, and other technologies of body management, before reintroducing them into their communities as radically transformed people (implying that their lives will now be better, more successful, happier, etc.). Such shows encourage people to pass for a younger age and to consider cosmetic surgery (especially breast implants and argumentation) as something women of all ages should seek and want. Though they are often entertaining and seductive in their voyeuristic appeal, it is important to recognize the role they play in the social construction of "beauty," the advertising of products and body-management technologies, and the social elations of power in society. In considering

In Six Chix, May 31, 2001. Reprinted with the author's permission.

these practices—from following fashion and buying clothes, accessories, and makeup to breast enhancement and all the practices in between—we need to keep in mind how much they cost, how they channel women's energies away from other (perhaps more productive) pursuits, and how they may affect the health and well-being of people and the planet.

These technologies of the body have global impact and appeal. Desire to script the body in accordance with cultural notions of attractiveness is worldwide. As discussed above, standards of "beauty" that vary across cultures are maintained by diverse practices that are both traditional to specific cultures as well as shaped by global media. Developments in Iran illustrate such practices as this country now has the world's highest number of rhinoplasties per capita (as well as a problematic number of botched surgeries). A 2013 report in the *Guardian* newspaper also cites an increased number of these surgeries among Iranian-American women.

The body and the various practices associated with maintaining the female body are probably the most salient aspects of what we understand as femininity, and they are crucial in social expressions of sexuality. Note how many bodily practices of contemporary femininity encourage women to stay small, not take up space, and stay young. Maturity in the form of body hair is unacceptable; we are encouraged to keep our bodies sleek, soft, and hairless—traits that some scholars identify with youth and powerlessness. The trend among some women to shave and remove pubic hair so that the genitalia appear prepubertal is an example of this. Such hair removal, mimicking the display of female genitalia in pornography, sends the message that the mature female body is "gross" or should be altered. It also sexualizes children's bodies.

About Body Image

WHAT DOES THE TERM *BODY IMAGE* MEAN?

Body image is defined by the following:

- How you see yourself when you look in the mirror.
- What you believe about your own appearance.
- How you feel about your body, including your height, weight, and shape.
- How you feel in your body, not just about your body.

WHAT DOES IT MEAN TO HAVE A HEALTHY BODY IMAGE?

Someone with a healthy body image has a clear perception of their body; understands that someone's physical appearance says very little about their value as a person; refuses to spend unreasonable amounts of time worrying about food, weight, and calories; and is comfortable and confident in their own skin.

IF SOMEONE HAS AN UNHEALTHY BODY IMAGE, DOES IT MEAN THAT THEY HAVE AN EATING DISORDER?

No. Many people feel poorly about their bodies from time to time, but it does not mean that they necessarily have an eating disorder. It is important to recognize that it is normal to struggle with how we feel about our bodies. It is also important to recognize the signs and symptoms someone might display if they have an eating disorder. For more information about eating disorders and how to tell if you or a friend might suffer from one, go to *http://www1.villanova.edu/villanova/ studentlife/counselingcenter/infosheets/eating_disorders.html.*

WHAT ARE THE MAJOR INFLUENCES ON HOW SOMEONE VIEWS THEIR BODY?

While there are endless pressures that influence the way we feel about our bodies, there are several major influences that help to shape a person's sense of themselves and their bodies.

They are:

- Peers.
- Media—just take a look at the shows that pervade television channels today . . . "America's Top Model" and "Make Me a Supermodel," that focus solely on someone's appearance.
- Family.
- Culture—Check out a great website like adiosbarbie.com to investigate how our culture contributes greatly to how we feel about ourselves and our bodies.

HOW CAN I MAKE MYSELF FEEL BETTER IF I'M HAVING A BAD BODY IMAGE DAY?

- Engage in physical activity—play tennis, go for a jog, dance around in your room to your favorite song.

- You're so lucky to have a healthy, strong functional body—wear some of your favorite clothes; wear clothes that you feel comfortable in and make you happy.
- Treat your body—paint your toenails, get a massage, or simply sit down and put your feet up; your body works hard for you each day and sometimes you forget to appreciate it.
- Mentally list at least three qualities and talents about which you are proud.
- Think of the reasons you like your friends—they probably don't have anything to do with their appearance, and neither are the reasons that your friends like you.
- Make plans with a friend that you have been meaning to catch up with to go for a walk or a cup of coffee.
- Take the step to tackle a long-term project—you've been putting it off . . . whether it's cleaning your room or signing up for a pottery class, there is no better time than right now.
- Think of your favorite body part and focus on why you like it.
- Take a few moments for deep breathing and relaxation—you can do this sitting waiting for class to start or on a bench outside; inhale deeply through your nose for a count of five, filling your lungs with cool air and positive energy, and then exhale slowly through your mouth.
- When you exercise, think of your bones and muscles getting stronger—think of this and your blood circulating throughout your body rather than focusing on calories and weight loss.
- At meals, eat healthy colorful foods—and, think of energy, vitamins, and nourishment you are fueling your body with.

BODY IMAGE SELF-EVALUATION QUIZ

Take this quiz to help measure how comfortable you are with your body and how accepting you are of yourself.

True or False	I can easily name my favorite body part (other than my hair or eyes).
True or False	I can look at myself in the mirror & see an attractive person looking back.
True or False	I am not preoccupied with when I can and cannot eat.
True or False	I don't need to count calories or fat grams to feel that I am eating healthfully.
True or False	I don't exercise to change my body shape, only to be healthy and happy.
True or False	I never smoke or use drugs to curb my appetite.
True or False	I feel comfortable eating around other people—male or female.
True or False	I don't harm my body when dealing with stress.
True or False	I don't compare the way I look to the way my friends look.
True or False	I don't think I am much bigger or smaller than my friends tell me I am.
True or False	I am comfortable being naked when alone.
True or False	I am comfortable being naked with my partner—even with the lights on.
True or False	I do not feel that I need a sexual partner in order to feel attractive.

The more questions you answered TRUE, the more likely you are to have a positive perception of your body. Keep retaking this quiz over time to gauge your changing body image. Hopefully, the change will be positive.

Source: *http://www1.villanova.edu/villanova/studentlife/health/promotion/goto/resources/bodyimage.html*

The *fourth* and final point regarding the "beauty" ideal is that while beauty standards and practices shape our bodies and lives, it is a huge aspect of consumerism and global capitalism that supports imperialist cultural practices worldwide. Although enormous profits accrue to the fashion, cosmetics, beauty, and entertainment industries yearly, they not only sell products, but they also sell ideas and values and transform communities. The underlying message for all of us, however, is that we are not good enough the way we are but need certain products to improve our looks and relationships. This does not help the development of positive self-esteem. We are bombarded with such messages to buy products to fix these kind of "flaws." As discussed in Chapter 5, advertising messages teach unattainable and unrealistic notions of body perfection that leave us thinking we are never quite good enough. Images present flawless young bodies that give the illusion of absolute perfection. In reality these images tend to be airbrushed and computer enhanced or completely computer generated. These digital representations integrate all the "positive" features associated with contemporary North American "beauty" in one image. Such images of perfect bodies are fabricated by a male-dominated culture and are reinforced by multi-billion-dollar industries organized around corporate profit making.

One of these industries concerns weight loss. Millions of dollars are spent every year by people who seek to cram their bodies into smaller sizes. Of course, many individuals want to make their bodies smaller out of a concern for better health and mobility, and the weight and exercise industries help them attain these goals. But we often do not recognize that you can be both fit and fat. Instead we fail to acknowledge the ways we have been taught to both despise fat and participate in consumerism out of a desire to more closely fit certain cultural standards. Again, there is a double standard here whereby fat women have a harder time than fat men in our culture. This is not to say that fat men have an easy time; certainly, as already mentioned, prejudice against large-size people of all genders is one of the last bulwarks of oppression in U.S. society. Many people have no qualms about blatantly expressing their dislike and disgust for fat people even when they might keep sexist or racist attitudes hidden. However, fat women have an especially difficult time because of the interaction between sexism and fat phobia.

LEARNING ACTIVITY   **Feminism and Cosmetic Surgery**

In recent years, technology has made cosmetic surgery more successful and more accessible for a large number of American women. Women are having nearly every body part resized and reconstructed. Televisions shows such as *The Swan, Extreme Makeover,* and *Nip/Tuck* have popularized the notion of creating a new self through surgery. Beyond nose and breast jobs, however, women are now also having all sorts of plastic surgery to have their labia reduced or their hymen "repaired." Put the word *labiaplasty* or *vaginoplasty* in your Web search engine. Visit the sites of some of the doctors who offer these forms of plastic surgery. What are these surgeries? Why do these sites suggest women might want these surgeries? Why do you think so many women are choosing these surgeries? Read Cressida J. Heyes and Meredith Jones' *Cosmetic Surgery: A Feminist Primer* (Ashgate, 2009) for feminist perspectives on cosmetic surgery.

In this way the beauty ideal supports the weight-loss industry and encourages looksism and fat oppression.

At the very same time that we are bombarded with messages about being thin, the food industry in the United States (the third largest industry nationally) has considerable clout. Never before have North Americans (and, increasingly, people in developing countries) been bombarded with advertising for cheap and often toxic (high in sugar, fat, salt, or preservatives) food to such a degree. Many of these agricultural products are subsidized by the U.S. government. In addition, children watch more than 10,000 food ads per year on television, 90 percent of which are for four types of "food": sugar-coated cereals, soft drinks, fast food, and candy. A study from the United Kingdom found that the more overweight a child was, the more she or he would eat when exposed to advertisements following a television show. Obese children increased food intake by 134 percent and normal-weight children by 84 percent. Chocolate was the food source of choice. The need for healthy nutrition is underscored by a study at Brigham and Women's Hospital in which researchers found that though as many as 1 in 4 children under the age of 14 years diet, these behaviors were not only ineffective but often tended to lead ultimately to weight gain.

EATING DISORDERS

Today, models weigh about 23 percent less than the average woman, and this fact alone sends many women into despair as they compare themselves against these mostly unattainable images. It is distressing that people often experience their bodies as sources of anxiety rather than joy and celebration. Such images encourage body loathing and can precipitate eating disorders and other unhealthy disordered thinking. For example, Marni Grossman, the author of "Beating Anorexia and Gaining Feminism," writes of the despair she felt in comparing her body to those of her girlfriends. Such competition and anxiety often continue as women age and are encouraged to measure bodies against constructed images of youthful "beauty."

Eating Disorder Information

The following organizations provide information about eating disorders. Visit their websites to learn more about anorexia, bulimia, and other forms of disordered eating.

Academy for Eating Disorders Telephone: 847-498-4274 Website: *www.aedweb.org*

National Association of Anorexia Nervosa and Associated Disorders Telephone: 877-355-7601 Website: *www.anad.org*

National Eating Disorder Information Center (Canada) Toll-free: 866-633-4220 Website: *www.nedic.ca*

National Eating Disorders Association Toll-free: 800-931-2237 Website: *www.NationalEatingDisorders.org*

Contemporary eating disorders are compulsive disorders that include a variety of behaviors. Among these are *anorexia nervosa* (self-starvation), *bulimia nervosa* (binge eating with self-induced vomiting and/or laxative use), *compulsive eating* (uncontrolled eating or binge eating), and *muscle dysmorphia* (fear of being inadequately muscled). Alongside these diagnostic categories are general eating-disordered behavior that may include occasional binge eating and fasting, overly compulsive food habits such as eating only certain foods, not being able to eat in public, and general problems associated with compulsive dieting and/or compulsive overexercising (sometimes called *anorexia athletica,* although at this time this is not recognized as a formal diagnosis). The latter catchall category of generalized disordered eating/exercising seems to be widespread among North American women.

These disorders are culturally mediated in that they are related to environmental conditions associated with the politics of gender and sexuality. It appears that the number of eating-disordered women in any given community is proportional to the number of individuals who are dieting to control weight. Dieting seems to trigger the onset of an eating disorder in vulnerable individuals. According to a British study, teenage girls who dieted even "modestly" were five times more likely to become anorexic or bulimic than those who did not diet. Those on strict diets were 18 times more likely to develop an eating disorder. The extent of this problem is illustrated by a 2011 study that found that by age 6, girls especially start to express concerns about their own weight or shape. About half of all elementary school girls (ages 6 to 12) are concerned about their weight or about becoming too fat. These fears and concerns are foundational in understanding eating disorders.

The reading "Beating Anorexia, Gaining Feminism" addresses the ways anorexics become very thin and emaciated by refusing to maintain a healthy body weight, have intense fears of gaining weight, and tend to strive for perfection. Author Marni Grossman survived the ordeal and learned important lessons about the politics of the body. She allowed her anger to propel herself beyond self-hatred toward empowerment. Bulimics also display intense body dissatisfaction. They eat large amounts of food in a short time (binge) and then make themselves vomit, or they purge with laxatives or overexercising, or they may purge through diuretics and/or amphetamines. Bulimics are more likely to be of normal weight than anorexics, although they both share emotions and thoughts associated with self-punishment, or feelings of being overwhelmed because they feel fat, or feelings of frustration and/or anger with other factors in their lives. Compulsive eating (which may involve binging) is understood as an addiction to food and often involves using food as comfort and includes eating to fill a void in life, hide emotions, or cope with problems. Compulsive eaters often have low self-esteem and feel shame about their weight. Individuals with muscle dysmorphia believe that their physiques are too small and unmuscular rather than too large. They participate in maladaptive exercise and dietary practices, and many use performance-enhancing substances. Although early studies focused on male bodybuilders, recent scholarship suggests that such symptoms can appear in the general population and that women are increasingly demonstrating this disorder. Similarly, while boys and men tend to use steroids more than women to increase athletic performance, new scholarship has shown that girls and women are also using steroids. Steroid use among women is more likely to be used to improve body image and muscle tone and control weight than for purely athletic reasons.

Eating disorders (with the exception of muscle dysmorphia) affect women primarily; the ratio of women to men among anorexia nervosa and bulimia sufferers is 10:1 and the figure is 3:1 for binge eating. In North America, these disorders primarily affect young (aged 15 to 25 years) women. Current statistics suggest that about 1 percent of female adolescents have anorexia, 4 percent have bulimia (with about half of the former also developing bulimic patterns), and approximately 3.5 percent experience binge eating in any 6-month period. Accurate numbers associated with generalized eating problems are unknown, although it is assumed that the number of women who indulge in disordered eating patterns of some kind is quite substantial.

While these disorders occur in all populations in the United States, white women and those with higher socioeconomic status are somewhat more likely to suffer these problems. As the reading by Greenwood and Dal Cin suggests, however, women of color are not immune from body dissatisfaction and potential eating disorders. This is corroborated by new data showing the prevalence of eating disorders as similar among white women and women of color, with the exception that anorexia nervosa is more common among white women. However, it is also important to understand reporting bias whereby reports tend to reflect the ways "incidence" is tied to resource availability for treatment in various communities. We do not know the incidence of unacknowledged or untreated eating disorders that occur in communities where treatment resources are scarce or unavailable. Finally, while eating disorders are associated with the developed global north and usually not manifested in countries with food scarcity, Asian countries have recently experienced a surge in the incidence of eating disorders as a result of increased development, especially urbanization.

There are often serious physical and emotional complications with these disorders, and up to 20 percent of people with serious eating disorders die from the disorder, usually of complications associated with heart problems and chemical imbalances, as well as suicide. With treatment, mortality rates fall to 2–3 percent; about 60 percent recover and maintain healthy weight and social relationships; 20 percent make only partial recoveries and remain compulsively focused on food and weight; and approximately 20 percent do not improve. The latter often live lives controlled by weight- and body-management issues, and they often experience depression, hopelessness, and loneliness. Chronic obesity that may follow compulsive eating also has important consequences for health and illness.

Many students who live in dorms and sororities report a high incidence of eating disorders; perhaps you have struggled with an eating disorder yourself or have had a close friend or sister similarly diagnosed. If the huge number of women who have various issues with food—always on a diet, overly concerned with weight issues, compulsive about what they do or do not eat—are also included in the figures on eating disorders, then the number of women with these problems increases exponentially. Indeed, although teenage boys are actually more likely to be overweight than girls, they are less likely to diet. A study published in the *American Journal of Health Promotion* found that 21 percent of the teenage girls in the study were overweight, 55 percent said they were dieters, and 35 percent were consistent dieters. Although more teenage boys in the study were overweight, only a quarter said they were dieters and only 12 percent were consistent dieters. Because food and bodies are central preoccupations in so many women's lives, we might ask, why women and why food?

First, women have long been associated with food and domestic pursuits; food preparation and focus on food are a socially accepted part of female cultural training. Given that

IDEAS FOR ACTIVISM

- Organize an eating disorders awareness event. Provide information about eating disorders and resources for help. Invite a therapist who specializes in treating eating disorders to speak. Create awareness posters to hang around your campus.
- Organize a letter-writing campaign to protest the representation of such a small range of women's shapes and sizes in a particular women's magazine.
- Organize a speak-out about beauty ideals.
- Organize a tattoo and piercing panel to discuss the politics of tattooing and piercing. Have a tattoo and piercing fashion show, and discuss the meaning of the various tattoos/piercings.

women have been relegated to the private sphere of the home more than the public world, food consumption is easily accessible and unquestioned. Second, food is something that nourishes and gives pleasure. In our culture, food has been associated with comfort and celebration, and it is easy to see how eating can be a way of dealing with the anxieties and unhappiness of life. Put these two together, and we get food as the object of compulsion; when we add the third factor, the "beauty" ideal, with all the anxieties associated with closely monitoring the size and shape of women's bodies, the result can be eating disorders.

Scholars also emphasize that eating disorders reflect the ways women desire self-control in the context of limited power and autonomy. In other words, young women turn to controlling their bodies and attempt to sculpt them to perfection because they are denied power and control in other areas of their lives. Central in understanding eating disorders, however, is the pressure in our society for women to measure up to cultural standards of beauty and attractiveness, what is often called the "culture of thinness." These standards, discussed throughout this chapter, infringe on all our lives whether we choose to comply with them or to resist them. Messages abound telling women that they are not good enough or beautiful enough, encouraging us to constantly change ourselves, often through the use of various products and practices. The result is that girls learn early on that they must aspire to some often-unattainable standard of physical perfection. Such bombardment distracts girls and women from other issues, "disciplining" them to focus energy on the body, affecting their self-esteem and constantly assaulting the psyche as the body ages. In this way, eating disorders can be read as cultural statements about gender.

NEGOTIATING "BEAUTY" IDEALS

Although many women strive to attain the "beauty" ideal on an ongoing, daily basis, some actively resist such cultural norms. These women are choosing to not participate in the beauty rituals, not support the industries that produce both images and products, and to create other definitions of beauty. Some women are actively appropriating these standards by highlighting and/or exaggerating the very norms and standards themselves. They are carving out their own notions of beauty through their use of fashion and cosmetics. For them, empowerment involves playing with existing cultural standards. Most women comply with some standards associated with the beauty ideal and resist others. We find a place that suits us, criticizing some standards and practices and conforming to others, usually learning to live with the various contradictions that this implies and hopefully appreciating the bodies we have (see the box "Learn to Love Your Body" below).

A question that might be raised in response to ideas about resisting beauty ideals and practices is: What's wrong with being beautiful? Feminists answer that it is not beauty that is a problem but, rather, the way that beauty has been constructed by the dominant culture. This construction excludes many "beautiful" women and helps maintain particular (and very restricted) notions of femininity. In "Is Fat a Feminist Issue?" Fikkan and Rothblum encourage us to understand the cultural loathing of fat that many women in the United States have internalized and to recognize weight-based stigma as a serious source of women's oppression.

Another common question is: Can you wear makeup and enjoy the adornments associated with femininity and still call yourself a feminist? Most feminists (especially those who identify as third wave) answer with a resounding yes. In fact, you can reclaim these trappings and go ultra-femme in celebration of your femininity and your right to self-expression. What is important from a feminist perspective is that these practices are *conscious*. In other words, when women take part in various reproductions of femininity, it is important to understand the bigger picture and be aware of the ways "beauty" ideals work to limit and objectify women, encourage competitiveness (Is she better looking than me? Who is the cutest woman here? How do I measure up?), and ultimately to lower women's self-worth. Understand also how many beauty products are tested on animals, how the packaging of cosmetics and other beauty products encourages the use of resources that end up polluting the environment, and how many fashion items are made by child and/or sweatshop labor and then exported overseas as examples of cultural imperialism. The point is for us to make conscious and informed choices about our relationships to the "beauty" ideal and to respect, love, and take care of our bodies.

Learn to Love Your Body

Do you ever stand in front of the mirror dreaming about where you'd get a few nips and tucks? Or feeling like life would be better if only you had smaller thighs, a flatter tummy, or there was simply less of you? These are all signs of a not-so-hot body image.

It's important that you feel good about who you are. And until you like yourself as is, trying to change your body shape will be a losing proposition. High self-esteem is important for a healthy, balanced lifestyle—and it's a definite must if successful weight loss is one of your goals. So it's time to smile back at that image in the mirror and value all the wonderful characteristics about the person reflected there. Try these techniques:

1. *Recognize your special qualities.* Make a list of all your positive qualities—not including your physical traits. Are you kind? Artistic? Honest? Good

(continued)

in business? Do you make people laugh? Post your list near the mirror or another place where you'll see it every day.

2. *Put your body back together.* Most of us with negative body images have dissected our bodies into good and bad parts. "I hate my thighs and butt." "My butt's okay, but my stomach is fat and my arms are flabby." Reconnect with your body by appreciating how it all works to keep you going. Try stretching or yoga—the fluid movements are great for getting in touch with the wonders of the human body.

3. *Remember the kid inside you.* Give yourself permission not to be perfect. Inside all of us is the kid we used to be—the kid who didn't have to be perfect and worry about everything. Remember that kid, and give yourself a break. Place a photo of yourself as a child in your bedroom or at your desk at work so that you can see it each day and remember to nurture yourself and laugh a little.

4. *Enjoy your food.* Eating is pleasurable. So enjoy it! Food gives us energy and sustains life. Don't deprive yourself or consider eating an evil act. If you allow yourself to enjoy some of the foods you like, you'll be less likely to overeat. In turn, your body won't feel bloated and uncomfortable.

5. *Indulge in body pleasures.* One step toward being kind to your body, and inevitably yourself, is to indulge yourself. Get a massage, take a long, hot bath, use lotions that smell good, or treat yourself to a manicure or pedicure.

6. *Speak positively.* Pay attention to your self-talk. It's amazing how often we put ourselves down throughout the day. Each time you catch yourself making critical comments, fight back by immediately complimenting yourself.

7. *See the world realistically.* It's common to compare ourselves to people in magazines or movies, but this can make you feel self-conscious. If you want to compare yourself to others, look at the real people around you. They come in different shapes and sizes—and none of them are airbrushed or highlighted.

8. *Dress in clothes that fit.* When we feel badly about our bodies, we often dress in shabby clothes, waiting until we lose weight before we buy something we like. But why? Feel good now! Find attractive clothes that fit your current size. Treating yourself will make you feel renewed.

9. *Be active.* Movement and exercise can make you and your body feel terrific. Not only does exercise help boost your mood, it stimulates your muscles, making you feel more alive and connected to your body.

10. *Thrive!* Living well will help you feel better about who you are and how you look. Strive to make your personal and professional life fulfilling. You are a unique, amazing person. A healthy, happy life can be all yours!

Source: www.thriveonline.com/shape/countdown/countdown.feature2.week7.html.

Breast Buds and the "Training" Bra

Joan Jacobs Brumberg (1997)

In every generation, small swellings around the nipples have announced the arrival of puberty. This development, known clinically as "breast buds," occurs before menarche and almost always provokes wonder and self-scrutiny. "I began to examine myself carefully, to search my armpits for hairs and my breasts for signs of swelling," wrote Kate Simon about coming of age in the Bronx at the time of World War I. Although Simon was "horrified" by the rapidity with which her chest developed, many girls, both in literature and real life, long for this important mark of maturity. In Jamaica Kincaid's fictional memoir of growing up in Antigua, *Annie John,* the main character, regarded her breasts as "treasured shrubs, needing only the proper combination of water and sunlight to make them flourish." In order to get their breasts to grow, Annie and her best friend, Gwen, lay in a pasture exposing their small bosoms to the moonlight.

Breasts are particularly important to girls in cultures or time periods that give powerful meaning or visual significance to that part of the body. Throughout history, different body parts have been eroticized in art, literature, photography, and film. In some eras, the ankle or upper arm was the ultimate statement of female sexuality. But breasts were the particular preoccupation of Americans in the years after World War II, when voluptuous stars, such as Jayne Mansfield, Jane Russell, and Marilyn Monroe, were popular box-office attractions. The mammary fixation of the 1950s extended beyond movie stars and shaped the experience of adolescents of both genders. In that era, boys seemed to prefer girls who were "busty," and American girls began to worry about breast size as well as about weight. This elaboration of the ideal of beauty raised expectations about what adolescent girls should look like. It also required them to put even more energy and resources into their body projects, beginning at an earlier age.

The story of how this happened is intertwined with the history of the bra, an undergarment that came into its own, as separate from the corset, in the early twentieth century. In 1900, a girl of twelve or thirteen typically wore a one-piece "waist" or camisole that had no cups or darts in front. As her breasts developed, she moved into different styles of the same garment, but these had more construction, such as stitching, tucks, and bones, that would accentuate the smallness of her waist and shape the bosom. In those days, before the arrival of the brassiere, there were no "cups." The bosom was worn low; there was absolutely no interest in uplift, and not a hint of cleavage.

The French word *brassière,* which actually means an infant's undergarment or harness, was used in *Vogue* as early as 1907. In the United States, the first boneless bra to leave the midriff bare was developed in 1913 by Mary Phelps Jacobs, a New York City debutante. Under the name Caresse Crosby, Jacobs marketed a bra made of two French lace handkerchiefs suspended from the shoulders. Many young women in the 1920s, such as Yvonne Blue, bought their first bras in order to achieve the kind of slim, boyish figure that the characteristic chemise (or flapper) dress required. The first bras were designed simply to flatten, but they were superseded by others intended to shape and control the breasts. Our current cup sizes (A, B, C, and D), as well as the idea of circular stitching to enhance the roundness of the breast, emerged in the 1930s.

Adult women, not adolescents, were the first market for bras. Sexually maturing girls simply moved into adult-size bras when they were ready—and if their parents had the money. Many women and girls in the early twentieth century still made their own underwear at home, and some read the advertisements for bras with real longing. When she began to develop breasts in the 1930s, Malvis Helmi, a midwestern farm girl, remembered feeling embarrassed whenever she wore an old summer dimity that pulled and gaped across her expanding chest. As a result, she spoke to her mother, considered the brassieres in the Sears, Roebuck catalog, and decided to purchase two for twenty-five cents. However, when her hardworking father saw the order form, he vetoed the idea and declared, "Our kind of people can't afford to spend money on such nonsense." Although her mother made her a makeshift bra, Malvis vowed that someday she would have store-bought brassieres. . . .

The transition from homemade to mass-produced bras was critical in how adolescent girls thought about their breasts. In general, mass-produced clothing fostered autonomy in girls because it took matters of style and taste outside the dominion of the mother, who had traditionally made and supervised a girl's wardrobe. But in the case of brassieres, buying probably had another effect. So long as clothing was made at home, the dimensions of the garment could be adjusted to the particular body intended to wear it. But with store-bought clothes, the body had to fit instantaneously into standard sizes that were constructed from a pattern representing a norm. When clothing failed to fit the body, particularly a part as intimate as the breasts, young women were apt to perceive that there was something wrong with their bodies. In this way, mass-produced bras in standard cup sizes probably increased, rather than diminished, adolescent self-consciousness about the breasts.

Until the 1950s, the budding breasts of American girls received no special attention from either bra manufacturers, doctors, or parents. Girls generally wore undershirts until they were sufficiently developed to fill an adult-size bra. Mothers and daughters traditionally handled this transformation in private, at home. But in the gyms and locker rooms of postwar junior high schools, girls began to look around to see who did and did not wear a bra. Many of these girls had begun menstruating and developing earlier than their mothers had, and this visual information was very powerful. In some circles, the ability to wear and fill a bra was central to an adolescent girl's status and sense of self. "I have a figure problem," a fourteen-year-old wrote to *Seventeen* in 1952: "All

of my friends are tall and shapely while my figure still remains up-and-down. Can you advise me?"

In an era distinguished by its worship of full-breasted women, interest in adolescent breasts came from all quarters: girls who wanted bras at an earlier age than ever before; mothers who believed that they should help a daughter acquire a "good" figure; doctors who valued maternity over all other female roles; and merchandisers who saw profits in convincing girls and their parents that adolescent breasts needed to be tended in special ways. All of this interest coalesced in the 1950s to make the brassiere as critical as the sanitary napkin in making a girl's transition into adulthood both modern and successful.

The old idea that brassieres were frivolous or unnecessary for young girls was replaced by a national discussion about their medical and psychological benefits. "My daughter who is well developed but not yet twelve wants to wear a bra," wrote a mother in Massachusetts to *Today's Health* in 1951. "I want her to wear an undervest instead because I think it is better not to have anything binding. What do you think about a preadolescent girl wearing a bra?" That same year a reader from Wilmington, Delaware, asked *Seventeen*: "Should a girl of fourteen wear a bra? There are some older women who insist we don't need them." The editor's answer was an unequivocal endorsement of early bras: "Just as soon as your breasts begin to show signs of development, you should start wearing a bra." By the early 1950s, "training" or "beginner" bras were available in AAA and AA sizes for girls whose chests were essentially flat but who wanted a bra nonetheless. Along with acne creams, advertisements for these brassieres were standard fare in magazines for girls.

Physicians provided a medical rationale for purchasing bras early. In 1952, in an article in *Parents' Magazine,* physician Frank H. Crowell endorsed bras for young girls and spelled out a theory and program of teenage breast management. "Unlike other organs such as the stomach and intestines which have ligaments that act as guywires or slings to hold them in place," Crowell claimed, the breast was simply "a growth developed from the skin and held up only by the skin." An adolescent girl needed a bra in order to prevent sagging breasts, stretched blood vessels, and poor circulation, all of which would create problems in nursing her future children. In addition, a "dropped" breast was "not so attractive," Crowell said, so it was important to get adolescents into bras early, before their breasts began to sag. The "training" that a training bra was supposed to accomplish was the first step toward motherhood and a sexually alluring figure, as it was defined in the 1950s.

. . .

Breasts were actually only one part of a larger body project encouraged by the foundation garment industry in postwar America. In this era, both physicians and entrepreneurs promoted a general philosophy of "junior figure control." Companies such as Warners, Maidenform, Formfit, Belle Mode, and Perfect Form (as well as popular magazines like *Good Housekeeping*) all encouraged the idea that young women needed both lightweight girdles and bras to "start the figure off to a beautiful future."

The concept of "support" was aided and abetted by new materials—such as nylon netting and two-way stretch fabrics—developed during the war but applied afterward to women's underwear. By the early 1950s, a reenergized corset and brassiere industry was poised for extraordinary profits. If "junior figure control" became the ideal among the nation's mothers and daughters, it would open up sales of bras and girdles to the largest generation of adolescents in American history, the so-called baby boomers. Once again, as in the case of menstruation and acne, the bodies of adolescent girls had the potential to deliver considerable profit.

There was virtually no resistance to the idea that American girls should wear bras and girdles in adolescence. Regardless of whether a girl was thin or heavy, "junior figure control" was in order, and that phrase became a pervasive sales mantra. "Even slim youthful figures will require foundation assistance," advised *Women's Wear Daily* in 1957. In both *Seventeen* and *Compact,* the two most popular magazines for the age group, high school girls were urged to purchase special foundation garments such as "Bobbie" bras and girdles by Formfit and "Adagio" by Maidenform that were "teen-proportioned" and designed, allegedly, with the help of adolescent consultants. The bras were available in pastel colors in a variety of special sizes, starting with AAA, and they were decorated with lace and ribbon to make them especially feminine. In addition to holding up stockings, girdles were intended to flatten the tummy

and also provide light, but firm, control for hips and buttocks. The advertisements for "Bobbie," in particular, suggested good things about girls who controlled their flesh in this way; they were pretty, had lots of friends, and drank Coca-Cola. As adults, they would have good figures and happy futures because they had chosen correct underwear in their youth.

By the mid-1950s, department stores and specialty shops had developed aggressive educational programs designed to spread the gospel of "junior figure control." In order to make young women "foundation conscious," Shillito's, a leading Cincinnati department store, tried to persuade girls and their mothers of the importance of having a professional fitting of the first bra. Through local newspaper advertisements, and also programs in home economics classes, Shillito's buyer, Edith Blincoe, promoted the idea that the purchase of bras and girdles required special expertise, which only department stores could provide. (*Seventeen* echoed her idea and advised a "trained fitter" for girls who wanted a "prettier" bosom and a "smoother" figure.) Blincoe acknowledged that teenage girls were already "100% bra conscious," and she hoped to develop the same level of attention to panty girdles. . . .

In home economics classes, and also at the local women's club, thousands of American girls saw informational films such as *Figure Forum* and *Facts About Your Figure,* made by the Warner Brassiere Company in the 1950s. Films like these stressed the need for appropriate foundation garments in youth and provided girls with scientific principles for selecting them. They also taught young women how to bend over and lean into their bras, a maneuver that most of us learned early and still do automatically. Most middle-class girls and their mothers embraced the code of "junior figure control" and spent time and money in pursuit of the correct garments. . . .

In the postwar world, the budding adolescent body was big business. Trade publications, such as *Women's Wear Daily,* gave special attention to sales strategies and trends in marketing to girls. In their reports from Cincinnati, Atlanta, and Houston, one thing was clear: wherever American girls purchased bras, they wanted to be treated as grown-ups, even if they wore only a AAA or AA cup. In Atlanta, at the Redwood Corset and Lingerie Shop, owner Sally Blye and her staff spoke persuasively to young customers about the importance of "uplift" in order "not to break muscle tissue." And at Houston's popular Teen Age Shop, specially trained salesgirls allowed young customers to look through the brassieres on their own, and then encouraged them to try on items in the dressing room without their mothers. Although many girls were shy at first, by the age of fourteen and fifteen most had lost their initial self-consciousness. "They take the merchandise and go right in [to the dressing room]," Blincoe said about her teenage clientele. Girls who could not be reached by store or school programs could send away to the Belle Mode Brassiere Company for free booklets about "junior figure control" with titles such as "The Modern Miss—Misfit or Miss Fit" and "How to Be Perfectly Charming." In the effort to help girls focus on their figures, Formfit, maker of the popular "Bobbies," offered a free purse-size booklet on calorie counting.

Given all this attention, it's not surprising that bras and breasts were a source of concern in adolescents' diaries written in the 1950s. Sandra Rubin got her first bra in 1951, when she was a twelve-year-old in Cleveland, but she did not try it on in a department store. Instead, her mother bought her a "braziere" while she was away on a trip and sent it home. "It's very fancy," Sandra wrote. "I almost died! I ran right upstairs to put it on." When she moved to New York City that September and entered Roosevelt Junior High School, Sandra got involved with a clique of seven girls who called themselves the "7Bs." Their name was not about their homeroom; it was about the cup size they wanted to be. . . .

Breasts, not weight, were the primary point of comparison among high school girls in the 1950s. Although Sandra Rubin called herself a "fat hog" after eating too much candy, her diary reportage was principally about the bosoms, rather than the waistlines, she saw at school. Those who had ample bosoms seemed to travel through the hallways in a veritable state of grace, at least from the perspective of girls who considered themselves flat-chested. "Busty" girls made desirable friends because they seemed sophisticated, and they attracted boys. In December 1959, when she planned a Friday-night pajama party, thirteen-year-old Ruth Teischman made a courageous move by inviting the "gorgeous"

Roslyn, a girl whom she wrote about frequently but usually only worshiped from afar. After a night of giggling and eating with her junior high school friends, Ruth revealed in her diary the source of Roslyn's power and beauty: "Roslyn is very big. (Bust of course.) I am very flat. I wish I would get bigger fast." Many girls in the 1950s perused the ads, usually in the back of women's magazines, for exercise programs and creams guaranteed to make their breasts grow, allegedly in short order.

The lament of the flat-chested girl—"I must, I must, I must develop my bust"—was on many private hit parades in the 1950s. There was a special intensity about breasts because of the attitudes of doctors, mothers, and advertisers, all of whom considered breast development critical to adult female identity and success. Although "junior figure control" increased pressure on the entire body, and many girls wore waist cinches as well as girdles, it was anxiety about breasts, more than any other body part, that characterized adolescent experience in these years. As a result, thousands, if not millions, of girls in early adolescence jumped the gun and bought "training bras" at the first sight of breast buds, or they bought padded bras to disguise their perceived inadequacy. In the 1950s, the bra was validated as a rite of passage: regardless of whether a girl was voluptuous or flat, she was likely to purchase her first bra at an earlier age than had her mother. This precocity was due, in part, to biology, but it was also a result of entrepreneurial interests aided and abetted by medical concern. By the 1950s, American society was so consumer-oriented that there were hardly any families, even among the poor, who would expect to make bras for their daughters the way earlier generations had made their own sanitary napkins.

Training bras were a boon to the foundation garment industry, but they also meant that girls' bodies were sexualized earlier. In contemporary America, girls of nine or ten are shepherded from undershirts into little underwear sets that come with tops that are protobrassieres. Although this may seem innocuous and natural, it is not the same as little girls "dressing up" in their mother's clothing. In our culture, traditional distinctions between adult clothing and juvenile clothing have narrowed considerably, so that mature women dress "down," in the garments of kids, just as often as little girls dress "up." While the age homogeneity of the contemporary wardrobe helps adult women feel less matronly, dressing little girls in adult clothing can have an insidious side effect. Because a bra shapes the breasts in accordance with fashion, it acts very much like an interpreter, translating functional anatomy into a sexual or erotic vocabulary. When we dress little girls in brassieres or bikinis, we imply adult behaviors and, unwittingly, we mark them as sexual objects. The training bras of the 1950s loom large in the history of adolescent girls because they foreshadowed the ways in which the nation's entrepreneurs would accommodate, and also encourage, precocious sexuality.

R E A D I N G  29

If Men Could Menstruate

Gloria Steinem (1978)

A white minority of the world has spent centuries conning us into thinking that a white skin makes people superior—even though the only thing it really does is make them more subject to ultraviolet rays and to wrinkles. Male human beings have built whole cultures around the idea that penis-envy is "natural" to women—though having such an unprotected organ might be said to make men vulnerable, and the power to give birth makes womb-envy at least as logical.

In short, the characteristics of the powerful, whatever they may be, are thought to be better than the characteristics of the powerless—and logic has nothing to do with it.

What would happen, for instance, if suddenly, magically, men could menstruate and women could not?

The answer is clear—menstruation would become an enviable, boast-worthy, masculine event:

Men would brag about how long and how much.

Boys would mark the onset of menses, the longed-for proof of manhood, with religious ritual and stag parties.

Congress would fund a National Institute of Dysmenorrhea to help stamp out monthly discomforts.

Sanitary supplies would be federally funded and free. (Of course, some men would still pay for the prestige of commercial brands such as John Wayne Tampons, Muhammad Ali's Rope-a-dope Pads, Joe Namath Jock Shields—"For Those Light Bachelor Days," and Robert "Baretta" Blake Maxi-Pads.)

Military men, right-wing politicians, and religious fundamentalists would cite menstruation ("*men*struation") as proof that only men could serve in the Army ("you have to give blood to take blood"), occupy political office ("can women be aggressive without that steadfast cycle governed by the planet Mars?"), be priests and ministers ("how could a woman give her blood for our sins?"), or rabbis ("without the monthly loss of impurities, women remain unclean").

Male radicals, left-wing politicians, and mystics, however, would insist that women are equal, just different; and that any woman could enter their ranks if only she were willing to self-inflict a major wound every month ("you *must* give blood for the revolution"), recognize the preeminence of menstrual issues, or subordinate her selfness to all men in their Cycle of Enlightenment.

Street guys would brag ("I'm a three-pad man") or answer praise from a buddy ("Man, you lookin' *good!*") by giving fives and saying, "Yeah, man, I'm on the rag!"

TV shows would treat the subject at length. ("Happy Days": Richie and Potsie try to convince Fonzie that he is still "The Fonz," though he has missed two periods in a row.) So would newspapers. (SHARK SCARE THREATENS MENSTRUATING MEN. JUDGE CITES MONTHLY STRESS

IN PARDONING RAPIST.) And movies. (Newman and Redford in "Blood Brothers"!)

Men would convince women that intercourse was *more* pleasurable at "that time of the month." Lesbians would be said to fear blood and therefore life itself—though probably only because they needed a good menstruating man.

Of course, male intellectuals would offer the most moral and logical arguments. How could a woman master any discipline that demanded a sense of time, space, mathematics, or measurement, for instance, without that in-built gift for measuring the cycles of the moon and planets—and thus for measuring anything at all? In the rarefied fields of philosophy and religion, could women compensate for missing the rhythm of the universe? Or for their lack of symbolic death-and-resurrection every month?

Liberal males in every field would try to be kind: the fact that "these people" have no gift for measuring life or connecting to the universe, the liberals would explain, should be punishment enough.

And how would women be trained to react? One can imagine traditional women agreeing to all these arguments with a staunch and smiling masochism. ("The ERA would force housewives to wound themselves every month": Phyllis Schlafly. "Your husband's blood is as sacred as that of Jesus—and so sexy, too!": Marabel Morgan.) Reformers and Queen Bees would try to imitate men, and *pretend* to have a monthly cycle. All feminists would explain endlessly that men, too, needed to be liberated from the false idea of Martian aggressiveness, just as women needed to escape the bonds of menses-envy. Radical feminists would add that the oppression of the nonmenstrual was the pattern for all other oppressions. ("Vampires were our first freedom fighters!") Cultural feminists would develop a bloodless imagery in art and literature. Socialist feminists would insist that only under capitalism would men be able to monopolize menstrual blood. . . . In fact, if men could menstruate, the power justifications could probably go on forever.

If we let them.

R E A D I N G   **30**

Prosthetic Power

Aimee Mullins (2009)

Aimee Mullins was born without fibular bones; both of her legs were amputated below the knee when she was an infant. She learned to walk on prosthetics, then to run, competing as a champion sprinter in college.

I was speaking to a group of kids at a children's museum, and I brought with me a bag full of legs and had them laid out on a table. Kids are naturally curious about what they don't know, or don't understand, or what is foreign to them. They only learn to be frightened of those differences when an adult influences them to behave that way and censors that natural curiosity. I pictured a first-grade teacher out in the lobby saying, "Now, whatever you do, don't stare at her legs."

But, of course, that's the point. That's why I was there—I wanted to invite them to look and explore. So I made a deal with the adults that the kids could come in, without any adults, for two minutes. The doors open; the kids descend on this table of legs, and they are poking and prodding, and they're wiggling toes, and they're trying to put their full weight on the sprinting leg to see what happens. And I said, "I woke up this morning and I decided I wanted to be able to jump over a house. If you could think of any animal, any superhero, any cartoon character, anything you can dream up right now, what kind of legs would you build me?"

Immediately a voice shouted, "Kangaroo!" "Should be a frog!" "It should be Go Go Gadget!" "It should be the Incredibles." And then one 8-year-old said, "Hey, why wouldn't you want to fly too?" And the whole room, including me, was like, "Yeah." Just like that, I went from being a woman these kids would have been trained to see as disabled to somebody who had potential that their bodies didn't have yet. Somebody who might even be super-abled. Interesting.

Eleven years ago, the Technology, Entertainment, Design (TED) conference was the launchpad to the next decade of my life's exploration. At the time, the legs I presented were groundbreaking in prosthetics. I had woven carbon fiber sprinting legs modeled after the hind leg of a cheetah, and also these very lifelike, intrinsically painted, silicone legs.

It was my opportunity to put a call out to innovators outside the traditional medical prosthetic community to bring their talent to the science and to the art of building legs—so we can stop compartmentalizing form, function, and aesthetic and assigning them different values.

This started an incredible journey. Curious encounters were happening to me; I'd been accepting invitations to speak on the design of the cheetah legs around the world. People would come up to me after my talk, and the conversation would go something like this: "You know, Aimee, you're very attractive. You don't look disabled." I thought, "Well, that's amazing, because I don't feel disabled." It opened my eyes to this conversation that could be explored about beauty. What does a beautiful woman have to look like? What is a sexy body? And interestingly, from an identity standpoint, what does it mean to have a disability? I mean, Pamela

Anderson has more prosthetic in her body than I do. Nobody calls her disabled.

Today, I have over a dozen pairs of prosthetic legs, and with them I have different negotiations of the terrain under my feet. And I can change my height—I have a variable of five different heights. Today, I'm six foot one. I had these legs made in England, and when I brought them home to Manhattan, a girl who has known me for years at my normal five foot eight went, "But you're so tall!" I said, "I know. Isn't it fun?" And she looked at me and she said, "But Aimee, that's not fair."

That's when I knew that the conversation with society has changed profoundly. It is no longer a conversation about overcoming deficiency. It's a conversation about augmentation. It's a conversation about potential. A prosthetic limb doesn't represent the need to replace loss anymore. It can stand as a symbol that wearers have the power to create whatever it is that they want to create in that space. So people society once considered disabled can now become the architects of their own identities and indeed continue to change those identities by designing their bodies from a place of empowerment. What is exciting is that by combining cutting-edge technology—robotics, bionics— with the age-old poetry, we are moving closer to understanding our collective humanity. If we want to discover the full potential in our humanity, we need to celebrate those heartbreaking strengths and those glorious disabilities we all have. It is our humanity and all the potential within it that makes us beautiful.

R E A D I N G **31**

Beating Anorexia and Gaining Feminism

Marni Grossman (2010)

Sometimes it feels as though feminism was my consolation prize for surviving an eating disorder. I beat anorexia, and all I got was this battered copy of *The Feminine Mystique* and a complimentary Ani DiFranco CD. . . .

My mother likes to brag that she was the first girl in her high school to wear pants. She took my sister and me in strollers to pro-choice rallies. She told me I could be whatever I wanted to be, and I believed her.

But for a long time, my feminism lay dormant because there were other things to think about. Good grades, for instance. Or the complicated flow-chart of alliances and long-held grudges that made up my circle of friends. There were calories to count. Food to avoid. Body mass index to calculate. Dulcolax or ex-lax! Razor blades bought in packs of ten and issues of *Vogue* magazine and Anne Sexton poems.

Anorexia changed everything, though. I tired of starving and bleeding and puking and crying. I wearied of living out my own personal reenactment of *The Bell Jar*. I got bored of my own bullshit. And then I became furious.

Social conscience is a funny thing. No one leaps out of the womb, arms raised, hands balled in fists, protesting injustice and decrying hypocrisy. And while I wish the facts were different, I delved head-long into feminism because I was sick of being hungry. I was sick of being silent and subdued. It hardly seemed fair. My girlfriends and I, we were all engaged in this elaborate, masochistic dance of self-loathing and self-denial. The boys, meanwhile, were speaking up. They were stepping up. They were seizing the scepter, grasping the keys to the kingdom, never once questioning whether or not they deserved it.

Why, then, weren't all the brilliant girls I knew kicking ass in science and making themselves heard? Like me, they were busy tallying up the entries in their food journals and straightening their hair. They were keeping their mouths shut because boys don't like girls who talk back. They were purging in the bathroom after lunch and slicing up their arms with the dull edge of car keys under their desks. *Reviving Ophelia* wasn't a cautionary tale for us. It was a how-to guide to being young, female, and fucked-up.

In the beginning there was this: I am ugly. My certainty on this point was absolute. Three little words that were imbued with such profundity, such truth. I felt it in my blood. My bones. My marrow.

Mostly I felt it in the pit of my stomach, that hole that never seemed to get full.

My nose is long and angular. It meanders leftward. My hair grows dark and thick against white white skin. It grows in places it ought not to. Gravity compels my breasts to swing low, to droop. One is bigger than the other. I am asymmetrical.

I am an Egon Schiele painting. Vaguely indecent. Compelling. Hunched over from years of back-breaking worry.

The other girls at school didn't look like this. They were tall and tan and toned. They invited word choices like *lithe* and *lissome*. They didn't sweat. They didn't need to shave their legs or pluck their eyebrows or bleach their mustaches. Their breasts were perky and well-behaved. They were sleek and hairless and lovely. Everything I needed to be but couldn't. Or so they seemed to me.

If I can't be beautiful, I thought, *I will be thin. I'll be the thinnest, in fact. I'll be tiny and adorable and very, very good.vvv*

Much has been written on the subject of starving. Reams and reams of gorgeous, heartbreaking prose by women more talented than I. Caroline Knapp, for example. Marya Hornbacher and Kathryn Harrison. They tell this story better than I ever could. And it's always the same story. It's always a variation on a played-out theme.

We think we discovered it. We think our tricks are unique. Feed the meal to the dog when no one is looking. Excuse yourself to the bathroom. Keep the water running to cover the sounds of half-digested pizza hitting water. Say you have a stomach flu. Tell them you're too nervous to eat today. Invent yourself an ulcer. But *Cosmo* already wrote that article. And we are not unique. We are legion. An army of the undead. An army of the sexless, the neutered. We are a lumpen mass of jutting limbs and squandered potential.

Life became a series of failures. Because when you are anorexic, you're always failing. You're always giving in to the temptation of a bag of M&Ms or a handful of popcorn at the movies. Even when you're asleep, you're guilty. You dream of lavish gourmet meals, and you wake up hungry. Hungry and desperately wanting.

You wanted so badly to be selfless. To be without need. You fail at this, too. Because though you'd never admit it, you want the most. You want to be a starving, pint-size martyr. You want someone to genuflect before your broken ninety-pound body.

I hoped that at my funeral someone would remark on how thin I looked. "You can see her ribs," they'd say admiringly. And in this way, I would win.

It sounds crazy. I know that. Death is not winning. Starving is not success. I know that and you know that. And yet.

I'm no anomaly. If this is madness, then it's a mass psychosis.

We fall for the mirage every time. We believe that thinness is next to godliness. We believe that less is always more. We believe that hunger is control and fullness chaos. We believe that cellulite is a moral failing and that washboard abs will bring about happiness and world peace. We believe this because they told us it was so. I didn't know this when I was sixteen. I know it now.

In her essay "Body Politic," Abra Fortune Chernik says, "gaining weight and getting my head out of the toilet bowl was the most political act I have ever committed." This quote has been cited hundreds of times. Every person who takes a women's studies class has read this essay. Professors put Chernik's piece on the syllabus because it rings true. It strikes a chord within every girl.

In insidious ways, we learned that our value is in our sex appeal, that our worth is our size-2 jeans. We were all raised to believe that, for women, thin and pretty are synonymous and if you're neither, you may as well not exist. Brains are irrelevant. Beauty reigns supreme. The patriarchy depends on our acceptance of this myth. It keeps us prone. Powerless before Cover-Girl and Trimspa and Lean Cuisine.

Putting down the laxatives and picking up Naomi Wolf was the most political act I have ever committed.

As I started to gain weight, I felt something inside me stir. Anger. Righteous indignation. The need to raise holy hell. And so I took to the library for answers.

My high school had a limited selection of feminist texts. In the months I spent recovering, I read them all. I read Nancy Friday and Susan Faludi and Elizabeth Wurtzel. I devoured Katha Pollitt and Betty Friedan, and I realized that my anger, selfish as it was, could—as theirs did—propel me into something wonderful. Feminism—warts and all—has a place. And while the media insists on forecasting the movement's imminent death, there are girls out there, desperate (as I was) to channel their anger into something more radical than self-hatred.

The Beauty Myth led to Susan Bordo. Susan Bordo led to bell hooks and Simone de Beauvoir. I wrote papers decrying the sexism in *The Taming of the Shrew* and *One Flew over the Cuckoo's Nest*. I created a heavy-handed art installation about the media's influence on female body image full of decoupaged magazine pictures and broken mirror shards. I went to college and became copresident of the Eating Disorder Reach-Out Service. I preached about the evils of the diet industry. I talked about air-brushing and read about fat activism.

But that was just the beginning. Organizing around issues of body image wasn't enough. Only the privileged, after all, starve themselves. What of women who didn't have that dubious luxury? What of trans women and sex workers and the girls toiling away in the maquiladoras? I declared a women's studies major. I went to work.

Some people receive a summons to do G-d's work. Me? I heard strains of Helen Reddy music. Feminism was calling.

There's an obvious flaw in this essay. It is disjointed. It's fragmentary. It does not flow. It's confusing and piecemeal and unpolished. There are too many incomplete sentences and too many beginning with conjunctions or ending with prepositions. I agonized about this. I asked friends how to fix it. I put it aside for days and came back to it with fresh eyes. But no solution came to me.

I decided not to "fix" it. If this piece is disjointed and fragmentary and piecemeal, it's because that is how I came to feminism. There was no straight line. It was confusing and unpolished. I made mistakes. I will make more mistakes. But I won't apologize. I won't gloss over the nasty bits or cloak my anger in pretty prose. Feminism is not about perfection. It's about the power of speaking one's truth. Regardless of how ugly or raw that truth may be.

Ethnicity and Body Consciousness

Dara N. Greenwood and Sonya Dal Cin (2012)

The increasing display of slim bodies in the mass media motivated increased interest in the possible psychological effects of such images on young women's self and body image. However, much of the research has focused on the experience of young White women and White media icons (either exclusively, e.g., Heinberg & Thompson, 1995, or predominantly, e.g.. Greenwood, 2009; Harrison, 1997). It has often been presumed that Black women inhabit a different cultural milieu—one that rejects, or deems irrelevant. White/thin beauty norms and where self-esteem is derived from non-media sources like church and family. In line with Crocker and Major's (1989) theory regarding stigmatized outgroups, Black women are thought to engage in adaptive disidentification from a dominant and historically oppressive White culture, drawing instead on positive in-group values. There is some empirical support for these ideas: Blaek women tend to report lower tendencies to stake self-worth in others' approval than White women (Crocker et al., 2003), lower internalization of thin beauty ideals (Jefferson & Stake, 2000), increased resistance to mainstream beauty norms (Rubin et al., 2002), and lower levels of body dissatisfaction than White women (Botta, 2000; Schooler et al., 2004).

However, meta-analytic studies have shown that differences between White and Black women in the realms of body concerns and eating disorder symptoms may be smaller than previously believed (Grabe & Hyde, 2006; Shaw et al., 2004). Further, the stereotype that Black women are *immune* to body image concerns may result in missed diagnoses of and treatment for eating disorders (e.g., Striegel-Moore & Smolak, 1996), and missed nuances in the complex relationship that all women have with their bodies vis-a-vis idealized images of beauty in the mass media. Fortunately, scholarship on media images and young women's body esteem has begun to incorporate the conditions in which Black women may experience heightened body concerns (e.g., Botta. 2000; Jefferson & Stake, 2000; Schooler et al., 2004). Less fortunately, the research picture is—in the words of one recent review—"both woefully sparse and, perhaps not surprisingly, equivocal" (Lopez-Guimerá et al., 2010, p. 22). Some of the latter may be due to wide diversity with regard to how media ideals are assessed and whether the work in question is correlational or experimental.

Typically, researchers have examined broad tendencies to internalize thin media ideals, selective exposure to certain kinds of television programs, or postviewing responses to specific, experimenter-selected targets. The present study contributes a new puzzle piece to this sparse literature by integrating across these approaches: we assess how young Black and White women relate to *specific* television personae that they designate as "favorites," in the context of their self and body image concerns. This approach enables us to capture a more naturalistic view of how young women engage with preferred female media icons in their everyday lives, and how those selections and attitudes are relevant to body image concerns.

CORRELATIONAL RESEARCH

Some studies find that although Black women are generally less likely to internalize thin ideal standards of beauty than White women, those who *do* internalize this standard show similar levels of body image concerns to White women (Jefferson & Stake, 2000; Shaw et al., 2004). Further, a recent large-scale survey of Black women also finds that, similar to research on White women, increased internalization of thin ideals as well as a tendency to compare one's body with that of television and movie stars predicted increased body image concerns (Rogers Wood & Petrie, 2010). Research on exposure to certain television programs/characters (vs. thin media ideals per se) finds that when Black women idealize White/thin characters (Botta, 2000) or selectively watch White-oriented programs (e.g., programs with predominantly White casts, Schooler et al., 2004), such tendencies are linked to increased body concerns or eating disorder symptomatology.

An interesting nuance to the aforementioned findings is that although both Black and White women are generally more likely to compare themselves with ethnically similar others, this comparison is linked to increased body image concerns for White women only (Jefferson & Stake, 2000). The authors argue that, "the beauty ideals that [African American] women internalize may be more balanced with regard to the attractiveness of their features, leading to fewer upward comparisons" (p. 406). In a related vein, selective exposure to Black-oriented television shows (vs. White-oriented) has been linked to more *positive* body image among Black women (Schooler et al., 2004). Schooler et al. offer a number of possible explanations for these findings, ranging from the greater diversity of body types among Black women on television to the possibility that social comparison with same race others may confer ingroup esteem: "Black women may see other Black women as allies, not as competitors, and may therefore find comparisons with other Black women, even with ideal media images, inspiring" (p. 44). Thus, rather than highlighting adaptive disidentification as protective, the authors note the potential power of adaptive assimilation.

Taken together, the results of correlational studies suggest that the negative associations of White beauty ideals on Black women may be limited to those Black women who are more receptive to White-oriented media ideals (and exposure to Black-oriented media might even be protective).

EXPERIMENTAL RESEARCH

The above conclusion is complicated by findings from experimental research, which suggest that increased self-relevance of media images may *negatively* impact Black women's body esteem. For example, Frisby (2004) exposed Black undergraduate women to White models and had them engage in a thought-listing task; although they tended to note the physical attractiveness of the White models in question (e.g., "she's so pretty"), they were less likely to experience wishful identification with these models (e.g., "I wish I looked like that"). This lack of White model idealization seemed to translate into a lack of effect on body esteem following exposure. This is consistent with the idea that Black women can appreciate White beauty ideals without viewing them as self-relevant/demoralizing targets of social comparison. However, in a subsequent study, Black women with existing body concerns reported lower levels of body esteem when exposed to a Black model (there was no decrease in body esteem for women shown a White model).

Similarly, Harrison and Fredrickson (2003) investigated whether different body norms (lean vs. nonlean) depicted in the media might affect White and non-White middle school students differently. They exposed White and non-White teens to clips of women's "lean sports" (those typically associated with a slim body ideal, e.g., ice skating, cheerleading), women's "nonlean" sports (e.g., soccer, basketball) and men's sports. The ethnicity of the sports models was varied throughout so that the only systematic differences were in body size/shape or gender. Results showed that postviewing self-objectification was highest for non-White girls exposed to nonlean female sports players and for While girls exposed to lean female sports players (no differences emerged, as expected, following exposure to male sports). Although teens' body mass did not appear to interact with experimental condition, the authors explain their findings in light of ethnic differences in body ideals: "participants of color seemed to disregard the comparatively skinny look of the lean athletes as personally irrelevant, but did link the larger fuller bodies of the nonlean athletes to thoughts of their own body shape and size, resulting in increased self-objectification" (p. 228). Thus, the results of the experimental studies suggest that Black women can experience the negative effects of exposure to beauty ideals, as long as the model (and hence the ideal) is seen as a self-relevant model for comparison.

WHERE DOES THIS LEAVE US?

Research suggests that Black women are less likely to rely on others' approval, less likely to idealize dominant (White, thin) norms, and less likely to experience body dissatisfaction compared with White women. In focus group research. Black women have explicitly noted the decreased self-relevance and impact of such beauty norms (Rubin et al., 2002). White, thin images may be deemed irrelevant targets for social comparison among Black women and thus may be less likely to lead to demoralizing self-assessments. As a participant in Rubin et al.'s (2002) study reflects, ". . . you gotta be thin, [W]hite . . . young. As a [B]lack woman, I look at those images and I don't see me" (p. 63).

However, it is important not to gloss over some very important exceptions in the literature that invite ongoing scholarship. First, Black women who *do* selectively engage with White-oriented media or internalize thin media ideals seem as susceptible to body dissatisfaction as their White counterparts (Jefferson & Slake, 2000; Rogers Wood & Petrie, 2010; Shaw et al., 2004; Schooler et al., 2004). Second, experimental research shows that making specific self-relevant comparisons is not always protective; Black and/or heavier targets of comparison may inspire body image concerns among Black women (Frisby, 2004; Harrison & Fredrickson, 2003).

None of the studies to date have examined ethnic differences with regard to affinity for specific characters (e.g., those which are considered favorites within the broader landscape of an individual's media use tendencies). Focusing on young women's favorite female media characters provides a more specific target of social comparison than scales that assess women's relationship to broadly construed media ideals. It also allows us to explore the kinds of media personae with whom young women consider it pleasurable to engage, rather than having them confront an image or icon that is not familiar or not typical of their media habits.

THE PRESENT STUDY

The vast majority of research on body image concerns is focused on static images in magazines or broad surveys regarding "internalization of thin ideals" (e.g., Thompson et al., 2004). Rarely, researchers have considered the potential impact of characters/figures with whom individuals develop more multidimensional, so-called parasocial bonds (Horton & Wohl, 1956). The latter is, in many ways, more similar to how people may connect with peers than the way in which they connect with fashion models. Of course, media figures we come "to know" on television often embody the same kinds of body ideals as fashion models—precisely why it is critical to study how young women's attitudes about favorite media figures is linked to body concerns. Allowing participants to generate their favorite characters enables us to understand how individuals' chronic body concerns may be linked to chronically accessible, liked, media figures.

Focusing on specific character affinities also has the potential to clarify any differences regarding how White and Black women relate to media characters as well as differences regarding how these media affinities predict body image concerns. Toward this end, we focus on two specific dimensions of character affinity: wishful identification (the desire to be like a favorite character), and perceived similarity (a sense of shared characteristics between the self and the character). Although we do not directly measure individuals' general tendencies to compare themselves with an idealized media figure, we ask them to report on how similar to and how much they *wish* they were similar to a favorite character. In this sense, we are eliciting both a potential social comparison target and a social comparison process, if only for the purposes of the survey.

Beyond this, we also provide increased granularity with regard to self-image by assessing whether approval-based self-worth (Crocker et al., 2003) predicts body image concerns over and above global self-esteem and media affinities across ethnicity. Finally, we probe the nature of Black and White women's favorite character choices (i.e., their ethnicity and body type) to determine whether character qualities are germane to idealization/identification tendencies and/or body concerns.

METHOD

Participants

Data were collected at a large midwestern university from Fall, 2007 through Spring, 2011. Data collection proceeded over multiple semesters to increase the number of Black American women in the sample.[1] Students participated either for course credit or for payment, depending on whether they were drawn from introductory Communication classes (credit) or from classes in the Department of African and African American Studies (DAAS; payment). Although recruiting from DAAS helped us increase the number of Black participants in the sample, it should be noted that both recruitment pools yielded Black and White participants. Further, it is unlikely that White or Black students in the introductory DAAS courses we recruited from were markedly different than other students on campus, given that these courses, although not required, fulfill specific College distribution requirements that all students must complete.

The original sample consisted of 110 White American participants and 41 Black American participants. However, inspection of favorite female character selections showed that eight participants chose characters for whom questions about appearance idealization or perceived similarity would be less relevant (e.g., cartoons, children), and one participant failed to identify a favorite female character. These participants were excluded. Further, one participant who reported a BMI of 50 (approximately 6 SDs above the mean; $M = 23.1$; $SD = 4.4$) was also excluded from the sample. The final sample thus consisted of 37 Black American participants and 104 White American participants. The mean age of the sample was 19.43 years ($SD = 2.13$).

Measures and Procedure

Measures are described in the order in which they appeared on the survey, which was administered online in a web survey format. Participants logged on using their school IDs but were assured that their identifying information was only being used for purposes of providing credit or money and that it would be deleted from the data set before any of their responses were analyzed. . . .

Self-esteem. We used Rosenberg's (1965) 10-item measure of self-esteem, which included items such as: "All in all, I am inclined to feel that I am a failure" (reverse-scored) and "I take a positive attitude toward myself." . . .

Others' approval. We used the others' approval subscale of Crocker et al.'s (2003) Contingencies of Self-Worth Scale (one of seven subscales used to capture domains in which individuals are more or less likely to stake their self-worth). The measure was devised and validated using a diverse sample of college students, and is comprised of five items such as, "What others think of me has no effect on what I think about myself" (reverse-scored) and "My self-esteem depends on the opinions others hold of me. . . .

Body Consciousness. The body surveillance subscale of the Objectified Body Consciousness Scale (McKinley & Hyde, 1996) was used to measure body image concerns.[2] This subscale taps the tendency to evaluate the body from a third party perspective and is negatively correlated with body esteem. . . .

Female character affinities. Participants were asked to list the name of their favorite female character/personality on television and the name of the program on which she appears. Next, they responded to questions designed to tap domains of perceived similarity and wishful identification. Specifically, individuals responded to three questions about how similar they perceived themselves to be to their favorite character's personality, life experiences, and physical appearance. . . .

Body Mass Index. Participants reported their height and weight at the end of the survey, along with other demographic information (e.g., age, ethnicity) so that BMI could be calculated.[3] . . .

DISCUSSION

The present study is the first to examine relationships among media ideals, self-worth, and body concerns for Black and White women by using participants' own favorite female media figures as targets. Although Black and White women reported equivalent levels of perceived similar to a favorite female media figure, Black women showed lower stake in others' approval, lower wishful identification with a favorite female television persona, and lower body surveillance than did White women. Interestingly, our analyses showed that ethnicity did not, in fact, moderate the links between character affinities or concern with others' approval and body surveillance. Women with greater discrepancies between how similar they felt to their chosen character and how much they wanted to *be like* that character reported the highest level of body surveillance. These findings are consistent with other research in which Black women show lower levels of media internalization and/or body concerns but do not differ from White women when it comes to the links among these variables (Jefferson & Stake, 2000; Shaw et al., 2004).

. . . Larger gaps between one's actual and ideal selves result in more emotional distress and dissatisfaction. Importantly, we found this interaction effect after controlling for self-reported BMI. This suggests that the perceived discrepancy is not driven by "objective" body size but rather a subjective positioning of the self relative to media ideals.

Our study is the first to demonstrate that to the extent that Black women *do* report approval concerns, they share the same vigilance re: body surveillance as White women do. Thus, women whose favorite media characters represented an as yet unattained ideal, and who were preoccupied with other people's evaluations, showed the greatest body monitoring tendencies. The study suggests that in attempting to understand women's thoughts and concerns about their bodies, not only is it important to understand how they feel about the real people in their every day life, but also to understand how they feel about the media icons who populate a more distant and often distorted (if emotionally compelling) landscape.

The fact that concern with others' approval was strongly associated with body concerns, after accounting for all other study variables, suggests that young women continue to conflate concern about being valued by others with physical appearance concerns. Moreover, findings suggest that women also continue to view the self from a third-party perspective, which takes its toll on mental health and happiness (Fredrickson & Roberts, 1997). Body surveillance tendencies signify a degree of (normative) preoccupation and worry over whether one's body is being approved by others. As noted earlier, although body surveillance itself does not necessarily imply chronic negative evaluations of the body, it has been found to correlate with lower levels of body esteem and higher levels of body shame. More work is needed to clarify the role that approval concerns play in young women's body image.

Our more fine-grained character analyses, controlling for both self-esteem and BMI, suggest there may be ethnic differences that matter when it comes to understanding how women select and relate to favorite female media characters. Specifically, although White women, compared with Black women, were not significantly more likely to have a favorite character who was thin, those who *did* choose thin characters showed increased wishful identification and body surveillance relative to Black women. A reverse trend emerged within-ethnicity for Black women: those with average/heavy (vs. thin) favorite characters reported increased body surveillance.

It is important to note that being average-size by television standards is not typically at odds with being glamorous (or, for that matter having a "normal" BMI. e.g., Katherine Heigl, Tyra Banks). More work is also needed to continue probing the qualities in media characters that attract young women's admiration, and potentially interfere with a healthy body image. Interestingly, recent work shows that Black women may experience body dissatisfaction and surveillance when deviating from a more curvaceous (vs. thin) standard compared with White women (Overstreet, Quinn, & Agocha, 2010). Additional research is needed to continue clarifying these important details.

Although favorite character body types were not meaningfully related to young women's ethnicity, they were meaningfully linked to character ethnicity (White vs. non-White). Our findings are consistent with previous scholarship suggesting that body norms for women of color are more diverse than the body norms for White women (e.g., Schooler et al., 2004). In the present study, popular non-White characters (e.g., America Ferrera, Tyra Banks) were more likely to have average or heavy body types than White characters (e.g., Jennifer Aniston, Lauren Conrad). Character ethnicity was also relevant to young women's choices and affinities. Specifically, White women were more likely to choose White versus non-White characters and to report greater wishful identification with those characters (and greater similarity to White characters than White women choosing non-White characters). Black women were more evenly split with respect to favorite character ethnicity and reported greater perceived similarity to non-White characters compared with White women. Finally, wishful identification was heightened among Black women with non-White (vs. White) favorite characters.

Taken together, the character analyses suggest that White women show increased affinity for White/thin characters with associated heightened body surveillance, whereas Black show increased affinity for non-White/average weight characters with associated heightened body surveillance. Rather than providing a protective assimilative buffer, as some work on Black women and body image has suggested (e.g., Jefferson & Stake, 2000; Schooler et al., 2004), affinity for self-relevant characters appears to be more versus less implicated in young women's body image concerns. Our results are thus more in line with experimental findings regarding exposure to particular media images (Frisby, 2004; Harrison & Fredrickson, 2003). . . .

Future research is needed to tease apart the impact and extent to which media figures' ethnicity and body type may be conflated with other variables (e.g., assertiveness, comedic talent). The ways in which various media icons explicitly reference and/or resist body image concerns would also be important to study. For example, what is the impact of Tyra Banks' now infamous response to allegedly unflattering tabloid bathing suit pictures, in which she donned the same bathing suit on her show and tearfully and defiantly dared anyone who disparages women for not fitting into a thin ideal to "kiss [her] fat ass"? Are such role models more prevalent among non-White than White media icons? Do powerful media figures like Tyra Banks ultimately send a mixed message regarding the importance of physical appearance by insisting on glamour and endorsing the modeling industry, despite her appropriate outrage at social pressures to be thin? Will Jennifer Hudson's recent, dramatic weight loss and role as a Weight Watchers spokeswoman make the thin ideal all the more compelling for women of color? These would all be important questions to continue asking and answering empirically.

A final key variable to consider for future research would be the extent to which Black women feel ethnically identified with their in-group (e.g., feeling good about belonging to one's ethnic group, seeking information about one's ethnic group). This construct has been found to be relevant to how Black women engage with both themselves and the media (e.g., Rogers Wood & Petrie, 2010; Schooler et al., 2004). Once again the picture is complex at best; some research has found that high ethnic identity is inversely linked to internalization of a thin ideal (Rogers Wood & Petrie, 2010). However, Schooler et al., (2004) found that young women with *lower* scores on ethnic identity show more *positive* self-image with respect to Black-oriented television exposure than women with higher ethnic identities (no association emerged for those with higher ethnic identity scores). The authors reason that Black women with less certain ingroup affiliations may be more likely to view Black television characters as positive role models. Clearly, there is great diversity with respect to how all women, irrespective of ethnic identity, engage with media figures. However, understanding the role of ethnic identity would help clarify when and for whom specific media figures function to boost versus deflate self and body image. . . .

REFERENCES

Botta. R. A. (2000). The mirror of television: A comparasion of black and white adolescent girls' body image disturbance. *Journal of Communication, 50*, 144–159, doi: 10.1111/j.1460-2466.2000.tb02857.x

Crocker, J., Luhtanen, R. K., Cooper. M, L., & Bouvrette, S. (2003). Contingencies of self-worth in college students: Theory and measurement. *Journal of Personality and Social Psychology, 85,* 894–908. doi: 10.1037/0D22-3514.85.5.894

Crocker, J., & Major, B. (1989). Social stigma and self-esteem: The self-proteetive properties of stigma. *Psychological Review, 96,* 608–630. doi: 10.I037/0033-295X.96.4.608

Fredrickson, B. L., & Roberts, T. (1997). Objectification theory: Toward understanding women's lived experiences and mental health risks. *Psychology of Women Quarterly, 21,* 173–206. doi:10.111/j.1471-6402.1997.tb00108.x

Frisby, C. M. (2004), Does race matter? Effects of idealized images on African American women's perceptions of body esteem. *Journal of Black Studies, 34,* 323–347. doi: 10.1177/0021934703258989

Gosling, S. D., Rentfrow, P. J., & Swann, W. B., Jr. (2003). A very brief measure of the Big Five personality domains. *Journal of Research in Personality, 37,* 504–528.

Grabe, S., & Hyde, J. S. (2006). Ethnicity and body dissatisfaction among women in the United States: A Meta-Analysis, *Psychological Bulletin, 132,* 622–640. doi; 10.1037/0033-2909.132.4.622

Harrison, K., & Fredrickson, B. L. (2003). Women's sports media, self objectification, and mental health in Black and White adolescent females. *Journal of Communication, 53,* 216–232. doi: 10.1111/j.1460-2466.2003.tb02587.x

Harrison, K. (1997). Does interpersonal attraction to thin media personalities promote eating disorders? *Journal of Broadcasting & Electronic Media, 41,* 478–500. doi: 10.1080/08838159709364422

Heinberg, L. J., & Thompson, J. K. (1995). Body image and televised images of thinness and attractiveness: A controlled laboratory investigation. *Journal of Social and Clinical Psychology, 14,* 325–338. doi: 10.1521/jscp.1995.14.4.325

Horton, D., & Wohl, R. R. (1956). Mass communication and para-social interaction: Observations on intimacy at a distance. *Psychiatry, 19,* 215–229.

Jefferson, D. L., & Stake, J. E. (2009). Appearance self-attitudes of African American and European American women: Media comparisons and internalization of beauty ideals. *Psychology of Women Quarterly, 33,* 396–409. doi:10.111 1/j. 1471-6402 .2009.01517.x

Lopez-Guimerá, G., Levine, M. P., Sanchez-Carracedo, D., & Fauquet, J. (2010). Influence of mass media on body image and eating disordered attitudes and behaviors in females: A Review of effects and processes. *Media Psychology, 13,* 387–416. dot: 10.1080/15213269.2010.525737

Mckinley, N. M., & Hyde, J. S. (1996). The Objectified Body Consciousness scale: Development and validation. *Psychology of Women Quarterly,* 20, 181–215. doi: 10.1111/j.1471-6402.1996.tb00467.x

McKinley, N. M. (2006). The developmental and cultural contexts of objectified body consciousness: A longitudinal analysis of two cohorts of women. *Developmental Psychology, 42,* 679–687. doi: 10.1037/0012-1649.42.4.679

Overstreet, N. M., Quints, D. M., & Agocha, V. B. (2010). Beyond thinness: The influence of a curvaceous body ideal on body dissatisfaction in Black and White women. *Sex Roles, 63,* 91–103. doi:10.1007/sl 1199-010-9792-4

Rogers Wood, N. A., & Petrie, T. A. (2010). Body dissatisfaction, ethnic identity, and disordered eating among African American women. *Journal of Counseling Psychology, 57,* 141–153. doi:10.1037/a0018922

Rosenberg, M. (1965). *Society and the adolescent self-image.* Princeton, NJ: Princeton University Press.

Rowley, S. J., Sellers, R. M., Chavous, T. M., & Smith, M. A. (1998). The relationship between racial identity and self-esteem in African American college and high school students. *Journal of Personality and Social Psychology, 74,* 715–724. doi: 10.1037/0022-3514.74.3.715

Rubin, L. R., Fitts, M. L., & Becker, A. E. (2003). "Whatever Feels Good in My Soul": Body ethics and aesthetics among African American and Latina Women. *Culture, Medicine and Psychiatiy, 27,* 49–75. doi:10.1023/A:1023679821086

Schooler, D., Ward, L. M., Merriweather, A., & Caruthers, A. (2004). Who's that girl: Television's role in the body image development of young White and Black women. *Psychology of Women Quarterly, 28,* 38–47.doi:10.1111/j.1471-6402.2004.00121.x

Shaw, H., Ramirez, L., Trost, A., Randall, P., & Stice, E. (2004). Body image and eating disturbances across ethnic groups: More similarities than differences. *Psychology of Addictive Behaviors, 18,* 12–18. doi:10.1037/0893-164X.18.1.12

Striegel-Moore, R., & Smolak, L. (1996). The role of race in the development oft eating disorders. L. Smolak, M. P. Levine, R. Striegel-Moore. *The developmental psychopathology of eating disorders: implications for research, prevention, and treatment* (pp. 259–284). Hillsdale, NJ, England: Lawrence Erlbaum Associates, Inc.

Stunkard, A. J., Sorensen, T., & Schulsinger, F. (1983). Use of the Danish adoption register for the study of obesity and thinness. In S. S. Kety, L. P. Rowland, R. L., Sidman & S. W. Matthysse (Eds.), *Genetics of Neurological and Psychiatric Disorders* (pp. 115–120). New York, NY: Raven.

Thompson, J. K., van den Berg, P., Roehrig, M., Guarda, A. S., & Heinberg, L. J. (2004). The sociocultural attitudes towards appearance scale-3 (SATAQ-3): development and validation. *International Journal of Eating Disorders, 35,* 293–304. doi: 10.1002/eat. 10257

NOTES

1. The present article uses the White and Black sub-sample (n = 80 White American participants; n = 13 African American participants) from an earlier article by the first author (Greenwood, 2009) but enables a more meaningful inspection of the role of ethnicity by adding participants (n = 24 White American participants: n = 25 African American participants).

2. Participants also responded to Body Shame subscale items but they were not the focus of inquiry for the present study.

3. BMI was calculated according to the Center for Disease Control and Prevention Website: (Height [inches]/Weight [lbs]^2) × 703

R E A D I N G **33**

What We Do for Love

Rose Weitz (2004)

Rapunzel's life turned around the day a prince climbed up her hair and into her stairless tower. The rest of us sometimes suspect that, as was true for Rapunzel, our hair offers us the key to finding a prince who'll bring us love and happiness. Yet surprisingly often, when we talk about hair and romance, we talk not only about love but also about power—the ability to obtain desired goals through controlling or influencing others. Power exists not only when a politician fixes an election or an army conquers a country, but also when we style our hair to get boyfriends or to keep men away, and when our boyfriends browbeat us into cutting our hair or growing it longer.

CATCHING A MAN

Hair plays a central role in romantic relationships, from start to finish. If we're in the mood for love (or sex), from the moment we meet someone, we begin an internal calculus, reckoning how attractive we find him and how attractive he seems to find us.

If he finds us attractive, our power will increase, for in any relationship, whoever wants the relationship most holds the least power.[1]

Attractiveness, of course, means many different things. A man might be attracted to a woman because of her income, interest in sports, or good sense of humor. But when it comes to dating—especially first dates—pretty women, like pretty girls, usually come out ahead. In a recent experiment, researchers placed bogus personal ads for two women, one a "beautiful waitress," the other an "average looking, successful lawyer." The waitress received almost three times more responses than the lawyer. (The reverse was true for men: the "successful lawyer" received four times more responses from women than did the "handsome cabdriver.") Other studies also have found that men choose their dates based more on women's looks than on women's earning potential, personality, or other factors.[2]

In a world where beautiful waitresses get more dates than do successful women lawyers, it makes perfect sense for women to use their looks to catch and keep men. Although some writers imply that women who do so are merely blindly obeying cultural rules for feminine appearance and behavior—acting as "docile bodies," in the words of the French philosopher Michel Foucault—most women are acutely aware of those rules and know exactly what they are doing and why.[3]

The first step in getting a man is catching his eye. A classic way to do so is with the "hair flip." Of course, the flip can be an innocent gesture, intended only to get the hair out of our eyes or move a tickling strand off our cheeks. But often it's consciously used to get men's attention while on dates, in classes, stopped at red lights, and elsewhere. If you want to see it in action, sit at any bar. Sooner or later a woman will look around the room, find a man who interests her, wait until he turns toward her, and then—ever so nonchalantly—flip her hair.

Hair flipping can be an amazingly studied act. In response to an e-mail query on the subject that I sent to students at my university, a white undergraduate female replied,

> I have very long hair and do use the hair flip, both consciously and unconsciously. When I do it [consciously], I check the room to see if anyone is looking in my direction, but never catch a guy's eye first. I just do it in his line of vision. [I] bend over slightly (pretending to get something from a bag or pick something up) so that some of my hair falls in front of my shoulders. Then I lean back and flip my hair out, and then shake my head so my hair sways a little. I make sure that the hair on the opposite side ends up in front of my shoulder. I keep that shoulder a little bit up with my head tilted and lean on the hand that I used to flip my hair.

Similarly, in the film *Legally Blonde*, the lead character, Elle, instructs her dumpy friend Paulette how to "bend and snap"—bending over so her hair will fall forward, then standing up while snapping her head and hair back to catch men's attention.

Other times the hair flip is less studied, but the motivation is the same. A Mexican-American student writes:

> I tend to flip my hair when I see an attractive male, but I do it unconsciously. I don't think, "Okay, here

he comes, so now I have to flip my hair." It's more of a nervous, attention-getting thing. When I see a good-looking guy and get that uneasy feeling in my stomach, I run my fingers through my hair and flip it to make it look fuller and to attract his eye as he passes. If there isn't enough room to flip my hair, I'll play with a strand of hair instead.

Whether conscious or unconscious, hair flipping works. In a world that expects women to speak in a low tone, keep eyes down, and sit quietly with legs together and elbows tucked in, the hair flip says, "Look at me." . . .

Even when a man finds neither long hair nor the flip inherently attractive, flipping hair can whet his interest. The gesture itself draws the eyes by taking up space and causing motion. Perhaps more important, men know the flip can be a form of flirtation. As a result, they pay close attention to any woman who flips her hair to see whether she's flirting with them, flirting with someone else, or simply getting the hair out of her eyes.

This use of the hair flip doesn't escape notice by women with short hair. An undergraduate writes:

> In Hispanic culture hair is very important for a woman. It defines our beauty and gives us power over men. Now that I cut my hair short, I miss the feeling of moving my hair around and the power it gave me. . . . It is kind of a challenge [to other women] when a woman flips her hair. [She's] telling me that she has beautiful healthy hair and is moving it to get attention from a male or envy from me.

The hair flip is especially aggravating for those black women whose hair will not grow long. As one black graduate student explains,

> As an African-American woman, I am very aware of non-African-American women "flipping" their hair. . . . I will speak only for myself here (but I think it's a pretty global feeling for many African-American women), but I often look at women who can flip their hair with envy, wishfulness, perhaps regret? . . . With my "natural" hair, if I run my fingers through it, it's going to be a mess [and won't] gracefully fall back into place.

She now wears long braided extensions and, she says, flips her hair "constantly."

In the same way that women use their hair's motion to catch men, they use its style and color. Cecilia told how she dyed her hair Kool-Aid bright to horrify others in her small Southern town. These days her hair decisions serve very different purposes:

> I can think of an occasion where I changed my hair while I was dating this guy. I had this feeling that he was losing attraction for me and I'd just been feeling the need to do something to my appearance. And my hair is always the easiest way to go. It's too expensive to buy a new wardrobe. There's nothing you can do about your face. So your hair, you can go and have something radically done to it and you'll look like a different person.

With this in mind, Cecilia cut off about seven inches of her hair:

> It was kind of a radical haircut, shaved, kind of asymmetrical, and [dyed] a reddish maroon color. When he saw me, [he] was like, "Whoa! . . . Oh, my God, look at it!" He just couldn't stop talking about it. . . . He said, "I don't know, there's just something about you. I really want to be with you."

When I ask how she felt about his rekindled interest in her, she replies, "I was pretty pleased with myself."

Few women would cut their hair asymmetrically and dye it maroon to capture a man's interest, but millions try to do so by dyeing their hair blonde. Of the 51 percent of women who dye their hair, about 40 percent dye it blonde.[4] (Most of the rest dye it brunette shades simply to cover any gray.) Several women I've talked to, when asked why they dye their hair blonde, responded by singing the old advertising ditty: "Is it true blondes have more fun?" These women, like many others, have found blonde hair a sure way to spark men's interest.

But being a blonde can be a mixed blessing: Remember Marilyn Monroe. To catch men's attention without being labeled dumb, passive, or "easy" (stereotypes that haunt all blondes, dyed or natural), about 20 percent of women who dye their hair instead choose shades of red. Red hair, they believe, draws men's interest while calling on a different set of stereotypes, telling men that they are smart, wild, and passionate.[5] Brenda, a quiet, petite twenty-eight-year-old, for many years envied her golden-blonde sister's popularity. A few years ago she began dyeing her hair red to "let people know I'm a competent person, independent, maybe a little hotheaded—or maybe a lot hotheaded, [even] fiery." Dyeing her hair red, she believes,

> *made* people see me. . . . Before I dyed my hair, my sister and I would go out and all these guys would ask her to dance and talk to her and ask for her number and I would just be standing there. And after I started dyeing my hair, I started getting noticed a little bit more. I also stopped waiting to be asked.

Brenda credits her marriage in part to her red hair; her husband approached her initially because he "always wanted to date a redhead."

Using our hair to look attractive is particularly important for those of us whose femininity is sometimes questioned. Since Jane Fonda began selling her fitness videos in 1982, women (or at least middle-class women) have been expected to look as though they "work out." Yet those whose broad shoulders and muscular arms and legs announce them as dedicated athletes are still often stigmatized as unfeminine, or denigrated as suspected lesbians. Since most true athletes can't have manicured nails (which can break during sports) or wear makeup (which can smear from sweat), those who want to look attractively feminine often rely on their hair. The tennis-playing Williams sisters and the U.S. women's soccer team won the hearts of Americans not only through their athletic skills but also because their beaded braids and ponytails, respectively, told us they were still feminine and heterosexual (an image bolstered by constant news coverage about the Williamses' fashion sense and the soccer players' boyfriends and husbands). Similarly, most professional female bodybuilders counterbalance their startlingly muscular bodies with long, curled, and dyed blonde hair. Those who don't do so risk losing contests, no matter how large and well-sculpted their muscles.[6]

Similar pressures weigh on black women. Although it is far less true today than in the past, many people—whites and blacks, men and women—still regard black women as less feminine and less attractive than white women. . . .

As a result of such attitudes, black women often feel especially obligated to do what they can to increase their attractiveness. Within the black community attractiveness still primarily centers on having light skin and long, straight hair.[7] Since there's little one can do about one's skin color, much of black women's attention to their looks focuses on their hair. Norma explains,

> If you are an African-American woman and you have long hair, you are automatically assumed to be pretty, unless your face is just awful! [But if you have short, tightly curled hair like mine,] African-American males [will] say "I'm not going out with her, her head is as bald as mine!" Or they will call [you] "nappy head."

To avoid such treatment without subjecting herself to the difficulties and expense of straightening her hair, Norma now wears a wig with shoulder-length straight hair. Her husband approves. Many other black women do the same, creating a substantial market in the black community for wigs (ads for which appear regularly in the major black magazines), while many others rely on purchased hair extensions.

But each of these options carries a price. In choosing straightened hair, wigs, or extensions over natural hair, black women obtain hair that *looks* good in exchange for hair that *feels* good to the touch. If your lover starts stroking your wig, it might fall off or come askew. If he strokes your extensions, expensive hair that took hours to attach may come out. If you've got a weave, his fingers will hit upon the web of thread holding the hair in. And if he tries to stroke your carefully coiffed straightened hair, not only will it lose its style, but it will feel stiff and oily or, if it hasn't been moisturized in a while, like brittle straw. Or it might just break off. To avoid these problems, black women teach the men and boys around them never to touch a woman's hair. Stephen, a twenty-three-year-old black student, told me:

> The same way you learn as a kid not to touch that cookie in the cookie jar, you learn not to touch that

hair. I remember once trying to touch my mother's hair and having her slap my hands away. . . .

> You learn at beauty parlors, too. When I was a kid, my mom would go to the beauty parlor every two weeks. And it would take six hours to do her hair sometimes, and we would have to sit around the whole time. So we saw how long it took and how important it was for them. And then you'd hear the stylists tell the little girls not to touch their hair afterwards. And you'd hear all the women talking about their own hair, and how they would have to sleep sitting up to keep from messing it. Or they'd say, "That man better not try to touch my head, I just paid $200 for this hair!"

When black women date either white men or the rare black man who hasn't been properly trained, the women keep the men's hands away by covering their hair before coming to bed, relying on quick maneuvers to keep their hair out of harm's way, saying they need to get their hair done and it's not fit to be touched, or saying they just had their hair done and don't want it ruined.[8]

Like black women, disabled women also can rely on their hair to make themselves seem more feminine and attractive. . . . In contemporary America disabled women are often ridiculed as unattractive and asexual, leaving them more likely than either disabled men or nondisabled women to remain single, to marry at later ages, and to get divorced.[9]

When I interviewed Debra, who became quadriplegic in a car accident when she was twenty, she was sitting in her kitchen. Her hair was immaculately styled: dyed and frosted shades of blonde, with perfectly placed bangs and neat waves falling below her shoulders.

Although Debra always cared about her appearance, her disability has heightened its importance for her. As she explains,

> When people first see someone in a wheelchair, the image they have [is] like a "bag of bones" or something toting urine. They expect the person to not have a high level of hygiene. . . . People will actually say things to me like "You are so much cleaner than I expected," and will give me shampoo as gifts because they assume I need the help. I'm trying to beat that image.

For Debra, keeping her hair nicely styled is a point of pride. It also offers her the pleasure of feeling more feminine and feeling at least partly in control of her body. Like other disabled and overweight women, this is particularly important for her because in other ways she can't make her body do what she wants. Controlling her hair also takes on special significance because it's difficult for her to find attractive, nicely fitting clothes suitable for someone who spends her days in a wheelchair and who can't dress herself.

. . .

But even able-bodied, slender white women take risks when they rely on their appearance to bolster their self-confidence and their attractiveness. Attractiveness offers only a fragile sort of power, achieved one day at a time through concentrated effort and expenditures of time and money. As a result, the occasional "bad hair day" can seem a catastrophe. From the moment we realize our hair just isn't going to cooperate, things start going badly. We spend extra time trying to style our hair in the morning, then have to run out the door because we're late. By the time we get to work or school, we're feeling both frazzled and self-conscious about our appearance. Throughout the day, a small voice in the back of our head may nag, berating us either for not having our act together or for worrying what others are thinking. As a result, we lose self-confidence and the ability to concentrate, as well as prospects for male approval. In the long run, too, if a man is interested in us only because of our looks, his interest likely won't last. (It may not even survive the morning after, when we awake with bleary eyes, no makeup, and "bed head.") And attractiveness must decline with age, as more than one middle-aged society woman dumped for a younger "trophy wife" has discovered.

HAIR IN RELATIONSHIPS

Once we are in a relationship, hair can bring pleasure to our partners and ourselves. If our hair is long enough, we can drape it over our partner's chest to form a silky curtain, or swing it from side to side to tease and caress him. And whether our hair is long or short, our partner can enjoy the pleasure of brushing it, washing it, smoothing his hands over it, or weaving his fingers through it. In addition, caring for our hair enables the men in our lives to show their love and affection without having to put their feelings into words.

Eva's relationship with her husband, Stanley, epitomizes this dynamic. After more than forty years of marriage, it's clear that he's still smitten. While I am interviewing Eva, Stanley seems unable to stay out of the room. Once in the room, his eyes linger on her. His hand grazes her hair and keeps drifting to her shoulder. Although to me Eva's hair seems ordinary, he makes more than one comment about its beauty.

Ever since he retired, Stanley has dyed Eva's hair for her. They describe this as a way to save time and money, and I'm sure it does. But they're retired and wealthy, so I'm convinced that Stanley cares for Eva's hair primarily as a way of caring for Eva.

Sometimes, though, the pleasures of hair turn to perils if our partners come to view our hair as an object for their own pleasure. Learning to do so begins early, when boys realize they can pull girls' braids in schoolyards and classes and touch girls' hair against their will, with few if any repercussions. Once in relationships, some boys and men will come to think of their girlfriend's or wife's hair as their property or as a reflection on them. When this happens, our hair becomes an object for a man to critique or control. For example, when Debra met her first boyfriend, a couple of years before her accident, her hair was waist-length. The boyfriend had previously dated a hairstylist who taught him how to style hair and gave him his own haircutting equipment. Although Debra wasn't happy about it, he quickly took charge of her hair and began cutting it shorter and shorter with each passing month. "It ended up being a control feature in our relationship," she says. "He always wanted it worn very spiky and short, and I hated that look." He also took control of dyeing her hair. "It ended up being a trust game," she recalls, "where he'd say, 'I'm going to go get a hair color, and you're not going to know what color it is. So you have to trust me that I will not make you ugly.' . . . In retrospect, the relationship really was very controlling."

At the extreme, men's control of women's hair can become violent. In a recent study, the sociologist Kathryn Farr looked at thirty consecutive reported cases of woman-battering that escalated to attempted homicides. In three of those cases, the police noted in the record that the man had cut the woman's hair by force during the attack. (The men may well have done so in additional cases without the police noting it.) The attitude of these men toward their wives and girlfriends comes through clearly in a fourth case that did not quite meet Farr's definition of attempted homicide. After the man in that case finished punching and kicking his girlfriend, he forced her to kneel on the floor and began cutting her hair. When she asked why he was doing this, he replied, "You belong to me and I can do anything I want."[10]

. . .

CELEBRATING INDEPENDENCE FROM MEN

In the same way we sometimes use our hair to attract men, we also can use our hair to proclaim our independence from a particular man or from men in general. Darla first met her husband on a blind date in 1949, when she was fifteen. Normally before a date Darla would wash her hair, set it, and leave it to dry in curlers for three hours before combing it out and styling it. This time, though, to show that she "was not the kind of girl who went out on blind dates, [and] was just not impressed with that idea at all," she didn't set her hair until right before he arrived.

When the doorbell rang, Darla went to greet her date with her hair in curlers and wrapped in a bandanna. She immediately realized she'd made a big mistake:

> Here was this young god standing there. Black wavy hair, way better [looking] than James Dean. And not only that, he was all dressed up. He had on a white shirt and tie. And there was nothing I could do about my hair.

To compensate for her hair faux pas, Darla excused herself so she could triple-check her makeup and swap her pedal-pushers for a pretty skirt. Then they went out, as if there were nothing unusual about going on a date wearing curlers:

> He did not say anything [about my hair]. And he didn't seem to be turned off. . . . I think he found me attractive. . . . The fact that I had my hair up in curlers didn't seem to bother him at all, which impressed me.

When he called for a second date, Darla made sure her hair looked great. They've now been married more than fifty years.

Although few of us would, like Darla, use our hair to signal our lack of interest in a man at the beginning of a relationship, many of us do so when a relationship breaks up. After Roxanne got divorced, she dated a man who loved her hair and who took great pleasure in braiding, brushing, and especially washing it. But they had "a very bad breakup," leading Roxanne to decide to cut her hair. When I ask her why, she replies by singing the lyric from *South Pacific:* "I'm gonna wash that man right out of my hair." As she explains, "I had to get rid of everything that he liked, and I started with my hair." She "felt great" afterward.

. . .

Although Roxanne used her hair to reject her former partners, she didn't want to reject men in general and continued to use her hair to attract men's attention. But other women use their hair, at least occasionally, to *reduce* men's interest in them. For example, LaDonna, a black woman who [has] described the attention her hair brought her as a child, usually enjoys the power her naturally long and wavy hair now gives her over black men. Nonetheless, her hair is a mixed blessing, because she can't control who will be attracted to it (her handsome neighbor or her married boss?) or why (because he simply likes long hair or because he thinks hair that looks "white" is superior?). As a result, she says, "It's kind of funny, because I know it [my hair] will get me attention, and I do things to make it look nice that I know will get me attention, but sometimes I don't wear my hair down because I *don't* want the attention. I don't feel like dealing with this."

Susan goes to even greater lengths to avoid male attention. She's probably the prettiest woman I interviewed, with the prettiest hair. Her blue eyes and cascade of naturally curling dark hair contrast attractively with her pale skin, giving her a girl-next-door sort of appeal that matches her outgoing nature. Susan met her husband, who is an Egyptian Muslim, when they were both studying in England. Once she began dating him, the other Arab men in the school seemed to consider her "fair game." So long as her boyfriend was around she felt safe, but her fears grew when he left the school six weeks before she did. During those weeks, she recalled, "The Arab men were all over me, constantly bugging me. . . . I was afraid I would get raped by one of them one night."

After they returned to the United States, Susan and her boyfriend married. As she began to learn more about Islam, her interest in it grew, and she decided to convert. A few months later they went to visit her husband's family home. Expecting the men there to treat her as they would any Muslim woman, she was appalled when they instead treated her as a "loose" American. To convince others that she was a chaste Muslim and to protect herself from sexual harassment or worse when her husband was absent, she began wearing a hijab (a traditional robe) and covering her hair in Muslim fashion. Her husband, aghast, told her that if he'd wanted a traditional Muslim bride, he would have married one. Moreover, in his city only the oldest women still wore head coverings, which were now considered old-fashioned, ugly, and "backward." It's not surprising, then, that, as Susan describes, "He flipped out. He got so upset. He *wants* my hair to show, because . . . he wants to show me off."

Still, feeling that her physical safety was at risk, Susan ignored his wishes and began covering her head. Her strategy succeeded:

> If you are not born Muslim and you are American, [and] you're not dressed the way they [Arab men] think is best for a Muslim women, and covering your head, . . . they'll think you're loose [and] treat you disrespectfully. . . . But when I put the hijab on and covered my head, . . . everybody changed how they treated me.

After they got back to the United States, Susan decided to continue veiling. Like other Muslim-American women who veil, she enjoyed the sense of empowerment the veil brought her by reminding her of her religion and her God.[11] And, even though she no longer felt physically at risk, she continued to appreciate the protection from men's eyes that the veil afforded her. Without the veil, she says, "You feel like you're naked. . . . Men would look at me and smile and I'd know that they thought I was beautiful. I don't want that. I just want my husband to think that."

Susan's husband objected even more vociferously to her desire to veil herself once they returned to the United States. After a series of fights, they compromised and agreed that she could cover most of her hair with a turban if he was with her in public, and could veil more completely if he wasn't.

For Susan, the fights and the eventual compromise were worth it. She recognizes that women gain rewards for displaying attractive hair, but feels that the power she gets from *covering* her hair is greater:

> Men open doors for you. Not just Arabic men but, even more, American men. What must be going through their heads is exactly what you are trying to put across: that I am . . . a person of God, someone who is chaste. And they're very helpful, very respectful. And I don't think it's that they think you are submissive, because I don't appear submissive. I talk, I stand tall. I'm by myself. It's not like I'm with my husband and I don't say anything.

Most tellingly, she notes, "It's hard for Americans to think that a woman could be empowered without using her body and beauty to do it. [But] my power comes from within."

At the same time, Susan has paid a price for her choice. Her husband remains unhappy about her veiling, which strains their marriage. She's also sentenced herself to a hot, uncomfortable head covering, given up the pleasure of playing with personal ornamentation, and foresworn the myriad benefits—in addition to those that occur within intimate relationships—that come to those who look attractive to the world in general.

Still, because Susan is married and doesn't work outside the home, she can afford to make this choice. Women who have paid jobs, on the other hand, must style their hair in ways that balance relationship issues with career requirements—or pay the consequences.

. . .

NO MORE BAD HAIR DAYS

There's no getting around it: As it was for Rapunzel, hair is central to our identities and our prospects. Whenever we cut our hair short or grow it long, cover the gray or leave it alone, dye it blonde or dye it turquoise, curl it or straighten it, we decide what image we want to present to the world. And the world responds in kind, deciding who we are and how to treat us based in part on what our hair looks like.

At one level, this is perfectly natural. Whenever we first meet someone, we need to figure out what sort of person he or she is (a threat? a potential friend? a new boss? a new client?), and often need to do so quickly. As a result, we use any clues available to decipher whether that person is wealthy, middle-class, or poor; friendly or aloof; athletic or bookish; and so on. Hair offers one of the most visible clues. This is why people who have no hair typically look less individualistic; although their bald heads are distinctive, their faces often seem vaguely alike.

But for all its naturalness, this process of defining ourselves and others through hair is also a product of culture. As we've seen, girls have to be taught to consider their hair central to their identities and to use their hair to manipulate both their self-identity and the image they project to others. And although it's probably true that humans are innately attracted to beauty, the definition of beautiful hair varies across time and culture—how many beautiful women these days sport six-inch-high beehives?—and so girls must learn how beauty is defined in their particular social world. Once they do, they quickly also learn that a wide variety of rewards accrue to those who most closely meet beauty norms.

In part because our hair plays such a large role in how we view ourselves and are viewed by others, it offers us many opportunities for pleasure. Each day our hair provides us with the means to create ourselves anew—at least until our perm, relaxer, or hair dye grows out. And in comparison to losing weight, affording a better-looking wardrobe, or finding true love, changing our lives by changing our hair seems downright easy. Styling our hair also offers the artistic and, at times, intellectual pleasure of sculpting a highly malleable substance. Often, too, hairstyling is a community affair, involving friends, relatives, or stylists and bringing us the pleasures of laughing, joking, working, talking, and sharing our lives with other women. What's more, the results of our efforts bring sensual and sexual pleasures to us and to our lovers, be they male or female.

But each of these pleasures of hair also carries dangers. As girls learn the importance of attractive hair (and of attractiveness in general); start spending time, energy, and money on their appearance; and come to evaluate both themselves and other girls on their appearance and on their ability to attract the opposite sex, they help perpetuate the idea that only a limited range of female appearance is acceptable. More insidiously, their actions make it seem as if focusing on appearance is something that girls do naturally, rather than something girls must learn to do. This in turn limits the life chances both of girls who succeed at attractiveness and of those who don't, for those who succeed sometimes must struggle to be seen as more than just a pretty image and those who fail are often denigrated not only as unattractive but also as lazy, unintelligent, and incompetent. At the same time, the focus on appearance teaches girls to view each other as competitors and limits the potential for true friendship between them.

By the time we reach adulthood, all of us have, at least to some extent, absorbed these lessons. Yet this does not mean that we docilely internalize them and blindly seek male approval for our appearance, as some writers seem to suggest.[12] Rather, each of us chooses daily how far she will go to meet beauty expectations. As we've seen, some of us choose hairstyles for convenience, some to project a professional image, some to reject notions of proper femininity or to reject male approval altogether. Moreover, those of us whose main goal in styling our hair is to attract men typically know perfectly well what we're doing. Far from meekly and unconsciously following cultural scripts, we actively use our appearance to get what we want: wearing long extensions, dyeing our hair blonde or red, flipping it off our shoulders to catch men's eyes, spiking it with gel to suggest sexy rebelliousness, and so on. In a world that still all too often holds women back and expects them to accept passively whatever life brings, those of us who manipulate our appearance to manipulate men and to create opportunities that might otherwise be denied us—whether getting a promotion or marrying well—can sometimes seem like rebels, resisting the narrow role in which others would place us.

That said, it would be equally wrong to overstate the extent to which, in manipulating our appearance, we manipulate our social position and so resist those who would constrain our lives and options.[13] Whether we wear our hair in blonde curls to attract men's interest or in short, professional styles to move ahead in the corporate world, we're still limited by social stereotypes regarding women's nature and capabilities. Although our hair can help us achieve our personal goals, it cannot change those stereotypes. Rather, such strategies *reinforce* stereotypes by reinforcing the idea that appearance is central to female identity. In the long run, therefore, they limit all girls' and women's opportunities. Even those hair strategies that seem most to embody resistance, like "lesbian power cuts" and voluntary baldness, have limited ability to change women's position since, like Afros, they either stigmatize their wearers and reduce their ability to achieve their goals or evolve into mere fashions that lack political effect.

The truth, then, lies somewhere in between these two positions. In our decisions about hair, we actively and rationally make choices based on a realistic assessment of how we can best obtain our goals, given cultural expectations regarding female appearance and given our personal resources. As this suggests, girls and women are far from free agents. If we ignore cultural expectations for female appearance we pay a price in lost wages, diminished marital prospects, lowered status, and so on. If we attempt to follow cultural expectations, we pay a price in time, money, and energy when we obsess about our hair; in low self-esteem when our hair fails us; and in low esteem from others when we are considered

little more than the sum total of our hair and our appearance.

. . .

Only when all girls and women are freed from stereotypical expectations about our natures and abilities will we also be freed from the bonds of the beauty culture. Again, we can see those effects already. Girls whose athletic, creative, or academic interests are nurtured, taking into account and valuing all levels of abilities; whose special talents are rewarded with approval from parents and teachers; who attend schools and universities where their particular skills and talents are appreciated; and who believe that their futures hold myriad intriguing possibilities are far less likely than other girls to center their identities on their appearance. In such environments, too, others are more likely to evaluate girls on their personality and achievements and less likely to evaluate them on their looks. By the same token, women whose social and economic positions are based not on their looks but on their intellect, personality, skills, talents, and achievements can afford to regard their hair as a personal pleasure rather than as a tool for pleasing or manipulating others.

Rapunzel had only one way to change her life: attracting a prince through her hair and her beauty. All of us these days have more options than that. Still, as it was for Rapunzel, our hair remains an almost magical substance: both uniquely public, open to others' interpretations, and uniquely personal, growing out of our bodies and molded (if imperfectly) to our individual desires. For this reason, hair will continue to serve as a marker of our individual identity throughout our lives. Yet our hair can also be simply fun: an idle amusement, a sensuous pleasure, an outlet for creativity, a means for bonding with others, and a way of playing with who we are and who we might become. The more control we gain over our lives as girls and women, the more freedom we will have to truly enjoy and celebrate our hair.

NOTES

1. On the social psychology of relationships, see Judith A. Howard, "Social Psychology of Identities," *Annual Review of Sociology* 26 (2000): 367–93.

Physical appearance also, of course, plays a role in romantic relationships between women. However, existing data on this topic are very mixed. Some studies suggest that lesbians find a broader range of appearance acceptable than do heterosexuals, and other studies indicate that mainstream appearance norms are equally important in the lesbian community. See Dawn Atkins, ed., *Looking Queer: Body Image and Identity in Lesbian, Bisexual, Gay, and Transgender Communities* (New York: Haworth, 1998); and Jeanine C. Cogan, "Lesbians Walk the Tightrope of Beauty: Thin Is In But Femme Is Out," *Journal of Lesbian Studies* 3, no. 4 (1999): 77–89. This topic deserves a fuller treatment than I can give in this [reading], and so I have chosen only to discuss heterosexual relationships here.

2. David M. Buss, Todd K. Shackelford, Lee A. Kirkpatrick, and Randy J. Larsen, "A Half Century of Mate Preferences: The Cultural Evolution of Values," *Journal of Marriage and the Family* 62 (2001): 491–503; Susan Sprecher, "The Importance to Males and Females of Physical Attractiveness, Earning Potential, and Expressiveness in Initial Attraction," *Sex Roles* 21 (1989): 591–607; Erich Goode, "Gender and Courtship Entitlement: Responses to Personal Ads," *Sex Roles* 34 (1996): 141–69.

3. Michel Foucault, *Discipline and Punish: The Birth of the Prison* (New York: Vintage, 1979), and *History of Sexuality* (New York: Pantheon, 1980). For critiques of feminist writings that emphasize women's docility, see Lyn Mikel Brown, *Raising Their Voices: The Politics of Girls' Anger* (Cambridge, Mass.: Harvard University Press, 1998); Kathy Davis, "Remaking the She-Devil: A Critical Look at Feminist Approaches to Beauty," *Hypatia* 6, no. 2 (1991): 21–42; and Lois McNay, "The Foucauldian Body and the Exclusion of Experience," *Hypatia* 6, no. 3 (1991): 125–39.

4. *DSN Retailing Today,* "Salon-Inspired Hair Products Weave Their Way into Mass Market," 40 (5): 17 (2001); and Victoria Wurdinger, "The Haircolor Report," *Drug and Cosmetic Industry* 161 (4): 38–47 (1997). In contrast, about 10 percent of men dye their hair (a sharp increase over previous years), with most doing so to impress other young men with their "coolness." See Dana Butcher, "More Than a Shave and a Haircut," *Global Cosmetic Industry* 166, no. 1 (2000): 45–48.

5. For stereotypes of blondes and redheads, see Wendy Cooper, *Hair: Sex, Society, and Symbolism* (New York: Stein and Day, 1971); Saul Feinman and

George W. Gill, "Sex Differences in Physical Attractiveness Preferences," *Journal of Social Psychology* 105 (1978): 43–52; Druann Maria Heckert and Amy Best, "Ugly Duckling to Swan: Labeling Theory and the Stigmatization of Red Hair," *Symbolic Interaction* 20 (1997): 365–84; Dennis E. Clayson and Micol R. C. Maughan, "Redheads and Blonds: Stereotypic Images," *Psychological Reports* 59 (1986): 811–16; and Diana J. Kyle and Heike I. M. Mahler, "The Effects of Hair Color and Cosmetic Use on Perceptions of a Female's Ability," *Psychology of Women Quarterly* 20 (1996): 447–55.

6. For further discussion of this process (referred to in the scholarly literature as a "feminine apologetic"), see Dan C. Hilliard, "Media Images of Male and Female Professional Athletes: An Interpretive Analysis of Magazine Articles," *Sociology of Sport Journal* 1 (1984): 251–62; and Maria R. Lowe, *Women of Steel: Female Body Builders and the Struggle for Self-Definition* (New Brunswick, N.J.: Rutgers University Press, 1998). Quote is from Lowe, 123–24.

7. For data on the prevalence and nature of attitudes toward black women, see Rose Weitz and Leonard Gordon, "Images of Black Women among Anglo College Students," *Sex Roles* 28 (1993): 19–45. Numerous books discuss attitudes toward black women's bodies and hair, including Ingrid Banks, *Hair Matters: Beauty, Power, and Black Women's Consciousness* (New York: New York University Press, 2000); Patricia Hill Collins, *Black Feminist Thought: Knowledge, Consciousness, and the Politics of Empowerment* (London: Routledge, 1991), 67–90; Maxine Craig, *Ain't I a Beauty Queen?: Black Women, Beauty, and the Politics of Race* (Berkeley: University of California Press, 2002); Noliwe M. Rooks, *Hair Raising: Beauty, Culture, and African American Women* (New Brunswick, N.J.: Rutgers University Press, 1996); and Ayana D. Byrd and Lori L. Tharps, *Hair Story: Untangling the Roots of Black Hair in America* (New York: St. Martin's Press, 2001).

8. Cherilyn Wright, "If You Let Me Make Love to You, Then Why Can't I Touch Your Hair?" in *Tenderheaded: A Comb-Bending Collection of Hair Stories,* edited by Juliette Harris and Pamela Johnson (New York: Pocket Books, 2001), 64–165.

9. Regarding the importance of fatness in African beauty contests, see Norimitsu Onishi, "Maradi Journal: On the Scale of Beauty, Weight Weighs Heavily," *New York Times,* February 12, 2001. Regarding stereotypes and experiences of disabled women,

see Michelle Fine and Adrienne Asch, eds., *Women with Disabilities: Essays in Psychology, Culture, and Politics* (Philadelphia: Temple University Press, 1988); Adrienne Asch and Michelle Fine, "Nurturance, Sexuality, and Women with Disabilities: The Example of Women and Literature," in *Disability Studies Reader,* edited by Lennard J. Davis (New York: Routledge, 1997); and William John Hanna and Betsy Rogovsky, "Women with Disabilities: Two Handicaps Plus," in *Perspectives on Disability,* 2nd ed., edited by Mark Nagler (Palo Alto, Calif.: Health Markets Research, 1993).

10. Kathryn Farr, Department of Sociology, Portland State University, personal communication with the author.

11. Jen'nan Ghazal Read and John P. Bartkowski, "To Veil or Not to Veil? A Case Study of Identity Negotiation among Muslim Women in Austin, Texas," *Gender & Society* 14 (2000): 395–417.

12. Writers who have been criticized for emphasizing women's docility include Sandra Lee Bartky, "Foucault, Femininity, and the Modernization of Patriarchal Power," in *Feminism and Foucault,* edited by Irene Diamond and Lee Quinby (Boston: Northeastern University Press, 1988), and Susan R. Bordo, "The Body and the Reproduction of Femininity: A Feminist Appropriation of Foucault," in *Gender/Body/ Knowledge,* edited by Alison M. Jaggar and Susan R. Bordo (New Brunswick, N.J.: Rutgers University Press, 1989).

13. Writers who have been criticized for overstating women's resistance include Lyn Mikel Brown, *Raising Their Voices: The Politics of Girls' Anger* (Cambridge, Mass.: Harvard University Press, 1998); Kathy Davis, "Remaking the She-Devil: A Critical Look at Feminist Approaches to Beauty," *Hypatia* 6, no. 2 (1991): 21–42; Kathy Davis, *Reshaping the Female Body: The Dilemma of Cosmetic Surgery* (New York: Routledge, 1995); and Lois McNay, "The Foucauldian Body and the Exclusion of Experience," *Hypatia* 6, no. 3 (1991): 125–39. Among those who have criticized such research are Scott Davies, "Leaps of Faith: Shifting Currents in Critical Sociology of Education," *American Journal of Sociology* 100 (1995): 1448–78; Joan Ringelheim, "Women and the Holocaust," *Signs: A Journal of Women in Society* 10 (1985): 741–61; and Myra Dinnerstein and Rose Weitz, "Jane Fonda, Barbara Bush and Other Aging Bodies: Femininity and the Limits of Resistance," *Feminist Issues* 14 (1994): 3–24.

R E A D I N G **34**

Hold That Nose

Lisa Miya-Jervis (2003)

I'm a Jew. I'm not even slightly religious. Aside from attending friends' bat mitzvahs, I've been to temple maybe twice. I don't know Hebrew; my junior-high self, given the option of religious education, easily chose to sleep in on Sunday mornings. My family skips around the Passover Haggadah to get to the food faster. Before I dated someone from an observant family, I wouldn't have known a mezuzah if it bit me on the butt. I was born assimilated.

But still, I'm a Jew, an ethnic Jew of a very specific variety: a godless, New York City–raised, neurotic middle-class girl from a solidly liberal-Democratic family, who attended largely Jewish, "progressive" schools. When I was growing up, almost everyone around me was Jewish; I was stunned when I found out that Jews make up only 2 percent of the American population. For me, being Jewish meant that on Christmas Day my family went out for Chinese food and took in the new Woody Allen movie. It also meant that I had a big honkin' nose.

And I still do. By virtue of my class and its sociopolitical trappings, I always knew I had the option to have my nose surgically altered. From adolescence on, I've had a standing offer from my mother to pay for a nose job.

"It's not such a big deal."

"Doctors do such individual-looking noses these days, it'll look really natural."

"It's not too late, you know," she would say to me for years after I flat-out refused to let someone break my nose, scrape part of it out, and reposition it into a smaller, less obtrusive shape. "I'll still pay." As if money were the reason I was resisting.

My mother thought a nose job was a good idea. See, she hadn't wanted one either. But when she was 16, her parents demanded that she get that honker "fixed," and they didn't take no for an answer. She insists that she's been glad ever since, although she usually rationalizes that it was good for her social life. (She even briefly dated a guy she met in the surgeon's waiting room, a boxer having his deviated septum corrected.)

Even my father is a believer. He says that without my mother's nose job, my sister and I wouldn't exist, because he never would have gone out with Mom. I take this with an entire salt lick. My father thinks that dressing up means wearing dark sneakers; that pants should be purchased every 20 years—and then only if the old ones are literally falling apart; and that haircuts should cost $10 and take as many minutes. The only thing he says about appearances is, "You have some crud . . ." as he picks a piece of lint off your sleeve. But he cared about the nose? Whatever.

Even though my mother is happy with her tidy little surgically altered nose, she wasn't going to put me through the same thing, and for that I am truly grateful. I'm also unspeakably glad that her comments stayed far from the "you'd be so pretty if you did" angle. I know a few people who weren't so lucky. Not that they were dragged kicking and screaming to the doctor's office; no, they were coerced and shamed into it. Seems it was their family's decision more than their own—usually older female relatives: mothers, grandmothers, aunts.

What's the motivation for that kind of pressure? Can it be that for all the strides made against racism and anti-Semitism, Americans still want to expunge their ethnicity from their looks? Were these mothers and grandmothers trying to fit their offspring into a more white, gentile mode? Possibly. Well, definitely. But on purpose? Probably not. Their lust for the button nose is probably more a desire for a typical femininity than for any specific de-ethnicizing.

But given the society in which we live, the proximity of WASPy white features to the ideal of beauty is no coincidence. I think that anyone who opts for a nose job today (or who pressures her daughter to get one) would say that the reason for the surgery is to look "better" or "prettier." But when we scratch the surface of what "prettier" means, we find that we might as well be saying "whiter" or "more gentile" (I would add "bland," but that's my personal opinion).

Or perhaps the reason is to become unobtrusive. The stereotypical Jewish woman is loud and pushy—qualities girls really aren't supposed to have. So is it possible that the nose job is supposed to usher in not only physical femininity but a psychological, traditional femininity as well? Bob your nose, and become feminine in both mind and body. (This certainly seems to be the way it has worked with Courtney Love, although her issue is class more than ethnicity. But it's undeniable that her new nose comes with a Versace-shilling, tamed persona, in stark contrast to her old messy, outspoken self.)

Even though I know plenty of women with their genetically determined schnozzes still intact, sometimes I still feel like an oddity. From what my mother tells me, nose jobs were as compulsory a rite of passage for her peers as multiple ear-piercings were for mine. Once, when I was still in high school, I went with my mother to a Planned Parenthood fundraiser, a cocktail party in a lovely apartment, with lovely food and drink, and a lovely short speech by Wendy Wasserstein. But I was confused: We were at a lefty charity event in Manhattan, and all the women had little WASP noses. (Most of them were blond, too, but that didn't really register. I guess hair dye is a more universal ritual.)

"Why are there no Jewish women here?" I whispered to my mother. She laughed, but I think she was genuinely shocked. "What do you mean?" she asked. "All of these women are Jewish." And then it hit me: It was wall-to-wall rhinoplasties. And worse, there was no reason to be surprised. These were women my mother's age or older who came of age in the late '50s or before, when anti-Semitism in this country was much more overt than it is today. Surface assimilation was practically the norm back then, and those honkers were way too, ahem, big a liability on the dating and social scenes. Nose jobs have declined since then. They're no longer among the top five plastic surgeries, edged out by liposuction and laser skin resurfacing.

I don't think it's a coincidence that, growing up in New York, I didn't consider my nose an "ethnic" feature. Almost everyone around me had that ethnicity, too. It wasn't until I graduated from college and moved to California that I realized how marked I was. I also realized how much I like being instantly recognizable to anyone who knows how to look. I once met another Jewish woman at a conference in California. In the middle of our conversation, she randomly asked, "You're Jewish, right?" I replied, "With this nose and this hair, you gotta ask?" We both laughed. The question was just a formality, and we both knew it.

Only once did I feel uneasy about being "identified." At my first job out of college, my boss asked, after I mentioned an upcoming trip to see my family, "So, are your parents just like people in Woody Allen movies?" I wondered if I had a sign on my forehead reading "Big Yid Here." His comment brought up all those insecurities American Jews have that, not coincidentally, Woody Allen loves to emphasize for comic effect: Am I *that* Jewish? I felt conspicuous, exposed. Still, I'm glad I have the sign on my face, even if it's located a tad lower than my forehead.

Judaism is the only identity in which culture and religion are supposedly bound closely: If you're Irish and not a practicing Catholic, you can still be fully Irish; being Buddhist doesn't specify race or ethnicity. To me, being a Jew is cultural, but it's tied only marginally—even hypothetically—to religion, and mostly to geography (New York Jews are different from California Jews, lemme tell ya). So what happens when identity becomes untied from religion? I don't know for sure. And that means I'll grab onto anything I need to keep that identity—including my nose.

R E A D I N G **35**

Is Fat a Feminist Issue? Exploring the Gendered Nature of Weight Bias

Janna L. Fikkan and Esther D. Rothblum (2011)

In the late 1970s and early 1980s, feminists began to draw increasing attention to the gendered nature of weight preoccupation and disordered eating, with Orbach's self-help book, *Fat Is a Feminist Issue* (1978), perhaps the best known of this genre. Helping women to see their private struggles with compulsive eating and hatred of their bodies as rooted in the social constraints placed on women's autonomy and patriarchal devaluation of all things feminine (including fat bodies) had a major impact on the field of psychotherapy and has spawned subsequent generations of feminist writing on the topic of women and weight. However, as critics noted then (e.g., Diamond 1985), the assumption that "fat" was indicative of pathology and, in Orbach's formulation, unconscious drives to defend against unwanted experiences (such as intimacy), was left largely intact. Additionally, the resolution of these psychological issues was seen as the pathway to permanent weight loss, thus also leaving unquestioned the assumption that thinness should still be a woman's goal.

By contrast, other writers at this time (e.g., Wooley et al. 1979) were starting to question the assumptions about fat as a medical or psychological problem to be solved. Wooley et al. (1979), followed by others (e.g., Brown 1985, 1989; Chrisler 1989), asserted that fat is a feminist issue because the culture at large allows for much less deviation from aesthetic ideals for women than it does for men, meaning that many more women than men end up feeling badly about their (normal and healthy) bodies, and thus engage their energies in all manner of corrective action, from restrictive dieting to eating disorders. Wooley et al. (1979) also noted that the "price paid" by women for having deviant bodies is more than psychological and emotional, and went on to cite some of the early research on weight bias. It is this "price," in the form of discrimination experienced by women due to weight, which is the point of departure for the current article.

The purpose of our review is to pool evidence from several disciplines and across multiple domains that demonstrates the disparate impact of weight bias on women. We conducted an internet search on gender and weight stigma, and also found additional references within those articles. We focus our review on studies of women or studies in which gender is examined as an independent variable. . . .

EMPLOYMENT AND INCOME

As we will review in this section, the literature on weight-based employment discrimination spans several disciplines and includes both experimental studies and analyses of trends in occupational attainment and compensation within large data sets. Common to most of the studies exploring this phenomenon is that fat women are more adversely impacted by weight-based employment discrimination than are men in a number of ways (Fikkan and Rothblum 2005; Griffin 2007) and are over 16 times more likely than men to perceive such discrimination, according to results from a large U.S. sample (Roehling et al. 2007). As detailed below, discrimination against fat women in the employment sphere occurs at multiple levels, including hiring, promotion, performance evaluation, and compensation.

Rothblum et al. (1988) assessed the impact of weight on job candidate desirability in an all-female college student sample and found that when raters read written descriptions of candidates' appearance,

fat women were rated more negatively than non-fat women on supervisory potential, self-discipline, professional appearance, personal hygiene, and ability to perform a physically strenuous job. When level of attractiveness was controlled, however, the negative stereotyping of fat applicants was considerably reduced, indicating that the bias against fat women may be mostly due to the presumed negative effect on physical attractiveness.

A recent study by Miller and Lundgren (2010), which also used a college student sample, examined whether a double standard existed for female political candidates based on weight. Consistent with the investigators' hypotheses, "obese" female candidates were evaluated more negatively overall and assessed more negatively in terms of reliability, dependability, honesty, ability to inspire, and ability to perform a strenuous job than were non-obese female applicants. Strikingly, not only was there an absence of the same penalty for obese male candidates, obese men were actually rated *more* positively than non-obese male candidates.

The stigma of being a fat woman is so pronounced that, in one study sample, non-fat men who were merely associated with a fat woman appeared to experience stigmatizing effects. Hebl and Mannix (2003) found in a sample of adult raters that non-fat male job applicants were judged more harshly when seen with a fat woman prior to being interviewed than were men seated next to a non-fat woman.

Given the differential treatment of fat women in the job market, it is not surprising that evidence continues to accumulate about the long-term effects of this discrimination. Longitudinal studies using large national data sets . . . have demonstrated trends of lower occupational attainment and lower hourly and lifetime earnings for fat women, even after controlling for other relevant variables, such as education and family socioeconomic status. . . .

Cawley (2004) . . . examined the relationship between weight and wages and found that the negative relationship between body weight and wages is most consistently found for "significantly overweight" White women, whom he estimates are paid on average 9% less than women of median weight. He proposes this wage difference is equal to that associated with roughly 3 years of prior work experience, 2 years of job tenure, or 1 year of education.

Baum and Ford (2004) . . . found a weight penalty for both men and women, with that for women roughly twice as large as that for men. Additionally, they found that being "overweight or obese" has a significant impact on women's wages, while only "obesity" negatively impacts the wages of men.

Finally, analysis . . . by Han and colleagues (Han, Norton and Stearns 2009) also found that "obesity" reduces the likelihood of employment among White women and reduces hourly wages for both White and Black women, whereas no effect is observed for men when other variables are controlled. They found this wage effect for women to increase with age (particularly after age 30) and to be larger in occupations requiring more social interactions than in other occupations. A second investigation by these authors (Han, Norton and Powell 2009) was conducted to examine both the direct effect of weight on wages and indirect effects through educational attainment and occupational sorting. . . . The authors concluded, in fact, that the total wage penalty for women's BMI is underestimated in other samples by approximately 19% without the inclusion of these indirect effects.

Given these collective findings of lower occupational attainment and lower earnings among fat women, we should also expect their lifetime earnings to reflect such discrimination. A study by Fonda and colleagues (Fonda et al. 2004) . . . indeed showed that "overweight" and "obese" women have a lower logged net worth at retirement-age than do their non-fat counterparts. This difference was attenuated to a non-significant level once potential covariates were controlled (e.g., sociodemographics, health, work, and marital status). For men, however, "overweight" and "obesity" were associated with *higher* logged net worth at retirement.

In addition to the main findings of employment-related discrimination against fat women, a few notable trends are worth highlighting. The first is that women, predominantly White women, tend to experience decreasing wages at much lower weights than do men, as found in the aforementioned analysis by Gregory and Ruhm (2009). For example, Maranto and Stenoien (2000), using data from the NLSY, found the negative effect of weight on salaries to be highly significant for White women in the "overweight" range and only marginally significant for Black women. White and Black men, on the other hand, experienced wage *premiums* for being "overweight" or "mildly obese" and only experienced wage penalties at the very highest weight levels (100% above standard weight for their height). In fact, White women in this sample were found to suffer a greater wage penalty for "mild obesity" (20% over standard weight for their height) than Black men did for weight that is 100% over standard weight.

Another consistent finding is that the penalties for fatness in women vary by occupational level and appear to most significantly impact a women attempting to move into higher prestige (and more highly compensated) occupations. . . .

A . . . absence of fat women was found by Roehling et al. (2009) in their study of top U.S. CEOs at Fortune 1000 companies. Women in general are underrepresented in this stratum of the corporate world, but fat women remarkably so. Whereas roughly two thirds of adult women in the U.S. are classified as "overweight" or "obese," only 10% of top US female CEOs fall into these weight categories. And though obese men are also quite rare among top CEOs, overweight men are actually overrepresented among them (61% of top US male CEOs are overweight, compared to 31% of an age-matched population sample).

In summary, there is ample evidence that weight-based employment discrimination is disproportionately experienced by women and that such discriminatory practices have a significant impact on their work experiences, occupational attainment and financial compensation. Recent findings that women may be experiencing the greatest wage penalty when they move from "below-average" in weight to just slightly over "ideal weight" highlights the extremely narrow range of body weights deemed acceptable for women and the pervasive emphasis placed on appearance in the evaluation of women in professional settings. Additionally, it appears that a woman's weight is even more of a liability as she attempts to move into higher-ranking professions.

EDUCATION

Given the disparities that have been documented between fat and non-fat women in the labor market, researchers have also examined whether these differences begin to emerge prior to entering the workforce. There is cross-sectional evidence that body weight and educational attainment are inversely related among White women, whereas the relationship is less consistent among men and women of color (Leigh et al. 1992). Although the direction of effect has often been presumed to be that lower levels of education lead to increases in weight, evidence from longitudinal studies has demonstrated that the educational outcomes of young women are also negatively impacted by prior weight status (Glass et al. 2010; Gortmaker et al. 1993).

Studies highlighting the impact of weight on educational outcomes began nearly 40 years ago with work by Canning and Mayer (1966) demonstrating that, among elite universities in the Northeastern U.S., students classified as "obese" were significantly more likely to be denied acceptance, and this was especially true for women. Based on additional research by these investigators (Canning and Mayer 1967) showing that, among high school students, there were no significant differences between those classified as obese and non-obese on standardized intelligence scores, grades, involvement in extracurricular activities, or interest and intent in pursuing higher education, they concluded that obese students were being discriminated against during in-person interviews by college admission boards primarily based on their weight status. This seminal work has since inspired additional research on how body weight plays a role in both the high school experiences of adolescents and college enrollment rates.

Falkner et al. (2001) conducted a cross-sectional study in a population-based sample of public school students in 7th, 9th, and 11th grades. They found that "obese" status was associated with adverse social and educational outcomes for both boys and girls, but that these associations were both greater in number and worse in severity for girls. After adjusting for the possible influence of confounding variables, they found that "obese" girls, in addition to having greater odds of reporting adverse social and emotional outcomes, were over two times as likely to perceive themselves as being below-average students and one-and-a-half times more likely to report having been held back a year in school. Despite this, these girls did not report lower educational aspirations or less confidence in expecting to be professionally successful in adulthood.

A series of more recent longitudinal studies by Crosnoe and colleagues (Crosnoe 2007; Crosnoe and Muller 2004; Crosnoe et al. 2008) found that the negative impact of body weight on educational outcomes for girls may be partly attributable to the social stigma they experience and the emotional consequences of this stigma. Using data from the National Longitudinal Study of Adolescent Health (Add Health), a nationally representative study of U.S. adolescents in grades 7–12, these researchers found that adolescents of both genders who were "at risk of obesity" (those in the 85th percentile or above in BMI for their age group and gender) had lower academic achievement than other students. This was particularly true in schools where the average BMI of the student body was lower and where there were higher rates of dating, contexts in which a heavier body might be both more noticeable and more of a social liability in the context of romantic activity. This led the authors to conclude that the impact of body weight on achievement may be mediated through lower self-appraisals in the context of higher stigma (Crosnoe and Muller 2004).

. . . Crosnoe (2007) found that adolescent girls classified as "obese" (at or above the 95th percentile of BMI for their age-gender group) were less likely to enter college after high school than their non-obese peers, especially when they attended schools in which obesity was relatively uncommon and even when controlling for numerous other factors (e.g., parental education, academic ability, etc.) that could conceivably be related to both obesity and educational attainment. Obesity was not related to boys' rates of college matriculation. Additionally, body weight for young women predicted an increase in internalizing symptoms, more alcohol and drug use, and academic disengagement. These psychosocial factors explained about one third of obese girls' lower odds of enrolling in college.

Finally, several other recent studies have replicated the general findings of the negative impact of women's weight on educational outcomes while also considering the role of race. Merten et al. (2008) examined the relationships between weight status . . . and depressive symptoms and status attainment (indexed by college enrollment, employment and job satisfaction). . . . They found that "obesity" among adolescent girls was associated with more depressive symptoms and lower status attainment in young adulthood when compared with girls with weight in the normative range, whereas obesity status among males was not associated with either outcome. These researchers found no difference in these relationships between White and Black adolescents.

However, two other studies did find that the impact of adolescent girls' weight on academic outcomes differs by race. . . . Sabia (2007) found evidence of a significant negative relationship between BMI and grade point average for White females between the ages of 14 and 17. He also found, while controlling for other relevant variables, that White females who *perceived* themselves to be overweight had lower grade point averages than those who did not perceive themselves to be overweight. The results for White females were consistent across statistical estimates, whereas evidence for a significant relationship between weight and academic achievement for nonwhite females and males was not consistent.

Collectively, these data point to yet another domain in which a higher body weight is more of a liability for females than for males, perhaps particularly so for certain ethnic groups. Additionally, understanding the discrepancies between fat and non-fat women in the labor market may be better understood by an appreciation for the different trajectories that begin in earlier stages of development and impact employment prospects.

ROMANTIC RELATIONSHIPS

Another area in which females are more heavily penalized for their weight than males is in the context of romantic relationships. The vast majority of this research has been conducted on heterosexual

relationships, which we will review first, followed by a discussion about what is known about women's weight in same-sex relationships.

Starting in early adolescence, young women who are at the higher end of the weight spectrum report fewer opportunities to date and less involvement in romantic relationships, relative to their thinner peers. . . . Halpern et al. 2005 . . . found that, after controlling for potential confounding variables (e.g., physical maturity, demographic characteristics, and prior relationship history), for each one-point increase in BMI, the likelihood of being in a romantic relationship decreased by 6–7%. Widerman and Hurst (1998) found a similar pattern among college-aged women, where being heavier was related to lower probability of being involved in a romantic relationship and less sexual experience, despite the women having similarly positive attitudes toward, and interest in, sexual relationships.

Whereas the preceding three studies only examined these relationships among females, studies that compare the experiences of males and females consistently find that having a heavier body weight is not as detrimental to the dating and sexual relationships of young men. Pearce et al. (2002), for example, found that, among students in grades 9–12, 50% of girls classified as "obese" reported having never dated, compared to only 20% of their average-weight peers. For boys, however, the percentage reporting no dating experience was virtually identical between "obese" boys (29%) and average-weight boys (30%).

A similar pattern of results is found for college students. In a study by Sheets and Ajmere (2005), women who were a standard deviation or more above the mean BMI for the women in their sample were half as likely to be dating as women one standard deviation or more below the mean BMI, with no significant differences in dating status observed between men in various weight categories. Among those in the sample who were coupled, weight was also inversely related to relationship satisfaction among women, but positively correlated with relationships satisfaction among men, indicating that the negative feedback women receive about their weight may both determine the likelihood of being in a relationship and the quality of relationships.

. . . Chen and Brown (2005) asked college students to rate the attractiveness of prospective partners and found that men were more likely to choose sexual partners on the basis of weight than were women. Male study participants rated "obese" women as less attractive than women who were missing a limb, in a wheelchair, mentally ill or had a sexually transmitted disease.

The finding that women's weight is more of a liability than men's in the sphere of romantic relationships has probably received the most attention in studies of so-called "marriage market" outcomes. This research has largely been done by economists using data from the National Longitudinal Study of Youth (NLSY) and the Panel Study on Income Dynamics (PSID). Findings consistently show that women who are fat have lower rates of both cohabitation (Mukhopadhyay 2008) and marriage (Averett and Korenman 1996; Averett et al. 2008; Conley and Glauber 2007; Fu and Goldman 1996) than thinner women and that, when they do marry, tend to marry partners with lower levels of education (Garn et al. 1989a; b), lower earnings (Averett and Korenman 1996; Conley and Glauber 2007;), of shorter stature (Oreffice and Quintana-Domeque 2010) and less physical attractiveness (Carmalt et al. 2008) than do thinner women, whereas these effects are either less or not observed at all for men's weight.

Thus, for fat women, heterosexual romantic relationships are yet another domain in which they fare worse, primarily because men are both more focused on, and critical of, the weight of their female partners, which may stem, in part, from the negative social judgment leveled at men who are associated with fat women (Hebl and Mannix 2003). The potential outcomes for fat women range from being excluded entirely from desired relationships, to forming relationships with less desirable partners, to the extreme case of being targeted as "easy marks" for sexual conquest (Gailey and Prohaska 2006; Prohaska and Gailey 2009).

There has been no research to date on the impact of body weight on the frequency or quality of relationships among lesbians. Yet this would be an interesting area to investigate, since studies have found lesbians to be . . . more satisfied with their bodies, diet less, and score lower on measures related to eating disorders than heterosexual women (Bergeron and Senn 1998; Gettelman and Thompson 1993; Herzog et al. 1992; Moore and Keel 2003; Owens et al. 2003; Share and Mintz 2002; Schneider et al. 1995; Siever 1994). This is despite the fact that some studies have found lesbians to weigh more than heterosexual women (e.g., Boehmer et al. 2007; Guille and Chrisler 1999; Herzog et al. 1992; Owens et al. 2003), even when compared with their heterosexual sisters (Rothblum and Factor 2001). . . .

MEDIA

Although a sizable body of research in the field of eating disorders has examined the impact of the ever-present *thin* female body in the media on both standards of attractiveness and eating disorder symptoms (see Greenberg and Worrell 2005, for a review), far fewer studies have explored the roles assigned to fat women in mass media. Indeed, one of the main challenges in analyzing the characterization of fat women in the media is that they are largely absent. One of the first studies examining prevalence of body types in prime time television was conducted by Kaufman in 1980, who found that 88% of the individuals shown in prime time television programming had thin or average body types and only 12% were "overweight or obese." Men with larger body sizes were depicted roughly twice as frequently (15% of the sample) as were women with larger bodies (8% of the sample).

More recent studies have replicated both the under-representation of all fat bodies, as compared with statistics from the general population, and the discrepancy between men and women. . . .

A study that examined both the distribution and associated characteristics of various body types on prime-time television found that only 14% of females and 24% of males were in the "overweight or obese" category, less than half the percentages in the general population. Although a number of unfavorable characteristics were associated with large body size for both genders (e.g., reduced likelihood of interacting with romantic partners), fat women were also less likely than their thinner counterparts to be judged as attractive, less likely to show physical affection, and more likely to be the object of humor, whereas these differences were not significant between weight categories for male characters (Greenberg et al. 2003).

The tendency for fat women, when they are included in mass media, to be cast primarily as foils for thinner characters has also been studied. Fouts and colleagues (Fouts and Burggraf 1999; 2000; Fouts and Vaughan 2002) have shown in studies of situation comedies shown on prime time television in the late 1990s that below-average weight women are over-represented, compared with the general population, and receive significantly more positive verbal comments from male characters with regards to body weight and shape than do heavier women (Fouts and Burggraf 1999). Conversely, heavier female characters receive significantly more derogatory comments from male characters and the majority of the time these comments are followed by audience reactions of laughter, "oohs," or giggles, implying that male commentary on fat female bodies is a socially acceptable behavior (Fouts and Burggraf 2000).

When they explored whether the same would be true for heavy male characters they found that, while fat men were also underrepresented compared to the population, there was a smaller discrepancy than that for women, and that it was the heavy male characters themselves who made comments about their own weight (again, followed by audience laughter) rather than a dynamic in which either females or other males made reference to their weight (Fouts and Vaughan 2002). Similar findings were also reported by Himes and Thompson (2007), who examined fat stigmatization messages presented in both television shows and movies between 1984 and 2004 and found that, although men and women were almost equally likely to be the targets of fat stigmatization, men were about three times more likely to make comments about someone's weight than were women.

In addition to often being the butt of jokes, as noted above, fat women are less likely to be portrayed as being the object of romantic interest. In a more in-depth analysis of two particular television situation comedies that featured fat female characters,

Giovanelli and Ostertag (2009) found that the fat women characters, although often present during discussions of the romantic or sexual adventures of other (thin) characters, either did not participate in these conversations by referring to their own sexual or romantic interests, or were depicted as pursuing love interests who had already been judged by others as clearly flawed and/or who were also the butt of jokes. Analysis of other media (i.e., popular movies and so-called "Chick Lit," a genre of fiction written by and for women) find that even when a fat woman is portrayed as a romantic lead, her weight is often as much of interest (comically, or otherwise) as any other aspect of the plot line (Frater 2009; Mendoza 2009).

In summary, the media contribute to the marginalization of fat woman either by rendering them invisible when presenting a "norm" of predominantly underweight women and/or by making fat women's weight the most salient characteristic about them as people and a target for remedy (through weight loss), pity, or comedy. Aside from the deleterious effect on consumers of the media, it can also be inferred that, given their scarcity in the industry, fat women likely face steep challenges to obtaining employment in this domain.

RACE AND ETHNICITY

Research has generally found some racial and ethnic minority groups in the U.S. to weigh more than White people but also to be more satisfied with their weight and body size. . . .

. . . Puhl et al. (2008) used data . . . which asked participants about daily or lifetime discrimination in interpersonal relationships based on age, gender, race, height or weight, ethnicity or nationality, physical disability, appearance other than height or weight, sexual orientation, religion, or other reason. Women (10.3%) were twice as likely as men (4.9%) to report weight-based discrimination, and weight discrimination was reported more frequently by Black women (23.9%) and Black men (12.7%), who also weighed more. In regression analyses, being younger, female, and having high BMI were predictors of weight discrimination, but there was no effect for race.

Wade and DiMaria (2003) found an interaction of race and weight when White college students were asked to rate vignettes of women that were accompanied by a photograph depicting the woman as either Black or White, and either fat or thin. The thinner White woman was rated more positively than the fatter White woman on attractiveness, friendliness, enthusiasm, occupational success, and mate potential, whereas there was no difference on trustworthiness or parenting skills. In contrast, the heavier Black woman was rated more positively than the thinner Black woman on friendliness, trustworthiness, parenting skills, and mate potential, while there was no difference on attractiveness, enthusiasm, or occupational success.

Latner et al. (2005) asked male and female college students to rate figure drawings of adults (men rated male targets and women rated female targets) who were depicted as average weight with no visible disability, holding crutches with braces on one leg, sitting in a wheelchair, missing a hand, having a facial disfigurement, or fat. Overall the fat figure drawing received the second-to-lowest rating, above the drawing of the adult missing a hand, and men gave the fat drawing lower ratings than did women. Black and Asian students rated the fat drawing more positively than did White students; there was no difference between Hispanic students and White students. In a gender by race/ethnicity interaction, Black women rated the fat drawing more positively than did White women.

A study by Hebl and Turchin (2005) examined differences in weight stigma between White and Black male college students by having them rate targets on seven dimensions. In addition to the male students stigmatizing heavy White men more than heavy Black men, there were also ethnic differences in the ratings given to female targets. Specifically, White men appeared to have a narrower range of acceptable weight for White women, rating both heavy and medium-sized women more negatively than thin women whereas Black men gave more positive ratings to both thin and medium-sized Black women than they gave to heavy Black women. Interestingly, body size did not influence men's evaluations of women of a different race, only their ratings of women within their own racial group.

In sum, Black and Hispanic women may weigh more than White women and in that regard be subjected more often to weight-related discrimination. On the other hand, research on Black and White women and men shows Black people to be more accepting of heavier weight. Reasons for this could include the greater prevalence of large body size among these groups, or a tendency among people of color to reject mainstream White values, including White standards of bodily attractiveness. Moreover, even if lower body weight is preferred for the sake of attractiveness, fatness is not necessarily associated with negative personal qualities. . . .

We caution against an overly optimistic reading of this phenomenon for two reasons. The first is that other sources of discrimination against Black women may simply overshadow those attributable to body size. The venues in which fat White women are most likely to be discriminated against, namely high status jobs and marriage to earners of high income, may be venues from which many women of color have been excluded due to other factors, making additional effects due to weight impossible to detect (Averett and Korenman 1999).

Second, some scholars have interpreted the apparent lack of size discrimination against Black women in particular as fitting with the racial stereotype of Black women as being large, strong, independent and nurturing of others (Beauboeuf-Lafontant 2003; Bowen et al. 1991). Such a stereotype, however, often masks the very real powerlessness and marginalization of Black women, as well as potentially invalidating the experiences of Black women who do experience body image distress, as well as discrimination due to body size (Neumark-Sztainer et al.1998).

CONCLUSION

The price paid by women as a result of weight-based discrimination is significant, cuts across multiple domains, and yet has received relatively little attention by feminist scholars when compared with other topics relating to weight (e.g., eating disorders and body image disturbance) or with other sources of discrimination impacting women. Although research on weight stigma has increased significantly in recent years, few researchers have addressed or attempted to assess the gendered nature of this bias (Griffin 2007 being a notable exception). As can be surmised from this review, however, there is substantial and consistent evidence that women suffer disproportionately from weight bias in a number of domains.

Given how extensively anti-fat bias impacts the lives of women, we question why feminist scholars have not paid more attention, why, as Hartley (2001) writes, ". . . the fat body has largely been ignored in feminist studies that attempt to theorize the female body" (p. 61). Whereas anorexic bodies have been conceptualized as a metaphor for cultural proscriptions on women, fat bodies too often get interpreted in terms of poor health, with blame placed squarely on the individual (LeBesco 2009). This discrepant treatment in the feminist literature parallels the treatment of eating disorders and fatness in the popular media. Saguy and Gruys (2010) have examined how news media (specifically, the *New York Times* and *Newsweek*) described anorexia versus "overweight" in the years 1995–2005. They state: ". . . the news media treats anorexics as *victims* of a terrible illness beyond their and their parents' control, while obesity is caused by bad individual behavior, including, in the case of children, parental neglect" (p. 232). They also point out that girls with anorexia are portrayed as White and from affluent families whereas fatness is associated with poor girls of color.

Since the publication of *Fat is a Feminist Issue* in the late 1970s, much of the writing by feminists on the subject of women's weight has concerned itself primarily with the question of whether fatness (often conflated with disordered eating or other forms of psychopathology) should be "treated" by feminist therapists (e.g., Chrisler 1989) and, much more often, with the subject of how thinness came to be prized as highly as it is in a patriarchal culture (e.g., Bordo 1993). We propose that it is not enough to note that the ever thinner cultural ideal means that practically every woman will feel badly about her body. Feminists also need to turn our collective attention to the reality that, because of the

pervasiveness and gendered nature of weight-based stigma, a majority of women stand to *suffer significant discrimination* because they do not conform to this ever-narrower standard.

Although the feminist movement has mobilized women to organize in opposition to other forms of discrimination that disproportionately impact women, there seems to be an exception when it comes to weight-based discrimination (Rothblum 1994). That a fat woman's experience would not receive the same level of attention, critique, and organized action only serves to further devalue her.

REFERENCES

Averett, S., & Korenman, S. (1996). The economic reality of the beauty myth. *Journal of Human Resources, 31,* 304–330. doi:10.2307/146065.

Averett, S., & Korenman, S. (1999). Black–white differences in social and economic consequences of obesity. *International Journal of Obesity, 23,* 166–173. doi:10.1038/sj.ijo.0800805.

Averett, S. L., Sikora, A., & Argys, L. M. (2008). For better or worse: Relationship status and body mass index. *Economics and Human Biology, 6,* 330–349. doi:10.1016/j.ehb.2008.07.003.

Baum, C. L., & Ford, W. F. (2004). The wage effects of obesity: A longitudinal study. *Health Economics, 13,* 885–899. doi:10.1002/hec.881.

Beauboeuf-Lafontant, T. (2003). Strong and large black women? Exploring relationships between deviant womanhood and weight. *Gender and Society, 17,* 111–121. doi:10.1177/0891243202238981.

Bergeron, S. M., & Senn, C. Y. (1998). Body image and sociocultural norms. *Psychology of Women Quarterly, 22,* 385–401. doi:10.1111/j.1471-6402.1998.tb00164.

Bertakis, K. D., & Azari, R. (2005). The impact of obesity on primary care visits. *Obesity Research, 13,* 1615–1623. doi:10.1038/oby.2005.198.

Boehmer, U., Bowen, D. J., & Bauer, G. R. (2007). Overweight and obesity in sexual-minority women: Evidence from population-based data. *American Journal of Public Health, 97,* 1134–1140. doi:10.2105/AJPH.2006.

Bordo, S. (1993). *Unbearable weight: Feminism, Western culture, and the body.* Berkeley: University of California Press.

Bowen, D., Tomoyasu, N., & Cauce, A. (1991). The triple threat: A discussion of gender, class and race differences in weight. *Women & Health, 17*(4), 123–143. doi:10.1300/J013v17n04_06.

Brown, L. S. (1985). Women, weight, and power: Feminist theoretical and therapeutic issues. *Women & Therapy, 4,* 61–71.

Brown, L. S. (1989). Fat-oppressive attitudes and the feminist therapist: Directions for change. *Women & Therapy, 8,* 19–29.

Canning, H., & Mayer, J. (1966). Obesity—its possible effect on college acceptance. *The New England Journal of Medicine, 275,* 1172–1174. doi:10.1056/NEJM196611242752107.

Canning, H., & Mayer, J. (1967). Obesity: An influence on high school performance? *American Journal of Clinical Nutrition, 20,* 352–354.

Carmalt, J. H., Cawley, J., Joyner, K., & Sobal, J. (2008). Body weight and matching with a physically attractive romantic partner. *Journal of Marriage and Family, 70,* 1287–1296. doi:10.1111/j.1741-3737.2008.00566.x.

Cawley, J. (2004). The impact of obesity on wages. *Journal of Human Resources, 39,* 451–474. doi:10.2307/3559022.

Chen, E. Y., & Brown, M. (2005). Obesity stigma in sexual relationships. *Obesity Research, 13,* 1393–1397. doi:10.1038/oby.2005.168.

Chrisler, J. C. (1989). Should feminist therapists do weight loss counseling? *Women & Therapy, 8*(3), 31–37. doi:10.1300/J015V08N03_05.

Conley, D., & Glauber, R. (2007). Gender, body mass, and socioeconomic status: New evidence from the PSID. *Advances in Health Economics and Health Services Research, 17,* 253–275. doi:10.1016/S0731-2199(06)17010-7.

Crosnoe, R. (2007). Gender, obesity, and education. *Sociology of Education, 80,* 241–260. doi:10.1177/003804070708000303.

Crosnoe, R., Mueller, A. S., & Frank, K. (2008). Gender, body size and social relations in American high schools. *Social Forces, 86,* 1189–1216.

Crosnoe, R., & Muller, C. (2004). Body mass index, academic achievement, and school context: Examining the educational experiences of adolescents at risk of obesity. *Journal of Health and Social Behavior, 45,* 393–407. doi:10.1177/002214650404500403.

Diamond, N. (1985). Thin is the feminist issue. *Feminist Review, 19,* 45–64.

Falkner, N. H., Neumark-Sztainer, D., Story, M., Jeffery, R. W., Beuhring, T., & Resnick, M. D. (2001). Social, educational, and psychological correlates of weight status in adolescents. *Obesity Research, 9,* 32–42. doi:10.1038/oby.2001.5.

Fikkan, J., & Rothblum, E. (2005). Weight bias in employment. In K. D. Brownell, R. M. Puhl, M. B. Schwartz, & L. Rudd (Eds.), *Weight bias: Nature, consequences and remedies* (pp. 15–28). New York: Guilford.

Fonda, S. J., Fultz, N. H., Jenkins, K. R., Wheeler, L. M., & Wray, L. A. (2004). Relationship of body mass and net worth for retirement-aged men and women. *Research on Aging, 26,* 153–176. doi:10.1177/0164027503258739.

Fouts, G., & Burggraf, K. (1999). Television situation comedies: Female body images and verbal reinforcements. *Sex Roles, 40,* 473–481. doi:10.1023/A:1018875711082.

Fouts, G., & Burggraf, K. (2000). Television situation comedies: Female weight, male negative comments, and audience reactions. *Sex Roles, 42,* 925–932. doi:10.1023/A:1007054618340.

Fouts, G., & Vaughan, K. (2002). Television situation comedies: Male weight, negative references, and audience reactions. *Sex Roles, 46,* 439–442. doi:10.1023/A:1020469715532.

Frater, L. (2009). Fat heroines in Chick-Lit: Gateway to acceptance in the mainstream? In E. Rothblum & S. Solovay (Eds.), *The fat studies reader* (pp. 235–240). New York: New York University Press.

Fu, H., & Goldman, N. (1996). Incorporating health into models of marriage choice: Demographic and sociological perspectives. *Journal of Marriage and the Family, 58,* 740–758. doi:10.2307/353733.

Gailey, J. A., & Prohaska, A. (2006). "Knocking off a fat girl": An exploration of hogging, male sexuality and neutralizations. *Deviant Behavior, 27,* 31–49. doi:10.1080/016396290968353.

Garn, S. M., Sullivan, T. V., & Hawthorne, V. M. (1989a). Educational level, fatness and fatness differences between husband and wives. *American Journal of Clinical Nutrition, 50,* 740–745.

Garn, S. M., Sullivan, T. V., & Hawthorne, V. M. (1989b). The education of one spouse and the fatness of the other spouse. *American Journal of Human Biology, 1,* 233–238. doi:10.1002/ajhb.1310010302.

Giovanelli, D., & Ostertag, S. (2009). Controlling the body: Media representations, body size, and self-discipline. In E. Rothblum & S. Solovay (Eds.), *The fat studies reader* (pp. 289–296). New York: New York University Press.

Glass, C. M., Haas, S. A., & Reither, E. N. (2010). The skinny on success: Body mass, gender and occupational standing across the life course. *Social Forces, 88,* 1777–1806.

Gortmaker, S. L., Must, A., Perrin, J. M., Sobol, A. M., & Dietz, W. H. (1993). Social and economic consequences of overweight in adolescence and young adulthood. *The New England Journal of Medicine, 329,* 1008–1012. doi:10.1056/NEJM199309303291406.

Gregory, C. A., & Ruhm, C. J. (2009). Where does the wage penalty bite? NBER Working Paper Series (Vol. w14984). Retrieved from http://www.nber.org/papers/w14894, May.

Greenberg, B. S., Eastin, M., Hofschire, L., Lachlan, K., & Brownell, K. D. (2003). Portrayals of overweight and obese individuals on commercial television. *American Journal of Public Health, 93,* 1342–1348. doi:10.2105/AJPH.93.8.1342.

Greenberg, B. S., & Worrell, T. R. (2005). The portrayal of weight in the media and its social impact. In K. D. Brownell, R. M. Puhl, M. B. Schwartz, & L. Rudd (Eds.), *Weight bias: Nature, consequences, and remedies* (pp. 42–53). New York: Guilford.

Griffin, A. W. (2007). Women and weight-based employment discrimination. *Cardozo Journal of Law and Gender, 13,* 631–662.

Guille, C., & Chrisler, J. C. (1999). Does feminism serve a protective function against eating disorders? *Journal of Lesbian Studies, 3*(4), 141–148. doi:10.1300/J155v03n04_18.

Halpern, C. T., Udry, J. R., Campbell, B., & Suchindran, C. (1999). Effects of body fat on weight concerns, dating and sexual activity: A longitudinal analysis of Black and White adolescent girls. *Developmental Psychology, 35,* 721–736. doi:10.1037//0012-1649.35.3.721.

Halpern, C. T., King, R. B., Oslak, S. G., & Udry, J. R. (2005). Body mass index, dieting, romance, and sexual activity in adolescent girls: Relationships over time. *Journal of Research on Adolescence, 15,* 535–559. doi:10.1111/j.1532-7795.2005.00110.x.

Han, E., Norton, E. C., & Powell, L. (2009). Direct and indirect effects of teenage body weight on adult wages. NBER Working Paper Series (Vol. w15027). Retrieved from http://ssrn.come/abstracts=1413591, June.

Han, E., Norton, E. C., & Stearns, S. C. (2009). Weight and wages: Fat versus lean paychecks. *Health Economics, 18,* 535–548. doi:10.1002/hec.1386.

Hartley, C. (2001). Letting ourselves go: Making room for the fat body in feminist scholarship. In J. E. Braziel & K. LeBesco (Eds.), *Bodies out of bounds: Fatness and transgression* (pp. 60–73). Berkeley: University of California Press.

Hebl, M. R., & Mason, M. F. (2003). Weighing the care: Patients' perceptions of physician care as a function of gender and weight. *International Journal of Obesity, 27,* 269–275. doi:10.1038/sj.ijo.802231.

Hebl, M. R., & Mannix, L. M. (2003). The weight of obesity in evaluating others: A mere proximity effect. *Personality and Social Psychology Bulletin, 29,* 28–38. doi:10.1177/0146167202238369.

Hebl, M. R., & Turchin, J. M. (2005). The stigma of obesity: What about men? *Basic and Applied Social Psychology, 27,* 267–275.doi:10.1207/s15324834basp2703_8.

Himes, S. M., & Thompson, J. K. (2007). Fat stigmatization in television shows and movies: A content analysis. *Obesity, 15,* 712–718. doi:10.1038/oby.2007.635.

Jambekar, S., Quinn, D. M., & Crocker, J. (2001). The effects of weight and achievement messages on the self-esteem of women. *Psychology of Women Quarterly, 25,* 48–56. doi:10.1111/14716402.00006.

Kaufman, L. (1980). Prime-time nutrition. *Journal of Communication, 30,* 37–46. doi:10.1111/j.1460-2466.1980.tb01989.x.

Kiefer, A., Sekaquaptewa, D., & Barczyk, A. (2006). When appearance concerns make women look bad: Solo status and body image concerns diminish women's academic performance. *Journal of Experimental Social Psychology, 42,* 78–86. doi:10.1016/j.jesp.2004.12.004.

Latner, J. D., Stunkard, A. J., & Wilson, G. T. (2005). Stigmatized students: Age, sex, and ethnicity effects in the stigmatization of obesity. *Obesity Research, 13,* 1226–1231. doi:10.1038/oby.2005.145.

LeBesco, K. (2009). Weight management, good health and the will to normality. In H. Malson & M. Burns (Eds.), *Critical feminist approaches to eating disorders* (pp. 147–155). London: Routledge.

Leigh, J. P., Fries, J. F., & Hubert, H. B. (1992). Gender and race differences in the correlation between body mass and education in the 1971-1975 NHANES I. *Journal of Epidemiology and Community Health, 46,* 191–196. doi:10.1136/jech.46.3.191.

Maranto, C. L., & Stenoien, A. F. (2000). Weight discrimination: A multidisciplinary analysis. *Employee Responsibilities and Rights Journal, 12,* 9–24. doi:10.1023/A:1007712500496.

Mendoza, K. R. (2009). Seeing through the layers: Fat suits and thin bodies in *The Nutty Professor* and *Shallow Hal.* In E. Rothblum & S. Solovay (Eds.), *The fat studies reader* (pp. 280–288). New York: New York University Press.

Merten, M. J., Wickrama, K. A. S., & Williams, A. L. (2008). Adolescent obesity and young adult psychosocial outcomes: Gender and racial differences. *Journal of Youth and Adolescence, 37,* 1111–1122. doi:10.1007/s10964-008-9281-z.

Miller, B. J., & Lundgren, J. D. (2010). An experimental study of the role of weight bias in candidate evaluation. *Obesity, 18,* 712–718.doi:10.1038/oby.2009.492.

Moore, F., & Keel, P. K. (2003). Influence of sexual orientation and age on disordered eating attitudes and behaviors in women. *International Journal of Eating Disorders, 34,* 370–374. doi:10.1002/eat.10198.

Mukhopadhyay, S. (2008). Do women value marriage more? The effect of obesity on cohabitation and marriage in the USA. *Review of Economics of the Household, 6,* 111–126. doi:10.1007/s11150-007-9025-y.

Neumark-Sztainer, D., Story, M., & Faibisch, L. (1998). Perceived stigmatization among overweight African American and Caucasian adolescent girls. *Journal of Adolescent Health, 23,* 264–270.

Orbach, S. (1978). *Fat is a feminist issue.* New York: Berkeley Books.

Oreffice, S., & Quintana-Domeque, C. (2010). Anthropometry and socioeconomics among couples: Evidence in the United States. *Economics and Human Biology, 8,* 373–384. doi:10.1016/j.ehb.2010.05.001.

Owens, L. K., Hughes, T. L., & Owens-Nicholson, D. (2003). The effects of sexual orientation on body image and attitudes about eating and weight. *Journal of Lesbian Studies, 7*(1), 15–33.doi:10.1300/J155v07n01_02.

Pearce, M. J., Boergers, J., & Prinstein, M. J. (2002). Adolescent obesity, overt and relational peer victimization, and romantic relationships. *Obesity Research, 10,* 386–393. doi:10.1038/oby.2002.53.

Prohaska, A., & Gailey, J. (2009). Fat women as "easy targets": Achieving masculinity through hogging. In E. D. Rothblum & S. Solovay (Eds.), *The fat studies reader* (pp. 158–166). New York: New York University Press.

Puhl, R., & Brownell, K. D. (2001). Bias, discrimination, and obesity. *Obesity Research, 9,* 788–805. doi:10.1038/oby.2001.108.

Puhl, R., Wharton, C., & Heuer, C. (2009). Weight bias among dietetics students: Implications for treatment practices. *Journal of the American Dietetic Association, 109,* 438–444. doi:10.1016/j.jada.2008.11.034.

Roehling, P. V., Roehling, M. V., Vandlen, J. D., Blazek, J., & Guy, W. C. (2009). Weight discrimination and glass ceiling effect among top US CEOs. *Equal Opportunities International, 28,* 179–196. doi:10.1108/02610150910937916.

Roehling, M. V., Roehling, P. V., & Pichler, S. (2007). The relationship between body weight and perceived weight-related employment discrimination: The role of sex and race. *Journal of Vocational Behavior, 71,* 300–318. doi:10.1016/j.jvb.2007.04.008.

Rothblum, E. D. (1992). The stigma of women's weight: Social and economic realities. *Feminism & Psychology, 2,* 61–73. doi:10.1177/0959353592021005.

Rothblum, E. D. (1994). "I'll die for the revolution, but don't ask me not to diet": Feminism and the continuing stigmatization of obesity. In P. Fallon, M. A. Katzman, & S. C. Wooley (Eds.), *Feminist perspectives on eating disorders* (pp. 53–76). New York: Guilford.

Rothblum, E. D., & Factor, R. (2001). Lesbians and their sisters as a control group: Demographic and mental health factors. *Psychological Science, 12,* 63–69. doi:10.1111/1467-9280.00311.

Rothblum, E. D., Miller, C. T., & Garbutt, B. (1988). Stereotypes of obese female job applicants. *International Journal of Eating Disorders, 7,* 277–283. doi:10.1002/1098-108X(198803)7:2<277::AID-EAT2260070213>3.0.CO;2-2.

Sabia, J. J. (2007). The effect of body weight on adolescent academic performance. *Southern Economic Journal, 73,* 871–900.

Saguy, A. C., & Gruys, K. (2010). Morality and health: News media constructions of "overweight" versus eating disorders. *Social Problems, 57,* 231–250. doi:10.1525/sp.2010.57.2.231.

Share, T., & Mintz, L. B. (2002). Differences between lesbians and heterosexual women in disordered eating and related attitudes. *Journal of Homosexuality, 42*(4), 89–106. doi:10.1300/J082v42n04_06.

Sheets, V., & Ajmere, K. (2005). Are romantic partners a source of college students' weight concern? *Eating Behaviors, 6,* 1–9.doi:10.1016/j.eatbeh.2004.08.008.

Siever, M. D. (1994). Sexual orientation and gender as factors in socioculturally acquired vulnerability to body dissatisfaction and eating disorders. *Journal of Consulting and Clinical Psychology, 62,* 252–260. doi:10.1037/0022-006X.62.2.252.

Silberstein, L. R., Mishkind, M. E., Striegel-Moore, R. H., Timko, C., & Rodin, J. (1989). Men and their bodies: A comparison of homosexual and heterosexual men. *Psychosomatic Medicine, 51,* 337–346.

Vartanian, L. R., & Shaprow, J. G. (2008). Effects of weight stigma on exercise motivation and behavior: A preliminary investigation among college-aged females. *Journal of Health Psychology, 13,* 131–138. doi:10.1177/1359105307084318.

Wade, T. J., & DiMaria, C. (2003). Weight halo effects: Individual differences in perceived life success as a function of women's race and weight. *Sex Roles, 48,* 461–465. doi:10.1023/A:1023582629538.

Widerman, M. W., & Hurst, S. R. (1998). Body size, physical attractiveness, and body image among young adult women: Relationships to sexual experience and sexual esteem. *Journal of Sex Research, 35,* 272–281. doi:10.1080/00224499809551943.

Wooley, O. W., Wooley, S. C., & Dyrenforth, S. R. (1979). Obesity and women II: A neglected feminist topic. *Women's Studies International Quarterly, 2,* 81–92. doi:10.1016/S0148-0685(79)93096-3l.

R E A D I N G **36**

Bodies and Bathrooms

Dan Frosch (2013)

Coy Mathis was born a boy. But after just a few years, biology succumbed to a more powerful force. A buzz cut grew into long hair. Jeans gave way to pink dresses. And the child's big cheeks trembled with tears when anyone referred to Coy as male. Halfway through kindergarten, after consulting with doctors, Coy's parents informed their child's school that Coy identified as a girl and should be treated as one—whether that meant using feminine pronouns to describe her or letting Coy wear her favorite dresses.

"It became really clear that it wasn't just about liking pink or feminine things," said Kathryn Mathis, Coy's mother, recounting how Coy had anxiety attacks when people treated her as a boy. "It was that she was trying so hard to show us that she was a girl."

In December, however, when Coy, 6, was a few months into the first grade, the Mathises angrily pulled her out of school after being told that she could no longer use the girls' bathroom but could instead use a gender-neutral restroom. A letter from a lawyer for the Fountain-Fort Carson school district explained that "as Coy grows older and his male genitals develop along with the rest of his body, at least some parents and students are likely to become uncomfortable with his continued use of the girls' restroom."

Now, Coy's case is at the heart of legal dispute that is likely to test Colorado's anti-discrimination law, which expanded protections for transgender people in 2008. The case is unfolding in this small town just south of Colorado Springs, as other states across the country seek to clarify their policies relating to transgender students. It is an issue that has become more commonplace in recent years as advocacy groups push to ensure that school districts are more attuned to the needs of transgender children.

According to the Transgender Legal Defense and Education Fund, which has filed a complaint with Colorado's civil rights division on the Mathises' behalf, 16 states and the District of Columbia offer some form of legal protections for transgender people. In many instances, those protections extend to schools, where the most mundane rituals like going to the bathroom and using a locker room can be especially traumatic for transgender students.

These days, even in states where no protections exist, school districts have become more amenable to meting out a solution when a dispute arises, said Michael D. Silverman, the group's executive director. Mr. Silverman cited a recent Kansas case handled by his group, in which a 10-year-old biologically male student wanted to be known by a female name and dress like a girl. The school, he said, ultimately agreed.

"In most cases, when you're dealing with children this age, nobody is usually fussing about this sort of thing," Mr. Silverman said. "The schools are much more willing to work with families to ensure that their child is successfully integrated."

Nonetheless, conflicts over gender identity are, understandably, sensitive territory for administrators, transgender students and their families. Last month in Batesville, Miss., a group of high school students protested after a transgender classmate was permitted to wear women's clothing. The students felt that their classmate was being given preferential treatment given the school district's gender-specific dress code, according to local news reports. The Massachusetts Department of Elementary and Secondary Education recently issued guidelines on the treatment of transgender students, two years after the legislature passed a law banning discrimination based on gender identity. The guidelines explain the new law and lay out scenarios that schools might encounter. "Our primary concern is to make sure that every child has a safe and supportive learning environment," said Jonathan Considine, a spokesman for the department. The guidelines point out that deciding how best to handle bathroom access for transgender students can be especially challenging. The department recommended that students be permitted to use bathrooms that conform to the gender they identify with and also suggested that schools create gender-neutral restrooms.

"I have been stunned over the last three years by the explosion of concerns and interest and outreach coming from educational professionals around transgender issues," said Eliza Byard, the executive director of the Gay, Lesbian and Straight Education Network.

Still, gay and transgender advocates say transgender students, while typically a small minority, are particularly vulnerable to bullying and harassment. In a 2012 study by Dr. Byard's organization, many elementary school students reported hearing comments from fellow students about how both boys and girls should act and look. About a third of teachers surveyed said that elementary school students who did not conform to gender norms would feel uncomfortable at their schools.

The Mathis case has drawn particular attention, advocates said, because Coy is so young and the Colorado school district had clashed with her parents over what was best. In that case, the state's civil rights division is looking into whether the district violated Colorado law by prohibiting Coy from using the girls' bathroom. A lawyer for the district, Kelly Dude, declined to comment. In recent public statements, the school district criticized the Mathises for widely publicizing Coy's situation while it was under review and said it had acted "reasonably and fairly" in the matter.

In a letter to Mr. Silverman, Mr. Dude wrote that Coy was allowed to wear girls' clothing to school and was referred to as female, as the Mathises had requested. Though Coy could no longer use the girls' restroom at her elementary school, Mr. Dude said she still had access to staff bathrooms and a gender-neutral restroom in the school's "health room." Mr. Silverman countered that the school district was, he said, "punishing a little girl for what may or may not happen down the road."

At the Mathises' home along a stretch of rolling hills, Coy's parents said they were still mystified over what prompted the school district to change its mind, especially because school administrators seemed so supportive at first. "It didn't make any sense to me," said Jeremy Mathis, a stocky Marine veteran and Coy's father, noting that Coy had made plenty of friends and grown noticeably happier since identifying as a girl. "This is elementary school, and you're singling out this one kid and saying she has to use a special bathroom?" In the meantime, Coy and her sister and brother—they are triplets—are being home-schooled. While torn about it, the Mathises said they would not return them to school until Coy is allowed to use the girls' bathroom again.

In the backyard, Coy played happily with her bike, dirt dusting her face and her pink, sparkly boots. She said she would rather be back in school with her friends but knows why she is not. "They're being mean to me," she said. "And they're telling me that I'm a boy when I'm really a girl."

Postscript: In June 2013 the Colorado Civil Rights Division ruled in favor of Coy. She can now use the girls' bathroom in public schools.

If the Clothes Fit: A Feminist Take on Fashion

Minh-Ha T. Pham (2011)

"My passion for fashion can sometimes seem a shameful secret life," wrote Princeton University English professor Elaine Showalter in 1997.

And indeed, after these words appeared in Vogue, more shame was heaped on her. Surely she must have "better things to do," said one colleague.

Fashion, like so many other things associated primarily with women, may be dismissed as trivial, but it shapes how we're read by others, especially on the levels of gender, class and race. In turn, how we're read determines how we are treated, especially in the workforce—whether we are hired, promoted and respected, and how well we are paid. That most ordinary and intimate of acts, getting dressed, has very real political and economic consequences.

If feminists ignore fashion, we are ceding our power to influence it. Fortunately, history has shown that feminists can, instead, harness fashion and use it for our own political purposes.

When the rhetoric of equality fell on deaf ears, suffragists in the late 19th and early 20th centuries made quite literal fashion statements. Green, white and violet jewelry was a favored suffragist accessory, but not because of any aesthetic imperative: The first letters of each color—G, W, V—was shorthand for give women votes.

A century later, in the 1980s, women appropriated men's styles of dress in an attempt to access the social and economic capital that lay on the other side of the glass ceiling. So-called career women practiced power dressing, wearing tailored skirt suits with huge shoulder pads, approximating the style and silhouette of the professional male executive.

Yet such adaptations of men's fashion and styles are rarely without small feminine touches. Sociologist Jan Felshin coined the term feminine apologetic to describe how the pearls or ruffles on a woman's professional attire serve as disclaimers: I may be powerful but I'm not masculine. Or (gasp!) a lesbian.

The fact that even the most politically and culturally commanding women must walk a razor's edge between looking powerful and still appearing "appropriately feminine" underscores visual theorist John Berger's concise description of mainstream society: "Men act and women appear." In other words, men are judged by their deeds; women, by their looks.

In U.S. politics, Hillary Clinton has experienced the damned-if-you-do, damned-if-you-don't double bind for strong women. If she wears a power pantsuit, it's a "desexualized uniform," but if she shows a hint of cleavage—as she famously did in 2007—it can ignite a media firestorm that eclipses her political platform.

While all women's fashion choices are more carefully policed than men's, women of color endure heightened scrutiny. Racist stereotypes that cast some women of color as "out of control" (the angry black woman, the hypersexual Latina) and others as easily controllable (the traditional Asian woman, the sexually available Indian squaw) serve women poorly in the workplace. Professional women of color thus consciously and unconsciously fashion themselves in ways that diminish their racial difference. One Asian woman interviewed by sociologist Rose Weitz for the academic journal *Gender & Society* admitted that she permed her hair for work "because she felt that she looked 'too Asian' with her naturally straight hair." A black woman interviewed by Charisse Jones and Kumea Shorter-Gooden for their book *Shifting: The Double Lives of Black Women in America* explains that "she never goes into an interview or a new job experience without first straightening her hair. . . . 'I don't want to be prejudged.'"

Away from the workplace, in everyday life, fashion policing of women is also racially stratified. Women of color who wear "ethnic dress" are often read as traditional, unmodern and, in some instances, conservative. When similar garments are worn by white women, they signify global cosmopolitanism, a multicultural coolness.

Fashion's cultural appropriation is nothing new. Sally Roesch Wagner uncovered an earlier moment of appropriation in her book, *Sisters in Spirit,* recounting the little-known history of the bloomer: the long baggy pants that narrowed at the ankles, usually associated with dress reformers in the mid-19th century. While prevailing fashion histories credit white New Yorker Elizabeth Smith (second cousin to Elizabeth Cady Stanton) with inventing the billowy pants and Amelia Bloomer with popularizing them, Wagner finds that Smith was influenced by Native Haudenosaunee women.

If fashion has been used to introduce new ways of expressing womanhood, it has also been a tether that keeps women's social, economic and political opportunities permanently attached to their appearances. At a time when makeover reality TV shows suggest that self-reinvention is not only desirable but almost required, and the ubiquity of social media encourages everyone to develop a "personal brand," the pressure on women to be fashionable has never been more pervasive. Even as the Internet has intensified the desire to be fashion-forward, it has also given outsiders unprecedented influence on the industry. In 2008, a fashion blog by an 11-year-old Midwestern girl named Tavi Gevinson went viral. Within two years, her reviews of new clothing lines were being closely followed by fashion movers and shakers, and famously aloof designers and editors invited Gevinson to their offices, runway shows and parties. Now a ripe old 15, she has used fashion as a springboard to her latest venture: editing an online teen magazine with a feminist point of view.

Today, fashion blogs that celebrate an array of non-normatively raced, gendered, sexed and sized bodies have emerged to challenge the dominant messages of gender, beauty and style. And bloggers are using their clout to speak out against offensive fashion and beauty products.

A blog-initiated campaign in 2010 convinced the cosmetics company MAC and the Rodarte design team to abandon their collection of nail polish and lipstick with names such as "Ghost Town," "Factory" and "Juarez" (referencing the Mexican border town notorious for the serial murders of women working in local factories). Similar online campaigns have also been waged against designers and magazines that employ blackfacing and yellowfacing, as well as against retailers like Abercrombie & Fitch and American Apparel that perpetuate racist, sexist and sizeist beauty ideals. In the age of interactive social media, consumers have at least one ear of the fashion establishment; we should continue to speak up. Wearing fashion does not have to mean that we allow it to wear us down.

DISCUSSION QUESTIONS FOR CHAPTER 4

1. How is gender inscribed on the body? How are bodies shaped to conform to gendered expectations? What are the connections between gendered and racialized bodies?

2. How are power relations reflected and reinforced in beauty norms?

3. How do beauty norms affect women and men differently? How does a focus on beauty for women serve to maintain women's subordinate status?

4. How do disabled bodies challenge dominant notions of beauty and desirability?

5. How are fat bodies stigmatized in ways that are gendered?

6. How do practices of body modification reinforce gendered bodies and gendered patterns of personal and social behavior?

SUGGESTIONS FOR FURTHER READING

Crawley, Sara, Lara Foley, and Constance Shehan. *Gendering Bodies.* Walnut Creek, CA: AltaMira Press, 2007.

Hobson, Janell. *Body as Evidence.* Albany: State University of New York Press, 2012.

Lorber, Judith, and Lisa Jean Moore. *Gendered Bodies: Feminist Perspectives,* Second Edition. New York: Oxford University Press, 2010.

Mintz, Susannah. *Unruly Bodies: Life Writing by Women with Disabilities.* Chapel Hill, NC: The University of North Carolina Press, 2007.

Orbach, Susie. *Bodies: Big Ideas/Small Books.* New York: Picador, 2009.

Rothblum, Esther, and Sondra Solovay. *The Fat Studies Reader.* New York: New York University Press, 2009.

CHAPTER **5**

Media and Culture

Although literature and the arts remain important cultural forms, popular culture—television, movies, music, print media, and the Internet—also plays a significant role in reflecting, reinforcing, and sometimes subverting the dominant systems and ideologies that help shape gender. Popular culture is very seductive; it reflects and creates societal needs, desires, anxieties, and hopes through consumption and participation. Popular culture also provides stories and narratives that shape our lives and identities. It gives us pleasure at the end of a long day and enables us to take our minds off work or other anxieties. In this regard, some scholars have suggested that popular culture regulates society by "soothing the masses," meaning that energy and opposition to the status quo are redirected in pursuit of the latest in athletic shoes or electronic gadgets.

Of course, popular culture creates huge multi-billion-dollar industries that themselves regulate society by providing markets for consumption, consolidating power and status among certain groups and individuals. Media conglomerates have merged technologies and fortunes, consolidating resources and forming powerful corporations that control the flow of information to the public. Over the last few decades globalization (those forces integrating communities and economies into a global marketplace) has created global media with powerful mass media corporations that both dominate domestic markets and influence national governments. The Walt Disney Company, for example, is the largest media conglomerate in the world with almost U.S. $50 billion in revenue and $5 billion in profits in 2012. Disney is closely followed by Comcast with more than $4 billion in profits and then Time Warner with almost $3 billion.

At the same time, corporations such as Disney spark resistance as women of color and LGBTQ individuals, for example, respond to their absence and misrepresentation in contemporary media. The FAAN (Fostering Activism and Alternatives Now!) Project is a media literacy and media activism project formed by young women of color in Philadelphia. They seek to critique and create media, with the goal of social change. Another organization is the Queer Women of Color Media Arts Project that creates, exhibits, and distributes new films that reflect the lives of queer women of color and address vital social justice issues that concern them. Blogs and zines, discussed below, and various online communities also provide feminist media activism, including cyberactivism, that seeks to empower and change society. The reading "Cyberactivism and the Role of Women in the Arab Uprisings" by Courtney Radsch is an example of this.

As emphasized in Chapter 4, popular culture plays a huge role in setting standards of beauty and encouraging certain bodily disciplinary practices. Popular culture *is* culture for many people; the various forms pop culture takes help shape identity and guide people's understandings of themselves and one another. This chapter addresses such issues by focusing on the Internet and cell/mobile phone technology and their relationship to television, movies, the music industry, and print media. In this discussion we emphasize issues of power and access, gender stereotyping, and obstacles to active participation in contemporary media that include both technological (obtaining the hardware) and social aspects (knowledge and relationship to cultural norms about technology and who should use it, as well as literacy skills). The final section of this chapter addresses literature and the arts.

DIGITAL TECHNOLOGIES

The Internet is a global system of interconnected private, public, academic, business, and governmental computer networks that serve billions of users worldwide. These are linked by electronic, wireless, and optical networking technologies and carry a wide range of information resources and services, such as the World Wide Web and infrastructure to support email. The Internet is central in enabling and accelerating interactions through Internet forums, instant messaging, and especially social networking and the use of personalized services tailored to users. Most traditional communications media, including music, film, and television, are being reshaped or redefined by the Internet, as are newspaper and other print media, by blogging and web feed features, for example, often accessed through mobile wireless technologies. Of course pornography and gambling industries have also taken advantage of the Internet and provide a significant source of advertising revenue for

MAKING THE NEWS A Guide to Getting the Media's Attention

1. Have a clear message. Decide what you are calling for and keep repeating it clearly and concisely. Don't dilute strong arguments by going off on tangents or harping on trivialities. Relate your cause to everyday concerns. For example, if you're campaigning for ethical investment, point out that it is financially viable *and* has a positive effect on the world. If you speak calmly and appeal to common understandings, radical ideas can appear not only sensible but even obvious.

2. Make media a priority. Effective campaigning means making media engagement a priority. I have often seen activists organize an event and then think about promoting it to the media. Put media at the center of your planning from the beginning.

3. Offer news. Something is news only if it is new. Discussions of opinions are not news—but you can make them news. When the University of London Union campaigned on fair trade, they couldn't make headlines simply by repeating its benefits. But by conducting a survey that showed that London students were among Britain's most enthusiastic fair trade buyers, they made a good news story. Don't forget to be imaginative!

(continued)

4. Watch your timing. If you are aiming for a weekly paper that goes to print on Tuesday afternoon, don't hold an event on Tuesday evening. Be where journalists are, both literally and metaphorically. It's difficult to get journalists to come to a protest outside a company's offices, but if you demonstrate outside the company's big annual meeting, business correspondents will already be there. Contact them in advance and there's a good chance they'll come over to speak with you.

5. Talk to journalists. It sounds obvious, but it is often overlooked. Issue a news release when you act or respond to events, but don't rely on the release alone. Get on the phone with the journalists who have received it. Be concise and brace yourself for disappointments—most of them will not be interested. But chances are you will find someone who wants to know more eventually.

6. Build contacts. Go back to journalists every time you have a story, especially those who seemed interested earlier. If you're concise and reliable, and give them good stories, they will soon be phoning you for comments. When this happens, make sure that someone is available. A good relationship with a few journalists is worth a thousand press releases.

7. Choose the right media. Who are you trying to influence? If you're aiming to shift local public opinion, the local press is, of course, vital. When the UK student group People and Planet launched their Green Education Declaration, they targeted specialist education media. The news was read by fewer people than if it had been in mainstream media, but that audience included the decision makers whom the initiative was targeting.

8. Keep it human. A single death is a tragedy; a million deaths is a statistic. For example, Disarm UCL is a group of students campaigning for an end to their university's arms investments. They discovered that a University College London graduate named Richard Wilson had written a book about his sister's death as a result of the arms trade. By involving Wilson in their campaign, they made the story more human and made it harder for their opponents to dismiss them as inexperienced and unrealistic.

9. Make it visual. A good image can make or break your chances of coverage. Photo stunts should be original and meaningful but not too complicated. A great example is students who dressed in military jackets and mortarboards to illustrate military influence on universities. With photos of protests, be careful about the background. I'm amazed how often people protest outside a shop or company without ensuring that the company's name is visible in shots of the demonstration. Specialist media will often use photos provided by campaigners, so it's worth finding someone who's good with a camera.

10. Keep going. Media liaison is hard work, especially when you are new to it. But don't give up! The more you do, the more contacts you will acquire and the more coverage you will get. Keep your press releases and your phone calls regular. It will all be worth it when you see the coverage making a difference to your campaign.

Source: Symon Hill, *Utne*, March–April 2009. Reprinted from *Red Pepper*.

other websites. Although many governments have attempted to restrict both industries' use of the Internet, in general, this has failed to stop their widespread popularity.

As of this writing (and of all the chapters in this book, this is the one where knowledge most quickly goes out of date), more than a third of the world's approximate 7 billion people have used the services of the Internet. Despite this scope, accessibility (to the Internet and other media) is one focus of this chapter, as is the relationship of new technologies to imperialism and global capitalist development. New media both support traditional imperialist practices as well as provide opportunities for subversion and resistance through online communities organized to improve the lives of marginalized people. Indeed, over the last couple of decades there have been several global policy directives like the World Summits on Information Society (WSIS) by, for example, the United Nations, the World Bank, and various nongovernmental organizations to improve women's access to information and communication technologies generally.

In terms of expansion of global capitalist development, online shopping opportunities are now challenging and in many cases surpassing traditional consumer behaviors with staggering profits for major corporations. Much of this commerce relies upon the cheap labor of millions, especially women, worldwide. Data mining allows companies to improve sales and profitability by creating customer profiles that contain information about demographics and online behaviors. Cloud computing merges business with social networking concepts by developing interactive communities that connect individuals based on shared business needs or experiences. Many provide specialized networking tools and applications that can be accessed via their websites, such as business directory and reviewing services. However, the Internet also provides market opportunities for artisans and craftspeople (through websites such as etsy.com).

It is also important to note the environmental consequences of the marketing of these technologies worldwide—especially in terms of "e-waste" and its relationship to global climate change. Consequences of electronic production and use include: (1) raw material extraction of nonrenewable natural resources, including coltan, a rare metal that is mostly found in the Democratic Republic of Congo, where its mining is currently helping finance a war; (2) material manufacturing that involves greater use of fossil fuels than other traditional manufacturing; (3) computer and accessory manufacturing, packaging, and transport that involve extensive use of plastics and Styrofoam; (4) energy use to deal with the explosion of e-data generated, transmitted, and stored; and (5) despite recycling efforts, problems associated with the rapid obsolescence of electronic products containing toxic metals that end up in landfills and pollute the earth and its water sources. A concern is that large amounts of e-waste are sent to China, India, and Africa, where many unprotected workers are exposed to hazardous materials such as mercury and lead in the process of burning electronics in search of copper and aluminum to resell.

An important feature of the Internet is that it allows greater flexibility in working hours and location, especially with the spread of unmetered high-speed connections and tools such as virtual private networks, Skype, and videoconferencing. The relatively low cost and nearly instantaneous sharing of ideas, knowledge, and skills has increased opportunities for collaborative work nationally and transnationally. Such collaboration occurs in a wide variety of areas, including scientific research, software development, conference planning, political activism, and creative writing. Publishing a web page or a blog or building a website involves little initial cost and many cost-free services are available. However, "cyberslacking" has been identified as a drain on business and other organizational resources. A 2013 report suggests the average employee who uses a computer at work spends about an hour a day surfing the Web.

The term *Web 2.0* is commonly associated with web applications that facilitate interactive information sharing, user-centered design, and collaboration. Web 2.0 sites provide opportunities for users to collaborate and interact as initiators of user-generated content in virtual communities. This can be compared to websites where users consume online content created for them. Web 2.0 innovations include applications such as mashups, which use or combine data from several sources to create new services, and folksonomies, or collaborative tagging or indexing, which allow users to collectively classify and find information. Most familiar applications include blogs, wikis, video-sharing sites, hosted services, and social networking sites. Facebook, for example, the most popular social network service and website, has more than 1 billion monthly active users (about one person for every 7 in the world) as well as 50 million pages and 10 million apps. Similarly Twitter and Tumblr offer social networking and microblogging with millions of users. LinkedIn is a business-oriented site offering opportunities for professional networking with 200 million active users, Yelp is a business directory service and review site with social networking features, and Flickr provides image and video hosting, creating an online community allowing users to embed images in blogs and social media. These technologies not only rely on expensive hardware, but also, ultimately, on literacy, a key issue worldwide as women are less likely than men to be able to access education, and thus are more likely to be illiterate.

Increasingly people access the Internet through mobile devices such as cell phones and tablets. Currently about 90 percent of U.S. adults have cell phones and 55 percent of these access the Internet through mobile smartphones (double the number just three years ago). Overall, about a fifth of all people with cell phones use their phones as the primary or only way they connect with the Internet. There are very few significant differences in terms of cell and smartphone usage by gender or ethnicity, although older (older than 65-year-olds) have lower rates. Of U.S. adults using smartphones, more than two-thirds access news and social networking sites, and about a third upload photos, listen to online personalized radio or other music, and play games. About 15 percent watch movies on their smartphones.

A 2013 study by the Pew Research Center found 78 percent of U.S. teenagers (younger than 18 years) have cell phones and of those, almost half have smartphones. In addition, three-quarters of teenagers (a significantly higher number than adults) access the Internet using mobile devices. Teenagers and young adults represent the leading edge of mobile connectivity, and the patterns of their technology signal future changes in the adult population. It is interesting, and frightening, to note that more people on earth have access to mobile or cell phones than toilets. A recent study estimated that out of the world's approximated 7 billion people, 6 billion have access to mobile phones. Far fewer—only 4.5 billion people—have access to working toilets. Of the 2.5 billion who don't have proper sanitation, more than 1 billion defecate in the open. Worldwide there are about a billion Google searches and 2 billion videos viewed on YouTube daily.

Certainly these technologies are changing the ways we interact with each other and how we anticipate friendship and community. A 2012 poll of multiple nations (that included Brazil, South Korea, China, India, the United Kingdom, and the United States), for example, revealed 84 percent of respondents saying they could not go a single day without their cell phones and a fifth admitting they check their phone every 10 minutes. Fifty percent of U.S. smartphone users in this sample said they slept with their phone next to them like a teddy bear or a spouse (a number that includes more than 80 percent of 18- to 24-year-olds). Is unlimited access to information and communication always beneficial? Is the opportunity to have hundreds of friends on social networking sites helping us build community? The answers to such questions are complex and the case can be made that these devices are providing more knowledge at our fingertips, yet knowledge that is unfiltered as well as voluminous and therefore more easily forgettable. Social networking sites provide opportunities for us to keep in touch with a broad range of people in important ways, yet the case can be made that these are "faux friendships" without the interpersonal intimacies of "real" face-to-face friendship. What are your thoughts on this?

Sherry Turkle, founder and director of the MIT Initiative on Technology and Self and someone at the forefront of technological innovation, recently gave her opinion on the future of social life in this rapidly changing time. We are "networked and we are together," she said. "But so lessened are our expectations of each other that we feel utterly alone. And there is the risk that we come to see others as objects to be accessed—and only for the parts we find useful, comforting, or amusing." Scholars and clinicians have underscored her reservations with identification of various forms of Internet addiction disorder whereby excessive computer use interferes with daily life in relatively serious ways. Although Internet users are more efficient at finding information and have developed strong visual acuity and eye-hand coordination, these practices appear to interfere with deeper level thought related to creativity. And, although cell phones are usually considered devices that connect people, a 2012 study at the University of Maryland found that cell phone use for both women and men reduced empathic and pro-social behavior (measured via willingness to aid a charity). Researchers suggested that cell phone use evokes perceptions of connectivity to others, thereby fulfilling the basic human need to belong and reducing the desire to indulge in pro-social behavior. The ultimate risk of heavy technology use is that it not only fragments our life though multiple, diverse, and often superficial stimulation, but that it also diminishes empathy by limiting how much people really engage (off-line) with one another.

More significantly, how are digital technologies changing our brains? What does it mean for someone who has spent since birth, large portions of her or his day in front of screens, interrupted constantly, and encouraged to juggle various streams of information? Some scientists say without hesitation that juggling multiple sources of information and responding to ongoing communication is changing how we think and behave. It appears that the technology is actually rewiring the brain as neural networks continue to develop through life. Scientists say our ability to focus is undermined by bursts of information that stimulate (through a dopamine surge) the primitive impulse to respond to immediate opportunities and threats. This is why people experience digital technologies as addictive and feel bored or anxious when they are not "connected" to their devices. Along with this surge comes stress hormones that also have powerful effects on the body. Educators explain children have reduced attention span, difficulties focusing, and increased problems with obesity as a direct consequence of the ways we structure life around digital devices.

Originally the Web was imagined as utopian spaces where gender, race, class, and sexuality were neutral forces or where alternative subjectivities could be performed. Although this potential still remains, virtual realities tend to reinforce current social standards about gender and other identities. This occurs in two ways. First, traditional standards are scripted through gendered and racialized content supported by advertising, entertainment, and pornography. This "content" is saturated with traditional ideas about gender, downloading music and videos, watching television shows and reading narratives about other people's lives and activities on social networking sites.

Advertisements accompany most websites and a large percentage of Internet traffic is pornography related. Currently the worldwide pornography industry revenue is more than U.S. $100 billion with about $14 billion in U.S. revenue (although these numbers are notoriously difficult to estimate). The pornography industry has larger revenues than Microsoft, Google, Amazon, eBay, Yahoo, Apple, and Netflix combined. In addition, pornography is often credited as fuel behind technological innovation and adoption. For example, pornography companies were attempting to perfect video streaming long before mainstream media in order to offer live sex performers that could be streamed directly to consumers. Live chat rooms between pornography consumers and performers also innovated much of the technology used today in other arenas. Today about a quarter of all search engine requests and more than a third of all Internet downloads are pornographic in nature. Estimates include about 30,000 viewers of Internet pornography every second with peak Internet pornography traffic during the work day between 9 am and 5 pm. Approximately a fifth of U.S. men admit to watching online pornography at work and between two-thirds and three-quarters of men aged 18 to 24 years visit pornography sites in a typical month.

Finally, of course, it is important to mention the levels of violence in online entertainment. Of particular concern are violent video games marketed to adolescent boys and the relationship between these activities and teen violence. This concern has precipitated hearings in the U.S. House of Representatives to discuss the regulation of certain games that depict the death, maiming, and harassment of people and animals. Violent video games tend to glorify violence, desensitize individuals to suffering, and may legitimize and trivialize violence and hate crimes against marginalized groups.

Second, despite the fact that Internet technologies provide new opportunities and help people connect across wide geographical expanses, these technologies are not available to everyone. Social class limits access to all information and communication technologies, irrespective of gender. The speed with which technology evolves or becomes obsolete (the "technology turnover" that pushes new gadget accessories through the marketplace at astonishing speeds) exacerbates these issues of equity associated with Internet technologies. According to a study published in 2013, there are few gender differences in Internet access in the United States, although in terms of usage women are more likely to use it for communication (email, blogs, and fan following) and participate in social networking sites. Men are more likely to use the Internet for recreation. Women participate in more streaming content, whereas men downloaded more. Men also have a higher use of Internet pornography and violent gaming, as discussed above. In this way, although in the global north a majority of women have access to the Internet, it is still a contested site where girls and women may experience marginalization, discrimination, abuse, and/or disempowerment. Online predation of girls and young women is an increasingly important problem as computers are installed in children's bedrooms and phones with Internet capabilities are owned by younger and younger individuals, making the Internet a central feature of teen and preteen life. It is estimated that one in five children is approached by an Internet predator, mostly through social networking sites.

Although a global perspective on women's access to the Internet reveals similar gendered usage, there are important gender and class differences associated with access. Where resources are scarce, the gap between those with resources, access, and skills, and those without, grows. This means that because women as a group are limited by poverty and lack of education, they are less likely to be able to access digital technologies. In addition, cultural differences also come into play as some communities encourage women's access to the Internet and some do not. In this way, women's access to media is limited by socioeconomic factors as well as literacy and numeracy skills, and "user" characteristics such as time constraints associated with family obligations.

Finally, at the same time that the Internet reinscribes power issues on multiple levels, as already mentioned, it provides opportunities for subversion and resistance. Its relevance as a political tool facilitating various forms of cyberactivism is now well known. For example, recent U.S. presidential campaigns have been notable for their success in organizing voters and soliciting donations through the Internet. Digital technologies are also increasingly employed in resistance against standing regimes outside the United States, as in the case of the 2012 Arab Spring uprisings. In particular, social networking sites such as Facebook and Twitter helped citizens organize protests, communicate grievances, and share information. The reading "Cyberactivism and the Role of Women in the Arab Uprisings" by Courtney Radsch focuses on Egypt, Tunisia, Bahrain, and Yemen and explores how women used such media and employed citizen journalism to counter state-dominated media. China's attempts to censor and filter material on the Internet also reflect the growing civic potential of online communities and cyberactivism generally. Indeed, this activism is responding to the explosion of mass media globally that have grown with the expansion of markets on local, national, and global scales. Media corporations have grown stronger in their reach of audiences and in their ability to shape production and distribution processes worldwide.

The content and organization of the Web also provides opportunities to dispute and create new knowledge. Many women have fought to make a place for themselves in the technological world, developing their own activist websites, blogs, and computer games.

LEARNING ACTIVITY　**Analyzing Social Media**

1. Become a Twitter follower of a celebrity for a few days. Then complete a gender analysis of her/his tweets: What issues are important to this celebrity? Who is the audience for the tweets? What is s/he trying to accomplish with these tweets? How does this celebrity perform gender in these tweets? Does s/he address gender issues in her/his tweets? Do the tweets reinforce or challenge gender norms? Do you think tweeting can be an effective form of feminist activism?

2. Search for YouTube videos on a topic related to feminism. Watch a selection of these videos and analyze them: Who is the intended audience? How does the video frame feminist issues? What is the goal of the video? How does the video make its argument? How would you assess the video's contribution to feminist dialogue? Can YouTube videos be an effective form of feminist activism?

3. Identify three feminist bloggers and read a selection of their blogs on feminist issues. Who is their audience? How do they construct their arguments to reach this audience? What kinds of comments get posted in response to their blogs? How effective do you think these blogs are as a form of feminist activism?

The reading in Chapter 13 by Moya Bailey and Alexis Pauline Gumbs on black feminist blogging ("We Are the Ones We've Been Waiting For") is also a case in point. Blogs allow opportunities for citizen journalism that allows people to critique and provide social commentary on their lives or the world around them. Blogging has also changed the face of publishing. Although bloggers are not usually formally trained and may not have professional credentials, they have been able to publish their opinions or beliefs about any number of subjects, appearing in school projects, on activism websites, and on political web pages, often with accompanying video. Similarly, wikis are knowledge databanks in which any user can add, edit, and create definitions for common words, concepts, histories, or biographies. It is important to note that though wikis can be good sources of common information, they are not always accurate and should not be confused with academic databases! These sites reflect a democratic construction of knowledge to which individuals can contribute (the website Wikipedia is one example).

TELEVISION

Television is one of the most influential forms of media because it is so pervasive and its presence is taken for granted in most households in the United States. Television impacts family life because it encourages passive interaction, often replacing alternative family interaction. In addition, television is a visual medium that broadcasts multiple images on a continual basis in digitized, high-density formats. The ways people watch television, however, are changing as viewers increasingly record shows rather than watch them in real time, watch parts of shows in other formats (for example, YouTube), and view television shows through computers and other mobile devices. However, although television viewing habits are increasingly diverse and fragmented, still these images come to be seen as representing the real world and influence people's understanding of others and the world around them. This is especially significant for children because it is estimated that most children, on the average, watch far more television than is good for them. Of course, the range and quality of television shows vary, and a case can be made for the benefits of educational television. Unfortunately, educational programming is only a small percentage of television viewing.

The explosion of cable and satellite availability has resulted in an unlimited number of television channels. Such choice, however, has not meant greater access to a wide range of alternative images of gender. Reality shows, and makeover shows, in particular, reinforce dominant notions of gender and standards of beauty, as do entertainment shows such as *American Idol* and *The Voice*. In addition, a host of shows such as *Teen Mom* and *Pregnant and Dating* provide sometimes contradictory messages about the challenges and benefits of unplanned pregnancies (although recent research suggests these shows may increase contraceptive usage). Shows incorporating shame and humiliation can be said to "discipline" an audience even while they present other people's misfortune as entertainment. Ultimately they are engaged in the selling of products.

Advertising sponsors control the content of most commercial television. During male sporting events, for example, the commercials are for beer, cars, electronic products, Internet commerce, and other products targeted at a male audience. During daytime soap operas or evening family sitcoms, on the other hand, the commercials are aimed at women and focus on beauty and household products. As a result, commercial sponsors have enormous influence over the content of television programming. If they want to sell a certain product, they are unlikely to air the commercial during a feature that could be interpreted as criticizing such products or consumerism generally. In this way, commercial sponsors shape television content.

Television messages about gender are often very traditional, even when they are attempting to capitalize on new trends. The popular show *Modern Family* is case in point. Although it depicts a secure, loving gay couple, for example, it reinscribes many stereotypes about gay men. Similarly, while it also presents a very likeable Latina struggling to cope with life in the United States, it supports stereotypes of the ditsy Latin woman in most episodes. In fact, the assumed differences between the genders very often drive the plot of television programming. The format of shows is also gendered. For example, daytime soap operas focus on relationships and family and employ rather fragmented narratives with plots weaving around without closure or resolution, enabling women to tune in and out as they go about multiple tasks. Daytime soaps are only part of the story. Shows with drama and overt sexuality such as the long-running *Grey's Anatomy* target an evening audience, as do crime and thriller shows such as *Persons of Interest* and *NCIS*. The popularity of the historical drama *Downton Abbey* represents not only the interest in romance and intrigue, fashion and stately homes, but a nostalgia for the past. Cable networks such as HBO and AMC feature dramatic series such as *Mad Men,* another show set in the past, that garner popular acclaim and then become profitable as boxed-set DVDs. *Mad Men* provides a critique of corporate masculinity through its focus on men employed in a 1960s advertising agency. Similarly, popular series like *Game of Thrones* offer sexualized violence and misogynous male characters alongside some dynamic female characters. Even Breaking *Bad,* a show with high hopes from a feminist perspective, provided fodder for debate about contradictory messages about gender. Scholars have pointed out that these shows reconcile women to male-dominated interpersonal relationships and help enforce gendered social relations. Others argue that these shows enable women viewers to actively critique blatant male-dominated situations in ways that help them reflect on their own lives.

A similar analysis can be made of evening family sitcoms. Shows such as *Modern Family* and *The Good Wife* are funny and entertaining because they are relatively predictable. The family or work group (as in *The Office*) is made up of characters with distinct personalities and recognizable habits; each week this "family" is thrown into some kind of crisis, and the plot of the show is to resolve that crisis back to situation as usual. Sometimes

LEARNING ACTIVITY   **Talking About Talk Shows**

Watch several television talk shows. Keep a journal describing the topic of the show, the guests, and the commercial sponsors. How would you characterize the host? What do you notice about the interactions among host, guests, and audience? In what ways does gender operate in the shows? Do you think the shows are in any way empowering for the guests, audience members, or television viewers? How do you think these shows reflect either dominant or subordinate American cultures? How do you think these shows contribute to public discourse?

it involves a group of roommates or neighbors as in the classics *Friends*, *Seinfeld, The Big Bang Theory,* or *New Girl.* For the most part, the messages are typical in terms of gender, race, class, and other differences, and they often involve humor that denigrates certain groups of people and ultimately maintains the status quo. As already mentioned, reality television is especially influential. The appeal of "reality" shows such as *The Bachelor, Survivor, The Biggest Loser, Hell's Kitchen,* and *Jersey Shore* rely on creative casting, scripting, and editing to make the shows seem spontaneous, incorporating character traits and personalities that viewers love to hate and adore. These shows also rely on a cult of the celebrity, rampant in popular culture.

The Ellen DeGeneres Show and gay-themed decorating and personal styling shows may have helped normalize gay life for the broader society even while they often relied on traditional stereotypes. Some television specifically feature empowered LGBTQ characters such as Pam De Beaufort and Tara Thornton in *True Blood*, Callie Torres and Arizona Robbins in *Grey's Anatomy*, and other LQBTQ mainstays in such shows as *The Good Wife, The New Normal, Lost Girl,* and *Lip Service.*

Increasingly, we are seeing shows and advertisements that resist traditional representations, or at least show them with a new twist. Empowering roles for women are actually more likely to appear in television than in the movies because the former expects a female audience, whereas the latter relies on young male viewers. In addition, changes in society's views of gender and other differences have made sponsors realize that they have a new marketing niche. Susan Douglas writes about the proliferation of empowered female characters in the reading "Enlightened Sexism." She points to such characters as Miranda Bailey, the strong African American surgeon on *Grey's Anatomy;* agent Scully on *The X-Files,* a white, no-nonsense, smart character out to solve crime; and one of the most influential people in the entertainment industry, Oprah Winfrey. Douglas makes the case for these representations as fantasies of power that are especially seductive for girls and young women in that they provide the illusion and post-feminist message that "all has been won." Douglas explains that such "enlightened sexism" embeds feminism into its representations and insists that because women are now equal to men, it is okay and merely entertainment to present the old, tired stereotypes under new glitter. Often, unfortunately, these new representations involve the same old package tied up in new ways; typically they involve women and men resisting some of the old norms while keeping most intact.

For example, although women are starting to be shown as competent, strong, athletic, and in control of their lives rather than ditsy housewives or sex symbols, they still are very physically attractive and are often highly sexualized. In the reading, "Don't Act Crazy, Mindy," Heather Havrilesky discusses the trend for smart leading women in television sitcoms to act like "volcanoes that could blow at any minute." She recognizes this is televisionland's shorthand for complicated, strong-willed women and makes the case for saner, more authentic characters.

Glee is still a relatively popular evening television show that provides a gay-friendly script and some empowering roles and messages about femininity while at the same time featuring young women who are again physically attractive and often highly sexualized even though they often portray high schools students. Other examples abound in crime drama such as *Law & Order: SVU* and *CSI.* These shows provide strong, intelligent women as primary characters, but at the same time these women fulfill the stereotypical standards of beauty. They can track down criminals using forensic science and look gorgeous while doing it. Unfortunately, most of the victims are female, too. Despite some empowered characters in shows like *CSI*, the focus on sexy female corpses ultimately associates women, queer cultures, and sexual subcultures with traditional and shallow stereotypes, negativity, and death.

Finally, news programs play an important role in shaping public opinion. Fox News, for example, is known for its support of conservative political opinion. Media scholars are particularly interested in the relationship between political ideologies and news media and especially the role of organizations like Fox News in supporting a conservative Republican agenda. One of the most influential pundits shaping popular opinion is Rush Limbaugh. With an estimated net worth of $350 million, Limbaugh is the outspoken, ultra-conservative host of *The Rush Limbaugh Show*, an A.M. radio show about U.S. politics, although he is a personality with cross-over appeal to television. The reading, "The New Networked Feminism," by Tom Watson discusses the organized feminist response to one of Limbaugh's misogynous outbursts that resulted in a dozen advertisers and two radio stations canceling his show. Satire news shows such as Jon Stewart's *The Daily Show* and Stephen Colbert's *The Colbert Report* provide alternative, more liberal takes on domestic and international news.

MOVIES

In her groundbreaking work on cinema, feminist film theorist Laura Mulvey identifies the "male gaze" as a primary motif for understanding gender in filmmaking. Mulvey argues that movies are essentially made through and for the male gaze and fulfill a voyeuristic desire for men to look at women as objects. Viewers are encouraged to "see" the movie through the eyes of the male protagonist who carries the plot forward. In other words, the focus is on the production of meaning in a film (including television and digital media), how it imagines a viewing subject, and the ways the mechanisms of cinematic production shape the representation of women and marginalized others, reinforcing intersecting systems of inequality and privilege. Mulvey makes the point that traditional feminine subjects in film are bearers of meaning not meaning making. Meaning making in Hollywood tends to incorporate heteronormative (centering of heterosexuality) themes that reinforce gender ranking through such genres as gangster films, action films, and westerns that celebrate heterosexual masculine power (with exceptions, of course, such as *Brokeback Mountain*). In other words, these films portray heterosexuality as the dominant theme representing masculinities.

Some feminist scholars have suggested the possibility for "subversive gazing" by viewers who refuse to gaze the way filmmakers expect and by making different kinds of movies. A key aspect of this criticism is recognizing the way identities are constructed and performed (in everyday life as well as in the movies) rather than essentialist and intrinsic to people. Coming from a black feminist perspective, bell hooks writes about the "oppositional gaze," encouraging women of color in film to reject stereotypical representations in film and actively critique them. In addition, film theorists are increasingly taking global or transnational perspectives, responding to critiques of Eurocentrism or the centering of a white, European, as well as straight and economically privileged perspective that has traditionally excluded disparate approaches across class, racial, and ethnic groups throughout the world. The Bollywood film genre, for example, a Hindi-language film industry in India, demonstrates the popularity of non-"Western" consciousness. Feminist film theorists such as Claire Johnson, hooks, and Mulvey emphasize that alternative (to traditional Hollywood) films can function as "counter cinema" by integrating alternative cinematic forms and images and by putting women and other marginalized people in charge of directing and producing films. Finally, the integration of lesbian/gay/queer politics in film attempts to destabilize traditional Hollywood themes. For example, the Queer Film Society, a consortium of LGBT film critics, historians, artists, and scholars, focuses on the production and celebration of queer images in world cinema. One of their mottos is "We're here, we're queer, we're watching movies."

Probably the best genre of film in which to observe gender is the romantic comedy or romantic drama. Romantic comedies have become the de facto film produced for female audiences that shape notions of multifaceted femininities. Their heteronormative formula reinforces myths about romantic love and marriage as the most important keys to women's happiness. This popular and seductive genre sometimes contains glimpses challenging heteropatriarchy (such as the blockbuster film *He's Just Not That Into You*). These films are packed with subtle and not-so-subtle notions of gender. For example, the now classic movie *Pretty Woman* is a contemporary retelling of the Cinderella story, in which a young woman waits for her Prince Charming to rescue her from her undesirable situation. In this case, the prostitute-with-a-heart-of-gold is swept away in a white limousine by the older rich man who procured her services and then fell in love with her. Some films like *Enchanted* are trying to challenge the idea that all women need to be saved by a handsome prince. The *Shrek* series of movies satirizes traditional fairy tale elements, with the princess choosing to become an ogre and exhibiting her own sense of self and agency. Yet even these films that seem to challenge masculinist assumptions still often reproduce patriarchal understandings. So while Fiona in *Shrek* forsakes traditional femininity, she still embraces the roles of wife and mother as the ultimate goals for women.

Other genres of films are also revealing in terms of norms about gender. Slasher films and horror movies are often spectacular in terms of their victimization of women. The killers in these movies, such as Norman Bates in the classic *Psycho* (a spin-off television show in 2013, *Bates Motel*, capitalizes on this plot and reveals his ambiguous childhood psyche), are often sexually disturbed and hound and kill women who arouse them. This is also the subtext of other old films such as *The Texas Chainsaw Massacre* movies and *Prom Night*.

LEARNING ACTIVITY   **Women Make Movies**

Very often the subjects that are important to women are ignored in popular filmmaking or are distorted by stereotypes or the male gaze. Despite lack of funding and major studio backing, independent women filmmakers worldwide persist in documenting the wide range of women's lives and experiences.

Visit the website of Women Make Movies at *www.wmm.com*. Browse the catalog and identify movies made by filmmakers outside the United States. What themes do they pursue? Are these themes also common in American women filmmakers' movies? In what ways do they also express cultural distinctions? How do these films differ from mainstream box office releases? Why is an organization like Women Make Movies important?

Often it is sexually active couples who are killed, either after sex or in anticipation of it. Another plot of horror movies is the crazed and demanding mother who drives her offspring to psychosis, as in *Carrie,* where the mother gives birth to the spawn of Satan. The "final girl" trope is also a staple of slasher films. She is the last girl left alive, the one who confronts the killer and presumably lives to tell the story. She's seen in classic films such as *Halloween, Friday the 13th, Scream, A Nightmare on Elm Street,* and *Hatchet.* Although both women and men claim to be entertained by these films, it is important to talk about the messages they portray about men, about women, and about the normalization of violence.

Pornography is an extreme example of the male gaze and the normalization of violence against women (discussed in Chapter 10). With its print media counterpart, pornography extends the sexualization and objectification of women's bodies for entertainment. In pornographic representations, women are often reduced to body parts and are shown deriving pleasure from being violated and dominated. Additionally, racism intersects with sexism in pornography when women of color are portrayed as the "exotic other" and are fetishized and portrayed in especially demeaning and animalistic ways. Although many feminists, ourselves included, oppose pornography, others, especially those described as "sex radicals," feel that pornography can be a form of sexual self-expression for women. They argue that women who participate in the production of pornography are taking control of their own sexuality and are profiting from control of their own bodies.

Advertisers have targeted young girls with stripper and porn-inspired merchandise that creates a very narrow definition of what constitutes sexiness for women. Such pressures encourage young women to identify with this objectification and sexualization and confuse it with notions of self-empowerment. As already discussed, young people often follow celebrity blogs that feature gossip and photos about their favorite movie and music celebrities. Although this "cult of the celebrity" is not something new in popular culture, the growth of the Internet has facilitated public fascination with famous people and also encourages young people to seek their few minutes of fame. It has been suggested that this celebration of fame not only shapes young people's ideas about self and body with unrealistic expectations, but has also facilitated the growth and interest in reality television.

Some of the more pervasive and lasting gender images in U.S. culture derive from Walt Disney feature films. As mentioned, Disney Corporation is the number one media conglomerate in the world in terms of revenue created. A key source of their profits lies in the fact that Disney heroines live not only on the big screen, but also as dolls in little girls' rooms, on their sheets and curtains, and on their lunchboxes and clothes. On the whole, Disney characters reflect white, middle-class, heteropatriarchal, and imperialist norms. More recent representations in Disney movies have attempted to be more inclusive, but still rely largely on these traditional norms. For example, new Disney heroines are empowered to make choices for themselves, but still tend to be represented in sexualized ways with Anglo features.

As women have made societal gains, Hollywood filmmaking has changed and become more inclusive of new norms about gender and other forms of social difference. Indeed, as Susan Douglas explains in the reading "Enlightened Sexism," film media contain multiple images of female empowerment and gay-friendly narratives. Douglas asks why these images of female empowerment are not aligned with the realities of most women's lives and makes the case for a seductive appropriation of feminism for corporate gain. These empowered characters are more likely to be white and economically privileged at the same time that narratives about them tend to rely on heterosexual romance. Notice also the dearth of people of color or LGBQT characters in leading roles in most films. Bringing a critical eye to the movies we watch helps us notice how films play a role in maintaining privilege and moves us from being passive recipients of the movies' message to active viewers who can offer informed analysis.

One of the biggest contemporary movie hits is the *Twilight Saga*: screenplays based upon novels by Stephanie Meyer. A case can be made that the movies provide examples of subversions of traditional gender and complex messages about female power and agency. However, as Alison Happel and Jennifer Esposito suggest in the reading "Vampires and Vixens," the movies sexualize violence with potentially negative consequences for teenage girls. The major theme of the movies, for example, concerns a girl's love for a boy who wants to kill her. Even though he tells her to avoid him, the main character, Bella, repeatedly risks violence through her pursuit of him. Happel and Esposito emphasize that Bella's body language is especially sexual in violent scenes. Another very popular young-adult novel turned movie is Suzanne Collins's book *The Hunger Games*. Declared a feminist narrative in its representation of a strong black girl in pursuit of social justice, the movie also shows the main character, Katniss, clever and competent with qualities usually given to boys, who risks death to save her sister and another girl child. She appears as the opposite to Bella of *Twilight* in that she is not love-obsessed, and unlike Hermione of the *Harry Potter* series, she is the lead character and not the sidekick. Still, despite these credentials, it is noted that Katniss makes few decisions of her own, is still protected by men, and blessed with lucky accidents; and when things get impossible, there are packages from the sky. Some critics have also noted that it is a prime example of a cultural product that should not be assumed to be feminist simply because it has a female creator and female protagonist. If you have read or watched *The Hunger Games*, what do you think?

CONTEMPORARY MUSIC AND MUSIC VIDEOS

Popular music genres such as rock, grunge, punk, metal, techno, and hip-hop are contemporary cultural forms targeted at youth. Often this music offers resistance to traditional cultural forms and contains a lot of teenage angst attractive to young people who are figuring out who they are in relation to their parents and other adults in positions of authority in their lives. In this way, such music serves as contemporary resistance and can work to mobilize people politically. Certainly music functions to help youth shape notions of identity. The various musical forms offer different kinds of identities from which people can pick and choose to sculpt their own sense of self. In this way, music has played, and continues to play, a key role in the consolidation of youth cultures in society. There is a huge music industry in the United States, and it works in tandem with television, film, video, radio, and, of course, advertising. The Internet and personalized music devices like the iPod and iTunes allow people to download music and create their own personalized collections rather than purchasing complete CDs. Similarly, personalized radio like Pandora and Slacker allows individuals to indicate and provide feedback on a song or artist they like and the service responds by playing selections that are musically similar. These technologies have changed industries and listening practices.

Just as rock music was an essential part of mobilizing the youth of the 1960s to rebel against traditional norms, oppose the war, and work for civil rights, hip-hop music and culture has been influential in recent decades as a critique of racial cultural politics. Originating in African American urban street culture of the late 1970s, rap was influenced by rhythm and blues and rock and quickly spread beyond its roots into television, fashion, film, and, in particular, music videos. At the same time that the rap music industry has been able to raise the issue of racism, poverty, and social violence in the context of its endorsement of black nationalism, rap has also perpetuated misogyny and violence in its orientation and musical lyrics. There are women performers in hip-hop and new female rappers are receiving much more attention, but their status in the industry is far below that of male bands. Aya de Leon reflects on this in her poem "If Women Ran Hip Hop." Women's success in hip-hop is illustrated by the success of such artists as Queen Latifah, Lil' Kim, and Missy Elliot. Elliott in particular is known not only as a writer and performer but also as a producer of other artists' music. These women continue in the footsteps of blues and soul artists such as Billie Holiday, Aretha Franklin, and Etta James.

About 30 years after the advent of rock music, the combination of music with visual images gave rise to the music video genre, which gained immense popularity in the 1980s with the prominence of MTV, a music video station that has now branched into specialized programming. Music videos are unique in blending television programming with commercials such that while the viewer is actually watching a commercial, the illusion is of programmatic entertainment. Music videos are essentially advertisements for record company products and focus on standard rock music, although different musical genres like country-western also have their own video formatting. Most music videos are fairly predictable in the ways they sexualize women, sometimes in violent ways. As in movies, women are generally present in music videos to be looked at. In fact, music videos featuring male musicians are aired in greater numbers than those featuring female musicians.

Nonetheless, we could also argue that the music video industry has allowed women performers to find their voice (literally) and to script music videos from their perspective. This opportunity gave women audience recognition and industry backing. Music videos also helped produce a feminine voice with the potential to disrupt traditional gendered perspectives. At its peak in the mid-1980s, MTV helped such women as Tina Turner, Cyndi Lauper, and Madonna find success. Madonna is especially interesting because she was cast simultaneously as both a feminist nightmare perpetuating gendered

IDEAS FOR ACTIVISM

- Write letters to encourage networks to air television shows that depict the broad diversity of women.
- Write letters to sponsors to complain about programs that degrade or stereotype women.
- Form a reading group to study novels by female authors.
- Create your own zine about a feminist issue that's important to you.
- Sponsor a media awareness event on campus to encourage other students to be aware of media portrayals of women. Use social media to promote awareness of women's issues.
- Create a YouTube video to promote your women and gender studies program.

stereotypes about sexualized women and an important role model for women who want to be active agents in their lives. Lady Gaga (Stefani Germanotta) is similarly positioned as an icon who simultaneously supports and resists female sexualization. Both Madonna and Lady Gaga have been regarded as returning the male gaze by staring right back at the patriarchy. Similarly, Beyoncé, for example, has declared her feminism with empowering songs like "Single Ladies (Put a Ring on It)" and Destiny's Child's classic "Independent Women." Sophie Weiner makes the case for Beyoncé as a celebrity who furthers the cause of social justice in "Beyoncé: Feminist Icon?" Other artists like Christina Aguilera and Pink are also celebrated for being both sexual and assertively feminist in much the same way.

Performing rock music has generally been seen as a male activity, despite the presence of women rockers from the genre's beginnings in the 1950s. The male-dominated record industry has tended to exclude women rockers and tried to force women musicians into stereotypical roles as singers and sex objects. But the advent of new, accessible technologies has allowed women greater control of their own music. Now, instead of needing a recording contract with one of the big labels, an aspiring rocker can write, record, produce, and distribute her own music. For years, independent artists sold most of their music out of the back of a van, but now the Internet has made global distribution possible for just about every musician—without a large budget, agent, manager, or record label. New technologies both inside and outside the music industry have provided more ways for women to express themselves. Opportunities for self-promotion on YouTube and various social networking sites have encouraged a new generation of women musicians. Musicians can display their music and image for free with minimal effort. This allows them to break out of expected norms and potentially avoid industry stereotyping. Online communities such as GoGirlsMusic and Women in Music also support and help launch new artists.

Other strategies for independence include "indie" artists and bands whose music is produced within networks of independent record labels and underground music venues that emerged in the United States and elsewhere in the 1980s and 1990s. Indie is also seen as a distinct genre of rock music with a specific artistic aesthetic that includes many female artists. Singer-songwriters such as Ani DiFranco, the Indigo Girls, Tracy Chapman, and Tori Amos were important in providing feminist music as also were the "riot grrl" feminist punk artists and bands of the 1980s. Many of these artists continue to serve as role models for young women seeking to gain a more independent place in contemporary music.

PRINT MEDIA

No discussion of popular culture is complete without a discussion of print media. These mass media forms include magazines, newspapers, comic books, and other periodicals that are usually simultaneously available online. Like other media, they are a mix of entertainment, education, and advertising. Fashion magazines are heavy on advertising, whereas comic books tend to be geared toward entertainment and rely more on product sales of the comic books themselves. Newspapers fall somewhere in between.

Women's magazines are an especially fruitful subject of study for examining how gender works in contemporary U.S. society. As discussed in Chapter 4, women's magazines are a central part of the multi-billion-dollar industries that produce cosmetics and

LEARNING ACTIVITY **Looking Good, Feeling Sexy, Getting a Man**

Collect a number of women's magazines, such as *Cosmopolitan, Vogue, Elle, Glamor, Redbook,* and *Woman's Day.* Read through the magazines and fill in the chart listing the number of articles you find about each topic. What do you observe from your analysis? What messages about gender are these magazines presenting?

Magazine Title	Makeup	Clothes	Hair	Sex/ Dating	Dieting	Food/ Recipes	Home Decoration	Work	Politics

fashion and help shape the social construction of "beauty." Alongside these advertising campaigns are bodily standards against which women are encouraged to measure themselves. Because almost no one measures up to these artificially created and often computer-generated standards, the message is to buy these products and your life will improve.

Generally, women's magazines can be divided into three distinct types. First are the fashion magazines that focus on beauty, attracting and satisfying men, self-improvement, and (occasionally) work and politics. Examples are *Vogue* (emphasizing fashion and makeup), *Cosmopolitan* (emphasizing sexuality and relationships with men), and *Self* (emphasizing self-improvement and employment), although the latter two are also heavy on beauty and fashion and the former is also preoccupied with sex. Most of these magazines have a white audience in mind; *Ebony* is one similar kind of magazine aimed at African American women. Note that there are also a number of junior magazines in this genre, such as *Seventeen,* aimed at teenage women. However, although its title suggests the magazine might be oriented toward 17-year-olds, it is mostly read by younger teenagers and even preadolescent girls. Given the focus of teen magazines on dating, fashion, and makeup, the effects of such copy and advertisements on young girls are significant.

The second genre of women's magazines includes those oriented toward the family, cooking, household maintenance and decoration, and keeping the man you already have. Examples include *Good Housekeeping, Redbook,* and *Better Homes and Gardens.* These magazines (especially those like *Good Housekeeping*) also include articles and advertising on fashion and cosmetics, although the representations of these products are different. Instead of the seductive model dressed in a shiny, revealing garment (as is usually featured on the cover of *Cosmo* or *Glamor*), *Redbook,* for example, usually features a less glamorous woman (although still very normatively beautiful) in more conservative clothes, surrounded by other graphics or captions featuring various desserts, crafts, and so forth. The focus is off sex and onto the home.

The third genre of women's magazines is the issue periodical that focuses on some issue or hobby that appeals to many women. *Parents* magazine is an example of an issue periodical aimed at women (although not exclusively). *Ms.* magazine is one aimed at

HISTORICAL MOMENT   *SI for Women*

By Lindsay Schnell

Featuring a variety of male athletes, marketed to men and written (mostly) by men, *Sports Illustrated (SI)* magazine has never done a consistent job of covering and featuring female athletes. It's easy to see why: *SI* primarily covers professional sports, and a small percentage of professional athletes are women. For years, female athletes struggled to get a fair shake in media coverage, often being touted more for their looks than their abilities on the playing field.

That all changed in the spring of 1999 with the debut of *Sports Illustrated for Women.* Featuring teen basketball phenom Seimone Augustus—who went on to star at Louisiana State University and become the number-one pick of the 2006 WNBA draft—on its first cover, *SI for Women* catered to female athletes of all ages and skill levels. The magazine offered tips on eating like a professional athlete, previews of college and professional teams, in-depth features on known and unknown females making an impact in the world of sport, and much more. One issue even had a sports horoscope for its readers! *SI for Women* also had an answer to its parent magazine's hottest-selling issue annually: a swimsuit issue of its own, with male athletes showing off the bodies they had worked so hard for. Finally, women had a sports magazine just for them that celebrated their athletic accomplishments instead of just their looks.

One of the earliest covers featured Julie Foudy, a member of the 1999 Women's World Cup soccer team. Foudy and her teammates became known across the nation after a thrilling 5–4 shootout victory over China in the Rose Bowl for the '99 Cup title. Brandi Chastain's "shot heard 'round the world" and subsequent act of ripping off her shirt and falling to her knees in ecstasy became one of the most iconic sports images of the twentieth century.

Coupled with the success of the '99 World Cup team, *SI for Women* helped athletes like soccer great Mia Hamm and basketball superstar Sheryl Swoopes become household names. Unfortunately, *SI for Women* wasn't a hot seller on the newsstands, and lasted just 18 issues. It folded in 2002, but in the two-and-a-half years that *SI for Women* was in print it helped give a face—or faces—to a generation hungry for strong female role models.

In 2008 Winter X Games star Gretchen Bleiler told *ESPN The Magazine*, "It sucks. When you're a woman in sports, people want you to show some skin." Though it's no longer in print, *SI for Women* helped prove female athletes didn't have to show skin to get some pub. And with female athletic participation at an all-time high since Title IX was passed in 1972, is there any better news we can give to our friends, teammates, sisters, and daughters?

feminists, as are *Bitch* and *Bust.* Examples of hobby-type periodicals include craft magazines on needlework or crochet and fitness magazines. There are many specialized issue periodicals aimed at men (such as hunting and fishing and outdoor activities periodicals, computer and other electronic-focused magazines, car and motorcycle magazines, and various sports periodicals). The best known of the latter is *Sports Illustrated,* famous also for its "swimsuit edition," which always produces record sales in its sexualization of female athletes' bodies (see the sidebar "*SI for Women*"). That there are more issue periodicals for men reflects the fact that this group is assumed to work and have specialized interests, and women are assumed to be preoccupied with looking good, working on relationships, and keeping a beautiful home.

Again, as in music, technology has also provided a way for women to express their voices through publishing. "Zines" are quick, cheap, cut-and-paste publications that have sprung up both in print and online formats in recent years. These publications, which range in quality, often provide a forum for alternative views on a wide variety of subjects,

WOMEN IN PRINT

by Nancy Barbour

Feminist consciousness-raising efforts in the late 1960s and early 1970s increased women's awareness that their personal experiences needed articulation in wider sociopolitical contexts. Like their first wave sisters before them, second wave feminists worked to spread their critical knowledge to greater numbers of women by distributing newsletters and pamphlets. The now famous book *Our Bodies, Ourselves* (1973), by the Boston Women's Health Book Collective, began as a 35-cent feminist pamphlet that aimed to demystify women's health and sexuality. But the women's movement faced resistance from mainstream publishers.

High-circulation magazines for "ladies" rejected feminist articles that addressed issues of real concern to women. Instead, they often published advertising "puffs"—articles that appear to be informative but are designed to sell an advertiser's product. Feminists understood that these publications, while marketed directly to women, were controlled and edited almost entirely by men. In 1970, more than 100 feminists descended upon the offices of *Ladies' Home Journal* and staged an 11-hour sit-in. They demanded that the magazine hire women to fill all editorial and advertising positions, that it hire a proportionate number of

(continued)

non-white women at all levels, and that it cease publishing advertisements that were degrading to women. The editor did not capitulate, but the August 1970 issue included an eight-page insert on "The New Feminism," written by protesters. In 1973, *LHJ* hired a woman as editor-in-chief.

Feminists recognized that they could not rely upon the traditional publishing industry to represent women's interests and experiences. In the 1970s, a number of small, independent feminist presses were established across the United States, some first operating out of homes and garages. Shameless Hussy Press, The Women's Press Collective, Out & Out Books, New Victoria Publishers, and CALYX Press were among the first feminist and lesbian publishers that specialized in poetry, art, fiction, and nonfiction, predominantly by and for women. Kitchen Table: Women of Color Press, started in 1980, was the first to be managed and run exclusively by women of color. Many well-known and widely published women writers were first discovered by independent feminist publishers. Some of these presses are still operating. Others have disappeared in the wake of domination by conglomerate corporate publishers.

Today, a handful of conglomerates controls 80% of the U.S. book market. Feminist publishers once relied upon independent women's and lesbian bookstores as their major retailers, but many of these stores were driven out of business by chain sellers. Big chain bookstores collaborate with the publishing giants to dictate which books will be prominently featured and which are destined for obscurity. High-visibility spaces—at the ends of shelves and on tables near the entrance and cash registers—are purchased by publishers to increase their books' visibility and sales. Small, independent, and nonprofit publishers rarely have the marketing budgets to participate in these pay-to-display schemes. Their books are typically relegated to bottom shelves in the far corners of chain bookstores—if the stores carry them at all.

Feminist presses continue to strive toward strengthening the presence of women writers in the literary canon. Visit these independent feminist publishers online, join their mailing lists, and ask your favorite bookstores to carry their titles.

CALYX Press: Independent, nonprofit publisher of fine art and literature by women from diverse backgrounds. *www.calyxpress.org*

The Feminist Press: Independent, nonprofit literary publisher that promotes freedom of expression and social justice. *www.feministpress.org*

Seal Press: Independent publisher of books about women's health, parenting, popular culture, sexuality, gender and transgender life, and much more. *www.sealpress.com*

Cleis Press: The largest independent queer publisher in the United States. *www.cleispress.com*

Aunt Lute Books: Multicultural women's press, publishing literature by traditionally underrepresented women, especially women of color. *www.auntlute.com*

Spinifex Press: Independent Australian feminist publisher of feminist books with an optimistic edge. Eighty percent of titles are also available as eBooks. *www.spinifexpress.com*

especially pop culture. As Alison Piepmeier notes in the reading "Bad Girl, Good Girl," zines provide an opportunity for young feminists to resist ideas in mainstream publications that sustain women's subordination. Piepmeier explores the ways zines have allowed girls and young women to both critique and embrace girlishness and femininity. She suggests zine authors focus on the pleasures of girlhood even while they critique racist, heteropatriarchal social structures. She discusses *Bust* magazine as an example.

LITERATURE AND THE ARTS

In the reading "Thinking About Shakespeare's Sister," Virginia Woolf responds to the question "Why has there been no female Shakespeare?" Similarly, in the early 1970s, Linda Nochlin wrote a feminist critique of art history that sought to answer the question "Why have there been no great women artists?" Woolf and Nochlin reached very similar conclusions. According to Nochlin, the reason there had been no great women artists was not that no woman had been capable of producing great art but that the social conditions of women's lives prevented such artistic endeavors.

Woolf wrote her essay in the late 1920s, but still today many critics and professors of literature raise the same questions about women's abilities to create great literature. Rarely, for example, does a seventeenth- or eighteenth-century British literature course give more than a passing nod to women authors of the periods. Quite often, literature majors graduate having read perhaps only Virginia Woolf, George Eliot, Jane Austen, or Emily Dickinson. The usual justification is that women simply have not written the great literature that men have or that to include women would mean leaving out the truly important works of the literary canon (those written by white men).

In her essay, Woolf argues that it would have been impossible due to social constraints for a woman to write the works of Shakespeare in the age of Shakespeare. Although women did write, even in the time of Shakespeare, their works were often neglected by the arbiters of the literary canon because they fell outside the narrowly constructed definitions of great literature. For example, women's novels often dealt with the subjects of women's lives—family, home, love—subjects not deemed lofty enough for the canon of literature. Additionally, women often did not follow accepted forms, writing in fragments rather than unified texts. As the canon was defined according to white male norms, women's writing and much of the writing of both women and men of color were omitted. Jane Austen is still a popular novelist despite having written her books two centuries ago. Her current popularity is based in part on the dramatization of her work in a series of blockbuster movies as well as the fact that Austen was both a romantic and a feminist. The still-relevant romantic plots in Austen's novels provide a foundation for her strong critique of sexism and classism. We include in this chapter Emily Dickinson's short poem "The Wife," with its lament about the wife who "rose to his requirement, dropped/The playthings of her life/To take the honorable work/Of woman and of wife." Writing in the mid-nineteenth century, Dickinson was very aware, as women still are today, of the duties and expectations of women as they become wives.

Yet, toward the end of the twentieth century, more women began to publish novels and poetry, and these have been slowly introduced into the canon. These works have dealt with the realities of women's lives and have received wide acclaim. For example, writers such as Toni Morrison (who received the Nobel Prize for literature), Alice Walker, and Maya Angelou have written about the dilemmas and triumphs faced by black women in

a white, male-dominated culture. Annie Dillard won a Pulitzer Prize at the age of 29 for her nature essays about a year spent living by Tinker Creek. Feminist playwrights such as Wendy Wasserstein, Suzan Lori-Parks, Lynn Nottage, Migdalia Cruz, and Eve Ensler; performance artists such as Lily Tomlin and Lori Anderson; and feminist comedians such as Suzanne Westenhoffer, Tracey Ullman, Wanda Sykes, and Margaret Cho have also been very influential in providing new scripts for women's lives. Audre Lorde talks about the importance of literature in "Poetry Is Not a Luxury." She describes poetry as opportunity to bring forth dreams, longings, and all that we dare make real. She implores us to speak and write the truths of our lives.

Just as female writers have been ignored, misrepresented, and trivialized, so too female artists and musicians have faced similar struggles. Women's art has often been labeled "crafts" rather than art. This is because women, who were often barred from entering the artistic establishment, have tended to create works of art that were useful and were excluded from the category of art. Often, female artists, like their sisters who were writing novels and poetry, used a male pen name and disguised their identity in order to have their work published or shown. With the influence of the women's movement, women's art is being reclaimed and introduced into the art history curriculum, although it is often taught in the context of "women's art." This emphasizes the ways the academy remains androcentric, with the contributions of "others" in separate courses. Female artists such as Frida Kahlo, Georgia O'Keeffe, and Judy Chicago have revitalized the art world by creating women-centered art and feminist critiques of masculine art forms. Similarly, graphic artists such as Barbara Kruger and mixed-media artists such as Jennifer Linton have incorporated feminist critiques of consumerism and desire. Photographers such as Cindy Sherman and Lorna Simpson have also raised important questions about the representation of women and other marginalized people in media and society. Joyce Wieland has famously created quilted art pieces using a traditionally feminine art form and Kiki Smith has sculpted feminist imagery focusing on bodily secretions such as blood and sweat. Finally, the "Guerilla Girls," an anonymous feminist group wearing gorilla masks, use the names of dead female

ACTIVIST PROFILE   **Maxine Hong Kingston**

As a young girl, Maxine Hong Kingston could not find herself in the images in the books she read. The public library in her hometown of Stockton, California, had no stories of Chinese Americans and very few that featured girls. For Kingston, this meant a significant need and open space for the telling of her stories.

Kingston was born in Stockton in 1940 to Chinese immigrant parents. Her mother was trained as a midwife in China, and her father was a scholar and teacher. Arriving in the United States, Tom Hong could not find work and eventually ended up working in a gambling business. Maxine was named after a successful blonde gambler who frequented her father's establishment.

Growing up in a Chinese American community, Kingston heard the stories of her culture that would later influence her own storytelling. By earning 11 scholarships, she was able to attend the University of California at Berkeley, where she earned a B.A. in literature. She married in 1962, and she and her new husband moved to Hawaii, where they both taught for the next 10 years.

In 1976 Kingston published her first book, *The Woman Warrior: Memoirs of a Girlhood Among Ghosts.* This story of a young Chinese American girl who finds her own voice won the National Book Critics Circle Award. Kingston's portrayal of the girl's struggle with silence was met with a great deal of criticism from many Chinese men who attacked Kingston's exploration of critical gender and race issues among Chinese Americans.

Kingston followed *Woman Warrior* with *China Men* in 1980, which also won the National Book Critics Circle Award. This book explored the lives of the men in Kingston's family who came to the United States, celebrating their achievements and documenting the prejudices and exploitation they faced. Her 1989 novel, *Tripmaster Monkey: His Fake Book,* continued her explorations of racism and oppression of Chinese Americans. Although some critics have accused Kingston of selling out because her stories have not reflected traditional notions of Chinese culture, she has maintained her right to tell her story in her own words with her own voice.

(continued)

The Fifth Book of Peace, published in 2003, uses her personal tragedy of losing her house, possessions, and an unfinished novel in the Oakland-Berkeley fire of 1991 as a metaphor for war. She asks repeatedly the questions "Why war? Why not peace?" In 2006, she edited *Veterans of War, Veterans of Piece,* a collection of essays written by survivors of war who participated in her healing workshops. She published her memoir, *I Love a Broad Margin to My Life,* in 2012.

artists to highlight the ways women and people of color are disproportionately excluded from the art world through posters, postcards, and public appearances.

The works of female composers and musicians (such as by Fanny Mendelssohn Hensel and Clara Schumann) have also been ignored as barriers to female achievement in this arena prevented recognition of their talents. Women of color faced almost insurmountable obstacles by virtue of both race and gender discrimination as well as the effects of class. It was mostly economically privileged women who were able to devote themselves to music. In 1893 Margaret Ruthven Lang was the first female composer in the United States to compose a piece performed by a major American symphony orchestra. Contemporary women composers still face challenges despite achievements by such women as Cynthia Wong, Yu-Hiu Chang, and Paola Prestini. Similarly, very few women have been given the opportunity to conduct orchestras until recently with the debut of contemporary female composers such as Marin Alsop, Emmanuelle Haïm, Julia Jones, Anu Tali, and Xian Zhang. Nadia Boulanger was the first woman to conduct a symphony orchestra in the early twentieth century and was known as one of the best music teachers of her time. Women were limited in music by the gendered nature of certain musical instruments that rendered them inappropriate for women. In fact, through the nineteenth century, only certain instruments such as the keyboard and harp were considered appropriate for women to play, and, even today, women are still directed away from some instruments and toward others. Despite these obstacles, they continue to produce literature and art and to redefine the canon. As in other male-dominated arenas, however, women have had to struggle to create a place for themselves. This place is ever-changing, providing women with opportunities for fame, empowerment, self-validation, and respect.

HISTORICAL MOMENT   **The NEA Four**

Chartered by the U.S. Congress in 1965, the National Endowment for the Arts (NEA) provides funding for artists to develop their work. In 1990 Congress passed legislation that forced the NEA to consider "standards of decency" in awarding grants. Four performance artists—Karen Finley, Holly Hughes, John Fleck, and Tim Miller—had been selected to receive NEA grants, but following charges by conservatives, particularly Senator Jesse Helms (R–North Carolina), that the artists' works were obscene, the NEA denied their grants. All but Finley are gay, and Finley herself is an outspoken feminist.

Finley's work deals with raw themes of women's lives. She gained notoriety for a performance in which she smeared herself with chocolate to represent the abuse of women. Latching onto this image, conservatives referred to Finley as "the chocolate-smeared woman." Her work is shocking, but she uses the shocking images to explore women's horrific experiences of misogyny, and she uses her body in her performances in ways that reflect how society uses her body against her will.

Hughes's work explores lesbian sexuality, and, in revoking her NEA grant, then-NEA chairman John Frohnmeyer specifically referenced Hughes's lesbianism as one of the reasons she had lost her grant. Some of her performances have included "Well of Horniness," "Lady Dick," and "Dress Suits to Hire."

Following the revocation of their grants, the four sued the U.S. government, and in 1992 a lower court ruled in favor of the plaintiffs, reinstating the grants. The government appealed in 1994 and lost again. Then, in a surprise move, the Clinton administration appealed the decision to the U.S. Supreme Court. In 1998 the Supreme Court overturned the lower court rulings and held that the "standards of decency" clause is constitutional. Since the ruling, the budget and staff of the NEA have been slashed, and artists like Finley and Hughes must seek funding from other sources to continue their performances.

If you're interested in finding out more about feminism and censorship, visit the website of Feminists for Free Expression at *www.ffeusa.org*.

Thinking About Shakespeare's Sister

Virginia Woolf (1929)

. . . [I]t is a perennial puzzle why no woman wrote a word of extraordinary literature when every other man, it seemed, was capable of song or sonnet. What were the conditions in which women lived, I asked myself; for fiction, imaginative work that is, is not dropped like a pebble upon the ground, as science may be; fiction is like a spider's web, attached ever so lightly perhaps, but still attached to life at all four corners. Often the attachment is scarcely perceptible; Shakespeare's plays, for instance, seem to hang there complete by themselves. But when the web is pulled askew, hooked up at the edge, torn in the middle, one remembers that these webs are not spun in midair by incorporeal creatures, but are the work of suffering human beings, and are attached to grossly material things, like health and money and the houses we live in.

I went therefore, to the shelf where the stories stand and took down one of the latest, Professor Trevelyan's *History of England.* Once more I looked up Women, found "position of," and turned to the pages indicated. "Wifebeating," I read "was a recognized right of man, and was practiced without shame by high as well as low. . . . Similarly," this historian goes on, "the daughter who refused to marry the gentleman of her parents' choice was liable to be locked up, beaten and flung about the room, without any shock being inflicted on public opinion. Marriage was not an affair of personal affection, but of family avarice, particularly in the 'chivalrous' upper classes. . . . Betrothal often took place while one or both of the parties was in the cradle, and marriage when they were scarcely out of the nurses' charge." That was about 1470, soon after Chaucer's time. The next reference to the position of women is some two hundred years later, in the time of the Stuarts. "It was still the exception for women of the upper and middle class to choose their own husbands, and when the husband had been assigned, he was lord and master, so far at least as law and custom could make him. Yet even so," Professor Trevelyan concludes, "neither Shakespeare's women nor those of authentic seventeenth-century memoirs, like the Verneys and the Hutchinsons, seem wanting in personality and character." Certainly, if we consider it, Cleopatra must have had a way with her; Lady Macbeth, one would suppose, had a will of her own; Rosalind, one might conclude, was an attractive girl. Professor Trevelyan is speaking no more than the truth when he remarks that Shakespeare's women do not seem wanting in personality and character. Not being a historian, one might go even further and say that women have burnt like beacons in all the works of all the poets from the beginning of time—Clytemnestra, Antigone, Cleopatra, Lady Macbeth, Phèdre, Cressida, Rosalind, Desdemona, the Duchess of Malfi, among the dramatists; then among the prose writers: Millamant, Clarissa, Becky Sharp, Anna Karenina, Emma Bovary, Madame de Guermantes—the names flock to mind, nor do they recall women "lacking in personality and character." Indeed, if woman had no existence save in fiction written by men, one would imagine her a person of the utmost importance, very various; heroic and mean; splendid and sordid; infinitely beautiful and hideous in the extreme; as great as a man, some think even greater. But this is woman in fiction. In fact, as Professor Trevelyan points out, she was locked up, beaten and flung about the room.

A very queer, composite being thus emerges. Imaginatively she is of the highest importance; practically she is completely insignificant. She pervades poetry from cover to cover; she is all but absent from history. She dominates the lives of kings and conquerors in fiction; in fact she was the slave of any boy whose parents forced a ring upon her finger.

Some of the most inspired words, some of the most profound thoughts in literature fall from her lips; in real life she could hardly read, could scarcely spell, and was the property of her husband.

. . .

Be that as it may, I could not help thinking, as I looked at the works of Shakespeare on the shelf . . . it would have been impossible, completely and entirely, for any woman to have written the plays of Shakespeare in the age of Shakespeare. Let me imagine, since facts are so hard to come by, what would have happened had Shakespeare had a wonderfully gifted sister, called Judith, let us say. Shakespeare himself went, very probably—his mother was an heiress—to the grammar school, where he may have learnt Latin—Ovid, Virgil and Horace—and the elements of grammar and logic. He was, it is well known, a wild boy who poached rabbits, perhaps shot a deer, and had, rather sooner than he should have done, to marry a woman in the neighbourhood, who bore him a child rather quicker than was right. That escapade sent him to seek his fortune in London. He had, it seemed, a taste for the theatre; he began by holding horses at the stage door. Very soon he got work in the theatre, became a successful actor, and lived at the hub of the universe, meeting everybody, knowing everybody, practising his art on the boards, exercising his wits in the streets, and even getting access to the palace of the queen. Meanwhile his extraordinarily gifted sister, let us suppose, remained at home. She was as adventurous, as imaginative, as agog to see the world as he was. But she was not sent to school. She had no chance of learning grammar and logic, let alone of reading Horace and Virgil. She picked up a book now and then, one of her brother's perhaps, and read a few pages. But then her parents came in and told her to mend the stockings or mind the stew and not moon about with books and papers. They would have spoken sharply but kindly, for they were substantial people who knew the conditions of life for a woman and loved their daughter—indeed, more likely than not she was the apple of her father's eye. Perhaps she scribbled some pages up in an apple loft on the sly, but was careful to hide them or set fire to them. Soon, however, before she was out of her teens, she was to be betrothed to the son of a neighbouring wool-stapler.

She cried out that marriage was hateful to her, and for that she was severely beaten by her father. Then he ceased to scold her. He begged her instead not to hurt him, not to shame him in this matter of her marriage. He would give her a chain of beads or a fine petticoat, he said; and there were tears in his eyes. How could she disobey him? How could she break his heart? The force of her own gift alone drove her to it. She made up a small parcel of her belongings, let herself down by a rope one summer's night and took the road to London. She was not seventeen. The birds that sang in the hedge were not more musical than she was. She had the quickest fancy, a gift like her brother's, for the tune of words. Like him, she had a taste for the theatre. She stood at the stage door; she wanted to act, she said. Men laughed in her face. The manager—a fat, loose-lipped man—guffawed. He bellowed something about poodles dancing and women acting—no woman, he said, could possibly be an actress. He hinted—you can imagine what. She could get no training in her craft. Could she even seek her dinner in a tavern or roam the streets at midnight? Yet her genius was for fiction and lusted to feed abundantly upon the lives of men and women and the study of their ways. At last—for she was very young, oddly like Shakespeare the poet in her face, with the same grey eyes and rounded brows—at last Nick Greene the actor-manager took pity on her; she found herself with child by that gentleman and so—who shall measure the heat and violence of the poet's heart when caught and tangled in a woman's body?—killed herself one winter's night and lies buried at some cross-roads where the omnibuses now stop outside the Elephant and Castle.

That, more or less, is how the story would run, I think, if a woman in Shakespeare's day had had Shakespeare's genius. . . .

This may be true or it may be false—who can say?—but what is true in it, so it seemed to me, reviewing the story of Shakespeare's sister as I had made it, is that any woman born with a great gift in the sixteenth century would certainly have gone crazed, shot herself, or ended her days in some lonely cottage outside the village, half witch, half wizard, feared and mocked at. For it needs little skill in psychology to be sure that a highly gifted girl who had tried to use her gift for poetry would have been so thwarted and hindered by other people, so tortured and pulled asunder by her own contrary instincts, that she must have lost her health and sanity to a certainty. No girl could have walked to London and stood at a stage door and forced her way into the presence of actor-managers without doing herself a violence and suffering an anguish which may have been irrational—for chastity may be a fetish invented by certain societies for unknown reasons—but were none the less inevitable. . . .

But for women, I thought, looking at the empty shelves, these difficulties were infinitely more formidable. In the first place, to have a room of her own, let alone a quiet room or a sound-proof room, was out of the question, unless her parents were exceptionally rich or very noble, even up to the beginning of the nineteenth century. Since her pin money, which depended on the good will of her father, was only enough to keep her clothed, she was debarred from such alleviations as came even to Keats or Tennyson or Carlyle, all poor men, from a walking tour, a little journey to France, from the separate lodging which, even if it were miserable enough, sheltered them from the claims and tyrannies of their families. Such material difficulties were formidable; but much worse were the immaterial. The indifference of the world which Keats and Flaubert and other men of genius have found so hard to bear was in her case not indifference but hostility. The world did not say to her as it said to them, Write if you choose; it makes no difference to me. The world said with a guffaw, Write? What's the good of your writing? . . .

R E A D I N G **39**

The Wife

Emily Dickinson (c. 1860)

She rose to his requirement, dropped
The playthings of her life
To take the honorable work
Of woman and of wife.

If aught she missed in her new day
Of amplitude, or awe,

Or first prospective, or the gold
In using wore away.

It lay unmentioned, as the sea
Develops pearl and weed,
But only to himself is known
The fathoms they abide.

R E A D I N G **40**

Rush Limbaugh and the New Networked Feminism

Tom Watson (2012)

So much for post-feminism.

The world of networked hurt that descended on the spiteful media enterprise that is Rush Limbaugh revealed a tenacious, super-wired coalition of active feminists prepared at a moment's notice to blow the lid off sexist attacks or regressive health policy.

When Limbaugh called Georgetown University law student Sandra Fluke a "slut" and "prostitute" in response to her testimony before Congress on contraception costs, he may well have been surprised by the strength of the response. But he shouldn't have been.

At latest count, 12 advertisers and two radio stations have pulled the plug on Limbaugh. Each was effectively targeted on Facebook and Twitter by an angry and vocal storm of thousands of people calling for direct action. The campaign was almost instantaneous, coordinated by no individual or organization, and entirely free of cost. Prominent feminist organizers told *Forbes* that it was social media's terrible swift sword, led once again by Twitter and Facebook-savvy women, that dealt Limbaugh the worst humiliation of his controversial career, and in many ways, revealed the most potent "non-organized" organization to take the field on the social commons in the age of Occupy Wall Street and Anonymous.

"Given that much of the increased vocabulary and awareness about gender in the national discussion comes through social media and from young people, I think that instances like this one should give those who claim that young people don't care about feminism pause!" says Rebecca Traister, a contributor to Salon and author of the important feminist history of the 2008 Presidential race, *Big Girls Don't Cry*. "Young people are the ones who know how to use social media in this way, and look at the kind of impact it's having."

"What's most interesting to me is that in the last two years or so specifically, women have been leading the charge online to campaign for themselves against this kind of abuse, largely thanks to advances in social networking," said media technologist Deanna Zandt, author of *Share This! How You Will Change the World with Social Networking.* "In the past, we'd have to wait for some organization to take up the cause—create a petition, launch an email campaign—and outside of traditional feminist movement types, those campaigns rarely reached widespread acceptance."

"Women aren't waiting to be told what to do or which petition to sign, they're just doing what we do best: talking and connecting," agreed Allison Fine, senior fellow for progressive think tank Demos.

It's the next chapter in many ways to the story that hit the public consciousness with the strong, active online reaction to the Susan G. Komen Foundation's decision to cut funding to Planned Parenthood a month ago. The response was quick, massive, and targeted. My own social graph (on both Facebook and Twitter) lit up like a summer fireworks display after sundown—stirring conversation, concentration around hashtags and shared media, and truly crowdsourced action.

"What we're seeing right now is a continuation of the networked response to the right-wing war on women's health that began with the Komen reaction a few weeks ago," said Fine. "It is across generations and extra-organizational with individual women using a variety of social media channels to connect with other women and create their own protests."

Yet it would also be a mistake to view the semi-organized reaction to Limbaugh as purely another battle between left and right on the American political spectrum. While Limbaugh's sexist words have to been seen in the light of a Republican Presidential race that has, inexplicably, placed an opposition to contraception and women's health at the center of its increasingly nasty public debate, the roots of El Rushbo's humiliation also run deeper than spectrum ideology and political parties.

You can see those roots, for instance, in the brilliantly-organized campaign in late 2010 against two prominent liberal voices: filmmaker Michael Moore and talk show host Keith Olbermann. Feminist blogger Sady Doyle took Moore to task for posting bail on behalf of WikiLeaks founder Julian Assange after rape accusations brought by two women in Sweden confined him to custody in England, and her supporters battled both Moore and Olbermann for being dismissive of those accusations and implying they were a set-up to derail Assange's exposure of U.S. government secrets.

Wrote Doyle in December, 2010 in a post that ignited a firestorm: "We are the progressive community. We are the left wing. We are women and men, we are from every sector of this community, and we believe that every rape accusation must be taken seriously, regardless of the *accused rapist's connections, power, influence, status, fame, or politics.*"

Thousands of activists then used the #mooreandme tag on Twitter to (successfully) demand apologies from Moore and Olbermann. That campaign disproves the assertion by Fox News political analyst Kirsten Powers in the Daily Beast that "the real fury seems reserved only for conservatives, while the men on the left get a wink and a nod as long as they are carrying water for the liberal cause."

But Powers does indeed have a point that casual misogyny among men in the media rather easily crosses ideological lines—and just as clearly, the new feminist moment online is in part a strong and serious pushback against a culture that divines a narrow, almost forgiving attitude toward violence and sexual assault against women. Among the feminist bloggers from more recent generations, tactics like the Slutwalk—and a strong effort to expose a culture of violence to the light of day—point to a renewed and yes, combative new stance. On the left, when prominent figures like Assange and Dominique Strauss-Kahn were accused of sexual violence, a new network of women stood ready to push back on political commentary that seemed to excuse or invalidate the charges. Feminist blogger Lindsay Beyerstein wrote that the target of these new protests was "the inaccurate stereotype that rape is an uncontrollable frenzy of lust that women provoke in men. That's like imagining all theft as an uncontrolled frenzy of consumerism."

When he used the word "slut" to describe Sandra Fluke—linking the need for contraceptives to a kind of rampant (and distasteful) sexual desire in women that society shouldn't pay for—Limbaugh casually played the flip side of the classic "she asked for it" defense of sexual assault. The Republican Party's most potent media figure may well have reckoned that talk radio's legendary reach and loyal conservative audience would easily sustain a few harmless raindrops of outrage on the roof.

But he was (perhaps fatally) wrong.

There was a powerful, decentralized social venture lurking on the digital network—totally empowered and working with a toolset as potent as Clear Channel's microphones.

"I think the feminists were always out there, but often isolated from one another or overwhelmed by the amount of work to be done and lack of time in a day," says feminist writer Kate Harding.

"Social media allows us to work together quickly and publicly for something like a boycott or twitter campaign—(mostly) without the distractions of in-group politics or disagreement on any number of other issues—and that creates an energy that makes it feel so much more like a unified movement, even when people are still quite loosely connected."

Philanthropy measurement guru and social ventures blogger Lucy Bernholz believes that the immediate feedback loop of the social networks drove both the Limbaugh and Komen protests—even without visible leadership or a budget.

"The dynamics of the media are such that if you're engaged about something, be it Komen or Limbaugh you can drive your action, measure it, and add it into a larger effort," said Bernholz. "If something resonates, you pass it on. If it doesn't, you try something else. It's like the supposed Facebook mantra 'code wins.' Everyone who participates in these networked action can see—and measure—immediately, what resonates with others and they can work fromt here."

Adds Kate Harding: "I think the public aspect is really important. #mooreandme, the Limbaugh boycott, the Komen/Planned Parenthood uproar all worked because there was somewhere to express ourselves visibly. Who knows how many feminists were sending letters and making phone calls over similar instances in the past? But without any way for an outside observer to measure it, the target of a boycott or letter-writing campaign was never forced to acknowledge that criticism publicly. When your brand's Facebook wall is overtaken by feminist outrage, you can't just write it off as a few man-hating cranks and continue on as usual."

After the 2008 campaign, Traister's book painted a rosy path for feminist organizing that seemed a stretch at the time, at least to me. In Hillary Clinton's failed campaign, she wrote, "women's liberation movement found thrilling new life."

Yet her words now seem prophetic—and indeed, the sheer breadth and strength of the wired feminist network is impressive.

"Some of what we're seeing now feels more coordinated in a way that fits with a maturation and increased confidence of online activism and with a media that, post-2008, is better trained to hear and report on this kind of response," says Traister. "That last part really matters, and is really relevant coming out of 2008: There is an increased sensitivity around gender and around race and around sexuality that I think was not part of the national conversation ten or even five years ago.

"That makes a difference when Rush Limbaugh calls someone a slut in 2012."

R E A D I N G 41

Poetry Is Not a Luxury

Audre Lorde (1982)

The quality of light by which we scrutinize our lives has direct bearing upon the product which we live, and upon the changes which we hope to bring about through those lives. It is within this light that we form those ideas by which we pursue our magic and make it realized. This is poetry as illumination, for it is through poetry that we give name to those ideas which are—until the poem—nameless and formless, about to be birthed, but already felt. That distillation of experience from which true poetry springs births thought as dream births concept, as feeling births idea, as knowledge births (precedes) understanding.

As we learn to bear the intimacy of scrutiny and to flourish within it, as we learn to use the products of that scrutiny for power within our living, those fears which rule our lives and form our silences begin to lose their control over us.

For each of us as women, there is a dark place within, where hidden and growing our true spirit rises, "beautiful/and tough as chestnut/stanchions against (y)our nightmare of weakness/"[1] and of impotence.

These places of possibility within ourselves are dark because they are ancient and hidden; they have survived and grown strong through that darkness. Within these deep places, each one of us holds an incredible reserve of creativity and power, of unexamined and unrecorded emotion and feeling. The woman's place of power within each of us is neither white nor surface; it is dark, it is ancient, and it is deep.

When we view living in the european mode only as a problem to be solved, we rely solely upon our ideas to make us free, for these were what the white fathers told us were precious.

But as we come more into touch with our own ancient, noneuropean consciousness of living as a situation to be experienced and interacted with, we learn more and more to cherish our feelings, and to respect those hidden sources of our power from where true knowledge and, therefore, lasting action comes.

At this point in time, I believe that women carry within ourselves the possibility for fusion of these two approaches so necessary for survival, and we come closest to this combination in our poetry. I speak here of poetry as a revelatory distillation of experience, not the sterile word play that, too often, the white fathers distorted the word *poetry* to mean—in order to cover a desperate wish for imagination without insight.

For women, then, poetry is not a luxury. It is a vital necessity of our existence. It forms the quality of the light within which we predicate our hopes and dreams toward survival and change, first made into language, then into idea, then into more tangible action. Poetry is the way we help give name to the nameless so it can be thought. The farthest horizons of our hopes and fears are cobbled by our poems, carved from the rock experiences of our daily lives.

As they become known to and accepted by us, our feelings and the honest exploration of them become sanctuaries and spawning grounds for the most radical and daring of ideas. They become a safe-house for that difference so necessary to change and the conceptualization of any meaningful action. Right now, I could name at least ten ideas I would have found intolerable or incomprehensible and frightening, except as they came after dreams and poems. This is not idle fantasy, but a disciplined attention to the true meaning of "it feels right to me." We can train ourselves to respect our feelings and to transpose them into a language so they can be shared. And where that language does not yet exist, it is our poetry which helps to fashion it. Poetry is not only dream and vision; it is the skeleton architecture of our lives. It lays the foundations for a future of change, a bridge across our fears of what has never been before.

Possibility is neither forever nor instant. It is not easy to sustain belief in its efficacy. We can sometimes work long and hard to establish one beachhead of real resistance to the deaths we are expected to live, only to have that beachhead assaulted or threatened by those canards we have been socialized to fear, or by the withdrawal of those approvals that we have been warned to seek for safety. Women see ourselves diminished or softened by the falsely benign accusations of childishness, of nonuniversality, of changeability, of sensuality. And who asks the question: Am I altering your aura, your ideas, your dreams, or am I merely moving you to temporary and reactive action? And even though the latter is no mean task, it is one that must be seen within the context of a need for true alteration of the very foundations of our lives.

The white fathers told us: I think, therefore I am. The Black mother within each of us—the poet—whispers in our dreams: I feel, therefore I can be free. Poetry coins the language to express and charter this revolutionary demand, the implementation of that freedom.

However, experience has taught us that action in the now is also necessary, always. Our children cannot dream unless they live, they cannot live unless they are nourished, and who else will feed them the real food without which their dreams will be no different from ours? "If you want us to change the world someday, we at least have to live long enough to grow up!" shouts the child.

Sometimes we drug ourselves with dreams of new ideas. The head will save us. The brain alone will set us free. But there are no new ideas still waiting in the wings to save us as women, as human. There are only old and forgotten ones, new combinations, extrapolations and recognitions from within ourselves—along with the renewed courage to try them out. And we must constantly encourage ourselves and each other to attempt the heretical actions that our dreams imply, and so many of our old ideas disparage. In the forefront of our move toward change, there is only poetry to hint at possibility made real. Our poems formulate the implications of ourselves, what we feel within and dare make real (or bring action into accordance with), our fears, our hopes, our most cherished terrors.

For within living structures defined by profit, by linear power, by institutional dehumanization, our feelings were not meant to survive. Kept around as unavoidable adjuncts or pleasant pastimes, feelings were expected to kneel to thought as women were expected to kneel to men. But women have survived. As poets. And there are no new pains. We have felt them all already. We have hidden that fact in the same place where we have hidden our power. They surface in our dreams, and it is our dreams that point the way to freedom. Those dreams are made realizable through our poems that give us the strength and courage to see, to feel, to speak, and to dare.

If what we need to dream, to move our spirits most deeply and directly toward and through promise, is discounted as a luxury, then we give up the core—the fountain—of our power, our womanness; we give up the future of our worlds.

For there are no new ideas. There are only new ways of making them felt—of examining what those ideas feel like being lived on Sunday morning at 7 A.M., after brunch, during wild love, making war, giving birth, mourning our dead—while we suffer the old longings, battle the old warnings and fears of being silent and impotent and alone, while we taste new possibilities and strengths.

NOTE

1. From "Black Mother Woman," first published in *From a Land Where Other People Live* (Broadside Press, Detroit, 1973), and collected in *Chosen Poems: Old and New* (W. W. Norton and Company, New York, 1982), p. 53.

Enlightened Sexism

Susan Douglas (2010)

How do we square the persistence of female inequality with all those images of female power we have seen in the media—the hands-on-her-hips, don't-even-think-about-messing-with-me Dr. Bailey on *Grey's Anatomy,* or S. Epatha Merkerson as the take-no-prisoners Lieutenant Anita Van Buren on *Law & Order,* Agent Scully on *The X-Files,* Brenda Leigh Johnson as "the chief" on *The Closer,* C.C.H. Pounder on *The Shield,* or even Geena Davis as the first female president in the short-lived series *Commander in Chief?* Advertisements tell women that they have achieved so much they should celebrate by buying themselves their own diamond ring for their right hand and urge their poor, flaccid husbands, crippled by an epidemic of emasculation and erectile dysfunction, to start mainlining Viagra or Cialis. Indeed, in films from *Dumb and Dumber* (1994) to *Superbad* (2007), guys are hopeless losers. In *Sex and the City,* with its characters who were successful professionals by day and Kama Sutra masters by night, there was no such thing as the double standard: women had as much sexual freedom, and maybe even more kinky sex, than men. *Cosmo* isn't for passive girls waiting for the right guy to find them; it's the magazine for the "Fun, Fearless Female" who is also proud to be, as one cover put it, a "Sex Genius." Have a look at *O!* The magazine is one giant, all-encompassing, throbbing zone of self-fulfillment for women where everything from pillows to celadon-colored notebooks (but only if purchased and used properly) are empowering and everything is possible. And why not? One of the most influential and successful moguls in the entertainment industry is none other than Oprah Winfrey herself.

Something's out of whack here. If you immerse yourself in the media fare of the past ten to fifteen years, what you see is a rather large gap between how the vast majority of girls and women live their lives, the choices they are forced to make, and what they see—and *don't* see—in the media. Ironically, it is just the opposite of the gap in the 1950s and '60s, when images of women as Watusi-dancing bimbettes on the beach or stay-at-home housewives who needed advice from Mr. Clean about how to wash a floor obscured the exploding number of women entering the workforce, joining the Peace Corps, and becoming involved in politics. Back then the media illusion was that the aspirations of girls and women weren't changing at all when they were. Now, the media illusion is that equality for girls and women is an accomplished fact when it isn't. Then the media were behind the curve; now, ironically, they're ahead. Have girls and women made a lot of progress since the 1970s? You bet. Women's college basketball, for example—its existence completely unimaginable when I was in school—is now nationally televised, and vulgar, boneheaded remarks about the players can get even a money machine like Don Imus fired, if only temporarily. But now we're all district attorneys, medical residents, chiefs of police, or rich, blond, So-Cal heiresses? Not so much.

Since the early 1990s, much of the media have come to overrepresent women as having made it—completely—in the professions, as having gained sexual equality with men, and having achieved a level of financial success and comfort enjoyed primarily by the Tiffany's-encrusted doyennes of Laguna Beach. At the same time, there has been a resurgence of retrograde dreck clogging our cultural arteries—*The Man Show, Maxim, Girls Gone Wild.*[1] But even this fare, which insists that young women should dress like strippers and have the mental capacities of a vole, was presented as empowering, because while the scantily clad or bare-breasted women may have *seemed* to be objectified, they were really on top, because now they had chosen to be sex objects and men were supposedly nothing more than their helpless, ogling, crotch-driven slaves.

What the media have been giving us, then, are little more than fantasies of power. They assure girls and women, repeatedly, that women's liberation is a fait accompli and that we are stronger, more successful, more sexually in control, more fearless, and more held in awe than we actually are. We can believe that any woman can become a CEO (or president), that women have achieved economic, professional, and political parity with men, and we can expunge any suggestions that there might be some of us who actually have to live on the national median income, which for women in 2008 was $36,000 a year, 23 percent less than that of their male counterparts. Yet the images we see on television, in the movies, and in advertising also insist that purchasing power and sexual power are much more gratifying than political or economic power. Buying stuff—the right stuff, a lot of stuff—emerged as the dominant way to empower ourselves.[2] Of course women in fictional TV shows can be in the highest positions of authority, but in real life—maybe not such a good idea. Instead, the wheedling, seductive message to young women is that being decorative is the highest form of power—when, of course, if it were, Dick Cheney would have gone to work every day in a sequined tutu.

. . .

So what's the matter with fantasies of female power? Haven't the media always provided escapist fantasies; isn't that, like, their job? And aren't many in the media—however belatedly—simply addressing women's demands for more representations of female achievement and control? Well, yes. But here's the odd, somewhat unintended consequence: under the guise of escapism and pleasure, we are getting images of imagined power that mask, and even erase, how much still remains to be done for girls and women, images that make sexism seem fine, even fun, and insist that feminism is now utterly pointless—even bad for you. And if we look at what is often being said about girls and women in these fantasies—what we can and should do, what we can and can't be—we will see that slithering just below the shiny mirage of power is the dark, sneaky serpent of sexism.

There has been a bit of a generational divide in how these fantasies are presented. Older women—I prefer the term "Vintage Females"—like myself have been given all those iron-clad women in the 10:00 P.M. strip: the lawyers, cops, and district attorneys on the entire *Law & Order* franchise; the senior partner Shirley Schmidt on *Boston Legal;* the steely (and busty) forensic scientists on the various *CSIs;* the ubiquitous female judges; and Brenda Leigh Johnson who, with her big hair and southern drawl, whipped her male chauvinist colleagues into shape ASAP on *The Closer.*

But many of us, especially mothers, have been less thrilled about the fantasies on offer for girls and younger women. For "millennials"—those young women and girls born in the late 1980s and 1990s who are the most attractive demographic for advertisers—the fantasies and appeals have been much more commercial and, not surprisingly, more retrograde. While they are the "girl power" generation, the bill of goods they are repeatedly sold is that true power comes from shopping, having the right logos, and being "hot." Power also comes from judging, dissing, and competing with other girls, especially over guys. I have watched these fantasies—often the opposite of the "role model" imagery presented to me—swirl around my daughter and, well, I have not been amused.

Things seemed okay back in the 1990s when she could watch shows like *Alex Mack,* featuring a girl with superhuman powers who morphed into something that looked like a blob of mercury and conducted industrial espionage, or *Shelby Wu,* a girl detective. But then she graduated to MTV: by this time, the network had stopped showing Talking Heads videos and, instead, offered up fare like *Sorority Life.* Here viewers got to track the progress of college girls pledging to a sorority, and to see which traits, behaviors, and hairdos got them in ("nice," "pretty," ponytails) and which ones kept them out ("like so bossy," "like so phony," any hairstyle that resembled a mullet). Even though the show was allegedly about college life, no books, newspapers, novels, debates about the existence of God, or discussion of any recent classroom lectures cluttered the scene or troubled the dialogue. These college girls were way too shallow for any of that.

My sympathetic response to my teenage daughter on the sofa, wrapped in a quilt, escaping for a bit into this drivel-filled world? A simple bellow: "Shut that crap off!"

. . .

As I stewed about the fantasies of power laid before my daughter and those laid before me, I was, of course, most struck at first by their generational differences, and how they pitted us against each other, especially around the issues of sexual display and rampant consumerism as alleged sources of power and control. But if you think about it, they simply buy us off in different ways, because both approaches contribute to the false assumption that for women, all has been won. The notion that there might, indeed, still be an urgency to feminist politics? You have totally got to be kidding.

. . . While these fantasies have been driven in part by girls' and women's desires, and have often provided a great deal of vicarious pleasure, they have also been driven by marketing—especially niche, target marketing—and the use of that heady mix of flattery and denigration to sell us everything from skin cream to running shoes. So it's time to take these fantasies to the interrogation room and shine a little light on them. . . . We need to understand, and unravel, the various forces that have given us, say, the fearless computer geek Chloe on *24,* without whom Jack Bauer would have been toast twenty-five times over, versus Jessica Simpson on *Newlyweds,* who didn't know how to turn on a stove (ha! ha! get it?).

One force is embedded feminism: the way in which women's achievements, or their desire for achievement, are simply part of the cultural landscape. Feminism is no longer "outside" of the media as it was in 1970, when women staged a sit-in at the stereotype-perpetuating *Ladies' Home Journal* or gave awards for the most sexist, offensive ads like those of National Airlines, which featured stewardesses purring, "I'm Cheryl. Fly Me" (and required flight attendants to wear "Fly Me" buttons). Today, feminist gains, attitudes, and achievements are woven into our cultural fabric.[3] . . . Joss Whedon created *Buffy the Vampire Slayer* because he embraced feminism and was tired of seeing all the girls in horror films as victims, instead of possible heroes.

But women whose kung fu skills are more awesome than Jackie Chan's? Or who tell a male coworker (or boss) to his face that he's less evolved than a junior in high school? This is a level of command-and-control barely enjoyed by four-star generals, let alone the nation's actual female population.

But the media's fantasies of power are also the product of another force that has gained considerable momentum since the early and mid-1990s: enlightened sexism.[4] Enlightened sexism is a response, deliberate or not, to the perceived threat of a new gender regime. It insists that women have made plenty of progress because of feminism—indeed, full equality has allegedly been achieved—so now it's okay, even amusing, to resurrect sexist stereotypes of girls and women.[5] After all, these images (think Pussycat Dolls, *The Bachelor, Are You Hot?,* the hour-and-a-half catfight in *Bride Wars*) can't possibly undermine women's equality at this late date, right? More to the point, enlightened sexism sells the line that it is precisely through women's calculated deployment of their faces, bodies, attire, and sexuality that they gain and enjoy true power—power that is fun, that men will not resent, and indeed will embrace. True power here has nothing to do with economic independence or professional achievement (that's a given): it has to do with getting men to lust after you and other women to envy you. Enlightened sexism is especially targeted to girls and young women and emphasizes that now that they "have it all," they should focus the bulk of their time and energy on their appearance, pleasing men, being hot, competing with other women, and shopping.

Enlightened sexism is a manufacturing process that is produced, week in and week out, by the media. . . . Enlightened sexism is feminist in its outward appearance (of course you can be or do anything you want) but sexist in its intent (hold on, girls, only up to a certain point, and not in any way that discomfits men or pushes feminist goals one more centimeter forward). While enlightened sexism seems to support women's equality, it is dedicated to the undoing of feminism.[6] In fact, because this equality might lead to "sameness"—way too scary—girls and women need to be reminded that they are still fundamentally female, and so must be emphatically feminine. Thus enlightened sexism takes the gains of the women's movement as a given, and then uses them as permission to resurrect retrograde images of girls and women as sex objects, bimbos, and hootchie mamas still defined by their appearance and their biological destiny. So in the age of enlightened sexism there has been an explosion in makeover, matchmaking, and modeling shows, a renewed emphasis on women's breasts (and a massive surge in the promotion of breast augmentation), an obsession with babies and motherhood in celebrity journalism (the rise of the creepy "bump patrol"), and a celebration of stay-at-home moms and "opting out" of the workforce.

. . .

But girls and women are not dupes, simply saying "whatever" to the sexism of *The Real World* or *The Swan* (in which contestants underwent up to fourteen often heroic cosmetic surgeries so they could compete in a beauty contest), as we could see in the outpouring of fury against the media coverage of Hillary Clinton's campaign, or as the ridicule my students heap on most MTV fare suggests. We enter into TV shows, movies, magazines, or Web sites and chat rooms to escape, to transport ourselves into another realm, yet we don't want to feel like we're totally suckered in either. This is where most of us are, in the complicated and contradictory terrain of negotiation.[7]

. . .

Thus, despite my own love of escaping into worlds in which women solve crimes, are good bosses, live in huge houses, can buy whatever they want, perform lifesaving surgeries, and find love, I am here to argue, forcefully, for the importance of Wariness, with a capital W. The media have played an important role in enabling us to have female cabinet members, in raising awareness about and condemning domestic violence, in helping Americans accept very different family formations than the one on *Leave It to Beaver*, even in imagining a woman president.

. . .

With *The Closer*, the surgeons on *Grey's Anatomy*, Dr. House's female boss, and all those technically savvy forensic scientists on the various *CSIs*, might we be tempted to think such political rollbacks are irrelevant and can't really touch us? Or, conversely, do the female obsessions with extreme makeovers and being the one to get the bachelor suggest that, at the end of the day, women really are best confined

to the kitchen and bedroom? A 2009 poll revealed that 60 percent of men and 50 percent of women "are convinced that there are no longer any barriers to women's advancement in the workplace."[8] The media may convey this, but data about the real jobs most women hold, and the persistence of discrimination against them, belie this happy illusion.

. . .

It is only through tracing the origins of these images of female power that we can begin to untangle how they have offered empowerment at the cost of eroding our self-esteem, and keeping millions in their place. Because still, despite everything, what courses through our culture is the belief—and fear—that once women have power, they turn into Cruella De Vil or Miranda Priestly in *The Devil Wears Prada*—evil, tyrannical, hated, unloved. And the great irony is that if some media fare is actually ahead of where most women are in society, it may be thwarting the very advances for women that it seeks to achieve.

But still we watch. There is plenty here to love, and even more to talk back to and make fun of. Because, while it's only a start, laughter—especially derisive laughter—may be the most empowering act of all. This is part of the ongoing, never-ending project of consciousness-raising. Then we can get down to business. And girls, there is plenty of unfinished business at hand.

NOTES

1. For an excellent rant against and analysis of this new sexist fare see Ariel Levy, *Female Chauvinist Pigs: Women and the Rise of Raunch Culture* (New York: Free Press, 2006).
2. See the superb essay by Yvonne Tasker and Diane Negra, "Feminist Politics and Postfeminist Culture," in their coedited collection, *Interrogating Postfeminism* (Durham, N.C.: Duke University Press, 2007), 2.
3. Rosalind Gill does a superb job of summarizing postfeminism in the media in *Gender and the Media* (Cambridge, U.K.: Polity Press, 2007), 40.
4. I am adapting this term from Sut Jhally and Justin Lewis's term "enlightened racism" from their book *Enlightened Racism: The Cosby Show, Audiences, and the Myth of the American Dream* (Boulder, CO: Westview Press, 1992).
5. This entire discussion of enlightened sexism is indebted to Angela McRobbie's pathbreaking work on

postfeminism. See, for example, "Notes on Postfeminism and Popular Culture: Bridget Jones and the New Gender Regime," in *All About the Girl,* ed. Anita Harris (New York: Routledge, 2004); see also Gill, *Gender and the Media.*

6. Angela McRobbie, *The Aftermath of Feminism,* 11. (London: Sage, 2009).

7. Stuart Hall, "Encoding/Decoding," in *Culture, Media, Language,* ed. Stuart Hall (New York: Routledge, 1980). And I want to thank my daughter, Ella, for pointing out that these days a negotiated reading of media texts is the preferred reading.

8. See the Rockefeller Foundation/*Time* magazine poll in Nancy Gibbs, "What Women Want Now," *Time,* October 26, 2009, 31.

R E A D I N G **43**

If Women Ran Hip Hop

Aya de Leon (2007)

If women ran hip hop
the beats & rhymes would be just as dope,
but there would never be a bad vibe when you walked
    in the place
& the clubs would be beautiful & smell good
& the music would never be too loud
but there would be free earplugs available anyway
& venues would have skylights and phat patios
and shows would run all day not just late at night
cuz if women ran hip-hop we would have nothing to
    be ashamed of
& there would be an African marketplace
with big shrines to Oya
Yoruba deity of the female warrior & entrepreneur
and women would sell & barter & prosper
If women ran hip hop
there would never be shootings
cuz there would be onsite conflict mediators
to help you work through all that negativity &
    hostility
& there would also be free condoms & dental dams
in pretty baskets throughout the place
as well as counselors to help you make the decision:
do I really want to have sex with him or her?
& there would be safe, reliable, low-cost 24 hour
    transportation home
& every venue would have on-site quality child care
where kids could sleep while grown folks danced
& all shows would be all ages

cause the economy of hip-hop wouldn't revolve
    around the sale of alcohol
If women ran hip hop
same gender-loving & transgender emcees
would be proportionally represented
& get mad love from everybody
& females would dress sexy if we wanted to celebrate
    our bodies
but it wouldn't be that important because
everyone would be paying attention to our minds,
    anyway
If women ran hip hop
men would be relieved because it's so draining
to keep up that front of toughness & power & control
    24-7
If women ran hip hop
the only folks dancing in cages would be dogs & cats
from the local animal shelter
excited about getting adopted by pet lovers in the crowd
If women ran hip-hop
there would be social workers available to refer gang-
    sta rappers
to 21-day detox programs where they could get clean
    & sober
from violence & misogyny
but best of all, if women ran hip hop
we would have the dopest female emcees ever
because all the young women afraid to bust
would unleash their brilliance on the world

Vampires and Vixens

Alison Happel and Jennifer Esposito (2010)

The movie *Twilight*, first in the *Twilight* Saga and directed by Catherine Hardwicke and produced by Summit Entertainment, was released in November of 2008. The screenplay was based on the 2005 novel of the same name, which was the first of four novels in a series written by Stephanie Meyer. Meyer's book series has sold more than 42 million copies worldwide, and it has been translated into 37 languages. The novel was adapted for the screen by Melissa Rosenburg in 2007. The popularity of the book series led to the overwhelmingly positive reception of the film. Following the books, the film was an immediate success; it grossed 70.5 million dollars on its opening weekend, and has since grossed over 310 million in box office sales (http://en.wikipedia.org/wiki/Twilight_(2008_film)).

The film has been very popular with young adults, and it has been marketed heavily to preteens and teenagers. Besides the usual movie marketing strategies, the marketers of *Twilight* invested heavily in online marketing that specifically targeted young adults. The advertising for *Twilight* was Web savvy, and it included easily accessible trailers of the movie, along with advertisements in heavily trafficked young adult online spaces such as Myspace, iTunes stores, Facebook, and YouTube. The age-specific marketing strategies, along with the popularity of the book series, have facilitated the tremendous popularity of the film. Indicative of its popularity among young adults, the film was nominated for seven MTV movie awards and won five of the awards in June of 2009. Given the film's popularity, and also its spawn of material goods and related products, we view the film as an important part of youth's lives and, thus, a site in need of critique. We need to understand the ways the film speaks to, for, and about youth. It is for these reasons we have chosen to review the film. We argue that, although this movie works to interrupt some stereotypical notions of gender, overall, it sexualizes violence. We see the movie as one way in which young girls are taught to romanticize sexualized violence and, as feminists within the field of Education, we believe it is vital for those of us working with youth to critically engage patriarchal messages being sold to young girls. In what follows, we articulate how popular culture is a site of education that has social and material consequences on youth's lives and how this film specifically bears dangerous lessons upon the lives of girls.

FILM SYNOPSIS

The *Twilight* Web site advertises the film as an "action-packed, modern day love story." It is the story of a 17-year-old White girl, Bella (played by Kristen Stewart), who moves to a small town in Washington to live with her dad (Billy Burke), who is the chief of police. She is immediately welcomed in her new high school by a diverse group of students who include her in a range of high school activities. Although she hangs out with her newly acquired friends, she is intrigued by the Cullen siblings, four White students who are mysterious and aloof. She meets Edward (Robert Pattinson), one of the brothers, in science class and she immediately feels an unexplainable attraction to him. Although Bella is captivated by Edward, he seems repulsed by her and avoids her. One morning before school, Bella is almost hit by a van in the parking lot, and Edward crosses the entire parking lot in seconds and, with his hand as a shield, stops the van from hitting her. Edward plays the classic hypermasculine hero in this scene and Bella is increasingly obsessed with him. In spite of his warnings to keep her distance, Bella starts to investigate how he saved her life. After much research, she discovers that he is a vampire. Bella confronts Edward with her newly found knowledge and he opens up to her by disclosing details about his life as a vampire. They start to fall in love.

Edward introduces Bella to his family. His family is unique in that, as vegetarians, they refuse to drink the blood of humans; rather, they satisfy their need for blood by only consuming the blood of animals. Although Edward has committed himself to not hunting and killing humans, Bella's scent is very tempting to him and he has to forcibly resist his instincts to kill her. After Bella meets Edward's family, three nomadic vampires arrive on the scene, and one of them, James (Cam Gigandet), smells Bella's scent and immediately wants to kill her and drink her blood. The three vampires leave because they are outnumbered, and the rest of the film chronicles how Edward's family protects Bella from James. In the final scene, James lures Bella into an old building, where he proceeds to bite her wrist in an attempt to kill her. Before he can inflict any more injuries, Edward saves her by fighting and killing James. For Bella to survive, Edward must suck Bella's blood to remove James' venom. It is very hard for him to stop once he tastes human blood, but he does because of his love for her. Bella is taken to the hospital once Edward saves her, and after her release from the hospital, Edward and Bella attend prom together. The movie ends with Bella telling Edward that she wants to become a vampire to be with him forever, but he refuses her request.

POPULAR CULTURE AS A SITE OF EDUCATION

Popular culture texts are important sites that teach people about themselves and others (Kellner 1995; Lipsitz 1998; Esposito and Love 2008). It is often through popular culture that people gain knowledge about groups to which they do not normally have access. This is especially true for marginalized groups who may not be often represented in mainstream popular culture. For example, representations of Native Americans in Hollywood films are sparse. Exceptions include *Dances with Wolves* (1990), *The Last of the Mohicans* (1992), and Disney's *Pocahontas* (1995). Because of the lack of representation of Native Americans, the representations in existence become that much more powerful as they educate viewers who may not have direct experience with particular marginalized populations. Popular culture, thus, serves as a source of information about things we may not learn about elsewhere.

From consumption of popular culture texts, we learn what it means to live particular identities like gender or race (Kellner 1995). These texts are crucial sites of education and, therefore, must be continually critiqued. Popular culture texts are constitutive (Hall 1988). These texts do not just reflect current understandings about the world. Instead, the texts help create the world. Consequently, as an institution, popular culture can exert tremendous power on creating particular versions of the world by privileging certain ideologies. It is, thus, imperative to continually critique films that have mass appeal especially to youth.

The popular culture text and its meaning do not stand alone (Fiske 1989). Thus, viewers are not passive in their consumption and interpretation of texts. The relationship between viewers and texts is an active process (Hall 1981) of negotiating one's view of the world with the text's views. We approach our reading of the film *Twilight* as feminist identified women. One author is White; one is Latina. Both are academics. We list these identities not to essentialize or fix meanings. For example, what exactly does it mean to live as a White feminist academic? Our identities are not stable, nor do they denote consistently particular ways of viewing the world. We divulge this information, however, to assert that our reading of the film is but one. In fact, youth may make entirely different interpretations of the text, thus, as Buckingham (1998) suggests, there are limitations to adult readings of youth culture. We recognize, however, that this reading is still crucial in an attempt to understand the power of popular culture texts.

POSTFEMINISM AND POPULAR CULTURE

There has always been contention within the feminist movement. When feminism is discussed in terms of a historical perspective, the movement is often simplistically divided into 3 waves. Sheila Tobias (1998) distinguishes first wave feminism as the time period 1850–1919 which culminated in women gaining the right to vote. The second wave is often marked by the publication of Betty Friedan's *Feminine Mystique* in 1963, and this wave has been deemed in popular culture as the *bra-burning* time of fighting against the objectification of women (1960s and 1970s). The third wave made claims to be a new generation of feminists. These women had benefited from their grandmother's and mother's activism and maintained that, because the political and social climate was different in the 1980s and 1990s than what it was during the 1960s and 1970s, their feminism espoused different goals and expectations. McRobbie (2004) articulates the 1990s as a period where feminists recognized the body as a site of political struggle. There was less focus on institutional apparatuses of power as feminists made claims to body politics. This turn away from political power structures (including patriarchy) has created what has been termed *postfeminism*. Although this term has wide variation depending upon discipline (and even within discipline), McRobbie (2004) defines postfeminism as:

> An active process by which feminist gains of the 1970s and 80s come to be undermined. It proposes that through an array of machinations, elements of contemporary popular culture are perniciously effective in regard to this undoing of feminism, while simultaneously appearing to be engaging in a well-informed and even well-intended response to feminism. (258)

Postfeminism suggests that the goals of feminism have been attained and, thus, there is no need for further collective mobilization around gender (Modleski 1991). Women are presumed to be free to articulate our desires for sex, power, and money without fear of retribution. The notion of choice discussed in terms of postfeminism takes the stance that women are free agents in their lives, thus, they are able to make choices free from sexist constraints and institutionalized oppression. The focus remains on the individual (the personal as split from the political), instead of how the individual is located within a heteropatriarchal culture (the personal is political).

It is the institution of popular culture that helps disseminate the proliferation of postfeminism's ideologies (McRobbie 2004). Some popular culture texts deliberately examine the issue of feminism to only illustrate how it is no longer a useful concept and that, instead, women have moved beyond a feminist critique of woman as object to celebrate the notion of choice or of woman as subject (McRobbie 2004). Kinser (2004) claims that a postfeminist discourse is seductive to young women because they can simultaneously acknowledge feminism while expressing relief that the feminist movement is no longer necessary. We must be cognizant of the ways that postfeminism "co-opts the motivating discourse of feminism but accepts a *sense* of empowerment as a substitute for the work toward and evidence of *authentic* empowerment" (Kinser 2004, 134). We utilize this cautionary lens in our analysis of *Twilight* as we examine and critique its post-feminist messages.

SEXUALIZED VIOLENCE AS EMPOWERMENT?: FEMINIST ANALYSIS OF *TWILIGHT*

Regardless of the quality of representation, *Twilight* includes a variety of people of different races/ethnicities. We do not intend to operate from within a binary of *good* versus *bad* representations. Issues of representation are more complicated than such a binary allows. Instead, we posit that representations of race and gender should be complicated as those identities do not denote static states of being. Instead, race and gender are shaped, constructed, and performed in specific social contexts and historical moments. Although *Twilight* is problematic in its representation of gender roles, it does try to be transgressive in terms of destabilizing stereotypical (or nonexistent) Hollywood representations of marginalized populations. For example, although Bella, the main character, attends high school in a small town (population 3,000) in Washington State, subcharacters include a Native American (Jacob) who attends school on a reservation, as well as an Asian American (Eric). Native Americans and Asian Americans are rarely included in Hollywood productions or, if included, are represented in ways that perpetuate stereotypes. *Twilight* also tried to destabilize the ways race is often coded as good versus evil. The "vegetarian" vampires (Edward and his family) are all White. The evil vampires are comprised of two White characters and one Black character. Although the Black man is hypersexualized (the only character shown with his shirt open to reveal his muscular body), he ultimately reveals a good side as he decides his two White vampire friends are just too evil to continue hanging around. He refuses to participate in the tracking of Bella and the fighting with Edward's family.

Twilight also is transgressive to a degree with its feminist messages. For example, a female friend of Bella's says, "I'm thinking Eric will ask me to the prom but he never does." Bella tells the girl to ask Eric herself, "Take control. You are a strong independent woman." The female friend asks incredulously, "I am?" A few weeks later, she tells Bella, "I'm going to the prom with Eric. I just asked him. I took control." Here, in true postfeminist fashion, the notion that a woman can choose to take control and be an agent of her own life is taken for granted. It is something Bella reminds us to do yet it is framed as if women should already know this and be taking charge of their own lives in this way. Yet, in one of the next scenes, viewers witness the girls shopping for prom dresses as the boys view them through the store window. The girls are being objectified, but it is only Bella who recognizes the problem with it as she says, "That's disgusting." Her friends, on the other hand, do not seem to mind being objectified. The lack of discussion of male privilege helps position Bella as a feminist who is taking things all too seriously. This is an excellent example of popular culture contributing to the postfeminist message that equality has already been achieved, so women really do not need to mobilize anymore least of all complain about being looked at by men.

However, the film shows us the sometimes brutal cost of unequal gendered relations in the next scene. Bella walks back from a bookstore by herself that night while her friends still shop for prom dresses. It appears there is a price to pay for her being smart and seeking knowledge. She happens upon four drunk boys who circle around her. Viewers brace themselves for what appears will be a rape. Bella is stunned and voiceless at first. Then she yells, "Don't touch me!" Before she starts to fight off the boys, Edward comes to her rescue. He tells her to get into the car and then shows his fangs to the boys, who instantly cower and back away. Bella's friends are genuinely concerned about her and believe something might have happened to her. When she and Edward pull up in his car, he takes responsibility for Bella and tells her friends it was his fault Bella is late. Her friends giggle and tell him, "It happens." Although it is implied by her friends' fears that something terrible might have happened to Bella, her friends seem jovial that Bella was spending time with Edward instead of them. Here, it seems as if it is okay for girls to give up their female friends to spend time with a boy.

Although there are, arguably, complicated messages concerning female power and agency within the movie, we argue that its basic premise upholds patriarchal ideology while employing certain assumptions of postfeminism. *Twilight's* main theme, Bella's love for a boy who wants to kill her, sexualizes violence. Throughout the movie, Edward warns Bella about the dangers of being around both him and his family, yet she continues to put her life in jeopardy because of her love for him. The movie is consistently sensual, and the eroticism seems to be heightened during scenes involving violence. Bella's body language during violent scenes throughout the movie is noticeably sexual; she often appears breathing heavily with her mouth open and her cheeks flushed. Also, the movie suggests that there is a correlation between her love for Edward, and how dangerous he is to her. This sexualization of violence is related to postfeminism in that postfeminism claims that women have the power and agency to choose any kind of relationship for themselves, even relationships that have the potential for danger and/or violence. Postfeminism's insistence on individualism and assumed equality is the foundation for the audience to view Bella's relationship with Edward as an innocuous choice that does not need to be contextualized in histories of violence against women. This ahistorical and decontextualized presentation of sexualized violence through the employment of postfeminism actually serves to uphold and perpetuate patriarchal (and highly dangerous) notions about love, sexuality, and gender roles. Because postfeminism assumes that women have already fought for equality and won, Bella's choice to be with Edward is seen as a personal choice that was made autonomously, and therefore should be respected and not challenged.

IMPLICATIONS FOR YOUTH

Twilight was released on November 21, 2008, only months before two popular hip hop/R&B artists, Chris Brown and Rihanna, were part of a domestic dispute that led to Brown threatening Rihanna with death and beating her almost unconscious. Brown's attack caused multiple contusions and bruises on Rihanna's body. Rumors circulated in the media that Rihanna ultimately forgave Brown, went back to the relationship, and even asked a judge to not issue a "No contact" order against Brown. Whether this is true or not does not matter. What matters is what young girls believed about the outcome of the incident. The media examined this case from a variety of different angles, including the fact that, given that Rihanna was a role model to so many young girls, some were concerned about what the incident might have taught them (and young boys) about domestic violence. Sadly, we think that the Chris Brown and Rihanna incident teaches girls the old adage that "boys will be boys." Like Belle in Disney's *Beauty and the Beast*, the incident encourages girls to help tame their beast, to make him into a better man. We believe *Twilight* encourages a similar message.

Within the United States, there are alarming rates of physical and sexual violence against both women and girls. According to the Rape, Abuse, and Incest National Network, the largest antisexual assault organization in the United States, one in six women will be a victim of sexual assault, and someone is sexually assaulted every two minutes within the United States (http://www.rainn.org/statistics). Although the producers of movies such as *Twilight* assumedly seek to provide harmless entertainment while also providing a seemingly innocuous message of girl power, we argue that the movie, instead, perpetuates notions of feminized helplessness

and sexualized violence. Bella is tough and smart when she is not in danger, but when her life is in jeopardy, Edward intervenes on multiple occasions for the classic masculine rescue. Also, throughout the movie, Bella is obsessed with a boy who wants to literally kill her, and the audience is encouraged to romanticize this. Instead of raising concern about domestic and sexual violence through a feminist storyline, the movie instead sexualizes violence by making Edward's killer instincts sexy and Bella's irrational intrigue understandable and even condoned by friends and family.

Because we understand education as broadly conceived, we believe that it is important to engage with messages that youth are receiving both inside and outside of the actual school walls. We believe that it is important for educators and parents to understand what is happening in students' lives, and popular culture is an important educative site for many students of all ages. The walls of the school building are porous, and there is a dialectical relationship between what is learned inside of the classroom, and what lessons are learned outside of the classroom. To reach and connect with students, educators must be critically engaged with various messages and texts that students are consuming (Kellner and Share 2006), and we believe it is crucial for adults to critically engage with potentially problematic texts that promote harmful messages and ideologies. Critical engagement with and through popular culture is an important way for educators to better understand and relate to their students.

REFERENCES

Buckingham, David. 1998. "Introduction: Fantasies of Empowerment? Radical Pedagogy and Popular Culture." Pp. 1–17 in *Teaching Popular Culture*. Edited by David Buckingham. London: UCL Press.

Esposito, Jennifer, and Bettina Love. 2008. "More than a Video Hoe: Hip Hop as a Site of Sex Education about Girls' Sexual Desires." Pp. 43–82 in *The Corporate Assault on Youth: Commercialism, Exploitation, and the End of Innocence*. Edited by Deron Boyles. New York: Peter Lang.

Hall, Stuart. 1981. "Notes on Deconstructing the Popular." Pp. 227–240 in *People's History and Socialist Theory*. Edited by Raphael Samuel. London: Routledge.

———. 1988. "New Ethnicities." Pp. 27–31 in *Black Film/British Cinema, ICA Documents 7*. Edited by Kobena Mercer. London: Institute of Contemporary Arts.

Fiske, John. 1989. *Reading the Popular*. Boston: Unwin Hyman.

Kellner, Douglas. 1995. *Media Culture: Cultural Studies, Identity and Politics Between the Modern and the Postmodern*. New York: Routledge.

Kellner, Douglas and Jeff Share. 2006. "Critical Media Literacy is Not an Option." *Learning Inquiry 1*: 59–69.

Kinser, Amber E. 2004. "Negotiating Spaces for/through Third Wave Feminism." *NWSA Journal 16*: 124–154.

Lipsitz, George. 1998. *Dangerous Crossroads: Popular Music, Postmodernism and the Poetics of Place*. New York: Verso.

McRobbie, Angela. 2004. "Post-Feminism and Popular Culture." *Feminist Media Studies 4*: 255–264.

Modleski, Tania. 1991. *Feminism Without Women: Culture and Criticism in a "Postfeminist" Age*. New York: Routledge.

Tobias, Sheila. 1998. *Faces of Feminism: An Activist's Reflections on the Women's Movement*. Boulder, CO: Westview Press.

R E A D I N G **45**

Don't Act Crazy, Mindy

Heather Havrilesky (2013)

At first glance, this looks like a great moment for women on television. Many smart and confident female characters have paraded onto the small screen over the past few years. But I'm bothered by one persistent caveat: that the more astute and capable many of these women are, the more likely it is that they're also completely nuts.

I don't mean complicated, difficult, thorny or complex. I mean that these women are portrayed as volcanoes that could blow at any minute. Worse, the very abilities and skills that make them singular and interesting come coupled with some hideous psychic deficiency.

On "Nurse Jackie," for example, the main character is an excellent R.N. in part because she's self-medicated into a state of extreme calm. On "The Killing," Detective Linden, the world-weary, cold-souled cop, is a tenacious investigator in part because she's obsessive and damaged and a pretty terrible mother. And then there's "Homeland," on which Carrie Mathison, the nearly clairvoyant C.I.A. agent, is bipolar, unhinged and has proved, in her pursuit of an undercover terrorist, to be recklessly promiscuous.

These aren't just complicating characteristics like, say, Don Draper's narcissism. The suggestion in all of these shows is that a female character's flaws are inextricably linked to her strengths. Take away this pill problem or that personality disorder, and the exceptional qualities vanish as well. And this is not always viewed as a tragedy—when Carrie undergoes electroconvulsive therapy, we breathe a sigh of relief and draw closer. Look how restful it is for her, enjoying a nice sandwich and sleeping peacefully in her childhood bed.

You'd think the outlook would be sunnier on some of the lighter TV dramas and comedies, which have also lately offered several strong and inspiring (if neurotic) female protagonists, from Annie Edison of "Community" to Leslie Knope of "Parks and Recreation." Yet here, too, an alarming number of accomplished women are also portrayed as spending most of their waking hours swooning like lovesick tweens —whether it's Emily on "Emily Owens, M.D." (a knowledgeable doctor who loses focus whenever her super-dreamy crush enters the room), the title character of "Whitney" (a garrulous photographer who is nonetheless fixated on her looks and her ability to keep attractive romantic rivals away from her man), or Mindy of "The Mindy Project" (a highly paid ob-gyn who's obsessed with being too old and not pretty enough to land a husband). Even a classical comedic heroine like Liz Lemon on "30 Rock" is frequently reduced to flailing and squirming like an overcaffeinated adolescent. The moral of many of these shows doesn't seem so far off from that of those fatalistic female-centric magazine features that seem to run every few months; something along the lines of, "You can't have it all, ladies, and you'll run yourself ragged if you even try."

We could take heart that at least women are depicted as being just as reckless and promiscuous and demanding and intense as their male counterparts, if their bad behavior weren't so often accompanied by a horror soundtrack and dizzying camera angles that encourage us to view them as unhinged. The crazed antics of male characters like Don Draper, Walter White or Dr. Gregory House are reliably treated as bold, fearless and even ultimately heroic (a daring remark saves the big account; a lunatic gesture scares off a murderous thug; an abrasive approach miraculously yields the answer that saves a young girl's life). Female characters rarely enjoy such romantic spin.

Their flaws are fatal, or at least obviously self-destructive, and they seem designed to invite censure. Time and again, we, the audience, are cast in the role of morally superior observers to these nut jobs. At times we might relate to a flash of anger, a fit of tears, a sudden urge to seduce a stranger in a bar, but we're constantly being warned that these behaviors aren't normal. They render these women out of step with the sane world.

When Nurse Jackie chokes down pills and cavorts with the pharmacist while her perfectly good husband waits around at home with the kids, we can see clearly where too much sass and independence might lead. When Detective Linden dumps her son in a hotel room for the umpteenth time and then he goes missing, or Dr. Yang's emotional frigidity on "Grey's Anatomy" leaves her stranded at the altar, or Nancy Botwin of "Weeds" sleeps with (and eventually marries) a Mexican drug boss, thereby endangering her kids, we're cued to shake our heads at the woeful choices of these otherwise-impressive women. When Carrie on "Homeland" chugs a tumbler of white wine, then fetches one of her black sequined tops out of the closet, we're meant to lament her knee-jerk lasciviousness. Her mania is something she needs to be cured of, or freed from —unlike, say, Monk, whose psychological tics are portrayed as the adorable kernel of his genius.

So why should instability in men and women be treated so differently? "If you don't pull it together, no one will ever love you," a talking Barbie doll tells Mindy during a fantasy on "The Mindy Project," reminding us exactly what's on the line here.

Don't act crazy, Mindy. Men don't like crazy.

Some would argue that we've come a long way since Desi treated Lucy like a petulant child or June Cleaver smiled beatifically at her plucky spawn. "Mary Tyler Moore," "Murphy Brown" and "Roseanne" all demonstrated that a smart woman can have a life outside of cooking, cleaning and begging to be put in her husband's show. They offered us female characters who failed to blend seamlessly with their surroundings—because they were willing to voice their doubts, confess their crushes, seek out sex and openly confront others.

But right around the time "Ally McBeal" hit the air, the attempts to unveil the truth of the female experience started to sail far past the intended mark. The independent woman took on a hysterical edge; she was not only opinionated but also wildly insecure, sexually ravenous or panic-stricken over her waning fertility. Surprising as it was that McBeal was once heralded as a post-feminist hero on the cover of Time in 1998, what's more surprising is that since then, we haven't come all that much further, baby.

Sure, there are lots of exceptions, like Tami Taylor, the self-possessed working mom of "Friday Night Lights," or Hannah Horvath, the outspoken memoirist of "Girls," or the intelligent women of "Mad Men," whose struggles and flaws at least parallel those of the men swarming around them. But alongside every coolheaded Peggy Olson, we get hotheaded train-wreck characters like Ivy Lynn of "Smash"—women who, like the ballerinas with lead weights around their ankles in Kurt Vonnegut Jr.'s short story "Harrison Bergeron," can show no strength without an accompanying impediment to weigh them down, whether it's self-destructive urges, tittering self-consciousness or compulsive pill-popping. Where Roseanne and Mary and Murphy matter-of-factly admitted and often even flaunted their flaws, these characters are too ashamed and apologetic (and repeatedly demeaned) to be taken seriously.

"Women have often felt insane when cleaving to the truth of our experience," Adrienne Rich once wrote. There's truth in these images of women, from the neurotic ob-gyn fixated on finding Mr. Right to the workaholic C.I.A. agent who feels adrift when she isn't obsessing about issues of national security 18 hours a day. But why must these characters also be certifiable? Give Mindy a tiny slice of Louis C.K.'s poker-faced smugness. Give Carrie Mathison one-tenth of Jack Bauer's overconfidence and irreproachability. Where's the taboo in that?

Women, with their tendency to "ask uncomfortable questions and make uncomfortable connections," as Rich puts it, are pathologized for the very traits that make them so formidable. Or as Emily Dickinson wrote:

Much Madness is divinest Sense—

To a discerning Eye—

Much Sense—the starkest Madness—

'Tis the Majority

In this, as All, prevail—

Assent—and you are sane—

Demur—you're straightway dangerous—

And handled with a Chain—

"All smart women are crazy," I once told an ex-boyfriend in a heated moment, in an attempt to depict his future options as split down the middle between easygoing dimwits and sharp women who were basically just me with different hairstyles. By "crazy," I only meant "opinionated" and "moody" and "not always as pliant as one might hope." I was translating my personality into language he might understand—he who used "psycho-chick" as a stand-in for "noncompliant female" and he whose idea of helpful counsel was "You're too smart for your own good," "my own good" presumably being some semivegetative state of acceptance which precluded uncomfortable discussions about our relationship.

Over the years, "crazy" became my own reductive shorthand for every complicated, strong-willed woman I met. "Crazy" summed up the good and the bad in me and in all of my friends. Whereas I might have started to recognize that we were no more crazy than anyone else in the world, instead I simply drew a larger and larger circle of crazy around us, lumping together anyone unafraid of confrontation, anyone who openly admitted her weaknesses, anyone who pursued agendas that might be out of step with the dominant cultural noise of the moment. "Crazy" became code for "interesting" and "courageous" and "worth knowing." I was trying to have a sense of humor about myself and those around me, trying to make room for stubbornness and vulnerability and uncomfortable questions.

But I realize now, after watching these crazy characters parade across my TV screen, that there's self-hatred in this act of self-subterfuge. "Our future depends on the sanity of each of us," Rich writes, "and we have a profound stake, beyond the personal, in the project of describing our reality as candidly and fully as we can to each other."

Maybe this era of "crazy" women on TV is an unfortunate way-station on the road from placid compliance to something more complex—something more like real life. Many so-called crazy women are just smart, that's all. They're not too smart for their own good, or for ours.

Beyoncé: Feminist Icon?

Sophie Weiner (2013)

Beyoncé has become an icon, and in no small part this is due to her willingness to use her gender as a creative tool. The argument over whether the singer is a bona fide feminist or just a pop star cashing in on "girl power" has raged for years, but whatever side of the debate you land on, her message of empowerment, commitment to her craft, and control over her image and performance are undeniable. In celebration of her latest feat—that flawless halftime performance in which she was backed by an all-female band—here's a collection of Beyoncé's most feminist moments to date.

BEYONCÉ'S SUPER BOWL HALFTIME SHOW

The most recent and relevant example of Beyoncé's feminism was her performance at the all-American spectacle of Sunday's Super Bowl. With its massive budget and Beyoncé's overpowering stage presence, the show delivered. Along with her solo songs, the reunion of her original group, Destiny's Child, highlighted the progress she's made as an artist. The foregrounding of female musicians was incredible as a symbol of resistance against an industry where male musicians are still the norm. At the paean to male achievement that is the Super Bowl, it was impossible to see the performance and not feel Beyoncé had somehow won the whole thing.

BEYONCÉ IN *GQ*

Beyoncé's recent *GQ* feature and cover are a great example of the dichotomy of her public existence. While the sexy cover agitated many by-the-book feminists, the article itself complicated her image and demonstrated her in-depth understanding of gender inequality, particularly within the music industry. The most on-point quote in the article addresses the economic inequality that affects women at every socio-economic level (and even more so for African American women):

> You know, equality is a myth, and for some reason, everyone accepts the fact that women don't make as much money as men do. I don't understand that. Why do we have to take a backseat?" she says in her film, which begins with her 2011 decision to sever her business relationship with her father. "I truly believe that women should be financially independent from their men. And let's face it, money gives men the power to run the show. It gives men the power to define value. They define what's sexy. And men define what's feminine. It's ridiculous.

"INDEPENDENT WOMAN PART 1"

Possibly the most obvious musical example of Beyoncé's support of female empowerment is the song her former girl group Destiny's Child recorded for the 2000 film version of *Charlie's Angels*, "Independent Woman Part 1." In a matter-of-fact manner, the song states the benefits of being a woman who isn't beholden to a male breadwinner—a theme that repeats itself throughout Beyoncé's work. In a remake of a TV show that originally glorified female submissiveness, this was a great fuck-you to the misogynist subject matter, and a pop song that has endured.

TELEPHONE

A frequently noted and frustrating tendency of our patriarchal society is its tendency to encourage women, or any minority in a competitive field, to undermine each other in order to be the example of their demographic in the American mainstream. Though "Telephone" is neither Beyoncé's nor Lady

Gaga's best song, it's a great example of two female artists refusing to accept that women in the cutthroat world of pop stardom cannot work together. The allusions to both *Thelma & Louise* and a gender-inverted *Pulp Fiction* reinforce the video's premise that girl power can reign supreme.

RUN THE WORLD (GIRLS)

Another on the list of feminist-Beyoncé controversies is her song that proclaims that girls run the world. Though she herself acknowledges in her *GQ* article and other places that this isn't our reality, art has its own impact, and releasing a song that carries this message, with the intention of having it played on every dance floor around the world, is a ballsy political step.

BEYONCÉ ACCEPTS THE FEMINIST LABEL

"I think I am a feminist, in a way," Beyoncé told *The Daily Mail* in 2010. "It's not something I consciously decided I was going to be; perhaps it's because I grew up in a singing group with other women, and that was so helpful to me," she told the magazine. "It kept me out of so much trouble and out of bad relationships. My friendships with my girls are just so much a part of me that there are things I am never going to do that would upset that bond. I never want to betray that friendship, because I love being a woman and I love being a friend to other women."

Feminist actions speak louder than labels, so to us, this quote says it all: Beyoncé arrived at her definition of feminism out of genuine concern for the situation of herself and the women around her. If living by her own morals is what has defined Beyoncé's feminism, we are all for it.

SURVIVOR

A rock-solid breakup jam and feminist anthem, "Survivor," the title track off Destiny's Child's 2001 album, gave hope to a generation that was growing up in an era with few alternatives to the simplistic and stereotypical gender roles presented by Britney Spears and N*Sync. The lyrics show a belief in women's ability to solve their own problems, assuring us that whatever rough situation we're in, we'll get through it—something we could all stand to be reminded of from time to time.

JAY-Z TOOK BEYONCÉ'S NAME, TOO

Finally, and most confoundingly, Beyoncé has just announced that her next world tour will be called the "Mrs. Carter Show," taking its name from her husband, Jay-Z. Though seen as a step backward by many feminist fans, others interpreted this decision as one of marketing savvy, pooling the massive fan base that both artists possess, or just as a winking dedication to the husband she very publicly loves—and who has taken her name as she has taken his.

Cyberactivism and the Role of Women in the Arab Uprisings

Courtney C. Radsch (2012)

"I, a girl, am going down to Tahrir Square, and I will stand alone. And I'll hold up a banner. Perhaps people will show some honor. I even wrote my number so maybe people will come down with me. No one came except . . . three guys and three armored cars of riot police . . . I'm making this video to give you one simply message: We want to go down to Tahrir Square on January 25. If we still have honor and want to live with dignity on this land, we have to go down on January 25. We'll go down and demand our rights, our fundamental human rights . . . If you think yourself a man, come with me on January 25th. Whoever says a women shouldn't go to protests because they will get beaten, let him have some honor and manhood and come with me on January 25th . . . Sitting at home and just following us on news or Facebook leads to our humiliation, leads to my own humiliation. If you have honor and dignity as a man, come . . . If you stay home, you deserve what will happen to you . . . and you'll be guilty, before your nation and your people . . . Go down to the street, send SMSs, post it post it on the 'net. Make people aware . . . It will make a difference, a big difference . . . never say there's no hope . . . so long you come down with us, there will be hope . . . don't think you can be safe any more! None of us are! Come down with us and demand your rights my rights, your family's rights."

Thus was the call to action that 26-year-old Asmaa Mahfouz made in a video she posted to YouTube on January 18, 2011, which went viral and turned her into a symbol of the Egyptian revolution. A day later, 32-year-old Tawakkol Karman organized a protest in solidarity with the Tunisian people in downtown Sana'a that drew thousands to the streets in an unprecedented public demonstration by women. Young women have been at the forefront of the revolutionary uprisings that have toppled regimes in Egypt, Tunisia, and Yemen, along with the more protracted struggles in Bahrain, Saudi Arabia, and Syria. They were among the Twitterati and citizen journalists who became leading news sources—the protesters who took to the streets and the cybersphere to demand that their entrenched leaders step down, and the citizens who paid the ultimate price, being beaten to death and murdered in those regimes' desperate attempts to cling to power.

This research . . . explores how young women used social media and cyberactivism to help shape the "Arab Spring" and its aftermath. The engagement of women with social media has coincided with a shift in the political landscape of the Middle East, and it is unlikely that they will ever retreat from the new arenas they have carved out for themselves. Throughout the region, women have taken to the streets in unprecedented numbers, translating digital advocacy and organization into physical mobilization and occupation of public spaces in a dialectic of online and offline activism that is particular to this era. They have used citizen journalism and social networking to counter the state-dominated media in their countries and influence mainstream media around the world. In the process, they are reconfiguring the public sphere in their countries, as well as the expectations of the public about the role women can and should play in the political lives of their countries.

Several of the women who participated in and led the Arab uprisings were cyberactivists prior to the convulsions of 2011, but many more were inspired to become activists by the events happening around them. Although women young and old took part, it was the younger generation that led the way online.

They helped organize virtual protests as well as street demonstrations and played bridging roles with the mainstream media, helping to ensure that the 24-hour news cycle always had a source at the ready. Twitter became a real-time newsfeed, connecting journalists directly with activists and becoming a key tool in the battle to frame the protests and set the news agenda, particularly in the international media like Al Jazeera and elite Western outlets. Media outlets repurposed citizen-generated videos on YouTube and photos on Flikr, while Facebook provided a platform for aggregating, organizing, disseminating, and building solidarity.

Women have played a central role in the creation of a virtual public sphere online via social media and blogs, but have also demanded greater access, representation, and participation in the physical public sphere, epitomized by the physical squares that represent the imaginary center of political life in their countries: Tahrir Square in Egypt and Benghazi, Libya; Taghir Square in Yemen; and the Pearl Roundabout in Bahrain. They tore down physical and social barriers between men and women, challenging cultural and religious norms and taboos and putting women's empowerment at the center of the struggle for political change. As one blogger put it, "The most encouraging feature of the current upheaval is the massive participation of women; not only the young educated women who uses (sic) the Internet but also the grassroots uneducated older women from rural cities."*

Among the iconic figures of these Arab revolutionary uprisings are several women who are inextricably linked with the new media platforms that have fundamentally shifted the balance of power. Not only have cyberactivism and social media platforms shifted the power dynamics of authoritarian Arab governments and their citizenry, but they have also reconfigured power relations between the youth who make up the majority of the population and the older generation of political elites who were overwhelmingly male and often implicated in the perpetuation of the status quo.

While women and men struggle valiantly to bring about political change, the cyberactivists stand out for their use of new media technologies and access to platforms that transcended national boundaries and created bridges with transnational media and activists groups. The importance of these cyberactivist platforms could be seen in the way they became part of the lexicon of dissent. Esraa Abdel Fattah was known as "Facebook girl" for her role in launching one of the most important opposition youth groups in Egypt, the April 6 Movement. Egypt's Mona Eltahawy, Libya's Danya Bashir, Bahrain's Zeinab al-Khawaja and Maryam al-Khawaja, and many others became known as the "Twitterrati" as influential media and pundits dubbed their Twitter accounts as "must-follows.". . .

CITIZEN JOURNALISM AND SYMBIOSIS WITH MAINSTREAM MEDIA

Many of these women cyberactivists chose citizen journalism as the primary mode of contestation in their battles with entrenched regimes. One young woman named Fatima, but better known by her blog name Arabicca, labeled 2011 the "Year of Citizen Journalism."[1] Citizen journalists radically shifted the media ecosystem and informational status quo by witnessing, putting on record, and imbuing political meaning to symbolic struggles to define quotidian resistance against social injustice, harassment, and censorship as part of a broader movement for political reform. As sociologist Pierre Bourdieu aptly observed, "The simple report, the very fact of reporting, of putting on record as a reporter, always implies a social construction of reality that can mobilize (or demobilize) individuals or groups."[2] Information and events do not inherently have political meaning or importance, but rather must be interpreted, framed, and contextualized before becoming imbued with significance and import, a process in which journalists play a central role. As one of Egypt's leading cyberactivists and citizen journalists astutely notes on the front page of his blog: "In a dictatorship,

---

* Dalia Ziada, "Egypt's Revolution—How Does It All Start?" *Dalia Ziada* (blog), February 3, 2011, http://daliaziada.blogspot.com/2011/02/jan25-egypts-revolution-how-does-it-all.html.

independent journalism by default becomes a form of activism, and the spread of information is essentially an act of agitation."[3]

Cyberactivists sought to influence domestic media and counter the pro-regime framing of the uprisings. Indeed, one of the primary goals and successes of citizen journalism in the lead-up to the Arab uprisings was creating awareness among people about their rights and the excesses of the Arab regimes. In Egypt, the state-run media refused to even cover the uprising in the early days or would blatantly misreport information, while in Bahrain the lack of independent media meant that the regime's framing of the conflict as sectarian in nature had no counterpoint except for citizen media. Because of lingering distrust of the mainstream media in Libya, cultivated over the 42 years of Ghaddafi's rule in which he controlled and manipulated the media, people rely on personal connections and relationships in assessing the trustworthiness of news and information. "Facebook is more trustworthy than the media," one young Libyan woman told me. Bahraini writer Lamees Dhaif embodies this shifting typology of journalism, blurring the lines between professional and citizen journalist as she continues to speak out in the media against the abuses of her government, even as she blogs and tweets to an audience far bigger than the largest circulation newspaper in her home country. She dismissed the Bahraini authorities' attempts to silence her, noting that she has almost 60,000 followers on Twitter and 43,000 subscribers to her blog, whereas the largest circulation newspaper in Bahrain prints only 12,000 copies daily. "So if they don't want me to write in newspapers, who cares," said Dhaif.

In Tunisia, bloggers like 27-year-old Lina Ben Mhenni played a critical role in breaking the mainstream media blackout on the protests that erupted around the country after the self-immolation of a fruit vendor in the southern city of Sidi Bouzid. She was one of the first people to write about the incident and turned her blog, Twitter, and Facebook page into a virtual newsroom.

On December 17, 2010, tweets about Tunisia started appearing following the death of 26-year-old Mohamed Bouazizi, who had set himself on fire in protest against the humiliation and harassment he

suffered at the hands of police as he tended to his stand; his story was familiar to many young men and women who heard about it via social media networks. Ben Mhenni, who blogs in Arabic, English, French, and German at *A Tunisian Girl*, called her friends for updates she then posted on social media and ended up deciding to go there herself to report. "I decided to share the grief of the inhabitants of Sidi Bouzid," she wrote on her blog.[4] Over the next several weeks she travelled the country, posting pictures and reports about the outbreak of street demonstrations and the violent responses by the regime. She relied on Twitter, Facebook, and her blog because, as she noted, only citizen media was covering the protests since the mainstream media only concerned itself with such uncontroversial news as the activities of the president and sports.[5]

Several Facebook pages were created in the wake of Bouazizi's suicide, such as the Arabic page "Mr. President, Tunisians are Setting Themselves on Fire," which garnered 2,500 fans within a day of its creation and 10,000 more a week later, helping to spread information about protests and providing an outlet for young Tunisians to express their anger.[6]

There were few foreign media in Tunisia at that time: *Al Jazeera* had one foreign correspondent on the ground, as did France24, while the U.S. media were completely absent. There were no American channels, and even the Arab and French channels heavily depended on social media content and YouTube video. There were reports that *Al Jazeera* relied on citizen-generated videos for more than 60 percent of its content during the weeks leading up to President Zine al-Abedine Ben Ali's ouster on January 14, 2011, although one senior media executive told me that in fact the station was 100 percent dependent on such content in the first couple of weeks of the uprising. Citizen journalists and bloggers like Ben Mhenni, therefore, played a critical role in reporting on the uprising and providing content to mainstream media.

As the uprising gathered strength, the regime engaged in a counter-information campaign and sought to discredit citizen media. Ben Mhenni, whose father was also a political activist, started blogging in 2007 and had already earned a reputation covering human rights issues and freedom of expression, so her credibility was established. She also knew how to bypass the censorship that rendered key social media sites, including YouTube and Flikr, inaccessible to those who were not as adroit at using circumvention tools. "The Tunisian government did not find another solution but to censor the websites disseminating the story and imposing a blockade on the city of Sidi Bouzid, where people are expressing their anger by protesting in the streets," she wrote on the activist blog Global Voices.[7] Tunisia was among the most sophisticated Internet censors in the world, leading Reporters without Borders to put the country on its list of "Internet Enemies" and Freedom House[8] to characterize its multilayered Internet censorship apparatus as "one of the world's most repressive."[9]

By 2011, 3.6 million Tunisians had Internet access and more than 1.8 million of them had a Facebook account. As one Tunisan *bloguese*[10] put it: "Everything happened on Facebook."[11] Twitter was also an important tool; the Tunisian share-of-voice among MENA Twitter users rose significantly as protests erupted throughout the country, rising from about five percent on December 17, 2010, to more than 70 percent the day before Ben Ali fled the country.[12] That is, everything that happened in the streets was recorded and posted online, which flooded social media networks with news of the uprising. "Women were present in every stage and each action of the uprising," Ben Mhenni told me. "They were present on the street [and] behind their screens."

. . .

Linking Cyberactivism with the Street

Cyberactivists recognize that their activism does not end at the computer screen, but must go hand-in-hand with other forms of political engagement and be translated into physical manifestations of political protest. "Cyberactivism is not just work behind the screen, it is also smelling the tear gas and facing the security forces live ammunition," noted Ben Mhenni in an interview. Many explicitly credited social media with changing the dynamics in authoritarian countries throughout the region, but acknowledged the offline work that must also go into human

rights and political reform work. Throughout the region people took to the streets to demand change in unprecedented numbers, and in each case women figured prominently.

According to reports about previous protests in Egypt, women only accounted for about 10 percent of the protesters, whereas they accounted for about 40 to 50 percent in Tahrir Square in the days leading up to the fall of Mubarak.[13] Since 2004, Egyptian women have actively staked a claim in cyberspace, even as they took to the streets as part of the Kefaya movement in 2004-2006, the April 6 Youth Movement in 2008, and others—but never in the numbers that participated in the revolution. The 18-day uprising included women on a scale not seen before, and in many ways the cyberactivist movement helped lay the groundwork and change the mindset of a new generation of Egyptian youth. Veiled and unveiled women participated in the protests, provided support to the hungry and the wounded, led chants against the regime and more recently against the ruling military Supreme Council of the Armed Forces (SCAF), opened their homes to protesters and cyberactivists, and slept in Tahrir Square together with their male compatriots. These women were not only secularists or liberals; the Muslim Sisters, the female wing of the *Ikhwan Muslimeen* (The Muslim Brotherhood), were also active. Muslim Sisters joined in the protests, discussing their ideas and leading collective actions, using their social media accounts to communicate their experiences and fight for their political ideals. As one activist noted: "The women of the Muslim Brotherhood, who are traditionally a silent group walking behind the chanting men, were joining with other people, discussing and exchanging with them—they were even up there, right at the front, leading cheers and chants. That is a radical shift."[14]

. . .

Inspiration and Mobilization

Women played a pivotal role in inspiring their fellow citizens to take part in the uprisings, whether through admiration or confrontation. In her YouTube message (quoted at the beginning of this paper), for example, Egypt's Asmaa Mahfouz played on the male sense of honor in calling for men to join her in the street, deriding men who stayed at home while "the more vulnerable sex" took to the streets and faced the riot police.

As they watched the fall of regimes in Tunisia and Egypt, Libyan youth started talking on Facebook about the need for revolution in their country. They wrote on each other's walls and started groups to inspire each other and build support for collective action. On February 17, 2011, a video of the protest in Benghazi spread like wildfire among the connected youth of Libya, who made sure it also got to the international media. "I must say that without Facebook and social media, there would not have been a revolution," one 23-year-old blogger from Misrata told me. "It was a revolution started on Facebook." Others inspired their fellow citizens with their fearlessness in the face of repression and willingness to traverse red lines.

. . .

SEXUAL VIOLENCE AS A FORM OF INTIMIDATION

Women face specific threats and violence that their male counterparts for the most part do not, and they have paid a steep price as regime defenders and authorities have used sexual violence in an attempt to silence and intimidate them. Gender-specific threats and sexual violence—including brutal beatings during protests, so-called "virginity tests,"[15] degrading and brutal treatment including torture during detainment, and character assassination—specifically exploit cultural taboos in which female victims are seen as having brought dishonor upon themselves. Sexual assault, including rape, has become a defining feature of the uprisings in Egypt and Libya, but has also been used by regimes throughout the region as a tactic against the women who participate in protests and seek to break down gender barriers and cultural taboos. Cyberactivists also face intimidation and sexual harassment in the virtual public sphere, as they become the subject of virulent reputation assassinations and defamation campaigns, and receive threats on their social media profiles and blogs. Online defamation campaigns

against women cyberactivists have been seen in Bahrain and Tunisia as well as Egypt. As women have come to play a central role in the uprisings, they have also become a target of the regime, which seeks to delegitimize their participation and calls for political reform by disparaging them and raising the potential costs of involvement.

In Egypt, for example, the police, security forces, and thugs harassed and assaulted women during the uprising, continuing the trend of targeting women that goes back to at least 2005, when there was a marked turn by the Egyptian government toward the use of violence against women. During the 2005 demonstrations against a proposed constitutional amendment, gangs of men allegedly hired by a member of the ruling National Democratic Party (NDP) attacked women journalists, including cyberactivists like Nora Younis, and female journalists, specifically targeting them in what Younis called a "sexist approach."[16]

"A woman is just a body and [the regime] felt that a woman, she will never go back to the streets and men would feel humiliated and not go out," she explained. But women stayed in the streets from 2005 onward, and during the protests were beaten and tear-gassed just like everyone else. One woman said the police were "particularly vicious to women. They target us. I've had my veil pulled off by one of them. In my own town of Menoufeya, a certain police officer would tell women who got arrested, 'You come in as virgins, and I'll make sure you leave as real women.'"[17] Thugs attacked, beat, and ripped the clothes off of professor Noha Radwan during a mass demonstration in Cairo and killed protester Sally Zahran by clubbing her with a baseball bat; police killed a woman named Amira and ran over Liza Mohamed Hasan.[18] Samira Ibrahim, 25, was the only one of at least seven women subjected to "virginity tests" by the military in spring 2011 who filed a case against her perpetrators.[19] In December 2011, amateur mobile phone videos captured the beating of a woman by Egyptian security forces, who tore off her abaya and exposed her blue bra. Video and photos of the assault quickly went viral and the "blue bra" girl became a symbol of the continuing military repression and violence against women as people tweeted and Facebooked the attack. U.S. journalist Lara Logan was sexually assaulted while covering the protests in Tahrir, and during the November 2011 parliamentary elections, Egyptian commentator Mona Eltahawy was arrested and sexually assaulted by police. But rather than remain silent, these women and their compatriots who lived to bear witness have taken to the airwaves and cyberspace to tell their stories, refusing to back down. "Oppression begets solidarity," one woman in Tahrir astutely observed.

. . .

In Egypt, a group of volunteers created Harassmap,[20] a crowdsource mapping project launched in 2010 to track incidents of sexual harassment in the streets of Cairo by location, type, and frequency and provide real-time information about areas women should avoid, and to change attitudes toward the problem in local communities.[21] Many people used this platform in the months following the uprising as sexual assaults became more common with the breakdown in security. In 2010, draft legislation that would criminalize sexual harassment was put in front of the Egyptian Parliament, but it was dissolved and replaced in the post-Mubarak era. Without the concerted effort by citizen journalists, cyberactivists, and women's rights organizations to document these cases and bring attention to the issue while building alliances with other concerned groups in the human rights community, it seems unlikely that Egypt would have made much progress in either changing mindsets or legal frameworks.

PUBLIC SPHERE

The Middle East is highly patriarchal, although the region varies in terms of women's formal participation in the public sphere. In Egypt, Bahrain, and Tunisia, women held parliamentary seats prior to the revolution and participated in economic life. In Yemen, Saudi Arabia, and Libya, however, women were largely relegated to the home and not visible in the public sphere. Mass participation by women in street protests and political demonstrations was rare if not unheard of prior to the 2011 uprisings, when women young and old took to the streets across the region, slept in the squares, and climbed atop of

the shoulders of men to rally the public. Pictures of middle-aged women tending their children in tents and stories of older women refusing the youth's protestations to go inside where they would be safer have become part of the revolutions' story.

But while women were relatively less visible in the streets and public squares prior to the Arab uprisings, over the past several years, young women have carved out a robust, participatory, and leadership role for themselves in cyberspace. In more conservative societies, women were able to "leave the confines of the four walls of her home," as one young Libyan put it, by going online, where they could access information, communicate with people outside of their physical social circles (they were often constrained by social mores and familial expectations from intermixing with men), and engage in collective action, from "liking" a Facebook post to coordinating donations among friends. "Cyberactivism has made activism on the street more acceptable," explained Yemeni activist Maria al-Masani.

It also enabled young women in the more conservative countries of Libya and Yemen to participate in the revolutions because there are fewer strictures on gender mixing and female comportment online, and anonymity is an option—whereas it is not in most cities and villages, where extended family ties mean that it can be difficult to escape prying eyes and ears. Several Libyan and Yemeni women said that cyberactivism empowered them to be active in a way they could not be in the physical world. "Women are equal on the Internet," more than one person told me. "In cyberactivism, men don't get in physical contact with women, so a lot of women are in cyberactivism because their father says he would not want his daughter to go to a demonstration, but if she's anonymously online then no one's going to object to that," explained Mansani, in an observation echoed by several other young women. An activist who wished to remain anonymous said her cousins would object to her cyberactivism, so she used a pseudonym; another explained that they would use codes to discuss what was happening on the ground in Libya because certain words like "NATO" were under surveillance. Libyan activist Sarah al-Firgani said new media pushed women to get involved more. "They were at home using Internet, they can speak freely and . . . it changed the look of women in their community, the men respect them more and see they have a role to play to beyond family and children," explained Firgani. "Women proved they can do what men can do, some women did more than what many men did."

. . .

The role of women in the public sphere has inalterably shifted over the past several months as women translated gains made in the virtual sphere to the embodied public sphere, of which squares in the capital cities were emblematic. Women participated in the Arab uprisings and reconstituted the role and position women occupy in the public sphere. While some countries, like Bahrain, Egypt, and Tunisia, had a handful of women parliamentarians prior to the revolutionary uprisings, others like Yemen and Saudi Arabia were virtual black holes in terms of women's public participation in the public sphere. Similarly, in Bahrain, Yemen, and Saudi Arabia, the virtual instantiations of contentious politics—as well as the dialectic of the embodied and virtual public spheres that reconstituted women's role and image in Arab politics and society—provided new mechanisms for the articulation of their identities and brought new issues to the public agenda. Although Arab states have highly variable rates of Internet connectivity, social media—particularly Facebook, Twitter, and YouTube—have become central facets of young women's daily lives. Even in Yemen, where Internet penetration is a mere 10 percent, youth have clamored to join Facebook. "Everyone knows everyone else through Facebook," according to Yemeni blogger Afrah Nasser, noting that it helped connect youth in various provinces so that they could unite in the revolution.

. . .

Cyberactivism is both reflexive and reactive. For many women, posting on Facebook or blogging was the first time they had ever expressed their personal feelings publicly. Cyberactivism was a form of empowerment, a way to exert control over one's personhood and identity, while gaining a sense of being able to *do* something in the face of a patriarchal hierarchy and an authoritarian state. "People are starting to say their views openly and freely because of social media, it has changed their mentality," according to Afrah Nasser. As a blogger named Israa explained in an interview prior to the Egyptian uprising, blogging was "a way to spread our ideas and concepts to people and make things that can change our facts and conditions." This sentiment was expressed by many women before, during, and after the revolutions. "The power of women is in their stories. They are not theories, they are real lives that, thanks to social networks, we are able to share and exchange," said Egyptian-American activist Mona Eltahawy.

New and alternative media have given women new tools for articulating their identity in the public sphere, putting issues that were of particular concern to them onto the public agenda, and making their opinions heard, from straightforward online blogging platforms in the mid-2000s to mobile and microblogging in 2007, to the explosive popularity of the social networking site Facebook by 2008. Women have even made gains within the conservative Muslim Brotherhood, as evidenced by the recent comments of Supreme Guide Mohamed Badie at an *Ikhwan* press conference entitled "Woman: From the Revolution to the Prosperity." "No one can deny the vital role the women played during the January 25 Revolution, whether as activists, mothers, or wives," he said in his opening speech, noting that they "partook with men in everything." Women, he said, "made history, and with their success they gave the whole world a lesson about how to fight injustice and tyranny."

. . .

POST-REVOLUTION: ORGANIZING, ELECTING, AND PARTICIPATING

Zeinab al-Khawaja, best known by her Twitter handle @AngryArabiya, is another iconic figure who has been active from the start of the uprising and continues to push the limits of political expression in Bahrain, earning her the wrath of the authorities and the admiration of people around the world who interact with her on Twitter. Her sister, Maryam al-Khawaja, went into exile and shuttles between Europe and Washington, D.C., as advocacy director of the Bahrain Centre for Human Rights, the leading human rights monitoring group in the country. Their father was beaten, tortured, and sentenced to life in prison at a sham military trial and eventually went on a hunger strike that at this writing had been going on for more than a month. Yet they both continue their advocacy, one from inside the country and one from outside, using cyberactivism to ensure the world does not forget about the ongoing protest movement in Bahrain.

In Libya, women seem to be more active than men in building civil society and, in particular, using social media to do so. New nongovernmental organizations, coalitions, and Facebook groups are sprouting up everywhere to deal with problems as local as the sewage in Lake Benghazi to those as complicated as the issue of federalism and elections. In many cases, young women said their organizations grew out of Facebook pages or groups they started with friends.

Ibtihad, a 26-year-old activist from Tripoli who was forced to leave Libya during the war, created a Facebook page with her friends because she felt she could not just sit and do nothing—she needed to take action. They began to lay the groundwork for an organization so that when she and her friends were able to return to Libya, they would have the foundation for a registered NGO. The Facebook group, which was open only to friends, adopted a policy of complete transparency and democracy. The 100 or so members of the group voted on everything, from the name to the logo to the program of work. They wrote a mission statement and bylaws, and when she returned in August 2011 they registered their new organization, which they named Phoenix, after the bird that rises again from the ashes, and the Arabic term that refers to beauty. They raised money from friends and acquaintances and posted an accounting online with pictures of everything they purchased with donated funds. After Ghaddafi's fall, as the country entered the transitional phase, Phoenix created a fan page that was open to all and took its online activism offline, holding information sessions and establishing a women's resource center. Such examples are common in Libya, where the youth have been inspired to lead their country to a better future in the post-Ghaddafi era. "We started

Phoenix because our parents didn't let us interact with anyone, and we were just trying to help, so we started this Facebook group and we started adding trusted friends" who had gone abroad to collect donations of money and clothes, Ibtihad said.

Young women throughout the region agree that a fundamental mind shift must take place in order for women to make real gains, as for some women, authoritarianism is experienced in the private as well as the public sphere. Dalia Ziada underscored the challenges that still remain in Egypt, noting that a poll of more than 1400 people she helped conduct revealed that not a single one wanted to see a woman president one day. In their personal lives, young women must juggle their studies and family responsibilities (some of them are mothers and wives), and negotiate cultural expectations about women's roles. Carving out time for cyberactivism seems to have taken on more importance as social media use expanded, and as the uprisings spread. . . .

The diminutive 15-year-old Arwa al-Taweel was among the first *Ikhwan* sisters to create a blog in 2005, and helped pave the way for its members to participate in the blogosphere, having encouraged and trained dozens, if not hundreds, of her fellow Ikhwan to blog, including several who participated in the revolution. Her blog, *Ana Keda*—an expression that she translated as meaning something to the effect of "That's How I Am" or "I Am Enough"—and later her tweets and Facebook updates became a venue for political activism and articulation of her Islamic faith and in many ways defined her, she told me. She became known as a blogger and cyberactivist, recognizable to strangers because she posted a photo on her blog. Blogging was both personal and political, but she shied away from the public critique of the *Ikhwan's* 2007 party platform in favor of more personal reflections on life, love, and poetry. But given her father's reputation and her own activism as a citizen journalist for *Al Jazeera Talk* and *Al Destor* and her active support for Gaza, the former could hardly be separated from the latter. In 2008 she told me she would refuse to stop being a cyberactivist if and when she got married, a promise she ended up keeping when she broke off her engagement with a man who wanted her to stay at home more often. Defying the traditional role of

Muslim Sister as stay-at-home wife, she vowed to travel and remain politically active, and last year found a husband who would support her. In the wake of the revolution she even professed an interest in running for parliament when she turned 30.[22]

The translation of online experiences and relationships into the "real world" blurred the lines between public and private life, and provided new and varied opportunities for women to expand their circles and interact with people they never could have otherwise. Such translation also contributed to attempts to claim control over the articulation of the female identity. Feminist reinterpretations clashed with conservative traditionalists seeking to maintain hegemonic control over the representation of women and their proper roles in society. Blogs and social media made the invisible visible, gave voice to the voiceless, and embodied a commitment to free expression and *itjihad*, or independent judgment. "This is a revolution of making our voice heard," said Afrah Nasser, noting that half of Yemen's population is under 18. "We are now creating a new form of political awareness in Yemen that has never been talked about before, [a] new form of politics," she added, pointing out that the fact she had been invited to speak at an international conference on Arab women and cyberactivism was proof of such change. In her country, women played an unprecedented leadership role in the uprisings, recognized by the awarding of the 2011 Nobel Peace Prize to Yemeni journalist and human rights activist Tawakkol Karman for her role in inspiring the democratic uprising in her country, which grew from 20 women journalists who gathered to protest the day Tunisia's president Ben Ali fled the country to tens of thousands in the weeks and months that followed.

. . .

Women have carved out new spaces for debate and discussion in the public sphere, both physically and rhetorically, through activism on the streets and online through agenda-setting and framing as they erased red lines that had previously kept topics like torture, political succession, and sexual harassment off limits. They are unlikely to retreat from the public sphere no matter the outcome of the revolutions. . . .

CONCLUDING THOUGHTS

Despite the region's democratic uprisings, many countries—including Bahrain, Saudi Arabia, Syria, and Yemen—experienced backsliding in Freedom House's 2012 annual survey of political rights and civil liberties because of crackdowns on pro-reform activists. Tunisia was a bright spot in a region that continues to rank among the least free in the world, moving from "Not Free" to "Partly Free" on the Freedom House 2012 survey amid the successful democratic consolidation that took place in the wake of Ben Ali's ouster last year. Egypt continued to rank as "Not Free" amid continued repression by the ruling military power. Thus the struggle to consolidate revolution and enact meaningful reforms remains a challenge that young women will continue to be involved in; they will undoubtedly continue to use new media technologies to participate in and influence the future trajectory of their countries.

The Arab Spring is not just a political revolution; it is a social, sexual, and potentially religious one as well. Women cyberactivists are upending traditional hierarchies, reinterpreting religious dogma, breaking taboos, and bringing new issues into the public sphere even as they push to redefine the cultural mores between public and private spheres.

The tension between privacy versus publicity, activism versus journalism, professional versus amateur, physical versus virtual, and conformity versus *itjihad* are at the epicenter of the revolutionary transformations underway throughout the region. Social media and the Internet enabled young women to play a central role in the revolutionary struggles underway in their countries, whether as revolutionaries, citizen journalists, or organizers. As Internet access increases, as mobile phones are increasingly able to connect online, and as social networking expands, cyberactivism will continue to be a central form of contestation even as new platforms and strategies develop. Ensuring that women receive education and training, as well as expanding their legal and political rights, will help consolidate the sociopolitical gains of the Arab uprisings. With the widespread recognition of the role young women played in the uprisings, there is little doubt they will work to secure their role in the post-authoritarian order that is in the process of emerging in the region.

REFERENCES

Bourdieu, Pierre. 1998. *On Television*. New York: New Press, distributed by W.W. Norton.

El-Dahshan, Mohamed. 2011. *Egyptian Women Eye Revolutionary Role*. Institute for War and Peace Reporting.

Freedom on the Net. 2011. New York: Freedom House.

Kelly, Sanja and Julia Breslin, eds. 2010. *Women's Rights in the Middle East and North Africa 2010: Progress Amid Resistance*. Lanham, MD: Freedom House.

Krahe, Dialika. 2011. "Visions of Female Identity in the New Egypt." *SpiegelOnline*, April 1. http://www.spiegel.de/international/world/0,1518,druck-754250,00.html.

Radsch, Courtney. 2008. "Core to Commonplace: The Evolution of Egypt's Blogosphere." *Arab Media & Society* Fall, no. 6.

Radsch, Courtney C. 2012. "Bloggers & Believers: Dynamics of Activism and Identity in the Muslim Brotherhood." In *Information Evolution in the Arab World*, edited by Adel Iskander, Leila Hudson, and Mimi Kirk. Washington, D.C.: Georgetown University Press.

NOTES

1. We spoke together in Denmark at a May 2011 conference titled "Cyberactivism Changing the World?"
2. Pierre Bourdieu, *On Television* (New York: New Press: Distributed by W.W. Norton, 1998), 21.
3. See the home page of *3arabawy* (blog), http://www.arabawy.org/.
4. Lina Ben Mhenni, "Manifestation pour Sidi Bouzid," *A Tunisian Girl* (blog), December 25, 2010, http://www.atunisiangirl.blogspot.com/2010/12/manifestation-pour-sidi-bouzid.html.
5. Lina Ben Mhenni, "Sidi Bouzid Brule!" *A Tunisian Girl* (blog), December 19, 2010, http://www.atunisiangirl.blogspot.com/2010/12/sidi-bouzid-brule.html.
6. Global Voices, "Tunisia: Unemployed Man's Suicide Attempt Sparks Riots," December 23, 2010, http://globalvoicesonline.org/2010/12/23/tunisia-unemployed-mans-suicide-attempt-sparks-riots/
7. Ibid.
8. Freedom House is a U.S.-based nongovernmental advocacy group that conducts research on democracy, political freedom, and human rights.
9. *Freedom on the Net* (New York: Freedom House, 2011), 324; *Internet Enemies* (Paris: Reporters Sans Frontières 2009).
10. The French term used for a female blogger.
11. Quoted in "Sidi Bouzid ou la révolte tunisienne organisée sur Facebook," *Le nouvel observateur*, April 1, 2011, http://tempsreel.nouvelobs.com/vu-sur-le-web/20110104.OBS5680/sidi-bouzid-ou-la-revolte-tunisienne-organisee-sur-facebook.html, translation by the author.
12. *Using Social Share of Voice to Anticipate Significant Events* (San Francisco: Topsy Labs, 2012), 4. Share-of-voice analysis measures the social volume of keywords mentioned on Twitter, in this case #Tunisia compared to other MENA countries.
13. "Women Make Their Power Felt in Egypt's Revolution," *The National*, 2011, http://www.thenational.ae/news/worldwide/middle-east/women-make-their-power-felt-in-egypts-revolution.
14. See Mohamed el-Dahshan, *Egyptian Women Eye Revolutionary Role* (Institute for War and Peace Reporting, 2011).
15. This is a procedure in which a woman is forcefully penetrated to see whether she bleeds in order determine if she is a virgin. At least seven women in Egypt were subjected to these "tests" by military officers who were not doctors following their arrests in Tahrir Square in March 2011.
16. Radsch, "Core to Commonplace," 2008.
17. Mohamed El Dahshan, "Egyptian Women Eye Revolutionary Role," Institute for War and Peace Reporting, March 8, 2011, http://iwpr.net/report-news/revolutionary-role-egyptian-women.
18. Nadine Naber, "Imperial Feminism, Islamophobia, and the Egyptian Revolution," *Jadaliyya*, February 11, 2011, http://www.jadaliyya.com/pages/index/616/imperial-feminism-islamophobia-and-the-egyptian-re.
19. On March 15, 2012, a military tribunal acquitted the army doctor accused of performing the so-called virginity tests in a ruling seen by many civil society activists as a setback for women's rights, and for human rights more generally.
20. See the Harassmap site at http://www.harassmap.org.
21. Author's conversation with Injy Galal and Rebecca Ciao, January 18, 2012, in Cairo.
22. Dialika Krahe, "Visions of Female Identity in the New Egypt," *SpiegelOnline*, 2011, http://www.spiegel.de/international/world/0,1518,druck-754250,00.html.

Bad Girl, Good Girl: Zines Doing Feminism

Alison Piepmeier (2009)

Grrrl zines don't simply expose the dangers of being a girl or woman in a patriarchal culture. They also often engage with familiar configurations of girlishness and femininity—playfully reclaiming and reworking them. To a certain extent, this has become an identifiable grrrl zine visual style: the kinderwhore or "kitten with a whip" aesthetic, in which girlish images are given a twist or are recontextualized in ways that change their meaning, making them tough or resistant.[1] For example, Sarah Dyer's famous anarchist Hello Kitty became an almost ubiquitous image in grrrl zines in the 1990s. There are countless examples of this phenomenon, from the celebration of children's book protagonist Pippi Longstocking in numerous grrrl zines to Cindy Crabb's use of girlish doodles, such as hearts, stars, and flowers, in conjunction with discussions of weighty subjects such as sexual assault. . . .

These reframings of femininity are examples of zines' "insubordinate creativity," and they function as challenges to corporate culture industries that position girlhood in terms of passivity and consumption.

To be sure, many grrrl zines are fronting these challenges in ways that embrace certain aspects of femininity. Rather than simply rejecting sexist culture, many zines are engaged in the project of identifying the pleasures of femininity. This work is sometimes seen as "not feminist enough" because it can be understood as complicit with patriarchal gender roles and, indeed, corporate culture; during the early 1990s heyday of the Riot Grrrl movement, "girl power" quickly became a marketing strategy, even while it was being developed as a tool of resistance. Although I understand this sort of skepticism about reclaiming femininity, I contend that this skepticism can quickly lead to a flattening of feminist resistance. According to this approach, the only appropriate feminist response to patriarchal tropes of femininity is outright rejection. Bell hooks asks,

"How do we create an oppositional worldview, a consciousness, an identity, a standpoint that exists not only as that struggle which also opposes dehumanization but as that movement which enables creative, expansive self-actualization?" She warns that in these efforts, "Opposition is not enough."[2] Like hooks, these zines and their creators suggest that a dichotomous framing of feminism's gender interventions, in which feminists are supposed to voice monolithic opposition to corporate culture, is inadequate. These zines are playing in the spaces between resistance and complicity and as such are creating third wave tactics.

One publication committed to the pleasures of femininity is *Bust* which began as a zine but is now a full-fledged professional magazine. Debbie Stoller, Laurie Henzel, and Marcelle Karp started the zine in 1993 because, as Stoller explained to me, they wanted a publication that was like *Sassy* for adult women. In particular, Stoller admired *Sassy*'s framing of girlhood as a positive space: "Whereas other teen girl magazines were saying things like, you're gonna get breasts and boys are gonna want to touch them and make sure they don't. You know, *Sassy* was kind of like, you're gonna get breasts and if someone touches them it's gonna feel really good, so pick a cute guy to do it, you know, just sort of embracing, trying to really show the positive things about being a teen girl and all the great new things you could do as a teen girl . . . rather than pretending it was always in such a negative light." She was well aware of the dangers and vulnerabilities that zines such as *Mend My Dress* (and magazines such as *Ms.*) documented, but she was searching for something different. She wanted *Bust* to create "an embraceable feminist culture that's positive, that gives us stuff that we can relate to, to talk about how difficult it is to be a woman and about how much culture is misogynist, but I wanna just try to present an alternative, just try to create an alternative that you can read and be happy and feel good about."[3]

The pleasures of girlhood and womanhood have been a theme in *Bust* since its inception. The publication has featured articles that celebrate such stereotypically feminine acts as flirting, shopping, developing your own sense of style, and lipstick. However, *Bust* also tries to broaden the terrain of fun for women, emphasizing the pleasures of more stereotypically male activities such as nonmonogamous sex, physical aggression, and swearing. As *Bust* demands pleasure for women, it also documents the cultural tension between appropriately performed womanhood and female pleasure. For instance, the second issue focused on fun, and the editors' letter offered the question, "As women, is it even acceptable for us to want to have fun? . . . we are expected to undergo a kind of pleasure-ectomy so that we may become the selfless keepers of compassion, moderation, serenity, and responsibility that is the definition of 'womanhood.'"[4] A few years later, the editors upped the ante in the "Bad Girl" issue of *Bust,* an issue that came to set the thematic course for the publication. This issue discussed the pursuit of pleasure, and the editors argued that what really makes a bad girl bad is "simply doing the one thing that is truly un-feminine: *acting on your desires.*"[5] *Bust* leverages two available cultural categories— the bad girl and the good girl—against each other, and the good girl, the one who has experienced the "pleasure-ectomy," gets pushed off the page. The bad girl becomes the primary iconographic terrain for the publication.

The bad girl is an agent rather than simply an object of desire, and *Bust*'s covers often highlight this social identity. In so doing, however, they often illustrate the tension between competing notions of femininity, the fact that, as they noted in the "Bad Girl" issue, "female badness seems to only be acceptable as long as it remains *attractive*—as long as it benefits someone else.[6] The cover of the zine's second issue challenges this emphasis on the bad girl as attractive. This cover features a cartoon of a giant female dog (note: bitch) with bared breasts, carrying a stereo, a beer, sex toys, movies, comics, and junk food. She is stomping through a theme park called "Fun City," her booming feet crushing some

of the tiny cartoon creatures below her who run for cover. She is not particularly attractive—she is, in fact, google-eyed, drooling, and dangerous—and this is at least partly the point. She is not the typical woman's magazine cover model, and therefore she doesn't function as an easily assimilable image for women to aspire to become. The discomfort this cover might produce in a reader is part of how zines work, keeping the reader from the passive consumption mindset produced by mainstream capitalist media.[7] It functions more specifically in this case to interrupt assumptions about femininity and force the reader to consider how femininity and pleasure interface.

Many other *Bust* covers enhance this tension, as well, such as the cover of the first "Sex" issue, which features a woman's enormous pregnant stomach with the word "SEX" scrawled across it, in Riot Grrrl fashion.[8] This is the pregnant woman not as beatific, sanitized symbol of maternal instinct but as sexy, bikini-wearing, defiant girl, insurgent and owning up to the act that led to the pregnancy in the first place. Again, *Bust* celebrates the bad girl as a figure who is so colorful and dramatic—even uncomfortably so—that she completely overshadows and upstages the more familiar, palatable models of appropriate femininity.

The *Bust* editors see celebrating femininity and the pleasures of femininity as a tactical political move. Stoller explained:

> When men's magazines were starting to come out, like *Details* (there was no *Maxim* yet), there was always emphasis in those magazines about men's pleasure and how fun it is to be a guy and all the great things you can do as a guy, and so that was very consciously an important part of what shaped our ideas for how to do *Bust,* that we wanted it to keep emphasizing the pleasures of being female and feminist and making it feel like it was a great, cool club to be a part of.[9]

Pleasure is an energy, a generative force and a connective one. . . . Pleasure helps create the embodied community of grrrl zines, and *Bust* is using it intentionally, as a way to mobilize their community of readers. Certainly, there are benefits for the publication: *Bust* grew from a zine to a magazine, in part, because the zine was fun to read and it promoted consumer culture as part of the enjoyment of being a woman. By the second year, the publication was running with glossy color covers, and by the time I spoke with Stoller and Henzel in 2006, they were selling nearly 100,000 copies per issue, with around 22,000 going to subscribers and the rest being sold in bookstores (the magazine is for sale in major retailers such as Barnes and Noble and Borders) and on newsstands. Even as it moved from zine to magazine status, *Bust* maintained much of its thematic focus—its celebration of the bad girl and of female pleasures in general.

Its magazine format is necessarily less intimate and inviting than the scruffy, informal publications that readers identify as "a present in the mail," and this has had consequences for the way the publication is perceived. One complication from *Bust*'s success came in 1999, when the publication was bought out by an Internet company that planned to grow the magazine but, as it turned out, "they weren't really that interested in running a magazine so the magazine was losing money with them even though it was looking great." When the stock market began to fall, the magazine's owners decided to find other investors to help grow *Bust,* but their big push for investment began with an article in the *New York Times,* which came out on September 10, 2001, the day before the terrorist attacks in New York City, Washington, D.C., and Pennsylvania. Stoller explained, "and then that was really kind of the end of it. Within a month, they closed the entire company down basically.[10]

Stoller, Henzel, and Karp were able to buy *Bust* back from its owners, a move they decided to make because they started receiving so many letters from readers expressing their love for the publication and asking what they could do to help. Stoller and Henzel explained what a frightening time that was: "We had nothing except for [the rights to publish a magazine called *Bust*]. We had no money in the bank, no money to publish the next magazine with," but their understanding of the publication and of their readership was so solid that, Stoller explained, "within six months we were able to start paying ourselves and our staff. Not very much at first, but it grew and grew."[11] It's worth noting here that, although

Bust struggled financially due to their magazine status, they benefited from an embodied community of readers who felt such attachment to the publication that they helped bring it back from ruin.

Another complication the publication has faced is that, as a successful, visible publication, *Bust* has been a lightning rod for both praise and criticism from feminists and others in a way that seems less likely within the smaller zine community. This, however, is part of what Stoller was striving for with *Bust*. She explained to me, "I never wanted it to be some well-kept secret, some little underground thing, cause that wasn't the function, the function was to reach as many people as possible and to have, to try to have an actual cultural influence."[12] The pleasures of womanhood became a successful marketing strategy for *Bust* as the pleasures of "being a guy" were for men's magazines like *Maxim.*

More than this, though, *Bust*'s deployment of pleasure also helps alter the terrain of femininity, not to mention feminism. Stoller explicitly identifies this intervention in the terrain of femininity as a form of feminist activism: "I really believe that the thing that is incredibly influential to the way we live our lives and what restricts us and what we think about ourselves is our culture and our values, and that if you can change, those are the things that really need to change."[13] It may be worth noting here that one of the ways in which self-identified third wave feminists have sought to distinguish themselves from the second wave is via this emphasis on pleasure. Several grrrl zine creators said, on conditions of anonymity, that reading more mainstream feminist publications identified with the second wave, notably *Ms.* magazine, was akin to "eating your green vegetables" or "doing your homework"—in other words, not fun.[14] *Bust* has made tactical interventions into mainstream notions of girlhood and womanhood using pleasure—the idea that it should be fun to be a girl or a woman—as their barometer for accepting or rejecting the parts of the culture with which they come into contact.

Zines that reclaim femininity are sometimes identified as enacting a version of cultural feminism, but I don't think it's useful to frame them in these terms.[15] Cultural feminism, usually defined as a feminism that celebrates women's unique perspective, is a somewhat outmoded category that doesn't capture the complexity of these zines' gender interventions. What these zines are doing is offering a contradictory stance: yes, girlhood and womanhood are dangerous, and, yes, they are culturally constructed for particular political ends, but I can do something different with them and enjoy them. On the one hand, this approach can be seen as politically suspect; indeed, in earlier writing I myself have labeled it "the feminist free-for-all" and have suggested that these sorts of actions represent the bankrupting of feminist politics.[16] But I question that stance now. Just because these zines don't offer a coherent political standpoint, just because they don't fully undermine mainstream gender performances, doesn't mean that they are complicit with cultures of domination. Again, I stress that the binary of resistant/complicit is inadequate to the task of assessing these zines (or texts more generally). In fact, I think the incompleteness I see in these zines, their "yes, but" approach to feminism and femininity, represents a valid theoretical stance, a tactical subjectivity that's keyed to this cultural moment and is characteristically third wave.

This "yes, but" approach encodes resistance and attempts to move the feminist discussion of female subjectivities beyond opposition. Johnson suggests that many young feminist scholars—and I would extend her insight to many grrrl zinesters as well—are so familiar with the discourses critical of racism, sexism, and homophobia that they do not mention them. She argues: "Our redirection does not constitute a turning away from . . . skepticism and critique . . . but a thoroughgoing acceptance of skepticism and critique as the givens of our approach, joined with a desire to go beyond them."[17] This is obviously not to say that young feminists or grrrl zinesters see racism, sexism, homophobia, or other oppressive systems as being gone; in fact, just the opposite. The cultural critique of these systems is the foundation on which they are building, but they don't necessarily stay in that space of critique, choosing, rather, to generate alternative subject positions and to tap into the pleasures of creation and cultural intervention.

There are potential problems with this approach, of course. One of the concerns regularly raised about third wave feminists is that, having come to

consciousness in a hyperindividualistic backlash culture, they often don't recognize pervasive problems or know how to address them. A related concern is that white zinesters, who make up the majority of those producing zines, often give only lip service to racism, ultimately replicating societal hierarchies around race and ethnicity. Ultimately, though, I think it would be reductive (and condescending) to understand the celebration of femininity and pleasure as merely a form of false consciousness or denial. Better to take seriously the desire to create what Stoller calls "an embraceable feminist culture that's positive," a desire that helps animate a community.

NOTES

1. Lily Burana, "Grrrls, Grrrls, Grrrls," *Entertainment Weekly* 429 (May 1, 1998), 76.
2. bell hooks, *Yearning: Race, Gender, and Cultural Politics* (Boston: South End Press, 1990), 15.
3. Debbie Stoller, personal interview.
4. Letter to the Editor, *Bust,* 1.2 (fall 1993), 2.
5. Editorial, *Bust* 7 (spring/summer 1996), 2.
6. Ibid.
7. Duncombe, *Notes from Underground,* 123.
8. *Bust* 1.4 (summer/fall 1994).
9. Stoller, personal interview.
10. Ibid.
11. Ibid.
12. Ibid. Circulation information from personal correspondence and Bust media kit, http://www.bust.com/2008mediakit.pdf. Interestingly, while Stoller always envisioned *Bust* as a magazine, Henzel, who has been the publication's creative director from the beginning, explained to me, "for the design part, I wasn't looking at real magazines as inspiration, I was really looking at zines. I was a big zine reader, so it had that feel because that's what I like. Obviously the early issues didn't look kind of the way they do now, and I wasn't looking at *Vanity Fair* and saying 'oooh,' it was a zine in my mind" (Henzel, personal interview).
13. Stoller, personal interview.
14. Personal interviews with four zine creators who asked not to be identified.
15. Kearney (*Girls Make Media*), in particular, labels grrrl zines in terms of cultural feminism.
16. Rory Dicker and Alison Piepmeier, "Introduction" to *Catching a Wave: Reclaiming Feminism for the 21st Century,* ed. Dicker and Piepmeier (Boston: Northeastern University Press, 2003), 17.

17. Merri Lisa Johnson, "Introduction: Ladies Love Your Box—The Rhetoric of Pleasure and Danger in Feminist Television Studies," in *Third Wave Feminism and Television: Jane Puts It in a Box,* ed. Johnson (New York: I. B. Tauris, 2007), 13

DISCUSSION QUESTIONS FOR CHAPTER 5

1. How do you think cultural forms shape gender? How might cultural forms function subversively to challenge traditional gender norms?

2. How is television an example of what Susan Douglas calls "enlightened sexism"? Give specific examples from current TV shows. How do these shows focus viewers' gaze away from continuing barriers to women's equality?

3. What pitfalls and possibilities do social media offer young women? How might social media be used for feminist activism?

4. How does pornography as a cultural form influence gender norms in U.S. society? How does race intersect with gender in pornography's representation of women?

5. Why do you think some critics suggest there has never been a female Shakespeare or a female da Vinci? Do you agree with this assessment? Why or why not?

SUGGESTIONS FOR FURTHER READING

Brake, Deborah. *Getting in the Game: Title IX and the Women's Sports Revolution.* New York: New York University Press, 2010.

Carson, Mina, Tisa Lewis, and Susan M. Shaw. *Girls Rock! Fifty Years of Women Making Music.* Lexington: University Press of Kentucky, 2004.

Dolan, Jill. *The Feminist Spectator in Action: Feminist Criticism for the Stage and Screen.* New York: Palgrave Macmillan, 2013.

Halberstam, J. Jack. *Gaga Feminism: Sex, Gender, and the End of Normal.* Boston: Beacon Press, 2012.

Jones, Amelia, ed. *The Feminism and Visual Culture Reader,* Second Edition. New York: Routledge, 2010.

Lee, Shayne. *Erotic Revolutionaries: Black Women, Sexuality, and Popular Culture.* Lanham, MD: Hamilton Books, 2010.

Karlyn, Kathleen Rowe. *Unruly Girls, Unrepentant Mothers: Redefining Feminism on Screen.* Austin: University of Texas Press, 2011.

Radner, Hilary, and Rebecca Stringer. *Feminism at the Movies: Understanding Gender in Contemporary Popular Cinema.* New York: Routledge, 2012.

C H A P T E R 6

Sex, Power, and Intimacy

Sexuality is a topic of great interest to most people. It entertains and intrigues and is a source of both personal happiness and frustration. It is also an aspect of our lives that is highly regulated as communities shape and control sexual desires and behaviors. Scholars emphasize that this control has emerged as a principal means of governing contemporary societies. Such regulation includes laws that condone certain relationships and sexual expressions. Regulation also involves "regimes of truth" discussed in earlier chapters, where power is more dispersed and individuals shape normative behaviors in themselves and others. A central aspect of such contemporary discourses on sexuality is the fundamental assumption that all adults should experience sexual desire. Asexual individuals who do not experience desire, and have no inclination to do so, radically challenge the prevailing normative culture. Karli June Cerankowski and Megan Milks locate asexuality as a viable sexual and social identity in their article, "New Orientations: Asexuality," emphasizing how it challenges feminist pro-sex rhetoric.

The flipside of this focus on the regulatory regimes of sexuality is that sex when freely chosen and practiced has the potential to be a liberating force. To enjoy and be in control of one's sexuality and to be able to seek a mutually fulfilling sexual relationship can be a very empowering experience. Feminists tend to value this notion of an empowered female sexuality, but may disagree about the definition of, and the path to, such empowerment, especially among adolescents. Certainly media literacy education and proficient sexuality education are central to enhancing adolescent girls' sexual empowerment. Sexual empowerment is a central theme of this chapter where we not only discuss the social construction of sexuality and provide key terms, but also focus on two themes: first, the politics of sexuality, and second, intimacy, romance, and interpersonal communication.

THE SOCIAL CONSTRUCTION OF SEXUALITY

Human sexuality involves erotic attractions, identity, and practices, and it is constructed by and through societal sexual scripts. In this sense, we perform sexuality just as we perform gender and other identities. *Sexual scripts* are guidelines for how we are supposed to feel and act as sexual persons. They are shaped by the communities and societies in which we participate and therefore are socially constructed (they emerge from communities and societies). The focus on these scripts is meant to emphasize the ways they create our understanding of "normal." People are not naturally anything, individuals' sexual desires and identities change over the course of their lives, and "normal" is a historically specific, constructed concept emerging out of human communities. In this way social scripts are socially produced and part of the discourses and broader regimes of truth that reflect social norms and practices; in other words, they provide frameworks and guidelines for sexual feelings and behaviors in particular communities at a particular time. Foundational in these scripts is the oppositional binary of heterosexuality and homosexuality that constructs normative sexuality and shapes sexual feelings and expression. By opposing heterosexuality to homosexuality, the former gains its credibility.

Sometimes there is embarrassment, shame, and confusion associated with sexual scripts, and they may easily become fraught with potential misunderstandings. As Jessica Valenti explains in "The Cult of Virginity," an excerpt from her book *The Purity Myth,* the contemporary focus on virginity as an indicator of female moral worth (the "good girl") is both problematic and confusing in an era when girls and young women are increasingly sexualized and yet simultaneously faced with abstinence movements aiming to control sexual activity. Surveys show that more than half of participating teens in "virginity pledges" become sexually active anyway, and the numbers who take precautions against pregnancy and STIs (sexually transmitted infections) was significantly lower than non-pledgers.

Sexual scripts, contextualized in specific communities and nations, shape how individuals come to develop a sense of their own sexual lives. We learn these subjective understandings by assimilating, rejecting, and ultimately negotiating the sexual scripts available to us. These subjective understandings are called *sexual self-schemas.* They can be defined as ideas and beliefs about sexual aspects of the self that are established from past and present experiences and which act to guide sexual feelings and behavior. What is desirable or acceptable to one person may be unacceptable or even disgusting to another.

Sexual identity is one aspect of sexual self-schemas that can be defined as a person's attraction to, or preference for, people of a certain gender. It is an individual's romantic and/or sexual (also called erotic) identity and behavior toward other people. Note that sexual identity does not necessarily require sexual experience or behavior. *Heterosexuality* is a sexual identity where romantic and/or sexual attachments are between people of the "opposite sex" (popularly termed *straight*). *Homosexuality* is a sexual identity where romantic and/or sexual attachments are between people of the "same sex." Because the term *homosexual* is stigmatized and because the term seems to emphasize sexual behavior, many communities have preferred the term *gay. Gay* and *homosexual* are terms inclusive of women, although they are used mainly to describe men. The term *lesbian* means the romantic and/or sexual attachment and identification between women, specifically. You might also hear the terms *dyke, butch,* and *femme. Dyke* is synonymous with lesbian, although it connotes a masculine or mannish lesbian. Like queer, dyke is a word that is used against lesbians as an insult and has been appropriated or reclaimed by lesbians with pride. This means that if you are not a member of the lesbian, gay, or queer communities, you should use these terms with care. Butch and femme are roles associated with gender that have been adopted by some lesbians, especially in the past. Butch means acting as the masculine partner, and femme means acting in a feminine role. Although today many lesbians avoid these role types because there is little incentive to mimic traditional heterosexual relationships, others enjoy these identities and appropriate them to suit themselves.

Bisexuality implies a sexual identification with both women and men. There are derogatory social connotations of bisexuality as hypersexualized that not only do these people have sex all the time, but they are doing it with both women and with men, simultaneously. Of course, to be bisexual does not imply this at all; it just means the choice of lover can be either a woman or a man. Nonetheless, these connotations reflect the fact that there are many stigmas associated with bisexuality from both the straight and the lesbian and gay communities. Although these identities are experienced and enjoyed by individuals, and therefore pragmatic for our understandings of sexuality, such definitions rely on fixed notions of "woman" or "man." In response, the term *polysexual*, defined as the attraction to multiple genders and sexual identities, is used intentionally to disrupt the binary implied in the above definitions. In other words, polysexual people are attracted to individuals from the full range of sexual identities. Importantly, however, the gendering of "people" is broader than the "woman" and "man" used above. Polysexuals are attracted to diverse sexual identities performed by a broad array of gender identities. In particular, this term critiques the heterosexual/homosexual binary implicit in the term *bisexuality*. Individuals who identify as polysexual may be attracted to transgender, two spirit, or those who identify as "genderqueer." They may also, however, still be attracted to cisgendered people of all sexual identities. Polysexuality as a sexual identity is different from *polyamory* (discussed below), defined as the desire to be intimately involved with more than one person at once. Polyamory does not imply that a person is attracted to a diversity of sexual identities, only that a person seeks multiple and simultaneous romantic encounters.

The word *queer,* traditionally meaning out of the ordinary or unusual, and historically an insult when used in the context of sexualities (most often as a derogatory term for effeminate and/or gay boys and men), has in recent times taken on new meaning. As already discussed in previous chapters, it has been reclaimed as a source of self-empowerment by those who reject the categories of straight, gay, lesbian, and bisexual, and who seek to live alternative sexual identities that are more fluid and less rigidly put into binary boxes. It is important, however, to emphasize that *queer* is not a synonym for LGBT (lesbian, gay, bisexual, trans) identity. It is a critique of "all things oppressively normal," especially conventional ideas about sex. In this sense, it embraces both gender and sexual difference. Nowadays this distinction is often lost and queer tends to be used as another alternative to lesbian and gay, thus creating a new (and perhaps more trendy) fixed category. Finally, *asexuality*, as already mentioned, involves a person who does not experience desire and attraction to others. As Cerankowski and Milks emphasize in their article, asexuality has been pathologized and medicalized and seen as a "deviance" or a "deficit." The authors question whether asexuality can be regarded as a "queer" orientation in its resistance to contemporary normative standards that expect adults to want to experience sexual desire. Note that asexuality is not about people who experience a decrease in sex drive and are distressed by it. Asexual people are those who do not experience sexual desire and are not distressed by this "lack."

Again, as emphasized in Chapter 3 and mentioned above, it is important to understand both the ways gender (the focus of Chapter 3) and sexuality (the focus of this chapter) are simultaneously distinct and intertwined. Leila Rupp's reading "A World of Difference" that discusses love and desire within the constraints of compulsory heterosexuality worldwide illustrates this point. She describes how some individuals who have been assigned female at birth cross the gender line and live as men who marry women. This occurs in societies where living as a lesbian in public is possible as well as in those where to do so is illegal. She writes that sometimes "biologically female transmen" married women and identified as lesbians and other times their desire to live as men in sexual relationships with women meant that they identified as heterosexuals. We know this is terribly confusing, but try to remember that gender is about femininity and masculinity, and sexual identity is about sexual desire and behaviors. It is possible to have multiple combinations of gendered individuals identifying with varying sexual scripts.

Finally, the term *coming out* refers to someone adopting a gay, lesbian, bisexual, or queer identity. Coming out is a psychological process that tends to involve two aspects: first, recognizing and identifying this to oneself, and second, declaring oneself in a "public" (broadly defined) way. In terms of this second aspect, individuals usually come out to affirming members in their own community before they (if ever) face a general public. Some never come out to families or coworkers for fear of rejection, reprisals, and retaliation. For some, coming out means becoming part of an identifiable political community; for others, it means functioning for the most part as something of an outsider in a straight world. The phrase *in the closet* means not being out at all. In the closet can imply that a person understands her/himself to be lesbian or gay but is not out to others. It can also imply that a person is in denial about her/his own sexuality and is not comfortable claiming a nonheterosexual identity. Given homophobia and the potential for bullying in many communities, it is easy to see how individuals are encouraged to police themselves and each other. It is important to emphasize that homophobia (fear or hatred of homosexuals, gays, lesbians, bisexuals, and/or queer people) can be especially hurtful to young people identifying as gay, lesbian, bisexual or queer. Indeed, gay youth are especially at risk for suicide, resulting in a relatively higher rate of suicides among these teens. Data show a higher rate of attempted suicides among girls and a higher rate of suicide deaths among boys. Suicidal behavior can be understood, in part, by examining risk factors—the conditions or experiences that increase the likelihood of suicide. Overall, risk factors are greater and more severe for lesbian, gay, bisexual, and queer youth, especially in situations where there is bullying and stigma. They experience higher rates of depression and substance abuse: factors associated with increased risk of suicide. They also are more likely than teens overall to lack family and community support. It is homophobia and institutionalized heterosexism that lead gay youth to kill themselves.

A focus on sexual scripts highlights the ways these discourses vary across cultures and through time and always concern issues of power (such as which groups get the authority to define "appropriate" sexual activity and the means to regulate it). *Compulsory heterosexuality,* the expectation that everyone should be heterosexual, is a central component of the regulation of sexual scripts worldwide. Also implicit in this script is the notion of *heteronormativity* or the assumption of heterosexuality as the norm or normative behavior in any given setting that regulates at the level of social policy. For example, historically in the United States, anti-miscegenation laws prevented people from different races from engaging in sexual relationships and the "Don't Ask, Don't

LEARNING ACTIVITY   **Queer Cinema**

The depictions of LGBTQ people in movies tell us a lot about how a culture frames non-dominant sexual relationships. The following movies were made in very different cultures and time periods.

- Watch several of these movies and think about what they tell us about how the culture and time period understood various sexual identities and sexual relationships. How have depictions of LGBTQ people in film changed or not over time?
- Do some research on the Web to learn about the people who produced and directed these films? Did these filmmakers have a political agenda?
- Read reviews of the films. How were the films received?
- How do you think the movement from lesbian and gay identity and politics to queer theory may affect how we analyze these films?

Movies:

- *Rope* (USA, 1948)
- *The Children's Hour* (USA, 1961)
- *Victim* (UK, 1961)
- *In a Year with Thirteen Moons* (Germany, 1978)
- *Making Love* (USA, 1982)
- *Personal Best* (USA, 1982)
- *The Hunger* (USA, 1983)
- *My Beautiful Laundrette* (UK, 1985)
- *The Color Purple* (USA, 1985)
- *The Kiss of the Spider Woman* (USA, 1985)
- *Desert Hearts* (USA, 1985)
- *I've Heard the Mermaids Singing* (Canada, 1987)
- *Torch Song Trilogy* (USA, 1988)
- *Paris Is Burning* (USA, 1990)
- *The Crying Game* (USA, 1992)
- *Longtime Companion* (USA, 1999)
- *My Own Private Idaho* (USA, 1991)
- *Philadelphia* (USA, 1993)

- *The Sum of Us* (Australia, 1994)
- *When Night Is Falling* (Canada, 1995)
- *The Incredibly True Adventures of Two Girls in Love* (USA, 1995)
- *Fire* (India, 1996)
- *The Watermelon Woman* (USA, 1996)
- *Happy Together* (Hong Kong, 1997)
- *Before Night Falls* (USA, 2000)
- *Hedwig and the Angry Inch* (USA, 2001)
- *Tropical Malady* (Thailand, 2004)
- *The Blossoming of Maximo Oliveros* (Philippines, 2005)
- *Brokeback Mountain* (USA, 2005)
- *Milk* (USA, 2008)
- *A Single Man* (USA, 2009)
- *The Kids Are All Right* (USA, 2010)

Tell" law prevented gays and lesbians from openly serving in the military. Current marriage laws in many states also provide examples of the institutionalization of sexual scripts endorsing compulsory heterosexuality into social policy. The current battle over gay marriage is case in point.

In this age of globalization, women's bodies and sexuality are increasingly the site of intense conflict as control of female sexuality carries symbolic value in many societies, both in the United States and worldwide. Imperialism and globalization have played significant

Rainbow History

1. At what New York bar did the modern gay liberation movement begin?
   a. Studio 54
   b. Stonewall
   c. Club 57
   d. Scandals

2. What were homosexuals required to wear to identify them in concentration camps during World War II?
   a. A yellow star
   b. A lavender H
   c. A pink star
   d. A pink triangle

3. What Greek letter symbolizes queer activism?
   a. Lambda
   b. Alpha
   c. Delta
   d. Sigma

4. What is the name of the religious organization that supports queer Catholics?
   a. Spirit
   b. Celebration
   c. Dignity
   d. Affirmation

5. What is the country's largest political organization working specifically for queer rights?
   a. Human Rights Campaign
   b. ACT-UP
   c. NOW
   d. Christian Coalition

6. In what year did the U.S. Congress vote to repeal "Don't Ask, Don't Tell," the military policy that prohibited gay and lesbian service members from being open about their sexual identity?
   a. 1968
   b. 1993
   c. 2001
   d. 2010

7. What show made television history by having the first gay lead character?
   a. *Soap*
   b. *Roseanne*
   c. *Ellen*
   d. *All in the Family*

8. Who was the first openly gay man elected in California (to the San Francisco Board of Supervisors in 1977)?
   a. Harvey Milk
   b. Barney Frank
   c. Allen Ginsburg
   d. Elton John

9. What was the first openly black lesbian novel published in the United States (1974)?
    a. Alice Walker's *The Color Purple*
    b. Ann Allen Shockley's *Loving Her*
    c. Gloria Naylor's *The Women of Brewster Place*
    d. Ntozake Shange's *Sassafrass, Cypress, and Indigo*

10. In 2004, which became the first state to legalize gay marriage?
    a. Iowa
    b. California
    c. Vermont
    d. Massachusetts

Answers: 1. b 2. d 3. a 4. c 5. a 6. d 7. c 8. a 9. b 10. d

roles in shaping sexual politics worldwide, in part through colonialism that functioned to organize sexual power by constructing the sexual norms and morality of indigenous societies as "exotic" and/or "uncivilized." Indeed, in terms of the colonization of the Americas, the depiction of colonized peoples as sexually perverse and/or sinful was fundamental to colonial projects. Colonialism tends to reorganize sexual relationships among indigenous communities and devalue those that are not organized around heteropatriarchy. In response to colonial rule, many nationalist movements in the Caribbean, Asia, and Africa after World War II protested and secured formal political independence. Unfortunately these gains did not necessarily ensure greater sexual autonomy for women who were often seen as the "mothers of the nation" and vital to maintaining the purity and sanctity of the nation. In addition, because women are often associated with national culture, controlling women's sexual behaviors under the guise of morality has become a question of national concern. Efforts to control women's sexual lives by religiously inspired fundamentalist social groups such as the Taliban of Afghanistan or the Religious Right in the United States are cases in point. Such forces have often criminalized LGBTQ issues in many regions of the world.

The economic, social, and cultural aspects of globalization also shape sexual identities by constraining people's sexual expressions and practices and normalizing particular sexual identities, delegitimizing and sometimes destroying local culture, and making sex into a commodity that can be bought and sold. These processes involve new media and the rapid circulation of cultural representations of sexuality worldwide, including pornography. Commodification and consumerism include increased demand for women's sexual labor, with growth in sex tourism and the global sex industry generally. However, globalization also provides opportunities for resistance and the possibilities of new sexual identities.

Certainly analyses of sexuality focusing on the United States must be contextualized in a global perspective and the struggle for sexual freedom must be understood within a broader struggle for social justice. This is a key point in Andrea Smith's reading "Dismantling Hierarchy, Queering Society." She emphasizes that any liberation struggle that does not challenge heteronormativity cannot challenge imperialism and white supremacy. This relationship between imperialism and sexuality is also a focus of Paula Gunn Allen's poem "Some Like Indians Endure." In this reading she makes connections between racism against native people and heterosexism. Both Indians and lesbians have endured and survived oppression, emphasizing the needs for social justice among these communities. Similarly, in the reading "A World of Difference," Leila Rupp writes that the multiple and diverse ways that women are able to love women worldwide concern women's rights to social justice. The right of subjects to control their sexual lives is a central component of liberation movements.

Sexual scripts vary across intersecting differences such as gender, race, class, age, ability, and so forth. This means that although gender is a significant dimension of sexual scripts, it must be understood as intersecting with other identities. Women with physical disabilities, for example, are often faced with stigma that asexualizes them and refuses to represent them as sexual beings. Kimberly Springer discusses intersections in her essay on the racialized constructions of heterosexuality for black women ("Queering Black Female Heterosexuality"). Gendered and racialized double standards of sexual conduct have condoned certain activities for men as opposed to women and for white women as opposed to black women and white men compared to black men. She suggests how the history of segregation and lynching and of caricaturing black women as asexual mammies and promiscuous "jezebels" is reproduced today as the "black woman-as-whore image in a new mass-media age." These examples emphasize how sexual scripts are heavily informed by multifaceted notions of gender.

As discussed in Chapter 3, feminine sexual scripts have often involved a double bind: To want sex is to risk being labeled promiscuous and to not want sex means potentially

World Report 2013: Lesbian, Gay, Bisexual, and Transgender Rights

Although the visibility of lesbian, gay, bisexual, and transgender people throughout the world continued to rise in 2013, their increased visibility was accompanied by attacks based on sexual orientation and gender identity. Human rights activists who sought to use the human rights framework to call to account states that participated in these rights abuses or condoned them also came under attack. In virtually every country in the world people suffered from *de jure* and *de facto* discrimination based on their actual or perceived sexual orientation. In some countries, sexual minorities lived with the very real threat of being deprived of their right to life and security of person. A small number of countries continued to impose the death penalty for private sexual acts between consenting adults.

. . .

The following examples from the Human Rights Watch's 2013 Report suggest the enormity of discrimination faced by lesbian, gay, bisexual, and transgender people worldwide, and highlight some of the progress made toward LGBT rights:

Armenia: On May 8 2012 unidentified people threw a homemade bomb at DIY, a Yerevan bar frequented by LGBT and women's rights activists. Graffiti identified LGBT people as targets. Deputy Speaker of Parliament Eduard Sharmazanov called the attack "right and justified." Police arrested two suspects who were released pending trial. Unidentified attackers destroyed bar property and made death threats against its owners in three subsequent May incidents. Police were called during each attack but intervened only once.

. . .

Honduras: Bias-motivated attacks on transgender people are a serious problem in Honduras. According to local rights advocates, more than 70 members of the lesbian, gay, bisexual, and transgender (LGBT) population were killed between September 2008 and March 2012.

The alleged involvement of members of the Honduran police in some of these violent abuses is of particular concern. Impunity for these cases has been the norm. . . .

Kuwait: In May and June 2012, the Kuwaiti police arrested hundreds of young people on spurious grounds which included "imitating the appearance of the opposite sex," practicing satanic rituals, engaging in lewd behavior and immoral activities, prostitution, and homosexuality. Many of these arrests took place during raids on private homes. A month earlier, the Justice Bloc, a Salafi parliamentary group, proposed establishing "a prosecutions office and a police force to combat crimes against public morality," which could potentially lead to an institutionalization of such crackdowns.

These crackdowns follow the arbitrary detention, ill-treatment, torture, sexual harassment, and sexual assault of scores of transgender women by the police since 2007. These arrests and abuses are a result of an amendment to article 198 of the penal code which criminalized "imitating the appearance of the opposite sex," imposing arbitrary restrictions upon individuals' rights to privacy and free expression.

Malaysia: In 2012, discrimination against lesbian, gay, bisexual, and transgender (LGBT) persons reached new levels of intensity. On June 25 2012, Prime Minister Najib publicly stated that LGBT activities do not "have a place in the country." On July 19, speaking before 11,000 imams and mosque committee members, he stated that "it is compulsory for us to fight" LGBT behavior.

. . .

Two October court rulings concerning transsexuals also caused alarm: in one, a transsexual was refused the right to change the gender recorded on her national identity card; and in the other it was ruled that Muslims born as males may not dress as females.

The government refuses to consider repeal of article 377B of the penal code which criminalizes adult consensual "carnal intercourse against the order of nature," or to replace article 377C on non-consensual sexual acts with a modern, gender-neutral law on rape.

. . .

Nigeria: Nigeria's criminal and penal codes punish consensual homosexual conduct with up to 14 years in prison. Sharia penal codes in many northern Nigerian states criminalize consensual homosexual conduct with caning, imprisonment, or death by stoning. In March (2012), a court in Nasarawa State sentenced two men to two-year prison terms for having sexual intercourse, and in September an Abuja court sentenced a man to three months in prison for sodomy.

In November 2011, the Senate passed sweepingly discriminatory legislation that would criminalize anyone who enters into or assists a same-sex marriage, or supports lesbian, gay, bisexual, or transgender groups or meetings. At this writing, the House of Representatives had passed the second reading of the bill. Similar legislation has stalled at least twice in the past amid opposition from domestic and international human rights groups.

. . .

Russia: By the end of 2012, legislation banning "homosexual propaganda" was in force in nine Russian provinces. The "propaganda" bans could be applied for such things as displaying a rainbow flag or a gay-friendly logo. In May, prominent Russian LGBT rights activist Nikolai Alekseev became the first person to be fined under the new St. Petersburg law after he picketed city hall with a poster declaring, "Homosexuality is not a perversion."

(continued)

In 2010, the European Court of Human Rights (ECtHR) had firmly rejected the Russian government's argument that there is no general consensus on issues relating to the treatment of "sexual minorities." In spite of the court's ruling, Moscow city authorities in both 2011 and 2012 banned the Gay Pride event.

. . .

Uganda: The notorious draft Anti-Homosexuality Bill, which proposes the death penalty for some consensual same-sex activities, remains tabled in parliament, threatening the rights of Uganda's LGBT people.

Zimbabwe: In Zimbabwe, where gays and lesbians frequently find themselves playing the role of "folk devils," gay-bashing follows the election cycle all too predictably, with President Robert Mugabe raising the specter of homosexuality as a way to deflect attention from the country's more pressing social, political, and economic problems. In 1995, as his regional stature was diminishing, Mugabe unleashed a vitriolic attack on gays, whom he said "offend against the law of nature and the morals of religious beliefs espoused by our society." In 2012, Mulikat Akande-Adeola, the majority leader of Nigeria's House of Representatives, was equally unequivocal when she supported a sweeping anti-LGBT bill when it passed its second reading: "It is alien to our society and culture and it must not be imported," she said. "Religion abhors it and our culture has no place for it."

Ukraine: On May 19 (2012), unidentified assailants defaced photographs at a Kiev exhibition depicting lesbian, gay, bisexual, and transgender (LGBT) families in Ukraine.

At a May 20 press conference, LGBT Pride organizers cancelled the march scheduled for that day in Kiev because police claimed they could not protect participants from potential violence from neo-Nazi and nationalist groups planning a protest at the same time and location.

After the press conference, five men beat Kiev Pride organizers Svyatoslav Sheremet and Maksim Kasyanchuk. The authorities opened a criminal investigation but failed to identify the suspects despite video recordings of the attack, and failed to consider the activists' sexual orientation or activism in the investigation.

In June, an unidentified man approached Kiev Pride head Taras Karasiichuk near his home, asked his sexual orientation, and beat him, breaking his jaw and giving him concussion. Investigators were unable to identify the attacker.

On July 2 and 9, neo-Nazis and nationalists verbally attacked and tore posters belonging to LGBT activists who were protesting in Kiev against two draft laws regarding "promotion of homosexuality" in the public domain and media. The first law, which imposes up to five years' imprisonment, was passed by parliament on October 2 in a first reading. The second law, claiming to "protect children," envisions administrative fines of up to US$1,500. On July 2, police intervened and detained one individual. On July 9, police who were present at the rally did not intervene. . . .

Source: Excerpted from The Human Rights Watch World Report 2013, *http://www.hrw.org/sites/default/files/reports /wr2013.pdf.*

being labeled frigid and a prude. For many women, sexuality is shrouded in shame and fear, and, rather than seeing themselves as subjects in their own erotic lives, women may understand themselves as objects, seen through the eyes of others. Valenti makes this point in "The Cult of Virginity" when she writes about the "ethics of passivity" that defines subjects by what they do not do. This can be compared to an ethics of autonomy or self-actualization involving the ability to initiate and enjoy being the center of one's erotic experience. Springer also advocates such autonomy and suggests black heterosexual women adopt the language of queer rights and make the case for enjoying sex "on our own terms." She advocates straight black women's refusal to acquiesce to sexist and racist representations. In addition, the relentless youth-oriented culture of contemporary U.S. society also sees "older" ("older than whom?" you may ask—note how this term encourages a mythical norm associated with young adulthood) people as less sexual, or interprets their sexuality as humorous or out of place. Much of these scripts are learned from the media and enacted in peer groups. Indeed, the increasing sexualization of young girls in media normalizes men's demands for younger sexual partners, teaches girls that to be acceptable they must be sexual, and robs children of their childhoods.

THE POLITICS OF SEXUALITY

The term *politics* used here implies issues associated with the distribution of power in sexual relationships. There are politics in sexual relationships because they occur in the context of a society that assigns power based on gender and other systems of inequality and privilege. As Andrea Smith emphasizes in the reading "Dismantling Hierarchy, Queering Society," the interconnections of systems are reflected in the concept of *heteropatriarchy:* the dominance associated with a gender binary system that presumes heterosexuality as a social norm. As mentioned above, this presumption is also called *heteronormativity.* Smith makes the case that heteropatriarchy "is the logic that makes social hierarchy seem natural." Her integration of queer politics into the analysis highlights the role of binary systems (such as straight versus gay or lesbian) in maintaining hierarchies and advocates a breaking down of these polarized categories. Smith's goal in her writing and activism is social transformation.

When people get together romantically, what results is more than the mingling of two idiosyncratic individuals. The politics of this relationship implies that people bring the baggage of their gendered lives into relationships. We negotiate gender and intersecting identities associated with systems of inequality and privilege that inform sexual scripts and shape our lives through internalized self-schemas. Although much of this is so familiar that it is thoroughly normalized and seen as completely natural, the experiences of differently gendered lives implies power, just as the intersection or confluence of all identities involves power on multiple levels.

As many feminists have pointed out, heterosexuality is organized in such a way that the power men have in society gets carried into relationships and can encourage women's subservience, sexually and emotionally. Practically, this might mean that a woman sees herself through the eyes of men, or a particular man, and strives to live up to his image of who she should be. It might mean that a woman feels that men, or again, a particular man, owns or has the right to control her body or sexuality, or that she should be the one to ease the emotional transitions of the household or tend to a man's daily needs— preparing his meals, cleaning his home, washing his clothes, raising his children—while still working outside the home. Even though a woman might choose this life and enjoy the role she has, feminists would argue that this is still an example of male domination in the private sphere where individual men benefit. They have their emotional and domestic

ACTIVIST PROFILE **Emma Goldman**

According to J. Edgar Hoover, she was one of the most dangerous women in America in the early twentieth century. Emma Goldman came to the United States from Russia as a teenager in 1885, but for a Jewish immigrant, America was not the land of opportunity she had envisioned. Rather, she found herself in slums and sweatshops, eking out a living. Goldman had witnessed the slaughter of idealist political anarchists in Russia, and in 1886 she saw the hangings of four Haymarket anarchists who had opposed Chicago's power elite. As a result of these experiences, Goldman was drawn to anarchism and became a revolutionary.

Goldman moved to New York, where she met anarchist Johann Most, who advocated the overthrow of capitalism. Most encouraged Goldman's public speaking, although she eventually began to distance herself from him, recognizing the need to work for practical and specific improvements such as higher wages and shorter working hours. In 1893 she was arrested and imprisoned for encouraging a crowd of unemployed men to take bread if they were starving.

In New York, Goldman also worked as a practical nurse in New York's ghettos where she witnessed the effects of lack of birth control and no access to abortion. She began a campaign to address this problem, and her views eventually influenced Margaret Sanger and Sanger's work to make contraception accessible. Goldman was even arrested for distributing birth control literature.

Goldman was particularly concerned about sexual politics within anarchism. She recognized that a political solution alone would not rectify the unequal relations between the sexes. Rather, she called for a transformation of values, particularly by women themselves—by asserting themselves as persons and not sex commodities, by refusing to give the right over her body to anyone, by refusing to have children unless she wants them.

Her involvement in no-conscription leagues and rallies against World War I led to her imprisonment and subsequent deportation to Russia. There she witnessed the Russian Revolution and then saw the corruption of the Bolsheviks as they amassed power. Her experience led her to reassess her earlier approval of violence as a means to social justice. Instead, she argued that violence begets counterrevolution.

Goldman remained active in Europe and continued to exercise influence in the United States. In 1922 *Nation* magazine named her one of the 12 greatest living women. In 1934 she was allowed to lecture in the United States, and in 1936 she went to Spain to participate in the Spanish Revolution. Goldman died in 1940 and was buried in Chicago near the Haymarket martyrs.

needs filled by women and are left free to work or play at what they want. Of course, their part of the bargain for these services is the expectation (whether it is fulfilled or not) that men should provide for women economically. This is an arrangement many women choose rationally.

We know that heterosexual relationships are a source of support and strength for many women; it is not heterosexuality that is faulted here but the context in which heterosexual coupling takes place. When heterosexual intimacies are grounded in unequal power relationships, it becomes more and more difficult for women and men to love in healthy ways. The politics of sexuality also come into play in lesbian/gay, bisexual, and queer relationships. Women, for example, may come together with the baggage of femininity to work out and often internalized homophobia as well. These relationships also have fewer clear models for successful partnering. An example of this is the "Are we on a date?" syndrome that occurs as two women attempt to deal with the boundaries between being platonic girlfriends and being romantically interested in each other. These relationships also occur in the context of heteronormativity and compulsory heterosexuality. For example, various institutions support and encourage heterosexual coupling and dating. Schools offer dances and proms, the entertainment industry generally assumes heterosexual dating, and there is a public holiday (Valentine's Day) that celebrates it. Even though gays and lesbians are thoroughly visible in popular media (although sometimes, as in the case of the depiction of lesbians, for the titillation of heterosexual men), these are overshadowed by the barrage of public displays of heterosexual intimacy on the Internet, on billboards, magazine covers, television shows and in the movies.

Finally, there is marriage, an institution that historically has recognized two committed people only if one is a woman and the other a man. In 2013, however, the U.S. Supreme Court found the Defense of Marriage Act (DOMA), which had made the case that marriage is only between a man and a woman, as unconstitutional. The ruling found that DOMA treated gay marriage in states where this was legal as "second-class marriages" in preventing those couples from receiving the same federal benefits. The ruling clears the way for individuals in same-sex marriages in states where there is marriage equality to receive many of the benefits of marriage entitled to heterosexual couples, such as Social Security benefits and immigration rights. As of this writing there are 17 U.S. states plus the District of Columbia which issue marriage licenses to lesbian and gay couples: Massachusetts, Connecticut, Iowa, Vermont, New Hampshire, New York, Washington, Maryland, Maine, Rhode Island, Delaware, Minnesota, California, New Jersey, Hawaii, New Mexico, Illinois, plus the Coquille Indian Tribe, the Suquamish Tribe, and the Little Traverse Bay Bands of Odawa Indians. In Utah and Oklahoma judges have issued rulings in favor of same sex marriage, but implementation has been stayed pending appeal. Same-sex marriage has been legalized through legislation, court ruling, and tribal council rulings and upheld by popular

LEARNING ACTIVITY **Reality TV**

Tune into some reality TV shows. As you watch, record observations about the behaviors, roles, and interactions of women and men. If all anyone knew about gender and heterosexual relationships was what she or he saw on reality TV, what would this person believe? How does race shape perception of these reality TV actors? Social class? Sexual identity?

Work with one or two other people in your class to devise an episode of a feminist reality TV show. What would the premise be? Into what situation would you place participants? What would the rules be? Would you have a winner? What would you call your show? Is feminist reality TV possible? Would anyone watch?

vote in a statewide referendum. Under domestic partnership laws couples usually sign a registry at the secretary of state's office and pay a fee for a domestic partnership contract that gives them similar legal rights and responsibilities as married heterosexual couples. Private employers are not required to offer health care and other benefits to domestic-partner couples, although state employees are usually covered in some form under this mandate. It is important to note that marriage equality is recognized only at the state level. Even though DOMA was struck down as unconstitutional in its treatment of gay couples legally married in a state (a violation of the Fifth Amendment), as of this writing all states get to define marriage for themselves and do not have to recognize gay marriages performed in other states.

Nonheterosexual couples often encounter obstacles when adopting children and gaining custody of and raising their biological children (products of previous heterosexual relationships, planned heterosexual encounters with the goal of conception, or artificial insemination). This is because these sexual identities are often constructed by society as an immoral and abnormal "choice" that could have negative consequences for children. It has generally been assumed by the dominant culture that children of homosexual parents will grow up to be homosexual, although all the evidence shows that this is indeed not the case. Despite research that suggests that lesbians make fine mothers and lesbian couples fine parents, there are strong social imperatives against lesbian child rearing. A related prejudice is the notion that gays, lesbians, bisexuals, and queer-identified people abuse or recruit children. These negative and misinformed stereotypes reinforce homophobia and help maintain heterosexism. Research shows overwhelmingly that it is heterosexual males who are the major predators of children. Nonetheless, because of these societal stigmas LBGQT parents encounter obstacles concerning voluntary parenting, and, in addition, are often not welcome in occupations involving children.

LEARNING ACTIVITY   **Heteronormativity: It's Everywhere**

Heterosexism is maintained by the illusion that heterosexuality is the norm. This illusion is partly kept in place by the visibility of heterosexuality and the invisibility of other forms of sexuality. To begin to think about the pervasiveness of heterosexuality, grab a clipboard, pen, and paper and keep a tally.

- Go to a card store and peruse the cards in the "love" and "anniversary" sections. How many depict heterosexual couples? How many depict same-sex couples? What options are there for customers who wish to buy a card for a same-sex partner?
- Look at the advertisements in one of your favorite magazines. How many pictures of heterosexual couples do you find? How many pictures of same-sex couples? If a photo is of a man or woman alone, do you automatically assume the person is heterosexual? Or is that assumption so deep-seated that you don't even think about it at all?
- Watch the commercials during your favorite hour of television. How many images of heterosexual couples do you see? Of same-sex couples?
- Go to the mall or a park and people-watch for an hour. How many heterosexual couples holding hands do you see? How many same-sex couples?

In this way, sexual self-schemas develop in a social context and are framed by the various workings of power in society. This section has emphasized how politics—the workings of power—influence and shape every aspect of sexual relationships. On the macro (societal) level these politics are often represented in the forms of public debates about sexuality (like marriage equality, reproductive rights, sex education, interpersonal violence) that are also experienced on the individual level. This micro (individual) level analysis is the topic of the next section of this chapter.

INTIMACIES

Courtship is an old-fashioned word, but it means that period when two people are attracted to each other, develop intimacy, enjoy each other's company, and identify as a couple. In contemporary U.S. society this period usually involves dating, although what "dating" means changes across time and place and is heavily influenced by popular culture and the technologies of the time. Cell phones and online dating sites, for example, have influenced communication in relationships, altering notions of public and private conversations, and encouraging the accessibility of individuals to each other. An essential aspect of courtship and dating is the development of romantic love: a mainstay of our culture and one of the most important mythologies of our time. *Romantic love* is about a couple coming together, sharing the excitement of an erotic relationship, and feeling united with the other in such a way that the object of their love is unique and irreplaceable. The clichés of love abound: Love is blind; love is painful; love means never having to say you're sorry; love conquers all; and so forth. "Gate C22," the poem by Ellen Bass, counters the idea that love happens only for young, "beautiful" people, and shows how expressions of love move us as humans.

Romantic love is a cultural phenomenon and not necessarily a basis for marriage. While of course romantic love and sexual attraction have always been present in marriage and other domestic relationships through time, its value as a prerequisite for most contemporary marriages in societies of the global north is a relatively modern notion. Indeed, there is a tight relationship between romantic love as an ideology and consumer culture as an industrial development. Prior to the twentieth century, dating as we know it did not exist. As dating developed after the turn of the twentieth century, it quickly became associated with consuming products and going places. The emerging movie industry glamorized romance and associated it with luxury products; the automobile industry provided

LEARNING ACTIVITY   **It's in the Cards**

Go to a local card shop and browse through the cards in the "love" or "romance" sections. What are their messages about heterosexual relationships? How do cards targeted toward women differ from cards targeted toward men?

Now get creative. Design a feminist romance greeting card. How does it differ from the ones you saw at the card shop? How do you think the recipient will feel about this card? Now, if you're really brave, send it to the one you love.

those who could afford it with the allure of travel, getaways, and private intimacy; and dance halls allowed close contact between men and women in public. Romance became a commodity that could be purchased, and it made great promises. Women were (and still are) encouraged to purchase certain products with the promise of romantic love. Fashion and makeup industries began revolving around the prospect of romantic love, and the norms associated with feminine beauty became tied to glamorous, romantic images. Romantic love came to be seen as women's special domain; women were encouraged to spend enormous emotional energy, time, and money in the pursuit and maintenance of romantic love.

Romantic love is fun; it can be the spice of life and perhaps one of the most entertaining features of women's lives. In particular, it often contrasts starkly with our working lives because romance is associated with leisure, entertainment, and escape. At the same time, however, romantic love and its pursuit have become the means by which women are encouraged to form relationships and the justification for tolerating inequities in interpersonal relationships, both straight and lesbian/queer. Many scholars suggest that romance is one of the key ways that sexism is maintained in society.

When it comes to sexuality, romantic love plays a large part in feminine sexual scripts. Research suggests that women as a social group seem to be more likely than men to make sense of sexual encounters in terms of the amount of intimacy experienced so that love becomes a rationale for sex. If I am in love, women might reason, sex is okay. Men as a social group seem more easily to accept sex for its own sake, with no emotional strings necessarily attached. In this way, sexual scripts for men have involved more of an *instrumental* (sex for its own sake) approach, whereas for women it tends to be more *expressive* (sex involving emotional attachments). There is evidence to suggest that women are moving in the direction of sex as an end in itself without the normative constraints of an emotional relationship. By and large, however, women as a group are still more likely than men to engage in sex as an act of love. *Polyamory* is the practice, desire, or acceptance of having more than one intimate relationship at a time with the knowledge and consent of everyone involved. It is distinct from both swinging (which emphasizes sex with others as merely recreational) and polysexuality (discussed above). Polyamory, often abbreviated as poly, is often described as "consensual, ethical, and responsible non-monogamy." The practice emphasizes ethics, honesty, and transparency.

As romantic relationships develop, individuals may become physically intimate and sexually active. These sexual practices can include kissing, hugging, petting, snuggling, caressing, oral sex (oral stimulation of genital area), penis in vagina sex, and anal sex (sexual stimulation of the anus with fingers, penis, or other object). Note how "foreplay" (in this case meaning heterosexual behaviors before "the act" of vaginal penetration) is often not defined as "sex," although, ironically, "foreplay" often is expressed as the sexual activity heterosexual women most enjoy. Lesbians do many of the same things as straight couples, although there is no penis–vagina sex. Some women, straight and lesbian, use dildos (penis-shaped objects that can be inserted into a bodily opening) when they are having sex or during masturbation (sexual self-stimulation), and some straight women use dildos to penetrate male partners during sexual intercourse.

In heterosexual relationships, sexual scripts tend to encourage men to be sexual initiators and sexually more dominant. Although this is not always the case, women who do initiate sex often run the risk of being labeled with terms that are synonymous with "slut." Having one person in the relationship more sexually assertive and the other more passive

LEARNING ACTIVITY **Cybersex**

The growth of technology has created a new form for sexual expression: cybersex. You can create a persona, meet someone online, and have cybersex—with no risk of disease, no commitment, no regrets in the morning. Right? Maybe, but maybe not. On the one hand, cybersex does present an opportunity for a different kind of sexual exploration. On the other, cybersex may raise real problems of isolation, harassment, addiction, and infidelity. Spend a little time surfing the Web for information about cybersex. Then make a list of the pros and cons. How might cybersex be different for women and men? What role does gender play in cybersex? What role does race play? How does sexual identity come into play? How do you think feminists might evaluate cybersex? Would they see it as potentially liberating for women? Or might it reinforce male sexual dominance?

Consider organizing a faculty panel to talk about these issues on your campus. Be sure to include a variety of disciplinary perspectives—women's and gender studies, sociology, psychology, ethnic studies, philosophy, communication, computer science, religion, anthropology, disability studies.

is different from sado-masochistic sexual practices (S and M) where one person takes a domineering role and the other becomes dominated. There are both heterosexuals and homosexuals who enjoy sado-masochistic practices. Although usually consensual, S and M can also be coercive, in which case it functions as a form of violence.

Emotional intimacy can be defined as sharing aspects of the self with others with the goal of mutual understanding. Intimacy can sometimes be a source of conflict in heterosexual relationships because women tend to be more skilled at intimacy than men. Traditionally, individuals who identify as women have been socialized to be emotional and emotionally expressive, and those who identify as men have been socialized to put their energy into shaping culture and society and to be more reserved about interpersonal emotional issues. As explained in Chapter 3, this does not mean, of course, that all women in sexual relationships demonstrate these traits or that all men do not. Instead these behaviors illustrate gendered sexual performances that we call "feminine" or "masculine" and which intersect with social learning associated with other identities. Although girls and women are more likely to be socialized to perform femininity, and boys and men masculinity (whatever that might mean in a given community), anyone can act in feminine ways and/or masculine ways in intimate relationships. We all know of boys or men who demonstrate more feminine traits and are more skilled at expressing emotions than some women even though this might not be the norm. Gender is a learned performance that shapes the experiences of intimacy in any given setting.

Some scholars have suggested that women are inherently better at connecting with others and that this skill is rooted in early childhood psychosexual development that reflects the fact that girls have a continuous relationship and identification with a maternal figure, unlike boys, who have to break from the mother to identify with the masculine. Others have focused on the social context of childhood skill acquisition. They suggest that the interpersonal skills girls learn at an early age are a result of social learning. Certainly

HISTORICAL MOMENT **The Faked Orgasm**

From "Venus Observed" by Ruth Davis in *Women: A Journal of Liberation,* 1972, Davis, CA.

In the early days of the second wave of the Women's Movement, women gathered in small consciousness-raising groups to talk about their experiences as women, and, of course, sooner or later, the conversation turned to sex. What surprised most women as they began to talk openly was that they were not the only ones ever to fake orgasm. While the sexual revolution was rolling on for men, opening greater and greater access to sexual exploits with lots of women, women were finding themselves continuing to fall into the role prescribed by their gender— pleasing men sexually even when they themselves were not being satisfied. But as the Women's Movement began to have an impact, women came to expect to be equal partners in the sexual revolution . . . and that meant no longer faking orgasms.

In 1968 Anne Koedt wrote "The Myth of the Vaginal Orgasm," denouncing Freud's construction of the vaginal orgasm as the truly mature sexual response and denigrating the clitoral orgasm as "infantile." She argued that by marginalizing the clitoris, Freud and other doctors and scientists had controlled women's sexuality and had made women feel sexually inadequate for not achieving vaginal orgasm. Soon, the "faked orgasm" became a metaphor for women's sexual exploitation.

And feminists offered a variety of solutions, from sex toys to celibacy. In 1970, Shulamith Firestone argued that sex, not social class, was the root of all oppression. In *The Dialectic of Sex,* she argued that reproductive technologies should be pursued to deliver women from the tyranny of their biology.

Germaine Greer, author of *The Female Eunuch,* contended that all women should become sexually liberated, and she advocated a strike, the withdrawal of women from sexual labor. She said that women should have the same sexual freedom as men and, if need be, should use men for sexual pleasure.

The debate about sexuality swirled among feminists through the 70s, encompassing issues ranging from pornography to rape, abortion to prostitution. And while the question of the dangers and/or pleasures of sex remained an open one, the raising of the question itself had made an important mark on the consciousness of American women.

Source: Ruth Rosen, *The World Split Open* (New York: Viking, 2000).

these skills are useful for women in terms of intimacy generally, and in terms of their role as keepers of heterosexual relationships in particular. For example, girls are more likely to play games that involve communication: talking and listening, as well as taking the role of the other through imaginary role-playing games. Boys, on the other hand, are more likely to play rule-bound games where the "rights" and "wrongs" of the game are predetermined rather than negotiated. As a result, girls learn to notice and are trained to be perceptive. They learn to be sensitive of others' feelings, and become more willing to do emotional work. Boys are often raised to repress and deny their inner thoughts and ignore their fears. As Michael Kimmel explains in "What's Up with Boys?" (his dialogue with Christina Hoff Sommers) in Chapter 3, boys are taught that feelings are feminine or are for sissies. Girls become more comfortable with intimacy, and boys learn to shy away from it because intimacy is often seen as synonymous with weakness. Boys learn to camouflage feelings under a veneer of calm and rationality because fears are not manly. Importantly, as boys grow up they learn to rely on women to take care of their emotional needs, and girls learn that this request is part of being a woman.

Because emotional intimacy is about self-disclosure and revealing oneself to others, when people are intimate with each other, they open themselves to vulnerability. In the process of becoming intimate, one person shares feelings and information about her/himself, and then the other person (if that person wants to maintain and develop intimacy) responds by sharing too. In turn each gives away little pieces of her/himself, and, in return, mutual trust, understanding, and friendship develop. Given the baggage of gender, however, what can happen is that one person does more of the giving away, and the other reveals less; one opens up to being vulnerable, and the other maintains personal power. The first person also takes on the role of helping the other share, drawing that person out, translating ordinary messages for their hidden emotional meanings, and investing greater amounts of energy into interpersonal communication. The first person has taken the role prescribed by femininity and the latter the role that masculinity endorses. The important point here is that intimacy is about power. Men who take on masculine scripts tend to be less able to open themselves up because of anxiety associated with being vulnerable and potentially losing personal power. Again, anyone can take on masculine or feminine sexual scripts.

Central in understanding masculine sexual scripts and issues around emotional intimacy is the mandate against homosexuality. Because boys and men may play rough and work closely together—touching each other physically in sports and other masculine pursuits—there are lots of opportunities for *homoeroticism* (arousal of sexual feelings through contact with people of the same sex). In response to this, strong norms against homosexuality (examples of "regimes of truth") regulate masculine behavior—norms fed by homophobia and enforced by such institutions as education, sports, media, family, the military, and the state. In the United States these norms tend to discourage men from showing affection with each other and thus discourage intimacy between men. They also encourage male bonding where women may function as objects in order for men to assert sexual potency as "real" heterosexuals. Examples of this include women as entertainment for various kinds of stag parties, women as pinups in places where men live and/or work together, and, in the extreme, gang rape. Homophobia serves to keep women apart too, of course. In particular, women are encouraged to give up the love of other women in order to gain the approval of men. However, compared with men, women in the United States tend to have more opportunities for intimacies between friends. This is also demonstrated in language about friendships: Women friends call each other "girlfriend" with no sexual innuendo, while men tend not to call their platonic male friends "boyfriend."

Copyright © 1992 by Nicole Hollander. Used by permission of Nicole Hollander.

A key aspect of intimacy, and thus sexuality, is interpersonal communication. Again, the ways we communicate in relationships have a lot to do with gender, as well as membership in other communities with specific norms about social interaction, including verbal language spoken and nonverbal language expressed. Feminine and masculine speech varies in the following ways: First, in terms of speech patterns, feminine speech is more polite, less profane and uses more standard forms. More fillers like "um," hedges like "sort of" and "I guess," and intensifiers like "really" and "very" are used. In addition, feminine speech involves tag questions on statements like "It's hot today, isn't it?" and often turns an imperative into a question: "Would you mind opening the door?" rather than "Open the door!" All these forms of speaking are less authoritative. Note again that although women in U.S. society are more likely to use feminine speech and men to use masculine speech, anyone can learn these speech patterns and they also vary by membership in other identities and communities. Indeed, women are often trained in masculine speech to function effectively in authority positions or careers in which an assertive communication style is necessary or most productive.

Second, feminine speech tends to use different intonations with a higher pitch that is recognized as less credible and assertive than a lower pitch. This speech has more emotional affect and is more likely to end with a raised pitch that sounds like a question and gives a hesitant quality to speaking.

Third, feminine speech differs from masculine speech in that the latter involves more direct interruptions of other speakers. Listening to real people talking, we find that although

IDEAS FOR ACTIVISM

- Work with various women's groups on your campus to develop, publish, and distribute a "Check Up on Your Relationship" brochure. This brochure should contain a checklist of signs for emotional/physical/sexual abuse and resources to get help.
- Organize and present a forum on healthy dating practices.
- Organize a clothes drive for your local women's shelter.
- Research gay rights, such as protection against discrimination in employment or housing, domestic partner benefits, or hate crimes legislation in your city or state. If you find that gay, lesbian, bisexual, or transgender people in your area do not enjoy full civil rights, write your government officials to encourage them to enact policies providing civil rights for queer people.
- Organize a National Coming Out Day celebration on your campus.
- Organize an event on your campus in recognition of World AIDS Day, which is December 1.
- Become a member of the Human Rights Campaign. For more information see *www.hrc.org*.

men and women interrupt at about the same rate in same-sex conversations (women interrupting women, and men interrupting men), in mixed groups men interrupt other speakers more than women do, and men are more likely to change the subject in the process, whereas women tend to interrupt to add to the story with their own experiences and thoughts. Although there are cultural differences around interruptions, it is clear that who interrupts and who gets interrupted is about power.

Fourth, feminine speech patterns involve more confirmation and reinforcement, such as "Yes, go on" or "I hear you" or "uh-huh." Examples of nonverbal confirmation of the speaker might include leaning forward, eye contact, and nodding, although these behaviors may vary (as does all social interaction) across communities.

Finally, feminine speech and masculine speech fulfill different functions. Feminine speech tends to work toward maintaining relationships, developing rapport, avoiding conflict, and maintaining cooperation. Masculine speech, on the other hand, is more likely oriented toward attracting and maintaining an audience, asserting power and dominance, and giving information. Given these gendered differences in communication, it is easy to see how problems might arise in interpersonal interaction generally and in sexual relationships in particular, and how these issues are related to the give-and-take of interpersonal power.

In this way, sexual intimacy is as much about sexual scripts taught and regulated by society as it is about physiology. Sexuality is wound up with our understandings of gender as well as other intersecting identities that shape our sense of ourselves as sexual persons. These social constructs encourage us to feel desire and enjoy certain sexual practices and relationships, and they guide the meanings we associate with our experiences.

The Cult of Virginity

Jessica Valenti (2009)

In the moments after I first had sex, my then-boyfriend—lying down next to me over his lint-covered blanket—grabbed a pen from his nightstand and drew a heart on the wall molding above his bed with our initials and the date inside. The only way you could see it was by lying flat on the bed with your head smashed up against the wall. Crooked necks aside, it was a sweet gesture, one that I'd forgotten about until I started writing this book.

The date seemed so important to us at the time, even though the event itself was hardly awe-inspiring. There was the expected fumbling, a joke about his fish-printed boxers, and ensuing condom difficulties. At one point, his best friend even called to see how things were going. I suppose romance and discretion are lost on sixteen-year-olds from Brooklyn. Yet we celebrated our "anniversary" every year until we broke up, when Josh left for college two years before me and met a girl with a lip ring.

I've often wondered what that date marks—the day I became a woman? Considering I still bought underwear in cutesy three-packs, and that I certainly hadn't mastered the art of speaking my mind, I've gotta go with no. Societal standards would have me believe that it was the day I became morally sullied, but I fail to see how anything that lasts less than five minutes can have such an indelible ethical impact—so it's not that, either.

Really, the only meaning it had (besides a little bit of pain and a lot of postcoital embarrassment) was the meaning that Josh and I ascribed to it. Or so I thought. I hadn't counted on the meaning my peers, my parents, and society would imbue it with on my behalf.

From that date on—in the small, incestuous world of high school friendships, nothing is a secret for long—I was a "sexually active teen," a term often used in tandem with phrases like "at risk,"

or alongside warnings about drug and alcohol use, regardless of how uncontroversial the sex itself may have been. Through the rest of high school, whenever I had a date, my peers assumed that I had had sex because my sexuality had been defined by that one moment when my virginity was lost. It meant that I was no longer discriminating, no longer "good." The perceived change in my social value wasn't lost on my parents, either; before I graduated high school, my mother found an empty condom wrapper in my bag and remarked that if I kept having sex, no one would want to marry me.

I realize that my experience isn't necessarily representative of most women's—everyone has their own story—but there are common themes in so many young women's sexual journeys. Sometimes it's shame. Sometimes its violence. Sometimes it's pleasure. And sometimes it's simply nothing to write home about.

The idea that virginity (or loss thereof) can profoundly affect women's lives is certainly nothing new. But what virginity is, what it was, and how it's being used now to punish women and roll back their rights is at the core of the purity myth. Because today, in a world where porn culture and reenergized abstinence movements collide, the moral panic myth about young women's supposed promiscuity is diverting attention from the real problem—that women are still being judged (sometimes to death) on something that doesn't really exist: virginity.

THE VIRGINITY MYSTERY

Before Hanne Blank wrote her book *Virgin: The Untouched History,* she had a bit of a problem. Blank was answering teens' questions on Scarleteen[1]—a sex education website she founded with writer

Heather Corinna so that young people could access information about sex online, other than porn and Net Nanny—when she discovered that she kept hitting a roadblock when it came to the topic of virginity.

"One of the questions that kept coming up was 'I did such-and-such. Am I still a virgin?'" Blank told me in an interview. "They desperately wanted an authoritative answer."

But she just didn't have one. So Blank decided to spend some time in Harvard's medical school library to find a definitive answer for her young web browsers.

"I spent about a week looking through everything I could—medical dictionaries, encyclopedias, anatomies—trying to find some sort of diagnostic standard for virginity," Blank said.

The problem was, there was no standard. Either a book wouldn't mention virginity at all or it would provide a definition that wasn't medical, but subjective.

"Then it dawned on me—I'm in arguably one of the best medical libraries in the world, scouring their stacks, and I'm not finding anything close to a medical definition for virginity. And I thought, *That's really weird. That's just flat-out strange.*"

Blank said she found it odd mostly because everyone, including doctors, talks about virginity as if they know what it is—but no one ever bothers to mention the truth: "People have been talking authoritatively about virginity for thousands of years, yet we don't even have a working medical definition for it!"

Blank now refers to virginity as "the state of having not had partnered sex." But if virginity is simply the first time someone has sex, then what is sex? If it's just heterosexual intercourse, then we'd have to come to the fairly ridiculous conclusion that all lesbians and gay men are virgins, and that different kinds of intimacy, like oral sex, mean nothing. And even using the straight-intercourse model of sex as a gauge, we'd have to get into the down-and-dirty conversation of what constitutes penetration.

Since I've become convinced that virginity is a sham being perpetrated against women, I decided to turn to other people to see how they "count" sex. Most say it's penetration. Some say it's oral sex. My

closest friend, Kate, a lesbian, has the best answer to date (a rule I've followed since she shared it with me): It isn't sex unless you've had an orgasm. That's a pleasure-based, non-heteronormative way of marking intimacy if I've ever heard one. Of course, this way of defining sex isn't likely to be very popular among the straight-male sect, given that some would probably end up not counting for many of their partners.

But any way you cut it, virginity is just too subjective to pretend we can define it.

Laura Carpenter, a professor at Vanderbilt University and the author of *Virginity Lost: An Intimate Portrait of First Sexual Experiences,* told me that she wrote her book, she was loath to even use the word "virginity," lest she propagate the notion that there's one concrete definition for it.[2]

"What is this thing, this social phenomenon? I think the emphasis put on virginity, particularly for women, causes a lot more harm than good," said Carpenter.[3]

This has much to do with the fact that "virgin" is almost always synonymous with "woman." Virgin sacrifices, popping cherries, white dresses, supposed vaginal tightness, you name it. Outside of the occasional reference to the male virgin in the form of a goofy movie about horny teenage boys, virginity is pretty much all about women. Even the dictionary definitions of "virgin" cite an "unmarried girl or woman" or a "religious woman, esp. a saint."[4] No such definition exists for men or boys.

It's this inextricable relationship between sexual purity and women—how we're either virgins or not virgins—that makes the very concept of virginity so dangerous and so necessary to do away with.

Admittedly, it would be hard to dismiss virginity as we know it altogether, considering the meaning it has in so many people's—especially women's— lives. When I suggest that virginity is a lie told to women, I don't aim to discount or make light of how important the current social idea of virginity is for people. Culture, religion, and social beliefs influence the role that virginity and sexuality play in women's lives—sometimes very positively. So, to be clear, when I argue for an end to the idea of virginity, it's because I believe sexual intimacy should be honored and respected, but that it shouldn't be revered at the expense of women's well-being, or seen as such an integral part of female identity that we end up defining ourselves by our sexuality.

I also can't discount that no matter what personal meaning each woman gives virginity, it's people who have social and political influence who ultimately get to decide what virginity means—at least, as it affects women on a large scale.

VIRGINITY: COMMODITY, MORALITY, OR FARCE?

It's hard to know when people started caring about virginity, but we do know that men, or male-led institutions, have always been the ones that get to define and assign value to virginity.

Blank posits that a long-standing historical interest in virginity is about establishing paternity (if a man marries a virgin, he can be reasonably sure the child she bears is his) and about using women's sexuality as a commodity. Either way, the notion has always been deeply entrenched in patriarchy and male ownership.

> Raising daughters of quality became another model of production, as valuable as breeding healthy sheep, weaving sturdy cloth, or bringing in a good harvest. . . . The gesture is now generally symbolic in the first world, but we nonetheless still observe the custom of the father "giving" his daughter in marriage. Up until the last century or so, however, when laws were liberalized to allow women to stand as full citizens in their own right, this represented a literal transfer of property from a father's household to a husband's.[5]

That's why women who had sex were (and still are, at times) referred to as "damaged goods"—because they were literally just that: something to be owned, traded, bought, and sold.

But long gone are the days when women were property . . . or so we'd like to think. It's not just wedding traditions or outdated laws that name women's virginity as a commodity; women's virginity, our sexuality, is still assigned a value by a movement with more power and influence in American society than we'd probably like to admit.

I like to call this movement the virginity movement. And it is a movement, indeed—with conservatives and evangelical Christians at the helm, and our government, school systems, and social institutions taking orders. Composed of antifeminist think tanks like the Independent Women's Forum and Concerned Women for America; abstinence-only "educators" and organizations; religious leaders; and legislators with regressive social values, the virginity movement is much more than just the same old sexism; it's a targeted and well-funded backlash that is rolling back women's rights using revamped and modernized definitions of purity, morality, and sexuality. Its goals are mired in old-school gender roles, and the tool it's using is young women's sexuality. (What better way to get people to pay attention to your cause than to frame it in terms of teenage girls' having, or not having, sex? It's salacious!)

And, like it or not, the members of the virginity movement are the people who are defining virginity—and, to a large extent, sexuality—in America. Now, instead of women's virginity being explicitly bought and sold with dowries and business deals, it's being defined as little more than a stand-in for actual morality.

It's genius, really. Shame women into being chaste and tell them that all they have to do to be "good" is not have sex. (Of course, chastity and purity, as defined by the virginity movement, are not just about abstaining sexually so much as they're about upholding a specific, passive model of womanhood.)

For women especially, virginity has become the easy answer—the morality quick fix. You can be vapid, stupid, and unethical, but so long as you've never had sex, you're a "good" (i.e., "moral") girl and therefore worthy of praise.

Present-day American society—whether through pop culture, religion, or institutions—conflates sexuality and morality constantly. Idolizing virginity as a stand-in for women's morality means that nothing else matters—not what we accomplish, not what we think, not what we care about and work for. Just if/how/whom we have sex with. That's all.

Just look at the women we venerate for not having sex: pageant queens who run on abstinence platforms, pop singers who share their virginal status, and religious women who "save themselves" for marriage. It's an interesting state of affairs when women have to simply do, well, *nothing* in order to be considered ethical role models. As Feministing .com commenter electron-Blue noted in response to the 2008 *New York Times Magazine* article, "Students of Virginity," on abstinence clubs at Ivy League colleges, "There were a WHOLE LOTTA us not having sex at Harvard . . . but none of us thought that that was special enough to start a club about it, for pete's sake."[6]

But for plenty of women across the country, it *is* special. Staying "pure" and "innocent" is touted as the greatest thing we can do. However, equating this inaction with morality not only is problematic because it continues to tie women's ethics to our bodies, but also is downright insulting because it suggests that women can't be moral actors. Instead, we're defined by what we don't do—our ethics are the ethics of passivity. (This model of ethics fits in perfectly with how the virginity movement defines the ideal woman.)

. . .

But it's not only abstinence education or conservative propaganda that are perpetuating this message; you need look no further than pop culture for stark examples of how young people—especially young women—are taught to use virginity as an easy ethical road map.

A 2007 episode of the MTV documentary series *True Life* featured celibate youth.[7] Among the teens choosing to abstain because of disease concerns and religious commitments was nineteen-year-old Kristin from Nashville, Tennessee. Kristin had cheated on her past boyfriends, and told the camera she'd decided to remain celibate until she feels she can be faithful to her current boyfriend. Clearly, Kristin's problem isn't sex—it's trust. But instead of dealing with the actual issues behind her relationship woes, this young woman was able to circumvent any real self-analysis by simply claiming to be abstinent. So long as she's chaste, she's good.

Or consider singer and reality television celebrity Jessica Simpson, who has made her career largely by playing on the sexy-virgin stereotype. Simpson, the daughter of a Baptist youth minister, started her singing career by touring Christian youth festivals and True Love Waits events. Even when she went mainstream, she publicly declared her virginity—stating that her father had given her a promise ring when she was twelve years old—and spoke of her intention to wait to have sex until marriage. Meanwhile, not surprisingly, Simpson was being marketed as a major sex symbol—all blond hair, breasts, and giggles. Especially giggles. Simpson's character (and I use the word "character" because it's hard to know what was actually her and not a finely honed image) was sold as the archetypal dumb blond. Thoughtless moments on *Newlyweds,* the MTV show that followed her short-lived marriage to singer Nick Lachey, became nationally known sound bites, such as Simpson's wondering aloud whether tuna was chicken or fish, since the can read "Chicken of the Sea."

Despite Simpson's public persona as an airhead (as recently as 2008, she was featured in a Macy's commercial as not understanding how to flick on a light switch), women are supposed to want to be her, not only because she's beautiful by conventional standards, but also because she adheres to the social structures that tell women that they exist purely for men: as a virgin, as a sex symbol, or, in Simpson's case, as both. It doesn't matter that Simpson reveals few of her actual thoughts or moral beliefs; it's enough that she's "pure," even if that purity means she's a bit of a dolt.

For those women who can't keep up the front as well as someone like Simpson, they suffer heaps of judgment—especially when they fall off the pedestal they're posed upon so perfectly. American pop culture, especially, has an interesting new trend of venerating and fetishizing "pure" young women—whether they're celebrities, beauty queens, or just everyday young woman—simply to bask in their eventual fall.

And no one embodies the "perfect" young American like beauty queens. They're pretty, overwhelmingly white, thin, and eager to please. And, of course, pageant queens are supposed to be pure as pure can be. In fact, until 1999, the Miss America pageant had a "purity rule" that barred divorced women and those who had obtained abortions from entering the contest—lest they sully the competition, I suppose.[8]

So in 2006, when two of those "perfect" girls made the news for being in scandalous photos on the Internet, supposed promiscuity, or a combination thereof, Americans were transfixed.

First, twenty-year-old Miss USA Tara Conner was nearly stripped of her title after reports surfaced that she frequented nightclubs, drank, and dated. Hardly unusual behavior for a young woman, regardless of how many tiaras she may have.

The *New York Daily News* could barely contain its slut-shaming glee when it reported on the story: "'She really is a small-town girl. She just went wild when she came to the city,' one nightlife veteran said. 'Tara just couldn't handle herself. They were sneaking those [nightclub] guys in and out of the apartment' . . . Conner still brought boyfriends home. . . . Soon she broke up with her hometown fiancé and started dating around in the Manhattan nightclub world. . . .'"[9]

Instead of having her crown taken away, however, Conner was publicly "forgiven" by Miss USA co-owner Donald Trump, who appeared at a press conference to publicly declare he was giving the young woman a second chance.[10] In case you had any doubts about whether this controversy was all tied up with male ownership and approval, consider the fact that Trump later reportedly considered giving his permission for Conner to pose for *Playboy* magazine. He played the role of dad, pimp, and owner, all rolled into one.[11]

Mere days later, Miss Nevada USA, twenty-two-year-old Katie Rees, was dethroned after pictures of her exposing one of her breasts and mooning the camera were uncovered.[12] When you're on a pedestal, you have a long way to fall.

. . .

Shaming young women for being sexual is nothing new, but it's curious to observe how the expectation of purity gets played out through the women who are supposed to epitomize the feminine ideal: the "desirable" virgin. After all, we rarely see women who aren't conventionally beautiful idolized for their abstinence. And no matter how "good" you are otherwise—even if you're an all-American beauty queen—if you're not virginal, you're shamed.

The desirable virgin is sexy but not sexual. She's young, white, and skinny. She's a cheerleader, a baby sitter; she's accessible and eager to please (remember those ethics of passivity!). She's never a woman of color. She's never a low-income girl or a fat girl. She's never disabled. "Virgin" is a designation for those who meet a certain standard of what women, especially younger women, are supposed to look like. As for how these young women are supposed to act? A blank slate is best.

NOTES

1. www.scarleteen.com
2. Laura M. Carpenter. *Virginity Lost: An Intimate Portrait of First Sexual Experiences* (New York: New York University Press, November 2005).
3. Laura M. Carpenter. Interview with the author, March 2008.
4. Dictionary.com definition of "virgin," http://dictionary.reference.com.
5. Hanne Blank. *Virgin: The Untouched History* (New York: Bloomsbury USA, 2007), 29.
6. Feministing.com. "Ivy Hymens: Why glorifying virginity is bad for women," March 31, 2008, www.feministing.com/archives/008913.html.
7. MTV. "True Life: I'm Celibate," July 2007, www.mtv.com/videos.
8. Denise Felder. "Miss America 'Purity Rule' Change Halted," September 14, 1999, www.ktvu.com/entertainment.
9. *New York Daily News.* "Miss USA Tara Conner Sex & Cocaine Shame," December 17, 2006, www.feministing.com/archives/006220.html.
10. Mark Coulton. "Trump deals disgraced Miss USA a new hand," *The Age,* December 21, 2006, www.theage.com.au.news.
11. Page Six. "Duck and Cover," *New York Post,* January 4, 2007, www.nypost.com/seven/01042007/gossip/pagesix/duck_and_cover_pagesix_.htm.
12. Fox News. "Miss Nevada Katie Rees Fired Over Raunchy Photos," December 22, 2006, www.foxnews.com.

READING (50)

Gate C22

Ellen Bass (2007)

At gate C22 in the Portland airport
a man in a broad-band leather hat kissed
a woman arriving from Orange County.
They kissed and kissed and kissed. Long after
the other passengers clicked the handles of their
    carry-ons
and wheeled briskly toward short-term parking,
the couple stood there, arms wrapped around
    each other
like he'd just staggered off the boat at Ellis Island,
like she'd been released at last from ICU, snapped
out of a coma, survived bone cancer, made it down
from Annapurna in only the clothes she was
    wearing.
Neither of them was young. His beard was gray.
She carried a few extra pounds you could
    imagine
her saying she had to lose. But they kissed lavish
kisses like the ocean in the early morning,
the way it gathers and swells, sucking
each rock under, swallowing it

again and again. We were all watching—
passengers waiting for the delayed flight
to San Jose, the stewardesses, the pilots,
the aproned woman icing Cinnabons, the man
    selling
sunglasses. We couldn't look away. We could
taste the kisses crushed in our mouths.
But the best part was his face. When he drew back
and looked at her, his smile soft with wonder, almost
as though he were a mother still open from
    giving birth,
as your mother must have looked at you, no matter
what happened after—if she beat you or left you or
you're lonely now—you once lay there, the varnix
not yet wiped off, and someone gazed at you
as if you were the first sunrise seen from the Earth.
The whole wing of the airport hushed,
all of us trying to slip into that woman's
    middle-aged body,
her plaid Bermuda shorts, sleeveless blouse, glasses,
little gold hoop earrings, tilting our heads up.

READING **51**

A World of Difference

Leila J. Rupp (2009)

LOVE AND DESIRE WITHIN THE CONSTRAINTS OF COMPULSORY HETEROSEXUALITY

In Lesotho, a small poor country in southern Africa where men tend to migrate to South Africa for employment, young women at school routinely form intimate and sexual bonds. Similar relationships exist among schoolgirls in Kenya and among Venda and Zulu schoolgirls in South Africa.[1] Slightly younger girls take on the role of "babies" to older girls' "mummies."[2] In a context in which bonds between men and women are fragile because of lengthy male absences and in which there is a taboo on discussion of sexuality between a woman who has borne a child and one who has not, mummy-baby relationships provide socialization into adult roles of domesticity, intimacy, and sexuality. The roles have roots in traditional cultural forms, including initiation ceremonies for girls and the practice of labia lengthening alone or in small groups, which provides an opportunity for autoerotic or mutual stimulation. But, as suggested by the use of the English words *mummy* and *baby* and the importance of schools in the formation of these relationships, they are also connected to the rise of a modern educational system. Some women maintain their relationships after school when they go to work in towns, and some young married women form new intimate ties after their marriages.

. . .

And it is not only schoolgirls who continue to love one another in sex-segregated spaces. Women in prison, women sex workers, and nuns, among others, have found love and sexual satisfaction in institutions designed for entirely other purposes. In examples from China, a scholar writes of meeting a woman in 1985 who had been repeatedly jailed in Shanghai for heterosexual delinquency. During one sentence, her cellmate, charged with lesbian behavior, "treated Za as her lover, touching her, petting her, and opening up to her the possibilities of sex between women.[3] Two prostitutes in Guangzhou, hired to engage in a threesome with a male client, enjoyed it so much that they became lovers. And two nuns in a Buddhist convent, denounced to the authorities for their relationship, confessed that the older nuns had introduced them to love between women. In all these ways, love and sex in sex-segregated spaces continues.

. . .

An Indian woman who takes the pseudonym Supriya, at sixteen the second wife of an alcoholic husband whose first wife, Lakshmi, could bear no children, writes of the loving relationship that developed between the two women. Lakshmi had suggested that her husband take another wife, and Lakshmi took care of Supriya's children while their mother worked as a servant to support the family. She also protected Supriya from their husband's advances, since he had sex with prostitutes and Supriya was afraid of contracting a venereal disease. The two women slept together near the children, who

considered both women their mothers, and their loving friendship became sexual as well.[4] Another Indian woman, interviewed when she was almost seventy, told of her relationship with her co-wife: "Gradually a friendship between us started to flourish. Inside the four walls of the home, we would rub each other's back and look at each other's bodies. We slept in the same bed with our feet locked together.[5]

An Indian lesbian living in the United States reports that when she was first involved with another girl as a teenager in India, she suggested to the other girl, "we should find a pair of brothers to marry so that we could live in the same house and continue our relationship. It seemed the closest thing to what we viewed as normal."[6] In a case reported in the Indian press in 1997, police arrested a young man and woman whom they suspected of having eloped under age, only to find that the young man was a woman. This was not the first time they had run off together, so their parents did not want them to come home. The families had already suggested that the girls marry two brothers, "which would ensure that they live in the same house"[7] And a documentary film made in New Delhi in 2003 tells the story of two women, one of them masculine, who announce that if they have to marry, they want to marry brothers so they can live together.[8]

Whether or not such negotiations go on in other societies with polygynous marriage or joint-family households—and there are suggestions that they do in the Islamic Arab world as well—it is clear that some women continue to make space for their love within the constraints of compulsory heterosexuality.[9]

MARRYING WOMEN

In 1996, the press in Malaysia reported that Azizah Abdul Rahman, a Malay woman, presented herself as a man and married another woman, Rohana. Reports focused on Azizah's looking "like a teenage boy" and wearing "a chocolate-colored pair of slacks and a purple t-shirt." Although it was Rohana's father who exposed Azizah, and Azizah claimed that they married only when Rohana threatened to end their relationship, Rohana told the press, "I did not marry Azizah because I am a lesbian." Although they had

had intercourse, Rohana denied knowing that Azizah had a female body. While in prison for a *zina*, a sex-related crime, Azizah, according to the press, returned "to womanhood." She claimed that she had married Rohana out of love and to prevent her from "slipping through her hands into somebody else's."[10]

A Thai woman in her late seventies recalled a female couple who married in her rural village in the 1980s. "They got married formally. They married like a man and a woman." Although the Thai government encourages people to register marriages, not everyone does so. And since weddings are not regulated by Buddhism either, same-sex marriages do occur. In this case, villagers helped with and attended the wedding between what they called "the woman" and "the woman who was a man." "The 'woman' was very beautiful. Both of their parents had the 'woman who was a man' move into the woman's family house" (as is customary for ethnic Thais). "Nobody said anything negative or mean to them."[11]

In the 1990s in a very poor rural region of India, Geeta, a woman from a *dalit,* or "untouchable," family who was married to an abusive husband, met Manju, an older woman whose masculinity had won her a great deal of respect and power in her village. They became friends at a residential school run by a women's organization devoted to equality and empowerment, and then they fell in love. As Geeta put it, "I do not know what happened to me when I met Manju but I forgot my man. I forgot that I had been married. We were attracted to each other that we immediately felt like husband and wife. . . . After that, we did not leave each other. . . . I knew I could lose my job. But I also knew it was impossible for me to stop. . . . I was in grip of magic."[12] Geeta accepted Manju as her husband at a Shiva temple, Manju's family welcomed Geeta as daughter-in-law, and Manju became both a second mother and a father to Geeta's daughter.

. . .

STILL CROSSING THE GENDER LINE

We have already encountered female-bodied women who secretly dressed as men and married women. But it is important to add that, even in societies in which a lesbian life in public became possible, some women continued to cross the gender line and marry women. In 1945 in New Zealand Mr. X, as the newspapers called him, was arrested for marrying a woman, and unlike in the earlier twentieth-century case of Percy Carcol Redwood, the question of sexual deviance came into play.[13] Mr. X told reporters that life as a woman had been difficult because of his masculinity and that he had successfully passed and worked as a man for twelve years, even having his breasts removed and registering for the armed forces during the Second World War. Since he felt and acted like a man, the relationship with his wife seemed normal, and both were happy with the situation. The media focused on his masculinity, not just in appearance—"tall, robust, broad-shouldered and husky-looking, with a mop of unruly black hair and a virile mien"—but also in behavior. His conversation was "frank and fearless," his room was messy, and he worked as a laborer and enjoyed male sports, including boxing.[14] Yet both Mr. X and his wife admitted to the police during the investigation that they were "of the Lesbian type."[15] Although Mr. X insisted that his feelings and actions were "natural and normal," the legal system and the media thought differently.[16] A Methodist minister proclaimed that Mr. X's "sexual maladjustment" demanded "some form of skilled psychological treatment," and the judge denounced the marriage as "an extraordinary perversion."[17] The couple was ordered to separate and seek psychiatric treatment.

. . .

In the twenty-first century, in at least some places in the world, it is possible, if not safe, to be openly transgendered. Manel is a biologically female transman from Sri Lanka who dresses, works, behaves, and identifies himself as a man. Manel described his family's reaction to him as he was growing up as a masculine girl: "My family is confounded by my behavior. My sisters could not bring me into our village society as a girl because of my manner of speech and behavior. The society I grew up in drew back in fear—is this a girl, is this a boy?"[18] His family explored the possibility of sex-reassignment surgery for him, and although Manel was not accepted by the doctors, he sees this as a positive move on his family's part. Manel found support through the Women's Support Group, the only lesbian, bisexual, and transgender organization in Sri Lanka. He said, "I only realized that homosexuality exists in Sri Lanka when I came here [to the Women's Support Group]. Because of this, the mentality I had about hospitals and wanting operations has gone away. I don't feel alone anymore." Although he was fascinated by lesbians in the Women's Support Group, he made clear that he could not live as a woman. "I am not homosexual. I don't know how to live as a homosexual, I don't understand it. I can't do women-with-women. I have my own unique method of sexual practice which suits the pleasures of my body."[19]

In contrast, Shanthi—who also grew up in Sri Lanka, dressed and behaved as a boy, and recognized her attraction to girls—has moved from wanting sex-reassignment surgery to embracing a lesbian identity. "I was told that the process involved constructing a penis from flesh taken from my body. I was told that it would be like a piece of meat. They do not construct testicles. I think this would be more mentally troublesome than my present state. I wouldn't be able to enjoy sex either. I have now reconciled myself to my choices as Buddhism has taught us to do."[20] Through exercise and weight training she developed a muscular frame with less body fat, and her relationship with a lesbian who perceives her as a woman has led her to accept that identity. "I will live as a lesbian and choose another lesbian as my partner."[21] Manel and Shanthi represent different possibilities for masculine female-bodied persons in the contemporary world.

The transgender movement in the United States makes clear how complicated the relationship can be between gender identities—whether one perceives oneself as male or female—and sexual identities—whether one identifies as homosexual, bisexual, or heterosexual. Oscar, a gay-identified transman from the San Francisco Bay Area who has had "top surgery" (the removal of breasts) and takes testosterone, explained the difference for him between his approach and the old model of erasing one's history as a woman: "So glad to have that behind us now, change the birth certificate, burn the photos, make up lies about when you were in the Boy Scouts, don't talk about it, don't show anybody the pictures. . . . I'm very grateful that in the last few years, a number of people have really seriously challenged all of the

above: That you don't have to, necessarily, identify as a man."[22] And his sexual identity is not based on the gender of the person he is involved with sexually or on his own body's vagina (since he has not, like many female-to-male transsexuals, had "bottom surgery," creation of a penis from the vagina). So neither dating a fem woman nor having penis-in-vagina sex with a man would make him heterosexual.

. . .

FEMALE MASCULINITY CONTINUED

If we consider the "troubling" rather than just the crossing of the gender line, we find a whole range of expressions of female masculinity in the contemporary world. Although the emergence of lesbian feminism throughout the "First World" in the 1970s and 1980s fostered the creation of a supposedly androgynous aesthetic along with the celebration of female values and a critique of masculinity, female masculinity remained and remains a central feature of many of the worlds in which women love women.

In a contemporary Thai nightclub, for example, Kot, with short hair and wearing men's pants and a button-down shirt over a white undershirt, explained what it means to be a *tom* (from the English word *tomboy*): "I always wanted to be a boy and even knew how to pee standing up."[23] When an old girlfriend slept with Kot's brother and then went back to Kot, the brother angrily called Kot a *kathoey,* a term meaning transgender or third sex. Kot's mother joked that since he was not using his penis much, he should give it to Kot. Kot's new girlfriend, a *dee* (from the English word *lady*) named Tee, also had boyfriends. With Kot, she would have sex only when she wanted it and the way she wanted it. For Kot, that is just how women are.

. . .

In Hong Kong, "TBs" (tomboys) go with "TBGs" (tomboys' girls).[24] The term *TB* originated in girls' schools, where masculine girls with crushes on other students were an accepted part of the social scene. The terms spread to the lesbian community, which emerged in the 1990s out of private gatherings in earlier decades. The use of *TB* avoided negative terms in circulation and could be used in public without alerting others to its meaning. TBs cut their hair short, wear men's clothes, and take care of their girlfriends in ways they perceive as masculine. In lesbian pubs, they drink beer and sing karaoke, choosing male pop songs. As Yin-shing, a TB, put it, "A TB must take care of her girlfriend; otherwise what's the point for her to keep a masculine appearance? . . . A masculine appearance means nothing if this TB does not take care of her girlfriend and cannot afford her girlfriend's daily expenses."[25] And in Hong Kong there is also the identity of "pure," which means "pure lesbian" and not TB or TBG. Hong Kong's integration into global society means that the Western notion of a non-gender-differentiated lesbian identity coexists with the gendered identities of TB and TBG.

. . .

In Japan, male-identified female-born *onabe* serve as sex workers in bars where they service heterosexually identified women. Featured in a documentary film, *Shinjuku Boys,* an *onabe* named Gaish described his/her sense of self: "I cannot make myself more feminine. I don't want to be a real man. If people think I'm in between, that's OK with me. I don't feel like a woman in my mind. . . . I've always been like this, it is natural to me." They dress and behave as men, some taking hormones to grow a beard and lower their voices. They make love to clients, keeping their clothes on. Said Tatsu, another *onabe* in the film, "I have heard lesbians take their clothes off, but we *onabe,* we hate that.''[26]

. . .

And consider the story of Phakamile and Cora, Black South African lesbians.[27] Phakamile is a working-class butch woman who lives in a small room attached to her parents' house in Soweto. She considers herself very masculine, despite her small size. She plays soccer and smokes tobacco and marijuana, all expressions of masculinity. Most lesbians in Soweto are butches who have relationships with women who identify as straight. Phakamile is in love with Cora, a middle-class woman who lives with her family in a house that has running water and electricity. Cora identifies as a "lesbian woman" but is not open with her family about her identity, although Phakamile spends the night with her often enough that her mother

confronted them about being lovers yet has accepted Phakamile as a family member. Cora is unusual in criticizing the butch-fem dynamic, a contentious issue between them. Phakamile says she proposed to Cora at a soccer game, where she was one of the star players, but Cora laughingly disagrees: "You know what . . . Phakamile, as butch as she is, I proposed to her. Really, really. Well, could see that . . . she was interested and she was afraid, and so I thought let me make things easier for her, you know and propose."[28]

As all these examples suggest, there are both similarities and differences between *toms* and *dees* or TBs and TBGs, on the one hand, and butches and fems in Western culture, on the other. Although dominant Western notions of lesbian identities have spread through the Internet, transnational gatherings, and personal contact through travel, local concepts of gender and sexual identities have by no means been erased by processes of globalization. Rather, local ideas of what it means to love and desire someone with a biologically alike body intertwine with Western concepts, and the product becomes local, in a metaphor developed by Tom Boellstorff, like a dubbed film.[29] The dynamic of female masculinity runs through all these stories, but how it operates in each case is shaped by the particular historical and social circumstances. These possibilities put contemporary U.S. notions of "lipstick lesbians," "bois," drag kings, transmen, and "gender-queer" in a broader transnational perspective.

FRIENDS IN LOVE

Of the women who loved women whom we have encountered across time and place, some did not differentiate themselves as masculine and feminine. Co-wives, female monastics, romantic friends, and sometimes schoolgirls seem instead to have eroticized sameness, not difference. We find the phenomenon of falling in love with someone just like oneself in lesbian feminism as it emerged in the United States, in Canada, in England, in parts of Europe, and elsewhere in the 1970s and 1980s.

Lesbians involved in both women's movements and early male-dominated gay movements, finding themselves marginalized or invisible, began to form their own groups and alternative institutions, such as bookstores, publishing and recording companies, support groups, and coffeehouses and restaurants.[30] Lesbian feminists claimed a heritage going back to Sappho and the Amazons, as indicated by the prominence of Sappho's name in book and magazine titles and by the double-bladed Amazon ax that became a prominent lesbian feminist symbol.

. . .

Within lesbian feminism, sexual desire for women and resistance to male domination almost equally defined what it meant to be a "woman-identified woman." Women who did not want to have sex with women but identified with the lesbian feminist community came to be known as "Political lesbians," described by an English group called the Leeds Revolutionary Feminists as "a woman-identified woman who does not fuck men. It does not mean compulsory sexual activity with women."[31] In Mexico, too, as women involved in the movement explained, "there were also lesbians who said 'I have come to be a lesbian through a political decision,' textbook lesbians."[32] Women came to lesbian feminism in different ways, sometimes out of their sexual desires and sometimes out of politics, which then led to new desires and a new identity.

. . .

Ara Jones, an African American woman who grew up working class in the South, saw her lesbianism as "a changeable thing."[33] Her first woman lover was a white woman with whom she fell "madly in love."[34] She began to identify both as a lesbian and as a feminist, but not as a lesbian feminist, because she saw that world as mostly white. Bisexual in behavior if not identity, she liked the sex she had with men better but had deeper emotional commitments to women, so she defined lesbianism as "a relationship in which two women's strongest emotions and affections are directed toward each other."[35] Yet sexual passion with women was important to her. After marrying and divorcing a man, she fell in love with a woman again. She saw herself as choosing lesbianism but also said, "I'm not straight," meaning she could choose to deny her desire for women but did not.[36]

. . .

STILL OTHER WAYS OF LOVING WOMEN

And all the preceding examples are just some of the ways that women or female-bodied individuals continue to love women.

. . .

Working-class Creole (Afro-Surinamese) women in Paramaribo, Suriname, form sexual relationships with other women while maintaining ties with men, sometimes husbands. This is called *"mati* work," meaning that it is not an identity but a form of activity. The relationship involves emotional and financial support, as well as sexual obligation. A thirty-seven-year-old mother of five, married to the father of two of her children, explained *mati* this way: "love between two women is stronger than between a man and a woman. . . . With a woman, you know what you like sexually and so does she."[37] Such relationships are accepted within the community without their having any special significance for women's sexual identities or intimate relationships with men.

In Carriacou, the Caribbean island made famous by Audre Lorde's autobiographical *Zami: A New Spelling of My Name,* women who love and have sex with other women are called *madivine* or *zami,* the word Lorde adopted. Lorde wrote, "How Carriacou women love each other is legend in Grenada, and so is their strength and their beauty."[38]

. . .

Throughout our journey, we have seen many and various ways that women love other women. Some find spaces in which their love can flourish, some cross the gender line to marry their lovers, some form intimate friendships or marriage-like relationships, some embrace gender blurring, some embrace femininity, some express their love in passionate language, some simply make love to one another with hands, objects, tongues, or vulvas.

In all these spaces, indigenous practices and understandings merge in a variety of ways with globalized concepts of what it means to be "gay" or "lesbian" or "bisexual" or "transgendered." Processes of development that open up the possibility of economic independence for women, increased access to education, urbanization and social mobility, loosening of political and religious regulation of women's lives—all these developments have an impact on the ways that societies conceptualize love between women and the possibilities for women's lives. And the result is a world of difference.

NOTES

1. Baraka, Nancy, with Ruth Morgan. 2005. "'I Want to Marry the Woman of My Choice without Fear of Being Stoned': Female Marriages and Bisexual Women in Kenya." In *Tommy Boys, Lesbian Men and Ancestral Wives: Female Same-Sex Practices in Africa,* edited by Ruth Morgan and Saskia Wieringa, 25–50. Johannesburg: Jacana Media. Blacking, John 1978. "Uses of the Kinship Idiom in Friendships at Some Venda and Zulu Schools." In *Social System and Tradition in Southern Africa,* edited by John Argyle and Eleanor Preston-Whyte, 101–17. Cape Town: Oxford University Press.

2. This discussion in based on: Gay, Judith. 1985. "'Mummies and Babies' and Friends and Lovers in Lesotho." *Journal of Homosexuality* 11(3–4): 97–116. Kendall. 1998. "'When a Woman Loves a Woman' in Lesotho: Love, Sex, and the (Western) Construction of Homophobia." In *Boy-Wives and Female Husbands: Studies in African Homosexualities,* edited by Stephen O. Murray and Will Roscoe, 223–41. New York: Palgrave. Epprecht, Marc. 2004. *Hungochani: The History of a Dissident Sexuality in Southern Africa.* Montreal: McGill-Queen's University Press.

3. Ruan, Fang Fu, and Vern L. Bullough. 1992. "Lesbianism in China." *Archives of Sexual Behavior* 21 217–26.

4. Vanita, Ruth. 2005a. "Born of Two Vaginas: Love and Reproduction between Co-wives in Some Medieval Indian Texts." *GLQ: A Journal of Lesbian and Gay Studies* 11(4): 547–77.

5. Bhaiya, Abha. 2007. "The Spring That Flowers between Women." In *Women's Sexualities and Masculinities in a Globalizing Asia,* edited by Saskia E. Wieringa, Evelyn Blackwood, and Abha Bhaiya, 69–76. New York: Palgrave Macmillan.

6. Quoted in Vanita 2005, 567.

7. Ibid., p. 567.

8. Ibid., p. 567.

9. Najmabadi, Afsaneh. 2005. *Women with Mustaches and Men without Beards: Gender and Sexual Anxieties of Iranian Modernity.* Berkeley: University of California Press.

10. Tan, beng hui. 1999. "Women's Sexuality and the Discourse on Asian Values: Cross-Dressing in Malaysia." In *Female Desires: Same-Sex Relations and Transgender Practices across Cultures,* edited by Evelyn Blackwood and Saskia E. Wieringa, 281–307. New York: Columbia University Press.

11. Sinnott, Megan. 2004. *Toms and Dees: Transgender Identity and Female Same-Sex Relationships in Thailand.* Honolulu: University of Hawaii Press.

12. Swarr, Amanda Lock, and Richa Nagar. 2004. "Dismantling Assumptions: Interrogating 'Lesbian' Struggles for Identity and Survival in India and South Africa." *Sings: Journal of Women in Culture and Society* 29: 491–516.

13. Glamuzina, Julie. 2001. "An Astounding Masquerade." *Journal of Lesbian Studies* 5: 63–84.

14. Ibid., p. 70.

15. Ibid., p. 72.

16. Ibid., p. 75.

17. Ibid., pp. 75–77.

18. Wijewardene, Shermal. 2007. "'But No One Has Explained to Me Who I Am Now . . .': 'Trans' Self-Perceptions in Sri Lanka." In *Women's Sexualities and Masculinities in a Globalizing Asia,* edited by Saskia E. Wieringa, Evelyn Blackwood, and Abha Bhaiya, 101–16. New York: Palgrave.

19. Ibid., p. 111.

20. Ibid., p. 113.

21. Ibid., p. 114.

22. Vidal-Ortiz, Salvador. 2002. "Queering Sexuality and Doing Gender: Transgender Men's Identification with Gender and Sexuality." In *Gendered Sexualities,* edited by Patricia Gagné and Richard Tewksbury, 181–233. Amsterdam: JAI.

23. Quoted in Sinnott 2004, 76.

24. Lai, Franco. 2007. "Lesbian Masculinities: Identity and Body Construction among Tomboys in Hong Kong." In *Women's Sexualities and Masculinities in a Globalizing Asia,* edited by Saskia E. Wieringa, Evelyn Blackwood, and Abha Bhaiya, 159–79. New York: Palgrave Macmillan.

25. Ibid., p. 170.

26. Wieringa, Saskia E. 2007. "Silence, Sin, and the System: Women's Same-Sex Practices in Japan." In *Women's Sexualities and Masculinities in a Globalizing Asia,* edited by Saskia E. Wieringa, Evelyn Blackwood, and Abha Bhaiya, 23–45. New York: Palgrave Macmillan.

27. Quoted in Swarr and Nagar 2004.

28. Ibid., p. 508.

29. Boellstorff developed the concept of "dubbing culture" with regard to gay life in Indonesia. Boellstorff, Tom. 2005. *The Gay Archipelago.* Princeton, NJ: Princeton University Press.

30. There is a great deal of literature of lesbian feminism. See for example Ross, Becki L. 1995. *The House That Jill Built: A Lesbian Nation in Formation.* Toronto: University of Toronto Press. Nash, Catherine. 2001. "Siting Lesbians: Urban Spaces and Sexuality." In *In a Queer Country: Gay and Lesbian Studies in the Canadian Context*, edited by Terry Goldie, 325–53. Vancouver: Arsenal Pulp (on Canada). Echols, Alice. 1989. *Daring to Be Bad: Radical Feminism in America, 1967–1975.* Minneapolis: University of Minnesota Press. Franzen, Trisha. 1993. "Differences and Identities: Feminism and the Albuquerque Lesbian Community." *Signs: Journal of Women in Culture and Society* 18: 891–906. Taylor, Verta, and Leila J. Rupp. 1993. "Women's Culture and Lesbian Feminist Activism: A Reconsideration of Cultural Feminism." *Signs: Journal of Women in Culture and Society* 19: 32–61. Whittier, Nancy. 1995. *Feminist Generations: The Persistence of the Radical Women's Movement.* Philadelphia: Temple University Press. Freeman, Susan K. 2000. "From the Lesbian Nation to the Cincinnati Lesbian Community: Moving toward a Politics of Location." *Journal of the History of Sexuality* 9(1–2): 137–74. Enke, Anne. 2007. *Finding the Movement: Sexuality, Contested Space, and Feminist Activism.* Durham, NC: Duke University Press. Stein 1997, (on the United States). Willett, Graham. 2000. *Living Out Loud: A History of Gay and Lesbian Activism in Australia.* St. Leonards: Allen & Unwin. (includes material on Australia), and Jennings 2007 discusses Britain.

31. Jennings, Rebecca. 2007. *A Lesbian History of Britain: Love and Sex between Women since 1500.* Oxford, UK: Greenwood World.

32. Mogrovejo, Norma. 1999. "Sexual Preference, the Ugly Duckling of Feminist Demands: The Lesbian Movement in Mexico." In *Female Desires: Same-Sex Relations and Transgender Practices across Cultures,* edited by Evelyn Blackwood and Saskia E. Wieringa, 308–35. New York: Columbia University Press.

33. Stein, Arlene. 1997. *Sex and Sensibility: Stories of a Lesbian Generation.* Berkeley: University of California Press.

34. Ibid., p. 58.

35. Ibid., pp. 58–59.

36. Ibid., p. 59.

37. Wekker, Gloria. 2006. *The Politics of Passion: Women's Sexual Culture in the Afro-Surinamese Diaspora.* New York: Columbia University Press.

———. 1999. "'What's Identity Got to Do with It?' Rethinking Identity in Light of the *Mati* Work in Suriname." In *Female Desires: Same-Sex Relations and Transgender Practices across Cultures,* edited by Evelyn Blackwood and Saskia E. Wieringa, 119–38. New York: Columbia University Press.

38. Lorde, Audre. 1982. *Zami: A New Spelling of My Name.* Watertown, MA: Persephone.

R E A D I N G

Some Like Indians Endure

Paula Gunn Allen (1998)

i have it in my mind that
dykes are indians

they're a lot like indians
they used to live as tribes
they owned tribal land
it was called the earth

they were massacred
lots of times

they always came back
like the grass
like the clouds
they got massacred again

they thought caringsharing
about the earth and each other
was a good thing
they rode horses

and sang to the moon

but i don't know
about what was so longago
and it's now that dykes
make me think i'm with indians
when i'm with dykes

because they bear
witness bitterly
because they reach
and hold
because they live every day
with despair laughing
in cities and country places
because earth hides them
because they know
the moon
because they gather together
enclosing
and spit in the eye of death
indian is an idea
some people have
of themselves
dyke is an idea some women
have of themselves
the place where we live now
is idea
because whiteman took
all the rest
because father
took all the rest
but the idea which
once you have it
you can't be taken
for somebody else
and have nowhere to go
like indians you can be
stubborn

the idea might move you on,
ponydrag behind
taking all your loves and
children maybe downstream

maybe beyond the cliffs
but it hangs in there
an idea
like indians
endures

it might even take your
whole village with it
stone by stone
or leave the stones
and find more
to build another village
someplace else

like indians
dykes have fewer and fewer
someplace elses to go
so it gets important
to know
about ideas and
to remember or uncover
the past
and how the people
traveled
all the while remembering
the idea they had
about who they were
indians, like dykes
do it all the time

dykes know all about dying
and that everything belongs
to the wind
like indians
they do terrible things
to each other
out of sheer cussedness
out of forgetting
out of despair
so dykes
are like indians
because everybody is related
to everybody
in pain
in terror
in guilt
in blood
in shame
in disappearance
that never quite manages
to be disappeared
we never go away
even if we're always
leaving

because the only home
is each other
they've occupied all
the rest
colonized it; an
idea about ourselves is all
we own

and dykes remind me of indians
like indians dykes
are supposed to die out
or forget
or drink all the time
or shatter
go away

to nowhere
to remember what will happen
if they don't

they don't anyway—even
though the worst happens

they remember and they
stay
because the moon remembers
because so does the sun
because the stars
remember
and the persistent stubborn grass
of the earth

R E A D I N G 53

New Orientations: Asexuality

Karli June Cerankowski and Megan Milks (2010)

Feminist studies, women's studies, gender studies, sexuality studies, gay and lesbian studies, queer studies, transgender studies . . . asexuality studies: Although asexuality may not necessarily belong to its own field of study (yet), and may not make an easy fit with any preexisting field of study, the emergence and proliferation of the asexual community pose interesting questions at the intersections of these fields that interrogate and analyze gender and sexuality. As we know, these fields are neither independent of one another nor are they easily conflated; and they are ever shifting, revising, expanding, subdividing, and branching off. Where, then, might we place the study of a "new," or at least newly enunciated, sexuality? How do we begin to analyze and contextualize a sexuality that by its very definition undermines perhaps the most fundamental assumption about human sexuality: that all people experience, or *should* experience, sexual desire:

. . .

Recognizing that asexuality has a meaning both plural and mutable, we believe it necessary to expand and complicate the scant amount of scientific research on the topic. In that vein, we would like to consider asexuality as it relates to identity, orientation, and the politics of an asexual movement, which has given a name and a new understanding to what has commonly been viewed as dysfunctional or repressed sexuality. As we trace the possibilities for the future study of asexuality, we would like to begin by introducing our readers to asexuality in general—its definition, community formation, and politics. Then, we briefly survey the literature on asexuality before turning to a few of the many implications, questions, and possibilities the study of asexuality poses for feminist and queer studies.

INTRODUCING THE ASEXUAL COMMUNITY

"Asexual: a person who does not experience sexual attraction." This definition is provided on the homepage of the Asexual Visibility and Education

Network (AVEN), a Web community where members from around the world communicate with each other via Web forums, often using these communication networks to arrange in-person meetings for social or political action.[1] It is around this definition that the asexual community has organized, but that is not to say that it is a homogeneous group of people, nor even that all asexual individuals agree with this definition. As mentioned, members of AVEN are located around the world, coming from different backgrounds; identifying with various genders, races, and classes; forming different types of relationships; and even variously identifying as romantic and aromantic, monogamous and polyamorous, gay, straight, bisexual, and lesbian. This variation is unsurprising given the community's large and growing membership. Since its founding in 2001, the online community has amassed just over 19,000 users worldwide, with the most significant growth occurring between 2006 and 2008 when membership more than doubled from the near 6,000 users accounted for in January 2006. AVEN founder David Jay states that when he adds that number to the sum of members using the forums in languages other than English (these forums can be linked from the AVEN site), he accounts for nearly 30,000 members worldwide.[2] Although, as with most online communities, it is difficult to know how many registered members are unique users, and in this case, it is difficult to know if these unique users identify as asexual, we suggest that the increasing numbers of registered AVEN users indicate that the community of self-identified asexuals and their allies is indeed growing.

. . .

As the AVEN community grows and becomes more visible, it is inevitable that asexuality will garner more public attention. Yet such interest is no longer restricted to daytime television talk shows, such as those represented in AVEN's archive. For example, Arts Engine Inc., an independent organization focused on creating "social-issue documentaries," is currently developing a feature-length documentary entitled *Asexuality: The Making of a Movement;* it purports to "explore asexuality as a sexual identity, a lifestyle and a budding social movement."[3] Several members of AVEN are a part

of the film, which promises to contribute new material for discussions on asexuality and representation. With this expanded attention, it seems only appropriate that asexuality is explored more extensively within academic discourse as well.

LOCATING ASEXUALITY IN ACADEMIC DISCOURSE

The modest attention human asexuality has received has come mainly from medical and psychological discourse, which has acknowledged asexuality only relatively recently, and then solely in pathologizing terms. In the 1980 third edition of *Diagnostic and Statistical Manual of Mental Disorders* (*DSM-III*), the American Psychiatric Association added the diagnostic category "inhibited sexual desire," later renamed Hypoactive Sexual Desire Disorder (HSDD) in the *DSM-IV* (1994) and defined as "persistently or recurrently deficient (or absent) sexual fantasies and desire for sexual activity."[4] Although there are cases in which these diagnoses must be taken seriously, cases that demand psychiatric or medical attention, the presumption that all cases of disinterest in sex are pathological is what has contributed to the pejorative flavor of the word "asexual," a view that the growing asexual community has been working with some success to change. In fact, the group has put together a small taskforce to "create a new definition (of HSDD) that's more friendly to asexual people," which they hope to include in the newest edition of the *DSM*.[5] We would like to emphasize this point: there is a marked difference between those who experience a decrease in sex drive or lack of sexual desire and are distressed by this and those who do not experience sexual desire and are not distressed by this supposed "lack." We are interested in the latter group here and in locating asexuality as a viable sexual and social identity.

The project of separating asexuality from presumptive pathology has been taken up in a handful of social sciences studies published in the past six years. Two studies by Anthony F. Bogaert, who works in social psychology, are groundbreaking in this respect. In his 2004 article based on preexisting questionnaire data, Bogaert suggests that approximately 1 percent of the population is asexual; this is the first known empirical study of asexuality. Later he asks in a conceptual article, published in 2006, whether asexuality, here defined as "a lack of any sexual attraction," should be viewed as a unique sexual orientation and argues that indeed it should. Bogaert's two articles have accomplished much in distancing asexuality from pathology. His work has since been expanded by psychologists Nicole Prause and Cynthia A. Graham, whose 2007 study is the first (that we have come across) to analyze responses produced by individuals who self-identify as asexual. In 2008, Kristin S. Scherrer, working within sociology, furthers Prause and Graham's study with one that also uses responses from asexual-identified individuals in an attempt to more fully understand the identity-based (as opposed to behavioral and desire-based) aspects of asexuality.[6]

In addition to these short studies, we note one book-length exploration of asexual relationships, published in 1993, that focuses specifically within the lesbian community. *Boston Marriages: Romantic but Asexual Relationships Among Contemporary Lesbians* is a collection of theoretical articles and personal stories edited and compiled by psychologist Esther D. Rothblum and psychotherapist Kathleen A. Brehony. Describing their research process, they suggest that thinking through asexual relationships forced them to confront their own biases about sex and intimacy: they write that they "hope that readers will be challenged to reconsider the very basis of what constitutes a lesbian relationship."[7] Indeed, the selections in the book open up interesting possibilities for rethinking intimacy in relationships, and although the focus is on lesbian relationships, such a project resonates across many populations and communities.

. . .

ASEXUAL FEMINISMS, FEMINIST ASEXUALITIES

In thinking about relationships and connections between asexuality and feminist studies, perhaps the key question to address is how the recognition of asexuality as an identity meets and potentially challenges feminist conceptions of sex and female sexuality. Although asexuality compels us to reconsider multiple approaches to the feminist project of liberating female sexuality, it is perhaps especially conversant with radical feminism, pro-sex feminism, and the oppositional discourse that characterizes both.

Summarizing the anti-porn/pro-sex "sex wars" of the 1980s, Elisa Click, in "Sex-Positive: Feminism, Queer Theory, and the Politics of Transgression," explains both radical feminism and pro-sex feminism in terms of their opposing, but similarly liberatory, views of female sexuality: where radical feminists sought out "a sexuality purified of male sexual violence and aggression," pro-sex feminists sought out "a politically incorrect sexuality" that would transgress normative boundaries. Both camps saw themselves as espousing transgressive, liberatory sexualities that, in the case of radical feminism, combated the repression of female sexuality by the patriarchy and, in the case of pro-sex feminism, saw "repression as produced by heterosexism and 'sex negativity.'" Although both sides were engaged in conceiving sexual practices "as Utopian political strategies," the discourse's divisive rhetoric oversimplified their rival approaches into an "anti-sex'" versus "pro-sex" dichotomy that Click challenges in her critique of contemporary pro-sex theories.[8]

The emergence of the asexual movement compels us to reconsider the ways in which female sexuality was and still is framed by the rhetoric of liberation in the feminist movement. The crucial problem of the discourse surrounding the anti-porn/pro-sex debates is that it situates female sexuality as either empowered or repressed: the attendant assumption is that anti- or asexuality is inherently repressive or dysfunctional. The asexual movement challenges that assumption, working to distance asexuality from pathology and in so doing challenging many of the basic tenets of pro-sex feminism—most obviously its privileging of transgressive female sexualities that are always already defined against repressive or "anti-sex" sexualities.

Even as the asexual movement boldly challenges sex-positive feminism's view of asexuality as repressive, however, it is not necessarily more easily aligned with radical feminism. Although radical feminists did produce a few concepts of feminist asexuality, it is unclear how the asexual movement might reckon with their politicization of asexuality as a way out of phallocentric sexuality. Thus far, asexual individuals have not politicized their (a) sexual practices in the same way that radical feminists such as Andrea Dworkin have.

So what might feminist theorists do with asexuality, and what might asexuals do with feminist theory? Although the distancing of asexuality from pathology retains political primacy for an intersection of asexuality and feminist theory, at least with respect to the asexual movement's goals of visibility and education, we want to also identify two impulses that we can see as potential approaches to a feminism that acknowledges asexuality. The first impulse is to look at asexuality as a way to critique the liberatory rhetoric by which sex is still to a large extent framed within feminism. The second impulse is to theorize modes of asexuality that are or can be feminist, likely beginning by extending the work of radical feminists.

One approach to thinking through asexuality from a feminist perspective is to consider how asexuality might critique the rhetoric of liberation in which sex is still steeped within feminism. The asexual movement's politicization of sex is at this point very basic, its nominal goal being visibility and education, with no gestures toward explicitly challenging norms. That is, asexuality thus far is not politicized in the same way that female sexuality has been. (Of course, this does not mean that the asexual movement is not heading in that direction.) Whether female sexuality is conceived of from a radical feminist or from a pro-sex perspective, both are too steeped in the rhetoric of liberation to make sense in a way that can be inclusive of asexual persons who are simply uninterested in having sex and who may not be actively or explicitly engaged in radical politics.

As Glick argues, the liberatory rhetoric of the sex wars has led to rivaling erotic chauvinisms that still to a certain extent exist within a contemporary sex-positive feminism that privileges subversive sex. In contrast, the asexual community has so far taken pains to strive for inclusivity, separating itself from any presumptions that asexual individuals are against sex or somehow "better" than "sexual" individuals. The asexual community thus may push the feminist movement to recognize and avoid creating hierarchies of sexual practices while also urging us to look carefully at the ways in which words such as "repressed" and "dysfunctional" are used rhetorically to justify such erotic chauvinism.

A second approach to thinking through asexuality from a feminist perspective might attempt to theorize asexuality as feminist. In doing so, we would do well to begin with theories of feminist asexuality and anti-sexuality that emerged from radical feminism. Dworkin, for instance, in *Intercourse,* holds up Joan of Arc as an example of someone who has, exercising feminist agency, dropped out of phallocentric sex.[9] In the early fifteenth century, Dworkin argues, Joan of Arc's anti-sexuality indicated freedom from the inferiority of a female subjectivity. Dworkin's use of the word "virginity" to describe Joan of Arc's sexuality is perhaps problematic when linked with theories of asexuality; however, Dworkin's virginity is understood not as pureness or innocence (a sexist and repressive configuration) but as resistance to sexism and misogyny (a feminist configuration).

Can Joan of Arc be considered asexual? The question takes us back to the definition of asexuality. It seems clear that AVEN's "official" formulation of asexuality as not a choice, but a biologically determined orientation (a definition that itself opens up the larger ongoing nature/nurture debate in studies of human sexuality), does not easily map on to a theory of asexuality as a chosen, feminist mode of resistance. In fact, AVEN repeatedly opposes asexuality to celibacy, in its literature, in the General FAQ, and on the AVENwiki. For example, in an informational brochure, AVEN claims, "Celibacy is a choice to abstain from sexual activity. Asexuality is not a choice, but rather a sexual orientation describing people who do not experience sexual attraction. While most asexual people do not form sexual relationships, some asexuals participate in sexual behavior for the pleasure of others."[10] This not only raises questions about choice versus fixed identity but also forces us to question to what extent the practice of or abstention from sex acts matters to the definition of asexuality.

Importantly, that definition is not fixed; nor is it agreed upon by self-identified asexuals. AVEN's AVENwiki contains several pages devoted to competing formulations of asexual identity. We do not have the space to detail them here, but one seems especially of note: the Collective Identity model. This model constructs asexuality as a collective identification: someone who has no sex drive but does not see herself as asexual is not asexual; but someone who does experience a sex drive but sees herself as asexual is asexual. In theorizing feminist asexuality, then, we might look to this model, which proposes that those who describe themselves as asexual have "*chosen* to actively disidentify with sexuality" (our emphasis).[11] This model, which seemingly contradicts AVEN's more widely held essentialist formulation, is perhaps the most likely model to dialogue with radical feminism. A feminist mode of asexuality, accordingly, might consider as asexual someone who is not intrinsically/biologically asexual (i.e., lacking a sexual drive) but who is sexually inactive, whether short-term or long-term, not through a religious or spiritual vow of celibacy but through feminist agency.

Whether we accept Dworkin's virginity as a feminist asexuality, it seems clear that the feminist movement has paid inadequate attention to asexuality as a viable feminist mode. The emergence of the asexual movement compels us to revisit feminist theories of sex and sexuality in ways that will likely complicate the politics of both the asexual and feminist movements. The asexual movement encourages the feminist movement to think further about how to theorize a feminist asexuality that cannot be dismissed as conservative, repressive, or antisexual. On the other side of things, revisiting feminist theories of sexual practice and sexuality may complicate AVEN's definition of "asexual" and bring more attention to the various ways of being asexual that already exist within the community. Further, in light of the important developments of feminist theorists of color, and with a nod toward queer scholarship, we are compelled to question the

isolation of sexuality as a solitary category of analysis to allow for the possibility of shifting meanings of asexuality across different racial, ethnic, cultural, and class contexts.

IS ASEXUALITY QUEER?

In the General FAQ on the AVEN Web site, this question is framed as such: "I think asexuality is inherently queer. Do you agree?" The response to this question provides a perfect example of the palpable ambivalence between queerness and asexuality: "This has been the subject of much debate and discussion. On the one hand 'queer' is 'anything that differs from the norm,' especially the norm of sexuality, and there are asexual people who consider the relationships they form to be completely unconventional and therefore queer. Other asexuals consider their relationships to be entirely conventional and do not identify as queer in any way."[12] This response hinges upon the definition of "queer" as nonnormative, and such a definition comes up against the ongoing conflicts and questions within queer studies: how do we define "queer" and can anyone be queer? Such questions are specifically linked to the focus on sex as part of the definition of queerness. There is an ongoing worry among queer theorists and activists that "queer" is becoming a blanket term for, as the AVEN definition suggests, any variation from the norm. In such a universalizing move, as Leo Bersani has argued, "queer" desexualizes the gay and lesbian movement. Building from Michael Warner's suggestion in his introduction to *Fear of a Queer Planet: Queer Politics and Social Theory* that queer struggles are able to challenge social institutions, Bersani suggests that such a challenge is impossible "unless we define how the sexual specificity of being queer (a specificity perhaps common to the myriad ways of being queer and the myriad conditions in which one is queer) gives queers a special aptitude for making that challenge." Although Bersani often returns to "an erotic desire for the same" as the definitive way of being queer, we think a more generous reading is possible, wherein asexuality is one of Bersani's sexually specific "myriad ways of being queer."[13] By its very definition, asexuality brings a focus to the presence or absence of sexual desire as a way to queer the normative conceptions about how sex is practiced and how relationships are (or are not) formed around that practice.

Warner's follow-up to Bersani's critique, however, raises some doubt about the happy reception of asexuals within queer communities. In *The Trouble with Normal: Sex, Politics, and the Ethics of Queer Life,* Warner advocates "a frank embrace of queer sex in all its apparent indignity" in an attempt to shift the politics of shame and to bring sexual specificity back into queer politics. We certainly do not disagree with such a politics, but the worry is that by the end of his book, the asexual is almost posed as a threat to the sexualized queer movement that Warner imagines.

. . .

Paradoxical as it may seem, is it possible that not desiring sex can be part of that radical sexual culture? In short, does the asexual person threaten to remove sex from politics all over again, or does she or he challenge the ways we think about sex and desire even within queer communities?

We would of course argue for the latter, as we suggest that asexuality as a practice and a politics radically challenges the prevailing sex-normative culture. If the asexual community is indeed a part of a radical sexual political movement, we believe that it is critical to continue the conversation about whether queer communities can provide at least a coalition site for community building and social activism, even while challenging queer conceptions of sex and relationships. In other words, does the asexual movement as a visible political entity require that the queer movement rethink its equivalence of radical sex with radical politics or, even more, its definition of what constitutes radical sex? Within this discussion of queerness, the questions of oppression and marginalization also arise. The reality is that asexuality is often pathologized and medicalized and also that asexual people are often told that they are inchoate, that they haven't yet fully developed and experienced their sexuality, or they are interrogated about past trauma and sexual abuse. Similarly, asexual individuals experience the alienation that comes from lacking sexual desire in a world that presumes sexual desire and that attaches great power to sexuality. How does this experience compare with that of queers living in a heterosexist world? The parallels to the historical treatment of homosexuality and other queer modes of being should be clear, but is that overlap enough to ally asexual persons with those who practice queer sex:

. . .

CONCLUSION

Admittedly, we more so raise questions here than provide answers. In doing so, we hope to open up a new field of interrogation in the study of human sexuality. It is with an affinity to our own academic interests, and with attention to the interests of the readers of *Feminist Studies,* that we have focused our dialogue primarily on feminist and queer theories. Although we do not suggest that asexuality is decidedly feminist or queer, we do think that the study of asexuality informs, and is fruitfully informed by, both feminist and queer studies. Additionally, we realize that we have only touched on a miniscule sample of feminist and queer writing and readily acknowledge the much larger realm of dialogic possibility that we cannot give mention to here.

NOTES
1. AVEN, "Asexual Visibility and Education Network," www.asexuality.org.
2. David Jay, e-mail message to Cerankowski, 14 Aug. 2009.
3. Arts Engine, Inc., "Arts Engine, Inc.: Asexuality," www.artsengine.net/asexuality.
4. *Diagnostic and Statistical Manual of Mental Disorders,* 4th ed. (Washington, D.C.: American Psychiatric Association, 1994), 539.
5. David Jay and Andrew H., "DSM Fireside Chat," www.youtube.com/watch? v=4z3uODyUe6U.
6. Anthony F. Bogaert, "Asexuality: Prevalence and Associated Factors in a National Probability Sample," *The Journal of Sex Research* 41, no. 3 (2004): 279–87; Anthony F. Bogaert, "Toward a Conceptual Understanding of Asexuality," *Review of General*

Psychology 10, no. 3 (2006): 243; Nicole Prause and Cynthia A. Graham, "Asexuality; Classification and Characterization," *Archives of Sexual Behavior* 36, no. 3 (2007): 341–56; Kristin S. Scherrer, "Coming to an Asexual Identity: Negotiating Identity, Negotiating Desire," *Sexualities* 11, no. 5 (2008): 621–40.

7. Esther D. Rothblum and Kathleen A. Brehony, "Introduction: Why Focus on Romantic but Asexual Relationships among Lesbians?" in *Boston Marriages: Romantic but Asexual Relationships among Contemporary Lesbians,* ed. Esther D. Rothblum and Kathleen A. Brehony (Amherst: University of Massachusetts Press, 1993), 12.

8. Elisa Glick, "Sex Positive: Feminism, Queer Theory, and the Politics of Transgression," *Feminist Review,* no. 64 (Spring 2000): 21, 20.

9. Andrea Dworkin, "Virginity," in her *Intercourse* (New York: Basic Books, 2006), 103–51.

10. AVEN, "Asexuality: Not Everyone Is Interested in Sex" (unpublished document circulated in San Francisco, 2008).

11. AVEN, "Collective Identity Model," www.asexuality.org/wiki/index.php?title= Collective_identity_model.

12. AVEN, "General FAQ," www.asexuality.org/home/general.html.

13. Leo Bersani, *Homos* (Cambridge: Harvard University Press, 1995), 72–73. Michael Warner, introduction to *Fear of a Queer Planet: Queer Politics and Social Theory,* ed. Michael Warner (Minneapolis: University of Minnesota Press, 1993), vii-xxxi.

R E A D I N G **54**

Dismantling Hierarchy, Queering Society

Andrea Smith (2010)

Queer politics calls us to go beyond a simple toleration for gay and lesbian communities to address how heteropatriarchy structures white supremacy, capitalism, and settler colonialism. By heteropatriarchy, I mean the way our society is fundamentally based on male dominance—a dominance inherently built on a gender binary system that presumes heterosexuality as a social norm.

To examine how heteropatriarchy is the building block of U.S. empire, we can turn to the writings of the Christian Right. For example, Prison Fellowship founder Charles Colson makes a connection between homosexuality and the nation-state in his analysis of the war on terror, claiming that one of the causes of terrorism is same-sex marriage:

Marriage is the traditional building block of human society, intended both to unite couples and bring children into the world. . . . There is a natural moral order for the family. . . . The family, led by a married mother and father, is the best available structure for both child-rearing and cultural health. Marriage is not a private institution designed solely for the individual gratification of its participants. If we fail to enact a Federal Marriage Amendment, we can expect not just more family breakdown, but also more criminals behind bars and more chaos in our streets. It's like handing moral weapons of mass destruction to those who would use America's depravity to recruit more snipers, more highjackers, and more suicide bombers. When radical Islamists see American women abusing Muslim men, as they did in the Abu Ghraib prison, and when they see news coverage of same-sex couples being "married" in U.S. towns, we make our kind of freedom abhorrent— the kind they see as a blot on Allah's creation. [We must preserve traditional marriage in order to] protect the United States from those who would use our depravity to destroy us.

The implicit assumption in this analysis is that the traditional heterosexual family is the building block of empire. Colson is linking the well-being of U.S. empire to the well-being of the heteropatriarchal family.

Heteropatriarchy is the logic that makes social hierarchy seem natural. Just as the patriarchs rule the family, the elites of the nation-state rule their citizens. For instance, prior to colonization many Native communities were not only nonpatriarchal, they were not socially hierarchical, generally speaking. Consequently, when colonists first came to this land they saw the necessity of instilling patriarchy in Native communities because they realized that indigenous peoples would not accept colonial domination if their own indigenous societies were not structured on the basis of social hierarchy.

Patriarchy in turn rests on a gender-binary system; hence it is not a coincidence that colonizers also targeted indigenous peoples who did not fit within this binary model. Many Native communities had multiple genders—some Native scholars are now even arguing that their communities may not have been gendered at all prior to colonization—although gender systems among Native communities varied.

Gender violence is a primary tool of colonialism and white supremacy. Colonizers did not just kill off indigenous peoples in this land—Native massacres were also accompanied by sexual mutilation and rape. The goal of colonialism is not just to kill colonized peoples—it's also to destroy their sense of being people. It is through sexual violence that a colonizing group attempts to render a colonized people as inherently rapable, their lands inherently invadable, and their resources inherently extractable. A queer analytic highlights the fact that colonialism operates through patriarchy.

Another reality that a queer activist approach reveals is that even social justice groups often rely on a politics of normalization. Queer politics has expanded our understanding of identity politics by not presuming fixed categories of people, but rather looking at how these identity categories can normalize who is acceptable and who is unacceptable, even within social justice movements. It has also demonstrated that many peoples can become "queered" in our society—that is, regardless of sexual/gender identity, they can become marked as inherently perverse and hence unworthy of social concern (such as sex workers, prisoners,

"terrorists," etc.). We often organize around those peoples who seem most "normal" or acceptable to the mainstream. Or we engage in an identity politics that is based on a vision of racial, cultural, or political purity that sidelines all those who deviate from the revolutionary "norm."

Because we have not challenged our society's sexist hierarchy (which, as I have explained, fundamentally privileges maleness and presumes heterosexuality), we have deeply internalized the notion that social hierarchy is natural and inevitable, thus undermining our ability to create movements for social change that do not replicate the structures of domination that we seek to eradicate. Whether it is the neocolonial middle managers of the nonprofit industrial complex or the revolutionary vanguard elite, the assumption is that patriarchs of any gender are required to manage and police the revolutionary family. Any liberation struggle that does not challenge heteronormativity cannot substantially challenge colonialism or white supremacy. Rather, as political scientist Cathy Cohen contends, such struggles will maintain colonialism based on a politics of secondary marginalization in which the most elite members of these groups will further their aspirations on the backs of those most marginalized within the community.

Fortunately, many indigenous and racial justice movements are beginning to see that addressing heteropatriarchy is essential to dismantling settler colonialism and white supremacy. The Native Youth Sexual Health Network, led by Jessica Yee, integrates queer analysis, indigenous feminism, and decolonization into its organizing praxis. Incite!, a national activist group led by radical feminists of color, similarly addresses the linkages between gender violence, heteropatriarchy, and state violence. And queer-of-color organizations such as the Audre Lorde Project have rejected centrist political approaches that demand accommodation from the state; rather, they seek to "queer" the state itself.

This queer interrogation of the "normal" is also present in more conservative communities. I see one such thread in evangelical circles—the emergent movement (or perhaps more broadly, the new evangelical movement). By describing the emergent movement as a queering of evangelicalism,

I don't necessarily mean that it offers an open critique of homophobia (although some emergent church leaders such as Brian McClaren have spoken out against homophobia). Rather, I see this movement as challenging of normalizing logics within evangelicalism. This movement has sought to challenge the meaning of evangelicalism as being based on doctrinal correctness, and instead to imagine it a more open-ended ongoing theological conversation. Certainly the Obama presidential campaign has inspired many evangelicals—even though they may hold conservative positions on homosexuality or abortion—to call for a politics that is more open-ended and engaged with larger social justice struggles. Perhaps because of this trend, evangelical leader John Stackhouse recently complained that the biggest change in evangelicalism is "the collapse of the Christian consensus against homosexual marriage." Unfortunately, many leftist organizers tend to dismiss or ignore these openings within evangelicalism, but at their own peril. Social transformation happens only through sustained dialogue with people across social, cultural, and political divides.

As I have shown here, I believe queer politics offers both a politics and a method for furthering social transformation. It is a politics that addresses how heteropatriarchy serves to naturalize all other social hierarchies, such as white supremacy and settler colonialism. It is also a method that organizes around a critique of the "normal" (in society as a whole or in social movements) and engages in open-ended, flexible, and ever-changing strategies for liberation.

R E A D I N G   55

Queering Black Female Heterosexuality

Kimberly Springer (2008)

How can black women say yes to sex when our religious institutions, public policy, home lives, media, musical forms, schools, and parents discuss black women's sexuality only as a set of negative consequences? When mentioned at all, the words I recall most associated with black female sexuality were edicts against being "too fast." "Oooh, that girl know she fas'!" my aunty would tut as the neighborhood "bad girl" swished on by. Just looking too long at a boy could provoke the reprimand "Girl, stop being so fas'." Notably, it was only us girls who were in danger of being labeled "fast." Women in church, passing through the hairdressers, and riding by in cars with known playas were simply dismissed. They were already gone; "respectable" women uttered "jezebel" in their wake. The culture that's embedded in these subtle and not-so-subtle passing judgments tries to take away my right to say yes to sex by making me feel like if I do, I'm giving in to centuries of stereotypes of the sexually lascivious black woman.

Public assumptions about black female sexuality mirror the contradiction we deal with daily: hypersexual or asexual. We use silence as a strategy to combat negative talk. Perhaps if we do not speak about black women and sex, the whole issue will go away? After all, for centuries black women tried to escape sexual scrutiny by passing unnoticed through white America as nurturing mammies. It's the nasty jezebels who give black people a bad name, and it's Mammy's duty to keep those fast women in check. The mammy and jezebel caricatures were forged in the complex and perverse race relations of the post–Civil War South.

. . .

After slavery, though black women were no longer needed to supply offspring for sale, persistent racial and economic segregation required the jezebel image. Perpetuating the myth of black women as hypersexual served to set white women on a pedestal and excuse white men's rape of black women. If black women were always ready and willing sexual partners, it was impossible to have sex with them against their will. . . .

Black female sexuality in pop culture has not moved very far from these stereotypes. What better place to see this continued history of the asexual mammy than in the films of Queen Latifah? Whether she's *Bringin' Down the House* or having a *Last Holiday,* she's the queen of teaching white people how to be more human at the expense of her own sexuality, save the improbably chaste and deferred romance with a hottie like LL Cool J.

. . .

As sociologist Patricia Hill Collins points out in her book *Black Sexual Politics,* the more things change, the more they remain the same. Collins describes the continuous link between the mammy and a contemporary image of the "black lady." Stereotypes about black women's sexuality have met with resistance, particularly among middle-class blacks in the nineteenth century who advocated racial uplift and self-determination. Proving that blacks could be good citizens required silence about sexuality and sexual pleasure. Between respectability and silence, black women found little space to determine who they were as sexual beings. Black women might never be "true ladies" capable of withdrawing from the workplace and into the home and motherhood. The realities of racism and sexism in terms of wages and employment meant that black families needed two incomes long before white Americans needed or wanted double paychecks. Still, though most black women had to work, they could endeavor to be respectable and asexual. Respectable black women were professionals, good mothers, dutiful daughters, and loyal wives. Each role depended on their being traditionally married and in a nuclear family. Most certainly, one was not a loose woman.

Just as nineteenth-century black leaders advocated respectability, modern-day public policies that belittle black women as "welfare queens," "hoochie mamas," and "black bitches" work to control and define the parameters of black women's sexuality.

If black women's sexuality—particularly poor and working-class black women's sexuality—is routinely described as the root of social ills, then once again black women are left with little room to maneuver if they want respect in America's classrooms, boardrooms, and religious sanctuaries. Collins claims that the ideal of the "black lady" is what black women have to achieve if they want to avoid undesirable labels like "bitchy," "promiscuous," and "overly fertile."

The nonsexual black lady has become a staple in television and film. She wears judicial robes (Judges Mablean Ephriam and Lynn Toler of *Divorce Court*), litigates with stern looks (district attorney Renee Radick in *Ally McBeal*), is a supermom who seems to rarely go to the office (Claire Huxtable on *The Cosby Show*), delegates homicides (Lieutenant Anita Van Buren in *Law and Order*), and ministers to a predominantly white, middle-class female audience (Oprah Winfrey).

. . .

Today in black communities, women's communities, the hiphop community, and popular culture, the main way of viewing black female sexuality is as victimized or deviant. No one could have anticipated the proliferation of the black woman-as-whore image in a new mass-media age that is increasingly the product of black decision makers. Fans and detractors these days uncritically call women who perform in music videos "hoes," "ho's," or "hoez." No matter how it's spelled, the intent is still the same: to malign black women who use their bodies in sexual ways. An equal-opportunity sexist might claim, "Video hoes aren't only black—there are Asian hoes, white hoes, Latin hoes, all kinds of hoes!" How very exciting and magnanimous—an age of racial equality when little girls of any race can be called hoes.

They wear very little clothing (it might be generous to call a thong "clothing"). The camera shots are either from above (for the best view of silicone breasts) or zoomed in (for a close-up on butts). And the butts! They jiggle! They quake! They make the beat go *boom,* papi!

. . .

Jezebel has become a video ho, video honey, or video vixen—depending on your consumer relationship to the women who participate in making music videos.

There are also female rappers willing to play the jezebel role to get ahead in the game. As Collins and others observe, they have added another stereotype to the mix: the Sapphire. Sapphire is loud and bitchy. She is abusive to black men and authority figures, especially her employer. Embodied in raunchy rappers like Lil' Kim, Trina, and Foxy Brown, this combination Jezebel/Sapphire is hot and always ready for sex . . . but she just might rip your dick off in the process. Is this empowerment?

Listening to people debate black women's sexualized participation in rap music videos, but seeing asexual black women only on film and television, what's a girl to do? Young black girls and teenagers are aspiring to be well-paid pole dancers. Black women, such as Melanie in the CW's sitcom *The Game,* think that the only way to attract and keep their man is to adopt a position of "stripper chic," which means clinging comically to a newly installed pole in the living room. Black female heterosexuality seems to move deeper and deeper into unhealthy territory that is less about personal satisfaction and more about *men's satisfaction.*

This acquiescence is akin to a nationwide black don't ask/don't tell policy. In her documentary film *Silence: In Search of Black Female Sexuality in America* (2004), director Mya B asks young black women how they learned about sex. They all give a similar, familiar answer: *not* in my parents' house.

. . .

There is, of course, an intergenerational aspect to silence around discussions of sexuality that cuts across race and ethnicity. Puritanical views on sexuality are not confined by race. In the case of the black community, however, our silence is further enforced by traumatic intersections of race, sexuality, and often violence. In other words, there are nuances to silence that will take more than merely urging openness in dialogue between mothers and daughters to address. Ending this silence around sexuality needs to be more than telling girls how not to get pregnant or catch STDs. Speaking about black women's sexuality today should be as much about pleasure as it is about resistance to denigration.

This "damned if you do, damned if you don't" approach to black women's sexuality is a *crisis situation.* It might not have Beyoncé ringin' the alarm, but until black women find a way to talk openly and honestly about our private sexual practices, the terms of black female sexuality will always be determined by everyone but black women. The women in the videos are merely the emissaries delivering a skewed message.

Also of urgent concern is black women's acceptance of negative representations of our sexuality. Is the disavowal that we are not like the video hoes on our screens any better than silence? Is even accepting the term "video ho" resignation that the insult is here to stay? Postmodern sexuality theorist Michel Foucault wrote about how people will serve as their own surveillance by policing their own thoughts and actions. Our silence about our sexuality becomes the border that we must not cross if we too want to assume the role of the black lady. Racism, sexism, classism, and heterosexism are the sentinels on that border, but there is very little for these guardians to do when we keep ourselves within the designated zone with our own silence or condemnation of other women. There are women, increasingly young women, who believe that if they do not behave in sexually promiscuous ways, they will be exempt from public scorn. Unfortunately, that is not the case. Just as we can all take a bit of pride in Oprah's achievements, we also are all implicated in the mockery and contempt heaped upon Janet Jackson. Clearly, the strategies we've used since the end of slavery have not worked. What have we been doing? Being silent in an effort to resist the normalization of deviant representations of black female sexuality is a failed tactic.

. . .

In 1982 at Barnard College, a controversial conference, "Towards a Politics of Sexuality," exposed the tensions and anxieties inherent in wrestling with sexuality. Coming out of the conference was a key book, *Pleasure and Danger: Exploring Female Sexuality,* edited by Carol Vance. Vance asks questions in her introduction that remain, for me, unanswered: "Can women be sexual actors? Can we act on our own behalf? Or are we purely victims?" When applied to women of color, these questions become even more pressing, given that our sexuality is what is used as the dark specter to keep white women in line. Can black women be sexual actors in a drama of our own construction? Will black women act on our own behalf . . . even if doing so includes fantasies that incorporate racist or sexist scenarios? Or are black women destined to always be victims of a racial and sexual history that overwhelms hope for transformation and liberation? . . .

We need new visions and new ways of talking about black female sexuality.

Historically, white women parlayed their experiences working with blacks for the abolition of slavery into the drive for women's voting rights. In the early 1970s, many social-change groups adopted the language of the Black Power movement. Why? Because the notion of power was potent and, dare I say, *virile* language. The notion of pride and refusing to be ashamed had a confrontational edge to it that Chicanos, women's libbers, Asians, American Indians, and gays recognized as a new direction: Rather than ask for integration into a corrupt system, why not demand the resources to build a new world according to one's own agenda?

In developing that vision, gays, lesbians, bisexuals, and transgender (LGBT) activists not only declared a form of gay pride, but also later would even co-opt the language of civil rights. We see it today in demands for same-sex marriage as a right. And while LGBT uses of civil rights language might rub some African Americans the wrong way, I would say it is time for blacks—specifically, black women—to take something back. Isn't it time for heterosexual black women to adopt the language of queerness to free us from Mammy's apron strings? Wouldn't the idea of coming out of the closet as enjoying sex on our own terms make Jezebel stop in her tracks to think about getting *herself* off, rather than being focused on getting her man off? It is time to queer black female *heterosexuality*. As it stands, black women acquiesce to certain representations as if taking crumbs from the table of sexual oppression. Our butts are in vogue, we're nastier than white women in the bedroom, we're wilder than Asian women—all stereotypes derived in a male fantasy land of "jungle" porn and no-strings-attached personal ads. A queer black female heterosexuality isn't about being a freak in the bedroom; it's about being a sexual person whose wants and needs are self-defined.

. . .

Queerness, then, is not an identity, but a position or stance. We can use "queer" as a verb instead of a noun. Queer is not someone or something to be treated. Queer is something that we can *do*. The black woman is the original Other, the figure against which white women's sexuality is defined. Aren't we already queer? To queer black female sexuality means to do what would be contrary, eccentric, strange, or unexpected. To be silent is, yes, unexpected in a world whose stereotype is of black women as loud and hypersexual. However, silence merely stifles *us*. Silence does not change the status quo.

Queering black female sexuality would mean straight black women need to:

1. Come out as black women who enjoy sex and find it pleasurable.
2. Protest the stereotypes of black female sexuality that do not reflect our experience.
3. Allow all black women—across class, sexual orientation, and physical ability—to express what we enjoy.
4. Know the difference between making love and fucking—and be willing to express our desires for both despite what the news, music videos, social mores, or any other source says we should want.
5. Know what it is to play with sexuality. What turns us on? Is it something taboo? Does our playfulness come from within?
6. Know that our bodies are our own—our bodies do not belong to the church, the state, our parents, our lovers, our husbands, and certainly not Black Entertainment Television (BET).

Queering black female heterosexuality goes beyond language. Black communities go 'round and 'round about the use of "nigger" with one another. Is it a revolutionary act of reclaiming an oppressive word? Or does it make us merely minstrels performing in the white man's show? Older and younger feminists debate the merits of embracing the labels of "bitch" and "dyke" as a bid for taking the malice out of the words. There are some black women who say, "Yes, I am a black bitch" or, "Yes, I am a ho." These claims do little to shift attitudes. If nothing else, we merely give our enemies artillery to continue to shoot us down or plaster our asses across cars in rap videos. How does the saying go? You act like a trick, you get played like a trick. Claiming queerness is linguistic, but ultimately about action that does not reinforce the stereotypes.

I am not suggesting a form of political lesbianism, which was a popular stance for some feminists who struggled against male domination in the 1970s. In addition to adopting a political position, queering black female sexuality means listening to transformative things that have already been said about black sexuality. Black lesbians and gay men have something to tell straight black women about sexuality if we care to listen. Poets such as Audre Lorde, writer/activists such as Keith Boykin, and cultural theorists such as Cathy Cohen and Dwight McBride offer insights about African American sexuality that move beyond boundaries of sexual orientation and that we would do well to heed. Cohen, for example, challenges queer politics for lacking an intersectional analysis. That is, queer theory largely ignores questions of race and class when those categories in particular are the straw men against which marginalization is defined, constructed, and maintained.

Queer theory isn't just for queers anymore, but calling on the wisdom of my black, gay sisters and brothers runs the risk of reducing them solely to their sexuality. Thus, the challenge for me in bringing an intersectional perspective to queering black female heterosexuality is to remain mindful of my own heterosexual privilege and the pitfalls of appropriating queerness as identity and not as a political position.

What I must also claim and declare are all the freaky tendencies that I consider sexy and sexual. Sexual encounters mined from Craigslist's Casual Encounters, where I both defy and play with stereotypes about black women's sexuality. Speaking frankly about sex with friends—gay, straight, bisexual, trans, male, and female. Enjoying the music and words of black women, such as Jill Scott, who are unabashed about their sexual desire and the complexity of defining nontraditional relationships—monogamous and otherwise. All of these sexual interventions/ adventures in daily existence play against my own conditioning to be a respectable, middle-class

young lady destined to become an asexual black lady. That biology is *not* my destiny.

There is no guarantee that straight black women adopting queerness will change how the dominant culture perceives black female sexuality. I do not think black women embracing our sexuality and being vocal about that will change how politicians attempt to use our sexuality as a scapegoat for society's ills, as they did with the "welfare queen" in the 1980s and 1990s. However, I do believe that queering black female sexuality, if enough of us participate in the project, will move us collectively toward a more enlightened way of being sexual beings unconstrained by racialized sexism. Instead of trying to enact a developmental approach (we were asexual mammies or hot-to-trot jezebels, but now we are ladies), claiming queerness will give us the latitude we need to explore who we want to be on a continuum. It is a choice that both black women as a group and black women as individuals must make.

. . .

It may not seem like much, but overcoming centuries of historical silence will create different perceptions about black women and sex that will reshape our culture, society, and public policies. In calling for heterosexual black women to queer their sexuality, I am expressing the fierce belief that . . . we can dramatically change how black female sexuality is viewed in America. More important, though, I believe we can change how black girls and women *live* and *experience* their sexuality: on their own terms and free from a past of exploitation. Historians often refer to the "long shadow" that slavery has cast over African Americans. While it is important to acknowledge the reverberations of this human atrocity in black family structure, economic disadvantage, and especially black sexuality, it is just as critical that we push along a dialogue that reinvents black sex in ways that do not merely reinstate the sexual exploitation that was inflicted and that some of us now freely adopt.

Can black women achieve a truly liberated black female sexuality? Yes. If we continue to say no to negative imagery—but that alone has not been effective. In addition, we must create and maintain black female sexuality queerly. Only then can we say, and only then will society hear, both yes and no freely and on our own terms.

DISCUSSION QUESTIONS FOR CHAPTER 6

1. How does an emphasis on purity and virginity serve to control women's sexuality and maintain patriarchy?

2. How is the personal political in heterosexual relationships generally?

3. How does socialization into gender affect intimacy in relationships?

4. How is contemporary culture's construction of female sexuality a perversion of feminist notions of a truly liberated female sexuality? How has contemporary culture coopted feminist rhetoric about sexuality in ways that actually reinforce male dominance and male-centered sexuality? What might liberated female sexuality mean for adolescent girls? For asexual people?

5. How would you describe women's and men's different ways of communicating? How do women's and men's different ways of communicating affect relationships?

6. How is romantic love related to consumerism? Give some examples.

SUGGESTIONS FOR FURTHER READING

Ascencio, Marysol. Latina/o Sexualities: *Probing Powers, Passions, Practices, and Policies.* Piscataway, NJ: Rutgers University Press, 2009.

Blank, Hanne. *Straight: The Surprisingly Short History of Heterosexuality.* Boston: Beacon Press, 2012.

Faderman, Lillian. *Surpassing the Love of Men: Romantic Friendship and Love Between Women from the Renaissance to the Present,* Third Edition. New York: Alyson Books, 2010.

Gray, Mary. *Out in the Country: Youth, Media, and Queer Visibility in Rural America.* New York: New York University Press, 2009.

Hockey, Jenny, Angela Meah, and Victoria Robinson. *Mundane Heterosexualities: From Theory to Practices.* New York: Palgrave Macmillan, 2010.

Lee, Shayne. *Erotic Revolutionaries: Black Women, Sexuality, and Popular Culture.* Lanham, MD: Hamilton Books, 2010.

Shildrick, Margrit. *Dangerous Discourses of Disability, Subjectivity and Sexuality.* New York: Palgrave Macmillan, 2009.

CHAPTER 7

Health and Reproductive Justice

HEALTH AND WELLNESS

Health is a central issue in women's lives. Ask parents what they wish for their newborns and they speak first about hoping the baby is healthy; quiz people about their hopes for the new year and they speak about staying healthy; listen to politicians debate their positions before an election and health care is almost always a key issue. In contemporary U.S. society, good health is generally understood as a requirement for happy and productive living. Because women are prominent as both providers and consumers of health care, health issues and the health care system affect us on many levels. To make sense of the complexities of women's relationships to health care systems, we discuss five themes: equity, androcentrism, medicalization, stereotyping, and corporate responsibility. After this discussion we address reproductive justice and focus specifically on contraceptive technologies and abortion debates in the United States.

First, despite the passage of President Barack Obama's health care reform in 2010, described below, medical institutions in the United States provide different levels of service based on health insurance status and the general ability to pay. This issue of equity affects all aspects of health care, including access to fertility, contraceptive, and abortion facilities. Poor women are less healthy than those who are better off, whether the benchmark is mortality, the prevalence of acute or chronic diseases, or mental health. This is the issue of *equity*. Some people have better health care than others because of a two-tiered system that has different outcomes for those who can pay or who have health insurance and those who cannot afford to pay and do not have health insurance through their jobs or are not covered by welfare programs. This is a special problem as health care costs continue to rise. Some states are providing less coverage for low-income people, a problem because the United States, unlike most industrialized societies in the global north, does not yet have a nationalized health care system.

The health care reform that we do have in the United States at the time of this writing is the Patient Protection and Affordable Care Act (PPACA), commonly called the "Affordable Care Act," or simply "Obamacare." Together with the Health Care Education Reconciliation Act, it represents the most significant government expansion and regulatory overhaul of the health care system in the United States since the passage of Medicare and Medicaid in 1965. PPACA is aimed at increasing health insurance coverage and reducing the overall costs of health care. It provides a number of mechanisms, including individual mandates, subsidies, and tax credits, to employers and individuals in order to increase the coverage rate. Additional reforms aim to improve health care outcomes and streamline the delivery of health care. The U.S. Supreme Court upheld the constitutionality of this law in 2012.

In particular, the PPACA stated that, with a few exceptions, an individual cannot "be excluded from participation in, be denied the benefits of, or be subjected to discrimination under any health program or activity, any part of which is receiving federal financial assistance." This means that public or private entities receiving federal funds (private insurance companies often receive federal funds) can not discriminate against women on the basis of national origin, ethnicity, age, or disability. "Gender rating," charging women more than men for health insurance, is disallowed for individual and employer plans with more than 100 employees. It is estimated that women with individual health insurance plans have been paying up to 48 percent higher premiums. The legislation also requires insurers to provide maternity coverage (about three-quarters of plans have not included this) and that companies with more than 50 employees provide breast-feeding mothers with breaks and room to express milk. In addition, midwives and birth centers are covered. Other key aspects of the health care reform important for women's health include promises for preventive care provisions, mental health coverage, increased coverage for Medicaid and SCHIP (State Children's Health Insurance Program), and increased access for individuals to group rates. In addition, young people can stay on parents' health insurance policies until age 26, Medicare patients get better coverage, preexisting conditions and lifetime caps on coverage are eliminated, and employers are not able to give lesser plans to lower-paid workers.

Despite these gains, extreme opposition to President Obama's health care reform efforts resulted in the absence of a public option and limits on abortion coverage. Still, these changes in health care make sure that everyone in the United States has some kind of health insurance coverage. This legislation is especially important for women because growth in health costs over the last decade have had a disproportionate effect due to women's lower incomes, higher rates of chronic health problems, and greater need for reproductive health services. As discussed above, discriminatory practices charging women higher rates than men and refusing to cover essential service associated with reproductive health have had important consequences for women's health and well-being. Not surprisingly given the divisiveness of health care dialogue in the United States, enactment of health care reform has been slow, and more than half of respondents in a recent survey reported neglecting health care needs because of cost.

Back in 2013 approximately 19 million women were uninsured. Such women were more likely to have inadequate access to care, get a lower standard of care in the health system, and have poorer health outcomes. They were more likely to postpone care and to forgo filling prescriptions than their insured counterparts and often delayed or skipped important preventive care such as mammograms and Pap tests. One study attributed nearly 45,000 excess annual deaths to lack of health care coverage. For example, a 2013 study found that insurance, or the lack of it, proved to be the most powerful predictor of women's late-stage cancer. The study showed that being uninsured raises a woman's risk of late diagnosis by 80 percent. In addition, uninsured children are at greater risk of experiencing health problems such as obesity, heart disease, and asthma that continue to affect them as (potentially uninsured) adults, resulting in increased costs for public health care services. Such adverse effects of health care inequity carry long-term implications for families and society.

LEARNING ACTIVITY **Women, Heart Disease, and Cancer in Your State**

- To learn more about the prevalence of heart disease among women in your state, visit the CDC's website at *http://apps.nccd.cdc.gov/giscvh2/* and click on your state.
- To learn about the prevalence of cancer in your state, go to *http://apps.nccd .cdc.gov/DCPC_INCA/DCPC_INCA.aspx* and select your state.

Women are more likely to be employed in part-time work or full-time work without health insurance benefits and, compared to men, are more likely to be covered as a "dependent" by another adult's employer-based insurance. As a result, women are more vulnerable to losing their insurance coverage if they divorce or become widowed, or if a spouse or partner loses a job, or the spouse or partner's employer drops family coverage or increases premium and out-of-pocket costs. In addition, of course, employment has not necessarily ensured access to health insurance as more than two-thirds of uninsured women live in families in which they or a partner are working full time. As discussed, these obstacles cause low-income women (who are disproportionately women of color) to postpone care and delay preventive procedures.

Health club memberships and healthy foods are outside the reach of many low-income people, who also are more likely to live in neighborhoods that provide unhealthy environments with unsafe water because of the presence of hazardous waste associated with industrial production and the dumping of toxic chemicals in neighborhoods with little economic and political power. As discussed in Chapter 2, *environmental racism* has fostered an *environmental justice* movement. Low-income women are more susceptible to chronic conditions as well as acute problems that might have been avoided had preventive care been available. This costs the state millions of dollars annually and is not a fiscally-responsible way to provide health care services. Women of color are especially at risk for not having health care coverage and for receiving substandard care when they enter the system. They have higher maternal and infant mortality rates, higher rates of HIV infection, and their reproductive health is threatened by limited access to basic reproductive health care, including family planning services and abortion care. Services such as these can be understood as human rights, emphasizing the importance of such rights for social justice. In the reading "From Rights to Justice," Zakiya Luna expands understandings of uses of human rights in the United States and illustrates how race and gender identities contribute to social movement organizing around reproductive issues. In particular, she discusses the ways collective action by women of color has changed the face of reproductive rights organizing in the United States.

Professional health-related organizations (such as the American Medical Association [AMA]), health maintenance organizations (HMOs), insurance companies, pharmaceutical companies, and corporations representing other medical products and practices have enormous influence over health politics. In addition, health is not just about medical services. Health conditions, including incidence and mortality rates, are related to such socioeconomic factors as poverty, poor nutrition, interpersonal violence, substandard housing, and lack of education. Many of the social issues that affect women on a daily basis and that contribute to increased tobacco use, chemical addictions, stress, and poor nutrition among women have their consequences in increased rates of heart disease, cancer, chronic obstructive pulmonary disease, diabetes, and obesity, to name just a few. Health problems are compounded by the aging of the population, such that by the year 2030, women (who are likely to have fewer economic resources than men) will represent approximately 81 percent of people who are older than 85.

Globally, women's health access is one of the most important issues determining justice and equity for women. The reading by Nancy Fugate Woods titled "A Global Health Imperative" makes this claim through a focus on the effects of globalization

HIV Among Women: Fact Sheet

FAST FACTS

- At the end of 2010, an estimated 25% of adults and adolescents aged 13 years or older living with a diagnosis of HIV in the United States were women.[a] But not all women are equally at risk for HIV infection. Women of color, especially black/African American women, are disproportionately affected by HIV infection compared with women of other races/ethnicities.
- New HIV infections among black/African American women decreased in 2010.

THE NUMBERS

While black/African American women continue to be far more affected by HIV than women of other races/ethnicities, recent data show early signs of an encouraging decrease in new HIV infections. CDC is cautiously optimistic that this is the beginning of a longer-term trend. CDC recommends that all people aged 13 to 64 get tested for HIV. Yet, 15% of women who are HIV-positive are unaware of their status.

NEW HIV INFECTIONS[b]

- In 2010, women accounted for an estimated 9,500, or 20%, of the estimated 47,500 new HIV infections in the United States. Most of these (8,000, or 84%) were from heterosexual contact with a person known to have, or to be a high risk for, HIV infection.
- In 2010, the fourth largest number of all new HIV infections among all people in the United States occurred among black/African American women with heterosexual contact (5,300 infections)[c] (see bar graph). Of the total number of new HIV infections among women in the United States in 2010, 64% occurred in blacks/African Americans, 18% were in whites, and 15% were in Hispanics/Latinas.[d]
- At some point in their lifetimes, an estimated 1 in 32 black/African American women will be diagnosed with HIV infection, compared with 1 in 106 Hispanic/Latino women and 1 in 526 white women.

(continued)

- In 2010, the rate of new HIV infections (per 100,000 population) among black/African American women was 20 times that of white women, and the rate among Hispanic/Latino women was 4 times the rate of white women. However, the number of new infections among black/African American women in 2010 (6,100) represented a decrease of 21% since 2008.
- Young women aged 25 to 44 accounted for the majority of new HIV infections among women in 2010.

HIV AND AIDS DIAGNOSES[e] AND DEATHS

- In 2011, an estimated 10,257 women aged 13 years or older received a diagnosis of HIV infection in the United States, down from 12,146 in 2008.
- Women accounted for 25% (7,949) of the estimated 32,052 AIDS diagnoses in 2011 and represent 20% (232,902) of the 1,155,792 cumulative AIDS diagnoses (including children) in the United States from the beginning of the epidemic through the end of 2011.
- In 2010, HIV was among the top 10 leading causes of death for black/African American women aged 15 to 64 and Hispanic/Latino women aged 25 to 44.

PREVENTION CHALLENGES

The following risk factors contribute to prevention challenges for women:

- Women may be **unaware of their partner's risk factors** for HIV (such as injection drug use or unprotected sex with men, with multiple partners, or with anyone who has, or is at a high risk for, HIV). Some women may not insist on condom use because they fear that their partner will leave them or even physically abuse them.
- **Unprotected vaginal sex** is a much higher risk for HIV for women than for men, and **unprotected anal sex** is riskier for women than unprotected vaginal sex. Abstaining from sex or having sex with only a mutually monogamous partner who does not have HIV, and using condoms correctly and consistently, reduce the risk for HIV transmission.
- Women who have experienced **sexual abuse** may be more likely than women with no abuse history to engage in high-risk sexual behaviors like exchanging sex for drugs, having multiple partners, or having sex with a partner who is physically abusive when asked to use a condom.
- A substantial number of HIV infections among women are attributable to **injection drug and other substance use**—either directly, through sharing drug injection equipment contaminated with HIV, or indirectly, through engaging in high-risk behaviors like unprotected sex, while under the influence of drugs or alcohol.
- Some **sexually transmitted diseases** greatly increase the likelihood of acquiring or transmitting HIV. Rates of gonorrhea and syphilis are higher among women of color than among white women.

[a] Unless otherwise noted, this fact sheet defines women as adult and adolescent females aged 13 and older.
[b] "New HIV infections" refers to HIV incidence, or the number of people who are newly infected with HIV within a given period of time, whether they are aware of their infection or not.
[c] Heterosexual contact with a person known to have, or to be at high risk for, HIV infection.
[d] Can be any race.
[e] HIV and AIDS diagnoses indicate that a person is diagnosed, but not when the person was infected.

on the status of girl children. As already discussed in previous chapters, globalization refers to the processes by which regional economies, societies, and cultures have become integrated through an interconnected global network of communication, transportation, and trade. Woods addresses the health status of girls in Sub-Saharan Africa and explores interventions at the level of social and health policy and health care delivery. The HIV/AIDS global pandemic is also an important illustration of issues of gender and racial/ethnic equity in this region of Africa and other parts of the world as well as in the United States.

By the end of 2010, according to the most recent data published by the U.S. Centers for Disease Control and Prevention, an estimated 25 percent of adolescents and adults living with an HIV diagnosis in the United States were women. In addition, women accounted for 20 percent of the new HIV infections. See the box "HIV Among Women" for more information. However, not all women are equally at risk for HIV infection. Women of color, especially African American women, were disproportionately affected. Indeed, the rate of new HIV infection for African American women was nearly 20 times that of white women and nearly 5 times that of Latinas. Even though new HIV infections among African American women fell in 2010 for the first time in many years, compared with members of other races and ethnicities they continue to account for a higher proportion of cases at all stages of HIV from new infections to deaths. Both African American women and men are at higher risk because of higher rates of poverty and less access to HIV-prevention education and affordable health care. These socioeconomic issues directly and indirectly increase the risk for HIV infection and affect the health of people living with, and at risk for, HIV. Late diagnosis of HIV infection, in particular, results in lack of early medical care and facilitates transmission to others. High prevalence means increased transmission and more rapid acceleration of a problem than in communities with low prevalence. Also the fact that African Americans tend to have sexual relations with partners of the same race/ethnicity means the smaller population encourages an increased risk of HIV infection.

In addition, all communities share consequences of the stigma, fear, discrimination, homophobia, and negative perceptions associated with HIV testing. This is especially problematic if people fear stigma more than infection, and choose to hide high-risk behavior rather than seek counseling and testing. Stigma and discrimination are key points in "Southern Discomfort," the reading by Carl Gaines. He explains that poverty and lack of access to preventative care and services are not the only explanations for the HIV epidemic. Conservative attitudes toward sexuality and lack of sex education, along with language and immigration barriers, are also important obstacles to controlling HIV infection, especially in the southern states of the United States.

Risk factors for all women, both in the United States and globally, include lack of power in relationships (as reflected by sexual violence against women; their lack of input into decisions such as whether a male partner wears a condom, visits a prostitute, or has multiple sexual partners, etc.), inadequate health care and HIV-prevention education, lack of education about body and sexuality, and the biological vulnerability of women during sexual intercourse that provides more sources of entry for the virus. Scholars suggest that many students in the United States are at risk for HIV infection when they have multiple sex partners, use condoms inconsistently, and combine alcohol and/or other drugs with their sexual experiences. Although students tend to be knowledgeable about HIV, this does not always lead to condom use.

For Better or For Worse®   **by Lynn Johnston**

Although there has been increased funding for HIV/AIDS prevention, treatment, and care in Africa and the Caribbean, a U.S. "global gag rule" on the U.S. Agency for International Development (USAID) population-control program under Presidents Reagan, George H. W. Bush, and George W. Bush restricted foreign nongovernmental organizations (NGOs) that received USAID family-planning funds from using their own, non-U.S. funds to provide legal abortion services, lobby their own governments for abortion law reform, or even provide accurate medical counseling or referrals regarding abortion. It coincided with another U.S. policy that blocked contributions to the United Nations Population Fund. This fund supports programs in some 150 countries to improve poor women's reproductive health, reduce infant mortality, address sex trafficking, and prevent the spread of HIV/AIDS. Such policies undermine funding for other related health issues (as well as health and infant screening, nutritional programs, and health education) and encourage narrow, often religious, and abstinence-based approaches to HIV/AIDS prevention that exclude condom use. Officially known as the "Mexico City Policy," the global gag rule is an indirect method of targeting reproductive justice worldwide. Under the rule, organizations that even so much as mention abortion services to their clients, even for purely educational purposes as part of comprehensive sexual health instruction, are totally ineligible for funding from the United States. Health clinics have been forced to choose between censoring the health programs they have developed to serve women's needs or being denied the funding they need to keep their doors open at all. This global gag rule was lifted by President Obama in 2009, although it can be reinstated by another President at a later date. It is important to consider the ways anti-choice policies in the United States are threatening the quality of women's lives around the world.

The second theme of this chapter is *androcentrism* or male centeredness (see Chapter 1). The male body is constructed as normative and medical research has tended to focus on men (mostly white men), overgeneralizing the results of this research to others. Baseline data for heart monitors, for example, were based on middle-aged white men, causing serious complications for patients who did not fit this description. Until recently, women often were not included in clinical trials to determine the safety and effectiveness of drugs and other medical devices because it was thought that women's hormonal cycling or other factors peculiar to being female might constitute variables that could skew trial results. It was declared that excluding women protected them, because a woman might be pregnant or the drug might prevent future fertility. Drug companies did not want to get sued. Recently it has become increasingly clear that research from male-only trials may not apply equally to women, or may not provide data on important effects of drugs on women. Originally, researchers believed most sex differences in terms of reactions to drugs were most likely a result of differences in hormones, height, and/or weight. Scientists now know that these differences are more complex. Differences in the livers of men and women may explain why most women seem to metabolize drugs differently than men, for example. There may also be sex differences in pain tolerance and the ways individuals respond to pain medications. Laurie Edward's reading "The Gender Gap in Pain" discusses the ways men and women respond differently to drugs as well as pain, both acute and chronic. Today the National Science Foundation (NSF) and National Institutes of Health (NIH) have implemented regulations to ensure researchers receiving funds are free of gender discrimination and other kinds of bias, although as Edwards emphasizes, the application of medical research to clinical practice moves slowly, and "changes in assumptions about gender evolve even more slowly."

More money is spent on diseases that are more likely to afflict men. Related to this is the notion of "anatomy is destiny" (an example of biological determinism, already discussed in other chapters) whereby female physiology, and especially reproductive anatomy, is seen as central in understanding women's behavior. These trends have a long history. Social norms about femininity, for instance, have guided medical and scientific ideas about women's health, and female reproductive organs have long been perceived as sources of some kind of special emotional as well as physical health. "Female hysteria," for example, was a once-common nineteenth-century medical diagnosis of women in the United States and Europe that was "treated" by various practices that included hysterectomy (surgical removal of the uterus). Women thought to be suffering from it exhibited a wide array of symptoms, including nervousness, sexual desire or lack of desire, anxiety, and irritability. Basically women who transgressed cultural notions of femininity and had a tendency to cause trouble were suspected of suffering from the condition.

Third, *medicalization* is the process whereby normal functions of the body come to be seen as indicative of disease. This affects women in two ways. One, because women have more episodic changes in their bodies as a result of childbearing (for example, menstruation, pregnancy, childbirth, lactation, and menopause), they are more at risk for medical personnel interpreting these natural processes as problematic. Note how this tends to reinforce the argument that biology is destiny. Two, medicalization supports business and medical technologies. It tends to work against preventive medicine and encourages sophisticated medical technologies to "fix" problems after they occur. Medical services are dominated by drug treatments and surgery, and controlled by pharmaceutical companies, HMOs, and such professional organizations as the American Medical Association.

Fourth, the practices of *gender and ethnic profiling* encompass how notions about gender, race/ethnicity, and other identities inform everyday understanding of health care occupations and influence how medical practitioners treat their patients. For example, patients still often assume that white-coated white male orderlies are doctors and call women doctors "nurse." Women patients tend to interact differently with the health care system and are treated differently, often to the detriment of health outcomes.

Such differential treatment may occur as a result of provider bias. Provider bias concerns the ways stereotypes about people influence how providers interpret identical behaviors and clinical findings. Research in provider bias suggests several key interrelated factors about ways stereotypes influence how providers interpret identical behaviors and clinical findings. First, providers' conscious beliefs may be inconsistent with their automatic, unconscious reactions to low-income and/or minority patients. Second, when providers make complex judgments quickly, with insufficient and imperfect information or little time to gather information, they may "fill in the gaps" with beliefs associated with patients' social categories. Third, providers tend to be more likely to rely on stereotypes for "outgroup members" or people that do not act or look like them; and finally, providers may unconsciously favor those they feel to be similar to themselves, regardless of their conscious beliefs and politics.

For example, research suggests that physicians generally are more likely to consider emotional factors when diagnosing women's problems, and they are more likely to assume that the cause of illness is psychosomatic when the patient involved is female, prescribing more anxiety-mediating and mood-altering medication for women than for men. Although overall about 1 in 10 people in the United States older than age 12 takes antidepressant medication, the rate varies with about 6 percent of men and more than 15 percent of women, with white women having the highest rate. It is also interesting to note that the rate of antidepressant use in the United States has increased nearly 400 percent in the last 25 years and, according to the Centers for Disease Control, it is the most frequently used medication by persons aged 18 to 44 years. In addition, a recent study found that blacks, Latinas/os, and women generally waited longer for care. Whites waited an average of 24 minutes, while blacks had to wait an average of 31 minutes and Latinas/os had to wait 33 minutes on average. Homophobia and transphobia prevent LGBQT individuals from receiving fully informed care that affects their options and access.

Finally, a focus on women's health must discuss the issue of *corporate responsibility* and the role of the state in guiding and establishing that responsibility. This relates to how national and transnational corporations with strong profit motives affect our lives in terms of environmental degradation and toxic exposure, food additives, and problematic medical practices, and the ways decisions at national and international levels affect these practices. Examples include concern with greenhouse gases and global climate change, use of pesticides and herbicides, genetically modified food and corporate control of bioresources, and growth hormones in beef and dairy food products. All these issues are related to the corporatization of life and the global economy, the stresses of life in postindustrial societies, and ultimately the quality of life on the planet.

There is increasing interest in exploring the role of stress in our lives, as well as the connections between mind and body in terms of illness. Scientists have long known about these connections and have emphasized that it is less stress per se (of work, relationships, trauma, etc.) that affects the immune system, but more how individuals interpret or make meaning of that stress. It seems that stresses we choose evoke different responses from those we cannot control, with feelings of helplessness being worse than the stressor itself. While stress affects everyone, there is differential impact based on where a person lives, the kind of work s/he performs, the food s/he can afford to eat, and so forth. These stresses and the discriminations associated with being a target group member are examples of what scholars call *structural violence*, discussed later in Chapter 10.

LEARNING ACTIVITY   **Breast Science**

Go to the web page of the Breast Cancer Fund at *www.breastcancerfund.org*. Follow the "Clear Science" link. What does science tell us about the complex causes of breast cancer? Which chemicals are linked to breast cancer? Which populations are most vulnerable to breast cancer? Now go to the website of the National Cancer Institute at *www.cancer.gov/cancertopics/types/breast*. What are the incidences and death rates of breast cancer in the United States? Identify five facts about breast cancer that are new to you.

As mentioned above, differential exposure to environmental problems on the part of marginalized peoples has fostered an environmental justice movement to resist these inequities that occur as a result of lack of economic, social, and political power. In particular, environmental racism reflects the fact that people of color in the United States are disproportionately exposed to toxic environments due to the dumping of chemical and other waste on Native American lands and in urban areas where more people of color live. Environmental waste tends not to be dumped in areas populated by people of high socioeconomic status or where property values are high. The dumping of radioactive waste at Yucca Mountain, Nevada, despite the impact of this on the Western Shoshone tribe that considers the mountain sacred, is a case in point. People in developing countries who work in factories and sweatshops within the global economy (especially young women, who are often hired because they are cheap, dispensable, and easily controlled workers) are particularly at risk for occupational disease. See, for example, the reading in Chapter 9 by Momo Chang on the occupational hazards to health endured by workers in the nail salon industry.

Breast cancer is one important health issue closely tied to environmental problems and therefore to corporate responsibility. According to a 2013 National Cancer Institute fact sheet, 1 in 8 women will be diagnosed with breast cancer over a lifetime (compared to 1 in 20 in 1960). The relative increase in women living longer does not explain this increase in breast cancer incidence. It is the most common form of cancer in women and the number-two cause of cancer death (lung and bronchial cancer causes the most deaths), except in the case of Latinas, for whom breast cancer is the number-one cause of cancer death. Approximately 40,000 women die from breast cancer every year; men also can have the disease. Although African American women are not more susceptible to breast cancer, African American women aged 35 to 44 years are more than twice as likely to die from it. This is because they tend to have more advanced tumors as a result of poorer screening and reduced access to health care services.

Breast cancer research works to find a "cure," despite the fact that a focus on environmental contributors could work effectively to prevent breast cancer. The pink ribbon campaign for the cure, while a formidable support for breast cancer research and the empowerment of survivors, inadequately addresses environmental links to breast cancer. This is especially important because less than 10 percent of breast cancer cases have a genetic cause. About half of all breast cancer cases cannot be explained by known risk factors, encouraging scientists to suspect toxic chemicals in the environment playing a role in breast cancer risk. In particular, it has been hypothesized that environmental estrogens may play a role in the increasing incidence of breast cancer, testicular cancer, and other problems of the human reproductive system.

Environmental estrogens (also known as xenoestrogens) mimic the effects of human estrogen or affect its level in the body indirectly by disrupting the ways human estrogen is produced or used. Although some are naturally occurring (for example, phytoestrogens in plants such as soybeans), the greatest concern is synthetic estrogens that are not easily broken down and can be stored in the body's fat cells. More than 30 years ago researchers showed that organochlorines, a family of compounds including the pesticide DDT and the industrial chemicals known as polychlorinated biphenyls (PCBs), could mimic human estrogen and induce mammary tumors in laboratory animals. Organochlorines are organic compounds containing chlorine bonded to carbon. Virtually unknown in nature, they are primarily products or by-products of the chemical industry. Their largest single use is in the manufacture of polyvinyl chloride (PVC) plastics, but they are also used in bleaching, disinfection, dry cleaning, fire prevention, refrigeration, and such pesticides as DDT and atrazine. Although PCBs and DDT were banned years ago, they are still with us because they persist in the environment. An EPA (Environmental Protection Agency) report on dioxin, another highly toxic organochlorine, reports that North Americans have far higher levels of dioxin in their systems than was previously thought, raising new questions about the chemical's relationship to breast cancer and other health problems. It is also known that the plastic chemical BPA (Bisphenol A) (present in cash register receipts, the lining of canned goods, and in sporting equipment and medical supplies) is carcinogenic (cancer-promoting) and can cause lowered male sperm count.

Focusing on environmental issues necessarily involves addressing the effects of U.S. corporations and businesses on environmental quality. Even if exposure to toxic chemicals in the environment was shown to be associated with only 10 to 20 percent of breast cancer cases (a very conservative estimate, because, as already mentioned, about half of all breast cancer cases cannot be explained by known risk factors), policy enforced by the U.S. government to control individual and corporate use of toxic chemicals could prevent between 9,000 and 36,000 women and men from contracting the disease every year. In this way the "cure" is much more within reach than is acknowledged. See the sidebar "Breast Science" for links to help you explore the complex causes of breast cancer in the United States.

These environmental toxins are also affecting men's health, of course, and not only because men are also diagnosed with breast cancer. In particular, as well as other cancer risks, environmental estrogens are linked to the decrease in testosterone levels among men today (other causes include increased weight and decreased smoking). In 2006, researchers reported that the average 50-year-old man has almost 20 percent less testosterone than his father did 20 years ago.

REPRODUCTIVE JUSTICE

Reproductive justice involves being able to have safe and affordable birthing and parenting options; reliable, safe, and affordable birth control technologies; freedom from forced sterilization; and the availability of abortion. In other words, a key aspect of reproductive justice is the extent to which people can control their reproduction and therefore shape the

"All I really want is control over my own body!"

quality and character of their lives. Worldwide, some 215 million women have an "unmet need" for family planning, meaning that they want to either space or limit births but do not have access or lack consistent access to reliable methods of birth control that fit their personal needs. Women with unmet need make up 82 percent of the estimated 75 million unintended pregnancies that occur each year. The remaining 18 percent are due to inconsistent method use or method failure. Providing all women with basic family planning services is first and foremost a matter of basic human rights and bodily integrity. However, despite the importance of reproductive freedom in the United States and worldwide, it is increasingly under attack. For women of color in the United States in particular, as the reading "From Rights to Justice" by Zakiya Luna emphasizes, resisting population control while simultaneously claiming the right to bodily self-determination, including the right to contraception and abortion or the right to have children, is at the heart of the struggle for reproductive justice. Finally, another key aspect of reproductive choice is the right to assisted reproductive technologies for infertile couples who want children. Jennifer Parks discusses these technologies in the reading "Rethinking Radical Politics in the Context of Assisted Reproductive Technology." In response to debates about whether these technologies are ultimately good or bad for women, she makes the case that they are neither inherently liberating nor entirely oppressive. Rather, the consequences of these technologies can be understood only by considering how they are actually taken up within specific communities. In the sections that follow, we discuss the politics of sterilization, contraceptive technologies, and issues surrounding abortion.

Sterilization Practices

Female sterilization includes tubal ligation, a surgical procedure in which the fallopian tubes are blocked ("having the tubes tied"), and hysterectomy, in which the uterus is removed. A less invasive alternative to tubal ligation is a springlike device called *Essure* that blocks the fallopian tubes. Although hysterectomy (the removal of the uterus) is usually performed for medical reasons not associated with a desire for sterilization, this procedure results in sterilization. Vasectomy is permanent birth control for men, or male sterilization. It is effective and safe and does not limit male sexual pleasure. Countless women freely choose sterilization as a form of permanent birth control, and it is a useful method of family planning for many. "Freely choose," however, assumes a range of options not available to some women. In other words, "freely choose" is difficult in a racist, class-based, and sexist society that does not provide all people with the same options from which to choose.

HISTORICAL MOMENT   **The Women's Health Movement**

From the beginnings of the medical industry, women often suffered from the humiliation and degradation of medical practitioners who treated women as hysterical and as hypochondriacs, who medicalized normal female body functions, and who prevented women from controlling their own health. In 1969, as the women's movement heightened consciousness about other issues, women also began to examine the ways they had been treated and the ways women's biology and health had been largely unexplored. In the spring of that year, several women participated in a workshop on "women and their bodies" at a Boston conference. As they vented their anger at the medical establishment, they also began to make plans to take action. Although most of them had no medical training, they spent the summer studying all facets of women's health and the health care system. Then they began giving courses on women's bodies wherever they could find an audience. These women became known as the Boston Women's Health Collective and published their notes and lectures in what would eventually be known as *Our Bodies, Ourselves.*

Their efforts resulted in a national women's health movement. In March 1971 800 women gathered for the first women's health conference in New York. Women patients began to question doctors' authority and to bring patient advocates to their medical appointments to take notes on their treatment by medical professionals. Feminists questioned established medical practices such as the gendered diagnosis and treatment of depression, the recommendation for radical mastectomies whenever breast cancer was found, and the high incidence of cesarean deliveries and hysterectomies.

Although the original members of the women's health movement tended to be well-educated, middle-class white women, the movement quickly expanded to work with poor women and women of color to address the inequities caused by the intersections of gender with race and social class. Together, these women worked on reproductive rights, recognizing that for many poor women and women of color, the right to abortion was not as paramount as the right to be free from forced sterilization. Their work shaped the agenda of the National Women's Health Network, founded in 1975 and dedicated to advancing the health of women of all races and social classes.

Source: Ruth Rosen, *The World Split Open: How the Modern Women's Movement Changed America* (New York: Viking, 2000).

As a result, women on welfare are more likely to be sterilized than women who are not on welfare, and women of color and women in nonindustrialized countries are disproportionately more likely to receive this procedure rather than being offered more expensive contraceptive options. Lingering here is the racist and classist idea that certain groups have more right to reproduce than others: a belief and social practice called *eugenics.* Policies providing support for sterilization that make it free or very accessible obviously no longer force women to be sterilized. Rather, policies like these make the option attractive at a time when other options are limited.

One of the unfortunate legacies of reproductive history is that some women have been sterilized against their will, usually articulated as "against their full, informed consent." In the 1970s it was learned that many poor women—especially women of color, and Native American women in particular, as well as women who were mentally disabled or incarcerated—had undergone forced sterilization. Situations varied, but often they included women not giving consent at all, not knowing what was happening, believing they were having a different procedure, being strongly pressured to consent, or being unable to read or to understand the options told to them. The latter was especially true for women who did not speak or read English. Forced sterilization is now against the law, although problems remain. One consequence of forced sterilization for women of color in the United States was suspicion of birth control technologies as another potential tool of genocide. For example, when the contraceptive pill was available in the 1960s, some women of color remembered this history of forced sterilization and resisted its marketing, fearing the pill was another way to limit the non-white population. This was especially significant since the pill was originally tested on women in Puerto Rico.

Parenting Options and Contraceptive Technologies

In considering reproductive choice, it is important to think about the motivations for having children as well as the motivations for limiting fertility. Most people, women and men, assume they will have children at some point in their lives, and, for some, reproduction and parenting are less of a choice than something that people just do. Although in many non-industrial societies children can be economic assets, in contemporary U.S. society, for the most part, children consume much more than they produce. Some women do see children as insurance in their old age, but generally today we have children for emotional reasons such as personal and marital fulfillment, and for social reasons such as carrying on the family name and fulfilling religious mandates.

Childbirth is an experience that has been shared by millions of women the world over. Women have historically helped other women at this time, strengthening family and kinship bonds and the ties of friendship. As the medical profession gained power and status and developed various technologies (forceps, for example), women's traditional authority associated with birthing was eclipsed by an increasing medicalization of birthing. Again, the medicalization of childbirth regards birthing as an irregular episode that requires medical procedures, often including invasive forms of "treatment." As these trends gained social power, women who could afford it started going to hospitals to birth their children instead of being attended at home by relatives, friends, or midwives. Unfortunately, in these early days, hospitals were relatively dangerous places where sanitation was questionable and women in childbirth were attended by doctors who knew far less about birthing than did midwives. As the twentieth century progressed and birthing in hospitals became routine, women gave birth lying down in the pelvic exam position with their feet in stirrups, sometimes with their arms strapped down; they were given drugs and episiotomies (an incision from the vagina toward the anus to prevent tearing) and were routinely shaved in the pubic area. By the late twentieth century, thanks to a strong consumer movement, women were giving birth under more humane conditions. Birthing centers now predominate in most hospitals, and doctors no longer perform and administer the routine procedures and drugs they used to. Nonetheless, a large number of pregnant women (especially women of color) do not receive any health care at all, and a larger number still receive inadequate health care, some resorting to emergency rooms to deliver babies and having their first contact with the medical establishment at this time. As you can imagine, this scenario results in increased complications and potential unhealthy babies, and costs society much more financially than if routine health screening and preventive health care had been available.

Why might women want to control their fertility? The first and obvious answer concerns health. Over a woman's reproductive life, she could potentially birth many children and be in a constant state of pregnancy and lactation. Such a regimen compromises maximum health. Second, birthing large numbers of children might be seen as irresponsible in the context of world population and a planet with finite resources. Third, birthing is expensive and the raising of children even more expensive. Fourth, given that women have primary responsibility for childcare and that in the global north and many other regions the organization of mothering tends to isolate women in their homes, it is important to consider the emotional effects of constant child rearing. And, finally, if women had unlimited children, the constant caretaking of these children would preempt women's ability to be involved in other productive work outside the home. This "indirect cost" concept involves the loss or limitation of financial autonomy, work-related or professional identity, and creative and ego development.

Although today women are as likely to have children as they ever were, three facts stand out. First, the average family size decreased as the twentieth century progressed. Second, women are having children later in life than they did in earlier times in our society. Both of these trends are related to changes in health care technologies that have raised health care standards and encouraged parenting at later ages, the availability of birth control and abortion, and the increase in women's education and participation in paid labor with subsequent postponement of marriage and child rearing. Third, there has been a significant increase in the number of children born to single women, especially among non-white populations since the 1970s. Specifically, according to the most recent U.S. Census data, about a third of all children live in a single-parent home and approximately 85 percent of single-parent households are headed by women. The percentage of U.S. households headed by a single parent has nearly doubled since 1970. Approximately 40 percent of all babies are born to unmarried women who may or may not be partnered. One in 10 babies is born to a teenage mother, although these rates have been falling since 1991 with the exception of a two-year increase between 2005 and 2007 (which coincided with increased funding for abstinence-only sex education programs). Half of young women who have babies in their teens do not earn a high school diploma by age 22. A third of their children will go on to become teen parents and are also more likely to do poorly in school and drop out. Teens of color are especially susceptible to early pregnancy.

Unwanted unwed births, especially among teenagers, may result from lack of knowledge and support about reproduction and contraception in the context of an increasing sexually active population, poverty and lack of opportunities for education and employment, failure of family and school systems to keep young people in school, the increased use of alcohol and other drugs, and increasing restrictions on access to abortion services. Some girls see motherhood as a rite of passage into adulthood, as a way to escape families of origin, or as a way to connect with another human being whom they may believe will love them unconditionally. Because the largest increase in unmarried births has been among women aged 25 years and older, these changes also reflect changing norms about raising a child out of wedlock, either alone or in a heterosexual or lesbian cohabiting, or living together, arrangement, and the fact that some women are wary of marriage and/or choose and have the resources to maintain families outside of legal marriage.

Birth control technologies have been around for a long time. Many preindustrial societies used suppositories coated in various substances that blocked the cervix or functioned as spermicides; the condom was used originally to prevent the spread of syphilis, although it was discovered that it functioned as a contraceptive; and the concept of the intrauterine device was first used by Bedouins who hoped to prevent camels from conceiving during long treks across the desert by inserting small pebbles into the uterus. Nineteenth-century couples in the United States used "coitus interruptus" (withdrawal before ejaculation), the rhythm method (sexual intercourse only during nonfertile times), condoms, and abstinence. Although technologies of one kind or another have been around for generations, the issue for women has been the control of, and access to, these technologies. Patriarchal societies have long understood that to control women's lives it is necessary to control women's reproductive options. In this way, information about, access to, and denial of birth control technologies are central aspects of women's role and status in society.

In 1873 the Comstock Act made it illegal to send any "obscene, lewd, and/or lascivious" materials through the mail, including contraceptive devices and information. In addition to banning contraceptives and "quack" medicines, this act also banned the distribution of information on abortion. The state and federal restrictions became known as the Comstock Laws. Women understood that the denial of contraception kept them in the domestic sphere and, more importantly, exposed them to repetitive and often dangerous pregnancies. In response, a social movement emerged that was organized around reproductive choice. Called "voluntary motherhood," this movement not only involved giving women access to birth control, but also worked to facilitate reproduction and parenting under the most safe, humane, and dignified conditions. Many of its followers sought to control male sexual behaviors and advocated a social purity politics that saw male "vice" (prostitution, sexually transmitted infections, and sexual abuse) as the problem. Margaret Sanger was a leader of this movement and in 1931 wrote *My Fight for Birth Control* about her decision to become involved in the struggle for reproductive choice.

One unfortunate aspect, however, was the early birth control movement's affiliation with an emerging eugenics movement that argued only the "fit" should be encouraged to reproduce. Birth control was therefore necessary to prevent the "unfit" from unlimited reproduction. The "unfit" included poor and immigrant populations, the "feeble-minded," and criminals. Using a rationale grounded in eugenics, birth control proponents were able to argue their case while receiving the support of those in power in society. Nonetheless, although contraceptive availability varied from state to state, it was not until a Supreme Court decision (*Griswold v. Connecticut*) in 1965 that married couples were allowed legal rights to birth control. The Court's ruling said that the prohibition of contraceptive use by married people was unconstitutional in that it violated the constitutional right to privacy. This legal right was extended to single people in 1972 and to minors in 1977.

Today there are a variety of contraceptive methods available. Their accessibility is limited by the availability of information about them, by cost, and by health care providers' sponsorship. As you read about these technologies, consider the following questions: Whose body is being affected? Who gets to deal with the side effects? Who is paying for these methods? Who will pay if these methods fail? Who will be hurt if these side effects become more serious? These questions are framed by racialized gender relations and the context of the U.S. economy and its health organizations.

Other than tubal ligation where women are surgically sterilized and vasectomy where men are surgically sterilized, birth control methods include, first, the intrauterine device (IUD), a small, t-shaped device made of flexible plastic that is inserted into the uterus

ACTIVIST PROFILE **SisterLove**

The beginnings of SisterLove can be traced to a small group of women in Atlanta who organized to educate women about HIV/AIDS, self-help, and safer sex. Founded in 1989, SisterLove "is on a mission to eradicate the adverse impact of HIV/AIDS and other reproductive health challenges upon women and their families through education, prevention, support and human rights advocacy in the United States and around the world."[1] A part of the reproductive justice movement, which centers the reproductive health needs of women of color, SisterLove focuses on HIV prevention and outreach to women of color in Atlanta.

The organization's "Healthy Love" workshop provides prevention strategies. The facilitators take their programs into communities and offer them in spaces where participants feel safe and comfortable. SisterLove's website explains, "The workshop encourages participants to be confident in approaching their own sexuality and to demand safe behaviors from themselves and their partners. It also provides the opportunity for women to explore, discuss and dispel the barriers to practicing safer sex. The HLW respects the cultural traditions of African-American women who, throughout time, have gathered to support one another in times of crisis and growth."[2] Another outreach program focuses on HIV prevention education with women attending historically black colleges and universities.

SisterLove also offers a "Bridge Leadership" program that connects the group to a variety of other reproductive justice organizations, including SisterSong, and supports collaborative projects. The organization also has a capacity-building project in South Africa to enhance the capacity and leadership capabilities of NGOs and community-based organizations working with women and youth to prevent HIV.

As staff member Omisegun Pennick reminds us, "Indeed, 30 years into the epidemic we still have to drive the conversation around the absolute inclusion of women, especially women of color, in the movement to eradicate HIV/AIDS throughout the globe. We have to actively engage researchers in remembering to include women of color when talking about Pre-Exposure Prophylaxis (PreP) and other clinical treatments. We must support the critical work of campaigns such as the 30 for 30 to ensure that a minimum of 30% of the national resources for HIV/AIDS are given to organizations that directly serve women. We have to rally at the local, regional, and national level to ensure that policies and plans such as the National AIDS Strategy directly include women."[3]

[1] *http://sisterlove.org/about-us/.*
[2] *http://sisterlove.org/our-work/health-education-prevention/.*
[3] *http://sisterloveinc.blogspot.com/.*

and prevents the implantation of a fertilized egg. IUDs are available only by prescription, must be inserted by a clinician, and are a popular form of reversible birth control. Trade names include *ParaGard* and *Mirena* (the latter is an IUD that contains hormones). IUDs generally last up to 10 years, can result in heavier periods (although IUDs with hormones claim to reduce menstrual cramping and flow), and may increase the risk of pelvic inflammatory disease among women with multiple sexual partners. It is important to remember that IUDs do not protect against HIV/AIDS and other sexually transmitted infections.

Second are hormone regulation contraceptive methods. The combined oral contraceptive pill (COCP), often referred to as the birth control pill or colloquially as "the pill," is an oral contraceptive that contains a combination of two hormones: progestin and estrogen. It became widely available in the United States in the 1960s and quickly became the most popular means of contraception despite such side effects as nausea, weight gain, breast tenderness, and headaches. Combination pills usually work by preventing a woman's ovaries from releasing eggs (ovulation). They also thicken the cervical mucus, which keeps sperm from joining with an egg. Extended cycle pills are COCPs designed to reduce or eliminate menstrual bleeding. They usually produce a period every three months. The progestin-only or "mini pill" contains no estrogen and has fewer side effects than the regular pill, and it works by thickening cervical mucus and/or preventing ovulation. Taking the pill daily maintains the level of hormone that is needed to prevent pregnancy and it is important that this pill is taken at exactly the same time every day. The birth control pill trademarked as *YAZ* was marketed to appeal to young women through its claims to treat emotional and physical premenstrual symptoms and control moderate acne. *YAZ* is currently involved in lawsuits worldwide with alleged health problems including blood clots, pulmonary embolism, stroke, gallbladder complications, and heart attacks caused by the medication.

Contraception options also include implants such as *Norplant,* a contraceptive device implanted under the skin of the upper arm that releases a small amount of the hormone progestin through the inserted capsules for up to 5 years. As a result of lawsuits associated with unanticipated side effects, the maker of *Norplant* no longer markets this device in the United States, although it is available worldwide. *Depo-Provera* also uses progestin that is injected into the muscle every 11 weeks. It inhibits the secretion of hormones that stimulate the ovaries and prevents ovulation. It also thickens cervical mucus to prevent the entrance of sperm into the uterus. Risks include loss of bone density and side effects generally associated with the pill, such as weight gain, irregular, heavy, or no bleeding, headaches, depression, and mood changes. In addition, it may take up to a year after discontinuing use of *Depo-Provera* before a woman is fertile again. Alongside implants and injections are contraceptive patches, such as *Ortho Evra*, placed on the arm, buttocks, or abdomen, that releases hormones. Since its introduction in 2002, there have been a substantial number of lawsuits by plaintiffs citing serious blood clot–related injuries associated with *Ortho Evra*. This resulted in a warning from the Food and Drug Administration (FDA) for *Ortho Evra* in 2005.

Vaginal rings are also relatively popular contraceptives in the United States. One device marketed under the name *NuvaRing* was approved in 2001. It is a flexible, transparent ring about 2 inches in diameter that women insert vaginally once a month. The ring releases a continuous dose of estrogen and progestin. The ring remains in the vagina for 21 days and is then removed, discarded, and a new ring inserted. None of these hormone methods protect against HIV/AIDS and other sexually transmitted infections.

Next are the barrier methods. The diaphragm, cervical cap, and shield are barrier devices that are inserted into the vagina before sexual intercourse, fit over the cervix, and prevent sperm from entering the uterus. These methods work in conjunction with spermicidal jelly that is placed along the rim of the device. Some women use them in conjunction with spermicidal foam that is inserted into the vagina with a small plunger. Unlike the other methods, spermicides are available at any drugstore, but the diaphragm or cervical cap must be obtained from a physician or clinic. Also available at drugstores are vaginal

Sexually Transmitted Infections

Every year more than 12 million cases of sexually transmitted infections (STIs) are reported in the United States. The health impact of STIs is particularly severe for women. Because the infections often cause few or no symptoms and may go untreated, women are at risk for complications from STIs, including ectopic (tubal) pregnancy, infertility, chronic pelvic pain, and poor pregnancy outcomes.

CHLAMYDIA

Chlamydia is the most common bacterial sexually transmitted disease in the United States. It causes an estimated 4 million infections annually, primarily among adolescents and young adults. In women, untreated infections can progress to involve the upper reproductive tract and may result in serious complications. About 75 percent of women infected with chlamydia have few or no symptoms, and without testing and treatment the infection may persist for as long as 15 months. Without treatment, 20–40 percent of women with chlamydia may develop pelvic inflammatory disease (PID).

PELVIC INFLAMMATORY DISEASE

PID refers to upper reproductive tract infection in women, which often develops when STIs go untreated or are inadequately treated. Each year, PID and its complications affect more than 750,000 women. PID can cause chronic pelvic pain or harm to the reproductive organs. Permanent damage to the fallopian tubes can result from a single episode of PID and is even more common after a second or third episode.

One potentially fatal complication of PID is ectopic pregnancy, an abnormal condition that occurs when a fertilized egg implants in a location other than the uterus, often in a fallopian tube. It is estimated that ectopic pregnancy has increased about fivefold over a 20-year period. Among African American women, ectopic pregnancy is the leading cause of pregnancy-related deaths.

GONORRHEA

Gonorrhea is a common bacterial STI that can be treated with antibiotics. Although gonorrhea rates among adults have declined, rates among adolescents have risen or remained unchanged. Adolescent females aged 15–19 have the highest rates of gonorrhea.

HUMAN IMMUNODEFICIENCY VIRUS

Human immunodeficiency virus (HIV) is the virus that causes AIDS. The risk of a woman acquiring or transmitting HIV is increased by the presence of other STIs. In particular, the presence of genital ulcers, such as those produced by syphilis

(continued)

and herpes, or the presence of an inflammatory STI, such as chlamydia or gonor-rhea, may make HIV transmission easier.

HERPES SIMPLEX VIRUS (HSV)

Genital herpes is a disease caused by herpes simplex virus (HSV). The disease may recur periodically and has no cure. Scientists have estimated that about 30 million persons in the United States may have genital HSV infection. Most infected persons never recognize the symptoms of genital herpes; some will have symptoms shortly after infection and never again. A minority of those infected will have recurrent episodes of genital sores. Many cases of genital herpes are acquired from people who do not know they are infected or who had no symptoms at the time of the sexual contact.

HUMAN PAPILLOMA VIRUS (HPV)

HPV is a virus that sometimes causes genital warts but in many cases infects people without causing noticeable symptoms. Concern about HPV has increased in recent years after several studies showed that HPV infection is associated with the development of cervical cancer. Infection with a high-risk type of HPV is one risk factor for cervical cancer, which causes 4,500 deaths among women each year.

SYPHILIS

Syphilis is a bacterial infection that can be cured with antibiotics. Female adolescents are twice as likely to have syphilis as male adolescents. African American women have syphilis rates that are seven times greater than the female population as a whole.

Such infections among infants are largely preventable if women receive appropriate diagnosis and treatment during prenatal care. Death of the fetus or newborn infant occurs in up to 40 percent of pregnant women who have untreated syphilis.

CONDOM EFFECTIVENESS AND RELIABILITY

When used consistently and correctly, latex condoms are very effective in preventing a variety of STDs, including HIV infection. Multiple studies have demonstrated a strong protective effect of condom use. Condom breakage rates are low in the United States—no higher than 2 per 100 condoms used. Most cases of condom failure result from incorrect or inconsistent use.

For further information, contact the Office of Women's Health, Centers for Disease Control and Prevention, 1600 Clifton Road, Atlanta, GA 30033; phone: 800-232-4636.

Source: www.cdc.gov/od/owh/whstd.htm.

sponges that are coated with spermicide, inserted into the vagina, and work to block the cervix and absorb sperm. All these barrier methods work best when used in conjunction with a condom and are much less effective when used alone. The male condom is a latex rubber tube that comes rolled up and is unrolled on the penis. The female condom is a floppy polyurethane tube with an inner ring at the closed end that fits over the cervix and an outer ring at the open end that hangs outside the vagina. Condoms block sperm from entering the vagina and, when used properly in conjunction with other barrier methods, are highly effective in preventing pregnancy. Another very important aspect of condoms is that they are the only form of contraception that offers prevention against sexually transmitted diseases (STDs) generally and HIV/AIDS in particular. All health care providers emphasize that individuals not in a mutually monogamous sexual relationship should always use condoms in conjunction with other methods.

Finally, emergency contraception (EC), commonly known as the "morning-after pill" or by the trade-name Plan B, used after unprotected heterosexual intercourse is now available. Plan B and its generic, *Next Choice*, were approved by the FDA in 1997. Plan B is most effective if taken within 12 hours, although it offers protection for 3 days with some protection for up to 5 days. EC provides a high dose of the same hormones as are in birth control pills to prevent ovulation and fertilization. A *New England Journal of Medicine* study reported that almost 2 million of the approximately 3 million unintended pregnancies a year might be prevented if EC was more readily available. In addition, a study in the *Journal of the American Medical Association* reported that women with easy access to EC were not more likely to engage in unprotected heterosexual contact or abandon the use of other forms of birth control. The FDA has approved Plan B for over-the-counter sales for individuals aged 17 years and older, but women still face barriers when trying to obtain the medication in some communities. Plan B is expensive and current prices make it too expensive for some women. A new EC, *EllaOne* (ulipristal acetate), is more effective than Plan B in being able to work effectively for 5 days after unprotected sex rather than 3, and to provide less than 2 percent chance of pregnancy, a fail rate nearly half that of Plan B. Note that EC is different from the drug mifeprex (the U.S. trade name for mifepristone), also known as RU-486 and discussed in the following section, that works by terminating an early pregnancy and is known as a "medical abortion." Emergency contraception does not terminate a pregnancy but prevents one from occurring. It is important to understand the ways these two medications serve two different purposes and work completely differently from one another. As mentioned, RU-486 results in a termination of a pregnancy and is used only after pregnancy is established (and no more than 49 days since a woman's last menstrual period). On the other hand, EC or Plan B is used to prevent pregnancy. It will not harm an existing pregnancy and does not cause an abortion.

Current debate on EC concerns "refusal clauses" or the rights of medical personnel to deny medication such as Plan B based on their personal ideology. Currently 47 states and the District of Columbia allow certain individuals or entities to refuse to provide women specific reproductive-health services, information, or referrals. Nine states have adopted restrictions on EC specifically. In addition, the 2013 position statement of the American College of Clinical Pharmacy "supports the prerogative of a pharmacist to decline to personally participate in situations involving the legally sanctioned provision and/or use of medical and related devices or services that conflict with that pharmacist's moral, ethical, or religious beliefs." As of this writing, six states (Arkansas, California, Georgia, Idaho, Mississippi, South Dakota) have passed laws allowing a pharmacist the right to refuse to dispense EC and other contraception drugs and contraceptives and five (Illinois, Massachusetts, North Carolina, Pennsylvania, Washington) have passed legislation requiring pharmacists to fill or transfer certain prescriptions.

Many (including pharmacists) are opposed to such a stance, especially when it denies rape victims access to medication that is legally their right. The National Abortion Federation reports that approximately 13,000 women in the United States become pregnant as a result of rape every year. Timely access to EC ensures rape survivors the right to avoid additional trauma associated with pregnancy. Polls also show that nearly 80 percent of U.S. women want hospitals, whether religiously affiliated or not, to offer EC to rape survivors. Critics of pharmacists' ability to refuse dispensing EC and other medication emphasize that although these health workers have the right to consider their own religious or political beliefs in determining what medical decisions they make for their own care, these beliefs should not determine the care they provide customers and patients. In addition, the State Pharmacy Boards of some states have professional guidelines requiring pharmacists to fill prescriptions without recourse to their personal beliefs. Currently, 16 states and the District of Columbia require emergency rooms to provide information about EC and most of these also require EC-related services to sexual assault victims.

Abortion

Although induced abortion, the removal of the fertilized ovum or fetus from the uterus, is only one aspect of reproductive justice, it has dominated discussion of this topic. This is unfortunate because reproductive rights are about much more than abortion. Nonetheless, this is one topic that generates unease and often heated discussion. *Pro-choice* advocates believe that abortion is women's choice, women should not be forced to have children against their will, a fertilized ovum should not have all the legal and moral rights of personhood, and all children should be wanted children. Pro-choice advocates tend to believe in a woman's right to have an abortion even though they might not make that decision for themselves. *Pro-life* advocates believe that human personhood begins at conception and a fertilized ovum or fetus has the right to full moral and legal rights of personhood. They believe that rights about the sanctity of human life outweigh the rights of mothers. Some pro-life advocates see abortion as murder and doctors and other health care workers who assist in providing abortion services as accomplices to a crime.

According to the most recent Gallup poll published in 2013, and 40 years after the Supreme Court issued its opinion in *Roe v. Wade* that legalized abortion, significantly more people want the landmark abortion decision kept in place rather than overturned (53 percent to 29 percent with 18 percent having no opinion). The poll also showed that 48 percent of Americans consider themselves "pro-choice" (defined as in favor of women's choice to access abortion facilities), 44 percent "pro-life" (against abortion under varying circumstances), and the rest uncertain. The Rasmussen poll conducted at a similar time showed 54 percent pro-choice and 38 percent pro-life. Rasmussen polls tend to show higher pro-choice sentiment than Gallup polls, most likely because they survey likely voters, whereas Gallup surveys the population as a whole. However, these are two of several consecutive polls since May 2009 showing more people in the United States are pro-life than pro-choice, with more women than men advocating pro-choice views. Gallup shows 50 percent of women and 47 percent of men identify as pro-choice. People's support for pro-choice policies varies by political party, but also by demographic characteristics. People in the United States with no religious affiliation and self-described liberals are the most likely to call themselves pro-choice, with roughly 8 in 10 choosing this label. Those with a college education and high-income earners are also nearly as oriented to the pro-choice position as are Democrats, followed by those who live in the eastern part of the United States, those who live in cities, and young adults generally. On the other end of the spectrum, religiously-affiliated individuals, low-income individuals, adults with no college education, and those who live in the southern part of the United States are more likely to join Republicans and conservatives as the least pro-choice. Overall, a solid majority of Americans (61 percent) believe abortion should generally be legal in the first three months of pregnancy, while 31 percent disagree. However, support for abortions after the first trimester drops off sharply. Gallup has found this pattern each time it has asked this question since 1996, indicating that people in the United States attach much greater value to the fetus as it approaches viability, starting in the second trimester. These data show that relatively few Americans are positioned at either extreme of the spectrum of beliefs—that abortion should be legal in all circumstances or illegal in all circumstances. Despite this "middle ground" position among most people, the public debate on abortion tends to be highly polarized.

Issues associated with feminist pro-choice politics include moral responsibilities associated with requiring the birth of unwanted children, because the forces attempting to deny women safe and legal abortions are the very same ones that call for reductions in

LEARNING ACTIVITY   **Framing the Debate**

The words we choose to talk about issues matter, and the frames we create for understanding reproductive rights shape the conversation. Below are some of the ways anti-choice activists frame the debate. Search on the Web, newspapers, TV, or social media to find examples of these frames. How do you think these frames shape the debate? How do advocates of reproductive justice frame the debate? What differences do these frames make?

"Abortion as murder"

"Fetal personhood"

"Partial-birth abortion"

"Abortion as holocaust/genocide"

"Rape exemptions"

"Abortion as harm to women"

"Sexual morality"

"Abstinence-only until marriage"

"The right to conscience"[1]

[1] These frames are identified in *http://www.politicalresearch.org/wp-content/uploads/downloads/2013/04/Defending-Reproductive-Justice-ARK-Final.pdf.*

the social, medical, educational, and economic support of poor children. Does "pro-life" include being "for life" of these children once they are born? "Pro-life" politicians often tend to vote against increased spending for services for women and families. The second issue raised includes the moral responsibilities involved in requiring women to be mothers against their will. If you do grant full personhood rights to a fertilized ovum or fetus, then at what point do these rights take priority over the rights of another fully established person, the mother? What of fathers' rights? Third, several studies have shown that between two-thirds and three-quarters of all women accessing abortions would have an illegal abortion if abortion were illegal. Illegal abortions have high mortality rates; issues do not go away just by making them illegal. Although most feminists consider themselves pro-choice, there are exceptions, most notably the Feminists for Life of America organization. Their motto is "Pro Woman Pro Life" and they advocate opposition to all forms of violence, characterizing abortion as violence against women as well as against the fetus.

In the years since *Roe v. Wade,* the Supreme Court ruling legalizing abortion in the United States, thousands of women's lives have been saved by access to legal abortion. It is estimated that before 1973, 1.2 million U.S. women resorted to illegal abortions each year and that botched illegal abortions caused as many as 5,000 annual deaths. Barriers to abortion endanger women's health by forcing women to delay the procedure, compelling them to carry unwanted pregnancies to term, and leading them to seek unsafe and illegal abortions.

About half of U.S. pregnancies—more than 3 million each year—are unintended and about 4 in 10 of these are terminated by abortion. By age 45, at least half of all American women will have experienced an unintended pregnancy and about one-third will have had an abortion. Almost 9 in 10 abortions occur in the first 12 weeks of pregnancy (the first trimester) and 62 percent of all abortions take place in the first 9 weeks. About 1.5 percent occur at 21 weeks or later. Women who have abortions come from all racial, ethnic, socio-economic, and religious backgrounds and their motivations vary. Among women obtaining abortions, approximately half of these are younger than 25 years and 18 percent are teenagers. About 61 percent of abortions are obtained by women who have one or more children. The abortion rate is highest among women who are 20 to 24 years old (33 percent of all abortions). African American women are three times more likely to have an abortion than white women, and Latinas are two and a half times as likely, reflecting in part socioeconomic issues associated with raising children and, possibly, reduced adoption opportunities for children of color compared with white children. Approximately two-thirds of all abortions are obtained by never-married women (although many may be cohabiting), and the same number (although not necessarily the same women) intend to have children in the future. See box "Facts About Abortion, Choice, and Women's Health" for more details.

In the United States, abortion was not limited by law or even opposed by the church until the nineteenth century. In 1800 there were no states with anti-abortion laws and abortion was a relatively common occurrence through the use of pills, powders, and mechanical devices. Generally, abortion was allowed before "quickening," understood as that time when the fetus's movements could be felt by the mother (usually between 3 and 4 months). Between 1821 and 1840, 10 states enacted laws that included provisions on abortion, although in five these applied only to abortions after quickening. Between 1840 and 1860 the numbers of abortions increased such that some scholars estimate one abortion for every five or six live births. According to James Mohr's *Abortion in America,* abortion became more popular with married women and those of the middle and upper classes. This alarmed physicians in the rapidly growing medical profession. Mohr explains that physicians' concerns centered on ethical issues, scientific reasons to question the importance of quickening, the dangers of abortion for women, and the desire of physicians to rid themselves of some competitors such as midwives and others who helped provide abortions. He suggests that physicians were the major force in the enactment of laws against abortion in the nineteenth century, working through the American Medical Association to campaign to get state legislatures to further restrict abortion. Between 1860 and 1880 more than 40 laws restricted abortion and remained largely intact for a century. Abortion became less visible and the Comstock Laws prevented information about them. Abortions continued by performing the procedure but calling it something else, and in some states they were performed to save a mother's health and life. Not surprisingly, illegal abortions were rampant and often unsafe. By 1860 the Catholic Church officially had ruled against abortion despite the fact that, as explained, religious objections were not at the root of anti-abortion legislation. By the mid-twentieth century resistance to abortion laws had increased such that in 1959 the American Law Institute proposed revisions used by a number of states. It is important to understand that the Supreme Court decisions of the 1970s were not a modern "weakening" of moral standards, but a return to what many Americans believed and practiced in the past.

In 1969 Planned Parenthood supported the repeal of anti-abortion laws. Then in 1970 Hawaii and New York repealed their abortion legislation, but a 1972 referendum in Michigan to do so was defeated. Change came in 1973 when the United States Supreme Court ruled in *Roe v. Wade* that a Texas anti-abortion statute was unconstitutional and overturned all states' bans on abortion. The ruling used the *Griswold v. Connecticut* decision in arguing that abortion must be considered part of privacy rights in deciding whether to have children. It did not, however, attempt to decide the religious or philosophical issue about when life begins. The Court did agree that, under the law, a fetus is not treated as a legal person with civil rights. The ruling went on to divide pregnancy into three equal stages, or trimesters, and explained the differential interventions that the state could make during these different periods. The *Roe v. Wade* ruling held that the U.S. Constitution protects a woman's decision to terminate her pregnancy and allowed first-trimester abortions on demand. It declared that only after the fetus is viable, capable of sustained survival outside the woman's body with or without artificial aid, may the states control abortion. Abortions necessary to preserve the life or health of the mother must be allowed, however, even after fetal viability. Prior to viability, states can regulate abortion, but only if the regulation does not impose a "substantial obstacle" in the path of women.

There has been a general chipping away of women's rights to abortion since *Roe v. Wade*. Subsequent legislative and legal challenges have made abortion access more difficult and dangerous, but there has been no ruling yet that says life begins at conception and therefore no overturning of *Roe v. Wade*. Activities limiting legal rights to abortion currently include laws restricting poor and young women's access, refusal clauses (like those discussed previously that allow pharmacists to choose not to dispense medication if such practices offend their religious or political beliefs), bans on rarely-occurring late term abortion methods that protect women's health, violent tactics that intimidate doctors and patients, and pregnancy crisis centers that mislead women by purporting to offer full services but work to mislead and dissuade women from accessing an abortion. These restrictions on safe, legal abortions are discussed below. If the Supreme Court were to overturn

Roe v. Wade, abortion policy would revert to the states. Currently four states (Louisiana, Mississippi, North Dakota, South Dakota) have laws imposing near-total criminal bans on abortion (sometimes known as "trigger" bans) if *Roe v. Wade* were to be overturned.

One of the first restrictions on abortion rights was the Hyde Amendment, sponsored by Henry Hyde, a Republican senator from Illinois. It was an amendment to the 1977 Health, Education, and Welfare Appropriations Act and gave states the right to prohibit the use of Medicaid funds for abortion, thus limiting abortion to those women who could afford to pay and restricting abortion for poor women. Note that this was accompanied by Supreme Court rulings (*Beal v. Doe,* 1977) that said that states could refuse to use Medicaid funds to pay for abortions and that Congress could forbid states to use federal funds (including Medicaid) to pay for abortion services (*Harris v. McRae,* 1980). The latter ruling also allowed states to deny funds even for medically necessary abortions.

Second, the 1989 *Webster v. Reproductive Health Services,* sponsored by Missouri State Attorney William Webster, upheld a state's right to prevent public facilities or public employees from assisting with abortions, to prevent counseling concerning abortion if public funds were involved, and to allow parental notification rights. The latter restricts abortion for young women as parental involvement laws require young women who seek abortion care to tell their parents or get their permission, regardless of their family circumstances.

Third, Planned Parenthood v. Casey, although upholding *Roe v. Wade* in 1992, also upheld the state's right to restrict abortion in various ways: parental notification, mandatory counseling and waiting periods, and limitations on public spending for abortion services. Refusal clauses and counseling bans limit women's access to honest information and medical care, making it virtually impossible for some women to access abortion services altogether. Refusal clauses permit a broad range of individuals and/or

LEARNING ACTIVITY   **Debating Reproductive Rights**

Select one of the following topics to research from various perspectives. Be sure to represent perspectives that both support and oppose the topic, and be sure to examine various feminist analyses of the topic. Present your findings to your classmates. You may want to present your findings in the form of a debate, a Q & A session, or a pros and cons list.

TOPICS

1. The morning-after pill
2. The right to have children (particularly for lesbians, women with disabilities, single women, and older women)
3. Assisted reproductive technologies
4. Abstinence-only education
5. Distributing condoms in public schools
6. Selective reduction (abortion of one or more fetuses when pregnancy results in multiple fetuses)

Facts About Abortion, Choice, and Women's Health

- Between 1973, when abortion was made legal in the United States, and 1990, the number of deaths per 100,000 legal abortion procedures declined tenfold. By 1990, the risk of death from legal abortion had declined to 0.3 death per 100,000. (This rate is half the risk of a tonsillectomy and one-hundredth the risk of an appendectomy.)
- The mortality rate associated with childbirth is 10 times higher than for legal abortion.
- Worldwide, 125,000 to 200,000 women die each year from complications related to unsafe and illegal abortions.
- In 87 percent of the counties in the United States, no physicians are willing or able to provide abortions.
- Only 12 percent of ob-gyn residency programs in the United States offer routine training in abortion procedures.
- Eighty-eight percent of abortions are performed before the end of the first trimester of pregnancy.
- Sixty-four percent of states prohibit most government funding for abortion, making access to the procedure impossible for many poor women.
- Thirty-eight states have enacted parental consent or notice requirements for minors seeking abortions.
- Abortion has no overall effect on the risk of breast cancer.
- Abortion does not increase the risk of complications during future pregnancies or deliveries.
- Emergency contraceptives reduce a woman's chance of becoming pregnant by 75 percent when taken within 72 hours of unprotected sex with a second dose 12 hours after the first.
- Emergency contraceptives do not cause abortions; they inhibit ovulation, fertilization, or implantation before a pregnancy occurs.
- Use of emergency contraceptives could reduce the number of unintended pregnancies and abortions by half annually.
- Eighty-nine percent of women aged 18 to 44 have not heard of or do not know the key facts critical to the use of emergency contraceptives.

Sources: NARAL Publications: *www.naral.org;* Reproductive Health and Rights Center: *www.choice.org.*

institutions—hospitals, hospital employees, health care providers, pharmacists, employers, and insurers—to refuse to provide, pay for, counsel, or even give referrals for medical treatment that they personally oppose. Counseling bans, also known as "gag rules," prohibit health care providers, including individuals, under certain circumstances, from counseling or referring women for abortion care, preventing doctors from treating their patients responsibly, and severely limiting women's ability to make informed decisions. In 2013 there were 21 states with laws prohibiting some or all state organizations that receive state funds from providing counseling or referring women for abortion services. There have also been state rulings that require pregnant women to be offered ultrasound images of her fetus before she can have an abortion (even in the case of pregnancy due to rape or incest) and shield physicians from lawsuits if they choose not to tell a pregnant patient that her fetus has a birth defect for fear she might opt for abortion. Other bills in Mississippi and Virginia have been debated that require women to have ultrasounds before abortions can be performed.

Congress has also imposed restrictions on abortion care for women who depend on the government for their health care needs, including women serving in the military. With very rare exceptions, almost all women who obtain health care through federal programs are subject to additional restrictions on their right to choose. Unlike women who can use their own funds or private health insurance to pay for abortion care, women insured by federal health plans often lack the means to pay for an abortion. These include low-income women who receive health care through Medicare or Medicaid, federal employees and military personnel and their dependents, and women in federal prisons.

Webster v. Reproductive Health Services and *Planned Parenthood v. Casey* both gave states the right to impose parental involvement laws. Attempts to mandate parental involvement often seem reasonable, but unfortunately may endanger vulnerable teenagers. Some young women cannot involve their parents because they come from homes where physical violence or emotional abuse is prevalent, because their pregnancies are the result of incest, or because they fear parental anger and disappointment. In these circumstances, some young women feel they cannot involve their parents in the decision to terminate a crisis pregnancy. Mandatory parental involvement laws (both notice and consent: "notice" requires notification of intent to terminate a pregnancy; "consent" requires the permission of one or both biological parents) do not solve the problem of troubled family communication; they only exacerbate a potentially dangerous situation. In other words, although in a perfect world it would be positive for parents to provide guidance at this time, we do not live in a perfect world and instead of protecting young women, these laws have been shown to have serious consequences such as illegal and self-induced abortion, family violence, and suicide. Most states have laws that make it harder for teens to make a responsible and safe decision in a difficult situation. For example, 23 states currently require parental consent, 15 require parental notice, and 11 have parental notice and/or consent laws but permit other adults to stand in for a parent.

The *fourth* "chipping away" of *Roe v. Wade* occurred in September 2000 when the FDA approved mifepristone (mifeprex), formerly known as RU-486, an antiprogesterone drug that blocks receptors of progesterone, a key hormone in the establishment and maintenance of human pregnancy. Used in conjunction with a prostaglandin such as misoprostol, mifepristone induces abortion when administered early in a pregnancy, providing women with a medical alternative to traditional aspiration (suction) abortion. This drug has proven to be a safe and effective option for women seeking an abortion during the first few weeks of pregnancy since its approval in France in 1988. FDA approval of RU-486 in the United States requires a doctor administer and supervise the use of the drug as an abortifacient. Research in Europe suggests that the availability of this drug has not increased abortion rates generally. In the United States, however, RU-486 has been the target for anti-choice lobbying and activism to block access to the drug. Such efforts resulted in the "RU-486 Suspension and Review Act" of 2003, 2005, and 2007, which failed to advance in each session. Again, refusal clauses concerning pharmacists' rights to deny medication based on their personal ideology are a central aspect of this debate.

IDEAS FOR ACTIVISM **Ten Things You Can Do to Protect Choice**

1. *Volunteer for a pro-choice organization.* Pro-choice organizations need volunteers. There are dozens of organizations working in various ways to help women get the services they need. For pro-choice organizations nationwide, check *www.choice.org.*
2. *Write a letter to a local clinic or abortion provider thanking them for putting themselves on the line for women.* Doctors and clinic workers hear vociferously from those opposed to abortion. Hearing a few words of thanks goes a long way.
3. *Monitor your local paper for articles about abortion.* Write a letter to the editor thanking them for accurate coverage or correcting them if coverage is biased.
4. *Find out how your elected representatives have voted on abortion.* Call and ask for their voting records, not just on bills relating to legality of abortion, but also on related issues such as funding for poor women, restrictions meant to impede a woman's access to services (such as waiting periods and informed consent), and contraceptives funding and/or insurance coverage. Whether or not you agree with the votes of your elected officials, write and let them know that this is an issue on which you make voting decisions. Anti-choice activists don't hesitate to do this; you should do it too.
5. *Talk to your children now about abortion. Explain why you believe it's a decision only a woman can make for herself.*
6. *If you have had an abortion, legal or illegal, consider discussing it with people in your life.* More than 40 percent of American women will have at least one abortion sometime during their lives. More openness about the subject might lead to less judgment, more understanding, and fewer attempts to make it illegal.
7. *Volunteer for a candidate whom you know to be pro-choice.*
8. *Be an escort at a clinic that provides abortions.*
9. *Vote!*
10. *Hold a house meeting to discuss choice with your friends.* You could show one or all of Dorothy Fadiman's excellent documentaries from the trilogy *From the Back Alleys to the Supreme Court and Beyond. When Abortion Was Illegal* is a good conversation starter. For information on obtaining these videos, contact the CARAL ProChoice Education Fund or *Concentric Media.*

Source: *www.choice.org.*

Fifth, in 2003, the U.S. Congress passed the Federal Abortion Ban, and President George W. Bush signed it into law. The ban outlaws certain second trimester abortions that leading medical and health organizations, doctors, medical school professors, and other experts have repeatedly declared under oath as necessary to protect women's health. These are performed when the life or health of the mother is at risk or when the baby is too malformed (for example, in severe cases of hydrocephalus where the baby cannot live and a normal delivery would kill the mother). In 2007 the U.S. Supreme Court upheld this first ever federal ban on an abortion procedure. Surprisingly, and reversing three decades of legal rulings, the federal ban does not allow an exception when women's health is in danger. The court's decision gives the go-ahead to the states to restrict abortion services (discussed below) and paves the way for new legislation to enact additional bans on abortion, including those that doctors say are safe and medically necessary.

Following this federal ban on abortion is the restriction of rare, late-term abortions at the state level. In 2010, for example, Nebraska passed the country's most restrictive abortion law that barred abortions after 20 weeks. In 2011, Alabama, Idaho, Indiana, Kansas, and Oklahoma followed suit; and in 2012, Arizona, Georgia, and Louisiana passed curbs of their own. If laws provide exceptions for the life or health of the woman, they may be considered constitutional under *Roe v. Wade*. Many scholars, however, have emphasized that the movement to limit rare, late-term abortions is a "straw-man" argument in which a perceived opponent is misrepresented in order to create the illusion of having refuted the argument by replacing it with a superficially similar, yet unequivalent, position (the "straw man"). The misrepresentation is the notion that late-term abortions occur frequently and willingly by women rather than rarely and usually as a result of a medical emergency. Such tactics have been used throughout history in polemical debates, particularly in cases of highly charged, emotional issues. With the exception of laws in Arizona, Idaho, and Georgia, many of these cases have not been challenged as unconstitutional (Idaho's law was found to be unconstitutional as of this writing). This is due in part because they do not really have a serious effect: As already discussed, less than 2 percent of abortions occur after 20 weeks. Still, their real effect is two-fold: misrepresentation and the energizing of a movement to limit women's reproductive freedom, and the hope among anti-choice activists to force these laws for consideration by the U.S. Supreme Court with the goal of overturning *Roe v. Wade*. As of this writing, the latter may occur as states moved to pass earlier bans. For example, in 2013 Arkansas passed a ban on all abortions after 12 weeks (despite the veto of its governor), and North Dakota proceeded to pass the most restrictive law on all abortions after 6 weeks. While the Arkansas law still does not affect many procedures, the North Dakota law, although seemingly unconstitutional, basically bans all abortions in the state. Again the goal is to put abortion back in front of the Supreme Court, get *Roe v. Wade* overturned, and return abortion policymaking power to the states.

The *sixth* "chipping away" of abortion rights occurred in April 2004 when President George W. Bush signed the Unborn Victims of Violence Act into law, giving the zygote, embryo, or fetus the same legal rights as a person and preparing the groundwork for further restrictions on abortion access. Also known as the Laci Peterson Law, in reference to the murder of a woman and her unborn child, this law creates the notion of double homicide in the case of the murder of a pregnant woman, although the law has jurisdiction only for homicides committed on federal property. This law is somewhat controversial for women's rights supporters. Though written to support survivors of violence by establishing that a fetus of any gestational age has equal personhood with a woman, it jeopardizes women's rights to safe and legal abortions.

Seventh, versions of the Child Interstate Abortion Notification Act passed the House of Representatives between 1998 and 2007, but none yet (as of this writing) has been sent to the President for signing. It seeks to make it a crime to take a minor woman (under 18 years of age) residing in a state with parental notification and/or consent laws across state lines to access an abortion. It also seeks to create a national requirement for parental notification for underage women wanting to terminate a pregnancy and requires a 24-hour waiting period for a minor's abortion. Doctors and others could be prosecuted under the legislation. Supporters of the bill declare it necessary to protect young women because an adult predator could impregnate a girl and then force her to have an abortion to hide the crime. Opponents say the bill is too far-reaching, explaining that it sets up more roadblocks for women who have the right to safe and legal abortion, and could further isolate young women by making it a crime for a family member or other caring adult to provide assistance. Major medical and public health organizations, including the American Medical Association and the American Academy of Pediatrics, oppose such efforts to prevent young women from receiving confidential health services.

Finally, restrictions on abortion occur as a result of requirements such as those passed in Michigan in 2012 where clinics providing a certain number of surgical abortions per year and publicly advertising outpatient abortion services be licensed as freestanding outpatient surgical facilities. Restrictions also include violence and harassment of medical personnel who provide legal abortion services. These violent tactics intimidate medical personnel and patients seeking reproductive health care. In May 2009, for example, Dr. George Tiller was murdered inside his church in Wichita, Kansas. He was killed because he was a doctor who provided abortion services. Such medical personnel providing legal services face ongoing threats of murder, violence, and intimidation. They continue to face harassment, bombings and arson, death threats, kidnapping, assault, and stalking. Patients visiting clinics may also be targeted, as anti-abortion extremists often use such tactics to block patients' access to medical care.

Abortion in the United States remains legal, but its availability and accessibility is limited. As "The Only Good Abortion Is My Abortion," the first essay by Maggie Koerth-Baker in the reading "Freedom to Choose: Four Essays on Abortion Rights," emphasizes, there is less resistance to "good" abortions (meaning acceptable, as in her case because of fetal damage and the inevitability of miscarriage). She makes the case that there is no reason to treat the decision she has to make any differently than the decisions made by other women. Such resistance to women's right to choose, however, varies by state. At the moment there are three states in the United States that have only one abortion clinic and almost 90 percent of counties have no abortion provider at all. In addition, approximately one in six hospital patients are treated at Catholic hospitals that adhere to religious directives restricting certain procedures. The second essay in "Freedom to Choose?," this time an article titled "Treatment Denied" by Molly M. Ginty, addresses this issue. Despite its legality, abortion is heavily restricted in many states.

One piece of legislation, however, was passed in 1994 to safeguard women's right to access their legal rights. After the public outcry associated with the public harassment, wounding, and death of abortion services providers, and the vandalism and bombing of various clinics, the Supreme Court ruled in *Madsen et al. v. Women's Health Center, Inc.* to allow a buffer zone around clinics to allow patients and employees access and to control noise around the premises. The same year, the Freedom of Access to Clinic Entrances (FACE) Act made it a federal crime to block access, harass, or incite violence in the context of abortion services. FACE provides federal protection against unlawful tactics used by abortion opponents. It provides civil remedies and criminal penalties for a range of violent, obstructive, or threatening conduct directed at reproductive-health providers or patients. Courts repeatedly have upheld the law as constitutional, and scholars describe FACE as a significant factor in reducing clinic violence. In addition, 16 states and the District of Columbia have laws that protect health care facilities, providers, and/or patients from blockades, harassment, and/or other violence. Finally, seven states have passed *Freedom of Choice Acts* that codify a woman's right to choose, making the protections of *Roe v. Wade* part of state law. These states include California, Connecticut, Hawaii, Maine, Maryland, Nevada, and Washington. The latter three states passed this through ballot initiatives.

In closing this chapter it is important to emphasize that only 12 percent of ob-gyn medical residency programs offer routine training in abortion procedures. There has also been a significant increase in Crisis Pregnancy Centers (CPCs) that claim to offer comprehensive services but are actually focused on reducing abortions. Currently it is estimated there are between 2,300 and 4,000 CPCs in the United States. Many of these are unregulated and unlicensed and may not be required to follow privacy-protection laws required of physicians and comprehensive health clinics. They have been well documented as operating in close proximity to health clinics, mimicking the style or names of clinics that offer abortion services, and functioning to actively dissuade women from seeking an abortion. They use deceptive tactics to mislead women about pregnancy-related issues, making false claims such as abortion causes breast cancer or mental illness or can lead to sterility. Many CPCs receive state and federal funding and a recent study found that 87 percent of CPCs that receive federal funding provide false and unscientific information about abortion. The last essay in "Freedom to Choose?," titled "The Anti-Abortion Clinic Across the Street," discusses the current proliferation of CPCs. In this article the author, Kathryn Joyce, also addresses the relationship between CPCs and the violent anti-choice movement that advocates clinic violence. Such problems have prompted several cities including Baltimore and Austin to propose legislation to prevent such activities and a federal bill (Stop Deceptive Advertising Women's Services Act) was reintroduced to Congress in 2010. Under this act it would be illegal for CPCs to falsely advertise their services. Such legislation is important in addressing the obstacles to and limitations of access that disproportionately affect poor women, women of color, and young women.

The Gender Gap in Pain

Laurie Edwards (2013)

To the list of differences between men and women, we can add one more: the drug-dose gender gap. Doctors and researchers increasingly understand that there can be striking variations in the way men and women respond to drugs, many of which are tested almost exclusively on males. Early this year, for instance, the Food and Drug Administration announced that it was cutting in half the prescribed dose of Ambien for women, who remained drowsy for longer than men after taking the drug.

Women have hormonal cycles, smaller organs, higher body fat composition—all of which are thought to play a role in how drugs affect our bodies. We also have basic differences in gene expression, which can make differences in the way we metabolize drugs. For example, men metabolize caffeine more quickly, while women metabolize certain antibiotics and anxiety medications more quickly. In some cases, drugs work less effectively depending on sex; women are less responsive to anesthesia and ibuprofen for instance. In other cases, women are at more risk for adverse—even lethal—side effects.

These differences are particularly important for the millions of women living with chronic pain. An estimated 25 percent of Americans experience chronic pain, and a disproportionate number of them are women. A review published in the Journal of Pain in 2009 found that women faced a substantially greater risk of developing pain conditions. They are twice as likely to have multiple sclerosis, two to three times more likely to develop rheumatoid arthritis and four times more likely to have chronic fatigue syndrome than men. As a whole, autoimmune diseases, which often include debilitating pain, strike women three times more frequently than men.

While hormonal, genetic and even environmental factors might influence the manifestation and progression of autoimmune diseases, we don't yet know the reason for this high prevalence in women.

Pain conditions are a particularly good example of the interplay between sex (our biological and chromosomal differences) and gender (the cultural roles and expectations attributed to a person). In 2011, the Institute of Medicine published a report on the public health impact of chronic pain, called "Relieving Pain in America." It found that not only did women appear to suffer more from pain, but that women's reports of pain were more likely to be dismissed.

This is a serious problem, because pain is subjective and self-reported, and diagnosis and treatment depend on the assumption that the person reporting symptoms is beyond doubt.

The oft-cited study "The Girl Who Cried Pain: A Bias Against Women in the Treatment of Pain" found that women were less likely to receive aggressive treatment when diagnosed, and were more likely to have their pain characterized as "emotional," "psychogenic" and therefore "not real."

Instead of appropriate care for physical pain, this can lead to treatment for mental health issues that might not even exist. The situation is further complicated by the fact that antidepressants are absorbed differently in women and vary in effectiveness, depending on hormonal cycles.

The routine attribution of abdominal pain from conditions like appendicitis or gastrointestinal disease to gynecological problems can also delay or complicate the diagnostic process. A 2008 study published in the *Journal Academic Emergency Medicine,* designed to gauge gender disparities among emergency room patients complaining of abdominal pain, found that even after adjusting for race, class and triage assessment, women were still 13 to 25 percent less likely than men to receive high-strength "opioid" pain medication. Those who did get opioid pain relievers waited an average of 16 minutes longer to receive them.

Conditions like fibromyalgia or chronic fatigue syndrome, for which definitive causes have not been identified and concrete diagnostic tests are not available, illustrate the problems associated with the perceived reliability of the female patient as narrator of her pain. Women are more likely to receive diagnoses of many of these more nebulous conditions—fibromyalgia, which affects about six million patients in the United States, is nine times more likely to be diagnosed in women than in men—and this discrepancy surely contributes to the widespread skepticism that still exists over the legitimacy of these disorders.

I am a sufferer of pain and chronic disease. Like many, I've had physical symptoms (in my case, respiratory problems and infections) explained away as emotional. My freshman year in college, I was in the emergency room, flanked by machines and struggling to breathe while doctors lobbed questions at me: Why wasn't I responding to the medication the way they expected I would? Was I just too anxious? Could I not handle stress, and was that making me sick?

I was 23 before I was given a correct diagnosis of a rare genetic lung disease called primary ciliary dyskinesia. I'd been sick since birth, but long diagnostic journeys are occupational hazards of living with conditions doctors don't often see. Still, my journey was unnecessarily protracted by my doctors' dismissal of my symptoms as those of a neurotic young woman.

For all the medical advances of the past few decades, we still know shockingly little about pain and how to control it. Sex-based research is a crucial part of understanding not just the underlying mechanisms of pain, but the most effective ways to treat it for men and women alike. The Institute of Medicine report found gaps in research, particularly in terms of effective treatments, as well as in the oversight of pain research. The report recommended that these problems be addressed and that strategies to resolve them be implemented by 2015.

Among those improvements must be a renewed focus on discovering why women respond differently to some drugs and diseases, as well as an emphasis on training physicians to better diagnose and manage women's pain. A report by the Campaign to End Chronic Pain in Women found that inadequate physician training in diagnosing and treating just six pain disorders that affect women either exclusively or predominantly, including fibromyalgia and chronic fatigue syndrome, added as much as $80 billion a year to America's health care bills.

Part of the reason the diagnosis and treatment of women's pain lag so much is simply the pace of medical research itself, which is slow to move from publication to clinical practice. Unfortunately, if anything, changes in assumptions about gender evolve even more slowly.

R E A D I N G   57

Southern Discomfort

Carl Gaines (2011)

When Juanita Davis, director of HIV prevention and education for the state of Mississippi, visits church or school groups to teach about the virus, she arrives armed with Mounds bars, 5th Avenue bars, and lots of Sugar Babies.

She brings the sweets not to bribe her audiences to pay attention, but rather to help illustrate, with physical analogies, the things she is not allowed to say in the places she visits. Imagine trying to teach HIV prevention without being able to say "penis," "condom," or "semen."

That's where the candy bars come in.

The fact that Davis must use candy as euphemisms for body parts, contraceptives, and bodily fluids says much about the environment in which she—and others—are trying to fight the next big wave of HIV/AIDS in America.

Like her peers battling the virus in a region cinched tight by the Bible Belt, Davis has to use ingenuity. By the time anyone changes the system, or age-old beliefs, too many more will get sick, and even die. That's why Davis is willing to try to break down barriers—one chocolate bar at a time.

"If we can give just a little information—once we talk about the statistics, for instance—people are more open [to the idea of learning how to avoid HIV]," Davis says. "If we can [talk through] that crack, they'll open the door."

The challenges specific to the Southern United States have made people in this area uniquely at risk for HIV and have resulted in the disproportionately high rates of infection, as well as the high percent of people living with HIV who are unaware of their status or who know they have it but who are too afraid to seek care.

Although only 36 percent of the U.S. population lives in the South, about half of all people living with HIV/AIDS in the country live in the region. The South has the highest rates of new HIV cases, almost half of new AIDS diagnoses, the largest numbers of adults and adolescents living with HIV/AIDS, the most people with AIDS diagnoses, and the most AIDS deaths.

The HIV/AIDS epidemic is raging across the Southern United States like an out-of-control fire.

Conservative attitudes about sex and sexuality are just one hurdle HIV fighters face in the South. Extreme poverty is another. Kathie Hiers, chief executive officer of AIDS Alabama, says, "[The South has] the most people living with HIV/AIDS, the most rural areas, the most people without health insurance, and the highest [overall] death rate."

She cites poverty as a key element in the spread of HIV across the South, pointing out that as the economy tanked across the country, people in the region had less distance to fall before hitting rock bottom.

Of the 17 states considered "Southern" [including Washington, D.C.] by the U.S. Census Bureau, 13 have poverty rates of 16 percent or more. In Mississippi, the poorest of the poor states, the poverty rate is 21 percent.

To witness what that life below the poverty line looks like, you only need to travel a short distance out of Jackson, the state capital.

Two hours northwest of Jackson you hit Greenville. As you drive to Greenville, the terrain dips down and flattens out into a seemingly endless sea of cotton fields that flow down to the Mississippi delta. Located smack inside the delta, Greenville is one of the poorest cities in the state.

Located in Washington County, the town has a population of 35,355 and is famous for its cotton and catfish, but many people have left the area in recent years. As a result, there is a sense of real isolation in this predominantly rural area. Several people don't have cars or access to the Internet.

Poverty not only keeps expensive medications out of the reach of people diagnosed with HIV in Greenville, it even keeps people from getting to a doctor in the first place.

"I was diagnosed in 1990 when the health department told me I had contracted HIV," says Dorothy Davis, a longtime Greenville resident. After informing Davis of her status, the health department sent her home. "I walked home from the health department not knowing how I got there—I was in a daze," she says. Due to her low income and lack of transportation, she had trouble getting care and treatment.

Over the years, Davis has tried to organize support groups for other people in the area who are HIV-positive. But even though there has been interest, it has been too hard to get people together.

Another woman living with HIV, in Cleveland, Mississippi—about an hour's drive from Greenville—wanted to attend Davis' support group, but she didn't have access to a car and she couldn't get there via public transportation. As far as Davis knows, the woman still hasn't been linked to any support network.

Robin T. Webb, executive director of A Brave New Day, a Jackson-based HIV/AIDS advocacy group, says lack of transportation is a major issue when it comes to fighting and living with the disease in the South. "Peer networking is not valued [in Mississippi]," Webb says. "If it were valued, there would be transportation."

Webb also points out another critical barrier: lack of understanding about support programs designed to help low-income people get care and treatment. This is true, he says, of both people living with HIV and the medical providers who treat them.

"People don't know what HOPWA and ADAP are," he says, referring to Housing Opportunities for Persons with AIDS and the AIDS Drug Assistance Program. Our country, he continues, has a habit of offering services but not educating people that they are available.

Davis is a case in point. When she was asked, she didn't know who paid for her HIV medications. She suspected that their cost was covered by her Social Security Disability Insurance. All she knew for sure was that when she went to the pharmacy, her prescriptions were there. She had never heard of ADAP.

Even if Dorothy Davis knew about ADAP, she might not be able to receive benefits from the program.

Another complicating factor when it comes to fighting HIV in the South is that even federal funds specifically allocated to help people with HIV may not be reaching those most in need. The distribution of special funds was set up when the epidemic was concentrated on the coasts and in the north. The disease has moved faster than the systems set up to tackle it have evolved.

For example, in 2008, Part A of the Ryan White HIV/AIDS Treatment Modernization Act provided $627 million nationwide for emergency assistance for people living with HIV. The bulk of this federal funding was directed to EMAs, or "eligible metropolitan areas."

To qualify, according to the Department of Health and Human Services, an area must have reported more than 2,000 AIDS cases in the most recent five years and have a population of at least 50,000. Under these constraints, many of the South's rural areas cannot secure funding.

As a result of the structure for distributing Ryan White funding, the bulk of money for HIV/AIDS care in the South comes from Medicaid, the U.S. government's health care program for low-income Americans. (This is true in many other parts of the country, including those also covered

by Ryan White funding.) To date, Medicare covers the health care of four in ten Americans with HIV/AIDS. In an effort to bring down costs and shorten budget deficits, however, Southern states in particular are limiting their Medicaid contributions and the services that the program covers. For example, in 2010 the U.S. Congress allocated $127 million in supplemental Medicaid to Mississippi, but the state's governor, Haley Barbour, won't distribute the money until fiscal year 2012.

"I appreciate the leadership of both houses for agreeing that these additional funds should be saved and spent in fiscal year 2012 when we face a budget shortfall of more than $600 million," Barbour said in an August 2010 statement.

Meanwhile, in December 2010, there were 837 people on AIDS Drug Assistance Program wait lists in Georgia and 511 people waiting in Louisiana. There were no wait lists in Mississippi.

Southern states already have relatively low Medicaid expenditures given their population sizes. In 2008, Alabama, with a population of 4.7 million people, paid $4.1 billion for the program, and Mississippi, with a population of 2.9 million, paid $3.8 billion. By comparison, New York, with a population of 19.2 million, paid more than any other state—$47.6 billion.

Many see the Patient Protection and Affordable Care Act, a.k.a. the nation's new health reform law, as a bright spot, widening the net of HIV-positive people eligible for services.

"I think that health care reform is going to help a lot," Hiers says. "When health care reform kicks in, we figure that about 80 percent of HIV-positive people [in the South] are going to get Medicaid."

Personal poverty, tight-fisted and impoverished state governments, and conservative attitudes toward sex have created a perfect storm of inadequate HIV care for many Southerners, but Mother Nature herself has also played a big role. Hurricanes Katrina and Rita slammed into Louisiana and Mississippi in 2005, and the fallout continues to undermine both prevention and treatment efforts.

The storms destroyed infrastructure, much of which has yet to be rebuilt, and this continues to make getting around difficult. Many people who were dislocated from their homes are still not settled into new ones. Medical records for countless people were washed away.

The BP oil spill in 2010 further wrecked the Gulf Coast economy, making addressing the needs of those in the area even more challenging.

Sergio Farfan, cochair of the Louisiana Latino Health Coalition for HIV/AIDS Awareness, who lives in Baton Rouge, was one of the first to return to New Orleans after Katrina. As the chaos surrounding the hurricane subsided, he says, Latinos streamed in to help clean up the devastation.

According to a 2006 study by Tulane University in New Orleans and the University of California at Berkeley, almost half of all reconstruction workers who came to New Orleans after Katrina were Latino—a quarter of them undocumented. "The health needs for the Latino community, [including the people with HIV], increased tremendously [after the hurricane]," Farfan says. The Mexican Consulate in New Orleans closed in 2002, but it reopened after Katrina to deal with the increased need.

Farfan says that it's hard to reach the Latino population due to the stigma surrounding HIV. Too few outreach and prevention programs have workers who can speak Spanish. And the clients come from different countries, so there are small cultural differences that need to be accounted for, but often aren't.

He also cites current immigration laws: When undocumented people go into hiding to avoid detection, they also become ineligible for free services from the state.

But for all these factors—poverty, lack of funds and services, squeamishness about sex, language and immigration barriers, walls of water and oil washing over parts of the region—the largest obstacles in the South to fighting HIV/AIDS remain stigma and discrimination.

Kathie Hiers of AIDS Alabama tells the story of a board president at an AIDS service organization she ran in Mobile years ago. When he found out he was HIV-positive, the man drove several hours to Birmingham for medical care in order to avoid being seen in his neighborhood seeking treatment. His care lapsed, and he died.

"There is religiously driven stigma," says Webb of A Brave New Day. "[As a result,] across the board

people aren't getting tested [for HIV]." They're also not getting educated about the virus.

The lack of participation by many religious groups, especially black churches, in the fight against AIDS is a source of frustration for Ruby Gray, a social worker for the past two years in Canton, Mississippi, who has worked in HIV prevention services for more than 20 years.

Despite the fact that through 2008, 70 percent of AIDS diagnoses in Mississippi occurred in the black community, Gray says, black churches often don't want to even acknowledge that the HIV/AIDS epidemic exists. "It's like everyone's turning their heads and it's not happening—but it is happening," she says.

Black churches often are unwilling to get involved in HIV/AIDS education, prevention, and treatment because of the connection between the disease and people's sexual orientation. "The [stigma] is tied to the idea of MSMs," says Gray, referring to men who have sex with men.

In the United States, HIV is associated with gay people, sex workers, and drug users. Webb says churches are eager to do HIV/AIDS outreach in Africa, but they are unwilling to broach the topic at home.

Gray spent five years trying to convince her pastor to incorporate some mention of HIV into his sermons and to have someone come in to speak. He finally said yes, and since then she hasn't had any further problems getting HIV/AIDS materials into her church.

Greenville resident Dorothy Davis also knows how difficult it can be to get black churches to talk about HIV/AIDS. She does peer-to-peer outreach, speaking at churches and schools about HIV when they'll let her in the door, which isn't often.

"Churches don't want to participate," she says. Davis recalls once being invited by a congregant to speak at a nondenominational church, only to show up and have the pastor, who had approved the presentation, tell her there wasn't time in the service for her talk.

That Davis, a vocal advocate for prevention, has her own prejudices about homosexuality is testament to how deeply rooted the stigma surrounding AIDS is. She says she contracted HIV from a boyfriend who, unknown to her, also had sex with men.

"If a person wants to be gay, then be gay," Davis says. "You get caught up in it, and it's a hard habit to break—like cigarettes or drug addiction." To underscore her point, Davis recounts the years she has spent trying, to no avail, to quit her own smoking habit.

She says that women like her "didn't have a choice, because we didn't know," which is why she's made it her mission to educate Southern women, and men, about risk factors. Though her views on gay sex are controversial (and may ultimately harm many gay men), the fact is that she's trying, in her own way, to move beyond issues of sexual orientation to help save lives.

It's a step more people need to take.

Davis proves that we don't have to support or agree with people in regard to sexual orientation, immigration status, or religious and political beliefs to fight for the right to stay healthy. Progress requires heightened awareness, better health education, and access to care and services. And people from all political backgrounds must bring that message to the public. In schools. In churches. At home.

Dorothy Davis, educator Juanita Davis, and advocates Kathie Hiers and Sergio Farfan are models of the positive change that can happen when citizens take matters into their own hands: even in the most challenging environments; even if they have to use a candy bar to sugarcoat the bittersweet truth.

R E A D I N G (58)

A Global Health Imperative

Nancy Fugate Woods (2009)

Without a lifespan view of women's health as affected by globalization and economic development in the world, we are unlikely to be successful in advancing women's health. The purposes of my presentation are to review what we know about the health status and chances for health for girl-children in the world, with a particular emphasis on what we are learning about their health in parts of the world in varying stages of economic development and to suggest policy lenses that allow us to see how to improve the health of girl-children. . . .

SEX AND GENDER DISPARITIES IN HEALTH

In the United States, increasing attention to women's health over the past three decades has brought agreement that women's health issues or problems include those that occur predominantly or solely in women, for example, breast cancer, menopause; those that occur disproportionately in women, for example,

domestic violence/abuse, osteoporosis, depression, irritable bowel disorder; and those conditions that reflect unequal health outcomes in women compared to men, for example, heart disease, lung cancer, AIDS (Institute of Medicine [IOM], 2001). Although sex, gender, and health disparities are not typically conjoined in the discourse about gender in the United States, I use the notion of sex and gender disparities in health as a lens for viewing the health and safety of the girl-child in this article. . . .

The origins of sex and gender disparities in health are multiple. In addition to the influence of biological sex (genetic and endocrine factors linked to females having two X chromosomes and males only one), a variety of social, cultural, and environmental conditions have been implicated in gender-related health disparities. Among these are social conditions associated with poverty, low social and socioeconomic status, racism, sexism, heterosexism; exposure to toxins from the physical and chemical environment; sociocultural and political stressors such as those related to marginalization; and personal behavior patterns including tobacco, alcohol, and other substance use and abuse. Critical intersections of sex, gender, race, ethnicity, class, and age shape the environments that influence girls' chances for health. Consideration of these intersections is essential when assessing the differential effects of proposed and/or existing policies, programs, and legislation on women and men (Canadian Institutes of Health Research, 2006).

GLOBALIZATION AND ECONOMIC DEVELOPMENT: FRAMEWORKS FOR UNDERSTANDING GENDER DISPARITIES IN HEALTH

Globalization can be defined as interactive coevolution of technological, economic, institutional, social, and environmental trends. The intensification of cross-national cultural, economic, political, social and technological, and health interactions stimulates transnational and local changes and integration of cultural, economic, environmental, political, and social processes. These, in turn, affect the proximal determinants of health, in some cases amplifying health disparities.

Globalization provides a context for understanding health in countries undergoing changes related to economic development. Huynen and colleagues (2005) have proposed a conceptual framework for viewing the influence of globalization and population health in which globalization processes of new global governance structures, global markets, global communication and diffusion of information, global mobility, cross-cultural interaction, and global environmental change affect the more distal determinants of health: health policy, economic development and trade, knowledge, social interactions, and ecosystem goods and services. In turn, these affect the proximal determinants of health, including health services; social, environmental, and lifestyle factors; and the physical environment, including food and water (Huynen et al., 2005). Some of the most important health effects at stake as proximal determinants of health are diet, inactivity, smoking, alcohol use, and illicit drugs. Equally important for the girl-child's

development, however, are the changes in lifestyle that affect their gender-related socialization and roles.

SOCIOCULTURAL FACTORS INFLUENCING THE HEALTH OF THE GIRL-CHILD

Gender disparities in health and mortality are, in part, a function of globalization and its effects on the distal and proximal determinants of health. In countries with developing economies, the challenges of debt repayment constrain governments' abilities to invest in infrastructure for health and education. Changing role expectations for women as well as for men and the migration to centers of employment may contribute to the dislocation of families and their girl-children. Although forces of globalization are operative, gender disparities in health are deeply rooted in the gender values of the culture, especially those in which males are valued more highly than females.

From the time of birth, the meaning of being born female shapes the remainder of the life of a girl-child. In societies in which women and girls are perceived as equal to men and boys, the imagery of the genders may be different, but similarly positive. Parents may be as thrilled to learn they have a daughter as to have a son. In contrast, in some countries, gender preference determines the birth rates for female versus male infants. One expects to see a slightly higher ratio of female to male births in any country (IOM, 2001). When this ratio is reversed, it may indicate that gender preference accorded to male children is enacted through selective abortion. . . . As many as 60 million and up to 100 million females are missing in the world's population owing to gender preference (Coale, 1991; United Nations, 1994). . . .

In addition to a sex difference in numbers of live births, one expects to see a population distribution in which female infants' more robust immune system affords them a better chance at survival as neonates and infants. When this ratio is tipped in favor of males, it may signify that infanticide—either active or passive—may be occurring. Evidence from the World Fertility Survey conducted in the 1980s in 24 developing countries revealed that for infants (up to one year), the female mortality rate was lower in all countries except two. When considering toddlers, 12 out of 24 countries had higher mortality rates for females. When considering 2- to 5-year-old children, 15 of the 24 countries showed a reversal of the mortality ratio in favor of males (Royston & Armstrong, 1989). . . .

Data suggest that the typical female biological advantage "may be eroded by the social disadvantage of being female," especially in poor resource settings in which children must compete for scarce resources (Fatallah, 2000). Thus poverty may contribute to the enactment of gender preference both before and after birth.

In addition to gender (son) preference of parents, girl-children's health is shaped profoundly by gender role socialization, as the imagery of girls and women and their value in their cultures is reflected in role expectations of them. The status of women in the society is at the heart of the matter for the health of girl-children.

. . .

A reflection of the value accorded to girls and women is observation of cultural practices that reinforce the low social status of women. Some young girls may be used as prostitutes or become victims of trafficking. Alternatively, puberty rites, including the use of genital mutilation (excision and infibulation) to control girls' sexual activity and secure their purity are an extreme reflection of the differential gender role socialization and objectification of girls as property.

The value accorded to and expectations of girls are reflected in behaviors within families. Nutritional disparity in some cultures in which girl-children or their mothers or both eat last may be operative. Also lack of access to health care or preferential treatment of male children in response to sickness may be implicated. Neglect or frank discrimination may occur.

Health of young girls and women is affected by culture, including their social status, level of education, socioeconomic level, reproductive roles and marriage, employment opportunities, ownership privileges, economic power, exposure to violence, environmental factors, and access to quality health services. Each of these is shaped, in part, by the imagery the culture has of the girl-child and the meaning of her eventual womanhood. These meanings are codified in laws that govern the ownership of property, opportunities for employment, ability to establish credit, purchase goods and services, and so on.

It is no accident that 70% of people living in poverty in the world are women and girls. Although women perform two-thirds of the world's working hours, they earn only 10% of the world's income (PLAN, 2008). Inheritance laws and the treatment of widows reflect restriction of property ownership to men in some societies.

Poverty has dramatic associations with gender: One-sixth of the world's young people live on less than $2 per day, and 122 million girls in Sub-Saharan Africa live on less than $1 per day. Poverty is associated with girls' employment in the informal sector in which low-skilled jobs, minimal pay, long working hours, and unequal power relations lead to exploitation of their labor (Levine, Lloyd, Greene, & Grown, 2008).

Nearly two-thirds of the out-of-school children of the world are girls. When girls are allowed to attend schools, they often are required to spend more time on domestic chores than their brothers, leading to their having limited time for study and play. Only 17% of Sub-Saharan African girls enroll in secondary school (Levine et al., 2008).

One in seven girls in developing countries marries before age 15, with nearly half expected to marry by age 20 in some countries of South Asia and Sub-Saharan Africa. Unwanted pregnancy and lack of abortion services harm the health of these young girls. As a result, one-quarter to one-half of births in some countries are attributable to girls less than 18 years of age. Early childbearing is associated with poverty and limited opportunity, thus perpetuating the cycle of poverty and threatening adolescent and young women's lives. South Asia and Sub-Saharan Africa account for more than 90% of all maternal deaths in the world (Levine et al., 2008).

In addition to poverty, violence against girls and young women poses significant health risks for them. Estimates that are up to 14,000 15- to 19-year-olds have been raped, with many as an act of war. Half of sexual assaults are perpetrated on 15- to 19-year-old girls. An estimated 75% of Sub-Saharan African youth (15 to 19) with HIV are women (Garcia–Moreno, Jansen, Ellsberg, Heise, & Watts, 2006).

Joyce Beebe Thompson (2005) pointed out that "women, through reproduction, carry the most important society-maintaining and enhancing roles, often with the least attention given to their health and well-being" (p. 476). Paradoxically, the female child is socialized to become the custodian of the family and its health, but in many societies, girls are not allowed to go to school or have only limited access to education.

At the heart of the matter is whether the girl-child is viewed as fully human—and as having inherent value and human rights. At the extreme is the practice of son preference with selective abortion and infibulation and nonresponse to women's allegations of violence toward them. Nonetheless, the view of the girl-child and her inherent humanness shapes the opportunities for girls' safety and health throughout her early years and the remainder of her lifespan.

HEALTH STATUS OF THE GIRL-CHILD: A LIFESPAN VIEW

Consideration of the health status of the girl-child in the world is significant because the lives of these young girls are inherently valuable. Moreover, the potential intergenerational effects of their health on that of subsequent generations, as well as the burden of disease in their own lives as they age, amplify the effects of their well-being as children (Save the Children, 2007).

. . .

During infancy and early childhood (birth through age 4), many of the sources of morbidity and mortality are linked to malnutrition, including low birth weights and growth faltering (Lartey, 2008). Protein-energy malnutrition in very young girl-children also leaves them with greater susceptibility to infection. During childhood (ages 5 through 14), stunting and problems with pelvic development may occur, leading to obstructed labor, structural damage to a young woman's pelvic organs, sepsis, and hemorrhage

when she gives birth during adolescence (ages 15 through 19). During adolescence, delayed menarche may reflect malnutrition. In young girl-children, a variety of micronutrient deficiencies in iron, iodine, and zinc can result in growth faltering as well as congenital anomalies, which have lifespan and inter-generational consequences. Iron-deficiency anemia compromises the adolescent or young woman's ability to tolerate hemorrhage. Iodine deficiency results in impaired school performance and impaired pregnancy outcomes and zinc in impaired immune function (IOM, 1996; Lartey, 2008).

Obstetric morbidity and mortality can produce birth trauma, with obstructed labor of very young mothers resulting in epilepsy or other neurological complications for infants. Obstructed labor is more commonly experienced as a consequence of pregnancy in very young girls (Mayor, 2004). Often early pregnancies occur as a result of rape, economically coerced sex, or very early marriage (IOM, 1996).

The lifelong consequence of obstructed labor can include fistulae (rectovaginal and vesicovaginal), with urinary or fecal incontinence or both as well as structural damage to reproductive organs. Often fistulae-linked incontinence leads to ostracism and social isolation for these young women (Fayoyin, 1993; Miller, Lester, Webster, & Cowan, 2005; Muleta, 2006). . . . Complications of pregnancy are the leading cause of death in women 15 to 19 years of age in the poorest countries of the world (Mayor, 2004). . . . Approximately 70,000 adolescents die each year in childbirth. . . .

Another source of gender disparities in health for the girl-child is genital cutting (mutilation), which can result in hemorrhage, sepsis, and death, as well as structural trauma associated with obstructed labor, urinary and lower and upper genital traction infections, and stenosis (Almroth et al., 2005; Ekenze, Exegwui, & Adiri, 2007; IOM, 1996; Satti et al., 2006). Genital mutilation is most prevalent in Sub-Saharan Africa, especially East African countries. Practices may vary from incisions made in the skin covering the clitoris to excision of the clitoris and labia and infibulation, in which the introitus is sutured together with only a small opening remaining for excretion of urine and menstrual blood (IOM, 1996).

An estimated 130 million women have undergone some form of genital mutilation, and up to 2 million women remain at risk of genital mutilation despite the passage of laws forbidding the practice in 15 of 28 African countries by mid-2006 (Levine et al., 2008; Satti et al., 2006). Young girls' experience following genital cutting/mutilation includes being confined to bed for a week or more.

HIV/AIDS among girl-children is a significant health challenge, with 73% of the world's people with AIDS living in Sub-Saharan Africa. Regions of the world with a high prevalence of heterosexual spread of AIDS is associated with a low status of women. Southern and Eastern African countries have the highest concentration. The proportion of people with HIV who are women varies across Africa, with 58% vs. 55% in North Africa and the Middle East. In contrast, 25% in Europe and 20% living in Sub-Saharan Africa are women. High HIV prevalence rates have significant implications for girl-children, as they influence experiences of orphans, stress on health care systems, availability of care and drug therapy against the background of limited agriculture, famine, and national economies (Yeboah, 2007).

Yeboah (2007) cautions that the web of gender construction, Eurocentrism and racism, government attitude, globalization and poverty, culture, environment, and natural resources and history all converge to stifle development in Sub-Saharan Africa because it is losing human capital, and scarce resources are being dedicated to AIDS care. Economic and social gains will be eroded by falling life expectancy as has been experienced in Botswana. At the heart of AIDS control are roles and expectations related to valuing gender (women), sexuality, economic and power relationships that in turn influence condom use, sexual partnerships, and general empowerment of women.

In addition to the reproductive health problems encountered by girls, the IOM Committee to Study Female Morbidity and Mortality in Sub-Saharan Africa (1996) also emphasized nonreproductive causes of morbidity for girl-children. Among these were mental health, and nervous system problems, chronic diseases, injuries, occupational and environmental health issues, and infectious diseases.

. . .

Exposure to war has significant effects on the mental health of displaced children as evident in a recent study of children in southern Darfur. Seventy-five percent of children met criteria for post-traumatic stress disorder (PTSD) and 38% met criteria for clinical depression. Twenty percent had significant symptoms of grief. Of the war experiences, abduction, hiding to protect oneself, being raped, and being forced to kill or hurt family members were most predictive of traumatic reactions. Being raped, seeing others raped, the death of a parent, being forced to fight, and having to hide to protect oneself were strongest predictors of depressive symptoms. War experiences such as abduction, death of parents, being forced to fight, and having to hide to protect oneself were strongest predictors of grief. Exposure to atrocities of war have significant impact on the mental health of children in general, including girl-children (Morgos, Worden, & Gupta, 2008).

. . .

Injuries, including falls, burns, drownings, and unintentional poisonings, constitute major sources of mortality and morbidity during early childhood, Sexual abuse, partner violence, and rape become more prominent during childhood and adolescence. Rape persists as a major source of morbidity for adolescent women, and suicide and motor vehicle deaths join other injuries during this period of the lifespan (IOM, 1996).

Occupational and environmental health issues for very young children include indoor air pollution from domestic sources such as cooking fires. Child labor joins the list of hazards for 5- to 14-year-olds, and economically coerced sex becomes a major occupational hazard for adolescents (IOM, 1996).

In addition to infectious diseases linked to heart disease, many of the tropical infection diseases such as malaria, chistosomiasis, dracunculiasis, onchocerciasis, trypansomiasis, trachoa, leishmaniasis, and leprosy are prevalent among some countries. They may be more prevalent among young girls due to their added risk of infection owing to malnutrition and their early occupational exposures, for example, to schistosomiasis. Not surprisingly, sexually transmitted diseases join the list of hazards for girl-children, with congenital transmission of HIV/AIDS, perinatal and neonatal transmission preceding transmission via sexual abuse for girls aged 5 to 14 and adolescents. Transmission through unprotected sexual activity, and especially through forced prostitution and rape, remains a threat throughout the remainder of the girl-child's lifespan (IOM, 1996).

. . .

HEALTH POLICY AND HEALTH SERVICES FOR THE GIRL-CHILD

A lifespan view of the health of the girl-child emphasizes the importance of the long view: healthy infants mature as healthy adults as reflected in their lifespan. Health policy for the girl-children of the world begins with attention to gender disparities from the time of birth. . . .

Health services for the girl-child begin with access to prenatal care and nutrition during pregnancy and early in life. Advocacy for safe motherhood is advocacy for the health of girl-children, particularly when coupled with family planning programs and social policy that support healthy pregnancy with adequate nutrition for pregnant women and that discourage early pregnancies. Preschool-aged children's health is critical to their ability to benefit from education, as illustrated by the success of Head Start programs in the United States.

Increasingly, the transition to puberty and adolescence is identified as a critical turning point for girl-children. This is a risky time for dropping out of school, becoming pregnant, being victimized by rape or sexual assault, and foreshortening possibilities for future development as a woman. Programs focused on this transitional period should include education about health, including fertility management, HIV/AIDS prevention, healthy nutrition, prevention of or coping with genital cutting/mutilation and its consequences, managing unwanted sexual advances, building equitable relationships, and other life skills that are direct and proximal determinants of health. Awareness of basic rights, such as voting, inheriting land, avoiding unwanted sexual advances and genital cutting/mutilation, and the right to gain justice

is essential. These social policies *are* health policies.

. . .

Finally, the physical environment, including safe and adequate sources of food and water, will be fostered by development in the area of sanitation and agricultural practices that assure sustainable food and water sources. Given the nature of girl-children's domestic and agricultural work, these are significant and have the potential to reduce the burden of diseases linked to infectious agents.

International efforts must include peacekeeping protections, post-trauma attention, reshaping social underpinnings of stigma in post-conflict areas, and increased attention to eliminating rape as a common atrocity of war. Eradication of poverty of nations is at the heart of the challenges to assuring the health and safety of the girl-child. Without investing in girls—in the home, educational systems, workplaces, communities, and societies—the future for the next generations will remain bleak.

. . .

Given the complexity of the challenges for advancing the health of girl-children, particularly those in parts of the world that are most challenged, what can one person do? How can we create a global imperative to advance the health of girls everywhere?

We can begin by linking to one other woman or man in our commitment to an activity we can undertake together, for example, research about girls' health, practice models or projects related to girls, or education of future health professionals or girls, themselves, about their health. Daily, in a small but meaningful way, we can inquire of men about their daughters and wives, reminding them of the significance of their health. We can work for legislation in our own countries with sensitivity to its global impact on girls, for example, laws regulating trafficking and marital rape. We can engage with and in government and global efforts to advance the health of girls in the world. We can engage girls in planning for their health and health care, for example, through engaging them in advisory groups to health care systems (Tlou, 2002).

Margaret Mead once was asked if one person's actions could transform the world. She answered that it was the only thing that ever has!

REFERENCES

Almroth, L., Bedri, H., El Musharaf, S., Satti, A., Idris, T., Hashim, M. S., et al. (2005). Urogenital complications among girls with genital mutilation: A hospital-based study in Khartoum. *African Journal of Reproductive Health, 9*, 118–124.

Canadian Institutes of Health Research. (2006). *Gender and sex-based analysis in health research: A guide for CIHR Peer Review Committees.* Retrieved July 1, 2008, from http://www.cihr-irsc.gc.ca/e/32019.html

Coale, A. J. (1991). Excess female mortality and the balance of the sexes in the population: An estimate of the number of "missing females." *Population and Development Review, 12*, 517–523.

Ekenze, S. O., Exegwui, H. U., & Adiri, C. O. (2007). Genital lesions complicating female genital cutting in infancy: A hospital based study in south-east Nigeria. *Annals of Tropical Pediatrics, 27*, 285–290.

Fatallah, M. F. (2000). The girl child. *International Journal of Gynecology and Obstetrics, 70*, 7–12.

Fayoyin, A. (1993). The menace of VVF in Nigeria. *Nigeria Population, 1993,* Oct–Dec, 6–7.

Garcia-Moreno, C., Jansen, H., Ellsberg, M., Heise, L., & Watts, C. (2006). Prevalence of intimate partner violence: Findings from the WHO multi-country study on women's health and domestic violence. *Lancet, 368,* 1260–1269.

Huynen, M., Martens, P., & Hilderink, H. (2005). The health impacts of globalization: A conceptual framework. *Global Health, 3*(1), 14.

Institute of Medicine (IOM) Committee to Study Female Morbidity and Mortality in Sub-Saharan Africa. (1996). *In her lifetime: Female morbidity and mortality in Sub-Saharan Africa.* Washington, DC: National Academy Press.

Institute of Medicine (IOM) Committee on Understanding the Biology of Sex and Gender Differences. (2001). *Exploring the biological contributions to human health: Does sex matter?* Washington, DC: National Academy Press.

Khan, K. S., Wojdyla, D., Say, L., Gülmezoglu, A. M., & Van Look, P. F. (2006). WHO analysis of causes of maternal deaths: A systematic review. *The Lancet, 367,* 1066–1074.

Lartey, A. (2008). Maternal and child nutrition in Sub-Saharan Africa: Challenges and interventions. *Proceedings of the Nutrition Society, 67,* 105–108.

Levine, R., Lloyd, C., Greene, M., & Grown, C. (2008). *Girls count: A global investment and action agenda.* Retrieved July 1, 2008, from http://www.icrw.org/docs/Girls_Count_a_Global_Investment_&_Action_Agenda.pdf

Mayor, S. (2004). Pregnancy and childbirth are leading causes of death in teenage girls in developing countries. *British Medical Journal, 328,* 1152.

Miller, S., Lester, F., Webster, M., & Cowan, B. (2005). Obstetric fistula: A preventable tragedy. *Journal of Midwifery and Women's Health, 50,* 286–294.

Muleta, M. (2006). Obstetric fistula in developing countries: A review article. *Journal of Obstetrics and Gynacology, Canada, 28,* 962–966.

Plan. (2008). *Because I am a girl: The state of the world's girls 2007.* Plan International Headquarters working survey, UIC. Retrieved July 1, 2008, from http://www.plan-international.org

Royston, E., & Armstrong, S. (Eds.). (1989). Preventing maternal deaths. *World Health Organization, 66,* 51.

Satti, A., Elmusharaf, S., Bedri, H., Idris, T., Hashim, M. S., Suliman, G. I., et al. (2006). Prevalence and determinants of the practice of genital mutilation of girls in Khartoum, Sudan. *Annals of Tropical Pediatrics, 26,* 303–310.

Save the Children. (2007). *State of the world's mothers.* Retrieved July 1, 2008, from http://www.savethechildren.org/campaigns/state-of-the-worlds-mothers-report/2007/

Thompson, J. B. (2005). International policies for achieving safe motherhood: Women's lives in the balance. *Health Care Women International, 26,* 472–483.

Tlou, S. D. (2002). What nurses can do to empower young girls. *International Nursing Review, 49*(2), 65–68.

United Nations. (1994). *Report of the International Conferences on Population and Development. A Conference, 171*(13), 28–29.

Yeboah, I. (2007). HIV/AIDS and the construction of Sub-Saharan Africa: Heuristic lessons from the social sciences for policy. *Social Science and Medicine, 64,* 1128–1150.

Rethinking Radical Politics in the Context of Assisted Reproductive Technology

Jennifer Parks (2009)

In 1970, radical feminist Shulamith Firestone published *The Dialectic of Sex: The Case for Feminist Revolution*. In this manifesto, Firestone reconsiders from a feminist perspective Karl Marx and Friedrich Engels' materialist theory of history. She claims that while they rightly identify class struggles as fundamental to history, they overlook the significance of what she calls "sex class." For Firestone, this most basic form of class oppression derives from men and women's differing reproductive roles. She argues that, just as the proletariat must seize the means of production in order to eliminate the oppressive economic class system, so must women seize the means of reproduction in order to eliminate the sexual class system, and to break the "tyranny of the biological family." As she envisions it: "The reproduction of the species by one sex for the benefit of both would be replaced by . . . artificial reproduction."[1]

In the 1980s, radical feminist critiques of reproductive technologies conversely argued for a moratorium on all reproductive technologies. Gena Corea and Janice Raymond[2] have argued that reproductive technologies serve to oppress and subordinate women, that they are the final frontier for the patriarchal usurpation of women's reproductive role, and that these technologies have turned women's bodies into sites for dangerous experimentation and research. As Raymond claims, "I contend that the best legal approach to reproductive technology and contracts that violate women's bodily integrity—such as IVF and its offshoots . . . is abolition, not regulation."[3]

This paper will explore this question of reproductive technology and radical politics. For, as Firestone indicated more than thirty years ago, practices of childbearing and rearing are fundamental to women's social and political status.[4] Taking Firestone,

Raymond, and Corea to have important insights into the benefits and harms of assisted reproductive technology (ART), I will argue that whether it is emancipatory or oppressive for women cannot be determined outside the context of its actual and current practice. . . .

I choose these particular radical feminists because their accounts—now several decades old—are touchstones for feminists who write on reproduction and assisted reproductive technologies. More contemporary feminist accounts of ART have continued to press this question of whether to understand the technologies as emancipatory for women, or as new ways for governments to intervene in, legislate, and control women's lives.[5] By appealing to the particular radical accounts offered by Firestone, Corea, and Raymond, however, one can better historically situate feminist approaches to ART and its implications for women's lives. It also helps one to appreciate better the degree to which what counts as "radical" has shifted, along with the circumstances that condition women's reproductive lives. For example, critics like Corea and Raymond could not have foreseen how ART would serve radically to alter some family formations or that material changes in women's work lives would so quickly raise the average age of women's reproduction.[6]

Consider the contemporary use of IVF or artificial insemination by donor (AID) by lesbians and disabled, single, minority, and post-menopausal women. The use of reproductive technologies by these groups has extended reproduction to women who have historically been denied access because of their "difference." Here, ART has radical potential, and has been used to radical purposes (that is, by perverting our traditional conceptions of motherhood and family). Conversely, these technologies have also been used to privilege the white, heterosexual, married, middle class family (as evidenced by Bobbi McCaughey, the now-famous woman from Iowa whom the media glorified for being the first successfully to gestate and birth septuplets).

Thus, any account of ART must consider both the radical and conservative agendas it is likely to serve (or has served), as well as the liberating and oppressive outcomes that may result. While over time it may become clear that a practice is overwhelmingly oppressive or dangerous for women, for the most part the dialectical nature of ART will make it fairly difficult to determine that a practice should be banned outright. For example, the practice of contract motherhood has both oppressive and liberating implications. Gay couples and people with disabilities have contracted with women to carry pregnancies for them, thus allowing for family formations that might not otherwise be achieved. At the same time, however, the practice may result in the exploitation and commodification of women and children, a serious problem that must not be overlooked. . . .

SHULAMITH FIRESTONE ON REPRODUCTION AND RADICAL POLITICS

Firestone begins *The Dialectic of Sex* by stating that "Sex class is so deep as to be indivisible."[7] Here she appropriates Marx and Engels' notion of class division to argue that there is another class division— sex class—that was not properly addressed by these radical thinkers. Indeed, she argues that nature produced women's fundamental inequality to men: women are biologically distinguished from men, and culturally distinguished from human. Women's role as those who bear and rear children for the human race has been "consolidated" and "institutionalized in the interests of men."[8] From an historical materialist perspective, reproduction of the species has carried great costs to women, not only emotionally, spiritually and culturally, but also in strictly material/physical terms: repeated and successive childbirth has resulted in women's constant "female troubles," early aging, and even death. Women have thus been the slave class that has maintained the

species so that men are free to go about their business in the public realm, while women themselves have been largely relegated to the private sphere of the home.

Firestone argues that band-aid fixes to this deep division of labor are not enough: her radical approach argues for a sexual revolution of the sort headed by women, owned by women, and empowering for women. Integral to her sexual revolution is what she refers to as "the freeing of women from the tyranny of their reproductive biology by every means available"[9]; that is, the development of technologies like ectogenesis to remove reproduction entirely from women's bodies.

Firestone is not naïve about the possibility that this sexual revolution may be co-opted by a masculinist capitalist system as yet another way to control women; but she claims that we cannot speculate about post-revolutionary systems and that "we shall assume flexibility and good intentions in those working out the change."[10] She bluntly notes the following regarding women's reproduction:

> *Pregnancy is barbaric.* I do not believe, as many women are now saying, that the reason pregnancy is viewed as not beautiful is due strictly to cultural perversion. The child's first response, "What's wrong with the Fat Lady?"; the husband's guilty waning of sexual desire; the woman's tears in front of the mirror at eight months—all are gut reactions, not to be dismissed as cultural habits. Pregnancy is the temporary deformation of the body of the individual for the sake of the species. Moreover, childbirth *hurts*. And it isn't good for you.

Ultimately, Firestone claims, giving birth is like "shitting a pumpkin."[11]

Firestone's call for a feminist revolution focuses on reproductive and familial change. As part of her call to radical change, she argues (in a Marxist vein) for the death of the traditional nuclear family and a radical restructuring of our social world. Thus, she is not simply naïve in her assertions that ART will liberate women, for she places it within the context of a revolution that includes sweeping social and political change.[12]

GENA COREA AND JANICE RAYMOND ON WOMEN AS BREEDERS

Not for another fifteen years would radical feminists take up this issue again, this time (in the mid-1980s) adopting a very different perspective from Firestone's. Corea, radical feminist theorist and activist for FINNRAGE (Feminist International Network on the New Reproductive and Genetic Technologies) argues that ART results in the oppression, subordination, and control of women and their bodies: the new reproductive and genetic technologies are nothing more than the arm of patriarchy. Furthermore, Corea sees no emancipatory possibilities in the various technologies given that they are created "in the interests of patriarchy, reducing women to Matter."[13] She criticizes liberal approaches to ART for asking the wrong questions, such as: "How can the maturation quality of eggs be improved before they are suctioned out of women's ovaries during surgery?" and "Does the fee paid to the surrogate mother constitute, for federal tax purposes, compensation or rental income?"[14] These are what she calls foreground questions, and they fail to address the background questions to which feminists must be sensitive. These include:

> At what costs to women are we channeled into biomedically manipulated reproduction? What are the implications for women as a social group when our numbers are reduced through sex predetermination technology? What is the real meaning of a woman's "consent" to in vitro fertilization in a society in which men as a social group control not just the choices open to women but also women's *motivation* to choose?[15]

Likewise, in *Women as Wombs,* Raymond argues that ART renders banal the very notion of choice, reducing it to the right to consume. She claims that:

> It is time to examine what choices men, and some women, defend as our right and what choices these same men and women will not defend as our right. Why is women's right to choose surrogacy widely defended at the same time that women's more substantive human, civil, and economic rights are being suppressed, at the same time that affirmative action

is being gutted, at the same time that there is still no Equal Rights Amendment to the Constitution? The choice to become a surrogate is hardly the freedom for which most women have been fighting.[16]

Firestone's call for a feminist revolution never came to fruition: the technological advances in reproduction occurred without corresponding cultural change. But it is still an open question whether ART will eventually bring about radical change or whether radical change is required before ART can be liberating. Indeed, it is not even clear as we practice these technologies whether they will lead to radical change in the way we view reproduction and the family unit or whether the technologies will only serve to strengthen the cultural norm of the traditional, heterosexual, male-headed nuclear family.

I argue, however, that this "either/or" question is an incorrect starting-point for any radical feminist account of ART. For these technologies are taking place within cultures that are not static and unchanging: cultural norms change, are in flux, such that ART is taking place within what Valerie Hartouni calls a "shifting reproductive landscape."[17] There is a dialectical nature to ART insofar as it simultaneously produces two contradictory images of what families are and can be: on one hand, it promotes a radical conception of family as unbounded by traditional, "age-appropriate," heterosexual limits; on the other hand, it reinforces the primacy of reproductive functioning that one typically associates with traditional heterosexual families. In what follows I will use the example of post-menopausal motherhood to argue for the dialectic of assisted reproductive technology. I choose this example because it is one application of ART against which many critics have expressed serious ethical concern, and because post-menopausal mothering directly challenges the traditional conception of motherhood.

THE APPLICATION OF ART TO POST-MENOPAUSAL WOMEN

The use of ART by post-menopausal women exemplifies the kind of reproductive dialectic to which I am referring. That older women have used (and are using) in vitro fertilization and egg donation to have children beyond the normal reproductive age means that there is both a strengthening and an eroding of the received (western) view of motherhood. I claim that there is a strengthening because opposition to this practice has been voiced in terms of its "unnaturalness" and "abnormality": postmenopausal reproduction tests our social norms concerning who can mother, and who (morally) ought to mother, and in direct response some critics characterize it as monstrous.[18] But at the same time, older women *are* becoming mothers: they appear, along with their younger counterparts, in clinics for prenatal checkups, in the shops buying baby clothes and baby furniture, and in the workplace. But beyond post-menopausal gestation, grandmothers—women well beyond the typical age of mothering—are raising their grandchildren, thus further normalizing the raising of children by older women.

Post-menopausal motherhood, and other nontraditional mothering practices, is quietly causing a cultural revolution of sorts: for as these "abnormal" mothering practices take hold, cultural conceptions of "the mother" will be forced to change. Furthermore, the norm of the traditional nuclear family must change in order to accommodate these women, since women of advanced age may require other women to aid in and take over the parental role should they die or become ill or frail, or their (often younger) spouses may have to take up that role.[19] If the number of same-sex couples raising children also continues to increase, our conception of "mother" may require radical redefinition.

Yet with the advent of ART we have seen legal developments that serve to strengthen our cultural norm of the heterosexual nuclear family: that is, one father, one mother, and their genetic offspring. A series of court cases over the last twenty years has been decided in favor of biological parents, so that our legal understanding of what it means to be a parent comes down to one's genetic connection to a child and/or one's marital status.

. . .

In a recent case, a two-year-old boy known as "Daniel B." was deemed to be the legal child of both the single woman who birthed him and the married genetic father whose embryo was mistakenly implanted in her. The single woman "Susan B." went to the same clinic where married couple "Robert and Denise" had created thirteen embryos using Robert's sperm and donor eggs; Denise had no biological connection with the resulting embryos. Susan B. was seeking donor sperm and egg in order to create embryos anonymously so that "there would be no paternity case against her, ever." Ten months after the birth of Daniel B., the clinic informed the married couple of the error, and they sought contact with Daniel. Despite the many complications associated with this case, the court ruled that Susan B. could be the only "real" mother, that Denise had no claim on Daniel because she has no biological relation to him, and that Robert had paternity rights because of his biological connection to the child. An appeal of this case is likely, and it is anticipated that there will be court hearings regarding the custody and visitation of Daniel.[20]

Here again we see the negative side of the dialectic: the attempt by law to maintain the traditional concept of the nuclear family. The courts continue to impose patriarchal rule: that is, the father's right to his offspring, the importance of one's genetic connection, and the moral rightness of the heterosexual, two parent norm. The question is: how should feminists respond to this unfolding and dynamic nature of ART? Where do we go from here?

. . .

The practice of ART is so deeply entrenched in western culture that it is unrealistic and unproductive to simply wish it away; and in any case, contra Corea and Raymond, it is not clear that women should *want* to eradicate it. Rather, we should do what we can to encourage the most radical (but least harmful) uses of ART so that its practice continues to chip away at the suffocating norm of the heterosexual, married, biologically related family unit. We should continue to get more women, minorities, gays, lesbians, and other marginalized people to participate in ART as physicians, lawyers, politicians, lawmakers, and clients.[21] While women should attempt to diversify ART, we need, of course, to be concerned about some of the reproductive practices that may pose unnecessary risks to women (like egg selling, for example) or that serve to further threaten individuals already marginalized by the technologies, such as persons with disabilities.[22]

Such changes are slowly and steadily occurring. As Lisa Jean Moore indicates in *Sperm Counts: Overcome by Man's Most Precious Fluid,* a cultural anxiety about fatherhood is increasingly expressed in the media given the rise in the use of sperm donors by single women. These women, single mothers by choice, in their thirties or forties, desire families and seek their pregnancies through sperm banks rather than waiting for "Mr. Right" to appear. As Moore points out, "The growth of single mothers by choice leads to some men fearing that participation in reproduction is being reduced to the anonymous and disembodied use of their sperm with no further rights to the baby once it is conceived."[23] Yet, as Moore points out, this anxiety is unfounded given the historical understanding of the father as absent provider; and it returns us to the notion that "real" (that is, biological) fathers are superior to other parent types.[24]

Furthermore, as a recent article in *Mother Jones* indicates,[25] ART has brought about new problems through the creation and cryopreservation of human embryos. The process of in vitro fertilization (IVF) is invasive and expensive for women, and involves some degree of physical risk. To access as many eggs as possible, the IVF client is given fertility drugs that cause hyperstimulation so that she will produce an unusually large number of eggs during her cycle; those eggs are fertilized in a petri dish and then a certain number of the resulting embryos are returned to the client's uterus in the hopes that at least one will implant.[26] Those embryos not required for the first IVF cycle are usually frozen and stored for future use, saving the female client a good deal of discomfort and risk, and lowering the cost of successive IVF cycles.

The number of cryopreserved human embryos in the United States has reached close to half a million— mostly because couples store them and then, if the embryos are not needed for successive IVF cycles, they are uncertain what to do with them. This is where the tensions surface. As one study indicates,

> Parents variously conceptualized frozen embryos as biological tissue, living entities, "virtual" children having interests that must be considered and protected, siblings of their living children, genetic or psychological insurance policies, and symbolic reminders of their past infertility. . . . Many seemed

afflicted by a kind of *Chinatown* syndrome, thinking of them simultaneously as: Children! Tissue! Children! Tissue![27]

Clearly there is inconsistency and tension in the current thinking surrounding these cryopreserved human embryos. The confusion and uncertainty expressed by clients, whether anti-abortion or not, who are storing their embryos indicates the dialectical nature of this problem. On one hand, the fact of the embryos' existence establishes—at least in some minds—their claim on a right to life; on the other hand, the glut of human embryos reminds us of the pressing need to develop treatments and therapies that may be advanced through the use of embryonic stem cell research. As one researcher notes,

> . . . [the embryos'] presence is perhaps an unanticipated side effect of the use of advanced reproductive technology. But there is nothing inherently negative or wrong about their existence, and as we turn our attention to them, we may find that indeed they could be a tremendous resource for science, the country, and for mankind [*sic*] for that matter.[28]

Like many other procedures occurring within the arena of ART, the practice of embryo cryopreservation brings out its dialectical nature, and resists any simple reading as lending itself to either radical or conservative politics. The very existence of these embryos points us toward both radical and conservative possibilities at the same time; what we will end up with as a result is yet to be determined.

As I have indicated thus far, we cannot objectively establish the radical or conservative nature of ART outside the context of its practice. Furthermore, I am arguing, these technologies are dialectical: they are producing contradictory effects—tensions—by their very practice. In this case, the tension lies between the uses of ART to maintain the norm of the heterosexual, nuclear, two-parent family while at the same time being used to create radical family formations.

. . .

In arguing for "radical" approaches and "radical" politics, I mean to claim that we should use ART to extend the concept of family so that it is more inclusive and better reflects the broad range of lifestyles and close relationships chosen by a broad range of citizens. I do not mean to suggest that we should embrace any and all technologies: radical politics should not be pursued at the cost of harm to offspring, serious threats to the dignity of persons with disabilities, or physical harm to women. But some interventions, like artificial insemination by donor, are relatively low risk for women and (as Lisa Jean Moore notes) serve, when they are used by marginalized women living in non-traditional family situations, to turn our notion of family on its head.

Additionally, one must understand that what gets defined as "radical" is not fixed or given—as I previously indicated, Valerie Hartouni claims that we reside within a "shifting reproductive landscape" where our cultural meanings and practices are constantly undergoing construction and revision. In talking about a new body politics, Cynthia Daniels similarly points out that

> Women's relation to the state remains deeply contradictory . . . although at times the courts and legislatures have been used to affirm masculine control over the female body, at other moments they have clearly stood as women's last, best defense against social coercion. Women's ability to resist efforts to restrict, regulate, or criminalize their behavior has depended on their ability to use the power of the state in their own defense—a state which is clearly divided between its support for fetal rights and its need to affirm women's formal rights to citizenship.[29]

Political, legal, and social contexts condition women's reproductive lives, but women's choices and actions have an impact upon those contexts. Women are not just *affected* by those conditions, but can also *affect* them. Thus, we cannot accurately predict the meaning or implications of ART absent an understanding of and appreciation for its dialectical nature.

With regard to the proliferation of ART, Hartouni prophetically claims that "it is necessary and inevitable and suggests that the issue with respect to the panoply of new reproductive practices and processes is not whether there new practices are good or bad; [but] rather, how we should think them and how they

will think us."[30] If a reproductive revolution is to occur, it will happen quietly and dialectically, not through the kind of total revolution that Firestone had envisioned. Indeed, the "revolution" may be happening as we speak, despite attempts to stem the tide of political, cultural, and familial change.

NOTES

1. S. Firestone. 1970. *The Dialectic of Sex: The Case for Feminist Revolution.* New York, NY: Morrow: 11.
2. J. Raymond. 1994. *Women as Wombs: Reproductive Technologies and the Battle Over Women's Freedom.* Melbourne, Australia: Spinifex Press; G. Corea. 1986. *The Mother Machine: Reproductive Technologies from Artificial Insemination to Artifical Wombs.* New York, NY: HarperTrade.
3. Ibid: 208.
4. For a recent account of the mutually constitutive relationship between maternal bodies and the medical care they have received, see R. Kukla. 2005. *Mass Hysteria: Medicine, Culture, and Mothers' Bodies.* New York, NY: Rowman & Littlefield Publishers.
5. As excellent examples of these contemporary feminist scholars, see C. Daniels. 1993. *At Women's Expense: State Power and the Politics of Fetal Rights.* Cambridge, MA: Harvard University Press; C. McLeod. 2007. For Dignity or Money: Feminists on the Commodification of Women's Reproductive Labour. In *The Oxford Handbook of Bioethics.* B. Steinbock, ed. Oxford: Oxford University Press: 258–281; and R. Rapp. 2000. *Testing Women, Testing the Fetus: The Social Impact of Amniocentesis in America.* New York: Routledge.
6. For example, Raymond and Corea could not have predicted that, within approximately 25 years of their writings, we would witness the uncoupling of gender and childbearing. The media spotlight is currently focusing on Thomas Beatie, a transgender man from Oregon who is pregnant with his own biological child. His wife was unable to conceive due to a hysterectomy; upon birthing his child, Beatie will be the child's father and his wife will be its mother. See "Labor of Love" available at http://www .advocate.com/exclusive_detail_ektid52947_asp [Accessed 2 April 2008].
7. Firestone, *op. cit.* note 1, p. 1.
8. Ibid: 205.
9. Ibid: 206.
10. Ibid: 206.

11. Ibid: 199. Here again, we see the need to be sensitive to historical and cultural contexts, given the more recent reclamation of pregnancy as beautiful, and pregnant women as desirable.

12. Firestone is one of the only feminists who supports ART from a radical perspective. Almost without exception, other feminist (and non-feminist) accounts that support ART tend to examine it from a liberal perspective.

13. Corea, *op. cit.* note 2, p. 2.

14. Ibid: 2.

15. Ibid: 3.

16. Raymond, *op. cit.* note 2, p. 85.

17. V. Hartouni. 1997. *Cultural Conceptions: On Reproductive Technologies and the Remaking of Life.* Minneapolis, MN: University of Minnesota Press.

18. Hartouni addresses the cultural construction of "monstrous mothers"; this strong disapprobation has been widely expressed in print as follows: The Canadian Royal Commission on New Reproductive Technologies. 1993. *Proceed with Care: Final Report of the Royal Commission on New Reproductive Technologies.* Ottawa, ON: Canadian Government Publishing for the Commission on New Reproductive Technologies: 1; Editorial. Too Old to Have a Baby? *Lancet* 1993; 341: 344–345. For an argument in favor of the use of ART by postmenopausal women, see J. Parks. 1999. On the Use of IVF by Postmenopausal Women. *Hypatia,* 1999; 14: 77–96.

19. One might consider the practice of "othermothering" that is engaged in by women in the African American community. See P.H. Collins. 1991. *Black Feminist Thought: Knowledge, Consciousness, and the Politics of Empowerment.* New York: Routledge. Collins points out that African American women put less emphasis on genetic ties to their offspring, sometimes opting instead to "mother" other women's children, putting their investment into their communities rather than concerning themselves only with their own genetic offspring. Also see H.R. Clinton. 1996. *It Takes a Village: And Other Lessons Children Teach Us.* New York: Simon & Schuster. Clinton also challenges us to consider more communal approaches to rearing children.

20. American Society of Reproductive Medicine (ASRM). 2003. California Court of Appeal Affirms "Split" Parentage in Embryo Mix-Up Case. Birmingham, AL. Available at: http://www.asrm.org/Media/ Legally Speaking/vol37no3.html [Accessed 20 November 2007].

21. While this is not intended to be a wholesale endorsement of ART for women, one needs to recognize that the technologies are not going to go away. If they are going to persist we should ensure that women who are marginalized by their skin color, sexuality, ability status, marital status, and age are not denied access to the technology. In the absence of strong arguments concerning why these groups should not be given the opportunity to parent (and to date I have not seen any), these women should have equal access to the good of having a child of their own. I am not arguing for a rise in the use of ART, but in the proportional use by marginalized groups, who may use the technology to develop nontraditional, and flourishing, families.

22. For a clear account of the harms associated with oocyte vending, see McLeod, *op. cit.* note 5. For accounts of the harms of reproductive and genetic technologies for persons with disabilities, see E. Parens & A. Asch. Special Supplement: The Disability Rights Critique of Prenatal Genetic Testing: Reflections and Recommendations. *Hastings Cent Rep* 1999; 29: S1–S22.

23. L.J. Moore. 2007. *Sperm Counts: Overcome by Man's Most Precious Fluid.* New York: New York University Press.

24. We need to give some thought to how our reproductive practices will affect the children born of them. Feminists have taken the lead in raising concerns about the implications of ART on the offspring that result, especially where technology is increasingly being used to create "designer" babies, and where some adults who were born of ART claim that a connection to their genetic donors is meaningful and important to them.

25. L. Mundy. Souls on Ice: America's Human Embryo Glut and the Unbearable Lightness of Almost Being. *Mother Jones* 2006; 27 August, 39–45.

26. This is why IVF is associated with an alarming increase in multiple births, since multiple embryos will often implant and the woman is then left with the decision either to terminate some of the embryos selectively or to take a risk and carry them all to term. In order to reduce the likelihood of multiple births, most European countries put a limit of two to three embryos that can be returned for implantation.

27. L. Mundy, *op. cit.* note 32, p. 41.

28. Ibid: 43.

29. C. Daniels, *op. cit.* note 6, p. 133.

30. Ibid: 132.

From Rights to Justice: Women of Color Changing the Face of US Reproductive Rights Organizing

Zakiya Luna (2009)

INTRODUCTION

During the 2008 presidential election, an independent funding organization released a television advertisement criticizing Democratic nominee Senator Barack Obama's refusal to sign the Illinois Born Alive Infants Protection Act.[1] In the television ad, images of babies from different racial backgrounds fill the screen. Then a young woman comes onto the screen and asks the viewer "Can you imagine not giving babies their basic human rights, no matter how they entered our world?"[2]

In both this contemporary example, and historically, the United States (US) government has acted ambivalent, if not hostile, toward the idea of human rights instead focusing on narrower civil rights. Additionally, US social movement organizations not explicitly engaged in *international* human rights activities have resisted integrating human rights into their work.[3] Yet, the aforementioned presidential election advertisement provides but one recent example of how "human rights" has entered the mainstream US discourse. Activists perceive that the concept of human rights can mobilize US audiences on domestic issues. Gaining wider interest in organizing around human rights, however, remains a challenge for organizers. This is primarily because many people outside (and even within) the respective US social movements believe that human rights are what people need in *other* countries.

Reproductive and sexual health rights within the US context remain an area of rights that even recent reflections on human rights in the US have not explored adequately.[4] This article focuses on the reproductive justice movement, focusing on a unique US organization, SisterSong Women of Color Reproductive Collective (SisterSong), has utilized a human rights framework in their work. Specifically, this project assesses how SisterSong moves beyond the narrower focus on civil and political rights (dominant in US social movements) to emphasize other aspects of human rights when organizing for women's sexual and reproductive rights. . . .

SEXUALITY AND REPRODUCTION AS SITES FOR HUMAN RIGHTS

Recent activism by feminists has focused on the idea of "women's rights as human rights." In this debate, multiple authors have challenged the private/public distinction.[5] They argue that placing the issues women face in the realm of the private sphere leads to them not being taken seriously as "real" human rights violations that result from explicit state action (such as imprisonment due to political views). Therefore, son preference, employment discrimination, domestic abuse and other violation occur with the state's tacit permission.[6] Additionally, by attributing these violations to culture, states absolve themselves of their responsibility in stopping these acts. Bunch argues, "Sex discrimination kills women daily. When combined with race, class, and other forms of oppression, it constitutes a deadly denial of women's right to life and liberty on a large scale throughout the world."[7] These scholars go so far as to question whether women are even human when they continue to face human rights violations prohibited by the UDHR in 1948.[8]

Reproduction is an important area of inquiry when analyzing human rights debates because "the physical territory of this political struggle over what constitutes women's human rights is women's bodies."[9]

Sociologist Bryan Turner proposes that debates over these rights emerge due to changing economic conditions in which women have led to women gaining more economic and social power. Changing social contracts have provided most people the right to choose partners without family and state interference but this freedom has led to heated contests around rights.[10] As people become more aware of their vulnerability, social groups attempt to control some of the most personal aspects of people's lives. What scholars such as Turner do not address is that, historically, women of racial minority backgrounds have had to endure disproportionate consequences resulting from these attempts at control. Thus, efforts by these groups to gain human rights may not look like those of people who face oppression based on only one oppressed status.

Historically, intersectional analyses offered by women of color have challenged feminist theory and activism that assumed that the shared oppression of women should take precedence over organizing against racism, classism, homophobia, or these multiple oppressions simultaneously.[11] This resulted in conflicts within the women's movement of the "second wave" of feminism, but also set the stage for a shift toward more holistic analyses of oppression and varied organizational approaches such as that of SisterSong's. Thus, part of the appeal of human rights for marginalized groups is the opportunity these ideas pose to restructure society while also allowing for recognition of multiple identities.

SISTERSONG: WORKING AT THE INTERSECTION OF SOCIAL MOVEMENTS

SisterSong's network of organizations frames the concern around women's control of their bodies in terms of needing reproductive justice rather than only reproductive rights. SisterSong explicitly integrates human rights discourse into its literature. Its work represents a shift for women advocating for control of their bodies, from a narrower focus on legal access and individual choice (the focus of mainstream reproductive women's organization such the National Organization for Women), to a broader analysis of structural constraints

on agency. SisterSong explains: "The intersectional theory of Reproductive Justice is described as the complete physical, mental, spiritual, political, social, environmental and economic well-being of women and girls, based on the full achievement and protection of women's human rights."[12] Of note is that achievement of reproductive justice is imagined as happening specifically through attaining human rights. The lack of widespread human rights law in the US should result in fewer opportunities to mobilize human rights discourse, which would result in weakened belief in the utility of human rights. This way of framing reproduction resonates and is leading to changes in reproductive rights organizing nationwide, despite activists having fewer common cultural references on which to draw to construct an effective frame. Thus, SisterSong offers an ideal case to extend scholarly understandings about social movements engaging with human rights discourses.

Earlier social movements such as the Black Power movement have been criticized for their sexist tendencies. In addition, among social movements that explicitly address sexism and gender, such as the "second wave" of feminism, criticisms of unexamined racism emerged.[13] Women of color continued to work in these movements, but also founded autonomous organizations that sought to address *both* racism and sexism. These autonomous organizations provided a foundation for multilayered analysis of how multiple oppressions result in different experiences for different groups of women. In addition to tension around race, class differences were another site of tension, as demonstrated by analysis emphasized by two different groups organizing around reproductive rights middle-class-supported National Abortion Rights Action League (now NARAL Pro-Choice America) and the more diverse Committee for Abortion Rights and Against Sterilization Abuse (CARASA). NARAL Pro-Choice America focused on access to abortion while some of their literature on poor women criticized their fertility by focusing on the "social costs of uncontrolled childbearing."[14] In contrast, the more diverse CARASA focused on abortion rights but vocally challenged the forced sterilization of poor women, which denied them the right to have children.

Decades before the creation of SisterSong, poor women, who were disproportionately of racial minority groups, launched a critique of the mainstream reproductive rights framework because it did not address how these women lacked control over their reproduction. Abortion, as a legal right, was (and is) emphasized by mainstream groups as a matter of individual choice whereas alternative groups focus on a range of reproductive rights that were dependent on structural support that human rights emphasize. Many of the autonomous reproduction-related organizations, like CARASA, no longer exist. Their successors, however, are now moving into the relatively unexpected direction of integrating human rights.

DATA AND METHODS

Influenced by activism for gender equality, civil rights and international human rights, SisterSong was founded in 1997 with 16 organizations and currently has over 80 member and affiliate organizations and hundreds of individual members. These organizations are primarily based in the contiguous US, although a few are based in Puerto Rico and Hawaii or have links with international organizations. The founding organizations were four organizations from each of the original "mini-communities" of SisterSong: Asian/Pacific Islander, Black/African American, Latina and Native American/Indigenous. Organizations included larger organizations such as the National Asian Women's Health Organization to local organizations such as Project Azuka Women's AIDS Project, which served African-American women. Later, SisterSong added a Middle Eastern/Arab American mini-community, a caucus for white allies and a caucus for men of color. These caucuses exist to support SisterSong's primary focus on organizing around women of color's reproductive health concerns. The collective is composed of member organizations and individual members from across the country. To join, members agree to SisterSong's nine Principles of Unity, which stresses coalition work with other organizations and protection of various types of rights (including reproductive and sexual rights) as part of human rights.

Currently, there are six people who staff the national office in Atlanta, including the National Coordinator, Loretta Ross, who used to direct the National Center for Human Rights Education. Working Committees address areas such as organizing, mobilizing, research and publicity. SisterSong holds a national membership meeting or conference every year with hundreds of attendees, some of whom attend with the aid of scholarships, which are provided with the aid of thousands of dollars in grants to SisterSong. Speakers include members from local organizations as well as nationally known experts such as former Attorney General Jocelyn Elders. SisterSong staff also provide trainings (e.g. "What is reproductive justice?") and consult with member organizations on how to incorporate reproductive justice into their projects. Funding comes from foundations, membership fees, and organizations including mainstream organization[s] such as Planned Parenthood, which has provided sponsorship for [the] conference.

This article draws on publicly available documents and interviews. Since 2004, SisterSong has published a newsletter (*Collective Voices*) on an annual or bi-annual basis. Current circulation stands at 18,000. The newsletter highlights multiple types of stories: news articles provide statistics on relevant topics, personal narratives reflect on involvement with member organizations or reproductive justice activism, and others explain the history of the collective. Some pieces are written by people identified as SisterSong staff or committee members, although many list the author as a member or remain unidentified.

The analysis focuses on the first eight newsletters distributed 2004–2007, which averaged 21 pages. Focusing on the formal documents explicitly produced for consumption by members and potential supporters allows an assessment of how activists construct the discourse of civil rights and human rights. I augment my analysis with data I have collected over two years through interviewing Sister-Song members, archival research, and conducting participant observation at local and national events (a national conference, a workshop at the US Social Forum, a Reproductive Justice 101 training, and a national membership meeting).

RESULTS AND DISCUSSION

Choosing Human Rights

With civil rights and women's rights being dominant and somewhat successful *separate* movements, trying to combine these efforts into one movement that then integrates human rights is a challenge both financially and strategically. Nonprofits, which often rely on foundation funding, have to overcome misconceptions to convince funding bodies these ideas are valid. With a rights discourse based on Constitutional values dominant in the US, providing funding to groups challenging the limits of that model would seem risky if not counter to the mission of the funders. Reflecting on its history of confronting resistance by funding agencies, a Sister-Song founder writes,

> [A] decade ago the concept of funding human rights work in the United States was novel to the foundation world because human rights meant only international funding, while "civil rights" was stretched to cover human rights abuses in the U.S. . . . a sizable number of foundations are raising more than $10 million to support U.S.- focused human rights work, an idea scorned a mere decade ago.[15]

This quote educates members less familiar with the history of human rights in the US on how human rights was a stigmatized discourse even in the early 1990s. Human rights was not unknown but, instead, scorned and therefore perceived negatively.

One interviewee, who oversees part of the legal program for a reproductive rights organization that often argues Supreme Court cases, noted the disjuncture between different groups:

> . . . The two groups can really work together . . . the rights-based groups have a strong understanding of how to get things going within the legal system, and I think that what we need to be more creative about is expanding that to include international bodies and human rights . . . using human rights mechanisms (Katherine Grainger, Center for Reproductive Rights, 2007 Personal Interview).

While there are benefits to a human-rights analysis, there are potential strategic drawbacks due to its marginalized position in the United States. An article in SisterSong's newsletter from a linked organization illuminates the logic of focusing on human rights despite a hostile climate faced by reproductive justice activists:

> A human rights framework both speaks to the need to demand rights, not ask for privileges and the need to connect with other women and struggles worldwide through using a universal, internationally agreed upon framework. . . . Limitations on ratification and when the U.S. government fails to ratify human rights treaties (as it has failed to do so on most treaties) prevent individuals in the United States from securing these human rights through legal claims. Nonetheless, as activists we continue to use the human rights framework as our standard which should hold governments accountable.[16]

Since members may be unfamiliar with human rights, stories such as this provide a context for the concept (international recognition), how the US government limits human rights within the US (failure to ratify treaties) and, most importantly, why SisterSong continues to use this framework despite what appears to be a futile battle. Part of what the organization does is educate its members on human rights, which, for many readers, may be a foreign idea. Alternatively, they may only think of human rights as a synonym for civil rights, which is how the US government has traditionally engaged with human rights. Additionally, these rights are to be understood as entitlements rather than privileges. Pieces such as this emphasize how human rights fits into the work of activism in the US and perhaps just as importantly, women's activism throughout the world. Recognition of the validity of international rights provides the ability to make rights claims, but US social movements are still able to engage with discourse and deploy it for their own purposes, namely holding up an ideal toward which to work.

Educating on Global-Local Rights

SisterSong wants people to gain rights, but recognizes that traditional legislation can work against marginalized members of society. In a front-page story about how reproductive justice relates to immigrant rights, SisterSong notes that the heightened legal consciousness of opposing groups can have an effect on communities to which some members of the wider membership belong:

> It is critical to understand that, as this legislation is pending approval, *the amount of public debate that is created by these proposals also trigger different types of behaviors from different groups of people* . . . US citizens who work in institutions such as schools, hospitals, and banks among others, *feel empowered to request immigration documents inappropriately, without guidelines and without legal authorization.* This was the case immediately after California voters authorized the passage of Proposition 187 in 1994 (a law that denied social services, health care and public education to illegal immigrants and was subsequently struck down by the federal court).[17]

SisterSong cautions members to recognize how, even if there is no legal authority, opposition may attempt to overstep legal boundaries. Scholarly literature on legal consciousness assumes such consciousness is a positive development, but here SisterSong shows negative impacts of a group using this consciousness to deprive other people of their human rights.

Another important point within this specific example is that even though citizens who oppose immigration felt empowered, they did not have legal standing to take these actions. Also important is that a court stepped in to limit the effect of legislation. This shows that the organization recognizes that local defeats to its movement in the legal system are part of a larger process in which success can happen at other levels of that same legal system.

Because this organization recognizes that women are part of multiple communities, it overtly links reproduction to multiple movements rather than having it be only a "women's issue." Some ways SisterSong does this are by having member organizations write updates on their own work that might, at first glance, seem unrelated but connect with reproduction. Additionally, in each issue of the collective's newsletter, there are updates on women's reproductive rights in other countries. Still, since the organization is based in the US, one of its most important activities is to educate readers on how to apply a human rights lens to multiple problems within the US.

The following excerpt provides an example of how SisterSong's inclusion of human rights in its analysis of reproduction allows it to critically examine additional social issues than are found in material from organization focused on legal access to abortion services. A piece that looks at Hurricane Katrina as a feminist issue also connects Katrina to global problems. Specifically, one column links what many people still see as a natural disaster to the conflict between Palestine and Israel:

> We also witnessed the incredible violations of the human rights of the Katrina survivors. Not only was their right to survive threatened by the painfully slow response of local, state and federal governments, but their right to stay united as families, their right to adequate and safe shelter, their right to social services, their right to accurate information, their right to health care and freedom from violence. All of these are human rights violations but the one that brings the Middle East most forcefully to mind is the violation of the right to return to one's home. For those of us with short-term memories, keep in mind that the Supreme Court ruled this year that governments have expanded powers of eminent domain that may be used to prevent some survivors from ever returning to their communities as land is turned over to corporate developers.[18]

The quote above demonstrates how the organization takes familiar contemporary issues (such as Katrina) links them to specific articles of human rights documents, and relates them to the US legal system's role in the violation of human rights of its own citizens. At first glance, Katrina appears unrelated to the Palestinian-Israeli conflict, but this piece highlights the role of powerful governments in both the US and Israel to underscore the similarities between a "natural" situation and a situation that people understand as a product of human relations. Since the government's handling of Katrina continued to frustrate people (particularly of color), readers would be able to empathize with people across the world with whom they would otherwise feel disconnected.

Even if rights are of limited use, activists recognize the mobilizing potential of rights and the positive consequences of having a right recognized. To encourage a broader view, the organization highlights human rights documents to explain gaps in the US legal system. Starting with the title, "Reproductive Rights are Human Rights," one piece is clearly linking reproductive rights to international human rights. Then it discusses the US' position on multiple UN treaties:

> Presently there is an important set of treaties the United States has failed to ratify which include the Convention on the Elimination of All Forms of Discrimination Against Women (better known as the Women's Human Rights Treaty or CEDAW), and the Convention on Violence Against Women. *Since the United States has not ratified either of these treaties, an important goal of the U.S. reproductive justice movement should be to pressure Congress to ratify these treaties, bringing the United States into compliance with the rest of the industrialized world.*[19]

Despite the limits of the US' rights system, Sister-Song encourages its readers to pressure Congress, which is embedded within the traditional rights system that often produces the problems against which members fight (e.g., prison policies or punitive welfare laws that disproportionately impact women of color). Activists who recognize the complexity and limits of gaining rights retain hope for, and work toward, rights. Since members understand themselves as specifically engaged in a social justice project, they have to focus on shifting the institutions that make up our society (including the legal system that confers rights). They do not foresee a problem with rights even though the current legal system is flawed. Despite egregious violations of their dignity, both individually and collectively, these activists retain a belief in the ability to rectify past wrongs through using some aspects of legal institutions (e.g. courts, formal complaint processes) as they challenge the nation within which that system sits.

Intersecting Identities: Beyond Race or Gender
Overall, SisterSong engages rights as a concept that mobilizes people but believes that rights are ultimately important for marginalized groups. However, codification of rights into law is not the only concern. The group was partially founded because of members' frustration with the mainstream pro-choice movement that operates assuming protecting *Roe v. Wade* should be the movement's principal concern. The problem with doing so is that focusing on this one piece of legislation can ignore how some policies, that disproportionately impact minority women (such as welfare reform), are about reproduction if examined through a broader human-rights lens. Thus, SisterSong knows about the role of laws and courts in affecting women's lives, but understands the limits of achieving narrow rights.

As previously noted, laws can shape identities and shift community relationships. Merry observes that "grassroots individuals take on human rights discourse through a double subjectivity as rights-bearers and injured kinsmen and survivors. There is not a merging and a blending, but two somewhat distinct sets of ideas and meanings that coexist."[20] Multiple writings by women of color activists document how, in previous social movements, they felt pressured to choose a racial *or* gender community for which to seek justice.[21] Keeping in mind the need to gain rights for multiple groups, but recognizing that it is these very groups that have "injured" members by insisting they only address one identity, SisterSong has found a workable solution in human rights. It describes connections between the types of rights for which human rights provide:

> *Reproductive Justice stresses both individuality and group rights.* We all have the same human rights, but may need different things to achieve them based on our intersectional location in life—our race, class, gender, sexual orientation and immigration status. *The ability of a woman to determine her reproductive destiny is directly tied to conditions in her community. The emphasis is on individuality without sacrificing collective or group identity.* As with the human rights framework, it does not grant privileges to some at the expense of others.[22]

Emphasizing the "intersectional location in life" is also where SisterSong is doing something different from organizations that only emphasize the legal right to abortion. SisterSong emphasizes links between oppressions that affect women who need protection from the injustices, but consider these women in relation to groups that need protection.

SisterSong's emphasis on US communities linked to a global community beyond the US poses a challenge to women's movement activists who largely rely on ideas of individual autonomy when discussing women's rights. Here, the article's author observes that the US women's movement is critiqued for having narrow focus that does not benefit all women, thus human rights brings the possibility of building a "true" women's movement in which all women are included. One article, describing SisterSong's impact on a coalition of mainstream pro-choice organizers, explains the organization's approach:

> By promoting the more inclusive human rights framework in reproductive justice organizing, SisterSong also helps the mainstream movement recognize the limits of the "choice" rhetoric, and truly build a movement to transform women's lives. This human rights-based framework is based on the early recognition among women of color organizers that we have the right to control our own bodies simply because we are human, and as social justice activists we have the obligation to ensure that those rights be protected.[23]

This excerpt demonstrates recognition of the importance of the rights gained by the "second wave" of feminism, but also the limits of solely focusing on the legal right to abortion. As Mark Tushnet and others discuss, rights framed in such individualistic terms do not reflect the complex interrelationships between groups. A critique of choice does just that by pointing out that a right to abortion does not change the reasons why many women get abortion[s], why some women's reproduction is encouraged and others discouraged, or the other rights women do not have that could make accessing this right easier— a right to economic stability; for example.

Abortion is one example of a right for which a social movement fought (and continues to) across multiple realms to maintain its legal status. As embattled as the right to abortion is, groups fight for and against its existence, buttressed by the

knowledge they are fighting for or against something that exists in practice and on the legal books, unlike a more idealistic or esoteric concept such as economic justice. Multiple authors in support of rights discuss how these rights are linked to concrete policy gain and legislation. Yet, SisterSong activists recognize the limits to such gains:

> [E]ven with *Roe* on the books, many women currently have limited, if any access to abortion services. The majority of poor and low-income women in the United States are denied access for a variety of reasons including abortion funding bans, bans on the provision of abortion services by government health care facilities, a shortage of abortion providers, and parental involvement laws.[24]

Cleary, being "on the books" is not enough for a law to be effective as the state may end up violated or curtailing it, even thought the state is ostensibly supposed to protect the human right of bodily integrity. Therefore, social movements have to fight for more than protection of existing laws. They have to encourage new ways of thinking that challenge current popular discourses.

An example of how SisterSong's embrace of human rights translates into grassroots organizing is the 2004 March for Women's Lives. The 2004 March initially focused on established ideas around which the National Organization for [Women] (and other major co-sponsors) had organized previous marches, namely access to abortion. NOW noted that its 1989 and 1992 "mass marches forced the issue of *abortion rights* into the forefront of political debate."[25] After planning for the 2004 March began, a representative from NOW approached SisterSong members at a membership meeting to seek its endorsement. After the plenary session at which members debated the proposal, SisterSong members agreed to endorse the March but with certain stipulations, the first of which was to change the name of the March to reflect their concerns:

> The March for Freedom of Choice was not a big enough thing for what we're talking about. Because I'd talked about [how] abortion or not to abort is not how women of color organize, because we feel that not only do we have to fight for the right to

have a child, but we have to fight for the right to parent the children that we have. . . . So, the March for Freedom of Choice wasn't working as a title.[26]

The original March co-sponsors complied with the request and changed the name to the March for Women's Lives. Ross' comment demonstrates that the abortion rights/reproductive choice frame the March organizers were using to mobilize support for the protest did not resonate with SisterSong members because it was experientially incommensurate. While abortion was a concern, another part of members' experiences not felt by middle-class white women was that the media has continually represented their choices to become mothers as irresponsible and pathological, as seen in debates around welfare reform and other controversial issues. Even though abortion and choice remained focal points, later material produced for the March began to highlight social justice and the variety of issues around which different groups supporting the March worked. For SisterSong, this meant engagement with the concept of "reproductive justice," which focuses on achievement of human rights.

Weeks later, the first email sent from the NOW listserve that gave updates on the March announced the name was changed

> To convey the sense of urgency before us and to explain in no uncertain terms that this March is about reproductive justice and freedom; access to reproductive health services, and family planning, which includes the right to practice birth control and the right to have children and determine one's family formation.[27]

Subsequent messages emphasized diversity of coalition support (including the NAACP) and the many ways that the march went beyond protection of the landmark *Roe* legislation. Organizers emphasized social justice and the linkages between identities and access to justice. After SisterSong joined the coalition, NOW's publicity material reflected a shift in framing, which was the result of SisterSong bringing in an analysis that considered race, gender and class within a context of human rights.

CONCLUSION

As civil rights operate in the US, they are limited because they do not require protection in the areas that other citizens do not have legal rights. In addition, those rights can be on the books but not achieved in practice. For example, all racial minorities have the same legal right to vote as whites and can sue a state if they are kept from exercising this right. Yet, since whites do not have economic stability protected (or even mentioned) in the Constitution, minorities cannot claim they are being denied their economic rights due to their racial identity because no one of any race has right to those rights. In the cases of the women with less class and/or racial privilege, achievement of specific rights around reproduction cannot be achieved until other human rights (such as economic rights) are achieved. They argue these concerns have not been taken up by the pro-choice movement fighting for reproductive rights, but are matters of reproductive justice when analyzed through a human rights lens. Immigration is not a traditional "women's issue" if gender is the only lens to analyze this contentious issue. Yet, it becomes a concern for reproductive justice advocates who consider how the specific social location and experience of immigrant (women) leads to particular experiences of violation of their reproductive rights that goes beyond inability to access abortion.

Examples such as these may fall outside the line of vision of many activists and scholars, but deeper analysis can contribute to our growing understanding of how the language of human rights is deployed in different local settings. This explains why an organization like SisterSong, which is focused on a long-term strategy of organizing a new movement for reproductive justice rather than specific legislative gains, could still perceive going against mainstream movement convention as a logical move. Because the rights for which SisterSong advocates do not currently exist within the US legal system, it advocates for a new system.

Problems with relying on the state for protection notwithstanding, rights codified into law remain conceptually and practically important for people, including the activists working to increase them. Evidence of flaws in the Constitutionally-based rights regime surrounds us daily; and eventually, even if adopted in full, we may find that human rights may not fare better in the US context. Yet, doing away with rights (as some suggest) cannot address the concrete problems oppressed groups face on a day-to-day basis. Thus, rights will retain their inspirational quality, but activists will continue to find ways to ensure individuals and states begin to take human rights seriously, creating the revolution for which earlier activists could only begin to hope.

Emphasizing the importance of human rights for achieving social justice in the US is not all-or-nothing for activists. In the case of SisterSong, the organization acknowledges the previous gains achieved through the narrower civil rights approaches of other movements, but also integrates a human rights analysis while balancing the rhetoric that both individual and group identities are in need of protection. This rectifies the limits of earlier movements that focused on racial justice at the expense of women on color's gender identities or that focused on gender at the expense of women of color's racial identities. To do this, the organization must also educate its members (and coalition collaborates who work in various movements) about those limitations and the relevance of human rights. Doing so moves the larger social movement sector toward creating the conditions of possibility that may allow for progress in human rights standards within the US.

To advance our understanding of social movements for human rights, we have to consider the multiple ways they operationalize human rights and how limits of other analyses encourage this embrace. Finally, we would be wise to avoid the same mistakes that these activists seek to avoid— namely a singular focus on identity or group status that does not resonate with the lived complexity of multifaceted identities.

NOTES

1. Supporters of the Act argued that it ensured fetuses from unsuccessful abortions were defined as people and provided medical treatment. Opponents argued it was redundant with federal legislation and a backdoor way to erode *Roe v. Wade.*
2. CNN Ticker 2008.
3. Mertus 2007.
4. Blau and Moncada 2006; Merry 2006; Blau, Brunsma, Moncada, and Zimmer 2008.
5. Binion 1995; Bunch 1990; Cook 1993; Kerr 1993a.
6. Kerr 1993b.
7. Bunch 1990, p. 489.
8. MacKinnon 2006.
9. Bunch 1990, p. 491.
10. Turner 2006, p. 70.
11. Combahee River Collective 1983.
12. Ross 2006, p. 1.
13. Bambara 1970; Combahee River Collective 1983; Roth 2004.
14. Ferree and Hess 1985, p. 88.
15. Diallo 2005, p. 11.
16. Levi 2006, p. 10.
17. Jimenez 2006, p. 1, emphasis added.
18. Ross 2005, p. 2.
19. SisterSong 2005, p. 17, emphasis added.
20. Merry 2006, p. 181.
21. One often-cited text that discusses these tensions around belonging to multiple (identity) communities is Moraga and Anzaldúa's 1981 anthology *This Bridge Called my Back: Radical Writings from of Women of Color.*
22. Shen 2006, p. 3, emphasis added.
23. SisterSong 2004, p. 12.
24. Shen 2006, p. 1.
25. National Organization for Women "History of Marches and Mass Action," emphasis added.
26. Global Feminisms Project 2006.
27. National Organization for Woman "March News."

REFERENCES

Anderson, Carol 2003, *Eyes Off the Prize: African Americans, the United Nations, and the Struggle for Human Rights, 1944–1955,* Cambridge, UK; New York: Cambridge University Press.

Bambara, Toni C. 1970, *The Black Woman: An Anthology*, New York: New American Library.

Binion, Gayle 1995, "Human rights: A feminist perspective" *Human Rights Quarterly* 17, (3): 509–26.

Blau, Judith R., et al. 2008, *The Leading Rogue State: The United States and Human Rights,* Boulder, CO: Paradigm Publishers.

Blau, Judith R., and Moncada, Alberto 2006, *Justice in the United States: human rights and the U.S. constitution*, Lanham: Rowman & Littlefield Publishers.

Bunch, Charlotte. 1990. "Women's Rights as Human Rights: Toward a Re-vision of Human Rights." *Human Rights Quarterly* 12, (4) (Nov.): 486–98.

CNN Ticker Producer Alexander Mooney. Http:// politicalticker.blogs.cnn.com/2008/09/16/obamas-abortion-record-under-fire-in-latest-independent-ad/. [cited September 12, 2008]. Available from http:// politicalticker.blogs.cnn.com/2008/09/16/obamas-abortion-record-under-fire-in-latest-independent-ad/.

Combahee River Collective 1983, "Combahee River Collective Statement," In *Home Girls: A black feminist anthology,* Barbara Smith (ed.), pp. 272–282. New York: Kitchen Table: Women of Color Press.

Cook, Rebecca 1993, "Gaining Redress Within a Human Rights Framework," In *Ours by Right: Women's rights as human rights*, Joanna Kerr (ed.), 13–15. London: Zed Books.

Diallo, Dazon D. 2005, "Surviving Grant Writing with a Smile," *Collective Voices, 1*, no. 3:11.

Donnelly, Jack 2007. *International Human Rights. Dilemmas in world politics.* 3rd ed. Boulder, Colo.: Westview Press.

Ferree, Myra Marx, Beth B. Hess, and Irwin Taylor Sanders 1985, *Controversy and Coalition: The New Feminist Movement.* Boston: Twayne Publishers.

Global Feminisms Project 2006. "Loretta Ross interviewed by Zakiya Luna," Institute for Research on Women and Gender, http://www.umich .edu/~glblfem/en/us.html.

Jimenez, Laura 2006, "Ningún ser humano es illegal: Immigration Reform, Human Rights and Reproductive Justice," *Collective Voices, 2*, no. 5:1–2.

Kerr, Joanna 1993a, "The Context and The Goal" In *Ours by right: Women's rights as human rights*, 3–9. London: Zed Books.

Kerr, Joanna 1993b. *Ours by Right: Women's rights as human rights*. London; Zed Books

Levi, Robin 2006, "Making the Silent Heard and the Invisible Visible," *Collective Voices, 2*, no. 5:10–12 and 13.

McCann, Michael 2006, "Law and Social Movements: Contemporary Perspectives," *Annual Review of Law and Social Science, 2*, 2.1–2.22.

Merry, Sally E. 2006, *Human Rights and Gender Violence: Translating International Law into Local Justice,* Chicago: University of Chicago Press.

Mertus, Julie 2007, "The Rejection of Human Rights Framings: The Case of LGBT Advocacy in the US," *Human Rights Quarterly 29*, (4): 1036–64.

Mertus, Julie 2004. *Bait and Switch: Human rights and U.S. foreign policy*. Global horizons series. New York: Routledge.

Moraga, Cherrie, and Anzaldua, Gloria 1981, *This Bridge Called My Back: Writings by Radical Women of Color*, Watertown, MA: Persephone Press.

National Organization for Women. "History of Marches and Mass Actions" http://www.now.org/history/ protests.html (accessed 6 July 2007).

National Organization for Women, 2003, "March news-131 Days Until The March for Women's Lives!," December 16, http://www.now.org/lists/march-news/ msg00000.html (accessed 6 July 2007).

Okin, Susan Moller. 1998. "Feminism, Women's Human Rights, and Cultural Differences." *Hypatia* 12, (2): 32–52.

Ross, Loretta 2006, "Understanding Reproductive Justice" online http://www.sistersong.net/ publications_and_articles/Understanding_RJ.pdf (accessed 27 July 2007).

Ross, Loretta 2005, "A Feminist Perspective on Katrina," *Collective Voices, 1*, no. 3:1–4.

Roth, Benita 2004, *Separate Roads to Feminism: Black, Chicana, and White feminist movements in America's Second Wave*, Cambridge, UK; New York: Cambridge University Press.

Shen, Evelyn 2006, "Reproductive Justice: Towards a Comprehensive Movement," *Collective Voices, 1*, no. 4:1–3.

SisterSong Women of Color Reproductive Health Collective 2005, "Reproductive Rights are Human Rights," *Collective Voices, 1*, no. 3:16–17.

SisterSong Women of Color Reproductive Health Collective, "Collective Voices," online http://www .sistersong.net/newspaper.html (accessed 27 July 2007).

Turner, Bryan S. 2006, *Vulnerability and Human Rights*, University Park, PA.: Pennsylvania State University Press.

Zoelle, Diana Grace 2000, *Globalizing Concern for Women's Human Rights: The Failure of The American Model*. New York: St. Martin's Press.

Freedom to Choose? Three Essays on Abortion Rights

The Only Good Abortion Is My Abortion

Maggie Koerth-Baker (2012)

As I write this, it is 1:17 a.m. on Wednesday, June 20th, 2012.

I am lying awake in bed, trying to decide whether or not to have an abortion.

Of course, we don't call it an abortion. We call it "a procedure" or a D&C. See, my potential abortion is one of the good abortions. I'm 31 years old. I'm married. These days, I'm pretty well off. I would very much like to stay pregnant right now. In fact, I have just spent the last year—following an earlier miscarriage—trying rather desperately to get pregnant.

Unfortunately, the doctors tell me that what I am now pregnant with is not going to survive. Last week, I had an ultrasound, I was almost six weeks along and looked okay. The only thing was that the heartbeat was slow. It wasn't a huge deal. Heartbeats start slow, usually around the sixth week, and then they speed up. But my doctor asked me to come back in this week for a follow up, just to be sure. That was Tuesday, yesterday. Still my today. The heart hasn't sped up. The fetus hasn't grown. The egg yolk is now bigger than the fetus, which usually indicates a chromosomal abnormality. Basically, this fetus is going to die. I am going to have a miscarriage. It's just a matter of when.

Because of these facts—all these facts—I get special privileges, compared to other women seeking abortion in the state of Minnesota.

Nobody has to tell my parents. I am not subject to a 24-hour waiting period. I do not have to sit passively while someone describes the gestational stage that my fetus is at, presents me with a laundry list of possible side-effects (some medically legit, some not), lectures me on all the other options that must have just slipped my mind, or forces me to look at enlarged, color photographs of healthy fetuses.

Because I have health insurance, I can afford a very nice OB/GYN whom I chose and who does not exercise her right to deny me this option. Thankfully, I don't live in a state where she can legally lie to me about the status of my fetus, to dissuade me from having an abortion.

Most importantly, from my perspective, I have the privilege of a private abortion in a nondescript medical office. I will not have to go to an abortion clinic. I will not have to walk by any protesters—not even Charlie, the one guy who is paid to protest every day outside Minneapolis' abortion clinic, where I have volunteered as an escort in the past.

Most of these privileges boil down to the fact that, as far as my doctor and my medical billing are concerned, this is not an elective procedure.

But here's the thing. It is elective.

I don't have to do this. I am making a decision. Plain and simple. An incredibly awful, heart-wrenching decision with positives and negatives no matter which option I choose.

Having an abortion would get this miscarriage over with quickly. Most likely, there would be less pain and less bleeding. That's a big deal. My last miscarriage happened at four weeks along. I woke up in the middle of the night wanting to scream and almost vomiting from the pain. I bled for nearly two weeks after that. My guess is that these effects are not weaker for a seven-week miscarriage. Finally, even if I wait this out, there's still a pretty decent chance that I end up having to get an abortion after all. It's not uncommon for miscarriages like this to take too long to start, or not finish completely on their own. With just enough bad luck, I might get to experience both options.

On the other hand, I'm scared. This is surgery. Surgery is scary. There are small but very real-feeling risks involved: reaction to anesthesia, infections, and in rare cases some women develop scar tissue in their uterus that can make it hard to get pregnant again. That might be the biggest fear for me, honestly. It took five months to get pregnant the first time. It was a year after that miscarriage before this pregnancy happened. I know that, for the most part, this is random chance. I have bad luck. But part of me is terrified of anything that might make this process harder than it already is. Also, psychologically, I'm still clinging to this pregnancy. I want the doctors to be wrong. I want to have one of those miracles where everything turns out to be okay and I am relieved to find that I haven't actually lost everything.

Right now, at 2:06 a.m., I'm leaning towards a compromise. I think I probably want the abortion. I don't think I want to have to jump from thinking I had a viable pregnancy to having an abortion in a span of two days. I have a list of questions to ask my doctor in the morning. This decision is entirely dependent upon her answers, but I think it's the right one for me.

That was a lot of TMI, I know. But I am telling you this to press a point.

I am making a decision.

The only thing that makes my abortion decision different from anyone else's abortion decision is that some people who are against abortion will think that my abortion is acceptable.

Some. Not all. Maybe not even most. I honestly have no idea. My life is not in danger, after all. I have not been raped. I merely think that I might not want to sit around, feeling the symptoms of pregnancy, for god knows how long, until a heartbeat stops and the ripping pain kicks in and the blood starts flowing on its own.

Let me be clear. I have options. It's just that they all suck. That's kind of how bad news related to pregnancy works.

If you are pregnant, and do not want to be, all of your options suck.

If you cannot seem to get pregnant, and want to be, all of your options suck.

If you are pregnant, and won't be soon, all of your options suck.

There is no universal good option. There is no universal bad option. But for each individual there is an option that is the least bad. Here is why I am pro-choice. If someone has to make a decision and the best they can hope for is the least-bad option, I don't believe I have any business making that choice for them.

My abortion is not a good abortion. It's just an abortion. And there's no reason to treat the decision I have to make any differently than the decisions made by any other woman.

Treatment Denied
Molly M. Ginty (2011)

Kathleen Prieskorn gasped in shock as her medical nightmare began. Still reeling from the heartbreak of an earlier miscarriage, Prieskorn was three months pregnant and working as a waitress when she felt a twinge, felt a trickle down her leg and realized she was miscarrying again.

She rushed to her doctor's office, "where I learned my amniotic sac had torn," says Prieskorn, who lives with her husband in Manchester, N.H. "But the nearest hospital had recently merged with a Catholic hospital—and because my doctor could still detect a fetal heartbeat, he wasn't allowed to give me a uterine evacuation that would help me complete my miscarriage."

To get treatment, Prieskorn, who has no car, had to instead travel 80 miles to the nearest hospital that would perform the procedure—expensive to do in an ambulance, because she had no health insurance. Her doctor handed her $400 of his own cash and she bundled into the back of a cab.

"During that trip, which seemed endless, I was not only devastated, but terrified," Prieskorn remembers. "I knew that if there were complications I could lose my uterus—and maybe even my life."

Ordeals like the one Prieskorn suffered are not isolated incidents: They could happen to a woman of any income level, religion or state now that Catholic institutions have become the largest not-for-profit source of health-care in the U.S., treating 1 in 6 hospital patients. And that's because Catholic hospitals are required to adhere to the Ethical and Religious Directives for Catholic Health Care Services—archconservative restrictions issued by the 258-member U.S. Conference of Catholic Bishops.

Because of the directives, doctors and nurses at Catholic-affiliated facilities are not allowed to perform procedures that the Catholic Church deems "intrinsically immoral, such as abortion and direct sterilization." Those medical personnel also cannot give rape survivors drugs to prevent pregnancy unless there is "no evidence that conception has already occurred." The only birth control they can dispense is advice about "natural family planning"—laborious daily charting of a woman's basal temperature and cervical mucus in order to abstain from sex when she is ovulating—which only 0.1 percent of women use.

The Catholic directives involve not just abortion and birth control but ectopic pregnancies, embryonic stem cell research, in-vitro fertilization, sterilizations and more. "The problem with [the directives]," says Susan Berke Fogel, an attorney at the National Health Law Program in Los Angeles, "is about substandard care becoming rampant in the U.S., threatening women's health and women's lives."

Catastrophe was only narrowly averted in 2009 when a 27-year-old, 11-weeks-pregnant patient in Arizona staggered into the emergency room of St. Joseph's Hospital and Medical Center in Phoenix with such severe pulmonary hypertension that her doctors determined she would die without an immediate abortion. The ethics committee voted to break hospital policy and advise the woman of her option of a lifesaving abortion. The woman chose to have doctors terminate the pregnancy.

But when the bishop overseeing the Phoenix diocese heard about this, he declared that St. Joseph's could no longer be a Catholic institution unless it agreed to follow Catholic "moral teachings." The Bishop forbade Catholic Mass in the hospital's chapel and excommunicated Sister Margaret McBride—the only nun on the ethics committee.

The Phoenix story drew national outrage, but lesser-known cases of religious doctrine affecting medical care are rampant. In Oregon, a bishop threw out a medical-center director from his diocese for refusing to stop sterilizing patients. In Arizona, a couple raced to a Catholic hospital ER after the wife miscarried one of a pair of fetuses, only to be sent to a secular facility after doctors determined that the twin fetus was still alive—though not viable. And in New York, doctors at a Catholic institution neglected to terminate an ectopic pregnancy (in which the fertilized egg begins to develop outside the uterus) even though the embryo could not possibly survive and the patient faced a potentially fatal rupture of her fallopian tube.

How did we get to the point where 258 right-wing bishops—all (supposedly) celibate male clerics—are prohibiting doctors from practicing medicine and denying women essential reproductive care? The debacle starts with anti-choice legislation. The U.S. Congress started to pass "conscience clauses" pushed by the Roman Catholic Church and anti-abortion forces in the immediate wake of the Roe v. Wade Supreme Court decision that legalized abortion in 1973. Today, these laws apply not only to physicians and nurses who oppose abortion, but to entire institutions whose "consciences" allow them to withhold medically indicated care.

Even as recently as 2008, the George W. Bush administration issued sweeping regulations to give health-care workers the right to refuse to take part in any procedure that "violates" their religious beliefs. The Obama administration moved to reverse this policy in February (making it explicit that contraception is not covered by conscience provisions), but 47 states and the District of Columbia now allow individuals or entities to refuse women reproductive health services, information or referrals.

You don't have to be a Catholic to end up at a Catholic hospital that refuses you lifesaving care. A Catholic facility might be the only one in your area, and when you expect treatment you may get dogma instead. "Religion in America should mean that the church runs the church," says Barry Lynn, the executive director of Washington, D.C.-based Americans United for Separation of Church and State. "It shouldn't mean the bishops are running your reproductive life."

The Anti-Abortion Clinic Across the Street
Kathryn Joyce (2010)

In 2010, when Scott Roeder stood trial for the murder of abortion provider Dr. George Tiller, he described his preparations for the crime. For years, Roeder had gathered information about Tiller's schedule and habits, not just by looking for his home in a gated community or through surreptitious attendance at his church, but also by showing up outside Tiller's Wichita, Kan., clinic, Women's Health Care Services, as a "sidewalk counselor."

At the same time that Roeder was "counseling" on the sidewalk—trying to talk women out of having abortions—he was beginning to determine if there was a "window of opportunity" that would leave the doctor exposed. He testified that for years he had been mulling over how and where Tiller could be murdered—at the clinic, could the doctor be hit with a car, or shot "sniper" style from a rooftop?

Just next door to Tiller's clinic is the crisis pregnancy center (CPC) Choices Medical Clinic. Choices, like many CPCs, appears to be a medical facility, but its main mission is dissuading women from having abortions. As a sidewalk counselor, Roeder tried to steer abortion patients away from Tiller's clinic and over to Choices—if he did, he explained in his testimony, that was considered a "success."

The deceptive tactics of many of the country's CPCs—which are estimated to total between 2,300 and 4,000 centers nationwide—have been well-documented: They often mislead women about whether they perform abortions, mimicking the style or names of abortion clinics and operating in close proximity to them. Some provide misinformation about women's pregnancy status or due date, or suggest unproven links between abortion and cancer, infertility or suicide. A 2006 congressional report requested by Rep. Henry Waxman (D-Calif.) found that 87 percent of CPCs that receive federal funding provide false information—prompting both local and proposed federal legislation to mandate truth-in-advertising standards for CPCs.

Despite these fraudulent practices, CPCs have received millions in funding from both federal and state coffers and enjoy support from certain politicians and churches. CPCs present a public persona that is woman-friendly, compassionate and "empowering"—a love-bombing alternative to public images of angry protestors berating women entering abortion clinics.

However, this image is belied by the reality at a number of the nation's most heavily-targeted abortion clinics, where neighboring CPCs have close ties with extremists and sidewalk counselors, who function as an outreach arm that works, with or without acknowledgement, to draw CPC clients in. In Roeder's testimony linking the work of anti-abortion sidewalk counselors—the unofficial foot soldiers of the CPC movement—with his own violent vigilantism, he bared the troubling intersection of some of these seemingly innocuous centers with a number of the anti-abortion movement's most notorious members.

CPCS have long had connections with the most extremist anti-abortion cohorts. The zealous anti-abortion group Operation Rescue, which doggedly pursued Dr. Tiller, has long urged its supporters to get involved with CPCs and sidewalk counseling. In its 1990s guide "How to Stop Abortion in Your Community," Operation Rescue of California (which later moved to Wichita and changed its name to simply Operation Rescue) recommended volunteering at the local CPC and sidewalk counseling "right at the doors of the abortion mill"—along with picketing at abortion doctors' homes, filing lawsuits and conducting clinic blockades (called "rescues" in anti-abortion parlance). The latter, they wrote, "helps buy time for the sidewalk counselors."

Just the presence of a CPC in the vicinity of an abortion clinic ups the potential for violence. A recent survey by the Feminist Majority Foundation of women's reproductive health clinics nationwide found 32.7 percent of clinics located near a CPC experienced one or more incidents of severe violence, compared to only 11.3 percent of clinics not near a CPC. (Severe violence includes clinic blockades and invasions, bombings, arson, bombing and arson threats, death threats, chemical attacks, stalking, physical violence and gunfire.)

A who's who of anti-abortion extremists have been involved with the CPC movement:

- Cheryl Sullenger, Operation Rescue's "senior policy director" in Wichita, who served two years in prison for conspiring to blow up an abortion clinic in California in 1988, began her path to radical activism at a CPC. As she told anti-abortion activists gathered in Omaha, Neb., for a training during Operation Rescue-organized protests in August 2009, "Very soon I realized that there were so many women that fell through the crisis pregnancy center safety net and never approached those places; they went straight to the abortion clinics. And I thought, 'Who is gonna go to the abortion clinic to help them?'" (Sullenger's phone number was found in Scott Roeder's car after he fled the Tiller murder scene.)
- Michael Bray, a convicted abortion-clinic bomber and author of the "justifiable homicide" tome A Time to Kill, cofounded the Bowie Crofton Pregnancy Clinic (a CPC) in 1982 in Bowie, Md. Bray is "lifetime chaplain" of the extremist group Army of God, whose adherents have been responsible for the murders of abortion doctors and for clinic bombings, including a fatal 1998 bombing in Birmingham, Ala.
- Chet Gallagher, a former police officer who has been arrested dozens of times for trespassing and abortion-clinic blockades organized by Operation Rescue, lent his anti-abortion star power to a fundraising benefit this past April for Gabriel's Corner, a Council Bluffs, Iowa, CPC. It was a brotherly act: The CPC is run by his sister, Christine Wilson. Wilson herself draws no lines between sidewalk counseling and CPCs, saying that CPCs exist as a resource to bolster the effectiveness of the counselors, who can intercept abortion-bound women and then take them across the street to close the sale.

- Joan Andrews Bell, a "justifiable homicide" supporter who spent five years in a Florida state prison for invading and vandalizing the Ladies Center clinic in Pensacola, Fla., and who has been arrested repeatedly since for clinic blockades, has long been involved with CPCs. Her husband, Chris, founded Good Counsel Homes, a string of five homes for unwed pregnant women in New York that also "responds to crisis pregnancy situations."
- James Kopp, the convicted murderer of abortion provider Dr. Barnett Slepian in 1998 (and the prime suspect in the attempted murders of four other doctors in Canada and New York), founded a CPC in San Francisco and worked for Chris Bell's Good Counsel Homes. Kopp has been affiliated with several of the most extremist groups in the country, including Operation Rescue and the Lambs of Christ, and is believed to be a member of the Army of God.

Vicki Saporta, president of the National Abortion Federation (NAF), argues that Kopp's escalation of tactics—from starting a CPC to engaging in blockades to making attempts on the lives of four abortion doctors to finally murdering Slepian—is not an uncommon progression. "Some of the anti-abortion extremists got their start in establishing CPCs," she says. "And one of the best examples is James Kopp. His evolution mirrored the evolution of the anti-choice movement."

Aid for Women, an abortion clinic in Kansas City, Kan., is where Scott Roeder got his start in anti-abortion extremism, repeatedly super-gluing the clinic locks and being part of the group of regular clinic protesters/sidewalk counselors.

Across the street is the Your Choice Pregnancy Resource Center, a CPC once owned by Eugene Frye—an anti-abortion veteran who was one of Roeder's most frequent visitors in prison and who told The Kansas City Star he was helping Tiller's assassin consider a "justifiable homicide" defense.

Frye, a 66-year-old contractor who has been arrested repeatedly since 1991 for various unlawful anti-abortion actions, including clinic blockades, can be found outside the Aid For Women clinic most Saturday mornings, including one in early August, leaning on a table-sized poster of a dismembered fetus and calling through a bullhorn to women entering the clinic, his voice audible for blocks around, "Mommy, I don't want to die. . . . Please don't let them kill me, Mommy. I'll be a good child."

Although Frye—whom clinic manager M. Jeffrey Pederson calls "the number one guy around here"—no longer owns Your Choice, there are still discernible ties between the center and clinic protesters. For years, Pederson has butted heads with Frye over property lines and harassment tactics, but the new owners of Your Choice—apartment lessors James, Gordon and Ruth Peterson—seem to want to distance themselves from protesters like Frye or other extremist faces outside the clinic. (Those include Army of God member and convicted conspirator in clinic arson attacks Jennifer McCoy, formerly a regular protester at Dr. Tiller's clinic, who now travels cross-state to protest at Aid For Women.)

"I'm not really supposed to be involved in [sidewalk counseling] as an employee here," says Robin Marriott, Your Choice's current director, who tells me she takes issue with "the screamers and yellers," and claims ignorance of the tenor of the Saturday protests put forth by Frye and others. "But I've tried to encourage churches. . . . to be [involved in sidewalk counseling]. I've said what we really need is sidewalk counselors."

Frye understands their reticence. "I think they'd like to see themselves as autonomous," says Frye. "They don't want to be associated with any violence. Scott Roeder used to come over here with us. He was here two weeks before he shot Dr. Tiller, and obviously they can see the connection: that he was from here."

Since Dr. Tiller's murder, extremists' activities have escalated at a number of abortion clinics nationwide. In Bellevue, Neb., the clinic of Dr. LeRoy Carhart has become the chief target of Wichita-based Operation Rescue, the group that conducted a seven-year campaign against Dr. Tiller (and in whose activities Scott Roeder claimed to have participated). In the heated atmosphere there, the involvement of extremists with the local CPC is laid bare.

In August 2009, Operation Rescue and Nebraska anti-choice group Rescue the Heartland staged a well-publicized "Keep It Closed" demonstration at Carhart's Abortion and Contraception Clinic of Nebraska (ACCON) to protest Carhart's plans to keep Tiller's clinic open. The neighboring CPC, A Woman's Touch Pregnancy Counseling Center, played a leading role in an Operation Rescue salvation story that has reached the level of anti-abortion mythology.

In the story, which I heard five versions of between Kansas City and Bellevue, a woman coming for her abortion appointment at Carhart's clinic was frightened off by clinic defenders shouting her name through a bullhorn. She was gently diverted by sidewalk counselors to the CPC, where she viewed an ultrasound picture and fell in love with her unborn child. (Free ultrasounds are one of CPCs' main lures these days.) The woman then requested that dozens of copies of the ultrasound be printed and distributed to the media and pro-choice clinic defenders. When Operation Rescue president Troy Newman waved the photos, pro-choicers shrunk from the picture like vampires from a cross, claimed Rescue the Heartland founder Larry Donlan. In some versions of the story, the woman has twins.

"It was a total set up," says Mary Carhart, Dr. Carhart's wife and colleague, of the tale. She says the woman didn't even have an appointment at the abortion clinic that day, and clinic defenders weren't carrying bullhorns. Reporters on the scene also expressed skepticism at the tale when they were denied an interview with the woman, or even her name. But the ease of Operation Rescue's coordinated publicity with A Woman's Touch is more proof to the Carharts of the connection between CPCs and anti-abortion protestors—something they've believed for years as they've watched their chief antagonists go in and out of the CPC, sometimes through the backdoor. Many routinely park their cars at A Woman's Touch and seem to use it as base camp for demonstrations.

Similar tactics were used in Wichita, says Carhart, who, for many years, traveled to Wichita monthly to work at Tiller's clinic. He noticed that those participating in demonstrations went in and out of the Wichita CPC next door to Dr. Tiller's clinic. "In fact, [protestors] would stand on the porch of the CPC and use a megaphone to yell at patients over the fence," he says. "And when we worked in Ohio, the protesters we had in Dayton bought the old gas station next to the clinic and converted it into a CPC. It's just an extension of their ways to try to deny women access to the services that are available."

The Bellevue CPC was started, in fact, by stalwart anti-abortion protester Liz Miller, whom the Carharts report has reappeared on the sidewalk in front of their clinic since ceasing full-time management of the center. Miller is still on its board of directors, though, along with attorney Matt Heffron, who glides smoothly between representing the CPC on property tax matters and representing one of ACCON's longtime chief protestors: Father Norman Weslin. A Catholic priest who founded a number of unwed mothers' homes and heads extremist anti-abortion "rescue" group the Lambs of Christ, Weslin is known for traveling around the country with Kopp, Donlan and other anti-abortion extremists to blockade abortion clinics. He was arrested in 2007 when he invaded Dr. Carhart's clinic for the second time.

Joan Aylor, the peer-counselor director for A Woman's Touch, further adds that the center was founded in 2002 "by a group of women . . . who had on their hearts to do something for abortion-minded women and to perhaps provide a little shelter for those sidewalk counselors—those brave people who are out there at all hours of the day, in whatever weather."

One of the other frequent protestors outside Carhart's clinic is Rescue the Heartland founder Donlan, a longtime anti-abortion extremist who drove one of Operation Rescue's raucous and graphic "Truth Trucks" through neighborhoods where Carhart's employees live—prompting the establishment of a nuisance law in Bellevue, transparently aimed at him. He also has written threatening letters to Carhart's employees, warning them that unless they resign their positions, he and his Rescue the Heartland group will begin a "campaign of exposure"—including circulating flyers with their photos and holding vigils in front of their houses and throughout their neighborhoods.

Meeting me outside ACCON one day, Donlan underscores the casual connection he has with A Woman's Touch, referring to it in terms of "we," "us" and "our"—an affiliation that he doesn't officially acknowledge, even as he was able to produce a client of A Woman's Touch to meet with me on short notice. At one point he notes, "It's not unreasonable to think that [abortion clinics] look at us [CPCs] as competition that's more successful."

But he demurs when asked about his official ties to A Woman's Touch. "I'm one of those people who will talk to a gal and if I can bring her over here [to the CPC]," he adds, "I'll do that, but that's as far as my affiliation goes."

Some anti-abortion leaders admit the partnership between themselves and CPCs is sometimes seamless, but sometimes strained.

"We, the church of Jesus Christ, are an army, and CPCs are triage, the Red Cross. They're always in the back of the lines, and they help the wounded to get well," explains Flip Benham, director of Operation Save America/Operation Rescue (not to be confused with the Operation Rescue in Wichita). Benham, who has been arrested many times for blockading clinics and is currently facing criminal charges for stalking an abortion doctor, himself began working with the Dallas CPC network Last Harvest Ministries in 1984.

He explains how Operation Save America (and its Las Vegas coordinator, Chet Gallagher) worked "hand in hand" with a local CPC, First Choice Pregnancy Center, to host Operation Save America's 2009 National Event in Las Vegas. He complains, however, that other CPCs try to keep the connection fuzzy—perhaps out of fear of lawsuits or loss of stature and funding.

A lot of "churches don't want to go further than the back lines," he tells me over the phone from the sidewalk outside an abortion clinic in Charlotte, N.C. The city is where, since Tiller's murder, Benham and Operation Save America have escalated protests against the three local abortion clinics and held a "siege." They've set up ladders to peer over the privacy fence and amplify their protests at the Family Reproductive Health abortion clinic. They also stand in the driveway, holding STOP signs up to entering patients, whom they attempt to direct to the local CPC, Pregnancy

Resource Center—often driving patients there themselves.

Benham and Operation Rescue have also printed and distributed WANTED posters with abortion doctors' photos at the doctors' homes and offices and in their neighborhoods—a terrorizing tactic that, when carried out in Pensacola, Fla. in the 1990s, preceded the earlier murders of two other abortion providers and a clinic volunteer. Those posters were ruled as true threats in a civil lawsuit, under the FACE Act (Freedom of Access to Clinic Entrances).

Meanwhile, the back lines—the CPCs—remain untainted by such activities. The back lines are "clean," says Benham. "So you'll see great financial support for CPCs. We, the people who are out front of the abortion mills, are the 'ugly,' 'dirty' pro-lifers. . . .You look at the reports in the media and you'll see that we are the people who blow up abortion mills, kill abortionists; we're the Timothy McVeighs. . . .When all arguments fail, they resort to ad hominem."

However, the borders between extremist side-walk counselors and even CPCs seeking to keep distance from them might not be that solid. As NAF's Saporta notes, while CPCs likely seek to "maintain a façade of some kind of legitimate medical facility" to keep receiving federal funds, abortion-clinic staff have recognized the faces of their regular protesters as CPC employees.

It's a demonstration of the labyrinthine connections in the anti-abortion world that seem to prove Dr. Carhart right when he argues that the camps are one and the same. "They have two different spheres. The underlying theory of both is never let the truth stand in the way of getting your point across. If you distort facts to women, there is no difference."

And if you distort facts to the public, which is providing funding for some of your activities, the public deserves to scrutinize both your activities and the company you keep.

What such scrutiny will uncover, Carhart predicts, is that "There is no difference. It's the same people."

DISCUSSION QUESTIONS FOR CHAPTER 7

1. How do patriarchal norms constitute a threat to women's health?

2. How are women treated differently in the health care system? What is the effect of this differential treatment? How does racism have an impact on the gendered experiences of women of color in the health care system? Have you ever had a negative experience based on gender in the health care system?

3. Why is a reproductive justice framework important, especially for women of color?

4. What have been the consequences of women's loss of control of their reproductive processes?

5. How does the chipping away of abortion rights threaten the achievements of *Roe v. Wade?*

SUGGESTIONS FOR FURTHER READING

Boston Women's Health Book Collective. *Our Bodies, Ourselves for the New Century.* New York: Simon & Schuster, 1998.

Chrisler, Joan C. *Reproductive Justice: A Global Concern.* Santa Barbara: Praeger, 2012.

Dubriwny, Tasha N. *The Vulnerable Empowered Woman: Feminism, Postfeminism, and Women's Health.* New Brunswick, NJ: Rutgers University Press, 2012.

Ehrenreich, Barbara, and Deirdre English. *Witches, Midwives, and Nurses: A History of Women Healers.* New York: Feminist Press, 2010.

Ehrenreich, Nancy, ed. *The Reproductive Rights Reader: Law, Medicine, and the Construction of Motherhood.* New York: NYU Press, 2008.

Goldberg, Michelle. *The Means of Reproduction: Sex, Power, and the Future of the World.* New York: Penguin, 2009.

Luce, Jacquelyne. *Beyond Expectation: Lesbian/Bi/Queer Women and Assisted Conception.* Toronto: University of Toronto Press, 2010.

Malson, Helen, and Maree Burns, eds. *Critical Feminist Approaches to Eating Dis/Orders.* New York: Routledge, 2009.

Tallis, Vicci. *Feminisms, HIV and AIDS: Subverting Power, Reducing Vulnerability.* New York: Palgrave Macmillan, 2012.

Weddington, Sarah. *A Question of Choice.* New York: Penguin, 1993.

CHAPTER 8

Family Systems,
Family Lives

The title of this chapter reflects the reality of the family as both a major societal institution and a place where individuals experience intimate relationships. Using the definition of institution as established patterns of social behavior organized around particular purposes, the family is constituted through general patterns of behavior that emerge because of the specific needs and desires of human beings and because of the societal conditions of our lives. At the institutional level, the family maintains patterns of privilege and inequity and is intimately connected to other institutions in society such as the economy, the political system, religion, and education, which together produce social discourses or "regimes of truth" that create meaning associated with family and its relationship to these institutions. At the level of experience, the family fulfills basic human needs and provides most of us with our first experiences of love and relationship as well as power and conflict. Families are complex entities, as the poem "My Grandmother Washes Her Feet in the Sink of the Bathroom at Sears" by Mohja Kahf illustrates. This poem demonstrates relationships among families, religion, and culture, emphasizing how young family members often serve as a bridge or translator between traditional cultures within families and contemporary institutions and practices.

Scholarship on the family has demonstrated that family forms are historically and culturally constructed in global context and that family is a place for the reproduction of power relations both nationally and transnationally. Families worldwide are increasingly shaped not only by social structures within each society, but also by uniquely global forces, including worldwide demographic shifts, transnational employment across national and political borders, regional and international violence, and worldwide culture systems. In this way, families are primary social units that maintain other institutions and reinforce existing patterns of domination. At the same time, however, family networks provide support systems that can reduce the indignities and/or challenge the inequities produced by various systems of inequality in society.

DEFINITIONS OF FAMILY

Families are part of what social scientists call kinship systems, or patterns of relationships that define family forms. In most societies worldwide people live together on the basis of kinship ties and responsibilities for raising children. Such ties involve rules about who has sexual access to whom, what labor should be done and by whom, and how power should be distributed. In virtually all societies there is a publicly announced contract and/or ritual that makes sexual and economic ties legitimate. Kinship systems vary widely around the world and determine matters such as family descent or claims to common ancestry (for example, through the line of the father [*patrilineal*], mother [*matrilineal*], both parents [*bilateral*], or either parent [*unilateral*] line) and distribution of wealth. Kinship rules also govern norms about the meanings of marriage and the numbers of marriage partners allowed. *Monogamy* involves one wife and one husband, *polygamy* means multiple spouses, and *cenogamy,* group marriage. *Polygyny,* multiple wives, is a more common form of polygamy than *polyandry,* or multiple husbands. In this way, families are central organizing principles among humans around the world and, as a result, the status and role of women in families are not only dependent on women's access to power in society generally, but also related to the status of families within a society—especially their access to economic resources.

In the United States, there is no "normal" family, though such tends to be constructed as the nuclear family of the middle-class, white, married, heterosexual couple with children. *Nuclear* family implies a married couple residing together with their children, and it can be distinguished from an *extended* family in which a group of related kin, in addition to parents and children, live together in the same household. U.S. Census Bureau data show nuclear families dropping below a quarter of all households and that multiple family forms

The World's Women: Women and Families

The world's population tripled in the period 1950–2010 to reach almost 7 billion.

- There are approximately 57 million more men than women in the world, yet in most countries there are more women than men.
- There is a "gender spiral," with more boys and men in younger age groups and more women in the older age groups.
- Fertility is steadily declining in all regions of the world, though it still remains high in some regions of Africa.
- Life expectancy is steadily rising, with women living longer than men.
- International migration is increasing. There are more and more women migrants, and in certain areas they outnumber men.
- The age at marriage for women continues to rise—and it remains high for men.
- In family life women overwhelmingly carry the workload, although in some countries the gap has narrowed significantly.

Source: http://unstats.un.org/unsd/demographic/products/Worldswomen/WW_full%20report_color.pdf.

are now the rule in U.S. society rather than the exception. Instead, frequently occurring family forms in the United States today include single-parent, blended families, families headed by lesbian and gay domestic partners, and other cohabiting couples with children. In addition, there has been an increase in multi-generational families over the last decades (now 16 percent of all families) that reflects economic forces, especially the job losses and home foreclosures of recent years, and the rise in numbers of immigrants, who, like their European counterparts from earlier centuries, are far more likely than native-born North Americans to live in multi-generational family households.

This diversity of family forms also more closely parallels U.S. families of the nineteenth century rather than in the recent past. In the premodern era before industrialization households were made up of various kin and unrelated adults and children, reflecting the ways an agricultural way of life meant that households contained many people—not just kin, but others who came to help work the land or maintain the household. These social, economic, and demographic facts underscore the myth of the nuclear family in the United States, either currently or in the distant past.

In other words, traditional "regimes of truth" about the normative family hide the reality of the wide diversity of family life in the United States. For example, there has been a significant drop in the number of legally married heterosexual couples in the last few decades, with more women never marrying, delaying marriage, cohabiting in heterosexual and gay relationships, and raising families alone. In addition, currently about 2 million children are raised by lesbian and gay parents, and one-third of lesbian and one-fifth of gay male households have children. Barely half of all U.S. adults are married (compared to almost three-quarters of all adults in the 1960s) and 40 to 50 percent of all marriages end in divorce. The median age of first marriage is 28 years for men and 26 years for women, up from 23 and 21 years, respectively, in 1980. The reading "Singled Out" by Tamara Winfrey Harris addresses marriage trends in the United States through a focus

LEARNING ACTIVITY   **What Makes a Family?**

Conduct an informal survey of the people on your dorm floor or in an organization to which you belong about the structure of their family of origin. Whom do they consider to be in their family? What relation do these people have to them? Did all of these people live in the same house? Who had primary responsibility for caring for them as children? Who was primarily responsible for the financial well-being of the family? For the emotional well-being of the family? Was the family closely connected to extended family? If so, which extended family members and in what ways?

Compare your findings with those of your classmates. What do your findings lead you to surmise about what makes a family? How closely do the families of your interviewees resemble the dominant notion of the nuclear family—a husband and wife (in their first marriage) and their two or three children? What do you think is the impact of our stereotype of the nuclear family on social policy? How do you think this stereotype affects real families dealing with the real problems of everyday family life?

Myths and Facts About Lesbian Families

Myth 1: Lesbians don't have lasting relationships.
Fact: Many lesbians are in long-term partnerships. Unfortunately, social supports and civil rights are not accorded to lesbian partnerships as they are to hetero-sexual marriages. As of this writing, 17 states (Massachusetts, Connecticut, Iowa, Vermont, New Hampshire, New York, Washington, Maryland, Maine, Rhode island, Delaware, Minnesota, California, New Jersey, Hawaii, New Mexico, Illinois) and the District of Columbia issue marriage licenses to gay couples. A number of other states recognize gay and lesbian relationships through civil unions or domestic partnerships that provide some or most of the benefits afforded married heterosexual couples. The federal government began recog-nizing same sex marriages in 2013.
Myth 2: Lesbians don't have children.
Fact: Between 8 and 10 million American children are being raised by lesbian or gay parents. Many lesbians have children from previous heterosexual relation-ships before they came out. Others have children through artificial insemina-tion, and others adopt children. Unfortunately, because the courts may believe stereotypes about lesbians, lesbian mothers still sometimes lose custody of their children in a divorce, despite research indicating the fitness of lesbian mothers. In some states, adoption is difficult for lesbians, and rarely can both partners in a lesbian relationship legally adopt a child together.
Myth 3: Children of lesbian parents develop psychological disorders.
Fact: Research indicates that there is no difference in the development or fre-quency of pathologies between children of heterosexual parents and children of homosexual parents. In fact, study after study suggests that children in lesbian

families are more similar to than different from children in heterosexual families. Studies of separation-individuation, behavior problems, self-concept, locus of control, moral judgment, and intelligence have revealed no major differences between children of lesbian mothers and children of heterosexual mothers.
Myth 4: Children of lesbian parents become gay themselves.
Fact: Research indicates no difference between children raised in lesbian families and children raised in heterosexual families with respect to gender identity, gender role behavior, and sexual orientation. Studies suggest that children in lesbian families develop along the same lines as children in heterosexual families; they are as likely to be happy with their gender, exhibit gender role behaviors, and be heterosexual as children of heterosexual mothers.

on black women who marry at lower rates than whites (even though most eventually do marry). Harris discusses how these figures support problematic stereotypes of the sassy independent black woman whom media have singled out to be blamed or pitied. In reality, educated black women are more likely to marry than their less-educated counterparts. As of 2008, 70 percent of black female college graduates were married, compared to 60 percent of high school graduates, and just 53 percent of black women who did not complete high school. Indeed, while African American women are less likely to marry than whites, their rates are higher for educated women. And, although marriage rates have decreased since 1980, they have decreased less for educated women than for anyone else. Furthermore, college-educated women of all races, once they do marry, are less likely to divorce. As a result, by age 30, and especially at ages 35 and 40, college-educated women are significantly *more* likely to be married than any other group. This represents a historic reversal of what has been called the "success" penalty for educated women writes sociologist Stephanie Coontz in *American Families*.

U.S. census data also show a dramatic increase of almost 15 percent in the last few years among cohabiting couples. Demographers believe the increase involves individuals delaying marriage because of the cost, avoiding marriage altogether, or moving in without a long-term plan because of short-term financial pressures. At the same time, the increase in the number of women not marrying, and the age of those who do, reflects the improved status of women in these countries where they have relative control over their reproductive and economic lives. Such data illustrate the complex role of economic factors in marriage trends. This is true, of course, for families worldwide where poverty often increases the incidence of marriage, especially among young women. It is the lack of opportunities, extreme poverty, and the importance placed upon female virginity that encourages girls to be married as children. And, even though countries may enact marriage laws to limit marriage to a minimum age such as 16 years, depending upon jurisdiction, traditional marriages of girls of younger ages are widespread in Sub-Saharan Africa as well as many regions of South Asia. Goods that may include livestock, cash, or other valuables received from the bride price of a daughter are often essential for sustaining the rest of the family. Child brides are also subject to interpersonal violence and health problems such as obstetric fistula. Organizations such as Human Rights Watch advocate for the end of these practices, as does Girls Not Brides, a global partnership of almost 200 nongovernmental organizations committed to addressing child marriage.

A 2013 Pew Research Center report based on U.S. census data shows that 40 percent of households with children younger than the age of 18 included mothers who provided the sole or primary source of income for the family (up from 11 percent in 1960). They attribute this growth to the increasing number of women in the workforce. In addition, the report emphasizes that the majority of these breadwinning mothers are single parents: 63 percent—or 8.6 million—are single mothers. Half of all U.S. children will live in a single-parent household at some point during their childhood. The Pew report also shows that 37 percent of their breadwinning mothers (about 5.1 million women) are married mothers who earn more than their husbands and are thus the primary breadwinners. It is important to note that the two groups in the Pew report (single and married mothers) differ greatly in income with the median total family income for homes with married mother breadwinners about $80,000, compared to $23,000 for families headed by single mothers. Not surprisingly, Pew also found that married mothers who outearn their husbands tend to be older, white, and college educated, while single mothers are more likely to be younger, black or Latina, and less likely to have a college degree. An increasingly large number of poor children live in single female-headed households. As the chart "Families and Poverty" shows, these families are approximately five times more likely to be in poverty than marrried couples, with 28 percent of single female–headed households living in poverty compared to 5 percent of married couples.

In this way, the diversity of families includes single parents, extended and multigenerational families, lesbian and gay families with and without children, people (single or not and with or without children) living in community with other adults, grandparents raising grandchildren or nieces and nephews, and so forth. These families represent all social classes, sexualities, and racial and ethnic groups, and one in five children in the United States speak a language other than English in their homes. Globally, family structure is affected by the consequences of the global economy as well as by militarism and colonial expansion. Examples include the effects on family life as a result of immigration patterns associated with exportation and consolidation of global capital and the consequences for women in families as a result of their labor in industries such as textiles or electronic components worldwide.

Despite such diversity among U.S. families, legislation has restricted the legality of unions beyond the male/husband and female/wife relationship, although as discussed in Chapter 6, in 2013 the Defense of Marriage Act (DOMA) was found unconstitutional in treating gay marriage in states where there is marriage equality as "second-class marriages," thus violating the Fifth Amendment. The U.S. Supreme Court set the stage for gay couples to receive the same federal benefits as straight couples in these states. The ruling clears the way for individuals in same-sex marriages in states where there is marriage equality to receive many of the benefits of marriage entitled to heterosexual couples, such as Social Security benefits and immigration rights. However, as of this writing, states are still able to define marriage for themselves and do not have to recognize gay marriages performed in other states. The first essay by Audrey Bilger in the reading "Marriage Equality: Three Essays" discusses this development. She makes the case that the opposition to gay marriage at this point in time is dying. Indeed, more than 50 percent of the U.S. population endorse marriage equality. It is estimated that a greater number of people in the United States currently support marriage equality than believe in evolution as a scientific principle. Gay and lesbian rights activists make the case that the values of gay couples are indistinguishable from those of their straight neighbors. They are no less loyal to their partners, they

"You just wait until your other mother gets home, young man!"

value and participate in family life, and they are just as committed to their neighborhoods and communities. They also pay the same taxes. As such the case is made for their right as citizens to the right that all straight people have: the right to legal marriage. Still, as already discussed in Chapter 6, gay marriage is restricted in the United States, although as of this writing there are currently 17 states plus the District of Columbia that provide marriage equality. (Massachusetts, Connecticut, Iowa, Vermont, New Hampshire, New York, Washington, Maryland, Maine, Rhode Island, Delaware, Minnesota, California, New Jersey, Hawaii, New Mexico, Illinois, and the District of Columbia, with, Colorado, Nevada, Oregon, and Wisconsin providing legal or "civil unions" for same-sex couples). Under domestic partnership laws couples usually sign a registry at the secretary of state's office and pay a fee for a domestic partnership contract that gives them similar legal rights and responsibilities as married heterosexual couples.

The reading "Marriage Equality: Three Essays" discusses these issues in the context of gay parenting, adoption, and custody legislation. The ongoing political debate concerning "family values" illustrates how supporters of the *status quo* (or existing power relations) in society have made the term *family values* synonymous with traditional definitions of the family and its role in society. This includes seeing women defined in terms of their domestic and reproductive roles, men as the rightful sources of power and authority, and married heterosexual families as the only legitimate family. Many people are offended by this narrow construction of family and its association with a repressive political agenda, and reject such values as *their* family values. Determining what kinds of families get to be counted as "real" families and determining whose "family values" are used as standards for judging others are heated topics of debate in the United States.

It is also important to note, however, that not all lesbian/gay/queer committed couples advocate marriage for themselves or necessarily endorse the legal recognition of gay marriage as a primary goal of the lesbian/gay/queer movements. They recognize the right to equal domestic partnerships and the basic economic benefits that come with that, but understand marriage as a key feature of a heterosexist culture that underpins the very discrimination they experience as non-heterosexual people. In other words, they resist legal marriage because of its role in maintaining the heteropatriarchy that justifies homophobia. They ask why mimic practices associated with an institution central to supporting heterosexism (the discrimination against non-heterosexual people)? The second essay by Daniel D'Addario in the reading "Marriage Equality: Three Essays" addresses this issue. He discusses the work of queer academics and activists who believe that gay marriage is the wrong fight. Their critique centers on the problems with marriage as an institution and suggests there should be options for couples other than marriage that he defines as "an institution that [problematically] blends church and state." In addition, as Gowri Vijayakumar in the final essay in this reading explains, often people in more affluent developed countries focus on gay marriage to the detriment of addressing issues such as violence, discrimination, and social exclusion. She emphasizes that often LGBQT equality gets positioned as "one of the great civilizational gifts the U.S. has to offer the seemingly poor, backward countries like India," even though India has a long history of sexual minority issues.

The notion of family—with all its connotations of love, security, connectedness, and nurturing—is a prime target for nostalgia in the twenty-first century. This is especially pertinent as economic forces transform the ways families function and we yearn for a return to the "traditional" family, with its unconditional love and acceptance, to escape from the complexities and harsh realities of society. Although many families do provide this respite, dominant ideologies about the family have idealized and sometimes glorified the family, and women's roles in the family, in ways that hide underlying conflict and violence. In addition, these ideologies present a false dichotomization between public (society) and private (family) spheres. Poor and non-white families have rarely enjoyed the security and privacy assumed in this split between family and society. For example, the state, in terms of both social welfare policies and criminal justice statutes, has a stronger impact on and more consequences for poor families than middle-class families. This is the topic of the next section: the connections between the family and other social institutions.

INSTITUTIONAL CONNECTIONS

The family interacts with other institutions in society and provides various experiences for family members. For example, economic forces shape women's family roles and help construct the balance between work and family responsibilities. As discussed in Chapter 9, women perform more than two-thirds of household labor—labor that is constructed as family work and often not seen as work. In addition, the family work that women do in the home is used to justify the kinds of work women are expected to perform in the labor force. It is no coincidence that women are congregated in a small number of occupations known for their caretaking, educating, and servicing responsibilities. In addition, the boundaries are more fluid between women's paid work and home life than between men's. This is structured into the very kinds of jobs women tend to perform, as well as part of the expectations associated with hiring women. These assumptions can be used against women very easily as they attempt to advance in careers. At the same time, the more rigid boundaries between work and home for male-dominated jobs mean that men have a more difficult time negotiating parenting responsibilities when they want to be more actively involved in their children's lives.

The economic system impacts families in many ways; in turn, families support and impact economic systems. Women care for and maintain male workers as well as socialize future generations of workers, thus supporting economic institutions that rely on workers to be fed, serviced, and able to fulfill certain work roles. Although in contemporary U.S. society some families are still productive units in that they produce goods directly for family consumption or for exchange on the market, most families are consumptive units in that they participate in the market economy through goods purchased for family consumption. As a result, advertisers target women as family shoppers. The family is a consumptive unit that provides the context for advertising, media, and other forms of entertainment. In these ways family systems are intimately connected to economic forces in society. Some scholars and activists are making the case for a return to the family as a productive, ecologically mindful unit that consumes local goods and supports local businesses.

The impact of shifting economies and changing technologies on families varies considerably by gender, class, sexuality, and race, such that a family's placement in the larger political economy directly influences diverse patterns of family organization. The ways economic systems affect family organization and life is demonstrated by the fact that African American children are twice as likely to enter U.S. foster care systems because of the conditions of poverty in their lives. This is the focus of the Gaylynn Burroughs reading in Chapter 11 titled "Too Poor to Parent?" Economic factors impact single-headed families such that households headed by women have about half the income and less than a third of the wealth (assets) of other U.S. households and are about three times as likely to be at or below the poverty level. Most recent census data show that the poverty rate for single mothers is twice as high as the rate for single fathers. As already mentioned, almost half of children living in single-headed households live in poverty. Race impacts this economic situation such that households headed by women of color are the most likely to experience poverty. It is well known that the most effective antipoverty program for families is one that includes educational opportunities, a living wage with benefits, and quality childcare.

In this way families are shaped by their relationship to systems of inequality in society. This means, for example, that working-class women's lack of flexible work scheduling affects how families are able to meet their needs, as does the lower pay of working-class women, making them less able to afford quality daycare. Similarly, higher unemployment among men of color as compared to white men impacts families and pushes women in family relationships with unemployed men to work outside the home full time while also taking care of young children. Jobs with different incomes and levels of authority and seniority affect access to such family-friendly benefits as flextime, on-site childcare, and company-sponsored tax breaks for childcare. For example, although unpaid parenting leave is a legal right of all U.S. employees, many companies provide better family benefits for their higher level and better-paid employees than they do for their lower level employees.

Around the world 169 countries guarantee paid maternity leave with 98 of these providing 14 or more weeks. The United States provides no paid parenting leave. In addition, almost half of employed private sector women workers lack a single paid sick day that they could use in a medical or family emergency. Institutional support for healthy parenting is a focus of the reading by Judith Warner titled "Family Way." She reviews books on mothering, comes to the conclusion that family-friendly policies are a necessity for effective child rearing, and makes suggestions for achieving these goals.

LEARNING ACTIVITY   **Families and Poverty**

To learn more about poverty and families in your area, go to the factfinder tool of the U.S. Census Bureau website at *www.factfinder2.census.gov.* Use the site's features to find out the median income of your area or the number of families in your state living in poverty.

Imagine that you are a single parent, the head of a family of four living in your area, and your take-home income is $1,500 per month. Create a budget for your family. Be sure to include rent, utilities, transportation, food, clothes, medical needs, school supplies, childcare, and other essentials. Find out what assistance you might qualify to receive and include that in your calculations. What does this activity suggest to you about the difficulties of living in poverty?

Families Below Poverty Level by Selected Characteristics

Characteristic	Number below poverty level (1,000)					Percent below poverty level				
	All races[1]	White alone	Black alone	Asian alone	His-panic[2]	All races[1]	White alone	Black alone	Asian alone	His-panic[2]
Total families	8,792	5,994	2,125	337	2,369	11.1	9.3	22.7	9.4	22.7
Age of householder:										
15 to 24 years old	1,096	708	328	26	283	34.2	30.1	52.6	21.7	36.2
25 to 34 years old	2,476	1,649	635	69	756	18.9	16.3	33.1	10.2	29.8
35 to 44 years old	2,072	1,437	491	76	681	12.1	10.7	21.9	7.9	23.5
45 to 54 years old	1,454	998	322	73	370	8.0	6.7	15.4	8.8	17.6
55 to 64 years old	894	644	192	31	154	6.5	5.6	14.2	5.5	13.4
65 years old and over	757	536	141	58	114	5.6	4.6	12.9	13.4	12.6
Region:										
Northeast	1,314	866	329	92	335	9.3	7.4	21.2	11.8	22.5
Midwest	1,827	1,227	485	55	208	10.5	8.1	28.6	12.7	25.7
South	3,717	2,432	1,127	71	892	12.5	10.5	21.4	8.7	22.4
West	1,934	1,470	184	120	935	11.0	10.2	21.7	7.7	22.5
Type of family:										
Married couple	3,409	2,694	366	230	1,054	5.8	5.4	8.6	7.9	16.0
Male householder, no spouse present	942	629	234	32	249	16.9	15.0	25.0	12.6	23.0
Female householder, not spouse present	4,441	2,671	1,524	76	1,066	29.9	27.3	36.7	16.9	38.8

[1] Includes other races, not shown separately.
[2] Hispanic persons may be any race.
Source: U.S. Census Bureau, *Income, Poverty, and Health Insurance Coverage in the United States: 2009,* Current Population Reports, P60–238, and Detailed Tables—Tables POV04 and POV44, September 2010. See also <http://www.census.gov/hhes /www/cpstables/032010/pov/toc.htm>.

The family experience is also affected by the state and its legal and political systems. As the reading "Lullabies Behind Bars" by Beth Schwartzapfel explains, prison systems shape experiences of family by incarcerated mothers who are disproportionately women of color. She discusses new programs that attempt to provide prison nurseries for mothers behind bars to encourage effective bonds between mothers and babies. More generally the government closely regulates families and provides certain benefits to legally married couples. Couples need a license from the state to marry, and the government says they may file a joint tax return, for instance. Lesbian and gay couples who jointly own property and share income and expenses may not have the privileges of marriage, joint tax filing, and domestic partner benefits. Benefits accrue to certain family members and not to people who, even though they might see themselves as family, are not recognized as such by the state. Lisa Miya-Jervis makes this very clear in the reading "Who Wants to Marry a Feminist?" She makes the case that in choosing marriage, feminists must understand the oppressive roots of marriage as an institution and actively work to "forge a new vision of what marriage is." Although an advanced industrial society, the United States has no national funding of daycare centers. This lack affects the social organization of the family and the experience of parenting. Federal and state policies also impact the family through legal statutes that regulate marriage and divorce legislation, reproductive choice, and violence in families.

Indeed, the family has connections to all societal institutions, and these connections help shape the kind and quality of experiences that we have as family members. Religion and the family are closely tied as social institutions. Religious socialization of children occurs in the family through religious and moral teachings, and religious institutions often shape societal understandings of families as well as provide rituals that help symbolize family and kin relations (such as baptisms, weddings, and funerals). Educational institutions rely on the family as a foundation for the socialization, care, and maintenance of children. Health systems rely on parents (and women in particular) to nurse and care for sick and elderly family members, as well as provide adequate nutrition and cleanliness to prevent disease. Military institutions need the family as a foundation for ideologies of combat and for socialization and support of military personnel. Sports and athletics are tied to the family through gender socialization, the purchase of certain equipment and opportunities, and the consumption and viewing of professional sports in the home. Although we might like to think of the family as an "oasis" apart from society, nothing could be further from the truth.

POWER AND FAMILY RELATIONSHIPS

At the direct level of experience, the family is the social unit where most people are raised, learn systems of belief, experience love and perhaps abuse and neglect, and generally grow to be a part of social communities. It is in the family where most of us internalize messages about ourselves, about others, and about our place in the world. Some learn that love comes with an abuse of power as large people hit little people, all in the name of love. Some also learn that love means getting our own way without responsibility—a lesson that may detract from the hopes of a civil society where individuals care about one another and the communities of which they are a part. Others learn that love is about trust, care, compassion, and responsibility.

ACTIVIST PROFILE **Hannah Solomon**

Hannah Greenbaum Solomon believed that "woman's sphere is the whole wide world" and her first responsibility was to her family. Solomon worked tirelessly in turn-of-the-century Chicago for social reform. Laboring alongside Jane Addams at Hull House, Solomon worked to improve child welfare. She reformed the Illinois Industrial School for Girls, established penny lunch stations in the public schools, and led efforts for slum clearance, low-cost housing, child labor laws, mothers' pensions, and public health measures.

In 1876 Solomon became the first Jewish member of the Chicago Woman's Club, where she developed a sense of women's ability to work together for social good. In 1893 she organized the Jewish Women's Congress at the Chicago World's Fair, which led to her founding the National Council of Jewish Women (NCJW) to enhance social welfare and justice. Solomon saw her commitment to justice as a part of her responsibility as a Jew, a woman, and an American.

Under Solomon's leadership, the NCJW sponsored programs for the blind, formed the Port and Dock Department to assist immigrant women in finding housing and jobs, established a permanent immigrant aid station on Ellis Island, supported Margaret Sanger's National Birth Control League, raised relief dollars during World War I, and participated in the presidential effort to create jobs during the Depression.

Solomon's legacy has continued in the NCJW since her death in 1942. Following World War II, the NCJW provided assistance to Holocaust survivors in Europe and Israel. During the McCarthy era, the NCJW organized the Freedom Campaign to protect civil liberties. Additionally, the organization was the first national group to sponsor Meals on Wheels, built the Hebrew University High School in Jerusalem, helped establish the Court Appointed Advocate Project (CASA) to protect the rights of children in court cases, and launched a national campaign to try to ensure that children were not harmed by changes in welfare law.

Currently, the National Council of Jewish Women has 90,000 members and continues the work of Hannah Solomon by bringing her vision of justice to bear in the world.

Family is where many of us first experience gender because societal understandings of the differences between girls and boys are transferred through early teachings by family members. Parents bring home baby girls and boys, dress them in gender-"appropriate" colors, give them different toys, and decorate their bedrooms in different ways that tend to facilitate and enforce cisgendered behaviors. As Chapter 3 emphasizes, the family is a primary institution for teaching about gender. In addition, experiences of gender are very much shaped by the gender composition of family members. A girl growing up in a family of brothers and a boy growing up with only women and girls in his family have different experiences of gender.

Central in any discussion of family is a focus on power. Power in families can be understood as access to resources (tangible or intangible) that allows certain family members to define the reality of others, have their needs met, and access more resources. In most U.S. families today, power is distributed according to age and gender. Older family members (although not always the aged, who often lose power in late life) tend to have more power than children and young people, who are often defined as "dependents." Men tend to have more power in the family than women do if this is measured in resource management and allocation and decision-making authority. Women, however, do have power if this is defined as day-to-day decisions about the running of the household and how certain household chores get done. Sociologists tend to emphasize that this latter sort of "power" is vulnerable to changes in broader family dynamics and subject to decisions by men in positions as major economic providers or heads of household.

The United States has among the highest marriage and the highest divorce rates of any industrialized country. Although a large number of people get divorced, this does not seem to indicate disillusionment with marriage because large numbers of people also remarry. Marriage traditionally has been based on gender relations that prescribe authority of husbands over wives and that entail certain norms and expectations that are sanctioned by the state. The traditional marriage contract assumes the husband will be the head of household with responsibilities to provide a family wage and the wife will take primary responsibility for the home and the raising of children and integrate her personal identity with that of her husband. As in "Mrs. John Smith" and "Dr. and Mrs. John Smith," Mrs. Smith easily can become someone who loses her identity to her husband. The declaration of "man and wife" in the traditional marriage ceremony illustrates how men continue to be men under this contract and women become wives.

As Lisa Miya-Jervis writes in "Who Wants to Marry a Feminist?" these norms are increasingly being challenged by contemporary couples who have moved from this traditional contract to one whereby women are expected to contribute financially and men are expected to fulfill family roles. Despite these modifications, husbands still tend to hold more power in families and women do the majority of physical and emotional family work. The rituals of marriage ceremonies illustrate these normative gender relations: the father "giving away" his daughter, representing the passage of the woman from one man's house to another; the wearing of white to symbolize purity and virginity; the engagement ring representing a woman already spoken for; and the throwing of rice to symbolize fertility and the woman's obligation to bear and raise children. Finally, as already mentioned, the traditions of naming are illustrative of power in families: Approximately 9 out of 10 women take the name of their husband and among those who keep their name, most give their children their husband's name and not their own. Indeed, among college-educated women in their 30s, the number keeping their names has dropped significantly since 1990 when almost a quarter of such women kept their own "maiden" names.

It is especially in the family where many girls and women experience gender oppression; in close relationship with men, they often experience gender domination. In other words, it is in the home and family where many girls and women feel the consequences of masculine power and privilege. Writing in 1910, socialist anarchist Emma Goldman saw marriage as an economic transaction that binds women into subservience to men (through love and personal and sexual services) and society (through unpaid housework). In the reading "Marriage and Love," she advocated "free love" that is unconstrained by marriage and relations with the state. Goldman believed love found in marriages occurred in spite of the institution of marriage and not because of it.

Sexism in interpersonal relationships among family members reduces female autonomy and lowers women's and girls' self-esteem. Consequences of masculine privilege in families can mean that men dominate women in relationships in subtle or not-so-subtle ways, expecting or taking for granted personal and sexual services, making and/or vetoing important family decisions, controlling money and expenditures, and so forth. In addition, power in family and marital relationships may lead to psychological, sexual, and/or physical abuse against women and children. Often the double standard of sexual conduct allows boys more freedom and autonomy compared to girls. Also, girls are very often expected to perform more household duties than boys, duties that may include cleaning up after their brothers or father. Studies have shown that boys spend about a third less time doing chores than their sisters and are more likely than girls to get paid or receive an allowance for doing the work. Mirroring the housework data for adults (see Chapter 9), chores such as dishwashing and cooking, often regarded as routine and performed for free, are more likely to be done by girls than boys. This sets up gender inequities in the family, impacts the amount of free time girls can enjoy, and sets a precedence for adult behavior.

LEARNING ACTIVITY   **Divorce Law: Who Benefits in My State?**

Research your state's divorce laws. How is property divided in a divorce? How is custody determined? How are alimony and child support determined? How do these laws affect women and children in actuality in your state? What are the poverty rates for divorced women and their children in your state? How many fathers do not pay child support as ordered by the court? How does your state deal with nonpaying fathers? What can you do to challenge the legal system in your state to be more responsive to women's and children's needs following divorce?

IDEAS FOR ACTIVISM

- Become a Court Appointed Special Advocate (CASA) for children.
- Offer to babysit for free for a single mother one evening a month.
- If your state has not approved same-sex marriage, lobby your state lawmakers.
- If you are planning your wedding, include a reading that supports marriage equality.
- Find out your university's family leave policies and childcare support for faculty/staff. Organize a campus campaign to improve these if needed.
- Become a Big Brother or Big Sister. To learn more: *www.bbbs.org*.
- Organize an educational activity on your campus around alternative family models.

In particular, the balance of power in marriage (or any domestic partnership) depends in part on how couples negotiate paid labor and family work in their relationships. Marriages or domestic partnerships can be structured according to different models that promote various ways that couples live and work together. These models include "head–complement," "junior partner/senior partner," and "equal partners"—relationships that each have different ways of negotiating paid work and family work, and, as a result, provide different balances of power within these relationships.

HISTORICAL MOMENT   **The Feminine Mystique**

In 1963 Betty Friedan, a housewife and former labor activist, published the results of a series of interviews she had conducted with women who had been educated at Smith College. Despite their picture-perfect lives, these women reported extreme despair and unhappiness and, unaware that others shared this experience, blamed themselves. To deal with this "problem that has no name," these women turned to a variety of strategies, ranging from using tranquilizers to having affairs to volunteering with church, school, and charitable organizations.

What had happened to these educated women? Following World War II, when women had found a prominent role in the workforce, a national myth emerged that the place for (middle-class, white) women was in the home. To conform to this ideal, women sublimated their dreams and desires and fell in line with "the feminine mystique."

When Friedan's book, *The Feminine Mystique,* appeared in 1963, it spoke loudly to the unspoken misery of millions of American housewives. In its first year, it sold 3 million copies. Unfortunately, during the era immediately following the repressive, anti-Communist McCarthy years, Friedan feared that were she to push the envelope in her book to include an analysis of race and social class, her work would be discredited. So, rather than choosing to address the more complex problems of working-class women and women of color and likely be dismissed, she chose to be heard and addressed the safer topic of middle-class housewives.

Despite its shortcomings, *The Feminine Mystique* found a readership that needed to know that they were not alone in believing that something was seriously wrong with their lives. Friedan suggested that that something wrong was a conspiracy of social institutions and culture that limited the lives of women. She challenged women to find meaningful and purposeful ways of living, particularly through careers.

While Friedan did not go so far as to question the need for men to move into equitable work in the home as she was encouraging women to move out into the workforce or to examine the social and economic, as well as psychological, forces at work in limiting women's lives, she did bring to national attention the problem of women's circumscribed existence and offered a call for women to begin to examine the limitations imposed on them.

Source: Ruth Rosen, *The World Split Open: How the Modern Women's Movement Changed America* (New York: Viking, 2000).

The "head–complement" model reflects the traditional marriage contract as discussed previously whereby the head/husband has responsibilities to provide a family wage and the complement/wife takes primary responsibility for the home and the raising of children. In addition the complement sees (usually her) role as complementing the head's role by being supportive and encouraging in both emotional and material ways. The balance of power in this family system is definitely tilted in the direction of the "head" of the head–complement couple. Power for the complement is to a large extent based on the goodwill of the head as well as the resources (educational and financial in particular) that the complement brings into the relationship. Although the complement does tend to have control over the day-to-day running of the household, this power may disappear with divorce or other internal family disruption.

As already mentioned, the percentage of married-couple households with children younger than 18 has declined to about a fifth of all households. Less than 5 percent of stay-at-home parents in the United States are fathers, although this number has tripled in the last decade. However, there is a trend in educated women choosing to give up their careers and live the head–complement lifestyle. This does not contradict the longitudinal trend of an increasing number of women with children entering the workplace since 1950; rather, it points to the slight decrease in this trend in the last 5 years specifically among affluent couples. These choices, addressed in the reading by Judith Warner, reflect the difficulties in juggling the demands of work and home and the fact that these families can afford for wives not to work outside the home.

The "junior partner/senior partner" model is one in which the traditional marriage contract has been modified. Both members of the couple work outside the home, although one member (usually the wife or female domestic partner), considers her work to be secondary to the senior partner's job. She also takes primary responsibility for the home and childcare. This means that the junior partner has taken on some of the provider role

"Son, your mother is a remarkable woman."

Reprinted with permission from Carol Simpson Labor Cartoons.

while still maintaining responsibility for the domestic role. In practice this might mean that if the senior partner is transferred or relocated because of (usually his) work, the junior partner experiences a disruption in her work to follow. If someone is contacted when the children come home from school sick, it is the junior partner. She might enter and leave the labor force based on the needs of the children and family. This model, the most frequently occurring structure for marriage or domestic partnerships today in the United States, encourages the *double day* of work for women, in which they work both inside and outside the home.

In terms of power, there is a more equitable sharing in this model than in the head–complement model because the junior partner is bringing resources into the family and has control over the day-to-day running of the household. Note in both models described here, the head and senior partner loses out to a greater or lesser degree on the joys associated with household work—especially the raising of children. Junior partners tend to fare better after divorce than the "complements" of the head–complement model. But junior partners do have the emotional stress and physical burdens of working two jobs. These stresses and burdens are affected by how much the senior partner helps out in the home.

The "equal partners" model is one in which the traditional marriage contract is completely disrupted. Neither partner is more likely to perform provider or domestic roles. In practice this might mean both jobs or careers are valued equally such that one does not take priority over the other and domestic responsibilities are shared equally. Alternatively, it might mean an intentional sharing of responsibilities such that one partner agrees to be the economic provider for a period of time and the other agrees to take on domestic responsibilities, although neither is valued more than the other, and this is negotiated rather than implied. In this model financial power is shared, and the burdens and joys of domestic work and childcare are also shared. Although this arrangement gives women the most power in marriage or domestic partnerships, not surprisingly it is a relatively infrequent arrangement among contemporary couples. This is because, first, most men in domestic relationships have been socialized to expect the privileges associated with having women service their everyday needs or raise their children, and most women expect to take on these responsibilities. Both men and women rarely question this taken-for-granted gendered division of labor. Second, men's jobs are more likely to involve a separation of home and work, and it is more difficult for them to integrate these aspects of their lives. Third, men tend to earn more money than women do on the average, and although it might be relatively easy to value women's paid work equally in theory, it is difficult to do so in practice if one job brings in a much higher salary than the other. For example, imagine an equal partner relationship between a dentist and a dental hygienist. These occupations are very gender segregated, with the majority of dentists being men and dental hygienists women. On average among dual-career families generally, wives contribute about one-third of family income. Although the couple may value each other's work equally, it might be difficult for a family to make decisions concerning relocation and so forth in favor of the one partner who works as the dental hygienist because she makes a small percentage of her partner's salary as a dentist.

It is important to emphasize that despite these various arrangements and the differential balance of power in marriage or domestic partnerships, for many women the family is where they feel most empowered. Many women find the responsibilities of maintaining a household or the challenges of child rearing fulfilling and come to see the family as a source of their competency and happiness. Sometimes this involves living in traditional family forms, and sometimes it means devising new ways of living in families. In this way the family is a positive source of connection, community, and/ or productive labor. These diverse experiences associated with family life suggest how family relationships are a complex tangle of compliance with and resistance against various forms of inequities. Mothering, in particular, is one experience that often brings women great joy and shapes their experiences of family relations at the very same time that in patriarchal societies it may function as a form of behavioral constraint. This is the topic to which we now turn.

MOTHERING

Scholars who research the family identify three types of childcare associated with mothering: activities to meet children's basic physical needs; work that attends to children's emotional, cognitive, and recreational needs; and activities for maintaining children's general well-being. Mothers tend to be involved with children more than fathers in all these ways except being involved with their recreational activities. The latter is especially true for fathers with male children, illustrating how gender informs parenting behaviors. Indeed, our understanding of motherhood is conflated with notions of innate, biologically programmed behavior and expectations of unconditional love and nurturance. In other words, even though the meanings associated with motherhood vary historically and culturally, women are expected to want to be mothers, and mothers are expected to take primary responsibility for the nurturing of children. Unlike the assumptions associated with "to father," "to mother" implies nurturing, comforting, and caretaking. You might mother a kitten or a friend without the assumption of having given birth to them. To have fathered a kitten implies paternity: You are its parent; you did not cuddle and take care of it. Similarly, to father a friend makes no sense in this context. In contemporary U.S. society, there is a cultural construction of "normal motherhood" that is class and race based, and sees mothers as devoted to, and sacrificing for, their children. These issues are addressed in Warner's reading, "Family Way." In addition, as global societies have developed and the expectations associated with the role of motherhood have been framed by patterns of consumption in postindustrial societies of the global north, the role of the "perfect" middle-class mother has transformed to include managing a child's life and providing social and educational opportunities as well as managing their own careers. This scenario may cause stress for both mothers and children.

This primary association between women and the nurturing aspects of mothering has brought joys and opportunities for empowerment as well as problems and hardships. It has justified the enormous amount of work women do in the home and encouraged girls to set their sights on babies rather than on other forms of productive work, or, more likely today, on both babies *and* jobs, without enough conversation about the sharing of responsibilities or an understanding of the often exhausting consequences of attempting to juggle the needs of families and careers. It has justified the types of labor women have traditionally done in the labor force as well as women's lower pay, it has kept women out of specific positions such as in the military where they might be involved in taking life rather than giving life, and it has encouraged all kinds of explanations for why men are, and should be, in control in society. For example, research published by sociologist

Shelley Correll asked volunteers to evaluate a pool of equally qualified job applicants and found that mothers were consistently viewed as less competent and less committed, and they were held to higher performance and punctuality standards than other female or male candidates. Mothers were 79 percent less likely to be hired and, if hired, would be offered a starting salary $11,000 lower than nonmothers. Fathers, by contrast, were offered the highest salaries of all. In addition, the nonmothers were more than twice as likely as equally qualified mothers to be called back for interviews.

The close relationship between womanhood and mothering has caused pain for women who are not able to have children as well as for those who have intentionally chosen to not have any. Mothering a disabled child brings its own challenges and joys: Ableism and the normatively abled notion of childhood construct institutional responses that affect the experience of mothering.

In this way, contemporary constructions of mothering, like the family, tend to be created around a mythical norm that reflects a white, abled, middle-class, heterosexual, and young adult experience. But, of course, mothers come in all types, shapes, and sizes, and reflect the wide diversity of women in the United States. Their understandings of their roles and their position within systems of inequality and privilege are such that mothering is a diverse experience. This is because society has varied expectations of mothers depending on class and culture and other differences at the same time that these differences create diverse attitudes toward the experience of mothering. For example, although society often expects poor mothers to work outside the home rather than accept welfare, middle-class mothers might be made to feel guilty for "abandoning" their babies to daycare centers. Because of class, ethnicity, and/or religious orientation, some women experience more ambivalence than others when it comes to combining work and family roles. About a third of all births in the United States are to single mothers, and many more women become single in the process of raising children. Motherhood for single mothers is often constructed through societal notions of stigma. Further, as the reading by Beth Schwartzapfel "Lullabies Behind Bars" explains, there are thousands of mothers in the United States who attempt to parent while they are incarcerated. These women experience stigma on an ongoing basis. According to Schwartzapfel, there are nearly 2 million U.S. children who have one or more parents in prison.

Interracial or LGBTQ couples or people who adopt a child of another race are often accused of not taking into account the best interests of their children. Of course, it is society that has these problems and the families are doing their best to cope. Lesbian mothers in particular have to deal with two mutually exclusive categories that have been constructed as contradictory: mother and lesbian. This illustrates the narrow understandings of motherhood as well as the stereotypes associated with being a mother and with being a lesbian. In addition, in most states lesbian mothers (although often mothering with a female partner who also parents) are legally understood as single mothers: women parenting with an absent father. As a result, they must deal with that stigma too.

In this way, North American families are increasingly diverse forms of social organization that are intricately connected to other institutions in society. The family is a basic social unit around which much of society is built; it is fundamental to the processes of meeting individual and social needs. The centrality of the family in U.S. society encourages us to think about the way the family reproduces and resists gender relations and what it means to each of us in our everyday lives.

Marriage and Love

Emma Goldman (1910)

The popular notion about marriage and love is that they are synonymous, that they spring from the same motives, and cover the same human needs. Like most popular notions this also rests not on actual facts, but on superstition.

Marriage and love have nothing in common; they are as far apart as the poles; are, in fact, antagonistic to each other. No doubt some marriages have been the result of love. Not, however, because love could assert itself only in marriage; much rather is it because few people can completely outgrow a convention. There are today large numbers of men and women to whom marriage is naught but a farce, but who submit to it for the sake of public opinion. At any rate, while it is true that some marriages are based on love, and while it is equally true that in some cases love continues in married life, I maintain that it does so regardless of marriage, and not because of it.

On the other hand, it is utterly false that love results from marriage. On rare occasions one does hear of a miraculous case of a married couple falling in love after marriage, but on close examination it will be found that it is a mere adjustment to the inevitable. Certainly the growing-used to each other is far away from the spontaneity, the intensity, and beauty of love, without which the intimacy of marriage must prove degrading to both the woman and the man.

Marriage is primarily an economic arrangement, an insurance pact. It differs from the ordinary life insurance agreement only in that it is more binding, more exacting. Its returns are insignificantly small compared with the investments. In taking out an insurance policy one pays for it in dollars and cents, always at liberty to discontinue payments. If, however, woman's premium is a husband, she pays for it with her name, her privacy, her self-respect, her very life, "until death doth part." Moreover, the marriage insurance condemns her to life-long dependency, to parasitism, to complete uselessness, individual as well as social. Man, too, pays his toll, but as his sphere is wider, marriage does not limit him as much as woman. He feels his chains more in an economic sense.

Thus Dante's motto over Inferno applies with equal force to marriage. "Ye who enter here leave all hope behind."

. . .

From infancy, almost, the average girl is told that marriage is her ultimate goal; therefore her training and education must be directed towards that end. Like the mute beast fattened for slaughter, she is prepared for that. Yet, strange to say, she is allowed to know much less about her function as wife and mother than the ordinary artisan of his trade. It is indecent and filthy for a respectable girl to know anything of the marital relation. Oh, for the inconsistency of respectability, that needs the marriage vow to turn something which is filthy into the purest and most sacred arrangement that none dare question or criticize. Yet that is exactly the attitude of the average upholder of marriage. The prospective wife and mother is kept in complete ignorance of her only asset in the competitive field—sex. Thus she enters into life-long relations with a man only to find herself shocked, repelled, outraged beyond measure by the most natural and healthy instinct, sex. It is safe to say that a large percentage of the unhappiness, misery, distress, and physical suffering of matrimony is due to the criminal ignorance in sex matters that is being extolled as a great virtue. Nor is it at all an exaggeration when I say that more than one home has been broken up because of this deplorable fact.

If, however, woman is free and big enough to learn the mystery of sex without the sanction of State or

Church, she will stand condemned as utterly unfit to become the wife of a "good" man, his goodness consisting of an empty brain and plenty of money. Can there be anything more outrageous than the idea that a healthy, grown woman, full of life and passion, must deny nature's demand, must subdue her most intense craving, undermine her health and break her spirit, must stunt her vision, abstain from the depth and glory of sex experience until a "good" man comes along to take her unto himself as a wife? That is precisely what marriage means. How can such an arrangement end except in failure? This is one, though not the least important, factor of marriage, which differentiates it from love.

Ours is a practical age. The time when Romeo and Juliet risked the wrath of their fathers for love, when Gretchen exposed herself to the gossip of her neighbors for love, is no more. If, on rare occasions, young people allow themselves the luxury of romance, they are taken in care by the elders, drilled and pounded until they become "sensible."

The moral lesson instilled in the girl is not whether the man has aroused her love, but rather it is, "How much?" The important and only God of practical American life: Can the man make a living? Can he support a wife? That is the only thing that justifies marriage. Gradually this saturates every thought of the girl; her dreams are not of moonlight and kisses, of laughter and tears; she dreams of shopping tours and bargain counters. This soul poverty and sordidness are the elements inherent in the marriage institution. The State and the Church approve of no other ideal, simply because it is the one that necessitates the State and Church control of men and women.

Doubtless there are people who continue to consider love above dollars and cents. Particularly is this true of that class whom economic necessity has forced to become self-supporting. The tremendous change in woman's position, wrought by that mighty factor, is indeed phenomenal when we reflect that it is but a short time since she has entered the industrial arena. Six million women wage workers; six million women, who have the equal right with men to be exploited, to be robbed, to go on strike; aye, to starve even. Anything more, my lord? Yes, six million wage workers in every walk of life, from

the highest brain work to the mines and railroad tracks; yes, even detectives and policemen. Surely the emancipation is complete.

Yet with all that, but a very small number of the vast army of women wage workers look upon work as a permanent issue, in the same light as does man. No matter how decrepit the latter, he has been taught to be independent, self-supporting. Oh, I know that no one is really independent in our economic treadmill; still, the poorest specimen of a man hates to be a parasite; to be known as such, at any rate.

The woman considers her position as worker transitory, to be thrown aside for the first bidder. That is why it is infinitely harder to organize women than men. "Why should I join a union? I am going to get married, to have a home." Has she not been taught from infancy to look upon that as her ultimate calling? She learns soon enough that the home, though not so large a prison as the factory, has more solid doors and bars. It has a keeper so faithful that naught can escape him. The most tragic part, however, is that the home no longer frees her from wage slavery; it only increases her task.

According to the latest statistics submitted before a Committee "on labor and wages, and congestion of population," ten percent of the wage workers in New York City alone are married, yet they must continue to work at the most poorly paid labor in the world. Add to this horrible aspect the drudgery of housework, and what remains of the protection and glory of the home? As a matter of fact, even the middle-class girl in marriage can not speak of her home, since it is the man who creates her sphere. It is not important whether the husband is a brute or a darling. What I wish to prove is that marriage guarantees woman a home only by the grace of her husband. There she moves about in *his* home, year after year, until her aspect of life and human affairs becomes as flat, narrow, and drab as her surroundings. Small wonder if she becomes a nag, petty, quarrelsome, gossipy, unbearable, thus driving the man from the house. She could not go, if she wanted to; there is no place to go. Besides, a short period of married life, of complete surrender of all faculties, absolutely incapacitates the average woman for the outside world. She becomes reckless in appearance, clumsy in her movements, dependent in her decisions, cowardly in her judgment, a weight and a bore, which most men grow to hate and despise. . . .

The institution of marriage makes a parasite of woman, an absolute dependent. It incapacitates her for life's struggle, annihilates her social consciousness, paralyzes her imagination, and then imposes its gracious protection, which is in reality a snare, a travesty on human character.

R E A D I N G **63**

Who Wants to Marry a Feminist?

Lisa Miya-Jervis (2000)

The winter I got engaged, a college friend was using some of my essays as course material for a Rhetoric 101 class she was teaching at a large Midwestern university. She couldn't wait to alert her students to my impending marriage. "They all think you're a lesbian," she told me. "One of them even asked if you hate men." I was blown over by the cliché of it all—how had we come to the end of the twentieth century with such ridiculous, outmoded notions even partially intact? But I was, at least, pleased that my friend was able to use my story to banish the stereotype once and (I hoped) for all in the minds of 30 corn-fed first-years. "To a man?" they reportedly gasped when told the news.

I'd been married less than a year when a customer at the bookstore where my husband works approached the counter to buy a copy of the feminist magazine I edit. "You know," a staffer told her while ringing up the purchase, "the woman who does this magazine is married to a guy who works here." The customer, supposedly a longtime reader, was outraged at the news—I believe the phrase "betrayal of feminism" was uttered—and vowed never to buy the magazine again. These two incidents may be extreme, but they are nonetheless indicative. Although we are far from rare, young married feminists are still, for some, something of a novelty—like a dressed-up dog. We can cause a surprised "Oh, would you look at that" or a disappointed "Take that damned hat off the dog, it's just not right."

Let's take the disappointment first. Marriage's bad reputation among feminists is certainly not without reason. We all know the institution's tarnished history: women as property passed from father to husband; monogamy as the simplest way to assure paternity and thus produce "legitimate" children; a husband's legal entitlement to his wife's domestic and sexual services. With marriage rates falling and social sanctions against cohabitation falling away, why would a feminist choose to take part in such a retro, potentially oppressive, bigotedly exclusive institution?

Well, there are a lot of reasons, actually. Foremost are the emotional ones: love, companionship, the pure joy that meeting your match brings with it. But, because I'm wary of the kind of muddled romanticizing that has ill-served women in their heterosexual dealings for most of recorded history, I have plenty of other reasons. To reject marriage simply because of its history is to give in to that history; to argue against marriage by saying that a wife's identity is necessarily subsumed by her husband's is to do nothing more than second the notion.

And wasn't it feminists who fought so hard to procure the basic rights that used to be obliterated by marriage? Because of the women's rights movement, we can maintain our own bank accounts; we can make our own health care choices; we can refuse sex with our husbands and prosecute them if they don't comply. In the feminist imagination, "wife" can still conjure up images of cookie-baking, cookie-cutter Donna Reeds whose own desires have been forced to take a backseat to their stultifying helpmate duties. But it's neither 1750 nor 1950, and

Donna Reed was a mythical figure even in her own time. Marriage, now, is potentially what we make it.

Which brings me to the "surprise" portion of our program. As long as the yeti of the antifeminist world—the hairy-legged man-hater (everyone claims to have seen her but actual evidence is sparse)—roams the earth, we need to counteract her image. And as long as wives are assumed—by anyone—to be obedient little women with no lives of their own, those of us who give the lie to this straw bride need to make ourselves as conspicuous as possible.

I want to take the good from marriage and leave the rest. I know it's not for everyone, but the "for as long as we both shall live" love and support thang really works for me. Sure, I didn't need the wedding to get that love and support, but neither does the fact of marriage automatically consign me and my man to traditional man-and-wife roles. Like so many relationships, married and un-, ours is a complex weave of support, independence, and sex. We achieve this privately—from the mundanities of you-have-to-cook-tonight-because-I-have-this-deadline-tomorrow to sleepy late-night discussions on more profound matters, like the meaning of life or how many steps it takes to link Kevin Bacon to John Gielgud by way of at least one vampire movie. But also publicly—with our name change, for example (explaining to folks like the Social Security Administration and whoever hands out passports that, yes, we both need new papers, because we each have added the other's name was, and I mean this quite seriously, a thrill). And it's this public nature of marriage that appeals. It's what allows me to take a stab at all this change I've been yammering about.

I won't pretend I meet with success all the time. Disrupting other people's expectations is hard, and sometimes it's neither possible nor desirable to wear the workings of one's relationship on one's sleeve. An appropriate cocktail party introduction is not, "This is my husband, Christopher, who knows how to truss a turkey, which I don't, and who, by the way, doesn't mind at all that I make more money than him. Oh, and did I mention that the last time our toilet got scrubbed, it wasn't by me?"

Plus, some people's perceptions can only change so much. My 90-year-old grandfather, who has been nothing but open-minded and incredibly supportive of my feminist work, persists in asking what my husband is going to do for food whenever I leave town on my own. Each time, I say the same thing: "Christopher knows perfectly well how to feed himself. In fact, he's cooking dinner for me right now." And then my grandfather gives a little surprised chuckle: those crazy kids, what will they think of next? And my accountant, who's been doing my taxes for years and knows my husband only as a Social Security number, automatically assigned Christopher the status of "taxpayer" and put me down as "spouse" on our first joint return. Yeah, it was a tad annoying, but so far it's the sum total of the eclipse of my identity by his. Not so bad, really.

By and large I do believe that we're culturally ready to accept changes in the way marriages are viewed. Increasing rates of cohabitation and the growing visibility of long-term same-sex partnerships are changing popular notions of relationships. Even trash TV holds promise: Fox's *Who Wants to Marry a Multi-Millionaire?* debacle laid bare many ugly things about American capitalism and media spectacle, but there was one fairly unexpected result. The show was presented as a display, however crass, of old-fashioned marital values—a trade of youth, beauty, and fecundity for wealth, security, and caretaking, complete with the groom's friends and family on hand for that lovely arranged-marriage feel. But it turned out to be nothing of the kind. The bride, as it happened, just wanted the lark of a free trip to Vegas, and the groom, a boost to his moribund show-biz career. That the concept saw the outside of a Fox conference room proves that modern marriage is in dire need of feminist attention. But the widely expressed outrage and disgust that followed the show are evidence that the general public is more than ready to discard the notion that a woman's ultimate goal is the altar.

It's true that the most important parts, the actual warp and weft of Christopher's and my relationship, could be achieved without a legal marriage (and I could have kept my third-wave street cred). In the end, though, the decision to marry or not to marry is—no matter how political the personal—an emotional one. I wanted to link my life to Christopher's, and, yes, I admit to taking advantage of the universally understood straight-shot-to-relationship-legitimacy that marriage offers. But it is a testament to the feminists who came before me, who offered up all those arguments about marriage's oppressive roots and worked tirelessly to ensure that my husband owns neither my body nor my paycheck, that I can indulge my emotion without fear of being caught in those roots. Instead, I can carry on their struggle and help forge a new vision of what marriage is.

R E A D I N G 64

Family Way

Judith Warner (2012)

Just as everyone was getting ready to throw out the Baby Bjorns and start practicing detachment parenting *à la française* comes a new book, from the esteemed philosopher Elisabeth Badinter, warning that French motherhood isn't all it's cracked up to be.

Sure, Badinter writes in *The Conflict*—a polemic that set off heated debate when it was published in France in 2010—French mothers enjoy some pretty great work-family protections, which permit them to keep their public and professional selves vibrantly alive after they have children. They quickly get themselves back in the saddle physically and sexually. They don't much go in for breast-feeding. Soundly rejecting the view that "the ideal mother is enmeshed with her child bodily and mentally," they drink and smoke throughout their pregnancies. And, out of fealty to the idea that "a mother cannot allow herself to be consumed by her baby to the point of destroying her desires as a woman," they make sure their *vie de couple* isn't rent asunder by the addition of needy children.

Thanks to what Badinter calls this "nonchalant approach to motherhood"—which she dates to the once widespread practice in France of sending newborns away to distant wet nurses (in whose care they often died)—French society, she says, has successfully framed motherhood, even working motherhood with multiple children, as an appealing prospect. Indeed, she notes, the country enjoys the highest birthrate of all European nations.

The special French legacy of maternal freedom and fun is now deeply threatened, however,

Badinter warns. A new wave of ideology—a silent "revolution" built on the "exalted" mother figure and a toxic, back-to-nature "new essentialism"—is bearing down on Frenchwomen, threatening them with exhortations to embrace their motherly instincts, reject disposable diapers and breast-feed. If Frenchwomen don't resist, she predicts, they'll soon lose not only their jobs but all the advantages of their cool-mother exceptionalism. "The reverence for all things natural glorifies an old concept of the maternal instinct and applauds masochism and sacrifice, constituting a supreme threat to women's emancipation and sexual equality," she writes.

Badinter doesn't point fingers across the Atlantic to blame us *Américaines* for this very un-French new threat to women's progress (except to note that the "ayatollahs of breast-feeding" associated with La Leche League first began their "ideological crusade" here), but no one who has lived through or witnessed American motherhood over the past couple of decades can read her depiction of a new generation of postfeminist mothers losing their sexuality, abandoning their adult identities and shelving their professional purpose in the pursuit of "some ideal notion of child rearing" without an uncomfortable shudder of self-recognition. As we know, Badinter's warnings about the dangers of excessive child-centeredness are in many ways well founded; it was, after all, a general exasperation with our hyperventilating mode of motherhood that led us, in the past Tiger Mother-dominated year or so, to start casting our eyes abroad for inspiration.

So why is it that her book, impressively researched, elegantly argued and forcefully written, feels, in the end, so profoundly wrong? Not just intellectually outmoded, not just emotionally somewhat off, but actually, for this reader—as I suspect will be the case for many American readers—downright offensive?

It isn't, I think, just a matter of what the French like to call our knee-jerk "puritanism," in this case a reluctance, perhaps, to embrace an argument that bashes breast-feeding on the grounds that a nursing mother "is not necessarily an object of desire for the father watching her," and by extension condemns the practice as one that "may well obliterate the woman-as-lover and endanger the couple." (As for Badinter's implied approval of mothers' freedom to smoke in "moderation" during and after their pregnancies: having shared a maternity ward with women who tucked cigarette packs into their newborns' bassinets before wheeling them into the garden for air, I'm inclined to see such acts more as signs of enslavement than of self-expression.)

It's rather that for Badinter, who happens to be a mother of three, motherhood itself—not just the construction or idea of motherhood, but the fact of childbearing and -rearing—is, in the end, women's greatest enemy. This is an old idea, dating to Simone de Beauvoir's classic *The Second Sex*, the book that, Badinter has said, turned her into a feminist. Rejecting motherhood was *undoubtedly* a liberating, and maybe necessary, choice for women who wanted to lead full lives in the desperately pro-natalist period after World War II, when *The Second Sex* was published. But in today's context—and particularly in a country like France, where generous work-family policies, however imperfect, are well developed and prized—anti-motherhood talk (Badinter writes of the "despotism of an insatiable child" and the "tyranny of maternal duty") seems not just outdated, but a little weird.

Certainly it's hard to imagine American women embracing Badinter's proposed solution to what she sees as the unsolvable conflict of mother-child interests: a system of "part-time motherhood" that may sound great on its surface—emphasizing state support and freedom from the "moral or social pressure" of all-consuming motherhood—but which seems to be predicated on mothers' having an emotional on/off switch, permitting them to disengage from their children at will. Can such a thing as part-time motherhood exist? In suggesting that it does, Badinter unwittingly reprises the argument made in America by the critics of working mothers, whose rhetoric has long put these moms' presumably part-time affections in opposition to the ever-on-demand attentiveness of at-home "full-time mothers."

Missing from Badinter's philosophical schema is any sort of intellectual middle path that, instead of pitting mothers against children, might lead to solutions that could benefit both. The importance of finding that middle path has been suggested for decades by social scientists whose research has consistently shown that when mothers are able to carry on satisfying lives, their children tend to do better as well. The evolutionary anthropologist Sarah Blaffer Hrdy, for one, has argued strongly, in her important book *Mother Nature* (the chief argument of which is badly misrepresented in *The Conflict*), that a life combining both nurturing and providing for family is not only the most satisfying, but also the most traditionally natural for mothers. Hrdy's research teaches that the split, or conflict, between a woman's nurturing maternal role and her out-in-the-world, family-provider role is a false one that flies in the face of the mothering practices of our primate ancestors, and that has been greatly aggravated by the work patterns of the modern industrialized world.

This sort of argument leads to the suggestion that it's as much, if not more, the culture of work as the culture of motherhood that must change for the promise of the women's movement to bear full fruit. This idea, unsexy though it is, provides the only realistic starting point from which to think our way toward greater progress in America, where meaningful work-family policies are all but nonexistent.

Thinking the way forward in a concrete, realistic American context is precisely what Madeleine M. Kunin's latest book, *The New Feminist Agenda: Defining the Next Revolution for Women, Work, and Family,* accomplishes. Kunin, a former Clinton administration ambassador to Switzerland who served as the first woman governor of Vermont, exhaustively catalogs where we are in terms of work-family balance (deeply out of whack) and where we need to go if we want to make the idea of merging motherhood with all the other necessary aspects of a woman's life a reality.

Kunin's is not a book of literary value, like Badinter's. The writing is unremarkable, and there are no big, interesting philosophical ideas. Yet whereas Badinter's argument is beautiful and essentially wrong, Kunin—Pollyanna-ish faith in the family-friendly nature of female politicians aside—is almost unimpeachably right, as she diagnoses what we in America need, why we've never gotten it, and how we may have some hope of achieving change in the future.

She notes that while many individual women have accomplished a great deal since the women's liberation movement of the 1970s, our society, collectively, has not adapted to acknowledge these accomplishments and respond to the changed needs of families. Despite the fact that only about 20 percent of American families with children under age 15 are now constructed along the old model of a working father and a stay-at-home mother, the United States is virtually alone in the world—or, more precisely, it's in the exclusive company of Liberia, Papua New Guinea and Swaziland—in not guaranteeing any form of paid leave for families with newborns. (Since 2011, when Australia left us behind, we've been the only country in the advanced industrialized world not to offer any guaranteed paid leave for newborn care.)

We're the only one of the world's 21 wealthiest nations in which paid sick days aren't required by law. Even Britain, our closest cultural cousin, now offers mothers a full year of (minimal) paid family leave, six months of which can be transferred to fathers. (Britain also has a policy guaranteeing employees the right to request a flexible work schedule; 80 percent of those requests, which must be denied in writing and can then be sent to an impartial tribunal, are granted.) And no other industrialized country can rival us for the Wild West quality of our underfunded, largely unregulated day care and early childhood education "system"—fully 12 percent of which is so poor, Kunin reports, that experts actually deem it harmful for the children who endure it.

The social cost of all this noncare: We have the highest rate of child poverty in the developed world, lagging test scores, a shameful incarceration rate and, Kunin adds, an American dream that's in decline. This is "not only an unjust waste of human potential," Kunin writes, "it is a dangerous economic policy that will impact the well-being of every American."

We've heard much of this before, and Kunin's reiteration of the usual evidence in favor of early childhood education and other family supports (they're good for the developing brain; they're cheaper than the cost of later putting adults in jail) feels old-hat, too. Her book is most interesting when it moves beyond such well-charted territory to demonstrate how certain states—including, notably, a few very conservative ones—were able (at least before the Great Recession) to implement ambitious and surprisingly forward-looking family-friendly policies.

California, New Jersey and Washington State instituted paid family leave. In the first two cases, lawmakers raised money through funding mechanisms already in place (state disability insurance programs, employee contributions to which increased so slightly that two-thirds of people surveyed in California subsequently didn't notice the change); Washington, which didn't have funding in place, had to delay implementation of its program after the economic downturn began. Conservative Oklahoma established universal voluntary free preschools by creating bipartisan support and enlisting the help of evangelicals.

From all this, and from the international examples she effectively details, Kunin draws some important lessons: First, presenting policies like family leave or universal preschool as a way to let women self-actualize is a nonstarter; for these ideas to have any hope of becoming a reality, they have to be all about the children. (Paid leave in Britain was achieved via arguments that centered not on gender equality but on keeping mothers in the work force as a way to end child poverty.) Second, feminists who want to fight for wide-ranging family-friendly policies must make far-reaching, sometimes unnatural-seeming alliances: join with groups like the AARP and the unions, and enlist the disabled, religious organizations, independents, political conservatives—and men. "The issue of accommodating both work and family has outgrown the parameters of our current perception of feminism," she writes. Third, language counts. Paid family leave passed in New Jersey, Kunin shows, in part because advocates called it "family leave insurance," not "paid family leave." "Everybody believes in insurance; not everybody believes you should be paid for not working," a New Jersey policy expert who worked on the law's messaging told her.

Finally, there has to be a way to turn public opinion—which according to Kunin is overwhelmingly favorable to paid sick days and family and medical leave—into something like a movement.

A movement as motivating, gut-compelling and passionate as the forces now arrayed for and against abortion rights. She acknowledges this is a tall order. "Could we hold a march for family/work policies in Washington? Would anybody come?" she asks shrewdly. "Or would they be too tired, too busy, too scared of losing their jobs to attend?"

It's a good question. How do you get today's moms, and all their equally overtaxed potential allies, to show up for a revolution? Perhaps we need a 21st-century Gloria Steinem, a multitasking, minivan-driving, media-savvy soccer mom (or dad) with just enough of a hint of glamour to make protest as appealing a prospect as Girls' Night Out.

R E A D I N G ⬭65⬭

Marriage Equality: Three Essays

Marriage Equality Is a Feminist Issue

Audrey Bilger (2012)

2012 was a huge year for marriage equality. In May, President Barack Obama declared support for the right of lesbians and gay men to marry—and then he resoundingly won re-election. Three new states approved gay marriage rights in ballot initiatives, and another defeated a constitutional ban.

In December . . . Washington state's first bride/bride, groom/groom couples said "I do." Polls continue to show dramatic upticks in support for this once deeply controversial issue, leading conservative pundit George Will to tell ABC news, "There is something like an emerging consensus. . . . Quite literally, the opposition to gay marriage is dying."

As we celebrate victories and anticipate upcoming developments, we should also step back to evaluate how the marriage debate has made it this far—and start giving a good deal of the credit to feminism. Take the two marriage equality cases that went before the Supreme Court in 2013, Hollingsworth v. Perry, which challenged

California's Proposition 8, and United States v. Windsor, which aimed to smack down the Defense of Marriage Act (DOMA). Neither can be viewed apart from feminist history.

Without ever using the word "feminism," the 2010 Prop 8 trial repeatedly evoked feminist advances. For example, historian Nancy Cott testified about how marriage changed to give women greater autonomy as citizens, crediting such changes to the "Women's Rights revolution."

In her testimony, Cott reviewed the history of marriage in the U.S. in terms of traditional ideas about "coverture": "Upon marriage, the wife was covered in effect by her husband's legal and economic identity," Cott explained. "She lost her independent legal and economic individuality." In traditional marriage, man and woman became one person, and that person—in the eyes of the law— was the man. Cott explained the rationale for male authority in marriage:

[It] had everything to do with the sexual division of labor. Because assumptions were, at the time, that men were suited to be providers, were suited for certain sorts of work; whereas, women, the weaker sex, were suited to be dependent, needed a stronger hand to guide them, to support them and protect them.

But, she pointed out, "Through the 20th century and into our era, the sexual division of labor is no longer necessary for the kinds of work people do in the world."

Justice Vaughn Walker took the history of heterosexual marriage into account when he ruled that Prop 8 is unconstitutional, emphatically declaring, "Gender no longer forms an essential part of marriage; marriage under law is a union of equals."

Marriage equality is, of course, about equal rights for lesbian and gay citizens, and I'm not arguing that the hard work of LGBT rights activists has been insignificant in moving the dial on this issue; however, without a presumption of married unions as equal partnerships—a direct legacy of feminist activism and effort—the idea of lesbian and gay marriage rights would be much harder to advocate. For opponents of same-sex marriage, the gender binary rules. So those who insist that a marriage can only take place between one man and one woman are asking the state to enforce complementary gender roles.

The story of 83-year-old Edie Windsor, the plaintiff in United States v. Windsor who sued the federal government for discrimination under DOMA, poignantly illustrates the perils of marriage inequality. Together for 47 years, Edie and Thea Spyer were legally married in Canada in 2007. When Thea passed away two years later, the federal government disregarded their legal marriage and forced Edie to pay more than $360,000 in estate taxes, thus treating Edie and Thea as legal "strangers." In spite of Edie's loving care of Thea, who battled multiple sclerosis in the last decades of her life, and in spite of the state of New York's willingness to recognize their legal marriage, DOMA enforced the one man/one woman definition of marriage.

Dan Savage, who renewed vows with his husband in Washington state, explained the importance of marriage for lesbian and gay couples in an interview with MSNBC's Chris Hayes:

> When you marry, you get to declare your next of kin. You get to choose. It's empowering to say, 'This person is my next of kin, not my parents, siblings or distant cousins who may be alive.'

Being able to choose one's next of kin, the person who will be acknowledged as family in the eyes of the law, presumes equality not just with heterosexual citizens but within that foundational union. Windsor, by every account (see for yourself in the documentary *Edie and Thea: A Very Long Engagement*), was Spyer's next of kin. Their roles toward one another were not defined by gender, and if Thea had been a man no one would have questioned her marriage. (No one, for example, would have brought up the issue of procreation-as-essential-in-marriage to an octogenarian heterosexual couple).

Even though marriage equality may still have a way to go, we need to acknowledge this new shift in acceptance as a step forward in the history of the institution. As Ms. Blog editor Michele Kort and I discovered when we collected stories for our anthology *Here Come the Brides! Reflections on Lesbian Love and Marriage*, lesbian wives call into question marriage as fundamentally patriarchal. And in the union of two men, when there's no woman to subordinate, the word "husband" gets a positive makeover. When lesbian and gay marriage becomes the law of the land, the idea of complementary gender roles (as opposed to chosen behavior) will begin to seem as outdated in personal relationships as feminism has long argued it ought to be in public life.

What does it matter if we bring feminism into our discussions of marriage equality? For one thing, it means that this struggle is not just about the rights of lesbians and gay men—as big a deal as that is. Whether you're straight or gay, if you're committed to the feminist principle that marriage is a union of two equals, then you need to take this fight personally. Or else the next marriage the state tries to redefine in traditional terms may be yours.

The Wrong Fight

Daniel D'Addario (2013)

The sea of red "equal" signs on Facebook . . . might lead the casual clicker to believe that all progressives are united in support of gay marriage. But there are a handful of holdouts.

Nancy Polikoff, a professor of law at American University, is among a small group of queer academics and activists who have opposed the growing drumbeat in favor of gay marriage. The author of *Beyond (Straight and Gay) Marriage* is among the proponents of a critique of "marriage equality" hinging on the pitfalls of marriage itself—Polikoff argues that there should be options for couples other than marriage, an institution that blends church and state.

Polikoff and some other academics and activists had hoped the conversation about marriage would go in a different direction, perhaps even abolishing the idea of "marriage" as a contract issued by the state.

Once gay people are just like everyone else, many of these critics argue, they won't be able to fight for new definitions of legally recognized unions that are less binding, or less restrictive. They imagined something different than being pulled into marriage, an institution often tied closely to the church, defined conservatively by the state, and celebrated as the ultimate achievement of any individual.

"What gets swept away is this interesting critique that came out of gay culture and the feminist movement. It's all been reduced to wedding cakes," said William Dobbs, who was active in the early years of ACT UP.

Had history bent a different way, the gay movement might still be fighting for measures of equality beyond marriage and more pertinent to broader social justice. At least, that's what Polikoff and those like her believe. The sex columnist Dan Savage disagrees.

"Some people took pride in that, that outlaw status," Savage told *Salon* [a liberal news and commentary website]. "The people who were into the outlaw thing, they felt like part of the tribe, but there were people in that tribe that felt they were not there by their own free choice. The minute that they got the option to walk away, they did. That's driving some of the people who identified as outlaws a bit crazy. They thought they were in a parade and they weren't; it was a forced march."

Polikoff, however, continues to fight against the tide, with her recent book advocating the end of marriage as an institution bestowing legal privileges. As the Supreme Court debates gay marriage, Polikoff, herself a lesbian, spoke to *Salon* about how the fight for marriage got so far so quickly—and why she and other critics from the left are hoping for more sweeping and systemic change in how we view marriage.

Salon: Can you talk a little about your background opposing marriage? Polikoff: I'd have to trace it to feminism in the 1970s and a critique of institution of marriage. There are these two essays by Tom Stoddard and Paula Ettelbrick that are relatively short and have gotten this iconic status over the years. Tom was executive director of Lambda Legal and Paula was legal director and they wrote this pair of essays, published in 1989. Paula and I were buddies and I was one of the people who worked on that piece with her. [Ettelbrick took an anti-marriage view with an essay titled "Since When Is Marriage a Path to Liberation?"]

My critique of marriage stems from the 1970s. As gay people began talking about this more, there were these questions about using the resources of fledgling legal groups on marriage. There was a significant contingent of people who identified as feminists who said, "This is the wrong approach, this isn't what we should be doing." That viewpoint carried the day for a long time. My point of view dates back to long before where we are now.

Solan: Are you married? Polikoff: I'm in a registered domestic partnership. We have the option to marry. We have not. D.C. has always allowed same-sex couples and different-sex couples and any two people living together in a committed familial relationship to register as domestic partners. D.C. did not eliminate its domestic partnership. Because D.C. had it as an option for more than same-sex couples—it wasn't a way station.

Solan: What changed the mainstream view of marriage among gay people from a lost cause to something to which so much energy should be devoted? Polikoff: Logistically, what happened was the Hawaii case [declaring, in 1993, that banning same-sex marriage violated the state Constitution], which was not brought by any gay rights organizations. It was brought by a lawyer in Hawaii. When that case was decided in 1993 by the Hawaii Supreme Court and said that state has to prove a really good reason for preventing gay couples from marrying: That was a game changer. That was the first time a state's highest court said this might be a violation of our Constitution. And gay people realized: We might be able to win marriage.

From that point on, gay rights legal groups did start committing resources. The case was going to keep being litigated in Hawaii, and it was going to go forward with or without help. If there was expertise in [gay-rights] organizations, they would want them to be done well. The Hawaii decision led to state actions and federal actions in terms of DOMA. DOMA is passed in 1996; that wouldn't have happened without the Hawaii decision.

During the same period, there was another shift going on about marriage. When Dan Quayle made the "Murphy Brown" speech [in which he decried the TV character's decision to become a single mother], the reaction was uniformly negative. People accused him from all sides of being out of touch with the times and unnecessarily disrespecting single women. There was universal disapproval of his statement. One year later, there was a cover story on the Atlantic magazine and the cover story was "Dan Quayle was right." Bill Clinton said there was a lot that was good about that speech. Suddenly the country is blaming social problems on the decline of marriage. David Blankenhorn's "Fatherless America" said lesbians raising children was "radical fatherlessness." They were blaming every social problem on the decline of lifelong heterosexual marriage.

And so the movement for same-sex marriage has been able to latch on to an ideology that identifies marriage as solution to all our social problems. That ideology lets off the hook income inequality, racism, discrimination and unemployment. It takes a look at all of the things many of us would identify as serious social problems that lead to real consequences and says none of those are the problem! For instance: "People aren't getting married before they have children." The movement for marriage equality has been able to piggyback onto that and say, "Let us marry, marriage is the bedrock institution of society and we want in! Can't we just agree—everyone should be married and everyone should be married before they have children." This strain from the 1990s allows conservatives to say this is a conservative issue.

Solan: Do you think marriage is inherently a sexist institution? Polikoff: If you were to look at the original purposes of marriage going back numerous centuries when marriage was really about property, I would say that was true. I wouldn't say that in the modern context of how people talk about marriage.

To me, the important thing is eliminating marriage as the dividing line between relationships that count in the law and relationships that don't. Marriage is an on-off switch for many legal consequences that matter to people. I'd like there to be more nuanced dividing lines as to who's in and who's out, for economically and emotionally interdependent units. If one person goes to work and is killed on the job, that unit is going to lose income it depended on. It shouldn't matter whether that's a unit based on marriage—what matters is there was an economically and emotionally interdependent household that has lost income. In many places, you get it if you're married, you don't get it if you're not. For family policy purposes, we need to be evaluating the areas where marriage is an on-off switch.

Solan: But this is hard to sell to the American public—especially in comparison to something as easily understood as marriage equality. Polikoff: In the current context, it's a lot harder to talk about in a sound bite, but how easy it is to discuss something in a sound bite has nothing to do with justice. I am proposing something less efficient than having a single on-off switch. The Supreme Court decided decades ago there are higher values than speed and efficiency when it comes to evaluating relationships. Husbands used to have control of every decision in marriage, and that was very efficient. I want this bright line to change because I don't think it's just.

Solan: Do you feel that the push for marriage equality has changed what it's like to be gay? Polikoff: In the current moment, it has come to stand in for full respect as a human being. Practically everyone wants to feel like they belong. For many gay people, they don't want to be outsiders. This is a way of demonstrating belonging to the larger community. The problem is, when you read many of the briefs, it makes it seem like the way you show you're a full adult citizen belonging to the community is by getting married. That is not how the lives of most heterosexuals operate, to the chagrin of right-wing supporters of same-sex marriage, and it hasn't been how the lives of homosexuals operate.

Marriage Equality and Beyond

Gowri Vijayakumar (2013)

A few days before my Facebook News Feed was flooded with red equal signs, I went to a short march in Bangalore. The Gender and Sexual Minorities Pride March demanded, among other things, "human rights and overall development" of a range of sexual minorities[1], focusing on the right to be included on the electoral rolls, access to social services for those below the poverty line, job skills support, low-cost health services, old-age pensions, loans, and housing support.

At the end of the march, I met a European woman, engaged in a spirited conversation with some of the participants. "In my country, we accept all groups," she told them. "You can marry whoever you want."

It wasn't the first time I'd come across cross-cultural discussions of marriage in my research in India. Once, I was sitting in a drop-in center for sexual minorities during a visit with a group of Swedish students. I ended up the de facto translator for their conversation with the eight or nine transgender [Indian] women who gathered around to talk. After they told their stories to the [Swedish] students, and I stammered and struggled through translating all the complicated local terms for various sexuality categories, the conversation turned to Sweden. "Can you find a good man in Sweden? Here, all the men run away after a while." "Can we come with you?" they joked. Then, the real question: "What's it like for people like us in Sweden?" The students paused, and then one of them spoke up. "I don't know about transgender people. But in Sweden everyone has the right to love whoever they want. We accept any kind of marriage."

This was the first time marriage had come up in the discussion. The trans people had been sharing stories of horrific violence, much of it from the police; political exclusion; and rejection by their families. They'd been talking about running away from home, about being raped and abused. But when it came to Sweden, the students seemed mainly to think of marriage as the overarching issue.

In my limited time working with sexual minority groups in India, I've often found myself in conversations like these. "What's it like for people like us in America? Are they accepted?" It's a question that gives me pause. Being from the US in India means people often share with you their wildly romanticized visions of a far-off place. And it's true—in many ways, being queer in the US is probably safer than it is in India. But I'm not sure the US is the paradise they imagine. I usually say that there are many similarities between what LGBTQ people in the US and sexual minorities in India face. I often end up providing some explanation of state law and federal law in the US, and how some states have marriage equality and some don't—then confusion ensues. And then I hear this kind of comment: "They can worry about marriage because they have addressed all the other issues. They're a rich country. We haven't gotten there yet."

I wish they were right. I wish the reason that marriage dominated mainstream accounts of LGBTQ politics in the US were that all the other issues had been addressed. Yet transgender respondents in a recent survey in California were twice as likely than the general population to be living below the poverty line, and they faced 14% unemployment. One in five transgender respondents had been homeless.[2] Across the US, same-sex couples are significantly more likely to be living below the poverty line than heterosexual couples. Poverty rates among lesbian couples are higher—6.9%—than poverty rates for different-sex married couples (5.4%) or gay male couples (4.0%). Poverty is highest among black lesbian couples (21.1%), compared to 4.3% among white lesbian couples and 14.4% among black gay couples.[3] A disproportionate twenty percent of homeless youth are gay or transgender.[4] And then there are the high levels of violence.[5] I wish we'd checked all of these things off the list, one by one, and now, with the bread and butter taken care of, we were turning to issues of marriage.

As the Obama administration positions itself as a global defender of LGBTQ rights,[6] there's an underlying implication that LGBTQ equality is one of the great civilizational gifts the US has to offer seemingly poor, backward countries like India, trapped in tradition and behind the curve. But Indian sexual minorities have a long, complex history. And in a context where poverty is visible and tangible and ubiquitous and impossible to ignore, it wouldn't make sense for sexual minority groups to deny the connection between gender, sexuality and poverty. People intuitively understand that economic and political and social and sexual issues are all part of the same puzzle. That's true everywhere, not just in India.

I'm a woman married to man, and I carry with me all the privileges that go with that. As an ally, I don't think it's my place to criticize people for wanting the same privilege I have access to. So when so many of my queer friends see marriage as a vehicle for their collective aspirations, I support them. But being in India has made it clear to me that marriage in rich countries has become a proxy for thinking through a wide range of issues like poverty, violence, discrimination, and social exclusion, particularly that facing LGBTQ people. So, while I hope the best for marriage equality, I hope I never see Americans walking around in India, telling people that now that we're getting closer to marriage equality, the work is complete.

NOTES

1. The Indian activists I've talked to prefer the term "sexual minorities," so I use it when referring to India rather than "LGBTQ" or "queer."
2. http://transgenderlawcenter.org/archives/860
3. http://williamsinstitute.law.ucla.edu/wp-content/uploads/Albelda-Badgett-Schneebaum-Gates-LGB-Poverty-Report-March-2009.pdf
4. http://www.americanprogress.org/wp-content/uploads/issues/2012/01/pdf/black_lgbt.pdf
5. http://www.hrc.org/files/assets/resources/Hatecrimesandviolenceagainstlgbtpeople_2009.pdf
6. http://www.state.gov/secretary/rm/2011/12/178368.htm

R E A D I N G **66**

Singled Out

Tamara Winfrey Harris (2012)

Steve Harvey is convinced you could use a few lessons in being "a lady." So he says in his relationship advice tome, *Act Like a Lady; Think Like a Man*, in a chapter titled "Strong, Independent—And Lonely—Women." Ladies are those who let men take the lead in picking a dinner spot. They don't ask a date in for a nightcap until he has earned "the cookie" (i.e. sex) after a 90-day probation period.

Ladies do not fix household items or mow the lawn. But "don't be afraid to make a meal or two—the kitchen is both your and his friend."

Though the comedian and radio personality avoids mentioning race explicitly in the book, it has been targeted to his largely African American fan base. . . . [T]his week [it] debuts on the big screen as *Think Like a Man*, featuring a heavy-hitting black cast including Gabrielle Union, Kevin Hart and Chris Brown. Harvey's work is but the latest in a narrative that focuses on single black women and the alleged missteps that keep them from marrying, and it is emblematic of the sexist and racist critique and regressive advice bombarding black women in the era of the "black marriage crisis."

According to a 2011 report by the Pew Research Center, barely half of U.S. adults are married—a record low. (In 1960, 72 percent of all adults were married; today, just 51 percent are.) And Americans are not alone. The role of marriage is evolving all over the world. Nevertheless, much ado is made of the fact that black Americans marry at lower rates than their white counterparts. According to 2010 census data, 47 percent of the black population age 15 and older have never been married, compared to about 26 percent of white Americans.

We are told this is cause for alarm—that the dearth of "strong black families" is to blame for poverty, high incarceration rates, poor educational performance by black children and a longer litany of ills. The media has embraced this notion of crisis, but their focus isn't so much the not-marrying of black people, but the not-marrying of black women. It is rare coverage that does not turn on the fact that black women are about half as likely to marry as their white counterparts. Experts offer a variety of explanations for this gap, including the lasting legacy of slavery; high incarceration rates of black males; demographics (there are simply more American black women than men); and the success gap: Black women outnumber black men in higher education more than 2 to 1, which often creates a wedge of opportunity and class.

But data reveal black *men* to be as uncoupled as their female counterparts and most black women *do*

wed (the percentage of black women over 35 who have never married is less than 39 percent); nevertheless, black women are singled out by the media to be pitied and blamed for their marital status. There has emerged a sort of what's-wrong-with-sisters-and-why-aren't-they-married industrial complex.

In 2009, ABC News' *Nightline* explored the phenomena of unmarried black women with the segment "Single, Black, Female—And Plenty of Company." The following year, the program hosted a panel discussion to answer the question, "Why Can't a Successful Black Woman Find a Man?" CNN has also fretted about the issue, wondering in 2010 whether black churches or single mothers are to blame for rampant black female singleness, and in 2011 whether a dearth of good black men is the problem and whether black women should give up on their male counterparts altogether.

Harvey's bestseller is but one of a glut of books aimed at setting black women on the right course. NPR contributor Jimi Izrael names the problem plaguing black women "the Denzel Principle" in his 2010 book by the same name. Black women have standards that are just too high, argues Izrael. They expect partners on a par with actor Denzel Washington or President Barack Obama. In his 2011 book, *Is Marriage for White People?*, Stanford Law School professor Ralph Richard Banks suggests that black women date nonblack men to level the romantic playing field.

It has also become de rigueur for R&B artists to weigh in on love and marriage during media tours. In a 2011 video interview with gossip site Necole-Bitchie.com, actor and crooner Tyrese warned black women not to "independent your way into loneliness." Barely a month later, R&B singer Robin Thicke weighed in on the black marriage question in an *Essence* interview, saying, "Maybe the women have to take better care of their men. Maybe you're being too stubborn. Maybe you're not saying you're sorry. You have to take good care of him, too. You have to give love to get love."

Maybe black women want too much. Maybe they don't know how to treat men or choose them. Maybe they are too independent. Surely there must be something wrong with them if they are not being chosen as wives. The media's eagerness to abet this narrative is as frustrating as society's willingness to digest it.

The message reveals a patriarchal view of male/female relationships that positions women as objects of conquest rather than agents who make their own choices. Women should bend themselves to be more attractive to men; they should be less—less educated, less independent, less discerning, less themselves. While it is not surprising that many of the most prominent voices on the issue are not women, but men, the hyper-focus on black women's marital status has its roots in a particular intersection of sexism and racism. Behind the relationship "advice" is the specter of Sapphire—the stereotype of the black woman as unfeminine, emasculating and unattractive—named for an overbearing character on *Amos 'n' Andy*. That black women are single in large numbers, that they are advancing in education and careers, that they head so many households, that they are independent is deemed proof of their deficiency as women. The

trumpeting of statistics and media bias also creates a narrowed picture of black womanhood, effectively erasing married women, women who don't wish to marry and queer women.

All this hand-wringing misses the point. What we should be focusing on—no matter what race—is how marriage's place in our culture is shifting and how that shift might affect public policy and gender roles. We miss an opportunity to discuss how we can remake marriage for a new century, just as gay couples have been doing, or learn to live without it as the centerpiece of our society. We miss a chance to talk about solving the success gap or reforming the criminal-justice system. Instead we fret about black women and encourage them to make concessions—to lower their standards, to give up claims on equality, to blame their faiths and their single mothers—a position that moves no one closer to healthy and successful relationships. That's the real crisis.

R E A D I N G (67)

Lullabies Behind Bars

Beth Schwartzapfel (2009)

It's the middle of the day, and Rachael Irwin, 27, scurries across the floor on her hands and knees, playing peekaboo with her 10-month-old daughter, Gabriella. The baby's big blue eyes dance with delight. Like many children her age, Gabriella is in day care. Unlike most children her age, though, Gabriella is in prison. She and her mother are participating in the Bedford Hills (N.Y.) Correctional Facility's nursery program, one of only nine programs in the country that allow incarcerated women to keep their babies with them after they give birth.

Nationwide, nearly 2 million kids have parents in prison. "These children are sort of victims by default," says Paige Ransford, research associate at the Center for Women in Politics and Public Policy at the University of Massachusetts Boston and coauthor

of the recent report "Parenting from Prison." Many of the children go live with grandparents or other relatives; 10 percent of incarcerated mothers report that their children are placed in foster care. About half are separated from their siblings. These children are more likely than their peers to experience social developmental difficulties and to be in trouble with the law later in life.

In the case of women who enter the system as mothers-to-be, the usual excitement of pregnancy is replaced with a sense of dread. The choices that, on the outside, are understood to be a woman's right—such as where and how to give birth, and whether or not to breastfeed—are transferred from the woman to bureaucrats and officers at the state Department of Corrections (DOC).

Of the 112,459 women incarcerated in the United States as of 2006, about 4,300—4 percent of women in state custody and 3 percent in federal—were pregnant when they entered prison. In the vast majority of cases, babies are removed from their mothers immediately after birth and placed with relatives or in foster care. However, a small but growing number of states are recognizing that the mother-child bond formed in the first few months of life is crucial to the child's development, and that the bond need not be broken.

"We're definitely seeing more states grapple with what it means to send women, some of whom are pregnant, to prison," says Sarah From, director of public policy and communications for the Women's Prison Association (WPA). Eight states now have programs to house female offenders together with their newborns, and West Virginia is slated to begin a program this year.

These programs vary widely in the length of time babies are allowed to stay with their incarcerated mothers and in the services they provide. South Dakota allows babies to stay for just 30 days—with the mother in her regular cell—while Washington state allows children to stay for up to three years with their mothers in a separate wing of the prison. The Washington facility offers a federal Early Head Start program for prenatal health and infant-toddler development, and partners with the nonprofit Prison Doula Project to provide doula services to the women during and after their pregnancies.

The Bedford Hills program is the oldest and largest in the country, with its own nursery wing and space for up to 29 mother-baby pairs. Women live with their babies in bright rooms stuffed with donated toys and clothes. During the day, while the women attend DOC-mandated drug counseling, anger management, vocational training, and parenting classes, their children attend a day care center staffed by inmates who have graduated from an intensive two-year early childhood associate training program.

Although the idea of babies living the first months of their lives behind bars is sad to contemplate, many experts say that separating them from their mothers is far worse. "If a woman is serving a short sentence and can look forward to a life with her child . . . so much research addresses the importance of that early bonding relationship," says Sylvia Mignon, associate professor and director of the graduate program in human services at UMass Boston and coauthor, with Ransford, of the "Parenting from Prison" report. "The reality is, an infant does not know that she is in prison. All she knows is that she's getting the warmth and love and attention of this wonderful being called mom." Among women serving sentences of more than a decade, however, there is no clear consensus on what's best for the child; the Bedford Hills program generally accepts only women serving sentences of five years or less. "We don't want to create a bond that's guaranteed to be broken," says the children's center program director, Bobby Blanchard.

Unlike in the general prison population, doors in the program's wing are never locked; inmates come and go freely in order to warm bottles, do laundry, and comfort crying children out of the earshot of other sleeping babies. Rooms are decorated with photographs and handmade posters that say things like "Loving yourself is something to be proud of!" Danielizz Negron, 23, rocks her four-month-old son, Jeremiah, while he naps in a stroller. She was six months pregnant when, after a year of fighting burglary charges, she accepted a plea deal and turned herself in. "If I had not known about this program, I would not have came in. I would have been in Mexico somewhere by now," she says, only half-joking.

As the number of prison nurseries continues to grow, some caution against becoming overly sanguine. They're wonderful programs, says the WPA's Sarah From, but our priority should be working in the community to put fewer women in prison rather than looking to build more prison nurseries.

My Grandmother Washes Her Feet in the Sink of the Bathroom at Sears

Mohja Kahf (2003)

My grandmother puts her feet in the sink
of the bathroom at Sears
to wash them in the ritual washing for prayer,
wudu,
because she has to pray in the store or miss
the mandatory prayer time for Muslims
She does it with great poise, balancing
herself with one plump matronly arm
against the automated hot-air hand dryer,
after having removed her support knee-highs
and laid them aside, folded in thirds,
and given me her purse and her packages to hold
so she can accomplish this august ritual
and get back to the ritual of shopping for housewares

Respectable Sears matrons shake their heads and frown
as they notice what my grandmother is doing,
an affront to American porcelain,
a contamination of American Standards
by something foreign and unhygienic
requiring civic action and possible use of disinfectant
    spray
They fluster about and flutter their hands and I can see
a clash of civilizations brewing in the Sears bathroom

My grandmother, though she speaks no English,
catches their meaning and her look in the mirror says,
I have washed my feet over Iznik tile in Istanbul
with water from the world's ancient irrigation systems
I have washed my feet in the bathhouses of Damascus
over painted bowls imported from China
among the best families of Aleppo
And if you Americans knew anything
about civilization and cleanliness,
you'd make wider washbins, anyway
My grandmother knows one culture—the right one,
as do these matrons of the Middle West. For them,
my grandmother might as well have been squatting
in the mud over a rusty tin in vaguely tropical squalor,

Mexican or Middle Eastern, it doesn't matter which,
when she lifts her well-groomed foot and puts it over
    the edge.
"You can't do that," one of the women protests,
turning to me, "Tell her she can't do that."
"We wash our feet five times a day,"
my grandmother declares hotly in Arabic.
"My feet are cleaner than their sink.
Worried about their sink, are they?
I should worry about my feet!"
My grandmother nudges me, "Go on, tell them."

Standing between the door and the mirror, I can see
at multiple angles, my grandmother and the other
    shoppers,
all of them decent and goodhearted women, diligent
in cleanliness, grooming, and decorum
Even now my grandmother, not to be rushed,
is delicately drying her pumps with tissues from her
    purse
For my grandmother always wears well-turned pumps
that match her purse, I think in case someone
from one of the best families of Aleppo
should run into her—here, in front of the Kenmore
    display

I smile at the midwestern women
as if my grandmother has just said something lovely
    about them
and shrug at my grandmother as if they
had just apologized through me
No one is fooled, but I

hold the door open for everyone
and we all emerge on the sales floor
and lose ourselves in the great common ground
of housewares on markdown.

Source: *E-mails from Scheherazad* (University Press of Florida, 2003)

DISCUSSION QUESTIONS FOR CHAPTER 8

1. What are some myths about the normative U.S. family? How do these myths help to perpetuate patriarchal power? How do they disadvantage most real families?

2. How are families both places of comfort, security, and nurture and at the same time places of domination, conflict, and violence?

3. How do social institutions reinforce power relations in the family? How does the family often reflect power relations of the dominant social order?

4. What conflicts do women face between work and family? How do other social institutions such as media, religion, education, and government create and reproduce this conflict? What alternatives do feminist critiques of traditional marriage and traditional notions of the workplace offer?

5. What are feminist arguments for and against marriage equality? What alternatives to marriage do some feminists offer and why?

SUGGESTIONS FOR FURTHER READING

Barker, Nicola. *Not the Marrying Kind: A Feminist Critique of Same-Sex Marriage.* New York: Palgrave Macmillan, 2013.

Coontz, Stephanie. *A Strange Stirring: The Feminine Mystique and American Women at the Dawn of the 1960s.* New York: Basic Books, 2011.

Frye, Joanne S. *Biting the Moon: A Memoir of Feminism and Motherhood.* Syracuse, NY: Syracuse University Press, 2012.

Hequembourg, Amy. *Lesbian Motherhood: Stories of Becoming.* New York: Harrington Park Press, 2007.

Hertz, Rosanna. *Single by Chance, Mothers by Choice: How Women Are Choosing Parenthood Without Marriage and Creating the New American Family.* New York: Oxford University Press, 2006.

Kinser, Amber. *Motherhood and Feminism.* Berkeley, CA: Seal Press, 2010.

Kotulski, Davina. *Love Warriors: The Rise of the Marriage Equality Movement and Why It Will Prevail.* New York: Alyson Books, 2010.

Kunin, Madeleine M. *The New Feminist Agenda: Defining the Next Revolution for Women, Work, and Family.* White River Junction, VT: Chelsea Green, 2012.

O'Reilly, Andrea. *Twenty-First-Century Motherhood: Experience, Identity, Policy, Agency.* New York: Columbia University Press, 2010.

Work Inside and Outside the Home

Worldwide, work, both paid and unpaid, and inside and outside the home, is a gendered phenomenon whereby certain activities are coded feminine and others masculine, and where the latter tends to be valued more. No matter who actually performs certain kinds of work like housework, it is devalued (even though when men perform household labor, especially child rearing, it is often noted and celebrated). But the reality is that humans who identify as women are much more likely to do such devalued labor, and to be paid less than those who identify as men for the work they do. So while work is a gendered analytic construct, and there are social discourses and "regimes of truth" that construct meaning for work activities, there are important material realities for individuals performing the tasks of human subsistence. Most people who identify as women work outside the home whether they are married or have children or not. Indeed, 40 percent of all families with children in the home have women as the *primary* breadwinner, and a major proportion of these are single women. If you factor in the work that women also do in the home, then women are working very hard. In other words, in the United States and around the world, women work long hours because work for them often involves unpaid domestic labor and care of dependent family members as well as paid labor. In addition, when they do get paid for their work, women tend to earn lower wages compared with men and are less likely to have control over the things they produce and the wages they receive. In this chapter we examine both domestic unpaid labor and women's employment in the labor force, the latter discussion focusing on the global economy and the changing nature and patterns of women's labor force participation, the dual economy, and the gender gap in wages.

UNPAID LABOR IN THE HOME

Work done in the home is often not considered work at all: It is something done in the name of love, or because, somehow, one group of humans is better programmed to do this than others. The humorist Dave Barry, for example, declares that 85 percent of men in the United States are "cleaning impaired," satirizing the supposed ineptitude or lack of participation in domestic activities on the part of men, (what Terrance Heath in the reading "Will Marriage Equality Lead to Equal Sharing of Housework?" calls the "bumbling dad" stereotype), as normalized or natural. The point, though, is that there is nothing natural about the fact that

LEARNING ACTIVITY **Housework and Technology**

The conventional wisdom would suggest that modern household inventions have saved time and energy for homemakers. But is that the case? Have technological innovations freed women from household chores? Or have they created more work for women in the home?

Take a look at Susan Strasser's *Never Done: A History of American Housework* and Ruth Schwartz Cowan's *More Work for Mother: The Ironies of Household Technologies from the Open Hearth to the Microwave*. What do they suggest about the role of household inventions?

Use these books and a search engine on the Web to research the following household appliances. Have they saved time and energy for women?

- Vacuum cleaner
- Stove
- Washing machine
- Dryer
- Refrigerator
- Microwave

Watch a couple of hours of daytime television and take note of the advertisements. What sorts of household products are advertised? What do the ads suggest about how these products can make women more efficient homemakers? Do you think these items really improve women's lives? What do these ads imply about women's responsibilities in the home? Do the ads suggest that men are equally responsible for housework? Do they suggest household technologies can help men become more efficient homemakers?

women on the average do more than two-thirds of all household work. The fact that they may be better at it is only because of years of practice. Social discourses about gender that associate women, the home, and domesticity reinforce the assumption that housework and childcare are women's work. This work, often termed "reproductive labor," includes care and domestic-related activities such as unpaid housework, the emotional care of family members, and the raising of children. Such labor tends to be undervalued as women's formal "productive" paid labor in the workforce is prioritized. This is clearly the case in analyses of the effects of *economic globalization,* where statistics often tend to disregard reproductive labor. Economic globalization can be defined as processes that integrate economies toward a global marketplace or a single world market as illustrated by the rapid growth of transnational corporations and complex networks of production and consumption. Reproductive labor is rarely included in a country's national statistics of productivity such as the GNP (gross national product) and GDP (gross domestic product). See the sidebar "Domestic Workers' Bill of Rights" below for more information about the transference of reproductive labor to the paid labor force.

In the reading "Maid to Order," Barbara Ehrenreich focuses on the politics of housework in contemporary U.S. society. She emphasizes that housework is not degrading because it involves manual labor but, instead, because it is embedded in degrading relationships that have the potential to reproduce male domination from one generation to

LEARNING ACTIVITY **Domestic Workers' Bill of Rights**

In 2010 New York became the first state to pass a domestic workers' bill of rights, giving nannies, housekeepers, and household cooks the same protections as other workers. The campaign by Domestic Workers United took 6 years of work, lobbying, and meetings. The group discovered that only 10 percent of domestic workers were provided with health insurance, 26 percent made less than minimum wage, and 33 percent had been verbally or physically abused by an employer. Ninety-three percent of New York's domestic workers are women, and 95 percent are people of color, and so those who are already marginalized and vulnerable are most affected by the lack of laws protecting domestic workers. To learn more, visit Domestic Workers United's website at *www .domesticworkersunited.org.*

To learn more about movements for domestic workers' rights worldwide, visit the website of the International Domestic Workers' Network at *www .domesticworkerrights.org* and the National Domestic Workers Alliance at *www .nationaldomesticworkersalliance.org*. What does New York's bill provide for domestic workers? Why are these conditions important for domestic workers? Where are there other campaigns for a domestic workers' bill of rights? What is the status of domestic workers' rights in your state?

the next. She notes that a contemporary solution to the housework problem among those who can afford it is to hire someone else to do the work. That "someone" is most likely a woman and very often a woman of color. Paid domestic work is one occupation traditionally held by women of color; it is also an occupation that is usually nonunionized and has low pay, little power, and few or no benefits. In addition, workers who used to contract services directly with employers are now being replaced by corporate cleaning services that control a good portion of the housecleaning business. Ehrenreich emphasizes that this new relationship between cleaners and those who can afford to employ them abolishes the traditional "mistress-maid" relationship and allows middle-class people who are sensitive to the political issues involved with hiring servants to avoid confronting these issues and feel less guilt.

As mentioned above, most researchers who study household labor define it as all tasks involved in cleaning and household maintenance, purchasing and preparing food, taking care of children and/or aging or sick family members, and garden and yard work. Family work also involves "kin keeping," discussed below, that includes taking care of the emotional needs of family members. Two major findings emerge in the data on housework. The first concerns the amount of time women and men spend on household work. A 2011 U.S. Bureau of Labor Statistics study shows that women on average spend about 15 hours and 17 minutes per week on household labor compared to men who spend about 9 hours and 34 minutes. On an average day 19 percent of men reported doing housework—such as cleaning or doing laundry—compared with 48 percent of women. Forty percent of men did food preparation or cleanup versus 66 percent of women. A 2009 study by Joni Hersch reported similar findings with married women completing an average of 97 minutes per day on housework broadly defined and unmarried women spending an average of 67 minutes a day. Hersch also found that housework had a negative impact on

Women and Agriculture

- Women make up 51 percent of the agricultural labor force worldwide.
- A study of the household division of labor in Bangladeshi villages found that women worked almost 12 hours a day—compared with the 8 to 10 hours a day worked by men in the same villages.
- In many regions, women spend up to 5 hours a day collecting fuelwood and water and up to 4 hours preparing food.
- In Africa and Asia, women work about 13 hours more than men each week.
- In Southeast Asia, women provide up to 90 percent of the labor for rice cultivation.
- In Africa, 90 percent of the work of gathering water and wood, for the household and for food preparation, is done by women.
- In Pakistan, 50 percent of rural women cultivate and harvest wheat.
- In the world's least developed countries, 23 percent of rural households are headed by women.
- In Sub-Saharan Africa, women produce up to 80 percent of basic foodstuffs both for household consumption and for sale.
- Women perform from 25 to 45 percent of agricultural field tasks in Colombia and Peru.
- Women constitute 53 percent of the agricultural labor in Egypt.
- Fewer than 10 percent of women farmers in India, Nepal, and Thailand own land.
- An analysis of credit schemes in five African countries found that women received less than 10 percent of the credit awarded to males who own small farms.
- Only 15 percent of the world's agricultural extension agents are women.

Sources: www.fao.org/gender/en/labb2-e.htm and www.fao.org/gender/en/agrib4-e.htm.

the salaries of women, regardless of their occupation. Interestingly, although most studies find that as women's earnings increase compared with their male partners, they gain more leverage over who does the housework, Australian research found that high-earning women completed relatively more housework than those women earning less. Women who contributed 70 percent or more of the weekly family income started doing more housework rather than less, putting in more time cleaning and cooking than women who contributed half of family finances. Researchers suggested that for these women, doing extra housework reflected their need to balance family dynamics by compensating for husbands who were not fulfilling traditional masculine roles.

In other words, although the amount of housework done by U.S. women has dropped considerably since the 1960s and the amount of housework done by men has increased, women are still doing considerably more housework than men. Married women currently perform about two-thirds of all household labor. As discussed in Chapter 8, daughters are also more likely to do household work than their brothers with consequences for their leisure and other activities. Couples with higher levels of education tend to have more equitable divisions of household labor. Terrance Heath addresses these issues in the reading "Will Marriage Equality Lead to Equal Sharing of Housework?" and reports that when it comes

to allocating their time, men spend about an additional 40 minutes on sports and leisure compared to women and an additional hour and 16 minutes performing work-related activities. In this reading he addresses the issue of marriage equality and explains that opponents to gay marriage also usually define themselves as supporters of traditional cultural norms endorsing a gender division of labor in the home. They are "defenders" of traditional gender performances, he writes, precisely because "they know same-sex marriage undermines the cultural norm that keeps the gender-based division of labor in the home." As a gay man raised and willing to do his share of household labor, Heath suggests that "you don't have to marry another dude to [support an egalitarian division of labor in the home]. You just have to pick up a mop more often, wash a few dishes, [and] change your share of diapers, etc."

In her 2005 reissue of *The Second Shift,* sociologist Arlie Russell Hochschild writes of the "70–30" gender split associated with household work. Similarly, Chloe Bird, also a sociologist, suggests that once married, women do about twice the amount of work in the home as their spouses, increasing their stress and anxiety. When women marry, unfortunately most gain an average of 14 hours a week of domestic labor, compared with men, who gain an average of 90 minutes. Husbands tend to create more work for wives than they perform. A study from the University of Michigan estimated this husband-created labor at about 7 hours a week. This can cause stress-related problems and mental and physical exhaustion for women trying to juggle family responsibilities and paid employment. Studies find that couples who are most contented have the most flexibility regarding work and commitment to sharing responsibilities. According to Neil Chethik in *VoiceMale,* a book on husbands and marriage, men who do more housework and childcare report a better sex life with their wives, who have more energy for sexual intimacy when they have fewer dishes to wash and lunches to make. Importantly, women are more content with male partners who take an active role in the home and this encourages sexual intimacy.

Cross-national comparisons of the gender gap in housework drawing on data in Japan, North America, Scandinavia, Russia, and Hungary by the Institute for Social Research

LEARNING ACTIVITY   **Who Does the Work at Your School and in Your Home?**

Use the following charts to discover who does various kinds of work at your school and in your home. Discuss your findings with your classmates. What patterns do you notice? What do your findings suggest about how systems of inequality function in the institution of work, both inside and outside the home?

WHO DOES THE WORK AT YOUR SCHOOL?

Job Description	White Men	White Women	Men of Color	Women of Color
Top administration				
Teaching				
Secretarial				
Groundskeeping				
Electrical/carpentry				
Janitorial				
Food preparation				
Security				
Intercollegiate coaching				

WHO DOES THE WORK IN YOUR HOME?

Job Description	Person in the Family Who Generally Does This Job	Sex of Person Who Generally Does This Job	Hours per Week Spent in Doing This Job
Laundry			
Mowing the lawn			
Maintaining the car			
Buying the groceries			
Cooking			
Vacuuming			
Washing dishes			
Making beds			
Cleaning bathroom			

(ISR) indicate that North American men are less egalitarian (meaning equally sharing power) than Scandinavians (Swedish men do an average of 24 hours of housework a week), but more egalitarian than Japanese men. Russian women do the least amount of housework, although they work the most total hours (employed plus domestic work), and Hungarian women do the most housework and have the least amount of leisure time.

All these comparative data must be interpreted with caution as questions are raised in terms of how household labor is defined, whether methods for reporting are standardized, and whether a discussion of "women doing less housework" means overall hours or as a proportion of total hours performed by women and men.

One of the most significant issues to consider in terms of the reliability of this house-work data is that much family work is difficult to measure. This is especially true of the work involved in "kin keeping": remembering birthdays, sending cards, preparing for holidays, organizing vacations, keeping in touch with relatives, and providing "spousal career support" by entertaining, volunteering, and networking. These tasks are time consuming and involve emotional work that is not easily quantified and is often invisible. Women tend to perform the bulk of this kin-keeping work. It is important to note that such work cannot easily be replaced with hired labor (which of course is usually the labor of another woman, often a woman of color, or poor woman). Finally, when it comes to household work, women seem to be better at multitasking, and, as a result, often underestimate the work they do because they are performing multiple tasks at the same time. As a general trend, however, researchers find both women and men over-report the amount of housework they do, with men over-reporting at almost twice the rate of women (about 150 percent compared to 68 percent).

The second major finding concerns the gendered division of household labor. This means that women and men (and girl and boy children) do different kinds of work in the home. According to 2011 U.S. Bureau of Labor Statistics data, on an average day women spend twice as much time preparing food and drink, three times as much time doing interior cleaning, and almost four times as much time doing laundry as did men. Men spend twice as much time doing activities related to lawn, garden, and houseplants, and twice as much time doing interior and exterior maintenance, repairs, and decoration as did women. In other words, women tend to do the repetitive, ongoing, daily kinds of tasks, and men are more likely to perform the less repetitive or seasonal tasks, especially if these tasks involve the use of tools or machines. Studies show that heterosexual couples are more likely to share cooking and childcare and less likely to share cleaning, the bulk of which is overwhelmingly performed by females (women and girl children). Some tasks are seen as more masculine and some as more feminine. In this way, gender plays a significant role in the types of housework men and women perform.

It is important to note that the "feminine," frequently performed tasks are less optional for families and are also more likely to be thought of as boring by both women and men. Among heterosexual couples who do share household work there seems to be a focus on "equally shared" rather than "equally divided" tasks. Equally shared means that couples negotiate who does what to provide equity rather than divide up all tasks and each do an equal amount (equally divided). Although equal sharing takes into account personal preferences, efficiency, and vested interest and often is more "workable," it can run the risk of replicating gender-stereotyped behaviors that ultimately lead to inequities in the division of labor in the home.

Many readers are probably remembering their father doing the housework or have a male partner who shares equally in domestic labor. According to several studies, men with a higher education are more likely to pick up and pitch in. Although there have been changes over the past decades with more men taking on household responsibilities and "helping out," it is important to note how the term *helping* assumes that it is someone else's responsibility. Nonetheless, it is important to state that housework, although often

HISTORICAL MOMENT   **Wages for Housework**

Women do two-thirds of the world's work but receive only 5 percent of the world's income. Worldwide, women's unpaid labor is estimated at $11 trillion. Early in the women's movement, feminists made the connection between women's unpaid labor and the profits accumulated by the businesses that relied on women's household and child-rearing work to support the waged laborers who produced goods and capital. They argued, then, that women should be compensated for the domestic labor that is taken for granted and yet depended on to maintain capitalist economies.

Several groups agitated for wages for housework, and in 1972 the International Wages for Housework (WFH) Campaign was organized by women in developing and industrialized countries to agitate for compensation for the unpaid work women do. They argued that this goal could best be reached by dismantling the military-industrial complex. In 1975 the International Black Women for Wages for Housework (IBWWFH) Campaign, an international network of women of color, formed to work for compensation for unwaged and low-waged work and to ensure that challenging racism was not separated from challenging sexism and other forms of discrimination.

Few American feminists advocated this position, although it constituted a significant position for feminists in Europe. Some feminists opposed the campaign, arguing that to pay women for housework would reinforce women's role in the home and strengthen the existing gendered division of labor.

Both the WFH and IBWWFH campaigns remained active into the early 2000s, advocating change in the ways women's work is valued and rewarded. They were involved in a campaign for pay equity and a global women's strike.

dreary and repetitive, can also be creative and more interesting than some paid labor. And, although raising children is among the hardest work of all, it is also full of rewards. Men who do not participate in household work and childcare miss the joys associated with this work even while they have the privilege of being free to do other things.

PAID LABOR

Trends and Legalities

The reading "A Brief History of Working Women" by sociologists Sharlene Hesse-Biber and Gregg Lee Carter overviews the changes in women's labor force participation over the past centuries for different groups of women. Briefly, as U.S. society became industrialized in the nineteenth century, the traditional subsistence economies of producing what families needed to survive from the home, taking in work (like spinning or washing), or working in others' homes or on their land were changed in favor of a more distinct separation between work and home. Factories were established, employees were congregated under one roof (and thus more easily controlled), and emerging technologies started mass-producing goods. Instead of making products in the home for family consumption, people were working outside the home and spending their earnings on these mass-produced goods. Urban centers grew up around these sites of production, and ordinary people tended to work long hours in often very poor conditions. These harsh conditions associated with women's wage labor coincided with continuing domestic servitude in the home. This double day of work was recognized by scholars over a hundred years ago and is still a central aspect of women's lives today.

At the same time that working-class women and children were working in factories, mines, and sweatshops, the middle-class home came to be seen as a haven from the cruel world, and middle-class women were increasingly associated with this sphere. From this developed the "cult of true womanhood"—prescriptions for white, middle-class femininity that included piety, purity, and domesticity. Although these notions of femininity could be achieved only by privileged white women given structural arrangements in society, such norms came to influence women generally. At the same time, some women were starting to enter higher education. With the founding of Oberlin Collegial Institute in 1833, other women's colleges such as Mount Holyoke, Bryn Mawr, and Wellesley were established as the century progressed. In addition, state universities (beginning with Utah in 1850) started admitting women. By the turn of the century, there were cohorts of (mostly privileged white) women who were educated to be full political persons and who helped shape the Progressive Era of the early twentieth century with a focus on reform and civic leadership. These women entered the labor force in relatively large numbers, and many chose a career over marriage and the family.

As the twentieth century progressed, more women entered the public sphere. The years of the Great Depression slowed women's advancement, and it was not until World War II that women were seen working in traditionally male roles in unprecedented numbers. The government encouraged this transition, and many women were, for the first time, enjoying decent wages. All this would end after the war as women were encouraged or forced to return to the home so that men could claim their jobs in the labor force. Childcare centers were dismantled, and the conservative messages of the 1950s encouraged women to stay home and partake in the rapidly emerging consumer society. The social and cultural upheavals of the 1960s and the civil rights and women's movements fought for legislation to help women gain more power in the workplace.

The most important legislative gains include, first, the Equal Pay Act of 1963, which protects men and women who perform substantially equal work in the same establishment from sex-based wage discrimination. This is the "equal pay for equal work" law. Second, Title VII of the Civil Rights Act of 1964 prohibits discrimination in employment based on race, color, religion, sex, and/or national origin in establishments with 15 or more employees. It makes it illegal for employers to discriminate against these protected classes in terms of the conditions and privileges of employment (hiring, firing, pay, promotion, etc.). Title VII said that gender could not be used as a criterion in employment except where there is a "*bona fide* occupational qualification," meaning it is illegal unless an employer can prove that gender is crucial to job performance (for example, hiring male janitors in men's bathrooms). For the most part, the law had little influence until 1972 with the enforcement of the Equal Employment Opportunity Commission that had been established in 1965. The courts have fine-tuned Title VII over the years, and it remains the most important legislation that protects working women and people of color. For example, in 2009 the Lilly Ledbetter Fair Pay Act, the first bill signed into law by U.S. President Barack Obama, amends Title VII by stating that the 180-day statute of limitations for filing an equal-pay lawsuit regarding pay discrimination resets with each new paycheck affected by that discriminatory action. This legislation overturns previous time limits imposed on discrimination claims. Lilly Ledbetter was a production supervisor at a Goodyear tire plant in Alabama who filed an equal-pay lawsuit regarding pay discrimination under Title VII, 6 months before her early retirement in 1998. The courts gave opposite verdicts and eventually the case went to the U.S. Supreme Court in 2007, which ruled that Ledbetter's complaint was null because of time limits. The 2009 Act amended this ruling.

In 1976 the Supreme Court expanded the interpretation of Title VII to include discrimination on the basis of pregnancy as sex discrimination, and in 1993 the Family and Medical Leave Act was passsed. It protected all workers by guaranteeing unpaid leave and protection of employment as a result of caring for a sick family member or the birth or adoption of a child. In 1986 the Supreme Court declared sexual harassment a form of sex discrimination and in 1993 broadened this ruling by stating that people suing on the basis of sexual harassment did not have to prove that they had suffered "concrete psychological harm." Sexual harassment legislation made a distinction between *quid pro quo* (sexual favors are required in return for various conditions of employment) and *hostile work environment* (no explicit demand for an exchange of sexual acts for work-related conditions but being subjected to a pattern of harassment as part of the work environment). In a poll conducted by the *Wall Street Journal* and NBC, 44 percent of working women said they had been discriminated against because of their gender and one-third said they had experienced sexual harassment. Scholars emphasize that such harassment denies employment opportunities and threatens physical safety and integrity. It is important to note that although some states have enforced state- and local-level legal protections against harassment targeted at LGBTQ individuals, currently 30 states have no protection. Trans people are especially prone to job discrimination and harassment and may have little to no recourse.

Third, the Age Discrimination in Employment Act that was enacted in 1968, and amended in 1978 and 1986, outlaws mandatory retirement and prohibits employers with 20 or more employees from discriminating on the basis of age, protecting individuals who are 40 years of age and older. In 2005 courts restricted this law by interpreting it narrowly. Generally groups suing under Title VII of the Civil Rights Act of 1964 do not need to prove intentional discrimination and can declare "disparate impact" and claim they were disproportionately harmed by an employer's policy or behavior. Many courts now refuse to allow older workers to bring disparate-impact claims and require them to prove intentional harm. Fourth, the Americans with Disabilities Act (ADA) of 1990 prohibits employment discrimination against qualified individuals with disabilities.

Finally, affirmative action policies that encouraged employers to take gender and race into account in terms of hiring were first initiated by President Kennedy in the 1960s. Since that time, affirmative action has helped diversify the workplace and encouraged the hiring of women and people of color. However, there is a lot of misunderstanding as well as serious hostility associated with affirmative action, as evidenced by the dismantling of affirmative action guidelines in many states. Basically, affirmative action creates positive steps to increase the representation of women and people of color in areas of employment, education, and government from which they may have been historically excluded. Affirmative action encourages the diversification of the job pool, but it does not encourage the hiring of unqualified women or people of color. It is a misunderstanding of these policies to think that white males now have a hard time getting jobs because they are being undercut by unqualified women or people of color.

The Dual Labor Market and the Changing Economy

At the beginning of the twenty-first century it is important to understand the changing nature of the workplace in the United States and the connections between U.S. corporate capitalism and the global economy. Capitalism is an economic system based on the pursuit of profit and the principle of private ownership. Such a system creates inequality because this profit comes in part from surplus value created from the labor of workers. In other words, workers produce more value than they receive in wages, this difference or surplus being reinvested into capital accumulation and corporate profit. The U.S. economy is able to maintain this profit accumulation through the perpetuation of a "dual labor market" that provides a "primary" market, with relatively high wages and employee benefits and protections for workers, and a "secondary" market, where workers (disproportionately women and people of color) receive lower wages, fewer benefits, and less opportunity for advancement. For example, employees in the beauty industry tend to be working in the secondary market. Along with low pay and few benefits, workers are often exposed to occupational health risks. The reading "Color Me Nontoxic" by Momo Chang discusses the health risks associated with women working in nail salons.

What Is Sexual Harassment?

Sexual harassment is legally defined as unwelcome sexual advances or requests for sexual favors. It also includes any verbal or physical conduct of a sexual nature when the following criteria are met:

- Submission is made explicitly or implicitly a term or condition of an individual's employment.
- Submission to or rejection of such conduct by an individual is used as the basis for employment decisions affecting that individual.
- Such conduct has the purpose or effect of substantially interfering with an individual's work performance or creating an intimidating, hostile, or offensive working environment.

Sexual harassment may include physical conduct, verbal conduct, or nonverbal conduct such as sexual gestures or pornographic pictures.

TWO TYPES OF SEXUAL HARASSMENT

Quid Pro Quo

Unwelcome sexual advances, requests for sexual favors, and other verbal or physical conduct of a sexual nature constitute quid pro quo sexual harassment when:

Submission to such conduct is made either explicitly or implicitly a term or condition of an individual's employment or submission to or rejection of such conduct by an individual is used as the basis for employment decisions affecting that individual.

Hostile Work Environment

In determining whether or not an environment is hostile, it must be determined whether or not the conduct unreasonably interfered with an individual's work performance or created an intimidating, hostile, or offensive work environment.

The Equal Employment Opportunity Commission (EEOC) suggests that the courts look at the following criteria:

- Whether the conduct was verbal, physical, or both
- How frequently the conduct was repeated
- Whether the conduct was hostile or patently offensive
- Whether the alleged harasser was a coworker or a supervisor
- Whether others joined in perpetrating the harassment
- Whether the harassment was directed at more than one individual
- Whether the remarks were hostile and derogatory
- Whether the harasser singled out the charging party
- Whether the charging party participated in the exchange
- The relationship between the charging party and alleged harasser

The Supreme Court established a two-pronged test for determining a hostile environment:

1. The conduct must "be severe or pervasive enough to create an objectively hostile or abusive environment that a reasonable person would find hostile or abusive."
2. The victim must "subjectively perceive the environment to be abusive."

Bernice Sandler of the National Association of Women in Education reports that surveys indicate that up to 30 percent of female college students and 70 percent of women in the workplace have been sexually harassed.

IDEAS FOR ACTIVISM

- Advocate with your elected representatives for an increase in the minimum wage.
- Encourage your school to analyze pay equity and to make corrections where needed.
- Write your elected representatives to encourage legislation and funding for childcare.
- Investigate exploitative employment practices of major national and multinational corporations and launch boycotts to demand improved conditions for workers.
- Encourage your elected representatives to support affirmative action.

Workers are routinely exposed to hazardous toxins that jeopardize health. The reading describes an entrepreneur, Uyen Nguyen, who opened a "green" nail salon that does not use toxic nail products. Similarly the reading "Virtuous Valentine? Think Again" by Hannah Levintova addresses the problematic work experiences of those involved in industries catering to products for Valentine's Day. The dual labor market also maintains profit through globalization strategies, discussed below.

In terms of the changing nature of the U.S. economy, three features stand out. First, new technologies (especially electronic communications) have revolutionized work and, in some cases, replaced workers and made some jobs obsolete. In cases where technology cannot replace workers, jobs have been exported overseas to take advantage of lower wages. Second, there has been a huge increase in the service sector and a shift from manufacturing to service-sector work. This has brought a change in the kinds of skills workers need in order to compete in this sector, reflecting the dual labor market and its distinctions between high-skilled service work (e.g., financial consultants, public relations) and low-paid and low-skilled service work (food service, child and elderly care). Women and people of color are more likely found in the latter part of the service sector, illustrating the ways the economy is a conduit for the maintenance of systems of inequality and privilege. Consequences of the dual labor market are discussed in the sections below on women's labor force participation and issues of pay equity.

Third, economies around the world are increasingly connected to, and positioned differently within, a global economy. As explained in other chapters, *globalization* refers to the processes by which regional economies, societies, and cultures have become integrated through an interconnected global network of communication, transportation, and trade. As mentioned above, economic globalization is a component of these processes and involves the integration of national economies toward a global marketplace or a single world market as illustrated by the rapid growth of transnational corporations and complex networks of production and consumption. Wealthy nations in the global north have more influence in this global marketplace, in part because of their influence on and with such institutions like the World Trade Organization (WTO) and the World Bank. The WTO is an international financial institution that provides loans to developing countries for capital programs with certain social and economic strings attached, too complex to go into here. Basically the WTO supervises and regulates international trade deals by providing frameworks for negotiating and formalizing trade agreements. The WTO currently has 153 members and is governed by a general council and a conference every two years. The World Bank is involved with loans and foreign investment and thus has power over international trade and economic globalization generally. China became a member of the World Bank in 1980 and is rapidly becoming a powerful economic force in contributing a significant proportion of economic global growth each year.

Global multinational corporations have grown in size and influence, and mergers have resulted in a smaller number of corporations controlling a larger part of the global market. They have immense power and influence and often no longer correspond to national borders, functioning outside the jurisdiction of nation states. Because many U.S.-based corporations rely on the cheaper, nonunionized labor force and looser environmental restrictions outside the United States, much manufacturing and increasingly service work is done overseas. As shown in the sidebar "Global Employment Trends for Women," such processes of economic globalization involve vast numbers of women traveling across state borders and serving as cheap labor. In addition it encourages the immigration of women in both the formal economy of globalization (electronics and garment work) and the informal economy (childcare, sex work, street vending) in the United States. As discussed in Chapter 11, the military has close ties to globalizing economies, creating what scholars call the military-industrial complex. Military operations and the presence of international military forces in developing countries serve in part to "stabilize" these nations and protect foreign business interests such as oil or other resources, often in the name of forging "peace" or "democracy."

The effects of the global economy include profound inequalities between rich and poor nations as well as between rich and poor citizens within individual countries. Often these inequalities are based on older inequities resulting from nineteenth- and early-twentieth-century colonization and imperialism. For individual women, although multinational corporations do give women a wage, they often upset subsistence economies and cause migration and cultural dislocation, which encourages increasing consumerism, sex trading, and the pollution of fragile environments. Women often work in poor and unhealthy conditions for little pay. In addition, many thousands of U.S. workers have lost their jobs as corporations have moved productive processes overseas. These events are not random but part of a broader pattern of global capitalist expansion. In "Virtuous Valentine? Think Again," Levintova illustrates all the above points in her example of the corporatization of Valentine's Day and the global implications of consumption during this holiday. In this short essay she examines the social, economic, and environmental politics associated with the production and purchase of flowers, chocolate, and greeting cards.

Women's Labor Force Participation

The major change in terms of trends in women's workforce participation has been the increase in the number of women who were in paid employment or looking for work as the last century progressed. The U.S. Bureau of Labor Statistics reports that this number grew from 5.3 million in 1900 to 18.4 million in 1950 and more than 70 million in 2013. Women made up 18 percent of the labor force in 1900, almost 30 percent in 1950, and almost 50 percent of all workers in 2013. About 58 percent of women in the United States are working in the labor force, and of these, about a third are women of color. Approximately 71 percent of U.S. mothers with children younger than age 18 and 55 percent of those with infant children are in the labor force. In addition, about two-thirds of mothers generally are breadwinners or co-breadwinners. Only approximately one in five families involves a stay-at-home mother who does not also work outside the home, and, as already mentioned in Chapter 8, according to a 2013 Pew Research Center study, 4 in 10 U.S. households with children younger than age 18 now include a mother who is either the sole or primary earner for her family. This means that women are not only more likely to be the primary caregivers in a family, but increasingly the primary breadwinners too. In terms of the latter, this reflects evolving family dynamics where it has become more acceptable and expected for married women to join the workforce, even those with young children, and especially for single women to raise children alone (of those 4 in 10 households mentioned above, two-thirds are headed by single mothers). It also reflects the economic recession in the United States with men disproportionately employed in industries such as construction and manufacturing that have been especially hard hit. Economics also shape attitudes about women working, along with a loosening of traditional norms about gender in recent decades. For example, about a third of mothers in the Pew study reported that their ideal situation would be to work full-time (compared to 20 percent of women who said this as recent as 2007).

The reading, "The Triumph of the Working Mother" by Stephanie Coontz, addresses the contemporary situation of U.S. mothers working in both the labor force and at home. She discusses the benefits for mothers in terms of physical and mental health, and especially

Global Employment Trends for Women, 2012

- Globally, gender gaps in the economic indicators of unemployment and employment trended towards convergence in the period 2002 to 2007, but with reversals coinciding with the period of the crisis from 2008 to 2012 in many regions. The gender gap in labour force participation, examined over a longer period of the last two decades, shows convergence in the 1990s, but little to no convergence in the 2000s, with increasing gaps in some regions like South Asia and Central and Eastern Europe. Demographic and behavioural change appears to have added to the impact of the crisis, to reverse convergence in regions harder hit by the crisis, such as the advanced economies and Central and Eastern Europe.
- Economic indicators of job quality, such as gender gaps in vulnerability and occupational segregation show significant gaps for 2012. An indicator for sectoral segregation could be observed over a long run period of two decades, and showed women crowding into services sectors, in both developed and developing countries. . . .

THE CRISIS

- The immediate context of this summary is the financial and economic crisis. The policy stimulus of 2009 gave way to austerity in 2011–12, that in 2012 led to a double dip in GDP growth in some countries. The 29 million net jobs lost during the global economic crisis have not been recovered. The Eurozone crisis combined with the "fiscal cliff" threat in the United States, have generated downside risks to growth. The IMF's downgrade of global GDP growth for 2013, from 3.8 to 3.6 per cent, has led the ILO to estimate that an additional 2.5 million jobs could be lost in 2013 as result.

GENDER GAPS IN UNEMPLOYMENT

- From 2002 to 2007, the gender gap in unemployment was constant at around 0.5 percentage points, with the female unemployment rate higher at 5.8 percent, compared to male unemployment at 5.3 percent (with 72 million women unemployed compared to their global employment of 1.2 billion in 2007 and 98 million men unemployed compared to their global employment of 1.8 billion). The crisis raised this gender gap to 0.7 percentage points for 2012 (destroying 13 million jobs for women), with projections showing no significant reduction in unemployment expected even by 2017.
- Analysis of regional trends shows that, over 2002 to 2007, women had higher unemployment rates than men in Africa, South and South-East Asia, and Latin America, while in East Asia, Central and Eastern Europe and more recently the advanced economies, there were negative gender gaps in unemployment rates (male unemployment rates higher than female rates). . . .
- The crisis appears to have worsened gender gaps in unemployment across all regions, regardless of whether they were on the front lines of the crisis like the advanced economies, or a degree removed like Asia and Africa. . . .

GENDER GAPS IN EMPLOYMENT

- The global gender gap in the employment-to-population ratio, between 2002 and 2007 inched down, but remained high at 24.6 points. The reduction in the gap from 2002 to 2007 was particularly strong in Latin America and the Caribbean, the advanced economies, Africa and the Middle East. The pre-crisis gap increased significantly in only one region, Central and Eastern Europe. This pre-crisis reduction of the gender gap in the employment-to-population ratio was based on historically higher employment growth rates for women of 1.8 percent, compared to men at 1.6 percent, from a low base for women. Again this held for all regions.
- However, the period of the crisis saw a reversal in the historically higher employment growth rates for women, lowering them below those for men by 0.1 percentage points, and with no projected return to the earlier trend even by 2017.

GENDER GAPS IN LABOUR FORCE PARTICIPATION

- The gender gap in the labour force participation rate decreased globally in the 1990s from 27.9 to 26.1 percentage points, with men's rates falling faster than women's, in all regions. However, in the last decade, between 2002 and 2012, this gap remained constant, with both men's and women's participation rates falling equally. Three broad reasons cited for the fall in participation rates are, most importantly education for younger age cohorts, aging, and a "discouraged worker" effect.
  . . .
- The labour force participation gap for women was driven by two contrasting developments. As women have become more and more educated, in particular in developing countries, their participation rates tended to increase thus allowing them to reap the full benefits of their higher productivity and capacity to generate income. At the same time, the higher education levels for adult women came at the expense of longer stays in the education system for younger female cohorts. This tended to decrease the labour force participation rates for young women, which—depending on the relative size of the youth cohort—even decreased the overall female participation rates in some regions.

GENDER GAPS IN VULNERABILITY

- Women also suffer from a difference in the quality of employment in comparison to men. Vulnerable employment, which comprises contributing family workers and own account workers (as opposed to wage and salaried workers), is more widespread for women than for men. In 2012, there was a global gender gap of 2.3 percentage points, with a larger share of women in vulnerable employment (50.4 per cent of employed women, compared to 48.1 percent of men).
- Regional vulnerability gaps varied, with North Africa at 24 percentage points, the Middle East and Sub-Saharan Africa at 15 points, and the Asian regions lying between zero and 10 percentage points. Only in the advanced economies, Central and Eastern Europe, and Latin America and the Caribbean, were a smaller share of women in vulnerable employment as compared to men.

(continued)

Within the category of the vulnerable, a larger share of men are own account workers, while a larger share of women are contributing family workers. The higher share of women in contributing family labour overrode the higher share of men in own account work, resulting in the gender gap in vulnerability.

GENDER GAPS IN SECTORAL SEGREGATION

- Women are more limited in their choices for employment across sectors. This sectoral segregation increased over time, with women moving out of agriculture in developing economies and out of industry in developed economies, and into services.
- In 2012, at the global level, a third of women were employed in agriculture, near half in services, and a sixth in industry. Women's industrial share only slightly rose over the last two decades as most women are moving out of agriculture and directly into services.
- In advanced economies, women's employment in industry halved, crowding more than 85 percent of them into services, primarily in education and health.

  . . .

GENDER GAPS IN OCCUPATIONAL SEGREGATION

- Occupational segregation has been pervasive over time, with some evidence of a decline in the gap in the previous decade, and a stalling in this convergence in the past decade. For a sample of both advanced and developing countries, men were over-represented in crafts, trades, plant and machine operations, and managerial and legislative occupations. In contrast women were over-represented in mid-skill occupations, like clerks, service workers, and shop and sales workers.
- The initial impact of the crisis, in the advanced economies, seemed to have affected men in trade-dependent sectors more than women in health and education. Conversely women were strongly hit in developing economies, in tradable sectors.

POLICIES TO ADDRESS GENDER GAPS

- As regards general policies, there is the need to expand social protection measures to reduce women's vulnerability, the need to invest in their skills and education, and policies to promote access to employment across the spectrum of sectors and occupations. In addition, these six policy guidelines focus on creating the right conditions to help households reduce the gender bias in their work decisions:

  (a) Reducing the burden of house work through better infrastructure— principally electricity, water, sanitation, mobility and school access

  (b) Reducing the burden of unpaid care work through provision of care services—child care (and in some demographic contexts, care for elderly) being especially correlated to women's participation in the labour force

> (c) Balancing the gender division of paid and unpaid work—mainly being programs to increase fathers' share of parenting
>
> (d) Changing the costs and benefits of gender specialisation—principally taxes and transfers to encourage dual earner families
>
> (e) Compensating for unequal employment opportunities based on gender—principally compensating for the adverse impact of career breaks through paid leave and right of return to post
>
> (f) Public campaigns to challenge gender stereotypes, and for proper implementation of legislation against discrimination.
>
> Source: *http://www.ilo.org/wcmsp5/groups/public—dgreports/—dcomm/documents/publication/wcms_195447.pdf.*

lower rates of depression, among women who work outside the home. Wives' employment also lowers couples' risk of divorce in the United States, unless wives are compelled to work outside the home out of economic necessity and against their wishes, in which case they have the least happy marriages. An interesting finding is that although employed mothers today spend less time with their children than homemakers, the former still spend more time with their children than stay-at-home mothers did in 1965. This reflects the increasing child-focused aspect of contemporary families. A key point made by Coontz is that this kind of labor force participation by parents requires affordable, accessible, and good-quality childcare. The United States is unique among developed countries in leaving daycare almost entirely to the private market and takes last place among developed nations for support of working families. Many families spend a substantial portion of monthly income on childcare. In addition, women are more likely to work part time than men are (25 percent compared to 11 percent) because of their caretaking responsibilities. Because unemployment, retirement, and other benefits are contingent on full-time work, women, for example, receive lower Social Security checks than men. This is because worker benefits are calculated on their 35 highest-earning years and women lose an average of 12 years out of the paid labor force. Scholars emphasize that these caregiving years should be taken out of the equation or given a monetary value.

Given the large number of women working in the labor force, what kinds of work are they doing? The answer is everything. Women are doing all kinds of work and can be found in all segments of the labor force. At the same time, however, women are much more likely to be found in some sectors than others and are crowded into a smaller number of fields than are men, many of which are characterized as secondary sector jobs in the dual labor market. One aspect of segregating women and men into different jobs is *horizontal segregation* (meaning segregation of women and men across different kinds of jobs). These jobs held by women are often called "pink-collar" and tend to reflect extensions of reproductive labor or unpaid work in the home. The horizontal segregation of women into "feminine" occupations (especially working with people, the aged, and the young, replicating unpaid labor in the home) that are valued less than "masculine" occupations (such as working with technology or machines) in part explains the gender gap in wages (discussed next).

As reported in the nearby table on occupations of employed women compiled by the U.S. Department of Labor with most recent data available, such horizontal segregation

20 Leading Occupations of Employed Women, 2010 Annual Averages
(employment in thousands)

Occupation	Percent Women	Women's Median Weekly Earnings
Total, 16 years and older (all employed women)	47.2%	$669
Secretaries and administrative assistants	96.1	657
Registered nurses	91.1	1,039
Elementary and middle school teachers	81.8	931
Cashiers	73.7	366
Retail salespersons	51.9	421
Nursing, psychiatric, and home health aides	88.2	427
Waiters and waitresses	71.1	381
First-line supervisors/managers of retail sales workers	43.9	578
Customer service representatives	66.6	586
Maids and housekeeping cleaners	89.0	376
Receptionists and information clerks	92.7	529
Childcare workers	94.7	398
Bookkeeping, accounting, and auditing clerks	90.9	628
First-line supervisors/managers of office and administrative support	68.7	726
Managers, all others	35.0	1,045
Accountants and auditors	60.1	953
Teacher assistants	92.4	485
Personal and home care aides	86.1	405
Office clerks, general	84.2	597
Cooks	40.5	381

Source: U.S. Department of Labor, Bureau of Labor Statistics, Annual Averages 2010.

reveals almost 96 percent of secretaries and administrative assistants, 91 percent of registered nurses, and almost 95 percent of childcare workers are women. Females congregate in clerical, retail, sales, and various service-sector jobs. In comparison, U.S. statistics show that only 1 in 7 engineers is female, between 2 and 5 percent of working women are employed in occupations associated with precision production, craft, and repair, and less than 2 percent of electricians are women. These "masculine" occupations tend to be valued more than "feminine" occupations and pay more money independent of who actually performs the work. Despite these traditional patterns, women's presence in certain once-male-dominated professions has increased. As we discuss later, in 1970, 9 percent of practicing physicians were female, compared with about 30 percent in 2013. Numbers are also increasing in dentistry. About a fifth of all dentists are women and they make up

Selected Nontraditional Occupations of Employed Women in 2010
(Numbers in thousands)

Occupation	Total Employed (Both Sexes)	Total Employed Women	Percent Female
Sales representatives, wholesale and manufacturing	1,284	321	25.0
Farmers and ranchers	713	175.4	24.6
Detectives and criminal investigators	159	36.2	22.8
Computer programmers	470	103.4	22
Butchers and other meat, poultry, and fish processing workers	331	70.2	21.2
Dishwashers	246	51.9	21.1
Computer software engineers	1,026	214.4	20.9
Chiropractors	57	11.5	20.2
Industrial engineers	159	31.8	20
Chefs and head cooks	337	64	19
Farm, ranch, and other agricultural managers	237	42.9	18.1
Announcers	52	9.4	18
Barbers	96	17.2	17.9
Grounds maintenance workers	1,195	69.3	5.8
Baggage porters, bellhops, and concierges	77	13.8	17.9
Clergy	429	75.1	17.5
Chemical engineers	50	8.6	17.3
Network and computer systems administrators	229	37.8	16.5
First-line supervisors/managers of police and detectives	103	15.9	15.4
Taxi drivers and chauffeurs	390	56.2	14.4
Service station attendants	77	10.4	13.5
Police and sheriff's patrol officers	714	92.8	13
Engineers, all other	334	43.1	12.9
Aerospace engineers	126	13.6	10.8
Computer hardware engineers	70	7.2	10.3
Broadcast and sound engineering technicians & radio operators	102	10.1	9.9
Civil engineers	318	30.8	9.7
Engineering managers	113	8.7	7.7
Electrical and electronic engineers	307	22.1	7.2
Television, video, and motion picture camera operators and editors & radio operators	54	3.9	7.2
Construction managers	1,083	73.6	6.8
Mechanical engineers	293	19.6	6.7
Railroad conductors and yardmasters	58	3.8	6.5

(continued)

Electronic home entertainment equipment installers and repairers	52	3.1	6
Aircraft pilots and flight engineers	110	5.7	5.2
Drivers/sales workers and truck drivers	3,028	139.3	4.6
Firefighters	301	10.8	3.6
Highway maintenance workers	110	2.7	2.5
Locomotive engineers and operators	57	1.5	2.6
Aircraft mechanics and service technicians	136	3.1	2.3
Electricians	691	10.4	1.5
Pipe layers, plumbers, pipe fitters, and steam fitters	526	7.9	1.5
Carpenters	1,242	17.4	1.4
Automotive body and related repairers	168	2	1.2
Logging workers	63	0.7	1.1
Roofers	214	2.1	1
Carpet, floor, and tile installers and finishers	209	1	0.5
Electrical power line installers and repairers	124	0.5	0.4
Bricklayers, block masons, and stone masons	162	0.2	0.1

Source: U.S. Department of Labor, Bureau of Labor Statistics, Annual Averages 2010. Women's Bureau August 2010

approximately 45 percent of the dental school students in 2013. Women attorneys make up about a third of all practicing attorneys, and approximately half of all law students. Similarly, female pharmacists also increased from 30 percent in 1985 to more than half of the profession in 2013.

One of the most female-segregated jobs is sex work such as prostitution, where women workers have often struggled to control the conditions of their work against the demoralization and abuse by customers, pimps, and police. The reading "Sex Work as a Test Case for African Feminism" by Marlise Richter focuses on this issue through the lens of sex-positive feminism. She discusses prostitution, the legalities surrounding it, and the history and current issues associated with the relationship between feminism, the women's movement, and prostitution, focusing specifically on the consequences of the decriminalization of sex work practices on sex workers themselves. She points out that the issue of sex worker rights is conspicuously absent among African feminism in particular, despite the prevalence of high rates of HIV among African sex workers. In particular, this reading explores escalation of punitive prostitution policies and growing sex workers' rights movements worldwide.

The term *blue collar* implies working class or involved with industrial, production, and factory work and can be contrasted with *white collar,* which means office or professional work and usually refers to middle-class occupations. Note the slippage between industrial work and male-segregated work such that blue collar means working class but also implies male-segregated work with its use of the word *blue* as opposed to *pink.* The Bureau of Labor Statistics reports the following occupations as the most

ACTIVIST PROFILE **Dolores Huerta**

Dolores Huerta is one of the most powerful and influential labor leaders in the United States. Born in Dawson, New Mexico, in 1930, Huerta grew up in Stockton, California, and eventually earned a teaching certificate from Stockton College. After one year of teaching, however, she quit to work with Community Service Organization (CSO). She thought she could do more to help the hungry children she saw at school by helping organize their farmworker parents.

While with CSO, she met César Chavez, and in 1962 they founded the United Farm Workers of America (UFW). Although Chavez was more comfortable in the fields organizing workers, Huerta became the voice of the union, becoming the first woman and first Chicana negotiator in labor history. The UFW met with great success in the 1965 Delano Grape Strike, which won the first collective bargaining agreement for farmworkers, and Huerta was instrumental in the negotiations. She also became consciously involved with the feminist movement when she met Gloria Steinem in 1968, although she had always focused on issues specific to women farmworkers.

In 1972 she co-chaired the California delegation to the Democratic Convention, and she led the struggle for unemployment insurance, collective bargaining rights, and immigration rights for farmworkers under the 1985 amnesty legalization program. She was the first Latina inducted into the National Women's Hall of Fame, and she received the National Organization for Women's Woman of Courage Award and the American Civil Liberties Union's Bill of Rights Award. She continues to struggle for farmworkers through the UFW and serve as a role model for Chicanas in their fight against discrimination.

male segregated: engineers, mechanics and drivers, carpenters and construction trades, firefighters, airline pilots and navigators, and forestry and logging work. You will note the obvious ways feminine jobs involve working with people, children, cleaning, and administrative support, whereas masculine employment tends to involve working with machines and inanimate objects. There are other differences too, such as that wages for the heavily male-segregated jobs tend to be higher than wages for the female-segregated, pink-collar work. That is because, as already mentioned, these jobs are valued more. Finally, unionized women workers earned about 25 percent more than nonunion women workers and received better health and pension benefits: Union membership narrows the gender wage gap. However, currently only about 11 percent of employed women in the United States are union members.

LEARNING ACTIVITY   **Working Women and Unions**

Visit the web page of the AFL-CIO at *www.aflcio.org* to learn more about women in the workforce. What are some of the key issues for working women identified by the AFL-CIO? What legislative issues does the AFL-CIO identify that would be beneficial to working women? What is a union? What benefits do unions provide? Why are unions important for working women? What steps would people take to form a union at their workplace?

Another important aspect of occupational segregation by gender is that there is gender segregation even within the same job type. This is termed *vertical segregation* (segregation *within* jobs), and, like horizontal segregation, it functions as a result of sexism and racism and other systems of inequality and privilege. For example, although the number of women physicians is increasing as already mentioned, women are still overwhelmingly found in certain specialties such as pediatrics, dermatology, and public health work, and are less likely to be found in surgical specialties, orthopedics, and more entrepreneurial positions. And, while women's presence has increased dramatically in some specialties, in 1970 only 5 percent of doctors in obstetrics and gynecology were female; by 2013 this number had risen to about 80 percent of obstetricians and 57 percent of pediatricians who are female (and these numbers increase if data include physician residents in training). Changes have occurred more slowly in other specialties where only about 7 percent of orthopedic surgeons were women in 2013. Observers note that the growing proportion of U.S. physicians in patient care who are female (currently about 30 percent of all physicians, although in 2013 they made up almost half of all first-year medical students) is improving the quality of medicine through more emotionally focused and patient-centered practice. The influx of women, however, is lowering physicians' average salaries overall. Female physicians on the average earn about a third less than male physicians, mostly because they enter the different specialties discussed above.

Similarly, female lawyers are less likely to be in criminal law and are more likely to practice family law and make about 80 percent of male lawyers' salaries. Male teachers are more likely to teach sciences and are more likely to be with older children; female professors are more typically in the humanities and the social sciences and found in smaller number in the physical and applied sciences and technical fields. Usually specialties and fields that men occupy are more prestigious and the salaries are higher. In this way, women and men do not just tend to perform different jobs, but the jobs that they do are valued differently and have different levels of status and power and bring different problems associated with integration and advancement. This differential is related to sexism in society generally as well as to other systems of inequality and privilege. Not surprisingly, when you look at women in these professions such as law, pharmacy, human and animal medicine, and dentistry, overwhelmingly men are more likely to own their own practices and run their own businesses. Women of color are the most underrepresented among these more entrepreneurial professionals. The reasons for this are largely economic as owning your own business takes wealth and capital.

Barriers to advancement in the labor force (what is often called the *glass ceiling*) have been challenged by individuals, the courts, and by the organized women's movement. And, although these barriers are beginning to come down, they are still holding strong in many areas. Women tend not to be promoted at the same rate as men and they also continue to face obstacles when trying to enter the most prestigious and best-paid occupations. Normative gendered and racialized social discourses about women's place come into play in these public arenas, often in very unconscious ways as well as through institutionalized practices that systematically provide obstacles for certain individuals. As the reading "The Sexist Truth About Office Romances" by Peggy Drexler suggests, there is a double standard of attitudes and expectations by gender at play in many occupational settings in the United States. Drexler emphasizes that while 4 out of 10 employees have dated someone from work, women are judged differently than men by both women and men. More negative judgments are directed against women, and it is often assumed that women are motivated by a desire to get ahead in their job.

Although U.S. women have made advancements in moving into middle-management business positions, data from 2013 show women's relative absence in top leadership positions. Only 20 (or 4 percent) of Fortune 500 companies have women CEOs (chief executive officer) or presidents and only 8 of these are actually in the top Fortune 100. Of the 20 high-earning executives (women still held only 8% of the highest-earning slots), only 3 are women of color. Women make up about 17 percent of Fortune 500 boards of directors, and this drops to just over 3 percent for women of color. Indeed, two thirds of all companies had no women of color on their board of directors at all. In addition, although women make up more than 60 percent of the nonprofit workforce (as opposed to the business for-profit workplace), they still lack access to top management positions, share of foundation dollars,

The Glass-Ceiling Index

If you are a working woman, you would do well to move to New Zealand—or if that is a little out of the way, you could try one of the Nordic countries. To mark International Women's Day, *The Economist* has compiled its own "glass-ceiling index" to show where women have the best chance of equal treatment at work. Based on data mainly from the OECD, it compares five indicators across 26 countries: the number of men and women respectively with tertiary education; female labour-force participation; the male-female wage gap; the proportion of women in senior jobs; and net child-care costs relative to the average wage. The first four are given equal weighting, the fifth a lower one, since not all working women have children. New Zealand scores high on all the indicators. Finland does best on education; Sweden has the highest female labour-force participation rate, at 78%; and Spain has the smallest wage gap, at 6%. The places not to be are South Korea and Japan, partly because so few women hold down senior jobs (though the new president of South Korea is a woman).

Economist.com

"Whatever happened to a good cry in the Ladies Room?"

Reprinted with permission from Carol Simpson Labor Cartoons.

and board positions. Women of color are relatively absent in the higher echelons of corporate power in all sectors. The reading "Power Plays" by Martha Burk explains six ways the corporate elite keeps women down and emphasizes power dynamics in the corporate world that continue to maintain the status quo.

Alongside consideration of the problems associated with the glass ceiling, it is important to recognize what researchers have called the *glass escalator* and the *glass precipice.* The glass escalator refers to the practices whereby men who go into traditionally female-dominated professions such as teaching, nursing, and social work are disproportionately advanced into management and administrative positions where they receive more prestige, pay, and power than women. The glass precipice is the process whereby women are encouraged into leadership positions in failing organizations and companies and are disproportionately set up to fail professionally.

Finally, it is interesting to look at how the development of certain occupations as female segregated has affected the status and conditions of work. For example, clerical work, although low prestige, was definitely a man's job until the turn of the twentieth century, when women quickly became associated with this work. This was due to the following factors: There was a large pool of women with few other opportunities; clerical work's low status made it easier for women to be accepted; typewriter manufacturers began promoting the typewriter as something women used; and the personal service aspect of the work fit gender norms about the feminine aspect of secretarial work. As more women entered this profession, the gap between clerical wages and blue-collar wages generally increased, and the status of the clerical profession fell. A more recent example is the field of pharmacology. Two trends—the increasing number of pharmacies attached to chain drugstores and the increasing number of female pharmacists—have been seen as the reasons why the status of pharmacology has fallen as a profession. It remains to be seen whether the increase of women in human and animal medicine, and in the sciences generally, will decrease the status of these professions.

To "Lean In" or Not to "Lean In"?

Jessica Valenti

Sheryl Sandberg's *Lean In*—a book advising women to embrace ambition—has been released to a backlash. . . .

Sandberg has been called out of touch, her book a "vanity project." She's been slammed as being too interested in building her brand and for advising women on work and family issues while having the temerity to employ a nanny.

What's remarkable about these criticisms is that they're not coming from the usual right-wing antifeminists, but from feminists themselves.

The feminist backlash against Sandberg, Facebook's chief operating officer and a former vice president at Google, reveals a big and recurring problem within the movement: We hold leaders to impossible standards, placing perfection over progress. And a movement that does more complaining than creating is bound to fail.

There are certainly substantive critiques to be made about Sandberg's book. *Lean In* is mostly tailored for married women with children and may not resonate with women who aren't upper-middle-class or elite, something Sandberg acknowledges up front: "The vast majority of women are not looking to lead in the workplace, but are struggling to make ends meet and take care of their families."

Critics have also knocked Sandberg for putting the onus on women to lift themselves up, rather than blaming society for being sexist. But in her book, she frequently identifies how internal and external forces keep women from advancing in their careers. She also supports structural change, citing economic inequalities, discrimination, and the lack of paid maternity leave and affordable child care as problems that need to be addressed.

And yet, swift and biting attacks have become the default for feminist discourse, so much so that writers at *Forbes,* at the *New Republic* and in *The Washington Post* didn't even read "Lean In" before writing about its presumed flaws. (Yes, Sandberg's TED Talk that inspired the book has been widely watched and publicized, but eagerness to get shots in shouldn't be more important than doing your homework.)

In this kind of culture, the snarkiest takedown wins. *New York Times* columnist Maureen Dowd has called Sandberg a "PowerPoint Pied Piper in Prada ankle boots." In *USA Today,* Joanne Bamberger wrote that Sandberg wants women to "pull themselves up by the Louboutin straps." (Sandberg does not discuss fashion or her shoe choices in the book.) Sandberg's foray into workplace inequities has been framed as a catfight between herself and Anne-Marie Slaughter, of the blockbuster *Atlantic* article "Why Women Can't Have It All." Melissa Gira Granteven implied in *The Post* that Sandberg wrote *Lean In* because of sheer selfishness: "She had it all—a husband, children, a beautiful home, a seat on the board of a billion-dollar company, a nine-figure net worth of her own. But there was one thing Sheryl Sandberg didn't have." Because if there's anything wealthy women are desperate for, it's the chance to lead a social movement.

The detractors underestimate how radical Sandberg's messages are for a mainstream audience. When was the last time you heard someone with a platform as big as hers argue that women should insist that their partners do an equal share of domestic work and child care?

(continued)

The view that Sandberg is too rich and powerful to advise working women is shortsighted; it assumes that any sort of success is antithetical to feminism. The truth is, feminism could use a powerful ally. Here's a nationally known woman calling herself a feminist, writing what will be a wildly popular book with feminist ideas, encouraging other women to be feminists. And we're worried she has too much influence? That she's too ... ambitious?

. . .

It's clear that when Sandberg sat down to write *Lean In,* she expected some of this resistance. In her introduction, she acknowledges that "it is much easier for me to lean in since my financial resources allow me to afford any help I need."

That's true. Few of us host dinners for Nobel Prize winners or count former Treasury secretaries among our mentors. But just because most women can't relate to Sandberg's life doesn't mean we can't learn from it. In fact, her achievements may make her a perfect feminist spokesperson. Sandberg's power as an evangelist and organizer of American elites is profound. Like it or not, a social justice movement needs power behind it—on the ground and from the boardroom.

Part of the hesitance to embrace powerful women is embedded in feminism itself, says Buzzfeed's Anna North. "Feminism is a movement founded on women's status as a marginalized group," North writes, "and as a woman moves closer to the centers of corporate or government power, she can come to seem like, for lack of a better word, the Man."

But shunning anything that has roots in powerful places or powerful people is a mistake. Will Sandberg's book or work speak to all women? No. But the last thing the feminist movement needs is a leader who universalizes women's experiences—this has been part of the problem with feminism in the past. No one woman can speak to the diversity and nuance of all women's lives. Instead of focusing on what Sandberg's book doesn't do, we should be thinking about what it could do.

. . .

Sandberg is providing feminists with an incredible opportunity to add to her ideas about women, work and ambition. Do we really want to discard it in favor of unproductive ideological one-upmanship?

I found it fitting that, toward the end of *Lean In,* Sandberg addresses how women cutting each other down can undercut our progress as individuals and as a movement.

"Every social movement struggles with dissension among its ranks, in part because advocates are passionate and unlikely to agree on every position and solution. There are so many of us who care deeply about these matters. We should strive to resolve our differences quickly, and when we disagree, stay focused on our shared goals. This is not a plea for less debate, but for more constructive debate."

I second that emotion.

Learning Activity: Read Sheryl Sandberg's book as well as feminist blogs and articles supporting and critiquing it. Then make your case: Is her book good for feminism and women or not?

Source: http://www.washingtonpost.com/opinions/dear-fellow-feminists-ripping-apart-sheryl-sandbergs-book-is-counterproductive/2013/03/01/fc71b984-81c0-11e2-a350-49866afab584_story.html.

Wages and Comparable Worth

The most disparate wage gap in the United States is that between those who head corporations and those who work for corporations. In 2014 the average CEO pay (around $12 million/year) was more than 200 times that of the average compensation of full-time, year-round workers in nonmanagerial jobs, not including the value of many perks CEOs receive, nor their pension benefits. A report from the Institute of Policy Studies emphasizes that this gap increases to 364 times when the top 20 U.S. companies are used (average CEO salary rises to approximately $36.4 million/year) and the average salary for all workers is employed (average salary falls to about $30,000/year). Such CEO compensation far exceeds leaders in other fields and in other countries. Top managers in the United States made three times more than those in similar European companies, even though the Europeans tended to have higher sales numbers than their U.S. counterparts. It is important to keep in mind that, as already discussed, only about 4 percent, or 20, of the top 500 U.S. companies are led by women, and almost all of these women are white.

The *gender wage gap* is an index of the status of women's earnings relative to men's and is expressed as a percentage and is calculated by dividing the median annual earnings for women by the median annual earnings for men. These data include only full-time, year-round workers and exclude all part-time or seasonal workers. Because a large number of women work part-time jobs, the inclusion of these would lower the numbers discussed below because part-time work tends to be lower paid and these workers receive fewer job-related benefits and are less likely to be unionized. According to 2010 data from the U.S. Bureau of Labor Statistics, the most current on record for women's median annual earnings, the gender wage gap or ratio of women's and men's median annual earnings was 77 percent for full-time, year-round workers. This means that for every dollar a man earns, a woman earns 77 cents. An alternative measure of the wage gap, the ratio of women's to men's median weekly earnings for full-time workers, was 82 percent in 2011. The difference between these two measures is that the former, which measures median annual earnings for full-time year-round workers, includes self-employed workers and excludes seasonal workers. The weekly measure excludes self-employed and includes seasonal workers. The figures are based on the same raw Bureau of Labor Statistics data. A 2013 report from the Institute for Women's Policy Research suggests that the progress in closing the gender wage gap has stalled—and actually backslid during 2012. They report a median weekly full-time earnings gender ratio of 81 and explain that this ratio declined one percentage point from 2011 figures.

Women of color, of course, earn less than this monolithic "woman," as do older women generally. African American women earn just 67.5 percent of all men's earnings and 62 percent of white men's annual median earnings. Similarly, Latinas earn 58 percent of all men's and 53 percent of white men's annual median income. Asian American women fare better with 90 percent of all men's and 82 percent of white men's annual median income. Figures from U.S. women's weekly earnings data in 2012 also show Asian American women who worked full-time with higher earnings than women of all other races and ethnicities, including white women. For example, Asian American women earned about $751 a week, white women $703, African American women $595, and Latinas $518. No data were available for American Indian women workers.

Women now earn the majority of college degrees and currently 37 percent of all employed women have a college degree, compared to only 11 percent in 1970. Now only approximately 7 percent have less than a high school diploma, compared to 34 percent of employed women in 1970. This education improves women's earnings as female full-time wage and salary workers aged 25 and older with only a high-school diploma had median weekly earnings of about $554 (men's median weekly earnings with the same educational attainment was $720). This represented 81 percent of the earnings for women with an associate's degree ($682) and 56 percent of those for women with a bachelor's degree or higher ($998). Women with Ph.D.s earned an approximate weekly salary of $1,371 compared to men with the same educational attainment at $1,734. In this way, despite the important gains for women as a result of education, the returns on this training are still lower for women than for men. Overall median annual earnings of female high-school graduates are about 34 percent less, women with bachelor's degrees and graduate degrees about 32 percent less, and women with a doctoral degree 29 percent less than their male counterparts. The main reason is that women and men choose different education and training that prepare them for different kinds of jobs (discussed in more detail below).

Since the Equal Pay Act was signed in 1963, the gender wage gap has been closing at a very slow rate. In 1963, women who worked full-time, year-round made 59 cents on average for every dollar earned by men. This means that the wage gap has narrowed by less than half a cent per year. If working women earned the same as men (those who work the same number of hours; have the same education, age, and union status; and live in the same region of the country), their annual family incomes would rise by more than $4,000 and poverty rates would be cut in half. The Institute for Policy Research reports that over a lifetime of work, the average 25-year-old woman who works full-time, year-round, until she retires at age 65 years will earn on the average almost a half million dollars less than the average working man. Currently about 15 percent of men and 5 percent of women earn $75,000 or more a year, whereas about a fifth of men and a tenth of women earn between $50,000 and $75,000 a year. Raising of the minimum wage would help all people and support many families whose members are employed, but still live in poverty.

So why do women earn less money than men on the average? The gender wage gap is explained by several factors. *First*, it is explained by the horizontal segregation of the labor force: Women and men tend to work in different kinds of jobs and the jobs women hold are valued and rewarded less. Such differences are not covered by the Equal Pay Act because women and men are engaged in different kinds of work. Indeed, when you compare similarly qualified and positioned men and women in the same occupation, the gender gap drops considerably, to about 4 percent, for example, in the case of computer engineers, and to 2 percent in the case of registered nurses, and only 1 percent in the case of elementary school teachers. In other words, whether you identify as a woman or a man, if you go into elementary teaching in the United States, your wages will be equally relatively low (although there are still differences: see vertical segregation below) compared to work in technology and engineering where both women and men will have relatively higher wages. The reality, of course, is that many more women go into elementary education than men (82 percent are women) and more men go into computer engineering than women (14 percent of engineers generally are women), hence the difference in median weekly or annual salaries by gender. In addition, the jobs that women tend to go into experience differential wage growth over a life cycle compared to those that men tend to enter (about 62 percent salary growth for computer engineers compared to 32 percent growth for registered nurses).

Second, the gap is explained by vertical segregation, or the ways women and men are in different specialties within the same occupation. Currently it is estimated that women tend to earn less than men in 99 percent of all occupations. Indeed, comparable wages

Studies show that women with "sexy" names like DAWN AND CHERYL ARE...

Less likely to be promoted to managerial jobs than women with names like...

BILL OR ROGER.

are a problem in every occupational category, even in occupations in which women considerably outnumber men. Women in professional and related occupations—sales and office occupations, for example—earned about a quarter less than their male counterparts. Female elementary and middle school teachers and registered nurses earned about 10 percent less than similarly employed men, despite comprising the majority of the field, and, as already noted, female physicians and attorneys earn less than male counterparts. This vertical segregation implies that women and other marginalized workers are in specialties or have work assignments within these professions that are less valued and rewarded than more "masculine" specialties and work assignments.

Finally, the gender pay gap is explained by overt and covert discrimination against women and other marginalized workers. After economists control for "human capital" variables (such as time spent in work, education, seniority, time since receipt of degree, prestige of institution awarding degree, etc.), there is still a proportion of unexplained variance between the wages of men and women in the same specialties or work assignments and within the same occupational category. Social discourses about gender, race, age, and social class work to create patterns of institutionalized inequalities that reinforce ideas concerning certain people's worth and the kinds of work those individuals should do.

Comparable worth, also known as pay equity, is one means to pay women and men in different occupations comparably. Basically, comparable worth works to compare different jobs on experience, skill, training, and job conditions and assigns relative points on these indices in order to determine their worth. There is no federal-level comparable worth legislation, although many states have enacted laws demanding comparable worth comparisons in determining pay for state workers. In addition, the courts have ruled both for and against workers who have brought comparable worth suits against various corporations. When the courts have ruled in favor of plaintiffs, it has often meant a considerable amount of money in back pay to compensate female workers for years of financial inequities.

In this way inequality in women's work lives has important consequences for inequality in other spheres of life. Because most women work both inside and outside the home and spend a considerable part of their lives working, it is of central importance to understand the conditions under which women work as well as to strive for equality in the workplace.

Will Marriage Equality Lead to Equal Sharing of Housework?

Terrance Heath (2013)

My mom turned to me one day and said something I've never forgotten since. I was in my teens, and was probably complaining about some chore that she wanted me to do, when she said to me, "There is no excuse for a young man in your generation not to know how to cook his own meals, wash his own clothes, and clean his own house. And before you leave this house, you *will* know how to do at least that much."

She meant it, and I did learn. My sister and I took turns doing *the exact same chores*. Today, I can cook, clean, and kiss boo-boos with the best of 'em. But apparently, many men from my generation on down can't, or just don't.

It's something I've written about before: even in the most progressive families, the lion's share of housework and childcare still falls to women.

Women spend a greater number of hours doing household and caregiving duties, which decreases the number of hours they can work for pay. Even for full-time workers, men worked on average 8.3 hours per day while women worked 7.8 hours per day in 2011.

The differences in the daily activities that men and women perform are captured by the U.S. Bureau of Labor Statistics' American Time Use Survey. The survey has 12 major categories of how we use our time, and women dominate eight of the 12 categories.

In 2011, the latest year available, we see the expected gender division in time use with women spending an average of two more hours per day than men doing the activities of personal care; household chores; purchasing goods and services; caring for and helping household and nonhousehold members; organizational, civic or religious activities; telephone calls, mail and email; and other activities not classified elsewhere in the survey.

How did men allocate their time? They spent an average of an additional 40 minutes per day on sports and leisure compared with women, four additional minutes on eating and drinking, two additional minutes on educational activities, and 1 hour and 16 minutes additional time working and performing work-related activities.

The two of the areas with the largest deficits for men were 47 fewer minutes per day on household activities and 22 fewer minutes on caring for and helping household and nonhousehold members.

I've got something that might help solve this problem: marriage equality. What's gay marriage got to do with this? What's the only thing that's keeping us defining housework as "woman's work"? As Anne York explains in the post quoted above: "It is only our cultural norm that is defining who does which task."

What's one of the top arguments against marriage equality? Opponents of marriage equality often define themselves as defenders of long-standing "cultural norms," because they know same-sex marriage undermines the cultural norm that keeps the gender-based division of labor in the home.

The threat of legal same-sex marriage, then, is actually doubled. It carries one step further the progress that's lead to women no longer having to "submit to their husbands"; they might *volunteer*, a'la the "surrendered wife" model, but not many women *have* to marry and thus "submit to their husbands" as a necessity for survival. Social progress changed the status of women, and the same people who oppose same-sex marriage would like to undo that progress to whatever degree they can. Legal same-sex marriage further cements those social changes, and makes it even harder to turn back the clock.

It's no coincidence that the political forces opposed to same-sex marriage or marriage equality also oppose gender equality and advocate returning to more strictly enforced gender roles. The Institute for Progressive Christianity recently published a paper titled "The Kingdom of God and the Witness of Gay Marriage," which includes among its premises:

Gay marriages demonstrate the possibility and desirability of gender equality in any marriage by modeling a relationship where the parties to the marriage do not distribute roles and responsibilities based on gender. This modeling supports the positive transformation of the curse of gender conflict, and subsequent patriarchal domination pronounced at the Fall from Paradise into gender egalitarianism.

Gay marriage's ascendancy and resilience in society participates in a fundamental shift of the culture's understanding of marriage. **That is, marriage is being transformed from a utilitarian arraignment grounded in the idea that women are sexual property to an egalitarian life journey with a partner who one chooses to develop and share mutual love, affection, respect, and support.**

. . . One of the most obvious issues to which gay marriage speaks is gender equality. One of the strongest and most relied upon objections to gay marriage from the Right is that it violates the concept of gender complementarity. Gender complementarity is the metaphysical claim that men's and women's social functions in the world are determined dichotomously by their biological sex, such that where men are convex women are concave.

. . . **Undergirding the concept of gender complementarity is the assumption that men are metaphysically meant to rule over women (ideally in the spirit of love, of course) and women are metaphysically meant to serve men[.]**

. . . Thus, from the gender complementarian perspective, those who act as though women and men gain equal spiritual, emotional, psychological, and existential satisfaction and dignity from leading and serving, and are meant to experience both of these sides of the human psyche, are disordered, as those who advocate this notion of equality and balance.

The possibility of gay marriage invites heterosexuals to view their intimate partners (or potential intimate partners) not through a lens of gendered otherness primarily—that is through the lens of gender complementarity—but through the lens of sameness, that is through the lens of sharing a common human dignity, as it was in the beginning.

As much as it may seem like a tangent, the above both reinforces the relationship between sexism and homophobia, and places gay & lesbian equality in general and marriage equality specifically in the context of earlier progressive social movements, all of which—from the abolitionist movement, to women's suffrage to the civil rights movement—had strong foundations in moral principles; progressive moral principles like those Pitt referenced in his column.

It's a cultural norm that's both overtly and co-vertly reinforced. One of the ways it's reinforced (and the one I find most annoying) is the "incompetent father" or "bumbling dad" stereotype. While we've made some progress in changing that old stereotype, it's still ubiquitous in our media. It's been an advertising staple practically forever, and it's still around today.

Although he's clever at times, he's not usually allowed to be smart. He has no idea that Shortcuts Make Long Delays. He's lazy, gluttonous and has miscellaneous other glaring vices. His children may love him, but they often don't respect him. However, he is still a sympathetic character; the source of his charm is his complete love and loyalty to his family, even if the main way he shows it is by fixing problems he caused himself.

His family is made up of at least one child nearing or in their teenage years, and a wife (usually much prettier than Dad) who spends her time Parenting The Husband. If he has one or more teenage daughters, at least one will be a Bratty Teenage Daughter or a Daddy's Girl; whether they are or not, the dad will be an Overprotective Dad in regards to the girl(s).

Often used as an enabler of several Double Standards. Sometimes, on the rare occasions that a mom does something dumb, she's cut more slack than she otherwise would be, since the Bumbling Dad is there to make her look better by comparison. On the other hand, if everyone just gets used to tolerating Dad's incompetence, they might still hold Mom to the standards of a competent adult—in fact, she may end up being held responsible for fixing his screw-ups. After all, somebody's got to be the grownup in a family, and you can't hold Dad accountable for not acting like one if he's just an idiot. The frustrating and stagnant sexual roles enforced by this trope are often pointed to by feminists as a sign of how sexism hurts men as well as women.

This trope is still mostly seen in sitcoms and cartoons, along with many commercials, especially ones aimed at kids. In anime, this type of character is taken more respectfully, since it usually consists of a goofier dad, more involved with his family than the stereotypical Salaryman. This is even more common when his children have no visible mother.

As gay dads, we confront this cultural norm on a regular basis. We confront it when someone sees one of us out with the boys and comments that "It must be mom's day off." If our kids are infants, we confront it even from well-meaning people. I'll never forget the elderly woman who approached me at the mall when [P]arker was a baby. We were shopping, and Parker was fussy, so I took him out of the store while the hubby continued shopping. I sat down on a bench, reached in to the diaper back, made a bottle, took Parker out of the baby carriage, and gave it to him. I'd just finished burping him when this elderly woman came up to me and said with a smile, "I just wanted to tell you that you handle that baby just marvelously."

My Southern manners kicked in, and I simply said "Thank you, ma'am." But as she turned and went on her way, in the back of my mind I thought "Is there some reason I *shouldn't* be good at this?" Then I realized, she was from a generation in which she probably *never* saw a man—a father—doing something as simple as taking care of his child. Not unless the child's mother was sick or dead or something. No wonder she was impressed.

Imagine if she'd stuck around for the diaper change!

My mom was undermining "cultural norms" by insisting on raising me to do most household tasks myself. She may not have realized it then, but she was also undermining cultural norms when she justified my braiding the hair of of my sister's dolls by telling my dad (who expressed concern that I was braiding a doll's hair) that I might have a daughter of my own someday and I might have to know how to do her hair.

It's almost like my mom was thinking of *this* dad.

The point is my mom had probably confronted the same thing that the elderly woman in the mall had confronted: generations of men not only raised to know nothing about taking care of their own homes and their own children, but to believe that doing so wasn't in their job description. My mom decided she was going to raise at least one man who wouldn't be quite so entrenched in a gender-based division of labor.

It happens that in our home there is no gender-based division of labor. We share the housework evenly. And if there is a deciding factor in who does what, its not based on gender but on who prefers to do it, who's better at it, or who has the time and flexibility.

It's interesting, because in our house we don't have gender-based division of labor to fall back on. That doesn't mean we don't have disagreements about housework. But it's based more on personal traits than gender. (For example, as I tell the hubby, it's not that clutter *doesn't* bother me. It just bothers him sooner than it bothers me.) For the most part, who does what in our house depends on who's free, and who prefers to do it. (Gardening, for example, I cede to him. But, I usually clean the downstairs bathroom, etc.)

Sometimes, it's a matter of consideration. For example, I'm going to come home late tomorrow, which means the hubby will have the boys by himself tomorrow night. Thus, before I go to bed tonight, I'll probably load and run the dishwasher, and pick up the toys, shoes, etc., scattered around the family room. So at least he can come home to an empty sink and a relatively tidy house. (It makes a difference when you're parenting solo.)

But the article reminded me of something else. One of the reasons for the opposition to same-sex marriage is the potential of marriage equality to call gender roles more into question.

So, yeah. That's a "cultural norm" that we undermine on a daily basis. It also means that our sons are not growing up with a gender-based division of labor. They see two men cooking, cleaning, taking care of children, etc., and they will learn to do the same. And maybe their future spouses won't be stuck with the lion's share of housework.

To my heterosexual brethren, I say this. You, too, can help change this old, tired, "cultural norm." And you don't have to marry another dude to do it. You just have to pick up a mop more often, wash a few dishes, change your share of diapers, etc.

In other words, be an equal partner in your marriage and family.

R E A D I N G   **70**

A Brief History of Working Women

Sharlene Hesse-Biber and Gregg Lee Carter (1999)

WOMEN WORKERS IN PRE-INDUSTRIAL AMERICA

Seven hundred and fifty thousand Europeans came to America between 1600 and 1700. The bulk of them were from Britain, but the colonies also saw significant numbers from Holland, France, and Germany. Many came as indentured servants, exchanging their labor for the cost of passage to the American colonies. Indentured servants often worked from five to ten years to pay back their creditors. As early as the 1600s, prior to the slave trade, some Africans also came to the colonies as indentured servants; they often worked side by side with white indentured servants. Women's lives in this country differed drastically, depending on their race, class, and marital status.

White Women

European women usually arrived in the New World with their families, as daughters and wives, under the auspices of fathers or husbands. In the pre-industrial economy of the American colonial period (from the seventeenth century to the early eighteenth century), work was closely identified with home and family life. The family was the primary economic unit, and family members were dependent on one another for basic sustenance. Men performed the agricultural work, while women's work was done chiefly in the home, which was a center of production in colonial America. In addition to cooking, cleaning, and caring for children, women did spinning and weaving, and made lace, soap, candles, and shoes. Indeed, they manufactured nearly all articles used in daily life. This work was highly valued, and the colonies relied on the production of these "cottage industries."

Single women remained within the domestic sphere, living with relatives, often as "assistant homemakers." For married women, the nature of their work depended on the economic circumstances of their husbands:

> In cash-poor homes and among frontier families, women bore the burden of filling most of the family's basic needs. They worked to reduce cash expenditures by growing vegetables in the kitchen

garden and making the family's clothes, candles, soap and household furnishings. If a husband were a craftsman or the proprietor of a shop or tavern, his wife and children might also work in the business, in addition to all the other tasks. In contrast, the wife of a successful farmer, plantation owner, or merchant did little actual work; instead, she supervised household servants and slaves who purchased or made the goods the family needed, cooked the meals, and maintained the house.

The social codes of colonial America did not exclude a woman from working outside the home, and many did so. Colonial women engaged in a great range of occupations, and as old documents are discovered and new histories of women's work are written, that range appears greater still. Women were innkeepers, shopkeepers, crafts workers, nurses, printers, teachers, and landholders. In the city of Boston during 1690, for example, women ran approximately 40 percent of all taverns. During that year, city officials also granted more than thirty women the right to saw lumber and manufacture potash. Women acted as physicians and midwives in all the early settlements, producing medicines, salves, and ointments. Many of the women who worked outside their homes were widows with dependent children, who took their husbands' places in family enterprises. It seems that at one time or another, colonial women engaged in many of the occupations practiced by men. Indeed, most models of the "patriarchal family economy" ill fit the historical evidence; for example, eighteenth-century diaries describe "a world in which wives as well as husbands traded with their neighbors" and "young women felt themselves responsible for their own support." Not surprisingly, however, women's wages in this period were significantly lower than those of men.

For poor women, there were special incentives to work outside the home. Local poor laws encouraged single poor women to work rather than become recipients of relief. The choice of jobs was much more limited, and many poor women became laundresses, house servants, or cooks. Again, however, female laborers were paid approximately 30 percent less than the lowest-paid unskilled, free, white male

workers and 20 percent less than hired-out male slaves.

The fact that some women worked in so-called "masculine fields"—that they were merchants, tavern owners, shopkeepers, and so on—has sometimes been interpreted to mean that the colonial period was a "golden age of equality" for women. Contemporary historians argue instead, however, that these jobs were exceptions to the rule, and that in fact "colonial times were characterized by a strict and simple division of labor between men and women, which assigned them to fields and house, or to the public and private spheres, respectively." The dominant ideology was still that a woman's place was at home, raising children. . . .

Women of Color

Historically, the experiences of women of color have differed dramatically from those of white women. If we consider only the present time period, it may appear that women of color and white women have certain experiences in common—relatively low economic position, being the target of discriminatory practices in education and in work, and overall marginality in the power structure. But women of color and white women have reached their present circumstances through very different histories. Although white women's status was clearly inferior to that of white men, they were treated with deference, and they shared in the status privileges of their husbands. African American women almost never had the option of choosing between work and leisure, as did some white women. They were not included in the image of the "colonial housewife." African American women were not considered "weak" females, but were treated more like beasts of burden. Thus these women of color suffered a double oppression of sexism and racism.

Nowhere is this double oppression more clearly demonstrated than within the institution of slavery, which became established in late seventeenth- and early eighteenth-century colonial society—largely as a result of the demand for cheap agricultural labor, especially within the Southern plantation economy. Historians estimate the slave population in the United States, Caribbean, and Brazil consisted of

9.5 million blacks. More than double that number are estimated to have died in transit to the New World. Slave women in the Southern colonies were without doubt the most exploited of all women. They were exploited not only as workers but as breeders of slaves. The following advertisement was typical of the time:

Negroes for Sale: A girl about twenty years of age (raised in Virginia) and her two female children, four and the other two years old—remarkably strong and healthy. Never having had a day's sickness with the exception of the smallpox in her life. She is prolific in her generating qualities and affords a rare opportunity to any person who wishes to raise a family of strong and healthy servants for their own use.

Slave women were also sometimes exploited as sex objects for white men. Like male slaves, they were considered intrinsically inferior. Slaves were property, not people. They faced severe cultural and legal restrictions: their family lives were controlled by their owners, their children were not their own, and their educational opportunities were almost nonexistent.

Sojourner Truth, formerly a slave and an activist in the abolitionist and women's rights movements, eloquently expressed the differences in treatment, under slavery, of black and white women: "That man over there says that women need to be helped into carriages and lifted over ditches, and to have the best place everywhere. Nobody ever helped me into carriages, or over mud puddles, or gives me any best place . . . and ain't I a woman?"

Before the Civil War, a black woman in one of the "cotton states," working on one of the larger plantations, would have been either a house servant or one of several million field hands who produced major cash crops. In the Southern plantation economy, we thus find a "bifurcated" concept of woman. The European woman became "the guardian of civilization," while the African American woman was "spared neither harsh labor nor harsh punishment," though the experience of slaves differed depending on the economic status and individual personality of the slave owner.

Even pregnancy did not deter some slavemasters from cruel treatment: "One particular method of whipping pregnant slaves was used throughout the South; they were made to lie face down in a specially dug depression in the ground, a practice that provided simultaneously for the protection of the fetus and the abuse of its mother."

Some white women benefited from such slave labor and shared with their husbands the role of oppressor, although the slave-mistress relationship was psychologically complex: "In their role as labor managers, mistresses lashed out at slave women not only to punish them, but also to vent their anger on victims even more wronged than themselves. We may speculate that, in the female slave, the white woman saw the source of her own misery, but she also saw herself—a woman without rights or recourse, subject to the whims of an egotistical man." Conflict between white and African American women often resulted in violence, in which "mistresses were likely to attack with any weapon available—knitting needles, tongs, a fork, butcher knife, ironing board, or pan of boiling water." Yet, while the relationship was often filled with strife, white and African American women "also shared a world of physical and emotional intimacy that is uncommon among women of antagonistic classes and different races."

Slavery was justified by notions of race involving the "biological superiority" of the colonists. It was assumed that Europeans in the colonies made up an easily identifiable and discrete biological and social entity—a "natural" community of class interests, racial attributes, political and social affinities, and superior culture. This was of course not exactly true, but given that the differences between white skin and black skin were more noticeable than many of the differences among Europeans themselves, and given that whites were in dominant positions politically and socially, it could easily *seem* to be true.

Slave families often resisted the oppressive workloads by banding together to help one another in the fields and to lessen the workloads of older, weaker, or sicker workers. The extended family was of vital importance under the slave system. African American mothers labored most of the day, some of them caring for white women's families, while their own children were left under the care of grandmothers and old or disabled slaves. While the two-parent, nuclear family may have been the most typical form of slave cohabitation, close relatives were often very much involved in family life. Stevenson's study suggests that in colonial and antebellum Virginia, the slave family was a "malleable extended family that, when possible, provided its members with nurture, education, socialization, material support, and recreation in the face of the potential social chaos that the slaveholder imposed."

Even though African American men were unable to own property, to provide protection and support for their children, or to work within the public sphere, there was a sexual division within the slave household. Men collected the firewood and made furniture—beds, tables, chairs—and other articles of wood, such as animal traps, butter paddles, and ax handles. They also wove baskets and made shoes. African American women grew, prepared, and preserved foods; spun thread, wove and dyed cloth, and sewed clothes; and made soap and candles.

In the North, while slavery was an accepted practice, it was not nearly as widespread. Many African American women worked as free laborers as domestic servants; others worked as spinners, weavers, and printers.

Native American Women

The work and family life experience of Native American women prior to European colonization differed depending on the region of the country and the type of tribal society. But in every Native American nation, women played very important roles in the economic life of their communities:

> They had to be resourceful in utilizing every aspect of the environment to sustain life and engaging in cultural exchanges to incorporate new productive techniques. They gathered wild plants for food, herbs for medicines and dyes, clay for pottery, bark and reeds for weaving cloth. In many nations, they also tilled the soil and sowed the seeds, cultivated and harvested, made cloth and clothing, dried vegetables, and ground grains for breads. In hunting

societies, they cured the meats and dried the skins. They also assisted in the hunt in some cultures.

As a general rule, men hunted and women engaged in agricultural work. The more important hunting was to a community's survival, the more extensive the male power within the community; the greater the dependence on agriculture, the greater the power and independence of women. Women had the responsibility for raising children and maintaining hearth and home. Men engaged in hunting, fishing, and warfare.

In the East especially, many Indian communities were predominantly agricultural. Women constituted the agricultural labor force within these communities. An English woman who was held captive by a Seneca tribe observed that

> Household duties were simple and Seneca women, unlike English wives and daughters, were not slaves to the spinning wheel or the needle. In the summer, the women went out each morning to the fields, accompanied by their children, to work cooperatively and in the company of friends and relatives, planting and tending the corn, beans, and squash at a pace to their individual rhythms and skills rather than to the demands of an overseer. They moved from field to field, completing the same tasks in each before returning to the first.

Women within agricultural communities would often maintain control over tools and land—as well as any surplus foods they gathered from the land. This often enabled them (especially elderly women who were heads of households) to garner some political clout within their tribal communities. For instance, if Iroquois women opposed war on certain occasions, they might refuse to let the men have the cornmeal they would have needed to feed their raiding parties or armies. These communities often had a matrilineal family structure (inheritance and family name were through the female line, with family connections through the mother) and matrilocal residence (upon marriage a man lived with his mother-in-law's relatives).

Through the lens of the white colonist, the work roles and family structure of Native American society appeared deviant and, in some cases, perverse.

After all, English society was characterized by a patriarchal family structure with patrilocal residence:

> To Europeans, Indian family patterns raised the specter of promiscuous women, freed from accountability to their fathers and husbands for the offspring they produced. . . . Equally incomprehensible—and thus perverse—to many Europeans were the work roles accepted by Indian men and women. In the world the English knew, farming was labor and farmers were male. Masculinity was linked, inexorably, to agriculture: household production and family reproduction defined femininity. That Indian men hunted was not a sufficient counterpoise, for, in the England of the seventeenth century, hunting was a sport, not an occupation. Many concluded that Indian men were effeminate, lazy; Indian women were beasts of burden, slaves to unmanly men.

European colonization and conquest pushed Native Americans off their land, depriving them of food and livelihood, culture and traditions. Disease or warfare demolished whole societies. Others were radically transformed, especially with regard to the traditional gender and work roles. Having used military force to remove Native Americans from their lands onto reservations, the U.S. government "began a systematic effort to destroy their cultures and replace them with the values and practices of middle-class whites."

Confined to relatively small reservations, Native American men could no longer hunt as extensively as before (nor, defeated by U.S. forces, could they any longer carry on warfare). They therefore needed to redefine their social roles and to find new economic activities. In many a Native American tribe, the men took over agriculture, traditionally the women's work. Family structure also changed, at the prompting of missionaries and others including government officials, to become more like that of the Europeans, with less emphasis on the matrilineal extended family and more on the nuclear family and the husband-wife relationship.

THE ARRIVAL OF INDUSTRIALIZATION

The transformation from an agrarian rural economy to an urban industrial society ushered in a new era in women's work. With the advent of industrialization, many of the products women made at home—clothes, shoes, candles—gradually came to be made instead in factories. For a while, women still performed the work at home, using the new machines. Merchants would contract for work to be done, supplying women with the machines and the raw materials to be made into finished articles. The most common of these manufacturing trades for women was sewing for the newly emerging clothing industry. Since women had always sewn for their families, this work was considered an extension of women's traditional role, and therefore a respectable activity. As the demand for goods increased, however, home production declined and gave way to the factory system, which was more efficient in meeting emerging needs.

The rise of factory production truly separated the home from the workplace. With the decline of the household unit as the center of industrial and economy activity, the importance of women's economic role also declined. Male and female spheres of activity became more separated, as did the definitions of men's and women's roles. Man's role continued to be primarily that of worker and provider; woman's role became primarily supportive. She was to maintain a smooth and orderly household, to be cheerful and warm, and thus to provide the husband with the support and services he needed to continue his work life. The industrial revolution created a set of social and economic conditions in which the basic lifestyle of white middle-class women more nearly approached society's expectations concerning woman's role. More and more middle-class women could now aspire to the status formerly reserved for the upper classes—that of "lady." The nineteenth-century concept of a lady was that of a fragile, idle, pure creature, submissive and subservient to her husband and to domestic needs. Her worth was based on her decorative value, a quality that embraced her beauty, her virtuous character, and her temperament. She was certainly not a paid employee. This ideal was later referred to as the "cult of true womanhood" because of its rigid, almost religious standards.

Biological and social arguments were also often used to justify women's exclusion from the labor force. Women were seen as too weak and delicate to participate in the rough work world of men. It was believed they lacked strength and stamina, that their brains were small, that the feminine perspective and sensitivity were liabilities in the marketplace. Such arguments rationalized women's accepting the roles of homemaker and mother almost exclusively, as the industrial revolution spread across the country.

During the early years of industrialization, however, because many men were still primarily occupied with agricultural work and were unavailable or unwilling to enter the early factories, male laborers were in short supply. American industry depended, then, on a steady supply of women workers. Yet how could society tolerate women's working in the factories, given the dominant ideology of the times, which dictated that a woman's place was at home? Single white women provided one answer. Their employment was viewed as a fulfillment of their family responsibilities, during an interlude before marriage.

The employment of young, single women in the early Lowell (Massachusetts) mills is a prime example of the reconciliation of ideology with the needs of industry. Francis Cabot Lowell devised a respectable route into employment for such women. Recruiting the daughters of farm families to work in his mill, which opened in 1821 in Lowell, he provided supervised boardinghouses, salaries sufficient to allow the young women to offer financial aid to their families or to save for their own trousseaux, and assurances to their families that the hard work and discipline of the mill would help prepare them for marriage and motherhood.

In the early industrial era, working conditions were arduous and hours were long. By the late 1830s, immigration began to supply a strongly competitive, permanent workforce willing to be employed for low wages in the factories, under increasingly mechanized and hazardous conditions. By the late 1850s, most of the better-educated, single, native-born women had left the mills, leaving newly immigrated women (both single and married) and men to fill these positions.

While women thus played a crucial role in the development of the textile industry, the first important manufacturing industry in America, women also found employment in many other occupations

during the process of industrialization. As railroads and other business enterprises expanded and consolidated, women went to work in these areas as well. In fact, the U.S. Labor Commissioner reported that by 1890 only 9 out of 360 general groups to which the country's industries had been assigned did not employ women.

By 1900, more than five million women or girls, or about one in every five of those 10 years old and over, had become a paid employee. The largest proportion (40%) remained close to home in domestic and personal service, but domestic service was on the decline for white working-class women at the turn of the century. About 25 percent (1.3 million) of employed women worked in the manufacturing industries: in cotton mills, in the manufacture of woolen and worsted goods, silk goods, hosiery, and knit wear. The third largest group of employed women (over 18%) were working on farms. Women in the trade and transportation industries (about 10%) worked as saleswomen, telegraph and telephone operators, stenographers, clerks, copyists, accountants, and bookkeepers. Women in the professions (about 9 percent, and typically young, educated, and single, of native-born parentage) were employed primarily in elementary and secondary teaching or nursing. Other professions—law, medicine, business, college teaching—tended to exclude women. The fastest growing of these occupational groups were manufacturing, trade, and transportation. In the last thirty years of the nineteenth century, the number of women working in trade and transportation rose from 19,000 to over half a million. These women also tended to be young, single, native-born Americans; immigrants and minority women were excluded from these white-collar positions.

. . .

By the turn of the century, the labor market had become clearly divided according to gender, race, and class. Fewer manufacturing jobs were being defined as suitable for white women, especially with the rising dominance of heavy industry employment for which female workers were considered too delicate. Working-class women were increasingly devalued by their continued participation in activities men had primarily taken over (such as factory work), because these activities were regarded as lacking in the Victorian virtue and purity called for by the "cult of true womanhood." As the economy expanded and prosperity came to more and more white middle-class families, middle-class women could "become ladies." A "woman's place" was still defined as at home. If these women did work outside the home, the appropriate occupation was a white-collar job (sales, clerical, and professional occupations). White women's occupations shifted from primarily domestic service—which became increasingly identified as "black women's work"—and from light manufacturing to the rapidly growing opportunities in office and sales work. These jobs were also considered more appropriate for feminine roles as defined by the cult of true womanhood. Women of color did not share in this occupational transformation. In 1910, for example, 90.5 percent of African American women worked as agricultural laborers or domestics, compared with 29.3 percent of white women.

The Legacy of Slavery

African American women were not part of the "cult of true womanhood." They were not sheltered or protected from the harsh realities, and "while many white daughters were raised in genteel refined circumstances, most black daughters were forced to deal with poverty, violence and a hostile outside world from childhood on." After emancipation, their employment and economic opportunities were limited, in part because the skills they had learned on the plantation transferred to relatively few jobs, and those only of low pay and status.

African American women's concentration in service work—especially domestic work—was largely a result of limited opportunities available to them following the Civil War. The only factory employment open to them was in the Southern tobacco and textile industries, and until World War I most African American working women were farm laborers, domestics, or laundresses. . . .

Despite the limited range of job opportunities, a relatively large proportion of African American women were employed. The legacy of slavery may partly account for the relatively high labor-force participation rate of African American women. Although women's labor-force participation rate is generally lower than men's, African American women's participation rate was historically much higher than that of white women. Thus, for example, white women's labor-force participation in 1890 was 16.3 percent, while African American women's rate was 39.7 percent.

WORLD WAR I AND THE DEPRESSION

World War I accelerated the entry of white women into new fields of industry. The pressure of war production and the shortage of male industrial workers necessitated the hiring of women for what had been male-dominated occupations. Women replaced men at jobs in factories and business offices, and, in general, they kept the nation going, fed, and clothed. The mechanization and routinization of industry during this period enabled women to quickly master the various new skills. For the most part, this wartime pattern involved a reshuffling of the existing female workforce, rather than an increase in the numbers of women employed. Although the popular myth is that homemakers abandoned their kitchens for machine shops or airplane hangars, only about 5 percent of women workers were new to the labor force during the war years. . . .

Thus the wartime labor shortage temporarily created new job opportunities for women workers, and at higher wages than they had previously earned. This was not necessarily the case for African American women, however. Although World War I opened up some factory jobs to them, these were typically limited to the most menial, least desirable, and often the most dangerous jobs—jobs already rejected by white women. These jobs included some of the most dangerous tasks in industry, such as carrying glass to hot ovens in glass factories and dyeing furs in the furrier industry.

World War I produced no substantial or lasting change in women's participation in the labor force. The employment rate of women in 1920 was actually a bit lower (20.4%) than in 1910 (20.9%). The labor unions, the government, and the society at large were not ready to accept a permanent shift in women's economic role. Instead, women filled an urgent need during the wartime years and were relegated to their former positions as soon as peace returned. As the reformer Mary Von Kleeck wrote, "When the immediate dangers . . . were passed, the prejudices came to life once more."

When the men returned from the war, they were given priority in hiring, and although a number of women left the labor force voluntarily, many were forced out by layoffs. Those remaining were employed in the low-paying, low-prestige positions women had always occupied and in those occupations that had become accepted as women's domain. . . .

The Great Depression of the 1930s threw millions out of work. The severe employment problems during this period intensified the general attitude that a woman with a job was taking that job away from a male breadwinner. Yet during the 1930s, an increasing number of women went to work for the first time. The increase was most marked among younger, married women, who worked at least until the first child, and among older, married women, who reentered the marketplace because of dire economic need or in response to changing patterns of consumer demand. Most jobs held by women were part-time, seasonal, and marginal. Women's labor-force participation increased slowly throughout this period and into the early 1940s . . . , except in the professions (including feminized professions such as elementary teaching, nursing, librarianship, and social work). The proportion of women in all professions declined from 14.2 percent to 12.3 percent during the Depression decade.

WORLD WAR II

The ordeal of World War II brought about tremendous change in the numbers and occupational distribution of working women. As during World War I, the shortage of male workers, who had gone off to fight, coupled with the mounting pressures of war production brought women into the workforce. A corresponding shift in attitudes about women's aptitudes and proper roles resulted. Women entered the munitions factories and other heavy industries to support the war effort. The War Manpower Commission instituted a massive advertising campaign to attract women to the war industries. Patriotic appeals were common.

. . .

Equal work did not mean equal pay for the women in these varied wartime occupations. Although the National War Labor Board issued a directive to industries that stipulated equal pay for equal work, most employers continued to pay women at a lower rate. Furthermore, women had little opportunity to advance in their new occupations.

World War II marked an important turning point in women's participation in the paid labor force. The social prohibition concerning married women working gave way under wartime pressure, and women wartime workers demonstrated that it was possible for women to maintain their households while also assuming the role of breadwinner with outside employment. More women than ever before learned to accommodate the simultaneous demands of family and work. The experience "pointed the way to a greater degree of choice for American women."

However, at the war's end, with the return of men to civilian life, there was a tremendous pressure on women to return to their former positions in the home. During this time, a new social ideology began to emerge; Betty Friedan later called it "the feminine mystique." This ideology drew in social workers, educators, journalists, and psychologists, all of whom tried to convince women that their place was again in the home. It was not until the "cult of true womanhood" advanced in the late 1800s to differentiate middle-class women from working-class women. As Friedan notes, in the fifteen years following World War II, the image of "women at home" rather than "at work" became a cherished and self-perpetuating core of contemporary American culture. A generation of young people were brought up to extol the values of home and family, and woman's role was defined as the domestic center around which all else revolved. Women were supposed to live like those in Norman Rockwell *Saturday Evening Post* illustrations. The idealized image was of smiling mothers baking cookies for their wholesome children, driving their station wagons loaded with freckled youngsters to an endless round of lessons and activities, returning with groceries and other consumer goods to the ranch houses they cared for with such pride. Women were supposed to revel in these roles and gladly leave the running of the world to men.

. . .

Yet, unlike the post–World War I period, after World War II women did not go back to the kitchens. Instead, women's labor-force participation continued to increase throughout the post–World War II decades, so that by the late 1960s, 40 percent of American women were in the labor force, and by the late 1990s, 60 percent were. Who were the women most likely to be part of this "new majority" of women at work?

AFTER WORLD WAR II:
THE RISE OF THE MARRIED WOMAN WORKER

Between 1890 and the beginning of World War II, single women comprised at least half the female labor force. The others were mostly married African American, immigrant, or working-class women.

The decade of the 1940s saw a change in the type of woman worker, as increasing numbers of married women left their homes to enter the world of paid work. . . . Although single women continued to have the highest labor-force participation rates among women, during the 1940s the percentage of married women in the workforce grew more rapidly than any other category. Between 1940 and 1950, single women workers were in short supply because of low birthrates in the 1930s. Furthermore, those single women available for work were marrying at younger ages and leaving the labor market to raise their families. On the other hand, ample numbers of older, married women were available, and these women (who had married younger, had had fewer children, and were living longer) were eager for paid employment.

In 1940, about 15 percent of married women were employed; by 1950, 24 percent. This increase has continued: by 1960, 32 percent of married women; in 1970, over 41 percent; in 1980, 50 percent; and by 1995, 61 percent. Indeed, as the twentieth century comes to a close, we can see that labor-force participation rates of single and married women have become almost identical. . . .

During the 1940s, 1950s, and 1960s, it was mainly older, married women entering the workforce. In 1957, for example, the labor-force participation rate among women aged forty-five to forty-nine years exceeded the rate for twenty- to twenty-four-year-old women. During the 1960s, young married mothers with preschool- or school-age children began to enter the workforce. This trend continued for the next three decades; by 1995, more than three-quarters of married women with children between six and seventeen years of age were employed, and, most significantly, almost two-thirds of those women with children under the age of six were in the labor force. . . . In short, whereas before 1970 the overwhelming majority of married women stopped working after they had children, today the overwhelming majority of married women do not.

WOMEN OF COLOR

Denied entrance to the factories during the rise of industrialization and, for much of the twentieth century, facing discriminatory hiring practices that closed off opportunities in the newly expanded office and sales jobs, many women of color entered domestic service. From 1910 to 1940, the proportion of white women employed in clerical and sales positions almost doubled, and there was a decline in the numbers of white women in domestic work. Private household work then became the province of African American women: the percentage of African American household workers increased from 38.5 percent in 1910 to 59.9 percent in 1940. . . . For the next three decades, African American women remained the single largest group in domestic service.

African American women's economic status improved dramatically from 1940 through the 1960s, as a result of an increase in light manufacturing jobs, as well as changes in technology. African American women moved from private household work into manufacturing and clerical work, and made significant gains in the professions. Whereas in 1940, 60 percent of employed African American females worked in private households, by the late 1960s only 20 percent did. Their job prospects continued to improve, and by the 1980s, almost half of all working African American women were doing so in "white-collar" jobs—clerical and sales positions, as well as professional jobs in business, health care, and education. Through the 1990s, the historic, job-prestige gap between African American and white working women continued to close. Almost two-thirds of working African American women had jobs in the white-collar world by 1996, compared with nearly three-quarters of working white women. . . .

Other Women of Color at Work

Each minority group has had a different experience in American society and has faced different opportunities and obstacles. Women in each group share with African American women the concerns of all minority women; they share with the men of their ethnic groups the problems of discrimination against that particular ethnic minority.

Native American Women

As we noted earlier, gender roles in Native American communities were disrupted during the conquest and oppression by whites. For example, Navajo society was traditionally matrilineal, with extended families the norm; Navajo women owned property and played an important role in family decisions. But beginning in the 1930s, government policy disrupted this system by giving land only to males. As they could no longer make a sufficient living off the land, more and more Navajo men had to seek employment off the reservations. Nuclear families became the norm. Navajo women became dependent on male providers. With the men away much of the time, these women are often isolated and powerless. They often face divorce or desertion and thus economic difficulties, because the community frowns on women seeking work off the reservation.

Such disruption of the traditional Native American society left Native American women in very grim economic circumstances. But in recent decades, more and more of them have gotten jobs. Native American women's labor-force participation rate in 1970 was 35 percent (compared to 43% for all women). This rate rose sharply to 55 percent by

the early 1990s and is now within a few percentage points of the rate for all women.

Like their African American counterparts over the past half century, Native American women have gradually moved out of low-skill farm and nonfarm work and domestic jobs into clerical, sales, professional, technical, and other "white-collar" jobs. In 1960, one in six working Native American women was employed as a domestic household worker; by the early 1990s only one in a hundred was. During the same period, the proportion of Native American women involved in agricultural work also went from ten to one in a hundred. Manufacturing work was increasingly replaced by white-collar work, reflecting the overall trends in the occupational structure; more specifically, while the percentage involved in factory work (much of it in textiles and traditional crafts) fell from 18.1 to 14.2, the percentage doing white-collar work soared from 28.9 to 61.3. Although many of these white-collar jobs are classified as "professional" (15.7% of all working Native American women) or "managerial" (9.4%), two-thirds of Native American women are still concentrated in the "secondary" sector of the labor market—which is characterized by low wages, few or no benefits, low mobility, and high instability. They are kept there because of the "stagnation of the reservation economy," discrimination, and their relatively low level of educational attainment. A significant number do not have a high school diploma (in 1990, more than one-third of all those over the age of 25, compared to one-fifth of white women).

Latina [Chicana] Women

. . . Large numbers of Chicanas migrated, usually with husband and children, from Mexico to the United States during the 1916–1920 labor shortage created by World War I. They found work in the sprawling "factory farms" of the Southwest, harvesting fruits, vegetables, and cotton in the Imperial and San Joaquin valleys of California, the Salt River valley of Arizona, and the Rio Grande valley of Texas. They also went to the Midwest, for instance to Michigan and Minnesota, to harvest sugar beets. Such migrant workers typically were exploited, spending long, tedious, and physically demanding hours in the fields for very low pay. Some became tenant farmers, which might seem a step up, except too often this system "created debt peonage; unable to pay the rent, tenants were unable to leave the land and remained virtually permanently indebted to their landlords."

During the 1920s, with a shortage of European immigration, new job opportunities opened up for Mexican Americans, and they began to migrate from rural, farm country to the urban, industrial centers, where they found work as domestics and factory workers. By 1930, one-third of working Chicanas were domestics and a quarter worked in manufacturing; at the time, the share employed in agriculture, forestry, and mining had fallen to 21 percent. Wage scales varied according to ethnicity, however. It was not uncommon to pay Chicana workers lower wages than "Anglo" (whites of European descent) women for doing the same job, whether as domestics, laundresses, or workers in the food-processing industries of the West and Southwest. Then the Depression years of the 1930s, with the general shortage of jobs, brought a backlash against Mexican American labor, and thousands of Mexicans were deported or pressured to leave.

World War II once again opened up the American labor market for Mexican migrants, as their labor was needed to offset wartime labor shortages. However, their treatment was deplorable by modern standards. In short, Mexican workers comprised a "reserve army" of exploited labor. Through the government-sponsored Bracero or "Manual Workers" program, Mexican workers were granted temporary work visas so that they could be employed on large corporate farms and elsewhere, but too often they were treated like slaves or prisoners.

World War II and the years following saw a massive shift in the occupational and geographical distribution of Chicana workers:

> Many left Texas for California, and the population became increasingly more urban. Women continued their move from the fields into garment factories throughout the Southwest. . . . [A] comparison of the 1930 and 1950 [census] data shows the magnitude of these shifts. For instance, the share of employed southwestern Chicanas working on farms dropped from 21 percent in 1930 to 6 percent in 1950, while the percentage in white-collar work doubled.

By the 1960s, the largest occupational category for Chicana workers was operatives, followed by clerical and service work. Chicanas became concentrated in particular industries—food processing, electronics (including telecommunications), and garments. Like their Native American counterparts, Chicana women have made some progress in entering professional and managerial occupations (primarily noncollege teaching, nursing, librarianship, and social work). In 1960, 8.6 percent were in these occupations; by 1980, 12.6 percent, and by the early 1990s 17.5 percent. However, like the Native Americans, Chicana women are still overwhelmingly found in the secondary labor market (75%)—much more so than women (60%) and men (32%) of white European heritage.

The dominant reasons behind the low occupational prestige of all minority groups are the same: discrimination and low educational attainment. In the case of Chicana women, over 15 percent "are illiterate by the standard measure (completion of less than five years of schooling)," but studies of functional illiteracy during the 1970s and 1980s suggest "much higher rates—perhaps as high as 56 percent." At the other end of the educational attainment spectrum, only 8.4 percent of Latina women have completed four or more years of college—compared with 21.0 percent of white women and 12.9 percent of blacks. However, education is only part of the formula for success in the U.S. occupational system: for when education is held constant, Latina women make only between 84 and 90 percent of what white women do.

Beyond lack of education, Chicana women face other important obstacles in the labor market. They have high rates of unemployment and underemployment. Many of the jobs they hold are seasonal and often nonunionized. This lack of advancement translates into higher poverty rates (23 percent for Chicana/os in the early 1990s). The median income for full-time Chicana workers is lower than that of any other U.S. racial-ethnic group. For Latina women (in general) with children and no husband present, the poverty rate is even worse: 49.4 percent compared with 26.6 percent of white women in this situation.

Increasingly, Chicana women, like many female workers of color around the globe, are doing service or assembly work for multi-national corporations, especially in the apparel, food-processing, and electronics industries. These women have often displaced men in assembly work because they can be paid less and many do not receive job benefits. The work hours are long, and women are often assigned monotonous tasks that are dangerous to their health.

. . .

Asian American Women

. . . Asian Americans are considered to be the "model minority." . . . However, this is as much myth as fact. While many among both the native-born and the recent arrivals have high levels of education and professional skills and can readily fit into the labor market, others lack such advantages, often finding work only as undocumented laborers in low-paying jobs with long work days, little or no job mobility, and no benefits.

> We are told we have overcome our oppression, and that therefore we are the model minority. Model refers to the cherished dictum of capitalism that "pulling hard on your bootstraps" brings due rewards. . . . Asian American success stories . . . do little to illuminate the actual conditions of the majority of Asian Americans. Such examples conceal the more typical Asian American experience of unemployment, underemployment and struggle to survive. The model minority myth thus classically scapegoats Asian Americans. It labels us in a way that dismisses the real problems that many do face, while at the same time pitting Asians against other oppressed people of color.

In 1996, 37.3 percent of Asian women who were 25 years and over had at least a bachelor's degree, compared with 23.2 percent of non-Latina whites. Filipina American women secured the highest college graduation rate of all women, a rate 50 percent greater than that of white males. Following closely behind are Chinese American and Japanese American women, who exceed both the white male and female college graduation rates. Yet, these educational achievements bring lower returns for Asian women than for whites. Census data reveal a gap between achievement and economic reward for Asian American women, who suffer from both race and sex discrimination within the labor market.

. . .

And it would be wrong to equate "Asian" with "well educated," because the majority of Asian women immigrating to the United States since 1980 have low levels of education. Though, as just noted, Asian women are much more likely to be college-educated than non-Latina white women, they are also much more likely—two and a half times more likely—to be grade-school dropouts: in 1996, 12.5 percent of Asian women had not gone beyond the eighth grade, compared to only 5.2 percent of their non-Latina white counterparts. This fact is linked to the other most obvious difference between Asian and white women . . . —the proportions working as "operators, fabricators, and laborers," where we find significantly more Asian women.

These women are most commonly employed as sewing machine operators at home or in small sweatshops in the Chinatowns of New York and San Francisco. Asian immigrant women are also heavily employed in the microelectronics industry. Women in general comprise 80 to 90 percent of assembly workers in this industry, and approximately "half of these assembly workers are recent immigrants from the Philippines, Vietnam, Korea, and South Asia." Within the microelectronics industry jobs are often "structured along racial and gender lines, with men and white workers earning higher wages and being much more likely to be promoted than women and workers of color." Karen Hossfeld's research on relationships between Third World immigrant women production workers and their white male managers in the high-tech Silicon Valley of California relates how immigrant women of color negotiate and often employ resistance to primarily white, middle-class management demands. One Filipina circuit board assembler in Silicon Valley puts it this way:

> The bosses here have this type of reasoning like a seesaw. One day it's "you're paid less because women are different than men," or "immigrants need less to get by." The next day it's "you're all just workers here—no special treatment just because you're female or foreigners."
>
> Well, they think they're pretty clever with their doubletalk, and that we're just a bunch of dumb aliens.

But it takes two to use a seesaw. What we are gradually figuring out here is how to use their own logic against them.

As clerical or administrative support workers, Asian American women are disproportionately represented as cashiers, file clerks, office machine operators, and typists. They are less likely to obtain employment as secretaries or receptionists. Noting that there is an "overrepresentation of college-educated women in clerical work," Woo suggests that education functions less as a path toward mobility into higher occupational categories, and more as "a hedge against jobs as service workers and as machine operatives or assembly workers."

Asian American women with a college education who obtain professional employment are often restricted to the less prestigious jobs within this category. Asian American women "are more likely to remain marginalized in their work organization, to encounter a 'glass ceiling,' and to earn less than white men, Asian American men, and white women with comparable educational backgrounds." They are least represented in those male-dominated positions of physician, lawyer, and judge, and are heavily concentrated in the more female-dominated occupations of nursing and teaching.

Asian women have been subjected to a range of stereotypes. The "Lotus Blossom" stereotype depicts them as submissive and demure sex objects: "good, faithful, uncomplaining, totally compliant, self-effacing, gracious servants who will do anything and everything to please, entertain, and make them feel comfortable and carefree." At the opposite extreme, the Dragon Lady stereotype portrays Asian women as "promiscuous and untrustworthy,"

> as the castrating Dragon Lady who, while puffing on her foot-long cigarette holder, could poison a man as easily as she could seduce him. "With her talon-like six-inch fingernails, her skin-tight satin dress slit to the thigh," the Dragon Lady is desirable, deceitful and dangerous.

Asian American feminist Germaine Wong notes how stereotypes concerning Asian women operate in the workplace, serving to deter their advancement into leadership roles and to increase their vulnerability to sexual harassment. Additionally, these stereotypes have fostered a demand for "X-rated films and pornographic materials featuring Asian women in bondage, for 'Oriental' bathhouse workers in U.S. cities, and for Asian mail-order brides."

In sum, the notion of Asian Americans as the "model minority" deviates considerably from sociological reality. While Asian American women as a group have achieved some "success" in terms of high educational attainment, they receive lower returns on this investment compared to the white population. They have not "escaped the stigmatization of being minority and recent immigrants in a discriminatory job market.

R E A D I N G **71**

The Triumph of the Working Mother

Stephanie Coontz 2013

Fifty years ago, Betty Friedan made a startling prediction in her controversial best seller, *The Feminine Mystique.* If American housewives would embark on lifelong careers, she claimed, they would be happier and healthier, their marriages would be more satisfying, and their children would thrive.

At the time, experts believed that a married woman should work only to kill time while searching for a husband or to fill time after the children had left home. A wife who pursued a career was considered a maladjusted woman who would damage her marriage and her kids.

Today, with almost two-thirds of married mothers employed and women the sole or main breadwinner in 40 percent of households according to a 2013 Pew study . . . , we can test these competing points of view.

Ms. Friedan wins on the question of whether working improves women's well-being. At all income levels, stay-at-home mothers report more sadness, anger, and episodes of diagnosed depression than their employed counterparts.

And the benefits of employment mount over a lifetime. A recent multiyear study by the sociologists Adrianne Frech and Sarah Damaske found that women who worked full time following the birth of their first child had better mental and physical health at age 40 than women who had not worked for pay. Low-wage jobs with urgent and inflexible time demands do raise the risk of depression, especially among new mothers. But in less stressful low-wage jobs, mothers who work relatively long hours during the first year following childbirth experience less depression than those who cut back to fewer hours.

Back in the 1960s and '70s, a wife taking a job raised the risk of divorce. Today, however, a wife's employment lowers the couple's risk of divorce. Among middle-class Americans, dual-earner couples report the highest marital quality. Things are less rosy for wives who do not want to work but are forced to by economic necessity, especially if their husbands don't pitch in at home. Such women have the least happy marriages in America.

Yet staying home doesn't necessarily help, because financial distress is an even more potent source of marital unhappiness and conflict than it used to be. In a 2012 Gallup poll, stay-at-home mothers in low-income families were less likely than employed moms at the same income level to report that they had smiled, laughed, or enjoyed themselves "yesterday."

What about the kids? As more wives took jobs between 1965 and 1985, the time mothers spent with children decreased. But since 1985, both mothers and fathers have increased their time with children. Employed moms spend fewer hours per week with their children than stay-at-home mothers, but they spend more time with their children than homemakers did in 1965!

And fathers nearly tripled their amount of time with children. A review of nearly 70 studies in the United States finds no significant negative effects of maternal employment on the intellectual achievement of young children. And in low-income families, children whose mothers had stable jobs had fewer behavior problems than children whose mothers experienced job instability or who did not work at all, according to another study. In Britain, researchers who controlled for mothers' education and household income found no negative effects of maternal employment for boys, while girls in two-earner families had fewer behavioral problems than girls in male breadwinner-female homemaker households. And a 2013 study of 75,000 Norwegian children found no behavioral problems linked to children's time in day care.

Of course, Britain offers 52 weeks of maternity leave, 39 of them paid, while Norway, unlike the United States, has strict standards for day care. Also, the same review that found no ill effects of maternal employment on young children in the United States did identify some added risks for adolescents, suggesting that society would benefit from more structured after-school programs for this age group. And a 2010 study found that some children had slightly lower cognitive achievement if mothers worked 30 hours or more a week in the first 9 months after their birth.

So while Friedan was right in her counterintuitive claim that maternal employment could be good for women and families, she failed to foresee that the United States, which pioneered public education for all and was on the verge of establishing a comprehensive child care system in 1971 (before President Richard M. Nixon vetoed the bill), would by the early 21st century have fallen to last place among developed nations in supports for working families. While the average working woman might be better off, we need to offer better maternity leave and child care for those more at risk.

After 50 years, shouldn't we stop debating whether we want mothers to work and start implementing the social policies and working conditions that will allow families to take full adva[n]... benefits of women's employment and t... its stresses?

READING (72)

Maid to Order

The Politics of Other Women's Work

Barbara Ehrenreich (2000)

In line with growing class polarization, the classic posture of submission is making a stealthy comeback. "We scrub your floors the old-fashioned way," boasts the brochure from Merry Maids, the largest of the residential-cleaning services that have sprung up in the last two decades, "on our hands and knees." This is not a posture that independent "cleaning ladies" willingly assume—preferring, like most people who clean their own homes, the sponge mop wielded from a standing position. In her comprehensive 1999 guide to homemaking, *Home Comforts,* Cheryl Mendelson warns: "Never ask hired housecleaners to clean your floors on their hands and knees; the request is likely to be regarded as degrading." But in a society in which 40 percent of the wealth is owned by 1 percent of households while the bottom 20 percent reports negative assets, the degradation of others is readily purchased. Kneepads entered American political discourse as a tool of the sexually subservient, but employees of Merry Maids, The Maids International, and other corporate cleaning services spend hours every day on these kinky devices, wiping up the drippings of the affluent.

I spent three weeks in September 1999 as an employee of The Maids International in Portland, Maine, cleaning, along with my fellow team members, approximately sixty houses containing a total of about 250 scrubbable floors—bathrooms, kitchens, and entryways requiring the hands-and-knees treatment. It's a different world down there below knee level, one that few adults voluntarily enter. Here you find elaborate dust structures held together by a scaffolding of dog hair; dried bits of pasta glued to the floor by their sauce; the congealed remains of gravies, jellies, contraceptive creams, vomit, and urine. Sometimes, too, you encounter some fragment of a human being: a child's legs, stamping by in disgust because the maids are still present when he gets home from school; more commonly, the Joan & David–clad feet and electrolyzed calves of the female homeowner. Look up and you may find this person staring at you, arms folded, in anticipation of an overlooked stain. In rare instances she may try to help in some vague, symbolic way, by moving the cockatoo's cage, for example, or apologizing for the leaves shed by a miniature indoor tree. Mostly, though, she will not see you at all and may even sit down with her mail at a table in the very room you are cleaning, where she would remain completely unaware of your existence unless you were to crawl under that table and start gnawing away at her ankles.

Housework, as you may recall from the feminist theories of the Sixties and Seventies, was supposed to be the great equalizer of women. Whatever else women did—jobs, school, child care—we also did housework, and if there were some women who hired others to do it for them, they seemed too privileged and rare to include in the theoretical calculus. All women were workers, and the home was their workplace—unpaid and unsupervised, to be sure, but a workplace no less than the offices and factories men repaired to every morning. If men thought of the home as a site of leisure and recreation—a "haven in a heartless world"—this was to ignore the invisible female proletariat that kept it cozy and humming. We were on the march now, or so we imagined, united against a society that devalued our labor even as it waxed mawkish over "the family" and "the home." Shoulder to shoulder and arm in arm, women were finally getting up off the floor.

In the most eye-catching elaboration of the home-as-workplace theme, Marxist feminists Maria Rosa Dallacosta and Selma James proposed in 1972 that the home was in fact an economically productive and significant workplace, an extension of the actual factory, since housework served to "reproduce the labor power" of others, particularly men. The male worker would hardly be in shape to punch in for his shift, after all, if some woman had not fed him, laundered his clothes, and cared for the children who were his contribution to the next generation of workers. If the home was a quasi-industrial workplace staffed by women for the ultimate benefit of the capitalists, then it followed that "wages for housework" was the obvious demand.

But when most American feminists, Marxist or otherwise, asked the Marxist question *cui bono?* they tended to come up with a far simpler answer—men. If women were the domestic proletariat, then men made up the class of domestic exploiters, free to lounge while their mates scrubbed. In consciousness-raising groups, we railed against husbands and boyfriends who refused to pick up after themselves, who were unaware of housework at all, unless of course it hadn't been done. The "dropped socks," left by a man for a woman to gather up and launder, joined lipstick and spike heels as emblems of gender oppression. And if, somewhere, a man had actually dropped a sock in the calm expectation that his wife would retrieve it, it was a sock heard round the world. Wherever second-wave feminism took root, battles broke out between lovers and spouses over sticky countertops, piled-up laundry, and whose turn it was to do the dishes.

The radical new idea was that housework was not only a relationship between a woman and a dust bunny or an unmade bed; it also defined a relationship between human beings, typically husbands and wives. This represented a marked departure from the more conservative Betty Friedan, who, in *The Feminine Mystique,* had never thought to enter the male sex into the equation, as either part of the housework problem or part of an eventual solution. She raged against a society that consigned its educated women to what she saw as essentially janitorial chores, beneath "the abilities of a woman of average or normal human intelligence," and, according to unidentified studies she cited, "peculiarly suited to the capacities of feeble-minded girls." But men are virtually exempt from housework in *The Feminine Mystique*—why drag them down too? At one point she even disparages a "Mrs. G.," who "somehow couldn't get her housework done before her husband came home at night and was so tired then that he had to do it." Educated women would just have to become more efficient so that housework could no longer "expand to fill the time available."

Or they could hire other women to do it—an option approved by Friedan in *The Feminine Mystique* as well as by the National Organization for Women [NOW], which she had helped launch. At the 1973 congressional hearings on whether to extend the Fair Labor Standards Act to household workers, NOW testified on the affirmative side, arguing that improved wages and working conditions would attract more women to the field, and offering the seemingly self-contradictory prediction that "the demand for household help inside the home will continue to increase as more women seek occupations outside the home." One NOW member added, on a personal note: "Like many young women today, I am in school in order to develop a rewarding career for myself. I also have a home to run and can fully conceive of the need for household help as my free time at home becomes more and more restricted. Women know [that] housework is dirty, tedious work, and they are willing to pay to have it done. . . ." On the aspirations of the women paid to do it, assuming that at least some of them were bright enough to entertain a few, neither Friedan nor these members of NOW had, at the time, a word to say.

So the insight that distinguished the more radical, post-Friedan cohort of feminists was that when we talk about housework, we are really talking, yet again, about power. Housework was not degrading because it was manual labor, as Friedan thought, but because it was embedded in degrading relationships and inevitably served to reinforce them. To make a mess that another person will have to deal with—the dropped socks, the toothpaste sprayed on the bathroom mirror, the dirty dishes left from a late-night snack—is to exert domination in one of its more silent and intimate forms. One person's arrogance— or indifference, or hurry—becomes another person's occasion for toil. And when the person who is cleaned up after is consistently male, while the person who cleans up is consistently female, you have a formula for reproducing male domination from one generation to the next.

Hence the feminist perception of housework as one more way by which men exploit women or, more neutrally stated, as "a symbolic enactment of gender relations." An early German women's liberation cartoon depicted a woman scrubbing on her hands and knees while her husband, apparently excited by this pose, approaches from behind, unzipping his fly. Hence, too, the second-wave feminists' revulsion at the hiring of maids, especially when they were women of color: At a feminist conference I attended in 1980, poet Audre Lorde chose to insult the all-too-white audience by accusing them of being present only because they had black housekeepers to look after their children at home. She had the wrong crowd; most of the assembled radical feminists would no sooner have employed a black maid than they would have attached Confederate flag stickers to the rear windows of their cars. But accusations like hers, repeated in countless conferences and meetings, reinforced our rejection of the servant option. There already were at least two able-bodied adults in the average home—a man and a woman—and the hope was that, after a few initial skirmishes, they would learn to share the housework graciously.

A couple of decades later, however, the average household still falls far short of that goal. True, women do less housework than they did before the feminist revolution and the rise of the two-income family: down from an average of 30 hours per week in 1965 to 17.5 hours in 1995, according to a July 1999 study by the University of Maryland. Some of that decline reflects a relaxation of standards rather than a redistribution of chores; women still do two thirds of whatever housework—including bill paying, pet care, tidying, and lawn care—gets done. The inequity is sharpest for the most despised of household chores, cleaning: in the thirty years between 1965 and 1995, men increased the time they spent scrubbing, vacuuming, and sweeping by 240 percent—all the way up to 1.7 hours per week—while women decreased their cleaning time by only 7 percent, to 6.7 hours per week. The averages conceal a variety of arrangements, of course, from minutely negotiated sharing to the most clichéd division of labor, as described by one woman to the *Washington Post:* "I take care of the inside, he takes care of the outside." But perhaps the most disturbing finding is that almost the entire increase in male participation took place between the 1970s and the mid-1980s. Fifteen years after the apparent cessation of hostilities, it is probably not too soon to announce the score: in the "chore wars" of the Seventies and Eighties, women gained a little ground, but overall, and after a few strategic concessions, men won.

Enter then, the cleaning lady as *dea ex machina,* restoring tranquillity as well as order to the home. Marriage counselors recommend her as an alternative to squabbling, as do many within the cleaning industry itself. A Chicago cleaning woman quotes one of her clients as saying that if she gives up the service, "my husband and I will be divorced in six months." When the trend toward hiring out was just beginning to take off, in 1988, the owner of a Merry Maids franchise in Arlington, Massachusetts, told the *Christian Science Monitor,* "I kid some women. I say, 'We even save marriages. In this new eighties period you expect more from the male partner, but very often you don't get the cooperation you would like to have. The alternative is to pay somebody to come in. . . .'" Another Merry Maids franchise owner has learned to capitalize more directly on housework-related spats; he closes between 30 and 35 percent of his sales by making follow-up calls Saturday mornings, which is "prime time for arguing over the fact that the house is a mess." The micro-defeat of feminism in the household opened a new door for women, only this time it was the servants' entrance.

In 1999, somewhere between 14 and 18 percent of households employed an outsider to do the cleaning, and the numbers have been rising dramatically. Mediamark Research reports a 53 percent increase, between 1995 and 1999, in the number of households using a hired cleaner or service once a month or more, and Maritz Marketing finds that 30 percent of the people who hired help in 1999 did so for the first time that year. Among my middle-class, professional women friends and acquaintances, including some who made important contributions to the early feminist analysis of housework, the employment of a maid is now nearly universal. This sudden emergence of a servant class is consistent with what some economists have called the "Brazilianization" of the American economy: We are dividing along the lines of traditional Latin American societies—into a tiny overclass and a huge underclass, with the latter available to perform intimate household services for the former. Or, to put it another way, the home, or at least the affluent home, is finally becoming what radical feminists in the Seventies only imagined it was—a true "workplace" for women and a tiny, though increasingly visible, part of the capitalist economy. And the question is: As the home becomes a workplace for someone else, is it still a place where you would want to live?

. . .

The trend toward outsourcing the work of the home seems, at the moment, unstoppable. Two hundred years ago women often manufactured soap, candles, cloth, and clothing in their own homes, and the complaints of some women at the turn of the twentieth century that they had been "robbed by the removal of creative work" from the home sound pointlessly reactionary today. Not only have the skilled crafts, like sewing and cooking from scratch, left the home but many of the "white collar" tasks are on their way out, too. For a fee, new firms such as the San Francisco–based Les Concierges and Cross It Off Your List in Manhattan will pick up dry cleaning, baby-sit pets, buy groceries, deliver dinner, even do the Christmas shopping. With other firms and individuals offering to buy your clothes, organize your financial files, straighten out your closets, and wait around in your home for the plumber to show up, why would anyone want to hold on to the toilet cleaning?

Absent a major souring of the economy, there is every reason to think that Americans will become increasingly reliant on paid housekeepers and that this reliance will extend ever further down into the middle class. For one thing, the "time bind" on working parents shows no sign of loosening; people are willing to work longer hours at the office to pay for the people—house-cleaners and baby-sitters—who are filling in for them at home. Children, once a handy source of household help, are now off at soccer practice or SAT prep classes; grandmother has relocated to a warmer climate or taken up a second career. Furthermore, despite the fact that people spend less time at home than ever, the square footage of new homes swelled by 33 percent between 1975 and 1998, to include "family rooms," home entertainment rooms, home offices, bedrooms, and often bathrooms for each family member. By the third quarter of 1999, 17 percent of new homes were larger than 3,000 square feet, which is usually considered the size threshold for household help, or the point at which a house becomes unmanageable to the people who live in it.

One more trend impels people to hire outside help, according to cleaning experts such as Aslett and Mendelson: fewer Americans know how to clean or even to "straighten up." I hear this from professional women defending their decision to hire a maid: "I'm just not very good at it myself" or "I wouldn't really know where to begin." Since most of us learn to clean from our parents (usually our mothers), any diminution of cleaning skills is transmitted from one generation to another, like a gene that can, in the appropriate environment, turn out to be disabling or lethal. Upper-middle-class children raised in the servant economy of the Nineties are bound to grow up as domestically incompetent as their parents and no less dependent on people to clean up after them. Mendelson sees this as a metaphysical loss, a "matter of no longer being physically centered in your environment." Having cleaned the rooms of many overly privileged teenagers in my stint with The Maids, I think the problem is a little more urgent than that. The American overclass is raising a generation of young people who will, without constant assistance, suffocate in their own detritus.

If there are moral losses, too, as Americans increasingly rely on paid household help, no one has been tactless enough to raise them. Almost everything we buy, after all, is the product of some other person's suffering and miserably underpaid labor. I clean my own house (though—full disclosure—I recently hired someone else to ready it for a short-term tenant), but I can hardly claim purity in any other area of consumption. I buy my jeans at The Gap, which is reputed to subcontract to sweatshops. I tend to favor decorative objects no doubt ripped off, by their purveyors, from scantily paid Third World craftspersons. Like everyone else, I eat salad greens just picked by migrant farm workers, some of them possibly children. And so on. We can try to minimize the pain that goes into feeding, clothing, and otherwise provisioning ourselves—by observing boycotts, checking for a union label, etc.—but there is no way to avoid it altogether without living in the wilderness on berries. Why should housework, among all the goods and services we consume, arouse any special angst?

And it does, as I have found in conversations with liberal-minded employers of maids, perhaps because we all sense that there are ways in which housework is different from other products and services. First, in its inevitable proximity to the activities that compose "private" life. The home that becomes a workplace for other people remains a home, even when that workplace has been minutely regulated by the corporate cleaning chains. Someone who has no qualms about purchasing rugs woven by child slaves in India or coffee picked by impoverished peasants in Guatemala might still hesitate to tell dinner guests that, surprisingly enough, his or her lovely home doubles as a sweatshop during the day. You can eschew the chain cleaning services of course, hire an independent cleaner at a generous hourly wage, and even encourage, at least in spirit, the unionization of the housecleaning industry. But this does not change the fact that someone is working in your home at a job she would almost certainly never have chosen for herself—if she'd had a college education, for example, or a little better luck along the way—and the place where she works, however enthusiastically or resentfully, is the same as the place where you sleep.

It is also the place where your children are raised, and what they learn pretty quickly is that some people are less worthy than others. Even better wages and working conditions won't erase the hierarchy between an employer and his or her domestic help, because the help is usually there only because the employer has "something better" to do with her time, as one report on the growth of cleaning services puts it, not noticing the obvious implication that the cleaning person herself has nothing better to do with her time. In a merely middle-class home, the message may be reinforced by a warning to the children that that's what they'll end up doing if they don't try harder in school. Housework, as radical feminists once proposed, defines a human relationship and, when unequally divided among social groups, reinforces preexisting inequalities. Dirt, in other words, tends to attach to the people who remove it—"garbagemen" and "cleaning ladies." Or, as cleaning entrepreneur Don Aslett told me with some bitterness—and this is a successful man, chairman of the board of an industrial cleaning service and frequent television guest—"The whole mentality out there is that if you clean, you're a scumball."

One of the "better" things employers of maids often want to do with their time is, of course, spend it with their children. But an underlying problem with post-nineteenth-century child-raising, as Deirdre English and I argued in our book *For Her Own Good* years ago, is precisely that it is unmoored in any kind of purposeful pursuit. Once "parenting" meant instructing the children in necessary chores; today it's more likely to center on one-sided conversations beginning with "So how was school today?" No one wants to put the kids to work again weeding and stitching; but in the void that is the modern home, relationships with children are often strained. A little "low-quality time" spent washing dishes or folding clothes together can provide a comfortable space for confidences—and give a child the dignity of knowing that he or she is a participant in, and not just the product of, the work of the home.

There is another lesson the servant economy teaches its beneficiaries and, most troubling, the children among them. To be cleaned up after is to achieve a certain magical weightlessness and immateriality. Almost everyone complains about violent video games, but paid housecleaning has the same consequence-abolishing effect: you blast the villain into a mist of blood droplets and move right along; you drop the socks knowing they will eventually levitate, laundered and folded, back to their normal dwelling place. The result is a kind of virtual existence, in which the trail of litter that follows you seems to evaporate all by itself. Spill syrup on the floor and the cleaning person will scrub it off when she comes on Wednesday. Leave *The Wall Street Journal* scattered around your airplane seat and the flight attendants will deal with it after you've deplaned. Spray toxins into the atmosphere from your factory's smokestacks and they will be filtered out eventually by the lungs of the breathing public. A servant economy breeds callousness and solipsism in the served, and it does so all the more effectively when the service is performed close up and routinely in the place where they live and reproduce.

Individual situations vary, of course, in ways that elude blanket judgment. Some people—the elderly and disabled, parents of new babies, asthmatics who require an allergen-free environment—may well need help performing what nursing-home staff call the "ADLs," or activities of daily living, and no shame should be attached to their dependency. In a more generous social order, housekeeping services would be subsidized for those who have health-related reasons to need them—a measure that would generate a surfeit of new jobs for the low-skilled people who now clean the homes of the affluent. And in a less-gender-divided social order, husbands and boyfriends would more readily do their share of the chores.

However we resolve the issue in our individual homes, the moral challenge is, put simply, to make work visible again: not only the scrubbing and vacuuming but all the hoeing, stacking, hammering, drilling, bending, and lifting that goes into creating and maintaining a livable habitat. In an ever more economically unequal culture, where so many of the affluent devote their lives to such ghostly pursuits as stock-trading, image-making, and opinion-polling, real work—in the old-fashioned sense of labor that engages hand as well as eye, that tires the body and directly alters the physical world—tends to vanish from sight. The feminists of my generation tried to bring some of it into the light of day, but, like busy professional women fleeing the house in the morning, they left the project unfinished, the debate broken off in midsentence, the noble intentions unfulfilled. Sooner or later, someone else will have to finish the job.

R E A D I N G   *73*

Color Me Nontoxic

Momo Chang (2010)

Walking into the Isabella Nail Bar in Oakland, California, on a rainy spring morning, I notice a remarkable difference between this salon and others that I've visited.

No bad nail salon smell.

Uyen Nguyen opened her shop in 2008, and it's one of a number of eco-friendly nail salons popping up around the country. It features formaldehyde-free polishes, organic lotions, and improved ventilation, among other things.

The mission behind Nguyen's salon, however, goes beyond saving the environment. Years ago, Nguyen's sister-in-law, who worked in nail salons for over 15 years, discovered that her baby had died in the womb when she was eight months pregnant. Nguyen believes the fetus died because her sister-in-law was exposed to toxic chemicals in salons, specifically while she was doing acrylic, or fake, nails.

The persistent chemical exposure is "a silent killer," Nguyen says, "so whatever I can do, I do. The cost [of opening a green salon] of course is more, but the long-term effects are worth it."

In 2007 *Time* magazine named nail salon work one of the worst jobs in the United States because of the toxic products used in most shops. Nevertheless, the industry has more than tripled in size during the past decade and rakes in $6 billion annually. There are now 350,000 manicurists in the United States; 96 percent are women and 42 percent are Asian or Pacific Islander, according to the industry magazine *Nails*. These workers are exposed to a constant dose of toxins for eight or more hours a day.

A study conducted in the Boston area by the University of Massachusetts, Lowell, with the nonprofit Viet-AID found that Vietnamese nail workers suffer from a host of health issues, including musculoskeletal disorders, breathing problems, headaches, and rashes. Though the U.S. government sets chemical exposure levels, the regulations aren't protecting workers, according to Cora Roelofs, the study's lead author.

"These workers are clearly overexposed," Roelofs says. "The [Occupational Safety and Health Administration] exposure limits are irrelevant in this work environment for many reasons—they are outdated, don't add together different chemicals that have the same effect, don't account for skin absorption, and were never meant to be protective against the myriad acute health effects experienced by these workers."

One of the most toxic chemicals found in salons is the carcinogen formaldehyde. Others are toluene and dibutyl phthalate, toxins known to cause birth defects and miscarriages. All are volatile organic compounds, which means they evaporate into air, and nail salon workers inhale them.

Some former workers have become advocates. Alisha Tran is a former manicurist who is now part of a research team with Asian Health Services and the Northern California Cancer Center. Tran works to convince salon workers to participate in the project, which entails wearing an air monitor badge that tests for chemicals in the air.

Tran became an advocate after she was sent to the emergency room twice within two months. Both times, she was working on someone's nails when her face and hands went numb. The second time Tran went to the hospital, the doctor who attended to her recommended that she leave her job.

"I quit two weeks later," Tran says.

Tran hopes that her research will prove to nail salon workers that their jobs put their health at risk. She says advocating can be tricky—she can't just tell people to leave their jobs because many have limited English skills and lack other options. And even if workers are concerned about chemicals, Tran says, they often fear that speaking up or asking to wear gloves will cause them to lose their jobs.

To ensure the safety of all nail salon workers, advocates believe the government should step in to regulate manufacturers, including banning more harmful chemicals, as the European Union has done. The U.S. cosmetics industry is allowed to sell products without even testing for safety, and manufacturers use known toxins—which they claim are safe—in small doses.

There's also currently no green certification for nail salons in the United States, though groups like the Asian Law Caucus are trying to set a standard in California, and a Seattle-area group is setting up standards as part of King County's EnviroStars green business program.

Without more laws to protect workers, more research into chemical exposure, and standards for green salons, people will have to rely on their own senses—and on entrepreneurs like Nguyen, whose goal isn't just to make a living, but also to make a statement.

Virtuous Valentine? Think Again.

Hannah Levintova (2012)

Valentine's Day skeptics are as prevalent as the holiday's loyalists: For every rose-toting lover, there's a cupid defector who most definitely does not want anything red, pink, or pastel-colored. After digging into the background behind the Valentine's Day industry, I'm pretty convinced that my own wry holiday spirit is merited—if not for this day's sky-high levels of consumption (expected to reach $17.6 billion this year) then, at the very least, for its environmental damage and poor labor practices. Below, a breakdown of the Valentine's Day trifecta: flowers, chocolate, and greeting cards. The results aren't pretty. So you can curse us for tainting your holiday—or thank us for enabling your cynicism.

Cut flowers: That bouquet you may be planning to gift today was most likely not grown in the United States. The floriculture industry taps out at $32.8 billion, and about $14 billion of that comes from the sale of fresh flowers. Around 63 percent of those imported blooms are imports from Colombia, and another 23 percent from Ecuador.*

The labor rights facts of this industry are truly depressing. In 2005, the International Labor Rights Forum found that 55 percent of women working in the Ecuadorian flower production trade (they constitute half the flower workforce) had been victim to sexual harassment in the workplace. Nineteen percent were forced to have sex with a supervisor or coworker. Compulsory pregnancy testing is also a serious industry issue. In Colombia, where women make up about

65 percent of flower workers, a survey conducted by the nation's flower industry union, Untraflores, found that about 80 percent of companies required women to take a pregnancy test as part of their job application process—presumably because they'd like to avoid providing paid maternity leave (required in Colombia). Another problem: In 2000, upwards of 48,000 children were found working in Ecuador's flower industry. Colombia wasn't much better. There have since been a number of hefty efforts at reform, and while Colombia's been improving, the US Department of Labor still confirms extensive child labor use in Ecuador.

The environmental picture is similarly bleak. Many growers in both countries have been accused of using high levels of toxic pesticides, fungicides, and fumigants to grow big, bug-free roses. These can pollute water sources and neighboring land—one insecticide used in Ecuadorian rose-growing, fenamiphos, for example, has been phased out of US use because of its high toxicity to a number of species.

Pesticides also affect flower workers. As *Mother Jones* has reported before, workers exposed to the many toxic pesticides used in flower-production experience major health problems—from blurred vision to abdominal pain and birth defects or other reproductive risks. And while there's little conclusive data on how much these pesticides can affect the eventual rose-owner, we do know that since roses aren't an edible import, their pesticide residues aren't regulated.

But you can still give guilt-free flowers to your sweetheart. VeriFlora is an eco-certification program that evaluates flower industry players for fair labor practices and sustainability efforts. Its "sustainably-grown" certified flowers are widely available at local florists and grocery stores.

Chocolate: As my colleague Jaeah Lee reported on another candy-heavy holiday—Halloween—most of

---

* The original version of this article stated that 63 percent of US cut flowers come from Colombia, and another 23 percent from Ecuador. Those percentages apply only to imported flowers, which according to the Society of American Florists make up between 85 and 98 percent of the most common US flowers. Thanks to commenter Max Fisher for noticing something was off.

the bon-bons that will be lovingly gifted and consumed this Valentines day come from West Africa, where child labor is rife, with over 500,000 children employed on cocoa farms in the Ivory Coast and Ghana alone.

The demands of the western world on the West African cocoa industry also contribute to biodiversity damage in the region. Ghana and the Ivory Coast produce almost 70 percent of the world's cocoa. They're also both located in the Upper Guinean forests, a tropical "biodiversity hotspot" which is home to more than half of the mammalian species in Africa, including several endangered ones. To meet growing industry demands, farmers have been expanding their cocoa farming by clearing forest territory, fragmenting coveted land in a way that disturbs the natural interactions of species and threatens their ultimate survival.

For ethical chocolate options, Shop to Stop Slavery has a nice list, as does the Rainforest Alliance— which has granted sustainability certification to a number of chocolate brands, most of which can be found at your local grocery store.

Greeting Cards: According to the EPA, the United States, with just 5 percent of the world's population, consumes 33 percent of its paper. The virgin-timber-based pulp and paper industry is also the largest consumer of fresh water in OECD countries and their largest water polluter, says Darby Hoover,

senior resource specialist at the Natural Resources Defense Council. Ink presents another eco stumbling block: Many greeting cards are printed with petroleum-based inks, which emit volatile organic compounds (VOCs) into the atmosphere. VOCs contribute to the development of ground level ozone, which is a main component of smog.

Greeting card companies have been making an effort to green the industry. Hallmark's website notes that about 85 percent of the cards they sell in North America are produced on at least 20 percent recycled paper, which they clearly note on the back. Some companies have been switching over to soy-based inks, but Hoover says that even these aren't "a slam-dunk" environmentally—they can contain other toxic ingredients, and are still a niche market. For greener cards, check out Conservatree's handy guide, which breaks down cards by occasion, company, and environmental attributes.

So whoever your Valentine may be, it might be worth trying one of the eco-friendly spins on holiday tradition listed above. Or, go with something zanier by donating to a cause in your Valentine's name (complete with free e-card), or crafting a card out of used materials with meaning, like an old magazine you both enjoyed, ticket stubs from a date, or the frayed takeout menu tacked to your fridge. The recipient just might be impressed with your creativity— not to mention your social conscience.

R E A D I N G   **75**

Power Plays

Six Ways the Male Corporate Elite Keeps Women Out

Martha Burk (2005)

Males, much more so than females, are conditioned almost from birth to view the world in terms of hierarchies, power relationships, and being winners.

In the business world, many symbols of power are built into the system, like merit badges in the Boy Scouts. In the early days of a career, power could get

you an office with a window, later the corner office or the reserved parking space. As the career progresses, the badges change; they're now the high-priced car, the $2,000 suit, the right club membership, fatter cigars, better brandy, the bigger expense account, and blonder, younger, thinner women. At the CEO level, corporate jets, unlimited expense accounts, a phalanx of "yes men," and obscenely high salaries and stock options are the norm.

So how can your average billionaire CEO deal-maker wring one more shred of superiority and one-upmanship out of this situation? He gets something money can't buy—such as belonging to a golf club that is so exclusive you can't apply for membership. And once you've got this thing, boy, are you reluctant to give it up.

When groups achieve a certain level of power and influence, sometimes their original purpose is subverted in favor of holding on to the status and the exclusivity that the group has achieved. Within that particular sphere, they are a *power elite*. And if the power sphere happens to be business related and male dominated, that's where the problem comes in for working women.

The power dynamic manifests itself in a number of ways:

Power re-creates itself in its own image. Psychologists have long known that we're most comfortable with people who are like us, both in appearance and ways of thinking. It has been well documented that managers like to hire people who look like themselves. In most of corporate America, that still means white and male. That's why laws against employment discrimination were passed in the first place—women and minority men just weren't on the radar screens of the folks doing the hiring and promoting. The so-called neutral processes in corporations were firmly enforcing a white-male quota system. That is still true—most companies have "diversity" in management only to the extent that it does not threaten the traditional balance.

Despite claims by some that women and minority men have taken all the jobs, the results of this re-creation process are fairly easy to see, even from casual observation. The numbers speak for themselves—and the higher you go in the hierarchy, the greater the enforcement of traditional quotas in favor of the dominant group. In most companies, there will be a fair number of women and minority men in the rank and file, fewer at lower management, and still fewer at middle management. At the very top level of the Fortune 500,

there are only nine female CEOs. Even in companies like Citigroup, where *women* are a 56 percent majority overall, *men* hold 56 percent of the "officials and managers" jobs. There is only one female top executive. She is paid 50 percent of the average for men at her level.

Power elites enforce norms and systems that guarantee continued power. At the highest levels of business, the board of directors is a major enforcer of the status quo—in both its own makeup and that of the top management of the company.

Consider what happens when an individual is chosen to be on a corporate board for the first time. He (or in rare cases, she) is usually nominated by the CEO or someone already on the board, and brought into a new environment with its own culture and skill set. The nominator has an interest in seeing this individual succeed, as it will reflect well on his judgment and business acumen. The newcomer, at the same time, wants to belong, wants to overcome any notion that he is unworthy or an impostor. So the new member is "trained" through mentoring and role modeling, quickly picking up on the board culture and the behavior and knowledge necessary to succeed.

It is not hard for the new individual to figure out what is expected. Boat rockers don't last as board members. So for a person in the minority (a woman or a man of color) there is actually a disincentive to advocate bringing others like herself into the circle, as she is likely to be accused of "pushing an agenda" and not behaving like a "team player."

Power creates a sense of entitlement. Most men at some level know that maleness is valued over femaleness in the culture, and we are all taught in subtle ways that males have first claim on jobs, sports, and opportunities. (Women of color are the first to admit their brothers are sexist, too.) But for the ordinary man, the cultural valuation of all things male does not translate into the sense of super-entitlement that corporate power elites exhibit. That comes from a corporate system where value is placed on its leaders that is far out of proportion to their actual worth.

Consider CEO pay. In 2003 the average CEO pay in large companies was more than 300 times that of the average worker (up from 42-to-1 in 1982). The rise in compensation for the top dogs outstripped rises in inflation, profits, and the S&P 500. Conservative journalist Robert Samuelson had this to say: "The scandal of CEO pay is not that it ascended to stratospheric levels . . . [but that] so few CEOs have publicly raised their voices in criticism or rebuke. . . . [T]here's a widespread self-serving silence. If they can't defend what they're doing, then maybe what they're doing is indefensible."

These words could as easily have applied to the controversy over membership in Augusta National Golf Club. CEOs did not raise their voices against the club's exclusion of women; there was a conspiracy of self-serving silence. It was obvious they believed themselves exempt from society's standards against discrimination, immune to criticism from the public or discipline from their companies, even in the face of employee unrest and questions at stockholder meetings.

Power creates invulnerability, leading to a flaunting of society's standards. As individuals become more powerful, they are increasingly surrounded by others whose job they control and who tell them how clever, smart, and right they are. Power elites are also increasingly insulated from the sanctions that ordinary people are subject to when they misbehave. In fact, breaking the rules to get where you are is excused as nothing more than hard-nosed business, shrewd politics, or the result of occupational pressure.

We've seen this again and again as sports and entertainment figures get a pass on cocaine possession or beating up their girlfriends, politicians get a pass on dallying with interns or taking "contributions" that result in big government contracts, and executives who lose billions and squander the retirements of thousands of workers get a slap on the wrist as they jump out of harm's way with the aid of their "golden parachutes."

Loyalty to power overshadows other loyalties, including gender and race. Statistics show that when it comes to income, black men gain more from being male than they lose from being black, particularly at high levels. It is also well known in business that after women reach a certain level, they are less likely to want to help other women advance. Two dynamics are likely at work here. As association with a certain group conveys more power, individuals begin to identify more with that group and less with other groups to which they belong. They also seek personal validation by the power group (almost everyone feels like an impostor at some level—women more so than men). In the business world this means behaving like the others. Holding on to the power—and gaining more of it—inevitably becomes more important than loyalty to what is now a less important group. Since the power group in corporate America is still overwhelmingly male and white, the less important group in the woman executive's case is other women.

In the majority male's case, however, the power group aligns perfectly with his race and gender group. So these loyalties, far from being lessened, are actually reinforced. He doesn't have to make a choice between his race and/or gender group and the power elite—he doesn't even have to think about it. When he promotes a member of his group up the executive ranks, or proposes a new board member who is not only like him but like the majority, he is never accused of "pushing an agenda." His candidate's credentials are never questioned because the nomination may be the result of a "special interest" mentality. In fact, it's the opposite; his nomination is seen as merely "normal." So not only is his choice reinforced, but also *his entitlement to make that particular choice.*

Group loyalty combined with power can trump good judgment and override individual moral codes. All Americans, male and female, are inculcated with a strong value for loyalty to one's group. In the great majority of cases, group loyalty is a good thing. It fosters team spirit for athletics, cohesiveness in military units, productivity in business, and dedication to the public good in community service organizations. But most of us know "loyalty" is perverted when it serves a purpose counter to society's values.

While we might stay in a group even if it occasionally took a stand we disagreed with, we wouldn't remain if the group stood for something society condemns (like discrimination) or if it conspired to break the law.

At the extremes, group loyalty can go terribly wrong. It can facilitate lawlessness under the cover of secrecy and lead to group actions and cover-ups of those actions that group members would never consider as individuals. Examples can range from illegal accounting schemes to harmful and sometimes fatal hazing by fraternity brothers, to gang rapes (too often by athletic team members), military atrocities, and terrorism. It is probably no accident that most of the excesses occur in male-dominated or exclusively male groups.

Obviously the average man does not participate in illegal, immoral, or harmful group actions. But the average man (much more so than the average woman) has been exposed, again and again, to the code of loyalty to a group that can lead to actions that are not in his best interests, nor in the best interests of society. It's about living in a culture that links masculinity to power, dominance and control. In everyday life it might never affect most, because they're not faced with the stark choice of taking a stand and doing what's right versus betraying an unspoken loyalty oath to the "brotherhood of men."

Women encounter these situations, too—it's just that they have not been conditioned to group allegiance in the same way, or to the same degree, that men have. It is also very rare that we hear of group actions by women that are comparable to fraternity hazings or gang rapes. But not necessarily because women are genetically predisposed to being kinder and gentler human beings, as many would argue. If women had had the same power, status, and conditioning that men have had over the centuries, we might see parallels in female group behavior. But these "antecedent conditions" have not existed historically, and they still don't exist, even in the most advanced societies. So we'll have to leave the genetic arguments to another planet or to another 10 millennia in the future.

R E A D I N G **76**

The Sexist Truth About Office Romances

Peggy Drexler (2013)

Joanie was a graphic designer in a small creative-services firm. When she started dating Scott, a good-looking and well-liked manager in another department, she wasn't surprised to find her romantic life the topic of office gossip. Everyone, it seemed, had an opinion about the relationship. But, then, in her office, everyone had an opinion about everything anyone else was doing.

What did surprise Joanie, however, was that so much of the gossip seemed to be negative chatter directed exclusively at her. Co-workers who would normally ask her to lunch began to exclude her from their outings. There were smirks in the halls. People who Joanie barely knew would ask her about Scott's whereabouts, almost in a mocking way. For Scott, meanwhile, work was business as usual. No one treated him any differently, made comments, or asked prodding questions about how he'd spent the weekend. "It was almost as if I was being punished," Joanie told me. "Except for what, I don't know. Dating Scott didn't get me any special treatment. I certainly wasn't sleeping my way to the top, or otherwise affecting anyone any more than he was."

According to a recent survey of 8,000 workers by the job-search website CareerBuilder.com, four out of 10 employees have dated someone at work; 17 percent have done it twice. It makes perfect sense: There are more singles in the workforce than ever before, spending more than half their waking hours on the job. With co-workers there's a familiarity and commonality, not to mention proximity and convenience. There's often plenty to talk about. Although the CareerBuilder survey also found that 72 percent of workers who have office relationships don't try to hide them—compared with 46 percent five years ago—interoffice dating, even among colleagues on equal levels or in different departments, is not without complications or negative reactions. And though both men and women who take part in office relationships are judged, women, it seems, bear that judgment far more.

A 2009 study published in the *Western Journal of Communication* found that most employees have negative perceptions of workplace romance, even though so many of them have taken part in it themselves, and largely direct their annoyance or anger at the woman.

Most researchers believe there are three primary motivating factors behind dating someone at work—love, ego, and job—and that how or whether colleagues accept an interoffice couple depends on what they view as the motivations behind it. As it turns out, those perceived motivations appear to vary depending on whether you're a man or a woman. The *WJC* study found that in most situations, employees believe that women are motivated by job—the prospect of some employment-related advantage—while men by the less professionally threatening love or ego. Which could help explain why Joanie's co-workers viewed her, and her relationship, with distrust, while largely letting Scott off the hook.

More so than males, female employees in an office relationship, even a lateral one, are more likely to be suspected of using their relationships to get ahead and of being loyal to their romantic partner above all else. Christine and Jake, two associate-level architects in a large firm, had been dating for three months when they were assigned to a project with a third co-worker, Jessica. Christine and Jessica had vastly different aesthetics, as well as ways of working. Christine didn't intend to use her relationship with Jake as an advantage to getting things done at work—nor did she believe he was giving

her special consideration—but the fact is that whenever there was a disagreement between the three, he always sided with her over Jessica. "I could tell Jessica resented me in particular, even though Jake was the one who was picking sides," Christine told me. "And I don't know that I blamed her for feeling that way, even though I never asked him to do that and it certainly wasn't why I started to date him in the first place."

Whether favoritism between couples at work is real or perceived may not even matter. One of the biggest reasons employers tend to discourage interoffice affairs is because they generate gossip—and gossip wastes time and fosters distrust and dissatisfaction. Women, meanwhile, are more likely than men to be the targets of that office gossip, according to a 2012 study published in the journal *Sex Roles*. That might explain why office gossip about a romantically involved couple would tend to target the woman over the man. Even those who are not dating superiors become subject to accusations of favoritism from co-workers when it comes to promotions, restructuring of teams, or financial bonuses. They become easy targets for those colleagues inclined to use office gossip as a means to undermine, or get ahead themselves.

Arianne and Brendan were both supervisors of their own departments at their financial advisory firm. Neither reported to the other, though they often worked together. After Arianne and Brendan had been dating for six months, Arianne's boss called her into his office. Some of Arianne's female reports had complained that Brendan had been treating them differently—at the behest, they suspected, of Arianne. It was untrue, but hard to convince her boss, or her reports, otherwise. She had, of course, complained about them to Brendan. But she hadn't asked him to take on her battles, and she didn't believe that he had—only that it was easy for her disgruntled reports to say that he had. The perception was all that mattered.

That's not to say women who date within the office always keep separate their personal and professional lives. Another reason women may feel the repercussions of office romance more deeply than men may be attributed to basic differences in gender. Although both men and women are emotional beings, women report feeling negative emotions more often than men, including anxiety and sadness, and to a more intense degree, according to a Florida State University study that looked at gender and emotion. This study also found that women express their feelings more readily than men and are more likely to talk about their feelings, specifically angry ones, with others.

As Joanie and Scott's relationship progressed, and their colleagues eventually realized that it had nothing to do with them, the gossip died down. But not before Joanie had learned an important lesson.

"Even if I could separate my professional life from my personal life, I realized it might have been too much to expect everyone else to," she said. "I couldn't just carry on as if things weren't different, because the truth is that they were. I'd made my bed, so to speak." Though she had the right to date whomever she wanted, she'd made a choice to date someone at work. "And if I had to work harder to prove that my love life wasn't impacting my work life?" she asked. "Well, so be it. Working harder isn't the worst thing that can happen."

READING 77

Sex Work as a Test Case for African Feminism

Marlise Richter (2012)

INTRODUCTION

I stopped to stare at the body showcased in the Amsterdam window and inadvertently shuddered. It was a white body—Eastern European-looking like the stereotype—with a white bra and G-string. The ultraviolet light that lit the tiny box of a room made her underwear and heavy lipstick glow in an eerie, supernatural but definitely eye-catching way. She was ostensibly chatting on her cellphone, her one leg up on the only chair in the box-like room, ignoring the group of male tourists that had gathered around her window, pointing. One brave one—brimming with testosterone—stepped forward and knocked on the ornate front door next to the box. The lady promptly finished her call and slipped in behind the velvet curtain that separated the window box and the room behind—I briefly caught a glimpse of a bed and a box of tissues—before the curtains were drawn shut to let the male customer in. I did not have time to see how long the transaction lasted, or how the male conqueror returned to

his mates from behind the curtain, probably getting "high 5s" and slaps on the back all-around. There were too many other window boxes to stare at in the "red light district" in De Wallen in Amsterdam. Free access to observe male fantasies played out in small square spaces—observable from the street. The spectators safe and anonymous, like in a zoo.

My trip to Amsterdam in 2009 perplexed me. I had been doing sex work research in southern Africa for a couple of years, and had become a passionate advocate for the decriminalisation of sex work. My conversations with sex workers in the inner-city Johannesburg district of Hillbrow, my work with the Sisonke Sex Worker Movement, the many, many reports of brutal attacks and rape of sex workers—mostly executed by police and clients—and the overwhelming HIV prevalence among sex workers in South Africa and the region have made one thing completely clear to me: the law is the biggest oppressor of sex workers at present. The current law that makes sex work illegal in South Africa also makes it possible for police to bribe, extort and mistreat sex workers; increases the stigma that attaches to sex work; compounds barriers to sex worker access to health and legal services; and empowers clients to do great harm to sex workers without fearing any legal consequences.

But the question is—is the only alternative to this criminalised system, those boxes in Amsterdam where sex work is legalised?

In this article, I explore the discomfort that some feminists feel when discussing this question by looking at the current debates about definitions of sex work and the ideological work that is employed to conflate sex work with social evils like child prostitution and human trafficking. I focus on how two strands of feminism—radical feminism and sex-positive feminism—have responded to the dilemma posed by sex work. I argue that an African, sex-positive feminist perspective would provide useful entry points into making feminist sense of the scenario described above. I conclude by showing that the type of feminism one identifies with would have no impact on the feminist imperative to support the decriminalisation of sex work.

SEX WORK, LAW AND SOCIAL CONTROL

During a writing workshop with female sex workers for submissions to the South African Law Reform Commission in 2008, my writing partner lifted her blouse to show me the scars of a knife slashing at her ribs. A cruel client's work. Another burst into tears when she recounted how the police threw her out of a speeding police car and she broke several bones. Every time I see her staggered walk on the streets of Hillbrow, bile of anger rises in my throat.

The law in South Africa currently makes every aspect of sex work a crime and a punishable offence. The law is as old and outdated as the hills—the current Sexual Offences Act is a remnant of the Immorality Act of 1927; the law that prohibited relationships across the colour bar and, later, same sex relationships under apartheid (Bodin and Richter, 2009). Very few people in South Africa would dispute that criminal law has no place in determining what race or gender the person should

be with whom you start a relationship or with whom you have sex. These sections of the criminal law were struck down as unconstitutional and slated as an antithesis to human rights very early on in South Africa's democracy. Our society seems mostly to be in agreement that the state should not interfere with the sexual, private lives of individuals—provided that they are adults, and that the sex is consensual. Nonetheless, many want to make an exception for sex work. Why is that?

DEFINITIONS OF SEX WORK

Sex work is the term preferred to prostitution and is indeed the language used by international organisations such as the United Nations, and more importantly: sex workers themselves (Naidoo, 2009). But while the terminology is clear, the definition and content are not. Most people have a very clear picture in their mind (usually based on a stereotype) when one talks about sex work but very few can verbalise a precise definition.

UNAIDS provides the following definition of sex work:

Female, male and transgender adults and young people who receive money or goods in exchange for sexual services, either regularly or occasionally (UNAIDS, 2009)

I believe that this definition is unworkable as it is too broad. It does not define "sexual services", whether "young people" include children, and whether "regularly or occasionally" means that this definition explicitly includes transactional sex.

The South African Law Reform Commission (SALRC) has been reviewing South Africa's sex work laws for almost a decade and has still not come to agreement on what to recommend to government. Its current definition is "the exchange of any financial or other reward, favour or compensation for the purpose of engaging in a sexual act" (South African Law Reform Commission, 2009, p. 9). The description of "reward" encompasses "both a monetary reward and other forms of compensation with pecuniary value, for example, clothing, food or accommodation" (South African Law Reform Commission, 2009, p. 16). The definitions of the SALRC and an earlier useful review of southern African laws on commercial sex work (Legal Assistance Centre, 2002) are unable to draw an unequivocal distinction between "sex work" and "transactional sex."

There is a graphic representation of the difficulties with pinning down meanings for "sex-for-reward" interactions. The sexual interactions described have an element of "reward" as provided for in the SALRC definition above. What makes the various scenarios so different that some parties could be prosecuted, while others not? Might it be because the women on the "illegitimate" side of the continuum are more dependent on the reward for their survival (and the survival of their dependants) than those on the "legitimate" side? Is it thus that class and financial status ultimately make the difference in terms of whether the state prosecutes women for sexual exchanges? Is it that rich women can have sex for whatever reason or reward they choose, but if poor women use sex as an informal livelihood strategy, they are deemed criminals? Is the difference related to the reward being given before the sexual act occurs or that the reward is explicitly negotiated before sex or that it is implicit in the interaction but not verbalised? Or is the only distinguishing factor that a scenario contains an individual who self-identifies as a sex worker, and that this should be grounds for prosecution?

I would argue that the difference between the scenarios is arbitrary and that no clear distinction between "sex-for-reward" interactions exists—least of all a difference that would hold up in court and would cause a woman to be jailed for it.

Sex workers across Africa make it clear that their profession relates to "sex that is paid for" and that it is a service that is rendered and their job should be respected (Naidoo, 2009, Legal Assistance Centre, 2002). Sex work researcher Johanna Busza identifies three main forms of "sexual exchange": sex work, transactional sex and survival sex (Busza, 2006a). The latter she argues is characterised by an attempt to alleviate extreme poverty. Sex work she sees as a "financial arrangement whereby a client pays a sex worker an agreed fee for sexual services,

which is a "professional" interaction. She notes that transactional sex—by contrast—is a financial arrangement "within other relationships often characterised by friendship, affection, or romantic attachment" (p. 135). Once again, the definitions are so nuanced and could be placed along a continuum, that it is not clear to me who should be put in jail and who should not—particularly so in southern Africa, where transactional sex is prevalent.

The most succinct definition of sex work I have come across is the following:

> *"Sex work is any agreement between two or more persons in which the objective is exclusively limited to the sexual act and ends with that, and which involves preliminary negotiations for a price. Hence there is a distinction from marriage contracts, sexual patronage and agreements concluded between lovers that could include presents in kind or money, but its value has no connection with the price of the sexual act and the agreement does not depend exclusively on sexual services."* (Source: Regional UNAIDS workshop on sex work in West and Central Africa, Abidjan, Cote d'Ivoire, 21–24 March 2000)

The contractual relationship between client and service provider and the upfront negotiation of price is clear, which none of the other definitions thus far have provided. However, the critiques of the other definitions still apply—even if we are able to better define who a "sex worker" is, what concrete grounds exist to prosecute them as criminals but not those who deliberately engage in other sexual exchanges for personal, financial gain, but where the reward may be implicit?

Perhaps what sex workers (and their sisters) do with sex is nobody's business except their own, and that terribly blunt instrument—the criminal law—has no place in this interaction and should rather focus its energies on murder, hijacking, rape and corruption?

WHAT SEX WORK IS NOT

One of the common denominators of the diverse definitions discussed above is the following: that sex work relates to adult, consensual sex. Sex work does not include the sale of sex by children. Under South African law—and across the region—the sale of sex by children is termed "commercial sexual exploitation" and carries high criminal penalties. The New Zealand's Prostitutes Collective puts it succinctly: "Children should be at the school. Not on the streets." (Healey, 2009)

Similarly, sex work is not human trafficking. The UN defines trafficking as follows:

> Trafficking in persons' shall mean the recruitment, transportation, transfer, harbouring or receipt of persons, by means of the threat or use of force or other forms of coercion, of abduction, of fraud, of deception, of the abuse of power or of a position of vulnerability or of the giving or receiving of payments or benefits to achieve the consent of a person having control over another person, for the purpose of exploitation. (Section 3A of the Protocol to Prevent, Suppress and Punish Trafficking in Persons, especially Women and Children, 2000

Thus, for a person to be regarded as having been trafficked, three minimum conditions have to be met: (1) the person should have been moved, (2) by means of force or coercion, and (3) for the express purpose of being exploited. Human trafficking is modern-day slavery and constitutes a gross human rights violation (Butcher, 2003). Adult, consensual sex work does not fulfil these conditions.

In the literature, child prostitutes, or people who have been trafficked are often referred to as "victims". The *Oxford English Dictionary* (8th ed) defines a victim as "a person injured or killed as a result of an event or circumstances." It also includes the synonyms "prey" or "dupe." The term "victim" often implies that the person had no choice in what happened to them—life dealt them a cruel blow and they were completely powerless in the face of it. Gender based violence advocates have long protested the labelling of women who have been raped as "rape victims." Many insist that this terminology erases the agency and tenacity of the women who have survived horrendous attacks, that "rape survivor" is preferred and celebrates the fortitude and strength of the survivor (Dunn, 2005). These critiques may also apply to the discourses of victimhood

with regard to child prostitution and trafficking, but I would like to make a different point: in calling sex workers "victims," or conflating sex work with trafficking or child prostitution, opponents of sex work try to remove the agency and choice of sex workers. A "victim" could be constructed as someone who is so bewildered or traumatised that they don't know what is good for themselves—indeed some "prostitution rehabilitation programmes" allege that they assist sex workers to deal with "Stockholm Syndrome." These campaigns ignore the following: taking up sex work to provide for yourself—and often your extended family—could be a resourceful strategy and a rational choice of livelihood activity, albeit that it could constitute a constrained choice in many circumstances.

In casting certain groups as "victims," the dialectic automatically sets up another group as heroic "saviours" (Doezema, 2000, Doezema, 2001). Examples include: some abolitionist feminist groups (often from the Global North) who endeavour to save sex workers from themselves by trying to eradicate sex work through criminal laws and international conventions; some misguided anti-trafficking campaigns—particularly when executed in the Global South—that initiate "Raid and Rescue" operations in brothels that leave many sex workers worse off than before; and religious-based interventions that attempt to "rehabilitate" sex workers and channel them into more worthy livelihoods like beading and sewing. These groups share the following characteristics: in casting sex workers as "victims" and themselves as "saviours," a power structure is created in which the "saviours" can superimpose their ideologies onto the bodies of the "victims" and be exempted from asking sex workers what they think or want. Such programmes can attract a lot of (often well-meaning) donor funding.

BUT ISN'T SEX WORK UNFEMINIST?

Before deciding what the most appropriate feminist response to sex work is, we have to pin down what "feminism" is. While a detailed discussion of various strands of feminism would be an impossible task in this article, the most salient point is that there are vigorous debates about what constitutes contemporary feminism(s). Yet, much of the overlap of different feminisms relates to the effects of male dominance on women and a "theory of power relations" (Ramazanoglu and Holland, 2002). With regard to various forms of African feminism, Desiree Lewis identifies the following commonalities: "a shared intellectual commitment to critiquing gender and imperialism coupled with a collective focus on a continental identity shaped by particular relations of subordination in the world economy and global social and cultural practices" (Lewis, 2001, page 4).

If the definition of feminism is an on-going debate, how feminism should relate to sex work is even more hotly contested. Priscilla Alexander describes the tension in what has been called the "Sex Wars" in the following way:

As feminists, we abhor the exploitation of women's sexuality by profiteers, and some of us feel instinctively, that prostitution supports an objectification of women's sexuality and of women, that is somehow related to the pervasive violence against us. In addition, we are defined, by ourselves and others, by our place in the age-old whore/Madonna dichotomy. However, there is a growing realisation among many feminists that the laws against prostitution, and the stigma imposed on sex work, keep all women from determining their own sexuality. (Alexander, 1996, page 342)

The tension in the Sex Wars ultimately centres on women's sexuality and how it relates to patriarchy. Catharine MacKinnon—an anti-sex work and anti-pornography feminist—describes sex work as inherently harmful and always a form of violence against women. In MacKinnon's view and those of other abolitionist or radical feminists, sex workers are trapped under the dominance of male clients and pimps, and are sexually exploited by them (Ahmed, 2011). This strand of feminist thought does not allow for sex worker agency or choice— sometimes maintaining that sex workers suffer from "false consciousness" (Barry, 1996) or "Stockholm Syndrome"—and that the industry should be

abolished by criminal sanction. Some effects of the view that "sex workers don't know what is good for them" include attempts in China to "rehabilitate" sex workers by sending them to labour re-education camps (Yardley, 2005), while more than a 1000 "marriage volunteers" from the Dera Sacha Sauda religious sect in India have pledged to marry sex workers in order "to stop the women from being exploited in brothels" and to help halt the spread of HIV and AIDS (BBC News, 2009).

One form of feminism that resists the abolitionist feminists' reading of sex work is sex-positive feminism. Carol Queen describes this intersection of sex radicalism and feminism:

[T]here is a community of people who are sex-positive, who don't denigrate, medicalize, or demonize any form of sexual expression except that which is not consensual. These "sex-positive feminists" [. . .] embrace the feminist analysis of gender inequality, but challenge the silence or conservative positions of [Andrea] Dworkin and [Catharine] MacKinnon-influenced feminism on sexual issues. (Queen, 2001, page 95)

While abolitionist feminists view female sexuality as being repressed by patriarchy, sex-positive feminists hold that this repression is produced by heterosexism and "sex negativity" (Glick, 2000, page 21) and that women's sexual autonomy and choice should be respected. Sex-positive feminists do not see anything inherently oppressive about sex work if it is regarded as "work," reflects women's choices and takes place within a human rights framework. Indeed, sex-positive feminists would view De Wallen in Amsterdam through a different lens: one that recognises a woman's choice to engage in sex work, to creatively manoeuvre and negotiate around men's sexual fantasies to make a living, and to render a service that is in demand.

The answer to the question posed above—is sex work unfeminist?—is therefore dependant on what form of feminism you identify with. However, I would argue that your view on feminism should not influence your position on how the law relates to sex work. One could be a staunch radical feminist and believe that sex work is deeply oppressive to all women, but still acknowledge that the sex industry will not be eradicated by the criminal law, that sex workers are worse off under a criminalised system, and that centuries of criminal and societal prohibition of sex work have not had any significant impact on the industry, except to make those who work in it vulnerable to violence, coercion, stigma and illness. Indeed, the criminalisation of sex work has far-reaching public health consequences in making sex workers, their clients and partners more vulnerable to HIV and other STIs (Richter et al., 2010). From this point of view, radical feminists should support the decriminalisation of sex work as heartily as sex-positive feminists do.

AFRICAN, SEX-POSITIVE FEMINISM AND SEX WORK

It is curious that, while the prevalence of female sex workers and proportion of female sex workers to the general population are higher in sub-Saharan Africa than in any other region of the world (Vandepitte et al., 2006), African feminisms have not grappled much with the issue of sex work. This is of particular concern against the backdrop of the staggering prevalence of HIV amongst sex workers in Africa—sex workers generally have a 10–20 fold higher HIV prevalence than the general population (Scorgie et al., 2011a)—and the on-going human rights violations against sex workers (Scorgie et al., 2011b, Arnott and Crago, 2009, Okal et al., 2011). Sex work and sex worker rights are conspicuously absent from most discussions on gender in Africa, and many feminists and gender practitioners avoid the issue like the plague—thus perpetuating the stigma and silence that surround the sex industry in Africa.

In concluding this article, I invite other African feminists to consider the growing literature on sex-positive feminism, and to apply and mould this to the African context. In particular, I would like to see feminists from all persuasions, gender activists, womanists, human rights advocates and AIDS workers grapple and wrestle with the issue of sex work. There is rich ground for discussion and debate on a matter that cuts across analyses based on class, race, migration and mobility, relative depravation, development economics, the law, sexual and reproductive health rights, and many others. Vital to these conversations and debates are the voices of sex workers—those who are most often silenced by law-enforcers and by feminists who deem they know best.

BIBLIOGRAPHY

Ahmed, A. 2011. *Feminism, Power, and Sex Work in the Context of HIV/AIDS: Consequences for Women's Health.* Harvard Journal of Law and Gender, 35, 225.

Alexander, P. 1996. *Prostitution - a difficult issue for feminists.* In: Jackson, S. & Scott, S. (eds.) Feminism and sexuality - a reader. New York: Columbia University Press.

Arnott, J. & Crago, A.-L. 2009. *Rights not Rescue: A Report on Female, Male, and Trans Sex Workers' Human Rights in Botswana, Namibia, and South Africa. Open Society Institute.*

Barry, K. 1996. *The Prostitution of Sexuality.* New York, New York University Press.

Author. 2009. Indian sect members vow to marry sex workers. BBC, 16 December.http:// news.bbc .co.uk/2/hi/south_asia/8416739.stms

Bodin, C. & Richter, M. 2009. *Adult, Consensual Sex Work In South Africa – The Cautionary Message Of Criminal Law And Sexual Morality.* South African Journal on Human Rights, 25, 179–197.

Busza, J. 2006a. For love or money: the role of exchange in young people's sexual relationships. In: Ingham, R. & Aggleton, P. (eds.) Promoting young people's sexual health - international perspectives. London, New York: Routledge

Busza, J. 2006b. Having the rug pulled from under your feet: one project's experience of the US policy reversal on sex work. Health Policy Plan, 21, 329–32.

Butcher, K. 2003. Confusion between prostitution and sex trafficking. Lancet, 361, 1983.

Doezema, J. 2000. Loose women or lost women? The re-emergence of the myth of white slavery in contemporary discourses of trafficking in women. Gender Issues, 18, 23–50.

Doezema, J. 2001. Ouch! Western Feminists' "Wounded Attachment" to the "Third World Prostitute". Feminist Review, 67, 16–38.

Dunkle, K. L., Jewkes, R., Nduna, M., Jama, N., Levin, J., Sikweyiya, Y. & Koss, M. P. 2007. Transactional sex with casual and main partners among young South African men in the rural Eastern

Cape: prevalence, predictors, and associations with gender-based violence. Soc Sci Med, 65, 1235–48.

Dunn, J. L. 2005. *"Victims" and "Survivors": Emerging Vocabularies of Motive for "Battered Women Who Stay"*. Sociological Inquiry, 75, 1–30.

Farley, M. 2004. *"Bad for the Body, Bad for the Heart": Prostitution Harms Women Even if Legalized or Decriminalized.* Violence Against Women, 10 1087–1125.

Farley, M., Baral, I., Kiremire, M. & Sezgin, U. 1998. *Prostitution in Five Countries: Violence and*

Post-Traumatic Stress Disorder. Feminism & Psychology, 8, 405–426.

Glick, E. 2000. *Sex Positive: Feminism, Queer Theory, and the Politics of Transgression.* Feminist Review, 64, 19–45

Healey, C. 2009. New Zealand's legal framework in relation to sex work. In: RICHTER, M. & MASSWE, D. (eds.) Consultation on HIV, Sex Work and the 2010 Soccer World Cup: Human Rights, Public Health, Soccer and beyond. Cape Town: Workshop Report.

Legal Assistance Centre. 2002.

DISCUSSION QUESTIONS FOR CHAPTER 9

1. How does women's unpaid labor in the home maintain systems of oppression?

2. How do racism and sexism intersect in the experiences of women in the paid labor force?

3. Why has legislation requiring equal pay and prohibiting discrimination failed to bring about equality for women in the workforce?

4. What problems and conflicts arise among women around issues of work? What roles do differences among women play in these problems and conflicts?

5. What changes do you think need to occur to create equitable systems of work for all women?

SUGGESTIONS FOR FURTHER READING

Bennetts, Leslie. *The Feminine Mistake: Are We Giving Up Too Much?* New York: Voice, 2007.

Burk, Martha. *Cult of Power: Sex Discrimination in Corporate America and What Can Be Done About It.* New York: Scribner, 2005.

Dunaway, Wilma, ed. *Gendered Commodity Chains: Seeing Women's Work and Households in Global Production.* Palo Alto, CA: Stanford University Press, 2013.

Federici, Silvia. *Revolution at Point Zero: Housework, Reproduction, and Feminist Struggle.* Oakland: PM Press, 2012.

Gottfried, Heidi. *Gender, Work, and Economy: Unpacking the Global Economy.* Cambridge: Polity, 2012.

Hirshman, Linda. *Get to Work: A Manifesto for Women of the World.* New York: Penguin, 2006.

Hochschild, Arlie, and Barbara Ehrenreich, eds. *Global Women: Nannies, Maids, and Sex Workers in the New Economy.* New York: Henry Holt, 2004.

Iversen, Torben, and Frances Rosenbluth. *Women, Work, and Politics: The Political Economy of Gender Inequality.* New Haven, CT: Yale University Press, 2010.

Kunin, Madeleine. *The New Feminist Agenda: Defining the Next Revolution for Women, Work, and Family.* White River Jct, VT: Chelsea Green Publishing, 2012.

CHAPTER 10

Resisting Gender
Violence

Gender violence in the United States and worldwide is an important public health and human rights issue. Violence, an assault on a person's control over her/his body and life, can take many forms and has varying consequences depending on the type of assault, its context and interpretation, the chronicity of violence, and the availability of support. *Gender violence* implies that harm evolves from the imbalance in power associated with masculinity and femininity. In most societies around the world, gender violence usually occurs when masculine entitlements produce power that manifests itself in harm and injury (physical, sexual, emotional/psychological) toward others. Overwhelmingly this gender power imbalance involves men's violence against women and other men. Women are especially vulnerable in intimate relationships; most violence against them occurs in their own homes. Women are 10 times more likely than men to be victimized by an intimate partner.

Because violence is about the exercise of power over another person, both men and women can perpetrate violence and it occurs in both heterosexual and lesbian/gay/queer relationships. However, men are most likely to suffer physical violence at the hands of other men, and males are especially at risk during childhood and adolescence for suffering physical abuse by female and male caretakers, and sexual abuse by other males. Given the norms about masculine invulnerability, it is often hard for boys and men to talk about sexual abuse and seek help. As a result, men are more likely than women to be in denial about such experiences, and some men who have been abused try to "master" the abuse by identifying with the source of their victimization and avoiding the weaknesses associated with being a "victim."

A range of gendered violence includes acts of intimidation and harassment (stalking; voyeurism; online/chat room, street, school, and workplace harassment; road rage; and obscene phone calls); forcing someone to watch or participate in pornography, prostitution, and other sex work; emotional/psychological, physical, and sexual abuse (that includes rape and attempted rape); and any other coercive act that harms and violates another person. Rates of violence against women in the United States are quite alarming, although compared to figures from the early 1990s, rates of rape and sexual assault have decreased somewhat. However, because intimate violence is so underreported, accurate statistics are difficult to collect. Recent laws such as rape shield laws, which prevent a victim's sexual history from being used by defense attorneys, and various state reform laws have helped survivors.

Mandatory arrest procedures in cases of domestic violence and the creation of temporary restraining orders have helped survivors of domestic abuse. In addition, the 1994 Violence Against Women Act (VAWA, passed as Title IV of the Violent Crime Control and Law Enforcement Act) provides some legal protections for women. Overall it is estimated that intimate partner violence against women in the United States costs the state and insurance companies, as well as communities, families, and individuals, more than $8 billion per year.

The 2011 National Crime Victimization Survey of the U.S. Bureau of Justice Statistics provides the most comprehensive and current statistics to date about gender-based violence. This survey reports that although the rate of intimate partner victimization declined over the last decade along with violent crime rates generally, an average of 24 people per minute are victims of rape, physical violence, or stalking by an intimate partner in the United States. Over the course of a year this amounts to more than 12 million people. Such numbers tell only part of the story as more than 1 million women are raped in a year and more than 6 million women and men are victims of stalking annually. These findings emphasize that sexual violence, stalking, and intimate partner violence are important and widespread public health problems in the United States. The term "intimate partner violence" describes physical, sexual, or psychological harm by a current or former partner or spouse. This type of violence can occur among heterosexual or same-sex couples and does not require sexual intimacy. Eighty-one percent of women and 35 percent of men who experienced rape, physical violence, or stalking by an intimate partner reported at least one impact related to the experiences, such as fear, concern for safety, injury, or having missed at least one day of work or school. Individuals who experienced rape or stalking by any perpetrator or physical violence by an intimate partner in their lifetime were more likely to report frequent headaches, chronic pain, difficulty with sleeping, activity limitations, and poor physical and mental health than those who did not experience these forms of violence. In other words, nearly 3 in 10 women and 1 in 10 men in the United States have experienced rape, physical violence, and/or stalking by a partner and report a related impact on their functioning. The next most likely assailant when it comes to physical and sexual violence is a friend and acquaintance. Overall, about 78 percent of all violent acts are committed by intimate partners, friends and acquaintances, or family members. About 22 percent of this violence is committed by strangers. Finally, women serving in the U.S. military are at special risk as a 2013 Pentagon report estimated that there are more than 70 sexual assaults involving military personnel every day. As discussed in Chapter 11, approximately 1 in 3 female soldiers experiences sexual assault while on duty, according to the U.S. Department of Defense.

Of all statistics, those associated with interpersonal violence are generally underreported and sometimes difficult to interpret. Different studies ask about victimization in different ways and get different results. Some studies ask about current abuse and some survey past histories; some ask only about physical abuse, while others include questions about emotional or psychological abuse and sexual abuse. It is important to consider whether consent for sexual intimacy can occur in a relationship where physical violence and intimidation are present.

According to national statistics published by the National Center for Victims of Crime, approximately one in five high school girls in the United States report being abused physically and/or sexually by a boyfriend, and 50 to 80 percent of teenagers report knowing others in violent relationships. Estimates of physical and sexual dating violence among high school students typically range from 1 in 10 to 1 in 4. Sometimes this dating violence occurs through text messaging, when many teens do not recognize controlling behavior

HISTORICAL MOMENT **The Violence Against Women Act of 1994**

For decades feminist activists had worked to gain recognition of the extent and severity of violence against women in the United States. On the whole, violence against women had not been fully recognized as a serious crime within the criminal justice system.

Often reports of sexual assault were greeted with skepticism or victim-blaming. Prior to feminist activism in the 1970s, women had to present evidence of resistance to sexual assault; rules of evidence allowed consideration of a victim's entire sexual history; and husbands were exempt from charges of raping their wives. Following the opening of the first rape crisis centers in 1972, grassroots advocacy managed not only to provide care and services to victims, but also to change these laws.

Generally, domestic violence was considered by law enforcement to be a "family matter," and so police, prosecutors, and judges were often reluctant to "interfere." The first domestic violence shelters opened in the mid-1970s, but not until the 1980s did this problem receive widespread attention. Thanks to activists, laws did change in the 1980s to codify domestic violence as criminal conduct, to provide increased penalties, to create civil protection orders, and to mandate training about domestic violence for law enforcement.

Following a Washington, D.C., meeting of representatives from various groups advocating for victims of sexual assault and domestic violence in the 1980s, activists turned their attention to ensuring federal legislation to protect women through interstate enforcement of protection orders, to provide funding for shelters and other programs for victims, and to provide prevention efforts. By demonstrating the need for these protections and programs, grassroots advocates and the National Organization for Women (NOW) Legal Defense Fund were able to develop bipartisan support in Congress and to pass the Violence Against Women Act (VAWA) in 1994. The four subtitles of the Act describe the target areas of concern: Safe Streets, Safe Homes for Women, Civil Rights for Women and Equal Justice for Women in the Courts, and Protections of Battered Immigrant Women and Children. VAWA changed rules of evidence, police procedures, penalties, and court procedures. It also authorized funding for prevention, education, and training.

Since 1994, VAWA has been reauthorized and modified several times. The Act was most recently reauthorized in 2013. For the first time, the law now includes protections for lesbian, gay, bisexual, and transgender survivors and allows tribal authorities to prosecute non-tribal members who commit crimes on tribal land. To find out more about VAWA, visit the website of the U.S. Department of Justice's Violence Against Women Office at *http://www.ovw.usdoj.gov*.

as abusive. This problem illustrates the ways communication technologies can influence dating violence by redefining boundaries between dating partners.

Although girls are more likely to be sexually abused than boys and the latter are more likely to be sexually abused by other males, both male and female adolescents report being targets of physical violence in relationships. Sometimes this involves mutual abuse, with both partners using violence against each other. However, it is clear that male and female adolescents use force for different reasons and with different results. Researchers have found that girls suffer more from relationship violence, emotionally and physically. They are more likely than males to have serious injuries and report being terrified. In contrast, male victims seldom fear violence by their girlfriends and often say the attacks did not hurt or that they found the violence amusing. Rape victims are about 4 times more likely to contemplate suicide and 13 times more likely to actually make a suicide attempt.

An important aspect of teen violence is bullying, where someone harasses verbally and/or physically another person perceived as weaker. Bullies seek power through aggression and direct their attacks at vulnerable targets. Boys are more likely to bully than girls and to bully other boys, although girls may of course also be perpetrators. Despite the most recent School Crime Supplement to the National Crime Victimization Survey, which reports that school crime has decreased in the last decade to include a drop in the rates of students reporting criminal victimization at school (now about 4 percent of all K–12 students), bullying has increased, especially cyberbullying. The National Institute of Child Health reports 6 out of 10 teenagers currently witness bullying in U.S. schools daily, and an estimated 1.6 million children in grades 6 through 10 are bullied at least once a week. More than two-thirds of students report general bullying as an ongoing problem in their school, 1 in 10 students drops out or changes schools because of repeated bullying, and more than 1 in 10 report school absences because of fear of bullying. Indeed, both the bully and the bullied are at greater risk of loneliness; lack of success in school; and becoming involved in drugs, alcohol, and tobacco. Almost half of all bullies had three or more police arrests by age 30. In addition, Asian American students are bullied in U.S. schools more than any other ethnic group, but particularly online. Indeed, cyberbullying is currently a serious social problem that may lead to tragic consequences, such as youths committing suicide after experiencing bullying and harassment. The prevalence of youths committing suicide due to long-term bullying has resulted in the term "bullycide." Gay youths or anyone who is perceived as "different" are likely targets. Finally, alongside these statistics on bullying and victimization of children and youths at school, is the tragic reality of school shootings, which have killed and severely wounded pupils and staff in schools across the United States. That these shooters are overwhelmingly white boys is sometimes overlooked by media and academics alike. A more thorough analysis of contemporary white masculinities, as well as the role of firearms and violent media in the cultural landscape, needs to be performed in order to better understand this phenomenon.

Online gender-based harassment targeted at people who speak out in favor of social justice is increasingly being understood as a rampant social problem in the United States as the public virtual space gets constructed as a masculine sphere where misogyny is rife. This is the point of the reading "How Some Men Harass Women Online and What Other Men Can Do to Stop It" by Ben Atherton-Zeman. He discusses the ways people writing about feminism and men's violence against women are silenced and controlled, in part through misogynous and brutal online threats of violence. Atherton-Zeman suggests 10 things to resist and transform this discourse. Such cyber threats are often one aspect of violence against LGBTQ individuals in particular. As the reading "Anti-LGBTQ Violence: Three Essays" by Tony Hobday, Michelangelo Signorile, and Hope Gillette emphasizes, violence against this population is especially problematic, in part because of the stigma of difference and socially accepted bigotry against LQBTQ persons. These essays discuss anti-LGBTQ violence in Russia, the United States, and in Latin America.

Another disturbing trend is the increase in stalking behavior directed at women (see the box in this chapter "Stalking Fact Sheet"). Stalking can be defined as the act of a person who, on more than one occasion, follows, pursues, or harasses another person, and, by actively engaging in a pattern of conduct, causes victims to believe the stalker will cause physical harm or mental distress to them. Behaviors include making unwanted phone calls, sending unsolicited or unwanted letters or emails, following or spying on the victim, showing up at places without a legitimate reason, waiting at places for the victim, leaving unwanted items, presents, or flowers, and posting information or spreading rumors about the victim on the Internet, in a public place, or by word of mouth. Approximately 13 percent of women on college campuses report being stalked and two-thirds of stalked women know their stalker. It is estimated that about 1 in 6 women will experience stalking in their lifetimes. All 50 states in the United States now have stalking laws. The most common consequence for women is fear and emotional and psychological trauma.

Violence against girls and women is a persistent problem all over the world and is increasingly understood as a human rights issue. The wars of the twentieth century and the new conflicts of the twenty-first, the increase in globalization and the scope of global commerce and communications have all facilitated an increase in violence against women and children, as approximately 1 in 3 women in the world is beaten, coerced into sex, and otherwise abused. In 2010 the International Violence Against Women Act (I-VAWA) was introduced into Congress and has still not yet passed. It would allocate more than a billion dollars over 5 years to make the prevention of gender-based violence a "strategic foreign-policy imperative."

Violence against indigenous girls and women is a problem worldwide. This violence involves economic exploitation and sexual abuse and exploitation, as well as gender-based violence in situations of armed violence, insecurity, and communal conflicts. Such gendered violence must be understood in the context of ongoing discrimination against indigenous peoples as well as their marginalization in terms of violation of individual and collective rights, poverty, and displacement. These problems occur despite United Nations Resolution 1325 on women and peace and security, adopted in 2000, which presents measures to protect women and girls from gender-based violence, particularly rape and other forms of sexual abuse, in situations of armed conflict. Still, some countries condone or legalize these crimes, and others accept such violence against women as necessary consequences of war and/or civil unrest and ethnic cleansing. Certainly increased militarism and military posturing among countries in the global north have important consequences for the safety of women and children in target societies, usually in the global south, facilitating prostitution and international sex trafficking in girls and women.

Sex trafficking in the United States is a focus of the reading with the same name by Rachel Chinapen. She writes about young women brought to Connecticut from such countries as Indonesia and Thailand and their coerced labor in the sex industry. This article emphasizes that sex trafficking does not occur only in places like Southeast Asia, but also in communities within the United States. Indeed, according to the Department of Justice thousands of people are trafficked into the United States every year and approximately 70 percent end up working in the sex industry. These problems exist despite the fact that there are U.S. laws against human trafficking at the federal level with the U.S. Trafficking Victims Protection Act (2000) and at state levels. The reading identifies legislation as well as law enforcement training, and survivor services. It also makes the distinction between human trafficking and sex trafficking specifically and emphasizes the importance of recognizing the difference between coerced sex trafficking and women who freely cross national borders to engage in sex work. Feminists of the global north have been guilty of sensationalizing the issue in their desire to "save" women from such sex work, often in ways that ignore the complexity of women's decisions and experiences in this work, and especially the differences between migrating sex workers and those who are coerced into such practices. Of course it is problematic to automatically assume "free choice" in these decisions, because "choices" are often made from limited options and reflect structural realities such as poverty and violence.

Gendered violence is specifically linked to processes of globalization, as already discussed, because these processes often heighten problems associated with gender inequities in relationships, families, and communities at the same time that they often increase women's poverty and therefore their vulnerability. Violence against women in Juarez, Mexico, for example, where countless women have disappeared and been raped and killed, can be explained in part by forces of globalization cheapening women's labor power and therefore their bodies in the context of the forces of prostitution, organized crime, police corruption, and drug trafficking. In addition, globalizing forces have encouraged the status of women to be used as a marker of the level of "civilization" of a society, just as cultural interventions have been justified in part in the name of improving the status of women (as was most recently shown with the U.S. attacks on Afghanistan as "liberating" women from the Taliban, discussed in the reading by Andrea Smith, "Beyond the Politics of Inclusion"). These developments often create complexity for feminist activism as women and men in these countries seeking to address nationalist, patriarchal problems can be interpreted as "traitors"; similarly, it causes problems for feminists in the global north whose activism can be interpreted as ethnocentric meddling or support for the militarist strategies of their own societies.

It is important in all these discussions to understand the tendency to "exoticize" global gendered violence as something that happens elsewhere and to avoid reading such problems as dowry-related violence or acid throwing (when acid is thrown at the face or person to maim or kill) as examples of crimes caused by customs and culture. These crimes are no more exotic or culturally based than atrocities perpetuated on women in the global north on a daily basis. For example, "Nirbhaya," the 23 year-old paramedic who died after being gang raped with unspeakable brutality on a bus in New Delhi, India, in late 2012, has become an icon of resistance and galvanized protests and calls for change in India. Although her tragic death has highlighted the problem of chronic gender violence in India and its relationship to cultural misogyny, it is important for those in the global north to understand that cultural misogyny is present in all our communities.

Any discussion attempting to address the issue of violence against women—either in the United States or worldwide—must involve several key points. *First*, violence against women must be understood in the context of socially constructed notions of gender. If boys are raised to hide emotion, see sensitivity as a weakness, and view sexual potency as wound up with interpersonal power, and girls are raised to be dependent and support masculine entitlement, then interpersonal violence should be no surprise. As Debra Anne Davis explains in the reading "Betrayed by the Angel," women are raised in ways that may encourage victimization. *Second*, violence is a power issue and must be seen as related to masculine dominance in society generally as represented in interpersonal relationships and in the control of political systems that address crime and create policy. Indeed, entitlements associated with masculinity produce a range that some scholars term the *rape spectrum*. This means that all sexist behaviors are arranged along a continuum from unexamined feelings of superiority over women, for example, on one

Anti-LGBTQ and HIV-Affected Hate Violence

REPORTED INCIDENTS:

- 2012 reports of anti-LGBTQ and HIV-affected hate violence stayed relatively consistent to 2011, with a 4% decrease (2,092 in 2011, 2,016 in 2012).

HATE VIOLENCE HOMICIDES:

In 2012 anti-LGBTQ and HIV-affected homicides decreased by 16.7% from 2011, (30 in 2011 to 25 in 2012). However, the total homicides for 2012 remains the fourth highest ever recorded by NCAVP (National Coalition of Anti-Violence Programs). Additionally, the disproportionate impact of homicides against people of color, transgender women, and gender nonconforming LGBTQ and HIV-affected people continued in 2012. 73.1% of all homicide victims in 2012 were people of color, yet LGBTQ and HIV-affected people of color only represented 53% of total survivors and victims. The overwhelming majority of homicide victims were Black/African American, (50%), 19.2% of victims were Latin@, 11.5% of victims were White and 3.9% of victims were Native American. 50% of total victims were transgender, all of whom identified as transgender women, yet transgender survivors and victims only represent 10.5% of total reports to NCAVP. 38.5% of homicide victims were men all of who identified as gay. Gay people represented 47.4% of victims, which mirrors the overall total of gay survivors and victims reported to NCAVP (45.3%).

MOST IMPACTED COMMUNITIES:

Transgender people were:

- 3.32 times as likely to experience police violence as compared to cisgender survivors and victims.
- 2.46 times as likely to experience physical violence by the police compared to cisgender survivors and victims.

Transgender people of color were:

- 2.59 times as likely to experience police violence compared to white cisgender survivors and victims.
- 2.37 times as likely to experience discrimination compared to white cisgender survivors and victims.

Transgender women were:

- 2.90 times as likely to experience police violence as compared to survivors and victims who were not transgender women.
- 2.71 times as likely to experience physical violence by the police as compared to survivors and victims who were not transgender women.
- 2.14 times as likely to experience discrimination as compared to survivors and victims who were not transgender women.

(continued)

Gay men were:

- 3.04 times as likely to report incidents of hate violence to the police as compared to survivors and victims who were not gay men.
- 1.56 times as likely to require medical attention compared to survivors and victims who were not gay men.

LGBTQ people of color were:

- 1.82 times as likely to experience physical violence as compared to white LGBTQ survivors and victims.
- 1.70 times as likely to experience discrimination as compared to white LGBTQ survivors and victims.

SURVIVOR AND VICTIM DEMOGRAPHICS:

Almost half of survivors and victims identified as gay (45.3%), and 20.6% of survivors and victims identified as lesbian. Bisexual survivors and victims represented 8.7% of total survivors in 2012. Gay and bisexual survivors and victims remained consistent with 2011, but lesbian survivors and victims decreased slightly (24% in 2011, and 20.6% in 2012). 30.4% of total hate violence survivors and victims identified as men, a considerable decrease from 50% in 2011. Women represented the second highest number of reports (25%), which is a decrease from 34% in 2011. Transgender identified survivors and victims represented 10.5% of overall survivors and victims, a decrease from 18% in 2011. Undocumented survivors represented 6.4% of total survivors, a slight decrease from 8% in 2011.

POLICE RESPONSE:

Only 56% of survivors reported their incidents to the police, a slight increase from 2011 (52%). Of survivors and victims' who reported to the police, 48% reported incidents of police misconduct to NCAVP, a considerable increase from 2011 (32%). While total number of survivors reporting to the police remains small, NCAVP finds that this number is growing incrementally over the years, 45.3% in 2010, 52% in 2011 and 56.5% in 2012. Of those who interacted with the police, 26.8% reported that the police attitudes were hostile, an increase from 2011 (18%).

POLICE CLASSIFICATION:

In 2012, 77.2% of hate violence incidents reported to the police were classified as bias crimes, a substantial increase from 2011 (55%).

DISABILITY:

In 2012 40% of survivors and victims reported having a disability, a substantial increase from 2011 (11%). Of those who reported having a disability, 52.8% of survivors and victims reported having a disability associated with their mental health. 35.8% of survivors and victims reported having a physical disability, 6.3% of survivors and victims reported having a learning disability, 2.8% of survivors reported being blind and 2.3% of survivors reported being deaf.

CHARACTERISTICS OF OFFENDERS:

Cisgender men made up the highest proportion of hate violence offenders in both 2011 and 2012, with a decrease in the number of cisgender men in 2012 (46% in 2012, 60% in 2011). Police made up 23.9% of unknown offenders, a considerable increase from 2011 (8%). In 2012, 63% of survivors reported one offender, a decrease from 2011 (78%). 19% of survivors reported 2–5 offenders, consistent with 2011 (20%). 16% of survivors reported 10 or more offenders, an increase from 2011 (10%).

CHARACTERISTICS OF INCIDENT SITES:

The most common site type remains private residence (38.6% in 2012, more than double the 18% reported in 2011). The second highest site type was the street (24.8% in 2012, an increase from 15% in 2011).

Source: Avp.org.

end to rape on the other. In this sense, all these behaviors, even though they are so very different in degree, are connected at some level.

In addition, scholars emphasize that these behaviors are often connected to "backlash" or resistance to gains made by women and other marginalized peoples. This is an important point made in the essays "Anti-LGBTQ Violence." Though many men today support these gains and are working on ways to address interpersonal power and violence, hoping to enjoy egalitarian relationships with women, some men have not responded well to these gains. They have responded with anger and feelings of powerlessness and insecurity. Interpersonal violence occurs as men attempt to reestablish power they believe they have lost as a direct result of the gains of women. As discussed in Chapter 2, hate crimes based upon identity are significant problems in contemporary society as people marked as "different" or marginal are targeted as victims of violence. Hate crimes target a victim because of his or her perceived membership in a certain social group and involve such criminal acts as damage to property or pets and offensive graffiti or letters (hate mail) as well as interpersonal violence such as physical and sexual assault, bullying, harassment, verbal abuse or insults, and murder. The series of essays making up the reading on anti-LGBTQ violence illustrate this poignant issue.

Third, gendered sexual violence is often related to the ways violence is eroticized and sexuality is connected to violence. Although pornography is the best example of this problem in its role in eroticizing power differences, women's magazines and advertising

Stalking Fact Sheet

WHAT IS STALKING?

While legal definitions of stalking vary from one jurisdiction to another, a good working definition of stalking is *a course of conduct directed at a specific person that would cause a reasonable person to feel fear.*

STALKING VICTIMIZATION

6.6 million people are stalked in one year in the United States.

1 in 6 women and 1 in 19 men have experienced stalking victimization at some point during their lifetime in which they felt very fearful or believed that they or someone close to them would be harmed or killed.

Using a less conservative definition of stalking, which considers any amount of fear (i.e., a little fearful, somewhat fearful, or very fearful), 1 in 4 women and 1 in 13 men reported being a victim of stalking in their lifetime.

The majority of stalking victims are stalked by someone they know. 66% of female victims and 41% of male victims of stalking are stalked by a current or former intimate partner.

More than half of female victims and more than 1/3 of male victims of stalking indicated that they were stalked before the age of 25.

About 1 in 5 female victims and 1 in 14 male victims experienced stalking between the ages of 11 and 17.

[Michele C. Black et al., "The National Intimate Partner and Sexual Violence Survey: 2010 Summary Report," (Atlanta, GA: National Center for Injury Prevention and Control, Centers for Disease Control and Prevention, 2011).]

46% of stalking victims experience at least one unwanted contact per week.

11% of stalking victims have been stalked for 5 years or more.

[Katrina Baum et al., "Stalking Victimization in the United States," (Washington, DC: Bureau of Justice Statistics, 2009).]

STALKING AND INTIMATE PARTNER FEMICIDE

76% of intimate partner femicide victims have been stalked by their intimate partner.

67% had been physically abused by their intimate partner.

89% of femicide victims who had been physically assaulted had also been stalked in the 12 months before their murder.

79% of abused femicide victims reported being stalked during the same period that they were abused.

54% of femicide victims reported stalking to police before they were killed by their stalkers.

[Judith McFarlane et al., "Stalking and Intimate Partner Femicide," *Homicide Studies* 3, no. 4 (1999).]

RECON STUDY OF STALKERS

2/3 of stalkers pursue their victims at least once per week, many daily, using more than one method.

78% of stalkers use more than one means of approach.

Weapons are used to harm or threaten victims in 1 out of 5 cases.

Almost 1/3 of stalkers have stalked before.

Intimate partner stalkers frequently approach their targets, and their behaviors escalate quickly.

[Kris Mohandie et al.,"The RECON Typology of Stalking: Reliability and Validity Based upon a Large Sample of North American Stalkers," *Journal of Forensic Sciences*, 51, no. 1 (2006).]

IMPACT OF STALKING ON VICTIMS

46% of stalking victims fear not knowing what will happen next.

29% of stalking victims fear the stalking will never stop.

1 in 8 employed stalking victims lose time from work as a result of their victimization and more than half lose 5 days of work or more.

1 in 7 stalking victims move as a result of their victimization.

[Baum et al.]

The prevalence of anxiety, insomnia, social dysfunction, and severe depression is much higher among stalking victims than the general population, especially if the stalking involves being followed or having one's property destroyed.

[Eric Blauuw et al., "The Toll of Stalking," *Journal of Interpersonal Violence*, 17, no. 1 (2002):50-63.]

STALKING LAWS

Stalking is a crime under the laws of 50 states, the District of Columbia, the U.S. Territories, and the Federal government.

Less than 1/3 of states classify stalking as a felony upon first offense.

More than 1/2 of states classify stalking as a felony upon second or subsequent offense or when the crime involves aggravating factors.

(continued)

Aggravating factors may include: possession of a deadly weapon, violation of a court order or condition of probation/parole, victim under 16 years, or same victim as prior occasions.

For a compilation of state, tribal, and federal laws visit www.victimsofcrime.org/src.

Source: Stalking Resource center
Last updated August 2012

generally are rampant with these themes. *Finally*, we must understand violence against women in terms of the normalization of violence in society. We live in societies where violence is used to solve problems every day, media are saturated with violence, militarism is a national policy, and rape is used as a weapon of war. Again, it is important to analyze the role of contemporary masculinity in these phenomena and consider the ways violent masculinity is normalized. What do you think would be the societal response if women and girls victimized men, boys, and other girls to the extent that men and boys routinely victimize girls, women, and each other?

Consider the following story told to us. The woman, a white professional in her early 30s, had been having a drink with her colleagues one early evening after work. A well-dressed man struck up a conversation with her, and they chatted a while. When she was leaving with her colleagues, the man asked if he could call her sometime, and she gave him her business card that listed only work information. He called her at work within the next week and asked her to have dinner with him, and, seeing no reason not to, she agreed to meet him at a particular restaurant after work. She was careful to explain to us that on both occasions, she was dressed in her professional work clothes and it was early evening in a public space. There was nothing provocative, she emphasized, about her clothes or her demeanor. At some point during the meal she started feeling uncomfortable. The man was very pushy; he chose and ordered her food for her and started telling her that if she wanted to date him, he had certain requirements about how his girlfriends dressed and acted. She panicked and felt a strong need to get away from him, so, at some point she quietly excused herself saying she needed to visit the ladies' room. She then did a quick exit and did not return to the table. Unfortunately, this was not the end of the story. The man found out where her home was and started to stalk her. One evening he forced his way into her apartment and beat her badly. Fortunately, he did not rape her. Although she took out a restraining order on him, he managed to gain entrance into her apartment building again and beat her senseless one more time in the hallway outside her apartment.

This story is a tragic illustration of misogyny and masculine entitlement. The man felt he had the right to define the reality of women in his life and expected them to be subordinate. He believed it was his entitlement. He was so full of rage that when a woman snubbed him, he would have to subdue her. In addition, the woman's telling of the story is illustrative of societal norms that blame women for their own victimization. When tearfully sharing her story, she had felt the shame and humiliation that comes with such

an experience; she wanted it to be known that she had not been "asking for it." He had given no indication that he was anything but clean-cut and upstanding, she was dressed appropriately, she took no risks other than accepting a date, she gave him only her work numbers, and she agreed to meet him in a public place. What more could she have done except be wary of all men she might meet?

Abused women are disproportionately represented among the homeless and suicide victims, and they have been denied insurance in some states because they are considered to have a "preexisting condition" (i.e., having resided with a batterer). It is important to remember that alongside the sheer physical and emotional costs of violence against women, the Centers for Disease Control and Prevention estimated that health-related financial costs of rape, physical assault, stalking, and homicide against women by intimate partners entail almost $6 billion annually. Women who are battered have more than twice the health care needs and costs than those who are never battered. This figure does not include lost wages and productivity. In the following sections we discuss sexual assault and rape, physical abuse, and incest and end with a discussion of pornography as an aspect of violence against women. Because many forms of pornography are legal, some people object to thinking about pornography in the context of sexual violence and claim instead that it is a legitimate type of entertainment. Despite these concerns, we have decided to discuss it in the context of sexual violence because pornography eroticizes unequal power relations between women and men and often involves representations of coercive sex. Men are the major consumers of pornography, and women's bodies tend to be the ones on display. Pornography thus represents a particular aspect of gender relations that reflects the issue of male sexual violence against women.

SEXUAL ASSAULT AND RAPE

Sexual assault can be defined as any sexual contact without consent that involves the use of force. Individuals may be sexually assaulted without being raped. Basically, rape is a form of sexual assault and sexual abuse, but sexual assault and abuse do not necessarily imply rape. More specifically, rape is the penetration of any bodily orifice by a penis or object without consent. Someone who is asleep, passed out, or incapacitated by alcohol or drugs cannot give consent. Silence, or lack of continued resistance, does not mean consent. Although rape can be broadly defined as sex without consent, it is understood as a crime of aggression because the focus is on hurting and dominating. The sexual abuse of children is often termed *molestation*, which may or may not involve rape. When children are molested or raped by family members, it is termed *incest*. Although the rates of rape are very high, sexual assault rates generally (which include but are not limited to rape) are even higher.

Women are often victims of *altruistic sex* (motivation for consent involves feeling sorry for the other person, or feeling guilty about resisting sexual advances) and *compliant sex* (where the consequences of not doing it are worse than doing it). Neither of these forms of sexual intimacy involve complete consent. Consent is a freely made choice that is clearly communicated. *Consensual sex* is negotiated through communication where individuals express their feelings and desires and are able to listen to and respect others' feelings and desires. Rape can happen to anyone—babies who are months old to women in their 90s, people of all races, ethnicities, and socioeconomic status. Both women and men are raped, but as already discussed, overwhelmingly it is a problem of men raping women and other men. Rape occurs relatively frequently in prisons; dominant men rape men they perceive as inferior. Often dominant inmates refer to the victims as "women." In this way, rape is about power, domination, and humiliation and must be understood in this context.

As already mentioned, most reported sexual assaults are against females, with 1 in 3 to 1 in 4 women experiencing sexual assault in their lifetime. In addition, half of all females raped are under the age of 18 years, and about one-fifth are younger than 12 years old. Offenders were armed with a gun, knife, or other weapon in about 11 percent of rape or sexual assault victimizations, according to the 2011 National Crime Victimization Survey. The percentage of reported rape or sexual assault victimizations that resulted in an arrest either at the scene or during a follow-up investigation decreased from 47 percent in the late 1990s to 31 percent in 2010. Overall, among both reported and not reported sexual assaults and rape, approximately 12 percent result in an arrest.

Among college women it is reported that women at a university with 10,000 female students could experience about 350 rapes a year with serious policy implications for college administrators. More than one-third of these college women say they have unwanted or uninvited sexual contacts, and about 10 percent had experienced rape. In about 9 out of 10 cases, offenders are known to the women. Survivors are more likely

LEARNING ACTIVITY   **How Safe Is Your Campus?**

Investigate the safety and security of your campus by asking these questions:

- How many acts of violence were reported on your campus last year?
- Does your campus have a security escort service?
- What resources does your campus provide to ensure safety?
- What training and educational opportunities about safety does your college provide?
- What specialized training about violence is offered to fraternities and sports teams on your campus?
- How does your school encourage the reporting of violence?
- What support services does your school offer to victims of violence?
- What is your school administration's official protocol for dealing with complaints of violence?
- How does your school's code of conduct address violence?
- Are there dark areas of your campus that need additional lighting?
- Are emergency phones available around your campus?

to report a rape or sexual assault when the assailant is someone they do not know, and indeed, among college women less than 5 percent of completed or attempted rapes are reported to law enforcement officials and about one-third of victims do not tell anyone. As already mentioned, the U.S. Bureau of Justice Statistics reports about 7 in 10 female rape or sexual assault victims identify offenders as an intimate, relative, friend, or acquaintance. In this way, acquaintance rape (often called date rape), in which each person is known to the other, is the most frequent form of rape, and is the most underreported.

Rapes on college campuses (especially gang rapes) may be committed by fraternity members, and may be part of male bonding rituals. This does not mean, of course, that all fraternities are dangerous places for women, only that the conditions for the abuse of women can occur in these male-only living spaces, especially when alcohol is present. About 70 to 80 percent of campus rapes generally involve alcohol or other drugs (with alcohol most pervasive among all drugs). The most common "date rape" or predatory drugs are rohypnol (commonly known as "roofies"), ketamine (commonly known as "special k"), and GHB (gamma hydroxybutyrate). These drugs are odorless when dissolved and are indiscernible when put in beverages. They metabolize quickly and make a person incapable of resisting sexual advances. Memory impairment is associated with these drugs, and a survivor may not be aware of such an attack until 8 to 12 hours after it has occurred. In addition, there may be little evidence to support the claim that drugs were used to facilitate the attack because of the speed at which these predatory drugs metabolize. It is imperative to be vigilant at social occasions where such attacks might happen; do not leave a drink unattended, get your own drinks from an unopened container, and watch out for your friends. A buddy system that includes a designated driver is essential!

Back in 1990 Congress passed the Campus Security Act, which mandated colleges and universities participating in federal student aid programs to complete and distribute security reports on campus practices and crime statistics. This was amended in 1992 to include the Campus Sexual Assault Victim's Bill of Rights to provide policies and statistics and to ensure basic rights to survivors of sexual assault. This act was amended again in 1998 to provide for more extensive security-related provisions, and, since then, the U.S. Department of Justice has given substantial grants to colleges and universities to address sexual and physical assault, harassment, and stalking on campus.

One specific form of intimate partner violence is marital rape. A national study reported that 10 percent of all sexual assault cases involve a husband or ex-husband, and the National Resource Center on Domestic Violence suggests that taking into account the underreporting that occurs as women are less likely to label such actions as rape, 10 to 14 percent of married women in the United States have been raped by their husbands. Historically, rape has been understood as a property crime against men as women were considered the property of husbands and fathers. As a result, it was considered impossible to violate something that was legally considered your property, and rape laws defined rape as forced intercourse with a woman who was not your wife. In 1993 marital rape became a crime in all 50 states, even though some states still do not consider it as serious as other forms of rape and include some forms of marital rape exemption (for example, if a spouse has an illness causing an inability to sexually respond, the other spouse may engage her/him in sexual relations without criminal liability). In addition, some states have lesser sentences for husbands than other rapists, and statutory rape laws often do not go into effect if a spouse is younger than the age of consent for that state.

Women who are raped by their husbands are often likely to be raped repeatedly. They experience not only vaginal rape, but also oral and anal rape. Researchers generally categorize marital rape into three types: force-only rape, when a husband uses only enough force to enact the rape; battering rape, in which rape occurs in the context of an ongoing physically abusive relationship; and sadistic/obsessive rape, where husbands use torture or perverse acts to humiliate and harm their wives. Pornography is often involved in the latter case. Women are at particularly high risk for being raped by their partners when they are married to domineering men who view them as "property," when they are pregnant, ill physically or mentally, or recovering from surgery, and when they are separated or divorced.

As will be discussed in Chapter 11, political institutions in the United States have historically supported men's access to women as sexual property, and the history of racism and the lynching of black men for fabricated rapes of white women have influenced how our society and the courts deal with the interaction of race and sexual violence. Although most rapes are *intraracial* (they occur within racial groups), women of color are especially vulnerable as victims of sexual violence because of their marginalized status. They also have less credibility in the courtroom when rape cases have gone to trial. Men of color accused of rape are more likely to get media attention, are more likely to get convicted, and receive longer sentences. While these differences result from the racism of society that sees black men in particular as more violent or dangerous, they also are related to class differences whereby men of color are generally less able to acquire superior legal counsel. As Andrea Smith explains in the reading "Beyond the

Politics of Inclusion," gender violence functions as a tool of racism and colonialism for women of color. She emphasizes the need to make the needs of marginalized women central in the anti-violence movement and implores writers and activists to understand the intersectionality of racism and sexism in social movements for ending violence and supporting racial justice.

Very often, women realize that a past sexual encounter was actually a rape, and, as a result, they begin to think about the experience differently. They may have left the encounter hurt, confused, or angry but without being able to articulate what happened. Survivors need to talk about what occurred and get support. It is never too late to get support from people who care. Feeling ashamed, dirty, or stupid is a typical reaction for those who have experienced sexual assault. It is not their/your/our fault.

Social myths about rape that encourage these feelings include the following:

- *Rape happens less frequently in our society than women believe. Feminists in particular blow this out of proportion by focusing on women's victimization, and women make up rape charges as a way to get attention.* This is false; rape happens at an alarming rate and is underreported. Rape is considered a crime against the state and rape survivors are witnesses to the crime. As a result, the credibility of the "witness" is challenged in rape cases, and women are often retraumatized as a result of rape trials. This is among the many reasons why rape is underreported, and, as a proportion of total rapes committed, charges are rarely pressed and assailants rarely convicted. The FBI reports that the rate of false reporting for rape and sexual assault is the same as for other violent crimes: less than 3 percent. Although feminists care about the victimization of women, we focus on surviving, becoming empowered, and making changes to stop rapes from happening.
- *Women are at least partly responsible for their victimization in terms of their appearance and behavior (encouraging women to feel guilty when they are raped).* This is false; rape is the only violent crime in which the victim is not *de facto* perceived as innocent. Consider the suggestion that a person who has just been robbed was asking to have his/her wallet stolen.
- *Men are not totally responsible for their actions. If a woman comes on to a man sexually, it is impossible for him to stop.* This is false; men are not driven by uncontrollable biological urges, and it is insulting to men to assume that this is how they behave. Likewise it is wrong to assume a woman has "to finish what she started." Everyone has the right to stop sexual behaviors at any time. Note how this myth is related to the previous one that blames the victim.

These myths not only support masculine privilege concerning sexuality and access to women and therefore support some men's tendency to sexually abuse women, but are also important means for controlling women's lives. Recall again the discussion of *sexual terrorism* in Chapter 2. Such terrorism limits women's activities and keeps people in line by the threat of potential sexual assault. Research on rapists in the early 1980s revealed that, although there are few psychological differences between men who have raped and those who have not, the former group were more likely to believe in the rape myths, were more misogynous and tolerant of the interpersonal domination of women generally, showed higher levels of sexual arousal around depictions of rape, and were more prone to use violence.

The Consequences of Intimate Partner Violence

The consequences of abuse are profound, extending beyond the health and happiness of individuals to affect the well-being of entire communities. Living in a violent relationship affects a woman's sense of self-esteem and her ability to participate in the world. Studies have shown that abused women are routinely restricted in the way they can gain access to information and services, take part in public life, and receive emotional support from friends and relatives. Not surprisingly, such women are often unable properly to look after themselves and their children or to pursue jobs and careers.

IMPACT ON HEALTH

A growing body of research evidence is revealing that sharing her life with an abusive partner can have a profound impact on a woman's health. Violence has been linked to a host of different health outcomes, both immediate and long term. The list below draws on the scientific literature to summarize the consequences that have been associated with intimate partner violence. Although violence can have direct health consequences, such as injury, being a victim of violence also increases a woman's risk of future ill health. As with the consequences of tobacco and alcohol use, being a victim of violence can be regarded as a risk factor for a variety of diseases and conditions.

. . .

Health Consequences of Intimate Partner Violence

Physical

- Abdominal/thoracic injuries
- Bruises and welts
- Chronic pain syndromes
- Disability
- Fibromyalgia
- Fractures
- Gastrointestinal disorders
- Irritable bowel syndrome
- Lacerations and abrasions
- Ocular damage
- Reduced physical functioning

Sexual and Reproductive

- Gynecological disorders
- Infertility
- Pelvic inflammatory disease
- Pregnancy complications/ miscarriage
- Sexual dysfunction
- Sexually transmitted diseases, including HIV/AIDS
- Unsafe abortion
- Unwanted pregnancy

Psychological and Behavioral

- Alcohol and drug abuse
- Depression and anxiety
- Eating and sleep disorders
- Feelings of shame and guilt
- Phobias and panic disorder
- Physical inactivity
- Poor self-esteem
- Post-traumatic stress disorder
- Psychosomatic disorders
- Smoking
- Suicidal behavior and self-harm
- Unsafe sexual behavior

Fatal Health Consequences

- AIDS-related mortality
- Maternal mortality
- Homicide
- Suicide

Source: World Report on Violence and Health, www.who.int/violence_injury_prevention/global_campaign/en/chap4.pdf.

PHYSICAL ABUSE

Although women are less likely than men to be victims of violent crimes overall, women are 5 to 8 times more likely to be victimized by an intimate partner. Intimate partner violence is primarily a crime against women and all races are equally vulnerable. The Department of Justice reports that about 96 percent of women experiencing nonfatal partner violence are victimized by a male, and about 85 percent of all victims are female. According to FBI statistics, every day about four women (approximately 1,500 a year) die in the United States as a result of domestic violence. Although about half a million reports of physical assault by intimates officially reach federal officials each year, it is estimated that 2 to 4 million women are abused each year, about one every 20 seconds or so. Women of all races and classes are abused, although rates are five times higher among families below poverty levels, and severe spouse abuse is twice as likely to be committed by unemployed men as by those working full time. These differences reflect economic vulnerability and lack of resources, as well as the ways these families have more contact with authorities like social services that increase opportunities for reporting. Women who are pregnant are especially at risk of violence. Approximately 17 percent of pregnant women report having been physically abused, and the results include miscarriages, stillbirths, and a two- to fourfold greater likelihood of bearing a low birth weight baby. Sadly, the impact of violence in families on children is severe. More than half of all female victims of intimate partner violence live in households with children younger than 12 years, and studies indicate that between 3 and 10 million children witness some form of domestic violence every year. Approximately half of men who abuse female partners also abuse the children in those homes. Of course, women may abuse their children, too. Violent juvenile offenders are four times more likely than nonoffenders to have grown up in homes where they saw violence. Children who have witnessed violence at home are also about five times more likely to commit or suffer violence when they become adults.

Women who are physically abused are also always emotionally abused because they experience emotional abuse by virtue of being physically terrorized. Mariah Lockwood writes poignantly about the emotional abuse of battered women in the poem "She Said." This reading illustrates the ways women internalize messages about femininity, love, marriage, and romance that can make them vulnerable to being dominated in interpersonal relationships. The poem also speaks of the importance of friendship and emotional support

IDEAS FOR ACTIVISM

- Volunteer at a local domestic violence shelter.
- Organize a food, clothing, and toiletries drive to benefit your local domestic violence shelter.
- Interrupt jokes about violence against women.
- Organize Domestic Violence Awareness Month (October) activities on your campus.
- Create and distribute materials about violence against women on your campus. Write a blog about gender-based violence.
- Organize a poetry slam to feature poems about gender-based violence.

Check Up on Your Relationship

DOES YOUR PARTNER

Constantly put you down?

Call you several times a night or show up to make sure you are where you said you would be?

Embarrass or make fun of you in front of your friends or family?

Make you feel like you are nothing without him/her?

Intimidate or threaten you? "If you do that again, I'll . . ."

Always say that it's your fault?

Pressure you to have sex when you don't want to?

Glare at you, give you the silent treatment, or grab, shove, kick, or hit you?

DO YOU

Always do what your partner wants instead of what you want?

Fear how your partner will act in public?

Constantly make excuses to other people for your partner's behavior?

Feel like you walk on eggshells to avoid your partner's anger?

Believe if you just tried harder, submitted more, that everything would be okay?

Stay with your partner because you fear what your partner would do if you broke up?

These indicators suggest potential abuse in your relationship. If you've answered yes to any of these questions, talk to a counselor about your relationship. Remember, when one person scares, hurts, or continually puts down the other person, it's abuse.

Source: Created by the President's Commission on the Status of Women, Oregon State University.

for battered women. Emotional abuse, however, does not always involve physical abuse. A man, for example, who constantly tells his partner that she is worthless, stupid, or ugly can emotionally abuse without being physically abusive. Sometimes the scars of emotional abuse take longer to heal than physical abuse and help explain why women might stay with abusive partners.

Why do some men physically abuse women or abuse other men? They abuse because they have internalized sexism and the right to dominate women (or others they perceive as subordinate or feminized) in their lives, have learned to use violence as a way to deal with conflict, and have repressed anger. Given this, how is it possible to explain why some women abuse men or abuse other women? Abusive behavior is an act of domination. Women too can internalize domination and can see men in their interpersonal relationships as subordinate to them, even though there is little support for that in society generally. Women in romantic relationships with other women can likewise negotiate dominance and subordination in their relationships and act this out. Battering is a problem in the LBGTQ community.

Why do people so often stay in abusive relationships? The research on this question suggests that when women leave abusive relationships they return about 5 to 7 times before actually leaving for good. There are several complex and interconnected reasons why survivors stay. First, emotional abuse often involves feelings of shame, guilt, and low self-esteem. Women in these situations (like rape survivors generally) often believe that the abuse is their fault. They may see themselves as worthless and have a difficult time believing that they deserve better. Low self-esteem encourages survivors to stay with or return to abusive partners. Second, some who are repeatedly abused become desensitized to the violence; they may see it as a relatively normal aspect of gender relationships and therefore something to tolerate.

A third reason people stay in abusive relationships is that abusers tend to physically isolate their partners from others. This often involves a pattern where survivors may be prevented from visiting or talking to family and friends, are left without transportation, and/or have no access to a telephone. Notice how, when women are abused, the shame associated with this situation can encourage them to isolate themselves. An outcome of this

The Cycle of Violence

Domestic violence may seem unpredictable, but it actually follows a typical pattern no matter when it occurs or who is involved. Understanding the cycle of violence and the thinking of the abuser helps survivors recognize they are not to blame for the violence they have suffered—and that *the abuser is the one responsible.*

1. *Tension building* The abuser might set up the victim so that she is bound to anger him. The victim, knowing her abuser is likely to erupt, is apologetic. She may even defend his actions.
2. *The abuse* The batterer behaves violently, inflicting pain and abuse on the victim.
3. *Guilt and fear of reprisal* After the violence, the abuser may have feelings of "guilt"—not normal guilt, in which he'd feel sorry for hurting another person, but actually a fear of getting caught. He might blame alcohol for his outburst.
4. *Blaming the victim* The abuser can't stand any kind of guilt feeling for long, so he quickly rationalizes his actions and blames the victim for causing him to hurt her. He might tell her that her behavior "asked for it."
5. *"Normalcy"* At this point, the batterer exhibits kind and loving behavior. Welcomed by both parties, an unusual calm will surround the relationship. He may bring gifts and promise the violence will never happen again.
6. *Fantasy/set-up* Batterers and abusers fantasize about their past and future abuses. These fantasies feed the abuser's anger. He begins to plan another attack by placing his victim in situations that he knows will anger him.

Source: Reprinted from *Take Care: A Guide for Violence-Free Living,* a publication of Raphael House of Portland.

ACTIVIST PROFILE   **INCITE! Women of Color Against Violence**

INCITE! Women of Color Against Violence demonstration, Color of Violence III Conference, New Orleans, LA, 2005.

In 2000 a group of radical feminists of color organized a conference, "The Color of Violence: Violence Against Women of Color," at the University of California, Santa Cruz. Initially, the gathering was to be small, focused on analyzing violence against women of color and strategizing ways to address violence against women of color. The response was overwhelming, and more than 2,000 women of color attended. Another 2,000 had to be turned away. At this conference, the focus turned to women of color who had survived violence and challenged mainstream conceptualizations of the anti–violence against women movement.

One result of this conference was the founding of INCITE! Women of Color Against Violence, a national grassroots activist organization of radical feminists of color working to end violence against women of color and their communities. Using direct action, critical dialogue, and grassroots organizing, INCITE! Women of Color Against Violence works with women of color to create projects that address issues of violence against women of color and their communities. INCITE! identifies violence against women of color "as a combination of violence *directed at* communities, such as police violence, war, and colonialism, and violence *within* communities, such as rape and domestic violence." Projects include "producing a women of color radio show, challenging the non-profitization of antiviolence and other social justice movements, organizing rallies on street harassment, training women of color on self-defense, organizing mothers on welfare, building and running a grassroots clinic."

INCITE! utilizes a framework of intersectional analysis to understand and work against violence against women of color who are located in the intersection of racism and sexism, as well as other forms of oppression. INCITE! also offers a challenge to the approach of many anti-violence organizations that are dominated by white women by placing women of color at the center of their analysis and work. INCITE!'s principles of unity guide the organization:

We at INCITE!:

- Maintain a space by and for women of color.
- Center our political analysis and community action in the struggle for liberation.
- Support sovereignty for indigenous people as central to the struggle for liberation.
- Oppose all forms of violence which oppress women of color and our communities.
- Recognize the state as the central organizer of violence which oppresses women of color and our communities.
- Recognize these expressions of violence against women of color as including colonialism, police brutality, immigration policies, reproductive control, etc.
- Link liberation struggles which oppose racism, sexism, classism, heterosexism, ableism, ageism, and all other forms of oppression.
- Support coalition building between women of color.
- Recognize and honor differences across cultures.
- Encourage creative models of community organizing and action.
- Promote shared leadership and decision-making.
- Recognize and resist the power of co-optation of our movements.
- Support these principles not only in our actions, but in the practices within our own organizations.
- Support the creation of organizational processes which encourage these principles and which effectively address oppressive individual and institutional practices within our own organizations.
- Discourage any solicitation of federal or state funding for INCITE! activities.

To learn more about INCITE! Women of Color Against Violence, visit the organization's website at *www.incite-national.org*.

isolation is that they do not get the reality check they need about their situation. Isolation thus helps keep self-esteem low, prevents support, and minimizes options in terms of leaving the abusive situation.

A fourth reason people stay is that they worry about what people will think, and this worry keeps them in abusive situations as a consequence of the shame they feel. Most women in abusive relationships worry about this to some extent, although middle-class women probably feel it the most. The myth that this is a lower-class problem and that it does not happen to "nice" families who appear to have everything going for them is part of the problem. And, indeed, the question about what people will think is a relevant one: Some churches tell abused women to submit to their husbands and hide the abuse, neighbors often look the other way, mothers worry about their children being stigmatized at school, and certainly there is embarrassment associated with admitting your husband or boyfriend hits you. For men this issue is even more pertinent, and the shame and embarrassment may be even greater for abused men.

A fifth reason survivors stay is that they cannot afford to leave. Women in this situation fear for the economic welfare of themselves and their children should they leave the abusive situation. These women tend to have less education and to have dependent children. They understand that the kind of paid work they could get would not be enough to support the family. Reason six is that some survivors believe that children need a father—and that even a bad father might be better than no father. Although this belief is erroneous in our view, it does keep women in abusive situations "for the sake of the children." Interestingly, the primary reason women do permanently leave an abusive relationship is also the children: When women see that their children are being hurt, this is the moment when they are most likely to leave for good.

Another reason people stay is that there is often nowhere to go. Although the increase in the numbers of crisis lines and emergency housing shelters is staggering given their absence only a few decades ago, some survivors still have a difficult time imagining an alternative to the abusive situation. This is especially true of those who live in rural areas and who are isolated from friends and family. Reason eight is that survivors may fear what might happen to abusive partners in the criminal system, especially if they are men of color. They may also believe their partner will change. Part of the cycle of violence noted by scholars in this area is the "honeymoon phase" after the violent episode. First comes the buildup of tension when violence is brewing, second is the violent episode, and third is the honeymoon phase when abusers tend to be especially remorseful—even horrified that they could have done such a thing—and ask for forgiveness. Given that the profile of many batterers is charm and manipulation, such behavior during this phase can be especially persuasive. Survivors are not making it up when they think their partner will change.

Finally, people stay because they believe their partner might kill them—or hurt or kill the children—should they leave. Again, a batterer's past violence is often enough to establish this as no idle threat. Men do kill in these situations and often after wives and girlfriends have fled and brought restraining orders against them.

INCEST

This topic is especially poignant as the poem by Grace Caroline Bridges, "Lisa's Ritual, Age 10," demonstrates. Incest is the sexual abuse (molestation, inappropriate touching, rape, being forced to watch or perform sexual acts on others) of children by a family member or someone with a kinship role in a child's life. There is now an evolving definition of incest that takes into account betrayals of trust and power imbalances, expanding the definition to include sexual abuse by anyone who has power or authority over the child. Perpetration might include baby-sitters, schoolteachers, Boy Scout leaders, priests/ministers, and family friends, as well as immediate and extended family members. It is estimated that in about 90 percent of cases where children are raped it is by someone they know. Studies suggest that 1 in every 3 to 5 girls have experienced some kind of childhood sexual abuse by the time they are 16 years old. For boys this number is 1 in 6 to 10, although this may be underestimated because boys are less likely to admit that they are survivors. Again, like other forms of abuse, incest crosses all ethnic, class, and religious lines. Power is always involved in incest, and, because children are the least powerful group in society, the effects on them can be devastating. Approximately

Violence Against Women: Selected Human Rights Documents

International human rights documents encompass formal written documents, such as conventions, declarations, conference statements, guidelines, resolutions, and recommendations. Treaties are legally binding on states that have ratified or acceded to them, and their implementation is observed by monitoring bodies, such as the Committee on the Elimination of Discrimination Against Women (CEDAW).

GLOBAL DOCUMENTS

The Universal Declaration of Human Rights (1948) has formed the basis for the development of international human rights conventions. Article 3 states that everyone has the right of life, liberty, and security of the person. According to article 5, no one shall be subjected to torture or to cruel, inhuman, or degrading treatment or punishment. Therefore, any form of violence against a woman that is a threat to her life, liberty, or security of person or that can be interpreted as torture or cruel, inhuman, or degrading treatment violates the principles of this Declaration.

The International Covenant on Economic, Social and Cultural Rights (1966), together with the *International Covenant on Civil and Political Rights,* prohibits discrimination on the basis of sex. Violence detrimentally affects women's health; therefore, it violates the right to the enjoyment of the highest attainable standard of physical and mental health (article 12). In addition, article 7 provides the right to the enjoyment of just and favorable conditions of work that ensure safe and healthy working conditions. This provision encompasses the prohibition of violence and harassment of women in the workplace.

The International Covenant on Civil and Political Rights (1966) prohibits all forms of violence. Article 6.1 protects the right to life. Article 7 prohibits torture and inhuman or degrading treatment or punishment. Article 9 guarantees the right to liberty and security of person.

The Convention Against Torture and Other Cruel, Inhuman or Degrading Treatment or Punishment (1984) provides protection for all persons, regardless of their sex, in a more detailed manner than the International Covenant on Civil and Political Rights. States should take effective measures to prevent acts of torture (article 2).

The Convention on the Elimination of All Forms of Discrimination Against Women (1979) is the most extensive international instrument dealing with the rights of women. Although violence against women is not specifically addressed in the Convention, except in relation to trafficking and prostitution (article 6), many of the anti-discrimination clauses protect women from violence. States parties have agreed to a policy of eliminating discrimination against women, and to adopt legislative and other measures prohibiting all discrimination against women (article 2). In 1992, CEDAW, which monitors the implementation of this Convention, formally included gender-based violence under gender-based discrimination.

(continued)

General Recommendation No. 19, adopted at the 11th session (June 1992), deals entirely with violence against women and the measures taken to eliminate such violence. As for health issues, it recommends that states should provide support services for all victims of gender-based violence, including refuges, specially trained health workers, and rehabilitation and counseling services.

The International Convention on the Elimination of All Forms of Racial Discrimination (1965) declares that states parties undertake to prohibit and to eliminate racial discrimination in all its forms and to guarantee the enjoyment of the right to security of the person and protection by the state against violence or bodily harm, whether inflicted by government officials or by any individual group or institution (article 5).

The four *1949 Geneva Conventions* and two additional Protocols form the cornerstone of international humanitarian law. The Geneva Conventions require that all persons taking no active part in hostilities shall be treated humanely, without adverse distinction on any of the usual grounds, including sex (article 3). They offer protection to all civilians against sexual violence, forced prostitution, sexual abuse, and rape.

Regarding international armed conflict, *Additional Protocol I* to the 1949 Geneva Conventions creates obligations for parties to a conflict to treat humanely persons under their control. It requires that women shall be protected against rape, forced prostitution, and indecent assault. *Additional Protocol II,* applicable during internal conflicts, also prohibits rape, enforced prostitution, and indecent assault.

The Convention on the Rights of the Child (1989) declares that states parties take appropriate legislative, administrative, social, and educational measures to protect the child from physical or mental violence, abuse, maltreatment, or exploitation (article 19). States shall act accordingly to prevent the exploitative use of children in prostitution or other unlawful sexual practices, and the exploitative use of children in pornographic performances and materials (article 34).

The International Convention on the Protection of the Rights of All Migrant Workers and Members of Their Families (adopted by the General Assembly in 1990 and put into force in 2003) asserts the right of migrant workers and their family members to liberty and security of person as proclaimed in other international instruments. They shall be entitled to effective protection by the state against violence, physical injury, threats, and intimidation, whether by public officials or by private individuals, groups, or institutions (article 16).

a third of all juvenile victims of sexual abuse are younger than 6 years old. Children who are abused often have low self-esteem and may find it difficult to trust.

Incest can be both direct and indirect. Direct forms include vaginal, oral, and rectal penetration; sexual rubbing; excessive, inappropriate hugging; body and mouth kissing; bouncing a child on a lap against an erection; and sexual bathing. Direct incest also includes forcing children to watch or perform these acts on others. Indirect incest includes sexualizing statements or joking, speaking to the child as a surrogate spouse, inappropriate references to a child's body, or staring at the child's body. Examples also include intentionally invading children's privacy in the bathroom or acting inappropriately jealous when adolescents start dating. These indirect forms of incest involve sexualizing children and violating their boundaries.

Often siblings indulge in relatively normal uncoerced sexual play with each other that disappears over time. When this involves a child who is several years older or one who uses threats or intimidation, the behavior can be characterized as incestuous. Indicators of abuse in childhood include excessive crying, anxiety, night fears and sleep disturbances, depression and withdrawal, clinging behaviors, and physical problems like urinary tract infections and trauma to the mouth and/or perineal area. Adolescent symptoms often include eating disorders, psychosomatic complaints, suicidal thoughts, and depression. Survivors of childhood sexual violence may get involved in self-destructive behaviors such as alcohol and drug abuse or cutting on their bodies as they turn their anger inward, or they may express their anger through acting out or promiscuous behavior. In particular, girls internalize their worthlessness and their role as sexual objects used by others; boys often have more anger because they were dominated, an anger that is sometimes projected onto their future sexual partners as well as onto themselves. Although it takes time, we can heal from being sexually violated.

PORNOGRAPHY

Pornography involves the sexualization and objectification of women's bodies and parts of bodies for entertainment value. There are many people, scholars and lay people, feminists and non-feminists alike, who resist considering pornography in the context of gender-based violence. Indeed, there are sex radical feminists who strongly endorse pornography and make the case for it as empowering to women, especially when women are in control of certain aspects of the sex industry. We intentionally use "sex radicals" and not "sex positive" to describe this feminist stance because the latter term inappropriately assumes that feminism generally is not sex positive. Such debates are alive and well in feminist studies and sometimes bring about some interesting coalitions among those who normally do not work together, such as feminists and conservative religious groups. However, although we recognize the potentially positive aspects of some pornography that is created in more egalitarian contexts, it is still important to emphasize that pornography involves, first, the sexual objectification of women and other marginalized people (whether they actually endorse and condone that or not, or are central in producing it), and, second, that pornography involves the eroticization of power in such a way that it historically and currently accompanies violent and misogynist behaviors. In other words, even if there is feminist disagreement over the first point (that pornography is objectification, and objectification does not serve social justice), the second point (that pornography is used as a tool of misogyny and domination in violent crime) means that it needs to be considered in any account of gender-based violence.

According to feminist legal scholar Catharine MacKinnon, who has written on and debated the issue of pornography at length, pornography can be defined as the graphic, sexually explicit subordination of women through pictures and/or words. She says pornography includes one or more of the following: women presented as dehumanized sexual objects, things, or commodities; shown as enjoying humiliation, pain, or sexual assault; tied up, mutilated, or physically hurt; depicted in postures or positions of sexual submission or servility; shown with body parts—including though not limited to vagina, breasts, or buttocks—exhibited such that women are reduced to those parts; women penetrated by animals or objects; and women presented in scenarios of degradation, humiliation, or torture, shown as filthy or inferior, bleeding, bruised, or hurt in a context that makes these conditions sexual. MacKinnon adds that the use of men, children, or transsexuals in the place of women is also pornography. Note the definition includes the caveat that because a person has consented to being harmed, abused, or subjected to coercion does not alter the degrading character of the behavior.

Just as there are degrees of objectification and normalization of violence in pop culture forms, so too in pornography there is a continuum from the soft porn of *Playboy* to the hard-core *Hustler* and along to illegal forms of representation such as child pornography and snuff films. Snuff films are illegal because women are actually murdered in the making of these films. The Internet is one of the largest sites for pornography. As already discussed, there are thousands of pornography sites on the Web, including those of "fantasy rape" that depict women being raped, and "sex" is still the top search word. In addition to Internet pornography there is the problem of Internet prostitution where technology is utilized for the global trafficking and the sexual exploitation of women and children as well as a tool for live cam pornography.

Many people condone pornography because they feel that it represents free speech, or because they feel that the women have chosen to be part of it, or because they like the articles in these magazines. This is especially true of soft porn like *Playboy*. Some people make a distinction between hard-core and soft porn and feel that the former is harmful and the latter relatively harmless. Some see pornography as a mark of sexual freedom and characterize those who would like to limit pornography as prudish. However, as already suggested, the case can be made that sexual freedom requires sexual justice and pornography is better understood as a violation of this justice rather than an expression of it. In this way, many oppose pornography as a violation of women's rights against objectification and sexualization for male pleasure, and believe that people's rights to consume such materials are no longer rights when they violate the rights of others.

Acts of violence and the threat of violence have profound and lasting effects on all women's lives. We tend to refer to those who have survived violence as "survivors" rather than "victims" to emphasize that it is possible to go on with our lives after such experiences, difficult though that might be. Understanding and preventing violence against women has become a worldwide effort, bringing women and men together to make everyone safer.

Beyond the Politics of Inclusion

Violence Against Women of Color and Human Rights

Andrea Smith (2004)

What was disturbing to so many U.S. citizens about the September 11, 2001, attacks on the World Trade Center is that these attacks disrupted their sense of safety at "home." Terrorism is something that happens in other countries; our "home," the U.S.A., is supposed to be a place of safety. Similarly, mainstream U.S. society believes that violence against women only occurs "out there" and is perpetrated by a few crazed men whom we simply need to lock up. However, the anti-violence movement has always contested this notion of safety at home. The notion that violence only happens "out there," inflicted by the stranger in the dark alley makes it difficult to recognize that the home is in fact the place of greatest danger for women. In response to this important piece of analysis, the anti-violence movement has, ironically, based its strategies on the premise that the criminal legal system is the primary tool with which to address violence against women. However, when one-half of women will be battered in their lifetimes and nearly one-half of women will be sexually assaulted in their lifetimes, it is clear that we live in a rape culture that prisons, themselves a site of violence and control, cannot change.

Similarly, the notion that terrorism happens in other countries makes it difficult to grasp that the United States is built on a history of genocide, slavery, and racism. Our "home" has never been a safe place for people of color. Because many mainstream feminist organizations are white-dominated, they often do see themselves as potential victims in Bush's war in the U.S. and abroad. However, those considered "alien" in the United States and hence deserving of repressive policies and overt attack are not only people of color. Since 9/11, many organizations in LGBT communities have reported sharp increases in attacks, demonstrating the extent to which gays and lesbians are often seen as "alien" because their sexuality seems to threaten the white nuclear family thought to be the building block of U.S. society.

Furthermore, many mainstream feminist organizations, particularly anti-violence organizations, have applauded the U.S. attacks on Afghanistan for "liberating" Arab women from the repressive policies of the Taliban. Apparently, bombing women in Afghanistan somehow elevates their status. However, the Revolutionary Association of the Women from Afghanistan (RAWA), the organization comprised of members most affected by the policies of the Taliban, has condemned U.S. intervention and has argued that women cannot expect an improvement in their status under the regime of the Northern Alliance with which the United States has allied itself. This support rests entirely on the problematic assumption that state violence can secure safety and liberation for women and other oppressed groups. Clearly, alternative approaches to provide true safety and security for women must be developed, both at "home" and abroad.

BEYOND INCLUSION: CENTERING WOMEN OF COLOR IN THE ANTI-VIOLENCE MOVEMENT

The central problem is that as the anti-violence movement has attempted to become more "inclusive" these attempts at multicultural interventions have unwittingly strengthened the white supremacy within the anti-violence movement. That is, inclusivity has come to mean taking on a domestic violence model that was developed largely with the interests of white, middle class women in mind, and simply adding to it a multicultural component. However, if we look at the histories of women of color in the United States, as I have done in other work, it is clear that gender violence functions as a tool for racism and colonialism for women of color in general (Smith 2002). The racial element of gender violence points to the necessity of an alternative approach that goes beyond mere inclusion to actually centering women of color in the organizing and analysis. That is, if we do not make any assumptions about what a domestic violence program should look like but, instead, ask what would it take to end violence against women of color, then what would this movement look like?

In fact, Beth Richie suggests we go beyond just centering women of color, to centering those most marginalized within the category of "women of color." She writes:

> We have to understand that the goal of our anti-violence work is not for diversity, and not inclusion. It is for liberation. If we're truly committed to ending violence against women, then we must start in the hardest places, the places like jails and prisons and other correctional facilities. The places where our work has not had an impact yet. . . . [W]e have to stop being the friendly colored girls as some of our anti-violence programs require us to be. We must not deny the part of ourselves and the part of our work that is least acceptable to the mainstream public. We must not let those who really object to all of us and our work co-opt some of us and the work we're trying to do. As if this anti-violence movement could ever really be legitimate in a patriarchal, racist society. . . . Ultimately the movement needs to be accountable not to those in power, but to the powerless. (Richie 2000)

When we center women of color in the analysis, it becomes clear that we must develop approaches that address interpersonal and state violence simultaneously. In addition, we find that by centering women of color in the analysis, we may actually build a movement that more effectively ends violence not just for women of color, but for all peoples.

HUMAN RIGHTS FRAMEWORK FOR ADDRESSING VIOLENCE

Developing strategies to address state violence, then, suggests the importance of developing a human rights approach toward ending violence. By human rights I mean those rights seen under international law to be inalienable and not dependent on any particular government structure. When we limit our struggles around changes in domestic legislation within the United States, we forget that the United States government itself perpetrates more violence against women than any other actor in the world. While we may use a variety of rhetorical and organizing tools, our overall strategy should not be premised on the notion that the United States should or will always continue to exist—to do so is to fundamentally sanction the continuing genocide of indigenous peoples on which this government is based.

One organization that avoids this problem is the American Indian Boarding School Healing Project, which organizes against gender violence from a human rights perspective. During the nineteenth century and into the twentieth century, American Indian children were abducted from their homes to attend Christian boarding schools as a matter of state policy that again demonstrates the links between sexual violence and state violence. This system was later imported to Canada in the form of the residential school system. Because the worst of the abuses happened to an older generation, there is simply not sufficient documentation or vocal outcry against boarding school abuses.

Responding to this need, the International Human Rights Association of American Minorities issued a report documenting the involvement of mainline churches and the federal government in the murder of over 50,000 Native children through the Canadian residential school system (Annet 2001). The list of offenses committed by church officials includes murder by beating, poisoning, hanging, starvation, strangulation, and medical experimentation. In addition, the report found that church, police, business, and government officials maintained pedophile rings using children from residential schools. Several schools are also charged with concealing on their grounds the unmarked graves of children who were murdered, particularly children killed after being born as a result of rapes of Native girls by priests and other church officials. While some churches in Canada have taken some minimal steps towards addressing their involvement in this genocidal policy, churches in the United States have not.

As a result of boarding school policies, an epidemic of child sexual abuse now exists in Native communities. The shame attached to abuse has allowed no space in which to address this problem. Consequently, child abuse passes from one generation to the next. The American Indian Boarding School Healing Project provides an entryway to addressing this history of child sexual abuse by framing it not primarily as an example of individual and community dysfunction, but instead as the continuing effect of human rights abuses perpetrated by state policy. This project seeks to take the shame away from talking about abuse and provide the space for communities to address the problem and heal.

A human rights approach can even be of assistance to traditional service providers for survivors of violence. The human rights approach provides an organizing strategy to protest John Ashcroft's dramatic cuts in funding for anti-violence programs, particularly indigenous programs. Adequate funding for indigenous-controlled programs and services is not a privilege for states to curtail in times of economic crises. Rather, as international human rights law dictates, states are mandated to address the continuing effects of human rights violations. Hence, the United States violates international human rights law when it de-funds anti-violence programs. For indigenous women and women of color in general, sexual and domestic violence are clearly the continuing effects of human rights violations perpetrated by U.S. state policy.

CONCLUSION

For too long, women of color have been forced to choose between racial justice and gender justice. Yet, it is precisely through sexism and gender violence that colonialism and white supremacy have been successful. This failure to see the intersectionality of racism and sexism in racial justice movements was evident at the UN World Conference Against Racism, where the types of racism that women of color face in reproductive rights policies, for example, failed to even register on the UN radar screen. Women of color are often suspicious of human rights strategies because white-dominated human rights organizations often pursue the imperialist agenda of organizing around the human rights violations of women in other countries while ignoring the human rights violations of women of color in the United States. Nonetheless, an anti-colonial human rights strategy can be helpful in highlighting the violence perpetrated by U.S. state policy and combating U.S. exceptionalism on the global scale—as well as right here at home.

REFERENCES

Annett, Kevin. 2001. "The Truth Commission into the Genocide in Canada." Accessed August 31, 2003 (http://annett55.freewebsites.com/genocide.pdf).

Richie, Beth. 2000. Plenary Address, "Color of Violence: Violence Against Women of Color" Conference, Santa Cruz, CA.

Smith, Andrea. 2002. "Better Dead than Pregnant: The Colonization of Native Women's Reproductive Health." In *Policing the National Body: Race, Gender, and Criminalization,* ed. Jael Silliman and Anannya Bhattacharjee. Cambridge: South End Press.

She Said

Mariah Lockwood (2010)

I married because he asked me
she said, a matrimonial Miss Manners
   aching to please
    fearful to disappoint
He might not ask again.

I dreamed candlelight, roses, she said,
shameful now, love's blush a pallor
rolled thin like dough, thinner,
   edges curling, splitting wide.
It started with words, she said,
a drizzle brushed from summer clothes

then streaming, torrents, hail
   denting life itself.

Imagine, concealer was my first friend
she said, cream over plums ripened deep,
sugar over salt lips cracked, smiling,
   hiding contraband fruit.
But you were my sweetest friend, she said,
when sadness leached to hollow shell
brittle, bleached, but strong, stronger
   alive meeting the tide, she said.

Sex Trafficking in the U.S.

Rachel Chinapen (2013)

During the day, Shandra Woworuntu was forced to service men at a brothel tucked away in New London [Connecticut]. At night, she was driven to hotels . . . and forced to service more men. Woworuntu was brought into the United States from Indonesia under false pretenses. She is now one of countless survivors of human trafficking in the country.

The $32 billion worldwide industry of human trafficking has been misperceived as something that occurs outside the United States, according to Alicia Kinsman, director of victim services at the International Institute of Connecticut. The institute works with foreign-born survivors, citizens and green card-holding survivors of human trafficking. . . . It's estimated that hundreds of thousands of people are trafficked—for both labor and sex—in

this country annually, according to The Polaris Project, a national anti-trafficking organization. "It's a rapidly growing criminal enterprise because it's a high-profit and low-risk crime," Kinsman said. "Criminals who were previously selling guns and drugs are now selling people because it's so hard to identify and prosecute."

The issue of human trafficking has gained attention at both the national and state levels. Many state and non-governmental agencies in Connecticut have zeroed in on the crime in the last few years. Agencies have dedicated resources to educating the public, training law enforcement, identifying cases and providing services to survivors. State legislators have worked to pass laws to enforce stricter penalties for traffickers and increase protection for survivors. [Since 2012, the University of Connecticut] identified 40 survivors in the state. [Since 2008, the state Department of] Children and Families [DCF] has identified 120 child survivors in the state. These numbers are likely underrepresented, as they only account for those who have been identified and served by an agency.

Woworuntu came to America in 2001 from Indonesia under the impression she would be working as a waitress in a major hotel. She paid $3,500 between airfare and administrative fees to obtain the job. When she got to New York, her passport and other identification were taken away, she said. She was taken to a brothel in Connecticut, far away from any neighbors, Woworuntu said. "They locked me up," Woworuntu said. "I couldn't open the door. I opened the window to try and jump from the second floor, but it was too high so I wouldn't escape." Woworuntu is one of tens of thousands of individuals who are trafficked into the United States. . . . But not all individuals who are trafficked come to the United States under false pretenses. Children in the states can be exposed to trafficking through boyfriends, older men and social media websites, Woworuntu said.

Many agencies have caught onto the issue of domestic trafficking and have begun preventative workshops and education initiatives. "Prevention and education is so key because it's giving these kids the tools and knowledge to protect themselves, and it's empowering them to know that they have that knowledge to protect themselves out in the community," said Nicole von Oy, U.S. training and outreach coordinator at Love 146—an international organization dedicated to the abolition of child exploitation and trafficking. Its U.S. office is in New Haven. Love 146 has held prevention education workshops in Connecticut high schools, group homes and care facilities since 2010. The workshops focus on four key elements: training of adults who work with at-risk children; intervention for victims; mentoring for survivors; and education for at-risk children. "If you were to really look at a list of risk factors, every girl is at risk," said von Oy. "However, there is a subpopulation of girls that are at risk that have been sexually abused, a history of trauma, domestic violence, experimenting with drugs."

Many police officers are still learning about the prevalence of sex trafficking within the state, according to Sgt. Tracy Baden of the New Britain Police Department. In 2006, Connecticut passed a law that required training programs about human trafficking for local police departments and prosecutors. "We find that a lot of girls and boys become runaways," Baden said. "They end up being pimped out, and end up being trafficked, and we see a lot of that. . . . I think police officers don't even realize how much it's happening right here." Children involved in the welfare system are at a higher risk because they are often more vulnerable, according to Stefania Agliano of DCF. Agliano said these children often come from a place where they faced trauma, abuse or neglect, and are seeking a connection or love. Still, it is important to note that all children are at risk because of the manipulative nature of traffickers. Traffickers can easily use social media to lure individuals from behind a computer screen, building "trusting" relationships with potential victims. . . . The complex relationship between a victim and a trafficker can hinder the ability of the victim to seek or receive help from the police. . . . "It's their comfort zone; it might be horribly abusive, but it's all they've ever known, and we have to get them comfortable in a whole new world," said survivor Jessica Richardson of Oregon.

Richardson met her trafficker when she was 17. He seemed to care, just what she was seeking after a rough couple of years. Her pimp created a false identity for her as a 22-year-old named Joanna. He had three to five girls, each serving 20 to 30 clients daily. She was a modern-day slave, but a police officer could easily have mistaken her for a prostitute.

"Part of this goes back to not being able to tell the difference between someone who is willingly in the sex industry and someone who is being exploited," Richardson said. "Short of being beaten and bloody all the time, in a dungeon, or a child, the only way to really find out is to build a relationship and build trust so they can tell you."

Baden, along with a handful of other officers, is now partnering with DCF to develop training for law enforcement officials on domestic minor sex trafficking in Connecticut. This consists of any commercial sex act involving a U.S. minor—pornography, prostitution or sex tourism, according to Love 146. More than 100,000 U.S. children are forced to engage in prostitution or pornography annually, the group says. These children often are marketed in pornography as college girls.

Training of law enforcement will be critical to the ability of patrol officers to identify the difference between a prostitute and a trafficking victim. As of 2010, Connecticut law prohibits law enforcement from prosecuting an individual younger than 16 for prostitution. While the training will focus on child sex trafficking, Agliano explained its overall importance. "Let's be clear that when you're making that arrest of a 35-year-old, you might only be meeting her in chapter 22 of her story," Agliano said. "We don't know everything that happened to her, and she might have been that 11-year-old."

Although Woworuntu was 24 when she was trafficked, she recalls one of the girls at a brothel as "so young." She eventually helped the girl escape through a bathroom window. "I went to a precinct in New York; they didn't listen to me. I went to another precinct; they didn't listen to me, too," Woworuntu recalled. She also remembered having to sleep on benches in the subway at one point. She had no identification and no money. It wasn't until she met a member of the Navy who believed her story and took her in that she found hope. He contacted the FBI and escorted her to a precinct, where an officer immediately took her case.

Not every survivor seeks law enforcement officials. Von Oy said that in some ways the situation can be compared to domestic violence. It may take seven to eight tries to get an individual out of the situation due to the control factors involved, according to von Oy. Additionally, for many, the idea of escape leaves them with questions about their basic survival needs.

After being beaten and trafficked around the West Coast, Richardson managed to flee her pimp in 2000. But even once she escaped, she knew no other way to make money except to take part in commercial sex acts. She continued to work in various forms of the sex industry on her own until she found herself pregnant. . . . Richardson's experience after fleeing her pimp is not unique. Many survivors find themselves with a lack of services and resources once they escape their enslavement. Survivors who have a record of prostitution have very limited job opportunities once they escape. Additionally, if there is a record of prostitution, they cannot seek victim compensation, according to Baden. Under state law, even when a survivor is identified by the FBI as a victim, their record is not cleared of prostitution charges.

In April [2013], legislators introduced a bill to try to correct legislation surrounding human trafficking. H.B. 6696 seeks to expunge the prostitution records of sex-trafficking survivors and enforce stronger penalties for johns.

[Fifty-five] female legislators joined in bipartisan support of H.B. 5666, which targets the pockets of traffickers with stronger profit and property forfeiture guidelines. Under this bill, third-degree prostitution and third-degree promotion of prostitution would be added to the list of crimes subject to forfeiture.

"The law needs to get better and better and better. It takes time," Woworuntu said. Woworuntu advocates for human-trafficking shelters for those who have nowhere to go. She remembers being put in a domestic violence shelter where men and women were mixed. She says shelters should have a 24-hour therapist on duty who is versed in human trafficking. "A survivor has trauma usually at the nighttime, the trafficker put them in the streets at night, it is trauma (that) comes at night," Woworuntu explained.

Marji Vitale, clinical director of youth and family services at the Bridge Family Center in West Hartford, said it is important for a therapist to have the background in treating trauma. In regard to a background on sex trafficking, Vitale sees some importance in that, too. "If a therapist doesn't have an understanding of why a person would stay in that situation, they might not understand . . . why they didn't just leave, and they might not understand the psychological hold offenders can have over their victims," Vitale said.

Von Oy agreed that services for survivors is a key component to healing. She says medical professionals that know how to work with survivors of trafficking, along with sensitivity about the wording used, will be important in treatment. Von Oy explained that educational services, such as General

Education Development programs, will help survivors obtain jobs and understand what they are capable of beyond commercial sex.

Richardson is now an advocate for abolishing human trafficking. Woworuntu settled in New York City and works with children with disabilities. Woworuntu has two children, 16 and 6. She says she spends a large portion of her time fighting human trafficking, including labor trafficking. "Working 24 hours, in sex trafficking . . . was like hell," Woworuntu said. "That was not what you want. That is not what you think is the right thing. I didn't know what trafficking was, but what I know, it wasn't right, it wasn't my dream."

Betrayed by the Angel

What Happens When Violence Knocks and Politeness Answers?

Debra Anne Davis (2004)

Mrs. W. arranged us alphabetically, so I spent my entire third-grade year sitting next to a sadist named Hank C. Every day, several times a day, whenever the teacher wasn't looking, Hank would jab his pencil into my arm. He was shorter than me, and I'd look down on his straight brown hair and he'd glance up at me with a crooked smile and then he'd do it: jab jab jab.

He'd get up from his seat often to sharpen the point; I'd sit in my seat in dread, listening to the churn of the pencil sharpener in the back of the room, knowing the pencil tip would be dulled not by paper but by my skin. I'd go home with little gray circles, some with dots of red in the center, Hank's own bull's-eye, all up and down my left arm. I remember it was my left arm because I can see myself sitting next to him, wearing one of the outfits, not just a dress, but an *outfit*—matching socks, hair ribbon, even underwear—that my mother would put me in each morning. I look at him and hope *maybe not this time, please no more,* and he glances at me (or doesn't—he got so good at it that after a while he could find my arm without looking) and: jab jab jab. Each time I hope he won't and each time he does.

Mostly I'd just endure. *This is what is happening; there's nothing I can do about it.* One day after school I decided that I couldn't take it anymore.

I decided that I would tell the teacher the very next time he did it. Of course I'd have to wait for him to do it again first. I felt relief.

When I went to school the next day, we had a substitute teacher instead of Mrs. W. I lost some of my resolve, but not all of it. Hank seemed in better spirits than usual. He started in soon after the bell rang while we were doing workbooks. Jab jab jab. I stood and walked to the front of the room, my lime green dress brushing against the gray metal of the teacher's desk. "Hank always pokes me with the pencil," I told the stranger. My voice was much smaller than I'd hoped. I'd said it like a whisper; I'd meant to sound mad.

"You go back to your seat and tell me if he does it again," she said. And that was it. I never could work up the nerve again to walk the 15 feet to the big desk and blurt out the nature of the boy's crime: Always, he pokes me. I continued going home each day with pencil wounds.

The problem, I think, was that I simply wasn't mad at him. When I went to tell the teacher, my voice wasn't loud in a burst of righteous anger; it was demure. I didn't want to bother her. Maybe I didn't want to see Hank punished. Maybe I didn't think I deserved not to be hurt. Maybe it just didn't seem that big an aberration. Even though no one else was being poked at every day, maybe this was just my lot in life.

I'm 25 years old. I'm alone in my apartment. I hear a knock. I open the door and see a face I don't know. The man scares me, I don't know why. My first impulse is to shut the door. But I stop myself: You can't do something like that. It's rude.

I don't invite him in, but suddenly he is pushing the door and stepping inside. I don't want him to come in; he hasn't waited to be invited. I push the door to close it, but I don't push very hard; I keep remembering that it's not polite to slam a door in someone's face.

He is inside. He slams the door shut himself and pushes me against the wall. My judgment: He is *very* rude. I make this conscious decision: Since he is being rude, it is okay for me to be rude back. I reach for the doorknob; I want to open the door and shove him outside and then slam the door in his face, rude or not, I don't care now. But frankly, I don't push him aside with much determination. I've made the mental choice to be rude, but I haven't been able to muster the physical bluntness the act requires.

Or maybe I realize the game is lost already. He is stronger than I am, I assume, as men have always been stronger. I have no real chance of pushing him aside. No real chance of it unless I am *very* angry. And I'm not very angry. I'm a little bit angry.

But, despite the fact that I didn't shove with much force, *he* is angry with *me*. I know why: It's because I've been rude to him. He is insulted. I am a bit ashamed.

We fall into our roles quite easily, two people who have never met each other, two people raised in the same culture, a man and a woman. As it turns out, a rapist and his victim.

I asked my students, college freshmen, these two questions once: What did your parents teach you that you will teach your own kids? What did they teach you that you won't teach your kids?

One young woman said, "My parents always told me to be kind to everyone. I won't teach my children that. It's not always good to be kind to everyone."

She was so young, but she knew this. Why did it take me so long to learn?

Working on this stuff makes me a little crazy. Sitting at my computer typing for hours about being raped and how it made me feel and makes me feel makes me distracted, jittery—both because I drink too much strong coffee and because writing goes beyond imagining into reliving.

I decided I needed to reread Virginia Woolf. I'd been making notes to myself for a while—"angel" or just "Woolf" scribbled on scraps of paper on my desk and in the front pocket of my backpack, to go buy the book, the book with the angel in it. (I could feel her hovering as I typed; I know the exact color and texture of her flowing gown.)

> What could be easier than to write articles and to buy Persian cats with the profits? But wait a moment. Articles have to be about something. Mine, I seem to remember, was about a novel by a famous man. And while I was writing this review, I discovered that if I were going to review books I should need to do battle with a certain phantom. And the phantom was a woman, and when I came to know her better I called her after the heroine of a famous poem. "The Angel in the House." It was she who used to come between me and my paper when I was writing reviews. It was she who bothered me and wasted my time and so tormented me that at last I killed her.
>
> —*"Professions for Women"*
> *Virginia Woolf (1931)*

There was TV. Reruns of reruns of *I Love Lucy* and *The Flintstones. I Dream of Jeannie. Bewitched.* I can't even think of a show from my youth that had a single female character who was smart, self-confident, and respected by others. My sister and I would lie on our stomachs, heads propped on fuzzy cotton pillows with leopard-skin covers, watching, indiscriminate, mildly entertained, for hours.

Samantha was smarter than Darrin, it was obvious, but she hid her intelligence just as she hid her magical powers, powers Darrin didn't have, powers that made him angry. Samantha's mother, Endora, used her powers with confidence and even flair, but she cackled and wore flowing bright green dresses and too much makeup; she was a mother-in-law. I was supposed to learn how to be like Samantha, not like Endora, and I did.

None of this is news, of course; we can all see those sexist stereotypes quite easily now. But just because I can see, understand, and believe that something is false, that it's not right, now, doesn't mean it won't continue to be a part of me, always.

(Barbara Eden calling Larry Hagman "Master." How many times did I hear *that?*)

"It's big," I say. I turn my head up. I smile. Why do I say this? I ask myself, even then. Well it is big. . . . And I want to flatter him, so he won't hurt me any more than he already plans to. I, yes, I am trying to flirt with him. I've learned about flirting and how it works and what it can do. (It can get people to like you, to do things for you, to treat you well.) It's a skill I have honed. And I'm using it now. To save my life. (And, hey, it worked! Unless of course he hadn't planned to kill me in the first place.)

He smiles down at me (I'm on my knees, naked, leaning against my own bed, my hands tied behind me, my head in his crotch) proudly.

You who come of a younger and happier generation may not have heard of her—you may not know what I mean by the Angel in the House. I will describe her as shortly as I can. She was intensely sympathetic. She was immensely charming. She was utterly unselfish. She excelled in the difficult arts of family life. She sacrificed herself daily. If there was chicken, she took the leg; if there was a draught she sat in it—in short she was so constituted that she never had a mind or a wish of her own, but preferred to sympathize always with the minds and wishes of others.

Back when he was pulling my jeans off, this is what happened: He kneeled behind me, reached around the waistband to the fly, and pulled until all the buttons popped open. Then he crawled back a few feet and began to pull the jeans off from the ankles—a stupid way to try to take someone else's pants off, but I didn't say anything.

He was having a little trouble because the pants weren't slipping off as, obviously, he'd envisioned they would. He tugged and then began yanking. "Stop fighting!" he growled at me. Ooh, *that* pissed me off! "I'm *not fighting!*" I sassed back at him. And I wasn't. How dare he! Accuse me, I mean. Of fighting.

Above all—I need not say it—she was pure. Her purity was supposed to be her chief beauty—her blushes, her great grace. In those days—the last of Queen Victoria—every house had its Angel. And when I came to write I encountered her with the very first words. The shadow of her wings fell on my page; I heard the rustling of her skirts in the room. Directly, that is to say, I took my pen in hand to review that novel by a famous man, she slipped behind me and whispered: "My dear, you are a young woman. You are writing about a book that has been written by a man. Be sympathetic; be tender; flatter; deceive; use all the arts and wiles of our sex. Never let anybody guess that you have a mind of your own. Above all, be pure."

One thing being raped did to me: It caused me to be sometimes rude to strangers. Not out of anger, though, but out of fear.

I was 25 when I was raped. I'm 35 now. This happened last week.

I was in a coffee shop, reading a textbook for a class I'm teaching. After a while, I took a little break and brought my now-empty cup back to the counter. There was a guy at the counter waiting for his drink. "What are you reading?" he asked. He had a big smile on his face, a friendly smile. He wasn't creepy; he was being friendly. I sensed these things. "It's a textbook," I answered. I was looking at the floor now, not at his face any longer.

"Oh! What class are you studying for?" he asked.

"It's a class I'm teaching," I said. Oh no.

"Where do you teach? At _____ College?"

"No," I said flatly and tried to smile a little. I felt nervous, pinned. I knew the conversation wasn't over, but I simply turned and went back to my little table. He stood there at the counter, probably watching me walk away and wondering why I wouldn't answer his question, why, against the unspoken code of our culture, I hadn't at least finished the exchange with a friendly word or a wave. But there was no way I would tell him (or *you,* notice) where I taught or what I taught or anything else about me. And there was no way I could explain this to him courteously; the whole exchange made me too nervous. I certainly wasn't angry at him, but I was a bit afraid. And right there in the coffee shop, I felt the presence of my angel, the rustling of her skirts: "Be sympathetic," I heard her reprimand me, sweetly. "Be tender. And pure." I couldn't be polite, but I did feel guilty.

Though I wasn't finished with my reading, when I got back to the table, I gathered up my things and left.

I turned upon her and caught her by the throat. I did my best to kill her. My excuse, if I were to be had up in a court of law, would be that I acted in self-defense. Had I not killed her she would have killed me.

He bent down to gently arrange the towel over my bare and oozing body, after it was all over with. "You were so good-looking, I just couldn't resist," he told me.

And for the first time in my life, I didn't enjoy being complimented on my physical appearance. Why, I wondered at that moment, had I ever wanted to be considered pretty—or kind, or good? Compliments mean nothing. Or worse, compliments mean this. What good does such a compliment do *me*?

Thus, whenever I felt the shadow of her wing or the radiance of her halo upon my page, I took up the inkpot and flung it at her. She died hard. Her fictitious nature was of great assistance to her. It is far harder to kill a phantom than a reality.

I haven't killed her. Yet. Maybe I need to go out and get an inkpot to fling at her. Hmm, I wonder how she'd hold up against a flying laptop. I can imagine hurling this 10-pound black plastic box at her (she's up in the corner, to my right). It easily tears through the soft blue, rough cotton of her ankle-length gown (she has a long, thin white lace apron tied around her waist). The computer crashes into the space where the walls and ceiling meet; she falls to the carpet. And then what? She's dead. And how do I feel about that? Guilty? Relieved? Well, I don't think I'd want to stuff my pockets with rocks and wade into a river. (Did Woolf ever really kill her angel? Or is it the angel that killed her?)

What I want to know is this: If I'm ever physically attacked again, will I fight to save myself? And will I be fighting out of righteous anger or out of unstrung fear?

What I need to know is this: Is the angel really the one who needs to die?

"I guess I'll get twenty years in the penitentiary for this," he says and waves his hand across the room at me.

Twenty years? Just for this? Just for doing this to me? Twenty years is a really long time.

In fact, he got 35 years. On a plea bargain. The police, the lawyers, the judge—the state, the legal system—even he, the criminal, the rapist, thought he deserved decades in jail for what he'd done to me. Why didn't I?

R E A D I N G 82

How Some Men Harass Women Online and What Other Men Can Do to Stop It

Ben Atherton-Zeman (2013)

When I write about feminism and men's violence against women, I often receive supportive comments. While some of the praise is earned, much of it gives me a lot of credit for doing very little.

When women write about those same topics, it's a different story. We men threaten women bloggers and writers with rape and murder. We call women "man-haters," verbally abuse them, hack into their email accounts and stalk them. We alter photos of women, putting cuts and bruises on their faces. Then we excuse ourselves, saying we were "just joking—can't you feminists take a joke?"

Racists harass people online; so do homophobes. Most people agree this is harassment. But my gender's online harassment of women seems to go unquestioned, even defended, in most circles. Yet men's online abuse of women has been well-documented by women such as Laurie Penney, Jennifer Pozner, Emily May and many other women.

"The sad part is that it works," says feminist blogger Soraya Chemaly. "I have spoken to many, many women writers who 'tone down' their voices or stop writing entirely as a result of threats. . . . I mean, who wants to wake up in the morning to 'Stupid, cunt' or 'I'll go from house to house shooting women like you.'"

"The death threat was pretty scary," says HollaBack! cofounder Emily May. "And there have been several rape threats. But it's mostly 'I want to rape you' or 'Somebody should rape you.' Most are not physical threats—they're more about how ugly I am, how nobody would bother raping me because I'm so fat and hideous. Once, after reading all these posts, I just sat in my living room and bawled like a 12-year-old."

Jennifer Pozner agrees. "Very rarely have I gotten negative feedback that doesn't include either a rape threat or calling me ugly and fat. Or sometimes they tell me I'm hot, but they hate what I'm saying—they'd rather watch me on TV with the mute on." Pozner's threats have not been limited to online: One man left a letter at her door saying he'd "find you and your mom and rape you both."

Chemaly adds, "The point of the harassment, like harassment on the street, is to make the public sphere seem dangerous and to portray women as provoking a violent response through their actions." Pozner agrees. "It's about the policing of women . . . using threats to keep us silent."

Richard Rogers and Vanessa Thorpe called for a stop to such harassment in the *Guardian* two years ago. But most men have remained silent, as we do with many forms of our gender's violence against women. Many of us blame the victim, suggesting things women can do differently to ameliorate the problem. We tell women to grow a thicker skin, not to "feed the trolls" and not to assume all men feel that way. Or we ride in on a white horse to "save" the poor damsels by insulting the insulters or

threatening violence against those who are threatening violence. This makes us feel better, but often does little to help the women being attacked or stop the violence from happening.

When men are harassed online, it's often because they are speaking out against rape culture. Comedian Jamie Kilstein reports receiving a few combative emails after questioning God's existence or challenging Glenn Beck—but he received "thousands" after challenging rape culture. "There is a cost for betraying one's privilege . . . [although] nowhere near the costs borne by the marginalized," says Don Bell of the National Organization for Men Against Sexism:

> Men could be silenced by the fear of being labeled as emasculated (weak), not linked to women sexually (gay), or dominated. . . . Men should be challenged to face their fears and risks because it is the right thing to do. Allying with women in support of feminist values—becoming pro-feminist—makes for better men and a better world.

Men's online abuse results in women hesitating to write, stopping writing altogether and fearing for their physical safety. Many women have told me that such abuse doesn't just happen when women are writing about feminism, it happens to them all the time. Amy Davis Roth blogged about atheism and was subjected to daily harassment as a result. Roth described a "typical day" as "Wake up. Make coffee. Block hateful messages on Twitter or other social media . . . Make art." Sarah Sentilles was disparaged and ridiculed when writing about theology, attacked for being "childish," her words called "chatter" despite her two doctorates.

In the early 90s, Rush Limbaugh popularized the term "feminazi." Across the country, we men opened our mouths to laugh, and closed our ears to feminist wisdom. In the name of "humor," male comics and pundits call women names and threaten them with violence—the rest of us don't challenge it, but further attack those who do. When we apologize, it's a fake apology, like comedian Daniel Tosh's.

Ironically, when women call men out on our harassment, they are harassed even more. I wrote a *Ms.* blog about Tosh last year and it drew some criticism but mostly praise. But when feminist blogger Cristy Cardinal wrote about it she was threatened with rape and murder and her email and Twitter accounts were hacked.

Yet, most men care deeply about the women and girls in our lives. It pains us to hear that you stop yourselves from writing online, walking outside or wearing certain clothing because of the harassment and violence our gender heaps upon you. We'd rather it never happened to you, so we often pretend it doesn't. We move from denial to anger at you for bringing it up, then from anger to bargaining—we question the statistics you cite, or distract with anecdotes of women who abuse men. We sometimes go through the whole Kubler-Ross cycle of death and dying before we're ready to move to "acceptance."

But some men do not seem to care about anyone but themselves. These men seem to take glee in making anonymous online threats, sometimes as part of a political movement that refuses to acknowledge men's violence against women as an epidemic. Instead, they see men as the real victims—of *feminism*. Their self-appointed victim status gives them the right to call women names, threaten and intimidate at will.

For me as a man, the "acceptance" stage involves really listening to what women's lives are actually like. It means getting sick to my stomach when I hear my friend Cristy Cardinal has been threatened, or admitting that I benefit from male privilege even if I don't harass women online myself. It means that when I laughed at Bill Maher calling Sarah Palin stupid or a bitch, I made writing and life that much harder for Soraya Chemaly.

The "acceptance" stage also means I'm ready to do something positive. It's not enough for me to simply not harass women myself—if I don't raise my voice when I see this, I'm letting the Limbaughs be the lone voices of my gender. So I'm proud to be part of a growing movement of men who are listening to women, learning from women, becoming active bystanders and "aspiring allies."

Clearly there's no one "right" way to intervene, but I've already heard several suggestions. Men, we can't remain silent any longer. Let us:

1. Listen to women's experience of online abuse and threats by men. Let us read articles about it. Instead of suggesting solutions, we can take in how hurtful the comments are.

2. Reach out to the target of the abuse. Ask her what she'd like you to do, if anything.

3. Write, "I think you're right," in Comments sections of articles, Facebook postings etc. of feminist women. Whether or not they've been harassed or attacked, agree with them and do so publicly.

4. When men harass women online, speak up. We can say something like, "As a man, your harassing comment offends me," in the Comments sections. Say how it hurts *you* rather than speaking on behalf of the target.

5. Name the specific silencing tactic being used: name-calling, focusing on a woman's appearance instead of her argument, etc.

6. Use humor. We can post something like, "Dude, put down your club—your caveman is showing!" Search online for feminist comedians of all genders who have done entire routines on this.

7. Watch for "professional trolls" from the "Men's Rights" or "Father's Rights" groups. They will often use terms such as "misandry" and refer to the feminist movement as anti-male or the domestic violence movement as an "industry."

8. Send supportive emails, letters, candygrams, etc. to feminist women. Thank them for the good work they are doing—not just when they are targets of online harassment, but all the time. "If you see someone doing good work, you can be sure they're being told they're fat and ugly," says Emily May. "Nice emails counterbalance the noise."

9. Flag Facebook posts (or pages) when they're abusive. If it's a comment, click on the X to hide the post. You then have the option to flag it as abusive.

10. If the perpetrator isn't an individual but a company, boycott the company. Write negative reviews of it on "Yelp" or other review sites, or suggest policy or legislative changes. (See the Ecological Model for Social Change for the philosophy behind this.)

What else would women like men to do? What would you like us *not* to do?. . .

Lisa's Ritual, Age 10

Grace Caroline Bridges (1994)

Afterwards when he has finished
lots of mouthwash helps
to get rid of her father's cigarette taste.
She runs a hot bath
   to soak away the pain
     like red dye leaking from her
      school dress in the washtub.

She doesn't cry
When the bathwater cools she adds more hot.
She brushes her teeth for a long time.

Then she finds the corner of her room,
curls against it. There the wall is
hard and smooth
as teacher's new chalk, white
as a clean bedsheet. Smells
fresh. Isn't sweaty, hairy, doesn't stick
to skin. Doesn't hurt much
when she presses her small backbone
into it. The wall is steady
while she falls away:
   first the hands lost

arms dissolving feet gone
  the legs dis- jointed
    body cracking down
      the center like a fault
     she falls inside
        slides down like
dust   like kitchen dirt
        slips off
the dustpan into
       noplace
  a place where
nothing happens,
nothing ever happened.

When she feels the cool
wall against her cheek
she doesn't want to
come back. Doesn't want to
think about it.
The wall is quiet, waiting.
It is tall like a promise
only better.

Anti-LGBTQ Violence: Three Essays

Anti-LGBT Violence Spreads Throughout Russian Regions

Tony Hobday (2013)

While parts of the globe are experiencing an increase of tolerance for LGBTQ people, and homophobia begins to dissipate, hatred and violence continue to ravage the territories that had once made up the Soviet Union. In recent months, regions of Russia have been rapidly adopting "propaganda of homosexuality" laws, legalizing discrimination against LGBTQ people, which seems to be leading to growing violence.

The author of the so-called "propaganda of homosexuality" legislation, Vitaly Milonov, is the United Russia city parliament deputy, and an Orthodox activist. The centuries-old domineering

Eastern Orthodox Christian denomination reigns the regions today, including Georgia, Ukraine and Russia, where LGBTQ rights are severely suffering. Heralding a seemingly unwavering "traditional" belief system, one based on "personal experiences of truth," Orthodoxy, for all intents and purpose, appears to be creating a second "Great Schism"— one that abandons global human rights continuity.

In fact, earlier this month Amnesty International released an in-depth report called, "Nothing to be Proud of: Discrimination Against LGBTQI People in Ukraine," denouncing the Ukrainian government for failing to follow international and European human rights law:

"Ukraine is failing to protect the basic rights of LGBTI people such as the right to be free from discrimination, the right to security of the person and the rights to freedom of peaceful assembly and expression," the report reads. "Ukraine has an international obligation to uphold the principle of non-discrimination and ensure that all individuals, including LGBTI people, are treated equally irrespective of their sexual orientation and gender identity in both law and fact."

The report also makes reference to last year's first-ever scheduled pride march in Kiev, Ukraine, which was cancelled following threats of violence when 2,000 anti-gay protesters showed up. Regardless, violence ensued May 20, 2012. Svytoslav Sheremet, the pride march organizer and president of the Gay Forum of Ukraine, was brutally attacked by seven men, some wearing surgical masks, after he announced the cancellation to the press.

"We may not have had a march, but only two of us were attacked, and we were able to start a lot of conversations in homes, with families and in the press. Politicians, educators and parents had to have the discussions that are so important and what will ultimately advance the cause," Sheremet told QSalt-Lake, a Utah LGBTQ newsmagazine in 2012, while visiting queer-rights groups in the United States, as part of a U.S. Department of State program to examine LGBT advocacy in America.

"Surprisingly, things have become far worse in Ukraine in the past decade because homosexuality isn't so hidden," Sheremet continued. "People want to come out and be open about who they are. Before, everyone was fine just keeping it all underground in a few gay bars, but as soon as people started to ask for equal protection, there was immediate backlash."

Despite the failed attempt at a pride march last year, Amnesty International and the Human Rights Watch are urging Kiev authorities to allow this year's march planned for May 25, 2013—despite the recent chaos that erupted May 17 in Tbilisi, Georgia, the capital city of the former Soviet state.

Though the Georgian government did give the green light on a gay-rights event to honor of International Day Against Homophobia, thousands of protesters gathered in the street, many of them members of the Orthodox Church, disrupting the event.

The tragic death of Vladislav Tornovoy, 23, on May 9 in Russia, and the subsequent ban of yet another pride event in the region, symbolized a formidable insurgence of hatred and violence against LGBTQ people in those areas. Tornovoy was brutally murdered and mutilated in Volgograd, just outside Moscow, for being gay—a mere six months following the beating death of Armen Ovcharuk, a young gay man who was killed while walking home from a gay nightclub in Kiev.

On May 17, commemorating the deaths of Tornovoy and Ovcharuk, and other victims of homophobic hate crimes, 150 LGBTQ people and their supporters rallied in St. Petersburg, Russia, making it the largest public LGBTQ demonstration in the city to date. The event was scheduled to last an hour, but police broke it up after only 10 minutes when approximately 100 protesters began throwing smoke pellets and small stones at the demonstrators.

Following the 2006 and 2007 bans on pride parades in Moscow, the European Court of Human Rights found in 2008 that the previous bans violated the European Convention on Human Rights in the areas of freedom of assembly and association. Despite the ruling, Moscow continues to deny approval of a pride parade each year.

In 2011, the Council of Europe's commissioner for human rights, Thomas Hammarberg, denounced Moscow's refusal to abide by the European Court's decision, saying, "The European Court of Human Rights has ruled in two judgments against unlawful restrictions or bans running counter to the exercise of freedom of assembly by LGBT persons in the context of the organization of Pride parades."

"Peaceful demonstrations cannot be banned simply because of hostile attitudes to the demonstrators or to the causes they advocate," Hammarberg continued. "The State also has a duty to protect the participants in peaceful demonstrations including when they hold unpopular views or belong to minorities."

A decision made by the Moscow City Court last June, however, bans gay pride parades in the city for the next 100 years.

Equality's Brutal Backlash

Michelangelo Signorile (2013)

A few months ago, I wrote about how my partner and I were called "disgusting" by a man on the street as we shared a quick goodbye kiss in the middle of the afternoon in the very gay Manhattan neighborhood of Chelsea. That has turned out to be less an aberration than a symptom of far more horrific things to come. We've seen reports of violent attack after violent attack in New York against gays in recent weeks, and now, this past weekend, we've experienced the brutal killing of 32-year-old Mark Carson in an alleged anti-gay shooting in Greenwich Village.

"You want to die tonight?" the alleged gunman reportedly said after repeatedly calling Carson and a male companion "faggots" while they were walking down the street, before fatally shooting Carson in the face.

This killing has kept me up the past two nights. It's sickening and enraging. And perhaps the shock I'm seeing expressed about it, particularly among younger LGBT people, underscores that many of us have been living with a false sense of security, intoxicated by the wins on marriage equality in the states and in the federal courts. It's way too easy to grow complacent, fed by the desire to have the fight done with as well as by the seductive message of some in the media who've simplistically declared victory for the LGBT rights movement.

Victory is very far off, however, if we can't walk the streets of even the most LGBT-friendly cities holding hands or expressing ourselves without fear of being taunted and violently assaulted. And for hundreds of thousands living in less tolerant places all across the country, openness has never been a reality. Until it is, we're nowhere near victory.

We may be seeing solid majorities in national polls supporting anti-discrimination laws for gay and transgender people, and even majorities supporting marriage equality. But the minorities are still substantial. And they are getting more desperate. For years, those who are anti-gay have been emboldened by the often hateful declarations of homophobic religious leaders and by the attacks by groups like the National Organization for Marriage, which have demeaned gays. After decades of struggle, we're finally beating them back in the courts, in legislatures and even at the ballot box. And perhaps the frustration and anger by those who oppose us is now further empowering the thugs who take their hate and rage to the streets.

It shouldn't come as a surprise then that in New York City, in a state that passed marriage equality in 2011, hate crimes against LGBT people so far in 2013 are almost double what were at this point in 2012. And 2012 itself was a notable year nationally, with outbreak of anti-LGBT violence in some of the country's most gay-friendly cities, like New York, Washington, Los Angeles, Dallas and Atlanta. 2011 saw the highest number of anti-LGBT murders ever reported, with transgender people the hardest-hit victims. At least 13 transgender Americans were reported to have been murdered in 2012 alone.

We sometimes forget that getting laws passed and getting court rulings declared is, comparatively, the easy part—as monumentally difficult as that has been and continues to be. One reason we in fact get the laws passed, in addition to protecting ourselves, is to change attitudes for future generations. But that part doesn't happen overnight and surely not without a backlash, which can sometimes be violent, as it has been in just about every other movement for equality. The hate is still out there and the haters are getting more desperate. Our worst enemies right now are complacency and the seductive message that we've "arrived."

Violence Against Transgender Women in Latin America

Hope Gillette (2013)

HIV prevalence among transgender women in Latin American countries is significantly higher (35 percent) when compared to the HIV incidence among the rest of the female population (less than 1 percent), reports the *Huffington Post UK*.

Transgender women in Latin America also face far more difficulties when it comes to accessing HIV prevention and care, as well as to medical services, due to transphobia, an unchecked form of discrimination, which makes these women targets for discrimination, violence and sexual abuse.

In a report entitled The Night Is Another Country: Impunity and violence against transgender women human rights defenders in Latin America, the International HIV/AIDS Alliance and partners have investigated transphobia in Latin American countries, revealing a disproportionate number of violent acts against transgender women which have gone undisciplined.

"Between 2005 and 2012 in Colombia, 60 transgender women were murdered without a single person having been brought to justice. In the same period 35 transgender people were killed in Guatemala with only one person undergoing legal proceedings," wrote Dr. Alvaro Bermejo, Executive Director, International HIV/AIDS Alliance in the *Huffington Post UK's* blog.

Other key findings of the report included:

- Approximately 80 percent of transgender activists interviewed reported violence or threats of violence from state officials including "extrajudicial executions, torture, cruel, inhuman and degrading treatment and arbitrary detentions that extend beyond the heading of hate crime."
- 79 percent of transgender murders in the world took place in Latin America for a total of 664 cases
- In Guatemala and Honduras, 60 percent of interviewed transgendered activists were subjected to arbitrary detention at some point in their lives

- 90 percent of violence against transgendered women was related to sex work

TRANSGENDER WOMEN, SEX WORK AND HIV

The high percentage of transgender women in sex work is directly related to the high incidence of HIV among the population, explained researchers. According to Bermejo, transgender women are often thrown out of their homes at a young age and excluded from an education. In order to make money, many feel they have no choice but to turn to the sex trade.

"About six months ago, I got in a car with a man who I know is a policeman," stated a transgender activist from Guatemala City, Guatemala, in a study report from the International HIV/AIDS Alliance. "He hired me to provide my sexual services, but afterwards he didn't want to pay and he wouldn't let me get out of the car. He shouted at me, 'Today you really are going to die, hueco!' I told him to kill me, because I knew that sooner or later I'd end up dead, because for me, life is a bonus."

Working in the sex trade puts many transgender women at risk for sexually transmitted diseases such as HIV, however, most Latin American countries do not recognized transgender people as a population, and therefore there are no laws protecting them or catering to their health care needs.

The majority of transgender women, states Bermejo, have no access to basic health care, and many clinics do not support their special needs. Not only are services limited, but due to the threat of violence against them, most transgender women look to keep their identities concealed, therefore rarely seeking medical attention.

"Because of the social exclusion that transgender women face and the context of violence and discrimination that surrounds them, it is virtually impossible to provide an effective HIV response focused on this at risk group," Bermejo stated in the blog.

REPORT RECOMMENDATIONS

To help bring much-needed HIV care to transgender women, the Alliance report notes the following issues need to be addressed:

- Arrests and trials must be made for those responsible for hate crimes against transgendered women
- Legal recognition of gender identity

- Targeting the transgendered community with health care efforts
- Ensure health care clinics and prisons allow transgendered women to use female-only facilities where the likelihood of abuse is minimal
- Acknowledging and protecting transgendered women from the risk of rape and abuse from both the public and from state employees

DISCUSSION QUESTIONS FOR CHAPTER 10

1. How do violence and the threat of violence exert social control on women? Do you ever fear gender-based violence? How do you think your gender affects your answer to this question?

2. Why do you think many feminists suggest that acts of violence against women are actually hate crimes? Do you think these acts should be classified as hate crimes?

3. Why do you think violence against women is so prevalent in society? Why do you think violence against women is primarily perpetrated by men?

4. How do myths about violence against women silence women and perpetuate sexist systems of oppression?

5. What are connections between violence against women and violence against LGBTQ people?

SUGGESTIONS FOR FURTHER READING

Abdulhadi, Rabab, Evelyn Alsultany, and Nadine Naber, eds. *Arab and Arab American Feminisms: Gender, Violence, and Belonging.* Syracuse, NY: Syracuse University Press, 2010.

Dominguez-Ruvalcaba, Hector, and Ignacio Corona. *Gender Violence at the U.S.-Mexico Border: Media Representation and Public Response.* Tucson, AZ: University of Arizona Press, 2010.

Edwards, Alice. *Violence Against Women Under International Human Rights Law.* New York: Cambridge University Press, 2010.

Hanhardt, Christina B. *Safe Space: Gay Neighborhood History and the Politics of Violence.* Durham, NC: Duke University Press, 2013.

Jung, Kyungia. *Practicing Feminism in South Korea: The Women's Movement against Sexual Violence.* New York: Routledge, 2013.

McGlynn, Clare, and Vanessa E. Munro, eds. *Rethinking Rape Law: International and Comparative Perspectives.* London: Routledge-Cavendish, 2010.

Meyersfeld, Bonita. *Domestic Violence and International Law.* Oxford, UK: Hart Publishing, 2010.

Renzetti, Claire M., Jeffrey L. Edleson, and Raquel Kennedy Bergen. *Sourcebook on Violence Against Women,* Second Edition. Thousand Oaks, CA: Sage Publications, 2010.

True, Jacqui. *The Political Economy of Violence against Women.* New York: Oxford University Press, 2012.

CHAPTER 11

State, Law, and Social Policy

As we have noted in earlier chapters, societal institutions are established patterns of social behavior organized around particular needs and purposes. Institutions structure aspects of life in families and communities, and also produce social discourses or "regimes of truth" that create meaning and construct our notions of knowledge and truth. Gender, race, class, and other identities associated with systems of inequality and privilege structure social institutions, creating different effects on different people. The state, the institution explored in this chapter, is a major social institution organized to maintain systems of legitimized power and authority in society. The state plays an important role in both teaching and enforcing social values. It is a very powerful institution that has profound implications for people's everyday lives. A key focus of this chapter is the interaction between the state and gender relations in society.

The *state* is an abstract concept that refers to all forms of social organization representing official power in society: the government, law and social policy, the courts and the criminal justice system, the military, and the police. The state determines how people are selected to govern others and controls the systems of governance they must use. With considerable authority in maintaining social order, the state influences how power is exercised within society. The definition of *state* here is different from state as a geographic region, such as California or Ohio.

Because the state is a conduit for various patterns of social inequity, it does not always fairly regulate and control social order. Historically, white women and women and men of color—and especially those with little economic privilege—have been treated poorly by the state. There are still many problems and challenges at all levels of the political system. However, the state has also been a tool for addressing historical forms of social, political, and economic inequalities through laws and social policy (as evidenced by civil rights and affirmative action legislation). In this way, the state works both to maintain sources of inequality and as an avenue for social justice. As already discussed in other chapters, the legal gains of the mid- and late-twentieth century have been important in improving the lives of women and people of color. Title IX of the Education Amendments of 1972, which prohibits sex discrimination of all kinds (not just concerning athletics) at institutions that receive federal funds, is a case in point.

LEARNING ACTIVITY   **Women and the United Nations (UN)**

Visit the website of United Nations Entity for Gender Equality and the Empowerment of Women at *http://www.unwomen.org/*. Follow the links to focus
areas to learn more about the UN's work with women. Then visit the UN's
WomenWatch site at *http://www.un.org/womenwatch* to learn more about the
UN's promotion of gender equality and empowerment of women. Follow the
link to Women of the World for region-specific information. Follow the link for
Statistics and Indicators for reports, databases, and archives relating to gender equality and women's human rights. What do you notice are the pressing
issues facing women worldwide? What is the United Nations doing to address
these issues?

As already discussed in Chapter 2, the state works with other institutions and assigns
roles and distributes resources. In particular, it regulates other institutions, provides guidelines for expected behaviors (roles), and channels resources and power. For example, it
regulates the family (such as the Family Leave Act that considers some families illegitimate
and thus ineligible for state benefits), education (such as Title IX), the economic system
(such as antitrust laws that prevent monopolies and anti-discrimination policies), and
religion (such as state rules for the separation of church and state). The state as nation-
state also participates in international policy-making that has important implications for
global economic development and military strategy. When the United States refuses to
ratify international treaties such as CEDAW (the Convention on the Elimination of All
Forms of Discrimination Against Women) or the Kyoto Treaty on environmental quality
because it seeks to protect U.S. statutes and corporations, it has significant impact globally.
The United States is often seen as a powerful symbol of urban secular decadence, with
the emancipation of women a central feature. This highlights the importance of gender-
sensitive conceptions of international aid and development.

Beyond national levels of state policy in the United States is the United Nations (UN),
which has tremendous influence on global politics. Scholars emphasize that even though
notions of women's "rescue" have been deployed to generate consent for military missions in Afghanistan, women's concerns remain peripheral to regional and international
politics. Although the right to gender equality has been affirmed in international law,
still many nations explicitly discriminate against women (including the United States).
UN Resolution 1325 on women and peace and security was adopted by the UN Security
Council in 2000 in response to this worldwide gender discrimination. As mentioned in
Chapter 10, this resolution addresses gender-based violence against girls and women,
especially in war zones. It also affirms the important role of women in the prevention and
resolution of conflicts, peace negotiations, peace-building, peacekeeping, humanitarian
response, and post-conflict reconstruction, and stresses the importance of women's equal
participation and full involvement in all efforts for the maintenance and promotion of
peace and security.

GOVERNMENT AND REPRESENTATION

Although the terms *government* and *state* tend to be used interchangeably, the government is actually one of the institutions that make up the state. The government creates laws and procedures that govern society and its citizens and is often referred to as the political system. Although the U.S. government is purported to be a democracy based on the principle of equal representation, the government is not representative of all people, and those who participate as elected officials do not necessarily represent all interests equitably. In addition, "citizen" is a constructed category that must be understood in historical context. Who is considered a U.S. citizen, for example, has changed over time along with the politics of immigration and the establishment of borders after the wars of the last centuries. The reading "Looking Beyond the Wall" by Robert Neustadt addresses the problem of undocumented migration across the Arizona–Mexico border. He is a professor who took a group of students on a class trip to the border. The reading shares students' experiences and makes the case for comprehensive immigration reform.

Women generally have had a complicated relationship to the Constitution. The liberal doctrine of representation first included women as rights-bearing citizens and represented them as members of the body politic. They came to be excluded for a variety of political reasons, justified in part because the dominant culture assumed that politics and citizenship were purely masculine domains. The founding fathers believed that women's political identity should be restricted because their presence in politics was immoral, corruptive, and potentially disruptive, and that women should be represented by fathers, husbands, or brothers. It was believed that women should be confined to the private sphere of the home where they would be dependent on men, and, as a result, they had no separate legal identity and were legal beings only through their relationship to a man. They had no claims to citizenship rights as women until well into the nineteenth century.

As you know from Chapter 1, the Seneca Falls convention in 1848 produced the Declaration of Sentiments and Resolutions that aimed to ensure citizenship rights for women. Women would have to wait until 1920 and the passage of the Nineteenth Amendment to the U.S. Constitution to receive the vote. In 1868, however, the Fourteenth Amendment was ratified, asserting that no state shall "make or enforce any law which will abridge the privileges or immunities of citizens of the United States, nor . . . deprive any person of life, liberty, or property without due process of law, nor deny to any person within its jurisdiction the equal protection of laws." This "person" was assumed to be male, and, as a result, women still could not vote, and the government did not (and, many people would argue, still does not) extend the same protection of the law to women as it does to men. Susan B. Anthony, one of the first feminists, who helped write the Declaration of Sentiments and Resolutions, wanted to test her belief that the Fourteenth Amendment should give women, as citizens, the right to vote. She voted in an election in Rochester, New York, and was fined. Hoping to push the case to the Supreme Court, Anthony refused to pay the fine. The case, however, was dropped in order to avoid this test of law. In the Anthony reading "Constitutional Argument," she argues her right to vote as a citizen under the terms guaranteed by the Fourteenth Amendment. This excerpt, published in 1898, is from a speech Anthony gave in 1873.

In 1923 the Equal Rights Amendment (ERA) was introduced into Congress to counter the inadequacies of the Fourteenth Amendment concerning women and citizenship. The ERA affirms that both women and men hold equally all of the rights guaranteed by the U.S. Constitution. It would provide a remedy for gender discrimination for both women and

MAN is the HUNTER. WOMAN is the CIVILIZING INFLUENCE,

AND WHEN WOMEN ABANDON THAT ROLE,

MEN BECOME...

CRANKY, AND START WARS.

men and, at the constitutional level, provide equal legal status to women for the first time in our country's history. It was rewritten in the 1940s to read: "Equality of rights under the law shall not be denied or abridged by the United States or by any state on account of sex"; and it eventually passed Congress (almost 50 years later) in 1972. Unfortunately, it failed to be ratified by the states and suffered a serious defeat in 1982. The most important effect of the ERA would have been to clarify the status of gender discrimination for the courts, whose decisions still show confusion about how to deal with such claims. For the first time, "sex" would have been a suspect classification like race. It would require the same high level of "strict scrutiny" and have to meet the same high level of justification—a "necessary" relation to a "compelling" state interest—as the classification of race.

Although survey after survey showed overwhelming public support for the ERA among women and men, it was officially defeated on June 30, 1982, when it failed to be ratified by the states. It fell three states short of the 38 states needed for ratification. Although the ERA continues to be introduced into each session of Congress, passage of the amendment has yet to regain the momentum it did during the 1970s (even though back in 1988 a Harris poll showed 78 percent approval). In order for the ERA to be fully amended, two-thirds of each house in Congress must pass it first, followed by its ratification by 38 states. As opposition to the ERA grew, some states retracted their prior ratification, and others, such as Illinois, changed laws in order to make ratification more difficult. Indiana became the thirty-fifth and last state to ratify the ERA in 1977, and the Republican Party removed ERA support from its platform. Many years later, ratification efforts continue, with women and men in many of the unratified states working under the "three-state strategy." This strategy argues that because there was no actual time limit for ratification in the original ERA, the amendment remains only three states short of official ratification. Currently 19 states have state ERAs or equal rights guarantees in their constitutions, and many groups are working together toward the legislation of the Equal Rights Amendment at all levels. These groups include the League of Women Voters U.S., American Association of University Women, Business & Professional Women/USA, National Organization for Women, National Women's Political Caucus, ERA Campaign, and the Equal Rights Amendment Organization.

Opponents of the ERA have mistakenly claimed that the amendment is anti-family, reporting that it would deny a woman's right to be supported by her husband and encourage women to desert motherhood. There was also worry that it would legislate abortion and gay and lesbian rights as well as send women into combat. In addition, anti-ERA sentiments

LEARNING ACTIVITY **The League of Women Voters**

The League of Women Voters was founded by Carrie Chapman Catt in 1920 during the convention of the National American Woman Suffrage Association, just 6 months before the Nineteenth Amendment was ratified. In its early years, the league advocated for collective bargaining, child labor laws, minimum wage, compulsory education, and equal opportunity for women in government and industry. Today the league is still involved in advocacy for justice, working on such issues as Medicare reform, campaign finance reform, and environmental preservation, as well as continuing the work begun more than 80 years ago to encourage women to use their political voices. To learn more about the League of Women Voters or to join the league, visit its website at *www.lwv.org*.

were voiced by business interests (such as members of the insurance industry) that profited from gender discrimination. The media sensationalized the issue and did not accurately report about what the ERA would and would not do, and conservative political organizations spent a lot of money and many hours organizing against it.

Most feminist leaders today agree that women would be better off if the ERA had been ratified in 1977. They would have received better opportunities for equality and would have been supported by stronger laws fighting gender discrimination in employment, education, and other areas of society. Some people feel that we no longer need a constitutional amendment because there have been piecemeal federal and state laws to protect against gender discrimination. However, as we have seen, federal laws are no longer as safe as they have been and can be repealed by a simple majority. Similarly, courts change policy as the makeup of the courts changes. A constitutional amendment requires three-quarters of the legislature to vote to repeal it. Although many people assume the continuity of women's rights, the U.S. Supreme Court is central in maintaining or potentially overturning several taken-for-granted rights. These rights include reproductive privacy, affirmative action, protection against gender-based discrimination, family and medical leave, and quality health care services.

An illustration of how the government has handled women and citizenship concerns the treatment of women who have married non-U.S. citizens. Prior to the mid-1920s, non-native-born women who married male U.S. citizens automatically became American, and native-born women who married male non-U.S. citizens automatically lost their citizenship and were expected to reside in their husband's country. They also lost their right to vote, once women had been given the vote in 1920. When laws were passed to retain women's citizenship in the mid-1920s, still only men were able to pass on citizenship to their children. Laws equalizing citizenship on these issues were eventually passed in the mid-1930s. Citizenship and who is classed as a citizen remains a highly volatile debate and often serves as a major conduit for inequality in many societies. This is illustrated in the reading "Looking Beyond the Wall" by Robert Neustadt, which addresses the problem of undocumented migration across the Arizona–Mexico border.

In addition to rights, citizenship entails such obligations as taxation, jury duty, and military service. Although women have shared taxation with men, in the past they have been prevented from service and/or exempted from jury duty because of their role as mothers and housewives. It was not until the 1970s that the Supreme Court declared that

ACTIVIST PROFILE   **Wilma Mankiller**

With her election as chief of the Cherokee Nation, Wilma Mankiller took both a step forward and a step backward. Although Mankiller was the first woman to serve as chief of a major Native American tribe in modern times, her election recalled the importance women had among the Cherokee before colonization by Europeans. Precontact Cherokee society was matrifocal and matrilineal. Women owned the property and maintained the home and were intimately involved in tribal governance.

Mankiller first became committed to involvement in Native American rights in 1969 when Native activists, including some of her own siblings, occupied Alcatraz island in San Francisco Bay. The 19-month occupation became a turning point in Mankiller's life. She became director of the Native American Youth Center in Oakland, California, and in 1973 she watched as her brother joined other Native American activists as they held off FBI agents for 72 days at Wounded Knee, South Dakota.

Following a divorce, Mankiller returned to her family's land in Oklahoma and began to work for the Cherokee Nation; as an economic stimulus coordinator, she had the task of encouraging Cherokee people to train in environmental health and science and then return to their communities to put their knowledge to use. In 1981 she became director of the Cherokee Nation Community Development Department, and her work was so successful that she attracted the attention of Chief Ross Swimmer, who asked her to run as his deputy chief in 1983.

Despite sexist rhetoric and verbal threats from opponents, Swimmer and Mankiller won. In 1985 Swimmer was named head of the Bureau of Indian Affairs by President

(continued)

Ronald Reagan, and Mankiller became chief of the Cherokee Nation. In 1987 Mankiller ran on her own and was elected chief in her own right. That year, *Ms.* magazine named her Woman of the Year. She was re-elected in 1991, winning by 83 percent of the vote. During her tenure as chief, Mankiller focused on addressing high unemployment and low education rates among Cherokee people, improving community health care, implementing housing initiatives and child and youth projects, and developing the economy of northeastern Oklahoma. She created the Institute for Cherokee Literacy, emphasizing the need for Cherokee people to retain their traditions. She did not run for re-election in 1995. In 1998 President Bill Clinton awarded her the Presidential Medal of Freedom. She died at her Oklahoma home in 2010.

juries had to be representative of the community. Even then juries were often racially biased such that it was not unusual for an African American to face a white jury. A 1986 Supreme Court ruling stated that juries could not be constituted on the basis of race, and a 1994 ruling declared that gender too could not be used as a basis for jury competence. The obligation for military service, which many women have wanted to share with men, is outlined in more detail later in the chapter. Of course, women have served in auxiliary roles as nurses, transport drivers, and dispatchers for many years and are now able to participate in combat positions within most divisions of the armed services.

Although women tend to be as involved as men in electoral politics (and sometimes even more involved) in terms of voting, showing support, and volunteering for campaigns, there are markedly fewer women involved in official political positions associated with campaigns. Women still constitute a relatively small number of candidates for local, state, and national offices, and their presence is greater at the local than the national level. As political offices get more visible, higher level, better paid, and more authoritative or powerful, there are fewer women in these positions. There are several explanations for this gap. Although some suggest that women are just not interested and that they lack the credentials, the main reasons are conflict between family and work roles, lack of political financing, and discrimination and sexist attitudes toward women in politics. The latter is illustrated in the reading "Name it. Change it" by Rachel Joy Larris and Rosalie Maggio, which presents a media guide for gender-neutral coverage of women candidates and politicians. The reading explains how social discourses about gender influence public opinion, and it makes the case that widespread sexism in media is one of the top problems facing women candidates. The reading provides guiding rules for gender neutrality in media.

As of this writing in 2014, 98 seats (18.3 percent) are held by women in the 113th U.S. Congress. This includes 78 women (17.9 percent) from 31 states in the House of Representatives (59 Democrats and 19 Republicans); and 20 women (20 percent: 16 Democrats and 4 Republicans) in the Senate. In addition, 3 Democratic women serve as Delegates to the House, representing Guam, the Virgin Islands, and Washington, D.C. Congresswoman Nancy Pelosi (D-CA), who was the first women speaker of the House, is (currently, as of this writing) minority leader. Rounding up percentages, we can say that women currently make up 18 percent of the U.S. Congress. Of these 98 women, 30 or 30.6 percent are women of color (28 Democrats and 2 Republicans), in addition to an African American delegate representing Washington, D.C., and a Caribbean American woman representing the Virgin

Where Women Rule: A Sample of Female Representatives in National Legislatures Worldwide

Simple statistics merely hint at complex stories. Rwandan genocide has increased the number of female representatives but so, it appears, has Scandinavian social democracy. The United States ranks 78th on the list. Why do you think so many other countries have more women representatives in their legislatures?

Rank	Country	Lower or Single House		
		Seats	Women	% W
1	Rwanda	80	45	56.3%
2	Andorra	28	14	50.0%
3	Cuba	612	299	48.9%
4	Sweden	349	156	44.7%
5	Seychelles	32	14	43.8%
6	Senegal	150	64	42.7%
7	Finland	200	85	42.5%
8	South Africa[1]	400	169	42.3%
9	Nicaragua	92	37	40.2%
10	Iceland	63	25	39.7%
11	Norway	169	67	39.6%
12	Mozambique	250	98	39.2%
13	Denmark	179	70	39.1%
14	Netherlands	150	58	38.7%
15	Costa Rica	57	22	38.6%
16	Timor-Leste	65	25	38.5%
17	Belgium	150	57	38.0%
18	Argentina	257	96	37.4%
19	Mexico	500	184	36.8%
20	Spain	350	126	36.0%
"	United Republic of Tanzania	350	126	36.0%
21	Uganda	386	135	35.0%
22	Angola	220	75	34.1%
23	Grenada	15	5	33.3%
24	Nepal	594	197	33.2%
"	Serbia	250	83	33.2%
25	Germany	620	204	32.9%
37	Afghanistan	249	69	27.7%
44	Iraq	325	82	25.2%
46	Australia	150	37	24.7%
"	Canada	308	76	24.7%
58	Pakistan	342	77	22.5%
"	United Kingdom	650	146	22.5%
69	Saudi Arabia	151	30	19.9%
78	United States of America	433	77	17.8%

[1]*South Africa: The figures on the distribution of seats do not include the 36 special rotating delegates appointed on an ad hoc basis, and all percentages given are therefore calculated on the basis of the 54 permanent seats.*

Islands. All these Congresswomen are in the House of Representatives, where they make up 4.5 percent of the total House. Only one woman of color has ever served in the U.S. Senate: Carol Moseley-Braun (D-IL), who served from 1993 to 1999.

In addition, women hold 1,783 of the 7,383 seats in the state legislature, making up 24.2 percent (1,136 Democrats and 632 Republicans). This breaks down to 20.8 percent of the U.S. state Senate seats and 25.4 percent of the state House seats. Overall since 1971, numbers of women serving in state legislatures have more than quintupled. Of these women state legislators, 367 (20.6 percent) are women of color (345 Democrats, 21 Republicans, and one Non-Partisan). They contribute 5 percent of the total U.S. state legislators.

Despite changes in the 113th Congress with the largest numbers ever of women generally, and women of color in particular, these statistics still illustrate male and white domination in society and challenge the extent to which women and people of color are represented. However, remember that females do not necessarily represent women's interests, just as people of color do not necessarily support issues that improve the status of non-white groups. Many feminists vote for men in political office over women candidates because they understand that a candidate's being female does not necessarily mean that her politics, or those of the party she represents, are pro-women.

As the reading by Eleanor Smeal, "The Feminist Factor," explains, the term *gender gap* refers to differences between women and men in political attitudes and voting choices. Smeal is president and founder of the Feminist Majority Foundation and has served as president of the National Organization for Women (NOW) twice. She explains in the reading that a gender gap is apparent in voting behavior, party identification, evaluations of presidential performances, and attitudes toward public policy issues. Polls find, for example, that compared with men, women are more likely to favor a more activist role for government; are more supportive of programs to guarantee health care and basic social services; more supportive of restrictions on firearms; more supportive of same-sex marriage; and more likely to favor legal abortion without restrictions.

In terms of the gender gap in voting specifically, the measurable difference in the proportions of women and men who voted suggest that on the average women tend to lean toward the Democratic Party more than men do since they are more concerned about such issues as education, welfare, health care, and the environment. Though there are exceptions, men are more likely as a group to vote for strong defense, anti-welfare, and anti–affirmative action policies: the stance of the Republican Party. This does not, of course, imply that all men are Republican, only that as a group, they are more likely to favor the issues put forward by this political party. More women than men voted Democrat in both recent presidential elections with 55 percent of the votes for President Barack Obama coming from women in 2012. Democratic wins over Republican candidates tend to change the political landscape in terms of women's issues, bringing a stronger focus on the needs and general welfare of women and children.

Women (and what might be called women's issues) are also not equally represented in U.S. law, although now a third of the justices on the highest court, the U.S. Supreme Court, are female. Its membership currently consists of the Chief Justice of the United States and 8 associate justices, all nominated by the president and appointed after confirmation by the U.S. Senate. As of this writing there are three women on the court: Ruth Bader Ginsburg, Sonia Sotomayor, and Elena Kagan. Only four women have ever served and Sotomayor is the first and only woman of color to serve.

The United States inherited British common law that utilized the doctrine of *femme couverte* (also known as *feme covert*), or covered women: Husband and wife were one person under law, and she was his sexual property. As a result, married women could not seek employment without the husband's consent, keep their own wages, own property, sue, exercise control over their children, and control their reproductive lives. As already discussed in Chapter 10, because husbands and wives were "one" in marriage, wives were sexual property of husbands, and rape within marriage was legally condoned. It was legally impossible to charge a husband with raping his wife because it would imply that the husband was raping himself. Although the Married Women's Property Act of 1848 allowed women to own and inherit property, the other constraints on their lives remained intact through the twentieth century. Even with the passage of these property acts, the law allowed the husband to control community property (jointly owned legally by husband and wife) until the 1970s.

Prior to the 1960s most states decriminalized violence in the family (meaning violence within families was not legally understood as criminal acts), and operated marital rape exemption laws. It was not until the 1980s and 1990s that women had legal protections against violence; these protections include legislation such as the rape shield laws, mandatory arrest procedures in cases of domestic violence, public notification programs about convicted sex offenders in communities, the creation of protective or temporary restraining orders, state rape reform laws, and the 1994 Violence Against Women Act. Also prior to the 1960s, women's reproductive lives were a function of state control because the state had criminalized access to contraceptive information and procedures. As discussed in Chapter 7, before the passage of *Griswold v. Connecticut* in 1965, women had no legal right to contraceptives, and before the early 1970s with the passage of state abortion rulings and *Roe v. Wade,* they had no legal right to an abortion. The issue of reproductive rights is still controversial, and the legal arena is the site for many of these battles today, especially in the area of parental notification and consent.

In terms of work and employment, *Muller v. Oregon* in 1908 reaffirmed the state's justification for limiting women's employment. This legislation approved Oregon's right to prevent women from working in factories or similar facilities for more than 10 hours a day based on the state's interest in protecting the reproductive functions of women. It was considered important for the "well-being of the race" that women's ability to contract freely be limited. As discussed in Chapter 9, by the 1960s various civil rights legislation was passed including the Equal Pay Act and Title VII, preventing employers from discriminating against women and people of color in employment. Affirmative action legislation of the 1970s and sexual harassment legislation of the 1980s further attempted to dismantle gender- and race-based inequities in the labor force. Challenges remain in this area, however, as systems of inequality still shape labor force experiences.

The state also affects women through the institution of marriage. Women had access to divorce in the nineteenth century, although divorce was much more difficult to obtain. In addition, divorce carried a considerable stigma, especially to the divorced wife. Prior to the advent of no-fault divorce in the 1970s (divorce on demand by either or both parties), partners had to sue for divorce. Grounds to sue were based on a spouse's violation of the marriage contract such as by cruelty, abandonment, or adultery, and the courts needed to prove that someone had committed a crime. This procedure was difficult and expensive for women; it also tended to involve a double standard of behavior based on gender. Nonetheless, because this procedure allowed wives to show that husbands were "guilty," wives might receive relatively generous compensation. With the advent of no-fault divorce, this has changed because no one is charged with blame.

HISTORICAL MOMENT   **Shirley Chisholm for President**

Shirley Chisholm was born to a mother from Barbados and a father from British Guiana. She grew up in Barbados and Brooklyn and graduated with honors from Brooklyn College with a major in sociology. Following graduation, she worked at the Mt. Calvary Childcare Center in Harlem and became active in local politics. She completed a master's in education at Columbia University in 1952 and then managed daycare centers.

Chisholm ran for a state assembly seat in 1964 and won, serving in the New York General Assembly until 1968. While in the New York legislature, she focused on issues of education and daycare. In 1968 she ran for and won a seat in the U.S. Congress representing New York's Twelfth Congressional District, becoming the first black woman in the House of Representatives. Chisholm quickly distinguished herself as an outspoken advocate for the poor and for women's and civil rights and against the war in Vietnam.

During a speech on equal rights for women before the House of Representatives in 1969, Chisholm pointed out, "More than half of the population of the United States is female. But women occupy only 2 percent of the managerial positions. They have not even reached the level of tokenism yet. No women sit on the AFL-CIO council or Supreme Court. There have been only two women who have held Cabinet rank, and at present there are none. Only two women now hold ambassadorial rank in the diplomatic corps. In Congress, we are down to 1 senator and 10 representatives. Considering that there are about $3\frac{1}{2}$ million more women in the United States than men, this situation is outrageous."

In January 1972, Chisholm announced her candidacy for the Democratic nomination for the presidency: "I stand before you today as a candidate for the Democratic nomination for the Presidency of the United States. I am not the candidate of Black America, although I am Black and proud. I am not the candidate of the women's movement of this country, although I am a woman, and I am equally proud of that. I am not the candidate of any political bosses or special interests. I am the candidate of the people."

Chisholm became the first woman considered for the presidential nomination. Although she was defeated, she did garner more than 150 votes from the delegates to the Democratic National Convention in Miami. She continued to serve in Congress until 1982. She wrote two books: *Unbossed and Unbought* and *The Good Fight*. She died January 1, 2005, at the age of 80.

Likewise, *alimony*, the payment that women have traditionally received as compensation for their unpaid roles as wives and mothers, has been reduced or eliminated through various legislation since 1970. Although eliminating alimony indicates a more gender-neutral situation where women are not simply viewed as dependent wives and mothers and may even have higher earnings than husbands, it has caused problems. This is because despite the gender-neutral language and intentions, society is stratified regarding gender, and women still tend to be financially subordinate to men. Although financial loss after divorce is significant for both men and women, women continue to bear the brunt of a breakup financially. This is because women tend to have lower salaries and therefore have less to live on, and also because women are more likely to have custody of children and endure more financial costs associated with single parenting. Financial hardship is often

"Uh, oh, Regina has her lawyer with her . . ."

Reprinted by permission of Dave Carpenter.

IDEAS FOR ACTIVISM

- Keep up with pending legislation with NOW's legislative update at *http://www.now.org/issues/legislat/*. Write letters and call your representatives to comment on important issues.
- Sign up to take action with Equality Now at *http://www.equalitynow.org/actions*.
- Work for a local candidate who supports human rights.
- Organize educational forums to examine political issues from perspectives of gender, race, class, and sexual identity.
- For more information about political issues of concern to women, visit the home page of the Feminist Majority Foundation at *www.feminist.org*. Follow the link to "Take Action" for ideas about what you can do to make a difference.

exacerbated by court-mandated child support that does not get paid to women. Some states have enforced legislation to track errant child-support monies and enforce payment. Yet, even though the law affects women in myriad ways, many women feel that law has little to do with their lives.

PUBLIC POLICY

State policies determine people's rights and privileges, and, as a result, the state has the power to exclude and discriminate against groups, and create policies in favor of certain other groups. By maintaining inequality, the state reflects the interests of the dominant groups in society and supports policies that work in their interests and reinforce their power. Native Americans, for example, have suffered because of state policies that required forced relocation, and African Americans have been harmed by Jim Crow laws that helped enforce segregation in the South and prevented African Americans from voting. As discussed in other chapters, there were miscegenation laws in the United States that prevented interracial marriage and aimed to maintain racial purity and superiority, and many states instigated laws that prevented African Americans from residing in certain communities and/or being in a town after sundown. Some of these laws were still on the books into the late-twentieth century.

An example of how policy reinforces systems of inequality is seen in lesbian and gay plaintiffs who are in the court system for child custody, contract, or property disputes. It is also evident in current discussions concerning gay marriage and civil unions. Homophobia in the system tends to work against gays and lesbians. As discussed in Chapter 8, the 1996 Defense of Marriage Act, which allowed states not to recognize gay unions performed in other states and prevented lesbians and gay men from enjoying the privilege of state recognition of marriage, was only overturned by the U.S. Supreme Court in 2013. As also mentioned, however, there are several states that recognize these partnerships as civil unions or domestic partnerships.

Welfare policy is especially illustrative of the ways the state is a conduit for the perpetuation of systems of inequality. Poverty in the United States is powerfully structured

Affirmative Action: Myths and Misconceptions

MYTH: Affirmative action is a form of reverse discrimination.
REALITY: Affirmative action does not mean giving preference to any group. In fact, it stands for just the opposite. Included in the concept of affirmative action is the idea that all individuals must be treated equally and that a position should be given to the candidate most qualified. However, a hiring committee *must* make a good-faith effort to create a pool of candidates that reflects the number of women and minorities who possess proper training for the position. Once the qualified candidates are identified, a candidate's ability to provide cultural diversity to a department, to serve as a role model, and to offer a range of perspectives should be major elements in the evaluation and selection progress.

MYTH: Affirmative action means establishing a "quota" system for women and minorities.
REALITY: There is a difference between goals and quotas. Ideally, the percentage of women and minorities working in the position should be similar to the percentage of women and minorities qualified for such positions. Affirmative action does not mean showing partiality but rather *reaching out to candidates and treating them with fairness and equity*. Quotas, on the other hand, are court assigned to redress a pattern of discriminatory hiring.

MYTH: Once you hire an affirmative action candidate, you can never fire him or her.
REALITY: The terms of employment are the same for women and minorities as they are for men and nonminorities. In fact, in terms of affirmative action principles, standards of achievement, job requirements, and job expectations should be applied equally to all individuals.

MYTH: To satisfy affirmative action responsibilities, all that needs to be done is to hire one or two women or minorities for dead-end jobs.
REALITY: This is called tokenism. Hiring women and minorities for positions that are terminal in terms of advancement does not satisfy the affirmative action goals. The same opportunities for employment and career advancement must exist for all individuals.

MYTH: Affirmative action will result in lowering the standards and reputation of a department.
REALITY: This will not happen if a qualified candidate is selected for a position. Diverse staff providing varying talents and points of view increases effectiveness and vitality and can lead to an enhanced reputation.

MYTH: Affirmative action and equal employment opportunity are the same things.
REALITY: Equal employment opportunity means that all individuals must be treated equally in the hiring process and in advancement once on the job. Each person is to be evaluated as an individual on his or her merits and not on a stereotypic conception of what members of specific groups are like. Affirmative action is a more proactive concept. It means that one will actively and aggressively seek to recruit women and minorities by making a positive and continuous effort in their recruitment, employment, retention, and promotion.

MYTH: Affirmative action means applying a double standard, one for white males and a somewhat lower one for women and minorities.

(continued)

> **REALITY:** Double standards are inconsistent with the principles and spirit of affirmative action. One standard should be applied to all candidates. This myth, of course, implies that women and minorities are inherently less qualified than white males.
> **MYTH:** Unqualified individuals are being hired and promoted for the sake of diversity/affirmative action.
> **REALITY:** Affirmative action plans that compromise valid job or educational qualifications are illegal. Plans must be flexible, realistic, reviewable, and fair. The U.S. Supreme Court has found that there are at least two permissible bases for voluntary affirmative action by employers under Title VII, the federal law that prohibits discrimination in employment on the basis of race, national origin, sex, or religion: (1) to remedy a clear and convincing history of past discrimination by the employer or union, and (2) to cure a manifest imbalance in the employer's workforce. Thus, affirmative action programs are intended to hire the most qualified individuals, while achieving equal opportunity for all.
>
> *Source: www.units.muohio.edu/oeeo/Myths.htm.*

by racial and gender inequities, and patterns of income and wealth are strongly skewed along these lines. The federal poverty level is used by the U.S. government to define who is poor. It's based on a family's annual cash income, rather than their total wealth, annual consumption, or their own assessment of well-being. For 2014, the federal poverty guideline is an annual income of $23,850 for a family of four. Add $4,060 for each additional person to compute the federal poverty level for larger families. Subtract $4,060 per person to compute it for smaller families. These are the guidelines for the 48 contiguous states. Guidelines for Alaska and Hawaii are a little higher, since it is more expensive to live there. The federal poverty level is updated every year. It also includes the poverty threshold, used by the U.S. Census Bureau to report how many people in the United States live in poverty each year. Currently about 47 million people, or 15 percent of the population, live below the poverty threshold: the highest number ever recorded. This means about one-fifth of all children and approximately 1 in 6 or 7 people in the United States lives below the poverty line. Poverty rose among all racial and ethnic groups, but stood at higher levels for African Americans (26 percent) and Latinos/as (25 percent) compared to whites at almost 10 percent. Worldwide poverty is a major problem with 2014 data from Oxfam International showing that almost half of the world's wealth is now owned by just one percent of the population whose combined wealth is approximately 110 trillion. The bottom half of the world's population (3.5 billion people) owns the same as the richest 85 people in the world.

Finally, about 20.5 million people in the United States live in "extreme poverty," which means their family's cash income is less than half of the poverty line, or about $10,000 a year for a family of four. Many of these families and individuals experience homelessness: a serious problem all over the United States. Between 1996 when welfare reform placed new limits on the amount of time a family could receive public assistance (discussed next) and 2013, the rate of extreme poverty has doubled. In this way poverty creates a special vulnerability for women with children—the ability of the state to take their children from them—as noted in the reading "Too Poor to Parent" by Gaylynn Burroughs.

"Regimes of truth" or social discourses (recall from other chapters that these are sets of beliefs and knowledge that support institutions in society) about who is deserving of wealth rely on the individualistic notion that success is a result of hard work and ambition; thus, anyone who works hard and pushes him- or herself should succeed economically. The corollary of this, of course, is that the fault associated with lack of economic success rests with the individual. This was referred to in Chapter 2 as the *bootstrap myth*. This myth avoids looking at structural aspects of the labor force and social systems that perpetuate classism and instead focuses on the individual.

The bootstrap myth helps explain the stigma associated with welfare in the United States and the many stereotypes associated with women on welfare—that they are lazy, cheat the system, and have babies to increase their welfare check. Women on welfare often face a triple whammy: They are women facing lower-paid work, they are mothers and have domestic responsibilities and childcare expenses, and they are single with only one paycheck. Indeed, if women earned as much as comparable men, then single women generally would see a rise in their incomes and a substantial drop in poverty rates. If we applied this comparable situation to single mothers, poverty rates would be cut almost in half, from 25 percent to 13 percent. Having a job does not necessarily lift women out of poverty. Having a job does not also guarantee sufficient retirement income, as the contemporary debate on Social Security reveals. Women will be disproportionately affected by Social Security reforms (and especially by any possible privatization of Social Security benefits).

In 1996 the passing of the Personal Responsibility and Work Opportunity Reconciliation Act (PRWORA) terminated the major source of welfare, Aid to Families with Dependent Children (AFDC), and replaced it with Temporary Assistance to Needy Families (TANF). No person could receive welfare for more than 5 years. In addition, welfare was transferred to the state through a block grant system, allowing some states to set their own agenda for distribution of funds. Critics of this and other policies of the 1990s have argued that not only have such policies failed to make low-income families self-sufficient, but they have kept wages low and undermined women's independence. Since this time, welfare "reform" bills have, for example, cut safety net programs for the poor, reduced spending on Medicare and Medicaid, and raised the number of hours mothers receiving welfare have to work outside the home, study, or be involved in training, from 30 to 40 hours, (at the same time that daycare in most states is totally inadequate). Communities of color experience some of the most devastating consequences of poverty, and welfare "reform" has increased the vulnerability of individuals (especially single mothers and children) in these communities. The Chapter 2 reading by Felice Yeskel, "Opening Pandora's Box: Adding Classism to the Agenda," addresses these issues. She, like others, makes the case that it is important to examine the argument that public assistance creates dependency: an argument generally made by people with a distorted picture of what it means to be poor. When survival is a constant struggle, people become ill-equipped to live in ways that facilitate steady employment. Imagine a mother who cannot afford to buy diapers for her child. No daycare will take a child without a supply of diapers. How might the mother go on a job interview without clothes and transportation, or an address beyond a homeless shelter to put on a resume. The idea that making poverty more unpleasant than it already is—coupled with lectures on ambition and self-reliance—might motivate people to improve their lot is flawed, because incentive tends usually not to be the problem. Meeting basic human needs would be a more productive solution.

A most obvious example of policies working to favor dominant groups is the practice often called "wealthfare," "welfare for the rich," or "aid to dependent corporations" (a play on words regarding AFDC) by some scholars. These policies reflect the ties political leaders have to the economic system and the ways the government subsidizes corporations and reduces taxes and other payments to the state for some corporations and businesses. Wealthfare involves five major types: direct grants; allowing publicly funded research and development to be used free by private for-profit corporations; discounted fees for public resources (such as grazing fees on public land); tax breaks for the wealthy; and corporate tax reductions and loopholes. It has been estimated that more than $200 billion in corporate welfare could be saved over the next five years as of this writing if policies reining in these favors were instigated. Neither Republican nor Democratic lawmakers want to do this because they fear losing donations to their respective parties.

Occupy Wall Street (OWS) is a leaderless resistance movement with people of many colors, genders, and political persuasions that originated in late 2011 to counter "wealthfare," among other issues. The main concerns raised by Occupy Wall Street are social and economic inequality, greed, and corruption, and especially the influence of corporate power on government and policy. The OWS slogan "We are the 99 percent" refers to income inequality and wealth distribution in the United States between the wealthiest 1 percent and the rest of the population. As of this writing OWS continues as a source of collective resistance to U.S. national and international policy, and especially policies associated with the alliances among the government-military-industrial/economic complex.

THE CRIMINAL JUSTICE SYSTEM

Laws can be defined as formal aspects of social control that determine what is permissible and what is forbidden in a society. The court system was created to maintain the law through adjudicating conflicts that may be unlawful and deciding punishments for people who have broken the law. The role of the police is to enforce these laws and keep public order. Prisons are responsible for punishing those who have broken the law and protecting society from people who have committed crimes. All these fit together to maintain the control of the state.

Although women are especially likely to be victims of certain crimes, such as rape and battering, they constitute a small proportion of people arrested for crimes (less than 20 percent) and a smaller number of those who are sent to prison (see learning activity "Women and Prison"). The reading "Delinquent Girls" by Andrea Doyle Hugmeyer focuses on the gendered paths to delinquency by girls in the United States and their differential treatment in court systems. This reading also advocates feminist interventions and programs that demonstrate positive outcomes for delinquent girls.

Women make up 23 percent of people on probation and 12 percent of the parole population. Unlike male incarceration, however, property and drug crimes (non-violent offenses) make up nearly two-thirds of the population of women in prison. Along with drug offenses, women are more likely to commit crimes of shoplifting, bad-check writing, and embezzlement, and less likely to be involved in arson, auto theft, burglary, and acts of vandalism. The crimes that women commit are gendered in that they involve less potential

LEARNING ACTIVITY   **Women and Prison**

To learn more about women in prison, visit *www.womenandprison.org,* a website created by incarcerated women. From this website, what do you learn about the gendered experiences of women in the criminal justice system? Why do these women argue that resistance to that system is necessary? What can you do to be an ally to incarcerated women around the world?

for violent armed confrontation. These "safer" crimes reflect women's need for money for drugs or other personal wants, and/or survival and family needs. Women are also more likely to engage in the public order crime of prostitution, of course. Both men and women engage in the exchange of sex for money, but women are more likely to be arrested, and men's arrests are more likely to involve the purchase of sex as "johns" or are related to business management as "pimps."

Overall, 80 percent of violent crime is committed by males. The disparity in rates is what is called the gender gap in crime commission. However, although women are much less likely to kill than men, they have a higher ratio of committing intimate partner murders than men. This does not mean that they are more likely to commit these crimes, far from it because they commit much less; but among the murders they do commit, intimate partner murder occurs more often, whereas for men it is both stranger and acquaintance murder as well as intimate partner murder. This reflects the fact that women are more likely to kill in self-defense in domestic violence situations.

Most of the homicides enacted by women are first-time offenses, involve male victims, and are most likely to have taken place in the home, with kitchen knives and other household implements rather than firearms. This evidence again suggests that much female homicide is done in self-defense. Although prior to the 1980s women who killed in self-defense almost always lost their plea, today juries are more understanding of the experiences of battered women. Even so, it is still sometimes very difficult for women to convince a jury that they were being abused, especially in terms of the question of "imminent danger" when an abused woman kills a partner when he is sleeping or not behaving violently at that moment. Defendants must meet two criteria for claiming justifiable homicide as self-defense: reasonable fear or perception of danger (such that killing was the only course of action to protect the defendant's life) and the confrontation of the defendant with deadly force by an assailant.

It is important to recognize that approximately 57 percent of incarcerated women have suffered severe and prolonged physical and/or sexual abuse. The Bureau of Justice Statistics reports that just under half of all women (and one-tenth of all men) in correctional facilities indicated physical and/or sexual abuse before their current sentence. A large number of these incidents occurred before the age of 18 years. In addition, women are subject to more sexual misconduct, both from other prisoners and the correctional staff, when they are in prison, according to the Institute on Women and Criminal Justice. The Government Accounting Office does not know the full extent of this problem, however, because of under-reporting and because female prisoners fear often retaliation.

Among men, poor men and men of color are more likely to be considered a danger to society and tend to receive the longest sentences because of social stigma, racism and discrimination, poverty, lack of education, and the consequences of these structural variables on access to good legal counsel. The highest levels of incarceration are among African American males in their 20s. Although incarceration rates for women of color are higher than those of white women, with their representation in the prison population higher than their representation in the total population, white women are currently being incarcerated at a higher rate of increase than women of color. In addition, nearly two-thirds of incarcerated women, both white women and women of color, are mothers. The reading in Chapter 8 by Beth Schwartzapfel ("Lullabies Behind Bars") focuses on the experiences of incarcerated mothers.

Finally, until 2009 when President Obama moved to grant political asylum to non-U.S. women who suffer severe physical or sexual abuse from which they are unable to escape, there had been a double standard in U.S. asylum law. Until that time asylum law provided protection for immigrants fleeing their country only if they were being persecuted because of race, religion, nationality, political opinion, or membership in a social group. Abuse was previously not considered grounds for asylum because abuse victims were not seen as members of a persecuted group under U.S. law. Although there were important advancements in asylum law during the Clinton presidency to protect women fleeing abusive husbands through policies to provide political asylum for women suffering severe domestic abuse in their homeland, this legislation was stalled by the Bush administration. The new granting of political asylum to abuse victims was a significant shift in policy that opened the way for physically and sexually abused women to seek the same protection that those fleeing female genital cutting already had under U.S. asylum law since 1996. All marginalized people (women and men) are at risk of being victimized by hate crimes, a constant problem in contemporary U.S. society. If sexual assaults and other sexual crimes were actually considered hate crimes, the increase in hate crimes nationwide would be dramatic.

THE MILITARY

The military, a branch of government constituted to defend against foreign and domestic conflict, is a central component of the state and political system. Militarism can be defined as the predominance of armed forces in state policies or the intent of a government or people for the maintenance of a strong military capability and its use to defend or promote (usually national) interests. Militarism is a central defining principle of many societies worldwide and is especially predominant in colonialist and imperialist societies intent on expansion and resource accumulation. It is important to understand the ways militarism functions as a mechanism of gendered power that perpetuates women's subordination within domestic, national, and international arenas. This includes women's experiences of war as combatants, victims, refugees, and survivors of violence, as well as workers (including sex workers) within the military-industrial complex. Contemporary wars of the late-twentieth and early-twenty-first centuries have utilized campaigns of fear and violence associated with nongovernmental agencies—or "terrorism"—that have changed the face of war and its responses. In the poem "First Morning in Exile," author Aleksandra Djajic-Horváth reflects on her experience of leaving Bosnia and Herzegovina after the war and being an exile, displaced and seeking respite from the war-torn conflict of that region. This reading speaks of the vulnerabilities of being an exile and is one example of the many ways war impacts women's lives.

As mentioned in Chapter 2, the military has strong ties to the economic system through a military-industrial complex that supports industries that manufacture weapons. Military presence overseas (as well as in civil wars) tends to be related to economic interests such as the need for oil or control of other resources, including the need for political "stability" in nations to maintain global corporate endeavors and strategic defense. The Pentagon has connections to other state entities, especially the government and its representatives. The military is a male-dominated arena, not only in terms of actual personnel who serve but in terms of the ways it is founded upon so-called masculine cultural traits such as violence, aggression, hierarchy, competition, and conflict. The military has a history of misogynistic and homophobic attitudes to enforce highly masculine codes of behavior. In the United States, military culture is integrated, often unknowingly, into our everyday lives, such as through camouflage fashions and ROTC on college campuses. Many scholars critique such normalization of militarism and call for a demilitarization of society.

Throughout most of history, women were not allowed to serve in the military except in such auxiliary forces as nursing. It was not until World War II that women who served in any military capacity were given formal status and not until 1976 that women were allowed into the military academies. In terms of race, the armed forces were officially segregated until 1948. Although between 2000 and 2005, the number of African American military personnel fell from almost a quarter to 14 percent after a substantial increase through the 1990s, current figures suggest that continuing economic recession and high unemployment are facilitating the increased recruitment of nonwhite military personnel, including African American women and men. Data from 2008 show the share of black recruits rose 2 percent, making up 95 percent of the total increase in recruits. Despite their relatively high numbers in the service, people of color are less likely than whites proportionately to be found in leadership positions. This is true for women of all races as well.

In 1981 the Supreme Court reaffirmed that it is constitutional to require registering men but not women for the draft. Currently, men are subject to conscription if a draft is in process and women are not, although women are allowed to serve if they wish. The rationale for the 1981 decision centered on the fact that women were not allowed in combat positions at that time, plus the notion that women have responsibilities in the home and family. After women's service in the Gulf War in 1991, there was pressure for President Clinton in 1993 to order a repeal of the ban on women in combat positions, and, as a result, many Navy and Air Force positions opened to women, although the Army and Marines continued to preclude women from combat positions in field artillery, armor, infantry, submarines, and special units. Then in January 2013 the longstanding ban that prevented women from participating in ground combat was lifted so that women for the first time had access to full parity and promotions. The U.S. military pledged to open full combat roles to female soldiers by January 2016, promising to "eliminate all unnecessary gender-based barriers." The Air Force has the highest percentage of women (19 percent), compared with 16 percent in the Navy, almost 14 percent in the Army and Coast Guard, and almost 7 percent in the Marines. Currently 18.5 percent of military women are officers (compared to 16.6 percent of military men), although only two female generals have attained the four-star rank. This is because officers must serve in ground combat to ascend to the top brass.

Women in Black: For Justice, Against War

Perhaps you've seen them—a small group of women dressed in black standing silently on a street corner or in some other public place and perhaps on your campus. They are Women in Black, part of a global network of women advocating for peace and opposing injustice, war, militarism, and other forms of violence. They are especially committed to challenging militarism in the governments of their own countries. Women in Black began in Israel in 1988, as Israeli women stood in weekly vigils to protest the Israeli occupation of the West Bank. They did not chant or march. Rather, they stood at a busy intersection with a simple sign that read "Stop the Occupation." Bypassers shouted at them, calling them "whores" and "traitors." They did not shout back but maintained a silent dignity. Eventually, Women in Black vigils were organized around the world to support the women in Israel. As war came to Croatia and Bosnia in 1992, Women in Black groups began to oppose the violence there. And so the movement has continued to spread as women around the world have responded to war. In both the Gulf War and the wars in Afghanistan and Iraq, women across the globe and in the United States have stood in protest. Any group of women anywhere can hold a Women in Black vigil against any form of violence, militarism, or war. Women in Black also engage in nonviolent and nonaggressive action—blocking roads or entering military bases. In 2001 the United Nations Development Fund for Women (UNIFEM) and International Alert awarded Women in Black the Millennium Peace Prize for Women. To find out if there is already a vigil in your area or to learn how to start your own vigil, visit *www.womeninblack.org*.

Women made up approximately 1 out of 10 soldiers involved in the most recent conflicts in Iraq and Afghanistan, with African American women overrepresented in this ratio (making up about a third of all women military personnel).

Sexualized violence and the harassment of women are recognized as a widespread problem within the U.S. armed services. The Department of Defense reports that 1 in 3 female soldiers is sexually assaulted while on duty: almost twice the rate at which civilian women are sexually assaulted. The Department of Defense opened the Sexual Assault and Prevention Response Office in 2005 and releases annual reports on military sexual trauma (MST), which encompasses both sexual assault and harassment. The number of patients receiving treatment for MST through the Veteran's Administration has doubled since 2007. The reading, "Struggling to Find a Home," by Patricia Leigh Brown discusses the ways MST is a common pathway to homelessness for female veterans. It is estimated that approximately 19,000 sexual assaults are committed annually, less than 14 percent of which are reported. About 7 percent of military rape cases see a conviction. This latter statistic spurred U.S. Senate hearings in 2013, which as of this writing, are facilitating reform efforts. In addition, a 2012 law finally enabled military health benefits to cover abortions stemming from rape. Other Pentagon recommendations for improvement include a transformation of sexist ideologies and practices and improvements in victim services (such as enhanced confidentiality, and the appointment within the Department of Defense to investigate and prosecute violent crimes), education to recognize and prevent abusive situations, increased funding of domestic violence shelters for military personnel, legislation to decrease the availability of firearms, and increased funding for research, treatment, and prevention.

Studies show women entering the military often have histories as abuse survivors and men have violent pasts. Misogynous military culture normalizes violence, pornography is often readily available, and prostitution is abundant around military bases. A key part of the problem is victim-blaming where women who do come forward are stigmatized and investigated. The prize-winning 2012 documentary *The Invisible War* addresses this problem and is used in military rape-prevention programs. However, as the torture of prisoners at the Abu Ghraib prison in Iraq in 2004 showed, women also can act in violent ways when assimilated into military culture.

The reading "Struggling to Find a Home" documents the plight of women veterans and makes the point that they are often lacking health care as well as other services that tend not to take into account the physical, mental, and reproductive health needs of women. As the reading explains, female veterans are more likely to be single parents and thus ineligible for transitional housing that exempts parents. In addition, less than a third of the Veteran Administration's medical centers have gynecologists on staff, for example. Families of service personnel are also at risk as unique stresses such as relocations, long work tours, frequent family separations, and dangerous work assignments increase the risk for family violence and encourage alcohol and drug use and abuse. As already mentioned, abused female military personnel (and civilian spouses fearful of jeopardizing husbands' prospects for continued service and promotion) often resist reporting incidents out of fear of lack of confidentiality, retaliation, and lack of available services.

Finally, the military has a long history of homophobia that has included the execution, persecution, and dismissal of gay soldiers. Although polls consistently show support for removing anti-gay bans, arguments in favor of such prejudice mirror those proposing racial segregation in earlier times. These include: The morale and fighting spirit of military personnel will drop if openly gay and lesbian personnel are present; and gays and lesbians pose a national security threat. Through the 1980s more than 15,000 military personnel were discharged because of homosexuality. By the mid-1990s President Clinton had created the "Don't Ask, Don't Tell" policy. It was supposed to be a compromise, although it had few supporters after 2001. Pentagon data showed women were disproportionately affected by "Don't Ask, Don't Tell" policies that required gay, lesbian, and bisexual service members to keep their sexual identity a secret or face a military discharge.

In December 2010, the House and Senate voted to repeal the policy, and the law was signed by President Obama. In 2013 the Pentagon expanded benefits to same-sex partners of military personnel to include a range of services offered at various posts and bases, but did still withhold medical and dental coverage and housing allowances. Full benefits required the 2013 repeal of the Defense of Marriage Act (DOMA) (as already discussed), the 1996 law that defined marriage as the union of a man and a woman. Because of the repeal of DOMA, military personnel now have full access to these services.

The state is a very powerful institution that has enormous effects upon women's everyday lives. It is important to understand how gender, race, and class mold and shape government, law, and policy, and how these institutions reflect and promote the needs of some groups over those of others.

Transgender Service Members and Veterans

Individuals who self-identify as transgender can include transsexuals, androgynous people, cross-dressers, gender queers and other gender non-conforming individuals whose gender identity and expression is different than their assigned sex at birth, or who break societal expectations and stereotypes related to gender. The military, however, narrowly defines transgender as individuals who have undergone sex reassignment surgery or whose gender presentation is visibly not aligned with socially accepted gender identity—definitions which exclude the diverse lived experiences of transgender individuals.

Unlike lesbian, gay and bisexual service members, transgender service members were not included in the DADT Repeal Act, and therefore cannot openly serve in the military. Additionally, transgender service members endure other forms of exclusion in the military. In the first place, individuals who have undergone genital surgery in order to change their gender are denied the opportunity to serve in the military at all. Furthermore, individuals diagnosed with "gender identity disorder" are also barred from serving in the military, which effectively excludes most open transgender individuals. Like lesbian, gay and bisexual service members, transgender service members are subject to harassment, hostile treatment and are generally unwelcome in the military.[1] They also may experience discrimination after service through institutions like the VA and many struggle with unemployment, homelessness and mental health disorders.[2]

- DOD regulations currently bar transgender service members from serving in the U.S. military. Specifically, DOD Instruction 6130.03 lists change of sex and hermaphroditism as medically disqualifying factors. The same regulation specifies "psychosexual" conditions such as "transsexualism" or "transvestism" as disqualifying mental conditions that preclude individuals meeting these criteria from serving in the military.[3] Conduct regulations can also affect transgender service members, such as prohibitions against cross-dressing.

- Unlike the U.S., other industrialized democracies (e.g. U.K., Israel) allow transgender individuals to serve openly in their militaries and some will pay for sex reassignment surgery (e.g. U.K., Canada).[4]
- Even though transgender individuals are not necessarily gay, lesbian, or bisexual, they are often assumed to be and were targeted disproportionately under DADT.[5] Although the DADT policy prohibited military leadership from questioning service members about their sexual orientation, 26% of active duty and transgender veterans report being asked about their sexual orientation; 14% report being asked by an officer. Transmen were more likely to be questioned than transwomen.[6]
- Transgender individuals, including veterans, report high rates of workplace discrimination. Over 90% of the transgender population report experiences of harassment, mistreatment, or discrimination at work or took actions such as hiding their identities to avoid it.[7]
- 26% of transgender veterans have experienced physical assault and 16% have been raped. Of transgender individuals who have experienced sexual assault, 64% have attempted suicide.[8]
- Almost one-third of transgender veterans believe they were not hired for a job specifically because they were transgender; almost 40% of transgender veterans are working for less than minimum wage.[9]
- 21% of transgender veterans have been homeless at some point in their lives.[10]
- Transgender veterans experience a host of mental health issues, and 40% have attempted suicide compared to 1.6% of the general population.[11]
- Transgender veterans are reluctant to seek healthcare, and many report negative experiences with healthcare institutions. 24% of transgender veterans report being refused medical treatment for being transgender, and 43% say they have postponed or neglected to seek medical care when they were sick for fear of discrimination or maltreatment.[12]
- While the VHA has made significant progress in the availability of medical care to transgender veterans, (including hormonal therapy, mental health care, preoperative evaluation, and medically necessary post-operative and long-term care following sex reassignment surgery), the VHA still will not perform or pay for sex reassignment surgery.[13]

[1] Karl Bryant and Kristen Schilt. 2008. "Transgender People in the U.S. Military: Summary and Analysis of the 2008 Transgender American Veterans Association Survey." Paper prepared for The Palm Center and the Transgender American Veterans Association (TAVA).
[2] Ibid.
[3] Department of Defense Instruction 6130.03, April 28, 2010. Available: http://www.dtic.mil/whs/directives/corres/pdf/613003p.pdf.
[4] At least ten countries allow transgender individuals to serve, including: Australia, Belgium, Canada, the Czech Republic, Israel, the Netherlands, Spain, Sweden, Thailand, and the United Kingdom (SLDN, http://www.sldn.org/pages/transgender-issues).
[5] Servicemembers Legal Defense Network. "Transgender Servicemembers." Available: http://www.sldn.org/pages/transgender-issues; Bryant and Schilt 2008.
[6] Bryant and Schilt 2008.
[7] Jaime M. Grant, Lisa A. Mottet, Justin Tanis, Jack Harrison, Jody L. Herman, and Mara Keisling. 2011. "Injustice At Every Turn: A Report Of The National Transgender Discrimination Survey." Washington, D.C.: National Center for Transgender Equality and National Gay and Lesbian Task Force.
[8] Bryan and Schilt 2008; Grant et al 2011.
[9] Bryant and Schilt 2008.
[10] Ibid.
[11] Based on survey data from the *National Transgender Discrimination Survey*, provided by the National Gay and Lesbian Task Force and National Center for Transgender Equality.
[12] Ibid.
[13] VHA Directive 2011-024 (June 9, 2011)

Source: Service Women's Action Network, servicewomen.org.

Constitutional Argument

Susan B. Anthony (1898)

Friends and Fellow-Citizens:—I stand before you under indictment for the alleged crime of having voted at the last presidential election, without having a lawful right to vote. It shall be my work this evening to prove to you that in thus doing, I not only committed no crime, but instead simply exercised my citizen's right, guaranteed to me and all United States citizens by the National Constitution beyond the power of any State to deny.

Our democratic-republican government is based on the idea of the natural right of every individual member thereof to a voice and a vote in making and executing the laws. We assert the province of government to be to secure the people in the enjoyment of their inalienable rights. We throw to the winds the old dogma that government can give rights. No one denies that before governments were organized each individual possessed the right to protect his own life, liberty and property. When 100 or 1,000,000 people enter into a free government, they do not barter away their natural rights; they simply pledge themselves to protect each other in the enjoyment of them through prescribed judicial and legislative tribunals. They agree to abandon the methods of brute force in the adjustment of their differences and adopt those of civilization. Nor can you find a word in any of the grand documents left us by the fathers which assumes for government the power to create or to confer rights. The Declaration of Independence, the United States Constitution, the constitutions of the several States and the organic laws of the Territories, all alike propose to *protect* the people in the exercise of their God-given rights. Not one of them pretends to bestow rights.

> All men are created equal, and endowed by the Creator with certain inalienable rights. Among these are life, liberty and the pursuit of happiness.

To secure these, governments are instituted among men, deriving their just powers from the consent of the governed.

Here is no shadow of government authority over rights, or exclusion of any class from their full and equal enjoyment. Here is pronounced the right of all men, and "consequently," as the Quaker preacher said, "of all women," to a voice in the government. And here, in this first paragraph of the Declaration, is the assertion of the natural right of all to the ballot; for how can "the consent of the governed" be given, if the right to vote be denied? Again:

> Whenever any form of government becomes destructive of these ends, it is the right of the people to alter or abolish it, and to institute a new government, laying its foundations on such principles, and organizing its powers in such form, as to them shall seem most likely to effect their safety and happiness.

Surely the right of the whole people to vote is here clearly implied; for however destructive to their happiness this government might become, a disfranchised class could neither alter nor abolish it, nor institute a new one, except by the old brute force method of insurrection and rebellion. One-half of the people of this nation today are utterly powerless to blot from the statute books an unjust law, or to write there a new and a just one. The women, dissatisfied as they are with this form of government, that enforces taxation without representation—that compels them to obey laws to which they never have given their consent—that imprisons and hangs them without a trial by a jury of their peers—that robs them, in marriage, of the custody of their own persons, wages and children—are this half of the people who are left wholly at the mercy of the other half, in direct violation of the spirit and letter of the declarations of the framers of this government, every one of which was based on the immutable principle of equal rights to all. By these declarations, kings, popes, priests, aristocrats, all were alike dethroned and placed on a common level, politically, with the lowliest born subject or serf. By them, too, men, as such, were deprived of their divine right to rule and placed on a political level with women. By the practice of these declarations all class and caste distinctions would be abolished, and slave, serf, plebeian, wife, woman, all alike rise from their subject position to the broader platform of equality.

The preamble of the Federal Constitution says:

We, the people of the United States, in order to form a more perfect union, establish justice, insure

domestic tranquillity, provide for the common defence, promote the general welfare and secure the blessings of liberty to ourselves and our posterity, do ordain and establish this Constitution for the United States of America.

It was we, the people, not we, the white male citizens, not we, the male citizens; but we, the whole people, who formed this Union. We formed it not to give the blessings of liberty but to secure them; not to the half of ourselves and the half of our posterity, but to the whole people—women as well as men. It is downright mockery to talk to women of their enjoyment of the blessings of liberty while they are denied the only means of securing them provided by this democratic-republican government—the ballot. . . .

R E A D I N G 86

The Feminist Factor

Eleanor Smeal (2013)

I've been thinking about the gender gap since the early 1970s, when I was doing graduate work on women's political attitudes. And in 1980, I proved its existence while analyzing job-approval polling, segmented by gender, for President Ronald Reagan, who opposed the Equal Rights Amendment (ERA). Women approved of him less than men—a statistic borne out in the election, in which there was an 8-point gap between women's votes for Reagan and men's. A team of us at NOW (the National Organization for Women), who were campaigning hard for the ERA, named it the gender gap, and we even had a ditty that we chanted toward politicians we opposed: "The gender gap will get you if you don't watch out!"

The gap—the measurable difference between the voting behavior and political attitudes of women and men—has grown considerably since then. It was decisive in November [2012], both in the presidential race and in maintaining a Democratic majority in the U.S. Senate.

To begin with, women (53 percent of all voters) cast some 8 million more votes for the president than men did. And 55 percent of those women chose Obama, compared to just 45 percent of men—for a 10-percent gender gap. If only men had voted, Mitt Romney would have won the presidency, 52 percent to 45 percent.

The gender gap and women's votes were also decisive in some key Senate races in which the Democratic candidate won, including Elizabeth Warren's in Massachusetts (a 12-percent gender gap) and Chris Murphy's in Connecticut (11 percent). If only men had voted in each of these races, the Republican candidate would have won.

Most importantly, this gender gap was crucial in the battleground states in which the presidential election was determined: In Ohio and Wisconsin, for example, the gender gap was 10 percent pro-Obama, and 8 percent and 10 percent, respectively, in favor of Democratic senatorial candidates Sherrod Brown and Tammy Baldwin. Even in states in which the gap was smaller, such as Virginia and Florida, it was large enough for Democrats to win the presidential and Senate contests.

But now it's time to add another metric beyond the gender gap to our postelection analysis: the "feminist factor." While there were many reasons for President Obama's decisive victory, the feminist factor may be one of the most significant.

We dubbed it that after analyzing an in-depth poll Ms. commissioned with the Communications Consortium Media Center and the Feminist Majority Foundation. Conducted Nov. 4–6, 2012, by Lake Research Partners, it found that 55 percent of women voters and even 30 percent of men voters consider themselves feminist.

These results are generally 9 points higher than they were in 2008, when the same question was posed to voters, and this upward trend is likely to continue given the strong identification with feminism by younger women and women of color.

Speaking of younger women, a solid majority of them (58 percent) identify as feminists—as did 54 percent of older women, nearly three-quarters (72 percent) of Democratic women and a respectable 38 percent of Republican women. The feminist factor cuts across race and ethnic lines, with a majority of Latina, African American and white women voters considering themselves feminists.

Most importantly, voters' views on feminism correlated with their choice of candidates. Among feminist women, some two-thirds (64 percent) voted for Obama, as did 54 percent of feminist-identified men. Looking at voters who identified as pro-choice, 61 percent cast their ballot for Obama.

While the votes of women—especially feminist women—were crucial in reelecting the president and a Democratic-majority Senate, they were not successful in electing a Democratic House majority. However, they probably could have done so if it weren't for severely gerrymandered districts that underrepresent Democrats (60 percent of whom are women), Latina/os, African Americans and women. Overall, Americans cast some 1.3 million more votes for House Democrats than House Republicans, but because of gerrymandering, they would need to win the popular vote in House elections

by more than 7 percent just to barely gain a House majority. (Thanks to Ian Millhiser of ThinkProgress for that analysis.)

Although feminists feel that the election was a victory for us in the War on Women—the term now commonly used by feminists and the media to describe initiatives in state legislatures and Congress that severely restrict women's rights in such areas as reproduction, violence and pay equity—we can't savor it for long. The 2012 election wins have prevented some of the worst attacks on women's rights from succeeding, but we won just a battle: The opposition to women's rights, especially at the state level, is certainly not going away. We have much to do if we are to realize the pro-choice, pro-women's rights agenda upon which President Obama and other candidates ran—an agenda that will move women and the nation forward.

Now is the time for feminists and feminist organizations to gear up and mobilize, making sure that the message we delivered in the 2012 election is actually received and results are delivered. We must work to prevent a backslide, as happened in the congressional and state elections in 2009 and 2010. . . .

Here is what we must do:

FIRST We must work to avert an economic crisis. As I write this, we just faced a "fiscal cliff," with another fight looming in Congress about raising the debt limit. Conservatives in Congress keep demanding benefits cuts in Social Security, Medicare and Medicaid—programs that women, especially, desperately need—so we cannot let this happen.

Congress must not balance the federal budget on the backs of the poor, the disabled or the elderly. There are plenty of cuts that can be realized without slashing benefits for programs that women rely upon. Just one example: The Affordable Care Act cuts some $716 billion out of Medicare over 10 years, but does so by reducing administrative costs and insurance company subsidies rather than cutting benefits to older recipients.

SECOND We must work to pass a series of other critical measures in Congress. For one, there's the federal Paycheck Fairness Act—filibustered by Senate Republicans in 2012—which increases protections for workers who sue employers for sex discrimination or even discuss their pay with coworkers.

We also must urge Congress to increase access to family planning and abortion, and keep intact the Affordable Care Act. Plus, we repeat: In these tough economic times, we must insist on keeping the protections of Medicare, Social Security and Medicaid.

But the next set of battles is not just at the national level.

THIRD We must organize to stop attacks on women's rights in many state legislatures, which are often led by their governors. We hardly had time to analyze the election results before those attacks started up again. One of the more egregious examples was when the lame-duck Michigan Legislature passed, and the governor signed into law, an extreme TRAP law (Targeted Regulations against Abortion Providers) in an effort to close abortion clinics.

Ohio's Legislature also used its lame-duck session to attack women's rights, introducing a very restrictive abortion law—which, fortunately, was withdrawn. But in Mississippi, the state is defending a newly passed TRAP law designed to close the only remaining abortion clinic in the state. And in Texas, a law that went into effect earlier this year is preventing Planned Parenthood—because it provides abortion services—from receiving any funding from the new Texas Women's Health Program, even though the health-care provider's services other than abortion aid some 50,000 women.

Clearly, the message of the gender gap and feminist factor weren't heard in Virginia, either. That state is in the process of implementing its new TRAP law, which the Republican anti-choice governor signed in late December, even though state voters favored President Obama and prochoice Democratic Senate candidate Tim Kaine (Kaine's gender gap was 7 percent, by the way). This action by the state just continues the extreme anti-abortion and anti-family-planning measures that seemed to dominate the Virginia Legislature in 2012.

FOURTH We must help build upon the wins in the equal-marriage movement for gay men and lesbians. Feminists were thrilled that four states voted in favor of same-sex marriage (with the gender gap being decisive in each state) . . . But, of course, we can't become complacent, and must still work to make equal marriage available in all 50 states.

FIFTH Feminists must seize the opening to push for more-stringent gun control. Considering the nationwide horror of the Sandy Hook massacre, there's probably no better time than now to bring this issue to congressional and state attention and support President Obama's gun-control initiatives. Too often women and children are the victims of gun violence, so it's no surprise that there is a massive gender gap on this issue, with women more strongly in favor of gun control. We cannot be ignored any longer on this issue: Enough is enough.

SIXTH We can't forget the women around the globe fighting against violence—from the girls in Pakistan such as Malala Yousafzai, battling the Taliban for the right to be educated; or the Pakistani women health-care workers assassinated just for doing their jobs; or Afghan girls and women bravely going to school and work or seeking health care despite threats and assassinations; or the women in India, victims of brutal gang rapes and facing everyday hostility.

One of the things we can do is work hard for the Senate to ratify the United Nations Convention on the Elimination of Discrimination Against Women (CEDAW) and pass the International Violence Against Women Act. It is disgraceful that the U.S. is one of only seven nations that has not ratified CEDAW, which requires a two-thirds vote, so the Democratic Senate must keep bringing it up until it is passed. The women of the world fighting horrific violence deserve our nation's full and unqualified support, and we feminists must demand it.

Finally, we'll keep pressing for the ratification of the Equal Rights Amendment to the U.S. Constitution. How can women and feminists accept anything less than full equality for women in the supreme law of our nation? Recognizing the power of the gender gap and the feminist factor, we can and must make it happen. Our strategy will be to increase cosponsors of the ERA in the new Congress and fight for its passage in the unratified states.

Full equality and full respect, nothing less and nothing more. We take that as the message of the 2012 elections as we continue to push forward.

Name It. Change It.

Rachel Joy Larris and Rosalie Maggio (2012)

Name It. Change It. is a nonpartisan joint project of the Women's Media Center and She Should Run. We work to identify, prevent, and end sexist media coverage of federal and gubernatorial women candidates, elected politicians, and high-profile public officials of all races. We monitor coverage by all members of the press—from bloggers to radio hosts to television pundits. Our goal, to quote Katie Couric, is to "make sexism as repugnant as racism."

Widespread sexism in the media is one of the top problems facing women. Our groundbreaking research from Lake Research Partners shows that sexist media coverage results in a drastic decrease of voter confidence in women candidates. This is similar to studies of bullying, in which people are less likely to identify with those negatively treated in public, due to the conscious or unconscious fear that such bullying or negative public characterization will then include them as bystanders and supporters. The ever-changing media landscape creates an unmonitored and often not fact-checked echo chamber, habitually allowing damaging comments to influence opinion without accountability.

Name It. Change It. was launched to hold media outlets accountable for their role in our government's gender disparity; women make up only 17 percent of Congress and 23 percent of state legislatures. Name It. Change It. identifies and publicizes sexist media coverage of women candidates and political leaders of all races. This project is also race-conscious in its understanding of stereotyping as it is used against various groups of women.

The Name It. Change It. project exists to reduce the incidence of sexist media references and replace the usual silence that follows such media offenses toward women candidates and public leaders with proactive and responsive tactics. We want to help members of the media identify sexism and stories biased against women so that sexism doesn't remain a barrier for women elected to office. We want to be a positive resource for members of the media who are seeking fair and accurate alternatives.

With our groundbreaking research, our case studies, our style guide of gender-neutral terms, and, finally, our Media Pledge of Gender Neutrality, we hope to reveal and reduce the problem that sexism creates for women in this country, whether they are seeking office or seeking representation, and that penalizes men by shrinking the pool of talented leaders.

We believe cultural change is possible. There is no doubt that the past few decades have shown an enormous amount of improvement in the standing of women in this country. But the goal of equality has not been achieved, and America's ratio of women representation lags behind that of many other countries. In fact, the U.S. ranks a shameful 78th in the world for representation of women in its national legislature. By addressing sexism in the political media, we believe we can improve all women's lives, from candidates to voters.

What Does This Mean For Members of Media?

During a political campaign, sexism might come from many different quarters. As our research shows, male opponents of women candidates receive an outsize benefit from gender-based attacks, giving them ample reason to use sexist language. Members of the media should be aware of this fact and note it for their audiences when candidate-to-candidate sexism appears.

But not all sexism is candidate-driven. Some of the strongest sexist language we've found has come from members of the media. Whether attacks come from opposing candidates or the media, the effect on the female candidate is the same. If anything, media use of sexism may be more disqualifying because it is perceived as coming from an objective, disinterested source.

Awareness is the strongest tool that both candidates and members of the media have in combating sexism. This means be aware of common sexism normalized by an unequal culture as well as of your own notions about gender, language and image, as well as how others express these notions. When a female candidate says she's been treated in a sexist manner, the most damaging response is a form of blaming the victim: "She's playing the gender card."

This guide shows the many ways women candidates and politicians are often stuck with "the gender card" and how it turns politics into a game in which democracy is the loser.

GUIDING RULES FOR GENDER NEUTRALITY

The Rule of Reversibility

"The most workable definition of equality for journalists is reversibility. Don't mention her young children unless you would also mention his, or describe her clothes unless you would describe his, or say she's shrill or attractive unless the same adjectives would be applied to a man. Don't say she's had facial surgery unless you say he dyes his hair or has hair plugs. Don't say she's just out of graduate school but he's a rising star. Don't say she has no professional training but he worked his way up. Don't ask her if she's running as a women's candidate unless you ask him if he's running as a men's candidate.

A good test of whether or not you as a reporter are taking sexism seriously is whether you would cite race, class, ethnicity, or religion in the same context."—*Gloria Steinem, Journalist and Co-Founder of the Women's Media Center*

Reversibility means abandoning or evaluating terms or story frames of women candidates that wouldn't be written about men. It means not citing sex with less seriousness or logical relation to content than you would cite race, class, ethnicity, or religion.

At the simplest level, do you use "Mr. Smith" on first reference, then "Smith" after that? Do you cite "Ms.," "Mrs.," or "Miss Smith" throughout? If you answered yes to both, you are granting Mr. Smith autonomy, but continuing to describe Ms. Smith by her marital status.

If terms are almost singularly applied to women but not to men, you probably shouldn't be using them. Sexism can also refer to the *type* of coverage, often about personality, appearance, or family, that is given to women politicians but not male politicians. See the chart for some examples.

Parallelism: When Everything Isn't Equal

Another type of sexism in media coverage is Parallelism. If a reporter is wondering whether it's offensive or inaccurate to say something about a group or person who may be subject to stereotyping, it's often helpful to make a parallel with another person or group who is less subject to stereotyping. It changes the context just enough to see the fairness or unfairness. Some examples of the effect come in word choice. For example, men have "brown hair," but women are "brunettes." Women in power are sometimes called "motherly," but men in power aren't "fatherly."

But other examples go beyond word choice to the very premise of a question posed to a candidate.

For example: If Sarah Palin had been a male vice presidential candidate, she probably wouldn't have been asked whether or not she could fulfill the job when she had young children, including one with special needs. Therefore, it wasn't okay to ask that question of or about Palin either—not unless it was also asked of or about her male equivalents.

For example: If Hillary Clinton had been a male presidential candidate of any race, her clothes and hair would have been far less written about. Therefore, it wasn't okay to discuss those in her case either, unless, of course, it was in the context of

CHART OF REVERSIBILITY

Said to Women	*Said to Men*
Cunt	NONE Girl / Woman
Whore	NONE Man Whore
Bitch	NONE
Slut	NONE
Prostitute	Player / Pimp
Man-Eater / Aggressive	Driven / Motivated
High-Strung / Temperamental	Powerful
Too Emotional	Sensitive / Caring
Mean Girl / Bully	Powerful / Decisive
Ice Queen / Cold	Hardworking / Commanding
Nagging / Shrill	Determined
Opinionated / Uppity	Knowledgeable / Passionate
Hot / Sexy / MILF	Handsome / Attractive
Ugly / Mannish / Dyke / Lesbian	NO ATTENTION GIVEN
Varicose Veins / Cankles / Wrinkled	Distinguished / Seasoned

General Menstruation Jokes

Moody / PMSing	Angry

General Comments on Appearance

Plunging Neckline / Short Skirt / High Heels / Hairstyle	Oh, look, he's wearing a red/blue tie "and an American flag pin"

discussing other male candidates' hair and clothing in the same article.

Note: Parallelism is not to be confused with the notion that if one side of a controversy or contest is criticized, the other must be criticized, too. If one candidate has a legitimate campaign issue, there may not be a "parallel" in the other candidate.

Takeaway

The media should treat women candidates exactly the same way they treat male candidates. If the same description, term, story, or question would seem ridiculous or "too feminine" for a male candidate for office, then it should not be used for a female candidate. To do so is to create different editorial standards by gender, which is sexist and inherently unfair.

CASE STUDIES

Now that we've provided guideposts on how media coverage is gendered, we shall examine two specific incidents in which two women candidates were victims of sexist attacks.

The Krystal Ball Example

In 2010, first-time candidate Krystal Ball ran for Congress in Virginia's 1st District against an incumbent. In October, with just about a month left to go in the campaign, racy photos of Ball at a costume party from 2004 appeared on a little-known conservative website, *Virginia Virtucon*. Although *Virginia Virtucon* eventually decided to take the post down, within days the photos were all over the Internet, including a slideshow run by Gawker with the frame.

"Krystal Ball dressed as a naughty Santa at a party 'right after college.' Her then-husband wore a dildo on his nose and leash around his neck. Years later, Krystal decided to run for Congress in Virginia. Guess what happened next?"

It didn't matter that most media outlets and pundits said the photos *shouldn't* hurt Ball's campaign, because by that point nearly every story about Ball was about the photos, not campaign points. Voters in Virginia's 1st District were bombarded with news stories asking whether they felt one of their candidates was a laughingstock.

It's possible Ball could have stayed a laughingstock. An image portraying a female politician as promiscuous is a hard stain to get away from, especially when media coverage amplifies the effect.

This is why the Name It. Change It. project was one of the few advising Ball to speak out about this smear. Based on our research, we knew that ignoring the issue wouldn't make it go away; it would only hurt Ball with voters. Even sympathetic media articles framed Ball as having been "stupid" for having pictures taken of her with her friends and family, gently tut-tutting something mostly 22-year-olds do.

[I]n October . . . 2010, Ball released a statement and began speaking out against the sexist coverage of her campaign.

On the day the photos were posted, I thought of Hillary Clinton. How she came out the next day after her private life was public and held her head high. Many advisors told me I was finished, that this was not what people wanted from their member of Congress. I decided that I had to fight. I had to come out publicly and raise my voice on this issue, even though I risked becoming some joke candidate named Krystal Ball. I also risked drawing more attention to the photos, which I still find tremendously embarrassing, but mostly because I'm shy, not because I think that what I did was wrong.

Against nearly all the advice I was given I decided to give interviews. Siobhan "Sam" Bennett, from Women's Campaign Forum, helped me to realize that the way to combat this was to take it head-on, to confront it.

In the end, Krystal Ball did not win her Congressional race, but by calling attention to sexist coverage, Name It. Change It. made the media focus on what's really important to voters—and it was not which candidate had the sexiest Facebook photos.

Janice Hahn and the YouTube Ad

In 2011, Democrat Janice Hahn was running in a special election to fill the seat for California's 36th Congressional district recently vacated by Democrat Jane Harman. A Los Angeles city councilmember, Hahn was running against Republican Craig Huey, a conservative political activist.

With the special election set to occur on July 12, and a month left to go in the campaign, the media coverage of the race was almost entirely taken over by a video produced by the SuperPAC Turn Right USA and directed by one of its founding members, Ladd Ehlinger, Jr.

In the video, a woman is dressed as a pole dancer and has a Janice Hahn "mask" with glowing red eyes. She dances provocatively while two African-American men dressed as gangsters sing, "Give us your cash, bitch, so we can shoot up the streets."

The reported basis for the ad, according to Turn Right USA, was that Hahn, as city councilmember, had supported programs that hired gang intervention specialists. While the ad was never aired as a paid TV spot, it was discussed endlessly throughout the media, and the sponsor, Ehlinger, spoke about it on national television.

The Women's Media Center, along with many other groups, was outraged by the ad's overtly sexist and racist content. We pointed out that the ad was also quite violent, ending with a rifle, the sound of shots, and the words "Keep her out of Congress." Considering that the shooting of Gabrielle Giffords had occurred earlier that year, the violent imagery hurled at Hahn was almost as disturbing as the blatant misogyny.

Huey at first declined to comment on the ad, claiming he had nothing to do with it. Later, he did denounce it, but made no move to ask Turn Right USA to take it down. Eventually it was viewed more than half a million times on YouTube during the campaign. Even though it was denounced from all quarters, it essentially dominated the final stages of the election.

In the end, Hahn won the special election, but the incident shows how a sexist ad can completely derail the campaign process.

RESEARCH ON MEDIA SEXISM

Key Findings—Sexism Has Consequences

- Sexism, even mild sexist language, has an impact on voters' likelihood to vote for a female candidate and on how favorably they feel toward a woman seeking office. It also affects perceptions of trustworthiness and effectiveness.
- Voters assume the sexist language comes from the woman's opponent, even when there is no indication in the newspaper stories or radio coverage that he or his campaign are involved. Her opponent pays some price—or will—for this type of negative coverage.
- Initially, after given a neutral profile of both a woman Congressional candidate and a man Congressional candidate, voters were more likely to say they would vote for the woman.
- If voters hear nonsexist, negative coverage of the woman and the man, the male candidate remains behind the woman.
- However, if voters hear sexist coverage of the woman candidate, the race becomes even.
- The effect of sexist language affects voters of all voting groups. The responses regain voters across the board.
- When the female candidate acknowledges and responds to sexist mistreatment by the media, it helps to repair the damage inflicted on her. She regains a clear lead over her opponent in the

horserace, she regains some lost ground in vote likelihood, and voters are more likely to view her favorably.
- Responding helps a female candidate even if the audience didn't hear the original slur.

What Our Research Shows

In September 2010, Lake Research Partners conducted a survey of 800 likely voters nationwide to see if sexist language affected voters' preferences. The survey was divided into a systematic experiment based on a hypothetical campaign. Half of the voters heard sexist coverage of the female candidate and negative but not sexist coverage of the male candidate. The other half heard coverage with an equally strong critique of the female candidate that lacked sexist language. All of the situations we tested occurred in real campaigns and all of the language was said by actual media against women running for Congress or governor.

First, survey respondents were presented with two generic candidate descriptions: one of a man, the other of a woman.

Jane Smith enjoys a reputation as a bipartisan reformer and is an advocate for small businesses and hardworking families. An economist by training, she graduated at the top of her class in law school. She grew up in a working-class neighborhood where she learned the value of hard work and discipline. As the daughter of a police officer and a nurse, she believes in fiscal responsibility, cracking down on criminals, and getting this economy working again.

Before running for Congress, she served two terms on city council, one as head of the Chamber of Commerce, and is in her third term in the state legislature. She currently serves as a ranking member of the Appropriations and the Joint Economic committees. She believes in free markets and personal responsibility. She is also a strong and tireless advocate for families who are unable to make ends meet in these tough economic times.

Smith married her high school sweetheart, Justin, a lawyer, and they have three grown children: Linda, Matt, and Jordon.

Dan Jones is known in the state legislature for his consistent voting record on issues like immigration, energy independence, and economic development. He is a staunch advocate for cutting unnecessary government regulations and is a believer in more fiscal discipline and accountability from Washington. He also believes in investing in our priorities like public education and expanding access to affordable health care for small business. He believes world-class education and affordable health care are key to our future economic competitiveness as a nation.

He successfully climbed the ranks of a Fortune 500 company before deciding to run for city comptroller and then was twice elected mayor of one of the largest cities in his state. He is currently serving his second term as state senator and majority leader, where he serves on the Appropriations Committee and the Governor's Economic Task Force.

Jones met his wife, Cecilia, after college, and they have two grown children: Christopher and Taylor.

After hearing the descriptions of the candidates, voters favored our hypothetical female candidate, Jane Smith, over Dan Jones by 11 points (43 percent Smith to 32 percent Jones), with support for Smith twice as strong as that for Dan Jones (18 percent to 9 percent). A quarter of the voters were undecided.

But after voters heard a mild sexist news story that referred to Jane Smith as a "mean girl" and an "ice queen," the ballot went from Smith being 11 points ahead to being 1 point behind. Sexist language reduced Jane's support among both men and women. Every single group of voters was affected by sexism.

We also tested what happened when even stronger sexist language was used against our hypothetical female candidate.

Further exploring her votes on health care and taxes, Jane Smith supported an article in the health care bill that said that any state that declared an emergency would get a $300 million grant. A talk radio host said she "may be the most expensive prostitute in the history of prostitution. She may be easy, but she's not cheap." Another noted radio host said, "Stupid Girl describes her vote pretty well."

Among voters overall, the ballot remained static after voters heard the stronger sexist language, with Smith and Jones tied. The over-the-top sexism further eroded Smith's advantage in the horserace among every subgroup except men and Democrats.

Such over-the-top language did get some pushback from men and younger voters, but not enough to make up for the initial losses from the milder "mean girl" and "ice queen" language.

VOTER LIKELIHOOD

	JANE SMITH		DAN JONES	
	Less Likely	*More Likely*	*Less Likely*	*More Likely*
Initial	22%	54%	30%	42%
Mild sexist	69%	17%	66%	16%
Mild control	57%	23%	60%	19%
Top sexist	66%	18%	64%	18%
Top control	57%	23%	63%	19%

Sexist language erodes voters' likelihood for voting for Smith.

Nearly seven in 10 voters reported being less likely to vote for Jane Smith after they heard her called an "ice queen" and a "mean girl," in addition to more overtly sexist language. Nonsexist language about Smith also eroded voters' likelihood of voting for her, but not to the extent of the sexist attacks. Republicans, Independents, and blue-collar voters were the most affected by the strong sexism, although sexist attacks lowered Jane Smith's favorability across the board more than nonsexist attacks. It especially had an effect on men's voting preference.

It's well-known that negative attacks create an unfavorable impression of both candidates, both the attacker and the target. You might think, then, that voters would react negatively to a candidate who uses overtly sexist language on his female opponent. The answer is that they do: sexist language used on a female candidate *does* hurt her opponent. In our research, Dan Jones' favorability suffered whether or not news stories about him were compared to sexist news stories about Smith. Jane Smith's favorability wore down when voters heard both the sexist and the nonsexist attacks on her, but there also seems to be an extra price paid for a male candidate who is perceived to be engaging in a sexist campaign.

Though described as coming from newspapers, voters clearly assume the sexist attacks come from her opponent. There was some backlash with Dan Jones' favorability decreasing more with sexist attacks, especially among men.

The key takeaway, however, was that sexism hurts women candidates' favorability more than the male candidate it's perceived as coming from. Voters' favorability toward each candidate plummeted after voters heard about Jane Smith being an ice queen and a mean girl. Nearly three-quarters felt unfavorably toward Smith, giving Jones a slight edge overall.

How Does Media Sexism Affect Women Candidates?

When voters are presented with a neutral description of a male and a female candidate, they start out believing the female candidate is more likely to care about people like them, share their values, and be trustworthy.

These results make sense in light of other research that shows voters have typically given women candidates a "virtue advantage"—having a slight edge in being seen as more honest and ethical than a male candidate.[1]

As one report noted, quoting a media consultant, "In my experience, voters are more likely to think that a woman candidate is in politics for the right reasons. [Voters] tend to start from a presumption that they are less corruptible and more honest and have more integrity than males."[2]

But the advantage of being put on a pedestal of "virtue" for female candidates is in reality more like standing on a knife's edge. Female candidates are punished more harshly by voters for any whiff of scandal.

Our research showed that voters' views of Smith were strongly impacted by the sexist language. After hearing the sexist attacks, Smith was seen as less empathetic and trustworthy and her values were questioned. Even more alarming was that after hearing the sexist attacks, voters also questioned her effectiveness, even though the critiques said nothing about her job performance. Sexism alone costs female candidates all the advantage of their gender

in a way that nonsexist critiques don't. When voters only heard nonsexist attacks, Jane Smith's positives dropped, but significantly less than they did for the sexist attacks.

Female candidates are also punished more harshly than male candidates for negative campaigning. When sexist attacks have occurred on them in the past, female candidates were typically advised not to respond for fear that making an issue out of sexism would only hurt them more. There was also a concern about amplifying a media frame that was detrimental to the candidate and potentially setting off a round of media stories that asked whether such attacks were sexist, completely moving away from any discussion of relevant issues in the campaign.

But our research found that this just isn't the case. Female candidates for office ignore sexist attacks at their peril. While sexist coverage of female candidates puts a damper on voters' likelihood to vote for them, a direct response makes up for lost ground.

What the Press Needs to Know About How Sexist Coverage Affects Women Candidates

If sexism, stemming either from the opposing candidate or from media coverage, is having a negative impact on a female candidate in voters' eyes, then what does the press need to know about those responding to sexism?

Our research shows the sexist attack doesn't have to be egregious to have a negative impact. But calling attention to the sexism does have an impact—a positive one.

We tested three kinds of responses to sexist attacks. In the first, the candidate called the attacks sexist outright, while in the second she called the topic inappropriate and attempted to go back to talking about the issues. Another test was to have an outside party, a media accountability group, call out the sexism on her behalf.

The result? Once voters heard the three responses to the sexist coverage, favorability toward Jane Smith rebounded. Voters responded similarly to each response, indicating that confronting sexism is valuable, whether done by the campaign or by outside groups. The responses effectively neutralized the erosion of Jane Smith's support caused by the sexist media treatment. Smith didn't regain back *all* of her support prior to the sexist attack, but she rebounded some, and ended up in a better poll position than if she hadn't responded at all.

The most interesting finding: when voters heard a candidate's response to a sexist incident, they still responded positively to the candidate even when they never heard the original slur. For years, women candidates have been advised not to respond to such incidents for fear of spreading the charges farther than the original event. Our research shows that there's a much higher potential cost to candidates who brush off even subtle sexism. This is why when the media pooh-pooh women candidates who complain about sexism, it actually compounds the problem for women.

Celinda Lake summarized her takeaway from the results thus: "Up until this research was conducted, I often advised women to ignore toxic media sexism. But now, women candidates are equipped with evidence that shows they can recover voter confidence from sexist media coverage by directly addressing it, and standing up for all current and future women leaders."

Reporters need to be aware that subtle sexism can actually be far more damaging to candidates than deliberate and outrageous sexism. It can be harder for candidates to respond directly to coverage that is subtly tilted against them, especially when the reporters aren't even aware they are being sexist!

[1]"Turning Point: The Changing Landscape for Women Candidates." Barbara Lee Family Foundation. 2010
[2] IBID, p. 35

R E A D I N G (**88**)

Too Poor to Parent?

Gaylynn Burroughs (2008)

When a recurrent plumbing problem in an upstairs unit caused raw sewage to seep into her New York City apartment, 22-year-old Lisa (not her real name) called social services for help. She had repeatedly asked her landlord to fix the problem, but he had been unresponsive. Now the smell was unbearable, and Lisa feared for the health and safety of her two young children.

When the caseworker arrived, she observed that the apartment had no lights and that food was spoiling in the refrigerator. Lisa explained that she did not have the money to pay her electric bill that month, but would have the money in a few weeks. She asked whether the caseworker could help get them into a family shelter. The caseworker promised she would help—but left Lisa in the apartment and took the children, who were then placed in foster care.

Months later, the apartment is cleaned up. Lisa still does not have her children.

Monique (also a pseudonym), too, lost her children to foster care despite all her efforts to keep her family united. The impoverished Georgia mother of three had been left by her boyfriend after discovering that their infant son needed heart surgery. Undeterred, she sent her older children to live with family out of state, while she moved to a shelter close to the hospital. When the baby recovered, she moved to New York and was reunited with her other kids.

Unemployed and without financial resources, Monique hoped to live with family, but when they couldn't take her in she looked for a shelter again. This time, though, she got caught up in endless red tape from the emergency housing *and* medical systems—the latter of which kept her waiting months for an appointment with a cardiologist and medication for her child.

Finally, settled in an apartment loaned by a friend, Monique began a job search, leaving the baby at home with a sitter—and that's when the *real* nightmare began. One day police found the baby alone and took him into protective custody. The next day, child-welfare officials charged Monique with inadequate guardianship *and* medical neglect (because the child hadn't seen a cardiologist or gotten his medication), and put all three children in foster care. Monique can now visit them only once a week, supervised, for just two hours.

It is probably fair to say that most women with children worry about their ability as mothers. Are they spending enough time with them? Are they disciplining them correctly? Are they feeding them properly? When should they take them to the doctor, and when is something not that serious? But one thing most women in the United States do not worry about is the possibility of the state removing children from their care. For a sizable subset of women, though—especially poor black mothers like Lisa and Monique—that possibility is very real.

Black children are the most overrepresented demographic in foster care nationwide. According to the U.S. Government Accounting Office (GAO), blacks make up 34 percent of the foster-care population, but only 15 percent of the general child population. In 2004, black children were twice as likely to enter foster care as white children. Even among other minority groups, black mothers are more likely to lose their children to the state than Hispanics or Asians—groups that are slightly underrepresented in foster care.

The reason for this disparity? Study after study reviewed by Northwestern University law professor Dorothy Roberts in her book *Shattered Bonds: The Color of Child Welfare* shows that poverty is the leading cause of children landing in foster care. According to one researcher, poor families are up to 22 times more likely to be involved in the child-welfare system than wealthier families. And nationwide, blacks are four times more likely than other groups to live in poverty.

But when state child-welfare workers come to remove children from black mothers' homes, they rarely cite poverty as the factor putting a child at risk. Instead, these mothers are told that they neglected their children by failing to provide adequate food, clothing, shelter, education or medical care. The failure is always personal, and these mothers and children are almost always made to suffer individually for the consequences of one of the United States' most pressing social problems.

Federal spending for foster care skyrocketed in the 1980s, but funding for antipoverty services to prevent foster-care placement—or speed reunification with birth parents—stagnated. As explained by child-welfare expert Martin Guggenheim, a professor at New York University School of Law, "Between 1981 and 1983, federal foster-care spending grew by more than 400 percent in real terms, while preventive and reunification spending grew by only 14 percent, and all other funds available for social services to the poor declined."

As a result of the failure to fund programs servicing poor families—helping them secure housing, jobs, health care, subsidized day care, mental health services and drug treatment programs—the number of poor children in foster care began to soar. In 1986, the foster care population numbered around 280,000 children. Just five years later, that number had jumped by 53 percent to 429,000. The latest data available shows an estimated 514,000 children in foster care.

Troubled not only by the number of children in foster care but by their longer stays in the system, Congress passed the Adoption and Safe Families Act (ASFA) in 1997. Its purpose is to achieve a permanent family environment more quickly for children in foster care, but the legislation accomplishes that goal by placing time limits on family reunification—thus encouraging adoption instead of the return of children to their parents.

Supporters of ASFA claim that the legislation is child-friendly because it measures time from the perspective of a child's development, and strives to place children in safe homes away from "bad parents" who are unlikely to stop putting their children in harm's way. Certainly there are situations in which temporarily placing a child in foster care, or even terminating parental rights, is the only responsible outcome. However, as Guggenheim points out, "ASFA makes no distinction between parents whose children were removed because of parental abuse and parents whose only crime is being too poor to raise their children in a clean and safe environment without additional benefits the government refuses to supply."

While ASFA was making it more difficult for some parents to win back their children, changes in federal antipoverty policies were making it more difficult for families struggling to keep their children. President Clinton's welfare reform in the mid-1990s eliminated federal cash assistance for single mothers and their children in favor of block grants to states, so individual states now have wide discretion to set benefit levels, establish work requirements for welfare assistance and create time limits for public assistance. For some women, the effect of welfare reform was a low-paying job or unemployment, coupled with the loss of a government safety net. Still poor, many of these women continued to lose their children because of the predictable consequences of poverty: lack of health care, inadequate housing and simply the inability to meet basic needs.

Yet public perception of parents accused of neglecting their children remains extremely negative, regardless of the actual allegations. Child-welfare workers in New York City, citing emergency conditions, routinely remove poor children from their homes without notifying the parents, without securing a court order and without informing parents of their legal rights. Sometimes they even remove children from school, day care or a friend's home without giving parental notice. It's not uncommon in court on Monday morning to meet frantic parents whose children were removed on Friday night and have still not learned where their children were taken. Someone must not think that these parents love their children and actually care to know.

The legal system often provides no haven for these parents. Based on even the flimsiest allegations, they are essentially presumed guilty and pressured to participate in various cookie-cutter services that often do not directly address the concerns that brought them to court. For example, after her children went into foster care, Lisa was asked to attend parenting classes, undergo a mental health evaluation, seek therapy and submit to random drug testing before her children could be returned. But child-welfare authorities did not assist her in repairing her home or finding a new apartment, nor have they gone after her landlord for allowing deplorable conditions. Lisa's poverty has led government authorities to pathologize her; she's automatically considered sick, careless or otherwise unfit if she attempts to parent while poor.

And what about children who are physically or sexually abused by their parents? A myth of child welfare is that foster care is full of such children, but in fact the majority of children who encounter the child welfare system have *not* been abused. At least 60 percent of child welfare cases in this country involve solely allegations of neglect.

Lacking private resources, poor women may also come to the attention of government authorities more often than other mothers do, as they must often rely on public services such as shelters, public hospitals and state welfare offices. That gives government workers more opportunities to judge, and report on, parental fitness. So poor mothers must cope not only with the daily frustrations of parenting but with the crushing gaze of the state, which is too willing to blame its own shortcomings in addressing child poverty on poor women and their "bad mothering."

. . .

Until the disparity in funding and services is addressed, and until this country comes to terms with its culpability in allowing widespread poverty to exist, poor black mothers will continue to lose their children to the state. And we will continue to label these women "bad mothers" to assuage our own guilt.

Looking Beyond the Wall

Robert Neustadt (2013)

On a crisp, cold November night, under a blanket of stars, we huddle by a fire. The steel border wall glows in the moonlight. Coyotes howl, bark and yip. Some students don't sleep that night. They lie awake, their nerves on edge. Before coming on this fieldtrip, we had read voluminously about the border. Now, camping within sight of the wall, many feel anxious in this unfamiliar environment.

We're here as part of a class I teach at Northern Arizona University. Our plan is to explore, from a multitude of angles and perspectives, the 2,000-mile border that divides Mexico and the U.S. Having read about the border, watched films, and discussed and analyzed immigration policy in terms of cost and effectiveness, we're on a five-day fieldtrip to explore both sides of the divide.

The next morning we walk across the border to Nogales, Sonora. No official asks to see our passports. We realize we have entered Mexico from the sign—*Welcome to Mexico*—and then visit an aid station for recently deported people. I approach a group standing in the shade and ask if they will share their experiences with us. An indigenous woman, her face scratched, her clothes dirty and torn, declines to speak. Fighting back tears, she gestures that, emotionally, she is not capable of talking. I invite a man in the group to speak. He says that he wants to ask us a favor. "If any of you become Border Patrol agents, please don't abuse migrants. We're not criminals, we just want to work and support our families." On hearing this, Ruth, the woman who couldn't speak before, interjects that she does want to say something.

She had been apprehended after four terrifying days in the desert. There was a sign in the cell: "If you are thirsty or hungry, or in need of medical assistance, notify a Border Patrol agent and you will receive assistance." She states that she did not receive help, only a cup of juice and two packages of peanut butter crackers. Her feet were so blistered that she was unable to walk until yesterday. Ruth has four children that she had left with a neighbor in an impoverished village in Oaxaca, nearly 1,500 miles to the south. She has no idea how, or if, she will get home. Ruth's children don't know where she is or what has happened—she doesn't want them to worry. I look up at my students and see tears streaming down their faces. In the spring, Ruth will try to cross the border again to cut lettuce in California. She says she has no choice. She has no money, nothing.

A student calls me over to talk. He almost didn't come on the trip because he didn't have the money to apply for a passport. A big guy, normally laughing and kidding, Corey feels he has been called to this place. "My mother gave me $100, I have it in my pocket. I don't need this money. I want to give it to this woman so that she can return to her kids in Oaxaca."

We meet other recently deported people at Grupos Beta, an aid station run by the Mexican government. One man tells us that he has been vomiting for four days, he cannot keep down any food or water. He doesn't know what to do. A couple tells us, in perfect English, that they had lived in New York for 15 years. They had returned to Mexico to see a dying grandmother, and hired a *coyote* (guide) to get back into the U.S., who told them that they would have to walk for only one hour. Border Patrol apprehended them on their fourth day in the desert. They were deported to separate cities, the wife to Nogales and the husband to Matamoros. To disorient migrants, and break their connections with smugglers, Border Patrol divides groups (though supposedly not families) and deports them to a different city than where they crossed. This couple, with children, had only recently found one another.

Some tell us that Border Patrol treated them well, though accounts of abuse are rampant. Another man told me that he saw a traveling companion get tased while hiding in a ditch. In a 2011 report, "Culture of Cruelty," the humanitarian group No More Deaths documents more than 30,000 incidents of abuse and mistreatment endured by individuals while in the custody of U.S. Immigration authorities. As we leave the aid station one of my students looks at me with tears in her eyes. "You didn't prepare us for this emotionally," she says. In spite of all that we had read, nothing can prepare you for an encounter with raw, wounded humanity.

Back on the Arizona side of the wall we meet "sound sculptor" Glenn Weyant. Glenn attaches microphones to the steel wall and plays it as a musical instrument. Recording the sound, he later mixes it on a laptop and then uploads the music to his website, sonicanta.com. Unlike a traditional musical instrument, Weyant explains, there is no correct or wrong technique—everyone can play a wall!

Glenn invites two students to choose implements (spoons, whisks, chopsticks, a cello bow) and asks them to play the wall. They can play what they want, however they want, but he encourages them to listen and to interact with each other musically. He then adds more students, two by two, until we are all playing. Two trucks idle on the dirt road behind us, we have an audience of Border Patrol. On the hill above, a contingent of National Guardsmen dressed in full combat gear, carrying M-16s, stands beneath a camouflaged tent and observe our concert. One waves at me. The music starts chaotically and as we continue to play we begin to communicate. We start to play rhythmic clusters, calling and responding to each other's phrases. We hit a samba-like groove. "I was beating my frustrations out," one student tells me. "Everything I had seen today, all of that sadness, I took it out on the wall." We drive away listening to a recording of Margaret Randall's poem, "Offended Turf," blended with Weyant's wall music on *Border Songs,* an album of immigration songs and poetry with proceeds going to No More

Deaths: "We are taking a chance our vibrations will change these molecules of hate," intones Randall. The wall growls and grinds and groans—the sound perfectly matches the complex emotions we feel: frustration, anger, and profound sadness.

One cannot see this hard steel barrier without asking how we have gotten to the point of walling people in and out of the country. The so-called "invasion" of undocumented people began in 1994 after the U.S. and Mexico signed the North American Free Trade Agreement (NAFTA). Subsequently, the U.S. flooded the Mexican economy with cheap, government-subsidized corn. It became impossible for small and mid-sized corn producers to make a profit and some 6 million people lost their livelihood. Suspecting that legions of immigrant families would seek work in the U.S., the government started building walls and implement border militarization to seal off the easy-to-cross urban centers of El Paso, San Diego, and Nogales. Recently, increased numbers of Central American people, especially Hondurans, are attempting to cross the border to flee abject poverty and violence.

Efforts to secure the border have increased over time. Between 2007 and 2011 alone, the U.S. spent over $4.7 billion on the border wall and the now abandoned "Virtual Fence." The Border Patrol, now the largest law enforcement agency in the country, has doubled in size in the last five years. The walls, and related strategies of "deterrence," intentionally funnel border crossers into remote and dangerous desert. According to Doris Meissner, former commissioner of the Immigration & Naturalization Service (INS), they "thought the number of people crossing the border through Arizona would go down to a trickle." Wrong. People are biologically driven to feed their children and care for loved ones. They will risk everything.

Since 1994, according to Kat Rodriguez, the director of the group Coalición de Derechos Humanos (the Human Rights Coalition), over 7,000 deceased human remains have been found in the borderlands. The number of total deaths is, in fact, almost certainly much higher since many migrants who die in the desert are never found. Many of those who die, furthermore, are never identified.

The morgue in Tucson currently houses nearly 800 unidentified dead migrants.

Recently, due to the decline in the U.S. economy, migration has dropped precipitously, though impoverished Mexicans and Central Americans continue to die in the borderlands. Border militarization—walls, helicopters, drones, high-tech monitoring devices, and Border Patrol agents—continue to push migrants into the desert. Last year alone, 179 migrants were found dead in the Arizona desert. Comprehensive immigration reform is a step in the right direction, but if it includes further border militarization, and virtually all of the current proposals do, it will also result in more death and suffering on the border.

We camp at the No More Deaths base near the small town of Arivaca. Early the next morning we hike through the desert, sidestepping cacti, chatting, laughing. Some of these kids have never hiked before. I am enjoying the crunch of gravel beneath my boots. Blue sky seems to bounce off of desert rocks. We curve around a bend in the trail and suddenly encounter a shrine with a white cross. Steve, a No More Deaths volunteer, points out the precise spot where a 14-year old girl from El Salvador died. Josseline Hernández Quinteros was attempting to join her mother in Los Angeles when she became ill after drinking stock pond water. Steve shows us how her legs were positioned, her feet had been soaking in a pothole of standing water.

This splendid desert wash suddenly takes on new meaning. We stand in silence, staring at the shrine and contemplate the place where she died. It's difficult to comprehend the magnitude of this tragedy. Students cry. Many hug. Some pray. Standing in this paradoxically beautiful place, listening to silence cut only by the occasional hum of insects, we mourn Josseline's death. In class, before this trip, we had read *The Death of Josseline: Immigration Stories from the Arizona-Mexico Borderlands* by Margaret Regan. It feels as if we knew Josseline. The students express dismay that Josseline's mother could not attend her daughter's funeral mass for fear of deportation. Several gather wildflowers and place them on her shrine. Corey hangs a rosary on the shrine. A student leaves a ring that she had worn for years. "I just felt like I had to offer something," she tells

me, "If Josseline had lived she would have been our age." We hike away from this spot and accompany NMD while they cache water on migrant trails in the desert. Students write messages of encouragement on the jugs. They feel empowered. Then, later that day, we discover slashed water bottles scattered in the desert. Clearly, some people do not agree with No More Death's mission.

The next day, we are finishing breakfast and a group of four migrants—wet and cold, dressed in black, their shoes shredded—walks into camp. They have been out for ten days, have not eaten in three. They had been drinking stock water until the day before when they encountered jugs of clean water left by NMD. A rail thin 22-year-old migrant has a swollen knee that can barely bend. NMD volunteers assess their physical condition and then cook and serve them breakfast. The guy with the injured knee, Israel, vomits after eating; the sudden ingestion proves too much of a shock to his system. A NMD medic administers small sips of electrolytes. Two students—Sol and Julie—agree to spend the day helping NMD volunteers at camp. Everyone has been jolted back to reality. After dinner we sit around a campfire. We play guitar and sing and look up at the stars and shiver. "There are no Mexican stars or American stars," says Charles Bowden on the *Border Songs* CD, "it's like a great biological unity with a meat cleaver of law cutting it in half." We imagine what it must be like for migrants who cross the desert with only the clothes on their back. Many of the students say that they almost dropped the class when they heard about the trip; now they thank me. One student, Rebecca, admits that before the trip she "hated immigrants because they cross our borders. But I don't think people should be dying out here," she adds. The group stares across the fire at her, trying to figure out if she really said what we think she said.

"Is everyone in here an American citizen?" asks an agent, while another commands a German shepherd to sniff our van. We are driving through a Border Patrol checkpoint. Two students, Ángel and Reyna, are permanent residents. The officer matches their Green Cards to their faces. We idle, and my Anglo students feel embarrassed by the scrutiny applied to two of their peers. Meanwhile, to the side of our van, a group of children and adults stand corralled under a brightly lit tent. It's the kind of tent you might rent for shade at an outdoor wedding. These people have been pulled from a vehicle—they are in the process of being detained.

In Tucson we meet with an off-duty Border Patrol agent. He speaks to us as an individual, clarifying that he is not authorized to speak for the agency. "Did you meet people who said that they were abused by Border Patrol?" asks the agent whom I'll call Wilson, "Well, I got to tell you, illegals lie a lot." He talks about drug runners and how he is trying to keep dope off of the streets. He feels sorry for migrants, but he simply focuses on his job. One student asks him, accusingly, why they don't feed people in detention. "Of course we feed them," Wilson, insists. "We give each adult two packages of crackers and a cup of juice every eight hours." Remembering Ruth's story, the students' faces contort with rage.

Another student remarks that people in Nogales complained of being roughed up by Border Patrol. "At times we have to be a little rough; it's called 'officer presence,'" says Wilson. "Since there are often more of them than there are of us, sometimes we have to throw some to the ground and handcuff them to make sure that the others don't try to run away." "How often do you work?" asks a student. "I'm a junior agent, so I don't get to go out to play as much. That's what we call going out on patrol," explains Wilson. We flash back to the stories deported people told us in Mexico. We think about the migrants we met in the desert. These people are not playing.

That afternoon, we enter the Tucson Federal Courthouse to attend an Operation Streamline hearing. In the Tucson sector the federal government prosecutes 70 detained people per day in a group hearing. Detainees sit, in the ornate wood-paneled courtroom, restrained with chains linking their ankle shackles, waists, and handcuffs. A line of 12 detained women sit in the middle of the room, in front of the observation gallery. A group of men fill the area to the left of the judge, and another group fills the entire left rear, an area designed for observers. The judge calls up five detainees at a time—they stand uncomfortably at microphones, each

shadowed by a lawyer who waits just behind. A student whispers to me that she must leave. She fears that she will be sick.

The judge asks each accused person to confirm his name, country of citizenship and then reads a script including the details of where and when they were detained after entering the United States illegally. Most listen through headphones while a simultaneous interpreter translates to Spanish. Many look confused as if they don't really understand the rapid-fire legalese. The judge asks each detainee if he knows that he has the right to a trial. "Sí." She asks them how they plead. Each person pleads *culpable* (guilty). The judge then reads a sentence, assigning a period of incarceration. A few receive time served, others 20 days, 30 days, 90 days, up to six months. This was all determined, and agreed upon, during a 15–30 minute meeting with a court-appointed lawyer the same morning.

Once convicted, they shuffle, their chains and shackles jangling, towards a door. The lawyers follow, occasionally placing a hand on their shoulder, sometimes hastily slipping a business card in the convicted person's handcuffed hand. A glove-wearing Border Patrol agent leads them out of the room and turns them over to guards for transport to prison. They shuffle right in front of us. One fellow lifts his handcuffed hands and manages a partial wave and smile as he passes by on his way to detention. We wonder why he waved. Perhaps he was hungry for human contact. Perhaps he felt it the polite thing to do.

Attorneys request special consideration for three cases. One detainee's wife had recently lost a baby. She was again pregnant and called him at work because she was bleeding. "He now knows," explains his lawyer, "that he should have called an ambulance, but he drove his wife to the hospital himself." The judge sentences him to 30 days. The last defendant of the day also asks for special dispensation. He has five children and a diabetic father that depend on him. Could the judge shorten his six-month sentence, so that he can care for his family? The judge answers that she cannot. If he would like to change his plea to innocent, she will allow him to do so. "You would not have to prove your innocence; the burden is on the government to prove your guilt. But you should be aware that if you go to trial and are convicted, you could spend 2–3 years in a federal penitentiary. Do you want to change your plea?" He declines and shuffles out of court. We leave the courthouse feeling stunned. It is mind-numbing to watch 70 people plead guilty in less than two hours.

Since 2005, the federal government has spent an estimated $5.5 billion incarcerating undocumented immigrants in the criminal justice system for illegal entry and re-entry. In Tucson alone, incarcerations, defense lawyers, and interpreters for Operation Streamline cost nearly $96 million per year. Private for-profit prison corporations such as GEO Group and Corrections Corporation of America (CCA) reap enormous profits from this system that criminalizes what was formerly a civil offense. The criminalization of undocumented immigration, then, provides economic incentives to some, at a great cost to taxpayers.

Back in Flagstaff, I am dropping off the students. I catch Rebecca's eye and mention the cold weather. "At least you have a jacket" she responds. I ask her what happened to her coat. "I gave it to a migrant," she says with a smile.

The next week we debrief in class and students confide that they are worried about the friends that they made, and left, in the medical tent at the NMD camp in the desert. They shake their heads and talk of living in different worlds. More than one student cries while reflecting on what we experienced. "We come home to warm showers and beds and we have no idea if these guys will make it, or die, or get caught by Border Patrol and end up in chains in Operation Streamline," says Sol. Before the trip Sol was planning on becoming a Border Patrol agent.

Students tell me, again and again, that before this trip, before they looked through and beyond the wall, that they had no idea the extent to which people are suffering on the border. It's as if we had been living behind a barrier that was blocking our view of a humanitarian catastrophe in our own backyard. "Now that we know," they tell me, "we must act." They have formed a student club on campus and are planning Immigration Awareness Week—a series of speakers, films, and art about the border and undocumented immigration. They want to share what they learned with their fellow students.

R E A D I N G **90**

Delinquent Girls

Andrea Doyle Hugmeyer (2011)

Issues of gender, female sexuality, and delinquency have been problematic in the juvenile justice system since its beginnings in 1899. In 1974, Congress passed the Juvenile Justice and Delinquency Prevention (JJDP) Act which focused heavily on the treatment of status offenders. Status offenses are laws and sanctions that apply to juvenile acts that are not considered criminal if committed by adults (Lundman, 2001). Status offenses vary across states, but the four major categories are running away, truancy, ungovernability, and underage liquor law violations

(Zhang, Katsiyannis, Barrett, & Willson, 2007). Although the JJDP Act was not written specifically to benefit young women, the act had a greater effect on girls because historically they have been arrested for more status offenses than boys. The JJDP Act mandated the deinstitutionalization of status offenders, which meant fewer girls were incarcerated.

Despite the implied benefit to delinquent girls after the passing of the JJDP Act, feminist criminologists point out that federally funded programs aimed at supporting delinquent girls were a low priority (Chesney-Lind & Irwin, 2005). With little community support, girls who were victims of abuse or family dysfunction still resorted to running away from home. Once found, they were taken in under the jurisdiction of the juvenile court and incarcerated. Throughout the 1970s, this pattern developed to such an extent that court officials demanded a return to incarceration for juvenile status offenders (Chesney-Lind & Irwin, 2005). Congress revisited the JJDP Act in 1980 and added additional legislation that allowed for the institutionalization of status offenders once again (Chesney-Lind & Shelden, 1998). It was not until 1992, when the JJDP Act was revisited again, that treatment and issues pertaining to juvenile delinquency and girls became a clear focus. The passing of the reauthorization of the JJDP Act in 1992 focused primarily on gender equality in the juvenile justice system and set the agenda for a national conversation about gender and delinquency.

The Reauthorization of the JJDP Act required states to assess existing programs for delinquent girls; determine needs for additional programming; develop a plan for providing gender-specific services to girls; and provide assurance that all youth are treated equitably (Chesney-Lind & Irwin, 2005). Federal funding was provided to states that took initiative on implementing these guidelines. The main benefit of the Reauthorization of the JJDP Act was that it provided a public forum illuminating the court's lack of treatment and programs for girls in the juvenile justice system (Chesney-Lind & Irwin, 2005).

FOR THEIR OWN PROTECTION

In 2004, the Office of Juvenile Justice and Delinquency Prevention (OJJDP) funded the Girls Study Group to research, review, and establish gender specific programming guidelines to benefit females (Zahn, Agnew, & Browne, 2009). Since the establishment of the Girls Study Group, the project has reviewed several programs aimed at preventing delinquency or rehabilitating female offenders, in addition to providing an extensive literature review of the history and research related to girls delinquency. Based on statistics provided by the OJJDP from 1985–2002, the Girls Study Group found a correlation between arrest rates and stricter policing action toward girls, explaining the rise of female delinquency rates in past years. Based on stereotypes about girls, police action impacts female delinquency rates by its exercise of greater social control over young women.

We see an effect of this stricter control from police authority in the different types of arrests experienced by girls compared with boys. Girls historically have had a higher rate of arrests for status offenses than boys have, suggesting that girls are being more closely controlled while committing fewer violent crimes than boys. This pattern likely results from the double standard of young female sexuality that has historically put girls at a disadvantage in the juvenile justice system (Alexander, 1995). A study in the 1970s, prior to the JJDP Act, revealed large numbers of girls incarcerated "for their own protection" (Rogers, 1972). One juvenile court judge claimed that it was best to lock the girls up in order to decrease their chances of getting pregnant at least until age 16 (Rogers, 1972). Sexist judicial attitudes regarding female promiscuity were often precursors to the treatment and sentencing of the offender (Vedder & Somerville, 1970; Rogers, 1972; Andrews & Cohn, 1974). Even today, judicial discretion and subjectivity differ between status offenses and criminal cases (Kurlychek & Johnson, 2004). Judges have much greater latitude in sentencing for status offenders, while criminal cases provide more structured sentencing rules. Without strict guidelines to follow, and with many status offense cases for female juveniles involving sexual misconduct, court personnel often rely on stereotypes, social sanctions, and a paternal judicial stance to treat female offenders (Feld, 2009; Tracy, Kempf-Leonard, & Ambramoske-James, 2009; Chesney-Lind & Shelden, 1998; Girls Inc., 1996).

The "power-control" theory of delinquency suggests another aspect of harsher social control and stressful life experiences for girls (Hagan, Simpson, & Gillis, 1985). This theory suggests that girls commit less delinquency than boys because parents more closely control the behavior of their daughters than their sons. Hagan and associates describe the patriarchal family as a prominent structure in the gender socialization that affects delinquent behaviors. They claim girls receive stricter control from parents during adolescence, resulting in passive and compliant daughters, while boys are encouraged to take risks and be deviant. Power-control theory also attempts to explain delinquency patterns by recognizing how gender relations are passed down generationally through familial relationships and note that in egalitarian households where the mother works outside of the home, girls' chance of delinquent behavior increases as a result of absent maternal control.

Feminist critics, however, argue against power-control theory's stereotypical gender assumptions and the implication that women's liberation and equality in the workplace increases female delinquency (Naffine, 1996; Chesney-Lind & Shelden, 1998). Power-control theory fails to consider nontraditional families in addition to blaming mothers for the delinquent behavior of youth (Tracy et al., 2009). In 1999, McCarthy, Hagan, and Woodward revised power-control theory, emphasizing that patriarchal families actually heighten levels of male delinquency more than female delinquency because of the dominant male characteristics in the household.

Gender is an integral aspect of life that explains a host of life chances, opportunities, and experiences for women and men in our society. An understanding of how girls live in our society can help identify reasons for their entrance into crime and the juvenile justice system. For example, in the 1970s feminist activists brought the issue of domestic violence into public conversation. As the topic became a concern and focus, research exposed connections between female delinquency and girls' history of physical and sexual abuse and now abuse is recognized as a major correlate of female delinquency. In a study exploring subgroups of female juvenile offenders, results indicated that the most violent group of female offenders was "more likely to suffer from child neglect, exposure to domestic violence, sexual abuse, physical abuse, and witnessing violence within their schools and communities" (Odgers, Moretti, Burnette, Chauhan, Waite, & Reppucci, 2007, p. 349). The exposure rate was at 100 percent

when neighborhood violence was also considered in this study. These results suggest that many girls in the juvenile justice system are victims as well as offenders, a significant attribute that should be considered for programming practices.

The way girls process traumatic abuse and violence differs from boys as well. Criminologist Robert Agnew (2009) claims that girls tend to blame themselves for the abuse and keep their feelings inside, resulting in feelings of anger, depression, and anxiety. Chronic exposure to traumatic events heightens risk-taking behaviors and the onset of Post Traumatic Stress Disorder (PTSD), a common ailment of delinquent girls (Ariga, Uehara, Takeuchi, Ishige, Nakano, & Mikuni, 2008). Mental health disorders offer justification or produce a coping mechanism for girls to self-medicate through drug use. Dembo, Schmeider, and Childs (2007) added to the recognition of drug use as a coping mechanism for delinquent girls in a study measuring the correlates of female and male juvenile offender abuse experiences. The authors found that being female and substance use were related to sexual victimization and the attempt to self-medicate the trauma experience (Dembo et al., 2007). Drug use, however, is not the only way females cope with their abusive situations. Running away from home is a common reaction for girls in those circumstances as well (Chesney-Lind & Shelden, 1998). Consequently, running away is one of the highest areas of arrest for female delinquents when compared to males. In 2007, female runaways were 9.2 percent of juvenile arrests, while only 3.1 percent for males (Tracy et al., 2009).

The effects of abuse do not stop once a girl enters the juvenile justice system. In fact, research has shown that institutionalizing females with histories of abuse has negative effects on behavior and mental health. The institutional characteristics of control, lack of personal agency, and feelings of powerlessness perpetuate the trauma of abused young women as well as foster feelings of dependency (Girshick, 2000). Furthermore, since a majority of delinquent girls enter the system with feelings of depression, confinement may trigger more depressive symptoms and initiate an ongoing cycle of trauma and stress (Ariga et al., 2008). This is an argument that originally helped push the movement to deinstitutionalize delinquents in the 1970s, prior to the passing of the original JJDP Act.

Finally, the message given to girls as they mature is that of dependence and subordination to males. Social institutions consistently convey ideas of sexism that affect the lives of young girls. The juvenile court system is only one piece of this social phenomenon that perpetuates the same ideology. Because law enforcement has a high employment of males (Reaves & Hickman, 2004) who are in positions of power and control in the girls' lives, the message that men are dominant over women is repeated. In addition, the vocational training offered to girls within juvenile facilities is often limited to skills like cosmetology and clerical work that are associated with underpaid and unstable jobs (Lahm, 2000; Hubbard & Mathews, 2008). In an overview of available community-based programs for girls in the U.S., "program descriptions revealed limited resources to make girls truly independent in terms of getting a job" (Chesney-Lind, Morash, & Stevens, 2008, p. 16). When girls are involved in gender-neutral job skills and activities like sports, such involvement provides a significant protection from delinquency and helps them to make choices independently and confidently (Booth, Farrell, & Varano, 2008).

REHABILITATION PROGRAMS

The factors that explain girls' lives leading up to delinquency and how they enter the court system may offer a foundation for creating programs to help rather than punish young women. Indeed, although feminist scholars advocate for programs to acknowledge the broader sociological concerns and oppressive systems that propel girls into crime, there are few successful programs acknowledging the inequalities and obstacles girls face when key rehabilitation practices are developed (Chesney-Lind et al., 2008; Hubbard & Mathews, 2008; Zahn, Day, Mihalic, & Tichavsky, 2009). This is evident despite the federal standards promoting gender-specific programming in the Reauthorization of the JJDP Act in 1992. The National Institute of Corrections has defined gender-specific programming and practice

as "[c]reating an environment through site selection, staff selection, program development, content, and material that reflects an understanding of the realities of women's lives and addresses the issues of the participants" (Bloom, Owen, & Covington, 2003, p. 2). Included in this definition are approaches that address social and cultural factors like poverty, race, class, and gender inequality as well as therapeutic interventions (Bloom et al., 2003).

Zahn and colleagues (2009) provide a summary of evaluation evidence for programs that specifically target girls and programs involving both genders. They acknowledge that gender-specific programs offered for girls do not have established methods and measures for the best evaluation, but there has been some evidence of the potential positive effects. Specifically, areas of education, employment, relationships with family and friends, self-esteem, and self-efficacy are important side effects of gender-specific programming, in addition to reducing recidivism. Chesney-Lind and her colleagues (2008) also did a comprehensive summary of gender-responsive programs in order to highlight successful characteristics of programs and areas of opportunity for future delinquency programs for girls. Their recent summary of gender-specific programs includes specific target areas identified in delinquency research that are ideal for gender-specific programs. These target areas include:

- Reaching girls during their "in risk" years (ages nine to 15);
- Emphasizing race or ethnicity;
- Preparing girls to address sexism, racism, or harassment;
- Addressing histories of abuse;
- Providing jobs for girls;
- Providing job training or career support;
- Teaching healthy sexuality;
- Including general health education;
- Providing housing assistance;
- Giving support among girls;
- Teaching leadership skills;
- Providing girls with long-term relationships with an adult/mentor;
- Not requiring parental involvement;
- And including follow up services

Key programs supported in both overviews (Chesney-Lind et al., 2008; Zahn et al., 2009) that have shown these effects and model gender-specific programming are Girls Inc. PEERsuasion, Reaffirming Young Sisters' Excellence (RYSE), Working to Insure and Nurture Girls' Success (WINGS), and Practical Academic Cultural Educational Center (PACE). More information about each program is listed below:

- Girls Inc. Friendly PEERsuasion
  - Offered in 4 major cities in the U.S. situated in "risky" neighborhoods.
  - Focuses on avoiding substance abuse and building leadership skills by teaching prevention to younger peer participants.
  - http://www.girlsinc.org/about/programs/friendly-peersuasion.html
- Reaffirming Young Sisters' Excellence (RYSE)
  - Location: Alameda County, California
  - Intensive probation program geared towards reducing recidivism in African-American and Chicana girls.
  - Includes home visits by probation officer, individualized case plans, life skills course, teen pregnancy services, counseling, and emergency monetary funds.
- Working to Insure and Nurture Girls' Success (WINGS)
  - Location: San Diego, California
  - Alternative probation program with individualized case plans and home visitations.
  - Includes an emphasis on mother-daughter relationships, counseling, anger management classes, career support, transportation, and academic help.
- Practical Academic Cultural Educational Center (PACE)
  - Location: 17 facilities across the state of Florida
  - Comprehensive day treatment program for delinquency prevention providing academic education, counseling, home visits and family relationship building, career planning, monthly community service projects, and up to 3 year follow-up services.
  - http://www.pacecenter.org/

For more information about gender equity in the juvenile justice system and current research regarding girls and delinquency, visit the Girls Study Group website (http://girlsstudygroup.rti.org/).

. . .

The original advocates for a separate court system for children were a group of reformists known as the child savers. The child savers are described as primarily middle and upper class white women with the time and means for philanthropic involvement (Platt, 1977). Although the movement for a juvenile court system started due to the efforts of women, it has taken a century to untangle the underlying restrictions regarding moral and social control that have been placed on women and girls. There is no better education and no better way to empower young women in society than to provide them an education centered on the teachings that value, empower, and support women and girls.

REFERENCES

Agnew, R. (2009). The contribution of mainstream theories to the explanation of female delinquency. In M. A. Zahn (Ed.), *The delinquent girl* (pp. 7–29). Philadelphia: Temple University Press.

Alexander, R. M. (1995). *The "girl problem."* Ithaca, NY: Cornell University Press.

Andrews Jr., R. H. & Cohn, A. H. (1974). Ungovernability: The unjustifiable jurisdiction. *Yale Law Journal*, 83, 1383–1409.

Ariga, M., Uehara, T., Takeuchi, K., Ishige, Y., Nakano, R., & Mikuni, M. (2008). Trauma exposure and posttraumatic stress disorder in delinquent female adolescents. *Journal of Child Psychology and Psychiatry*, 49, 79–87.

Bloom, B., Owen, B., & Covington, S. (2003). *A summary of research, practice, and guiding principles for women offenders.* Washington, DC: National Institute of Corrections.

Booth, J. A., Farrell, A., & Varano, S. P. (2008). Social control, serious delinquency, and risky behavior: A gendered analysis. *Crime and Delinquency*, 54, 423–456.

Chesney-Lind, M. & Shelden, R. G. (1998). *Girls, delinquency, and juvenile justice,* 2nd ed. Belmont: Thompson/Wadsworth.

Chesney-Lind, M. & Irwin, K. (2008). Still the "best place to conquer girls": Girls and the juvenile justice system. In R. G. Shelden & D. Macallair, *Juvenile justice in America* (pp. 115–136). Long Grove, IL: Waveland Press.

Chesney-Lind, M., Morash, M., & Stevens, T. (2008). Girls' troubles, girls' delinquency, and gender responsive programming: A review. *The Australian and New Zealand Journal of Criminology*, 41, 1–27.

Dembo, R., Schmeider, J., & Childs, K. (2007). Correlates of male and female juvenile offender abuse experiences. *Journal of Child Sexual Abuse*, 16, 75–94.

Feld, B. (2009). Violent girls or relabeled status offenders? An alternative interpretation of the data. *Crime and Delinquency*, 55, 241–265.

Girls, Inc. (1996). *Prevention and parity: Girls in juvenile justice.* Indianapolis: Girls Incorporated National Resource Center.

Girshick, L. B. (2000). *No safe haven: Stories of women in prison.* Boston: Northeastern University Press.

Hagan, J., Gillis, A. R., & Simpson, J. (1985). The class structure of gender and delinquency: Toward a power-control theory of common delinquent behavior. *American Journal of Sociology*, 90, 1151–1178.

Ho, C., Kingree, J. B., & Thompson, M. P. (2006). Associations between juvenile delinquency and weight-related variables: Analysis from a national sample of high school students. *International Journal of Eating Disorders*, 39, 477–483.

Hooks, B. (2000). *Feminist theory: From margin to center.* Cambridge, MA: South End Press.

Hubbard, D. J. & Matthews, B. (2008). Moving ahead: Five essential elements for working effectively with girls. *Journal of Criminal Justice*, 36, 494–502.

Kurlychek, M. C. & Johnson, B. D. (2004). The juvenile penalty: A comparison of juvenile and young adult sentencing outcomes in criminal court. *Criminology*, 42, 485–517.

Lahm, K. F. (2000). Equal or equitable: An exploration of education and vocational programs available for male and female offenders. *Federal Probation*, 66, 39–46.

Lundman, R. J. (2001). *Prevention and control of juvenile delinquency.* New York: Oxford University Press.

McCarthy, B., Hagan, J., & Woodward, T. S. (1999). In the company of women: Structure and agency in a revised power-control theory of gender and delinquency. *Criminology*, 37, 761–789.

Naffine, N. (1996). *Feminism and criminology.* Philadelphia: Temple University Press.

Odgers, C. L., Moretti, M. M., Burnette, M. L., Chauhan, P., Waite, D., & Reppucci, N. D. (2007). A latent variable modeling approach to identifying subtypes of serious and violent female juvenile offenders. *Aggressive Behavior,* 33, 339–352.

Platt, A. M. (1977). *The child savers: The invention of delinquency.* Chicago: University of Chicago Press.

Reaves, B. A. & Hickman, M. J. (2004). *Law enforcement management and administrative statistics, 2000: Data for individual state and local agencies with 100 or more officers.* Washington, DC: Department of Justice Programs, Bureau of Justice Statistics.

Rogers, K. (1972). "For her own protection . . .": Conditions of incarceration for female juvenile offenders in the state of connecticut. *Law and Society Review,* Winter, 223–246.

Tracy, P. E., Kempf-Leonard, K., & Ambramoske-James, S. (2009). Gender differences in delinquency and juvenile justice processing: Evidence from national data. *Crime and Delinquency*, 55, 171–215.

Vedder, C. B. & Somerville, D. B. (1970). *The delinquent girl.* Springfield, IL: Thomas.

Zahn, M. A., Day, J. D., Mihalic, S. F., & Tichavsky, L. (2009). Determining what works for girls in the juvenile justice system: A summary of evaluation evidence. *Crime and Delinquency,* 55, 266–293.

Zahn, M. A., Agnew, R., & Browne, A. (2009). Introduction. In M. A. Zahn (Ed.), *The delinquent girl* (pp. 1–6). Philadelphia: Temple University Press.

Zhang, D., Katsiyannis, A., Barrett, D. E., & Willson, V. (2007). Truancy offenders in the juvenile justice system: Examinations of first and second referrals. *Remedial and Special Education,* 28, 244–256.

Struggling to Find a Home

Patricia Leigh Brown (2013)

In the caverns of her memory, Tiffany Jackson recalls the job she held, fleetingly, after leaving the military, when she still wore stylish flats and blouses with butterfly collars and worked in a high-rise with a million-dollar view.

Two years later, she had descended into anger and alcohol and left her job. She started hanging out with people who were using cocaine and became an addict herself, huddling against the wind on Skid Row here.

"You feel helpless to stop it," she said of the cascade of events in which she went from having her own apartment to sleeping in seedy hotels and then, for a year, in the streets, where she joined the growing ranks of homeless female veterans.

Even as the Pentagon lifts the ban on women in combat roles, returning servicewomen are facing a battlefield of a different kind: they are now the fastest growing segment of the homeless population, an often-invisible group bouncing between sofa and air mattress, overnighting in public storage lockers, living in cars and learning to park inconspicuously on the outskirts of shopping centers to avoid the violence of the streets.

While male returnees become homeless largely because of substance abuse and mental illness, experts say that female veterans face those problems and more, including the search for family housing and an even harder time finding well-paying jobs. But a common pathway to homelessness for women, researchers and psychologists said, is military sexual trauma, or M.S.T., from assaults or harassment during their service, which can lead to post-traumatic stress disorder.

Sexual trauma set Ms. Jackson on her path. At first she thought she could put "the incident" behind her: that cool August evening outside Suwon Air Base in South Korea when, she said, a serviceman grabbed her by the throat in the ladies' room of a bar and savagely raped her on the urine-soaked floor. But during the seven years she drifted in and out of homelessness, she found she could not forget.

Of 141,000 veterans nationwide who spent at least one night in a shelter in 2011, nearly 10 percent were women, according to the latest figures available from the Department of Housing and Urban Development, up from 7.5 percent in 2009. In part it is a reflection of the changing nature of the American military, where women now constitute 14 percent of active-duty forces and 18 percent of the Army National Guard and the Reserves.

But female veterans also face a complex "web of vulnerability," said Dr. Donna L. Washington, a professor of medicine at U.C.L.A. and a physician at the West Los Angeles Veterans Affairs medical center, who has studied the ways the women become homeless, including poverty and military sexual trauma.

Female veterans are far more likely to be single parents than men. Yet more than 60 percent of transitional housing programs receiving grants from the Department of Veterans Affairs did not accept children, or restricted their age and number, according to a 2011 report by the Government Accountability Office.

The lack of jobs for female veterans also contributes to homelessness. Jennifer Cortez, 26, who excelled as an Army sergeant, training and mentoring other soldiers, has had difficulty finding work since leaving active duty in 2011. She wakes up on an air mattress on her mother's living room floor, beneath the 12 medals she garnered in eight years, including two tours in Iraq. Job listings at minimum wage leave her feeling bewildered. "You think, wow, really?" she said. "I served my country. So sweeping the floor is kind of hard."

Not wanting to burden her family, she has lived briefly in her car, the only personal space she has.

Some homeless veterans marshal boot-camp survival skills, like Nancy Mitchell, of Missouri, 53, an Army veteran who spent years, off and on, living in a tent.

"That's how we done it in basic," she said.

DOUBLE BETRAYAL OF ASSAULT

Of more than two dozen female veterans interviewed by *The New York Times*, 16 said that they had been sexually assaulted in the service, and another said that she had been stalked. A study by Dr. Washington and colleagues found that 53 percent of homeless female veterans had experienced military sexual trauma, and that many women entered the military to escape family conflict and abuse.

For those hoping to better their lives, being sexually assaulted while serving their country is "a double betrayal of trust," said Lori S. Katz, director of the Women's Health Clinic at the V.A. Long Beach Healthcare System and co-founder of Renew, an innovative treatment program for female veterans with M.S.T. Reverberations from such experiences often set off a downward spiral for women into alcohol and substance abuse, depression and domestic violence, she added.

"It just pulls the skin off you," said Patricia Goodman-Allen, a therapist in North Carolina and former Army Reserve officer who said she once retreated to a mobile home deep in the woods after such an assault.

Ms. Jackson won full disability compensation for post-traumatic stress as a disabling aftermath of her sexual trauma, although she was at first denied military benefits.

She grew up in a tough section of Compton, Calif., and served as a heavy equipment operator in the Army, exhilarated by her sense of mastery in a male-dominated environment. But after the rape—which she kept to herself, not even telling her family—her behavior changed. She assaulted a sergeant, resulting in disciplinary actions. Back home, she lost her job in sales after she passed out, drunk, during a business phone call. "It looked like I really had my stuff together," she said. "But I was dying inside."

She served three years in prison for drug dealing and finally confided in a prison psychiatrist, who helped her see that many of her bad decisions had been rooted in the sexual trauma.

"I realized I needed help," she says today, stable finally at 32 and snug in her mother's home in Palmdale, north of Los Angeles. "But to me breaking down was soft."

Her lawyer, Melissa Tyner, with the nonprofit Inner City Law Center here, said that many female veterans, like Ms. Jackson, associate the V.A. with a military that failed to protect them and thus forgo needed therapy. Other women who did not serve overseas said they did not realize they were veterans. "This makes them much less stable and therefore less likely to be housed," she said.

California, home to a quarter of the nation's veterans, is also home to a quarter of its homeless veterans. In Greater Los Angeles, a 2011 survey found 909 homeless women among them, a 50 percent increase since 2009.

Lauren Felber was one. Her decision to enter the military was a self-preservation instinct: she said she was molested by her father throughout her youth. "He's dead now," she said curtly. She thought the Army would make her strong.

When Ms. Felber returned, a debilitating complication from shingles made attempts to work, including bartending and construction jobs, painful. She became addicted to painkillers including methadone. Her welcome staying on friends' couches ran out, and she headed to Pershing Square, in downtown Los Angeles, resplendent with fountains and soaring palms. She slept on the steps. Sidewalk habitués schooled her on the ins and outs of free food. "On the street, everyone's hustling, selling something, even if it's friendship," she said.

Ms. Felber spent seven months in Rotary House, a shelter run by Volunteers of America. In her journal she wrote, "I walk the streets of Skid Row and see myself in the faces of the obsolete."

But life is finally on the upswing: she recently moved into an apartment through a program that provides permanent housing and other services, called Housing and Urban Development—Veterans Affairs Supportive Housing program, or HUD-Vash. Having a place of her own, Ms. Felber said, felt so unreal that she piled blankets and slept on the floor, as she had on the streets. But gradually, walking around the bare rooms, she felt "an overwhelming sense of awe and gratitude."

"I am fighting the fear of losing it," she added, "while I place each new item, making it a home."

FAMILY COMPLICATIONS

Returning veterans face a Catch-22: Congress authorized the V.A. to take care of them, but not their families. Women wait an average of four months to secure stable housing, leaving those with children at higher risk for homelessness. Monica Figueroa, 22, a former Army parachutist, lived in a family member's auto body shop in the Los Angeles area, bathing her baby, Alexander, in a sink used for oil and solvents until, with help, they found temporary housing.

Michelle Mathis, 30, a single mother of three, has bounced among seven temporary places since returning home in 2005 with a traumatic brain injury. Ms. Mathis, who served as a chemical specialist in Iraq, relies on a GPS device to help her remember the way to the grocery store and her children's school.

She said she did not feel safe in a shelter with her children, so they live in a room rented from a friend who is herself facing eviction. The only place Ms. Mathis said she truly felt at home was with fellow veterans at the V.A. medical center. Because she cannot afford child care, she sees her doctors with her year-old son Makai in tow.

Transitional housing has traditionally been in dormitory settings, which worked when returnees were mostly single men. But a March 2012 report by the Department of Veterans Affairs Office of Inspector General found bedrooms and bathrooms without locks.

Dr. Susan Angell, the executive director for Veterans Homeless Initiatives for the V.A., said that each site was individual and required a different approach, whether it meant putting up walls or installing card readers to beef up security. "There is no blanket solution," she said. "It has to fit the environment. We really want the best and safest environment for any veteran that comes to us for care."

Pledging to end veteran homelessness by 2015, the government is pouring millions of dollars into permanent voucher programs, like HUD-Vash, for the most chronically homeless veterans. Thirteen percent of those receiving vouchers are women, nearly a third of them with children, Dr. Angell said.

A newer V.A. program, with $300 million allocated by Congress, is aimed at prevention, providing short-term emergency money to help with down payments, utility bills and other issues. The government's motivation is financial as well as patriotic: the V.A. estimates that the cost of care for a homeless veteran, including hospitalizations and reimbursement for community-based shelters, is three times greater than for a housed veteran. A pilot project providing free drop-in child care is under way at three V.A. medical centers.

Senator Patty Murray, Democrat of Washington, a member of the Senate Veterans Affairs Committee, recently introduced legislation that would reimburse for child care in transitional housing for the first time.

AN EMOTIONAL BATTALION

But change in Washington can be glacial. And a sturdy roof is not always enough. On the outskirts of Long Beach, Calif., a national nonprofit group, U.S. Vets, created living quarters for at-risk families at Villages at Cabrillo, former naval housing, with a special program for homeless female veterans.

But the directors soon grew perplexed by the large number of women who were struggling to make it on their own.

"We began to understand that so many of them suffered from sexual trauma," said Steve Peck, the group's president and chief executive. "Their inability to cope with those feelings made it impossible for them to put one foot in front of the other."

The result was Renew, a collaboration with the V.A.'s Long Beach center. It incorporates psychotherapy, journal writing and yoga, and it accepts women who have been screened for military sexual trauma. Each class of a dozen women lives together for 12 weeks while spending eight-hour days at a women's mental health clinic, "where you can cry and not have to encounter a bunch of men with your mascara running," as Dr. Katz put it.

With Dr. Katz and other guides, the women formed an emotional battalion, squaring off against unseen enemies: fear, loneliness, distrust, anger and, most insidious of all, the hardened heart.

At the program's graduation in December, held in a therapy room, nine women spoke movingly of choosing strength over fragility. Cindi, an officer in the Air Force with a master's degree, said she had been bullied and ostracized by a female superior. After leaving the military, she had tumbled into a violent marriage and did not want her last name used for her own safety. She had been couch-surfing for a while.

She grew up in a household brimming with neglect. In her workbook, Cindi drew an image of water boiling on a stove, representing her traumas, more powerful than her self-regard.

After years of disappointment, Cindi was finally ready to forge new ground.

"I am more than the sum of my experiences," she read from her journal, seeming to evoke the story of every homeless veteran sister. "I am more than my past."

R E A D I N G **92**

First Morning in Exile

Aleksandra Djajic-Horváth

The first morning in exile
It all happened very quickly:
buying a plane ticket
going to the airport
a charter that was late
a three-hour flight.
And then—
a passport officer
confirms my identity
not exactly with goodwill and speed
(in my passport
destroyed cities lurk
and he simply cannot
so early in the morning
on an empty stomach . . .).

His well-fed sleepy fingers
hunt for me through the circuits
of the invisible powerful net
but my face does not appear—
I am still not on the list of those
who want to blow up the world
and after a long search
—resigned and tired
from the night shift
and last night's beer—
he lets me slip into
his blessed world
of short espresso
short memory
and long sound sleep.

DISCUSSION QUESTIONS FOR CHAPTER 11

1. How do governmental laws and policies maintain social inequality?

2. How does the early American assumption that citizens were white men perpetuate contemporary social inequities?

3. How do the failures of the U.S. military with regard to women soldiers reflect gendered assumptions and maintain a system of patriarchy within the military?

4. What myths about gender and race reinforce discrimination in the military, the welfare system, and the criminal justice system?

5. What would a truly just governmental system look like?

SUGGESTIONS FOR FURTHER READING

Burk, Martha. *Your Voice, Your Vote: The Savvy Women's Guide to Power, Politics, and the Change We Need.* Austin, TX: AU Publishing, 2012.

Enloe, Cynthia. *Globalization and Militarism: Feminists Make the Link.* Lanham, MD: Rowman & Littlefield, 2007.

Kaufman, Joyce, and Kristen Williams. *Women and War: Gender Identity and Activism in Times of Conflict.* Sterling, VA: Kumarian Press, 2010.

MacKinnon, Catharine. *Women's Lives, Men's Laws.* Cambridge, MA: Belknap Press, 2007.

Monahan, Evelyn, and Rosemary Neidel-Greenlee. *A Few Good Women: America's Military Women from World War I to the Wars in Iraq and Afghanistan.* New York: Knopf, 2010.

Murray, Rainbow, ed. *Cracking the Highest Glass Ceiling: A Global Comparison of Women's Campaigns for Executive Office.* Santa Barbara, CA: Praeger, 2010.

Sharpe, Gilly. *Offending Girls: Young Women and Youth Justice.* Abingdon, UK: Willan Publishing, 2010.

CHAPTER 12

Religion and Spirituality

Religion is a complex and complicating feature of women's lives. Although many women feel empowered by religion because it offers them a place of belonging, comfort, acceptance, and encouragement, others feel oppressed by religion because it excludes and sometimes degrades women. In this way, as this chapter will explore, religion remains a significant personal and political force in women's lives. Many of the social and cultural battles raging in American society are cast in religious terms—abortion, marriage equality, sex education, racial violence, domestic violence, to name a few—and many women organize their lives around their religious convictions.

The Southern Baptist controversy illustrates the experiences of many women in religious traditions. Throughout the 1980s and early 1990s, Southern Baptists, the nation's largest Protestant denomination with more than 14 million members, were embroiled in a controversy between fundamentalist and moderate leaders. The Baptist battles began over the issue of inerrancy (the notion that the Bible is without error in history, science, or doctrine) but quickly expanded to include, and then emphasize, social issues such as abortion, homosexuality, and the role of women in the home and church. As the fundamentalists grew in political power, they led the Southern Baptist Convention to pass resolutions excluding women from pastoral leadership in the churches and encouraging wives to submit to their husbands. Fundamentalist victory, however, did not come without a long, bitter conflict in which many women, particularly women in ministry, left the denomination. Other women decided to stay and focus their efforts on the autonomous local churches that carried on in the Baptist tradition of dissent, unbound by convention resolutions. Other women supported the denomination's stance and founded "women's studies" programs at the seminaries. These programs are anti-feminist and limit women's ministry to women and children.

Many moderate women became involved in alternative Baptist organizations that grew out of the controversy and promised women more visibility, opportunity, and support as seminary professors and denominational leaders. The women who found positions as seminary professors often faced resistance from students and misunderstanding from colleagues. Some became associate pastors in moderate Baptist churches, but very few were offered senior pastor positions. Women in the congregation heard the rhetoric of equality,

LEARNING ACTIVITY   **Women of Faith**

Interview three women who actively participate in a religious community. Ask about their experiences as women in their faith. Use the following questions or develop your own interview protocol.

- What is your religious community's stance on women's roles in home, society, and the religious community itself?
- What roles do women fulfill in your religious community?
- In what activities do you participate in your religious community?
- In what ways has your religious community been empowering for you as a woman? Has your religious community ever been oppressive to you as a woman?
- What do you gain by your participation in your religious community?
- How might your religious community better serve women?

Gather the data obtained by several other students in your class and examine your findings. Do you see any common themes arising from your interviews? What do your data suggest about these women's experiences in their faith communities? Can you make any generalizations from the data about how women experience religion as both empowering and oppressive?

but it came from the lips of the men who held the top positions in the churches and newly formed Baptist organizations. Women who were affirmed in their callings to pastoral ministry enrolled in new seminaries that offered little in the way of curricula focused on women.

The willingness of so many moderate Southern Baptist women to stay in Baptist churches despite the anti-woman actions of the Southern Baptist Convention indicates the powerful pull of religion. Even women who strongly opposed the policy of the Southern Baptist Convention often became active participants in other Christian denominations; few left Christianity entirely. This simultaneous push and pull of religion, as exemplified by the experience of Southern Baptist women, merits careful feminist analysis. As a force that can both oppress and empower, religion has a dramatic potential to work politically— either to continue women's oppression or to support women's liberation. Understanding this complex dynamic involves a close reading of the discourse of religion. As Ashley F. Miller points out in the reading, "The Non-Religious Patriarchy: Why Losing Religion Has Not Meant Losing White Male Dominance," the atheist movement in the United States has failed to support women and people of color even as it has critiqued religious subordination and oppression of those people.

RELIGION AS OPPRESSIVE TO WOMEN

Southern Baptists are not alone in Christianity, nor is Christianity alone in world religions, in functioning as an oppressive force to women. This section discusses four ways that religion as belief and institutional practice has helped subordinate women. First, central to religion's oppressive function is the premise of a divinely ordained order of creation in

IDEAS FOR ACTIVISM

- Invite a group of women pastors, ministers, priests, and rabbis to participate in a panel discussion of women in ministry.
- Organize a women's spirituality group.
- Organize an educational event to explore women in the world's religions. If possible, invite practitioners of various faiths to speak about women in their religious tradition.
- Investigate the official stance of your own religious tradition on women's roles and women's issues. Where there is room for improvement, write religious leaders to express your opinion.
- Organize an event to commemorate the women who died in the "burning times."

which females are deemed inferior and men not only are seen as superior to women but also closer to God. As discussed in the next section, gendered language about the deity reinforces male domination of women. The notion of women's inferiority is often supported by creation myths that embed woman's inferior status in the religious community's narrative of identity; these are the stories a religious community tells about itself in order to make itself known to both members and the outside community. For example, a common interpretation of the second Hebrew myth of creation (although feminist biblical scholars take issue with this interpretation) is that Eve is created after Adam because she is to serve him and be his subordinate. Later in the Christian testament, writers argue that woman's secondary status is a result of Eve's role as temptress in the fall of humanity. As Elizabeth Cady Stanton pointed out in the reading "Introduction to *The Woman's Bible*" over a hundred years ago, the Bible has most often been used to maintain the oppression of women by excluding them from particular roles in church, family, and society. This deep-seated misogyny also plays a significant role in the religious oppression of sexual minorities. To a great extent, religious prohibitions on same-sex relationships are about maintaining gender distinctions and gender roles in support of male domination. Same-sex relationships challenge these distinctions and roles by denying that there is an essential "male role" or "female role" in the home or in sexuality. This is especially disturbing in homosexual male relationships because of the shame that patriarchy associates with men being "used" like women or taking on stereotypically female roles in sexual relationships. In other words, the problem in the popular religious imagination is the association of gay male sex with the feminizing of men. To be a gay male is to be like a woman, and the worst thing for a man is to be like a woman.

Second, women's lower status is further maintained by excluding women from sacred rituals. Among the different world religions women have not been allowed to celebrate the Eucharist, pray in public, dance sacred dances, hear confession, make sacrifices, baptize, enter the holy of holies, read sacred scriptures aloud in public, preach, lead prayers, or teach men. One argument for the exclusion of women from priesthood has been that the priest stands as a representative of God, and a woman cannot represent God because she is female. The underlying assumption is that men are more Godlike than women. When worshippers see only men as representatives of God, it reinforces the notion that men are more Godlike, and women's exclusion continues.

LEARNING ACTIVITY   **That Old-Time TV Religion**

Watch several episodes of religious programming on television, such as the *700 Club* and two or three televised worship services. Who are the key personalities? What is their message? In the worship services, who is speaking? Who is singing? Who is leading? What messages about gender are conveyed, not only in the words themselves but also in the roles played by different people? What messages about race, class, sexual identity, and/or ability are conveyed? Do you think these shows are helpful to people? Why or why not? Are they helpful to women? Who do you think benefits from these shows? Are there ways in which these shows reinforce the subordination of women and other nondominant groups? Keep a log of your observations to share with your classmates.

Third, religions maintain women's oppression very directly through church laws that require wives to submit to their husbands, regulate women's sexuality, and create highly defined gender performances for women and men. For example, these laws may keep women in abusive relationships or prevent them from having access to birth control and/or abortion. Women may be told by church authorities that their role in the home is to be the support person for the husband and to submit to his divinely ordained authority in the home. Then, when abuse occurs, a woman may be told that she is to continue to submit because that is her role and that God will change her husband because of her obedience to God's commandments. The husband's abusive behavior then becomes the wife's responsibility because his changing is contingent upon her submission. This situation is exacerbated by a prohibition on divorce in some denominations, preventing women from permanently leaving abusive or dysfunctional marriages.

Finally, historically and currently, religions also exercise power over women through church- and state-sanctioned control. During its early years, Christianity taught a spiritual unity that integrated the oppressiveness of Roman laws and gave women some status in the church (although women's place was still subordinate and Jesus' teachings about equality did not manifest in the teachings and practices of the church). Some women found solace in devotional life of the convent where they could live a religious life as well as hold leadership positions and avoid the constraints of traditional femininity that included marriage and childbearing. In the "burning times" (between the eleventh and fourteenth centuries), tens of thousands of women in Europe were murdered as witches. For many of these women, "witchcraft" was simply the practice of traditional healing and spirituality and the refusal to profess Christianity. For other women, the charge of witchcraft had nothing to do with religious practices and everything to do with accusations rooted in jealousy, greed, and fear of female sexuality. But in the frenzy of the times, defending oneself against an accusation of witchcraft was practically impossible, and an accusation alone generally meant death. In 2012, the Vatican ordered a crackdown on the Leadership Conference of Women Religious, the umbrella organization for most nuns in the United States, for its "radical feminist" themes. Apparently, according to the Vatican, the nuns are putting too much emphasis on social justice issues such as poverty and hunger and not enough on moral issues such as abortion and homosexuality.

Other examples include the ways Christian imperialism has proved destructive for women and men of color and reinforced racism and ethnocentrism, despite the fact that in the Bible the Apostle Paul in his letter to the Galations said that in Jesus Christ there is "neither Jew nor Greek, slave nor free, male nor female," interpreted as everyone is equal in the sight of God and should be treated so. The genocide of Native Americans was conducted with the underlying belief that it was the God-given destiny of Europeans to conquer the native peoples of the Americas. Without understanding African cultures, Christian missionaries insisted that indigenous African peoples adopt Western ways. The legacy of Christian racism continued in the American South, where many Christians defended slavery based on their reading of scripture. Following Reconstruction, hate groups such as the Ku Klux Klan arose, calling for continued dominance by white, anglo Christians. This continues today with the messages of such groups as the Christian Identity Movement and the Aryan Nation (as well as the Klan). In Germany, thousands of Christians joined in Hitler's plan to build a master race and contributed directly to the genocide of 6 million Jews. In the 1950s and 1960s, while many Christians worked tirelessly for the civil rights movement and African American churches in particular became sites of resistance to racism, many others defended segregation and participated in acts of racial hatred. Only in 2000 did Bob Jones University, a fundamentalist institution of higher education in South Carolina, repeal its rule against interracial dating. Despite the many advances in the twentieth century, the twenty-first century began with the continuing problems of racism and intolerance by many who profess Christianity. It continues with an association between the executive branch of government and policies providing a conduit for structured inequalities. The reading "Feminist Questions of Christianity" by Caryn D. Riswold addresses a number of the difficult questions feminism raises for Christianity and examines why feminists should even care at all about Christianity.

In India, some Hindus believe self-immolation is the highest form of wifely devotion and leads to the spiritual salvation of a dead husband. The wife who commits *sati* by placing herself on the burning pyre with her husband's body is then revered as a goddess. While the practice was outlawed by British colonizers in the nineteenth century, around 40 cases of *sati* have been documented since Indian independence in 1947. While Indian feminists have argued against the practice, a number of women and men have argued that women should have the right to commit *sati*. Karen McCarthy Brown explains the story of Roop Kanwar, an 18-year-old woman who was burned alive on her husband's funeral pyre, as central in understanding fundamentalism in her essay titled "Fundamentalism and the Control of Women."

Currently the Religious Right, a political movement of religious conservatives in the United States that has received support from the political establishment, is attempting to exert control over women by influencing the U.S. legal system. Faith-based initiatives that provide government funds to religious institutions tend to blur the line between church and state, and often serve to reduce women's choice and autonomy. Religious influence on social policy has managed to chip away at abortion rights by convincing lawmakers to pass various restrictions on abortion. For many years, the Religious Right was also successful in preventing marriage equality for gay and lesbian couples, although recent gains have led Religious Right leaders to admit marriage equality seems likely to continue to move forward, despite their opposition. In mid-2013, leaders of Exodus International, an organization that attempted to make gay and lesbian Christians straight through prayer and reparative therapy, formally apologized for the damage it had done to gay and lesbian people and shut down the organization.

The reading by Morny Joy discusses the complicated intersections between religion and women's rights, and Nadja E. L. Norton's poem shows how religion compromises women's rights and calls on people to use their spirituality to bring about social change.

Sharia is the sacred law of Islam that has been interpreted and integrated into some societies (such as Iran and Saudi Arabia) in ways that control women's lives. However, modernist, traditionalist, and fundamentalist Muslims (and those within different geographic regions) differ in their interpretations and the scope they give sharia. Sharia deals with many public concerns addressed by secular law (such as economics) as well as personal and community issues that include family and sexuality. The Muslim practice of wearing the veil (*hijab*) presents an especially complex example of the simultaneously oppressive and empowering role of religion in women's lives. From the perspective of the global north, the practice of veiling is often viewed as absolutely oppressing. Although many Muslim women are critical of coercive practices associated with veiling, they also see choosing to wear the headscarf as an empowering practice of ethnic and cultural identity in the face of the influence of the global north. Muslim women often explain that they feel safer when veiled in public. The headscarf indicates that a woman is devout and virtuous, and therefore Muslim men will not objectify and sexualize a veiled woman. In fact, very often these women express sympathy for North American women, who must constantly fear sexual assault in public places. The headscarf, they claim, protects them and therefore allows them the freedom to move about publicly without fear, and, in some cases, it allows them to claim their identity and take a stand against the hegemonic forces of the imperialism of the global north. In this discussion it is important to recognize the differences between the teachings of the Quran and the interpretation of these teachings in some Muslim societies with the goal of keeping women subordinate to men. As the interview with Syafa Almirzanah explains in the reading "The Prophet's Daughters," Islam is not a monolithic religion. Rather, more conservative and more progressive Muslims, respectively, interpret the Quran in their different ways, and indeed more progressive Muslims interpret the Quran to promote women's value and equality.

RELIGION AS EMPOWERING TO WOMEN

Despite religion's long history of oppression, women have also experienced profound support, encouragement, and satisfaction in religion. This section focuses on those aspects of empowerment. First, for many women religion provides an environment in which they experience real community with other women. Women in traditional marriages who work in the home may find their only real social outlet in the church, mosque, or synagogue. Here they build connections with other women and participate in personally meaningful experiences in a community context.

Second, religion may provide women with opportunities for building and exercising leadership skills within religious organizations. Particularly for women in traditional families, this allows them to develop skills they might not learn otherwise. For example, although Southern Baptists have generally excluded women from pastoral leadership in the churches, Woman's Missionary Union (WMU), auxiliary to the Southern Baptist Convention, has provided thousands of women with the opportunity to become lay leaders in their churches, as well as in associational, state, and national WMU organizations. WMU is a missions education organization for women. In local church WMU organizations, women plan, budget, and implement programs for education and action. WMU curriculum materials teach young girls that they can do anything God calls them to do. The subversive power of this message is clear in talking to Southern Baptist women in ministry. Many of them report first experiencing their call to ministry in a WMU organization. Similarly, Catholic women have been empowered through convent experiences, in which they exercise leadership and enjoy community with other women.

Third, leadership within the church or religious organization may facilitate women's power within their local or regional communities as well as encourage their participation in various forms of social activism. For example, in Santeria, a Caribbean religion, women who are healers, or *santeras,* have great personal power and hold immense social power in their communities. These women willingly enter into altered states of consciousness and allow the spirits to use them to bring about healing. When a person visits a santera, the santera sees all the spirits with that person, and the santera is often able to reveal to the person what she or he needs to do. This ability puts the santera in an extremely powerful position, especially when the person consulting her is a politician or government official, as is often the case. Furthermore, as Caribbean women visit santeras, they see women who wield power in their culture and who can act as role models for them.

Another example of the role of religion in encouraging social activism is that of Jesse Daniel Ames, who helped organize the antilynching movement in the early part of the twentieth century. She worked through women's missions organizations in Methodist and

HISTORICAL MOMENT   **Becoming a Bishop**

Until 1984, no black woman had been elected bishop of a major religious denomination in the United States, but in that year, the Western Jurisdictional Conference of the United Methodist Church elected Leontine Kelly its first African American woman bishop and only the church's second female bishop.

Both Kelly's father and brother were Methodist ministers. Kelly married and had three children but divorced in the early 1950s. She remarried a Methodist minister in 1956 and returned to college to earn a bachelor's degree and become a social studies teacher. Kelly was drawn to preaching and became a certified lay preacher. When her husband died in 1969, she accepted the church's invitation for her to become pastor. She earned a master of divinity (MDiv) from Wesley Theological Seminary in 1976 and became an ordained minister in the Methodist Church. From 1977 to 1983 she was pastor of Asbury–Church Hill United Methodist Church in Richmond, Virginia, and then became assistant general secretary of evangelism for the United Methodist General Board of Discipleship.

Kelly's nomination to the post of bishop by a group of California clergywomen was not without controversy. Some thought her unfit for the position because she was a black woman. Others opposed her nomination because she was divorced. Nonetheless, she was elected and then named bishop for the San Francisco Bay area, making her the chief administrator and spiritual leader for more than 100,000 United Methodists in Northern California and Nevada. She remained at that post for 4 years until her retirement in 1988.

In the fall of 2000, the United Methodist Church elected three African American women as bishops, the first since Leontine Kelly: Violet Fisher, Linda Lee, and Beverly Shamana. Kelly commented, "I will always be the first African American woman bishop of the United Methodist Church, but praise God I am no longer the only."

Baptist churches in the South. Black churches were at the heart of the 1950s and 1960s civil rights movement in which many early leaders of second wave feminism had their first experiences of political organizing. A key component of Judaism is social justice, and Jewish women have long been actively involved in anti-defamation, anti-racist, anti-sexist, and anti-heterosexist work. Ernestine Louise Rose, who fought for women's rights and against slavery during the 1840s and 1850s, challenged New York state lawmakers in 1854 to allow women to retain their own property and have equal guardianship of children with their husbands. When male politicians urged women to postpone their quest for suffrage and focus on the rights of former slaves, Rose declared, "Emancipation from every kind of bondage is my principle." She also spoke out against anti-Semitism and set the tone for twentieth-century Jewish feminists' critique of Judaism's traditional attitudes toward women. More recently, feminist Mormon women have taken to the Internet as activists calling for social change. Websites include Feminist Mormon Housewives, Exponent, and Women Advocating for Voice and Equality (WAVE). Through their activism, these women seek to challenge the church's stances on feminist issues and reclaim the power they believe women held in earlier generations of Mormonism.

Finally, for many women, religion provides a place in which they find a sense of worth as a valued person. The poem "God Says Yes to Me" by Kaylin Haught illustrates an accepting, loving God that has the potential to empower women. In the early twenty-first century, many women participate in revivals of ancient woman-centered religions and have become empowered through the revaluing of the feminine implicit in this spirituality. *Wicca,* or witchcraft (although not the witches we popularly think of at Halloween), is a Goddess- and nature-oriented religion whose origins predate both Judaism and Christianity. Current Wiccan practice involves the celebration of the feminine, connection with nature, and the practice of healing. As Wiccan practitioner Starhawk suggests, witchcraft encourages women to be strong, confident, and independent and to love the Goddess, the earth, and other human beings. This notion of witchcraft is very different from the cultural norms associated with witches that are propagated in society.

WOMEN AND GOD-LANGUAGE

Many theorists contend that one of the most powerful influences in molding gender and maintaining gender oppression is language. The language religions use to talk about the divine is especially powerful in shaping the ways we think about men and women. Any language we use to talk about deities is of necessity metaphorical. We create images that can only partially represent the full reality of this concept. Unfortunately, those images sometimes become understood in literal rather than metaphorical ways. So, instead of thinking, for example, of God *as* Father, we may come to think God *is* Father. Throughout Jewish and Christian history, the preponderance of images for God have been masculine—Father, King, Lord, Judge, Master—and the effect has been that many people imagine God as male even though, intellectually, they might know this is not true. God is often imagined as white too.

In ancient times, the image of the Great Mother Goddess was primary in many cultures, but as war-centered patriarchal cultures developed, the life-giving Goddess had to be defeated by the warring God. In ancient Babylonian mythology, Tiamat was the Great Mother, but she was eventually slaughtered by her son Marduk, the God of war. Yahweh, the God of the ancient Israelites, was originally a consort of the Canaanite Mother Goddess, but, as the Israelites moved toward a patriarchal monotheism (belief in just one God), Yahweh became prominent as the Great Father God, and worship of the Goddess was harshly condemned by Yahweh's priests. The prominence of a single masculine image of deity then became reflected in the exclusion of women from the priesthood and eventually from the concept of Israel itself.

In response to the hegemony of masculine images of God, feminist theologians have constructed alternative feminine images of deity. Some theologians, such as Virginia Mollenkott, have returned to the Jewish and Christian testaments to point out the existence of feminine images within scripture. Other theologians, such as Sallie McFague, have challenged people to develop new models of God such as God as mother, God as lover, and God as companion. And yet other women have returned to the ancient images of the Goddess herself.

The political nature of the decision to challenge normative God-language does not go unnoticed by traditionalists wishing to cling to male images. The Southern Baptist

LEARNING ACTIVITY **How Well Do You Know the Goddess?**

Match the Goddess to her name.

_____ 1. Odudua

a. Egyptian mother Goddess and Goddess of the underworld, the queen of heaven and mother of light.

_____ 2. Coatlicue

b. "Queen of Heaven." Assyrian creator of life, mother and guardian. Goddess of fertility, love, sexuality, and justice.

_____ 3. Izanami-no-kami

c. Celtic creator of life. Mother Goddess of the earth and moon. The mother of all heroes or deities.

_____ 4. Demeter

d. Scandinavian creator of life. Leader of the Valkyries.

_____ 5. Tho-og

e. "Great, Invincible, and Magnificent Founder and Savior, Commander and Guide, Legislator and Queen." Creator and mother Goddess of Anatolia.

_____ 6. Kali

f. The mother of Hawaii. Mother and guardian, mother of Pele and the Hawaiian people.

_____ 7. Astarte

g. Creator of life who brings fertility and love. Goddess of the Yoruba people of Nigeria.

_____ 8. Kokyan Wuhti

h. Tibetan primordial being. The eternal mother who is self-formed. She is the preexisting space.

_____ 9. Freyja

i. "The Great Mother Goddess." Mesopotamian Goddess of justice, earth, nature, and goodness.

_____ 10. Haumea

j. Hindu Goddess. She who gives life and also destroys it. The symbol of eternal time.

_____ 11. Po Ino Nogar

k. "Spider Grandmother." Hopi creator of life. Beneficent deity who created humans, plants, and animals.

_____ 12. Hathor

l. "Serpent Skirt." Mother Goddess of all Aztec deities of Mexico, the ruler of life and death.

_____ 13. Anu

m. Greek mother and guardian. One of the twelve great Greek Olympian deities. She has power over the productivity of the earth and the social order of humans.

_____ 14. Asherah

n. "Female-Who-Invites." Japanese creator of life, earth and nature, heaven and hell.

_____ 15. Artemis Ephesus

o. "Great One." Vietnamese creator of life. World fertility Goddess who brings rice to the people and protects the fields and harvests.

Answers: 1. g; 2. l; 3. n; 4. m; 5. h; 6. j; 7. b; 8. k; 9. d; 10. f; 11. o; 12. a; 13. c; 14. i; 15. e

Source: Martha Ann and Dorothy Myers Imel, *Goddesses in World Mythology: A Biographical Dictionary* (New York: Oxford University Press, 1993).

LEARNING ACTIVITY   **Exploring New Metaphors for Deity**

Metaphors are images drawn from familiar human experiences, used in fresh ways to help explore realities that are not easily accessible in our everyday experience. All language about deity is metaphorical because no one image or analogy can capture the essence of deity. Throughout the history of Jewish and Christian faiths, in particular, deity has been variously imaged as Father, Shepherd, King, Lord, and Master. Originally, these metaphors helped many people explore and grapple with different aspects of the nature of deity. Many contemporary theologians, however, suggest the need for new metaphors for deity, shocking metaphors that will cause people to think about deity in new ways. Theologian Sallie McFague contends, "The best metaphors give both a shock and a shock of recognition." In good metaphors, we see something about reality, and we see it in new ways.

What are some of the metaphors for deity with which you are familiar? In what ways have those metaphors been helpful? In what ways are those metaphors limiting? What do you perceive as the consequences of taking these metaphors literally? Are there some metaphors you think have outlived their usefulness?

Following are a number of new metaphors for deity that are being utilized in current theological discussion. What do you think of these metaphors? In what new ways do they cause you to think about deity? What new ideas about deity do they suggest to you? In what ways do they call you to reappraise images of deity?

- God as mother
- God as lover
- God as companion
- God as gambler
- The earth as God's body

Can you think of any shocking new metaphors that help you think about deity in original ways?

Convention issued a statement declaring that God is not *like* a father, but God *is* Father. And a group of mainline churchwomen created a furor within their denominations when at a conference they chose to call God "Sophia," a biblical, but feminine, name for deity.

REINTERPRETING, RECONSTRUCTING, AND DECOLONIZING TRADITIONS

For those feminist women who have chosen to remain in religious traditions, the task of reworking oppressive elements has been great. Theology itself has been constructed with male experience as normative and has not taken into account the experiences of both men and women. Since the 1960s, feminist theologians have undertaken the task of rethinking traditional theological notions from the perspective of women's experiences. For example, the traditional notion of sin expressed in the story of the Fall in Genesis is that of pride and the centrality of the self. Redemption in the Christian testament then involves the restoration of what humans lack—sacrificial love. Yet the normative experience for women is not pride and self-centeredness, given that women are generally socialized to be self-negating for the sake of their families, and, in fact, encouraging women to be self-sacrificing as a form of redemption simply exacerbates women's situation. Feminist theology, as Alicia Ostriker suggests in her poem "Everywoman Her Own Theology," brings women's experiences to the center and reconstructs theological concepts in keeping with those experiences.

Because of the predominance of Christianity in the United States, the Bible and its various interpretations play a large role in shaping women's lives. Given this importance, feminist re-examinations of religion are on a continuum from reinterpretation to reconstruction. *Reinterpretation* involves recognizing the passages that are particularly problematic for women and highlighting and reintegrating the passages that extol equality between women and men. Proponents of such reinterpretation include Christian feminists who maintain a positive view of scripture as they continue to accept scripture as an authority in their lives. The goal of *reconstruction,* however, is to move beyond reinterpretation and recognize the patriarchal underpinnings of various interpretations and the ways they have been used to oppress women.

As an example of a reconstructionist account, Christian testament scholar Elisabeth Schüssler Fiorenza encourages readers of scripture to look for the presence of women in the margins and around the edges of the text. She calls for biblical readers to re-create the narratives of women that were left out of (but hinted at) in the text. In a similar fashion,

". . . and so, then I said, 'You think that just because I'm a woman I can't preach, just because I'm a woman I can't hold office in the convention, just because I'm a woman I can't do evangelism, just because I'm a woman I can't teach theology!' And he said, 'Yes.'"

Reprinted with permission from Norma Young.

ACTIVIST PROFILE   **Nannie Helen Burroughs**

Nannie Helen Burroughs was only 21 years old when she delivered her stirring speech, "How the Sisters Are Hindered from Helping," at the 1900 National Baptist Convention in Richmond, Virginia. This speech proved to be instrumental in the formation of the Women's Convention Auxiliary to the National Baptist Convention, the largest African American women's organization in the country at that time. The Women's Convention promptly elected Burroughs its corresponding secretary and continued to re-elect her every year from 1900 to 1948. In 1948 she became the convention's president and served in that role until her death in 1961.

Burroughs was also a tireless activist—challenging lynching and segregation, denouncing employment discrimination, opposing European colonization of Africa, and promoting women's suffrage. After the Nineteenth Amendment was passed, she founded the National League of Republican Colored Women and worked to encourage African American women to become politically involved. She also established the Women's Industrial Club, which offered short-term housing to African American women and taught them basic domestic skills. The club also offered moderately priced lunches for downtown office workers. During the Depression, Burroughs formed Cooperative Industrial, Inc., which provided free facilities for a medical clinic, hair salon, and variety store.

One of Burroughs's driving passions was the education of African American women. In 1909, with the support of the National Baptist Convention, she opened the National Trade and Professional School for Women and Girls in Washington, D.C., and served as the institution's president. The school emphasized a close connection between education and religion. Its curriculum focused on the development of practical and professional skills and included a program in black history in which every student was required to take a course. Burroughs's motto for the school was "We specialize in the wholly impossible." In 1964 the school was renamed the Nannie Burroughs School. In 1975 Mayor Walter E. Washington proclaimed May 10 Nannie Helen Burroughs Day in the District of Columbia in recognition of Burroughs's courage in advocating for education for African American women despite societal norms.

the reading "Standing Again at Sinai" by Jewish feminist scholar Judith Plaskow calls for a reconceptualization of notions of God, Torah, and Israel that are inclusive of women. Other reconstructions of scripture include "womanist" biblical interpretations of women of color that analyze the Bible in light of both sexism and racism. In these accounts the Bible itself is subject to scrutiny in terms of its expressions of justice and injustice. Readers of the Bible with this perspective focus on the moral and ethical imperatives of justice contained therein and with an eye toward struggle for liberation for women of color.

Women have begun to challenge and reconstruct religious traditions as well as scripture. For example, Jewish women have developed feminist haggadahs, texts containing the ritual for celebrating the Passover seder. These feminist haggadahs commemorate the women of the Exodus, the liberation of the Israelites from slavery in Egypt. In one haggadah, the four sons of the traditional ceremony become four daughters, and the lives of the women celebrating Passover are inserted in the ceremony to create a living history and a new story.

Perhaps one of the most contentious reconstructions of religious traditions is the ordination of women. Although feminist church historians have recovered a long tradition of women as rabbis, priests, pastors, bishops, and evangelists, most Christian denominations did not ordain women until the latter part of the twentieth century. Many still do not. One exception to this is the Quakers, who have a long and unique history of women's equality in the congregation. Although Quakers do not ordain anyone, some groups of Quakers do record ministers, and women have always been among the recorded. In silent Quaker meetings, women as well as men are assumed to be able to receive and speak a word from God. Beginning in the 1960s, many mainline Protestant churches began to ordain women ministers, although men still make up the larger percentage of senior pastors in almost every denomination. The Episcopal church elected The Most Rev. Dr. Katharine Jefferts Schori as its presiding bishop in 2006. Roman Catholics still prohibit women from becoming priests, although there is a growing movement within Catholicism, particularly American Catholicism, to change this policy. The Church of England first ordained women as priests in 1994, but the Church voted in 2012 to continue its exclusion of women as bishops. Several churches, such as the United Church of Christ, the Unitarian Universalist Association, and the Episcopal Church, ordain openly gay and lesbian clergy, although in the case of the Episcopal church, this has caused tension between churches in the worldwide Anglican fellowship inside and outside the United States because many of the latter resist such ordination of gay clergy. In 2004, the church invested the Right Reverend V. Gene Robinson, an out gay man, bishop of the diocese of New Hampshire and in 2010 consecrated The Right Reverend Mary Douglas Glasspool as its first openly lesbian bishop.

Particularly for women in the global south and women of color in the United States, neither reinterpreting nor reconstructing go far enough in examining and challenging the colonial underpinnings of religious traditions. Postcolonial feminist theologians confront and call out the legacies of empire in religious texts and practices and the ways religions have been used as colonizing influences. For example, writers such as Musa Dube of Botswana point to colonial beliefs in "God, gold, and glory" as intersecting theological and economic supports for the conquest of Africa and its subsequent pillaging by colonizers. In the reading "Decolonizing Religious Beliefs," Sylvia Marcos examines how indigenous women in Latin America have begun to develop their own spirituality, recapturing older religious traditions as a way to "decolonize" themselves from the influences of the religious traditions their people were forced to adopt during the colonial period.

Islamic feminists seek to recover the Qur'anic tradition of gender equality. They argue that patriarchy is not inherent in the religion but is a result of the ways patriarchal contexts and histories have taken precedence in Qur'anic interpretation. They also note that until recently Qur'anic interpretation had only been done by men. The goal of Qur'anic interpretation, they say, is to identify the unchanging principle in the text and implement it in the present. In so doing, they explain, Islamic feminists will recover Islam's foundational gender equality.

CREATING NEW SPIRITUAL TRADITIONS

Although some feminists believe in the reinterpretation and reconstruction of scriptures and choose to work within existing denominations, others prefer to create their own empowering religious texts and organizations. For some, traditional religious scriptures are so essentially androcentric, or male centered, that they can reproduce only patriarchal social relations. They see no possibility of liberation for women in scripture because even reconstruction of biblical texts cannot change the patriarchal core of, for example, the Bible. Rather, these reconstructions simply perpetuate the patriarchal order. Feminist philosopher Mary Daly argued that patriarchal language is not accidental or incidental to the Bible but is an essential element of it, rendering the Bible useless in the liberation of women. Women such as Daly look beyond traditional scripture for spiritual insight and understanding. Wiccan groups, discussed previously, fall into this category too.

In this way, although many women have expressed their spirituality within formal religious traditions, many others have created new forms of spiritual expression outside churches, synagogues, and mosques. Women's spirituality is an empowering force that has taken such various forms as meditation, poetry, art, prayer, ritual, and social action. Spirituality enables women to experience connection with creation, with other human beings, and with the divine within themselves.

For many feminists, spirituality is a central force in their politics. The awareness of the interconnectedness of all things motivates feminist action toward justice and peace and encourages women to work together across differences. Nature-based spiritualities affirm the connections among all living things and seek to protect the natural environment on which we all depend. Feminist spirituality values and affirms the diversity that makes up the unity of creation, and it challenges women to restructure the systems of power that create and maintain injustice. As feminist author Marge Piercy writes:

> Praise our choices, sisters, for each doorway
> open to us was taken by squads of fighting
> women who paid years of trouble and struggle,
> who paid their wombs, their sleep, their lives
> that we might walk through these gates upright.
> Doorways are sacred to women for we
> are the doorways of life and we must choose
> what comes in and what goes out. Freedom
> is our real abundance.*

---

* "The sabbath of mutual respect," *The Moon Is Always Female* (New York: Knopf, 1980).

Introduction to *The Woman's Bible*

Elizabeth Cady Stanton (1895)

From the inauguration of the movement for woman's emancipation the Bible has been used to hold [woman] in the "divinely ordained sphere," prescribed in the Old and New Testaments.

The canon and civil law; church and state; priests and legislators; all political parties and religious denominations have alike taught that woman was made after man, of man, and for man, an inferior being, subject to man. Creeds, codes, Scriptures and statutes, are all based on this idea. The fashions, forms, ceremonies and customs of society, church ordinances and discipline all grow out of this idea.

. . .

The Bible teaches that woman brought sin and death into the world, that she precipitated the fall of the race, that she was arraigned before the judgment seat of Heaven, tried, condemned and sentenced. Marriage for her was to be a condition of bondage, maternity a period of suffering and anguish, and in silence and subjection, she was to play the role of a dependent on man's bounty for all her material wants, and for all the information she might desire on the vital questions of the hour, she was commanded to ask her husband at home. Here is the Bible position of woman briefly summed up.

. . .

These familiar texts are quoted by clergymen in their pulpits, by statesmen in the halls of legislation, by lawyers in the courts, and are echoed by the press of all civilized nations, and accepted by woman herself as "The Word of God." So perverted is the religious element in her nature, that with faith and works she is the chief support of the church and clergy; the very powers that make her emancipation impossible. When, in the early part of the Nineteenth Century, women began to protest against their civil and political degradation, they were referred to the Bible for an answer. When they protested against their unequal position in the church, they were referred to the Bible for an answer.

This led to a general and critical study of the Scriptures. Some, having made a fetish of these books and believing them to be the veritable "Word of God," with liberal translations, interpretations, allegories and symbols, glossed over the most objectionable features of the various books and clung to them as divinely inspired. Others, seeing the family resemblance between the Mosaic code, the canon law, and the old English common law, came to the conclusion that all alike emanated from the same source; wholly human in their origin and inspired by the natural love of domination in the historians. Others, bewildered with their doubts and fears, came to no conclusion. While their clergymen told them on the one hand that they owed all the blessings and freedom they enjoyed to the Bible, on the other, they said it clearly marked out their circumscribed sphere of action: that the demands for political and civil rights were irreligious, dangerous to the stability of the home, the state and the church. Clerical appeals were circulated from time to time conjuring members of their churches to take no part in the anti-slavery or woman suffrage movements, as they were infidel in their tendencies, undermining the very foundations of society. No wonder the majority of women stood still, and with bowed heads, accepted the situation.

God Says Yes to Me

Kaylin Haught (1995)

I asked God if it was okay to be melodramatic
and she said yes
I asked her if it was okay to be short
and she said it sure is
I asked her if I could wear nail polish
or not wear nail polish
and she said honey
she calls me that sometimes
she said you can do just exactly

what you want to
Thanks God I said
And is it even okay if I don't paragraph
my letters
Sweetcakes God said
who knows where she picked that up
what I'm telling you is
Yes Yes Yes

Fundamentalism and the Control of Women

Karen McCarthy Brown (1994)

Religious fundamentalism is very difficult to define; yet many of us—scholars and journalists in particular—think we know it when we see it. For those attuned to gender as a category of analysis, a stab of recognition is often occasioned by the presence of high degrees of religiously sanctioned control of women. In conservative religious movements around the world, women are veiled or otherwise covered; confined to the home or in some other way strictly limited in their access to the public sphere; prohibited from testifying in a court of law, owning property, or initiating divorce; and they are very often denied the authority to make their own reproductive choices.

I propose to take up the thread of the control of women and follow it into the center of the maze of contemporary fundamentalism. Yet I will not argue, as might be expected, that the need to control women is the main motivation for the rise of fundamentalism, but rather that aggravation of this age-old, widespread need is an inevitable side effect of a type of stress peculiar to our age.

I will suggest that the varieties of fundamentalism found throughout the world today are extreme responses to the failed promise of Enlightenment rationalism. Fundamentalism, in my view, is the religion of the stressed and the disoriented, of those for whom the world is overwhelming. More to the point, it is the religion of those at once seduced and betrayed by the promise that we human beings can comprehend and control our world. Bitterly disappointed by the politics of rationalized bureaucracies, the limitations of science, and the perversions of industrialization, fundamentalists seek to reject the modern world, while nevertheless holding onto its habits of mind: clarity, certitude, and control. Given these habits, fundamentalists necessarily operate with a limited view of human activity (including religious activity), one confined largely to consciousness and choice. They deny the power of those parts of the human psyche that are inaccessible to consciousness yet play a central role in orienting us in the world. Most of all they seek to control the fearsome, mute power of the flesh. This characteristic ensures that fundamentalism will always involve the control of women, for women generally carry the greater burden of human fleshliness.

This essay is an exploratory one. Its topic is huge and it ranges widely, crossing over into several academic disciplines other than my own. Occasionally I am forced to paint with a broad stroke and a quick hand. Writing that is preliminary and suggestive can be risky, but the connections I see between religious fundamentalism and other, larger aspects of our contemporary world seem compelling enough to lead me to take that risk. My argument begins close to home, in the United States, with Christian anti-abortion activism.

THE ANTI-ABORTION MOVEMENT IN THE UNITED STATES

The "pro-life movement" emerged in the 1970s as a new type of religio-political organization. It was a bottom-up movement that used sophisticated, top-down technology. In the early stages of the movement, the organizing work was done around kitchen tables. But the envelopes stuffed at those tables were sent to addresses on computer-generated mailing lists, the product of advanced market-research techniques. This blend of grass-roots organization and advanced technology quickly brought a minority movement[1] to a position of significant political power. The combination of traditional and modern methods also reveals an ambivalence toward the ways of the modern world that I will later argue is characteristic of fundamentalist movements.

Many observers have noted an inconsistency in the pro-life position. The very groups who launch an emotional defense of the fetus's right to life are curiously indifferent to children outside the womb. As a rule, pro-lifers do not support social programs focused on issues such as child abuse, day care, foster care, or juvenile drug use. They oppose

welfare programs in general and have taken no leadership in educational reform beyond concern with sex education, public school prayer, and the theory of evolution. Furthermore, their so-called pro-life argument is deeply compromised by staunch support for increased military spending and for the death penalty. It seems clear that the pro-life position is not a consistent theological or philosophical stance. A quite different kind of consistency emerges from the full range of this group's social policy positions. Their overriding concern is that of maintaining strong and clear social boundaries—boundaries between nation-states, between law-abiding citizens and criminals, between the righteous and the sinful, between life and death, and not coincidentally, between men and women. This is a group centrally concerned with social order and social control.

Beyond the trigger of the 1973 Supreme Court decision in *Roe v. Wade,* stresses with a broader historical range have contributed to a focus on boundary maintenance in the anti-abortion movement. The upheavals of the 1960s created the immediate historical context of the anti-abortion movement of the 1970s. Student activists of the 1960s questioned the authority of parents, educators, and politicians. Black activists challenged the cherished American myths of equal opportunity and equal protection under the law. And the Vietnam War not only raised questions about U.S. military prowess but also planted doubts about the moral valence of the international presence and policy of the United States. These are very specific reasons why Americans in the 1970s might have felt that the social and moral orders were becoming dangerously befuddled.

. . .

A WORLD SUDDENLY TOO BIG

From the mid-nineteenth century into the early decades of the twentieth, the writings of travelers, missionaries, and, eventually, anthropologists were popular bedside reading materials in the United States. Americans were fascinated by exotic "others." They were concerned about their own place in this expanding, newly complex world. Most of these books did more than titillate. With their implicit or explicit social Darwinism, they also carried deeply comforting messages of progress and of Western superiority. Such messages, coming from many sources, infused an air of optimism into an otherwise disorienting age. During the same general time span, the seeds of American fundamentalism were sown and came to fruition.

Some of the social forces that shaped this period—expanding knowledge of and contact with the larger world, and increased communication—had emerged over a relatively long period of time. Others, such as the burgeoning of cities, the dramatic increase in immigrant populations, and a series of shifts in women's roles, had occurred more recently.[2] All of these forces came together in the second half of the nineteenth century to contribute to a general sense of vertigo; the world was becoming too big, too complicated, and too chaotic to comprehend. Most important, each individual's own place in it was uncertain. Religion, given its basic orientational role in human life, emerged as a natural arena for dealing with the resulting stress.

From that period until this in the United States, conservative Christians have come under a double attack. On one level, they have had to deal with the general stress of the times; and on the other, with the direct challenge of Enlightenment rationalism in the form of biblical higher criticism and evolutionary theory. The reaction of some groups of Christians has been ironic: they have responded to the threat by mimicking Enlightenment rationalism. The religion-versus-science debate pits against one another groups who share a common intellectual style: each claims to possess the truth. Believers, like rationalists, stress consciousness, clarity, and control.[3] Morality is codified; sacred narratives are taken literally and sometimes attempts are made to support them with "scientific evidence"; all sorts of truths are listed and enumerated; scripture becomes inerrant. Furthermore, conscious consent to membership in the community of belief, on the model of "making a decision for Christ," becomes increasingly important.

These are the religious groups we call fundamentalists. Their central aim is to make of their religion an Archimedean point in the midst of a changing world. But to do so, they must limit their religion's responsiveness to its social environment; and as a result they are left with little flexibility to respond to the complexity of their own feelings or to the challenge of a changing world. Sometimes they fall into aggressively defending brittle truths. This is what makes fundamentalism in the contemporary world problematic and, in some cases, dangerous.

. . .

FUNDAMENTALISM CROSS-CULTURALLY

Up to this point, I have been concerned with Christian fundamentalism in the United States, but in the process I have focused on dimensions of the story that serve, without denying the significance of local variations, to characterize fundamentalism around the globe. Religious fundamentalism is born in times and places where, for a variety of reasons, the world suddenly seems too complex to comprehend; and one's place in it, too precarious to provide genuine security.

One example is modern India, where the cult that developed around the recent immolation of a young woman on her husband's funeral pyre has been described as an instance of fundamentalism. John Hawley demonstrates that the background for the *sati* of Roop Kanwar was emerging Hindu nationalism in India augmented by a multitude of local destabilizing forces in Deorala, the site of the immolation. Furthermore, as Hawley and other authors have pointed out, Deorala is not a truly deprived area, and its residents are not traditionalists out of contact with the larger realities of modern India. I would therefore suggest, along with Hawley, that fundamentalism is not primarily a religion of the marginalized, as some have argued. Its more salient feature is that it develops among people caught off balance. Hence, fundamentalist groups often arise in situations where social, cultural, and economic power is up for grabs; many, like these groups now being referred to as Hindu fundamentalists, arise in postcolonial situations. Far from being essentially marginal to the societies in which they exist, fundamentalists are often directly involved in the political and economic issues of their time and place. And they often have a significant, if precarious, stake in them.

For the Rajputs in Deorala, traditional sources of pride and authority are being challenged by increasing contact with the cities of Jaipur and Delhi, and through them, all of India. These Rajputs are experiencing the disorientation of having to depend on economic and political systems beyond their control. Marwari merchants and industrialists, financial backers of the cult of the goddess Sati, are destabilized in another way. As their economic role expands throughout India, they risk their livelihood in a wider, less familiar, and less predictable world than the one in which earlier generations operated. The Marwari focus on the district around Jhunjhunu with its important Sati shrine gives them their emotionally saturated Archimedean point. The case of the Marwari businessmen suggests, even more directly than does that of the Rajputs, that fundamentalism is not a religion of the marginalized, but of the disoriented.

In the contemporary Indian context, rallying around the *sati* of Roop Kanwar (like anti-abortion activity in the United States) reasserts social control and demonstrates moral worth. It strengthens gender boundaries and provides an example of undiluted, innocent virtue that vicariously underwrites the virtue of Rajputs and Marwaris in general. Furthermore, as in the United States, insecurity about social control and moral rectitude is displaced onto the body of a woman. But in the *sati* ritual described by Hawley, the drive to kill the devouring, fleshly goddess and to enshrine the pure, spiritual one is much more painfully literal.

Both men and women attended the *sati* of Roop Kanwar, and both men and women subsequently revere her. At first glance this may seem difficult to understand, but the complicity of Indian women in the practice of *sati* has to be considered on more than one level. At the deepest level its explanation lies in the fear of women's will and women's flesh that men and women share, and in the relief that both feel when these forces are kept in check. But on another level there are explanations of a much more practical nature. Most Indian women's economic security heavily depends on marriage. A woman doing homage at a Sati shrine thus signals to her husband and to the world at large, as well as to herself, that she intends to be good and to do good, according to her society's standards. Thus she chooses to ignore any anger or fear she might feel about the practice, in the name of living a secure and ordered life. It is a herculean task for women to try to define the meaning and worth of their lives in terms different from those that prevail in their community. So some security can always be found in surrendering to, and even helping to strengthen, the accepted gender norms.

. . .

THE FAILED PROMISE OF ENLIGHTENMENT RATIONALISM

Modern communications, transnational economic pressures, and wars waged from the opposite side of the globe have brought many populations intimate knowledge of the vastness and complexity of their worlds. In the late twentieth century, the others in relation to whom we must define ourselves are more available to our experience and imagination than ever before; yet few if any of us have a satisfactory model for understanding ourselves within this complex, stressful world.

We all live in and are defined by a world too big and unstable for intellect or belief to comprehend, and we all react to intimations—as well as a few pieces of hard evidence[4]—of the failed promise of the Enlightenment. Academics, politicians, and ordinary folk the world over are immersed in this challenge and most commonly react to it (as fundamentalists do) by assuming that, with sufficient effort, the chaos can be first comprehended and then managed. In this way fundamentalists are simply extreme versions of the rest of us.

An emphasis on the control of women is characteristic of fundamentalism, but there is some of it everywhere in the world. The anti-abortion movement in the United States arises out of a much broader context in which, among other signals of misogyny, public power and authority have been denied to women for centuries. And the Sati cult could not have become an issue in Indian nationalism if in general Indian women were not seen as sources of pollution as well as of blessing—as a result of which they have been subject to a variety of social controls through the ages. When the mind and the spirit are cut off from the body, women become magnets for the fear raised by everything in life that seems out of control. The degree to which control is exercised over women is therefore a key to the profundity of stresses felt by most persons and groups. Fundamentalism is a product of extreme social stress.

Religion, whose primary function is to provide a comprehensible model of the world and to locate the individual safely and meaningfully within it, is an obvious place for this type of stress to express itself and seek redress. But as long as religions deal with this stress by positing a world that can be directly known, and in which it is possible to determine one's own fate, they only reinforce the controlling tendencies of Enlightenment rationalism and do nothing to move us beyond it to whatever comes next. We should be suspicious of any religion that claims too much certainty or draws the social boundaries too firmly. In this period marked by the gradual breakdown of Enlightenment rationalism and Euro-American hegemony in the world, something more is necessary. We need help in accepting ourselves as organic creatures enmeshed in our world rather than continuing to posture as cerebral masters granted dominion over it. This requires that we learn to trust the wisdom of our mute flesh and accept the limitations inherent in our humanity. If we could do this, it would radically diminish our scapegoating of women and all the other "others" who provide a convenient screen on which to project fears.

The resurgence of religion that we are experiencing at the turn of this millennium should not be viewed in an entirely negative light. If any system of orientation in the world can help us now, it seems likely to be a religious one. There is no small comfort in knowing that, as the grand ambitions spawned by the Enlightenment falter in the present age, what is likely to emerge is not what several generations of social scientists predicted. It is not civilization marching toward increasing secularization and rationalization. What is slowly being revealed is the hubris of reason's pretense in trying to take over religion's role.

NOTES

1. From the beginning of the anti-abortion movement to the present, opinion polls have consistently shown that the majority of people in the United States favor a woman's right to have an abortion.

2. Betty A. DeBerg, *Ungodly Women: Gender and the First Wave of American Fundamentalism* (Minneapolis: Fortress Press, 1990), has an excellent discussion of the general changes—and particularly the changes in women's roles—attendant to the formation of fundamentalism in the United States. . . .

3. Often the only kind of control that fundamentalists can exercise over a chaotic and threatening world rests in their claim to have a privileged understanding of the deeper meaning of the chaos. Fundamentalists who engage in "end-time" thinking thus sometimes find themselves in the position of welcoming the signs of modern social decay because these signal the approach of the time when God will call home the chosen few.

4. The growing ecological crisis is one of the most tangible pieces of this evidence; it also reinforces the point that reason alone is an insufficient problem-solving tool, because we are incapable of holding in consciousness the full range of the interconnectedness of things.

R E A D I N G   96

Women's Rights and Religion

Morny Joy (2013)

FUNDAMENTALISMS AND WOMEN'S RIGHTS

This article can be only a brief introductory survey of the fundamentalist challenge to the marked progress in women's rights as it evolved in the second half of the twentieth century.[1] At the Beijing World Conference on Women (1995), organized with the support of the United Nations (UN), women's gains in rights were consolidated, despite a highly organized opposition. Amrita Basu adds a sobering comment of the manner in which a fundamentalist coalition acted to prevent further progress.

Parallel to the evolution of transnational women's movements, and equally important, has been the phenomenal growth of transnational networks of the religious right. We saw this in the 1994 Cairo conference on population and development, and again in the Beijing [women's] conference of 1995. In both these contexts one found a thoroughly transnational alliance of groups on the religious right, not only official organizations but also members of non-state organizations, including religious bodies like the Catholic Church.[2]

Judith Butler describes her astonishment when she learned of the maneuverings on the part of the Vatican in the lead-up to the Beijing Women's Conference. "The Vatican not only denounced the term 'gender' as a code for homosexuality, but insisted that the platform language return to using the notion of sex in an apparent effort to secure a link between femininity and maternity as a naturally and divinely ordained necessity."[3] Joan Scott, an American historian and gender theorist, also reports on another occurrence in the United States around the same time, when a subcommittee of the US House of Representatives entertained submissions that warned morality and family values were under attack by "gender feminists."[4] Both the Vatican and fundamentalist Christian religious groups in the United States had seemingly been informed of Butler's work questioning traditional gender roles in her book *Gender Trouble*.[5] In their depiction of this threatening situation, the opponents of "gender" insisted that "gender feminists" regarded manhood and womanhood, motherhood and fatherhood, heterosexuality, marriage, and family as "culturally created, and originated by men to oppress women."[6] The Vatican's machinations, in which it collaborated with known global fundamentalist movements, did not work.[7] The UN did achieve consensus on language and documents retained the term *gender*,[8] as well as reiterating its commitment to women's rights, especially in relation to sexuality and reproduction. The interventions by a fundamentalist coalition and the Vatican at the UN conference, however, marked the beginning of concerted activity to thwart the further passing of progressive motions/conventions.

Courtney Howland is forthright about the challenge this presents, noting that "religious fundamentalism is premised on the notion that religious law takes precedence over all other law and defines, inter alia, relations between different religions and between men and women. Thus some states have argued, in the context of human rights treaties, that religious law takes precedence over international human rights law even when the state has not entered reservations to the treaty on this basis."[9] Such have been the subsequent negative effects of this well-organized lobby that a number of activists have contemplated abandoning the UN as an effective agency for implementing resolutions for women's rights.[10] In this context, religion and rights remain adamantly opposed, with certain conservative forces remaining most vehement in their objections.

FURTHER COMPLICATIONS

In addition to the opposition to rights from fundamentalist interests, rights have come under attack from postcolonial theorists and critical theorists. Both share similar positions regarding what they view as a prevalent form of essentialism intrinsic to the human rights platform. They also take issue with the Western categories and ideals they view as being imposed unilaterally.

Speaking from a postcolonial and critical perspective, Inderpal Grewal has strong reservations about the human rights project. First, she views the whole rights undertaking as dependent on a Western linear view of progress. "Human rights is . . . based on linear notions of progress by relying on notions of the South as Other and utilizing North/South inequalities to claim that the North has human rights (with a few aberrations) and the South needs to achieve them."[11] In this connection, Grewal also lambasts the assumed "moral superiority" of US global feminism in its operations to save the abused women of the world, disregarding the obvious faults in their own country where rights are concerned.[12]

Grewal charges that the language of women's rights is based on a Western understanding of the individual as the subject of human rights. "The hegemonic forms of Western feminisms [with their emphasis on individual rights] have been able, through universalizing discourses, to propose the notion of common agendas for all women globally, and to mobilize such discourses through the transnational culture of international law that can serve the interests of women globally."[13] This presumes a commonality among all women, so that local political and social anomalies of a structural or institutional nature are overlooked.[14] Finally, Grewal laments that, in some countries, the institutions or agencies to which women must appeal for redress are the very bodies that are responsible for the activities that have violated their rights. This alone would seem to defeat the actual purpose of the exercise.

As a remedial measure, Grewal recommends an approach that pays attention to regional contexts, in particular the socioeconomic, political, and cultural conditions that are inevitably interrelated in unique combinations in each locale. As a result, human rights and their violations can never be solely defined or implemented by a Northern-generated model—or by any unreconstructed universal formula, for that matter. Nonetheless, Grewal allows, despite all her misgivings, that "to the extent that some women will be able to use the language of universal rights and become subjects of the universal regimes, women's rights as human rights could be effective."[15] But she remains wary that, by becoming constituted as a subject in accordance with an international framework, one will be constricted by the regulations of modernity and the nation-state.

Grewal, however, does not acknowledge the rebukes that have come from American women themselves, calling their own nation to account for the same attitudes and actions that Grewal herself indicts. Wendy Brown, a critical theorist of politics, has indicted America for assuming certain universals that have all the characteristics of essentialist claims in relation to human rights and feminism. She intensified her rebukes in the light of 9/11. Brown is particularly scathing in her denunciation of the appeal to human rights, within a rhetoric of liberation, employed by George W. Bush, and Donald Rumsfeld in the retributive "war on terror." According to Brown, "It is not only that Rumsfeld has co-opted the language of human rights for imperialist aims abroad and antidemocratic ones at home, but that insofar as the 'liberation' of Afghanistan and Iraq promised to deliver human rights to those oppressed populations it is hard both to parse

cynical from sincere deployments of human rights discourse and to separate human rights campaigns from legitimating liberal imperialism."[16]

In the face of such distortion of rights, however, Brown ponders how rights could be used in the service of alleviating unjust suffering of other human beings. She observes: "If the global problem today is defined as terrible human suffering consequent to limited individual rights against abusive state powers, then human rights may be the best tactic."[17] Yet this statement needs to be put in perspective, particularly in light of the title of her paper, "'The Most We Can Hope For . . .'? Human Rights and the Politics of Fatalism." Brown views rights as only one possible means of redress, allowing that other political remedies may be required to counter the predatory ways of "superpower imperialism."[18] From this perspective, human rights is both a limited and limiting strategy, and her final plea is that progressives should try to work toward more than just rights if they are to change the present political regime. Brown's analysis could also provide the basis for rethinking women's rights as not only a means to relieve suffering but also as a call to engage with the political systems that do not recognize their rights.

There has also been a remarkable change of attitude on this issue in the work of Judith Butler, a critical thinker and debunker of all false pretensions to essentialisms of any variety. I have discussed this development elsewhere, but it remains relevant to the issue at hand.[19] In *Bodies That Matter,* Butler admits that in her earlier work *Gender Trouble* she may have played somewhat fast and loose with the notion of gender as performance, particularly as it was interpreted as an optional mode of identity that could be assumed at will.[20] She recognized that the physical body was vulnerable to harm and oppression and that claims could be made on its behalf for protection from abuse and violence. In a 2001 interview, "The End of Sexual Difference," Butler takes this a step farther. Here, she first acknowledges that gender will always remain a contentious site that needs to be constantly questioned. This is because certain societies, groups, and religions, in particular, will continue to employ it not only in a regulative manner, but even as invariable and nonnegotiable. Aware of the inroads that have been made by fundamentalists, however, and the attempts made to reframe, restrain, and even cancel many of the rights that had been hard-won by former generations of women, she allows: "Although many feminists have come to the conclusion that the universal is always a cover for a certain epistemological imperialism, insensitive to cultural texture and difference, the rhetorical power of claiming universality for say, rights of sexual autonomy and related rights of sexual orientation within the human rights domain appears indisputable."[21] Butler has also reflected on the nature of the universal and the inevitable problems that arise with its use. In acknowledging that there will always be cultural variables that work against any universal claim, she nonetheless observes: "This is not to say that there ought to be no reference to the universal or that it has become, for us, an impossibility. On the contrary. All it means is that there are cultural conditions for its articulation that are not always the same, and that the term gains its meaning for us precisely through these decidedly less than universal cultural conditions for its articulation."[22] The reclamation of rights, albeit highly qualified, by these two formidable critics, in the light of present oppositional forces that are mainly motivated by political expediency or religious zealotry, initiates a possibility not only of rethinking the project of rights in relation to women but also constructive ways of responding to the hostility of the opponents. . . .

FINAL OBSERVATIONS

By way of concluding, I would like to offer two views, promoted by women scholars as ways that religion and rights could be reconsidered, and that speak to the issues discussed in the course of my essay. One approach, taken by Madhavi Sunder in an article titled "Piercing the Veil," advises women to claim their rights in the face all forms of religious oppression. Her description of those who participate in the movement is as follows:

> These individuals reject the binary approach of the Enlightenment, which forces individuals to choose between religious liberty (on a leader's terms) in the private sphere and equality (without a

normative community) in the public sphere. Rather they articulate a vision of human flourishing that requires freedom *within* the context of religious and cultural community. This vision includes not only a right to equal treatment in one's cultural or religious community, but also a right to engage in those communities on one's own terms.[23]

I discern in Sunder's strategy a position of renegotiation for women who find themselves in religious traditions that are today resorting to fundamentalist dictates and trying to silence moderate, let alone progressive, voices of women on reform. Sunder then continues to describe the modifications that she would like to see. She supports those "cultural dissenters or individuals within a community [who seek] to modernize, broaden, the traditional terms of cultural membership, [and who challenge the traditional liberal understandings of liberty and equality as premised on a 'thin' theory of the self." She posits that traditional liberalism takes too lightly the difficulties of women who cannot easily exit from their community, or those who may not wish to. Instead of complete rejection, she advocates reform of both religion and rights: "I read in the rise of cultural dissent that human flourishing requires not only a liberty right to normative community, but access to a community free of the fear of discrimination within it."[24] Such a position challenges primarily the traditional public/private distinction, but it also takes into account the need for a "thicker" understanding of subjectivity—one that includes religion. . . .

Further insight is provided by Mahnaz Afkhami, former Iranian Minister of State for Women's Affairs and a veteran activist of thirty years or more. She addresses the dualism that pits individual rights against the community and places them as mutually exclusive:

> We must move beyond the theory of women's human rights as a theory of equality before the law, of women's individual space, or a "room of one's own," to the theory of the architecture of the future society where the universality of rights and relativity of means merge to operationalize an optimally successful coexistence of community and individuality. This architectural theory will point to a

dynamic design where broadly conceived human relations evolve with the requirements of the times as they satisfy he needs of both community and individuality.[25]

It is worth noting that Afkhami's program does contain a proviso that is deemed necessary for its success: "We must insist that no one, man or woman, may claim a right to a monopoly of interpretation of God to human beings or a right to force others to accept a particular ruling about any religion. The upshot of this position is that women ought not to be forced to choose between freedom and God. The same applies on the part of tradition."[26]

Sunder's and Afkhami's statements are indicative of contemporary women who do not wish to settle for the status quo, but instead are struggling to express ideas and strategies that could help in time to move beyond the present impasse. None of their recommendations will be uncomplicated to implement—and they do not necessarily all sit easily together—but they are suggestive of a start that holds promise. In one sense, I think such developments will be necessary, for I foresee a time when secular feminists and women from liberal and moderate religious backgrounds from the different religions and regions of the world, particularly in international bodies and in NGOs, will need to form strategic coalitions. This move will help to moderate the influence of fundamentalist forces that have so effectively mobilized to obstruct and to prevent any further advances in the area of women's rights.

NOTES

1. Devaki Jain, *Women, Development, and the UN: A Sixty-Year Quest for Equality and Justice* (Bloomington: Indiana University Press, 2005); and Leila J. Rupp, *Worlds of Women: The Making of an International Women's Movement* (Princeton, NJ: Princeton University Press, 1998).
2. Amrita Basu, "Women's Movements and the Challenge of Transnationalism," accessed January 26, 2013, http://www3.amherst.edu/~mrhunt/womencrossingbasu.html.
3. Judith Butler, "The End of Sexual Difference?" in *Feminist Consequences: Theory for a New Century,* ed. Elisabeth Bronfen and Misha Kavka (New York: Columbia University Press, 2001), 423.
4. Joan Wallach Scott, *Gender and the Politics of History* (1988; reprint, New York: Columbia University Press, 1999), ix.
5. Judith Butler, *Gender Trouble: Feminism and the Subversion of Identity* (New York: Routledge, 1990).
6. Scott, *Gender and the Politics of History,* ix.
7. As Bayes and Tohidi relate, "in Beijing, the coalition of Catholic countries that joined the Vatican included Guatemala, Honduras, Ecuador, Peru, Bolivia, and the Philippines. These were joined by the Muslim countries of Iran, Sudan, Libya, Egypt, and Kuwait. . . . During the 1995–2000 period, other Catholic Muslim cooperative efforts occurred." See Jane H. Bayes and Nahereh Tohidi, eds., *Globalization, Gender, and Religion* (New York: Palgrave, 2001), 3. While the Vatican itself could not be termed *fundamentalist,* it did not hesitate to join with countries that supported fundamentalist forms of religion.
8. For further comments, see Butler, "The End of Sexual Difference?" 430. Devaki Jain nonetheless reflected that while the term *gender* had been helpful as an analytical tool, it could deflect attention from the actual struggles of women (*Women, Development, and the UN,* 157).
9. Courtney W. Howland, "Women and Religious Fundamentalism," in *Women and International Human Rights Law,* ed. Kelly D. Asian and Dorean M. Koenig (New York: Transnational Publishers, 1999), 616.
10. Anastasia Posadskaya-Vanderbeck, "International and Post-socialist Women's Rights Advocacy: Points of Convergence and Tension," in *The Future of Women's Rights: Global Visions and Strategies,* ed. Joanna Kerr, Ellen Sprenger, and Alison Symington (London: Zed Books, 2004), 187.
11. Inderpal Grewal, "'Women's Rights as Human Rights': Feminist Practices, Global Feminism, and Human Rights Regimes in Transnationality," *Citizenship Studies* 3, no. 3 (1999): 337–54, quotation on 338.
12. ibid., 344.
13. ibid., 340.
14. ibid., 341–42.
15. Ibid., 351.
16. Wendy Brown, "'The Most We Can Hope For . . .'? Human Rights and the Politics of Fatalism," *South Atlantic Quarterly* 103, nos. 2–3 (2004): 451–63, quotation on 460.
17. Ibid., 461.
18. Ibid.
19. Joy, "Gender and Religion."

20. Judith Butler, *Bodies That Matter: On the Discursive Limits of "Sex"* (New York: Routledge, 1993), and Butler, *Gender Trouble*.

21. Butler, "End of Sexual Difference?" 423. More recently, Butler has also become extremely vocal about human rights in regard to the treatment of "political prisoners at Guantanamo, and also Israel's treatment of the Palestinian people. In an interview she stated, "It seems to me that if we don't want a universal right to be an imposition of a Western culture on everyone, then we have to understand that what is 'universal' is constantly being made, it is constantly being articulated and rearticulated, under conditions of cultural translation, where different governments and nongovernmental organizations are involved in complex questions regarding, say what

would the right to personal liberty look like? Or what would the right to bodily integrity look like?" Judith Butler, "Peace Is a Resistance to the Terrible Satisfactions of War," May 2003, http://www.believermag.com/issues/200305/?read=interview_butler.

22. Butler, "End of Sexual Difference?" 430.

23. Madhavi Sunder, "Piercing the Veil," in *Just Advocacy? Women's Human Rights, Transnational Feminisms, and the Politics of Representation,* ed. Wendy Hesford and Wendy Kozol (New Brunswick, NJ: Rutgers University Press, 2005), 268.

24. Ibid.

25. Mabnaz Afkhami, "Rights of Passage: Women Shaping the Twenty-First Century," in Kerr, Sprenger, and Symington, *Future of Women's Rights,* 66.

26. Ibid., 65.

R E A D I N G 97

Decolonizing Religious Beliefs

Sylvia Marcos (2009)

The indigenous women's movement has started to propose its own "indigenous spirituality." Documents, declarations, and proposals that were generated at the First Indigenous Women's Summit of the Americas, as well as at other key meetings that have gathered since, reveal an indigenous spiritual component that differs from the hegemonic influences of the largely Christian, Catholic background of the women's respective countries. The principles of this indigenous spirituality also depart from the more recent influences of feminist and Latin American ecofeminist liberation theologies. Participants' discourses, live presentations, and addresses brought to light other expressions of their religious background. Catholicism—as a colonizing enterprise—has deeply permeated the indigenous traditions of the Americas, making it almost impossible to separate "pure" indigenous religious traditions from Catholic images, rites, and symbols.

. . .

Working, as some authors have suggested, from the "cracks of epistemic differences," I characterize

the indigenous women's movement as undertaking a "de-colonial" effort.[1] These women are actively recapturing ancestral spiritualities in order to decolonize the religious universes they were forced to adopt during the historical colonial enterprise.[2]

. . .

THE MODERNITY OF ANCIENT SPIRITUALITY

The Latin American continent has long been known as a stronghold of Catholicism. Even today, the Vatican counts Latin America as one of the regions boasting the greatest numbers of Catholics in the world.[3] Among indigenous social movements, claiming the right to develop and define their own spirituality is a novel attitude, yet one that indigenous people voice with increasing intensity.[4] Beyond claiming a right to food and shelter, a decent livelihood, and ownership of their territory and its resources, the indigenous are turning an internal gaze toward their traditional culture. They are also daring to question the most ingrained sequels of Catholic colonization and rejecting the contempt and disdain with which the Catholic majority views their spirituality, beliefs, and practices. . . .

Despite conflicting perspectives held by scholars and other commentators, indigenous social movements are the most visible transformational force in the Latin American continent.[5] Indigenous peoples no longer accept the image that was imposed on them from the exterior. They want to create their own identity; they refuse to be museum objects. It is not a question of reviving the past. Indigenous cultures are alive, and the only way for them to survive is to reinvent themselves, re-creating their identity while maintaining their differences.[6] . . . Indigenous women are claiming this ancestral wisdom, cosmovision, and spirituality, but theirs is a selective process and they are contesting issues within tradition that constrain or hamper their space as women. Meanwhile, those who have an enhanced position as women within their spiritual ancestral communities are held onto dearly, with the community ensuring their survival.

. . .

WHAT DOES INDIGENOUS SPIRITUALITY MEAN?

When the indigenous women use the word *spirituality*, they give it a meaning that clearly sets it apart from Catholic and other Christian traditions that arrived in the Americas at the time of the conquest and the ensuing colonization: "We indigenous Mexican women . . . take our decision to practice freely our spirituality that is different from a religion but in the same manner we respect everyone else's beliefs."[7] This stance is strongly influenced by an approach that espouses transnational sociopolitical practices. Indigenous movements and in particular the women in them are being increasingly exposed to a globalizing world. The presence of a Maori elder at the summit, as well as the frequent participation of Mexican indigenous women in indigenous peoples' meetings around the world, have favored new attitudes of openness, understanding, and coalition beyond their own traditional cultural boundaries.

Through the lens of indigenous spirituality, we can glimpse the cosmovision that pervades the worlds of indigenous women.

. . .

A WORLD CONSTRUCTED BY FLUID DUAL OPPOSITIONS, BEYOND MUTUALLY EXCLUSIVE CATEGORIES

To be able to comprehend contemporary indigenous spirituality it is important to review some of the tenets of Mesoamerican ancestral "embodied thought."[8] Duality is the centerpiece of spirituality understood as a cosmic vision of life. Duality—not dualism—is a pervasive perception in indigenous thought and spirituality. The pervasiveness of a perception without equivalent in Western thought could, perhaps, largely explain the persistent barrier to penetrating and comprehending indigenous worlds. According to Mesoamerican cosmology, the dual unity of the feminine and masculine is fundamental to the creation of the cosmos, as well as its (re)generation, and sustenance. The fusion of feminine and masculine in one bipolar principle is a recurring feature of almost every Mesoamerican community today. Divinities themselves are gendered feminine and masculine. There is no concept of a virile god (for example, the image of a white-bearded man as the Christian God has sometimes been represented) but rather a mother/father dual protector/creator. In Nahua culture, this dual god/goddess is called *Ometeotl,* from *ome,* "two," and *teotl,* "god." Yet Ometeotl does not mean "two gods" but rather "god Two" or, better, "divinity of Duality." The name results from the fusion of *Omecihuatl* (*cihuatl* meaning woman or lady) and *Ometecuhtli* (*tecuhtli,* man or lord), that is, of the Lady and of the Lord of Duality.

The protecting *Ometeotl* has to be alternately placated and sustained. Like all divine beings, it was not conceived as purely beneficial. Rather, it oscillated—like all other dualities—between opposite poles and thus could be supportive or destructive. In addition, a multiplicity of goddesses and gods entered into diverse relations of reciprocity with the people. . . .

Duality, defined as a complementary duality of opposites, is the essential ordering force of the universe and is also reflected in the ordering of time. Time is marked by two calendars, one ritual based and the other astronomical. The ritual calendar is linked to the human gestational cycle. The other is an agricultural calendar that prescribes the periods for seeding, sowing, and planting corn. Maize (corn) is conceived of as the earthly matter from which all beings in the universe are made.[9] Human gestation and agricultural cycles are understood within this concept of time-duality, as are feminine and masculine, but dualities extend far beyond these spheres. For instance, life and death, above and below, light and dark, and beneficence and malevolence are considered dual aspects of the same reality. Neither pole invalidates the other. Both are in constant mutual interaction, flowing into each other. Mutually exclusive categories are not part of the epistemic background of this worldview, whose plasticity is still reflected in the ways indigenous women deal with life and conflict. They seldom remain mired in a position that would deny the opposite. Their philosophical background allows them both to resist impositions and to appropriate modern elements into their spirituality. Fluidity and selectivity in adopting novel attitudes and values speak of the ongoing reconfiguration of their world of reference.

. . .

DUALITY AND GENDER

In the indigenous Mesoamerican world, gender is constructed within the pervasive concept of duality.[10] Gender, that is, the masculine/feminine duality, is the root metaphor for the whole cosmos. Everything is identified as either feminine or masculine, and this applies to natural phenomena such as rain, hail, lightning, and clouds; living beings, such as animals, plants, and humans; and even to periods of time, such as days, months, and years.[11] All these entities have a feminine or masculine "breath" or "weight." It is evident, then, that this perception of gender corresponds to a duality of complementary opposites, a duality, in turn, that is the fabric of the cosmos. Duality is the linking and ordering force

that creates a coherent reference for indigenous peoples, the knitting thread that weaves together all apparent disparities.[12]

. . .

Yet, despite the reverential espousal of the ancestral concept of gender duality and complementarity, contemporary indigenous women express some reticence and even rejection of some aspects of it. Their arguments are based on how it is lived today in many indigenous communities. For example, in the summit document dedicated to "Gender from the Vision of Indigenous Women," Maria Estela Jocón, a Mayan Guatemalan wise women, remarks that duality today "is something we should question, it is a big question mark, because as theory it is present in our cosmovision and in our customary laws, as theory, but in practice you see many situations where only the man decides . . . mass media, schools, and many other issues have influenced this principle of Duality so it is a bit shaky now" (*Summit Doc. Género* 7).[13] Alma Lopez, a young indigenous self-identified feminist, who is a *regidora* in her community, believes that the concept of duality of complementary opposites has been lost, noting that "the philosophical principles that I would recover from my culture would be equity, and complementarity between women and men, women and women, and between men and men. Today the controversial complementarity of Mayan culture does not exist."[14]

However, beyond the reticence or even outright negations of the contemporary and lived practices of inherited philosophical principles, indigenous women are still claiming them, still want to be inspired by them, and propose to re-inscribe them in their contemporary struggles for gender justice. They deem it necessary not only to recapture their ancestral cultural roots and beliefs but also to think of them as a potent resource in their quest for gender justice and equity.

As another summit document explains, "Today, there are big differences between the condition of women in relation to that of men. This does not mean that it was always like this. In this case there is the possibility of returning to our roots and recovering the space that is due to women, based on indigenous cosmovision" (*Memoria* 133).[15]

. . .

EQUILIBRIUM AS GENDER EQUITY

Equilibrium, as conceived in indigenous spirituality, is not the static repose of two equal weights or masses. Rather, it is a force that constantly modifies the relation between dual or opposite pairs. Like duality itself, equilibrium, or balance, permeates not only relations between men and women but also relations among deities, between deities and humans, and among elements of nature. The constant search for this balance was vital to the preservation of order in every area, from daily life to the activity of the cosmos. Equilibrium is as fundamental as duality itself.

Duality, thus, is not a binary ordering of "static poles." Balance in this view can best be understood as an agent that constantly modifies the terms of dualities and thereby bestows a singular quality on the complementary pairs of opposites that permeate all indigenous thought (as seen in the summit documents and declarations). Equilibrium is constantly reestablishing its own balance. It endows duality with a flexibility or plasticity that makes it flow, impeding stratification. There is not an exclusively feminine or exclusively masculine being. Rather, beings possess these forces in different nuances or combinations. The imperceptible "load" or "charge" that all beings have—whether rocks, animals, or people—is feminine or masculine. Frequently, entities possess both feminine and masculine capacities simultaneously in different gradations that perpetually change and shift.[16]

The gender documents created at the summit were direct transcriptions from the focus group discussions. The following rich and spontaneous evaluations of equilibrium express the indigenous manner of conceiving gender equity:

> We understand the practice of gender perspective to be a respectful relationship . . . of balance, of equilibrium—what in the Western world would be equity. (*Summit Doc. Género* 6)[17]

> Equilibrium means taking care of life . . . when community values of our environment and social community are respected, there is equilibrium. (*Memoria* 132)[18]

> Between one extreme and the other there is a center. The extremes and their center are not absolute, but depend on a multiplicity of factors . . . variable and not at all exact. . . . [Duality] is equilibrium at its maximum expression. (*Memoria* 231)[19]

Indigenous women refer to equilibrium as the attainable ideal for the whole cosmos, and as the best way to express their own views on gender equity.

THE SPIRITUALITY OF IMMANENCE

In the fluid, dual universe of indigenous spiritualities, the sacred domain is pervasive. Strong continuities exist between the natural and supernatural worlds, whose sacred beings are interconnected closely with humans, who in turn propitiate this interdependence in all their activities.

. . .

In striking contrast with indigenous spirituality, the dominant tradition in Christian theology stresses "classical theism," defined as centered on a metaphysical concept of God as ontologically transcendent and independent from the world. This concept of God has met with increasing criticism, particularly among ecofeminist and process theologians.[20] In indigenous spirituality, the relationship to the supernatural world lies elsewhere:

> The cosmic vision of life is to be connected with the surroundings, and all the surroundings have life, so they become SACRED: we encounter earth, mountains, valleys, caves, plants, animals, stones, water, air, moon, sun, stars. Spirituality is born from this perspective and conception in which all beings that exist in Mother Nature have life and are interrelated. Spirituality is linked to a sense of COMMUNITY in which all beings are interrelated and complementary. (*Memoria* 128)[21]

Ivone Gevara, a Brazilian ecofeminist theologian, recalls how an Aymara indigenous woman responded to Gevara's theological perspective: "With ecofeminism I am not ashamed anymore of expressing beliefs from my own culture. I do not need to emphasize that they have Christian elements for them to be considered good . . . they simply are valuable."[22]

Ecofeminist theology promotes complex and novel positions centered on a respect for earth and reverence for nature. Many indigenous women perceive this feminist theology to be easier to understand and closer to *the standpoint of* their indigenous spirituality than Catholic theism. These bridges between Christian and indigenous spiritualities become more intelligible when we reflect on the main characteristics that shape indigenous spirituality's relationship to nature: its divine dimensions, the personification of deities in humans, the fluidity between immanent and transcendent, and the fusion with the supernatural that women can and should enact. There is no exclusive relationship to a transcendent being called God; there is no mistrust of the flesh and the body; there is sanctity in matter: "We recover indigenous cosmovision as our 'scientific heritage,' recognizing the elders as ancient carriers of wisdom" (*Memoria* 60).[23] Similarly, they explain "that the indigenous women of different cultures and civilizations of Abya Yala do not forget that they are daughters of the land, of the sun, of the wind and of fire and that their continuous relation[s] with the cosmic elements strengthen their political participation in favor of indigenous women and indigenous peoples" (*Memoria* 63).[24]

The woman's body, a fluid and permeable corporeality, is conflated with Earth as a sacred place; they regard themselves as an integral part of this sacred Earth. The spirit is not the opposite of matter and neither is the soul of the flesh.

EMBODIED RELIGIOUS THOUGHT

According to dominant Western epistemic traditions, the very concept of body is formed in opposition to mind. The body is defined as the place of biological data, of the material, of the immanent. Since the seventeenth century, the body has also been conceptualized as that which marks the boundaries between the interior self and the external world.[25] In Mesoamerican spiritual traditions, however, the body has characteristics that vastly differ from those of the Western anatomical or biological body. Exterior and interior are not separated by the hermetic barrier of the skin. Between the outside and the inside, permanent and continuous exchange occurs. To gain a keener understanding of how the body is conceptualized in indigenous traditions,

we must think of it as a vortex, in whirling, spiral-like movement that fuses and expels, absorbs and discards, and through this motion is in permanent contact with all elements in the cosmos.

A SPIRITUALITY OF COLLECTIVITY AND THE INTERCONNECTEDNESS OF ALL BEINGS

For indigenous peoples, then the world is not "out there," established outside of and apart from them. It is within them and even "through" them. Actions and their circumstances are much more interwoven than is the case in Western thought, in which the "I" can be analytically abstracted from its surroundings. Furthermore, the body's porosity reflects the essential porosity of the cosmos, a permeability of the entire "material" world that defines an order of existence characterized by a continuous interchange between the material and the immaterial. The cosmos literally emerges, in this conceptualization, as the complement of a permeable corporeality. It is from this very ample perspective that the controversial term *complementarity* should be revisited according to its usage by indigenous women. From their perspective, it is not only feminine and masculine that are complementary. As *Comandanta* Esther insisted in her address to the Mexican Congress, complementarity embraces everything in nature. She explained that earth is life, is nature, and we are all part of it. This simple phrase expresses the interconnectedness of all beings in the Mesoamerican cosmos. Beings are not separable from one another. This principle engenders a very particular form of human collectivity with little tendency to individuation. . . .

"Spirituality" . . . is born from this vision and concept according to which all beings that exist in Mother Nature are interrelated. Spirituality is linked to a communitarian sense for which all beings are interrelated and complement each other in their existence (*Memoria* 128). Among the examples of several pervasive spiritual and cosmological references reproduced by the indigenous women of the Americas, this one seems to be at the core: the interconnectedness of everyone and everything in the universe.

. . .

In recent years, indigenous peoples have intensified their struggle to break free from the chains of colonialism and its oppressive spiritual legacy. Indigenous women's initiatives to recover their ancestral religious legacy constitute a decolonizing effort. Through a deconstruction of past captivities, they re-create a horizon of ancestrally inspired spirituality. They lay claim to an ethics of recovery while rejecting the violence and subjugation suffered by their ancestors within the religious and cultural domain. "We only come to ask for justice," the organized indigenous women have repeatedly declared. Yes, justice is their demand: material, social, and political justice. They also seek recognition of and respect for their cosmological beliefs as an integral part of their feminist vision.

NOTES

1. Walter Mignolo coins these phrases in "From Central Asia to the Caucasus and Anatolia: Transcultural Subjectivity and De-colonial Thinking," *Postcolonial Studies* 10, no. 1 (2007): 111–20.

2. Historically, identification with "indigenous" ethnicity, traditions, languages, and attire has elicited elite derision throughout the Americas. The emergence of active indigenous movements all over the Latin American world, however, has opened new spaces for "positive" discrimination. In other words, political and economic spaces now exist that have been reserved for indigenous identities. As a middle-class intellectual and university professor who never suffered the discriminations and offensive behaviors to which the indigenous peoples have been constantly exposed since European conquest and colonial times, my ethical stand is to refrain from either "speaking on behalf" or taking advantage of any preferential treatment now available. It happens sometimes though that I am assimilated to my indigenous friends, and when this is the case, I feel extremely honored.

3. During the past twenty years, the Catholic population has been decreasing consistently. Today in Mexico, roughly 82 percent of the population identifies as Catholic in contrast to 96.5 percent two decades ago. Among the impoverished and dispossessed of Mexico are many Catholics, among whom stand sixty-two distinct indigenous groups in the country.

4. This theme resounds around the world with other indigenous peoples. See the Maori claims in Linda Tuhiwai Smith, *Decolonizing Methodologies: Research and Indigenous Peoples* (New York: Zed Books, 1999).

5. José Gil Olmos, interview with Alain Touraine, "Mexico en riesgo de caer en el caos y caciquismo," *La Jornada,* November 6, 2000, 3.

6. José Gil Olmos, interview with Yvon Le Bot, "Moderno y creativo el movimiento de indígenas en América," *La Jornada,* March 26, 2000, 3.

7. "Las mujeres indígenas mexicanas . . . tomamos nuestras decisiones para ejercer libremente nuestra espiritualidad que es diferente a una religión y de igual manera se respeta la creencia de cada quien." *Mensaje de las Mujeres Indígenas Mexicanas a los Monseñores de la Comisión Espiscopal de Obispos,* December 1–2, 2002, Oaxaca, Mexico, 1, copy in author's possession.

8. Sylvia Marcos, "Embodied Religious Thought: Gender Categories in Mesoamerica," *Religion* 28(1998): 371–82.

9. Sylvia Marcos, *Taken from the Lips: Gender and Eros in Mesoamerica* (Leiden: Brill, 2006).

10. Marcos, "Embodied Religious Thought," and Marcos, *Taken from the Lips.*

11. Alfredo Lopez Austin, *The Human Body and Ideology* (Salt Lake City: University of Utah Press, 1988).

12. See, for example, Noemí Quezada, *Sexualidad Amor y Erotismo: México y préhispanico y México Colonial* (México: IIA–Universidad Nacional Autónoma de México y Plaza Valdez, 1997); and Sylvia Marcos, "La construcción del género en Mesoamerica: Un reto Epistemológico," paper presented at the 13th Congreso Internacional de Ciencias Antropologicas y Etnológicas, Mexico, August 4, 1993.

13. "La Dualidad hoy en dia es cuestionate, es un signo de interrogación grandisimo, porque como teoría existe en nuestra cosmovisión y en nuestras costumbres, como teoría, pero en la practica se ven muchas situaciones donde solamente el hombre decide. . . . Los medios de comunicación, la escuela y muchos otros elementos han influido para que ese principio de la Dualidad esté un poquito tambaleant."

14. "Los principios filosóficos que yo recuperaría de mi cultura son la equidad, la complementariedad entre hombres y mujeres, entre mujeres y mujeres, entre hombres y hombres. . . . Actualmente esa famosa complementariedad de la cultura maya no existe." Quoted in Bastian Duarte and Angela Ixkic, "Conversación con Alma Lopez, Autoridad Guatemalteca: La Doble Mirada del Género y la Etnicidad," in *Estudios Latinoamericanos,* nueva epoca, 9, no. 18 (2002): 176–82, quotation on 178.

15. "En la actualidad existen grandes diferencias entre la situación de la mujer con relación a la del hombre, no significa que siempre fue así, en este caso existe al posibilidad de retomar las raíces y recuperar el espacio que le corresponde a la mujer basado en la cosmovisión indígena."

16. Lopez Austin, *Human Body and Ideology*.

17. "Se entiende así la practica de enfoque de género como una relación respetuosa, . . . de balance, de equilibrio-lo que en occidente sería de equidad."

18. "El equilibrio es velar por la vida. . . . Cuando los valores de la comunidad, de nuestro medio social y de nuestro entorno son respetados hay equilibrio."

19. "Entre extremo y extremo se encuentra el centro. Los extremos de la escala, asi como su centro, no son cualidades absolutas, sino dependen de multitud de factores . . . variables y en absoluto exactos . . . [la Dualidad] es el equilibrio, en su maxima expresión."

20. Catherine Keller, *From a Broken Web: Separation, Sexism, and Self* (1986; reprint, Boston: Beacon Press, 2002); and Ivone Gevara, "Epistemologia Ecofeminista," in *Ecofeminismo: Tendencias e Debates* (Mandragora, Sao Bernado do Campo: Universidad de Metodista de Sao Paulo, 2001), 18–27.

21. "La visión cósmica de la vida es estar conectado con el entorno y todo los que hay en el entorno tiene vida, por lo que adquiere un valor SAGRADO: encontramos tierra cerros, planicies, cuevas, plantas, animales, piedras, agua, aire, luna sol, estrellas. La espiritualidad nace de esta visión y concepción en la que todos los seres que hay en la Madre Naturaleza tienen vida y se interrelacionan. La espiritualidad está ligada al sentido *comunitario*, donde los seres se interrelacionan y se complementan."

22. Quoted in Gevara, "Epistemologia Ecofeminista," 21.

23. "Retomamos la cosmovisión indígena o ciencia de los Pueblos indígenas, reconociendo a los ancianos y ancianas como portadores de sabiduría ancestral" (*Memoria* 31).

24. "Que las mujeres indígenas de las diferentes culturas y civilizaciones de Abya Yala no se olviden que son hijas de la tierra del sol, del viento y del fuego y que su relación continua con los elementos cosmogónicos fortalecerán su participación política a favor de las Mujeres indígenas y de los Pueblos indígenas" (*Memoria* 34).

25. Susan R. Bordo and Alison M. Jaggar, eds., *Gender/Body/Knowledge* (New Brunswick, NJ: Rutgers University Press, 1989), 4.

R E A D I N G   98

The Prophet's Daughters

An Interview with Syafa Almirzanah (2009)

Syafa Almirzanah, a professor of comparative religion at Islamic University Sunan Kalijaga in Yogyakarta, Indonesia, could have continued her studies anywhere in the Muslim world, but she chose Catholic Theological Union in Chicago. . . .

"Dialogue is, for me, a must," she says. "In my tradition it is the obligation of Muslims to learn from others, to get knowledge from everywhere."

Almirzanah has been active in interreligious dialogue in both her home country of Indonesia and in the United States. She feels comfortable with Catholicism, she says, because of the many similarities between it and Islam.

One unfortunate similarity is the way scholars from both traditions have misused faith to repress women.

Almirzanah hopes that by learning about the history and theology of Islam—and by participating in interreligious dialogue—Muslims will embrace more female-friendly interpretations of the religion.

"I think one of the most important things in dialogue is having the courage to criticize our own tradition. We must learn from others, then come back and look at our tradition with a new horizon," Almirzanah says. "Learning from others enriches our traditions. We can be better Muslims and better Christians."

What does the Qur'an have to say about women?
The Qur'an is very positive about women. In the story of Creation, women and men are created from

the same cells, so usually scholars say that means that men and women are the same before God.

The problem is that different Muslims understand the Qur'an in different ways. Islam is not the monolithic religion people think it is, just as Christianity is not monolithic.

If you read the Bible, you cannot ignore the context. When God revealed himself, it was not in a vacuum. People who receive the revelation of God have different backgrounds, experiences, and contexts, so they respond to it differently.

The same is true in Islamic tradition. Some more traditional Muslims only focus on what's written in the text and don't pay attention to the context of the verses; other more modern Muslims look at why God revealed a particular verse and how the community at that time understood it.

The verse on polygamy, for example, says that you can marry one or two or three or four women. More fundamentalist or traditional Muslims use this verse to justify having more than one wife, but actually the verse does not stop there. It continues: "If you cannot do justice, just marry one." They ignore that crucial part of the verse. This verse was revealed after a war, and there were a lot of widows and orphans, so men were allowed to marry multiple women in order to take care of them.

You also must look at verses in relation to other verses. The Qur'an says elsewhere that even if you wanted to, you could not do justice to more than one wife. So actually Islam and the Qur'an ban polygamy. It says if you cannot do justice, just marry one woman, but it also says you can never really do justice to more than one wife.

How were women treated during the seventh century in the Arabian Peninsula at the time of Muhammad?
This is also debatable. Scholars usually compare what it was like for women before Islam and after Islam.

Most scholars say that pre-Islamic times were worse for women. They say that before Islam men could marry more than four women. A Muslim scholar will argue that Muhammad limited polygamy and advocated the ideal marriage of one man and one woman. This is progress because some say that husbands could even sell women before Islam.

But there are also many scholars who write that before Islam women's conditions were not really bad because they were free and had rights. One author says that before Islam a lot of women were involved in war and managed businesses. There is evidence of cultures where husbands came into their wives' homes when they married, and the children would belong to the women's tribe. Our Prophet's first wife was a businesswoman, and she came from a very noble tribe, though she may be the exception.

I personally think it was almost like it is today. In certain communities where people are poor and have no access to education, of course women may not have the same opportunities as women who have rich families and live in an urban society. I can say that there were some good attitudes toward women before Islam, but Islam increased those good attitudes.

How did Muhammad treat his wives?
The first wife of the Prophet was a businesswoman. His youngest wife, Aisha, was a scholar and one of the interpreters of what the Prophet was saying. Because she was very close to the Prophet, a lot of people asked Aisha about what they should do in matters of love or matters of *Sharia,* or Muslim law. She also was involved in battle.

The Prophet didn't teach that women should just stay at home. These rules were introduced by the Prophet's companions after his death. The Qur'an gives women the right to pursue an education and be involved in worldly matters.

I think we need to get traditional Muslims to look at history, even at our Prophet's wives, and see that they were very active. Why should we now have to stay at home?

There is a verse that says men are above women, but *above* here does not mean women are naturally inferior. It means men are responsible for family welfare because they work outside the home and earn money—as they were in Muhammad's time.

Today, a woman can go outside of the home, work, and earn money, so she has the same status as a man. She also has responsibilities for her family, so for a more modern scholar, men are not above women.

How do more traditional Muslim scholars explain away the prominence of Muhammad's wives?

They say that his wives were exceptions. Most of the interpreters of the Qur'an have been men, so there is a lot of submission of women in Muslim teachings. When I was doing my graduate studies, my adviser told me that some of the interpreters were men who really hated women.

A lot of the misogynistic hadiths—the sayings of the Prophet—do not come from trusted sources, though.

Hadiths tell scholars about the life of the Prophet and the context of the revelations but aren't actually revelations themselves. They are passed on through generations of people from Muhammad's contemporaries, so scholars have to make sure there is a common link back to the time of the Prophet. In order to evaluate whether the Prophet said something, we have to study the transmission of the tradition and who it came from.

We have very strict requirements to accept that a saying really came from the Prophet. Most of the misogynistic hadiths come only from one source. These cannot be used as a resource for an edict. But some people choose the one that matches their thinking rather than the one that has the best source.

Who are other notable female figures in Islam beyond Muhammad's wives?

There are a lot. The ninth-century scholar Ibn Sa'd wrote biographies of important Islamic figures, and he had a whole book of women in Islamic history.

There are also women saints. Rabia al-Adawiyya is a very famous Sufi, or Muslim mystic. She was a pioneer for the idea of love for God in Islamic mysticism. She has a well-known prayer: "God, if I pray to you only so you do not put me in hell, just put me in hell, and if I pray to you only so I can go to paradise, don't put me in paradise, but if I pray to you only because I love you, don't hide your face from me."

Rabia is said to be in the rank of men because she was close to or one with God. A lot of Muslim women look at her as an example—the ideal mystic woman. She didn't marry, but there are a lot of

women mystics who did marry. Some are the wives or daughters of male mystics. Sufi men had women teachers. A teacher of the famous Sufi Iban Arabi said, "I am his spiritual mother."

As in Christian spirituality, there are a lot of Muslim women mystics who are highly regarded. Mystics go beyond the text into the essence of the story. When you do that, every religion can meet, and men and women can meet. It is very conducive to dialogue.

Christian women sometimes struggle with male images of God. Is God thought of as male in Islam?

God is often described as having both a feminine and masculine aspect. One scholar compared it to yin and yang. In the Islamic tradition we call it *Jalal* and *Jamal*. *Jalal* is the might of God, and *Jamal* is the beauty of God. God has both of these aspects, feminine and masculine.

Yin and yang always are together, so women and men should be together. Man is not better than woman, and woman is not better than man. In Islam women and men should cooperate. Even in the Muslim Creation story, Eve is not the cause of the fall.

Still, the pronoun for God is a male pronoun, and that is a problem that feminists discuss. There are also certain verses in the Qur'an that only use a male pronoun, so Muslim feminists say that the male pronoun refers to both genders. For example, verses such as "you have to pray every day" use the male pronoun, but this doesn't mean that praying is only for males.

What does it mean to be a Muslim feminist?

Quite simply, I define it as someone who supports women's rights. There are a lot of male feminists who support the equal status of women, especially in Indonesia and Egypt. Some governments also promote equal rights.

Generally, what is the status of women in the Muslim world today?

As I said, Islam isn't a monolithic religion. The place of women depends a lot on the social, political, and cultural conditions of the community. Islam in

Indonesia is very different from Islam in Saudi Arabia, for example.

In Indonesia it's common for women to study and be in politics, but still there is resistance. We had a female president before our current president. When she was to be appointed president, fundamentalist groups opposed it because they said that Islam prohibited women from leading them. She became our president anyway. There are no verses that prohibit a woman from being president.

Still, many believe that women's responsibilities are domestic tasks such as cooking and taking care of children. Even my in-laws still believe that. They wouldn't let my husband cook.

When a woman's husband comes home from his job, she is supposed to serve him. But both my husband and I work outside the home, so why should I serve him? I always say, "I am not his servant. I am his wife." If I serve him on an occasion, it's not because it's my responsibility; it's because I love him.

We also have to understand there are women themselves who really believe in the fundamentalist interpretation. They believe that they should be at home and that they might have to accept being a second wife because this is what Islam teaches.

How much of that is due to religion and how much is due to culture?

I think it has to do with both. Culture is there, but certain interpretations of religion are there, too. There is a certain interpretation of Islam that says women should stay at home, not go anywhere, and take care of the family.

This is why women have to study what Islam actually teaches about women and our position. Our Prophet cooked and even sewed his clothes himself. There is nothing to be ashamed of in that.

We have to improve Muslims' understanding of the Qur'an. A lot of laypeople are Muslim because their family is Muslim, and they have never really studied their own tradition. They depend on their religious leader: Whatever he says, they will follow it. We cannot just do that; we have to know the sources of Islam ourselves.

There are a number of schools of thought for Islamic law. I was taught that you don't have to follow one of them, but the most important thing is to know why they say what they do.

How can women's positions in the Muslim world improve?

There are a lot of ways to improve our status, but I think the key, again, is education. Unfortunately, there are still a lot of people who do not have access to it. A lot of families in my country still pay only for boys and not girls to study if they have limited resources.

I have a brother, and my father let me go to school even to the highest levels, but that's often not the case at the university level. As a professor in Indonesia, I do see a lot of female students studying theology, though.

. . .

What issues do Christian and Muslim women share?

I think Muslim and Christian women have the same struggle to gain equal positions to men within our traditions. Most of the interpreters in the Catholic tradition are male, just as in Islam. That's one of the reasons they underestimate women, and there are misinterpretations of both religions.

For example, Jesus had female followers, but the Catholic tradition doesn't really consider them to be apostles. From my perspective, the women of those days were Jesus' apostles. In Islam we also have women companions to the Prophet Muhammad. But for some reason, in both cases, these women have been forgotten.

Muslim and Christian women can work together. We need to interpret verses for ourselves and criticize the old male interpretations. We should study together and go deeper into the traditions to find out what our traditions are actually saying about the position of women.

Standing Again at Sinai

Judith Plaskow (1990)

EXPLORING THE TERRAIN OF SILENCE

. . . The central Jewish categories of Torah, Israel, and God are all constructed from male perspectives. Torah is revelation as men perceived it, the story of Israel told from their standpoint, the law unfolded according to their needs. Israel is the male collectivity, the children of a Jacob who had a daughter, but whose sons became the twelve tribes. God is named in the male image, a father and warrior much like his male offspring, who confirms and sanctifies the silence of his daughters. Exploring these categories, we explore the parameters of women's silence.

In Torah, Jewish teaching, women are not absent, but they are cast in stories told by men. As characters in narrative, women may be vividly characterized, as objects of legislation, singled out for attention. But women's presence in Torah does not negate their silence, for women do not decide the questions with which Jewish sources deal. When the law treats of women, it is often because their "abnormality" demands it. If women are central to plot, the plots are not about them. Women's interests and intentions must be unearthed from texts with other purposes, for both law and narrative serve to obscure them.

The most striking examples of women's silence come from texts in which women are most central, for there the normative character of maleness is especially jarring. In the family narratives of Genesis, for example, women figure prominently. The matriarchs of Genesis are all strong women. As independent personalities, fiercely concerned for their children, they often seem to have an intuitive knowledge of God's plans for their sons. Indeed, it appears from the stories of Sarah and Rebekah that they understand God better than their husbands. God defends Sarah when she casts out Hagar, telling Abraham

to obey his wife (Gen. 21:12). Rebekah, knowing it is God's intent, helps deceive Isaac into accepting Jacob as his heir (Gen. 25:23; 27:5–17). Yet despite their intuitions, and despite their wiliness and resourcefulness, it is not the women who receive the covenant or who pass on its lineage. The establishment of patrilineal descent and the patriarchal family takes precedence over the matriarch's stories. Their relationship to God, in some way presupposed by the text, remains an undigested element in the narrative. What was the full theophany to Rebekah, and how is it related to the covenant with Isaac? The writer does not tell us; it is not sufficiently important. And so the covenant remains the covenant with Isaac, while Rebekah's experience floats at the margin of the story.

The establishment of patrilineal descent and patriarchal control, a subtext in Genesis, is an important theme in the legislation associated with Sinai. Here again, women figure prominently, but only as objects of male concerns. The laws pertaining to women place them firmly under the control of first fathers, then husbands, so that men can have male heirs they know are theirs. Legislation concerning adultery (Deut. 22:22, also Num. 5:11–31) and virginity (Deut. 22:13–21) speaks of women, but only to control female sexuality to male advantage. The *crime* of adultery is sleeping with another man's wife, and a man can bring his wife to trial even on suspicion of adultery, a right that is not reciprocal. Sleeping with a betrothed virgin constitutes adultery. A man who sleeps with a virgin who is not betrothed must simply marry her. A girl whose lack of virginity shames her father on her wedding night can be stoned to death for harlotry. A virgin who is raped must marry her assailant. The subject of these laws is women, but the interest behind them is the purity of the male line.

The process of projecting and defining women as objects of male concerns is expressed most fully not in the Bible, however, but in the Mishnah, an important second-century legal code. Part of the Mishnah's Order of Women (one of its six divisions) develops laws discussed in the Torah concerning certain problematic aspects of female sexuality. The subject of the division is the transfer of women—the regulation of women who are in states of transition, whose uncertain status threatens the stasis of the community. The woman who is about to enter into a marriage or who has just left one requires close attention. The law must regularize her irregularity, facilitate her transition to the normal state of wife and motherhood, at which point she no longer poses a problem. . . .

Thus Torah—"Jewish" sources, "Jewish" teaching—puts itself forward as *Jewish* teaching but speaks in the voice of only half the Jewish people. This scandal is compounded by another: The omission is neither mourned nor regretted; it is not even noticed. True, the rabbis were aware of the harshness of certain laws pertaining to women and sought to mitigate their effects. They tried to find ways to force a recalcitrant husband to divorce his wife, for example. But the framework that necessitated such mitigations went unquestioned. Women's Otherness was left intact. The Jewish passion for justice did not extend to Jewish women. As Cynthia Ozick puts it, one great "Thou shalt not"—"Thou shalt not lessen the humanity of women"—is missing from the Torah.

For this great omission, there is no historical redress. Indeed, where one might expect redress, the problem is compounded. The prophets, those great champions of justice, couch their pleas for justice in the language of patriarchal marriage. Israel in her youth is a devoted bride, subordinate and obedient to her husband/God (for example, Jer. 2:2). Idolatrous Israel is a harlot and adulteress, a faithless woman whoring after false gods (for example, Hos. 2, 3). Transferring the hierarchy of male and female to God and his people, the prophets enshrine in metaphor the legal subordination of women. Those who might have named and challenged women's marginalization thus ignore and extend it.

The prophetic metaphors mark an end and a beginning. They confront us with the injustice of Torah; they link that injustice to other central Jewish ideas. If exploring Torah means exploring a terrain of women's silence, this is no less true of the categories of Israel or God.

Israel, the bride, the harlot, the people that is female (that is, subordinate) in relation to God is nonetheless male in communal self-perception. The covenant community is the community of the circumcised (Gen. 17:10), the community defined as male heads of household. Women are named through a filter of male experience: that is the essence of their silence. But women's experiences are not recorded or taken seriously because women are not perceived as normative Jews. They are part of but do not define the community of Israel.

The same evidence that speaks to women's silence in the tradition, to the partiality of Torah, also reflects an understanding of Israel as a community of males. In the narratives of Genesis, for example, the covenant moves from father to son, from Abraham to Isaac to Jacob to Joseph. The matriarchs' relation to their husbands' God is sometimes assumed, sometimes passed over, but the women do not constitute the covenant people. Women's relation to the community is also ambiguous and unclear in biblical legislation. The law is couched in male grammatical forms, and its content too presupposes a male nation. "You shall not covet your neighbor's wife" (Ex. 20:17). Probably we cannot deduce from this verse that women are free to covet! Yet the injunction assumes that women's obedience is owed to fathers and husbands, who are the primary group addressed.

The silence of women goes deeper, however, than who defines Torah or Israel. It also finds its way into language about God. Our language about divinity is first of all male language; it is selective and partial. The God who supposedly transcends sexuality, who is presumably one and whole, comes to us through language that is incomplete and narrow. The images we use to describe God, the qualities we attribute to God, draw on male pronouns and experience and convey a sense of power and authority that is clearly male. The God at the surface of Jewish consciousness is a God with a voice of thunder, a God who as lord and king rules his people and leads them into battle, a God who forgives like a father when we turn to him. The female images that exist in the Bible and (particularly the mystical) tradition form an underground stream that occasionally reminds us of the inadequacy of our imagery without transforming its overwhelmingly male nature.

This male imagery is comforting and familiar—comforting because familiar—but it is an integral part of a system that consigns women to the margins. Since the experience of God cannot be directly conveyed in language, imagery for God is a vehicle that suggests what is actually impossible to describe. Religious experiences are expressed in a vocabulary drawn from the significant and valuable in a particular culture. To speak of God is to speak of what we most value. In attributing certain qualities to God, we both attempt to point to God and offer God's qualities to be emulated and admired. To say that God is just, for example, is to say both that God acts justly and that God demands justice. Justice belongs to God but is also ours to pursue. Similarly with maleness, to image God as male is to value the quality and those who have it. It is to define God in the image of the normative community and to bless men—but not women—with a central attribute of God.

But our images of God are not simply male images; they are images of a certain kind. The prophetic metaphors for the relation between God and Israel are metaphors borrowed from the patriarchal family—images of dominance softened by affection. God as husband and father of Israel demands obedience and monogamous love. He repays faithfulness with mercy and loving-kindness, but punishes waywardness, just as the wayward daughter can be stoned at her father's door (Deut. 22:21). When these family images are combined with political images of king and warrior, they reinforce a particular model of power and dominance. God is the power over us, the One out there over against us, the sovereign warrior with righteousness on his side. Family and political models of dominance and submission are recapitulated and rendered plausible by the dominance and submission of God and Israel. The silence and submission of women becomes part of a greater pattern that makes it appear fitting and right.

. . .

Clearly, the implications of Jewish feminism reach beyond the goal of equality to transform the bases of Jewish life. Feminism demands a new understanding of Torah, Israel, and God. It demands an understanding of Torah that begins by acknowledging the injustice of Torah and then goes on to create a Torah that is whole. The silence of women reverberates through the tradition, distorting the shape of narrative and skewing the content of the law. Only the deliberate recovery of women's hidden voices, the unearthing and invention of women's Torah, can give us Jewish teachings that are the product of the whole Jewish people and that reflect more fully its experiences of God.

Feminism demands an understanding of Israel that includes the whole of Israel and thus allows women to speak and name our experience for ourselves. It demands we replace a normative male voice with a chorus of divergent voices, describing Jewish reality in different accents and tones. Feminism impels us to rethink issues of community and diversity, to explore the ways in which one people can acknowledge and celebrate the varied experiences of its members. What would it mean for women *as women* to be equal participants in the Jewish community? How can we talk about difference without creating Others?

Feminism demands new ways of talking about God that reflect and grow out of the redefinition of Jewish humanity. The exclusively male naming of God supported and was rendered meaningful by a cultural and religious situation that is passing away. The emergence of women allows and necessitates that the long-suppressed femaleness of God be recovered and explored and reintegrated into the Godhead. But feminism presses us beyond the issue of gender to examine the nature of the God with male names. How can we move beyond images of domination to a God present *in* community rather than over it? How can we forge a God-language that expresses women's experience?

Everywoman Her Own Theology

Alicia Suskin Ostriker (1986)

I am nailing them up to the cathedral door
Like Martin Luther. Actually, no,
I don't want to resemble that *Schmutzkopf*
(See Erik Erikson and N. O. Brown
On the Reformer's anal aberrations,
Not to mention his hatred of Jews and peasants),
So I am thumbtacking these ninety-five
Theses to the bulletin board in my kitchen.

My proposals, or should I say requirements,
Include at least one image of a god,
Virile, beard optional, one of a goddess,
Nubile, breast size approximating mine,
One divine baby, one lion, one lamb,
All nude as figs, all dancing wildly,
All shining. Reproducible
In marble, metal, in fact any material.

Ethically, I am looking for
An absolute endorsement of loving-kindness.
No loopholes except maybe mosquitoes.

Virtue and sin will henceforth be discouraged,
Along with suffering and martyrdom.
There will be no concept of infidels;
Consequently the faithful must entertain
Themselves some other way than killing infidels.

And so forth and so on. I understand
This piece of paper is going to be
Spattered with wine one night at a party
And covered over with newer pieces of paper.
That is how it goes with bulletin boards.
Nevertheless it will be there.
Like an invitation, like a chalk pentangle,
It will emanate certain occult vibrations.

If something sacred wants to swoop from the
        universe
Through a ceiling, and materialize,
Folding its silver wings,
In a kitchen, and bump its chest against mine,
My paper will tell this being where to find me.

Feminist Questions of Christianity

Caryn D. Riswold (2009)

Feminists are often suspicious of Christianity and have a lot of questions about a religion led by men that worships a male God. In what way can this religion be good for women and men who are interested in an equal humanity? History provides many examples of the ways that Christianity has served to support and justify patriarchal ideas like wifely submission and women's second-class status. With the weight of this evidence, feminists wonder why they should continue to care about Christianity. Perhaps it is only another patriarchal institution that needs to be dismantled.

The questions in this reading capture this critical attitude toward Christianity, and the answers provide some information about the religion in a way that takes the questions seriously, often recognizing where the suspicions are well grounded.

. . .

WHY SHOULD FEMINISTS CARE ABOUT CHRISTIANITY?

Feminists should care about Christianity because it is simultaneously a religion with an egalitarian vision that has been and should continue to be liberating for women, and because it has been a major institution of patriarchy that remains a pervasive cultural force needing criticism. The first two waves of feminism demonstrated how various institutions of patriarchy promoted injustice and inequality especially for women, and they helped bring about positive change in many of them. The work of criticizing the negative elements of Christianity while uncovering its positive legacy must continue today with third-wave feminist insights and strategies.

One reason that feminists should care about Christianity is that it impacts women's lives in a significant way. It was during the second wave of feminism that activists and scholars began turning their attention to religion in a more sustained and sophisticated way than the suffragists had in the previous century. In the United States, this meant paying particular attention to Christianity. Early feminist theological works challenging the church as well as its ideas were written by Valerie Saiving and Mary Daly. Saiving offered the first critique of basic Christian ideas about sin, while Daly mounted a serious case against the Catholic Church for its treatment of women throughout history. They saw that like government, education, and the professional world, religion was a powerful tool of patriarchy that needed challenge and reform.

Because Christianity is a religion that helps perpetuate patriarchy, whether or not a woman participates in a religious community, whether or not she is religious at all, religion affects her life because it shapes society. In any society, the dominance of one religion necessarily affects the culture and the laws that impact everyone. Despite the legal separation of church and state that defines religious freedom in the United States, Christianity is a dominant cultural force: every president to date has been a Christian; the vast majority of Supreme Court justices to date have been Christian.[1] This is one reason why, whether religious or not, feminists need to engage in the critical examination necessary to understand Christianity.

Effects of this cultural dominance of Christianity are seen in several events from recent years: Controversy erupted in several states when pharmacists refused to fill prescriptions for emergency contraception, written by medical doctors, on the claim that it violated their religious beliefs against contraception and/or abortion. Much of the anti-choice and anti-abortion activism in America has its roots in Christian communities; the 2008 election saw the passage of Proposition 8 in California, which revoked the right of gay and lesbian Americans in that state to marry. This resulted in widespread protests and demonstrations targeting Mormons and evangelical Christian churches, groups who publically support outlawing gay marriage and who helped fund the Proposition 8 campaign. These examples show what many feminists consider to be the negative, sexist, and homophobic legacy of Christianity. Because it is a patriarchal institution, in practice as well as in its belief, that supports legal and political maneuvers to limits on rights based on gender, it necessarily commands attention from feminists. But that is not the only reason.

Feminists should care about Christianity because it provides life and spiritual sustenance for many women. This has been true from the days that Jesus talked with, healed, and dined with women, and it is still true today. Feminist biblical scholars like Elisabeth Schüssler Fiorenza help Christians more fully understand the relevance of Jesus' own actions with regard to women. She suggests that there were feminist impulses within Judaism that Jesus amplified in his teaching and ministry. Scholars of the Pauline literature show some of the egalitarian impulses of that early Christian community, and how they were sidelined as the church grew and gained power into the fourth century. The inclusion of commendations and greetings for women like Phoebe ("minister of the church"), Prisca ("who work[s] with me in Christ Jesus"), and Junia ("prominent among the apostles") at the conclusion of Paul's letter to the Romans (Romans 16:1, 3, 7), for example, suggests a gender ideology different from what many see in texts from 1 Timothy and Ephesians that restrict women's public and teaching authority. Patriarchy ultimately defined the institution of Christianity due in no small measure to the cultural and philosophical influences of the society in which it emerged and took formal shape. Historians like Karen Torjesen, however, have meticulously shown how traditions such as women priests were in fact part of Christianity from the beginning.

Beyond the early formative years and texts of Christianity, women's voices show how the religion continued to provide a source of life and liberation even as patriarchy took an entrenched hold on it. Medieval women mystics and martyrs give powerful testimony to the way visions of God and Jesus sustained them throughout their lives. Julian of Norwich's intimate descriptions of the Mother Jesus and Catherine of Siena's passionate engagement with the politics of the thirteenth-century church provide models of women who seized their voice because of their religious experiences. Surviving narratives from slaves in the American historical record reveal further how biblical stories like the exodus provided the spark of hope that God was on the side of the enslaved, how Jesus was seen as the one who suffered like they did, and that there was liberation and new life awaiting them.

If there is something good in Christianity, which legions of women and men throughout history and in the world today suggest, then feminist scholars have reason to pay attention to it. If there continues to be something problematic in the religion, which legions of critics and scholars suggest, then feminists have an obligation to engage it critically. This obligation includes bringing the most serious critical feminist tools to bear on Christian beliefs and practices. This can contribute to chipping away the patriarchal mantle and liberating a core message that early on declared that ethnicity, sex, and status do not ultimately determine one's fate: "There is no longer Jew or Greek, there is no longer slave or free, there is no longer male and female; for all of you are one in Christ Jesus" (Galatians 3:28).

. . .

HOW HAS CHRISTIANITY BEEN A PROBLEM FOR WOMEN?

. . .

A brief look into the history of Christianity shows how its view of women sits at the root of much social and theological sexism. Tertullian, while instructing women and men on how to dress in the third century, told women that they were the devil's gateway, the means by which evil entered the world. He articulated the part of traditional Christian anthropology that views women as responsible for sin and evil entering the world because of Eve's actions in the Garden of Eden story of Genesis 3. This idea of some ancient and primordial human decision has had a tremendous influence not only on Christianity's view of women but on dominant Western cultural ideas about women and men.

In addition, ancient misunderstandings of biology were woven into medieval Scholastic texts in a way that continues to misshape our understandings of sex and gender. Saint Thomas Aquinas's theological views of human nature reflected his thirteenth-century understanding of the process of procreation, borrowed from Aristotle: man supplies the form and the ideal representation of human being, and woman is merely the matter and the place where the form grows. To put it more crudely, with ejaculation, the man implants a very tiny person (the homunculus) into the woman who is little more than the warm place for the tiny person to grow. The nineteenth-century discovery of the ovum and subsequent realizations about how procreation actually takes place rendered this understanding of human beings irrelevant. In many ways, however, the assumptions and dualisms about men and women derived from it remain in place. Aristotelian biology and Aquinas's theological adoption of it provided a foundation for claims about male superiority that still exist: Men are superior, women are inferior; men are stronger, women are weaker; men are active and women are passive; men provide, women receive; men create, women participate.

Ideas like these from the intellectual history of Christianity reveal where some of the roots of sexism and misogyny lie. Feminists who have an understanding of this can simultaneously point out the errors insofar as they exist, and they can push the religion and society toward better articulations of what it means to be human. Knowing specifically why Christianity has been a problem for women with these historical notes enables feminists to participate in fixing the problem.

The social and political implications of Christianity also deserve attention insofar as the religion has been oppressive for women both inside and outside the church. In the Western world, Christianity has been the religion of the dominant classes, and as such it has provided ideological basis for many of its oppressive practices. Biblical texts have been used to support the notion that wives must submit to their husbands, and that slaves should obey their masters. Arguments presented in the early twentieth century against women gaining the right to vote in places like Britain and the United States relied heavily on assumptions drawn from Christian ideas about men and women, like those described above. The idea that women were fully dependent on and represented by their husbands under the law stems in part from a reading of Genesis 2, where the woman is made from the rib of the man. The subsequent claim that women are physically inferior to men is also connected to the flawed biology and philosophical presumptions about form and matter from Aristotle and Aquinas. Dualisms borrowed in part from gnostic and Platonic philosophy also influenced the increasingly patriarchal Christianity to value spiritual over physical, free over slave, form over matter, and male over female. Patriarchy still depends on this mode of thinking to maintain the unquestioned dominance of men over women.

Despite some core theological commitments to peace, justice, and compassion, Christianity has also justified violence against women, officially as well as subtly. This is where feminist critique of sexism in Christian theology becomes essential. Official sanction of violence against women occurred with the persecution and subsequent execution of women as witches in the fifteenth and sixteenth centuries. This enterprise was supported by a declaration from Pope Innocent VIII, and led by Heinrich Kramer and Jacob Sprenger, who authored the *Malleus Mallificarum* (the *Hammer against Witches*) in 1486. This text, a manual for finding and dealing with witches, excessively focused on women's sexuality and women's involvement in things mysterious to many men, like miscarriages and stillbirths. It reflected the Christian theological views of women and sex promoted by Tertullian, Augustine, and Aquinas as described above. These Christian thinkers fundamentally

believed that women were inferior beings more susceptible to the influence of the devil in part because of the demands of their bodies.

Historians conservatively estimate that sixty thousand people were executed during the medieval witch persecutions, a majority of them women; and some scholars estimate that millions were brought to trial.[2] This massive tragedy was among other things a culmination of generations of misogyny and misunderstanding about women perpetuated in large part by the Christian church.

Such sexism still exists today when well-intentioned pastors and Christian neighbors counsel women to endure mistreatment at their husband's hands in the spirit of turning the other cheek, or pressure a woman to prematurely forgive her rapist, or persuade a woman not to file charges against an abuser because of how it will affect his life.

. . .

Theological justification for counsel like this comes in part from biblical texts ("wives be subject to your husbands as you are to the Lord," Ephesians 5:22) as well as from sexist religious culture. Carole R. Bohn has called this a "theology of ownership" that has promoted male dominion over all things, again based on a reading of the Genesis texts. In cases of child abuse by priests, a theology of ownership again paves the way for destructive actions. Once experiences like these are revealed and taken seriously, such justifications can be delegitimized. The more that women find the courage and support to tell their stories and hold their religious leaders to account, the fewer women and children there will be who receive such warped counsel. As the movement built on the very criterion of taking women's experience seriously, feminism has a crucial role to play in making such truths known and such actions and theological claims unacceptable within Christianity, holding it accountable to wider cultural parameters and critique.

. . .

HAS CHRISTIANITY BEEN OPPRESSIVE ONLY ON THE BASIS OF GENDER?

One of the more shameful legacies of the Christian tradition has been its use as the ideological basis for the persecution of Jews and Muslims. In addition,

Christianity has provided religious justification for the careless misuse of the earth's natural resources. Each of these realities is taken seriously by third-wave feminists, who are attuned not only to oppression on the basis of gender but also to justice throughout the global and multifaith human community. Looking at examples of how Christianity has been oppressive in other ways also reveals how initiatives to correct these problems have emerged.

The Holocaust was in part made possible by centuries of Christian anti-Semitism, itself a gross misconstrual of the religion's relationship to Judaism. At the heart of the matter is the very difficult question of whether Christianity is inherently anti-Jewish because of its supersessionist tendencies. Supersessionism is the belief that Christianity supersedes, completes, and fulfills Judaism. It is the belief that once Christianity arrived, Judaism was no longer needed because Jesus was the messiah, the promised deliverer of the Jews; and anyone who didn't understand that was simply wrong. Since the beginning, Christians have had to walk a very fine line by maintaining a connection to Judaism while adhering to their claims that Jesus is God incarnate. Early Christianity was full of unfortunate tendencies to belittle Jews for their supposed ignorance because they did not accept Jesus as their savior. In Romans, for example, Paul speaks directly about the Jews when he says, "I can testify that they have a zeal for God, but it is not enlightened" (Romans 10:2).

Such problematic views did not end with the early centuries. In fact, they were in some ways solidified and entrenched. In 1543, Martin Luther wrote "On the Jews and Their Lies," which reflected his own move from a theological anti-Judaism to a racist anti-Semitism. For among other things, he lambasted the Jews for refusing to accept Jesus as their savior (a theological point) and called them a lazy and irrational people (a racist point).[3]

The Nazis in Germany were the fullest and most complex expression of a long history of anti-Semitism. The Christian churches in Europe retain a shameful legacy of nonintervention and collaboration in the mistreatment and murder of millions of Jews.[4] The weight of history clearly indicts Christianity for failing its Jewish neighbors, but glimmers of hope for a better future have since emerged. The World Council of Churches (WCC), founded in 1948 in part as a reaction to the world's collective failure in the Holocaust, holds as one of its chief purposes to "engage in Christian service by serving human need, breaking down barriers between people, seeking justice and peace."[5] Seminars on human rights, religions of the world, and interfaith community building are now regularly offered at the WCC ecumenical institute at Bossey in Switzerland. In addition, the Second Vatican Council of the Roman Catholic Church in the 1960s held discussions and produced official documents that took seriously the need for the Church to repair its relationship with Judaism. *Nostra Aetate* spoke of the "spiritual patrimony common to Christians and Jews" and rejected "any discrimination against men or harassment of them because of their race, color, condition of life, or religion."[6] These are just a few examples of the ways that Christianity has addressed the problems of its tenuous relationship with Judaism throughout history.

Christianity's relationship with Islam has a similarly violent and troubled past. The early twentieth-century *Catholic Encyclopedia* described the Crusades as "expeditions under-taken, in fulfillment of a solemn vow, to deliver the Holy Places from Mohammedan tyranny."[7] Christian beliefs here gave way to violent interaction with nations and people of other faiths. Various church-sanctioned military expeditions during the eleventh, twelfth, and thirteenth centuries resulted in shifting political boundaries and widespread resentment against Christianity. In addition, "viewed from the aspect of their purposes the Crusades were failures. They made no permanent conquest of the Holy Land . . . Their cost in lives and treasure was enormous. Though initiated in a high spirit of devotion, their conduct was disgraced throughout by quarrels, divided motives, and low standards of personal conduct."[8]

The impetus for this action was at least in part a misunderstanding of the religion of Islam, reflected by Christians' not only misnaming it with terms like "Mohammedan" but also believing it to be inherently tyrannical. These misunderstandings along with the history of aggressive colonialism working to ensure Christian domination of the world inform an increasingly complex relationship between the

Christian-dominated West and the Islamic-defined Middle East, well into the twentieth and twenty-first centuries.

Today much of Christianity better understands its familial relationship with both Judaism and Islam, and faithful scholars and leaders have worked to outline the necessity for and consequences of cooperation among the religions and their adherents. The National Council of Churches in the U.S. strengthens interfaith relations through various events and projects, and the Council on American-Islamic Relations today has ongoing interfaith outreach with Christian churches and their members. All this work is even more crucial in a world where *Muslim* is too often wrongly associated with *terrorist,* and the civil rights of Muslims in the U.S. have been under constant threat since the terrorist attacks of September 11, 2001.[9] Islamic feminist movements have also emerged in this context, taking seriously women's experiences both within their religion and as citizens of countries ravaged by sectarian violence and international military occupation. Third-wave feminism needs to engage these issues in order to fully participate in movements for peace and justice around the world.

A final example takes seriously the Christian theological justification for human misuse of the earth. Often because of an interpretation of Genesis 1:28 that exhorts humans to subdue the earth, the Christian tradition has viewed humans as the most important part of creation. Along with that, the rest of the earth is secondary and subjected completely to the whims and wishes of human beings. The consequences of viewing humans as masters of the universe was famously connected to Christianity by Lynn White Jr. in his 1967 article, "The Historical Roots of Our Ecologic Crisis" in the magazine *Science*. In response to environmental awareness and activism that emerged over the past two generations, Christian churches, groups, and leaders are moving to articulate the trusteeship of creation that is given to humans by God. Leading second-wave feminist theologian Rosemary Radford Ruether has written "an ecofeminist theology of earth healing" that draws together resources from the Christian tradition to identify both its contributions to the destruction of the planet and the resources it provides for healing the earth.

Third-wave feminists can see how, with regard to Jews, Muslims, and the earth, Christianity has been oppressive in a variety of ways. Feminism is a key critical voice that raises questions about power dynamics, about privilege and oppression in relationships with others, and about environmental exploitation. This is because patriarchy depends on and feeds off of racism, classism, and heterosexism as well as global capitalism, environmental racism, and religious discrimination. Third-wave feminism is keenly interested in the global reality of human life, which includes a multifaith community as well as responsibility for the effects of human participation in the ecosystem. If Christianity is not held to higher standards of relating to outsiders, insiders, and the planet, it will continue to support the destruction and division brought about by patriarchy.

. . .

HOW HAS CHRISTIANITY AFFECTED WOMEN'S LIVES IN A POSITIVE WAY?

Christianity has provided both a set of beliefs and a place that have been good for women individually and collectively. While the oppressive and sexist tendencies of the religion are well documented and discussed, its empowering dimension is often overlooked by feminist critics. History, theology, and practice are instructive on this topic. Historically, Christians created a community that welcomed the marginalized and served the poor, and this practice can be found resurging today. Theologically, Christianity provides a basis for egalitarian and just human relationships. In practice, Christian churches have been and still are places where women have found and fostered community, developed leadership skills, and transformed the societies in which they live.

The early Christian community was viewed by the dominant class as a radical and threatening sect because of its claims about Jesus, and because it welcomed women, slaves, and members of the lower social classes. Based in part on stories of Jesus' speaking to women in public (John 4), women's presence throughout his ministry (Luke 8), and his compassion for marginalized people (Matthew 9: 10–12), the Christian community was founded on the belief in a compassionate God who demonstrated on many occasions compassionate care for the poor and oppressed. In this way, early Christians continued the narrative that originated with the Israelite people's belief in God as the one who liberated the Israelites from slavery in Egypt, and who sustained them while exiled in Babylon.

In response to the worsening conditions of daily life for multitudes of people throughout Latin America, this belief in a God who opts for the poor and marginalized was revitalized as a core principle of Christianity in 1968. Inspired by the Second Vatican Council, Latin American bishops gathered at Medellín, Colombia, for a conference and Gustavo Gutiérrez emerged as a leading voice of what became liberation theology. Gutiérrez and the liberation movement insisted that Christianity was a religion that had become excessively focused on the afterlife and needed to become a religion more focused on the quality of life this world: "When we struggle for a just world in which there is not servitude, oppression, or slavery, we are signifying the coming of the messiah."[10] This opened up and affirmed entirely new forms of activism devoted to economic and social justice around the world. What liberation theology did was "shift the gaze" (to borrow Gutiérrez's phrase) of Christianity toward more careful attention to the injustices in human life here and now. This included justice for women.

. . .

Practically speaking, Christian churches have been hubs of ordinary women's leadership, sometimes in spite of official denominational pronouncements to the contrary. Cheryl Townsend Gilkes's descriptive book title articulates a reality that many people know to be true: *If It Wasn't for the Women*. Gilkes takes this phrase from a conversation she had with a bookstore manager who declared: "If it wasn't for the women, you wouldn't have a church!"[11] Many women social activists throughout history have taken their cue from their Christian identity. This is not only a modern phenomenon, as some medieval women's writing demonstrates. Catherine of Siena spoke out when she wrote to Pope Gregory XI in 1376 about the corrupt state of the church, urging the return of the papacy to Rome as well as the reform of its excessive focus on worldly things.

Despite official limits on women's leadership in Christianity, women have a long history of finding ways to change their communities and their church.

In American history, women who headed up the antilynching movement and the temperance and prohibition movements honed their organizational and leadership skills in their churches. In a society where women were not permitted to hold elective office, to vote, or to own property in their own names, Christian churches were places where women designed, implemented, and led programs and projects in their local communities. Ida B. Wells-Barnett wrote, spoke, and organized protests against lynching in the late nineteenth century. Another female social activist at the time, with whom Barnett publically sparred, was Frances Willard, president of the Women's Christian Temperance Union. There are many examples of social change led by women who gained practical leadership skills in their Christian churches, and who took many of their ideological commitments to community service, compassion, justice, and peace from that tradition.

. . .

HOW ARE FEMINISTS CHANGING THE FACT THAT CHRISTIANITY HAS BEEN ANTI-FEMINIST, IF NOT ANTI-WOMAN?

Feminists have been changing the sexist and misogynist tendencies of Christianity for generations. Examples from the first wave, the second wave, and the third wave of feminism demonstrate clearly how Christianity is in places becoming a pro-feminist and pro-woman religion. Continuing these efforts now is essential for the well-being of women and men around the world.

In the modern world, significant attempts to critically engage the Christian tradition gained public attention with the writings of abolitionist women and suffragists like Sarah Grimke, Elizabeth Cady Stanton, and Matilda Joslyn Gage. Grimke wrote *Letters on the Equality of the Sexes* in 1838, and in these letters she criticized sexist interpretations of a variety of biblical texts in order to make her case for the equality of men and women. She modestly pointed out one of the disadvantages to women, saying, "When we are admitted to the honor of studying Greek and Hebrew, we shall produce some various readings of the Bible a little different from those we have now." And despite her lack of advanced education, she was able to recognize that Jesus put forth ideas for all to follow "without any reference to sex or condition."[12]

Stanton's and Gage's efforts to construct *The Woman's Bible* appeared in two volumes in 1895 and 1898, representing another significant shot at patriarchally dominated schools of biblical interpretation. The effort itself, while not wholly successful, was monumental in scope, especially in its context. The legacy of *The Woman's Bible* is mixed because of the anti-Semitism present throughout, and the less-than-professional methodology used when Stanton physically cut out passages from the Bible. Because of several factors, it was not substantial enough to have a lasting impression on the field of biblical studies. Stanton and Gage were not trained scholars in the field of biblical commentary (a nineteenth-century woman rarely was, as Grimke had pointed out) and therefore were not able to break through. Gage went on to write a text with greater impact called *Woman, Church, and State* in 1893, in which she laid out the many ways the church has contributed to maintaining sexism and women's second-class citizenship. The strategies these nineteenth century women employed reflect their key insight that getting to the heart of religious justifications for sexism must be part of combating it.

Two important feminist theological works in the second-wave feminism were more substantial in their impact and marked an irrevocable shift in Christian theology. Valerie Saiving's article called "The Human Situation," published in the *Journal of Religion* in 1960, directly addressed the flaws in theological giant Reinhold Neibuhr's discussions of human nature and sin. Saiving showed how Niebuhr's focus on pride as the central human sin was steeped in androcentric thinking and did not resonate with women's experiences. On the contrary, Saiving argued, women suffer from socially conditioned passivity. Their sin is, in fact, too little pride and not enough self-assertion. She pointed out that Christian exhortations for the faithful to humble themselves do not take into account those whom Christianity already

humiliates. She showed definitively how Christian theology provided divine justification for the social reality of sexism and the second-class status of women. Saiving's argument influenced not only the specific field of Christian theological anthropology which discusses sin in particular, but also the entire Christian tradition which had up to that point been able to think and act based solely on male human experience.

A concurrent social development inspired by second-wave feminism was the emerging understanding in the medical sciences that testing and research on any number of diseases and conditions could no longer be done solely with male subjects. A conference on women's health and women's bodies in 1969 led to the formation of the Boston Women's Health Collective, and the publication of the groundbreaking book *Our Bodies, Ourselves* in 1971. Thus, activists in theology and in the sciences reached these conclusions about expanding their understanding of "human" experience around the same time because of second-wave feminism. No research on the human condition, spiritually or biologically, could be done in the same way after these breakthroughs in understanding "human" experience.

Another second-wave feminist theologian, Mary Daly, influenced the Christian tradition of thinking and speaking about God. In 1973 Daly encapsulated the problem of male images of God, about which she had been speaking and writing for many years. Drawing the connection between theology and sociology, Daly stated that "if God is male, then the male is god."[13] She showed how theological ideas have sociological roots as well as consequences. In fact, using theories of religion from Peter Berger and others, Daly showed that a group ascribes to its deity the attributes that it finds to be the highest and the most ideal. In patriarchy, that is first and foremost the male. Christian theology that has taken place after Mary Daly, whether it agrees with her or not, has had to reckon with the undeniable implications of exclusively male images and language for God.

Many theologians have picked up precisely on that challenge and have constructed feminist liturgies as well as participating in reshaping cross-denominational worship resources. The Inclusive Language Lectionary project in 1983 represented the National Council of Churches' belief that "All persons are equally loved, judged, and accepted by God . . . God is more than male or female, and is more than can be described in historically and culturally limiting terms."[14] This is one example of putting into practice the theological claim made by Daly and others that exclusive male imagery and language for God is problematic. It also shows how Christian theologians, feminist or not, understand the problem of sexism. At the same time, the New Revised Standard Version of the Bible (NRSV), which was completed in 1989, openly addressed "the danger of linguistic sexism arising from the inherent bias of the English language toward the masculine gender, a bias that in the case of the Bible has often restricted or obscured the meaning of the original text."[15] These two pan-Christian efforts in particular show how feminists and supporters of anti-sexism work have been directly changing the fact that Christianity has been anti-woman and anti-feminist.

Feminist theology in the third wave is more complex and continues to unfold around us today. Reflecting the third wave's intersectional focus on race, class, gender, sexuality, and ecology among other things, the later ecofeminist work of Rosemary Radford Ruether, the work of womanist theologian Delores S. Williams, and the thinking of mujerista theologian Ada María Isasi-Díaz set the stage for the more diffuse and complex relationship between feminism and Christianity with which we now live. Ruether's 1992 book *Gaia and God* spells out the responsibilities of Christianity to move toward a more ecologically minded theology; Williams, along with scholars like Jacquelyn Grant, inspired a generation of black (i.e. womanist) activists to engage the Christian tradition from their particular "tridimensional" experience at the intersection of race, class, and gender; Isasi-Díaz recenters Christian theology and ethics on the struggles that define Hispanic women's lives, recasting moral agency *en la lucha* (in the struggle).

While the battles for the ordination and equality of women in Christian churches defined much of the second wave, struggles for gay and lesbian Christians for full access to legal rights and church practices like marriage and ordination have begun to characterize one way that the third wave of feminism

continues to change Christianity. Daniel Helminiak's basic text, *What the Bible Really Says about Homosexuality,* as well as the work of Episcopal bishop John Shelby Spong and church activists like Lutheran pastor Anita C. Hill continue to reframe Christian understandings of inclusion and social justice.

As third-wave feminists continue to challenge the multifaceted sexism of Christianity, they are moving their attention to the global religious context. Attending to the reality of women's lives around the world becomes more important as Christianity grows in Latin America and Africa, and as the world understands more thoroughly than ever before the multireligious nature of the global community. These are the ways that third-wave feminist activism is moving its own advocacy work firmly into the new millennium, and the ways that it needs to continue to reform Christianity for a new generation.

NOTES

1. Kosmin, Barry A., et al. "The American Religious Identification Survey." (2001), 10. The Graduate Center at the City University of New York. http://www.gc.cuny.edu/faculty/research_studies/aris.pdf/.

2. Clark, Elizabeth A., and Herbert Richardson. "Woman as Witch: Witchcraft Persecutions in the Old and New World." In *Women and Religion: The Original Sourcebook of Women in Christian Thought,* edited by Elizabeth A. Clark and Herbert Richardson, 119–43. Rev. ed. San Francisco: HarperSanFrancisco, 1996.

3. Luther, Martin. "On the Jews and Their Lies." (1543). In *Luther's Works* 47:123–306. Edited by Frank Sherman. Philadelphia: Fortress, 1971.

4. Barnett, Victoria. "The Role of the Churches: Compliance and Confrontation." In *The Holocaust and the Christian World: Reflections on the Past, Challenges for the Future,* edited by Carol Rittner et al., 55–58. New York: Continuum, 2000.

5. World Council of Churches. "Who Are We?" http://www.oikoumene.org/en/who-are-we.html/.

6. Second Vatican Council. *Declaration on the Relationship of the Church to Non-Christian Religions (Nostra Aetate),* 660–668. www.vatican.va/archive/hist_councils/ ii_vatican_council/documents/vat-ii_decl_19651028_nostra-aetate_en.html.

7. Bréhier, Louis. "Crusades." In *The Catholic Encyclopedia.* Vol. 4. New York: Robert Appleton Company, 1908. http://www.newadvent.org/cathen/04543c.htm.

8. Walker, Williston. *A History of the Christian Church.* 3rd rev. ed. by Robert T. Handy. New York: Scribners, 1970.

9. The CAIR produces annual reports as well as periodic statements on legal issues, public opinion, and issues relevant to Muslims in America: http://www.cair.com/AmericanMuslims/ReportsandSurveys.aspx/.

10. Gutiérrez, Gustavo. "Toward a Theology of Liberation."(1968). In *Liberation Theology: A Documentary History,* edited by Alfred T. Hennelly, 62–76. Maryknoll, NY: Orbis, 1995.

11. Gilkes, Cheryl Townsend. *If It Wasn't for the Women: Black Women's Experience and Womanist Culture in Church and Community.* Maryknoll, NY: Orbis, 2001.

12. Grimke, Sarah, and Elizabeth Ann Bartlett. *Letters on the Equality of the Sexes and Other Essays.* Edited with an introduction by Elizabeth Ann Bartlett, 242. New Haven: Yale University Press, 1988.

13. Daly, Mary. *Beyond God the Father: Toward a Philosophy of Women's Liberation,* 19. Boston: Beacon, 1973.

14. Gold, Victor Roland et al. *An Inclusive-Language Lectionary.* 3 vols. Philadelphia: Westminster, 1983–1985.

15. Attridge, Harold, general editor. "To the Reader." In *The HarperCollins Study Bible: New Revised Standard Version, including the Apocryphal/ Deuterocanonical Books.* Fully revised and updated. Student edition. San Francisco: HarperSanFrancisco, 2006.

R E A D I N G   (**102**)

The Non-Religious Patriarchy: Why Losing Religion Has Not Meant Losing White Male Dominance

Ashley F. Miller (2013)

From the beginning, the non-religious movement has had women and African-Americans as prominent members. Women like Elizabeth Cady Stanton and Susan B. Anthony were non-religious—Stanton so much so that she got written out of history for her outspoken critiques of religion—and African-Americans like Frederick Douglass, W.E.B. Du Bois, and Asa Philip Randolph all spoke out strongly against organized religion and the harm it did to African-Americans. Langston Hughes, Zora Neale Hurston, and James L. Farmer, Jr. all also identified as freethinkers. Despite being dominated by white men, the non-religious, humanist movement had a strong, vocal minority of women and African-Americans and was strongly involved in political causes like ending slavery and getting women the vote. As time has passed, however, the movement has continued to be dominated by white men who hold traditional privilege and power, in much the same way that they do throughout society.

Despite the fact that the non-religious, atheist, and humanist movements began as a backlash against both Christian beliefs, which they considered false, and social injustice, which they believed to be caused by organized religion, the movement is *still* dominated by white men and white men's concerns. The movement is only 30 percent women and 15 percent people of color and focuses more on Biblical Criticism and debunking the supernatural than on social justice causes.

A great deal of research has been done into the patriarchal underpinnings of many of the major world religions; in the United States, this is primarily Christian sects. While many of the churches in the United States have slowly made reform in the nature of the relationship of women to religion and to the church, progress is slow. However, despite the fact that there are no *theological* underpinnings to support the patriarchy in the movement, the atheist movement has struggled to fight the larger *cultural* underpinnings of the patriarchal hegemony.

Likewise, the atheist movement has failed to appeal to people of color and incorporate their concerns. Although atheists are predominately liberal and claim to be pro-equality for all races, genders, and sexualities, the movement has failed to attract those people they claim to support—despite the fact that organized religion often subjugates and oppresses those same people, they are not finding their way to the atheist movement. . . .

SKEPTIC, HUMANIST, AND ATHEIST MOVEMENTS

Although the terms are often used interchangeably, there are important differences between those who label themselves "Humanists," "Atheists," and "Skeptics." Broadly speaking, secular humanists focus on morality and being "good without god," atheists focus on arguing against organized religion, and skeptics focus on debunking supernatural beliefs. Many people identify with all three, others identify with only one, but the demographics of all three movements are very similar and have similar aims. This article will refer to these three subgroups collectively as "the atheist movement" and focus on its presence and history in the United States.

Atheism has recently experienced a resurgence known as the New Atheist movement and led by bestselling books like Christopher Hitchens's *God Is Not Great* and Richard Dawkins's *The God Delusion*. Exploration of and research on the atheist experience has expanded to match.[1] This expansion has also included a burgeoning online social network and community that has connected atheists and secularists across the country and around the world; people who had previously been isolated by their minority view now use the Internet to create communities with people who have similar values.[2]

Research has explored the atheist experience as well as the degree to which atheists are the victims of prejudice and bias.[3] Some research has found that atheists are the most reviled minority group in America today, less trusted than homosexuals or Muslims.[4] Consequently, the majority of the scholarly literature on atheism concerns anti-atheist bias and how to combat it. The expanded interest

in atheists, their experiences, and anti-atheist sentiment in the United States has included little research or exploration of the experience of atheist women and African-Americans.

INTERSECTIONALITY AS AN APPROACH

Intersectionality is a research approach to study "the relationships among multiple dimensions and modalities of social relationships and subject formations."[5] The goal of an intersectional approach is to understand the interaction of societal concepts like race, class, gender, and sexuality and how they affect the "vectors of oppression and privilege."[6] The intersection of these different constructs not only reveals oppressions, but also offers insights into how different positions in society affect the people who occupy those positions. Not only do these insights help us to conceptualize problems, but they also offer us the opportunity to effect change informed by that insight.

Traditionally, the intersectional approach has focused primarily on race, class, gender, and sexuality, but this article seeks to add religion to that approach. In the same way that race, class, gender, and sexuality offer privileges to the majority, so too does religion. In the United States, this privilege goes to the Christians, whose god is referenced in the Pledge of Allegiance, on every piece of money, and embraced by politicians at large to win votes from the American public. Those who are not Christian are not considered fully American—"guns, freedom, Jesus" are what makes an American.

This article applies an intersectional analysis to women and people of color in the secular humanist and skeptic movements. This complicated, multi-layered feminist and intersectional analysis helps to unpack the questions: Why are women and people of color underrepresented in the atheist movement? Does the movement appeal more to white men than to others? Does religion have a special hold on women and people of color? Does the movement fail to reach out to those who are not white men? Does the movement isolate women and people of color? What can be done to bring more women and people of color to the atheist movement?

Religion's role in the patriarchy

Western culture depends heavily on the patriarchal structure that allowed for white male dominance of women and people of color. "Patriarchy is a theory that attempts to explain this widespread gender stratification as an effect of social organization rather than the result of some natural or biological fact" and to unpack why "there remains a near total domination of women by men at both the micro level of intimate relationships and the macro level of government, law, and religion."[7] Patriarchy is not limited to the system that controls women but is "always linked into other systems of inequality and privilege, including but certainly not limited to age, ability, education, race, sexual orientation, and class."[8]

According to Gerda Lerner,[9] the development of male-dominated society and slavery depended on the cultural move from hunter–gatherer societies to agricultural ones. Men took advantage of childbirth as a means of controlling women, which led to acceptance of people as property more generally. As time passed, religion and religious law developed around the male-dominated society, making women's subjugation not just acceptable, but the only acceptable option.

In the West, this structure was dependent on two ideas: one, the Aristotelian idea that women were flawed versions of men that could never reach the perfection of the male form, and two, the religious idea that a male God ruled over men who ruled over women.[10] The Judeo-Christian tradition meant that society functions based on the idea that the divine right of kings came from the divine right of Adam over Eve.[11] Through these developments, "the subordination of women comes to be seen as 'natural', hence it becomes invisible. It is this which finally establishes patriarchy firmly as an actuality and as an ideology."[12]

Religion's move in the direction of the patriarchy does not mean that religion was the cause of patriarchy. While it is now a tool for the continuation of male domination, it is possible, even probable, that changes in religion from fertility goddesses and polytheism to male-headed monotheism reflected a change in the culture, rather than the change in culture reflecting a change in religion. In other words, the shift "may be more prescriptive than descriptive.

It may tell us more about what the upper class of royal servants, bureaucrats, and warriors wanted the population to believe than what the population actually did believe."[13] As much as atheists may now assert that "religion poisons everything,"[14] religion developed as a function of the culture, not the other way around. Patriarchy uses religion as a tool for self-perpetuation, and so the fight against religion in the name of feminism is a logical one, but when you take religion away from the culture, you are still left with a patriarchal system. Which brings us to the atheist movement's patriarchal problem with women and people of color.

Race and gender in the atheist movement

Female atheists are a minority within a minority. Although the non-affiliated or "nones" are the fastest-growing demographic in the United States, having doubled to more than 15 percent since 1990, only 2 percent of the population identifies as atheist.[15] And while women make up a slight majority of the U.S. population, they are only 40 percent of the "nones"[16] and only 30 percent of the atheists.[17] As a whole, women in America think religion is more important than men do, are more likely to go to church, and are more likely to become religious after being raised secular.[18]

The numbers for African-Americans and African-American women are even more religious—92 percent of African-Americans identify as Christian and African-American women are the most religious demographic in the country.[19] Atheism simply does not attract as many women as it does men with the result that, as with lesbians and African-Americans in the lesbian, gay, bisexual, and transgender (LGBT) movement, women are a minority within a minority that is dominated by white men.

This leads to the question: Why is the atheist movement so dominated by white men? The answer is this: there is a social cost to being an atheist that is more easily borne by those with privilege than by those who are already minorities. Women and people of color, occupying a fundamental minority position in society, will thus suffer far greater social costs by identifying with atheism than white men. People are drawn to religion for reasons beyond belief—organized religion offers cultural and social capital and identity for people, especially for those who are disenfranchised already. Atheism means abandoning not just a belief system (which is, incidentally, the primary thing the atheist movement focuses on) but also an entire social system.

There are several kinds of social costs that come with identity as an atheist. As previously mentioned, atheists are among the most reviled minority groups in the United States. Before taking into account any other reason, it is necessary to acknowledge that being out as an atheist comes with negative consequences, regardless of one's age, class, race, gender, or sexuality. Atheists face discrimination both legally and in terms of social shunning in the United States[20] because of stereotypes of being immoral, criminal, evil, and unfeeling, even though all evidence points to the contrary.[21] Female atheists and atheists of color will endure the net effect of these consequences but still have additional obstacles facing them.

One reason is the difference in earning power between men and women, white people and black people, and the lack of a social safety net for low-wage earners. According to Sikivu Hutchinson, "The domino effect of socioeconomic instability and diminishing job and education returns has apparently bolstered the influence of organized religion on African-American communities."[22] The church provides economic resources to those who are not being supported by their communities or by the government. In the United States, the highly disparate incomes of those at the top and those at the bottom and the lack of a strong social safety net mean that there is a large population of people who are struggling to get by and take care of themselves and their families. These people are disproportionately black and female. The church offers the safety net that the government and society at large does not, making leaving the church not just a risk of social discrimination but a very real material loss of support like daycare and food. "This is especially true in African American communities where single parent female-headed households predominate."[23]

The church also offers a way of maintaining identities that are valued by society—it makes black men more masculine, women more feminine, and black women more innocent. "Patriarchy entitles men to reject organized religion with few implications for their gender-defined roles . . . men do not run the risk of compromising their *masculinity* if they question, don't participate in, and/or actively reject organized religion,"[24] but women are faced with the possibility of being seen as not feminine, or worse, "fallen" in the eyes of the religious culture around them.

Furthermore, minority culture especially places high value on women being religious, often because they are seen as the arbiters of morality and the sole caretaker of children. When atheists are seen as fundamentally immoral, a woman who chooses to be an atheist is also choosing to imbue her children and the children of the community with immorality; this is doubly true for black women who are more likely to be the sole caretaker of children. Beyond that, the church is a deep part of mainstream identity, but even more so a part of black identity—churches in black communities represent a greater facet of the community's racial identity than churches in white communities. "Insofar as atheism is an implicit rejection of both black patriarchy and authentic blackness, those who dare to come out of the closet as atheists are potential race traitors."[25] On the other hand, white people do not face the threat of seeming "less white" by rejecting belief, nor do men face the risk of seeming less masculine by embracing what is portrayed as an emotionless, scientific, masculine lack of belief.

There is a strong belief in the African-American community that church is one of the few ways that men can protect themselves from falling into drugs and going to prison and how women can redeem themselves for being unmarried with children.[26] Rather than address the systematic problems that cause the high incarceration rates of black men or provide social support that would reduce the stigma and financial difficulties faced by single mothers and without strong governmental programs to help them, the black community historically has turned to the church.[27] When you are disenfranchised by the culture at large and the only place that will discuss and address concerns that face your community is a church, the church is going to be where you turn.

Historically, as well, the church has served either in practice or symbolically in the fights for civil rights, the end of slavery, and the cause of women's suffrage. "Organized religion enabled African-Americans to achieve self-determination and community under conditions of racial apartheid" as well as creating the ability for black people to become insiders to the dominant culture of Christianity.[28] Oppressed groups often participate in their own means of oppression in an attempt for individuals to gain more individual power[29]—perhaps Christianity subjugated African-Americans, but it also offered a means of critiquing social systems in place. "American blacks rejected as exemplars the slave-owning freethinkers of the Enlightenment in favor of a biblical Jesus who spoke to the humanity of the most dispossessed elements of society."[30] Additionally, church was often the only or safest place for the community to discuss issues of social justice and community organizing.

Beyond this, the atheist movement fails to address or analyze the problem in meaningful ways. Within the critiques of organized religion, there is "little analysis of the relationship between economic disenfranchisement, race, gender, and religiosity" meaning that such critiques inevitably are of "limited cultural relevance for people of color."[31] Likewise, such critiques often fail to engage with the reasons that religion can be a very useful thing to women and people of color, in a strictly utilitarian way, even while it oppresses them. The atheistic, science-and-objective truth above all point of view means that the experiences of those without the luxury of choice or who cannot place more importance on philosophy than taking care of their families are both not explored and treated as inferior. Religion is not simply about a belief system, and treating it as though it is, is only possible with a blindness to all of the social benefits it provides, even while acknowledging all of the injuries it creates as well. From the position of privilege many in the atheist movement occupy, the focus is always on what is false rather than on what helps one to survive. This is not to say that organized religion is a net good, or something not worth fighting against, but rather to say that ignoring the reality of how religion helps people means being unable to offer meaningful alternatives to it.

There is a pervasive belief that "objective" science holds all of the answers without an acknowledgement that most values and causes are supported by philosophy and personal worldviews as well.[32] A white male scientist is naturally going to be interested in causes related to being a white male scientist and blind to or ignorant of causes not related to that.

It is a systematic bias. As a movement founded primarily by white male scientists who felt ostracized, the atheist movement has a difficult time acknowledging that science has its problems both historically and as the sole foundation of a worldview and that being white confers special privileges, as does being male. Ironically, their deep commitment to skepticism often fails to include a skepticism aimed at their own worldview.

The movement "likes to talk about the European Enlightenment as if nothing bad could ever legitimately be said about it"[33] despite the fact that the Enlightenment was responsible for scientific rationalization and implementation of terrible programs that exploited and hurt people of color and women. Historically, science has been responsible for: terrible programs of eugenics, claims of biological race, and sex differences that have sense been proven to be untrue, justification of slavery, scientific experiments on people of color, forced sterilization of women who committed the crimes of being poor, unmarried, or not white, forced imprisonment of women who were sexual or became involved with someone of a different race, and the list goes on. Science has been responsible for a great many crimes against humanity, and the majority of these crimes have been committed against those least able to defend themselves. There is a natural distrust from people who have faced generations of horror at the hands of scientists and science and the atheist movement's focus on science above all, with no recognition of the problematic history, makes it difficult for many to trust it.

In addition to the fact that church offers so many benefits to women and people of color that the movement offers no alternative for, the atheist movement often fails to create a welcoming environment. Even without addressing the fact that the movement does not make an effort to emulate the community support of church, it also does not treat the issue of welcoming women and people of color as an important one.

These explanations, however, are not the only ones found in the popular atheist books and websites, which often focus on "the supposed emotionalism of women versus the rationality of men" and women's nature as "naturally timorous and thus less inclined to question or challenge organized religion."[34]

The bestselling atheist books and most popular atheist websites are all written by men. Though not as numerous as those written by men, there are a large number of books and websites written by atheist women, but these books and websites do not become as popular as those written by men. The women who do have large readerships online are generally, simply by virtue of the demographics of the movement at large, writing for a male-dominated audience; Jen McCreight, writer of a popular feminist atheist blog, has an audience that is only 27 percent female.[35] This is especially problematic because so much of the atheist community is experienced not in person but through online communities and atheist texts.[36]

The atheist community is particularly reliant on the Internet as the home of its community. Because atheists make up a small percentage of the population at large, and an even smaller part of the population in rural areas and the South, the Internet has given them a means of connecting to those who are not geographically convenient.[37] For minorities, the availability or an online community is even more important. If you are a woman or an African-American, the social cost of simply coming out in your community as an atheist is prohibitive; forming an online social network allows one to find similar people without any public activity that might reveal behavior that they are embarrassed of. As Emily Brennan puts it, "Feeling isolated from religious friends and families and excluded from what it means to be African-American, people turn to these sites to seek out advice and understanding."[38]

The rise of atheism in the public consciousness and the rise of awareness of prejudice and hatred toward atheists are largely dependent on the birth and growth of online networking and communities for non-believers. According to Cimino and Smith, the online community is the key to the rise in visibility of atheists (2011, 2012). Interestingly, in their qualitative research into online communities, Cimino and Smith did not mention a single female atheist, though they mentioned over a dozen male atheists. Their research has thus overlooked a significant segment of the atheist population.

The online atheist community does have vocal female participants. In the past year, there have been several widespread online uproars started by women complaining about their treatment at the hands of the male-dominated atheist community. In what has come to be known as "Elevatorgate," Rebecca Watson, one of the most well-known atheist women, complained about the behavior of another conference attendee who followed her alone onto an elevator at 4 a.m. and asked her back to his room; she said that this was not the way to make women feel comfortable at atheist events. An online forum, reddit, discussed her blog and the response was swift and furious and became a major in-group fight. Richard Dawkins himself joined the debate to accuse Watson of overreacting and suggesting she should not be upset because she had not been physically harmed.[39] Very ugly, anti-woman things were said about Watson, now referred to by a subset of the atheist movement as "twatson," personally and about women who supported her.

"Elevatorgate" was followed at the end of 2011 by a discussion that became known as "redditgate." A fifteen-year-old woman on reddit posted a picture of herself with an atheist book her religious mother had given her and was immediately swamped with comments about her appearance and sex appeal. There were many "jokes" about statutory and anal rape. There was, predictably, an outcry from feminists in the online community and a counter-outcry from those who felt that it was not a problem that atheists on reddit were joking about anally raping a fifteen-year-old who was interested in getting involved in the atheist community.[40]

While these incidents are not necessarily representative of the atheist woman's online experience, community-wide online discussions about gender discrimination occur relatively regularly and some of the key contributors are women. The lack of scholarly attention to women atheists and their experiences in the atheist community and movement is problematic. It is problematic for the atheist movement in terms of attracting more female members; it is problematic for the women in the movement who are being rendered invisible; and it is problematic for researchers and writers who are not getting documenting and analyzing the full range of atheist communities and experiences. What is the atheist woman's experience in these important online communities? Do atheist women have a voice online, are they heard when they speak, or are they often ignored, mocked, and confronted with "jokes" about rape?

While the movement can be openly misogynistic, it is generally only tacitly racist. The movement is not generally interested in the issues that affect people of color or in promoting diversity within the movement, but racial epithets or claims of genetic inferiority of people of color are almost universally denounced, while calling women dykes, twats, and saying they are intellectually inferior to men is fairly common. In some ways, this makes having a conversation about race in the movement more difficult because the problem is more invisible. If no one is calling black people names or saying they cannot join, what's the problem? This refusal to recognize that there is a problem or belief that acknowledging race makes one racist leads to further alienation of people of color.

HOW TO MOVE FORWARD

Not all people or organizations fail to notice these problems; there is a small, vocal group within the movement that points out the failures of the movement to reach out to minorities and women. And though the most vocal are women and minorities, there are many white men in power who are also promoting the cause. Fred Edwords (2012) offers a critique, listing the problems that the atheist movement is failing to address to make itself relevant:

> Why, for example, would someone living in the inner city—dealing with the hard issues of economic survival, epidemics of drug abuse and AIDS, violent crime, urban blight, and other social problems—find it useful or even interesting to work her or his way through a cumbersome public transit system (designed to keep those from minority and poor neighborhoods balkanized) to reach the middle-class white suburbs and attend a humanist lecture or discussion about some abstract philosophical, scientific, or cultural matter or engage in social action on a mere symbolic issue like ceremonial deism? After only a moment's thought, the utter irrelevancy of many humanist gatherings to minority concerns becomes staggering.

When the vast majority of events appeal primarily to the concerns of white men without taking into account the concerns of other populations and how atheism, humanism, and skepticism can help those communities, the movement and organizations therein need to recognize that oftentimes their focus is on issues that are not universal. The problem is scope—"Liberation is not a matter of fighting against white racism, sexism, and classism, but of throwing off the shackles of superstition"[41] never mind that racism, sexism, and classism are structures just as illogical and unsupportable as religion. This leads to self-marginalization of the atheist community by making themselves irrelevant to the community at large.

Refusing to focus on more than the interests the movement currently focuses on is often referred to as mission drift, without recognizing that the current focus is driven by cultural forces and the white male patriarchal paradigm. The movement also needs to recognize that focusing on issues that affect minorities and women is not addressing "special" concerns, but human concerns that affect everyone. The saying is trite but useful in this case: everyone does better when everyone does better; social justice issues are not issues just for "other people." Even Gerda Lerner, in 1986, describes the fight against the patriarchy as a skeptical issue: "To step outside of patriarchal thought means: Being skeptical toward every known system of thought; being critical of all assumptions, ordering values, and definitions" (p. 228).

Sikivu Hutchinson recommends that the movement offers clear alternatives to supernatural beliefs, uses the moral values to critique socioeconomic problems, and creates atheist communities within communities of color. She could not be more correct. Atheism and humanism lead to a set of moral values that are not just useful for intellectual discussion but for the application to real-world problems that face women and people of color. Biblical scholarship and discussion of beliefs are, of course, important, but so are discussions of how to help those in need through a belief system that does not involve gods.

But the movement also needs to be proactive in supporting community efforts, even when those efforts might involve working with churches in the community. De-stigmatization of atheism in communities of color will go a long way toward helping minority communities see that one can still be black and an atheist. Mercedes Diane Griffin says that to "walk away from the only support system they have ever known, even when it comes with the price of intellectual stagnation, and repressive life options is not an easy one" and this "needs to be counteracted by developing a structured support system."[42] That support network needs to be less judgmental and more visible in communities of color.

Finally, there needs to be an attempt to reach out and work with other social justice movements that have historically been reluctant to work with atheists due to the stigma attached to non-believers. LGBT groups, feminist groups, and equal rights organizations all have a history of being reluctant to have vocal non-theists in their movement or have made attempts to hide historical figures who were atheists. Groups like Foundation Beyond Belief have made strides in making atheist participation in charity more public, but atheists need to make a strong effort to be seen as positive contributors to other causes. Religion is a cause of great suffering for the LGBT, women, and people of color, and these communities could be greatly served by embracing a humanistic, loving outlook that does not include a judgmental god or religion. However, often for PR reasons, these groups are reluctant to ally themselves with atheists. Atheists need to do everything they can to engage with them anyway.

This is not to say there have not been positive changes in the movement. An excellent example of an organization making progress on this front is the Richard Dawkins Foundation, which is providing free daycare at conferences so that women with young children have more opportunity to go. More conferences are also providing scholarships or reduced fees to make it easier for those with lower incomes to attend conferences. Many conferences, with a few notable exceptions, are making sexual harassment policies part of their conference guidelines. These are steps in the right direction, but a greater effort of being welcoming online, of reaching out to diverse people, of addressing issues pertaining to people who are not white men as mainstream issues rather than "special" ones is needed before true progress can be made.

NOTES

1. Cimino, Richard, and Christopher Smith, "The New Atheism and the Formation of the Imagined Secularist Community," *Journal of Media and Religion* 10, no. 1 (2011): 24–38, doi: 10. 1080/15348423.2011.549391.

2. Cimino, Richard, and Christopher Smith, "Secular Humanism and Atheism Beyond Progressive Secularism," *Sociology of Religion* 68, no. 4 (December 21, 2007): 407–424, doi: 10.1093/socrel/68.4.407; Cimino and Smith, "The New Atheism and the Formation of the Imagined Secularist Community,"; King, Lisa J., "Gender Issues in Online Communities," *The CPSR Newsletter* 18, no. 1 (Winter 2000), http://cpsr.org/prevsite/publications/newsletters/issues/2000/Winter2000/king.html/; Smith, Christopher, and Richard Cimino, "Atheisms Unbound: The Role of the New Media in the Formation of a Secularist Identity," *Secularism and Nonreligion* 1 (February 21, 2012): 17–31.

3. Caldwell-Harris, Catherine L., et al., "Exploring the Atheist Personality: Well-being, Awe, and Magical Thinking in Atheists, Buddhists, and Christians," *Mental Health, Religion & Culture* 14, no. 7 (2010): 659–672, doi: 10.1080/13674676.2010.509847; Edgell, Penny, Joseph Gerteis, and Douglas Hartmann, "Atheists As 'Other': Moral Boundaries and Cultural Membership in American Society," *American Sociological Review* 71, no. 2 (April 1, 2006): 211–234, doi: 10.1177/ 000312240607100203; Gervais, Will M., "Finding the Faithless: Perceived Atheist Prevalence Reduces Anti-Atheist Prejudice," *Personality and Social Psychology Bulletin* 37, no. 4 (April 1, 2011): 543–556, doi: 10.1177/0146167211399583; Gervais, Will M., Azim F. Shariff, and Ara Norenzayan, "Do You Believe in Atheists? Distrust Is Central to Anti-atheist Prejudice," *Journal of Personality and Social Psychology* 101, no. 6 (2011): 1189–1206, doi: 10.1037/a0025882; Goodman, Kathleen M., and John A. Mueller, "Invisible, Marginalized, and Stigmatized: Understanding and Addressing the Needs of Atheist Students," *New Directions for Student Services* 2009, no. 125 (March 1, 2009): 55–63, doi: 10.1002/ss.308; Smith, Jesse M., "Becoming an Atheist in America: Constructing Identity and Meaning from the Rejection of Theism," *Sociology of Religion* 72, no. 2 (June 20, 2011): 215–237, doi: 10.1093/socrel/srq082; Swan, Lawton K., and Martin Heesacker, "Anti-Atheist Bias in the United States: Testing Two Critical Assumptions," *Secularism and Nonreligion* 1 (February 22, 2012): 32–42.

4. Edgell, Gerteis, and Hartmann, "Atheists As 'Other'," 217.

5. McCall, Leslie, "The Complexity of Intersectionality," *Signs* 30, no. 3 (March 1, 2005): 1771–1800.

6. Ritzer, George, and Jeff Stepnisky, *Contemporary Sociological Theory and Its Classical Roots: The Basks,* 4th ed. (McGraw-Hill Humanities/Social Sciences/Languages, 2012), 204.

7. Ritzer, George and J. Michael Ryan, eds., "Patriarchy," *The Concise Encyclopedia of Sociology* (Wiley-Blackwell, January 25, 2011), 441.

8. Ibid.

9. *Women and History. 1. The Creation of Patriarchy* (Oxford University Press, 1986).

10. Ibid.

11. Filmer, Robert, "Patriarcha; or the Natural Power of Kings," *Constitution.org*, 1680, http:// www .constitution.org/eng/patriarcha.htm.

12. Lerner, *Women and History. 1. The Creation of Patriarchy,* 10.

13. Ibid., 158.

14. Hitchens, Christopher, *God Is Not Great: How Religion Poisons Everything* (Twelve, 2009).

15. Kosmin, Barry A., et al., *American Nones: The Profile of the No Religion Population/ARIS 2008,* ARIS 2008 (Institute for the Study of Secularism in Society & Culture, 2008), http://commons.trincoll .edu/aris/publications/american-nones-the-profile-of-the-no-religion-population/.

16. Ibid.

17. Pew Forum on Religion & Public Life, *U.S. Religious Landscape Survey* (Pew Research Center, June 23, 2008), http://religions.pewforum.org/reports.

18. Kosmin et al., *American Nones: The Profile of the No Religion Population/ARIS 2008;* Winseman, "Religion and Gender: A Congregation Divided," *Gallup,* December 3, 2002, http://www.gallup.com/ poll/7336/Religion-Gender-Congregation-Divided .aspx; Winseman, Albert L., "Religion and Gender: A Congregation Divided, Part II," *Gallup,* December 10, 2002, http://www.gallup.com/poll/7390/ Religion-Gender-Congregation-Divided-Part.aspx; Winseman, Albert L., "Religion and Gender: A Congregation Divided, Part III," *Gallup,* December 17, 2002, http://www.gallup.com/poll/7429/Religion-Gender-Congregation-Divided-Part-III.aspx.

19. Barna Group, "How the Faith of African-Americans Has Changed," *The Barna Group,* 2009, http://www .barna.org/barna-update/article/5-barna-update/286-how-the-faith-of-african-americans-has-changed.

20. Boyle, K., *Freedom of Religion and Belief: A World Report* (Routledge, 1997), http://books.go-ogle .com/books?hl=en&lr=&id=MFUZkWWgOtMC &oi=fnd&pg=PPl&dq=%22religion+or+belief .+The+terms+%E2%80%98belief+%E2%80%99 +and+%E2%80%98religion%E2%80%99+are+to+ be+broadly+construed.+Article+18%22+&ots=e_ AzCYMhsm&sig=uf0YlTunO3XYnb8n X2KjcG3aahw.

21. Zuckerman, P., "Atheism, Secularity, and Well-Being: How the Findings of Social Science Counter Negative Stereotypes and Assumptions," *Sociology Compass* 3, no. 6 (2009): 949–971.

22. *Moral Combat: Black Atheists, Gender Politics, and the Values Wars* (Infidel Books, 2011), 18.

23. Ibid., 31.

24. Ibid., 33.

25. Ibid., 20.

26. Davis, Reginald F., *The Black Church: Relevant or Irrelevant in the 21st Century?* (Smyth & Helwys Publishing, 2010); Wallace J. M., Jr., "Is Religion Good for Adolescent Health?," *A National Study of American High School Seniors. (Philadelphia, PA: University of Pennsylvania, Program for Research on Religion and Urban Civil Society, 2002),* CRRUCS Report 66, http://www.baylorisr.org/ wp-content/uploads/ISR_Adolescent_Health.pdf.

27. Hutchinson, *Moral Combat.*

28. Ibid, 205.

29. Lerner, *Women and History. 1. The Creation of Patriarchy,* 217.

30. Edwords, Fred, "The Hidden Hues of Humanism," *The Humanist,* 2012, http://thehumanist.org/march-April-2012/the-hidden-hues-of-humanism/.

31. Hutchinson, *Moral Combat,* 199.

32. Pigliucci, Massimo, *Denying Evolution: Creationism, Scientism, and the Nature of Science,* 1st ed. (Sinauer Associates, 2002).

33. Edwords, "The Hidden Hues of Humanism."

34. Hutchinson, *Moral Combat,* 27.

35. McCreight, Jennifer, "Blag Hag 2010 Census Results," *Blag Hag,* February 14, 2010, http://www.blaghag .com/2010/02/blag-hag-2010-census-results.html.

36. Cimino, Richard, and Christopher Smith, "The New Atheism and the Formation of the Imagined Secularist Community."

37. Smith and Cimino, "Atheisms Unbound."

38. "African-American Atheists," *The New York Times,* November 25, 2011, sec. Fashion & Style, http://www.nytimes.com/2011/11/27/fashion/ african-american-atheists.html.

39. Watson, Rebecca, "The Privilege Delusion," *Skepchick,* July 5, 2011, http://skepchick.org/2011/07/the-privilege-delusion/.

40. Watson, Rebecca, "Reddit Makes Me Hate Atheists," *Skepchick*, December 27, 2011, http://skepchick.org/2011/12/reddit-makes-me-hate-atheists/.

41. Hutchinson, *Moral Combat*, 218.

42. Griffin, Mercedes Diane, "The Color of Humanism: My Story as an African American Humanist and Activist," *Unscripted*, October 21, 2010, http://unorthodoxparadox.blogspot.com/2010/10/color-of-humanism-my-story-as-african.html.

DISCUSSION QUESTIONS FOR CHAPTER 12

1. Why do you think the control of women is a central component in many religions?

2. How do you think religion has been both empowering and oppressive for women?

3. How do you think the availability of a greater variety of images of God might impact religion and religion's influence on social life?

4. How might women work toward reform from within religious traditions? Why might some women feel the need to abandon religious traditions completely?

5. How have negative stereotypes of witchcraft served to perpetuate the oppression of women? Why do you think practices of women's spirituality were (and still are) perceived as such a threat?

6. How do nondominant religious traditions challenge the influence of hegemonic Christianity in U.S. society?

SUGGESTIONS FOR FURTHER READING

Campbell, Susan. *Dating Jesus: A Story of Fundamentalism, Feminism, and the American Girl.* Boston: Beacon Press, 2010.

Coleman, Monica A. *Ain't I a Womanist, Too?: Third Wave Womanist Religious Thought.* Minneapolis: Fortress Press, 2013.

Haberman, Bonna Devora. *Israeli Feminism Liberating Judaism: Blood and Ink.* Lanham, MD: Lexington Books, 2012.

Hayes, Diana. *Standing in the Shoes My Mother Made: A Womanist Theology.* Minneapolis: Fortress Press, 2010.

Joyce, Kathryn. *Quiverfull: Inside the Christian Patriarchy Movement.* Boston: Beacon Press, 2010.

Kidd, Sue. *The Dance of the Dissident Daughter: A Woman's Journey from Christian Tradition to the Sacred Feminine.* New York: HarperOne, 2006.

Nomani, Asra. *Standing Alone: An American Woman's Struggle for the Soul of Islam.* New York: HarperOne, 2006.

Ostman, Cami and Susan Tive, eds. *Beyond Belief: The Secret Lives of Women in Extreme Religions.* Berkeley, CA: Seal Press, 2013.

Stuckey, Johanna H. *Women's Spirituality: Contemporary Feminist Approaches to Judaism, Christianity, Islam, and Goddess Worship.* Toronto: Inanna Publications, 2010.

Activism, Change, and Feminist Futures

THE PROMISE OF FEMINIST EDUCATION

In Chapter 1 we discussed the goals of women's and gender studies as a discipline. These objectives include, first, an understanding of the social construction of gender: the ways gendered personhood is mapped on to physical bodies; second, the analysis of intersections of gender with other systems of inequality, including the effects of imperialism and globalization; and third, a familiarity with the status of women and other marginalized people, and individual and collective actions for change. A fourth objective of women's and gender studies is that you will start thinking about patterns of privilege and discrimination in your own life and understand your position vis-à-vis systems of inequality. We hope you will learn to think critically about how societal institutions affect individual lives—especially your own. We hope you will gain new insights and confidence and that new knowledge will empower you.

Feminist educators attempt to give students more inclusive and socially just forms of knowledge and to support teachers using their power in nonexploitive ways. Women's and gender studies usually involves nonhierarchical, egalitarian classrooms where teachers respect students and hope to learn from them as well as teach them. The focus is on the importance of the student voice and experience and the encouragement for personal and social change. Most women's and gender studies classes, however, are within colleges that do not necessarily share the same goals and objectives. Many feminist educators operate within the social and economic constraints of educational institutions that view "counter-hegemonic" education—that is, education that challenges the status quo—as problematic and/or subversive. Despite these constraints, feminist education, with its progressive and transformative possibilities, is an important feature on most campuses.

For many students, and perhaps for you too, the term *feminism* is still problematic. Many people object to the political biases associated with feminist education and believe knowledge should be objective and devoid of political values. It is important to emphasize that all knowledge is associated with power, as knowledge arises from communities with certain positions, resources, and understandings of the world. This means that all knowledge (and not just feminist knowledge) is ideological in that it is always associated with history and politics. To declare an unbiased objectivity or value neutrality is to ignore or mask the workings of power that are present in all forms of knowledge. Although feminist education is more explicit than other forms of knowledge in speaking of its relationship to power in society, this does not mean it is more biased or ideological than other forms of knowledge. It is important to note that some knowledge's claim to being objective, unbiased, and value neutral (these words essentially imply the same thing) is related to the claim to a scientific "truth." Feminist knowledge emphasizes that science is a human product and therefore hardly unbiased or value free either: All truth claims are relative and must be understood in the context of history, culture, and politics. This means that all knowledge, whether feminist or not, is "political."

Many people support the justice-based goals of feminism but do not identify with the label. "Fear of Feminism: Why Young Women Get the Willies," the classic reading by Lisa Marie Hogeland that is still relevant after some 20 years, addresses this issue. She examines the continuing resistance to feminism as a political standpoint and as a set of values that inform how we live our lives. She makes the important distinction between *gender consciousness* and *feminist consciousness,* explains why one does not necessarily imply the other, and discusses the fear of reprisals and consequences associated with a feminist consciousness.

ACTIVISM

We live in a complex time. White women have made significant progress over the past decades and are integrated into most societal institutions in the United States. Although the progress of women of color lags behind the gains made by white women, it too is beginning to be seen. Yet the big picture is far from rosy, as society has not transformed its core values in ways feminists throughout the last century hoped. And, as women experience more public power, they are encouraged to internalize more private constraints concerning the body and sexuality. In addition, an equitable sharing of power and resources in terms of gender, race, class, and other differences has not been actualized. Indeed, those whose differences, in terms of bodies and behavior, identify them as outside normative expectations are exposed to stigma and discrimination and endure both interpersonal violence (such as harassment and assault) and structural violence (such as poverty and homelessness). Wars rage around the world, violence is increasing in all walks of life, and the balance of power in the world seems fragile and in the hands of relatively few (often egocentric, delusional) men. If this wasn't bad enough, global climate change is affecting all communities, human and nonhuman alike. Global capitalism, which has allowed the privileged to lead lives of relative security, has deleterious consequences on humanity in many regions of the world. These are the issues around which individual and collective feminist activism, both in the United States and worldwide, coalesce.

Key issues addressed by feminism that you might be dealing with include access to affordable higher education and preparation for work and professional careers at a time of economic recession and high unemployment. Currently more than half of all bachelor's degrees are earned by women, and there is an increasing number of women (especially low-income women) compared with men in institutions of higher education. Scholars emphasize that such figures must not be interpreted as lack of opportunities for men, or failure on their part, except to acknowledge how lack of socioeconomic resources affects working-class men.

Still, as you are aware, having a college degree does not always guarantee employment. This is especially true for those individuals who challenge gender conformity, although such problems do not start only after college. As the reading "Transgender Inclusion" by Kim Case, Heather Kanenberg, Stephen Arch Erich, and Josephine Tittsworth explains, transgender students face a host of obstacles on many college campuses. The reading discusses student activism to change policy, in part through faculty–student alliances working to change university nondiscrimination policies.

Other key issues often mentioned as being at the forefront of students' minds are ways to balance work and family at a time when women are increasingly wanting to combine a career and motherhood. Access to affordable childcare and equitable sharing of domestic responsibilities are also high priorities for families as are affordable health care and reproductive services. You might also wonder about the development of the Internet and virtual realities and the effects of these new ways of communication and entertainment on children and families. Do you think smartphones are actually making us smarter or not? How are these technologies affecting our relationships and everyday lives? What are your thoughts about your level of media literacy? What is your relationship to contemporary media and how do you see it intersecting with feminism? Alongside concern about media in society, contemporary students question faith in politicians and government officials to make the best choices for them. Finally, perhaps you are concerned about globalization and increasing levels of consumerism in the United States. If you care about environmental degradation and the need for sustainability, what kinds of things can you do—or are you already doing? These are the questions many college students talk and write about—and these are the issues that feminism attempts to address. Whether people consider themselves feminists or not is less important than empowerment and collective action around these and other issues that might be important to you: LGBQT issues and discrimination, sexual freedom, and safety from physical, emotional, and sexual abuse. The box, "How to Learn the Modern Art of Protest," gives you some ideas about collective action that can be used to address these issues.

Many believe there is increasing prosperity in the United States, even though the gap between the rich and the poor is among the largest in industrialized nations and is increasing. Despite the widespread belief that the United States remains a more mobile society than some (meaning people can move out of poverty or move into more wealth), economists show that the typical child starting out in poverty here has less chance at prosperity than one in continental Europe or Canada. The United States and United Kingdom stand out as the least mobile among postindustrial societies. It is estimated that the top 1 percent of people in the United States own about 40 percent of the country's wealth, and 90 percent of new wealth in the last three decades has gone to 5 percent of the U.S. population. U.S. census data show more than 20 million people live in extreme poverty, and one in five children goes to bed hungry. Economists and sociologists emphasize that personal debt is a major problem in the United States—it is currently at about 120 percent of personal income. Despite this, U.S. workers tend to work about 9 weeks more a year than their European counterparts. The picture is one of great optimism and yet simultaneous despair. Perhaps we can address the rage, cynicism, and often mean-spiritedness of this historical moment and come up with a transformational politics that encourages a consciousness shift and extends generosity and compassion toward others. Any movement for justice-based equalities must have a strong moral foundation based on love, human dignity, and community.

LEARNING ACTIVITY   **Feminist.com**

Visit the website *www.feminist.com* and follow the link to the activism page. There you'll find links to action alerts and legislative updates for a number of feminist organizations, including the National Organization for Women (NOW), Code Pink, Feminist Majority, the League of Women Voters, the White House Project, and Planned Parenthood. Follow these links to learn what actions you can take. Find links to articles, speeches, and other websites on feminist.com's resource page, and, for feminist spins on current events, check out the site's news page.

As Audre Lorde, one of the most eloquent writers of the feminist second wave, once declared, "Silence will not protect you." Lorde wrote about the need to be part of social change efforts, and she encouraged us to speak out and address the problems in our lives and communities. And, as the reading by Byron Hurt, "Feminist Men," implies, speaking out and addressing inequities involves learning how to be an ally to people who are different from you and who do not enjoy the privileges you enjoy. Hurt writes about why black men should be embracing the "f" word (feminism) and emphasizes the necessity of men joining with women to make this world better for everyone. In this sense, coalitions are a central aspect of social change efforts.

In the past four decades there has been significant resistance to the status quo, or established power, in U.S. society, despite enormous backlash from the conservative right and other groups that seeks to maintain this power. As already mentioned in previous chapters, backlash can be defined as organized resistance to something that has gained popularity, prominence, or influence. In particular, there has been backlash to feminist advancements by groups seeking to prevent what they perceive as a loss of power and influence as a result of this movement for social justice. In 1991 Susan Faludi wrote *Backlash* to address the "undeclared war against women" that critiqued feminism as out of touch and elitist, among other things. This critique of feminist activism tended to center on the myths laid out in Chapter 1 and was often religion-based. Today, as Susan Douglas explains in the reading in Chapter 5, contemporary backlash also involves "enlightened sexism" and appropriation of the language of feminism. Examples include media portrayals of sassy, powerful women and messages that gender equality is an accomplished fact.

The strength of feminist justice-based movements involves their multi-issue and multistrategic approaches. *Multi-issue* means organizing on many fronts over a variety of different issues that include political, legal, and judicial changes, educational reform, welfare rights, elimination of violence, workplace reform, and reproductive issues. Basically all the issues in this text are components of a multi-issue approach to feminism. *Multistrategic* means relying on working coalitions that mobilize around certain shared issues and involve different strategies toward a shared goal.

Although human rights frameworks encourage coalitions to apply human rights standards associated with justice and human dignity to individual and community problems, they also promote a broad array of activist strategies from voting and policy changes, like the inclusion of LGBTQ issues in nondiscrimination statements in higher education, as already discussed, to art and music. The Russian feminist punk band Pussy Riot, which

How to Learn the Modern Art of Protest

INSTRUCTIONS

1. Focus on your target audience. Convincing people who already support you is a waste of time. Trying to change those diametrically opposed to you is pointless. Figure out who hasn't made up their mind yet but could be swayed to your side. Their support can help you get what you want.

2. Come up with an attention grabbing idea. PETA always gets on the news because they do outrageous things like having naked women go out in public to protest fur coats. The modern art of protest is all about media friendly events. Anything you decide to do should stop traffic. Otherwise the media won't care.

3. Organize your supporters. Gather together others who believe as you do. Enlist them to help you in your protest. Email, Facebook, Twitter, chat rooms and phone trees can all help you recruit followers.

4. Schedule your protest for the greatest impact. If your protest takes place on a busy news day it is less likely to be covered by the media. Late mornings and early afternoons on weekends tend to be the slowest time for news. Consider scheduling your protest then. If your protest would make a great live shot on the TV news then do it during the local morning news from 5 a.m. to 7 a.m. or afternoon broadcasts from 4 p.m. to 7 p.m.

5. Advertise your intentions. Write out a media release and be sure every media outlet in town gets it. Send both email and regular mail copies to everyone. Follow up with phone calls the day before the protest. The media release should be straightforward and simple. State your intentions and details of who, what, where and when. Contact people and their phone numbers should be prominent in the media release.

6. Be media friendly. During your event have designated people looking for reporters. Approach them and ask if they need any elements for their story. Provide easy access to people to interview, video opportunities and information. Have a focused message. Do not try to tell them everything. Keep your argument simple and straightforward.

7. Follow up. Watch the news and read the newspaper to see how much buzz you created. Put pressure on those whom you are protesting and let them know you will do it again if your demands are not met. If you make progress approach the media with a story about your results. If little changed protest again. This time top yourself and come up with something even more memorable.

TIPS & WARNINGS

- Be careful not to protest in the same way too often. The media will get bored quickly and ignore you. Be creative and choose your protests wisely.
- Understand the consequences of breaking the law during your protest. It is always best to obey the law, but historically some protesters have achieved change by being conscientious objectors. If you are planning to get arrested be sure you understand what will happen to you as a result of your arrest.

Source: Kent Ninomiya, *eHow.com.*

caused a scandal in Russia in 2012 when they sang a protest song in opposition to Russian President Vladimir Putin and the growing political power of the Russian Orthodox Church, are illustrative of the activist power of music. Their story is shared in the reading "What Pussy Riot Taught the World" by Michael Petrou.

Similarly, in the reading "We Are the Ones We've Been Waiting For," Moya Bailey and Alexis Pauline Gumbs write about the contemporary U.S. black feminist movement and its use of the Internet and blogosphere to connect scholars and activists, provide networking opportunities, and organize activism. The "Quirky Black Girl" social network site, for example, encourages a diverse group to share experiences and post videos and music while "building bravery and challenging each other's thinking." This reading emphasizes the multiple strategies of feminist activism that include online organization and activism.

As discussed in Chapter 1, some *liberal* or reformist activists have worked within the system and advocated change from within. Their approach locates the source of inequality in barriers to inclusion and advancement, and they have worked to change women's working lives through comparable worth, sexual harassment policy, and parenting leaves. Legal attacks on abortion rights have been deflected by the work of liberal feminists working within the courts, and affirmative action and other civil rights legislation have similarly been the focus of scholars, activists, and politicians working in the public sphere. These organizations tend to be hierarchical with a centralized governing structure (president, advisory board, officers, and so forth) and local chapters around the country. Other strategies for change take a *radical* approach (for example, radical or cultural feminism) and attempt to transform the system rather than to adapt the existing system. Together these various strategies work to advocate justice-based forms of equality. Contemporary feminism (both self-identified third wave activism and others) uses both liberal and radical strategies to address problems and promote change.

Although differences in strategy are sometimes a source of divisiveness among activists and feminists, they are also a source of strength in being able to work on multiple issues from multiple approaches. Indeed, any given issue lends itself to both reformist and radical approaches. LGBTQ rights, for example, is something that can be tackled in the courts and in the voting booths as organizations work toward legislation to create domestic partner rights or community civil protections. At the same time, consciousness-raising activities and grassroots demonstrations, such as candlelight vigils for victims of hate crimes and Queer Pride parades, work on the local level. Together, different strategies improve the quality of life. This is what is meant by *multistrategic.*

One important aspect to consider is that simply increasing women's participation and leadership does not necessarily imply a more egalitarian or feminist future. As you know, there are white women and women and men of color who are opposed to strategies for improving the general well-being of disenfranchised peoples. Changing the personnel— replacing men with women, for example—does not necessarily secure a different kind of future. Although in practice liberal feminism is more sophisticated than, for example, simply considering female leaders merely because they are women, it has been criticized for promoting women into positions of power and authority irrespective of their stance on the social relations of gender, race, class, and other differences. Still, the encouragement of women into leadership positions is a central aspect of feminist change.

Contemporary U.S. feminism is concerned with issues that are increasingly global, inevitable in the context of a global economy and militarism worldwide. These concerns

The World's Most Powerful Women 2013

For the 10th annual Forbes Power Women list, the mission is to redefine power. Forbes selected 100 women who go beyond the traditional classifications of the power elite (political and economic might). They are actually shifting our very idea of clout and authority and transforming the world and in exhilarating and novel ways. This annual snapshot of the 100 women with impact are top politicians and CEOs, activist billionaires and celebrities who matter. In roughly equal measure you'll find next gen entrepreneurs, technologists and philanthropists—all ranked by dollars, media momentum and impact. . . .

In 2013 the list featured eight heads of state—including our No. 1 for the eighth time, German Chancellor Angela Merkel—who run nations with a combined GDP of $9.9 trillion. The 24 corporate CEOs control $893 billion in revenues and of 16% of the women here have founded their own companies, including two new billionaires to the list, Tory Burch and Spanx's Sara Blakely. Speaking of, the 2013 class has 14 billionaires. 100 women on the 2013 list have major reach: a combined Twitter following of over 153 million. Following are the Top 10.

THE TOP 10 MOST POWERFUL WOMEN

Angela Merkel, Chancellor, Germany

The world's most powerful woman is the backbone of the 27-member European Union and carries the fate of the euro on her shoulders. Merkel's hard-line austerity prescription for easing the European debt crisis has been challenged by both hard-hit southern countries and the more affluent north, most particularly French President Francois Hollande. Merkel has served as chancellor since 2005, the first woman in the position, but her biggest challenge may still lie ahead: she is running for a third term this fall's general elections. 2013 SPOTLIGHT: Merkel has earned the top spot on the FORBES list of Most Powerful Women In The World for eight of the past 10 years.

Dilma Rousseff, President, Brazil

Now at the midpoint of her first term, the former revolutionary sits atop the world's seventh-largest national economy (GDP $2.4 trillion). Despite Brazil's size, Rousseff is tasked with pulling the country out of its slowest two years of growth in more than a decade. Her emphasis on entrepreneurship has inspired a new generation of startups, however many criticize the leader for favoring pro-development policy over more humanitarian concerns. 2013 SPOTLIGHT: Rousseff has a new ally in the first-ever Brazilian director-general of the World Trade Organization, Roberto Azevedo, who was confirmed in Geneva in early May.

Melinda Gates, Cochair, Bill & Melinda Gates Foundation, U.S.

Primary goals for the Bill and Melinda Gates Foundation this year have been to eradicate polio worldwide by 2018 and get modern contraceptives to another

120 million women by 2020; the Foundation has committed $140 million annually to this cause. In 2012 a particular emphasis was placed on devising tools for quantifying the success of initiatives as governments increasingly look for proof of the efficacy of the programs they pay for. "Some of the projects we fund will fail," the Gates say on the Foundation website of their own financial commitments. "We not only accept that, we expect it because we think an essential role of philanthropy is to make bets on promising solutions that governments and businesses can't afford to make." 2013 SPOTLIGHT: The Gates Foundation gave away $3.4 billion last year, the vast majority to global health programs, and has made more than $26 billion in grant commitments since the Foundation's 2000 founding.

Michelle Obama, First Lady, U.S.

The Harvard grad and former corporate attorney (and husband Barack Obama's boss) actively uses her platform as first lady to fight childhood obesity and promote healthier eating and lifestyles. With 67% of Americans viewing Michelle Obama in a positive light, she's more popular than her husband by far (47%)—likely because she spends more time laughing on TV than running the country. This year alone she's appeared on the shows of Katie Couric and Jimmy Fallon and announced the Best Picture for the Academy Awards. 2013 SPOTLIGHT: At a keynote address in March, she kept it real, saying "It wasn't that long ago that I was juggling a demanding job with two small children and a husband who traveled."

Hillary Clinton, Former Secretary of State, U.S.

The whole world is watching: Will Hillary run? Clinton has a CV full of firsts: She is the only first lady to become a U.S. senator turned viable presidential candidate turned secretary of state. Now a private citizen, she holds her position as one of the most powerful women on the planet with all bets on that she will be the 2016 Democratic presidential candidate and likely next leader of the free world. The polls don't lie. Sixty-five percent of Democrats say they'll vote Team Hillary, while another poll has her beating the two Republican forerunners by 52%. Her only speed bump now is the Benghazi controversy. And while Bill Clinton calls speculation about his wife's intention to run as "the worst expenditure of our time," she's done little to quiet the chatter, including hitting the speaking circuit last month at an estimated $200,000 fee per event and inking a reported $14 million book deal. 2013 SPOTLIGHT: Super PAC Ready for Hillary, launched in April, has nearly 150,000 Facebook likes, over 60,000 Twitter followers and more than 1,000 financial contributions.

Sheryl Sandberg, COO, Facebook, U.S.

Facebook's COO incited a new conversation on feminism in the workplace with her March 2013 book, *Lean In: Women, Work and the Will to Lead.*

(continued)

The manifesto sold nearly 150,000 copies in its first week and has held the top non-fiction spot on bestseller lists since. But Sandberg's biggest success of the year may have happened right in Menlo Park. After adding ads to its mobile news feed, Facebook earned more U.S. mobile revenue than any other publisher in 2012, with an 18.4% share of the entire market. The April release of "Home," the new Facebook phone, will reportedly allow companies to send advertising directly to users' smartphones even if the home screen is locked. 2013 SPOT-LIGHT: One year after Facebook's initial public offering, the company's stock is down roughly 30%.

Christine Lagarde, Managing director, I.M.F., France

The first woman to run the 188-country financial organization spent much of her first two years on the job battling the debt crisis in Europe and calling for ailing global economies to accelerate steps for stable growth. Her push for debt-sharing between EU nations and an increase in rescue funds has faced resistance from fellow power woman Angela Merkel, chancellor of Germany. French-born Lagarde was a labor and antitrust attorney in the U.S. before a six-year stint as French finance minister. 2013 SPOTLIGHT: Tongues are wagging that she may make a run for the French presidency.

Janet Napolitano, Secretary, Homeland Security, U.S.

Helms the third largest department in U.S. politics, overseeing a budget of $48 billion, a staff of 240,000 and 22 agencies, including FEMA, Customs, INS, the Secret Service and cyber security, which she describes as the fastest-growing threat to the country. Napolitano describes her leadership style as "keep[ing] your eye on long-term vision while dealing with the crisis du jour." 2013 SPOTLIGHT: At the Forbes Women's Summit in May, Napolitano said, "At such a critical time for our country, the participation of women in our political process has never been more important." She took on the position as the first female head of Homeland Security after serving as the third female governor of Arizona from 2003 to 2009.

Sonia Gandhi, President, Indian National Congress party, India

As the longest-serving chief of India's ruling political party, Gandhi has the reins of the world's second-most-populous country and tenth-largest economy. Rumors persist over a rift between her and Prime Minister Manmohan Singh, with many expecting Singh to leave office before the 2014 general elections. Son Rahul is next in line to take over India's most famous political dynasty. 2013 SPOTLIGHT: In May it was announced that women commandos of the elite Special Protection Group may soon be guarding Gandhi, her daughter Priyanka Vadra, and Prime Minister Manmohan Singh's wife, Gursharan Kaur.

Indra Nooyi, CEO, PepsiCo, U.S.

Nooyi has been busy pushing changes through PepsiCo this year. For starters, she boosted quarterly results—revenue jumped 1.2% to $13 billion—with higher prices and sales of the company's snacks like Doritos and Cheetos. Under her urging, PepsiCo is researching a new sweetener that could result in trading places with rival No. 1 Coca-Cola. 2013 SPOTLIGHT: Her total compensation dropped 17% after the company phased out option awards for top executives and offered stock awards for long-term performance.

Caroline Howard, Forbes Staff

have resulted in the sponsorship of numerous international conferences and have promoted education about women's issues all over the world. And, as communication technologies have advanced, the difficulties of global organization have lessened. Transnational feminist groups have worked against militarism, global capitalism, and racism, as well as supported issues identified by indigenous women around the world. This activism was demonstrated in 1995 with the United Nations Fourth World Conference on Women held in Beijing, China (the first conference was held in Mexico City in 1975, the second in Copenhagen in 1980, and the third in Nairobi in 1985). More than 30,000 women attended the Beijing conference and helped create the internationally endorsed Platform for Action. This platform is a call for concrete action involving human rights of women and girls as part of universal human rights, the eradication of poverty of women, the removal of obstacles to women's full participation in public life and decision making, the elimination of all forms

IDEAS FOR ACTIVISM

- Organize an activism awareness educational event on your campus. Invite local activists to speak about their activism. Provide opportunities for students to volunteer for a wide variety of projects in your area.
- Find out about your school's recycling program. If there's not one in place, advocate with administrators to begin one. If one is in place, try to find ways to help it function more effectively and to encourage more participation in recycling. If recycling services are not provided in your local community, advocate with city and county officials to begin providing these services.
- Find out what the major environmental issues are in your state and what legislative steps need to be taken to address these concerns. Then organize a letter-writing campaign to encourage legislators to enact laws protecting the environment.
- Identify a major polluter in your community and organize a nonviolent protest outside that business demanding environmental reforms.
- Sponsor a workshop on conflict management and nonviolence for campus and community members.

of violence against women, the assurance of women's access to educational and health services, and actions to promote women's economic autonomy. Since the Beijing conference in 1995, conventions under the leadership of the United Nations Commission on the Status of Women (CSW) continue to provide "progress reports" and re-formalize the platform in light of global changes since the conference. As of this writing, the most recent 57th session of CSW took place in New York in March, 2013, with a priority theme focusing on the elimination and prevention of all forms of violence against women and girls. Activism continues for U.S. ratification of the Convention on the Elimination of All Forms of Discrimination Against Women (CEDAW) and for other struggles to improve women's lives worldwide.

UN Millennium Development Goals

1. Eradicate extreme poverty and hunger

    Target 1.A:
    Halve, between 1990 and 2015, the proportion of people whose income is less than $1.25 a day
    - The target of reducing extreme poverty rates by half was met five years ahead of the 2015 deadline.
    - The global poverty rate at $1.25 a day fell in 2010 to less than half the 1990 rate. However, projections indicate that in 2015 almost one billion people will still be living on less than $1.25 per day.

    Target 1.B:
    Achieve full and productive employment and decent work for all, including women and young people
    - Globally, 456 million workers lived below the $1.25 a day poverty line in 2011—a reduction of 233 million since 2000, heavily influenced by progress in East Asia.
    - Vulnerable employment—insecure, poorly paid jobs—accounted for an estimated 58 percent of all employment in developing regions in 2011, down from 67 percent in 1991, with women and youth more likely to hold such positions.
    - More than 80 percent of working women in sub-Saharan Africa, Oceania, and Southern Asia held vulnerable jobs in 2011.

    Target 1.C:
    Halve, between 1990 and 2015, the proportion of people who suffer from hunger
    - About 850 million people, or nearly 15 percent of the global population, are estimated to be undernourished.
    - Despite some progress, nearly one in five children under age five in the developing world is underweight.
    - Children in rural areas are nearly twice as likely to be underweight as those in urban areas.
    - More than 42 million people have been uprooted by conflict or persecution.

2. Achieve universal primary education
   Ensure that, by 2015, children everywhere, boys and girls alike, will be able to complete a full course of primary schooling
   - Enrolment in primary education in developing regions reached 90 percent in 2010, up from 82 percent in 1999, which means more kids than ever are attending primary school.
   - In 2010, 61 million children of primary school age were out of school. More than half of them (33 million) were in sub-Saharan Africa and a further one fifth (13 million) in Southern Asia.
   - Even as countries with the toughest challenges have made large strides, progress on primary school enrolment has slowed since 2004, dimming hopes for achieving universal primary education by 2015.
   - With more children completing primary education, the demand for secondary education is growing. In 2010, there were 71 million young adolescents (typically aged 12–15 years) out of school around the world.
   - Gender gaps in youth literacy rates are also narrowing. Globally, there were 95 literate young women for every 100 young men in 2010, compared with 90 women in 1990.

3. Promote gender equality and empower women
   Eliminate gender disparity in primary and secondary education, preferably by 2005, and in all levels of education no later than 2015
   - The world has achieved parity in primary education between girls and boys, but for girls in some regions, education remains elusive.
   - The ratio between the enrolment rate of girls and that of boys grew from 91 in 1999 to 97 in 2010 for all developing regions. The gender parity index value of 97 falls within the plus-or-minus 3-point margin of 100 percent, the accepted measure for parity.
   - Gender inequality persists and women continue to face discrimination in access to education, work and economic assets, and participation in government.
   - Globally, women's share in paid jobs outside of the agricultural sector increased only slightly from 35 percent in 1990 to 40 percent in 2010.
   - Violence against women continues to undermine efforts to reach all goals.
   - Poverty is a major barrier to secondary education, especially among older girls.
   - Women are largely relegated to more vulnerable forms of employment.
   - Globally, women occupy only 25 percent of senior management positions and, in 2008/2009, were on average paid 23 percent less than men.
   - Business ownership is concentrated in men's hands throughout the developing world.

4. Reduce child mortality
   Reduce by two thirds, between 1990 and 2015, the under-five mortality rate
   - Despite population growth, the number of deaths in children under five worldwide declined from 12.4 million in 1990 to 6.9 million in 2011, which translates into about 14,000 fewer children dying each day.

(continued)

- Despite determined progress, an increasing proportion of child deaths are in sub-Saharan Africa.
- As the rate of under-five deaths overall declines, the proportion that occurs during the first month after birth is increasing.
- Mortality is more likely to strike children in rural areas.
- Children born into poverty are almost twice as likely to die before the age of five as those from wealthier families.
- Children of educated mothers—even mothers with only primary schooling—are more likely to survive than children of mothers with no education.

5. Improve maternal health

Target 5.A:
Reduce by three quarters the maternal mortality ratio
- Maternal mortality has nearly halved since 1990. An estimated 287,000 maternal deaths occurred in 2010 worldwide, a decline of 47 percent from 1990, but levels are far removed from the 2015 target.
- The maternal mortality ratio in developing regions is still 15 times higher than in the developed regions.
- The rural-urban gap in skilled care during childbirth has narrowed.

Target 5.B:
Achieve universal access to reproductive health
- More women are receiving antenatal care.
- More pregnant women are receiving care with the recommended frequency, but gaps still exist in regions most in need.
- Fewer teens are having children in most developing regions, but progress has slowed.
- The large increase in contraceptive use in the 1990s was not matched in the 2000s.
- The unmet need for family planning remains persistently high in regions with low levels of contraceptive use.
- Official Development Assistance for reproductive health care and family planning remains low.

6. Combat HIV/AIDS, malaria, and other diseases

Target 6.A:
Have halted by 2015 and begun to reverse the spread of HIV/AIDS
- New HIV infections continue to decline in the hardest-hit regions.
- More people than ever are living with HIV due to fewer AIDS-related deaths and the continued large number of new infections.
- Comprehensive knowledge of HIV transmission remains low among young people, along with condom use.

Target 6.B:
Achieve, by 2010, universal access to treatment for HIV/AIDS for all those who need it
- Access to treatment for people living with HIV increased in all regions.
- At the end of 2011, 8 million people were receiving antiretroviral therapy for HIV or AIDS in developing regions. This total constitutes an increase of over 1.4 million people from December 2009, and the largest one-year increase ever.

Target 6.C:
Have halted by 2015 and begun to reverse the incidence of malaria and other major diseases

- The global estimated incidence of malaria has decreased by 17 percent since 2000, and malaria-specific mortality rates by 25 percent.
- Countries with improved access to malaria control interventions saw child mortality rates fall by about 20 percent.
- Thanks to increased funding, more children are sleeping under insecticide-treated bed nets in sub-Saharan Africa.
- The anti-tuberculosis drive is closing in on a 50 percent cut in the 1990 death rate and more TB patients are being successfully treated.

7. Ensure environmental sustainability

Target 7.A:
Integrate the principles of sustainable development into country policies and programmes and reverse the loss of environmental resources

- Forest area increase in Asia is helping to slow, but not reverse, global losses worldwide.
- Of all developing regions, South America and Africa saw the largest net losses of forest areas between 2000 and 2010.
- In the 25 years since the adoption of the Montreal Protocol on Substances that Deplete the Ozone Layer, there has been a reduction of over 98 percent in the consumption of ozone-depleting substances.
- At Rio+20, the United Nations Conference on Sustainable Development, world leaders approved an agreement entitled "The Future We Want," and more than $513 billion was pledged towards sustainable development initiatives.

Target 7.B:
Reduce biodiversity loss, achieving, by 2010, a significant reduction in the rate of loss

- More areas of the earth's surface are protected. Since 1990, protected areas have increased in number by 58 percent.
- Growth in protected areas varies across countries and territories and not all protected areas cover key biodiversity sites.
- By 2010, protected areas covered 12.7 percent of the world's land area but only 1.6 percent of total ocean area.

Target 7.C:
Halve, by 2015, the proportion of the population without sustainable access to safe drinking water and basic sanitation

- The world has met the target of halving the proportion of people without access to improved sources of water, five years ahead of schedule.
- Between 1990 and 2010, more than two billion people gained access to improved drinking water sources.
- The proportion of people using an improved water source rose from 76 percent in 1990 to 89 percent in 2010.
- Over 40 percent of all people without improved drinking water live in sub-Saharan Africa.

(continued)

- Eleven percent of the global population—783 million people—remains without access to an improved source of drinking water and, at the current pace, 605 million people will still lack coverage in 2015.
- Access to improved sanitation facilities increased from 36 percent in 1990 to 56 percent in 2010 in the developing regions as a whole. The greatest progress was achieved in Eastern and Southern Asia.
- Despite progress, 2.5 billion in developing countries still lack access to improved sanitation facilities.

8. Develop a global partnership for development

Target 8.A:
Develop further an open, rule-based, predictable, non-discriminatory trading and financial system
- Despite the pledges by G20 members to resist protectionist measures initiated as a result of the global financial crisis, only a small percentage of trade restrictions introduced since the end of 2008 have been eliminated. The protectionist measures taken so far have affected almost 3 percent of global trade.

Target 8.B:
Address the special needs of least developed countries
- Tariffs imposed by developed countries on products from developing countries have remained largely unchanged since 2004, except for agricultural products.
- Bilateral aid to sub-Saharan Africa fell by almost 1 percent in 2011.
- There has been some success of debt relief initiatives reducing the external debt of heavily indebted poor countries (HIPCs) but 20 developing countries remain at high risk of debt distress.

Target 8.C:
Address the special needs of landlocked developing countries and small island developing States
- Aid to landlocked developing countries fell in 2010 for the first time in a decade, while aid to small island developing States increased substantially.

Target 8.D:
Deal comprehensively with the debt problems of developing countries
- At this time, it appears developing countries weathered the 2009 economic downtown and in 2011 the debt to GDP ratio decreased for many developing countries. Vulnerabilities remain. Expected slower growth in 2012 and 2013 may weaken debt ratios.

Target 8.E:
In cooperation with pharmaceutical companies, provide access to affordable essential drugs in developing countries
- Resources available for providing essential medicines through some disease-specific global health funds increased in 2011, despite the global economic downturn.
- There has been little improvement in recent years in improving availability and affordability of essential medicines in developing countries.

Target 8.F:
In cooperation with the private sector, make available benefits of new technologies, especially information and communications
- 74 percent of inhabitants of developed countries are Internet users, compared with only 26 percent of inhabitants in developing countries.
- The number of mobile cellular subscriptions worldwide by the end of 2011 reached 6 billion.

By the year 2015 all 189 United Nations Member States have pledged to meet the above goals.

Source: http://www.un.org/millenniumgoals/.

FUTURE VISIONS

How might the future look? How will our knowledge of gender-, race-, and class-based inequalities be used? Does our future hold the promise of prosperity and peace or economic unrest and increased militarization? Will technology save us or hasten our destruction? Will feminist values be a part of future social transformation? Future visions are metaphors for the present; we anticipate the future in light of how we make sense of the present and have come to understand the past. This approach encourages us to look at the present mindfully, so that we are aware of its politics, and creatively, so that we can see the possibility for change. In her playful poem "Warning," Jenny Joseph looks to the future to offer some guidance in the present.

There are some social trends that have implications for the future. Given the higher fertility rates among the non-white population as well as immigration figures, whites in the United States will eventually become a relatively smaller percentage of the population until they are no longer a majority, and the proportion of mixed-race individuals will increase. Latinas/os are the largest growing group, estimated to increase from the current 16 percent of the U.S. population to more than 20 percent by 2025. In addition, the rise in births between 1946 and 1960 (the baby boomer cohort) and the decline through the 1970s means a large percentage of the population will be older than 65 years old within the next couple of decades. Census reports suggest that by 2030 there will be about 70 million older persons (65 years and older): more than twice their number in 2000 and reaching approximately 20 percent of the population. Currently, persons 65 years and older represent about 13 percent of the population. And, although some people have always lived to be 80, 90, and 100 years old, the number of aged will grow in response to better nutrition and health care among certain segments of the population. As the baby boomers age, they will create stress on medical and social systems. They might also influence family systems as several generations of aged family members could require care at the same time. This is complicated by the fact that families are becoming smaller, women are marrying later if at all, and many women are the primary breadwinners and raising children alone. Ties between stepfamilies and other nonfamilial or "chosen family" ties are most likely going to become more important in terms of care and support.

ACTIVIST PROFILE **Andrea Smith**

Cherokee academic and activist Andrea Smith was born in California and received her BA in comparative religions from Harvard, her MDiv from Union Theological Seminary, and her PhD in History of Consciousness from the University of California, Santa Cruz. She is currently associate professor of media and cultural studies at the University of California, Riverside.

While living in Chicago after college, Andrea attended an American Indian Movement conference and was challenged to put work back into her community. A woman working with Women of All Red Nations (WARN) encouraged conference attendees to return to their communities and start a WARN chapter, and so Andrea did. While she had already been involved with activist causes, WARN marked a turning point for more focused activism. As she struggled to understand how to deal with global oppression, she decided to go to seminary. While she was there, her mentor, Dr. James Cone, a leader in black liberation theology, encouraged her to continue her education in a doctoral program. Andrea says her exposure to liberation theology, after having grown up in fundamentalist Christianity, allowed her to see how she could be a person of faith committed to ending global oppression.

Initially Andrea thought her stay in the academy would be short-lived, but she discovered that she could do both academia and activism, and so she made higher education her home base for her struggle to help end oppression. She says the academy gave her a place to think critically about her activism and develop effective strategies for change.

Andrea's greatest passion for change centers on ending violence against women of color. She is a co-founder of INCITE! Women of Color Against Violence (see Chapter 10 activist profile). She is author of *Conquest: Sexual Violence and American Indian Genocide.* Smith also authored *Native Americans and the Christian Right: The Gendered Politics of Unlikely Alliances* and is co-editor of INCITE!'s two anthologies, *The Revolution Will Not Be Funded: Beyond the Non-Profit Industrial Complex* and *Color of Violence.* Andrea is also a founding member of the Boarding School Healing Project, which works to document boarding school abuses and help Native Americans recover from that abuse.

In her teaching, she seeks to create an environment in which students can hear and critically reflect on issues of difference, power, and oppression. Often her students choose to do activism projects in her classes, and so she is teaching another generation of young activists who can also work to bring about an end to global oppression.

In our society, where the profit motive runs much of our everyday lives, where many citizens have lost respect for political and governmental institutions and are working longer hours and may feel disconnected from families and communities, the issue of integrity is something to consider. The definition of integrity has two parts: one, it is a moral positioning about the distinction between right and wrong, and two, it is a consistent stance on this morality such

Principles of Environmental Justice

1. Environmental justice affirms the sacredness of Mother Earth, ecological unity and the interdependence of all species, and the right to be free from ecological destruction.
2. Environmental justice demands that public policy be based on mutual respect and justice for all peoples, free from any form of discrimination or bias.
3. Environmental justice mandates the right to ethical, balanced, and responsible uses of land and renewable resources in the interest of a sustainable planet for humans and other living things.
4. Environmental justice calls for universal protection from nuclear testing, extraction, production and disposal of toxic/hazardous wastes and poisons that threaten the fundamental right to clean air, land, water, and food.
5. Environmental justice affirms the fundamental right to political, economic, cultural, and environmental self-determination of all peoples.
6. Environmental justice demands the cessation of the production of all toxins, hazardous wastes, and radioactive materials, and that all past and current producers be held strictly accountable to the people for detoxification and containment at the point of production.
7. Environmental justice demands the right to participate as equal partners at every level of decision making, including needs assessment, planning, implementation, enforcement, and evaluation.
8. Environmental justice affirms the right of all workers to a safe and healthy work environment, without being forced to choose between an unsafe livelihood and unemployment. It also affirms the right of those who work at home to be free from environmental hazards.
9. Environmental justice protects the right of victims of environmental injustice to receive full compensation and reparations for damages as well as quality health care.
10. Environmental justice considers governmental acts of environmental injustice a violation of international law, the Universal Declaration on Human Rights, and the United Nations Convention on Genocide.
11. Environmental justice must recognize a special legal and natural relationship of Native Peoples to the U.S. government through treaties, agreements, compacts, and covenants affirming sovereignty and self-determination.
12. Environmental justice affirms the need for urban and rural ecological policies to clean up and rebuild our cities and rural areas in balance with nature, honoring the cultural integrity of all our communities, and providing fair access for all to the full range of resources.
13. Environmental justice calls for the strict enforcement of principles of informed consent and a halt to the testing of experimental reproductive and medical procedures and vaccinations on people of color.
14. Environmental justice opposes the destructive operations of multinational corporations.
15. Environmental justice opposes military occupation; repression and exploitation of lands, peoples and cultures, and other life forms.
16. Environmental justice calls for the education of present and future generations that emphasizes social and environmental issues, based on our experience and an appreciation of our diverse cultural perspectives.

(continued)

17. Environmental justice requires that we, as individuals, make personal and consumer choices to consume as little of Mother Earth's resources and to produce as little waste as possible; and make the conscious decision to challenge and reprioritize our lifestyles to ensure the health of the natural world for present and future generations.

Source: People of Color Environmental Leadership Summit, 1991. *www.umich.edu/˜jrazer/nre/whatis .html.*

that we act out what we believe and attempt to live our ideals. "Do as I say and not as I do" is an example of the very opposite of integrity. What might it mean to live with feminist-inspired integrity as well as envision a future where feminist integrity is central? We understand that this notion of feminist integrity is rather a nebulous concept and invite you to consider what it might mean for your life. We'll discuss seven implications here.

First, it is important to set feminist priorities and keep them. In a society where sound bites and multiple, fragmented pieces of information vie to be legitimate sources of knowledge, we must recognize that some things are more important than others. Priorities are essential. Postmodernism might have deconstructed notions of truth to the point where some argue that there is no such thing as the truth; yet some things are truer than others. Figure out your truths and priorities based upon your own values and politics. Decide where to put your energy and figure out which battles are worth fighting. This also means developing personal resilience to weather the ups and downs (and, for some, the deeper trauma) of our lives. Survivors act not only from self-interest, but also in the interest of others. Having a relaxed

Women Working for Peace

The International Peace Bureau (IPB) is the world's oldest and most comprehensive international peace federation. Founded in 1892, the organization won the Nobel Peace Prize in 1910. Its role is to support peace and disarmament initiatives. Current priorities include the abolition of nuclear weapons, conflict prevention and resolution, human rights, and women and peace. To learn more about the IPB, visit the website at *www.ipb.org*.

The Women's International League for Peace and Freedom (WILPF), founded in 1915 to protest the war in Europe, suggests ways to end war and to prevent war in the future; as well, it seeks to educate and mobilize women for action. The goals of the WILPF are political solutions to international conflicts, disarmament, promotion of women to full and equal participation in all society's activities, economic and social justice within and among states, elimination of racism and all forms of discrimination and exploitation, respect of fundamental human rights, and the right to development in a sustainable environment. For more information, including action alerts and readings, visit the WILPF homepage at *www.wilpf.org*.

awareness and the confidence that it brings allows us to prioritize and use our energy for things that really matter. Refusing to be controlled by improper laws or social standards, yet choosing to abide by them for the sake of others and with an eye to changing these structures, is what Bernie Siegel in *Love, Medicine and Miracles* calls "cooperative nonconformity."

Second, it is important that we live in and envision a society that balances personal freedom and identity with public and collective responsibility. Transformational politics call for living with communal values that teach how to honor the needs of the individual as well as the group. The United States is a culture that values individualism very highly and often forgets that although the Constitution says you have the right to do something, we also

Female Nobel Peace Laureates

Fifteen women have been honored with the Nobel Peace Prize for their work for justice:

Baroness Bertha Von Suttner (1905) Austrian honored for her writing and work opposing war.

Jane Addams (1931) International President, Women's International League for Peace and Freedom.

Emily Greene Balch (1946) Honored for her pacifism and work for peace through a variety of organizations.

Betty Williams and Mairead Corrigan (1976) Founders of the Northern Ireland Peace Movement to bring together Protestants and Catholics to work for peace together.

Mother Teresa (1979) Honored for her "work in bringing help to suffering humanity" and her respect for individual human dignity.

Alva Myrdal (1982) Honored with Alfonso Garcia Robles for their work with the United Nations on disarmament.

Aung San Suu Kyi (1991) Burmese activist honored for nonviolent work for human rights in working for independence in Myanmar.

Rigoberta Menchú Tum (1992) Honored for her work for "ethno-cultural reconciliation based on respect for the rights of indigenous peoples."

Jody Williams (1997) Honored for her work with the International Campaign to Ban Landmines.

Shirin Ebadi (2003) Honored for her efforts to promote democracy and human rights.

Wangari Maathai (2004) Honored for her contribution to sustainable development, democracy, and peace.

Ellen Johnson Sirleaf, Leymah Gbowee, and Tawakkol Karman (2011) Honored for their nonviolent struggle for the safety of women and for women's rights to full participation in peace-building work.

Source: http://www.nobelprize.org/nobel_prizes/peace/laureates/.

have the right to criticize you for it. Similarly, we might question the limitations associated with certain rights. Is your right still a right if it violates our rights or hurts a community? And, just because the Constitution says something is your right, that does not necessarily make that act a moral choice. Just because we can do something doesn't mean we have to do it. Although the Constitution exists to protect choices and rights, it does not tell us which choices and rights are best.

Third, recognize that corporate capitalism does not function in everybody's interests. In this sense, economic *freedom* must not be confused with economic *democracy*. Because we can choose between 20 different kinds of breakfast cereal does not mean we have economic or political democracy where we actually all can afford to buy the cereal or live in neighborhoods where there actually are 20 different kinds of cereal available. Many of us have learned that capitalist societies are synonymous with democracies and that other economic systems are somehow undemocratic in principle. We live in a society that attempts a political democracy at the same time that economic democracy, or financial equity for all peoples, is limited. Unfortunately, capitalism has had negative effects on both physical and human environments, works hand in hand with imperialism and militarism, and has exacerbated global inequality. Poverty is probably the most serious social problem in the United States and worldwide. Starvation and hunger are often a result of inequity and politics, not a shortage of food. Consumerism has changed families and communities by encouraging people to accumulate material possessions beyond their immediate needs. Perhaps a motto for the future might be "pack lightly."

Fourth, a present and future with a core value of feminist integrity is one that understands the limitations of technology as well as its liberating aspects. The future vision must be one of sustainability: finding ways to live in the present so that we do not eliminate options for the future. It is important to balance economic, environmental, and community needs in ways that do not jeopardize sustainability. This means being in control of technology so that it is used ethically and productively, an issue that is related to the previous point about capitalist expansion. Corporations have invested heavily in new technologies that do not always work for the collective good. Certainly the recent oil spills with their poignant consequences for human and nonhuman communities is a case in point, as also is the problem of global climate change and water shortages that are caused by industrialization and global capitalist expansion. As the reading "Fracking Is a Feminist Issue" by Rebecca Clarren explains, the technology called hydraulic fracturing, which is commonly called fracking, mines natural gas trapped in sand and shale formations. After wells are drilled, chemical additives, water, and sand are injected under high pressure to break the rock and release the gas. Clarren discusses the potentially toxic consequences of this domestic natural gas boom for families and communities.

Closely related to understanding the limits of technology is our fifth notion of feminist integrity: the need to advocate a sustainable physical environment. There is only one world and we share it; there is an interdependence of all species. Given this, it makes no sense to destroy our home through behaviors that bring about global climate change, environmental pollution, and species eradication. A source of clean and sustainable energy to replace reliance on oil and other fossil fuels is imperative at this moment. Sustainable environmental practices start with addressing issues associated with capitalist global expansion and technological development, as discussed previously. Is it possible to own the rivers and other natural resources of the land? What does it mean to turn precious resources into commodities and what might be the consequences? Could we imagine such resources as sustainable communal property held in trust to be used in equitable ways by future generations? If this were possible, might we see air pollution, for example, as a violation of community property rights? Central here is the need for *environmental justice* because the poor and communities of color have suffered disproportionately in terms of environmental pollution and degradation. As already discussed, environmental justice calls for protection from nuclear testing, extraction, production, and disposal of toxic and hazardous wastes and poisons that threaten the fundamental right to clean air, land, water, and food. It also demands that workers have the right to safe and healthy work environments without being forced to choose between unsafe livelihood and unemployment.

Sixth, a peaceful and sustainable future is one that respects human dignity, celebrates difference and diversity, and yet recognizes that diversity does not necessarily involve equality. It is not enough to be tolerant of the differences among us, although that would be a good start; it is necessary to recognize everyone's right to a piece of the pie and work toward equality of outcome and not just equality of access. Natalie Merchant's song lyrics, "Wonder," speak to the rights of individuals to make their own way in the world. The song celebrates the differences among us—including those with disabilities—and emphasizes that thriving involves love, patience, and faith. These lyrics speak about human dignity and individual rights to live a productive life. We believe we must create social movements that derive from an ethic of caring, empathy, and compassion for all people.

Seventh and finally, we believe it is important to have a sense of humor and to take the time to play and celebrate. As socialist labor reformer Emma Goldman once said, "If I can't dance, it's not my revolution!"

A justice-based politics of integrity embraces equality for all peoples. It is an ethic that has the potential to help create a peaceful and sustainable future, improving the quality of our lives and the future of our planet. An ethic that respects and values all forms of life and seeks ways to distribute resources equitably is one that moves away from dominance and uses peaceful solutions to environmental, societal, and global problems. As a blueprint for the future, a focus on justice and equality has much to offer. The struggle has begun and there is no end in sight!

Feminist Men

Byron Hurt (2011)

The word turns off a lot of men (insert snarky comment about man-hating feminazis here)—and women. But here's why black men should be embracing the "f" word.

When I was a little boy, my mother and father used to argue a lot. Some mornings, I would wake up to the alarming sound of my parents arguing loudly. The disagreement would continue until my father would yell with finality, "That is it! I'm not talking about this anymore!" The dispute would end right there. My mother never got the last word.

My dad's yelling made me shrink in fear; I wanted to do something to make him stop raging against my mother. In those moments, I felt powerless because I was too small to confront my father. I learned early that he had an unfair advantage because of his gender. His size, strength and power intimidated my mother. I never saw my father hit her, but I did witness how injurious his verbal jabs could be when they landed on my mom's psyche.

My father didn't always mistreat my mother, but when he did, I identified with her pain, not his bullying. When he hurt her, he hurt me, too. My mother and I had a special bond. She was funny, smart, loving and beautiful. She was a great listener who made me feel special and important. And whenever the going got tough, she was my rock and my foundation.

One morning, after my father yelled at my mom during an argument, she and I stood in the bathroom together, alone, getting ready for the day ahead of us. The tension in the house was as thick as a cloud of dark smoke. I could tell that my mother was upset. "I love you, Ma, but I just wish that you had a little more spunk when you argue with Daddy," I said, low enough so my father couldn't hear me. She looked at me, rubbed my back and forced a smile.

I so badly wanted my mother to stand up for herself. I didn't understand why she had to submit to him whenever they fought. Who was he to lay down the law in the household? What made him so special?

I grew to resent my father's dominance in the household, even though I loved him as dearly as I loved my mother. His anger and intimidation shut down my mother, sister and me from freely expressing our opinions whenever they didn't sit well with his own. Something about the inequity in their relationship felt unjust to me, but at that young age, I couldn't articulate why.

One day, as we sat at the kitchen table after another of their many spats, my mother told me, "Byron, don't ever treat a woman the way your father treats me." I wish I had listened to her advice.

As I grew older and got into my own relationships with girls and women, I sometimes behaved as I saw my father behave. I, too, became defensive and verbally abusive whenever the girl or woman I was dating criticized or challenged me. I would belittle my girlfriends by scrutinizing their weight or their choices in clothes. In one particular college relationship, I often used my physical size to intimidate my petite girlfriend, standing over her and yelling to get my point across during arguments.

I had internalized what I had seen in my home and was slowly becoming what I had disdained as a young boy. Although my mother attempted to teach me better, I, like a lot of boys and men, felt entitled to mistreat the female gender when it benefited me to do so.

After graduating from college, I needed a job. I learned about a new outreach program that was set to launch. It was called the Mentors in Violence Prevention Project. As a student-athlete, I had done community outreach, and the MVP Project seemed like a good gig until I got a real job in my field: journalism.

Founded by Jackson Katz, the MVP Project was designed to use the status of athletes to make gender violence socially unacceptable. When I met with Katz, I didn't realize that the project was a domestic violence prevention program. Had I known that, I wouldn't have gone in for the job interview.

So when Katz explained that they were looking to hire a man to help institutionalize curricula about preventing gender violence at high schools and colleges around the country, I almost walked out the door. But during my interview, Katz asked me an interesting question. "Byron, how does African-American men's violence against African-American women uplift the African-American community?"

No one had ever asked me that question before. As an African-American man who was deeply concerned about race issues, I had never given much thought about how emotional abuse, battering, sexual assault, street harassment and rape could affect *an entire community,* just as racism does.

The following day, I attended a workshop about preventing gender violence, facilitated by Katz. There, he posed a question to all of the men in the room: "Men, what things do you do to protect yourself from being raped or sexually assaulted?"

Not one man, including myself, could quickly answer the question. Finally, one man raised his hand and said, "Nothing." Then Katz asked the women, "What things do you do to protect yourself from being raped or sexually assaulted?" Nearly all of the women in the room raised their hand. One by one, each woman testified:

"I don't make eye contact with men when
    I walk down the street," said one.
"I don't put my drink down at parties," said
    another.
"I use the buddy system when I go to parties."
"I cross the street when I see a group of guys
    walking in my direction."
"I use my keys as a potential weapon."
"I carry mace or pepper spray."
"I watch what I wear."

The women went on for several minutes, until their side of the blackboard was completely filled with responses. The men's side of the blackboard was blank. I was stunned. I had never heard a group of women say these things before. I thought about all of the women in my life—including my mother, sister and girlfriend—and realized that I had a lot to learn about gender.

Days after that workshop, Katz offered me the job as a mentor-training specialist, and I accepted his offer. Although I didn't know much about gender issues from an academic standpoint, I quickly learned on the job. I read books and essays by bell hooks, Patricia Hill Collins, Angela Davis and other feminist writers.

Like most guys, I had bought into the stereotype that all feminists were white, lesbian, unattractive male bashers who hated all men. But after reading the work of these black feminists, I realized that this was far from the truth. After digging into their work, I came to really respect the intelligence, courage and honesty of these women.

Feminists did not hate men. In fact, they loved men. But just as my father had silenced my mother during their arguments to avoid hearing her gripes, men silenced feminists by belittling them in order to dodge hearing the truth about who we are.

I learned that feminists offered an important critique about a male-dominated society that routinely, and globally, treated women like second-class citizens. They spoke the truth, and even though I was a man, their truth spoke to me. Through feminism, I developed a language that helped me better articulate things that I had experienced growing up as a male.

Feminist writings about patriarchy, racism, capitalism and structural sexism resonated with me because I had witnessed firsthand the kind of male dominance they challenged. I saw it as a child in my home and perpetuated it as an adult. Their analysis of male culture and male behavior helped me put my father's patriarchy into a much larger social context, and also helped me understand myself better.

I decided that I loved feminists and embraced feminism. Not only does feminism give woman a voice, but it also clears the way for men to free themselves from the stranglehold of traditional masculinity. When we hurt the women in our lives, we hurt ourselves, and we hurt our community, too.

As I became an adult, my father's behavior toward my mother changed. As he aged he mellowed, and stopped being so argumentative and verbally abusive. My mother grew to assert herself more whenever they disagreed.

It shocked me to hear her get in the last word as my father listened without getting angry. That was quite a reversal. Neither of them would consider themselves to be feminists, but I believe they both learned over time how to be fuller individuals who treated each other with mutual respect. By the time my father died from cancer in 2007, he was proudly sporting the baseball cap around town that I had given him that read, "End Violence Against Women." Who says men can't be feminists?

R E A D I N G   **104**

Fear of Feminism
Why Young Women Get the Willies

Lisa Marie Hogeland (1994)

I began thinking about young women's fear of feminism, as I always do in the fall, while I prepared to begin another year of teaching courses in English and women's studies. I was further prodded when former students of mine, now graduate students elsewhere and teaching for the first time, phoned in to complain about their young women students' resistance to feminism. It occurred to me that my response—"Of course young women are afraid of feminism"—was not especially helpful. This essay is an attempt to trace out what that "of course" really means; much of it is based on my experience with college students, but many of the observations apply to other young women as well.

Some people may argue that young women have far less to lose by becoming feminists than do older women: they have a smaller stake in the system and fewer ties to it. At the same time, though, young women today have been profoundly affected by the demonization of feminism during the 12 years of Reagan and Bush—the time when they formed their understanding of political possibility and public life. Older women may see the backlash as temporary and changeable; younger women may see it as how things are. The economic situation for college students worsened over those 12 years as well, with less student aid available, so that young women may experience their situation as extremely precarious—too precarious to risk feminism.

My young women students often interpret critiques of marriage—a staple of feminist analysis for centuries—as evidence of their authors' dysfunctional families. This demonstrates another reality they have grown up with: the increased tendency to pathologize any kind of oppositional politics. Twelve years of the rhetoric of "special interests versus family values" have created a climate in which passionate political commitments seem crazy. In this climate, the logical reasons why all women fear feminism take on particular meaning and importance for young women.

To understand what women fear when they fear feminism—and what they don't—it is helpful to draw a distinction between gender consciousness and feminist consciousness. One measure of feminism's success over the past three decades is that women's gender consciousness—our self-awareness as women—is extremely high. Gender consciousness takes two forms: awareness of women's vulnerability and celebration of women's difference. Fear of crime is at an all-time high in the United States; one of the driving forces behind this fear may well be women's sense of special vulnerability to the epidemic of men's violence. Feminists have fostered this awareness of violence against women, and it is to our credit that we have made our analysis so powerful; at the same time, however, we must attend to ways this awareness can be deployed for nonfeminist and even antifeminist purposes, and most especially to ways it can be used to serve a racist agenda. Feminists have also fostered an awareness of women's difference from men and made it possible for women (including nonfeminists) to have an appreciation of things pertaining to women—perhaps most visibly the kinds of "women's culture" commodified in the mass media (soap operas and romance, self-help books, talk shows, and the like). Our public culture in the U.S. presents myriad opportunities for women to take pleasure in being women—most often, however, that pleasure is used as an advertising or marketing strategy.

Gender consciousness is a necessary precondition for feminist consciousness, but they are not the same. The difference lies in the link between gender and politics. Feminism politicizes gender consciousness, inserts it into a systematic analysis of histories and structures of domination and privilege. Feminism asks questions—difficult and complicated questions, often with contradictory and confusing answers—about how gender consciousness can be used both for and against women, how vulnerability and difference help and hinder women's self-determination and freedom. Fear of feminism, then, is not a fear of gender, but rather a fear of politics. Fear of politics can be understood as a fear of living in consequences, a fear of reprisals.

The fear of political reprisals is very realistic. There are powerful interests opposed to feminism—let's be clear about that. It is not in the interests of white supremacy that white women insist on abortion rights, that women of color insist on an end to involuntary sterilization, that all women insist on reproductive self-determination. It is not in the interests of capitalism that women demand economic rights or comparable worth. It is not in the interests of many individual men or many institutions that women demand a nonexploitative sexual autonomy—the right to say and mean both no and yes on our own terms. What would our mass culture look like if it didn't sell women's bodies—even aside from pornography? It is not in the interests of heterosexist patriarchy that women challenge our

understandings of events headlined MAN KILLED FAMILY BECAUSE HE LOVED THEM, that women challenge the notion of men's violence against women and children as deriving from "love" rather than power. It is not in the interests of any of the systems of domination in which we are enmeshed that we see how these systems work—that we understand men's violence, male domination, race and class supremacy, as systems of permission for both individual and institutional exercises of power, rather than merely as individual pathologies. It is not in the interests of white supremacist capitalist patriarchy that women ally across differences.

Allying across differences is difficult work, and is often thwarted by homophobia—by fears both of lesbians and of being named a lesbian by association. Feminism requires that we confront that homophobia constantly. I want to suggest another and perhaps more subtle and insidious way that fear of feminism is shaped by the institution of heterosexuality. Think about the lives of young women—think about your own. What are the arenas for selfhood for young women in this culture? How do they discover and construct their identities? What teaches them who they are, who they want to be, who they might be? Our culture allows women so little scope for development, for exploration, for testing the boundaries of what they can do and who they can be, that romantic and sexual relationships become the primary, too often the only, arena for selfhood.

Young women who have not yet begun careers or community involvements too often have no public life, and the smallness of private life, of romance as an arena for selfhood, is particularly acute for them. Intimate relationships become the testing ground for identity, a reality that has enormously damaging consequences for teenage girls in particular (the pressures both toward and on sex and romance, together with the culturally induced destruction of girls' self-esteem at puberty, have everything to do with teenage pregnancy). The feminist insistence that the personal is political may seem to threaten rather than empower a girl's fragile, emergent self as she develops into a sexual and relational being.

Young women may believe that a feminist identity puts them out of the pool for many men, limits the options of who they might become with a partner, how they might decide to live. They may not be wrong either: how many young men feminists or feminist sympathizers do you know? A politics that may require making demands on a partner, or that may motivate particular choices in partners, can appear to foreclose rather than to open up options for identity, especially for women who haven't yet discovered that all relationships require negotiation and struggle. When you live on Noah's ark, anything that might make it more difficult to find a partner can seem to threaten your very survival. To make our case, feminists have to combat not just homophobia, but also the rule of the couple, the politics of Noah's ark in the age of "family values." This does not mean that heterosexual feminist women must give up their intimate relationships, but it does mean that feminists must continually analyze those pressures, be clear about how they operate in our lives, and try to find ways around and through them for ourselves, each other, and other women.

For women who are survivors of men's violence—perhaps most notably for incest and rape survivors—the shift feminism enables, from individual pathology to systematic analysis, is empowering rather than threatening. For women who have not experienced men's violence in these ways, the shift to a systematic analysis requires them to ally themselves with survivors—itself a recognition that *it could happen to me.* Young women who have not been victims of men's violence hate being asked to identify with it; they see the threat to their emergent sense of autonomy and freedom not in the fact of men's violence, but in feminist analyses that make them identify with it. This can also be true for older women, but it may be lessened by the simple statistics of women's life experience: the longer you live, the more likely you are to have experienced men's violence or to know women who are survivors of it, and thus to have a sense of the range and scope of that violence.

My women students, feminist and nonfeminist alike, are perfectly aware of the risks of going unescorted to the library at night. At the same time, they are appalled by my suggesting that such gender-based restrictions on their access to university facilities deny them an equal education. It's not that men's violence isn't real to them—but that they

are unwilling to trace out its consequences and to understand its complexities. College women, however precarious their economic situation, and even despite the extent of sexual harassment and date rape on campuses all over the country, still insist on believing that women's equality has been achieved. And, in fact, to the extent that colleges and universities are doing their jobs—giving women students something like an equal education—young women may experience relatively little overt or firsthand discrimination. Sexism may come to seem more the exception than the rule in some academic settings—and thus more attributable to individual sickness than to systems of domination.

Women of all ages fear the existential situation of feminism, what we learned from Simone de Beauvoir, what we learned from radical feminists in the 1970s, what we learned from feminist women of color in the 1980s: feminism has consequences. Once you have your "click!" moment, the world shifts, and it shifts in some terrifying ways. Not just heterosexism drives this fear of political commitment—it's not just fear of limiting one's partner-pool. It's also about limiting oneself—about the fear of commitment to something larger than the self that asks us to examine the consequences of our actions. Women fear anger, and change, and challenge—who doesn't? Women fear taking a public stand, entering public discourse, demanding—and perhaps getting—attention. And for what? To be called a "feminazi"? To be denounced as traitors to women's "essential nature"?

The challenge to the public-private division that feminism represents is profoundly threatening to young women who just want to be left alone, to all women who believe they can hide from feminist issues by not being feminists. The central feminist tenet that the personal is political is profoundly threatening to young women who don't want to be called to account. It is far easier to rest in silence, as if silence were neutrality, and as if neutrality were safety. Neither wholly cynical nor wholly apathetic, women who fear feminism fear living in consequences. Think harder, act more carefully; feminism requires that you enter a world supersaturated with meaning, with implications. And for privileged women in particular, the notion that one's own privilege comes at someone else's expense—that my privilege *is* your oppression—is profoundly threatening.

Fear of feminism is also fear of complexity, fear of thinking, fear of ideas—we live, after all, in a profoundly anti-intellectual culture. Feminism is one of the few movements in the U.S. that produce nonacademic intellectuals—readers, writers, thinkers, and theorists outside the academy, who combine and refine their knowledge with their practice. What other movement is housed so substantially in bookstores? All radical movements for change struggle against the anti-intellectualism of U.S. culture, the same anti-intellectualism, fatalism, and disengagement that make even voting too much work for most U.S. citizens. Feminism is work—intellectual work as surely as it is activist work—and it can be very easy for women who have been feminists for a long time to forget how hard-won their insights are, how much reading and talking and thinking and work produced them. In this political climate, such insights may be even more hard-won.

Feminism requires an expansion of the self—an expansion of empathy, interest, intelligence, and responsibility across differences, histories, cultures, ethnicities, sexual identities, othernesses. The differences between women, as Audre Lorde pointed out over and over again, are our most precious resources in thinking and acting toward change. Fear of difference is itself a fear of consequences: it is less other women's difference that we fear than our own implication in the hierarchy of differences, our own accountability to other women's oppression. It is easier to rest in gender consciousness, in one's own difference, than to undertake the personal and political analysis required to trace out one's own position in multiple and overlapping systems of domination.

Women have real reasons to fear feminism, and we do young women no service if we suggest to them that feminism itself is safe. It is not. To stand opposed to your culture, to be critical of institutions, behaviors, discourses—when it is so clearly *not* in your immediate interest to do so—asks a lot of a young person, of any person. At its best, the feminist challenging of individualism, of narrow notions of freedom, is transformative, exhilarating, empowering. When we do our best work in selling feminism to the unconverted, we make clear not only its necessity, but also its pleasures: the joys of intellectual and political work, the moral power of living in consequences, the surprises of coalition, the rewards of doing what is difficult. Feminism offers an arena for selfhood beyond personal relationships but not disconnected from them. It offers—and requires—courage, intelligence, boldness, sensitivity, relationality, complexity, a sense of purpose, and, lest we forget, a sense of humor as well. Of course young women are afraid of feminism—shouldn't they be?

R E A D I N G **105**

Fracking Is a Feminist Issue

Rebecca Clarren (2013)

AT NIGHT, BARB JARMOSKA looks out the window of her rural house and sees the flickering of flares in what was once an inky, endless sky. These 20 acres in Montoursville, Pa.—land her grandfather bought, where she once rode horses through mountains of tall pine and swam in the creek with her grand kids—are now an industrial landscape. Since 2009, she says, as many as 40 natural-gas wells have been drilled within a 5-mile radius of her home.

Due in large part to the embrace of a technology called hydraulic fracturing (commonly called *fracking),* previously inaccessible deposits of natural gas trapped in tight sands and shale formations are now being mined. After a well is drilled, tens of thousands of gallons of chemical additives, water and sand are injected under great pressure to crack rock and stimulate gas flow.

The potential for contamination terrifies Jarmoska. "Can I drink my water? Can I breathe my air? Will my horses die?" Jarmoska asks. "I worry about it every day."

Today, many Americans share their neighborhoods with drill rigs, ponds of wastewater, pipelines, truck traffic and compressor stations. Some gas wells are drilled, fracked and flared within 150 feet of homes and schools. The Energy Information Administration estimates that there are more than half a million natural-gas wells in 31 states, and that more than 630,000 oil and gas wells could be fracked in the coming decades.

Americans "should welcome" the domestic gas boom, President Barack Obama said at a campaign event in Ohio last summer, adding during his 2013 State of the Union address that his administration "will keep cutting red tape and speeding up new oil and gas permits." However, this rush to develop natural gas is taking place without key environmental safeguards. Congress has exempted fracking from the Safe Drinking Water Act and aspects of the Clean Air Act and Clean Water Act. A subcommittee created in 2011 by the secretary of energy to study the impacts of fracking doesn't include a single medical expert.

Between 30 and 70 percent of fracturing fluid remains underground indefinitely, according to studies by the Environmental Protection Agency (EPA) and the oil and gas industry. Critics fear that over the long term residual toxic fluids may contaminate groundwater. The EPA is currently studying the issue, but results won't be available for at least a year. Meanwhile, industry spokespeople say there's no proof that fracking contaminates drinking water, and yet claims of such pollution have been settled out of court, the records are predominantly sealed.

Fracking has ignited a wildfire of debate and activism. Vermont has banned it outright, and 348 local communities have passed measures to curtail or block it. As is the case with so many environmental movements, women are assuming a key role,

fighting to ensure that domestic energy isn't coming at the cost of our health.

On the Blackfeet Indian Reservation in Montana, native women are working to convince their leaders to stop supporting fracking on tribal lands. Women in Pennsylvania, Ohio and Illinois are joining anti-fracking coalitions. In a New York effort led by biologist and author Sandra Steingraber, a letter sent to Gov. Andrew Cuomo asking him to wait for studies to conclude before considering lifting a fracking moratorium was signed by hundreds of medical, environmental and political leaders, including Gloria Steinem and breast-cancer advocacy groups. Outside the U.S., South African women decry plans to frack the pristine Karoo region.

The majority of states that allow fracking do not require companies to disclose the quantity or the chemicals used during fracking, making it nearly impossible to link them to specific diseases. Theo Colborn and researchers at the Endocrine Disruption Exchange in Colorado pored through industry and government documents to assemble a list of generic chemicals that may be used during hydraulic fracturing, and her findings—published in the scientific journal *Human & Ecological Risk Assessment* in 2011—are scary. Of 353 chemicals for which they could find health information, nearly half could affect the brain and nervous system, a quarter may cause cancer and nearly 40 percent could affect the endocrine system, which regulates sexual development, pregnancy and many aspects of childhood development.

The oil and gas industry and its supporters say there's little reason for concern because they use such low concentrations of these chemicals, but scientists like Colborn aren't assured. Fetal and early childhood exposures to very low levels of endocrine-disrupting chemicals can have lifelong effects such as infertility and early puberty in girls.

What's more, after a well has been fracked, about one-third of the fluid flows back to the surface to sit in tanks or pits, and this "produced water" contains not only the chemicals injected into the ground but heavy metals and radioactive material found in deep geological layers. That water is either reused for another fracking, injected back or evaporated—passively or with aerators. Aeration can send radioactive material drifting onto nearby homes and schoolyards, says environmental scientist Alisa Rich, Ph.D., MPH, from the University of North Texas Health Science Center.

"The people who live nearby aren't aware of their exposure—it's forced on them," says Rich, who published a study of such ponds in Texas in *New Solutions: A Journal of Environmental and Occupational Health Policy.* "Many scientists, including myself, don't believe that the current method used for mining natural gas is safe for the public, workers or the environment."

A Pennsylvania group hosts a "List of the Harmed" on its website, where citizens who live near gas operations detail such complaints as rashes, headaches, asthma, insomnia, dizziness and rare tumors. But without published epidemiological studies, such claims are impossible to validate.

"On the one end of the spectrum, environmental advocacy groups say there has to be a moratorium and on the other end industry says it's safe, safe, safe and there's no cause for concern," says Trevor Penning, director of the University of Pennsylvania's Center for Excellence in Environmental Toxicology. Penning's center, working with Columbia University, is conducting the first epidemiological study to determine whether there is an association between water quality and the health of people who live near fracking operations. Results could be published within 18 months.

Until then, the activism will go on. "Fracking is a feminist issue," insists Steingraber, who cofounded the anti-fracking group Concerned Health Professionals of New York. "More than bedrock is fractured during gas extraction: It's our land, our water, our air. There's an inherent violence and lack of consent."

R E A D I N G   **106**

Wonder

Natalie Merchant (1995)

Doctors have come from distant cities
Just to see me
Stand over my bed
Disbelieving what they're seeing

They say I must be one of the wonders
Of god's own creation
And as far as they can see they can offer
No explanation

Newspapers ask intimate questions
Want confessions
They reach into my head
To steal the glory of my story

They say I must be one of the wonders
Of god's own creation

And as far as they can see they can offer
No explanation

O, I believe
Fate smiled and destiny
Laughed as she came to my cradle
Know this child will be able
Laughed as my body she lifted
Know this child will be gifted
With love, with patience and with faith
She'll make her way

People see me
I'm a challenge to your balance
I'm over your heads
How I confound you and astound you
To know I must be one of the wonders

Of god's own creation
And as far as you can see you can offer me
No explanation

O, I believe
Fate smiled and destiny
Laughed as she came to my cradle

Know this child will be able
Laughed as she came to my mother
Know this child will not suffer
Laughed as my body she lifted
Know this child will be gifted
With love, with patience and with faith
She'll make her way

R E A D I N G **107**

What Pussy Riot Taught the World

Michael Petrou (2013)

After seven months in jail, one member of Pussy Riot is still eager to court controversy

Yekaterina Samutsevich is a member of arguably the most famous musical ensemble ever to come out of Russia, but when not wearing a fluorescent balaclava and shouting, she's easy to miss in a crowd. Samutsevich is short and walks quickly, leaning forward with a hunched and self-effacing shrug in her shoulders. She wears a faded sweatshirt over an equally faded T-shirt and has her hair cut in the long-banged style that a teenaged skateboarder might have worn two decades ago. She seems a lot younger than her 30 years.

Her band, Pussy Riot, gained worldwide notoriety—and in Russia, a great deal of infamy—when its members stormed Moscow's Cathedral of Christ the Saviour to stage a "punk prayer" protest song to show their opposition to Vladimir Putin and the increasingly close ties between the Russian president and the country's Orthodox Church, which she says is an anti-feminist institution.

In the end, they were barely able to start before security was on them. Samutsevich didn't even get her guitar out of its case—which probably saved her from a lengthier incarceration. She was convicted of "hooliganism motivated by religious hatred" and sentenced to two years in prison. But her sentence

was suspended on appeal, and she was released in October, after almost seven months in jail. Her bandmates Nadezhda Tolokonnikova and Maria Alyokhina are still serving out their two-year sentences.

Sitting in a Moscow café with walls covered in photos of Soviet-era women heroes, and drinking hot chocolate in rapid spoonfuls, Samutsevich argues that the Russian authorities' harsh response is part of a bigger campaign to slander and punish political artists. Some 20 Russians who took part in a sanctioned anti-Putin protest in Moscow's Bolotnaya Square last May have been charged with "mass unrest" and assaulting police. Most are currently in jail or under house arrest. One man, Maxim Luzyanin, co-operated with police and pleaded guilty. He has been sentenced to 4½ years in jail. Alexei Navalny, a protest-movement leader who has exposed numerous cases of corruption among Russia's political elite, is also fighting charges of embezzlement. Many analysts believe these cases are politically motivated. Dissidents in Russia tend to encounter legal problems of one type or another.

Pussy Riot is comprised of around 10 women. Samutsevich, who studied at Moscow's Rodchenko School of Photography and Multimedia, met some of the other band members at art exhibitions. She says they were inspired by the feminist punk movement of the 1970s, and the American '90s band Bikini Kill. They chose the name "Pussy Riot" because of its intrinsic contrast: "pussy" objectifies women as soft and passive; "riot" is a reaction against that.

The band wanted to pursue the "art of activism" by staging creative and unexpected public events. They were particularly active during the run-up to last year's presidential election that saw Putin returned to power. Last January, in Red Square, the band performed a song titled Putin's Pissed Himself. "We ruined the campaign a little bit," she says. "It might have been some kind of personal grudge."

Samutsevich says protesting inside the Cathedral of Christ the Saviour wasn't a random act or the result of a flippant decision. They thought a lot about it. Patriarch Kirill, head of the Russian Orthodox Church, had called Putin's presidency a "miracle of God," and describes feminism as a dangerous phenomenon. "We needed to do it where Patriarch Kirill had stood," she says.

Pussy Riot members didn't expect such a strong state reaction. Some of them had been detained previously but were always released. Performing in a church might have been one step too far across an invisible line. But it's more likely that a legal case against them was inevitable. Still, Samutsevich says she has no regrets. "People ask us all the time if we would do it again," she says. "Yes, we would."

Samutsevich does worry about Tolokonnikova and Alyokhina, her jailed bandmates, and as the interview winds up, she guides the conversation back to them. Both have young children. Tolokonnikova was recently denied parole because she didn't show remorse and refused to participate in some prison activities, such as the "Miss Charm Prison Camp 14" beauty contest. The judge did not allow the defence to make a closing argument. In her statement, which Tolokonnikova wrote but could not present, she said she would not admit guilt and lie for the sake of parole.

She added: "I am truly grateful to the people I have encountered in my life behind barbed wire. Thanks to some of them, I will never call my time in prison time lost I will surely use my experience in [the penal colony] in my future work and, although this will not happen until completion of my sentence, I will implement it in projects that will be stronger and politically larger in scale than everything that has happened to me before."

R E A D I N G **108**

We Are the Ones We've Been Waiting For

Moya Bailey and Alexis Pauline Gumbs (2010)

For black feminists in the U.S., it has always been uncertain whether and how our words will survive. Who would have thought that the line "we are the ones we've been waiting for," from June Jordan's 1980 "Poem for South African Women," would have ended up in a speech by a successful presidential candidate—Barack Obama—and then [be] dispersed, unattributed, on countless mugs, T-shirts, key chains and posters? Who would have thought that classic literary devices such as dramatic irony, used by enslaved 18th-century poet Phillis Wheatley to ensure her words would be published despite unspeakable odds, would be the same devices that convinced Black literary critics her work was "not black enough" for more than a century?

When Black feminism's words do live on, it is not by accident, default or simple popularity: It is often because Black feminists scraped coins together to publish them, as when Black women's social clubs raised the funds for Ida B. Wells to put out her 1890s anti-lynching and anti-rape pamphlets. Similarly, nearly a century later, in the late 1980s, Barbara Smith risked bankruptcy to continue funding Kitchen Table, an autonomous press for writing by women of color.

We—the 1980s babies who authored this article—treasure this grassroots legacy, while knowing that Black feminism still lives on unstable ground. So from these roots, a new(er) generation of Black feminist voices coming out of academia are using free and direct means of publication—the Internet and its social media—to spread our visions and provoke on ongoing dialogue.

The Black feminist blogosphere that we are connected to includes more than 100 sites. To name just a couple created by Black feminist Ph.D. students at the University of Maryland, there are women's studies student Renina Jarmon's blog Model Minority: Thugs + Feminists + Boom Bap, which takes Black feminist theory to the streets, and Jessica M. Johnson's blog African Diaspora, Ph.D., which "honors the activists, artists, teachers, researchers, librarians, bloggers and others who bring depth to our work."

These sites defy the voices of cynics who have lamented since before we were born that when Black feminism moved into the academy it moved away from its activist roots. We know that the work of Black feminist critical practice has never been contained within the walls of universities, and has consistently lived in popular media outlets, including pamphlets, stickers and open letters. Thus, we, work with interactive modes of inquiry that challenge the ownership of knowledge within the university.

For instance, we're involved with Eternal Summer of the Black Feminist Mind, a blog that hosts a series of virtual and in-person "potlucks" that brings together participants from Durham, N.C., to Washington, D.C., and from Chicago to Nairobi, Kenya, to discuss Black feminist theory. In this way, we can take the research we've gained on the university's dime and use it to fortify and inform popular conversations based in activist communities.

Then there's the blog FireWalkers, a list-serv-linked network of African Diaspora women who do feminist activism and research both within and out-side of the academy. Taking our name from Beverly Guy-Sheftall's *Word of Fire,* we cross the artificial line between the politics of Black liberation and women's liberation, sometimes catching fire from both sides yet continuing to move forward with purpose. With our scholarship we hope to evolve the conversations in the Black and feminist communities into a more holistic understanding of each other.

Our websites also challenge the dominance of mainstream publishing. For instance, when the mainstream media gave little attention to a series of violent acts against Black women in the fall of 2007, Black feminist University of Chicago graduate student Fallon Wilson and activist Izetta Mobley used the Web to launch the Be Bold Be Red Be Brave: Ending Violence Against Women of Color campaign. Students, faculty, community organizers and other concerned individuals nationwide posted photos of rallies and vigils in which they wore red to protest a media that seemed only able to see racist and gendered violence as separate issues, not linked, and occurring only one sensationalist moment at a time. The site quotes Audre Lorde's words, "When we speak we are afraid our words will not be heard or welcomed. But when we are silent, we are still afraid. So it is better to speak."

Another important aspect of these networking endeavors is the social—long a key part of Black feminist movements. Black feminists have created alternative rituals and understandings of beauty, love, friendship, celebration and mourning as a way to critique, reject and replace dominant norms. We're inspired by the 1977 statement by the Combahee River Collective, a Black feminist socialist collective in the Boston area, which wrote about how valuable it was to have "found each other."

So we, Alexis and Moya, decided to create a social network called Quirky Black Girls, which allows a diverse group of self-identified QBGs to post our own videos, music and imagery, all the while building bravery and challenging each other's thinking. We maintain a blog, a site on social networking service Ning, a Facebook group and a Black speculative fiction reading group, and we organize regular in-person arcade nights, jam sessions, cook-outs and more. We put the network in an explicitly Black feminist frame by reflecting weekly with the group on specific quotes from the Combahee River Collective Statement and Audre Lorde's journals.

The two of us have found that our Web activism carries into our very relationships and the way we speak. When the Black women's blogosphere grieved over the brutal multiple rape of a 20-year-old who was in her apartment and went unaided by neighbors who listened for four hours, we communicated through list-servs and blogs to create action plans in our neighborhoods. We discussed our desire for responses that didn't involve the police and instead affirmed our faith in each other. Many ideas were spawned, including baking cupcakes in our apartment buildings and sharing them with fellow renters in order to dissolve the culture of anonymity and ambivalence an apartment complex can create.

In another action, after noticing the absence of children and their parents from activist events, Black feminists—along with other folks of color and white allies—felt the need to create child-care collectives. Online tools like Google groups and riseup.net helped us create a network of volunteers to provide this child care.

And finally, out of our desire to see, hear and feel Black women artists who create work that resonates in our souls, we are using Google Wave technology to plan a Quirky Black Girl Festival for 2012. The power of connecting people who might otherwise feel isolated and alone, but for the song that gets them through the day or that painting that rejuvenates the spirit, is a magic that the Internet seems born to do.

Our projects to create online and in person spaces for Black feminist conversation honor and supplement the rich tapestry of Black feminism that has come before us. We are the new thread connecting patches in a well-worn quilt, both tactile and virtual. We believe that our ancestors knew we were coming, and that our elders, communities, students and future comrades have demands on us that require a fully interactive frame. We are the ones we've been waiting for.

R E A D I N G   **109**

Warning

Jenny Joseph (1992)

When I am an old woman I shall wear purple
With a red hat which doesn't go, and doesn't suit me.
And I shall spend my pension on brandy and
    summer gloves
And satin sandals, and say we've no money for
    butter.
I shall sit down on the pavement when I'm tired
And gobble up samples in shops and press alarm bells

And run my stick along the public railings
And make up for the sobriety of my youth.
I shall go out in my slippers in the rain
And pick the flowers in other people's gardens
And learn to spit.

You can wear terrible shirts and grow more fat
And eat three pounds of sausages at a go
Or only bread and pickle for a week
And hoard pens and pencils and beermats and things
    in boxes.

But now we must have clothes that keep us dry
And pay our rent and not swear in the street
And set a good example for the children.
We must have friends to dinner and read the papers.
But maybe I ought to practise a little now?
So people who know me are not too shocked or
    surprised
When suddenly I am old, and start to wear purple.

DISCUSSION QUESTIONS FOR CHAPTER 13

1. How does a feminist classroom differ from a non-feminist classroom? What impact do these differences have on students?

2. What activist work must be done to build a truly inclusive, peaceful, healthy, and egalitarian community?

3. Why are peace and environmental justice important feminist issues?

4. What is the significance of a "transformational politics" for feminist activism?

5. How can feminist activists build inclusive alliances and coalitions for social change?

SUGGESTIONS FOR FURTHER READING

Aptheker, Bettina. *Intimate Politics: How I Grew Up Red, Fought for Free Speech, and Became a Feminist Rebel.* Berkeley, CA: Seal Press, 2006.

Braithwaite, Ann, Susan Heald, Susanne Luhmann, and Sharon Rosenberg. *Troubling Women's Studies: Pasts, Presents, and Possibilities.* Toronto: Sumach Press, 2005.

Daly, Mary. *Amazon Grace: Re-Calling the Courage to Sin Big.* New York: Palgrave Macmillan, 2006.

de Haan, Francisca, Margaret Allen, June Purvis, and Krassimira Daskalova, eds. *Women's Activism: Global Perspectives from the 1890s to the Present.* New York: Routledge, 2013.

Finley, Laura, and Emily Reynolds Stringer. *Beyond Burning Bras: Feminist Activist for Everyone.* Santa Barbara, CA: Praeger, 2010.

Hewitt, Nancy A., ed. *No Permanent Waves: Recasting Histories of U.S. Feminisms.* Piscataway, NJ: Rutgers University Press, 2010.

James, Stanlie M., Frances Smith Foster, and Beverly Guy-Sheftall, eds. *Still Brave: The Evolution of Black Women's Studies.* New York: The Feminist Press, 2009.

Roces, Mina, and Louise Edwards, eds. *Women's Movements in Asia: Feminisms and Transnational Activism.* New York: Routledge, 2010.

Unger, Nancy C. *Beyond Nature's Housekeepers: American Women in Environmental History.* New York: Oxford University Press USA, 2012.

Credits

Reading 1 Adrienne Rich, "Claiming an Education" from *On Lies, Secrets and Silence: Selected Prose 1966–1978*. Copyright © 1979 by W.W. Norton & Company, Inc. Used by permission of W.W. Norton & Company, Inc. **Reading 2a** Beverly Guy-Sheftall, "Forty Years of Women's Studies" from *Ms.* (Spring 2009): 56–57. Copyright © 2009. Reprinted with the permission of Ms. Magazine. **Reading 2b** Bonnie Thornton Dill, "Intersections" from Ms. (Spring 2009): 65. Copyright © 2009. Reprinted with the permission of Ms. Magazine. **Reading 3** Rosalyn Baxandall and Linda Gordon, "No More Miss America" from "*Dear Sisters: Dispatches from the Women's Liberation Movement*." Reproduced with permission of Basic Books in the format Republish in a book via Copyright Clearance Center. **Reading 4** Jennifer Baumgardner and Amy Richards, "A Day Without Feminism" from *Manifesto: Young Women, Feminism and the Future*. Copyright © 2000 by Jennifer Baumgardner and Amy Richards. Reprinted by permission of Farrar, Straus & Giroux, LLC. **Reading 5** bell hooks, "Feminist Politics: Where We Stand" from *Feminism Is for Everyone*. Copyright © 2000 by bell hooks. Reprinted with the permission of South End Press. **Reading 6** Rachel Graham Cody, "The Power and the Gloria" (2012). Reprinted by permission of the author. **Reading 7** C. V. Harquail, "Facebook for Women vs. Facebook Designed by Feminists: Different vs. Revolutionary" from Authentic Organizations blog, October 10, 2010, http://authenticorganizations.com/harquail/2010/10/05/facebook-for-women-vs-facebook-designed-by-feminists-different-vs-revolutionary/. Reprinted by permission of the author. **Reading 8** Anna Quindlen, "Still Needing the F Word." Copyright © 2003 by Anna Quindlen. Reprinted with the permission of International Creative Management, Inc. **Reading 9** Marge Piercy, "My Heroines" from *On the Issues* (July 20, 2010). Reprinted with the permission of *On the Issues Magazine*, www.ontheissuesmagazine.com. **Reading 10** Patricia Hill Collins, "Toward a New Vision: Race, Class, and Gender as Categories of Analysis and Connection" from *Race, Sex, and Class 1* (Fall 1993). Article published in the *Race, Sex, and Class* journal Vol. 1, #1, Fall 1993. Reprinted with the permission of Jean Belkir, Editor. **Reading 11** Vivian M. May, "Intersectionality." Copyright ©2012 by Vivian M. May. Reproduced by permission of Taylor and Francis Group, LLC, a division of Informa plc. **Reading 12** Audre Lorde, "There Is No Hierarchy of Oppressions" from *I Am Your Sister: Collected and Unpublished Writings of Audre Lorde*, edited by Rudolph P. Byrd, Johnnetta Betsch Cole, and Beverly Guy-Sheftall. Copyright © 1999, 2009 by Audre Lorde. Reprinted by permission of the Charlotte Sheedy Literary Agency. **Reading 13** Peggy McIntosh, "White Privilege and Male Privilege: Unpacking the Invisible Knapsack" from *Peace and Freedom* (July/August

1989): 10–12. Copyright © 1988 by Peggy McIntosh. May not be duplicated without permission of the author. mmcintosh@wellesley.edu. **Reading 14** Evin Taylor, "Cisgender Privilege" from *Gender Outlaws*. Copyright © 2010 by Kate Bornstein. Reprinted by permission of Seal Press, a member of the Perseus Books Group. **Reading 15** Felice Yeskel, "Opening Pandora's Box: Adding Classism to the Agenda" from *The Diversity Factor* (Winter 2007). Copyright © 2007 Class Action, www.classism.org, a national nonprofit co-founded by the late Felice Yeskel. Reprinted with permission. **Reading 16** Ellie Mamber, "Don't Laugh, It's Serious, She Says" from *The Poet's Job: To Go Too Far*, edited by Margaret Honton. Copyright © 1985. Reprinted with the permission of the author. **Reading 17** Susan Wendell, "The Social Construction of Disability" from *The Rejected Body*. Copyright © 1996. Reprinted with the permission of Routledge, Inc., a member of Taylor and Francis Group, LLC, a division of Informa plc. **Reading 18** June Jordan, "Report from the Bahamas" from *On Call: Political Essays*. Copyright © 2013 by June Jordan. Reprinted with the permission of the June M Jordan Literary Estate Trust, www.junejordan.com. **Reading 19** Maya Angelou, "Our Grandmothers" from I SHALL NOT BE MOVED. Copyright © 1990 by Maya Angelou. Used by permission of Random House, Inc. **Reading 20** Anne Fausto-Sterling, "The Five Sexes, Revisited" from *The Sciences* (July/August 2000): 18. Copyright © 2000. Reprinted by permission of the author. **Reading 21** Judith Lorber, "The Social Construction of Gender" from *Paradoxes of Gender*. Copyright © 1994 by Yale University. Reprinted with the permission of Yale University Press. **Reading 22** Cornelia Fine, "Unraveling Hardwiring" from *Delusions of Gender: How Our Minds, Society, and Neurosexism Create Difference*. Copyright © 2010 by Cordelia Fine. Used by permission of W.W. Norton & Company, Inc. **Reading 23** Evenlyn Blackwood, "Trans Identities and Contingent Masculinities: Being Tombois in Everyday Practice" from *Feminist Studies* 35, no 3 (Fall 2009).Copyright © 2009 by Evelyn Blackwood. Reprinted with the permission of the suthor. **Reading 24** Michael Kimmel and Christina Hoff Sommers, "What Up with Boys?". Feburary 20, 2013. Reprinted by permission of the authors. **Reading 25** Nellie Wong, "When I Was Growing Up" from *This Bridge Called My Back: Writings by Radical Women of Color*, edited by Cherrie Moraga and Gloria Anzaldua. Reprinted with the permission of Nellie Wong. **Reading 26** Isis H. Settles, Jennifer S. Pratt-Hyatt, and NiCole T. Buchanan, "Through the Lens of Race: Black and White Women's Perspective of Womanhood" from *Psychology of Women Quarterly* 32, no 4 (December 2008): 454–468. Reprinted by Permission of SAGE Publications. **Reading 27** Deborah L. Brake, "Wrestling with Gender: Constructing

Index